Goldmine

C MEDY

RECORD

PRICE GUIDE

Ronald L. Smith

Published by

**krause
publications**

700 E. State Street • Iola, WI 54990-0001
Telephone: 715/445-2214

Please call or write for our free catalog of music publications.
Our toll-free number to place an order or obtain a free catalog is 800-258-0929
or please use our regular business telephone 715-445-2214
for editorial comment and further information.

Library of Congress Catalog Number: 95-82429
ISBN: 0-87341-444-6

Printed in the United States of America

Contents

Introduction

WHAT'S IN THE BOOK—AND WHAT ISN'T

What's in this book?

Comedy albums: whatever record stores put in their "comedy" bin and what most catalogs list as "comedy."

They're listed by comedian. An appendix in the back lists albums that might be better known by the title ("The First Family") and who it is filed under.

Records are listed in chronological order under each comedian.

Only complete albums (ten-inch and twelve-inch, plus CDs) are included. If a comedian didn't make a full album, check the back for the Compilation Albums list.

What's not in this book?

"Spoken Word," the literary and educational albums (from Caedmon, Spoken Arts, CMS, etc.) of Mark Twain stories, Edward Lear poems, and so on, as well as "audio book" cassettes sold in bookstores.

Novelty albums such as The Chipmunks and The Muppets, which are usually filed under "Children's Recordings."

Vocalists who are amusing but filed under "Country" (Roger Miller), "Rock" (The Bonzo Dog Band), or "Jazz" (Slim Gaillard).

When in doubt, the records are included. (Weird Al Yankovic is sometimes in "Rock" and Anna Russell in "Classical," but they're here.)

Cassettes aren't included. They aren't collectible and it's impractical to list all the obscure, cheaply done tapes sold via mail or in comedy clubs. Vinyl and CD are the marks of the pro.

Imports aren't here, although British stars who have released at least one album in America have a supplementary note on their other albums.

Test pressings, acetates and DJ copies aren't listed unless they contain important rare material or are from a major name.

Radio station discs of syndicated programming featuring interviews with comedians and clips from their work, such as *Earth News*, *Dr. Demento*, *The Comedy Show with Jack Carney*, *National Lampoon Radio Hour*, *The Ralph Emery Show*, *Programmer's Digest*, *The Comedy Hour*, and *Lew Irwin Reports*, aren't listed. It would be impossible to list all of them, and the odds of collectors finding them are slim.

Every effort has been made to include *every* comedy record, but sometimes an album could not be authenticated, or the pressing was so small, obscure, and impossible to find that to list it would be pointless. In deference to fans' needs, notes on major stars sometimes refer to important 45s, 78s and "non-comedy" albums.

For space considerations, not every "one shot wonder" is listed. Rest assured, if it isn't here, it isn't valuable, and probably isn't funny either. Self-pressed albums and cruise ship items, from Ann Moore to Mal Kennedy, have also largely been eliminated.

CRITICAL RATINGS

The "star" system (first pioneered by Ronzoni pastina) should help readers make a quick evaluation. Unlike movie/video guides where a fleet of writers contribute reviews, every record in this book was reviewed by the author. Space limitations prevent detailed comments for every obscure record.

****   **Excellent (an important album and sure-fire fun)**

***   **Good (recommended to most anyone)**

**   **Average (some laughs, more for fans of the comedian or the genre)**

*   **Poor (t'ain't funny, McGee)**

The star system reflects "general" tastes. Ethnic, regional, lowbrow, or high-brow comedy can be hysterical for a certain group, and boring or even infuriating to another.

The system doesn't take into account environment (many times an album is a lot funnier if a whole room full of listeners is laughing) or price (plunk down $20 and "it better be good"). Every effort has been made to take into account the difference between a fun album worth picking up for $5 and something that, given collector's prices, ends up costing $50 an hour. Although ... $50 an hour for comedy might be better therapy than $50 spent on a psychiatrist.

PRICE GUIDE

"Caveat Emptor" doesn't mean Dick Cavett is hungry. It means "buyer beware." Prices of albums fluctuate wildly.

Why?

The seller. A busy record shop with low rent and a high turnover marks $5 on what a "collectors" store charges $15. Some stores are willing to wait for "the right buyer." Many mail order firms feel it's not worth wrapping and sending a record for under $10 or $20 and don't mind warehousing their stock.

Another twist: A dealer who mainly stocks rock albums may put a high price on "hip" Firesign Theater albums and a low one on a Catskill comic. A dealer with a classical or jazz clientele may put a low price on any comedy album that filters in from an auction lot or estate sale just to get rid of it.

Pricing is subjective: Some dealers sell an obscure comic's album cheap because "nobody's heard of him"; another charges double because "only a collector would want it—and collectors will pay anything to complete their collection!"

One New York dealer puts a $2 price on a country album because "nobody here likes corn." Down the street, another dealer makes it $20 precisely because "around here, country is rare!"

Dealers have different philosophies on CD reissues. Some believe the original vinyl is worth nothing. Others say vinyl is more enduring and "archival" than a CD that "might oxidize in a few years."

The prices quoted here reflect two standards. The low price is what you'll see at a reasonable record store or flea marketeer's table. The high price is what a collector's shop or a mail order firm might try to get.

Another way of looking at it is that the low price reflects a good copy of the record; the high price a sealed one.

In the case of a CD reissue, the lone price means that usually the original vinyl doesn't fetch more than the CD.

The prices I quote reflect what I've seen in mail order ads and during visits to dozens of different record shops in New York, Los Angeles, Las Vegas, Miami, Boston, Chicago, and other cities around the country.

If you need a rule for buying and selling records, this is as good as any: If you go to buy records, the prices in this book are in dollars. If you go to sell them, they're in pesos.

The best way to sell records is to know a collector who craves them, or (if you have enough discs to make it worthwhile) take out an ad in a collector magazine. A used record store that sells an album for $10 will pay you anywhere from $1 to $5 depending on how sure they are they'll resell it.

COMEDY RECORDS: A BRIEF HISTORY

Recorded comedy is a unique art form and it has served many valuable functions.

Early comedy cylinders preserved a performer's work for a greater audience than any stage star could reach. Cal Stewart's "Uncle Josh" series was a hit at the turn of the century. By 1915 Americans could buy a flat, two-sided 78 rpm disc for under a dollar and soon "Cohen on the Telephone" (as recorded by Joe Hayman, Monroe Silver, Barney Bernard, and other dialect comics) and "The Two Black Crows" (Moran and Mack) were big sellers.

Radio caused a temporary setback to the popularity of comedy records. With so much audio humor available free, there was little need for it on disc. Through the '40s "the art of the monologue" was confined to the very few comedy stars who relished the spoken word and specialized in a unique voice or cadence (such as W. C. Fields and his "Temperance Lecture").

Comedy on disc was supplied mostly by novelty songs, with Spike Jones leading the way. Record companies now believed that only loony tunes could sell, and that nobody would want to buy a spoken album that couldn't be heard "over and over."

The late '50s changed all that. It was the time of the "comedy album boom," which reflected the new nightclub scene. Risqué comics and hip comics (from Belle Barth to Lord Buckley, with Lenny Bruce in both categories) could not be heard on radio or TV—only in small nightclubs. As in the days of vaudeville, monologue albums flourished, giving these performers a much wider audience than the intimate lounges in sophisticated cities.

Another reason for the boom was new technology. Comedians such as Stan Freberg and Eddie Lawrence could record one track on top of another, creating new forms of aural humor. It also enabled obscure performers (such as Tom Lehrer, Benny Bell, and Dickie Goodman) to cheaply press up their own material and earn a cult following without touring or TV exposure.

In the late '50s, comedy albums were often called "party" records—because those not near a nightclub, or not wanting to deal with the expense, could have a "live comedian" in their living room via an inexpensive disc. And with TV in the early '60s restricted to only a few channels, a comedy album was a definite alternative to video.

The surprising "best-seller" comedy album emerged between 1958 and 1963, making stars of Shelley Berman, Bob Newhart, and Allan Sherman. With no topical monology or political satire on TV, Mort Sahl and Dick Gregory issued albums regularly. With no daring sitcoms, Vaughn Meader's "First Family" brought popularity to an odd hybrid comic form—sketch humor on disc.

The majority of entries in this book come from this "golden age" of comedy, the late '50s and '60s.

New comedy will continue to emerge on CD; digital sound suits musical satirists and people are still willing to listen to a monologist with a unique way of speaking comic truths. Many of today's comedians were inspired by listening to the classic albums from the previous generation. Comedy that expresses truths about human nature and the world around us always endures. The proof of that is on disc, where you can still laugh at monologue material from 1915.

A&P PLAYERS

- I LOVE JIMMY CARTER (A&P Records AP 1001) *1/2 $4 $8

Peter Livingston and Andrew Piotrowski wrote this feeble and tiresome 1976 "soap opera" parody of Jimmy Carter and his family. The cover drawing gives Carter a "Mary Hartman" braided wig, but the humor isn't in the offbeat style of that then-popular comic soap opera. Here's Jimmy in bed with his wife:

"Here I come! Wait a minute. Stop. Them peanut shells. Damn. I told you a hundred times ... despite the fact that our lives are based on a solid foundation of peanuts, much as I delight in your peanut-flavored kisses, your peanut-flavored lips, sweet honey, peanuts is welcome anywhere, anytime in our white house, but never sweet nut, never in bed, you may depend on that!"

PATSY ABBOTT

- HAVE I HAD YOU BEFORE? (CHESS 1450) *1/2 $5 $10
- SUCK UP, YOU'RE BEHIND (ABBOTT LP 1000) *1/2 $5 $10
- YIDDISH SONGS MAMA NEVER TAUGHT ME (ROULETTE S 25267) $8 $12

Abbott, born Goldie Schwartz in the Bronx, sang with Teddy King's orchestra and toured with Mickey Katz in "Borscht Capades." In 1958 she opened "Patsy's Place" in Miami and spent many years telling Yiddish-accented stories and risqué jokes to local funseekers.

Like Rusty Warren, Abbott likes to "liven things up" with corny songs. Instead of jokes, she prefers pushy ringsider banter. Unlike Rusty, Patsy tends to shift into Yiddish and pause to translate between the two languages. Typical of the tummling is her Jewish-accented punning on the "Suck Up" album: "You got 'appiness ... you got a-piness... you got a penis ... he's got a penis. All god's children gotta penis. I ain't got a penis! You put the accent on the wrong syllable." This sets the audience to snickering, so she goes into some prepared schtick. Talking about the nuclear age, she shouts "We have too much fallout! Ay, you know what you do in case of fallout? You put it back in again with shorter strokes. Put your head between your knees and kiss your tokus good-bye!"

The songs on her Roulette album are sung in Yiddish. The music is bouncy, with lots of percussion and brass, but unlike some Yiddish performers, Patsy's delivery isn't funny on its own. Some cuts sound pretty dirty, though: "Fuchin," for example. Others include "Berel Der Bluzzer," "Shittarayn," and "Noch a Bissel."

ABBOTT AND COSTELLO

- ABBOTT AND COSTELLO ON RADIO (Nostalgia Lane NL 1001) *** $5 $10
- ABBOTT AND COSTELLO RADIO TREASURY (Nostalgia Lane NL PB 7071) *** $8 $20
- WHO'S ON FIRST (Radiola MR 1038) **** $5 $10

"On Radio" compiles some of Bud and Lou's silliest word-confusion routines, including "The Board Routine," "Who's on First," and "Hertz U-Drive." Side Two is the December 12, 1946, episode of their radio show. They're on a hunting trip, and that means the terrible puns of their "tick" bit: "Gnats annoy the animals. Of course, some of them have ticks. There's deer's ticks." "Deer ticks? Who wound 'em up?" "Listen please, when I say deer ticks, I don't mean deer ticks. The ticks bother the deer." "Tics bothered me in school: arithmatics, mathematics...." "Lou, hundreds of animals in the woods have ticks." "That must be a pretty sound, when hundreds of animals get together and start ticking at once." "No, Costello, listen to me. Deer have ticks. Elk have ticks. One time my father shot a moose with ticks. Now you know what I'm talking about?" "Sure, your father's moose ticks!"

Radiola's collection is similar, with a side of routines including "Who's on First," "The Story of Moby Dick," "Hertz U-Drive" and "In Alaska." In the latter, Bud asks, "Uncle Mike is in Alaska, isn't he? Nome?" "Sure I know him, he's my Uncle Mike, ain't he?" "I mean Nome in Alaska!" "I'd know him anyplace!" Side Two is a complete radio show from November 9, 1944.

The double set "Treasury" has four radio shows: November 4, 1944; April 5, 1945; June 14, 1945; and an undated episode from 1943. The November 4 show, at the race track, has their "horse's fodder" routine. On April 5, the boys journey to the Andrews Sisters ranch, but argue over a rented car: "It's Hertz U-Drive all over the country!" "I don't want to drive all over the country and get hurt! If it hurts, you drive!" June 14th's Father's Day broadcast includes a visit to a department store. Bud suggests Lou buy a down pillow for Dad, with predictable results: "It's filled up with down." "Up with down?" "Certainly. You see that pillow up there? That's down." "How can it be down if it's up there?" And up and down it goes. Peter Lorre is the guest on the 1943 show. After catching the flu and enduring Bud's assertion that "when the flu flies we must flee," it's time to visit ghoulish Dr. Lorre. "He's a great doctor, Costello. He'll see that you get some rest and peace." "That's it—I don't want to rest in peace!"

- BEST OF ABBOTT AND COSTELLO (Murray Hill M58039) *** $10 $20
- HEY AAABOTT! (Murray Hill 899981) **1/2 $10 $20

"Best of" is a mixed bag offering examples of the team's radio, TV, and film humor. The three-record set opens with a collection of routines culled from the Abbott and Costello TV series: "Slowly I Turned" (with Sidney Fields as the demented stranger), "Loafing" (Bud's proud that his entire family of loafers kneaded dough), Lou's frustration in trying to reach "Alexander 4444," etc. There are three complete radio shows, sampling material from the NBC years (through 1946) and the ABC years (through 1951): November 11, 1943; October 5, 1944; May 5, 1948. Lucille Ball is the guest on the 1943 show, and Bela Lugosi appears on the one from 1948, the year Lugosi starred with the boys in "Abbott and Costello Meet Frankenstein." In this episode, he plays the owner of a haunted house, and a purveyor of some hideous jokes. "Just a minute Lugosi," says Abbott, "you've got a dead man in your cellar." "Yes, I know. He lives here." "But he's dead, why don't you throw him out?" "I can't. His rent is paid up till June first ...

if you want me, I'll be in the morgue, lying on my slab." "Don't look now Abbott, but I think he's a little slab-happy." The final disc offers a one-hour radio version of *Buck Privates*, their first starring movie.

The three-record "Hey Aaabott" contains a lot of duplication. Two records are nothing more than a repackage of Nostalgia Lane's "Radio Treasury" album. The remaining disc collects TV show material including "Who's on First," "Slowly I Turned," and "Fluegel Street," where citizens go berserk at the mere mention of the Susquehanna Hat Company. The shrill laugh track obscures some of the lines.

- BUCK PRIVATES (Radiola MR 1135) *** $4 $8
- CHRISTMAS STOCKING (Holiday HDY 1939) ** $3 $7
- BEST OF ABBOTT AND COSTELLO (Radiex 6) ** $5 $15
- WHO'S ON FIRST (Memorabilia MLP-731) **1/2 $5 $10
- ABBOTT & COSTELLO (Metacom 0300331) **1/2 $8

"Buck Privates," aired October 13, 1941, and is an hour-long radio version of Bud and Lou's blockbuster movie.

"Christmas Stocking" offers standard routines on one side ("Who's on First," etc.) and a December 12, 1946, radio show on the other.

"Best of" clips a few routines from the Abbott and Costello TV show. "Who's on First" survives, but a sketch in which sneaky carnival con Bud plays "hide the lemon" must be seen as well as heard. Side Two is "The Best of Amos and Andy."

The Memorabilia album is a poor buy, duplicating Nostalgia Lane's "Abbott and Costello on Radio" album minus about twenty minutes of routines. "The Hunting Trip" radio show episode is stretched over two sides, with only "Who's on First" as an added bonus. Metacom's CD compilation, usually sold via mail and bookstores, also has "Who's on First" and "The Hunting Trip."

NOTES: The boys are on several compilation albums. "Jest Like Old Times" (Radiola #1) has their "Mustard Routine." They do a bit about tailoring (and dyeing) on "The Edgar Bergen Show" (Radiola MR 1034). "Golden Age of Comedy" (RCA Victor LPV 580) has "Laugh, Laugh, Laugh" a rare 78 the duo made that's loaded with quickies ("Where do all the bugs go in the winter?" "Search me." "No thanks, just asking!"). A rousing chorus urges: "Laugh, Laugh, Laugh ... things have been worse before." Bud and Lou were right. The song was recorded the day after Pearl Harbor was bombed, December 8, 1941. It would be many years before the team recorded another single (a Decca 45, "Jack and the Beanstalk").

Abbott is heard on the album "Conversations in Hollywood" (Citadel 6002) giving a philosophical, dry-eyed account of his life: "You have the old show biz philosophy, ride on with the crest of the wave, up and down ... in other words, they always say the curtain must come up and the show must go on. And if you're not there, the show still goes on, so what's the difference."

ACE TRUCKING COMPANY

- ACE TRUCKING (RCA VICTOR LSP 4268) **1/2 $7 $15

At the time of this 1970 record, the San Francisco improv group consisted of Patti Deutsch, Michael Mislove, Bill Saluga, George Terry, and Fred Willard. Saluga later gained brief fame with his bit about a windy, friendly little Southerner ("Ohhh, you can call me Ray, or you can call me Jay, or you can call me R. J. ...") and even issued a 12-inch disco tune.

Ad-lib sketches are a lot funnier live. It's the tension and excitement of seeing the performers really work that makes the audience laugh nervously, or uproariously when there's unexpected success. But on vinyl, the spontaneity is lost and all that's left are the frail quips. The audience wants a honeymoon sketch. The groom gets a big laugh for ad-libbing to the bellboy, "You're waiting for a tip. And she's waiting for a tip." When the audience suggests a topic like constipation, the comics ad-lib word association and a phrase like "uptight" drives everyone into hysterics. Like the life of the party, you hadda be there.

The better sketches here are the few polished ones that were evolved from improvisation and nourished into complete routines. These include "Electric Chair" and "Paqua Velva."

ERNESTO ACHER

- MISCHIEF WITH MOZART (Stradivari SCD 6096) * $7

In this feeble rip-off of P. D. Q. Bach, ten classical selections are paired with ten pop tunes for what is billed as "a mischievous look at the classics! Humorous take-offs." For "A Little Hebrew Music," for example, Mozart's "Eine Kleine Nachtmusik" is interpolated with "Hava Nagila." There is no wit or art in this; anyone playing with the tuning knob on a radio can do the same thing by switching from a classical station to a pop one. Conductor Ernesto Acher and the Buenos Aires Philharmonic needed a stylish arranger for this 1987 CD—one with a sense of humor.

DON ADAMS

- DON ADAMS (Signature SM 1010, reissued as THE DETECTIVE [Roulette SR 25317]) ** $10 $20

Adams (the former Donald Yarmy) had a long stand-up career prior to *Get Smart*, and his Signature album from the early '60s has a bit that earned him some derision from *Time* magazine in their notorious article on the craze for "sicknik" comics. It's about a plane crash: "Sitting in the audience tonight are some relatives of the victims of the terrible plane crash at La Guardia ... Mr. Thompson who lost a wife and two children ... Mr. Thompson, would you stand up and take a bow please ... let's give him a nice hand, folks. No tears ... just take your bow and shut up."

The title track is a parody of movies in which a sleuth gathers all the suspects in a room and cleverly deduces the murderer: "You can't be the inspector. You must be the murderer. And if you're the murderer, then you're the inspector. And if you're the inspector ... I must be on the wrong case." Other self-contained bits on this very mild album include: "Television Ideas," "Bengal Lancers," and "Football Coach."

- THE ROVING REPORTER (GNP Crescendo GNP 91) ∗∗ $5 $10

An unidentified straight man plays "roving reporter" to Adams as he assumes various guises: "Big Mouthpiece," "Movie Star," "Killer," "Columbus," etc. Adams does some slightly askew routines, including an interview with Hitler, and a bit on a bank robber who gleefully murders bystanders and eventually the interviewer. Others offer typical character comedy, benefiting from Adams's pompous nasal voice of impervious authority. Here's Adams as a lawyer:

"You think justice will triumph?" a reporter asks. "No, I think we'll win." "The District Attorney has exposed Mrs. Glick as a liar, a cheat, a thief." "Well, none of us are perfect." "He says she's a homicidal maniac." "He certainly has a big mouth ... look at those legs. The dimpled knee, the well-turned calf, the slim ankle. Now I ask you, are those the legs of a homicidal maniac?"

- GET SMART (United Artists UAL 3533) ∗∗∗ $10 $20
- LIVE (United Artists UAL 3604/UAS 6604) ∗∗∗ $10 $20

As overconfident but inept Maxwell Smart crouches, cornered in a warehouse by enemy agents, he spends thirty minutes recalling his greatest moments in crime solving. Darn nice of UA to give a little production value to what is basically a set of voicetracks from the *Get Smart* show. A good job was done in finding segments of verbal humor that make sense on disc. One classic is Max and Harry Hoo (Joey Forman doing a Charlie Chan parody) discovering a body. "Moment please," says Harry, "much can be learned from man by what he carry on person. Please to examine pockets, Mr. Smart." "Wallet, handkerchief, comb, keys to my apartment ..." "One moment, Mr. Smart, victim had key to your apartment in his pocket?" "Oh, you wanted me to search *his* pocket!"

Adams's 1968 live album is a smooth, entertaining show that includes a long, well-honed airline bit, and a selection of golf stories, including odd quickies: "I had a wonderful experience on the golf course today. I had a hole in nothing. Missed the ball and sank the divot." He does some audience participation routines similar in tone to his friend Don Rickles; picking a hapless sap from the audience and bringing him onstage to play opposite him in a dialogue sketch.

Oddly, one bit is a word-for-word copy of Jackie Mason material. He tells Mason's joke about his mother, who is so hard of hearing that she ends up with eighteen children (her husband says "Do you want to go to sleep or what?" She says "What?"). And he uses Mason's opener about the previous act ("I'm not that great that I can afford to follow another stiff. I worked at a club a few weeks ago where the act before me, she was so bad, right in the middle of my act, they started booing her. They couldn't forget how lousy she was ... some people walked out on her while I was still performing." I asked Jackie about it and he shrugged: "I've never seen anybody comparatively successful steal so blatantly. It's offensive and disgusting, I'm amazed that with all his stardom he'd stoop to stealing my jokes word for word, but frankly, it hasn't hurt my career. The audience is buying our personalities, not one joke or routine."

Aside from the unsettling four or five minutes of copying, Adams's personality, the wise guy who needs to get smart, shines throughout this, his best album.

Adams also appears on the collector's album "The World's Funniest Press Conference" (see entry under Buddy Hackett). He narrates a children's story "E.A. Hass: Incognito Mosquito" (Caedmon 1749).

EDIE ADAMS

- EDIE ADAMS SINGS? (MGM 3751) ∗∗1/2 $8 $25

With Henry Mancini conducting the orchestra, Adams re-interprets some classic pop tunes with a droll, hip edge.

The hearty "Whiffenpoof Song" is given a ridiculous Marilyn Monroe-like reading with sexy whispers and lilting laughter. She mimics the overboard style of '50s torch singers with jazzed up versions of "School Days" and "All of a Sudden My Heart Sings" that are so overdramatized, she climbs up the scale like a frightened cat up a tree. For the classic McDonald & Eddy duet "Indian Love Call," Adams is abetted by thumping jungle drums and bellowing calls from husband Ernie Kovacs. On "Singing in the Rain," thunder begins to sound and soon soggy Adams is sniffling, singing off-key, and coming down with a head cold.

For fans of subtle musical satire, this was pretty poison back in the early '60s. For those with a knowledge (and hatred) of the tunes and the singers that sang them, this one will still hold up.

JOEY ADAMS

- CINDY AND I (MGM E 3784) ∗1/2 $4 $12

Joey Adams had written a string of books in the late '50s and had a mild hit with one in particular, *Cindy and I*. That yielded this album, recorded without an audience. It's a low-budget version of *The Bickersons*, with Joey giving uninspired readings (the lack of live laughs probably caused that) and Cindy loading up on the arch smarm that would serve her decades later as a gossip columnist. The wisecracks are cold and unfunny: "I don't know, I've tried every diet there is." "Yeah, between meals." "Yeah, well I know how I can get rid of 110 pounds immediately." "How?" "Dump you!"

STANLEY ADAMS

- CHANUKAH CAROLS (Sight and Sound LPM 6404) ∗∗ $5 $10

Hefty, raucous Adams growls and overacts through this collection of kosherized Christmas carols and folk songs. There's a lot of Yiddish (a glossary appears on the back cover) but a number of cuts should provide some shock humor to fans looking for something besides Allan Sherman and Mickey Katz. These include "Twas The Night Before Chanukah," "The Eight Days of Chanukah," and the predictable parody of "Jingle Bells" that now concerns matzoh balls: "Matzoh balls, matzoh balls, in the chicken soup! Mama makes you eat 'em till your stomach starts to droop. Matzoh balls, matzoh balls, have another cup. If matzoh balls don't kill you, your number isn't up! Dashing through the Bronx in a one-horse Chevrolet. To Mama's house we fly for a heiseh glass of tea. Over the bridge we speed, like a vilde yold. We gotta get there quick before the matzoh balls get cold!"

KIP ADDOTTA

- I HOPE I'M NOT OUT OF LINE (LAFF A 215) ** $4 $10
- COMEDIAN OF THE UNITED STATES (LAFF A 232) ** $4 $10
- WHITE BOY RAPP (LAFF 230 S) ** $4 $8
- LIFE IN THE SLAW LANE (RHINO RNLP 70826) ** $4 $10

Addotta made his first album in 1981 for Laff. It has the requisite quota of bathroom humor, like his discussion of urinals and why men should wear underwear:

"There's a reason for underwear. You see when a man is finished relieving himself, I don't care if he shakes it. I don't care if he twists it. I don't care if he wrings it out or beats it on the side of the bowl. There's always three drops left! Now I hope I'm not out of line, but that's what underwear's for! You shouldn't have to tell people these things."

His second album, "Comedian of the United States" offers monologue bits and two forgettable and indifferently performed raps ("White Boy Rapp" and "Big Cockroach"). The lone bright spot is "Wet Dream," a painfully pun-filled narrative with music: "My Barracuda was in the shop, so I was in a rented Stingray and it was overheating. So I pulled into a Shell station ... I knew the owner. He used to play for the Dolphins. I said, "Hi, Gil!" You have to yell. He's hard of herring."

"Wet Dream" is also on the mini-album "White Boy Rapp," featuring the title track, a less than funky cover of "Chantilly Lace," and five minutes of stand-up.

The title track of Addotta's 1986 "Life in the Slaw Lane" tried to duplicate the minor success of "Wet Dream." This rap collects a ton of food puns: "Sure, they'd sown their wild oats, but just barley, if you peas. Finally Peaches had given him an ultimatoe. She said I'm hip to your chive, and if you don't stop smoking that herb, I'm gonna leaf you. For Basil. Ya fruit."

The other songs don't make it. Kip's monotonous voice and smug tone kill whatever mild humor they might have. He sings about yuppies, egomaniacs, drunks, and couch potatoes, and becomes these obnoxious characters. The recognition humor isn't strong enough to overcome the nausea.

AGGIE JIM

- HOW CAN YOU TELL AN AGGIE? (Rainbow R 3700) ** $3 $8

Leisurely anecdotes predominate on this Texas album of (contrary to the title) all-purpose Southern humor: "I reckin' you heard about the Aggie. The professor asked him in school one day to spell Mississippi. He said, "You mean the state or the river?"

SPIRO T. AGNEW

- THE GREAT COMEDY ALBUM (Flying Dutchman FDS 137) * $3 $8

The then vice president of the United States is subject to a practical joke here. So are listeners who spend a lot for it. Will Jordan (as Richard Nixon and as Ed Sullivan) introduces each side of the album, which is nothing more than Agnew speeches with a laugh track.

FRANKLYN AJAYE

- FRANKLYN AJAYE (A&M 4405) ** $4 $8
- I AM A COMEDIAN, SERIOUSLY (3642) ** $4 $8
- DON'T SMOKE DOPE FRY YOUR HAIR (Little David LD 1011) ** $4 $8

In the mid '70s, nightclub audiences saw the rise of young minority performers, from the Hispanic Freddie Prinz to the black comic Franklin Ajaye. These performers had trouble with their comic identity. Assimilated just enough to talk without an accent and to have had contact and acceptance with young whites, they couldn't come on like angry young men, couldn't honestly revert to comic ethnic accents, but weren't comfortable doing raceless humor either.

Ajaye, like young blacks on mid '70s TV sitcoms, such as Lionel Jefferson (*All in the Family*) and Lamont Sanford (*Sanford and Son*), isn't really funky or funny. From the second album, here's an attempt by Ajaye to do some patter about black issues in front of a white comedy club crowd: "Some of the big black dudes on campus would intimidate some of the little white students. They'd butt in front of lines at registration. They'd just walk up and say 'Get back, Whitey.' And the white guy would stand there [using a Richard Dreyfus type of tempered, tolerant voice] 'Nice guy, isn't he? They've been oppressed, you know. We've got to make allowances.' I tried that one time, jumped up in front of a dude: 'Get back Whitey.' Jumped in front of the only white dude who wasn't afraid of niggers. Boy. Talk about tap dancing."

Now and then there's a telling one-liner ("You can tell Diana Ross is making it big now 'cause she's makin' records niggers can't dance to") but mostly the monologues are an uncomfortable jangle of half-hearted funk posturing and mild observations about school, girls, and so on.

AL ALBERTS AND LIFERS CHORUS

- SING SING SING ALONG (Jubilee JGM 2040) * $3 $7

Somebody must have really hated Mitch Miller's "Sing Along" albums and wished that all the middle-aged male singers were put away in jail.

That's the only logic behind this terrible one-joke album—twelve folk songs with new lyrics about life in prison! To "Merrily We Roll Along" there's: "Farewell, warden. Farewell, warden. We hate your guts, and how! Merrily we climb the wall, merrily we climb the wall, merrily we climb the wall, we're breakin' out tonight!" And to "When The Saints Go Marching In," there's: "They broke my nose. With a rubber hose! And I'll never smell again. Don't wanna be in that number when the guards come marching in."

ALESIA AND BLAKE

- FORGIVE ME FATHER FOR I HAVE SINNED (LAFF A 171) *1/2 $4 $8

Frank Alesia's partner "Timothy" Blake is a pretty blonde woman adept at playing hippie chicks (this album arrived in the early '70s), dizzy quiz show hostesses, and breathy bubble heads. Alesia tends to play off her like Mike Nichols or Woody Allen, with wan, mild-mannered confusion.

Some of their routines sound like updated Nichols and May, but without the edge, humor, or profundity. A hippie chick goes to the confessional and confounds a nervous priest with her frank sex talk, but typical for a Laff album, the emphasis is more on titillation than comedy. And here, a man dials the wrong number and gets a girl waiting for an obscene phone call:

"Listen, where have you been, I've been waiting for over an hour and a half! You're late! Let's get started, go ahead ... talk about my body, ... say something about the way I walk!" "Well, okay. You got a nice stride. I dunno...." "Pretend we're in the game room! What are we gonna do?" "We could play billiards...." "Listen! I've been waiting around an hour and a half for this call ... throw me down on the ground, caress my body from head to toe ... touch my white creamy skin ... oh I love it!"

Now and then the duo have a good idea for a bit, or show a flair for Nichols and May irony ("Going Back to Religion," where want ads try to entice people to join various churches). On another record label they may have been inspired to do better, but this was it for Alesia and Blake.

LOU ALEXANDER

- EARTH SHATTERING (United Artists) UAS 6718) ** $5 $10

Son of burlesque comic Jo Jo Gostel, mild-mannered Alexander offers fairly easygoing observations: "Horoscopes ... the book says people born in January are gentle. February people are honest. March people are sincere. April people are trustworthy and so on and so on. Now what I don't understand is: where the hell do all the rotten people come from?"

Most of the time the material is pretty heavy handed in its irony: "Dynamite was invented by Alfred Nobel. It's so incongruous. Here's a guy who comes up with the first big bomb in history that can cause more damage than anything in the world, and in his honor, they give out the Nobel Peace prize!"

Joey Bishop offered his endorsement on the back cover: "I enjoyed the album tremendously and I'm sure the public will too."

DAYTON ALLEN

- WHY NOT? (Grand Award GA 33-424) *** $10 $20

A comedy writer for Fred Allen and a cartoon voice specialist (Deputy Dawg, Heckle and Jeckle), Dayton Allen in 1958 became a comedy regular on Steve Allen's *Tonight Show*, starting a fad for his "Why not!" catchphrase.

Allen's voice and humor resemble a cross between 1930s Ed Wynn and 1980s Steve Martin. He's whimsical, silly, and often weird. His "What, me worry?" catchphrase was "Why not?" delivered with exaggerated optimism, so much so that it sounded more like a parody of positive thinkers : "Whoooooy nawt!" It began accidentally, when, during a "Man in the Street" interview he was stumped for an ad-libbed answer to a question and delivered his taunting question-wisecrack in return.

This early '60s album collects interviews from the *Tonight Show* with Steve Allen as straight man. Typical of the cute, corny exchanges is this bit, with Dayton as a criminologist. Steve asks:

"What makes a criminal tick?"

"A criminal tick? I don't know about criminal ticks. I seen some gangster cockroaches and very mean fleas, but never a criminal tick!" One liners: "The only way to combat criminals is by not voting for them.... The man who kills his entire family would probably someday commit a serious crime."

NOTES: Dayton Allen can be heard as a supporting player on many comedy albums. He plays Jimmy Carter in the parody LP "Just Plains Folks" and imitates Groucho Marx on one of Steve Allen's "Funny Fone Calls" albums.

FRED ALLEN

- COMEDY GEMS (Chase and Sanborn Promo Album) *** $10 $25
- FRED ALLEN LOOKS AT LIFE (Bagdad 6969) *** $10 $25
- COMEDY HIGHLIGHTS (Nostalgia Lane NLR 1023) ** $5 $10

Born John Florence Sullivan, Fred Allen juggled, told jokes during the act, and ended up writing and performing them for decades on radio. He invented "The Mighty Allen Art Players" and "Allen's Alley," and his dry wit influenced Dick Cavett and Johnny Carson.

"Gems" is an excellent but obscure compilation of highlights. It's a transcript of the November 14, 1965, tribute radio broadcast made by Edgar Bergen. In an "Allen's Alley" segment, Fred asks his loony panel for cures for the common cold. He visits Bing Crosby and Maurice Evans, and insults Jack Benny: "Benny was born ignorant and he's been losing ground ever since." Fred's version of Gilbert and Sullivan operettas "The Pinafore" (with Leo Durocher) and "Mikado" (transplanted to Manhattan) are here, as well as "Picadilly," a parody of "Oklahoma" featuring Bea Lillie.

Allen and Tallulah Bankhead satirize "happy talk" radio couples. After ripping the sponsor's products, Fred slaps his child: "That'll teach you, sneaking up on your parents with one tooth like an old Elk!" Tallulah asks, "Can the kid help it if she looks like you?" Finally he shoots his canary, his wife, and even the kid. Very few radio comics could've gotten away with a cynical, "sick" sketch like that. Even recently, when the bit was lifted for the compilation album "Golden Age of Comedy" (Evolution Records), the murder finale was censored.

The Bagdad double-set released in 1971 offers a lot of golden moments, but on some of them the sound is either speeded up or slowed down.

Fred interviews an eagle trainer whose bird gets loose in the studio (how many talk shows have since booked such acts hoping for things to get out of control?). Bert Lahr and Frank Sinatra drop by for some comedy, Fred sings the "Umpire Song" from his "HMS Pinafore" baseball parody, and there are sketches featuring Fred as detective One Long Pan and Inspector Bungo. He always pauses to give out with a typical one-liner observation: "the skunk: a possum with a motive!"

Nostalgia Lane's disc is the same as the first two sides of the double LP set "Fred Allen Looks at Life." There's no mention of this, and no one even bothered to remaster the material to correct the chipmunkish speed defects. The eagle owner is here, plus Bert Lahr.

- DOWN IN ALLEN'S ALLEY (Radiola #8) *** $7 $15
- TEXACO STAR THEATER (Radiola MR-1083) ** $5 $10
- THE FAMOUS FRED ALLEN SHOW (Memorabilia MLP 712) **1/2 $4 $8
- THE FRED ALLEN SHOW (Radiola MR 1146) *** $5 $10
- THE FRED ALLEN SHOW (Mar-Bren Records 741) *** $5 $10
- LINIT BATH CLUB REVUE (Radio Archives LP 1002) ** $8 $15
- SALAD BOWL REVUE (Radio Archives LP-1004) ** $8 $15

"Down in Allen's Alley" offers four different "Allen's Alley" segments. Fred routinely strolled down the alley to meet charming ethnic characters like Mrs. Nussbaum (Minerva Pious), who converted everything into Semitic terms ("You were expectin' maybe Emperor Shapirohito?"). Kenny Delmar played the great mouth from the South, Senator Claghorn ("Ah say, ahm from the deep South. My family's treadin' water in the Gulf Stream!"). Delmar's catchphrase, "That's a joke, son!" was very popular; his swaggering style stolen "in tribute" to the Warner Bros. cartoon rooster Foghorn Leghorn. The other two main alley denizens were special favorites of Allen, reflecting his own roots. There was New Englander Titus Moody ("Moody by name, moody by nature") played by Parker Fennelly, and the Irishman Ajax Cassidy (Peter Donald), given to such remarks as "Me boy, as a child I was subnormal and proud of it!" The flip side of the hour-long album will interest comedy buffs: Allen offers a 1949 look at "The State of American Humor," reporting on the origins of comedy, the wit of Josh Billings and Will Rogers, and the style of humor currently on radio.

Texaco's hour-long broadcast (May 10, 1942) has Marlene Dietrich as guest, joining Fred in a long sketch about the Yukon. There's strange humor here as Fred fumes over Marline's attraction to a stranger named Hymie: "You've been brought up to luxury: flannel underwear and soap. What can Hymie give you?" "Someday he'll own that Good Humor Wagon...." "I got the biggest saloon in the Yukon. I can give you anything Hymie can give you. Except tutti-frutti." "I'm a gold digger. Up here in the Yukon men are a dime a dozen." "Them are the little ones, Knell." It's an average show with a lot of padding, including many musical numbers.

Memorabilia has one 1940 show stretched over both sides of the album. It does have Frank Sinatra (crooning "It Might as Well Be Spring" and bantering a few gags) plus an Allen's Alley ("How is the traffic dilemma affecting you?")

Radiola's "Fred Allen Show" and Mar-Bren's entry both have the April 11, 1948, episode with guest Basil Rathbone, who actually sings a bogus radio commercial ("When you're buying frozen fruit, what's the fruit that's sure to suit? It's a frosted goodie, the fastest selling: Fagel's Frozen Watermelon!"). Later Fred plays the Oriental detective One Long Pan in a murder mystery. Radiola adds the April 25, 1948, show costarring an etiquette-conscious Leo Durocher, while Mar-Bren has the better October 28, 1945, show with Fred going to court with Charlie McCarthy: "Close that knothole you're talking through McCarthy, or I'll pull your arms off and use them for chopsticks." "Go peddle your margarine, Baggy Face." "If I give you a hotfoot from the knees down you'll be charcoal!"

Radio Archives concentrates on the shows Allen did in the early '30s. Fred hadn't yet hit his stride with unique one-liners and bright character comedy, but ardent fans will get a chuckle or two from his always literate approach.

On the Linit album, he plays an efficiency expert: "You remember The Dollar Store? Place was going to pieces till I stepped in ... I built it up to a Five and Ten."

NOTES: Fred Allen's feuds with Jack Benny have been collected on three albums listed in the Jack Benny section. Three short skits with Fred Allen appear on "Golden Age of Comedy" (Evolution 3013). An "Allen's Alley" segment and a few moments between Fred and Jack turn up on "Son of Jest Like Old Times" (Radiola #2). Fred Allen narrates "The Magnificent Rogue" (see W. C. Fields). A "Fred Allen Show" turns up on the boxed set "The Great Radio Comedians" (Murray Hill M5419x).

ROCKY ALLEN

- A PIECE OF THE ROCK (Critique 01624154232) *

A New York DJ fond of "scam" (i.e. crank and practical joke) phone calls, Allen admits that it took "960 hours of broadcasting ... to scrape sixty minutes for this recording." And that's the bottom of the barrel. He calls some fool, bickers for two minutes, reveals it's a radio prank, and the victim chortles "that's great!" Other stale DJ routines (like fake quiz shows and belaboring the-man-in-the-street interviews) are even more boring. Shamelessly self-promoting celebs (such as Geraldo Rivera and Susan Lucci) are heard reading a few promo lines for Rocky just to get on the air for an extra thirty seconds. Their names are listed on the album. Profits for the CD go to charity; giving it one star is being charitable.

STEVE ALLEN

• MAN IN THE STREET (Signature 1004) ***	$10	$25
• FUNNY FONE CALLS (Dot 3472) ***	$10	$20
reissued Casablanca 811-366-1-ML	$5	$15
• MORE FUNNY FONE CALLS (Dot 3473) ***1/2	$10	$20
reissued Casablanca 811- 367-1-ML	$5	$15

Although considered one of America's great wits, Steve Allen told me, "My dominant gift is for the composition of music. I write several songs a week and I have done that for a half a century." That may explain why of the nearly forty albums he's made, only a few are comedy. Steve's albums are all based on audio tracks from his talk show years.

"Man in the Street" was a favorite part of *The Tonight Show* with the regular appearances of grossly nervous Don Knotts, flamboyant Louis Nye, and haplessly blank-faced Tom Poston. Peter Ustinov makes a guest appearance on "Why Did You Grow a Beard?" There are plenty of chuckles here, although Louis Nye has his problems in answering the question "What Makes You Laugh?"

"Hi ho, Steverino ... my sense of humor is different from other people's. I've found that I just don't laugh at the same things everybody else laughs at." "What does everybody else laugh at?" "At me."

The phone call albums were originally released in 1963. Thanks to Steve Allen's stream-of-consciousness ad-libs before, during, and after dialing, these practical jokes are always entertaining. He even lets guest stars get in on the fun. The first album has Louis Nye and Mel Brooks, who ends up shouting to a caller, "You're too funny, will you just shut up a minute?" Allen tries to call an audience member's mother, only to have the woman insist she doesn't know an Art Goldstein: "Art? I have a son *Arthur* Goldstein...."

On the second album Steve gets into a wild exchange with a flirtatious lady who's obviously been drinking. When Steve inquires, "What do you do?" She snaps back, "That's a little personal, doncha think?" But then she gets personal. Bill Dana is on hand to bedevil a phone operator by insisting he's locked in a phone booth. Jack Lemmon nervously calls the auto club claiming his car just dropped into a swimming pool. And Shelley Berman discovers that the girl he's been trying to invite to a swinging party is only fifteen years old. "We could go to an all night party Saturday night—and then go to church." Jerry Lewis, never better, drives a caterer crazy in a twelve-minute put-on, and Steve caps the show by calling up Johnny Carson, who indulges in some cautious, "friendly enemies" ad-libbing with his competition.

NOTES: Steve Allen made a few 45 singles that have appeared on albums: "Very Square Dance" is available on "Laugh of the Party" (Coral CRL 57017). "What is a Freem" is a nonsense parody of Arthur Godfrey's sappy "What is a Boy/What is a Girl" hit, with lines like "A freem is stupidity with a bone in its mouth." It's on "Fun Time" (Coral CRL 57072). "Schmock, Schmock" is on "Hollywood Hi-Fi" (Brunswick 81013).

In response to a (naive) query for this book, Steve emphasized that his album "What Is a Subud" (Hanover) is not funny, like "What Is a Freem": "The Subud album was simply a tape-recorded interview I did with a fellow who was at the time the American head of the Subud religious-philosophical movement. Because of the album a lot of true believers assumed that I was a member of the fold, but that was not the case. In any event, it wasn't a funny album. At least not intentionally."

Allen also recorded two singles of "Hip Fables" (Brunswick 80231 and 80228), two singles with Jayne Meadows ("What Is a Wife/What Is a Husband" Coral 9-61552 and "Flattery/I Remember it Well" Signature 12003). There is also a rare 78: "But Baby/But Officer" (Brunswick 80230). He plays backup piano on the full-length hip fables comedy album by Al Collins. Allen has read excerpts from his various books on cassette.

In the early '50s, Steve had his own nightly CBS radio show. Some samples of it are on a promotional album issued by CBS, "Five Exciting New Radio Shows," which also features excerpts from *Horatio Hornblower*, *The Frank Fontaine Show*, *Gunsmoke*, and *December Bride*. He interviews a serviceman, who says "I'd like to say hello to the folks back home and my girlfriend Joyce." "They're all rooming together, are they? Where's home, Sergeant?" "Woonsocket, Rhode Island." (Applause.) "Let me see, you said Woonsocket and a lot of people screamed. Are you from Rhode Island, or have you had your woon socked?"

WOODY ALLEN

- WOODY ALLEN (Colpix CP/SCP 518 re-released as THE WACKY WORLD OF WOODY ALLEN on Bell Records, re-released as part of two-record sets listed separately) **** $10 $20
- WOODY ALLEN VOLUME 2 (Colpix CP 488, re-released as part of a two-record set listed separately) **** $10 $20
- WOODY ALLEN THREE (Capitol ST 2986, re-released as part of a two-record set listed separately) **** $10 $20

Woody Allen's stand-up years were very painful. The former Allen Konigsberg remembers "I'd feel this fear in my stomach every morning, the minute I woke up, and it would be there until I went on at eleven o'clock at night." No wonder he shifted to films. But out of this pain came three great albums.

Recorded in 1964 at Mr. Kelly's in Chicago, "Woody Allen" has a huge black and white photo of sorrowful, mousy Woody on the front—and recipes on the back for "Baked Wild Rice," "Monday's Oxtail Ragout," "Eggplant Casserole," and others. It's loaded with one-liners about Allen's hideous past, including childhood baseball games ("I used to steal second base—and feel guilty and go back"). He gets up to his college days ("I was thrown out of NYU ... on my metaphysics final I looked within the soul of the boy sitting next to me") and his marriage ("... or as it was known: "The Ox-Bow Incident").

"Volume Two" has a pop art portrait of Allen on the front cover, and on the back, photos from *What's New Pussycat* and private life (Woody in the graduating class picture of Public School 99 in 1949). This 1965 release is broken up into bands. He's experimenting with short comic stories here, like "The Moose," a brilliant shaggy moose story about a costume party, and "Science Fiction," a fantasy about superior beings from another planet invading the Earth to get their laundry done.

Also highlights: an anecdote about being with Hemingway and Gertrude Stein in Paris (later reworked into "A Twenties Memory" and published in his first book, *Getting Even*) and a wonderfully created kidnap yarn. Woody's father is told to leave the ransom money in a hollow tree in New Jersey: "He had no trouble raising the money, but he got a hernia carrying the hollow tree."

Though he made a few appearances after, Allen's stand-up career climaxed in 1968 with the release of Volume 3. It shows the comedian at the height of his powers, with nowhere else to go but to more challenging media. There are one-liners, surreal stories (the nightmare world of deliberately malfunctioning toasters and an anti-Semitic talking elevator), and moments of intensely personal humor (Woody describes how to "prolong the moment of ecstasy" by thinking about baseball during sex).

The nervous comic is even relaxed enough to banter with the audience for a "question and answer" session. A woman asks, "Have you ever been picked up by a homosexual?" Allen says, "No sir ... any further queries?" Later, "Is that a hand up? And a good hand, I might add. Five fingers all placed in the right order. Shouldn't the thumb be on the end, though?" The segment is unavailable on the compilation reissue of the concert, though it certainly displays another dimension to Allen's career in stand-up.

- WOODY ALLEN : THE NIGHTCLUB YEARS (United Artists UAS 9968) **** $10 $20
- WOODY ALLEN: STAND-UP COMIC 1964-1968 (United Artists UA LA 849J2, re-released as Casablanca NBLP 2-7145) **** $10 $20

"The Nightclub Years," released in 1972, was the first attempt to compile the best from Allen's three albums. The light-brown cover portrait of Allen bears one of his classic expressions of depression and alarm. The timings were as follows: Side One (20:54), Side Two (21:55), Side Three (24:04), Side Four (25:55).

In 1978, the three albums were re-edited for "Stand-Up Comic." The new compilation timings were the following: Side One (15:03), Side Two (15:41), Side Three (21:25), Side Four (18:10).

The first compilation had been fairly chronological. Sides One and Two were mostly from the March 1964 disc (a final five-minute fragment was from 1968). Side Three was the April 1965 date, and Side Four condensed the August 1968 concert. The revised double album changes the order somewhat: Side Three is 1968 and Side Four is 1965. In the re-release on Casablanca, Side One is 1968, Side Two is 1965, and the last two records are 1964!

This may all seem immensely trivial, but as long as Woody Allen bothered to make these changes, they are faithfully reported here.

What exactly did Woody Allen edit? Well, "Nightclub Years" for example, contains a long routine about the time Woody rode the subway, going to a birthday party dressed as Superman. He tries to rescue Hermina Jaffe (she had the sexiest overbite in Brooklyn) from the clutches of Guy de Maupassant Rabinowitz (whose parents, in the Roosevelt-Dewey election, had voted for Hitler). The story ends with courageous Woody failing to curb "Guy De" as the doors to the subway close on his Superman cape and drag him through the subway tunnel ("which is safer than riding inside the cars"). On "Stand-Up Comic" the entire bit is snipped out and the album is six minutes shorter on that side.

Allen also snipped bits and pieces from his 1968 show. Originally issued on Capitol and lasting thirty-six minutes, including a long question and answer ad-lib segment, it was chopped down to twenty-six minutes for the "Night Club Years" reissue and then chopped to twenty-one and a half minutes for "Stand-Up Comic," with Woody rethinking what was worth keeping.

By 1991 Woody's attitude had changed to the point that he probably could've edited it all down to a 45 rpm single: "It sounds pretty terrible to me when I listen to it. I sound pretty repulsive and obnoxious ... all those stupid girl-chasing jokes and sex jokes and, you know, self-deprecating stuff ... all that bullshit about being short and unloved."

NOTES: Woody Allen's double set is on domestic cassette. A CD was issued by EMI in England and as an import turns up often in major record stores. Soundtrack albums were released for some of Allen's films, some including dialogue: "What's Up Tiger Lily?" (Kama Sutra 8053) and "Play It Again Sam" (Paramount 1004). Allen can also be heard on "That Was the Week That Was" (Radiola MR 1123) doing a few gags never committed to disc before: "I had a bad marriage. My wife and I thought we were in love, but it turned out to be benign." Diehards may want to hear him play clarinet on the Eddie Davis CD "The Bunk Project" (Music Masters 650982).

ALLEN AND GRIER

- BETTER TO BE RICH THAN ETHNIC (FM Records FMLP 305) * $3 $7

Belting loud and obvious tunes got this male (Allen) and female (Grier) folkie duo noticed back in 1963, but only momentarily at New York's Bitter End and Chicago's Gate O' Horn. This studio album (guitar accompaniment only, no audience) covers a dozen songs, most written by John and Kay Holmes. The Kingston Trio recorded funnier songs on their straight albums and weren't prone to cloying overacting.

"Hyena Baby" is a parody of rock songs complete with annoying yodels and squeals and "Basketball Bill" a toothless satire of corruption. Bill threw the big game: "There's a moral for all young athletes. If it's money that you want to get, don't shave points in a basketball game. Shave on television for Gillette!" Dumb but kind of funny is "Celebrities Cake Walk," a set of lyrics with punned names in it: "with a frightful torrent of Claude Rains, Gale Storm came from Mae West. A Merv Griffin with Warren Beatty eyes flew to Conway Twitty's nest. The wind blew through the Natalie Wood, it slapped the John Birch trees, it wrecked the Yma Sumac and scattered Chuck Berries."

ALLEN AND ROSSI (with Bernie Allen)

- SEX IS ... (Cappo CPS 1001) *1/2 $5 $10

In the early '70s fans of "Allen and Rossi" were surprised when a new record appeared from the long disbanded duo. A close look revealed that the pudgy, older-looking "Allen" wasn't Marty, but Bernie Allen. Bernie, an ex-luncheonette owner and cab driver, got into show biz when customer Rocky Graziano enjoyed his wisecracks. Bernie was known for a stand-up bit as a stereotypical German telling risqué jokes about the old "fokker" he used to fly. He brought blue material to this version of Allen and Rossi, which led to sternly disapproving reviews in *Variety*.

The album is a succotash of corn and sleaze, including a segment in which Steve interviews "gay" Bernie.

When Steve got the chance to reteam with Marty Allen, he dropped Bernie instantly.

ALLEN AND ROSSI (with Marty Allen)

- HELLO DERE (ABC Paramount ABC 2270) ** $5 $10
- ONE MORE TIME HELLO DERE (ABC Paramount ABC S 445) ** $5 $10
- TOO FUNNY FOR WORDS (Reprise R 6104) *** $8 $15

The most popular nightclub comics of the early '60s, ready to be the new Martin and Lewis, Steve Rossi was the nice looking Italian singer and Marty Allen the childlike Jewish badboy. "Hello Dere" was a gold record in 1962. Badboy Marty Allen steps onstage and in his nasal, naughty voice recites: "Double your pleasure, double your fun. Get yourself two broads instead of just one." And then, "Roses are reddish, violets are bluish, if it wasn't for Christmas, the whole world'd be Jewish."

Steve Rossi quickly puts an end to the nonsense with some serious questions: "What do you think about the Taft-Hartley bill?" Allen: "I think we oughta pay it." As was to become their stock style, Rossi is straight man to Marty Allen's various characters, such as Wine Tester, Japanese Ball Player, and Christopher Columbus:

"Hello dere, my name is Christopher Columbus." "When were you born?" "On Columbus Day!" "What are you famous for?" "I'm a great lover." "What do you mean by that?" "Ever hear of the nights of Columbus?" "Who did you make love to?" "Nina, Pinta, and Santa Maria." "Those are ships." "It wasn't easy."

Major cuts on the second album include "The Lion Tamer," "The Golfer" and "The Punch Drunk Fighter." From the latter, some typically pat patter: "Tell me, how many fights have you had?" "Hundreds." "How many did you lose?" "Hundreds!" "How do you explain that?" "You can't win 'em all." "What is the first thing you think about when you get in the ring?" "How to get out." Steve Rossi gets to solo on the song "Because You're Mine."

In the early '60s, silliness and lighthearted comedy were coming into style (Bill Dana's Jose Jimenez, Vaughn Meader's harmless "First Family" album, discs from childlike comics Bill Cosby and The Smothers Brothers, etc.). In clubs, this naive humor, spiked with risqué gags, was just the right formula, and mop-haired little Marty Allen and his shy catchphrase "Hello Dere" couldn't be topped. At least, not for a few years.

"Too Funny," with Allen assuming a dozen interview disguises, is better recorded than the 1962 and 1963 ABC discs, and the jokes come a bit faster. Allen is varied as a bullfighter, folksinger, football coach, mechanical man, Japanese teenager, CIA chief, and so on. Of course it's still vintage Allen and Rossi: "Do you come from a large family?" "I got eighteen brothers and twelve sisters." "What does your father do?" "I don't know, but whatever it is he better cut it out."

- IN PERSON (Mercury SR 60979) **1/2 $5 $10
- GREAT SOCIETY (Mercury SR 61015) ** $4 $8

Allen and Rossi's first Mercury album has the standard interview material like "Marty the Spy," "Marty the Boy Scout" and "Marty the Indian": "Sir, I don't believe I have your name." "What's *your* name?" "Steve Rossi." "No, you don't have my name...." "Haven't I seen your face before?" "Yeah, on a nickel." "You mean the one with the buffalo on the back?" "That's my wife!" "... Do you hunt deer?" "Yes, darling ... don't ask me if I hunt bear."

"Great Society" is atypical for the duo—a set of thirty blackouts recorded live in a studio with a supporting cast including Dyanne Thorne and Carol McKinley. Marty slaps on a Southern accent to play LBJ, and takes a few other roles in quickies as well, including Martin Luther King, Jr. Here's the blackout with King:

"Rev. King, as sheriff of this here town, I have no jurisdiction to hold you in this here jailhouse. I will tell you one thing before you leave. Down the street to the right the Ku Klux Klan is waiting for you, and down the street to the left is the FBI."

"Can I have a minute to think it over?"

- BATMAN AND RUBIN (Mercury SR 61077) ** $10 $25
- TRUTH ABOUT THE GREEN HORNET (Roulette 507) *1/2 $5 $10
- DEDICATED TO OUR ARMED FORCES (Roulette 508) ** $8 $15

After trying political satire with "The Great Society" album, in 1966 and 1967 the team tried the other extreme of catering more toward a teenage audience, since kids always responded to Marty the Little Monster. By this time the momentum was with the new top comedy teams, The Smothers Brothers, and Rowan and Martin.

The "Batman and Rubin" album is the most noteworthy of the later albums, only because Batman creator Bob Kane actually wrote it, lampooning his own comic strip. The sketches aren't much. Batman (Rossi) must deal with a schlemiel partner, Rubin (Allen):

"Quick, Rubin, we haven't a second to lose. To the batpoles!"

"Oy, holy icicles! That's cold! Sure you didn't want to be a fireman when you were a kid?"

"Come on, Rubin, stop clowning!"

Or start! The album was released the same year as the duo's movie *Last of the Secret Agents.*

Allen and Rossi's *Green Hornet* parody (with supporting players Sterling Yates and Sharon Dale) is quick (under ten minutes per side) and sloppily done as the duo ad-lib out of character to the sparse but snickering studio audience. Allen puts on an Asian accent as Ca-Toe, sidekick to the Green Horn-Nut:

"How do you learn to do Kung-Fu?" "You break things like telephone poles with your bare hands and bare feet." "Will that help me protect myself?" "Sure, if you're ever attacked by telephone poles...." "Tell me, Ca-Toe, were you ever in the army?" "Yeah, I practice Kung-Fu in army and almost kill myself." "What happened?" "I salute general and crack my skull in half...." "Great. Now here's what I want you to do. I want you to get out of my life!" "If I do, you'll be stuck with this album!"

The title of Allen and Rossi's last album was true. Their profits were donated to the USO. Rossi takes up time with two solo song medleys plus the schmaltzy "See the Funny Clown." Together they reprise some of their older material and then simply reprise old jokes:

"You're a winetaster?" "No, I'm your Avon representative." "You look like you drink a lot." "You'd drink too if you had my problem." "What's your problem?" "I'm an alcoholic...." "What's the difference between an Irish wedding and an Irish wake?" "One less drunk."

The duo broke up by the end of the decade, with Rossi teaming with aging Joe E. Ross briefly, Slappy White (see "Rossi and White"), and Bernie Allen. In 1983 Allen and Rossi reteamed.

NOTES: "Punch Drunk Fighter" from "One More Time Hello Dere" is on "25 Years of Recorded Comedy" (Warner Bros 3BX 3131). Allen alone is on "Zingers from The Hollywood Squares" (Event Ev 6903) : "Oscar Wilde once said of it, it's the perfect type of a perfect pleasure, yet it leaves you unsatisfied. What was he referring to?" "A legitimate massage parlor!" They issued a few singles including "Little Sir Echo" (ABC 10393) and "Sway" (Calla 110). Their Batman parody album has extra interest from Batman fans and comic book collectors.

SHELDON ALLMAN

- FOLK SONGS FOR THE 21ST CENTURY (HiFi R 415) *1/2 $7 $15
- SING ALONG WITH DRAC (Delfi DFLP 1213) **1/2 $10 $25
- DRUNKS (Delfi DFLP 12170) * $7 $15

Circa 1961 Sheldon Allman released a quickie album of songs keyed to a fad for sci-fi movies and the current "race for space." The simple pop-jazz songs and mild lyrics aren't very impressive, most sounding about at the level of a Dr. Seuss cartoon special.

Allman's jolly, slightly gooey baritone (similar to Thurl Ravenscroft) lends some fun to the upbeat numbers like "Schizophrenic Baby" and the rock rave-up "Radioactive Mama," but nothing here is very memorable. One of the better tunes is the cheerful, lightly sick "Crawl Out Through the Fallout." Belting it out with the enthusiasm of a Jack Jones he ends: "If you cannot find the way just listen for my song. I'll love you all your life, although that may not be too long. Crawl out through the fallout, baby. To my lovin' arms. While those ICBM's keep us free. When ya hear me call out, baby, kick the wall out! And crawl out through the fallout back to me!"

"Sing Along with Drac," an early '60s bid to join Zacherly and others in the horror novelty craze, is eerie and offbeat. A jazz combo plus organ backs Allman as he sings in a deliberately dark, deeply sleepy voice (with a faint Transylvanian, Peter Lorre, or Karloff accent, depending on the song). New lyrics are grafted to slow, intimate tunes including "A Cottage for Sale," "They Can't Take That Away from Me," and "Among My Souvenirs." The result will strike some fans of the genre as monotonous; others will consider it a nicely numbing narcotic. "These Foolish Things Remind Me of You" now includes:

"The blood-stained towels that lie there on the tiling. Your head is in the sink and still it's smiling. But I won't leave a clue. These ghoulish things behind me were you.... Your eyes. Your ears. Your curly hair. I said a little prayer as I just tossed them anywhere. Your hands and feet, I threw into the river. I made a good luck charm out of your liver. But oh, how the ghost of you clings. These ghoulish things behind me were you."

Dry and deadpan Allman was a contrast to all the cheerfully manic monster parodists.

Allman does saloon interviews and candid microphone-style put-ons for "Drunks." One tedious routine has Allman deliberately locked in a bar's phone booth with a sullen man who eventually gets annoyed enough to start cursing (expletives censored with buzzing noises). Also, for fun, Allman sits at a bar and tells different drinking companions that he walked in on his wife making love with another guy. And it was their anniversary, too, and he'd bought her a $40 present, which now sits all wrapped up on the bar. None of them have anything bright to say, although one man does think he should now give her a ballpoint pen instead.

BILLY ALLYN

• MIRTHQUAKE (Combo 900) **	$4	$10
• EARTHY MIRTH (Dooto DTL 826) *1/2	$4	$10
• LAFF OF THE PARTY (Dooto DTL 824) *1/2	$4	$10

Billy Allyn was just another black comic in the Dooto stable. On his first, for Combo, the laid-back Allyn goes through the motions: "This preacher, he wanted to open up a new church, and he went to the congregation. He put all his initials behind his name 'cause he wanted to make an impression. He put B.S. M.S.P.H.D. ... One nosy sister, she walked up to him and said, 'Rev, what does that B.S. M.S.P.H.D. mean?' He said, 'Well, sister, you know what B.S. means.' She said, 'Yes.' 'Well, M.S.P.H.D. means "More of same, piled higher and deeper."' He wanted a bigger church so he said, 'All you members got to get out here and work, and you got to work and work like beavers.' One sister jumped up in the corner and said, 'But reverend, beavers work with their tails.' He said, 'All reet then!'"

The sound quality on the Dooto albums doesn't help his slightly mumbly delivery or the familiar jokes. On "Laff of the Party" he says: "I saw a girl the other day. I said, 'Do you like cocktails?' She said, 'Yeah, tell one.' Like, speaking about things like that, a friend of mine got married. Honeymoon. First night. The wife said, 'How about it, John?' He didn't say nothing. She said, 'John, how about it.' He said, 'How about what?' She said, 'How about us gettin' some sleep!'"

JEFF ALTMAN

• THE WASHINGTON HILLBILLIES (Casablanca NBLP 7052) *1/2	$3	$7
• I'LL FLIP YOU LIKE A CHEESE OMELETTE (Mercury/Polygram) **		$8

A "First Family" attempt during the Jimmy Carter years, the script is written to formula, including the news conference:

"Jack Feinberg, the Jewish Daily Forward ... who do you intend to appoint as Ambassador of Israel?"

"Henny Youngman ... first of all, he's a lot funnier than Dr. Kissinger and I like his timing better...."

"Many people think you are still not well-versed in affairs of state. How do you feel about that?"

"I feel that's totally unjustified. Presently I'm personally involved in the planning and implementation of viable programs for a number of State Fairs...."

Altman went on to TV commercials, stand-up, and eventually released a CD. Influenced by Jonathan Winters (Jeff told me how much he admired how onstage and off, Jonny's mind "keeps turning" with comic ideas), there's a lot of "you hadda be there" humor here. Jeff has to be seen—the way this mild, normal looking guy suddenly goes berserk with funny faces and high-energy schtick. Fans do get Altman's trademark bit. Hiking his pants up to his chest, he imitates his quivering, raging father: "I'll sink you like a three-foot putt, ya little bastard, I'll hit you so hard your kids'll be born dizzy ... I'll flip you like a cheese omelette."

AMERICAN COMEDY NETWORK

• OUTRAGEOUS RADIO (Compose 99052) *1/2	$8

The network, a dozen or more writers and performers, supplies high-energy low-mentality songs and gags to radio personalities too pinheaded to even attempt their own. Now and then there's about five seconds of amusement (a mock commercial with Roseanne Barr pushing her perfume "Derriere," a Stevie Nicks sound-alike mumbling unintelligibly) but the premise is always bludgeoned for an extra minute and it's impossible to tolerate more than a few cuts at a time of the predictable, deliberate wackiness.

"The Good Morning Song" for example consists of a saccharine choir chirping "good morning" until they all harmonize with: "... you look like hell!" An ad for "Smokers Airlines" includes the jingle: "We put the tar in tarmac, we put our heart in your heart attack. It's no joke—when you're going up in smoke you're goin' Smokers Airlines." And a fast food parody ad declares: "When you get that craving for mushrooms, molds, or any other kind of parasitic lower plant life ... come on down to The Fungus Hut! We have deep fried toadstools, mold shakes, and for dessert, hot mushroom pies ... Yeaaaah!"

AMOS AND ANDY

• AMOS AND ANDY STORY (Radiola 2 MR 2526) **1/2	$10	$20

Freeman Gosden and Charles Correll were Amos Jones and Andy Brown, radio's top comedy team. Their black dialect ("I gonna 'splain it to ya") amused generations, and stars like Johnny Carson and Dean Martin enjoyed dropping a catchphrase now and then. Through the years, some questioned the "racist" idea of whites imitating blacks. Others had no problem since the show demonstrated such warm character comedy (and set the standard and style for most radio and early TV sitcoms to follow).

The debate over Amos and Andy continues: Were the two white men making fun of blacks or celebrating their language and lifestyle? "The Amos and Andy Story" is as good a place to decide as any. The double set collects some of their earliest and latest broadcasts, including four complete fifteen-minute shows from 1929; a half hour show (October 10, 1948); a September 23, 1954, broadcast; and two 78 rpm records ("I'se Regusted" and "Presidential Election"). Also included is a docudrama, "The Life Story of Amos 'n Andy," a special 25th Anniversary show recorded on February 14, 1953. An interesting moment re-creates how the duo refined their actual speaking voices for the parts: one trying to get hoarser, the other being coached to let his voice ooze down an octave. Finally, the duo think they're ready to go on the air: "I think we done got somethin' here."

- AMOS AND ANDY BEST LOVED SHOWS (Murray Hill 89763) **1/2 $10 $25
- AMOS AND ANDY CLASSICS (Murray Hill 53622) **1/2 $10 $25
- LEGENDARY AMOS AND ANDY (MURRAY HILL 58616) **1/2 $10 $25
- RARE AMOS AND ANDY (Murray Hill 62206) **1/2 $10 $25

Murray Hill's boxed sets offer three records each. "Best Loved" has six different half hour shows broadcast July 12, 1946; July 6, 1948; October 10, 1948; October 17, 1948; November 16, 1952; and February 14, 1953 (the "Anniversary" Show). "Classics" includes favorite episodes "Kingfish Adopts Andy," "Andy Seeks a Mail Order Bride," and "Sapphire Discovers Someone Has Given Her a Mink Coat." The "Legendary" set includes the time Andy went to work as a department store Santa, and two tales of Sapphire: the time her boss proposed to her, and the day Kingfish tried to buy her a gold bracelet. "Rare" features "Andy Plays Sailor" (May 25, 1945), "Secret Honeymoon" (October 28, 1945), and "Andy Photographs Robbers" (March 6, 1949) among others.

- AMOS AND ANDY (Radiola MR 1074 and CD MR 1074) **1/2 $8
- RAREST AMOS AND ANDY (Radiola MR 1134) **1/2 $5 $10
- THE CHRISTMAS SHOW (Radiola MR 1004) **1/2 $5 $10
- AMOS AND ANDY (Radio Greats R 6101) **1/2 $5 $10
- AMOS AND ANDY (Yorkshire LP 714) **1/2 $5 $10
- AMOS AND ANDY 1943 (Memorabilia MLP 707) **1/2 $4 $8
- AMOS AND ANDY 1949 (Memorabilia MLP 708) **1/2 $4 $8
- AMOS AND ANDY 1955 (Memorabilia MLP 709) **1/2 $4 $8
- AMOS AND ANDY (Mar-Bren MBR 742) **1/2 $5 $10
- ORIGINAL RADIO BROADCASTS (Golden Age GA 5036) **1/2 $5 $8
- AMOS AND ANDY (Nostalgia Lane NLR 1024) **1/2 $5 $10

Among the single discs of shows, Radiola's "Amos and Andy" is among the best, offering episodes from October 31, 1948, and April 3, 1949. It was reissued on CD.

Four fifteen-minute shows appear on the "Rare" Radiola disc, including "The Marriage of Andrew Brown," which unfortunately is incomplete, with a cliffhanger ending to be continued. The disc also includes a 1936 show with guest Walter Huston, and the 1941 Christmas Show.

Memorabilia breaks up their episodes by year. The Mar-Bren set shows are from April 3, 1949, and November 17, 1944. The Golden Age album is February 23, 1945, and March 2, 1945. Nostalgia Lane's offerings are November 11, 1947, and January 13, 1948.

NOTES: The compilation album "Jest Like Old Times" (Radiola #1) offers three long excerpts from *Amos and Andy* shows: "How Kingfish Met Andy," "Andy's Introduction to Madame Queen," and a typical plot where Kingfish tries to swindle Andy for $100. A dull 78 rpm single from 1929, "The Dairy," turns up on "Golden Age of Comedy" (RCA Victor LPV 580), and an *Amos and Andy* show is on the flip side of an Abbott and Costello record from Radiex (Radiex 6). A half hour episode appears on "The Great Radio Comedians" (Murray Hill M5419X).

MOREY AMSTERDAM

- YUK-A-PUK (Signature 1023, reissued as THE NEXT ONE WILL KILL YOU (Roulette R 25196) **1/2
                                                                                                $10 $20

Long before *The Dick Van Dyke Show*, Morey Amsterdam was billed as "the human joke machine" of stand-up. He also had some hit songs, including "Yuk-a-Puk." The Signature album was recorded sans audience. It's a bit odd, but Amsterdam does a good job of timing his jokes for anticipated laughter, and keeping a conversational style as if only expecting a chuckle or two in return. The vaudeville-styled yucks are chuckle bait at best. He does a set of drunk jokes, psychiatrist bits, and in one segment decides to try monology as a baby:

"I am a baby. I am three months old. I would've been seven months old but my folks lived in Hackensack for two years. Not much of a joke, but what do you expect from a baby? I was born on Thanksgiving. Everybody thought I was a turkey. When I was born I was no stranger to Momma and Poppa, they knew my name right away. Some name. My momma's name was Anna, and my poppa's name is Ben. So they called me Ben-Anna. Very appealing. Of course I'm luckier than my friend. His father's name is Ferdinand and his mother's name is Liza, so they call him Ferd– well, you know."

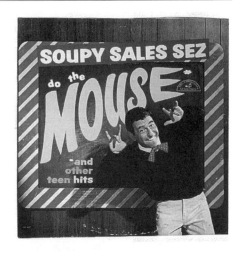

KID STUFF

"Get them young, and they're fans for life." If you
heard any of these albums as a kid, you'll find
'em still pretty funny now: Morey Amsterdam,
Soupy Sales, and The Three Stooges (with Joe
DeRita).

A PROFESSOR AND A PHILOSOPHER

Eddie Lawrence's albums are among the most prized by cultists and collectors. The odd Professor
Backwards made only one album, sought for its rarity, his comic talents, and the notoriety he received
as one of show biz's few murdered comedians. Chevy Chase on Saturday Night Live gleefully announced that Professor Backwards's last word was: "Pleh!"

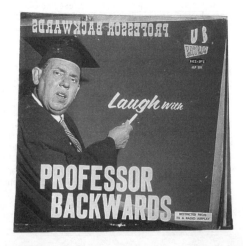

Novelty tunes break things up, with Amsterdam's theme song "Yuk-a-Puk" included. The lyrics here are different from his original 78 rpm single: "It's easy to grin when your ship comes in, and life is a happy lot. But the man who's worthwhile is the man who can smile when his shorts creep up in a knot. Yuk-a-puk, yuk-a-puk, yuk-a-puk."

The original Signature album has a full-color cover shot of Morey with his cello, and album notes by Morey himself. The Roulette reissue, trying to cash in on his TV sitcom success, has a close-up of Amsterdam near a dart-spiked dart board. It's in deference to the dart board prominently on the wall of the writer's office on *The Dick Van Dyke Show*.

- FUNNY YOU SHOULD ASK (MARSH MLP 101M) *** $10 $20

With Richard Deacon as straight man, and Rose Marie making two cameo appearances, Amsterdam portrays famous men from history, including P. T. Barnum, Buffalo Bill, and Christopher Columbus:

"Mr. Columbus, now that you've returned to us after having been a statue in Columbus Circle in New York for so many years, what's the first thing you'd like to do?" "I'd like to kill about three million pigeons...." "Mr. Columbus, how did you happen to discover America?" "Oooh! So big! How could I miss it!" "That's charming. Wasn't it really because you thought the world was round?" "That's right. I think the world is round, everybody else say the world is flat. But we're all wrong. The world is crooked...." "How did you ever get the money for your famous voyage?" "I wrote a check." "But in those days there was no such thing as writing checks." "That's why every year on Columbus Day they close up all the banks."

Vaudeville-corny, but always fast and fun, Deacon is the perfect stodgy deadpan foil to the puckish little Morey. Dick Van Dyke drew the cover portrait of Amsterdam.

- UNCLE MOREY'S MIXED UP STORIES FOR SMART KIDS (Golden LP 164)*** $12 $25

Recorded at the time of the *Dick Van Dyke Show*, Morey's stories could have amused that show's "Little Ritchie," or any other "smart kid" with a love of silly quips. Amsterdam rewrites "Bo Peep," "The Three Little Pigs," "Cinderella," "Carmen," and "Ali Babi" with typical gags. There's even sprightly music and some singing. Typical of the fun: "Rip Van Winkle didn't have a hair on his head. Not even eyebrows. If you looked at Rip from a few feet away it looked like his neck was blowing bubble gum. He was so bald he had to carry his dandruff around in his hand. And boy was he lazy. Rip would stay up all night so he wouldn't have to wash his face in the morning. Or he would take a snooze before he went to sleep. That was so he wouldn't be too tired when he was resting up for his nap. And boy was he absent-minded. He used to kiss the dirty dishes good night and throw his wife in the sink."

NOTES: Morey also appears on Max Asnas's album "Corned Beef Confucius" (Kimberly 2006). Amsterdam issued several novelty 45s, including "Cheese and Crackers" (Columbia), "Oh That'll Be Joyful" b/w "Halabaloo Kalafer Dofer" (MGM), and "Sue Me" (RCA). His 78s from the '40s include "Yuk a Puk" (Apollo), "Why Oh Why Did I Ever Leave Wyoming" (Lissen), and "Ugly Will from Uglyville" (Lissen). A three-78 set, "Party Songs," was issued by Crown and includes "Melodrama," "With His Wonderful Irish Brogue," "Saloon," "True Mon True," "Your Baby Has Gone Down the Drainpipe," and "How Does It Feel."

BONNIE ANDERSON

- UNPREDICTABLE: WRECKS THE WRECK (Art 36) $5 $10
- WRECKS THE WRECK AGAIN (Art 67) $5 $10

LEONA ANDERSON

- MUSIC TO SUFFER BY (Unique LP 115) ** $8 $20

Billed as "The World's Most Horrible Singer," Anderson was the kid sister of Bronco Billy Anderson. She appeared in silent films, notably "Mud and Sand" with Stan Laurel. Later she did a stage act that parodied vocalists. Here she accentuates a low note with a crowing caw ("I Love Paris"), hops, skips, and jumps on a note that's supposed to slide gracefully ("The Indian Love Call" and Chloe"), and turns a seductive ballad (the "Habanera from Carmen") into an off-key mess. This doesn't mean the result is hilarious. About ten seconds of any song is enough. There should've been more full-fledged novelty cuts like the bolero-style "Rats in My Room." On that one she croaks: "Every day I've got more rats in my room. Guess I better get some cats in my room so they can handle all those rats in my room. Cheese! I love to taste some cheese. I could accomplish that with ease, except my cupboard's always empty and bare. Because those dirty little rrrrats have been there!"

ANGELINA

- Confidential (Davis 112) ** $6 $15

One of the lesser vocalists on the Davis label of off-color songstresses, Angelina blandly croons risqué oldies by Andy Razaf: "Vice Versa," "Working Girl," "What a Man!" and, with Spencer Williams, "Electrician Blues." A real jazz singer could've raved some life into these tunes, but tranquil Angelina doesn't seem to even understand the double entendres on "Electrician Blues," like: "... my front lights aren't working and my double sockets are loose. Come look at my meter. Think I gotta have some juice ... last night I had no trouble and my fan was goin' fine. Stopped and I discovered a short circuit in my line."

ANSPACH AND SILVER

- BEWARE OF GREEKS BEARING GIFTS (Musicor MXS 3173) * $3 $7

The writer/producer team of Bob Booker and George Foster should've known better. When Jackie Kennedy married Aristotle Onassis, the American public didn't find anything remotely funny about it. And how many jokes could be concocted about an obscenely rich man and an ex-president's wife?

Recorded almost on the fifth anniversary of JFK's assassination (November 24, 1968), the album stars Joe Silver and Susan Anspach, who displays all the comic instincts of a Shredded Wheat biscuit. Typical of the stretched out blackout sketches is the scene in which a Brink's courier arrives at Jackie's door:

"Madam: (sound effects of heavy coins) Five bags American currency. (More coins clinking.) Twelve bags sterling silver. (Clinking coins, groaning as he lifts them.) Thirty-five bars of gold bullion." "See how generous he is? All I asked for was a quarter for the ladies room."

ANTHONY AND ROBERTS

- PEED OFF (Dingo D-2001) *1/2 $4 $8

Mike Anthony and Bert Roberts were billed as "The Madcaps" in the '60s, but there's nothing zany about their familiar (i.e. old) adult patter and song parodies. The ringsider banter is predictable, too: "What do you do, sir?" "He's a pimp." "That is not nice." "He's a nookie bookie!" "That's better. What kind of work do ya do?..." "He drives a truck." "Oh yeah? A dairy queen! A milkman in high heels!"

DANNY APOLINAR

- COME BY SUNDAY (Stereoddities 1904) $5 $10

Apolinar, called "a cross between Jerry Lewis and Pat Suzuki" by Dorothy Kilgallen, doesn't do much comedy even though the album jacket is loaded with news columnists' praise for his funny routines. The 1964 disc offers songs ("The Lady is a Tramp," "Got a Lot of Livin' to Do," "Thank Heaven for Little Girls," etc.) done only slightly better than Jerry Lewis could do them. "I'd Rather Cha Cha Than Eat" is one of the few comedy tunes. Apolinar also issued "A Spot in the Sun" (Entertainment Associates 101) in 1968. In the '90s Apolinar continued to play the piano and sing at his own restaurant, "The Sea Palace" in New York.

EVE ARDEN

- OUR MISS BROOKS (Radio Archives 100) *1/2 $5 $10
- OUR MISS BROOKS (Memorabilia 728) *1/2 $4 $8

Eve Arden played the wisecracking English teacher Miss Connie Brooks both on radio and TV. Mild, silly sitcoms like this seem to survive better on television. On radio, concentrating on the lines is hardly worth the effort. On the Memorabilia album Miss Brooks comes to school with "all the enthusiasm of a sailor returning to his submarine after a two week vacation at Bali Bali." The record is loaded with that type of sarcasm. When student Walter Denton pipes up with a wrong answer, Miss Brooks sasses, "Why Walter, I didn't know you had it in you, and I wish you'd put it back."

A December 5, 1949, episode of *Our Miss Brooks* appears on the flip side of an album by Harold "Great Gildersleeve" Peary (Radiola 1020), and a November 21, 1948, episode is coupled with a *My Friend Irma* show (no record company info on the label).

ALAN ARKIN

- ONCE OVER LIGHTLY (Elektra 21) ** $5 $15

In 1955 Arkin was a folksinger and about two-thirds of the dozen songs are serious ("Kisses Sweeter Than Wine," "Colorado Trail," etc.) A few are decidedly peculiar. The folk song "Tom with a Grin" is about a strange fellow who steals a sheepskin so he can wear britches "with the fleshy side out and the woolly side in." Then there's "The Mad Count," about a fellow who was "mad as any loon," prone to dancing "with a broomstick for a partner." There's also "Anne Boleyn," with some black comedy about how she's now wandering around "with her head tucked underneath her arm." Arkin updates the old folk song a bit. When her ghost appears, "The sentries think that it's a baseball Annie's carrying in, and when they've had a few they shout, 'Hey is Brooklyn going to win?' For they think she's Pee-Wee Reese, instead of poor old Anne Boleyn."

Arkin would later join "The Tarriers" and cowrite the unfortunately immortal "Banana Boat Song" (the one with the shouts of "Day-o, Day-o" in it). He's also on a Vanguard album "The Best of the Baby Sitters." He can be heard doing comedy sketches on a few of The Second City albums, and playing instrumentals on one from risqué folkie Ed McCurdy.

ALICE ARTHUR

- A NATURAL TEN (Columbia JC 36800) ** $4 $8

Thanks to the flashy album cover, unknowing store owners thought Arthur was a black singer and stuck her 1980 album in the disco or R&B music section; *knowing* store owners figured her album belonged there anyway, since her main topics for comedy are black singers. As Diana Ross, she mimics the singer's wan ballad style and raves about her latest promotional item: "My new Diana Ross doll. It sings, it acts, and if you slap it, it goes: "Berry Gordy! Berry Gordy! Save me! Save me!"

Later she talks about Barry White, "the 450 pound sex symbol. Can you imagine Barry White's bed? If it was a water bed they'd probably call it Lake Michigan. But I love him. I was at his first concert in Madison Square Garden. When he walked out onto the stage nobody in the audience could figure out whether he was coming to move the piano or play it!"

MAX ASNAS

- CORNED BEEF CONFUCIUS (KIMBERLY 2006) *1/2 $5 $15

Asnas, owner of New York's Stage Deli, was a beloved figure among show biz types, and like Yogi Berra in baseball, many gags were attributed to him. Supposedly Max once waited on three customers seated together. One said "Be sure when you bring the water, the glass is clean." When Max returned with his tray he said, "OK, which one wanted the clean glass?"

On this disc, poorly recorded live in the noisy deli, Jack E. Leonard tosses insults while Myron Cohen and Morey Amsterdam recall Max Asnas anecdotes and tell some one-liners. They all try to prompt the gravel-voiced, almost incomprehensible deli owner into telling some of his favorite jokes and ad-libbing some Asnas-isms. The comedians strain to keep things lively while Asnas mumbles, and dishes and silverware clatter. The record succeeds in one way: It gives some idea of what it might have been like to kibbitz with old-time comics over seltzer and sandwiches at their favorite joint.

MICHAEL ASPINALL

- THE SURPRISING SOPRANO (London OS 26537) * $4 $10

The surprise is that this soprano is a man. Billed as "a musical satirist," Aspinall enjoys lightly tweaking the "follies and foibles" of divas. Unlike the broader (in all senses) Anna Russell, Aspinall has a good voice and resists campiness. As he sings lieder ("Der Erlkonig"), Victorian songs ("The Cuckoo"), and classics from opera ("Vissi d'arte" from "Tosca") the jokes are his fey overenunciation, too cheery enthusiasm, and melodramatic trilling or vibrato. The audience giggles accordingly.

DAVE ASTOR

- WILL THE REAL DAVE ASTOR PLEASE STAND UP (Columbia CL1877/CS 8677) **1/2 $7 $15

In the early '60s Astor was a promising young comic working Mr. Kelly's in Chicago and The Blue Angel in New York. His delivery is quick and articulate, with just a trace of chichi affectation. The *New York Times* declared, "he will very probably take his place in the first rank of cabaret comics." It didn't work out, but this album displays the promise. Astor has a thinking man's approach to the basic jokes:

"Alcohol is good for you. My grandfather proved it irrevocably. He drank two quarts of booze every mature day of his life and lived to the age of 103. I was at the cremation. That fire would not go out.... Psychiatrists tell us one out of every five people is completely disturbed—and the reason is the other four are nuts.... Don't invest all your money in just one or two stocks. That's the danger. I know a man who put all his money in just two stocks, a paper-towel company and a revolving-door outfit. He was wiped out before he could turn around."

ALAN ATKINS

- SPIRO SAYS ABOUT FACE (A1-At Records AA-1) * $3 $8

On this dull studio album, sans audience, actors lifelessly go through some minor sketches attacking Spiro Agnew. At home, Agnew's wife asks what part of the turkey he wants for his Thanksgiving dinner. Punch line: "I'll have my favorite. The right wing."

Agnew's foot-in-mouth comments and bull-headed pomposity made him an inviting target for comics. Almost any anti-Agnew joke could get a laugh. But the ones here could only produce snickers among manic Agnew haters. Like the gag about a new toy on the market, the Spiro Agnew doll: "Wind it up and it becomes obnoxious."

Periodically, actual Spiro Agnew gaffes are read out loud with snotty comments after: "Spiro said on September 24, 1968, 'My golf game is so bad everything else I do looks good by comparison.' Not quite, sir, not quite."

GEORGE ATKINS AND HANK LEVINE

- SING ALONG WITH JFK (Reprise 6083) *1/2 $5 $15
- WASHINGTON IS FOR THE BIRDS (Reprise 6212) *** $7 $20

A little more ambitious than the average purveyors of "break-in" humor, Atkins and Levine tried to cut up politicians' speeches to create songs!

"Sing Along with JFK" doesn't quite have the technique down. Here, in a "call and response" style similar to a Mitch Miller "sing-along," Kennedy "recites" lyrics (clipped from his speeches) and a choir sings the line with grand élan. One cut is on the CD "Hollywood Hi-Fi" (Brunswick 81013).

On "Begin Anew for Two," for example, Kennedy says: "Let us begin." The chorus sings it. "Begin anew." Kennedy declares, "Civility is not a sign of weakness." The chorus wavers through that, too. And the rest of the speech goes the same way. The result is not exactly funny. In fact, parroting Kennedy's words musically ends up more an annoying mockery than anything else.

A few years later, though, the technique was perfected. "Washington Is for the Birds" has some amazing tracks. They aren't necessarily hilarious, but smart and creative novelties. One of the best is the opening cut, "Lady." On this, Lyndon Johnson's ballad to his wife, Johnson talk-sings, via nicely done tape splices, "Lady, I like the way you talk. Lady, I like the way you walk. I like the way, the way you do business! The might of past empires is little compared to ours. Lady, I want to talk to you today. Lady, there must be no delay ... so Lady, let us be on our way!"

Another stand-out cut is "You Don't Have Nixon to Kick Around Anymore." Backing vocalists sing this minor key lament with Dick Nixon talking through it a la some bad Brenda Lee ballad: "I made a flub. I made a flub. I lost the election. Just think how much you're gonna be missing. You don't have Nixon to kick around anymore." The original music is pretty good and so is the orchestration.

ROY ATWELL

- FAIRY TALES (Colpix CP 301) ** $5 $10

Atwell's specialties were tongue-twisters, spoonerisms, and a comic stutter. Sandy Baron wrote the script for this mild album of stories. An old-time performer who was a classmate of Cecil B. DeMille at New York's Sargeant School of Acting, Atwell was active in stage musicals (from 1907) and silent films, and went back to Broadway in the 1930s for *On to Foretune* and *Strike Me Pink*. He was also a regular on radio with Joe Penner. He died at the age of eighty-three on January 6, 1962.

PHIL AUSTIN

- ROLLER MAIDENS (Epic KE 32489) *1/2 $5 $15

A member of Firesign Theater, Austin went solo for this 1974 album. On the cover it looks like he's trying to be Jim Morrison: he's topless, posing with a moon and star sparkling on his chest. Only Morrison wouldn't have sung the cornball country rock tracks here. There's also a self-indulgent, long and aimless acid-tinged script about "Dick Private, Private Detective" (no competition for Nick Danger). The detective finds a clue: "String cheese. Fresno. Armenians. See, it all started to add up...." He's still clueless and only Firesign fans will have the patience to sit still for this. Austin fans will find their hero on 45s ("Duckman" Decca 31920) and audio books (notably "Tales of the Old Detective" from Audio Partners).

AVA

- A NIGHT WITH AVA (Borderline Records) ** $8 $15
- AVA MISBEHAVES (Borderline Records) ** $8 $15

A semi-sophisticated piano bar singer, Ava Williams was popular in the late '40s, on the bill with The Ink Spots and Jackie Gleason. She worked regularly in the '50s as well, and spent six years at Philadelphia's "Cambridge Club" and five in the "Jewel Room" at the Bostonion Hotel.

A bit jaded on these vintage albums, she doesn't seem to have her heart in her work anymore. She's more concerned with her lilting vibrato than the risqué lyrics, wishing she was Julie London and not Ruth Wallis. Her parody of "Secret Love": "Once I had a secret love, I wore a nylon negligee. When our night of love was through, I told him he didn't have to pay. When he asked me why my love was free, I told him Sealy Mattress sponsors me. Last night we were on Channel 4. Now our secret love's no secret anymore."

Though tired of tossing bright cracks at a dimly lit audience, her classy call-girl delivery lets her get away with some jokes that were wheezes even then, such as her line about being a streetwalker in Venice. She dares to talk about seeing a druggist: "My pleasure's men ... I came in for talcum powder." He says, 'Walk this way.' I said, 'If I could walk that way I wouldn't need the talcum powder.'"

ROY AWBREY

- LAUGH IT UP (Roy Awbrey RA-1) ** $5 $10
- COCK AND BULL TALES (Jubilee 2038) ** $5 $10
- BALD BILL (Stereo Fidelity 16800) ** $5 $10

"Triple threat" Awbrey not only told jokes, but resorted to pantomime and even used an electronic accordion for sound effects. His biggest fan was himself. The liner notes for his self-released "Laugh It Up" album declare, "Sensational is the word for Roy ... three acts all condensed into one: Wizard of the Accordion, Tops in Gags, and King of Pantomime." He's all right, but the albums would be more memorable if they featured his latter talent more than the former two.

JIM BACKUS

- DIRTY OLD MAN (Dore 332) ** $7 $15

Backus, plagued with health problems in his later years, is plagued with poor sound quality and the dubious guest appearances of Hudson and Landry on this 1970s disc. The disposable schtick with the duo hardly deserves to be preserved on wax. As a rich, Thurston Howell type, he's interviewed about a safari:

"I bagged that rhino you see there on the wall." "Aren't rhinos on the endangered species list?" "I think you can safely say that one is...." "Isn't going on safari terribly expensive?" "Expensive? It's outrageously expensive. That's why I love it—keeps the riff raff out of the jungle."

Some of the material is saved by the unique Backus voice, and his array of snickering laughs and eccentric mumbles. Soloing as Mr. Kelsey, an obnoxious airline passenger, Backus gives his listeners some idea of his sense of humor beyond the scripts of *Gilligan's Island*:

"I'm president of Kelsey's Nuts and Bolts. Got a little factory just outside of Ashtabula, Ohio, and in the winter it's cold enough to freeze your bolts! Not to mention ... heh heh ... lemme show you a picture of my wife. Uh oh, that's my membership card to the Benevolent Order of the Albino Beavers ... here's a picture of my wife, a dainty little heifer ... you can see that she's got Early American features. She's a dead ringer for Benjamin Franklin. And you see the kid between her legs is Mandrake, that's our only child, thank God."

The title cut "censors" crude dialogue with "nutty" sound effects. When Backus mutters, "I'll be dipped in —" the end of the sentence is replaced by a barrage of razzes, whoops, and whistles. This leaves something to the imagination, and a lot to be desired for laughs.

NOTES: Backus made occasional novelty singles including "Delicious" (Jubilee, reissued on Dr. Demento's 20th Anniversary CD set) and "I Was a Teenage Reindeer" (Dico). "Delicious" is a fairly famous laughing record. He and his lady sample champagne, snickering "Delicious!" until the laughs get louder and longer. His non-comedy albums include "The Little Prince" for Pip Records, and "Magoo in Hi-Fi" for RCA Victor, which has some of Magoo's mild mumblings as he demonstrates the wonders of hi-fi sound for his late '50s audience. He's not on half the album, which is given over to the "Mother Goose Suite" of music and piercing solos from a guest soprano. Backus made a children's LP for Wonderland Records (WLP 318) based on his cartoon character, Mr. Magoo.

HERMOINE BADDELEY

- A TASTE OF HERMOINE (Prestige/Lively Arts 30002) ** $8 $20

Without an audience, Baddeley sings cabaret material and presents monologue portraits of rich sophisticates. These are designed to be "droll," raising a polite titter or an appreciative nod rather than full-blooded laughs. Among the better ballads there's "You," a parody of inane, sickening love songs: "When you're far away I feel you're not here ... You are you, how can you not be you?" Another oddity, reflecting the Christine Jorgenson scandal, is "I Changed My Sex a Week Ago Today": "I don't know what the dressmaker will say. For whichever way it was, she'll have to alter it because my underpants were cut a different way." She achieved her greatest fame late in life as Mrs. Naugatuck on *Maude*, from 1974 to 1977. She died in 1986.

ROSS BAGDASARIAN

- THE MIXED UP WORLD OF BAGDASARIAN (Liberty LST 7451) *1/2 $5 $10

Bagdasarian, a part-time actor (*Rear Window*) was better known as "David Seville," creator of the novelty hit "The Witch Doctor" and later "The Chipmunk Song."

On his own, he's true to the album title: "mixed up." The liner notes ask "Is it comedy or pathos?" That question is raised by the schmaltzy songs like "Gotta Get to Your House." He spoonerizes as an anxious boy heading for a date with his girlfriend: "pretty pink hair, big brown dress!" Similar is "The Prom," a boy's nervous babble while waltzing. There are straight ethnic instrumentals and also "Come On-a My House," which was inexplicably a hit for Rosemary Clooney. There's something pretty sick about any song that wheedles, "Come on-a my house, my house, I'm gonna give you candy!" He wrote it with William Saroyan. Bagdasarian died in 1972.

WENDY BAGWELL

- AND THAT'S A FACT WITH MY HAND UP (Canaan 8331) ** $5 $10
- THIS, THAT AND THE OTHER (Canaan 9679) ** $5 $10
- YOU WON'T BELIEVE THIS (Canaan 9699) ** $5 $10
- BUST OUT LAFFIN' (Canaan 9765) ** $5 $10
- THE KNOWN COMIC (Canaan 9869) ** $5 $10

Religious humor from a pretty unlikely name. Bagwell might be odd enough, but this "Wendy" is a man. He sings gospel songs and offers country-tinged, easygoing, long conversational stories and monologues in a husky voice. From "Bust Out Laffin,'" an anecdote about rattlesnakes: "We was out in Ft. Worth, Texas ... and I had this great big ol' Texan come up to me, and he said, 'Brother Wendy,' he said, 'I can tell you somethin' about them rattlesnakes that'll help you one day, boy. Did you know that a rattlesnake won't bother you as long as you carry a lighted flashlight?' I said, 'No, don't reckin' he will if you carry it fast enough!'"

HARRISON BAKER

- LAST OF THE WELL COMEDIANS (RCA Victor LSP 2349) *1/2 $6 $12

An innocuous comedian, Baker stands up and delivers a pretty colorless monologue of uninspired gags:

"About an hour ago I was standing outside the club and I met a gorgeous girl ... what a dress she was wearing. I couldn't tell where the low neckline ended and her open-toed shoes began. She looked like the type of girl who would go out on Saturday night and sow her wild oats. Then go to church Sunday morning and pray for a crop failure. But I've come to the conclusion that women are entirely too expensive. And they say money can't buy love. Maybe not, but it certainly puts you in a wonderful bargaining position."

Most anyone could tell these gags with the same pleasant and perfunctory style and get a few giggles. Oddly, this was recorded in 1960 at The Hungry i, a place with a reputation for more cutting comedy.

ROBERT BAKER

- PARDON ME FOR BEING SO FRIENDLY BUT THIS IS MY FIRST LSD TRIP
  (GNP Crescendo 2027) *1/2 $7 $15

This relic from the '60s isn't worth "tripping" over. Baker, a gay-sounding stand-up, overacts his hipness as he recites non-poems and tries to sound blown away by the weirdness around him. Like, wow, aren't nursery rhymes wild: "The dish ran AWAY with THE SPOON!" Later he does a gay version of "The Lone Ranger": "Loney? This is Tonty! I'm absolutely furious with you! What's the big idea of riding off like that? Hi-yo Silver away ... but Robin, he

IS the boy wonder! Listen, I'm coming home. Want me to stop at Cost Plus and pick up anything? We need a new set of his and his towels ... keep the campfire burning, you kemo sabe you!"

Baker's delivery is annoyingly amateur as he breaks up, loses his place, and interrupts himself. His various voices are irritating as well. There are a lot of drug bits, most of them now ridiculous. At the time, of course, mentioning drug buzzwords generated hip laughter: "Hello, Mrs. Belladonna. Can amphetamine come out and play? You think she's coming down? What's LSD doing? Standing in front of the mirror, looking for his face? Tell him it's the reflection that's real, and he's the illusion. That'll blow his mind. Any message? Just tell 'em Sweet Cocaine was in the neighborhood and said hi."

LUCILLE BALL

- I LOVE LUCY (Radiola MR 1090) **1/2 $5 $10

Lucy fans get a chance to hear a half hour episode from her radio series *My Favorite Husband*. Her husband is not manic Hispanic Desi Arnaz but the blandly ordinary Richard Denning. Gale Gordon, Shirley Mitchell, and Bea Benaderet are in the cast. The script is dull and Lucy is better seen than heard, especially in a moment where she and her friend Iris discover that she can't get into her tight dress: "OK, Pull." "Oooh!" "Pull some more!" "I'm pulling! It's too bad we don't have a big shoe horn. Hold your breath! There!" "I did it! Let's go down and show George." "Hold it, girl, you have a bad case of gap-osis. You aren't zipped up the side." "Oh, I thought it was too easy." "There's something in the way." "What?" "You!"

The flip side is a Philip Morris-sponsored radio version of *I Love Lucy* from February 27, 1951. Desi narrates his story of typical sitcom doings, from a dripping shower that keeps him and Lucy up at night, to bickering with their new neighbors, Fred and Ethel Mertz. It too doesn't work very well without the visuals: hearing the loud drip of a faucet is not the same as imagining Lucy's facial reactions to it. Still, it's certainly a collector's item.

NOTES: The Friar's roast for Lucy and Desi (November 23, 1958) has some mild gags about the duo from Parkyakarkus, Milton Berle, Dean Martin, Tony Martin, Art Linkletter, and George Burns. This isn't raunchy (in deference to the presence of Lucy). As George Burns says: "With both Desi and Lucy up here I can't even get risqué because I'm sure Desi would resent it. I can't even tell any sexy jokes with Desi and Lu up here, because when you've been married a long time, sex sort of loses its humor. You don't have to go by me, you can ask Gracie. Maybe I'm not good on the stage, but when the lights are out, I get a lot of laughs."

KAYE BALLARD

- LIVE? (also released as KAYE BALLARD SWINGS United Artists 3043) ** $8 $20
- BOO HOO HA HA (United Artists 3165/6165) $8 $20

Ballard began her career with an act that mixed stand-up and many satirical and absurdist songs. "Boo Hoo Ha Ha" is mostly straight, but her first album is a combo of very familiar jokes, anecdotes about Italian family life, some madcap cabaret posturing (including a sudden impression of Señor Wences), and a few novelty tunes including "Teeny Tiny" and "I Just Kissed My Nose Goodnight."

The most interesting cut is a parody of "Autumn Leaves": "The autumn leaves passed by my window. And then the trees and then the buildings." It turns out that Kaye is in the middle of a hurricane. She pines, "The river overflowed. I must prove my love. A raft comes floating by. Just room for one...." The climax: "I will miss you most of all, my darling ... as autumn leaves start to fall."

The guy who wrote the new lyrics for his friend Kaye? Lenny Bruce.

Ballard also appears in the ensemble cast of "How to Pick a Wedlock" (Vanguard 9005). She's on many Broadway cast albums and on various straight albums including "Gershwin Rarities" (Walden 302), "The Fanny Brice Story" (MGM SES 3704), "Jerome Kern Revisited" (Painted Smiles PSCD 121 and 134), and more recently her solo show "Hey, Ma!" (DRG 91498).

KAYE BALLARD AND ARTHUR SIEGEL

- GOOD GRIEF, CHARLIE BROWN! PEANUTS
   (Columbia CL 1743/CS8543, reissued as Harmony HL 11230) *1/2 $6 $12

Now that the TV cartoon specials are so well known, it's hard to accept Ballard's Lucy and especially Siegel's Charlie. Their grown-up voices make Charles Schultz's childlike neurosis sound more like Jules Feiffer: "You can learn a lot about life from watching bugs. This little bug had built the most beautiful home you'd ever seen. And suddenly he lost it, just like that." "What happened?" "I kicked it over." These mini-vignettes, stark readings from the comic strip, are very stagy. There's no audience and the pause between each one for disjointed, beatnik jazz percussion does not help.

THE BALL BUSTERS

- NO JERK'N OFF (Dilligaf D 00012) ** $8
- NO HANG UPS (Dilligaf D 00072) * $8

Only hard-core fans of crank phone calls and dumb double entendres will enjoy the pinhead antics on the first CD, released in 1994. The pranksters call up a hardware store looking for "a power tool" and various sizes of screws, harangue an eighty-year-old by telling him he has a small penis, and annoy a bored woman named Lipshitz, who evidently is used to juveniles making fun of her name:

"Hello. You're Lipshitz." "Yes." "Well if your lip shits, then my ass talks." "Good." (Hangs up).

Once in a while the callers get into an amusing, ridiculous exchange, but not often enough to make listening to this worthwhile. Someone actually had a halfway good idea in calling up a phone sex hotline as a maddeningly goofy loser:

"Hi, this is Candy ... what are you wearing, Johnny?" "I'm wearing my Spider-Man pajamas. What are you wearing?" "I'm wearing a white crotchless G-string ... Oh, Johnny, you're getting me really wet." "You should dry off. You could catch a cold...." "Excuse me?"

Usually the witless Ball Busters can't maintain the joke, deteriorate into insults, or hang up—if they haven't been hung up on first. It's more of the same on the follow-up disc from 1995, as hapless, helpful receptionists and secretaries endure abusive idiocy.

DAVID BANKS

- I USED TO BE A BUS DRIVER (RCA APL 1-1828) ** $5 $10

Banks was a stand-up who ended up driving a bus for six years. Then he went to work for Columbia Records in the promo department, and later produced two albums for Richard Pryor. Seeing Pryor so successful inspired Banks to try again.

On this 1976 album he sounds more like gravel-voiced Redd Foxx as he tells a ringsider, "You ugly, nigger, with a face like that you could look through a keyhole and bust a blister on a brick! Little tunafish-faced black bastard, you could go in the jungle and be anything you wanna be except a hunter. You could go in the coal yard and be anything you wanna be except the engineer. You's an ugly, black, ignorant nigger!"

Most of the material is standard. He tells the Flip Wilson story about the bus driver who sees a woman and her baby come on board. "That's an ugly baby!" he exclaims. The lady is incensed, and tells a drunk sitting next to her that she's going to give the bus driver a piece of her mind. "Go ahead," the drunk says, "I'll hold your monkey!"

HEYWOOD BANKS

- IF PIGS HAD WINGS (Big Mouth) ** $7

Banks broke into comedy in the late '80s, winning a Johnnie Walker Red contest by beating on a toaster and singing a ballad about his love for toast. This self-done CD did little to advance his career.

DR. MURRAY BANKS

- HOW TO LIVE WITH YOURSELF (Murmil MB 101) ** $5 $10
- JUST IN CASE YOU THINK YOU'RE NORMAL (Murmil MB 102) ** $5 $10
- THE DRAMA OF SEX (Murmil MB 103) $5 $10
- JEWISH STORIES MIT PSYCHOLOGY (Murmil MB 104) ** $5 $10
- MORE JEWISH STORIES (Murmil MB 105) ** $5 $10
- A LESSON IN LOVE (Murmil MB 106) $5 $10
- HOW TO QUIT SMOKING IN SEX DAYS OR DROP DEAD IN SEVEN (Murmil MB 107) $5 $10
- ANYONE WHO GOES TO A PSYCHIATRIST SHOULD HAVE HIS HEAD EXAMINED
  (Murmil MB 108) $5 $10
- WHAT YOU CAN LEARN FROM THE KINSEY REPORT (Audio Masterworks 1210) ** $5 $10

Psychologist Dr. Murray Banks was, in addition to his private practice, a professor at Long Island University and an after dinner speaker and lecturer. His easygoing albums mix conversation, anecdotal stories, and jokes. The professionally personable Banks supposedly delivered his lecture, "How to live with yourself ... or what to do until the psychiatrist comes," five thousand times. It's full of anecdotal gags: "I received a letter the other day from a girl. She wrote me, 'Dear Dr. Banks, I'm 19 years old. I stayed out till 2 o'clock in the morning last Saturday night. My mother objected. Did I do wrong?' I wrote back and said 'Try to remember.'"

Banks's '60s era LPs were evidently sold mostly at his lectures and by mail. His 1956 album for Audio Masterworks has a few jokes during the lecture, but isn't really a comedy album.

SADIE BANKS

- SONGS MOTHER NEVER HEARD ME SING (Rivoli R-11) *1/2 $7 $15

Banks, a contemporary of Sophie Tucker, appeared on Broadway as early as 1915, and was in burlesque through the '20s. "Give It to Him" is typical of her off-color song/monology:

"To my fullest satisfaction I have learned that men love action. That doesn't mean ya gotta go about it at race-horse speed. I'm a lady who features leisure, even when I'm having pleasure. And I go for giving my man what a man should need ... why hold out your best possession? Give it to him!"

Banks's delivery is anything but sexy. Rather than Mae West, or even Tucker, she sounds more like a noodgy soprano George Jessel. She covers ancient recitation tunes like "Don't Advertise that Man," "If I Had a Million Dollars," and "Naggin' Won't Hold Your Man."

JOHN BARBOUR

- IT'S TOUGH TO BE WHITE (World Pacific 1834) **1/2 $7 $15
- I MET A MAN I DIDN'T LIKE (Dore 336) **1/2 $5 $10

Dick Gregory wrote the album notes for "It's Tough to Be White," calling Canada's Barbour "one of the brightest, sharpest young comics around." He used a deceptively low-key, conversational approach onstage. His take on cigarette commercials: "Nine out of ten doctors prefer Camel cigarette smokers to operate on." Political satire: "In Canada our largest selling periodical happens to be *MAD Magazine*. Down here you call it *Time*." Social satire: "San Francisco's forty percent Catholic and sixty percent homosexual. And the Catholics aren't reproducing as fast. Which is a paradox 'cause homosexuals practice birth control.... In Canada we never refer to them as homosexuals. We call them Mounties. 'Cause they always get their man."

Barbour went on to write for sitcoms, host local TV shows in Los Angeles, and make nightclub appearances. He was a host on *Real People*. In 1978 he released a second album on Dore, once more with celebrity endorsements (Burt Reynolds, Neil Simon, and Joan Rivers). He still could knock off an offbeat one-liner: "I came from a broken home, my mother wanted to put me up for adoption—when I was a fetus."

Like Dick Cavett, another comic who came along at the same time, Barbour was clever in stand-up, but had too much of an intellectual approach and lacked a charismatic one-to-one personality. Off the glaring stand-up stage, his humor sparkled better in interview and quiz show settings.

PETE BARBUTTI

- HERE'S PETE BARBUTTI (Vee Jay VJ 1133) **1/2 $10 $20
- THE VERY FUNNY SIDE OF PETE BARBUTTI (Decca DL 75008) *** $5 $10
- AT THE SAHARA (Contrast 2001) ** $5 $10

Jazz musician/comedian Barbutti has always been known for his offbeat, hip routines that blend laid-back ad-libs and prepared material. He got his break on *The Steve Allen Show* in the early '60s, and through the '80s guested on *The Tonight Show* a dozen times a year as a kind of jazz version of Victor Borge, doodling on the piano, and knocking off musical jokes, songs, and throwaways.

Barbutti's first album, released circa 1962, is disjointed, with a lot of quickies and embryonic versions of his "Kordeen School," "Bullfighting," "Communication," and "Airlines" routines. These are available in better, complete versions on the Decca record released four years later. The only notable material not available on the Decca disc are the musical parodies, including a long segment on the styles of lounge singers.

"Very Funny Side" offers Pete's offbeat-corny routine about Polish bullfighting: "... the arena becomes very solemn, for the local clergy appears and he consecrates the animal. And everyone stands up and shouts "Holy cow!" Wanna hear something worse? Then the people complain, because no matter where you put them, they're sitting behind a Pole!"

There's also "Kordeen School," his popular musical satire about a sharpie selling accordion lessons, and "Communication," a report on the custom of banging on pipes to get heat from an apartment janitor. This leads to comments on other communication quirks, like speaking to animals: "When we communicate with a lower form of life, we say everything in our native tongue as opposed to the animal. Like, if you have a German Shepherd dog, you seldom bark in German. If you have a Persian cat, you seldom meow in Persian. But you say everything twice ... you say "Come on boy, come on boy, nice boy, nice boy, whatsamatta boy, whatsamatta boy ... ever notice that, sir? Ever notice that, sir?"

At the turn of the '80s, Barbutti released an album on a local Las Vegas label. There are no big yocks here, just lighthearted conversational material as Barbutti talks, for example, about the case of the San Francisco nymphomaniac who blamed a fall from a cable car for her condition. Also included are "Deep Throat," "Las Vegas Living," "Ethnic Humor," and "Nurses." "Nurses are easy," he says, "because they know where everything is." Barbutti never went for knockout belly laughs, but his audience prefers walking away with a dizzy smile rather than a sore stomach.

BILL BARNER

- WARM PATTER FOR A HOT PLATTER (Duo D1) *1/2 $4 $8
- LAUGHS IT UP (Art 38) *1/2 $4 $8
- TROLLEY BAR PARTY (Art 52) *1/2 $4 $8
- NIGHT OUT (Art 56) *1/2 $4 $8
- TRUCKS IN (Art 88) *1/2 $4 $8
- WONDERFUL WACKY WORLD (Art 106) *1/2 $4 $8

Barner was best known in the Florida area. His nasal voice is more distinctive than his standard adult patter on the Duo album: "First thing I do when I check into a hotel is print 'Ladies' on my door. That's sneaky but I meet a lot of girls. I checked in at the desk and said, 'Pardon me sir, but do I register with you?' He said, 'Stick around, Ralph, we'll see.' I went right up there and knocked on the door. The girl said, 'Yes?' I didn't even ask her. Opened the door and there she was, barefoot right up to here, wearin' nothing but a smile. I soon wiped that off. And I wouldn't call this girl skinny, but if she stood sideways and stuck out her tongue she'd look like a zipper."

BARNES AND BARNES

- FISH HEADS: BARNES AND BARNES GREATEST HITS (Rhino RNDF 282) ** $15 $20
- THE BEST OF BARNES AND BARNES: ZABAGABEE (Rhino RNLP 70836) *1/2 $8

Barnes and Barnes (Robert Haimer and ex-child actor Billy Mumy) have produced many albums, but like their ancestors from Frank Zappa to The Bonzo Dog Band, most are categorized as rock albums, not comedy discs.

"Greatest Hits" is a picture disc cut into the shape of a fish head. It gets a half of a rating star for that alone. The disc has "Fish Heads," a sick but cute novelty song that became popular among the ten-year-olds listening to the *Dr. Demento* radio show. The entire composition of the song is two Chipmunk-type vocalists enunciating: "Fish heads, fish yeads, roly-poly fish heads ... eat them up. YUM!" to a very simple melody.

The boys went on to release more records for both Rhino and Epic, more heavy on the Zappa sneers than goofy comedy.

The later comedy-novelty anthology includes "Fish Heads," of course, along with childishly fake Zappa novelties "Party in My Pants" and "Pizza Face." The overdone "Cemetery Girls" is considerably less fun than Alice Cooper or Bloodrock, while the straight-rocking "Pussy Whipped" doesn't try to match the subject matter to a suitable vocal. Some song titles are better than the songs: "Life Is Safer When You're Sleeping."

SANDY BARON

- OUT OF THE MOUTHS OF BABES (Shell 1712) ** $5 $10
- THE RACE RACE (Roulette) *1/2 $5 $10
- I NEVER LET SCHOOL INTERFERE WITH MY EDUCATION (Capitol T 2613) *1/2 $5 $10

Baron (nee Berenofsky) appeared on TV often in the '60s (*Hey Landlord, That Was the Week That Was*) and was one of several to try to become the new Lenny Bruce with well-meaning, crusading social satire. He even appeared in various stage versions of *Lenny*.

He was twenty-four when he did "Babes," a kiddie interview LP with the usual delightfully precocious tots. He asks, "What is a Republican and a Democrat?" "Well, uh, a Democrat is for Christmas and a Republican is for Chanukah." Baron never listed this disc among his "official" comedy LPs.

"Race Race" from 1964 was a well-intentioned studio disc filled with obvious satire. Baron impersonates a variety of stereotypical whites—well-intentioned liberals and outright bigots—and ultimately wishes adults could be as color blind as the five-year-old child who tells his black playmate Roosevelt about a strange conversation he overheard:

"My father was sayin' to my mother that we have to move into a different neighborhood 'cause *them* are movin' in. I don't know who them are, I just know that them is dangerous. 'Cause my father says one of them wants to marry my sister, and one of them is a bad influence on me. I think it's my teacher! He's a bad influence on me.... Then he said that we have to move out 'cause most important, they're a different color than us, Roosevelt. I don't know who they are. You know who I think it is? Remember last week when we saw the movie about the Martians? Remember they were a different color than us? I think them is the Martians."

Dick Gregory and Jules Feiffer provided the album notes.

Baron's 1967 album of monology and sketches examines dating, smoking, exams, and the problems of teachers and students. The anecdotes are average: "I wanted to get my first car. I got $300, and the used car salesman had black patent leather hair and a little mustache and a pinkie ring. I thought of him as Sam Slime, see. And the car he sold me was a 1948 Lemon ... to me it was fantastic! The best way I can describe it to ya. I went out into the country. By accident I hit a horse. And they shot the car!"

- GOD SAVE THE QUEENS (A&M SP 4355) *1/2 $7 $15
- HOW I FOUND GOD, ZEN, YOGA ... (20th Century Fox T 537) ** $5 $10

In 1973, when Baron was starring as Cliff Gorman's replacement in "Lenny," he issued an album of gay humor. Not gay himself, Baron was trying to be a crusading social comic a la Lenny, and deserves some credit for trying something new, even if the album title and the cover's pastel hues implied that all homosexuals were drag queens. Dick Gregory, Bette Midler, and Alan King supplied album notes. They should've helped out with the sketches; they aren't very funny. There's literally no punch line to the story of the parents who come to their son's home and wonder about his lovelife.

The album ends with a pretentious "Fairy Tale" about a gay prince who is miserable in his kingdom until he discovers magic: "They call the magic 'pride.' All you have to do is open the closet door." Baron's heart was in the right place, and the actors who play gays avoid stereotyped lisping, but the comedy is no place to be found.

In 1977 he finally released a stand-up album instead of studio sketches. Brief endorsements came from Richard Pryor ("This honky's crazy") and Joan Rivers ("I loved the album, but don't go by my taste"). Cowritten with Paul Krassner, this album takes a look at the bewildering fad obsessions with EST, TM, and other therapies and con-sciousness-raising theories. Baron tries for Lenny Brucian observation gags. On Arthur Janov's Primal Scream technique: "Janov was a psychiatrist, they say. What he is, is a proctologist! You put a thumb up somebody's ass they will tell you about reality! They will scream!"

ROSEANNE BARR

- I ENJOY BEING A GIRL (Hollywood HR 610002) *1/2 $7

Barr's 1990 CD was released after her controversial mangling of the national anthem at a baseball game. (And before she became Roseanne Arnold and then just Roseanne). President George Bush was among the many who called her singing, and crotch-grabbing parody of ball players, a disgrace.

She gets even with about ten ear-splitting minutes of singing. It's a one-joke gag, self-indulgent and bratty, but no one ever said Roseanne knows the meaning of self-discipline. Other portions of the show, originally an HBO special, waste time with egocentric rants and contemptuous preening in front of the crowd. That leaves less than a half hour for her sarcastic housewife grousing, which is Roseanne at her best. She insists that the only thing men can do better than women is read a map: "'Cause only the male mind could conceive of one inch equaling a hundred miles."

DAVE BARRY

- LAUGHS FOR LOSERS (Liberty 3176) ** $5 $10
- WILL THE REAL HOWARD HUGHES PLEASE STAND UP? (Double Shot DSS 5006) ** $4 $8

A fairly standard '60s comic with routines about women drivers, drinking, and Las Vegas, Barry (on the Liberty album he gives his real last name as Siegel) offers a laid-back delivery that makes the gags easier to take. Combining wife jokes and Vegas jokes on his 1960 Liberty album: "I brought my wife with me to Las Vegas. You know how you pack a lot of things you don't need...." On women drivers: "She never stops for a red light. She says if you've seen one or two you've seen 'em all."

Barry's 1972 album on Howard Hughes is a series of sketches with support from Selma Diamond, Stanley Ralph Ross, and Eddy Carroll. The gags are hack-simple: "Mr. Hughes, are you a self-made man?" "Well, my mother and father did have a little to do with it." "Well then you were born with money." "Oh yes. When the doctor first brought me into the world he held me upside down and slapped me." "And?" "Two nickels and a dime fell out of my navel."

Barry imitated the voices of Bugs Bunny, Daffy Duck, and others for children's singles on the Little Golden Records label, and in 1956 issued "Do It Yourself Psychiatry," a 45 rpm extended play single on Key Records. Recorded before a live audience, he uses an Elmer Fudd voice for a segment of case histories: "Case histowee #6. Patient is afwaid of a bunch of gwapes ... at the sight of a bunch of gwapes, patient goes into tewiffic psychotic wage. Diagnosis: clusterphobia."

BELLE BARTH

- IF I EMBARRASS YOU TELL YOUR FRIENDS (After Hours LAH 69) *** $5 $10
- IN PERSON (Laugh Time LT 901) ** $7 $15
- WILD WILD WILD WILD WORLD (Record Productions LP 14,000,001) ** $7 $15
- HER NEW ACT (Riot R 301) **1/2 $6 $12
- HELL'S BELLE (Laff A 115) ** $6 $12
- THE CUSTOMER COMES FIRST (Lobo 109, Laff A 109) ** $6 $12
- I DON'T MEAN TO BE VULGAR BUT IF IT'S PROFITABLE (Surprise 169) ** $7 $15
- BOOK OF KNOWLEDGE/MEMORIAL ALBUM (LAFF A 180) ** $6 $12

One of the most famous of the red hot mamas who told dirty jokes on novelty records of the '60s, Belle sang a la Sophie Tucker before combining bawdy songs with snappy patter. "If I Embarrass You" was a famous and popular party record with plenty of one-liners, songs, and Jewish dialect stories like this one:

"An old man lost all his money. Seventy years old, hasn't got a dime. Who does he blame? His wife. He says, 'If you vere a good wife, you'd go out and voik for me....' She says, 'What could I do?' He says, 'You could be a whoo-eh.' 'I could be a whoo-eh?' 'You could try.' She comes back the next morning all stooped over, dirty, disheveled. He says, 'You made out?' She says, 'Certainly I made out. I made twenty four dollars and ten cents.' He says, 'What's the ten cents?' She says, 'Everybody gave me ten cents.'"

Her other early albums on small labels are almost at the same level, the standard jokes interrupted by snatches of raunchy, ridiculous songs or poems. On "In Person" her version of "Return to Sorrento" starts: "Vito matta cuanto bello ... who threw the douche bag in my Jello?"

"Wild World" has fuzzy sound quality, but the gags are frisky. She gets tumultuous yocks from this one: "Tomorrow Ben Casey does a four-hour spectacular: gonna circumcise the Green Giant." On other current events: "The Beatles? Now we have a female group called The Locusts. They don't sing, but they eat The Beatles!"

Generally, the Riot, Surprise, and Laff releases are the easiest Barth albums to find, and both Riot and Surprise offer good examples of Barth's resonant voice and redolent material. From the Riot album, a very typical Barth story that she delivers with her combination of school teacher sweetness and (at the punch line) Brooklyn bombast:

"A little boy went to the barber shop ... he was afraid of the barber. So what does the barber do? He gives the kid a little cookie. The kid's lookin' down, he's pickin' like this. And the barber says, 'You have a little hair on your cookie?' He says, 'I'm only seven years old, ya schmuck!'"

Aging by the time she got to Laff, the albums include some awful imitations of Sophie Tucker ("Bill Bailey" on the "Hell's Belle" disc) and some dull old gags told from memory. She died in 1971.

BELLE BARTH AND PEARL WILLIAMS

- BATTLE OF THE MOTHERS (Riot R 305) ** $5 $10
- RETURN BATTLE (Riot R 308) ** $5 $10

One side each of Barth and Williams, culled from previously released material.

FRED BARTON

- MISS GULCH RETURNS (Miss Gulch Records) *1/2 $6 $15

Almira Gulch was the nasty old lady who bedeviled Dorothy in the *Wizard of Oz* when she was still in Kansas. Fred Barton, a New York cabaret performer, is obsessed with her. He likes to dress up in "Miss Gulch" drag and sing campy songs about her. Songs like "I'm a Bitch," rave: "In a royal bitchy mood I could spoil frozen food. That's by walking through the kitch ... that old crappiness is my happiness ... isn't it queer, isn't it rich, I'm a bitch!" A 1987 release on his own label.

JOAN BARTON

- LOW LIGHTS AND LAUGHS (Warner Brothers WS 1481) **1/2 $5 $10

Daring for a major label in 1962, "Low Lights and Laughs" collects off-color comedy classics. Diffusing them slightly is Barton's sanitary, Dorothy Provine-ish delivery. Double entendre songs include "The Most Fun I Had without Laughing," "Am I Doing It Right?" "She Had to Go and Lose It at the Astor," and the nicely purred "I'm a Big Girl Now." Joan's leering lilt and put-on sophistication is certainly different from the technique old blues singers used on "Kitchen Man," the double entendre classic: "His frankfurters are oh so sweet, how I love his sausage meat ... oh how that boy can open clams. No one else can touch my hams ..." and finally, "When I eat his donut, all I leave is just the hole. And anytime he wants to, he can use my sugar bowl."

THE BARTON BROTHERS

- JEWISH COMEDY SONGS (APOLLO LP 475, also released as COCKEYE JENNY) ** $7 $20
- YIDDISH AMERICAN COMEDY (Rivoli 5) *** $7 $20
- STORIES OUR JEWISH MOTHER FORGOT TO TELL US (Jubilee 2061) ** $7 $20

The Barton Brothers were one of the most hilarious duos in Jewish comedy, remembered affectionately by those who saw them in the '50s and '60s. The Apollo album has their famous novelty songs "Joe and Paul" (a parody of radio commercials), "Minnie the Flapper," "Tzouris," and "Cockeyed Jenny." It's seventy-five percent in Yiddish, but there's no denying that the music alone is bright and bouncy, and the vocals sound funny no matter what the lyrics are. "Tzouris" has some dialogue between the choruses. "Heyyyyy, Lucky," one of them says with irritating good humor. "What, I'm lucky!" the other kvetches, explaining that he just lost his wife. His cheerful pal insists, "Tomorrow you'll go out into the world, you'll live again, laugh again, love again. You must love again!" "I know," says the miserable one, "but what am I gonna do TONIGHT?"

Their other two albums are mostly in English, but lack those classic songs. The Rivoli album does have some good novelty songs, as well as long music and dialogue sketches. "Little Red Riding Hood" and "Midnight Ride of Paul Revere" are bizarre combinations of traditional Jewish schtick and Stan Freberg.

"De British fired the first volley of cannonballs," the announcer cries on "Paul Revere's Ride." A scrappy Jewish voice shouts, "Ve vere ready ... balls they're throwing at us? We'll give 'em balls! Volleyballs, baseballs, matzoh balls. Blood ran like borscht ... then the moils went to work and cut them to pieces. Go ahead and start up! We hit them with last season's bagels! Balls they'll throw at us?"

A chorus of "Glory Glory Hallelujah" mixes with freilach dance music during the frenzied finale. Songs include "Activity" (a famous number many comics have done about Catskill exercise programs) and "Golf" about a Jew's first visit to the course: "Full of little holes. Eighteen of them. Why don't they fix it? And right away it cost me a hundred dollars for a couple of sticks: a driver, a nudnik, a smashie, a nooblick, and a putzer ... the first hole I lost my golf ball, the second hole I lost my partner, third I found my partner trying to sell my golf ball."

On the Jubilee album the boys offer classic, sometimes risqué stories instead of their usual songs.

ELI BASSE

- BASSE ACKWARDS (Stereoddities CB-1) ** $7 $15
- GARDEN OF YEDEN (Rivoli 17, Monogram 818) **1/2 $5 $10

Basse, born in England but raised in Brooklyn, wrote jokes for many comics, including Joe E. Lewis ("Whether you're rich or poor it's nice to have money") and authored many popular Yiddish novelty tunes.

"Garden of Yeden" contains many of these, mostly sung in English. "Number 4 Hoomintash Lane" is here, along with "Litvak Polka" and "Since Hannah Came Back from Havana." Much of the humor is involved in applying Jewish lyrics to unlikely rhumba, polka, and boogie-woogie beats. Against a rollicking jazz instrumental, love-sick Basse roars, "Don't keep me waiting. The boids and the bees are mating. It's springtime in the Bronx and the herrings are marinating!"

The Stereoddities album has a few sketches in addition to the songs: "Hand Me Down My Mercurochrome 'Cause My Horse Has Just Been Scratched," "Psychiatrist Papa," "Rosie," "Politics," "Matilda," and "It's Better than Being a Millionaire." His "The Girl in the New Oldsmobile" is filled with jaunty patter lyrics similar to Benny Bell's style: "Oh the girl in the new Oldsmobile, she looked more like an old Pontiac. Her fenders were bent, her rear-end had a dent, and her bumper just dragged in the back ... she was built like a Chevy but five times as heavy and just like a Model T Ford, she huffed and she puffed like her gasoline was stuffed. She was just a big ass-matic broad...."

Basse also wrote novelty tunes for Stereoddities' main comic, Woody Woodbury. "Allergic" and "I'm Returning All Your Presents" appear on Woodbury's "Saloonatics" album. Basse died in 1979.

BRUCE BAUM

- BORN TO BE RAISED (Horn HR 4003) *1/2 $4 $8

A pudgy David Crosby look-alike prone to desperate prop comedy, Baum was considerably slimmer in 1981 when he put on a diaper and tried to get some attention with his pouty "baby man" character. The album has the soggy "Ballad of Baby Man" and other grating novelties, including "Mother Goose on 45" (nursery rhymes bawled out evidently in parody of simpleminded disco tunes). He actually had a minor hit with his parody of "Bette Davis Eyes," now called "Marty Feldman Eyes." Baum's off-key shouting doesn't help the simple ugly-girl lines: "She'll woo you. Then she'll moon you, and forget to pull her pants up. She's obnoxious, and she knows this. And she knows how to blow her nose up ... she's got Marty Feldman eyes."

BILLY BAXTER AND PATRICIA BRIGHT

- LIFE WITH LIZ AND DICK (Roulette R 25292) *1/2 $4 $8

Patricia Bright plays Liz Taylor, and British comic Billy Baxter plays Richard Burton on this gentle topical comedy album. The various sketches include Jack Burns, Avery Schreiber, and Paul Sand.

There are jokes about the duo's idle rich lifestyle ("What do you say we both get up and take a nice brisk walk around the room?"), as well as dialogue about their loving and their quarrels:

"You ham!" "Don't call me a ham—fatty!" "Fatty? I've never been so insulted in all my life!" "Oh yes you have." "That does it. I'm not staying in this house with you another minute. I'm going home to my agent.... Richard, this is our first fight! Isn't that wonderful?" "What's so wonderful about it?" "We promised *Life* magazine an exclusive on that!"

Baxter recorded a novelty song album, "Billy Baxter and His Carnaby St. Vaudeville Band" (ABC ABCS-581). It didn't exactly follow "Winchester Cathedral" or Herman's Hermits to the charts. The "sassy" arrangements, complete with handclaps and campy ukulele, bludgeon the humor out of old vaudeville tunes "When I'm Cleaning Windows," "Why Build a Wall 'Round a Graveyard" and "I've Never Seen a Straight Banana."

ORSON BEAN

- ORSON BEAN AT THE HUNGRY i (Fantasy 7009) *** $10 $20
- I ATE THE BALONEY (Columbia CS 9743) *** $6 $12

Before he was blacklisted during the McCarthy era witchhunts, Orson Bean (born Dallas Burrows) was one of the nation's hottest young comedy stars. Though best remembered now as a panelist on *To Tell the Truth* and a costar on *Dr. Quinn, Medicine Woman*, Bean still deserves a place in the stand-up Hall of Fame for his unique persona. Very few stand-ups took the stage in a cheerful, optimistic way, offering cute and whimsical material. As he told me, "The most important thing in my life has always been to be happy. I spent most of my life trying to find out how to be the happiest bastard who ever lived.... I think that just shows in your work."

This late '50s Fantasy album, available on both black and red vinyl, contains a number of complete sketches, as well as the shaggy dog stories that were to become Bean's trademark, from "The Trial of 'Erbert Cranshaw" (a man arrested for having an affair with an ostrich) to a report on a football game between ants and elephants: "An ant had the ball, a regulation one pounder, and was streaking downfield. The elephants were in hot pursuit, but the blocking was magnificent! The ant with the ball reaches the five yard line, is about to make a touchdown, when one of the elephants, the fastest on the team, caught up to the ant with the ball, steps on him, and squashes him to death. A low murmur of disapproval spread through the crowd. The umpire ran out onto the field and said, 'Why'd you step on him for?' The elephant said, 'I was only trying to trip him!'"

A special four-page reprint from *MAD Magazine* was slipped into the record sleeve, "Making a Paper Eucalyptus Tree." The complete routine is illustrated by cult favorite Wally Wood and includes an instruction manual for do-it-yourselfers.

In the mid-60s, during his run on *To Tell the Truth*, he released "Baloney," a classic for fans of silly shaggy dog stories. It duplicates material from the first (the ostrich bit, gags on Chinese restaurants, and the flesh-eating "goo goo"), but there's plenty of fresh tales and comic or serio-comic tunes. "The Ballad of George Fink" is descended from W. C. Fields and the British Music Hall tradition of wacky, deliberately rhymeless ballads. The Sousa march "El Capitan" now acts out the drama between a virginal girl and her insistent beau. "In Which I Switch" is a long, sadly sweet poem about a loser.

The material is often charming, reflecting well that rarity on the stand-up stage—the low-pressure, likable comedian.

NOTES: Bean also appears on the original cast album of "Ilya Darling" (United Artists UAS 8901), "Subways Are for Sleeping" (Columbia KOS 2130), and the budget children's album "You're a Good Man Charlie Brown" (Leo 90).

LEW BEDELL

- A TRIBUTE TO JOE FRISCO (Dore 103) *1/2 $4 $8
- OH MIGHTY GAME OF GOLF (Dore 320) *1/2 $4 $8
- WHO THE HELL IS LEW BEDELL (Dore 323) *1/2 $4 $8

The most unusual album from Bedell, who is the owner of Dore Records, is "A Tribute to Joe Frisco." For some reason, some twenty years after Joe Frisco's death, Bedell decided to go into a studio and tell a bunch of anecdotes about him. There's no audience, so he simply goes from joke to joke without a pause for laughs, imitating Frisco's stutter on every punch line.

Frisco's reputation will survive this tribute, which contains gags like this: "They tell the story that one time a group of people were around a television set watching a fight on TV. And everybody was commenting how they thought the one fighter was throwing the fight. And someone recalled, yeah, that he had been mixed up in a number of fixed fights. So Joe's comment was "Heh heh, that's, heh-heh, true he'd, heh-heh, taken so many dives he's, heh-heh, beginning to, heh, look like Esther Williams.""

BENNY BELL

• JEWISH COMEDY (Bell) **1/2	$8	$20
• JEWISH-AMERICAN NOVELTY TUNES (Bell, reissued as PINCUS THE PEDDLER, Zion 234) ***	$8	$20
• KOSHER COMEDY (Kosher Comedy) **	$8	$20
• KOSHER COMEDY (Madison 120) **	$7	$15
• TO THE BRIDE (Zion 252) **	$8	$20
• KOSHER COMEDY (Zion 126) **	$8	$20
• LAUGH ALONG WITH PINCUS (Madison 523) **1/2	$7	$15
• SHOW TIME (Bell 303) **1/2	$8	$20
• SHAVING CREAM (Vanguard VSD 79357) ***	$8	$20

Two little cults exist for Benny Bell (born Ben Zamberg). Many love his peppy Jewish novelty tunes from the late '40s and '50s. Others crave his harmless bawdy numbers like "Shaving Cream." Benny told me he eventually had to choose between his two identities. Orthodox store owners were aghast knowing he did risqué comedy, so he chose to stay with antic Semitism, some in Yiddish, some in English.

Collectors have their problems, since Benny reissued his songs on various compilations, duplicating and deleting tunes at his own whim, sometimes overloading a disc with more Yiddish than English. Since he was Brooklyn-based, with small pressings, his material is hard to find beyond the East Coast.

"Jewish Comedy" is a set of two ten-inch albums. Most of the material is in Yiddish, including "Blessing the Bride," "Marie, Scram," "Shlimozzle" and "Bullvess." Some of the cuts are pure instrumentals, like "Yiddish Mazurka" and "Sophisticated Fraylech."

Several of Bell's classics are on the 1958 "Jewish American Novelty Tunes," including "Pincus the Peddler." To a bouncy melody, Benny describes the adventures of an unlucky Brooklynite about to be deported back to Slabutka. There's humorous descriptions of the homefolk: "My poppa was a plumber who doubled as a drummer. I never really saw that fella wear a frown. His whiskers were the longest, the toughest, and the strongest. How well they kept his pants from falling down." Then there are anecdotes about the "dirty rotten woman" who has him sent back for doing something as harmless as kicking her down the cellar and breaking "the nicest girdle that she ever had."

Other cuts include "Pincus in the Mountains," "Sammy from Miami," and "In Old Romania" (a cute version of "Romania Romania" where Benny exults, "Romania, Romania, Romania, it was so beautiful I could hardly explain ya.") The Zion reissue of 1959 has a spiffy front cover photo of Benny as a peddler.

The original "Kosher Comedy" (on the "Kosher Comedy" label) was issued in 1956. The Madison version arrived in 1960. Cuts on both discs are almost completely in Yiddish. Likewise with Zion's "Kosher Comedy" and "To the Bride."

"Laughing Along" is the easiest to find (re-released in 1972) and has the classics "Pincus the Peddler" and "Why Buy a Cow When Milk is Cheap." The songs are much better than the spoken sketches and monologues, which tend to rely on hokey gags: "No matter how young a prune may be, it's always full of wrinkles."

"Show Time" has whiz-bang humor and the nearly classic "Shiskebab," a variation on the more famous "Shaving Cream." Here, to a slightly different melody, Benny gets as close to a "no-no" word as he can. Sample lyric: "I once bought a small bag of popcorn. I hope that the man gets a fit. Instead of a bag filled with popcorn—he gave me a bag filled with Shi-shkebab, Shi-shkebab."

Other lewd cuts include "Ikey and Mikey," "She's Still Got It," and "Noses Run in My Family," which seems to be about something other than noses: "My cousin has a hard one that really takes the cake. My nephew has a soft one that wiggles like a snake."

The jokes, told one after another with canned laughter and carousel music, are harmless enough: "A pretty young girl sent her panties to the laundry and pinned a note on them that read, 'Dear Landryman, please use Sparkle Suds. Please.' Two days later the panties came back nice and clean with another note attached that read: 'Dear Young Lady, please use toilet paper. Please!'"

"Shaving Cream" was a hit when reissued in 1975. Paul Wynn (guest vocalizing) offers what could be obscene lines, saved by a sappy, straight-faced chorus: "I have a sad story to tell you. It may hurt your feelings a bit. Last night when I walked into my bathroom, I stepped in a big pile of ... Shhhhhaving cream. Be nice and clean. Shave every day and you'll always look keen."

Other winning wordplay songs here include "Take a Ship for Yourself" and "Everybody Likes My Fanny." All are sung by Benny Bell in his inimitable nasal croon. Bell did record his own version of "Shaving Cream" a few years after Wynn's 1946 recording, but when it came time for the reissue, he decided to include Paul Wynn's as a gesture of friendship.

ALAN C. BEMIS

• FRESH AS A HADDOCK (Droll Yankees 6)	$4	$8
• STORIES FOR GENTLEMEN (Droll Yankees 3)	$4	$8

LITTLE DISCS, BIG PRICES

Most "ten-inchers" are expensive, especially rarities like "And Awaaay We Go" by Jackie Gleason, Robert Benchley's "Best," and the ultra obscure "Write If You Get Work" from Bob & Ray.

CULTIVATING A CULT

These ten-inchers are gold for fans who know of 1940s Broadway great Willie Howard, or Brother Theodore, New York's late-night denizen of deathly humor from the 1950s through the 1990s. (And his 90s!)

New England humorist Bemis performs solo on "Fresh as a Haddock." The other disc includes storytellers Leon Nickerson and Russell F. Bacon. Bemis can also be heard swapping tales on a few albums starring Francis Colburn.

ROBERT BENCHLEY

- BENCHLEY'S BEST (Audio Rarities LPA 110) ** $15 $30

One of the few satirists whose work could actually be described as "droll," Robert Benchley's comic essays have been gathered on spoken word albums read by Henry Morgan (Listening Library 3316) and Bob Elliot (Caedmon). This, a ten-inch obscurity from the '50s, has Benchley himself lecturing on swing music and describing "How to Start a Vacation." He also does some whimsical travelogues:

"We are now nearing the city of Pung-Drunk, India. We notice a native family clustered around a crude hut. There is a baby playing in the dirt. He is n-a-k-e-d. Or as they say in India, naked. The child has his mother's eyes, his mother's nose, and his mother's mouth. Which leaves his mother with a pretty blank expression...."

"We are now passing through a Ubangi settlement in Africa. These quaint Ubangis think it's a thing of beauty to stretch their lips to enormous proportions. Their mouths attain these large dimensions since from childhood it is their custom to drink double-thick malteds through the wrong end of a bugle. As we stroll through the village we see a group of children playing in the shade of their mothers' lips."

WILLIAM BENDIX

- THE LIFE OF RILEY (Memorabilia MLP 711) ** $4 $8
- THE LIFE OF RILEY (Radiola MR 1119) ** $5 $10

Bendix's *Life of Riley* had a long radio run and was on TV 1953-1958. Radiola's hour-long "Lux Radio Theater" version (May 8, 1950) doesn't have the snap of the actual, shorter radio show. Bendix has plenty of time to utter his catchphrase, "What a revoltin' development THIS is." Fans have to wait for a really good line. Riley, trying to borrow money from a fair-weather friend: "He wouldn't lend me the money. He said it would ruin our friendship. Even when I told him I hated him he wouldn't give me the money." Fans can sympathize when he says, "I'm doin' the best I can with the brains I've got."

Memorabilia's mild episode takes place around Thanksgiving, with Riley mumbling through a turkey order at Al's meat market:

"You know in our house, all four of us like the drumstick and nobody likes the, uh, uh, whatchamacallit. So this year Al promised to give me a turkey with four drumsticks."

"How is that possible? One turkey with four drumsticks?"

"Yeah, well, with Al it's easy. Some other customer will get a turkey with no drumsticks and two whatchamacallits."

Bendix released a non-comedy album, "William Bendix Sings and Tells Famous Pirate Stories" (Cricket 30).

TY BENNETT

- QUEEN FOR A DAY (Half and Half 34 1/2) ** $7 $15

Bennett began his drag comedy career at the Jockey Club in Atlantic City in 1947, and about a dozen years later issued this album pressed in Union, New Jersey.

JACK BENNY

- GREATEST ORIGINAL RADIO BROADCASTS (MF Records MF 214) *** $12 $25
- JACK BENNY 1933 (Mark 56 #764) ** $5 $10
- JACK BENNY 1936 (Mark 56 #765) ** $5 $10
- JACK BENNY 1940 (Mark 56 #766) ** $5 $10
- JACK BENNY 1944 (Mark 56 #767) ** $5 $10
- THE JACK BENNY SHOW (Yorkshire LP 716) ** $5 $10
- THE JACK BENNY SHOW (Radiola MR 1147) *** $5 $10
- THE HORN BLOWS AT MIDNIGHT (Radiola MR 1068) ** $4 $8
- JACK BENNY ORIGINAL RADIO BROADCAST (Nostalgia Lane NLR 1003) **1/2 $5 $10
- JACK BENNY (Metacom 0300332) ** $8
- JACK BENNY AND HIS FRIENDS (Broadcast Tribute BTRIB 0004) **1/2 $7 $15
- THE JACK BENNY STORY (Radiola 2MR 4546) **1/2 $8 $20

The quality of Benny's shows remained solid through the years, so most any album will have some good laughs. Radiola's two half-hour episodes have weak guests in Andy Devine and Frank Fontaine. Their radio version of "Horn Blows at Midnight" was done in 1949. Nostalgia Lane has 1948 and 1950 shows with Fred Allen and Ronald Colman. Metacom is one of few CD offerings. The two episodes are "Jack Goes to the Doctor" and "Dinner at Don's."

Fans splurging for the 1978 three-record set from MF get six complete half-hour episodes with some solid guests: Ronald Colman, Van Johnson, Boris Karloff, and Humphrey Bogart and Lauren Bacall. Jack and Lauren are rehearsing a love scene as Bogart walks in:

Benny: "By the way, what should I call you, Lauren or Miss Bacall?"

Bogart: "Mrs. Bogart ... what's this sketch you're rehearsing?" Bacall: "To Have and Have Not. We're rehearsing the big scene we had together."

Bogart: "Oh? Which one of you's playin' my part?"

The Karloff episode demonstrates Benny's surreal side. It has some odd lines.

"Haven't you any children?" Benny asks Karloff.

"No," Karloff answers solemnly, "I married a smudgepot."

"Oh, then you haven't any children."

"No ... but we're lousy with oranges."

Ultimately the nightmare has Benny about to be executed.

"I can't walk that last mile!" Benny cries. The guard answers, "You won't have to, we'll bring the electric chair in here. We have a long cord, you know ... we have one of those new electric chairs. You pop up when you're done."

A two-record "Jack Benny Story" has two complete shows, including a 1953 visit to his vault; plus segments including parodies of "The Whistler" and "Snows of Kilimanjaro"; plus sketch-visits from Mel Blanc as Professor LeBlanc and the mono-syllabic Mexican named Cy. There's running commentary culled from an interview with Benny in his later years. Among his comments: "If through some miracle I could be again thirty-nine ... my answer would be only if I feel as good as I feel now ... when I was thirty-nine I had too many things to worry about."

"Broadcast Tribute" has episodes from Jack's show with guests Charles Boyer and Ingrid Bergman, and Maurice Chevalier. Tacked on at the end in order to justify the album jacket's claim, is a radio clip of Dinah Shore introducing Marlene Dietrich, who sings "Lili Marlene." Neither actually appear with Jack.

NOTES: Benny narrated "Remember the Golden Age of Radio" (Longines Symphonette SY5183), which has been released in several different versions, from a boxed set to individual albums. He's on "Son of Jest Like Old Times" (Radiola 2), "Golden Age of Comedy" (Evolution 3013), "Magic Moments from *The Tonight Show*" (Casablanca SPNB 1296), and "The Minstrel Men" (Colpix CL 434). Oddities include the souvenir record "Tom May 80th Birthday Dinner," recorded June 3, 1963; a pair of promos for State Farm Insurance; and "Jack Benny Plays the Bee" (Capitol T3241), also issued as "Fiddles with the Classics" (Capitol 8108) costarring Isaac Stern and Mel Blanc. A straight interview appears on "Conversations in Hollywood #2" (Citadel CT 6029). A double-set Friars tribute album is available.

Fans can look for some "album jacket" novelties. Jack is playing the violin dressed up as Santa Claus for "Dennis Day Sings Christmas" (Design DLPX-1) but despite the back cover billing ("Jack Benny and Dennis Day") Jack makes only a brief token appearance on the album. Jack supplies the album notes for an album of jazz and pop tunes, "The Beguiling Miss Frances Bergen" (Columbia CL 873). "Frances sings soft, low, and sexy ... her voice is soothing, her interpretation unusual, and her phrasing fascinating." And she was married to Edgar Bergen.

Benny has some cute moments as "The Taxpayer" on "Three Billion Millionaires" (UXL 4, distributed by United Artists), an album produced to celebrate the United Nations. He also lets his straight man get the biggest laugh: "And to help the United Nations, all the performers on this record appear without getting paid. Mr. Benny? Mr. Benny?"

JACK BENNY AND FRED ALLEN

- THE RADIO FIGHT OF THE CENTURY (Radiola 2MR 2930) *** $5 $10
- THE RADIO FEUD CONTINUES (Radiola MR 1111) *1/2 $5 $10

The good-natured feud between Fred Allen and Jack Benny delighted radio audiences for nearly twenty years. Clips cover many classic battles and one sketch has the duo recalling their (imaginary) days as a vaudeville team. Guest stars Bob Hope and Henry Morgan try to mediate the duo's arguments and a highlight is the aural slapstick of "King for a Day," with Benny trying to keep his pants on during a quiz show parody gone awry. At one point, Benny satirizes "Allen's Alley" by doing his own version, "Benny's Boulevard." Fred returns the favor by doing "The Pinch Penny Program" and imitating Jack.

The scraped-up bits and pieces for the sequel LP could make listeners feud with Radiola. The hour includes a dull fifteen-minute live broadcast from the premiere of the movie *Love Thy Neighbor*. Henny Youngman announces the celebrities as they arrive. The banter is forgettable, even Jack and Fred's when they arrive:

"The billing should be Fred Allen and Jack Benny." "Oh no, it shouldn't. My name should be first because in the picture I'm on longer than you are." "You aren't on longer, Benny, it just seems longer."

Another fifteen-minute promotion centers on the movie *Buck Benny Rides Again* and again, it's mostly guest stars babbling, and musical interludes. The only segment in which Benny and Allen have any time together is a fifteen-minute excerpt from "The Grape Nuts Program" of December 27, 1942, and it's not one of their better efforts.

BEA BEA BENSON

- LET IT ALL HANG OUT (Laff 138) *1/2 $4 $8
- OPEN AND ENTER (Laff 176) *1/2 $4 $8

Benson, with blonde wig and black painted-on eyebrows, plays the part of an aging floozie and snickers at her own jokes. Her elbow-in-the-ribs delivery makes her whiz-bang gags even more crass and charmless. From the first album:

"Girls, I used to be so damned skinny I had to tease ma' hair to keep ma' pants up! Huh! That's what Twiggy has to do. She's a born loser, that Twiggy. She puts her brassiere on backwards and it still fits 'er! Hah! Borrrrn loser! Some gal went out and bought a brassiere one day and brought it home. Her husband said, 'Why'd ya buy that thing—ya got nuthin' to put in it.' She said, 'You wear shorts, don't ya?' Hu-hah! How do ya like that, girls? What do you call a guy that doesn't wear any shorts? A reeeeal swinger! I don't wear brassieres myself, I wear spray-on starch. Try it fellas, it might help you too! Hah!"

GERTRUDE BERG

- HOW TO BE A JEWISH MOTHER (Amy 8007) *** $10 $25

On May 16, 1965, Gertrude Berg, along with David Ross, Michael Baseleon, and Jill Kraft, recorded a studio album based on the "training manual" by Dan Greenburg, which was a big-selling novelty book at the time. Berg, the beloved star/writer of the long-running *The Goldbergs*, gives her lines gentle irony rather than the crassness now associated with "Jewish mother" comedy. Typical of the gags is the segment in which an announcer offers instructions, acted out by Berg: "Give your son Marvin two sport shirts as a present. The first time he wears one of them, look at him sadly and say ... 'The other one you didn't like?'"

EDGAR BERGEN

- THE CHASE AND SANBORN SHOW (Mark 56 # 615) ** $5 $10
- EDGAR BERGEN AND CHARLIE MCCARTHY (Murray Hill M 60130) **1/2 $10 $30
- THE EDGAR BERGEN CHARLIE MCCARTHY SHOW (Radiola MR 1034) **1/2 $5 $10
- CHARLIE MCCARTHY RIDES AGAIN (Radiola MR 1157) **1/2 $5 $10
- FRACTURED FAIRY TALES (Radiola MR 1096) ** $5 $10

A ventriloquist with a successful radio show sounds like a bad joke, but with good jokes and a distinctive sounding dummy with a very human temperament, "The Bergen and McCarthy Show" ran from 1937 to 1956. Some might even read something deeper into the duo—the adult battling his own id. Charlie was the violent wise guy ("Lemme at 'im, I wanna hang one on 'im!"); Bergen was the gentle, imploring voice of reason.

The Mark 56 album collects excerpts from various programs. Bergen tells Charlie several fairy tales, including Rapunzel, Achilles, and Androcles the Lion. There's plenty of Charlie's sass. Bergen: "As Achilles lay dying, do you know what he said?" Charlie: "My feet are killing me."

A few segments let Mortimer Snerd shine, if that's possible. Bergen's other star dummy, the dull-witted hayseed, can't fathom anything, especially politics. Bergen asks: "How do you feel about the Taft-Hartley Bill?" Mortimer: "I think we should pay it."

Six-year-old Candy Bergen (whom announcer Ray Noble refers to as "Little Dextrose"), makes an appearance, and she has some dialogue with her "brother" Charlie.

Candy: "Daddy resents the idea that you support him."

Charlie: "Does he deny it?"

Candy: "No, but he resents it."

Fans who want to splurge will want the three-LP set from Murray Hill, but it won't be easy to find. Evidently it was withdrawn quickly due to problems with legal clearance. There's not that much to hunt for, actually. The first record is the same as the "Chase and Sanborn Show" Mark 56 album. Another record has two Christmas shows. That leaves one album of otherwise "lost" material, which includes routines with Bergen's female puppet Effie Klinker, and a show highlighting fussy Edward Everett Horton as a psychiatrist getting a lot of vaudevillian gag answers from Charlie:

Horton: "Do you suffer from headaches?"

Charlie: "Well I don't enjoy them!"

Horton: "Do you have a fear of high places?"

Charlie: "Only when I get stuck with the check."

Radiola's discs are the most accessible. MR 1034 is a winner with Abbott and Costello, plus Edward Everett Horton on one side (a 1942 show) and Marilyn Monroe the guest for the flip side's 1952 program. She's planning on marrying Charlie, and he's delighted with her outfit. "I'm wearing my wedding dress," she coos, "something borrowed." "You didn't borrow enough!"

The world is spared when Charlie fails his blood test: "No blood. Just sap!"

The sequel (MR 1157) has a good pairing as well, with Abbott and Costello returning, and Gene Tierney and Linda Darnell on the flip side.

NOTES: Bergen recorded an obscure disc, "Lessons in Ventriloquism" (Juro 591). As an oddity, it sometimes fetches $10 or more. The Charlie McCarthy battles with W. C. Fields can be heard on "Fields on Radio" (Columbia CS 9890) and "Great Radio Feuds" (Columbia KC 332540) among others. Charlie battles Fred Allen on "Vintage Radio Broadcasts" and "Comedy Gems," a broadcast from November 14, 1965 (see the Fred Allen listing). Bergen guests on "Ingrid Bergman on Radio" (Radiola 1154). A quick sketch, Charlie's destruction of Bergen's Oriental rug, is on Radiola's "Jest Like Old Times." A half hour show appears on the boxed set "Great Radio Comedians" (Murray Hill MH 5419X).

MILTON BERLE

- STARRING MILTON BERLE (Mark 56 # 788) **1/2 $4 $8
- UNCLE MILTIE ON RADIO (Radiola MR 1064) **1/2 $5 $10

Mr. Television did some radio work, and Mark 56 has excerpts from *The Milton Berle Show* with supporting comics Al Kelly, Arnold Stang, Jack Gilford, and Joe Besser. Manic Besser jousts with Berle as an income tax expert:

"Besser, don't tell me that you are the world's greatest authority on income tax." "Why certainly, you crazy, you! You're such a crazy! Last year I myself paid an income tax of $50,000." "Besser, you never worked a day in your life, how did you ever arrive at an amount like that?" "I copied off of the man in front of me!" "Besser, do you know what tangibles are?" "Yes. Little oranges!" "Besser, how does the government compute taxes?" "They take your year's salary ... that's it! They take your year's salary!"

Radiola offers a complete show (September 16, 1947) on one side. Berle gets off plenty of Berle-esque one-liners ("As the president of Standard Oil said to the president of Mobil Oil: your gas is as good as mine"). Side Two is stronger, collecting excerpts from many shows. This is prime Berle, brash and hokey: "I love Atlantic City ... especially at night when the piers are lit up. You can see a lot of beautiful things on the Boardwalk. But they're all with soldiers. But they're all with soldiers! Did you come in here for entertainment or revenge? The last time I was here my girl, who weighs three hundred pounds, won the beauty contest. She was voted Miss America. And parts of Canada, too. Boy, it's so tough to get a room here, I tried to check into the Jefferson Hotel and the clerk told me it was so crowded Jefferson was sleeping at the Claridge ... I'm very popular down here. I have a lot of fans. And on hot days I sell 'em for a nickel apiece. I'm pitching but you're not catching...."

NOTES: Berle released a non-music album, "Songs My Mother Loved" (Roulette 25018) and recorded novelty singles on RCA including "Bibbidy-Bobbidy-Boo" and "I'll Kiwl You a Miwl-Yun Times."

"Milton Berle's Mad Mad World of Comedy" (Publishing Mills) is an audio book featuring comedy clips plus interesting Berle interviews with George Burns, Phyllis Diller, Pat Buttram, and Jim "Fibber McGee" Jordan. Via mail order in 1996, Berle issued a CD called "Funniest Roasts of the Century" (Laugh Dome LD 2201-2) featuring himself and mostly dead comics (Jackie Vernon, Pat Buttram, Dick Shawn, and others who can't quibble about royalties) in clips from Friar's and similar roasts.

SHELLEY BERMAN

- INSIDE SHELLEY BERMAN (Verve MGV 15003) ★★★★ $4 $12

Before there was Woody Allen, there was Shelley Berman, the master of modern neuroses. An actor with roots in improvisational theater, Berman devised carefully polished and presented set pieces, some using the telephone for a prop. Berman's stern sense of decorum and his "concert" style of performing routines that were actually one-man "plays" changed the way nightclub comedy was perceived. He was an artist, one of the first to make stand-up an art.

This 1960 album is historic and classic, the first comedy record to be certified gold; the album that proved comedy on disc could sell. And it was art. It is amazing to realize that at a time when nightclub comedy was mostly wife jokes and schtick, Berman became so tremendously popular with stiffly presented, thoughtful, if not cerebral, routines.

The album opens with Berman's ten-minute airline routine, a virtuoso performance that captures every fear of this first generation of airplane passengers. A Borge-esque bit of wordplay muses on plurals: "It seems to me that the plural of yo-yo should be yo-yi. How about one sheriff, several sheriffim? One goof. A group of geef ... two jacki...." After an excruciating bit about a phone caller trying to alert authorities to a woman hanging from a window ledge, he does his famous "Morning After the Night Before." A drunk wakes up to discover that he made a fool of himself at a party and worse: "How did I break a window? I see. Were you very fond of that cat ... it's lucky the only thing I threw through the window was a cat ... oh ... she's a very good sport, your mother."

He even squeezes laughs out of a lecture on buttermilk. Berman gets worked up into a neurotic buttermilk lather, describing buttermilk drinking as "a little pornographic." After years of musing, including philosophical journeys into Zen, he has a revelation: "It is not the buttermilk that bothers me. It's the way the glass looks when you're through drinking it that makes me sick. That ugly white map inside of that glass...."

Berman's "Buttermilk" routine became one of his most famous. It "typed" the comic as the neurotic intellectual who can get bent out of shape over any facet of modern living. And, after the sleepy '50s, there were many in the audience similarly afflicted. Here was the brave new '60s, with changing sexual and racial attitudes, the bomb, and tremendous insecurity. Berman covered the traumas on an intense, raw, and personal level. His first comedy album best-seller remains fresh and gripping.

- OUTSIDE SHELLEY BERMAN (Verve MGVS 6107) ★★★★ $5 $10
- THE EDGE OF SHELLEY BERMAN (Verve MGVS 6161) ★★ $6 $12

"Outside" has some important material. "Franz Kafka on the Telephone" is dazzling, especially since few in the audience had heard of the tortured author. The bit is about a man caught up in a maze of bureaucratic phone operators while trying to call his girlfriend. More literate humor: Berman's description of a University of Chicago student: "If you give him a glass of water, he says, 'This is a glass of water. But is it a glass of water? And if it is a glass of water, WHY is it a glass of water?' And eventually he dies of thirst."

Drawing on his experience as an actor, Berman unveils his tour de force. "Father and Son" is a moving, touching, gently humorous portrait of a gruff but loving old deli man counseling his son who wants to leave home to become an actor in New York. For nearly an entire album side, the old Jewish father counsels, criticizes, and ultimately embraces his son. A warm, winning departure from Berman's sick and/or cerebral exercises, it's even more remarkable considering that it is not, as the audience assumed, based on Berman's life at all. Berman says his father was not nearly as supportive. This isn't autobiography. It's wishful thinking.

Berman displays another side of his talent in an audience participation bit. Playing an authority on children, he invites the audience to stump him with questions. He proves that he can improvise as well as anyone.

"Where do babies really come from?"

"If your child has asked you this question, where babies come from, we've had some success with pointing."

"How do you stop a child from swearing?"

"There are only two dirty words I will permit: tinkle and doody. That is because I believe the medical terms are obscene."

Soon after becoming the darling of the intellectuals, the neurotic comic naturally became "fed up" and decided to do more natural bits about average people. He wanted to do more "Father and Son" style bits with warmer humor. Consequently, there is no "edge" to his "Edge" album. One little playlet is a father's lecture to a daughter going out on a first date: "When he takes you home, Annie," the father lectures, "he's gonna wanna kiss you good night. Now I'm gonna give you an order. You come across, understand ... give him the kiss. That's his business. The second kiss Annie, that's your business. The third kiss: my business!"

The comic unveils a new character, an average schmuck who is awkward, pitiful, and cloddish. He's the nerd who calls up Shirley, his would-be girlfriend, trying to find out why she won't go out with him anymore: "Just tell me what it is ya don't like about me ... oh boy, uh, well, arright, I'm glad ya said it. Is there anything else? Arright, okay. Ya what else ... ya what else ... ya what else...." Another sketch with this character is about his lack of male friends. Unfortunately, Berman's best is so overpowering, both the neurotic material and "Father and Son," that the mild material here suffers by comparison.

- PERSONAL APPEARANCE (Verve V/V6 15027) **** $7 $15
- NEW SIDES (Verve V/V6 15036) ***1/2 $7 $15

Berman returns to peak form on "Personal Appearance," a blistering album with all the energy of a throbbing, exposed nerve. Berman comes out with a tensely enunciated story that would make him an instant candidate for a padded cell. With the conviction of a Poe or Kafka, but the twisted delivery of the tortured comedian he is, Berman reports on "a singular abnormal experience" preying on his mind: a paper napkin that kept slipping off his lap. Things get surreal from there. The next routine is one of his blackest portraits of angst, a phone call from a man trapped in a hotel room with no windows, no lights, and no door.

Berman's "Conventioneer" phone call achieves his desired blend of human comedy and bristling satire as he portrays an average drunken salesman alternately giddy, confused, tearful, and horny, calling his wife long distance. His bit about finding a black speck in his milk recalls his "Buttermilk" sketch, only here the manic victim of life's frustrations gets his revenge by devising a wide-eyed and calculated strategy for survival. Later Berman lets his raw nerves quiver through a crackling description of life's moments of agony.

For an encore, Berman does a devastating routine on dentists. It begins with a description of the waiting room, "a smartly furnished chamber of horrors" and the patients who sit "each one huddled, an island unto himself, quiet, nobody communicating ... and you sit there suffering your own personal chagrin." He ends up in the chair, paralyzed with fear, nervous about the X-rays, in agony from the pain, and fearing death by drowning in his own drool.

This is, simply on the passion of the performance, Berman's greatest album. Add the quality of the material, and it becomes a masterwork of stand-up art.

"New Sides" has two of Berman's best routines, a black comedy sketch about a traveling salesman nearly bleeding to death as he finds, time after time, to find a doctor willing to make a house call, and "The Complete Neurosis," about a seemingly calm neurotic ("I don't fly into a rage if my shoelaces aren't the same length on both sides") who has only one problem: he can't remember his name.

As for neurosis, it doesn't get much better or worse than on the intimate confession of bedtime perversity: "I was seized with an absolutely uncontrollable desire to – take off the pillow case ... the way I nuzzle it ... is it fair to go to bed with something night after night and never say a kind word to it? Well ... I'm not a brutish man, I'm a gentle man, I didn't just rip it off, I inched it up, the way a man should ... pretty little thing." But when the pillow displays a flaw (a tag saying "Do Not Remove This Tag Under Penalty Of Law") he rips the tag off. Tormented, he tells the audience, "I want to give myself up!"

Berman has a charming, light moment demonstrating the Jew's harp, and presents a few lesser sketches: a return of his doltish Every-jerk character (this time the poor soul calls up a finance company after hearing a commercial that says "you have a friend here") and a call from a dog owner who has lost his pet. Still, there is more thought-provoking satire here than on a dozen other comedy albums.

- SEX LIFE OF THE PRIMATE (Verve V/V6 15043) *** $10 $20

Berman's only studio sketch album, this last hurrah includes Jerry Stiller, Anne Meara, and Lovelady Powell. The improv-based sketches are uneven, some excellent, some ordinary. The long sketches include Anne Meara as the union representative of "Associated Wives of America," informing Berman of the latest rules and regulations, Lovelady Powell interviewing Berman on his marriage to a gorilla, and a dating sketch between Meara and Berman. They are diverting but lack the manic killer instinct of Berman's own monology. The best, a near classic, is a ten-minute routine about sex education in the classroom. Powell is the teacher and her kids are asking typically confused questions: "The male fish. Does he just fertilize his wife's roes, or does he just plunk any old roe?" "The word is fertilize ... Kevin, give us a summary of what we've learned so far...." "... the male fish swims over the roe, and drops fertilizer over the roe...." "Howard has a question." "How was I born? My father can't swim."

Recurring sets of "Cleans and Dirtys" provide quick laughs as Berman covers semantics: "Desk is a clean. Drawers is a dirty ... Lake Superior is a clean. Lake Titicaca is a dirty ... Nail is a clean. Screw is a dirty ... Chaucer is a clean. Lenny Bruce is a dirty ... Japanese Beetle is a clean. Spanish Fly is a dirty...."

Stiller and Meara perform their solo piece "Hate," one of stand-up's best husband and wife quarrel routines.

- GREAT MOMENTS IN COMEDY (Verve 15048) *** $5 $10
- LET ME TELL YOU A FUNNY STORY (Metro M 546) *** $7 $15

"Great Moments" is a "best of" but it's better to simply get "Inside" and "Outside." The Metro "best of" offers specially recorded new introductions. Berman says it took only ten minutes for him to create his bit about the neurotic who can't remember his name. His remark, "I realized I could cash in on my neurotic tendencies" is an understatement. Perhaps the most telling revelation occurs not in the introduction to "The Morning After the Night Before," but in its editing. Berman reveals that cat owners were upset that the drunk kills the cat. Now, thanks to the editing of a few lines from the original record, it seems as though the cat is still alive.

- LIVE AGAIN! (Chuckle 33732) *** $8

The "comeback" CD of 1995 offers mostly classic material, which should be a delight to the average fan unable to find the old albums. "The Department Store" (a woman hanging from a ledge), "Embarrassing Moments," and "Father and Son" return, along with the neurotic ("remember me, the fellow who used to be afraid of fear itself") who can't remember his own name.

It's a relief that Shelley's newer material is amusing, if not as biting, as the classics. "International Conference" is a cute, old-fashioned exercise in dialect humor and nonsense words, and "Hotels" borrows from his novelty book. Now and then he makes nostalgic references to the past material, and a self-effacing comment or two about changing times (he says that in an era where anything goes, he's still edgy about using a word like "condominium"). The audience is warmly responsive, as they should be for a living legend who has contributed art to stand-up. Despite the popularity of "observational" material, Berman's return proves that the "old-fashioned" style of set pieces and polished monology is not only "classic," but more than valid today.

NOTES: Berman's ledge routine appears on "25 Years of Recorded Comedy" (Warner Brothers 3BX 3131). The rarest Berman album is not a comedy disc but the original Broadway cast album "A Family Affair" (United Artists UAL 4099). It didn't last long on Broadway and is the target of original cast album collectors as well as Berman fans. It has some good songs; "Right Girls" is bombastic and amusing as Berman describes some of his failed dates. "Revenge" is even better since it's more typical of Berman's stand-up personality (there's even a phone call monologue thrown in).

Another rarity is "A Funny Thing Happened on the Way to the Conventions," made for Gulf Oil.

HERSCHEL BERNARDI

- CHOCOLATE COVERED MATZOHS: AN EVENING WITH HERSCHEL BERNARDI
  (Vanguard VRS 9074, CD: OVC 6023) **1/2 $8

In the early '60s, before taking over for Zero Mostel in "Fiddler on the Roof," Bernardi often made concert appearances as a singer and monologist, singing Jewish folk songs and telling warm, anecdotal stories about family life and assimilation. In a ten-minute monologue about the change from the old country to the new, Bernardi tells the story about a Jew who changed his name to C. D. Allen: "A friend asks, 'Your name is C. D. Allen? Where did you get a name like C. D. Allen?' He says, 'Well, everybody around me was changing their name, I got disgusted, I was standing on the street corner, I look up at the sign, it said Allen Street, so I changed it to Allen.' 'Oh, Allen, Allen Street. Where did you get the C. D.?' 'Corner Delancey.'"

Another highlight is a long routine on his own family life, also rich in character comedy. A few folk songs are included also, from the joyful "Chiri Bim" to the elegantly moving "Tumbalalaika" and "The Miller's Tears."

Bernardi appears briefly on Mel Henke's comedy album. He's on several Broadway cast albums, including "Bajour," "Zorba," and his own collection of "Fiddler on the Roof" songs.

SANDRA BERNHARD

- WITHOUT YOU I'M NOTHING (Enigma 7733692) * $12

"Performance artist" Bernhard's albums are not really comedy, though most stores put them in the comedy rack. Comedy fans can forget "I'm Your Woman" (Mercury 8248261M1); average rock tunes prefaced by melodramatic, often pretentious monologues. The most interesting thing about it is the cover photo. The shot of Bernhard, in lace bra and slip, heaving a guitar into the air is intoxicating. The full face back cover photo is sobering.

Only Bernhard fans will be able to stand "Without You," a self-indulgent eighty-minute CD (two record set). Bernhard spends a lot of time prattling about her own legend, playing the primping prima donna, and dispensing painfully theatrical, over-enunciated monologues with all the restraint of a freshman drama class student. She doesn't seem to be able to utter a sentence without lapsing into italics. The songs are worse, parodies (hopefully) of grating cabaret and show tunes.

"Excuses for Bad Behavior" (550 Music/Epic BK 57693, 1994) reverts to soft rock, including a ballad version of "Sympathy for the Devil." Anticipating those who prefer her bitchy humor to her songs, she stops the music briefly for a nasty two-minute impersonation of one of her own fans complaining about the lack of confessions and angst on the record.

DICK BERNIE AND COMPANY

- LIVE BURLESQUE LIVE (United Artists UAS 6613) **1/2 $7 $15

One of several "re-creations" of burlesque on record, this 1967 effort offers a few jazzy instrumental numbers and some fairly well done sketches from Bernie and his group, most of them concentrating more on corn than porn:

"Say, Dick, I haven't seen you around for a while, where have you been?" "Well, it's embarrassing. I've been in jail for thirty days." "What did you do?" "I drove through two red lights." "They cannot put you in jail for thirty days for driving through two red lights!" "These red lights were on the back of a police car. I got in front of the judge, I tried to plead insanity. I told the judge I was a fish!" "What happened?" "He sent me up the river, put me in the can. But now I'm up on a charge, I don't think I'll beat it." "What is the charge?" "You won't believe this. Statutory rape!" "Statutory rape?" "I wanna tell you something, if I knew it was a statue I wouldn't have tried it."

Other routines include "School Days" and a version of "Who's on First."

BERNIE BERNS

- BERNIE GOES TO WASHINGTON (Jubilee 2047) *1/2 $4 $8

The album notes explain what Bernie Berns has in mind: "Imagine the First Family with a Jewish accent."

The joke is hearing John F. Kennedy speaking in an Irish accent, yet peppering his talk with Yiddish terms and Jewish references. Kennedy on the phone: "Please, uh, get me the Hebrew Home of The Aged in Hyannisport. Hello, Tante? How is my favorite aunt this morning. Yes, I received the tallis this morning. No, I won't forget. How can I? If not for you I would not be able to read Hebrew at all ... and if I was a good boy and learned my lessons you would buy me a malted and a pretzel. Even if I was a bad boy you'd buy me a malted and a pretzel."

Berns doesn't have much of a Kennedy accent or a script on this strained concept album. He also released "Disha Bernie" on the Attey label.

BERT AND I

- BERT AND I (Bert and I 1) ** $5 $10
- MORE BERT AND I (Bert and I 2) ** $5 $10
- RETURN OF BERT AND I (Bert and I 5) ** $5 $10
- BERT AND I STEM INFLATION (Bert and I 11) ** $5 $10
- BERT AND I ON STAGE (Bert and I 12) ** $5 $10

"Bert and I" (Robert Bryan and Marshall Dodge) were a pair of Yale University students who put out an independent album of New England Yankee humor in 1959. It sold well and allowed the two men to pursue their destinies. Bryan became an Anglican minister and Dodge continued with monology until his death in a 1983 car accident.

Most of their material is adapted from nineteenth century literature and anecdotal folk tales. Told with a dry, offhand delivery similar to Fred Allen's or Allen's "Titus Moody" character, these stories barely raise a smile more than a belly laugh. From the first album, here's the story of a hunting trip:

"... All day long he walked without firing a shot. He was all set to head in, just about sundown, when he spied a fox behind a rock ... taking careful aim, he almost squeezed the trigger when he sighted another fox twenty feet away from the first. Well, he aimed somewhere in between. The shot hit a rock, split it in two and killed both foxes. The kick from the gun knocked him into the stream behind him. When he came to, his right hand was on a beaver's tail, his left hand on an otter's head, and his trouser pockets were so full of trout that a button popped off his fly and killed a partridge."

Dodge and Bryan often alternated in reciting monologues, but worked as a team on some routines. Some ancient vaudeville recited with tighty grim New England accents on "The Return of Bert and I":

"Sorry to hear that you're buryin' your Pa." "Got to. He's dead." "They say he was a self-made man." "If he was, it sure relieves the Almighty of considerable responsibility." "You the gravedigger?" "Yeah." "Isn't that grave too shallow?" "Maybe, but he ain't never gonna get out." "How come this graveyard has no fence around it?" "Why put a fence up when them on the inside can't get out, and them on the outside ain't in any hurry to get in?"

It's pretty much the same album after album.

BEVERLY HILLBILLIES

- THE BEVERLY HILLBILLIES (Columbia CS 9202, reissued as
    Harmony HS 11269 and on CD: Columbia 7296) ** $8

This album offers *The Beverly Hillbillies* cast singing comical songs that almost reach the level of humor on the show itself. On "Beverly Hills" Buddy and the gang report on the "strange" ways of the natives: "They'll go out in a pasture where the grass is slick, lay down a ball and hit it with a stick. Don't make no sense, bless my soul. They spend all day tryin' to lose it in a hole!"

There are songs on practically every phase of the sitcom, including the swimming pool, Granny's tonic, and Jethro's comic stupidity, which leads to the wistful refrain, "I gotta have a long talk with that boy" from Uncle Jed. Naturally, there's "The Ballad of Jed Clampett." For ardent fans it makes for an interesting novelty souvenir. Buddy Ebsen (MGM), Irene Ryan (Nashwood), and Donna Douglas (Arlen) issued singles during the series' run.

BEYOND THE FRINGE

- BEYOND THE FRINGE (Capitol SW 1792, CD reissue Angel ZDM 077776477121) **1/2 $8
- BEYOND THE FRINGE '64 (Capitol W 2072) **1/2 $10 $25

Peter Cook, Dudley Moore, Alan Bennett, and Jonathan Miller were the four-member troupe who leaped to stardom via the "Beyond the Fringe" revue. Barely out of school when the show opened in London on May 10, 1961, the group's satires were considered daring, cheeky, and irreverent fun. They influenced many other groups but now their material seems dated and mild. The religious humor of "Take a Pew" survives as cute; hardly daring. A priest cautions:

"Life? Life is rather like opening a tin of sardines. We're all of us looking for the key. Some of us think we've found the key, don't we? We roll back the lid of the sardine tin of life. We reveal the sardines, the riches of life therein. We get them out. We enjoy them. You know, there's always a little piece in the corner you can't get out. I wonder, is there a little piece in the corner of your life? I know there is in mine."

The old British political references may bewilder people who think "Beaverbrook" and "Mountbatten" are coat and umbrella companies. The most enduring bits are "Aftermyth of War" and "Sitting on the Bench." The former is a richly sardonic ten-minute look at Britain's early passivity and latter failures during World War II. Peter Cook is the officer who tells a soldier, "The war's not going very well ... I want you to lay down your life, Perkins. We need a futile gesture at this stage ... Good-bye, Perkins."

"Sitting on the Bench" is a Peter Cook monologue about becoming a coal miner. The only question on the job application was "Who are you ... and I got seventy-five percent on that." Another routine, "So That's the Way You Like It," is a Shakespearean satire that may be too close to the original for unschooled listeners. Those who get some of the lame recognition humor ("Saucy, Worscter!") may not want it. Dudley Moore is showcased playing some forgettable opera and music parodies on the piano.

The 1964 version has more American-based material, including commentary on the civil rights problem: "What's all this black muslin I hear they're wearing?" There's still plenty of gags about the British class system: "I don't want to see lust, rape, incest, and sodomy," says stuffy Lord Cobbold, the Duke, "I can get all that at home."

The first "Fringe" is now available on CD.

THE BICKERSONS

* THE BICKERSONS (Radiola MR 1115) *** $5 $10
* RETURN OF THE BICKERSONS (Radiola/Murray Hill 3MH36721) *** $9 $20
* THE BICKERSONS REMATCH (Columbia G 30523, $10 $20
    a reissue of THE BICKERSONS [Columbia CS 8492] **** $5 $10
    and THE BICKERSONS FIGHT BACK [Columbia CS 8683]) **** $5 $10

Writer Phil Rapp's ultimate quarreling married couple were played on radio and TV by Don Ameche and Francis Langford. Lew Parker and Marsha Hunt sometimes filled in. The single Radiola disc uses material from 1947-48 appearances on *Old Gold Time*. The scripts always tried to keep up a polished flow of give and take, even if there was a vaudevillian tilt to the humor: "The cat got out three times last night." "He won't get out tonight." "Where did you put him?" "In the birdcage." "In the birdcage! Where's the canary?" "In the cat."

"Return" is a three-record set. Originally produced for the Publishers Central Bureau/Outlet Books mail-order company, it was released in 1987. It's for fans who never grow tired of Blanche's complaints and John's weary comebacks:

"You throw away money on silly things! Didn't you pay $22 for that fire extinguisher? We had it a whole year and never used it once."

"I'll set fire to the house in the morning."

Although the very idea of humor in husband and wife bickering may seem a distasteful subject, and there might be questions over the stereotyped lazy, drinking hubby and his whining, pecking wife, there's no doubt the Bickerson sketches were well-written and excellently acted. Frances Langford gave Blanche some warmth and Ameche gave John one of the most hysterical snores in comedy history. In 1960 and 1961, Phil Rapp brought The Bickersons back for records that contain most of his best jokes.

Here's a quick sample of prime Bickerson material, cooking and boiling to a climax. Blanche expects an anniversary gift, but is demure about it:

"I hope you didn't spend a lot of money." "I didn't spend a lot of money." "Why not?" "Because I didn't have a lot of money. Just a little old beach bathrobe, it cost eight dollars." "Married eight years and you spend eight dollars! A dollar a year for washing your shirts, cooking your meals, darning your socks, raising your children—" "We haven't got any children." "Well what do you want for a dollar a year!"

NOTES: Frances Langford issued many straight records, including "Old Songs for Old Friends" (Capitol T 1865); Ameche's radio work appears on "W. C. Fields on Radio" (Columbia) and "The Spike Jones Show" (Radiola).

BIG DADDY

* BIG DADDY (Rhino RNLP 852) ** $5 $10
* MEANWHILE BACK IN THE STATES (Rhino RNLP 854) **1/2 $5 $10
* CUTTING THEIR OWN GROOVE (Rhino R2 70733) *** $8

This quirky band is filed equally under comedy, novelty, oldies, and rock. The Big Daddy style is to rearrange modern hit songs into '50s style songs. It's a one-joke idea, but is cleverly executed as the duo match a new song to a specific style, such as Buddy Holly, The Coasters, or Elvis Presley. If the listener knows both the recent tune and the style used to grease it for parody, the recognition humor can produce a bent, wide smile.

There's some good humor on the second album (the comedy highlight turns the somberly whining "Always on My Mind" into a snickering "Big Bopper" style put-on) but the group hit their stride on their first CD, "Cutting Their Own Groove." "Graceland" is now sung by an Elvis Presley type, not Paul Simon. A Frankie Avalon sound-alike juxtaposes the innocent "Venus" with Madonna's "Like a Virgin." The biggest chuckles come from the falsetto and doo-wopped destruction of "Memory" from *Cats*; a Coasters version of Kris Kristofferson's "Help Make It Through the Night" ("Get in the sack, don't talk back!"); and Sinead O'Connor's hit "Nothing Compares 2 U" handled by a sound-alike for Little Richard. The latter has some musical jokes (it begins with a bit of "The Star Spangled Banner," alluding to Sinead's protest over the use of the anthem to open shows) and downright sass, as "Little Richard" effeminately keeps the song's gender intact: "I put my arms around every boy I see, but they just remind me of you!"

ARTHUR BLAKE

• CURTAIN TIME (Star-Crest 1001) **1/2		$10	$25

An impressionist popular in the '40s and '50s, Blake (real name: Arthur Clark, Jr.) specialized in women (Tallulah Bankhead, Katherine Hepburn, Bette Davis) and arch men (Noel Coward and Clifton Webb). The album will delight the cabaret/camp element, but there's enough wit and oddity to interest others. A highlight on this disc (also released as "The Best of Arthur Blake") is Blake's re-creation of "Sorry Wrong Number" (complete with soap opera organ) as Raymond Burr and Peter Lorre plot to murder Barbara Stanwyck. There's snickery risqué humor as Stanwyck cries out "Hello, operator? Operator ... I was asleep and I woke with a jerk. No, no one you know. Operator, my finger got caught in the wrong hole ..."). Some of Blake's choices will be lost on modern listeners: Eleanor Roosevelt, Ethel and Lionel Barrymore, Zasu Pitts, Frank Morgan, Louella Parsons, and so on. Blake does Louella Parsons, Bette Davis, Noel Coward, and Tallulah Bankhead on 1962's "Jayne Mansfield Busts Up Las Vegas (20th Century Fox SFX 3049, reissued via World Record Club import TP 262). He duets with her a few times, but mostly helps with brief comedy introductions to her songs. Long retired, Blake died in 1985 at the age of seventy.

NAN BLAKSTONE

• AN EVENING WITH NAN BLAKSTONE (Gala 1000) **1/2		$12	$20
• AN EVENING WITH NAN BLAKSTONE VOL. 2 (Gala 1002) **1/2		$12	$20
• SOPHISTICATED SONGS (Jubilee 2000) **		$10	$20
• NEW HUSH HUSH ALBUM (Jubilee LP 1) **		$10	$20

Nan Blakstone had a lot of personality, enough to make her mild double entendre tunes more entertaining than the lyrics might warrant. Her sultry jazz-tinged phrasing and lively ad-libbing suggest how effective she must have been live in sophisticated lounges in the '40s.

Jubilee's ten-inchers were collections of 78s from the late '30s. "New Hush Hush" has her scat-singing "Blakstone's Secret Passion" and getting chuckles with "Blakstone's Torch Song," a gold digger's lament that ends up with parody lyrics based on "Sunday, Monday and Always." Her old, rich hubby isn't ready for the grave: "I thought that I'd get mink, but all I got was Fink. Sunday, Monday and always. Although his motor's gone, Fink still carries on. Sunday, Monday and always."

Blakstone's first Gala album of 78s features: "Sex Rears Its Ugly Head," "Little Richard's Getting Bigger," "Who Brought Me Home," and "Lady Godiva" among others. The second has highlights with "The Elevator Song," "Get Yourself a Past," "Blakstone's Admission of Being a Good Girl," and "Catherine, Madcap Empress of Russia."

Some of Blakstone's better material on Jubilee ten-inchers was reissued as one side of the slightly more accessible album "Dwight Fiske and Nan Blakstone." Clear-sounding copies of Blakstone discs are not easy to find, especially after so many decades. For those who prefer subtlety and have an ear for cabaret jazz, she surpasses Ruth Wallis and is at least the equal of Fiske and Charlie Drew. She died in 1951.

MEL BLANC

• A HUMOROUS LOOK AT COMMERCIALS (MBA) **		$7	$15
• SUPERFUN (MBA) *1/2		$7	$15

The creator of so many Warner Brothers cartoon character voices, Mel Blanc appears on many children's albums for Capitol, Decca, and Peter Pan. He also recorded a ten-inch novelty song disc, "Party Panic" (Capitol 436).

Aside from cartoon voices, Blanc was a busy man on radio, having his own show for a while and supporting Jack Benny right through the TV era. On Radiola's "The Jack Benny Story" he performs his popular routine as Cy, the Mexican who speaks one word at a time ("sí!").

He had his own company, Mel Blanc Associates, and "Humorous Look" was released to amuse clients and interest them in doing business. It's a copy of the 1966 lecture he delivered to ad executives on the history of advertising:

"Believe this or not. The first advertising was done by a sexually frustrated caveman. His initial attempt at advertising for a mate was done by standing in front of his cave and shouting, (Yosemite Sam voice) 'I wanna woman! I gotta have a woman!' This understandably produced no results. So he took the creative approach. Advertising with impact. He picked up a rock and gave the next girl he saw a smack on the head. Then he dragged her to his cave and fulfilled his desires. As primitive as this was, it has been said that advertising has changed very little since then."

A few years later he tried to pitch "Superfun: The Radio Comedy Service" to radio stations and ad people. Once again he pressed up samples on his own MBA label. The cast he assembled is impressive: Len Weinrib, Arte Johnson, Howard Morris, Gary Owens, Jesse White, Dave Ketchum, Pat Carroll, Naomi Lewis, Leo De Lyon, and Sid Melton. The comedy material isn't impressive. Among the blackouts intended for disc jockeys to use is this quickie: "Hi, this is Frank Sinatra. Thanks for playing all my records." The big joke is that it's a woman's voice. And from Gary Owens: "This is the off-stage announcer telling you, for their size, elephants don't really smell bad. Now, back to the records."

BLOWFLY

• WEIRD WORLD OF BLOWFLY (Weird World 2020) **		$5	$10
• BLOWFLY ON TV (Weird World 2021) **		$5	$10

- BLOWFLY ON TOUR (Weird World 2022) ** $5 $10
- ZODIAC (Weird World 2023) ** $5 $10
- BLOWFLY AT THE MOVIES (Weird World 2024) ** $5 $10
- BUTTERFLY (Weird World 2025) ** $5 $10
- OLDIES BUT GOODIES (Weird World 2026) **1/2 $5 $10
- BLOWFLY'S PARTY (Weird World 2034) ** $5 $10
- RAPPIN' DANCIN' AND LAUGHIN' (Weird World 2035) ** $5 $10
- PORNO FREAK (Weird World 2036) ** $5 $10
- ELECTRONIC BANANA (Oops 102) ** $5 $10
- IN THE TEMPLE OF DOOM (Oops 103) ** $5 $10
- ON TOUR 86 (Oops 104) ** $5 $10
- BLOWFLY'S FREAK PARTY (Oops 105) ** $5 $10
- FRESH JUICE (Oops 106) ** $5 $10
- ZODIAC/BLOWFLY (2 LP CD reissue House of Funk 1003) ** $8
- BLOWFLY X-RATED (BCM Records B.C. 50-2069-42) ** $20

Clarence Reid had a few minor hits under his own name, but he's carved out a longer and more colorful career over the years as "Blowfly."

A black party record favorite, some of Blowfly's early album covers sport the most unappetizing topless models ever seen. Blowfly's comedy is at Doug Clark level—much of it just a harmless celebration of dirty words and dirty acts.

"Oldies but Goodies" is nicely done (for fans of dirty comedy only, of course). It's basic dirty word parodies of popular '50s tunes. "Blue Moon," given a doo-wop version similar to The Marcel's classic arrangement, is renamed "Blue Balls." The lyrics are predictable: "Blue balls, you have my ass in a knot. I guess I'll get myself a shot. Why don't you leave me alone?" "All Shook Up" becomes "All F---ed Up," and "Get a Job" becomes "Blow Job." The formula of funny (if childish) dirty word song parodies (and some originals) would continue on and on. The later albums for Oops are better sonically, with the music on the original tunes equal in quality to both clean and dirty rap and R&B songs on major labels.

Some will find the repetitive beat and the indiscriminate cursing and sex talk more numbing than funny, but fans who like funky music and dirty jokes rate Blowfly the best in the business.

In 1990 Blowfly issued his last five albums (on the Oops label) on a three-CD or five-LP boxed set, "Blowfly X-Rated" (BCM Records B.C. 50-2069-42) complete with a souvenir T-shirt.

BOB AND PAPERSACK

- LIVE AT THE CLUB CHECKMATE (Chux CLP 1001) *1/2 $6 $12

The black comedy team of straight man Bob Lawrence and excitably funky James Lairy never got much beyond the Chicago area, where this disc was recorded in 1969. The humor on this badly recorded album generally involves Bob's stern Demond Wilson-style attempts to educate his frisky and silly friend. Some of their act is jokeless character comedy. Other times they'll rehash an old routine like this: "In order to play golf you gotta have a bag." "Don't worry 'bout dat! I got dat!" "But yo' bag gotta have some balls in it." "Don't worry about dat, I got dat!" "Your bag's gotta have at least twelve balls in it." "Huh? Dat many?" "How about a half a dozen?" "Hoo! Can I get by wit two?"

BOB AND RAY

- WRITE IF YOU GET WORK (Unicorn UN 1001) *** $20 $40
- ON A PLATTER (RCA VICTOR LSP 1773) *** $20 $50
- STEREO SPECTACULAR (RCA VICTOR LSP 2131) ** $20 $40

Bob Elliott and Ray Goulding were popular radio satirists who managed to survive from the '50s to the '80s, despite TV. They appeared on TV, even on Broadway, but radio suited them best as they satirized old soap operas and interview programs and created subtle mock-commercials. They have a loyal cult. Those outside it sometimes don't understand the humor in Bob and Ray's realistic, tongue-in-cheek approach that gently pokes at the pathetic absurdities of everyday existence, often by being deliberately homely or lame.

The ten-incher from 1954 on the Boston-based Unicorn label is quite rare. It has some deliberately odd non sequiturs that gratify their fans and annoy others. A radio commercial for a movie called *Grub, the Story of Food*, enthuses: "*Grub, the Story of Food!* See 1500 screaming babies waiting for their strained spinach. See tons and tons of frozen food! Women fought for ... Men died for ... Grub.... Repulsive Pictures' latest release, filmed in various shades of gray. Be sure to see *Grub, the Story of Food*. Produced by the same studio which gave you the moving vehicle, *Crosstown Bus*."

Other bits: "Mary McGoon," "Mr. Treat Chaser of Lost Persons," "Epic," "Tahiti," "O Sweaters," "The Crying Garter Man," and "Fonsicle Cigarettes."

RCA's 1960 "Platter" is high priced not only due to the Bob and Ray cult, but also fetishists who crave the era's "Living Stereo" pressings. Those who have to pay a high price for this mild and subtle comedy might be disappointed. There's "Charles the Poet," satirizing a Nick Kenny type of heartfelt versifier; the duo's popular routine about Wally Ballou interviewing a Cranberry grower; and a dentist bit filled with then-novel stereo effects. After jackhammer noises and polishing: "There's a tooth you can be proud of. You can see that at night." Some of the bits were daring stylistically. Now fans are used to Monty Python and others doing "non-comedy," but here's an early example of deliberate dullness: "Two Face West." For five minutes a pair of cowboys are unable to get off their horses: "Ho! Whoa ... I can't do it, I just can't do it...." "Now you're on my horse." Similarly, the duo fumble monotonously with their speeches during the "Shoddy Showmanship Awards." ("You want to get at it." "No, go ahead." "All right.") The "Stereo Spectacular" from 1958 is a sampler record with cuts from RCA albums by Abbe Lane, Julie Andrews, Lena Horne, etc. The team introduce the songs and have about ten minutes for their own comedy, most of it centered on a mock-interview with nutsy Dr. Ahkbar, whose aural experiments include getting bagpipers to march in circles, fastening a man to a pendulum so he ticks from side to side, and playing with a fly that buzzes all around the room. Considering the usual asking price, this disc will be disappointing to all but the duo's hard-core fans.

- THE TWO AND ONLY (Columbia S 30412) **** $7 $15

In 1970 Bob and Ray came to Broadway with a rich variety of their most popular routines and characters. Newsman Wally Ballou single-mindedly does a soft human interest man-in-the-street interview with a cranberry bog owner while the sounds of screams, gunfire, and a crime in progress go on nearby. A fellow irritates a waiter by insisting on ordering from the children's menu, and the duo perform their classic interview in which a disinterested, superficial interviewer is matched with an equally uninteresting and short-sighted guest—an expert on the Komodo dragon.

"The Komodo dragon is the world's largest living lizard...."

"They're of the lizard family, aren't they?"

"Yes. They are the world's largest living lizard. There are two Komodo dragons at the National Zoo in Washington...."

"Well now, if we wanted to take the kiddies to see a Komodo dragon, where would we go to take the kiddies to see a Komodo dragon?"

The few facts about the Komodo dragon are repeated endlessly, but like a fine Laurel and Hardy routine, this labor of futility is so likably and absurdly presented, the audience predicts the responses and laughs. Similar is another gem featuring a representative from the maddeningly "Slow Talkers of America." Another classic is the contrast between a defeated politician's blunt concession speech ("I'm never gonna run again!") and a newsman's analysis of it:

"His jeremiad, his threnody, call it what you will, can only be taken for what it is: an atrabilious amphigory."

The album is really "The Best" of Bob and Ray—delightful, deceptively simple, and deadly accurate in its dissection of the dolts, despicables, dimwits, and dizzies that make up the proud species of human beings on earth.

- MARY BACKSTAYGE NOBLE WIFE (Radiola/Goulding-Elliot-Graybar) *1/2 $7 $15
- VINTAGE BOB AND RAY (Genesis GS 1047) ** $10 $20
- BOB & RAY PRESENT WALLY BALLOU (Genesis GS 1065) ** $7 $15

Various albums of old radio show material have surfaced. The Radiola disc takes mundane slices of life from the team's long-running parody of soap operas. No doubt David Letterman's joy in "lame" humor came from Bob & Ray, who at one point decide to open a fast food chain called "The House of Toast." A bit too much of this disc is steeped in faithfully re-enacted clichés: "Join us next time when we'll hear Greg Marlowe say: 'Out in the kitchen, Mary, I'd like to see you for a minute.'"

1973's collection, "Vintage Bob and Ray" offers twenty three-minute sketches from their old *Monitor* radio show on NBC. To the average listener unfamiliar with Bob and Ray, much of the stuff will seem jokeless and bewildering. Bob and Ray fans may be amused to hear familiar characters like Mr. Trace (Keener Than Most Persons), Word Carr, Mr. Science, and Wally Ballou, but this is still a surprisingly uneven collection. The ideas are funnier in theory than in practice, like the "Reunited Sister and Brother" who, after seventy years, meet on a broadcast and have nothing much to say to each other beyond "hello."

Wally Ballou, the newsman/interviewer so oblivious to actual news, is the subject of an hour-long collection of twenty-one vignettes issued in 1976. Once again, he visits a dummy factory, a tranquilizer factory, an adult tap-dancing class, and even finds it worthwhile to interview a man who stabs paper with a stick for the sanitation department: "... Now he's going to demonstrate ..." "This is a little crinkly cup, tough to get at, particularly on cement." "... He's chasing it. Can't get it." "No. I'm gonna have to pick it up with my hand." "Well, this is Wally Ballou on the street, returning it to the studio."

NOTES: Bob and Ray worked for many ad agencies, including their own, and many promo albums exist that contain the particular client's semi-funny radio ads. Among others: "Bob and Ray for EPA," "Gulistan Carpet, A Garden of Roses for Spring," "Glidden: Paint the Town Spred," and several albums for the Radio Advertising Bureau. Collectors routinely pay $15 or more for these, as well as *Monitor* albums—transcription discs issued to radio stations in the '50s. *Monitor* was a magazine show that featured the duo. The transcription for April 28, 1955 (RCA F8-MP-3439) offers headline news, a poem from Phyllis McGinley, and "special features" like a visit to a "record your own voice booth" in Times Square and a German band in Munich. It's up to Bob and Ray to provide much-needed comic relief. Bob interviews Ray as "The Animal Lady," who is quick to point out, "I'm called the Animal Lady not because of my features, but because of the subject in which I deal." Bob has questions from listeners who own civits and tapirs. The Animal Lady answers, "I don't know what to say ... I wish you had mentioned a few of these questions to me before I went on the air and made a fool of myself!"

A lot of Bob and Ray material has been released in audiocassette-only collections from Radioart, notably "Classic Bob & Ray" Volume One and Two, and the Grammy-nominated "Bob and Ray: A Night of Two Stars."

BARONESS BOBO

- THERE'S A MOUSE IN MY PANTS (Laff 154) *1/2 $4 $8

Like most Laff Records comics, black transvestite Miss Bobo takes a familiar joke and embellishes it for several minutes, adding funky description and overacting the characters. The album title is based on his favorite long story:

"This little boy is named Johnny. This little girl used to beat him up every damn day. Wasn't a day passed that she didn't beat him up and pull his pants down. His mother told him, 'Listen, the next time she's ready to pull your pants down, you tell her you got a mouse in your pants 'cause all little girls are scared of mice. You tell her you got a mouse in your pants!'" Several minutes of storytelling later, the children have their confrontation: "She grabbed at his pants to rip 'em and pull 'em down. He said, 'Mary, you better watch it! I got a mouse in my pants!' Mary said, 'Oh! A mouse! Did you say a mouse?' He say, 'Yes, I got a mouse in my pants!' She pulled up her dress and pulled down her pants and said, 'Sic 'em pussy! Sic 'em!'"

ERIC BOGOSIAN

- ERIC BOGOSIAN (Neutral 10) * $5 $10
- SEX, DRUGS, ROCK AND ROLL (SBK Records CDP 04757) *1/2 $8

Bogosian's 1983 Neutral album offers "Voices of America," a long, long piece duplicating the obnoxiousness of FM radio disc jockeys, radio news, and commercials. It's accurate, but not funny. Which is why he's called a "performance artist" more often than a satirist or a comedian. On the flip side there's "Men Inside," a tiresome bit of stark theatrical cliché and excess. Even Billy Crystal wouldn't stand in the spotlight and, in a child's voice, start piping melodrama: "Hey Dad, guess what I did today? I ran as fast as I could, and I threw a rock at a bird and I killed it. Pretty good, huh Dad? Dad, when I grow up am I gonna be just like you? I wanna be just like you, Dad, I wanna be tall and strong and never make any mistakes."

Things aren't much better on 1990's "Sex, Drugs and Rock and Roll." On one cut Bogosian mimics the spiel of a subway bum for three minutes. It's letter perfect and painfully accurate: "Sorry my clothes aren't clean, I'm sorry I'm homeless, I'm sorry I don't have a job, I'm sorry I have to interrupt your afternoon, but I have no choice." Sorry, but it's not funny, and neither are most of the unpleasant characters he impersonates. Bogosian invites most of the adjectives normally associated with performance artists: self-indulgent, undisciplined, pretentious, tedious. The CD goes on for seventy-four minutes.

A sample of Bogosian appears on the compilation album "The Uproar Tapes." He has also issued audiocassettes and books.

DAVY BOLD

- BOLD HUMOR (Norman NL 100) **1/2 $5 $10
- A BOLD KNIGHT (Norman NL 103) **1/2 $5 $10
- HOW BOLD CAN YOU GET? (Norman NS 213) **1/2 $5 $10

Davy Bold was a quiet, unpretentious, adult-oriented nightclub comic. He ran "The Celebrity Club" in St. Louis. For anyone who really cares, it is Davy Bold, as owner-emcee, who introduces Henny Youngman on Youngman's "Primitive Sounds" album. Quite often, Bold was his own star comic, and if his material isn't that different from the other risqué comics of the early 60s, at least it's presented in a pleasant, understated way. All were recorded for a local label run by Norman Wienstroer.

On the first album he eyes a ringsider and muses (rather than raucously shouts), "There's a lady in a V neck dress. What does the V stand for? Virgin. It must be an old dress." Leisurely describing the audience the night before, he notes, "One gal raised her hand and said, 'Dave, can I sing a song with you?' I said, 'Are you a professional?' She said, 'Not if I like a guy.'"

This is a nice example of a content "small time" comedian working with a receptive local audience. There are even a few songs, like "The Half-Fast Waltz" and the silly "It Looks Like Rain in Cherry Blossom Lane," the latter turning up in a band version with sound effects on his third album.

Fans of whiz-bang corn will like his recitation of song titles on the "Bold Knight" album: "If I Had It to Do All Over Again I'd Do It All Over You," "Malcolm Get the Talcum, You're the Chap for Me," "I Can't Get Over a Girl Like You So Get Up and Answer the Phone Yourself," "He Took Her into the Fog and Mist."

Bold died in 1978, at the age of 55.

JOE BOLOGNA AND RENEE TAYLOR

- BOY AM I GLAD WE JOINED THE INDIANS (Jubilee JGM 2067) ** $5 $10

Bologna and Rudy DeLuca (a Mel Brooks film cowriter these days) wrote this silly studio LP of historical sketches, acted out by a supporting cast, mostly in Jewish accents. Robin Hood, Paul Revere, and The Wright Brothers are kosherized, as are Ponce De Leon and his wife:

"Poncellah ... Vat's wrong vit vanting to be young again? Ven I vas young de world vas mein oyster." "Oy ven you vere young you looked like an oyster." "... The Fountain of Youth! Poncellah ... take a look on me. What do you see?" "An old lady." "Now ... (splashes water) Did you notice any change?" "Yes. Definitely ... Now you're a wet old lady."

And, thanks to this album, we know that Thomas Edison and his wife were Jewish. "I've invented the electric light!" he cries. She answers, "Shut it off, you're wasting electricity."

ERMA BOMBECK
- THE FAMILY THAT PLAYS TOGETHER GETS ON EACH OTHER'S NERVES
(Warner Bros. BSK 3082) ** $5 $10

In 1977 the popular columnist of housewife humor recorded this LP edited from lecture appearances/readings from her columns. Though her subject matter can be trivial and her tone (both in print and on record) stuffy and old-fashioned, average housewives deserve to have a spokeswoman. Once in a while she has a good one-liner: "If you want to get rid of stinking odors in the kitchen, stop cooking." There's lots of recognition humor for older ladies: "I've never identified with women who can cross their legs in hot weather." Audiocassettes covering selections from Bombeck's best-sellers are available in bookstores. Bombeck died in 1996 at the age of 69.

BRYCE BOND
- BACHELOR APARTMENT (Strand SL 1019, also released as
SEDUCTION BACHELOR STYLE, Lobo 102) * $4 $15

Bond was a disc jockey who pulled the usual stunts DJs did in the early '60s, like staying awake for 127 hours straight. When the comedy LP boom of the era was on, and the small Strand label tried to cash in, "They said hey, put together an album, so I said OK."

"Bachelor Apartment" isn't much. In a studio, Bond and his partner Bernadette enact various scenes involving cheesy Lotharios. In one sixteen-minute sketch Bond maneuvers a nasal-voiced dimwit up to his apartment and keeps coaxing: "Let me take some of these clothes off ... it's gettin' warm in here." When he goes too far, the girl gets huffy: "Pardon me! Will you get your hands off of them?" "I'm sorry, they are so beautiful...." "I'd watch it if I was you." "What are they, 42s?" "Oh very funny, ha ha ha."

Not really. But it seems like the album was aimed at immature guys leering and snickering while "overhearing" one of their pals trying to pull the wool (skirt) over a girl's eyes. Talk about cons—Bond told me he only got "a $200 advance. I know the thing sold well over $372,000. I was supposed to get twenty cents an album. I got rooked. The money manipulation game."

The album title and cover give this extra collectibility for fans of '50s kitsch.

Bond, who made non-comedy albums for Folkways and other labels (a 1964 album called "Common Sense Philosophy" was issued by Beacon), is now, in his words, "A spiritual healer. It was a great transformation from one dimension to another. I have private consultations where I do spiritual healings."

BOOK AND MARTINO
- INTERVIEW WITH COUNT DRACULA (REC 1250) * $4 $8

This self-produced album is all that remains of obscure Brooklyn comedy team Raymond T. Book and Vito Martino. They received mild endorsements on the back cover from Hiram Kasten and Allan Bellmont, comics who emceed at New York (Dangerfield's) and Brooklyn (Pips) comedy clubs in the '80s. The disc is amazingly dull, from a ten-minute routine in which frustrated Rocco Linguini tries to get a phone number from information, to the pathetic title cut featuring a horribly corny Lugosi imitation and not a single quotable line. Most of this is a studio album sans audience, but on the audience tracks, there is more glass-tinkling and ambient noise than laughter.

TUBBY BOOTS
- TUBBY BOOTS GOES TOPLESS (Syllen 1001) *1/2 $7 $15
- THIN MAY BE IN, BUT FAT'S WHERE IT'S AT (Syllen 1002) *1/2 $7 $15
- OUT OF THIS WORLD (Syllen 1004) *1/2 $7 $15

Tubby Boots, son of the vaudeville team of Boots and Barton, was pudgy and bulgy enough to have almost female-looking breasts. For a gag, which became a trademark used on several of his album jackets, he'd put stripper's twirling tassels on and squeeze them together. He's a raucous tummler working the Florida crowd. On "Thin May Be In..." he tells the crowd, "no matter what I say or what I do, you came to see me, I did not go looking for you! The minute you walked through that door your reputation was shot to hell!" On "Goes Topless" he talks about his weight: "I'm built like a moose and hung like a mouse! I walk around the house all day with a Pepsi-Cola, pouring it on my schmuck, yelling, 'Come alive, we're in the Pepsi generation!' The goyim think that's dirty. A schmuck? That's a guy that gets out of the shower to take a leak!"

VICTOR BORGE
- A VICTOR BORGE PROGRAM (Columbia CL 6013) **1/2 $8 $20
- COMEDY IN MUSIC (Columbia CL 554) ** $8
- CAUGHT IN THE ACT (Columbia CL 646) **1/2 $8
- LIVE (!) (Sony Masterworks MDK 48482) **1/2 $8
- BORGE'S BACK
(MGM 3995, also released as GREAT MOMENTS IN COMEDY, Verve V 15044) *** $10 $20

A beloved entertainer known for his eccentric asides and bits of musical satires, Borge (born Borge Rosenbaum in Denmark) learned to tell jokes phonetically when he first appeared on radio. He would later set a Guiness World Record for the longest running one-man show in Broadway history, *Comedy in Music*, which ran from 1953 to 1956.

Borge's "Program," a ten-incher recorded circa 1951, offers "Phonetic Punctuation" as the comic highlight among several straight selections. On "Lesson in Composition" he samples various compositions and offers some light-hearted cracks. He disregards Shostakovich after playing a blizzard of notes: "I think we better wait till he gets sober."

Recorded in 1953, "Comedy in Music" and "Caught in the Act" use material from Borge's Broadway show, though they were recorded at The Plymouth Theater in Boston. They don't always succeed, since Borge's sight gags are so much a part of his whimsical humor. Straight instrumentals dominate an entire side of "Comedy in Music." There are some cute asides from time to time: "Bach had approximately twenty to thirty children. I guess that goes for Mrs. Bach too. It takes time to raise about twenty-five to thirty kids. I know, I have two myself. Mine are twins, though. Both of them. Can't think of their names. They don't come when I call them anyway."

"Caught in the Act" has more routines, including "Phonetics," his classic sound-effect lecture that makes punctuation audible. He also reports on his family history: "My father invented the burglar alarm. Which unfortunately was stolen from him." There's a long routine on a Mozart opera and plenty of instrumental humor as he twists "Tea for Two" till it comes out as "Malagueña" and skids "The Skater's Waltz" into "The Third Man Theme Song." Relaxed listeners will enjoy savoring the gentle jests, silliness, and sophistication of the master concert comedian at work.

Both albums were issued on CD. Then in 1992, Sony Legacy issued the seventy-four-minute CD "Victor Borge Live (!)," which is the complete "Caught in the Act" album, and twenty-six minutes of humor from "Comedy in Music."

"Borge's Back," from 1962, is cleanly recorded and edited to remove some of the frustrating visual humor and bewildering audience laughter. It's dotted with whimsical Borge asides ("Bernstein won an award yesterday for explaining the music of Igor Stravinsky. To Igor Stravinsky.") The album also offers one of Borge's most popular routines, in which he raises the number on words, so that "create would be crenine, and so fifth...."

NOTES: Borge's music-oriented Columbia ten-inch album is a rarity: "Brahms, Bizet and Borge" (CL 2538). So is "Victor Borge Plays and Conducts Concert Favorites (CL 1305). Borge can be heard on children's albums like "Piccolo Saxie and Company" (Columbia CL 1233) and "Hans Christian Andersen" (Decca 734406).

He recorded two albums in Europe that were re-released in 1972 as the two-LP set "Victor Borge at His Best" (PRT RECORDS COMP 5). They have more modern Borge material, including his duets with soprano Marylyn Mulvey ("She has sung in many operas—and not in just as many") and fresher one-liners: "Why are there threepedals on this piano? Who do they think I am!" One disc was done in the studio with anecdotal entries on Bach, Beethoven, and Handel from his book *My Favourite Intervals* (in America, known as *My Favorite Intermissions*). Just to confuse matters, "My Favorite Intervals" is also available as a double-record import (Pye NSPD 502), both sides based on the book.

The most expensive Borge disc was list-priced at $100: a one-sided album called "To Denmark the Legend" for the Scandinavia Scholarship Fund. Borge discusses Scandinavia during the war, and adds a slight touch of ironic humor now and then: "... on the 9th of April, 1940, this evil spirit broke into Denmark. Uninvited. Unwanted. Unwelcome, and, most crudely, before breakfast."

Borge's management company issued a Borge concert on video and audiocassette (mostly via mail order). A Borge excerpt appears on "Great Stars of Vaudeville" (Columbia CSS 1509).

JOHANN SEBASTIAN BORK

• HONKEYCHORD (Electric Lemon PLP 1915) **	$5	$10
• BORK LIVE (Electric Lemon PLP 1917) **	$5	$10
• MUSICAL MENOPAUSE (Electric Lemon PLP 1920) **	$5	$10

J. S. Bork, sort of an acid-casualty relative of P. D. Q. Bach, released his late '70s albums on the appropriately named Electric Lemon label. Bork sometimes offers ragtime or pop-fizzed versions of the classics. Other times, in a quasi-German/Swedish accent, he parodies recent hits.

Bork tries to be "eccentric" but often is just annoying. On "Menopause" he spends nearly three minutes rehearsing a ragtag choir's version of "I'd Like to Teach the World to Sing (In Perfect Harmony)." The joke is that they won't learn and aren't in harmony. Punch line: "Vell, I guess I don't use de choir very often."

RAE BOURBON

• AN EVENING IN COPENHAGEN (Jewel UTC 1) **	$5	$10
• YOU'RE STEPPING ON MY EYELASHES (Jewel UTC 2) **	$5	$10
• DON'T CALL ME MADAM (Jewel UTC 3) **	$5	$10
• A GIRL OF THE GOLDEN WEST (Jewel UTC 4) **	$5	$10
• BOURBON 100 PROOF (Jewel UTC 5) **	$5	$10
• ONE ON THE AISLE: CLAQUE CLAQUE (Jewel UTC 6) **	$5	$10
• LET ME TELL YOU ABOUT MY OPERATION (Jewel UTC 7) **	$5	$10
• AROUND THE WORLD IN 80 WAYS (Jewel UTC 8) **	$5	$10
• HOLLYWOOD EXPOSE (Jewel UTC 9) **	$5	$10
• LADIES OF BURLESQUE (Jewel UTC 10) **	$5	$10
• A TRICK AIN'T ALWAYS A TREAT (Jewel JB 3001) **	$5	$10

A female impersonator evidently influenced by Sophie Tucker's face and figure, and Joe E. Lewis's humor, Rae Bourbon starred in clubs throughout the 1950s. Hard times evidently found him in the late '60s. He was incarcerated in a Texas prison and died in 1971 at the age of seventy-eight.

His first six releases were ten-inchers (and if that strikes you as a straight line, then Rae's just up your alley). Some albums have no audience, mixing chatty anecdotes with phone call monologues and off-color songs. From the "Copenhagen" album, a typical dumb ditty: "Mr. Wong has got the biggest tong in China. And they say that there's really nothing finer ... other Tongs have mascots for which they are renowned, but Mr. Wong likes to have his dragon around."

"Claque Claque" is a bit different. As a drag version of Anna Russell, he offers opera parodies and lectures. As Rae says, "operas are enough to drive you out of your mind," especially the Wagner kind: "he beat everything out on an old banged up drum ... all about this wonderful big lesbian named Brunhilde."

Bourbon's "Don't Call Me Madam" album includes a routine called "The Neighbor's Party," which won a rave quote from Errol Flynn: "This is so real, and so funny, you think it is happening to you." In the monologue Rae puts on the voice of a brusque housewife who insults her husband periodically while phoning the cops about a wild party across the street: "Harry, what do you mean walking through the living room stark naked! You're not showing me a thing ... walking around the house naked! You look like a broken-down eunuch! You might as well be one for the good you do me ... pull the shade down! I don't want people to think I only married you for your money."

Bourbon's albums have mild cult appeal for fans of the genre. There are some minor differences between pressings: some of the originals have a blank back cover; later ones offer notes and listings of all available albums. The original "An Evening in Copenhagen" had no photo of Bourbon, or even his name, just a portrait of a unicorn on the front and back cover. In some major cities, notably San Francisco and New York, Rae's albums fetch a few dollars more.

DON BOWMAN

- DON BOWMAN (RCA Victor LPM/LSP 2831) ** $5 $10
- FUNNY WAY TO MAKE AN ALBUM (RCA Victor LPM/LSP 3495) ** $5 $10
- ALMOST ALIVE (RCA Victor LPM/LSP 3646) ** $5 $10
- FUNNY FOLK FLOPS (RCA Victor LSP/LPM 3920) ** $5 $10
- FROM MEXICO (RCA Victor LPM/LSP 3795) ** $5 $10
- OUR MAN IN TROUBLE (RCA Victor LPM/LSP 2831) ** $5 $10
- FRESH FROM THE FUNNY FARM (RCA Victor LPM/LSP 3345) ** $5 $10
- SUPPORT YOUR LOCAL PRISON (RCA Victor LSP 4230) ** $5 $10
- WHISPERING COUNTRY (RCA LSP 4295) ** $5 $10
- ALL NEW (Mega 311015) $4 $8
- STILL FIGHTING MENTAL HEALTH (Lone Star L 4605) $4 $8

Bowman was part of RCA's roster of country comics in the late '60s when he was in his 30s. He sings novelty songs in a doleful hard-luck voice—like Roger Miller after a good beating. On "Fresh from the Funny Farm" he sings about a sad love life ("I Fell Out of Love with Love"), drinking ("Plastered"), and having a hangover while reading a Dear John note: "Well it wouldn't've been so bad if I hadn't felt so bad, but I felt so bad, mostly in my head. When I read what your letter said. Wish I'd stayed in bed."

On "Funny Way to Make An Album" he indulges in some homely sick comedy. "Freddy Four Toes" is about a man who had a lawn mower accident: "Well I turned on the starter and pulled the cord and that power mower tore out across my yard. Where the flower bed was there's a six foot hole. Chopped down the front porch and the telly-phone pole ... the thing turned on me, took a bite out of my foot and chased me up a tree."

Bowman varies things with a monologue now and then.

KENT BOWMAN

- PIDGIN ENGLISH CHILDREN'S STORIES (Hula 502) $4 $8
- HAU KEA: SNOW WHITE (Hula 526) $4 $8
- KA'UMANUA (Hula 516) *1/2 $4 $8
- NO TALK STINK (Hula 545) *1/2 $4 $8

Honolulu businessman Bowman was also an after dinner speaker and emcee. Sometimes on these mid-60s albums he utilizes a Hawaiian dialect character, "Ka'umanua." As one can guess from the scat pun, he's doing old risqué jokes and not "true Hawaiian humor" as the cover advertises.

From the "No Talk Stink" album, "Ka'umanua" addresses his constituents: "Every election I come in fronna you, all I ask you do is sweep me into office with the rest of the rubbish ... Everybody cheer. I get applause ringing from the rafters ... My opponent get the votes and all I get is the clap. Ladies and gentlemens ... I'm gonna repeal the law on rape ... I notice some weak snickers from the men and some silence from the waheenees ... I'm gon change the law around. It's gonna be called "Assault with a Friendly Weapon." You can't blame the guys on Waikiki ... the hot pants, hoo wee! If the shorts get any shorter the waheenees will have trouble sitting down and men get in trouble for standing up."

"No Talk" and "Ka'umanua" are for adults only, but the other two are just about opposite: children's tales retold in Hawaiian dialect.

BOBBY BRADDOCK

- HARDPORE CORNOGRAPHY (RCA MHL18524) ** $5 $10

Like Ray Stevens, Braddock writes "straight" country tunes as well as novelty tunes. This LP is mostly comedy. "Dolly Parton's Hits" is cute, though obvious even by country standards ("B-b-b-bouncing up the charts, super bullet 46 ... nothing can compare with Dolly Parton's hits!") "I Lobster but Never Flounder" was given a better reading by Pinkard and Bowden.

OSCAR BRAND

• ABSOLUTE NONSENSE (Riverside RLP 12-825) **	$5	$10
• BAWDY SONGS (Audio Fidelity AFLP 1906) **	$5	$10
• BAWDY SONGS VOL. 2 (Audio Fidelity AFLP 1806) **	$5	$10
• BAWDY SONGS VOL. 3 (Audio Fidelity AFLP 1824) **	$5	$10
• BAWDY SONGS VOL. 4 (Audio Fidelity AFSD 5847) **	$5	$10
• BAWDY GOES TO COLLEGE (Audio Fidelity AFSD 5952) **	$5	$10
• 20 GREAT HITS (Audio Fidelity 20-402) **	$5	$10
• BAWDY SEA SHANTIES (Audio Fidelity AFSD 5884) **	$5	$10
• ROLLICKING SEA SHANTIES (Audio Fidelity AFSD 5966) **	$5	$10
• BAWDY HOOTENANNY (Audio Fidelity AFSD 6121) **	$5	$10
• BAWDY SING ALONG (Audio Fidelity AFSD 5972) **	$5	$10
• FOR DOCTORS ONLY (Elektra EKL 204) *1/2	$4	$8
• BOATING SONGS (Elektra 7183) *1/2	$4	$8
• COUGH (Elektra 7242) *1/2	$4	$8
• EVERY INCH A SAILOR (Elektra 7169) *1/2	$4	$8
• OUT OF THE BLUE (Elektra 7178) *1/2	$4	$8
• SNOW JOB (Elektra 7228) *1/2	$4	$8
• SONGS FOR GOLFERS (Elektra 7237) *1/2	$4	$8
• TELL IT TO THE MARINES (Elektra 7174) *1/2	$4	$8
• UP IN THE AIR (Elektra 7198) *1/2	$4	$8
• WILD BLUE YONDER (Elektra 7198) *1/2	$4	$8
• SINGS FOR ADULTS (ABC Paramount ABC 388)	$5	$10
• BRAND X (Roulette SR 420) **	$5	$10
• GIVE 'IM THE HOOK (Riverside RLP 12-832) *1/2	$4	$8
• LAUGHING AMERICA (Tradition TLP 1014) **	$5	$10
• PIE IN THE SKY (Tradition TLP 1022) **	$5	$10

Brand majored in abnormal psychology at Brooklyn College and ended up hosting a folk music show on WNYC radio for over thirty years.

Back in the early '60s, record stores were loaded with Oscar Brand's novelty collections of semi-vulgar folk tunes. The "Bawdy" series was very popular since they were the only sexy tunes allowed in shops. Many go back to Chaucer's time with their merry insinuation and nonsense words. From the first Bawdy album, Brand sings of a promiscuous maiden: "A few months went by, young Mary she grew fatter. And all of the neighbors were wondering who'd been at her. With his whack folly diddle dido and his whack folly diddle day."

Brand never uses a four-letter Anglo-Saxon word. Add the redeeming value of preserving "historic" old ribaldry, and his blandly innocuous airy tenor delivery, and it's not surprising he was allowed to make disc after disc. The surprise is who kept buying them, since they get awfully repetitive. Each album does have a few amusing cuts, and some of them are a bit more modern. "Bawdy Volume Four" has "I Used to Work in Chicago," a classic double entendre song: "A lady came up for a house dress, I asked her what kind she wished. Jumper said she. Jump her I did ... a lady came up for some pastry, I asked her what kind she wished. Layer she said. Lay her I did ... A lady came up for a sleeper. I asked her which berth she wished. Upper she said. Up her I went."

Sometimes Brand issued straight albums, and once in a while collections of humorous, but not bawdy, folk tunes ("Laughing America") or vaudeville pieces ("Give 'im the Hook"). They have historical, not hysterical, interest, especially not when he sings them. Brand's voice is simply too bland.

ANDY BRECKMAN

- DON'T GET KILLED (Gadfly 121089) $7

A lispy folkie with a lot of annoying non-tunes, Breckman writes like the poor man's Loudon Wainwright or the homeless man's Marshall Crenshaw. He sounds like an amateurish goofball on this 1990 CD. Recorded in front of indulgent audiences in Baltimore, Ann Arbor, and Edmonton, Canada, he strums a guitar as he sings his deliberately tilted tunes. Like: "I'm doin' OK. I had a good day ... I gotta say. I had a real good day. I didn't throw up. I didn't throw up. About a quarter to four I almost threw up. But I didn't throw up. I had a real good day."

DAVID BRENNER

- EXCUSE ME, ARE YOU READING THAT PAPER? (MCA 5457) **1/2 $5 $10

Brenner, like Robert Klein and Billy Crystal, is just hip enough to amuse thirty- and forty-year-olds, but full of enough old show-biz schmaltz to seem like a grandson to any old Vegas audience.

His 1983 album reflects his dual nature. In his monologues, he has some wise guy lines: "It is now a $50 fine if you get caught honking your horn in Manhattan. Meanwhile you can expose yourself on the subway and it doesn't cost you a dime. Unless you spit. Then it's $25. So if you're gonna spit, you might as well whip it out, have a little fun for the money." But stopping the monologues cold are studio inserts—formally recited anecdotes from his book, *Soft Pretzels with Mustard*. On these slices of family life, Brenner is so intent on being earnest and sincere that he sounds like he's delivering a eulogy. Some, such as the story about a crabby neighbor sweeping dead pigeons onto the Brenner family property like a hockey player scoring a goal, would have been memorable told live in concert, not dramatized with sound effects.

FANNY BRICE

- BABY SNOOKS (Yorkshir 717) ** $5 $10
- BABY SNOOKS (Memorabilia 720) ** $5 $10
- BABY SNOOKS (Mar-Bren 746) ** $5 $10
- BABY SNOOKS AND DADDY (Radiola MR 1039) **1/2 $5 $10
- RETURN OF BABY SNOOKS (Radiola 2MR 158159) **1/2 $7 $15
- THE ORIGINAL FUNNY GIRL (Audio Fidelity AFLP 707) ** $5 $10

A popular singer (the Streisand musical *Funny Girl* was based on her life), Brice is best known in comedy via her alter ego, "Baby Snooks." As the brat, she and her "Daddy" (Hanley Stafford) were very popular on radio during the 1940s. (She died in 1951). Fans will find each album loaded with coyness and cacophony. On the Memorabilia album, Snooks cheerfully buries a baby in the sand and nearly kills him. This alarms Daddy, but his irritated scolding is met by blamelessly cute logic.

"The child might have suffocated with his head in the sand. How did you expect him to get air?" "I put a hole in his trunks." "That's wonderful! Nobody can breathe through their trunks!" "Elephants can." "Very funny."

If it is, get 'em all. The first Radiola album deserves special note, since in addition to a full hour of Snooks's antics (in vignettes from 1939 to 1950) there's a guest appearance by Tallulah Bankhead. She is not amused by the child: "Please, take those sweaty little paws off my gown or I'll slug you one." "Gee, you wouldn't hit a little girl, would ya?" "No, but if you're as obnoxious as you look I may boot you one ... what do you want to ask me?" "How can I get to be a big actress like you?" "Don't be ridiculous my dear, no one can be like me. Sometimes I even have trouble."

"The Return of Baby Snooks" is a two-record, two-hour set with a small respite—twenty minutes of non-Snooks Brice in songs (including "Second Hand Rose") and sketches (she does some Yiddish dialect comedy opposite Bob Hope).

Audio Fidelity's album offers Brice's straight songs (notably "My Man"), a few of her early Jewish novelty tunes ("Oy, How I Hate that Fellow Nathan" and "Becky Is Back in the Ballet") and the six-minute monologue "Mrs. Cohen at the Beach."

A brief Snooks routine, involving a visit to the opera, turns up on "Jest Like Old Times" (Radiola #1). An annoying novelty tune of hers, "I'm an Indian," from 1929, is on "Golden Age of Comedy" (RCA Victor LPV 580). Many straight albums of her material are available, as well as a Baby Snooks children's album from Capitol. "Makin Whoopee" (Pro Arte CDD 460) splits nine of her old 78s, including "Mrs. Cohen at the Beach," "Becky Is Back in the Ballet," "I'm an Indian," "My Man," and "Second Hand Rose," with a half hour of Eddie Cantor songs.

BRILL AND FOSTER

- THE OTHER FAMILY (Laurie LC 5000) ** $5 $10
- JAMES BLONDE: THE MAN FROM TANTE (Colpix CPL 495) **1/2 $7 $15
- THE MISSING TAPES (Laurie LCS 5002) ** $4 $8

Marty Brill and Larry Foster made three attempts to cash in on fads. Sometimes they were novel, sometimes successful, sometimes not. Their novel first notion was to get "First Family" buyers to also purchase "The Other Family," all about Khrushchev. If Jackie Kennedy could give TV cameras a tour of the White House, here's dumpy Mrs. K. touring "The Red House" with an admiring interviewer:

"That's a lovely housedress you are wearing. I especially love the print and the apron ... and those lovely shoes ... what do you call them?"

"Brown Oxfords with ripple soles and heels."

Khrushchev, at a press conference, defends himself against the charge of brainwashing his people: "We do not brainwash. Do you understand? We do not brainwash. Repeat after me: we do not brainwash."

Given the quickness of the release, this is a competent knock-off. A few years later, amid the "spy craze" for James Bond and *The Man from U.N.C.L.E.*, the duo's "Man from TANTE" was a kind of Semitic *Get Smart*.

The 1965 studio LP is a half-hour sitcom. It even has a plot (a list of B'nai B'rith pledges has been stolen and hidden in a matzoh). The characters parody James Bond personnel: Miss Money Penny becomes Penny Candy, "M" is a woman (Mother), and Dr. No becomes Dr. Nu. Instead of Pussy Galore, there's "Sissy Alot," and she's so tempting that "from the moment you see her, you'll have only one thought in your head: you have to make Sissy."

The pleasantly silly jokes resemble Mel Brooks/*Get Smart* gags. "No guns!" M tells her son James, "it's a dangerous thing. You could hurt an eye, you could kill yourself or even worse." "All the other agents have guns." "Let their mothers worry!"

The Watergate scandal led Brill to try again, but his Nixon sounds more like Regis Philbin with throat problems. Foster plays Henry Kissinger and the cast also features Dick Capri, Connie Silver, and Ken Friedman. Nixon decides to meet in the Pentagon men's room:

Kissinger: This is the only place in Washington where anybody really knows what they're doing. And I figured we'd have absolute privacy here without secret surveillance...

Nixon: Why I'll bet this very room is where we'll find the biggest leaks in Washington!

Marty Brill started out as a folk singer and in 1957 issued "Roving Balladeer" (Mercury MG 20178).

ALBERT BROOKS

- COMEDY MINUS ONE (ABC ABCX-800, CD Reissue) ** $8
- A STAR IS BOUGHT (Asylum 7E 1035) ** $10 $20

In 1973, Brooks was making offbeat talk show appearances. Hip, suave, and smug, he challenged audiences' patience by reciting from the phone book, pretending to be an inept ventriloquist, and so on. A little too smart for the crowd (yes, his real name is Albert Einstein), it was the much broader Andy Kaufman and Steve Martin who became stars via "non-comedy." Still, Brooks was a "comedian's comedian" and still has a cult following.

"Comedy Minus One" has an extremely long kvetch about the problems of being a hip, urban comic opening for a rock act in Texas, but strikes gold with "Re-Writing the National Anthem," a glib, musical satire. He imagines various idiots auditioning their songs, from a Broadway hack who bangs out, "Hey! World! Look at Us!" to the Michigan amateur who offers the ultimate in logical lyrics: "While we stand here wait-ting, for the ballgame to start...." With the enclosed script, listeners can indeed read lines and play along with Brooks and guest George Jessel, savoring the canned laughs.

Brooks's second album, circa 1975, takes on the record industry—a hip insider parody of how to sell a record album. Documentary style, Monkees Peter Tork and Mickey Dolenz, Linda Ronstadt, Rob Reiner, and even label president David Geffen recall counseling Albert. After each slightly arch and slightly too tongue-in-cheek spoken segment, there's a different mock "hit single."

Brooks's put-on style works best on "The Englishman German Jew Blues," where he annoyingly keeps interrupting bluesman Albert King to try to cure his blues ("Al, stop being such a gloomy Gus"). He also tries to hit the charts with "Phone Call to Americans," a smug lampoon of patriotic narration-novelty singles, and even by putting lyrics to "Bolero," which naturally gets out of hand: "I never felt like this before, like I'm the sea and you're the shore. And as my surf begins to pound, you promise not to make a sound ... my tide coming in! Ha whooaaah! Oh Lord, this must be the place!"

Other cuts are too close to the originals to be that effective, like "Party from Outer Space," a *real* comedian's disdainful parody of Dickie Goodman's "Flying Saucer" novelty singles. The climax, his complete "Albert Brooks Show" is an accurate re-creation of '40s radio shows of the Jack Benny variety. Brooks plays an excitable comic trying to put on a show while interrupted by "zany" comedy characters (Daws Butler, Pat Carroll, and Sheldon Leonard) and a bandleader or two. It's lathered in laugh track and tastes sour. If Albert is actually paying an affectionate tribute or wishing he was around in the golden days of radio, it doesn't show. Harry Shearer cowrote the album and he gives it that "Credibility Gap" perfection of execution—the sound effects and music on target.

Fans will want to make sure the album includes the "personally autographed 8 x10 glossy!" Which, heh heh, is a picture of the smirking Brooks with the stamped line: "Hi - To single any one of you out individually would be a big mistake. Best wishes, Albert Brooks."

FOSTER BROOKS

- THE LOVABLE LUSH (Decca DL 7-5395) **1/2 $5 $10
- LIVE FROM LAS VEGAS (Lush LR 1001) ** $5 $10
- FOSTER BROOKS ROASTS (Roast Records RR 1002) *1/2 $5 $10

Brooks, a DJ and newscaster, developed a new career late in life as a Vegas opening act. He did a drunk routine. Not the falling down Red Skelton drunk or the elegantly high Dean Martin. Brooks was closer to the real thing; unpleasantly gaseous and prone towards mildly off-color wisecracks. Bill Cosby thought Brooks did a great satire on drunks and booked him on his 1972 variety series. He evidently helped him get a record deal and even wrote the album notes: "... Buy this record and play it for a drunken friend of yours and say to them 'here you are.'"

Brooks, the bleary boozer, belches and stutters and declares, "I must say that I have a very good re-reason for bein' loaded tonight. I been drinkin' all day!" Listeners can certainly debate whether that's glorifying alcoholism or not. Being a "lovable lush," he gets away with corny-risqué jokes like this: "Every morning I have my Tang. I suppose a lot of you folks get up in the morning and have a glass of orange Tang, but I make my own. I make it out of prunes. Orange Tang is alright, but I kind of go for a little prune Tang now and then."

"Live from Las Vegas" is a bit self-indulgent. One side is live comedy at the Desert Inn; the other "but seriously" schmaltz (recitations of poems, the singing of "And I Love Her So" and "My Way") that no doubt touched his Vegas audiences. (Brooks also issued a double-set album of straight songs). The comedy is weak; too many old generic-comic Vegas jokes: "Yesterday, we were out in the car, and my wife said, 'Hon, I don't have my credit card, would you give me a few dollars, I want to buy a brassiere.' Well, something funny I thought just crossed my mind. I thought

I'd say it, I didn't mean anything by it. I said to her, 'What do you want to buy a brassiere for? You haven't got anything to put in it.' She said, 'You buy shorts, don't ya?'"

"Roasts" has cuts from Brooks's TV appearances at roasts for Carroll O'Connor, Dean Martin, Johnny Carson, and so on. They weren't meant to be strung together and it gets annoying hearing him do the same schtick so often: stopping, stuttering and staggering through each line, gaseously lowering his voice and burping out the words. The gags written for him are as good as any for this type of thing. As he jokes about various celebs: "(Carson) was discussing bay– discussing bayyyyy– discussing baking, and asked Diahann Carroll to show him her brownies ... I have not missed a *Tonight Show*, which is a heck of a lot more than Johnny can say."

MEL BROOKS

- MEL BROOKS' GREATEST HITS (Asylum 5E-501) *** $7 $15

Brooks's early movies had memorable songs and this 1978 disc has them all, from the outrageous "Springtime for Hitler," to "High Anxiety," a satire on swing vocalists. There's also the grotesque humor of "Putting on the Ritz" sung by the Frankenstein monster in a tormented harelip voice, and the title track from *Blazing Saddles*, with Frankie Laine giving his all to blindly inane heroic lyrics: "He made his blazing saddle a torch to lead the way."

Although most of these require some appreciation of the films, "Hope for the Best, Expect the Worst," from *The Twelve Chairs*, stands on its own. The melody, from Brahms's "Hungarian Dance Number 4" is bittersweet and the lyrics, in the best Jewish tradition of laughter and irony, find bitter humor in fate: "I knew a man who saved a fortune that was splendid. Then he died the day he planned to go an spend it." The chorus declares "live while you're alive, no one will survive."

Collectors can round up the original soundtracks from RCA ("The Producers"), United Artists ("Silent Movie"), ABC ("Young Frankenstein"), Warner Bros. ("History of The World"), etc. There's usually a mix of dialogue and music, including some numbers not on the Greatest Hits album (Dick Shawn's "Love Power" is only on "The Producers" soundtrack). "The Producers" has album notes from Peter Sellers. "Silent Movie" includes a fold-out poster. Most have prices inflated by the demand from general soundtrack collectors.

NOTES: Brooks recorded "The Hitler Rap" (on Island Records's subsidiary Antilles AN 810) at the time of his film "To Be or Not To Be." On the twelve-inch single (seven-minute rap) he's a funky Hitler rapping in black dialect: "To all those mothers in the Fatherland, I said, 'Achtung, baby I got me a plan.' They said, 'Watcha got Adolf, watchoo gonna do?' I said, 'How about this one, World War II!'"

For the Philadelphia label WMOT, Brooks released a twelve-inch disco single, "It's Good to Be the King" (WMOT Records, 4W9 02761) at the time of "History of the World Part I." Brooks almost saves the bad music with his funky rap. He isn't afraid of no "gilly-o-teen." Not when he's having so much fun bein' King!

Brooks turns up on "Zingers from the Hollywood Squares" (Event EV 6903). He's asked "Next to his family, what does an Eskimo prize most?" He answers: "You know it's very cold, the big problem is the fishing, the lines freeze, they make many knots not to lose the fish, and they freeze their knots off 'cause it's very cold there!"

MEL BROOKS AND DICK CAVETT

- THE BEST OF THE BREWMASTER (Columbia Special Products 259) *** $10 $20

The album was subtitled "My Tongue Just Threw a Party for My Mouth. Certain irrelevant conversations between the 2500-year-old Brewmaster and the Man from Ballantine." The promo disc collects sixteen mildly comical commercials, including:

"Sir, we think that today's Ballantine beer is the best beer yet. I wonder, were you around when the very first beer was invented?..."

"It was in the year 4 and a half months. It wasn't even a year yet when beer was invented. I'll never forget that beer. It was mainly foam. It was so much foam that you had to drink for two days before you got to the beer!"

"Whereas with Ballantine Beer?"

"With Ballantine there's just enough foam and just enough beer. And it's loaded with all kinds of wonderful flavors. It's the beer with spirit. Are you the Man from Ballantine?"

"Yes, I am."

"Why am I telling you this, you should be telling me! You're some dummy!"

A Mel Brooks-Dick Cavett radio ad for "Circus Nuts" appears on "Radio Plays the Plaza," a 1969 promo from the Radio Advertising Bureau. Brooks plays a Jewish-accented cowboy who gives Cavett some information while munching on nuts: "Cowpunching is to take your fist and smash a cow in between the eyes until he falls down. 'Cause you can't take guff from a cow!"

BROTHER EATMORE See CHA CHA HOGAN

JULIE BROWN

- GODDESS IN PROGRESS (Rhino RNEP 610) *** $5 $10
- TRAPPED IN THE BODY OF A WHITE GIRL (Sire WB 25634) *1/2 $8

Julie Brown's 1984 Rhino mini-album (five cuts) takes on several tough targets for satire and skewers them brilliantly. In "'Cause I'm a Blond" she portrays an infuriatingly self-absorbed, ditsy blonde bimbo who giggles and says, "I can't spell VW, but I got a Porsche" and sneers, "Don't you wish you were me?" Unless Brown is absolutely dead center the listener would just be irritated. Same thing with "I Like 'Em Big and Stupid," which seems to be in praise of dumb guys. Another highlight is the full-blown "The Homecoming Queen's Got a Gun."

Brown's persona became more tacky, screechy, overboard, and overbearing over the years, and her major label debut three years later is a major disappointment. Designed to plumb Cyndi Lauper/Tracey Ullman territory, some songs ("Boys Are a Drug" and "Shut Up and Kiss Me") are just mainstream rockers. Julie's vocals have none of the sexy nuance of the Rhino album. They're all high-pitched and bitchy. On her first disc, she could impersonate obnoxious types without becoming obnoxious herself. The original "I Like 'Em Big and Stupid" was tongue in cheek. This one is overbearingly snotty. The title cut offers reverse racism as Julie makes fun of herself for not being as hip and cool as black women. (She may have thought better of it after MTV's "Downtown Julie Brown" appeared). The song's racial stereotyping of both those dancin' blacks and wimpy whites is an offensive earache.

Brown moved on to video specials and TV work, sometimes showing flashes of brilliance: the 1991 Showtime special where she parodied Madonna as "Medusa."

MICHAEL BROWN

- SINGS HIS OWN SONGS (Trio EB 2534, reissued Jubilee 2010) ** $10 $20
- ALARUMS AND EXCURSIONS (Impulse 24) ** $10 $20

Brown's first album, a 1954 ten-incher, features album notes by Julius Monk and contains much of the material he wrote for various New York cabaret revues. The cuts include "The Third Avenue El," "The Washingtons Are Doing Okay," "The Son of a Man and a Mermaid," "Lola Montez," "If I Were Free," "Louisiana Spring," and "The Monkey Coachman." The only cut duplicated on both discs is "Lizzie Borden." As an interpreter of his own work, he's blandly efficient at best.

"Lizzie Borden" is typical of his formula—matching black comedy lyrics to sprightly music. He cheerfully sings: "You can't chop your papa up in Massachusetts, not even if it's planned as a surprise. No you can't chop your papa up in Massachusetts, you know how neighbors love to criticize." This 1954 version, sung at a bouncy pace with The Norman Paris Trio, is the only cut that still has any punch to it. The others vary between dated fluff, sentiment (such as the ode to the departed elevated subway), and very ordinary straight tunes.

Trying to capitalize on the early '60s rage for folk music, Brown recut "Lizzie Borden" with some twang and a female chorus throwing a "yee-hah" in now and then. The back cover on this 1962 album declares, "The New Wave of Folk Music Is On Impulse," but Brown's sophisticated cabaret fans didn't appreciate the corny trappings and real folk fans probably found cuts such as "I Like a Funeral" too coy: "I like a funeral, a real good funeral! If there's a funeral I'll be there or I'll bust. For at a funeral, a funeral, an ideal funeral, you are rid of one more friend you couldn't trust!" Other topics include criminal Ruth Snyder and the John Birch Society.

ROSEMARY BROWN

- ROSEMARY BROWN PSYCHES AGAIN! (Enharmonic EN 82-005) * $5 $10

This is, literally, a brilliantly and beautifully produced record: it's stamped in silvery-clear vinyl. Better to hold it up to the light than slap it onto a turntable. The verbose album notes insist that Brown has been in contact with the netherworld and now offers works inspired by her conversations with the great masters.

The music "inspired" by Bach, Scott Joplin, and Mozart is not gimmicked a la P. D. Q. Bach or Hoffnung. It's just very ordinary stuff written in their styles. Why it's labeled "comedy" on the album jacket is difficult to figure out. Albums in the classical section on "the humorous" music of Mozart or Beethoven are funnier.

The only vaguely comic cut is "The Buttocks Pressing Song" supposedly written by Kodaly. An anemic chorus sings, "Let us all our buttocks press, taking care to use finesse ... he who will the buttocks press, should use caution, more or less, or he'll have no great success wooing yet a lovely lass."

The big joke on the flip side—"Johann Bach and Johannes Brahms discuss the musical merits of Rosemary Brown's efforts"—is that there's nothing but silence.

TOMMY BROWN

- I AIN'T LYING (T&L 1100) ** $5 $10
- I AIN'T LYING VOL. 2 (T&L 1101) ** $5 $10
- RATED X (T&L 1103) ** $5 $10
- SOUL BROTHER (T&L 1104) ** $5 $10

Georgia's Tommy Brown was a singer ("Cryin' Tommy Brown") before he turned up in Chicago doing comedy for a local label.

Brown is fond of shouting out his catchphrase: "I ain't lyin'." He also tends to shout out his recitations of old sex jokes, but the audience on these early '60s albums likes it. From the first album: "Man walks into a house of horizontal refreshments. Said, 'I want me a girl.' So the house lady, the madam, sent him upstairs with a big stallion. Five minutes later he's back downstairs. Says, 'She don't wanna do it like I wanna do it.' So she sent him upstairs with a little petite chick. Five minutes he's back downstairs, says, 'She don't wanna do it like I wanna do it.' House lady says, 'I been in this business twenty years, I'll fix him.' Ran upstairs, closed the door, locked it, looked at him, says, 'Now how you wanna do it?' He says, 'On credit.' I ain't lyin!"

LENNY BRUCE

- INTERVIEWS FOR OUR TIME (Fantasy 7001) **1/2 $8 $20
- THE SICK HUMOR OF LENNY BRUCE (Fantasy 7003) **** $8 $20

Though his early Fantasy work is on CD, real cultists need the vinyl, for the large-size covers, for whatever special joy there is in playing records over CDs, for the red vinyl in the first pressings, and certainly as a wistful wish for having been there when they first came out.

In 1958 Lenny Bruce made his album debut sharing a disc with Henry Jacobs and Woody Leifer, who did "Interview with Dr. Sholem Stein" and "Shorty Petterstein." He didn't like the idea.

Collectors pay high prices for the original album, not for the usual neurotic need for a first pressing or the bonus of red vinyl, but because of the back cover. Bruce demanded his name be removed from the album (the notes were so vague one might have believed Bruce was "Sholem Stein" or "Shorty Petterstein"). The original with a light tan cover photo (subsequent editions are tinted blue) has Bruce's name blacked out all through the back cover. (Trivia note: the man on the album cover is Max Weiss, co-owner of Fantasy Records at the time. The women are Peggy Watkins and Irmine Droeger.)

As for the album itself, there's "Father Flotski's Triumph," Lenny's hip prison satire (the better version is on his "American" album); his famous shaggy dog story about a genie working in an old Jewish candy store; and an unusual studio cut, "March of High Fidelity." Lenny liked to riff in front of a live audience, but here he was ahead of his time doing some satiric audio science fiction, complete with sound effects. At the time, Bruce's hip bit about a drugged out musician meeting Lawrence Welk was the main attraction.

Lenny sealed his reputation as a "sick comic" by deliberately titling his first solo album "Sick Humor" and taking the cover shot at a graveyard picnic. Inside, "Non Skeddo Airlines" was in horrific taste, especially at the time. It's about "John Graham. He blew up a plane with forty people and his mother. For this the state sent him to the gas chamber, proving actually that the American people are losing their sense of humor." He imagines the mad bomber coolly planting the weapon on his annoying mother, and later makes the audience roar by turning the victims into idiots (the ditsy stewardess) and pests (a nasty little boy passenger). The pilot is uniquely moronic: "Fifteen people just fell out! Are we gonna get yelled at! There goes six more. Good-byyyye!" Today, especially with Bruce's hilarious characterizations, the routine is "delightfully" sick, but in the '50s, uptight audiences couldn't deal with this kind of black humor. Lenny knew people had the urge to laugh at a funeral. He wanted to know why they also felt so guilty about it.

"Sick Humor" also includes Lenny's bit on Hitler trying to change his image via a good agent (this, with World War II still a fairly fresh sore); a jazz poem, "Psychopathia Sexualis," about a man in love with his horse; and the notorious "Religions Inc.," which dealt with the commercialism of religion, among other things. A long distance call to the new Pope is totally irreverent: "Hello Johnny, what's shakin' baby ... the puff of white smoke knocked me out. We got an eight-page ad with Viceroy." It's been theorized that it wasn't really the "obscenity" in Bruce's routines that drew the heat. Authorities just used it as the best way to silence him for his satires on religion.

- I AM NOT A NUT, ELECT ME (Fantasy 7007) **** $8 $20
- AMERICAN (Fantasy 7011) **** $8 $20

Lenny was still amused by the "sick comic" tag at this point. He irritated his detractors by printing the bad notices on the back of "I Am Not a Nut." The album is actually one of his least "sick," with one side filled by the nineteen-minute "Palladium" routine, Lenny's dissection of the rise and frantic fall of a small-time schtick comic. It's still a favorite among fellow comedians. Other bits include "White Collar Drunks," which is a parody of the racial drama *The Defiant Ones*; and his dissection of another film, *The Esther Costello Story*, where in a weird moment of drama, a deaf and blind girl is raped—and then able to see and hear: "So what's the moral?" Lenny was a natural comic who could break people up just recounting his experiences, and he does that on "The Phone Company," "Bronchitis," and his appearance on *The Steve Allen Show*.

"American" offers passionate social satire, excruciating insights on the human comedy, and brilliantly inventive "sick" humor. Breaking down the barrier between the comic and his audience, talking to them like friends and peers, Lenny talks about his painful divorce and the pathetic loneliness he found on the road in "Lima, Ohio." Many of his best routines are here as well.

On "How to Relax Your Colored Friends at Parties," with Andre Previn playing the piano background, Bruce presents a devastating look at well-meaning liberals. The wicked "Airplane Glue" vignette is Lenny's flight of fancy describing a kid becoming "the Louis Pasteur of junkiedom" when he discovers this new high. There's the sick joke story about a lost boy in the woods, an enigmatic anecdote about Shelley Berman's need for quiet onstage, and the finale, his wild prison movie parody "Father Flotski's Triumph," with its "yaddee yaddah" catchphrase.

- LENNY BRUCE IS OUT AGAIN (Philles 4010) *** $20 $100

Similar to "The Berkeley Concert," this album, produced by Phil Spector, is a Bruce ramble on law, language, and how law and order began. There's a bit on the Ku Klux Klan and sizzling one-liners on the Black plight in the South ("we pissed away a million dollars on Radio Free Europe and never gave them a nickel"). Lenny rolls into one of his last great routines, "Thank You Masked Man."

"Out Again" was not released in great quantity. It was a defiant album released at a time when Lenny was spending more time in jail or in hospitals than on the stage. Collectors recall seeing two different back covers. One has the "frying pan" photo later used on the "Berkeley Concert" album for Reprise. The better known back cover features a letter from The Rev. Sidney Lanier of St. Clement's Church in New York declaring Lenny a serious satirist and not at all obscene.

LENNY, JONNY, AND MORT

At a time when wife jokes were the norm, and comics wore tuxedoes onstage, Lenny Bruce, Mort Sahl, and Jonathan Winters combined to change stand-up forever. None of them told jokes. Lenny and Mort favored an intimate, conversational style, and Jonny broke barriers with wild improv and caricature. They were all satirists. Almost everyone since has been influenced by them. Their albums remain among the most valuable—in every meaning of the word.

TOO HIP FOR THE ROOM

Will Jordan, now best known for his mimicry, was a pioneering "sick" humorist. James Komack went on to produce TV sitcoms. Like Lenny Bruce, ex-schtick comic Murray Roman turned on, turned out hip records, then OD'd.

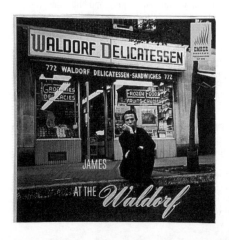

Some collectors want the record label printed in red ink as well as the one in black ink. Especially rare is the version Bruce issued on his own before it was released to stores on the Philles label. To capitalize on the national exposure of a Steve Allen talk show date, he printed up some copies. This version has the printed words LENNY BRUCE IS OUT AGAIN crudely laid out and on the bottom: $5.00 to Lenny Bruce 8825 Hollywood Blv. L.A. 69 CAL. There is no Philles logo or serial number. Some collectors insist there are a few differences in the actual content of the "self-pressed" version and the one Philles released.

- LENNY BRUCE ORIGINALS 1 (Fantasy FCD 60 023) **** $8
- LENNY BRUCE ORIGINALS 2 (Fantasy FCD 60 024) **** $8
- THE BEST OF LENNY BRUCE (Fantasy 7012) *** $7 $15
- THE REAL LENNY BRUCE (Fantasy F 79003) **** $10 $25

Fantasy released the first "Best of" in the mid-60s, and "The Real Lenny Bruce," a double set version, a decade later. The latter contains one cut unavailable on the other Fantasy albums—the cute novelty rap tune "My Werewolf Mama." The only other reason to hunt for it is the six full pages of album notes by Ralph Gleason, containing some interesting annotations on the bits. Like: there really was a Val Parnell who booked for the Palladium; Sally Marr (Lenny's mother) can be heard laughing on "Religions Inc."; and who Arthur Shields, Helen Noga, Hal McIntyre, and Julian Eltinge are. Lenny tended to toss in the names of many obscure actors, actresses, managers, and jazz musicians.

In 1992 Fantasy issued the original four albums on two CDs: "The Originals." A good change was substituting the "Father Flotski's Triumph" from the "Thank You Masked Man" album for the original track on "American." But Fantasy might have done fans a service by removing the non-Lenny tracks (the Shorty Petterstein material on the "Interviews" album) and inserting some of the material now in limbo: "Werewolf Mama," and the title track from "Thank You Masked Man."

- LENNY BRUCE AT THE CURRAN THEATER
   (Fantasy 34201, also available as Murray Hill 52952) *** $12 $40
- CARNEGIE HALL (United Artists UAS 9800, originally released as
   a single album, THE MIDNIGHT CONCERT UAL 3580, $8 $20
   and then reissued with a different cover as UAS 6794, $6 $15
   reissued on CD by World Pacific CDP 724383402021) **** $16

These two 1961 performances are posthumously released three-record sets. Though about nine months apart, they have little in common (except that both shows were recorded under rotten weather conditions.) Lenny was in vibrantly good spirits for the Carnegie Hall concert in New York on February 4, 1961. By November 19, 1961, at Curran, he was struggling under the pressure of his arrests/entrapments.

"Carnegie Hall" (first sliced up and issued as a single disc, then issued on three LPs and now two CDs) shows a transition Bruce was trying to make between "bits" and free-form rapping and ad-libs. He does some favorites ("Tits and Ass," "Christ and Moses") but presents them amid antic schtick (the squealing feedback on his microphone sends him into a Bela Lugosi impression) and riffs on whatever was bugging him at the moment. Some of it (homosexuality, the flag, communism, his fellow comics, and his ominous detractors) almost sounds like what you'd expect to hear from a brilliant, manic comic on the therapist's couch.

By the "Curran Concert," therapy wasn't working. Bruce admits, "I don't do bits anymore, so if you're drugged I don't do any bits, that's it, I wanna cook and free-form it all the way." He was simply too impatient, and in too much pain to concentrate on so much prepared material. That makes for some stretches that are sparse on laughs, especially when Bruce gropes his way through semantics and the legal mazes that are tying him into knots. It's dramatic autobiography, though, especially when he obsesses on his tormentor, Judge Axelrod, and intimately admits a comic, psychotic revenge fantasy: "My ex-old lady ... a shiksa that's well trained ... natural redhead ..." is going to meet the judge accidentally, get him aroused, seduce him, and make a tape recording of it. Bruce's cultists are with him all the way, and Lenny has enough humor left to satirize having been on so long. He likens it to Judy Garland's line to her "big nelly queen audience"—"Don't worry, if we have to we'll stay here all night, we'll sing 'em all." But then he realizes that "the line really did me in. 'Cause I never wanna go home ... nobody wants to go back to their room alone ... 'cause I never wanna go home unless I can say, "Ma, can I have a glass of water." No comic was as nakedly vulnerable onstage as Lenny Bruce.

- LENNY BRUCE: LIVE! BUSTED! (Viper's Nest CD STB 2511) *** $8

The album notes give no background on this historic recording. Instead, the writer attempts to prove how hip he is by dropping inane references to cartoon character El Kabong and cartoon producer Jay Ward (here misnamed Jay North). Along with this are tired rants that bash Mort Sahl, declare "Moses probably sounded a lot like Lenny," and pontificate on what the '60's "assimilated Judaism" and the "con/hipster" are really all about.

What this actually is, is Lenny Bruce getting busted at the Gate of Horn in Chicago in December of 1962. Lenny had triumphed the year before (his Carnegie Hall concert) then taken busts that left him confused and bitter (the Curran concert). Now, he was like a wounded lone wolf—very dangerous, very hurt, very unpredictable. What else can you expect from a harried, junk-sick guy hauling himself out onstage in a pajama top and denim pants, apologizing for his mismatched socks?

His act now dubbed "Let the Buyer Beware," Lenny was now doing blunt, challenging material. Despite the law, he curses regularly without any real care for the consequences. Instead of scratching at legal terminology as he did at Curran, he's hammering at favorite themes: "Sex is Dirty?" "Infidelity," "Christ and Moses." Lenny's speech is slurred, his attention wanders, his anger sometimes makes him speak a truth without any comic coating, leaving the audience quietly tense.

A fighter with nothing to lose, he puts on mad bursts of improv. He punches out a few sure-fire shots to kill the crowd ("How to Relax Colored People"). He flicks a mean jab: "Is it bizarre that married guys have to jerk off more than anyone else? 'Cause your old ladies won't ball ya and you can't chippie?"

In the end you actually hear what happens, how the police come toward him ("Oh shit ... out the back way!" Lenny snickers), how they identify themselves, and how Lenny mutters, "I knew that. Yeah...." As they take him away, the music over the speakers strikes up a sad jazz riff of "My Old Flame."

- WARNING (Lenny Bruce) *** $20 $100

On March 8, 1962, a San Francisco trial jury found Lenny Bruce not guilty of obscenity. The case had dragged on through two judges (Judge Axelrod, the subject of Lenny's ire in a bit on the "Curran Concert" album, and ultimately Judge Horn). During the trial, most of the attention centered around Lenny's use of one word ("cocksucker") and the obscenity of one bit ("To Is a Preposition, Come Is a Verb").

Lenny released a ten-inch album at this time; the taped material included what was used in evidence at the trial. On the cover there's a picture of Lenny in a policeman's uniform and these typewritten words: "WARNING. Sale of this album may subject seller to arrest for violation of the endemic obscenity laws; the sole exception being San Francisco, California (where the community standards may be lower)." Then on the bottom: "Lenny Bruce, 8825 Hollywood Blvd., Hollywood, California 90069."

The documented result of the trial is on the back: "The People of the State of California, Action O. F-54134, Charge 176-MPC (Amended) to 311.6 (Penal Code). Lenny Bruce, Defendent. Hon. Clayton W. Horn Judge Presiding Dept. No. 11 Date: March 8, 1962. Verdict Jury: NOT GUILTY. The court orders the action dismissed and the defendant discharged."

Some of the material surfaced years later on the Douglas album "To Is a Preposition" (aka "What I Was Arrested For"). It begins with the "Pretty Bizarre Show" and "Dirty Toilet" bits (as they're called on the Douglas album), but goes into more semantic detail: "Now if the bedroom is dirty to you, then you are a true atheist, because if you have any of the mores, the superstitions, if anyone in this audience believes that God made his body, and your body is dirty, the fault lies with the manufacturer. It's that cold, Jim. Yeah. You can do anything with a body that God made— and then you want to get definitive about the parts he made—I don't see that anywhere in any reference to any Bible. Made it all, it's all clean. Or all dirty. But the ambivalence comes from the religious leaders, who are celibates. The religious leaders are what should be. They say. They do not involve themselves with the physical. If we are good, we will be like our rabbi, our nun, our priest, and absolve, and finally put down the carnal and stop the race ... Let me tell you the truth. The truth is what is. If what is, you have to sleep, eight, ten hours a day, that is the truth. A lie will be: people need no sleep at all. Truth is what is. If every politician from the beginning is crooked, there is no crooked. But if you are concerned with a lie, what should be, and what should be is a fantasy. A terrible, terrible lie that someone gave the people long ago. This is what should be, and no one ever saw what should be, that you don't need any sleep and you can go seven years without sleep. So all the people were made to measure up to that dirty lie. No, there's no crooked politician, there is never a lie. Because there is never a truth."

Side Two offers one of Lenny's typically unique bits careening between anecdote and fantasy. Lenny describes sending off some elaborate hoax letters to the Thomas Burns detective agency and then talks about Solomon Ostrow, who killed six people in a synagogue in 1924.

The record ends with his "To Is a Preposition" routine. The Douglas version cuts the tape after Lenny flippantly announces: "If anyone in this room or the world finds those two words decadent, obscene, immoral, amoral, asexual, if the words "to come" really make you feel uncomfortable ... you probably can't come."

There was one line left off, and it's here: "'Cause that's the purpose of life. To re-create it."

- BERKELEY CONCERT (Bizarre/Reprise 6329, CD reissue 733952) *** $14
- LAW, LANGUAGE AND LENNY BRUCE (Spector/Warner SP 9101)*** $15 $40

Though released more than a decade apart, these two posthumous albums are both from 1965, and duplicate some material, including the difference between men and women ("A chick can't fall down and break her arm and go to bed with you thirty seconds later ... guys can have a head-on collision with Greyhound buses ... on the way to the hospital make a play for the nurse") and the theory that Jack Ruby killed Lee Harvey Oswald in a Jewish macho attempt to change a weak self-image.

Both albums contain Bruce's theory on the origin of Jews in show business: the Jews, trying to work less, were "being charming for the Pharaoh ... Let's watch the Jew be charming." Both albums are uneven, loaded with examples of Bruce's naiveté, his childlike attempts at simplifying morality, the Vietnam war, and the legal system. Both have more semantic lectures and legal jargon than the average listener would care to hear. But both have brilliant moments.

"Law and Language" has some essential bits, including his Eichmann rap, and the sure-fire offensiveness (even if he cautiously spells out the words instead of says them) of why Jewish judges are easier on smut than Christians: "To a Jew, f-u-c-k and s-h-i-t have the same value on a dirty word graph. A Jew has no concept that "f-u-c-k" is worth ninety points and "s-h-i-t" ten. And the reason for that is that both priests and rabbis s-h-i-t, but only one f-u-c-k's."

"Berkeley Concert," a two-record set issued as a single CD, has always been a good seller with fans. It may be that the cover shot of the bearded Lenny and the "Berkeley" reference makes it seem like the most modern and the most essential. In vinyl it was in print a lot longer than the only other "major label" full-length show, UA's "Midnight Concert."

Bruce muses on Mark Eden bust developing kits, midgets, and the rise of Zig Zag rolling papers. There are even a few one-liners: "Bela Lugosi ... the worst advertisement for rehabilitation. He was a dope fiend for seven years, he cleaned up and dropped dead." "Lyndon Johnson—it took him six months to learn how to say Negro." Among his better lecture routines, there's his description of how laws began: "We'll sleep in area c, we'll eat in area b. We'll throw a crap in area c ... if anyone throws any crap on us while we're sleeping, they get thrown in the craphouse." We get a vague idea of how Lenny might have mellowed as he got older, become more reflective, if not confused. Rock has replaced jazz by now and women are beginning to liberate. On the latter: "Dig what I miss ... lipstick and powder. I like 'em with paint on 'em." He begins to wrestle with concepts of masculine and feminine: "Guys are like dogs ... keep comin' back. Ladies are like cats. Yell at a cat one time, they're gone." He was still seething with ideas, with curiosity, with vivid humor. These records prove that. There was still hope.

- TO IS A PREPOSITION, COME IS A VERB $15 $30
  (re-released as WHAT I WAS ARRESTED FOR, Douglas KZ 30872) **** $10 $20
- THE ESSENTIAL LENNY BRUCE: POLITICS (Douglas SD 788) *** $15 $30
- THANK YOU MASKED MAN (Fantasy 7017) *** $15 $40

Each of these posthumous releases is worth hearing, but "To Is a Preposition" is essential. Today most of it seems less offensive than what's on morning radio. Bruce is at his zaniest with off-the-wall topics like "The Perverse Act," asking the desperate question, "Is there one other pervert that one time in your life, you did piss in the sink?" From there, Bruce creates a wild story of a guy in a room with no toilet, who tries to use the sink, only to be attacked by his roommate ("I'd kill you for that ... are you out of your mind?"). He ends up on a window ledge, and firemen, a priest, and eventually the man's mother try to prevent his apparent suicide.

Lenny does his "Tits and Ass" routine, a half-serious dissection of "Dirty Toilet" humor ("take this toilet and boil it..."), and is even good natured about judges and lawyers busting him for obscenity, and then using the dirty words in court ("he said blah blah blah!"). There's his famous opening shock bit ("I'm going to piss on you ...") and the comedy-jazz riff "To Come." The most accessible Bruce album for the uninitiated, it's loaded with memorable routines delivered with great charisma. Lenny was never given enough credit for simply being able to say things funny ("I just do it and that's all").

The "Politics" album was an interesting experiment. Taking a hodge-podge of "Berkeley Concert" era material, the record company collaged sound effects, political speeches (from Nixon, Johnson, etc.) and music, either to camouflage the poor quality of the tapes or stretch to get enough audio for a full album. Bruce purists obviously want pure stream-of-Lenny, and prefer him social not political, but the record does have some solid, "dangerous" comic logic bits (if pot leads to junkiedom, bingo in the Church produces gamblers) and some sex bits (like his anti-condom "to wear a balloon ... is dumb"). The collage is sometimes effective. When Bruce does his bit about LBJ stuttering in his ludicrous Southern accent, the real LBJ is heard babbling "ah, ah, ah-ah wanna talk."

And there's his memorable quote on liberals: "I'm so understanding, I can't understand anyone not understanding me, as understanding as I am."

Fantasy's search of the vaults produced the full twelve-minute version of the Lawrence Welk-jazz musician satire from Lenny's first album, a funny, offbeat six-minute bit on a monster rising at Coney Island; and an interesting revelation: the Firesign Theater-ish "Captain Whackencracker," an experimental bit Lenny did in his hotel room with a tape recorder. Using different voices, he creates a sinister kiddie show, where a coughing, corrupt host plays cartoons in which foxes gouge the eyes out of elephants. Then he urges the kiddies to go out into traffic and play chicken with oncoming trucks. The centerpiece is the title track, different from the Lone Ranger bit on "Lenny Bruce Is Out Again," and different from the best version (the one that became a cartoon short—one of Bruce's last projects).

- THE LENNY BRUCE PERFORMANCE FILM (Rhino 2949) **** $15

In 1992, Rhino issued Lenny's legendary August, 1965, "Performance" film on video as a boxed set with an added CD soundtrack version. His brilliant "Thank You Masked Man" cartoon is an added attraction. The video is indispensable, the only visual example of how Lenny worked in a nightclub. The CD isn't bad on its own, though some find it too monotonous on his legal problems. He does talk about his obscenity case and examines prosecution claims that he made gratuitous references to hot lead enemas, flashers in bushes, Eleanor Roosevelt's tits, pissing in the sink, sex with chickens, etc. After each perfunctory citation of obscenity, Lenny does the actual routine. With deceptive skill, he manages to slide into these bits so that they seem more spontaneous than counterevidence.

The strain on Lenny is evident, but he is hardly a "shell" of his former self, too bitter and obsessed with his drug and obscenity busts to be funny. He even tosses in some anecdotal bits, including one about nightclub gangsters (a variation on his "Shelley Berman" routine) and even a version of "Father Flotski's Triumph."

The CD has a bonus track: a seventeen-minute cut called "Christian & Jews." It's a bit ragged, both in the editing (it was obviously stitched together from various unreleased performances), and in Lenny's rambling. It leads through a lot of topics to the familiar rap about Christ's death: "We did it. I did it. My family. I found a note in the basement. It's now on exhibit at the Smithsonian. It said, 'We killed him....'"

NOTES: Collectors hunt for the red-vinyl Fantasy original releases and the "Interviews of Our Time" original cover with censor's black markings on the back. There are white label promo albums from Fantasy on red vinyl that also intrigue fans. Bruce fans might note Blue Thumb's two-LP set original Broadway cast recording of "Lenny" starring Cliff Gorman, and the United Artists album "Lenny" from the Dustin Hoffman film. Lenny's early days as a schtick comic may be heard briefly on "Arthur Godfrey's Talent Scouts" (Radiola MR1084). He wasn't exactly ordinary even then—frying minds with Barry Fitzgerald talking German in an Irish accent, a teutonic Humphrey Bogart ("Aw-wwright Rreggeh, drrop der shmegger"), and for the finale, Lenny sings in German as Frankie Laine.

An abbreviated "Law, Language and Lenny Bruce" was issued as a 33-1/3 EP promotional DJ item (Warner Spector PRO 598). The compilation "Great Moments from the *Tonight Show*" (Casablanca SPNB 1296) takes Lenny's "Airplane Glue" routine from his appearance with Steve Allen. The compilation "25 Years of Record Comedy" (Warner 3BX 3131) includes "Religions Inc."

Some Bruce fans want to be so complete they need the incomplete: the abridged, single disc version of "The Midnight Concert." United Artists issued it twice. The more interesting first printing (UAL 3580) has a picture of the Midnight show poster on the cover and a performance shot on the back. The second has a bland, silvery cover.

"Why Did Lenny Bruce Die" (Capitol KAO 2630), appearing in 1966, was a courageous documentary using Lawrence Schiller's taped interviews with now-regretful law enforcement officials, as well as friends, Bruce's mother, ex-wife Honey, and even eight-year old daughter Kitty singing "Yesterday."

WILLIE BRYANT

- THE FUNNIEST DREAM ON RECORD (Interlude 711) ** $6 $12

Not long after "The First Family" became a hit, this album appeared about "The First Family On the Other Side of the Tracks." Yes, the album jacket shows a black family walking over from "Soulsville St." to "Whitesville Boulevard," and into the White House.

Instead of an album about John Fitzgerald Kennedy, here's the story of Roosevelt Lincoln Canady who literally dreams that he's won the election. Or as a black newscaster says: "I'll leave you with this: God bless the child that's got his own."

President Canady meets with a member of the now-oppressed "White Citizen's Council." The white man tries to be friendly: "Boy, am I happy for you." President Canady says, "Let me get you straight ... you really struck out with that 'boy' jazz." "Oh, I meant no harm sir...sir, we're havin' trouble with the new colored board of education ... they won't let our white kids go to school with them colored kids."

Most of the jokes and situations have less of a Dick Gregory or Lenny Bruce sense of satire and simply go for the easy laugh. One of the president's aides talks about a new legal holiday in honor of a great Negro leader: "I'm not talkin' about your birthday, brother. I'm talkin' about the birthday of an all-time leader, a real soul brother, a leader from coast to coast: it's the birthday of Ray Charles."

The cast includes some singers and DJs that may have been known to some inner city listeners: Tommy Smalls, Lonnie Rochon, Chuck Mann, and Leonard Reed. Effie Smith appears in one sketch segment, as does Johnnie Lee, who played Calhoun on the old *Amos and Andy* TV series.

BUCHANAN AND GOODMAN See DICKIE GOODMAN

ART BUCHWALD

- SEX AND THE COLLEGE BOY (Capitol T 2205) *1/2 $10 $20

There's a very good reason why Buchwald is a columnist, not a stand-up comedian. He has a droning voice and a tired New York accent. His cadence sounds seasick, and after five or ten minutes of it, the listener may look up and wonder if the record is warped. Humor writers tend to be wry, their comedy laced up tartly with cleverly colorful descriptions. A reader sitting comfortably can savor these. But when read out loud, it usually comes off smug and self-serving. The title cut is some nonsense about a sex survey. Equally annoying is the lengthy, obvious monologue about how bad guys (World War II's Japan and Germany) are now friends and how good guys (World War II's Russia) are now bad guys. Now and then there's a quick example of Buchwald's wit, including this: "I covered the campaign and the one question the people still ask me is, 'Was the press really fair to Goldwater?' And I'm one of the people who think the press wasn't fair to Goldwater. For one thing, we quoted him."

LORD BUCKLEY

- THE BEST OF LORD BUCKLEY (Crestview CRV 801, portions $20 $50
  originally released as EUPHORIA on Vaya Records 101 and 102, $25 $75
  later reissued as HIS ROYAL HIPNESS, Directions CD 71001) *** $8

"The immaculately hip aristocrat," Buckley was an offbeat original, a jazz monologist who was equally effective using a British-sounding voice or black dialect "hipsomatic." He delivered charismatic comic Bible lessons, semi-serious histories of famous people, and poems reinterpreted in modern lingo. It was all mind blowing at the time (1950 to the year of his death, 1960) and still is today.

The Vaya (Crestview reissue) material was recorded in a studio in 1951. His best routines were the affectionate retelling of the glories of Jesus Christ ("The Naz") and the masterful "Jonah and the Whale," a great example of dialect humor. Lessers on the six-cut Crestview compilation are "The Hip Gahn," "Nero," and a pair of one-joke items: hip versions of "Gettysburg Address" and "Marc Antony's Funeral Oration."

The double set "Euphoria" is extremely hard to find, but it does have some key material not available on the "Best of." Volume One contains "The Naz" and "Mark Antony's Funeral Oration" on Side One, "Nero" and "Murder" on Side Two.

"Murder" is a strange drama with spooky organ music and disconcerting percussion: "there are two characters in this scene. One is a man. And the other ... a woman! The woman's head is not on her body! In the man's hand is a long, keen bloody knife! With the blood not yet congealed ..." Buckley inhabits the crazed conscience of the man as he moans, "I killed her because ... I loved her!" Finally someone calls, "Henry ... Henry! Henry, I want you to put on your pants and go outside and clean the hen house before breakfast." Is it all a dream? Whatever it is, it's closer to the dark world of Brother Theodore than the world of mystic colored lights the Lord usually played with.

"Euphoria Volume Two" features "Jonah and the Whale" and "The Gasser" on Side One, and on Side Two "The Hip Gahn" and a set of fables, "The Dog and the Wolf," "The Grasshopper and the Ant," "The Mouse and the Lion," and "The Lion's Breath." Typical of the fables is "The Dog and the Wolf." Buckley reports, "This lean, hungry wolf met a great big fat groovy house dog goofin' in the woods. And the wolf said, 'My, my, Jack, how fat and groovy you look ... as for me, as you can see, man, I'm in a bad bind ... I ain't had a good Sunday dinner for heaven knows how long. I can't hardly keep from starvin' to death.' Well, the house dog say ... 'You come with me to my head cat's house, the cat that own me, and then you get the same score I do.' Wolf lick his chops and say, 'Man, that'll be crazy....' But when he discovers that the dog has a collar, and spends most of his time a leashed pet, the wolf says, 'Well, I'm gonna plant you know and dig you later.'"

The CD version includes the six original cuts from the Crestview "Best of" plus "The Gasser" and a twenty-five-second bonus, Lord Buckley (accompanied by piano) declaring, "People! People are the true flowers of life! And it has been a most precious pleasure to have temporarily strolled in your garden."

* HIPSTERS, FLIPSTERS, AND FINGER POPPIN' DADDIES,
  KNOCK ME YOUR LOBES (RCA Victor 3246) *** $25 $100

This 1955 ten-incher has five cuts: "Friends, Romans, Countrymen," "Hiawatha," "To Swing or Not to Swing," "Boston Tea Party," and "Is This the Sticker."

While the front cover is just a silly cartoon of various friends, Romans, and countrymen, the back at least has notes from Buckley himself, who offers some autobiographical details. It's unfortunate that this expensive record isn't that interesting. Several cuts are just typical "hipsomatic" silliness, speeches rewritten to be jazz cool but not all that comic. "To Swing or Not To Swing," Buckley's take on Hamlet, does have a certain ludicrous appeal. Here the melancholy Dane wonders, "Shall I knock on the Pearlies, or dig the sweet sack of my pad, or sound the tall cat with the scythe? Ay, there's the drag!"

Buckley fans will enjoy his versions of history ("Boston Tea Party" and "Hiawatha") but the key cut is the finale, a bizarre voodoo jazz riff, "Is This the Sticker," about phantoms, bad dreams, "gut thunder," blood, and "mad kicks." Agitated violins accompany Buckley's melodrama, which is so loaded with hipsomatic slang that on the first listen (and on several subsequent ones) it's not easy to follow. "Is This the Sticker" is available on the "Lord Buckley Live" cassette tape (see notes section) and "Friends, Romans, Countrymen" appeared on RCA's "Golden Age" compilation.

* BLOWING HIS MIND (World Pacific 1849) **1/2 $20 $40
* IN CONCERT (World Pacific 1815, also released as WAY OUT HUMOR,
  World Pacific 1279) **1/2 $20 $40
* BUCKLEY'S BEST (World Pacific WPS 21879) **1/2 $15 $30

World Pacific has Buckley live, but although it's great to hear The Lord getting laughs, his better material is generally elsewhere. "Blowing His Mind" has stream-of-consciousness material: "Subconscious Mind," "Fire Chief," "Let it Down," "Murder," and three long sketches, "The Gasser," "Scrooge," and "Maharaja." The history lesson on Vasco De Gama ("The Gasser") is an incoherent travelogue through Florida to Mexico. Or as he says in a letter back to King Ferdinand, "Your Majesty ... I been hung up and jammed up and framed up and backed up and stacked up and macked up and racked up, but I never dug no jazz like this last riff you put me on." "Maharaja" is a fable (with bongo drums) of a sly liar keeping himself tight with his king. "Scrooge" sounds like Amos and Andy on dangerous drugs. There isn't as much humor on this album as there is bizarre storytelling.

The cuts on the 1959 "In Concert" are "Supermarket," "Horse's Mouth," "Black Cross," "My Own Railroad," "God's Own Drunk," "Willie the Shake," and "The Naz." Buckley uses his familiar formula and William Shakespeare really shakes: "Willie the Shake ... shook everybody. They gave him a nickel's worth of ink and five cents worth of paper. He sat down, wrote up such a breeze, that's all there was, Jack, there was no more ... here's a stud that's so powerful and so great they dig him up every six months a year, yeah that's him, put him back." The classic cut is the live version of "The Naz," complete with gospel singers in the background.

"Buckley's Best" is uneven: "Supermarket," "The Naz," "The Gasser," "Subconscious Mind," "Willie the Shake," "Martin's Horse," "God's Own Drunk."

* BAD RAPPING OF THE MARQUIS DE SADE (World Pacific WPS 21889) ** $15 $30
* A MOST IMMACULATELY HIP ARISTOCRAT (Straight STS 1054, $10 $20
  CD reissue: Enigma Straight 733982) *** $8

In the early '70s Buckley, along with Lenny Bruce, was rediscovered. These two albums dug up previously unreleased material. Both have fairly different versions of "The Bad Rapping of the Marquis de Sade," Buckley's humorous defense of the notorious sadist and libertine. The funniest thing about it is the periodic catchphrase, "Dey bad rapped 'im ever' step de way!" The World Pacific album has a nice eight minutes on "The Chastity Belt," seven minutes on

"The H-Bomb," and a hipsomatic version of Robert W. Service's "The Ballad of Dan McGroo" ("A bunch of the studs was swingin' it up at the old Red Dog Saloon. And a cat he was rockin' the eight eight and blowin' How High the Moon."). None of these cuts are essential to non-cultists.

Frank Zappa edited the Buckley tapes for his "Straight" label (distributed by Reprise) and he found a few gems, including a lively retelling of Poe's "The Raven" complete with a logical interpretation of its meaning: "When you don't want the bird, when you don't need the bird, when you don't have no possible use for the bird—that's when ya get it!" The Lord evidently enjoyed making home tapes, and "Governor Slugwell" and "The Train" are a pair of magical dabblings. Both offer exciting storytelling, loaded with his improbable sound effects ranging from brass band mimicry to the chugging "bibbity bibbity huppity huppity" of an oncoming train.

The album has been released in the CD format by Enigma, and later redistributed by Rhino.

NOTES: Buckley is one of the "Three Bs" in the world of comedy album rarities (Lenny Bruce and Bob & Ray are the others). In The Lord's case, the original Vaya discs and the RCA album are the main prizes. Import versions of the World Pacific albums (on the Demon Verbals label) have helped collectors somewhat.

Buckley issued three 45 rpm singles in 1956: "Flight of the Saucer, Parts 1 & 2" (Hip Records HI 270), "Gettysburg Address" (one side straight, the other hipsomatic; Hip HI 301) and "James Dean's Message to the Teenagers" backed with "Speak for Yourself, John" (Hip HI 302). The hip "Gettysburg Address" and "James Dean" are available on a cassette called "Lord Buckley Live" released in 1992 by Shambhala Lion Editions (an audio book company selling mainly to bookstores). Other cuts on the tape are from the Vaya and RCA discs: "The Hip Ghan," "The Gettysburg Address," "God's Own Drunk," "Is This the Sticker?" "The Naz," "Trouble," "Murder," "Scrooge," and "The Gasser." One outtake from the RCA sessions was included: "Baa Baa Blacksheep." According to Buckley's biographer, Oliver Trager, there are actually a half dozen unissued tracks from those 1955 sessions, including versions of "The Raven" and "Jonah and the Whale," as well as obscurities "Ace in the Hole," "Meeting of Marc Antony and Cleopatra," and "Pursuit of Morpheus." Buckley's son Richard compiled this tape, but surprisingly offered no notes on Buckley or the routines.

"Euphoria" was issued in a red vinyl version (Vaya CPM 10-1715LP). Aside from the Demon Verbals import reissues ("Blowing His Mind" VERB 3, "Lord Buckley in Concert" VERB 4, "Bad Rapping of the Marquis de Sade" VERB 6, and "A Most Immaculately Hip Aristocrat" VERB 8) there's an obscure British album called "The Parabolic Revelations of the Late Lord Buckley" (Pye/Nonesuch PPL 208) issued in 1963. Contents, based on 1952 tapes, include "Jonah and the Whale," "Georgia Sweet and Kind," "The Naz," "Chastity Belt," "Governor Gulpwell," and "Murder."

According to William Karl Thomas's book, *Lenny Bruce: The Making of a Prophet*, Buckley recorded an anonymous version of "The Farting Contest" (see Windersphere and Boomer). None of the versions reviewed for this book contain this apocryphal performance. A lot of authentic rarities have circulated among ardent collectors. These include outtakes of the 1956 Hip Records session (including "His Majesty the Policeman" and "Lonesome Road"), a broadcast over WERE-FM in Cleveland in 1957, a KPFA-FM interview from 1959, plus live concerts everywhere from "The Lighthouse" in Hermosa Beach to Henry Miller's house.

An acetate from 1950 features an oddity called "Moronic Father and His Idiot Son." There's piano backing for the experimental riff, as Buckley plays the doting father and the goofily demented son who can barely utter a coherent word. "My big beautiful, beautiful gorgeous son! How many fathers would be so fortunate as to have a son who stands for three hours in the house, looking at what? The moooooooon!" A true black comedy, the father is only mildly concerned that his son has set fire to the garage, which also serves as the servants' quarters!

THE BUFFALO BILLS

- SHUT THE DOOR! THEY'RE COMIN' THROUGH THE WINDOW (RCA Victor LSP 3401) ** $7 $15

No relation to the football team, these Bills were popular in the early '60s and released a few "straight" albums, as well as this all-novelty song collection in 1965 featuring "Sam, You Made the Pants Too Long," "Josephine Please No Lean on the Bell," "Barney Google," "Mad Dogs and Englishmen," "Does the Spearmint Lose Its Flavor," and "Too Fat Polka." With a few exceptions (there are some shrieks of laughter on "Cigareetes, Whusky and Wild Women") the fellows sing as straight as any barbershop quartet. Of more collector interest is the frantic Jack Davis cover painting.

ANDY BUMATAI

- LIVE IN WAIKIKI (Mountain Apple MAC 100) *1/2 $4 $8
- HAWAII'S FIRST STAND-UP COMIC (Mountain Apple MAC 1004) *1/2 $4 $8
- ALOHA (Bluewater 700) *1/2
- ALL IN THE OHANA (Bluewater 701) *1/2 $4 $8
- LIVE AT THE ROYAL HAWAIIAN (Bluewater 702) *1/2 $4 $8

Billed as "Hawaii's first stand-up comic" (at least the first Hawaiian comic to work the mainland comedy clubs with any success), Bumatai (rhymes with "zoom a pie") opened for Kenny Loggins, Lionel Ritchie, and Natalie Cole. Most of his gags have little to do with Hawaii: "You know you're on a diet when cat food commercials make you hungry." He's not too different from any other comedy club denizen. From the "First Stand-Up Comic" album, on current events: "Iran and hostages. Do you ever notice they only pick people who can't fight back? Airline passengers, people who freak if they're served a cold entree. They come at these people with Uzis. I'd like to hear of them attacking the Hell's Angels in San Bernardino! The news broadcast would say: The terrorists were found hung by portions of their anatomy, with signs that read 'Islamic Jihad My Ass' around their necks."

BUM BAR BASTARDS

- TUBE BAR (Detonator 304142) * $7

The Bastards (John Elmo and Jim Davidson) place calls to The Tube Bar in Jersey City to annoy the feisty bar owner. All they have to do is call up and start cursing, and he curses back. And it's about as entertaining as hearing two kids tease a barking dog. The predictable curses and threats get tiresome very quickly. Regularly the duo pull the old "fake name" gag of asking for "Al Kaholic," "Ben Dover" or "Phil Myass." It's hard to believe the bar owner isn't playing along when he keeps falling for it. Dirty songs sung in speeded-up chipmunk voices and "guests" like a foul-mouthed woman named Judy break up the monotony.

THE BUNCH

- THE BUNCH (RCA Victor LSP 3629) ** $7 $15

Julian Barry, who went on to write the Broadway show *Lenny*, wrote the script for this album lampooning the best-seller and 1966 movie about 1930s Vassar women, *The Group*. It's strictly for those who remember the movie and enjoy arch, tongue-in-cheek joking. Linda Lavin has turned out to be the most prominent member of the cast of budding stars used here. The others in the bunch were Sally Gracie, Diana Kagan, Renee Taylor, and Mary Louise Wilson.

Much of the script satirizes the liberal, well-meaning, but muddled ladies:

"I think that we should all just go over and fight in the war in Spain!"

"Oh? They're having a war? Gee, I mean, I know those people like to argue a lot...."

"... they're havin' a sort of Civil War ... on the one hand is the peasants, and on the other the bad people! But ... the real danger is the Germans. Now y'all remember them. They're just usin' this Civil War as a kind of out-of-town tryout ... see that German dictator, what's his name?"

"I've heard of him ... Moozerella?"

"... I thought Moozerella is a cheese."

"No, Leiderkranz is a cheese."

"I beg to differ, kiddies, but Leiderkranz was a German general in the War of the Roses."

"... I'm a little too busy to drop everything to fight against a guy who may be a cheese."

VICTOR BUONO

- HEAVY! (Dore LP 325) *** $5 $10

Quite literally a heavy, Buono initially was the Laird Cregar of the '60s, specializing in playing neurotic movie menaces. Later he was often a comic villain ("King Tut" on *Batman*, a nasty landlord on *The Odd Couple*. He demonstrated another side when he went on talk shows reading comical poems about fatness. These are collected in this performance before a packed audience.

"To most people the idea of being fat is tragic," Buono says, "There are times when it could be tragic if I allowed it to be. Such as when one is at the beach and one hears a childish voice sing out "Mamma, look, a man with titties!"

Buono's poems alternately deflate and celebrate fatness. An example: "I'm fat, I'm fat. That's all there is to that. You might think it etiquette to say that I am "heavy set" or just big boned, ya wanna bet? I'm fat, I'm fat, I'm fat! Portly, chubby, plump and stout: everyone's a diplomat. Why not let it all hang out. Go ahead and call me fat! So please, don't think you're being kind by pretending to be blind – just take a look at my ... physique. There's only one word: FAT." Which could be funny if you have the right viewpoint, and if you forget that the unhealthily proportioned Buono died while still relatively young.

GEORGE BURNS

- AN EVENING WITH GEORGE BURNS (Dove Audio) **1/2 $8

Originally, "An Evening with George Burns" was only available as an import (DJM 8004), a two-record set coproduced by Randy Newman. In the early '70s, after Groucho Marx had some success with a one-man show, Burns tried one. At the time, the impact was minimal. He was perceived as merely an old vaudevillian with some amusing stories and one too many bad old songs. But after making "The Sunshine Boys" and becoming a living legend as much for his longevity as his laugh lines, Burns's one man shows of the late '80s and '90s became events. The seventy-two-minute CD of George's New York performance at The Shubert Theater (introduction by Jack Benny) has some forgettable songs, some cute anecdotes about his career, and plenty of typical Burns: "I smoke between fifteen and twenty cigars a day. Well, at my age I've got to hold on to something." George Burns passed away in 1996 at the ripe old age of 100.

NOTES: Burns's musical albums sometimes had a few novelty songs on them. In the late '60s he recorded "George Burns Sings" (Buddah, reissued on CD by Special Music) and there's some slight humor in his raspy version of "I Can't Get No Satisfaction." The Mercury album "I Wish I Was Eighteen Again" has the song that became his signature tune, the wistful soft shoe ditty, "The Only Way to Go." It sounds better without the campy siren whistles and backing vocalists here. Burns is on a "Roast" album for Harry Joe Brown (see listing under George Jessel). Burns and Allen do a studio recorded routine on "Great Stars of Vaudeville" Columbia Special Products (CSS 1509) and Epic's "Show Business" compilation. A fine sample of their humor is on "Jest Like Old Times" (Radiola). Burns narrates of "Kings of Comedy" (Longines Symphonette SyS 5282) and appears on "My Favorite Story" (20th Century Fox TFM 3106).

BURNS AND ALLEN

- BURNS AND ALLEN (Nostalgia Lane PBO 157) **1/2 $4 $8
- THE BURNS AND ALLEN SHOW (Radiola MR 1028) **1/2 $5 $10
- THE NEW BURNS AND ALLEN SHOW (Radiola MR 1142) **1/2 $5 $10
- BURNS AND ALLEN SHOW (Memorabilia M 722) ** $4 $8
- GEORGE BURNS AND GRACIE ALLEN VOL 1 (Mark 56 # 614) **1/2 $4 $8
- ORIGINAL BROADCASTS: 1937 (Mark 56 # 735) ** $4 $8
- BURNS AND ALLEN (Murray Hill 59095) ** $15 $30
- BURNS AND ALLEN (Murray Hill 898047) ** $15 $30
- BURNS AND ALLEN (Metacom 0300333) ** $8

George Burns met Gracie Allen in 1923 and originally Gracie played it straight and George told the jokes. Once they straightened that out, the duo became radio and TV favorites until Gracie retired in 1959.

Nostalgia Lane takes two episodes from the old radio show. On the November 1, 1945, show Gracie plays matchmaker and in the process recalls dating George: "I knew the first time I kissed you that you'd been kissed before. You were dynamite." "Really?" "Sure, you kissed almost as good as I did." A week later, November 8, 1945, George hopes to play a lead role in a new Betty Grable film. Louella Parsons cameos a comment: "In my humble opinion, a picture starring George Burns should have everything. It'll need it."

Radiola's first Burns and Allen album has a complete (undated) half-hour show about George's jealousy over an old high school boyfriend of Gracie's: "George, you're getting excited for no reason at all. This is something you've built up in your own head and there's really nothing in it." Side Two collects six ditsy routines filled with corny gags like the one about Cousin Audubon Allen:

"He has two birdbaths in his backyard."

"Two of them?"

"George, don't you know that birds are male and female?"

"Well, Cousin Audubon made quite a bit of money selling articles to the Birdlover's Gazette. Such as ... 'Improved an Owl's Grammar.'"

"How did he do that?"

"He taught it to say 'whom.'"

The "New" Burns and Allen album offers two episodes (October 21, 1941, and December 16, 1941) steeped in the Burns and Allen formula. Here, Gracie and her maid go into the kitchen:

"I wonder if that cake in the oven is ready yet. Oh look, my cake is all ruined." "Well no wonder, you're supposed to put the icing on the cake after you bake it." "Oh, that isn't icing. All the candles melted."

The other labels have similarly inane material, but no dates are given for the broadcasts. On the first Mark 56 album Gracie imagines George becoming a doctor: "I can see him dashing around in his delivery truck, delivery babies. Giving tall people hypos and short people lopos ..." And on the 1937 disc, with Tony Martin a guest on one of the two episodes, Gracie talks of visiting New York City: "Tonight I'm going sight-seeing, then take in a movie, walk up and down Broadway, then go into a cafe in Greenwich Village, and then drive out to the beach for a clambake." "I suppose that's not tiring." "Oh no, they have somebody there to open the clams for you."

Murray Hill issued three-record sets. Number 59095 has album notes by Burns himself and includes episodes guest starring Fred Astaire and Rita Hayworth. Number 898047 mixes soundtracks from TV with full-length radio shows.

Metacom's 1994 CD compilation features two episodes: "George Inherits $5,000" and "Jack Joins George at College."

BURNS AND CARLIN

- AT THE PLAYBOY CLUB TONIGHT (Era EL 103)

Jack Burns and George Carlin were a team in the early '60s. This album, with the original cover, is worth more than the reissues, which don't mention Burns at all. See "The Original George Carlin." Burns went on to team with Avery Schreiber.

BURNS AND SCHREIBER

- IN ONE HEAD AND OUT THE OTHER (Columbia C 32442) **1/2 $5 $10
- PURE B.S. (Little David LD 1006) *** $5 $10
- THE WATERGATE COMEDY HOUR (Hidden ST 11202) **1/2 $4 $8

A popular comedy duo of the '60s, Jack Burns often played a slick, obnoxious know-it-all with Avery Schreiber as the chubby, good-natured realist who could gently let the air out of his pomposity.

Both the Columbia and Atlantic albums feature the duo's most popular routine, "The Cab Driver and the Conventioneer." Burns is the hyper, jabbering out-of-towner who bugs the cabbie with his bragging: "I guess there's still some life in the old trooper, huh?" "Yeah," Schreiber admits amiably. "Huh?" Burns barks. "Yeah." "Huh?" Yeah!" The team got a lot of mileage out of the "Huh" "Yeah" routine, a kind of "catchphrase" that quickly identified the personalities of the two characters. But the thrust of the routine was always deeper. The Burns character was, according to the first album, "the new emerging bigot." And way before Carroll O'Connor's Archie Bunker, Burns and Schreiber were satirizing the stupid intolerance to be found in everyday conversation with seemingly average people.

"I don't care about the color of a man's skin," Burns rambles, "I was the first guy to scream when they took *Amos and Andy* off the air ... by the way, your name on the nameplate there. You're of the Judeo-Hebraic persuasion?"

"You mean I'm a Jew."

"Hey, I don't go in for name calling ... But I'll tell you what I hate, I hate those people who make derogatory remarks about someone's ancestry ... he's a dago, he's a wop, he's a hebe. You know who says that the most? Your hunkies."

The Columbia album is basically the cab driver routine over one complete side (thirteen minutes). The other side offers Burns in another familiar character, "The Faith Healer," another long (eleven minutes) routine. The Atlantic album, which appeared in 1973 after the duo had split for many years and reunited for a TV series, has more variety. There's nine minutes for the cab driver bit, fourteen for the faith healer, and a full half-hour's worth of additional routines, including a look at a vice cop who entraps gays by casually taking baths in the sinks at men's rooms, and their "Dial-a-Friend" routine with Avery as an automated machine.

The "Watergate" album has cast members Ann Elder, Fannie Flagg (as Martha Mitchell), Bob Ridgely (amusing as Dick Cavett), Jack Riley, and Frank Welker (Richard Nixon). It's not too sharp and sometimes it's really silly. Burns and Schreiber turn up primarily in a six-and-a-half-minute re-creation of the Watergate break-in. Jack is the leader of the Cubans doing the job. He asks if they all have their binoculars and everyone responds, "Sí," except Schreiber. He cries "Sue!" "Sue? What the hell is Sue?" "Sue is someone I see on the seventh floor with my binoculars! She got big 'hugs!' Arriba!"

The duo appear on The Second City's "The Cosa Nostra Story" and "Second City Writhes Again" albums and are in the cast of "Life with Liz and Dick" by Baxter and Bright.

ABE BURROWS

- GIRL WITH THE THREE BLUE EYES (Decca DL 5288) *1/2 $10 $20
- ABE BURROWS SINGS? (Columbia CL 6128) ** $10 $20

Burrows (Abram Borowitz) is today best remembered as the lyricist for "Guys and Dolls," "How to Succeed in Business Without Really Trying," and "Cactus Flower." In the '50s "The Bald-Headed Baritone from Brooklyn" was a witty panelist on quiz shows and sometimes sang novelty tunes.

On these obscure ten-inch albums he seems like a stone-age Allan Sherman (adept at unpretentious Brooklyn-Jewish accented humor) or Irving Taylor (fond of satirizing the day's romantic ballads).

The Decca album has a theme. Burrows sits at the piano and tries to satirize all different "type" songs in popular music. This includes a cheerful love song: "Heaven above! I'm in love! With the girl with the three blue eyes!" Lacking Tom Lehrer's killer instinct, he pretty much leaves it at that: "What makes her different? Is it the way she walks? Or the way she shakes her pert little skirt? Or the way she talks? I'm singin' nothin' but blue skies! Cupid gave me a shove, and I'm in love. With the girl with the three blue, not one, not two, but three blue eyes!"

The dated satires, once perhaps considered "mad" and "outrageous" are toothless now. Some cuts sound more like *real* bad songs from the '50s than parodies. One opens: "I may be sick in the hospital, but I'm not sick of you."

The Allan Sherman side is evident on the Columbia album. On "The Gypsy's Violin" he adds Jewish realism to Hungarian mysticism: "A gypsy's heart is yearning. A gypsy's blood is churning. A gypsy's brain is learning. A gypsy's roast is burning. There are tears on the strings of a gypsy's violin and tears fall on the bow as he cries. Poor, poor gypsy! Now you cannot play until your violin dries!"

BUTTERBEANS AND SUSIE

- BUTTERBEANS & SUSIE (Classic Jazz 29) $8

Jody Edwards and Susie Edwards were a legendary black vaudeville team, married onstage in 1916. They sang blues tunes, sometimes comically bickering or taunting each other in mid-selection, and performed sketches. They gave Moms Mabley her first important break and influenced Pigmeat Markham as well. They recorded for Okeh from 1924 to 1930. After thirty years of touring small clubs, they recorded this album. The emphasis is on songs, not comedy, including Susie's straight ballads. There's some byplay, but not much, on two self-penned numbers, "A Married Man's a Fool" and "Get Yourself a Monkey Man." Butterbeans' asides show some of the indignant growling that Pigmeat Markham would later use effectively. The album is often placed in the comedy bin, but has a lot fewer laughs than jazz bin denizens Slim Gaillard, Louis Jordan, and Fats Waller. Various import labels can supply some of the 1920s tunes, notably the Denmark album from Contact Records, "Daddy's Got the Mojo" released in 1989 (BT 2009) and "Elevator Papa Switchboard Mama," a twenty-three-cut CD from England's JSP Records (CD 329).

RED BUTTONS

- LOVE DADDY (Wonderland LP 277) * $5 $10

In 1972 Buttons recorded an album of the nonsense poems he wrote for his daughter Amy. Unlike a Danny Kaye or an Ed Wynn, Red doesn't come across as a particularly warm or funny-voiced narrator, which is essential for kiddie comedy. Red would leave a poem as a surprise present. Like: "Bald Henrietta was so funny to see. She looked like a melon climbing a tree. When the sun hit her head, it got very red. And made a hot spot for a cold bumblebee. Love, Daddy!"

Somebody at Wonderland should've told him it wasn't necessary to repeat "Love, Daddy!" after every single poem.

Red's novelty hits from the '50s, "Strange Things Are Happening (Ho Ho, Hee Hee)" and "The Ho Ho Song," both appear on the compilation album "Fun House" (Harmony Columbia HL 7224), which includes songs by Abe Burrows, Art Carney, and Molly Goldberg.

PAT BUTTRAM

- OFF HIS ROCKER (Warner W 1455) *** $5 $10
- WE WUZ POOR (Ovation 1418) ** $5 $10
- AS I LOOK INTO YOUR FACES (Dore 102) **1/2 $5 $10

Buttram had his own radio show in the '60s and was an after dinner speaker. His Warner album arrived in 1962, pre-*Green Acres*. At the time he was best known as Gene Autry's old sidekick. With writing help from pros Hal Kanter and Milt Josefsberg, he offers pleasant country comedy, observations on modern life (including the trends of morbid teen tunes like "Tell Laura I Love Her" and the latest in funeral arrangements), and a homely definition now and then: "An hors d'oerve is an unfamiliar creature curled up on a cracker and stabbed with a toothpick to make sure it's dead."

"We Wuz Poor" from 1970 (sporting compliments from Richard Nixon and Lorne Greene) is mild and short, barely eleven minutes per side. He mentions that his first record was "on the Oral Roberts label, but you couldn't play the damn record, the hole kept healin' up." Having played the huckster Mr. Haney on *Green Acres*, he has no shame in swiping whiz-bang jokes that have been on everybody's records. He even lifts a Woody Allen gag: "My grandfather, on his deathbed, sold me this watch." Mostly he talks about his *Green Acres* star: "Eva Gabor wanted to be here tonight but she has a chest cold. Boy, those germs really know how to live, don't they?"

Pat narrates the Dore album, which collects some of his sly after dinner remarks at various celebrity functions. Honoring Steve Allen, Pat gets big laughs for each line as he declares, "As a straight dramatic actor he made his debut playing the part of Benny Goodman and he rocketed clarinet playing to the height of obscurity. Yessir, friends, he's the kind of a man who would've become a success in any business he'd chosen to enter. He could've been a great bad lawyer. He could've been the man who designed the Edsel. He could've been a male nurse for Governor Earl Long."

Buttram appears on one side of a promotional album for the Siegler Heater Company around 1960, addressing the firm's salespeople with a speech of anecdote-filled inspiration.

BUTTRAM AND CRANE

- LAFFTER SWEET AND PROFANE (KNX) ** $10 $20

This album was recorded "for file and reference purposes" by KNX Radio when Buttram was the afternoon host and Bob *"Hogan's Heroes"* Crane the station's morning man. One side has some of Pat's toastmaster speeches, including gags roasting film producer Jack Warner: "I want to thank Mr. Warner for inviting me here. He's one of our fine after dinner speakers. In fact he'll talk for two hours if anybody opens a lunch box. He started in the business as an entertainer. You get an idea why he gave that up. He's now in the production and management end of it. In fact, it's been said Mr. Warner can take a star and overnight make him an unknown."

The flip side has highlights from Crane's radio show, which was pretty hip for its time. Nichols and May give a brief introduction. Crane glibly jokes about his sponsor's product (to the off-mike laughter from the crew) and conducts laid-back interviews with stars George Jessel, Pat Boone, and Jonathan Winters. They improvise a bit with Crane as an actor and Winters as a movie producer. Crane insists, "My agent told me that I was very good." "Did he? What's good about ya?" "You really want to know?" "I really want to know. I'm that interested ..." "The agent said to me you're a very big man." "That's right, I am. Physically and mentally. I'm overweight, overtaxed, overtired and I'm over the hill. It's that simple, kid. Seventy-five pills a day, sixteen syringes and five bottles of juice—that's what keeps me going!"

SID CAESAR

- 25 YEARS OF LIFE: THANKS FOR THE MEMORY (Life Magazine MBOL-5804) ** $15 $25

This ten-inch album was recorded in 1961, evidently highlights from a *Life* magazine 25th anniversary TV special and a promo item for magazine execs or subscribers. Caesar and Peggy Cass star on one side in a long domestic sketch about "The Average American Family." It's full of slice-of-life humor.

Peggy: My shoulder, I was takin' the laundry downstairs to hang out on the line. Ooh, I think I wrenched it.

Sid: What happened? Wh-when did this happen?

Peggy: Oh, a week ago.

Sid: A week ago and you didn't say anything? You listen to me, Helen. If that pain in your shoulder don't go away in five or six days, I'm tellin' you, right now, I'm taking you down to the drugstore and I'm gonna ask the pharmacist what to rub on!

The flip side offers Bob Hope's opening monologue and production numbers with The Ray Charles Singers and Mary Martin.

Caesar appears as one of "The Three Haircuts" singing "You're So Rare to Me" on RCA's compilation album "Golden Age of Comedy." On Evolution's album also titled "Golden Age of Comedy" there's a brief sketch costarring Imogene Coca.

CAJUN PETE

- TALES OF THE BAYOU (Mercury MG 20633) ** $5 $10

Cajun Pete (a catchier name than Irvine Vidacovich) offers "storytelling as only the Bayou country of Louisiana can produce." Actually, most of the jokes are familiar Southern classics, not necessarily of Cajun origin. Pete, evidently Mercury's answer to Capitol's Justin Wilson, isn't quite as colorful—more of an after dinner speaker than a comedian, but he gets the job done. But watch out for groaners, like the long, long pun story about a "halo statue." (Which turns out to be the dialect way a Cajun answers the phone: "Halo. Statue?").

ROY CALHOUNE

- THE TICKLISH SIDE OF ROY CALHOUNE (RSP 1580) * $5 $10

Calhoune's early '70s self-pressed album could win a "worst cover drawing" award. The charcoal sketch makes him look like somebody's fourteen-year-old grandson. But his act isn't for doting grandmas. He's an amateur who uses everybody else's dirty jokes, like the one about the mugger who accosts an old Jewish lady and gropes her for money: "He says, 'You know, you're right lady, you don't got a damn dime.' She says, 'Don't stop now, I'll sign a check!'" And there's the one about the hooker who can't understand how her Japanese client can keep going hour after hour: "She gets up, she looks underneath the bed, and there's five more Japs!"

Calhoune prolongs these stories more than necessary and makes them noxious with unbearably stereotypical accents.

CALYPSO GENE See GENE FARMER

GODFREY CAMBRIDGE

- HERE'S GODFREY READY OR NOT (Epic FLM/FLS13101) *** $8 $20
- THEM COTTON PICKIN' DAYS ARE OVER (Epic FLM 13102) *** $8 $20
- TOYS WITH THE WORLD (Epic FLM/FLS 13108) *** $8 $20
- GODFREY CAMBRIDGE SHOW LIVE AT THE ALADDIN (Epic FLM 13115 FLS 15115) *** $8 $20

Cambridge was one of the pioneering black comedians of the early '60s. Dick Gregory was sharply satirical. Bill Cosby proved his equality with nonracial material. Cambridge combined both. He was a likable comic who could do Vegas routines (topless dancers, movies, gambling, etc.) but mixed in lampooning gags about racial problems using a "like it is" style.

On "Live at the Aladdin," Cambridge ushers the ringsiders in:

"Come right in, this is what is known as good race relations! I like the dress—very nice. I like to see white people in colorful clothes; it takes the pressure off of us! All I gotta do is put on a red shirt, man. Everybody says, 'See that, I told you them people like bright colors!' I also say drink up, because I encourage white people to get drunk because it also takes the pressure off of me! You get drunk, they just say, 'You're drunk.' I get drunk, I blow it for a whole race: 'See Mary, just came outta the South, don't know how to act ... my God those people are awful.'"

Typical of Cambridge's more standard, Vegas-oriented comedy is this from "Here's Godfrey Cambridge, Ready or Not." Godfrey talks about different women around the world and how they react after sex:

"A Latin woman will say, 'That was good! If you ever look at another woman again, I scratch your eyes out.' And a German woman is practical. She will say, 'Ach! Dat vas goot!' A French woman is solicitous. She will say, 'Ah, mon cherie, did I please you?' And an English woman will say, 'Feeling better?'

"And an American woman will say: 'Honey? What you say your first name was?'"

The albums were recorded within a few years of each other and are pretty interchangeable. "Ready or Not" sports liner notes by Lena Horne, Harry Belafonte, Steve Allen, and Abe Burrows, and has some key routines: "The Rent-a-Negro Plan," and "Arthur Uncle," a long serio-comic satire of Mantan Moreland, Stepin Fetchit, and Willie Best (Cambridge mentions them by name), who in the '60s had to defend themselves for their stereotypical work a generation earlier. The "Aladdin" album has some proud dialect comedy, from his talk of how Worcestershire sauce was named by a black man ("Wuss dis here sauce?") to the anecdote about how Yuma, Arizona got its name. "Toys with the World" has "Why Lord," a classic moment of comic agony. It's a talk with God:

"'Lord! Why did you make me so dark!' And the Lord says, 'My boy—' and he was wrong from the get-go, ya know, he says ... 'the reason I made you so dark is that when you're running through the jungle the sun would not give you sunstroke.' He says ... 'Lord! Why did you make my hair so coarse!' He said, 'Well ... so that when you're running through the jungle in quest of the wild beast ... your hair would not get caught in the brambles.' He said, 'Lord, why did you make my legs so long?' He said, '... so that when you're loping through the jungle ... you would run very fast and swiftly.' He said, 'My son, do you have any further questions?'

"He said, 'Yeah, Lord! What the hell am I doin' here in Cleveland!'"

Cambridge appears for about three minutes on the audio documentary "The Age of Anxiety" (Radiola MR 1151). Evidently culled from a TV appearance, he does a bit on the aggravations of trying to move into a whites-only apartment building.

MOLLY CAMP

- MOLLY CAMP SINGS (RCA Victor LPM 3649) *1/2 $7 $15

This 1966 album was evidently an attempt to amuse listeners who bought albums by both Allan Sherman and Mrs. Miller. Molly slightly alters pop songs and sings 'em in an elderly Yiddish accent. The Beatles' "Yesterday" comes out: "Yesterday, all mine troubles seemed too far avay. Now it looks they're here to stay. Oy, I believe in yesterday." Only the fast cuts, like "How Does That Grab You, Darlin'?" are really campy, as Camp gets carried away with being a spry Jewish granny. Molly isn't a bad singer, really, and most of the time she doesn't turn the accent into something grotesque a la Mickey Katz, so the result is no worse (and no funnier) than what any talented, if misguided, woman might sing in a Catskill resort.

ARCHIE CAMPBELL

• MANY TALENTS OF ARCHIE CAMPBELL (Nashville NLP 2064) **	$5	$10
• BEDTIME STORIES FOR ADULTS ONLY (Starday 167, also issued as THE GOOD HUMOR MAN, Starday 377) **	$5	$10
• THE JOKER IS WILD (Starday 223) **	$5	$10
• HAVE A LAUGH ON ME (RCA Victor LSP 3504) **	$5	$10
• THE COCKFIGHT AND OTHER TAIL TALES (RCA Victor LSP 3699) **	$5	$10
• BEST OF ARCHIE CAMPBELL (RCA Victor LSP 4280) **1/2	$5	$10
• ARCHIE CAMPBELL (Elektra 1075) **1/2	$5	$10

Archie Campbell was an unassuming, amusing storyteller who favored classic set pieces ("That's Good, That's Bad" on the "Many Talents" album) as well as shaggy dog stories that go on for several minutes to a corny punch line.

Campbell's first albums are hard to find on either coast. Campbell's style is already set, conversational, and folksy. "Many Talents" offers several serious songs recorded in a studio and written by Campbell ("The Master's Hand," "Sergeant York," etc.) as well as a live side of comedy that includes a dissection of "Jack and Jill" (who must've been going up the hill to get drunk, since they came tumbling down) and the well-known "W. C." story that became a cause celebre when Jack Paar read it on the old *Tonight Show.*

On "The Joker Is Wild" he sprinkles old one-liners in with general observation: "I'm glad to see Red here tonight ... I'm glad to report this one thing. Red's doing a lot better. Red doesn't drink anymore. He doesn't drink any less. But he doesn't drink any more, either. Seriously, he doesn't drink as much as he used to. He's so nervous he spills most of it."

Campbell was known for spoonerisms. "The Cockfight," an album of comic songs, has "Home on the Range" loudly wailed as "Rome on the Hange." He also offered spoonerism routines, rewriting fairy tales "Rindercella" and "Beeping Sleuty" (both can be had on "The Best of Archie Campbell").

Campbell's 1976 album for Elektra revives his classic "Rindercella" routine: "Now Rindercella lived with her mugly other and two sad blisters. Now in this same corn funtry there was a very pransom hince. Now this pransom hince was gonna have a bancy fawl, and he invited the people for riles amound." There's also "Hockey Here Tonight" (what Andy Griffith did for football Archie does in misunderstanding hockey) and some countrified vaudeville, including an "anticipation" routine with straight man Fred Smith that was first done by the black team of Fluornoy and Miller and later Mantan Moreland with various partners.

Campbell appears as straight man to Junior Samples on the album "Bull Session at Bulls Gap" (Chart CHS 1007).

DON CANNON

• DON CANNON'S GREATEST BITS (Gorilla 84595) *	$4	$8

Philadelphia's version of a comic morning disc jockey, Don Cannon of WIBG offers a collection of phone calls, schtick, and radio commercials, most of it forced and labored. One of the "greatest bits" immortalized here was the time he played Rod Stewart's "Maggie May" and inserted frog noises. At least trivia buffs who wonder what happened to Kyu Sakamoto (singer of the 1963 hit "Sukiyaki") get the unfunny answer as Don places a call to Japan: "Hello, Kyu Sakamoto?" "Yes, this is Kyu Sakamoto speaking." "This really Kyu Sakamoto?" "Yes." "This is Dan Cannon, I'm in the United States, in Philadelphia. I'm a big fan of yours, Kyu." "So." "You don't care, do you, Kyu. Kyu, I just wondered, your record, 'Sukiyaki?'" "Oh." "I played your record on the radio...." "Thank you. Thank you so much." "Listen, it's been eleven years since you've had a hit ... Are you still performing in Japan?" "Yes. TV, radio and stage ..." "Is it true Kyu means number nine." "Kyu means nine. I have nine brothers." "Ohhh. So! Hey, that's far out ... thank you very much for talking to me!"

JUDY CANOVA

• JUDY CANOVA (Camden CAL 662, reissued as Ju-Dee LP) ***	$8	$15

Beloved country comedienne Judy Canova is remembered on this 1961 disc via old radio sketches costarring Mel Blanc, Hans Conreid, Joe Kearns, Verna Felton, and Sheldon Leonard. The dialogue may be as plain as a haystack, but there are a few sharp needles here and there. In fact, this segment featuring Judy and Mel as a slow-talking, worn out Ma and Pa combo could easily have gotten the same laughs twenty years later if it was performed as a *Carol Burnett Show* TV sketch:

"Wake up, ya lazy critter." "I'm too tired to get up." "What makes ya so tired?" "I'm all pooped out. I walked clean from the barn yesterday." "Well, that hadn't oughta tire you out. It's only a few feet." "I know, Maw, but the wind was against me. Maw, I didn't sleep good last night. I was cold." "Well sir, I was cold in bed, too." "Well, I give you that hot water bottle last night. Didn't that warm ya up?" "No. And I drunk the whole thing." "Maw, has anything happened whilst I been asleep?" "Yeah, Paw, Uncle George fell down the well." "Is he all right now?" "I reckin' so. He stopped hollerin' for help yesterday."

Canova is available performing songs on several albums, including "Country Cousin" (Crown CLP 239), "Featuring Judy Canova" (Viking VK 8802), "Judy Canova and the Hoosier Hot Shots" (Hurrah Records 1051) and "Miss Country USA" (Craftsmen C 8062).

EDDIE CANTOR

- EDDIE CANTOR SHOW (Memorabilia MLP 702) ** $4 $8
- EDDIE CANTOR SHOW (Memorabilia MLP 703) ** $5 $8
- THE SHOW THAT NEVER AIRED (Original Cast OC 9347) ** $8
- CARNEGIE HALL CONCERT (Original Cast OC 92172) ** $10
- EDDIE CANTOR RADIO SHOW 1942-43 (Original Cast OC 9494) ** $20

As a singer, some of Cantor's work is in the Jolson category: peppy and amusing for those who enjoy nostalgia. As a comic, with his piping and petulant voice, Cantor doesn't age well. On his radio show he was mostly a straight man. On Memorabilia MLP 703, with Cesar Romero instructing him on dance:

"When you dance the samba, first the lady throws out her shoulder. Then the lady throws out her hips." "That's the lady. What part do I throw out?" "Eddie, with your parts I'd throw them all out." "Look, Cesar, I don't really need your help. The samba will come naturally to me. After all, I'm a Latin myself." "You are a Latin? Why, Eddie, I happen to know that you were born in Little Young New York." "Little Old New York." "It was young when you were born."

In addition to Cesar Romero, there are songs from Dinah Shore and a "Mad Russian" routine.

On the MLP 702 album, Jack Benny is one of the guests. Eddie has a question: "Just how old are you?" "Well, officially I tell everyone I'm 37. But I can't lie to you, Eddie. I'm 32." "You look like that and you're 32? Jack, don't try for 64!"

Cantor's October 23, 1940, broadcast was pre-empted by a presidential speech. Rather than disappoint the studio audience, Cantor performed anyway. The fifty-minute "Show that Never Aired" offers plenty of songs, but not much comedy. The six-minute routine that highlights the show will be of special interest to Abbott and Costello fans. It features A&C's nemesis Sid Fields as "Mr. Guffy," doing the same kind of argumentative bit he did on the boys' TV show a decade later: "Call me a crook, go on!" "You're not a crook, you never stole anything in your life." "Oh, I spent five years in Sing Sing for nothing."

Six episodes from Cantor's show appear on the three-CD set, "Eddie Cantor Radio Show 1942-43." The celebrity lineup is weak, with John Charles Thomas, Hattie McDaniel, Ida Lupino, Adolphe Menjou, and Bonita Granville. Modern listeners might get a kick out of hearing Edward G. Robinson and Cary Grant, but their shows suffer from indifferent gag-writing. Cantor to Cary: "I just noticed how tall you are. Gosh, I imagine you have a lot of trouble doing love scenes with a short leading lady." "Well, I tell ya, for me to kiss a movie star comfortably she's got to be about six feet tall." "Then we oughta team up." "How do you mean?" "While you're kissing the skyscraper girls, I'll take care of the basement trade."

On "The Original Complete Carnegie Hall Concert" CD, Cantor says, "This should be a very nostalgic evening." And it is, with his recollections of the good old times and his classic old songs. Previously fans had to make do with a song-filled abbreviation of the concert on LP, "A Date with Eddie Cantor" (Audio Fidelity AFLP 702).

An Eddie Cantor album was issued by Mark 56 (#757) and several straight albums are available, including one on RCA Camden. Cantor appears on various compilation albums. He's Jimmy Durante's foil on "Son of Jest Like Old Times" (Radiola) and plays straight with the Mad Russian on Evolution's "Golden Age of Comedy." Cantor's dreary 78 rpm "Tips on the Stock Market" (Recorded Oct. 29, 1929) is on RCA's "Golden Age of Comedy" compilation. Various CDs from Pro Arte, Columbia, and RCA offer Cantor songs (some of them novelty numbers).

THE CAPITOL STEPS

- THE CAPITOL STEPS LIVE (Capitol Steps) * $4 $8
- WE ARM THE WORLD (Capitol Steps) * $4 $8
- THANK GOD I'M A CONTRA BOY (Capitol Steps) * $3 $7
- WORKIN' 9 to 10 (Capitol Steps) * $3 $7
- SHAMLET (Capitol Steps) * $7
- STAND BY YOUR DAN (Capitol Steps) * $7
- DANNY'S FIRST NOEL (Capitol Steps) * $7
- GEORGIE ON MY MIND (Capitol Steps) * $7
- SHEIK, RATTLE AND ROLL (Capitol Steps) * $7
- 76 BAD LOANS (Capitol Steps) * $8
- FOOLS ON THE HILL (Capitol Steps) * $8
- JOY OF SAX (Capitol Steps) * $8
- ALL I WANT FOR CHRISTMAS (Capitol Steps) * $8
- LORD OF THE FRIES (Capitol Steps) * $8
- BRAVE NEWT WORLD (Capitol Steps) * $8

Combining the worst characteristics of cabaret and Mark Russell, The Capitol Steps are a coy group of young ladies and gents who try to compensate for their predictable parody lyrics with a lot of bright and bouncy overacting. Their first album, recorded at the Shoreham Hotel in Washington, DC, was released in 1984. They've kept 'em all in print, at least on cassette, which lessens their value.

Unlike Russell, the Steps don't restrict themselves to public domain cornball folk songs. So on the first album they can take Stephen Sondheim's "Send In the Clowns" and turn it into this parody, with Ronald Reagan crowing over his victory over Walter Mondale: "Can I run again? It's such fun to win! Can I run against Fritz one more time? We pulverized him! He must have a clone. Please, send in his clone!" Exit.

The format hasn't changed much over the years, though production values have gotten better. The parodies remain trivial. On "76 Bad Loans," "Moon River" becomes a momentarily amusing ode to CNN reporter Wolf Blitzer: "Wolf Blitzer, heartthrob of the gulf. My foxy little wolf—you dog! My Wolf whistles at big missiles like Edward R. Murrow you furrow your brow ... You're built like a steel armament. My furry little gent. No wimp like Arthur Kent! Wolf Blitzer, scud stud!"

The first Bill Clinton collection, 1993's "Joy of Sax," is leaden, with Mike Tifford's mediocre impression worse when he sings. It seems that once a song is matched to a parody title ("All of Me" becomes Bill Clinton's salute to the vice president, "Al and Me," and Gore's belief in the environment turns "Secret Agent Man" into "Secret Ozone Man") no effort is made to create funny lyrics. And 1995's "Newt" album is still loaded with corny, toothless parodies. "Bye Bye Blackbird" sasses the Republican efforts to reduce funding for the NEA and PBS: "Pack up all those feathered clothes, hit the road Pointy Nose, Bye Bye Big Bird!"

The first four albums, up to 1987's "Workin' 9 to 10," were released on cassette or vinyl only; the 1988 "Shamlet" marked the beginning of the cassette or CD only era.

AL CAPP

- ON CAMPUS (Jubilee JGS 2072) **1/2 $8 $20

The creator of "Lil Abner," Al Capp was a popular raconteur on talk shows, delighting and infuriating viewers with opinionated statements, generally taking a conservative approach. Capp doesn't deliver a monologue here. He answers questions from the audience given to him earlier and offers prepared essays on everything from washroom driers to intelligent life in outer space. Typical of the hit-and-miss material is this segment on sex and students:

"Mr. Capp, are opinions of eighteen-year-old students valuable?" "Yes ... on subjects they know something about, such as puberty and hubcaps. But nothing else ..." "What do you think of sex before marriage?" "All I know is it's great before breakfast. It's lovely after lunch and it's divine during dinner...." "What do you think about our two o'clock Saturday night curfew?" "I say if you can't score by two o'clock, there's no point in giving an extra hour or so to make a damn fool of yourself."

There's also a ten-inch album, "Interview with Al Capp" (Folkways FC 7353).

RON CAREY

- THE SLIGHTLY IRREVERENT COMEDY OF RON CAREY (RSVP ES 8003)   **1/2 $8

Ron Carey, remembered as Officer Levitt on the TV series *Barney Miller*, and Mel Brooks's foil in the film *High Anxiety*, (with the catchphrase of "I got it! I got it—I don't got it") was a stand-up back in the mid-60s. The twist: he did religious humor, mostly about Catholicism. This 1967 album actually is only "slightly irreverent," but back then it was probably irreverent enough to keep it and Carey from the public's ears and eyes. It's now out on CD.

Carey's look at indoctrination at a monastery recalls George Carlin's "Indian Sergeant" routine: "I'm gonna make real men out of ya! Tough men ... strong men ... now take off your shirts, your pants, and your jackets and put on your little brown dresses ... knock off the prayin'! Line up you guys, chins in! Heads bowed! And stand meek!"

GEORGE CARLIN

- THE ORIGINAL GEORGE CARLIN (Era E 600, originally $4 $8
  released as AT THE PLAYBOY CLUB TONIGHT [Era EL 103] $10 $20
  reissued as KILLER CARLIN [Laff A 219, Uproar 3664-2]) **1/2 $8

Carlin's first album was recorded circa 1960 with his partner Jack Burns. As a tribute to Lenny Bruce, who helped the duo get work, Carlin does Lenny's "Djinni in the Candy Store" routine. On the following track, Carlin does a great impression of Mort Sahl: "Right? Good? Thank you. Right. Forward. Good. OK, so. Lotta trouble in the world ... things are so bad I hear Brubeck has canceled his tour ... I wanna talk more about that."

Burns and Carlin do several sketches together, including an average boxing interview ("Killer Carlin") and a kiddie show parody ("Captain Jack and Jolly George") loaded with hip references: "Little girls, send for your Lolita kit ... you get an autographed picture of Vladimir Nabokov, and a little instruction booklet. If you do the exercises prescribed (that's kind of fun in itself, girls) in just two weeks you'll be walking and talking and acting like girls twice your age. And you can pick up a little cash after school ..."

It's an uneven mix: some slick and the rest schtick. The duo don't work well as a true "team." It's interesting as a look at Carlin's beginnings.

The original "At the Playboy Club Tonight" version is five or ten bucks higher than the others thanks to the cover photo of the duo flanked by Playboy bunnies. The reissues have Carlin alone on the cover.

- THE THIRD DEGARMO OPEN (DeGarmo) ** $6 $12
- TAKE OFFS AND PUT ONS (RCA VICTOR LSP-3772 $8 $20
  reissued as RCA Camden CAS 2566) *** $7 $15

The DeGarmo Open was a golf tournament, and Carlin was evidently the entertainment booked for the event's dinner. On this promotional/souvenir item Carlin goes perfunctorily through his paces. It's just another gig. A large number of advertising people are in his audience and Carlin spends most of this approximately twenty-minute record on TV commercial parodies. Only a few would ever turn up on any official Carlin record. A parody of a Dash laundry commercial: "'Pardon me, young man, are you finished repairing my washing machine?' 'Obviously madam, you are using a high suds detoigent in your top loading automatic. Or else ya got a big bra, because something is stuffin' up your lint filter here. Your machine didn't overflow, it threw up!'"

George is much more enthusiastic on "Takes Offs and Put Ons," his first real solo album (from 1967). The original cover has about forty-four different subway photo machine portraits of young George bending his rubbery face outlandishly. The reissue is just a portrait sketch. A slick, promising newcomer at the time, Carlin had plenty of safe sure-fire routines, like the one about the Indian sergeant drilling his troops:

"All right, all the tall guys over by the trees. Fat guys down behind the rocks. You with the beads, outta line! Boy, there's one in every village. All right, knock off the horseplay ... you guys over there playin' with the horse, will ya knock it off ... couple of announcements here. The fertility rites have been called off due to the recent cold wave. There will be a rain dance Friday night—weather permitting." Carlin covers quiz shows (with imbecilic contestant Congolia Breckenridge), radio disc jockeys, and TV news reports. The latter includes his bit as sportscaster Biff Burns (name later changed to Biff Barf) and as "hippie-dippy weatherman" Al Sleet, who declares: "Tonight's low: 35. Tomorrow's high: whenever I get up!"

- AM AND FM (Little David 7214) *** $4 $8
- CLASS CLOWN (Little David 1004) ***1/2 $4 $8
- OCCUPATION FOOLE (Little David LD 1005) ***1/2 $4 $8
- CLASSIC GOLD (double CD reissue of these three albums Eardrum 7-92219-2) *** $16

Carlin's 1972 "AM and FM" marked his emergence as a hippie stand-up. He explains his recent problems: "I got fired last year in Las Vegas from the Frontier Hotel for saying shit—in a town where the big game is called crap. That's some kind of a double standard." Half the album is a "farewell" performance of older "safe" material, like a bit on "Let's Make a Deal" and the radio parody "Son of WINO." George told me his favorite albums were "Class Clown" and "Occupation Foole" from 1972 and 1973, both filled with comic recollections of his youth. Fans love 'em because they're both filled with "words you can never say on television." "Class Clown" features the original "Seven words you can never say on television" routine. "And tits doesn't even belong on the list, you know? Man! It's such a friendly sounding word ... sounds like a snack, doesn't it? Yes, I know, it is."

On "Occupation Foole" George amends the list slightly in an eleven-minute exercise. He notes, "snatch, box, and pussy all have other meanings, even in a Walt Disney movie: we're gonna snatch that pussy and put it in a box ... but twat stands alone!"

- TOLEDO WINDOW BOX (Little David LD 3003 and 901291Y) **1/2 $5 $10
- AN EVENING WITH WALLY LANDO (Little David LD 1008) **1/2 $5 $10
- ON THE ROAD (Little David LD 1075) **1/2 $5 $10
- INDECENT EXPOSURE (Little David 1076) *** $4 $8
- THE CARLIN COLLECTION (Little David 902311) *** $4 $8

Carlin is a bit predictable on his mid '70s albums. On "Window Box" he says, "My job essentially is thinking up goofy shit." This includes ten minutes on drugs, plus a riff on Snow White: "Snow White ... smack or coke ... Happy was into grass ... Sleepy was into reds. Grumpy, too much speed. Sneezy was a full-blown coke freak. Doc was the connection. Dopey was into everything ... Bashful. He didn't use drugs—he was paranoid on his own."

At the time, George had critics either pronouncing him the new Lenny Bruce or dismissing him as a Lenny wanna-be. He does seem to be struggling with the ghost of Lenny as he riffs on Lenny topics, including God and homosexuality. On the latter: "What's normal, let's see, if you're standing in a room stripped, and it's dark, and you're hugging a person and rubbing 'em up and down and suddenly the light goes on and it's the same sex ... it felt OK ... so maybe it was normal." For gross-out humor, there's another report on farts, plus a treatise on snot, a subject Lenny Bruce also covered in a routine.

"Lando" is a low key 1975 album. Carlin isn't using his usual exaggerated, talking-to-doped-idiots voice of wonder. And he doesn't have much to say, ending up sounding like Andy Rooney: "Ya ever dial someone on the phone and forget who you're calling ... Ya ever look at yourself in store windows when you're passing stores ... Ya ever look at the crowds in old movies and wonder if they're dead yet ... Ya ever try to throw away an old waste basket?"

There's an embryonic version of his "Baseball vs Football" routine and some old reliables: "Teenage Masturbation" ("If God had intended us not to masturbate he would've made our arms shorter") and more dirty words ("take a piss ... you don't take a piss, you leave it!").

1977's "On the Road" comes with a "libretto." Every routine is written out on an enclosed booklet. Not surprisingly, a cold reading of the lines shows how much added humor is breathed into the material by Carlin's voices and comic cadence. The transcript can't capture the fun of George emphasizing each word: "Jeez, I hope I don't die ... won't come when you want. It's always off a little. What, now? Here on the freeway? Um hmmm. Thought surely I'd be home lying down ..."

There's no "essential Carlin" here, but some fun bits here and there, including his thoughts on the perfect murder: "You pick one guy up by his ankles and you kill another guy with him, and they both die and there's no murder weapon."

"Indecent Exposure" and "The Carlin Collection" were both "best of" compilations.

- A PLACE FOR MY STUFF (Atlantic SD 19326) **1/2 $5 $10

Once again, Carlin tells his audience his job is "thinking up goofy shit," and then proves it with some very silly hippie Andy Rooney material: "Hey, have you noticed that you never seem to get laid much on Thanksgiving? I think it's because all the coats are on the bed." There's an endless riff on people who say "have a nice day" and a dumb four minutes on how the job of cereal is to "just sit in the milk." The title track is a redundant rumination about stuff:

"Everybody's got a little place for their stuff. This is my stuff, that's your stuff, that'll be his stuff over there. That's all you need in life, a little place for your stuff. That's all your house is. A place to keep your stuff. If you didn't have so much stuff, you wouldn't need a house ... a house is just a pile of stuff with a cover on it."

Carlin often sounds like he's "talking down" to his audience. These repetitive, simple bits seem aimed at pinheads. More interesting is Carlin's "Interview with Jesus," with some Lenny Bruce lines: "What can you tell us about the last supper?" "Well, first of all, if I'd known I was gonna be crucified I woulda had a bigger meal. Ya never wanna be crucified on an empty stomach."

• CARLIN ON CAMPUS (Eardrum ED100) **	$5	$10
• PLAYIN' WITH YOUR HEAD (Eardrum 905231) **1/2	$5	$0

Carlin's 1985-86 LPs were based on cable TV concerts and are available in video versions. "Carlin on Campus" is weak. George simply doesn't have much to say here, scraping the bottom of the barrel for humor about the invention of the flamethrower, smoking breakfast cereal, rain dance techniques, and the correct way to get into a car. Flashes of the old Carlin turn up on "Cars and Driving," as recognition humor sparks the audience to laughter: "Have you noticed—anybody going slower than you is an idiot—and anyone going faster than you is a moron?" The highlight is his completed contrast between "Baseball and Football," first sketched on his "Wally Lando" album.

"Playin' with Your Head" has more than enough of Carlin's cute but predictable word-gaming (he does a long, long routine on the different ways people say "hello" and "good-bye"), but there's also more sardonic anger and starkness than Carlin has allowed before, including a furious assault on the nation's sports obsession. On football: "I would let all forty-five guys play at the same time ... leave the injured on the field ... let the Red Cross get those assholes." Lacrosse is "a faggot college activity" and car racing is just for the "five rednecks who win all the time ... driving five hundred miles in a circle does not impress me." His anger extends to the audience, which is rare for him. Hardly "hippie-dippy" cheerful, he spots a guy in the audience wearing an earring and growls, "How about a sanitary napkin! Do you have one of them on by any chance ... are you gay? Well, bend over and let's find out."

Reaching fifty, thinning hair pulled back tight, face weathered with wrinkles, Carlin seemed to be allowing himself to move away from the amiable, child-like funny-faced hippie character he'd used for so many, many years.

• WHAT AM I DOING IN NEW JERSEY? (Eardrum 909721) ***		$8
• PARENTAL ADVISORY, EXPLICIT LYRICS (Eardrum 915932) **1/2		$8
• JAMMIN' IN NEW YORK (Eardrum 922212) **		$8

Nearly half of Carlin's 1988 "New Jersey" album is a rollicking, furious report on cars and driving, including a sarcastic, grimacing look at bumper stickers: "The three most puke-inducing words that man has yet to come up with: 'Baby On Board.' I don't know what yuppie thought of that idea. I don't know. 'Baby on Board.' Who gives a f---! I certainly don't! You know what these morons are actually saying? They're actually saying to you: 'We know you're a shitty driver most of the time but because our child is nearby we expect you to straighten up for a little while.' You know what I do? I run 'em into a goddamn utility pole! Run 'em into a tree! Bounce that kid around a little bit, let him grow up with a sense of reality for Chrissakes! Life doesn't change because you post a sign!"

Carlin's a rasping, raging lecturer driven by a new-found sense of urgency. A segment on "offensive language" on the "Parental Advisory" album doesn't even bother with jokes. It's just Carlin spitting out a roll call of his most hated new age clichés: "I will not 'kick back, mellow out' or 'be on a roll.' I will not 'go for it,' and I will not 'check it out.' I don't even know 'what it is.' And when I leave here, I definitely will not 'boogie.' I promise not to refer to anyone as a 'class act, a beautiful person, or a happy camper.' I will also not be saying 'what a guy.' And you will not hear me refer to anyone's 'lifestyle' ..."

Later he offers a stinging (but again, jokeless) lecture on sneaky phrase manipulations ("toilet paper" to "bathroom tissue," "shell shock" to "battle fatigue") and ends up wondering if puking will some day be renamed "an involuntary personal protein spill." It's a tough set, but like-minded listeners will be gratified when curmudgeonly George hits on a favorite target for abuse. And occasionally there's a line that's vintage iconoclastic Carlin.

The soundtrack to Carlin's 1992 HBO special, "Jammin' in New York," is angry and furious, but mostly a misfire. There's a belabored semantic routine on "Airline Announcements" and some stern one-liners that would draw boos if Andrew Dice Clay said them. Too angry to use comic exaggeration, he simply attacks: "I'm tired of these golfing cocksuckers ... It's time to reclaim the golf courses from the wealthy and turn them over to the homeless! Golf is an arrogant, elitist game and it takes up entirely too much room in this country." Fortunately, as in the cases of Dick Gregory, Lenny Bruce, and other "cult" stars of that type, there are as many Carlin fans who see him to get "the word" as ones who only want funny words. Even if he's not always hilarious, he's still usually compelling, and both insightful and inciteful.

NOTES: Carlin appears on "Here's Johnny" (Casablanca SPNB 1296) and "Comic Relief" (Rhino 70704).

JUDY CARNE AND ARTE JOHNSON

• LAUGH-IN 69 (Warner/Reprise 6335) **	$8	$20

When Rowan and Martin left the cast, Judy Carne and Arte Johnson were the headliners on *Laugh-In.* Underneath their dual top billing were Ruth Buzzi, Henry Gibson, and Goldie Hawn. Fans of the show will find some nostalgia in the rapid-fire brew of quick sketches and junior high school level jokes.

There are gags about Burbank: "Know when the Burbank Zoo closes? At six o'clock, when everyone wants their dog back." And there are bits of dialogue: "Goldie, what do you think of Karl Marx?" "Well, uh, I like him, but I like Harpo better!" And it doesn't get much better or worse.

EDDIE CARROLL

- ON FRATERNITY ROW (Duo D-3) *1/2 $4 $8

Eddie and "The Kidney-Stone Trio" (at the time people were enjoying The Kirby Stone Four) sing forgettable novelty songs ("I Hate Banjos") with Dixieland backing. In between, Carroll tells some classic old jokes, like the one about the man facing a Latin firing squad. The head of the squad "lines up the firing squad and he gives the order. 'Ready! Aim!' And just before he gives the final command, in a last moment of defiance, the prisoner hollers out, 'Fidel Castro stinks!' The captain rushes up to the prisoner and says, 'Say listen, are you looking for trouble?'"

JEAN CARROLL

- GIRL IN A HOT STEAM BATH (Columbia CL 1511) **1/2 $10 $25

Stand-up comediennes were a rarity in the '40s and '50s. Jean Carroll was one of the first, and an inspiration for many, including Lily Tomlin. She was once part of a song and dance team with Buddy Howe. "After Burns and Allen," she recalled, "we were the big thing."

Carroll, unlike other pioneering female comics like Phyllis Diller, Joan Rivers, or Totie Fields, uses little self-deprecating humor. She sounds very much like any moderate '50s comedian of the Milt Kamen-Alan King school. She tells anecdotes about the suburbs, her family, and shopping.

JASPER CARROTT

- IN AMERICA (Rhino RNLP 817) *1/2 $4 $8

British comic Carrott (no, not his real name) tells conversational anecdotes about the differences between America and Britain. Most show the difference between funny and boring. And yes, he describes American drivers blowing their horns at him because ... "I'm drivin' the wrong bloody way!"

Nothing here sounds very different from what some dull but chatty Englishman would tell Johnny Carson during a deadly five minutes on The Tonight Show. He describes a bumper sticker he saw: "Honk for Jesus. Yeah! Now in England, honk means to throw up! Honk for Jesus? Bleeeaaah! Oh, you love Jesus too! Bleeaaah! You get things like 'Honk if You're Horny.' No way ... and people say, 'Oh, come 'round and pick us up. Don't ring the bell, just honk.' By the time you picked four people up, you don't want to go out, do ya? Bleeaaaah! Bleeahhhh!"

Carrott is well represented on import albums, and there is an import CD available as well: "Classic Canned Carrott" (Dover).

JOHNNY CARSON

- INTRODUCTION TO NEW YORK AND THE WORLD'S FAIR (Columbia CS 8990) $10 $20

Carson was successful in Vegas and delivered monologues on The Tonight Show for thirty years, but he never released a stand-up album. This semi-comic studio release was intended as "an amusing guide to some of the highlights of New York including the 1964-65 Worlds Fair."

Johnny reviews the facts, adding off-the-cuff gags: "When old friends arrive in New York they ask, 'Where do I stay?' My answer is always the same: 'Not at my place.' New York has over one hundred thousand hotel and motel rooms, more than twice as many as any city in the world. You can make reservations three different ways. One through your travel agent, two through the World's Fair Housing Bureau, and three directly through the hotel or motel. You'll find hotels listed in the Yellow Pages—under "Wheeee!" Over seventy-eight million people are expected to attend the Fair, so make your reservations early, or you may be forced to double up with someone. Of course, that's what makes New York the entertainment capital of the world."

- HERE'S JOHNNY: MAGIC MOMENTS FROM THE TONIGHT SHOW (Casablanca SPNB 1296) *** $6 $12
- HEEEEERE'S JOHNNY AND GUESTS FRIAR'S ROAST (Pornographic) **1/2 $20 $40

In 1974, Casablanca released this two-disc album based on Carson's tenth anniversary broadcast. He was against putting out the record and his instincts were right. It didn't sell; people were used to getting Carson free every night. Comedy fans have to pick through the musical numbers (Glen Campbell, Aretha Franklin, Judy Garland, Sammy Davis Jr., and so on). The Smothers Brothers do "Cabbage," Groucho Marx sings "Fathers Day," George Carlin and Jack Benny have solos, and there's a segment from Lenny Bruce's appearance when Steve Allen was the host.

There's only a fragment of an opening monologue included here. It's evidently from 1972, when Carson had recently married third wife Joanna Holland: "Look," he tells the applauding audience, "you really must stop, 'cause I have to leave the applause sign back in my honeymoon suite ... now Ed, I want to talk to you. Enough is enough ... it was not necessary to stand in my room on my wedding night going 'Hi-yooo!' But anyway ... to tell you the truth, I didn't get much sleep last night. My wife woke up with a nightmare. She was dreaming it was our first night together and Joey Bishop was standing in for me ... a little excitement last night ... there was an earthquake. There was a tremor. I thought Ed had fallen out of bed! But I knew it couldn't have been you. How can you fall off the floor? Ed said he slept like a log all night, and it's true. He slept in my fireplace!"

There's a seven-minute Art Fern "Tea-Time Movie," the classic "Copper Clappers" tongue-twister routine with Jack Webb, and a cute routine where Carson plays straight to Jay "Tonto" Silverheels: "One day Kemo Sabe let me peek under mask. No big deal." In a rare moment, Johnny croons "Our Love Is Here to Stay" with Pearl Bailey. "You got a good voice, boy!" Pearl says.

The Friar's Roast bootleg is not for Carson. The roast is for Don Rickles. Jack E. Leonard was the emcee. Johnny has one segment, as do Flip Wilson, Jackie Vernon, Ed and Norm Crosby. It's Johnny without having to worry about network censors: "I am one of Don's very close friends. And I think that's important to Don—because queers need friends! Let's get it out into the open. About eight years ago when I first met Don, the entire top of his head was covered with thick curly black hair. He was going down on Kay Arman, and that's enough to make Smokey the Bear turn queer! Now I know what you're probably saying. You call Don Rickles a homosexual, but he's married. Don was married three years ago, when he was thirty-eight years old. I look at it this way: any fellow who has to put platform fronts in his condom has got a hangup somewhere along the line.... Now I've seen Don entertain fifty times and I've always enjoyed his joke. His act has all the subtlety of an elephant's prick ... he's about as thrilling as watching Kate Smith take a douche."

NOTES: "Johnny Carson's Half a Century of NBC Comedy," was a two-hour radio special circa Thanksgiving 1982, issued to radio stations as a double disc set. Johnny perfunctorily narrates the clips, which are heavy on familiar old radio bits long available on disc and well known to anyone with a few radio compilation albums. These include Jack Benny's encounter with the Mexican named Cy, and Abbott and Costello's "Who's on First," to Fred Allen visiting "Allen's Alley." Once in a while the producers actually bother to make use of the NBC tape vault. The Ernie Kovacs "Question Man" parody (long available on disc) is prefaced with a rarer clip of the stilted original, "The Answer Man." The record of Stan Freberg's "Dragnet" parody is contrasted with Johnny's own "copper clapper caper" routine done with Jack Webb. Johnny declares toward the end of the show, "Laughter is the common denominator of our lives.... The more we learn to laugh with each other, the more we'll learn to live with each other."

JACK CARTER

- BROADWAY ALA CARTER (AAMCO ALP 319) $4 $8

Comedy collectors be warned. Buried in the fine print of the liner notes are the words "album of sparkling tunes." Only if you buy the record will you discover that they're oldies like "Red Red Robin" and "Me and My Shadow." Unlike the albums by comedians Dick Van Dyke, Red Skelton, and Danny Thomas, this one doesn't make it clear that it's music, not comedy. It's listed here in case someone has doubts.

JOEY CARTER

- LITTLE BELLY LAUGHS (Epic LN 3801/BN 605) ** $5 $10

The title is not just a parody of Carter's Little Liver Pills, it's accurate. Carter doesn't get big laughs. He follows the formula of Charlie Manna and Bob Newhart in doing mini-sketches and interview routines, but his delivery isn't sharp and his personality adds little to the material. He has some promising ideas (like a Jewish Lone Ranger having a radio casting call for a new Tonto) but he doesn't do much with them. One of his better routines envisions the director of a "History of Mankind" Bible epic at work:

"All right, cast. George, get those people in Asia quiet, will ya? For those of you who have lost your scripts, turn to the Bible, page one. I want the Adam and Eve people on set number one and I want the apes coming out of the sea. That's an alternate opening for the art houses. Good. All right. Where's Adam? You're Adam, right? Where's the girl? Well, get a rib from him, then. That's good, OK, start raising Cain! OK, now Abel, have a little fight, slug him, good boy. All right ... let's have a flood for Noah ... do me a favor, take the life preserver off, please."

LOU CARTER

- LOU CARTER (GC 3010) ** $5 $10
- WRITES AGAIN (GC 3044) *1/2 $5 $10
- HOW DEEP IS WHICH OCEAN? (Columbia CL 1503) *1/2 $5 $10

Originally a musician with Jimmy Dorsey, Carter guested on *The Perry Como Show* as "Louie, The Song-Writing Cabbie" and issued two albums for Golden Crest. They're dated, but those in the mood for tunes crooned with a mellow voice and slight Brooklyn accent might be amused. Those who aren't listening carefully may miss the gentle silliness in the seemingly romantic lyrics. Typical is "I Caught a Cold In My Heart" from the first album:

"I felt a draft from the way that you laughed. Then I caught a cold in my heart. The song of the breeze has become just a sneeze since I called a cold in my heart. Your love was like a burning light, you turned it on and off. And then I realized somehow this heart of mine could cough. We had a tiff, now I'm left with a handkerchief, 'cause I cold a caught in my heart."

The follow-up "Louie Writes Again" features a "musical comedy" on Side One: "Aqueduct Alley." Perhaps influenced by "The Tenement Symphony" and similar fare, it's loaded with sentiment. It is music of the spheres—in this case a bathosphere. The other side has more typical fare: "The Pig Wit' the Apple in His Mouf," and "Split Your Sangwich Wit' a Stranger."

"How Deep Is Which Ocean?" is an interesting idea: answering the questions posed in various straight songs. Among the cuts: "This Is the Thing Called Love," "You Can Keep Her Down on the Farm," "That's Why I Was Born," and the title track. Unfortunately the lyrics are gently satiric at best. On the title track he tries to answer how deep the ocean is: "Take the depth of the beautiful Atlantic. It can only be measured socially. Sporting fish set to sail with a prince of whale, enjoy a spot of Boston tea. When they ask you how deep the Irish Sea is, where the folks shy away from water sports. Change the fathoms to feet add the weight of the fleet then subtract the empty quarts. You see a blue sea that they call The Red Sea. Don't show alarm, it's only a harmless blunder. But if the Dead Sea is really a dead sea, just figure it to be six feet under."

BILL CARTY

- BLASTS OFF (Stereoddities CC 1) ** $4 $8

- CARTY PARTY (Stereoddities 1906) ** $4 $8

Carty's gags are no different from ones on any '60s party album. At least he goes through his paces with a quick, Henny Youngman-style delivery, which makes the familiar gags painless. He hardly takes more than one breath to spiel out this one:

"Here's to Pittsburgh. A very friendly city. Friendly. Where else can you walk into a bar, have a complete stranger come up to you, offer to buy you a few drinks, take you to his home overnight, and in the morning if you wake up and you're broke, help you out with a few dollars. Didn't happen to me up there. It happened to my sister."

LOU CARY

- BACCALA (M&R 1024) *1/2 $5 $10
- BACCALA STRIKES AGAIN (Baccala BAC 0002) *1/2 $4 $8
- THE NEW GENERATION (Baccala BAC 0001) *1/2 $4 $8

Cary is in Pat Cooper territory, strenuously giving his middle-aged supper club audiences complaints about modern times with an angry Brooklyn-Italian accent. From "Baccala," a complaint about changing saints:

"We don't even know who to pray to anymore. Poor St. Christopher, the poor man, all he did was drive in a car, they knocked him off the books! They were gonna do the same thing to Saint Gennaro but the guys from Mulberry Street went to Rome! And they told the Pope, 'You leave him alone, he's with us!'"

And from "The New Generation," observations on teens: "I wanna tell ya what's happening in the world today. Fuh-get about it ... de way these kids dance today! 'Member the good old days of the Glenn Miller Band ... when you danced wit a girl ... today it's altogether different ... the boyfriend at one end, the girlfriend at the other end, two hundred kids in between. And they're all in the Twilight Zone ... and the songs they sing: 'Pooosh pooosh in de booosh!' You can't tell dem nothing! The girls ya gotta see them! No bras, no panties! And the way they move all night long, that's why the men are gettin' heart attacks today! We can't take it any longaaahh!"

JOHNNY CASH

- EVERYBODY LOVES A NUT (Columbia CL 2492/CS 9292) ** $5 $10

For a change of pace, the man who always wears black lightens up for a program of bent country ballads. The contrast between Cash's somewhat grim and seemingly off-key voice and the wacky music and lyrics is amusing. There's the sick and silly Shel Silverstein song "Boa Constrictor," and the sprightly musical satire, "The One on the Right Is on the Left." The self-penned "Please Don't Play Red River Valley" is his warning to an amateur harmonic player: "Well, I see you done pretty good on your new harmonica. But don't you think you oughta learn about one more tune you know? See ya hold it like you was gonna eat a handful of popcorn, and sometimes you suck in and sometimes you blow." Some dealers price it high because a) it's out of print, b) country fans want it too, or c) the Jack Davis cartoon cover. Or d) all of the above, because they read it in this book.

THE CATCH CLUB

- I'LL TELL MY MOTHER (Capitol ST 1726) * $3 $7

The album notes insist "explosive laughter and applause" greeted Dave Reznick, Ted Rusoff, and Larry Pack when they harmonized on fey old songs by John Blow, Purcell, Arne, and others. Back in 1962 when this extraordinarily pretentious album was recorded, folks were buying albums of ancient ribaldry (by Oscar Brand and Ed McCurdy among others). But not this one. The Catch Club ruins any surviving humor in these tunes by carrying on like amateurs auditioning for Gilbert & Sullivan. When this poncing glee club sing the tunes as rounds, stepping on each other's lines, it's impossible to understand the lyrics, which aren't that interesting anyway. The title track in its entirety: "'I'll tell my mother,' my Jennie cries, and then a poor languishing lover dies, by my faith, I believe the gypsy lies, for all she is so grave and wise. She longs to be tickled, oh she longs to be tickled!"

DICK CAVETT

- THE COMEDY SHOW (Olympia Broadcast Network) $6 $20

Cavett hosted a radio show in the late '80s featuring cuts from comedy albums and sometimes an interview with a guest. One Halloween show featured Brother Theodore, for example. (And in the course of the interview, a nice mention of the author, who had accompanied him to the taping). Every week a two-hour show was shipped to radio stations on two LPs. These shows were not pressed in great quantity and were only circulated to participating radio stations. Collector interest varies with the guest star.

Die-hard fans might want the 1958 version of "Cyrano" Cavett, recorded with other Yale students (Yale Dramatic 6530).

SAM CHALPIN

- MY FATHER THE POP SINGER (ATCO 33 191) *1/2 $7 $15

A one-joke idea: rock songs performed by an old Jewish man. Cuts on the 1966 album include "Satisfaction," "I Want to Hold Your Hand," "Michelle," "Bang Bang," and "Leader of the Pack." Sixty-five-year-old Sam Chalpin is authentic, sounding slightly similar to George Jessel, his accent as much Bronx as it is Jewish, his voice as off-key as any candy store owner mockingly singing along to the radio. A few seconds of any cut here is plenty. Ironically, the same year RCA offered a similar album from an aging Jewish woman, Molly Camp.

LIGHTNIN' CHANCE

• WON'T THAT BLOW YOUR HAT IN THE CREEK (Warner Bros 1444) *1/2 $5 $10

Minnie Pearl supplies the album notes for this 1962 album. Why Warner Bros. took a chance on Chance is hard to figure. Even top country comedians, including Minnie Pearl, couldn't get on a major label. Thirty-seven year-old Lightnin' (he got his nickname for talking slow; the notes don't mention his first name, Floyd) was unknown outside Nashville, and even there had better credentials as a bass player on country albums. For his debut he offers mild anecdotes, some of them with whiskers. This one got big laughs. It's his recollection of school days and a principal about to give him some discipline:

"I reached up on top of the lockers and got one of those great big ol' geography books, ya know? I slipped it down in my britches and hid it pretty good. I knew what was gonna happen the minute I got down there. He had a paddle that was a good two foot. He bent me over his desk. 'Course I didn't mind it too much, I had the geography book in my britches, ya know, I knew it wasn't gonna hurt bad, but some little devil done drove a nail in that paddle. He rared back with that paddle, and that paddle had the nail in it, and he whopped me, and that nail went through England and Africa, back through Cuba and Miami. It hit my hometown, I dang near passed out, buddy."

CAROL CHANNING

• CAROL CHANNING ON TOUR (Vanguard VRS 9059, reissued as 51 West 16009) ** $6 $12

The only Channing album placed in the humor section, this audio glimpse of her nightclub act centers on musical comedy material. Some of it is fairly straight ("Little Girl from Little Rock," "The Old Yahoo Step," "Diamonds Are a Girl's Best Friend"). There are also some dumb novelty numbers like "Calypso Pete."

Less than half the album is spoken material. The highlight is a satiric swipe at Judy Garland via a pseudo-sincere speech to the audience ("here is little me trying to sing for you") and the overwrought ballad, "Somewhere There's a Little Bluebird." She also does Tallulah Bankhead singing "Happy Birthday" and an impression of Sophie Tucker who, she claims, gave her this advice on performing in Las Vegas: "When you're in the Casino, Carol, it won't help you to dress sexy! Believe me baby, to the boys around the crap table, a low cut dress is just another place to lose the dice!"

THE CHARACTERS

• SMASH FLOPS (Pip 1900, also issued as Lemon 1905) * $8 $15

A dumb idea for an album: a mock-collection of songs from the loser's side. For example, we all remember the immortal "Lucky Lindy," paying tribute to Lindbergh's flight across the Atlantic. But how many were aware of "When Amelia Earhart Flies Home?" It could've been a hit if she hadn't disappeared: "Get your ticker tape ready and tear up your confetti 'cause there's gonna be a big parade! What a celebration there'll be throughout the nation when her tedious journey is made. She'll be the first girl to do it! To fly around the world! So don't forget who flew it! Have that bunting unfurled. When Amelia Earhart circles the globe and comes flying home again."

Similar stupid songs with indifferent lyrics cover "When the Hindenberg Lands Today," "We're Depending on You, General Custer," "Congratulations, Tom Dewey," etc. The songs were composed by Milton Larsen and Richard M. Sherman (the latter well-known for writing Disney hits with his brother Robert). The Characters sing most of the selections, but five are credited to The Crown City Four. That Foursome recorded their own album, "Sing a Song of Sickness," also written by Larsen and Sherman.

CHEVY CHASE

• CHEVY CHASE (Arista AL 9519) *1/2 $4 $8

Only Chase's most devoted fans would care about this album of indulgences. His songs that make fun of tedious and obnoxious tendencies in R&B, funk, and rap end up just as tedious and obnoxious.

He puts on various voices, including a funky Randy Newman type for a parody of "Short People" that offers mock praise: "They look further away than they really are, they don't crowd your space, you can get a dozen in a car ... just want more Short People."

One of the better cuts takes a swipe at the popularity of the simpleminded reggae tune "I Shot the Sheriff." Here, more murders should mean more fun: "I shot the sheriff, and I also shot the deputy. I shot the bailiff after toking all the P.C.P. All around in my hometown I'm shooting everyone. That's right! I drop a lude, get in the nude, I take the knife and gun—I can't stop having fun."

NOTES: Chevy Chasers might want the album he made as drummer and backing vocalist for Chameleon Church. Also in the band was National Lampoonist Tony Scheuren. Their self-titled album was released by M-G-M (SE 4574).

CHINGA CHAVIN

• COUNTRY PORN (Country Porn Records no number, CD reissue Fruit of the Tune 666) ** $8
• LIVE AND POLITICALLY ERECT (Fruit of the Tune 1010) ** $8

In the early '70s, Nick Chavin was part of a folk trio with Kinky Friedman and an unknown singer named Janis Joplin. He lucked out when Bob Guccione helped him bankroll the "Country Porn" album in 1976. The song titles seemed to promise a raunchy version of Dr. Hook or a really kinky Friedman. The lyrics were a disappointment, the music mild Tex-Mex country corn, and the guy couldn't sing. But about fifty thousand took a chance on it when they saw it offered via mail order ads. Now it's back on CD.

A few cuts are still amusing. Once. The extremely dated "Asshole from El Paso" is a kick at Merle Haggard's much-hated (at the time) redneck creed "Okie from Muskogee." Chinga declares: "I'm proud to be an asshole from El Paso, a place where sweet young virgins are deflowered. You walk right down the street knee deep in horseshit. And braceros still get twenty cents an hour."

The 1993 live album has deliberately titillating titles like "Mamma's Turning Tricks to Throw My Bail," "Everybody Calls Her a Slut But I Love Her," and "Sadomasochistic Transvestite Queen." The mild raunch isn't much worse than stuff on "legit" albums from Shel Silverstein to Pinkard & Bowden. Now and then, the older, wiser Chinga actually writes a lyric with some depth beyond the "dirty ditty." On "Sex Partners," he describes a relationship where good sex just wasn't enough. With some pretty good rhymes, he nostalgically hollers: "We had the stuff that true love grows on, but as soon as we put our clothes on, everything got very off the wall. We split up and I beg your pardon, but sometimes I get a hard-on thinkin' about the way we used to ball."

The albums are often considered comedy but would be less disappointing if discovered in the country bin. Chavin, of the Manhattan ad agency Chavin-Lambert, has been smart enough not to quit the day job.

CHEECH AND CHONG

- CHEECH AND CHONG (Ode Sp 77010, reissued as Warner Bros. 3250) **1/2 $4 $8
- BIG BAMBU (Ode 77014, reissued as Warner Bros. 3251) *1/2 $5 $10
- LOS COCHINOS (Ode 77019, reissued as Warner Bros. 3252) * $4 $8
- WEDDING ALBUM (Ode 77025, reissued as Warner Bros. 3252) *1/2 $4 $8

Tommy Chong and Cheech Marin weren't liked by critics. They did recognition humor. But only their audience of hippies, ethnics, high schoolers, and beer and drug abusers could recognize it.

Just as Bob and Ray's work mystifies those who aren't exactly tuned into the wavelength, Cheech and Chong only appeal to those who recognize (or are) the various geeks and goofs impersonated.

Their debut album features "Waiting for Dave," a nice bit of Bob and Ray "non-comedy." A drug dealer is trying to make a connection. "It's Dave," the dealer hisses, "let me in, man." Chong answers dumbly, "Dave? Dave's not here." "No man, I'm Dave! Dave!" "Dave?" "Yeah, man, it's Dave!" "Dave's not here." For five minutes it's agonized frustration, worse than Bob and Ray trying to deal with one of the "Slow Talkers of America."

Another highlight is "Trippin' in Court," where a dim-witted druggie makes a fool of himself by standing in front of the judge and announcing woozily, "I don't need acid, man, I don't need marijuana," the substances he was busted for. "Cuz I'm hooked on downers!" In the background the other criminals snicker. "Cruisin' with Pedro" is another familiar story for druggies, all about the paranoia of thinking the cops are about to make a bust.

Cheech and Chong do deserve their criticism. They tend to be redundant. The scruffy characters they impersonate are not very sympathetic and often verge on repulsive. Often their acting is atrocious.

The Cheech and Chong formula continues album after album. "Big Bambu" is notable for the album cover (the duplication of a rolling paper company's product) and "Let's Make a Dope Deal," a pretty obvious quiz show parody.

"Los Cochinos" has another amusing cover for collectors (Cheech and Chong in a car—the inner sleeve enabling them to "drive" forward when taking the record out) but there isn't much inside that's as amusing. "Up His Nose" is particularly obnoxious and anti-Semitic as Cheech, in a rottenly inept Jewish accent, reports on his little boy who shoves money and bagels up his nose. There's also an interminable twelve minutes for the Pedro character and his uptight friend, and a painful three minutes accurately depicting hippie idiots fighting in their apartment: "Just stay outta my room, man." "Yeah? I don't have ta...." "What happened to the rest of the baloney, man?" "I ate it!"

"Basketball Jones," a demented song in which a black falsettos over the joys of basketball ("My momma bought me a bassetball, an' I loooved dat bassetball ... dat bassetball wuz like a bassetball ta me ..."), is available on the "Greatest Hit" album.

"Wedding Album," filled with nauseating pictures of the scruffy duo dressed up in tuxedos, has some juvenile, squeamy routines like "Championship Wrestling," in which a couple's slurpy kisses are announced like a sporting match: "Now they're givin' it to each other ... he's givin' it everything he's got."

- SLEEPING BEAUTY (Warner Bros. BSK 3254) *1/2 $5 $10
- LET'S MAKE A NEW DOPE DEAL (Warner Bros. HS 3391) * $4 $8
- CHEECH AND CHONG'S GREATEST HIT (Warner Bros. BSK 3614) **1/2 $8
- GET OUT OF MY ROOM (MCA 5677) * $4 $8

Cheech and Chong made only two albums in the late '70s (1976 and 1980). "Sleeping Beauty" has a collectible pill-shaped album cover, but the title cut overdoses in sixteen boring minutes. It's a drug-induced fairy tale that wanders on and on with stereotyped gays, lame English accents, and a poisonous plot. Slightly more amusing is "The Big Sniff," a look at death in a dog pound and an attempted escape by a pack of dogs. "T.W.A.T.," a well-produced action movie parody with sound effects and music about the "tactical women's alert team" is marred by juvenile dialogue and obvious punnery: "Muff Productions presents ... a crack unit of highly trained specialists dedicated to protect and serve the Department of the Interior ... ready to open up at a moment's notice ..." Teens ready to drop MAD for Hustler will be amused.

"Let's Make a New Dope Deal" has a new version of their none-too-interesting dope quiz TV show. Several cuts ("Queer Wars" and "Disco Disco") are gay parodies. They lampoon dopey soul music on "Bloat On," in which a vocalist is enraptured by the ingredients in a Big Mac. On the other extreme, there's a screaming punk version of "Rudolph the Red-Nosed Reindeer."

"Greatest Hit" offers most of Cheech and Chong's better routines—concentrating almost exclusively on their first three records.

In 1985 the team resurfaced on MCA. They unfortunately didn't change a bit. They never even bothered to vary things with a live concert album. They're again dead in the studio, duplicating the repulsive and stupid utterances of mindless snoids. Three segments called "Dorm Radio" let the listener overhear idiots bickering and whining and posturing with each other. The songs include "I'm Not Home Right Now" (about phone machines) and a nasal, screeching Chicano version of Bruce Springsteen's "Born in the U.S.A." renamed "Born in East L.A."

The team split up soon after this one, with both taking solo movie projects. Cheech also issued a kiddie CD, "My Name Is Cheech the School Bus Driver" (BMG Kids/Ode).

CHICKENMAN

- THE BEST OF CHICKENMAN (Atco) ** $10 $20
- CHICKENMAN RETURNS (Chicago Radio Syndicate SCRS 1001) ** $10 $20
  PUFFY SLEEVES AND OTHER EXQUISITE FOOLISHNESS
  (The Complete Collection of *Time* Magazine Radio Commercials DR6179,
  promo only, 1975-1978)

There's a small cult for the "Chickenman" comedy serial that originated in Chicago on WCFL radio in the mid-60s. Many fans swap tapes, and one album was put on disc by the Chicago Radio Syndicate, but Atco has the only official album of highlights. The campy caped crusader gets his outfit from a costume store (it was either the chicken outfit or a teddy bear suit) and takes off on his capers. As Chickenman, Dick Orkin favors a mock-heroic voice that falls somewhere between Adam West and Gary Owens. The script isn't much. After he crashes through a window to help a woman in distress:

"How do you do, I'm the wonderful white-winged warrior and I think I'm bleeding to death." "*You're* the most fantastic crime fighter the world has ever known?" "Yes. Notice the great white wings?" "Yes, I also notice blue jeans and sneakers." "I didn't have time to change completely ... these are my secret identity clothes." "You have a secret identity?" "Do you think I'd tell you? It wouldn't be a secret if I went around blabbin' to everybody."

THE CHOSEN FEW PLAYERS

- THE SHORTEST DAY (Award AS 30) * $4 $8

For some reason, the Israeli war triumph in 1967 was considered a good subject for satire. There should have been pride in seeing the stereotype of the ineffectual Jew destroyed as Israel's tough, courageous army triumphed. Instead, this album (and Lou Jacobi's "The Yiddish Are Coming) perpetuated the joke. A blackout skit:

"Look out, here comes an Egyptian tank from the North and an Israeli tank from the South. Are they? Yes! Yes! They're gonna have a head-on collision! The Arab is crawling out of his tank, let's hear what he's saying."

Arab: I surrender! I surrender!

Now the Israeli is climbing out of his tank.

Israeli: Never mind surrender! Who's your insurance agent? I got viplash! Viplash!"

"The Chosen Few Players" were Laser Goldblatt, Danny Davis, Larry Foster, and Lou Spencer.

BARRETT CLARK AND ALIX ELIAS

- THAT FUNNY SMOKING ALBUM (Judson D 1000) ** $6 $12

A 1964 topical album, the men (Barrett Clark, Stefan Gierasch, Ron Leibman) and women (Alix Elias and Minerva Pious) engage in predictable sketches with very little bite. The idea is not to offend smokers or nonsmokers. A blustery smoker announces, "I don't smoke anymore. Of course, I don't smoke any less!" A character meant to be Christine Keeler (known for a government sex scandal in England) declares that smoking is "a disgusting vice and should be prohibited by law."

Long sketches include "The Pact," about a couple who bicker about trying to quit smoking. They get on each other's nerves so badly that the woman walks out. She vows to go buy a carton of cigarettes and end the frustration. Her mate decides he wants cigarettes too, so they happily leave together, once more in total agreement. In "Cigarettes Anonymous," Minerva Pious describes breaking the habit: "The air smells sweeter. Food tastes better. Outside of a tendency to switch, and a little compulsion to slap the children now and then, I feel wonderful."

DICK CLARK

- RADIO'S UNCENSORED BLOOPERS (Atlantic 80188-1) * $4 $8

Around 1983-85, TV went blooper crazy with endless specials and series, from Steve Allen, to Don Rickles and Steve Lawrence, to Ed McMahon and Dick Clark. There weren't enough bloopers to go around, and that's obvious here as Clark introduces Top 40 disc jockeys and radio newscasters repeating themselves and/or making unfunny mistakes in copy reading that cause them to break up in helpless mirth.

If one of these moments is actually funny, the narration by Clark kills it. A famous Lowell Thomas giggling attack (available on several Kermit Schafer collections) is ruined as Clark interrupts with a whispered, "And remember, he's on the air, live!" Clark starts deliberately chuckling. His microphone is left open. As Thomas giggles and tries to get back to his news report, Clark is heard laughing in the background. And again he interrupts with, "It's live, on the air! He can't stop obviously! Hee hee heee ..."

Clark dominates this overproduced album, elaborately introducing each boring, obvious blooper, announcing the names of the disc jockeys, and forcing phony snickers after every cut as if he too can't believe what he just heard. The record lasts over forty minutes, but it would only last ten minutes without the elaborate synthesizer noises, drum beats, and "wacky" music before and after.

DOUG CLARK

• NUTS TO YOU (Gross 101) **	$10	$20
• ON CAMPUS (Gross 102) **1/2	$7	$18
• HOMECOMING (Gross 103) **	$7	$18
• RUSH WEEK (Gross 104) **1/2	$7	$18
• PANTY RAID (Gross 105) **1/2	$7	$18
• SUMMER SESSION (Gross 106) **1/2	$7	$18
• HELL NIGHT (Gross 107) **1/2	$7	$18
• FREAK OUT (Gross 108) **1/2	$7	$18
• WITH A HAT ON (Gross 109) **1/2	$7	$18

Blacks and hip college kids loved to sneak Doug Clark albums on the turntable during the early '60s. He and the "Hot Nuts" band knocked out dirty ditties and paused for rote readings of limericks and sappy sex jokes. The laid-back delivery of Doug Clark helps make the gags a little funnier than they are on paper. On the early albums, his charmingly inept recitations sound like he's reading them for the first time—and after two bottles of Ripple.

From "On Campus," Doug half-sings a limerick: "There once was a man named Glass, who had two nuts made of brass. When he rubbed them together, they played 'Stormy Weather.' And lightning shot out of his ass." The album features "Roly Poly" and "Barnacle Bill the Sailor."

Most albums maintain that level and are interchangeable. "Rush Week" is most notable for a parody of "Big John" ("Big Jugs"), Clark's laconic reading of the old porno poem "Everybody but Me," and the classic "Canal Street."

"Summer Session" is notable for the quick tune "Baby Lemme Bang Your Box," a nice '50s rocker, and "Gonna Hang My Balls from a Tree," which has the same kind of funky-silly charm as The Coasters' "In Old Mexico." Sample lyric in between the idiotic chorus: "Next time I saw her she was playin' a tune—in the orchestra pit on a meat bassoon. Fourth time I saw her she was slidin' down the rail, warming up dessert for her boyfriend's meal."

"Hell Night" is also more song-filled than other discs, with "Ring Dang Doo," "Sweet Sue" and "All Work and No Play." It's one of the few albums that features a female member of The Nuts. She sings two songs and sits in on a few of the round robin joke sessions where Doug and the other Nuts trade semi-moronic limericks.

The final album, "With a Hat On," is the crudest, which might be a recommendation for some.

JACKIE CLARK

• JACKIE CLARK (Musicor MS 3166) **1/2	$6	$12

A "nice boy" comic, Jackie has a pleasant conversational style that went over very well in the Catskills circa 1966:

"Television sets are becoming very popular in automobiles these days. My uncle has a television set in his automobile, but it led into a little trouble. You see, he was sitting in the car watching television while his wife was driving on the thruway at sixty miles per hour. And then the commercial came on, and he stepped out to go to the bathroom."

Clark also sings a few old favorites, "Cohen Owes Me Ninety Seven Dollars" (by Irving Berlin) and the ever popular "Don't Hit Your Gran'ma with a Shovel – It Makes a Bad Impression on Her Mind." The liner notes are a lot stronger than the genial family-oriented material. Alan King notes, "Jackie Clark is good enough to be an enemy." Singer Tony Martin says, "Jackie Clark is my Charlie Chaplin." Clark died in 1979 at the age of 51.

JIM H. CLARK

• THE WILD WILD WORLD OF JIM H. CLARK (Explosive C 368) *1/2	$5	$10

Clark tries to yock it up on this '60s album of nightclub whizbang: "Got up this morning feeling like a twenty-year-old. But I couldn't find one, so I went back to bed ... I call her Jell-O 'cause she's easy to make! Of course she calls me oatmeal 'cause I'm done in three minutes. Laugh it up!" Before he recorded this solo album, Clark spent nine years as a member of "The Nock-A-Bouts," recording one comedy album.

ANDREW "DICE" CLAY

• DICE (Def American 9 242142) **	$8

For his 1989 premiere, Clay was offering to low-class white audiences what Eddie Murphy was offering to black audiences: a particular brand of street corner wise guy goofing and posturing. Anyone not from the neighborhood, get lost.

There were two problems with Clay, though.

While smiling Eddie could get away with racist and sexist humor a bit more easily (though Asians probably didn't care for his "rice dick" lines and gays began to openly protest the AIDS jokes), the media was shocked, repulsed, and scared by Clay's white thug persona, this at a time when guys who acted like him were attacking minorities who strayed into white areas of Howard Beach or Bensonhurst.

The other problem, more glaring to his peers, was that Clay displayed little talent beyond stealing his attitude from Henry Winkler's "Fonz" sitcom character, his cadence from veteran risqué comic Pearl Williams, and his jokes from

REGIONAL APPEAL – MAYBE

Travel broadens a record collection. Outside Chicago (Bob and Papersack), Miami (Houston and Dorsey, ooh, this is an autographed copy!), or Dallas (Kuntz and Kuntz) you won't find these albums. But do you want 'em? Some dealers in big cities deliberately put high prices on "rare" regional discs.

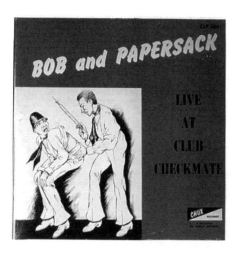

RARE AND VALUABLE? TO WHO?

AH, the subjectivity of pricing records. How many people know or care that Mae Questel (the "Mrs. Portnoy" of this failed topical album) is the voice of Betty Boop and Olive Oyl? What are the odds of finding an Allan Sherman fan anxious to pay big bucks for imitator Stan Ross? And is it boxing fans, comedy buffs, or poetry devotees that would pay top dollar for an album by the formerly-known-as Cassius Clay?

Belle Barth and Sylvia Stoun. Some of Clay's "Mother Goose rhymes" originally appeared on various party albums recorded at least twenty or twenty-five years earlier, like: "Little Miss Muffet sat on a tuffet eating her curds and whey. Along came a spider, he sat down beside her. He said, "Ay, what's in the bowl, bitch?"

When Clay tries to be a little more original, whether in recalling his dirty school days or love of masturbation, he does earn a few legitimate shock laughs, especially for those who happen to enjoy unapologetic thug humor in the Leo Gorcey tradition. When he's ridiculously crude, as opposed to just dirty, he can be funny. Even his misogyny and xenophobia can be funny if used in the "safety valve" style of Don Rickles. Trouble is, Clay never used enough comic hyperbole to hide his very serious rage, and there's a thin line between "recognition humor" and what could almost be a hate speech delivered behind closed doors.

- THE DAY THE LAUGHTER DIED (Def American 9242872) * $15
- DICE RULES (Def American 9265552) *1/2 $8

Clay was the most controversial comedian in America when the double CD "Laughter Died" came out in 1990. Riding on his own arrogance, buoyed by sold-out concerts attended by screaming raging fans, he issued this appropriately titled fiasco. Two hours of Clay is too much, especially when so much of it is pointless cursing and the anecdotal bravado that one might overhear in any subway men's room.

Unlike his main rival at the time, Sam Kinison, Clay rarely showed any vulnerability or made himself the butt of his jokes. Sam, the self-proclaimed "beast of burden," could be laughed at as he howled about his failed relationships. But Clay? There is no end to his posturing, snideness, and hard-headed thug ego. Clay drones on and on: "That's the beauty of this act. Do you know that? Do you know what I'm sayin'? You don't? That's 'cause you're a jerkoff."

"Dice Rules" sometimes has a moment of angry truth, or a line that most listeners could agree with, but there's no real laugh since Clay overuses attitude instead of wit.

- 40 TOO LONG (Def American 9268542) ** $8
- THE DAY THE LAUGHTER DIED PART II (American 9454732) * $8

"40 Too Long" arrived in the summer of 1992, and at sixty minutes, could be retitled "On Too Long." Clay's love affair with himself means that every literally overblown exhalation of cigarette smoke and every meandering remark to a ringsider must be preserved for posterity. He's still getting shock laughs just by calling women at ringside gutter names. Clay's still stealing from old dirty albums, but at least he uses them at appropriate moments. Noticing a muscular guy in the audience, he incorporates an ancient gag into his insults: "Your wife told me about you, Muscles! Big shoulders, big arms, big thighs. No dick ... 220 pounds of dynamite with a quarter inch ... fuse!"

Once in a while Clay's shock humor works, like his ludicrously raunchy gags about Jay Leno's chin (Jay wasn't booking him obviously), but he has to overbake it with too much blather.

By 1993, the year of Part II, nobody was colder than Clay, and he knew it. Which only made him more bitter and less funny than ever. Radio personality Howard Stern was the new favorite among angry blue collar and no collar white males. The title is stingingly honest: the laughter did die for Clay, and as he sulks and curses in front of a small crowd at Dangerfield's, there is a lot of embarrassing silence and mild, uncomfortable chuckles.

Clay starts shouting "Chink" at a ringsider, and when this alone fails to get laughs from more than two people in the whole audience, he becomes boneheadedly defensive: "I can't call him a Chink? Well, what is he? He's not Colombian. He's not Japanese. He's not black. He's a Chink. All of a sudden you can't call 'em Chinks? Every weekend with my friends: 'Hey, you wanna get some Chinks? Let's go get some good Chinks.' It's a nickname. Like 'jerk.'"

CASSIUS CLAY
- I AM THE GREATEST (Columbia CS 8893/CL 2093) ** $10 $35

When Muhammad Ali (then Cassius Clay) emerged on the boxing scene, he was as notorious for his rhymes and outrageous humor as well as his fists and footwork. Comic bragging predominates this collection of poems. He recites of himself, "This kid's great! He's got speed and endurance. But if you sign to fight him, increase your insurance! This kid's got a left, this kid's got a right. If he hits you once, you're asleep for the night!"

Today it's common for athletes to brag, but at the time, Clay was something new. As for the brilliance of his poetry—the liner notes are from the noted poet Marianne Moore!

Aside from the poems, which might be nostalgic for fans, there are some one-liners and even a sketch or two. Actors (uncredited) in a scene from the future:

"Daddy, why are all the flags flying today." "It's a national holiday, son. It's Cassius Clay's birthday." "Cassius Clay, is he the man who chopped down the cherry tree?" "No, he's the man who chopped down Sonny Liston...." "Mommy, how long ago he do that?" "Over 150 years ago." "He must've been a great man." "Why do you say 'must've been?' He's alive today—the oldest living ex-President!"

Clay issued various novelty singles, including "Will the Real Sonny Liston Please Fall Down" (Columbia 75717); the later Muhammad Ali issued a children's album, "Ali and His Gang vs Mr. Tooth Decay" (Cornucopia FV 1001).

JOHN CLEESE
- THE COMPLETE FAWLTY TOWERS (BBC 22003) *** $12 $20

John Cleese was brilliant as Basil Fawlty, the perpetually frustrated proprietor of the tatty holiday hotel Fawlty Towers. Once fans could only get the soundtracks, either in this boxed set of four records or individually ("Fawlty Towers," "Second Sitting," "A La Carte," and "At Your Service"). Now, via videocassette, the full spectrum of Cleese's great comic character can be enjoyed in all its fist shaking, lip curling, haplessly grinning glory.

CLEMENTS AND STEVENS

- THE WEIRD AND THE BEARD (Fraternity F 1012) * $5 $10

Disc jockey humor has generally been stupid and annoying, and this '60s album is an early example. Bearded Dale Stevens of Cincinnati's WNOP and straight man Jack Clements do some idiotic routines, like "Arf Arf," five minutes of a cliché psychiatrist talking to a man who can't help barking every ten seconds.

"Arf arf AAAAAARF! Arrf arrrf arrrrf!" "Down!" "Arrrrrf arrrf AAAARF! Arrrf ..." "Get off ... you're shedding." "Arrrrfff!" "Why don't you come in next Thursday?" "Can you make it Friday? I don't want to miss Huckleberry Hound." "OK, make it Friday." "Arrrf AAAAARF!"

Another dreadful sketch is an interview with a rock and roll star: "Wanna plug my latest record? Don't you play rock and roll?" "Well, to be honest, I feel it's deplorable music." "You don't like Fabian, Frankie Avalon, or Elvis?" "No, I don't think they have any talent." "You fat slob! You old fogey...." "That's a little strong—" "It's your generation made the H-Bomb and taught us kids how to drink ... I hope all you parents will take gas and die. Teenagers arise!" "Watch your step—ohh, what a horrible way to go. He fell into his own echo chamber."

KATE CLINTON

- MAKING LIGHT (Whyscrack 101) **1/2 $5 $10
- MAKING WAVES (Whyscrack 102) **1/2 $5 $10
- LIVE (Whyscrack 103) **1/2 $5 $10
- BABES IN JOYLAND (Whyscrack 104) **1/2 $8

Stereotypically, "lesbian feminist" is not a term that generally denotes a person with a great sense of humor. An exception is Kate Clinton, who has a likable stage persona and offers amusing, conversational observations. She began making albums in the late '80s.

She's prone toward knowing one-liners: "Thank you all for coming out," she tells her predominantly lesbian audience on the "Babes in Joyland" 1991 CD.

On the "Live at the Great American Music Hall" album, she lightly touches on lesbianism and religion: "The most terrifying commandment I ever heard was good old number nine: Thou shalt not covet thy neighbor's wife. I heard that commandment and I thought it had my name on it.... I knew I would personally be doing a lot of hell time.... The Pope. Great guy. Pope John-Paul George Ringo. What an exciting guy. Your Extreme Round-Headedness. See, I don't know about you, but I cannot respect a man who flies around the world kissing airports."

Her CD is readily available, but Clinton's first three albums are not easy to find outside of California and New York. The second album was pressed on blue vinyl, and her third in red vinyl.

DEL CLOSE

- DO IT YOURSELF PSYCHOANALYSIS (Hanover 5002) **1/2 $10 $25
- HOW TO SPEAK HIP (Mercury G 1245) **1/2 $10 $25

A legend in the Chicago area, especially among fans of The Second City, Del Close has been a pivotal member of several improv troupes. He appears on a few Second City albums, as well as the album from "The Premise" and Julius Monk's "Pieces of Eight" revue.

"Do It Yourself Psychoanalysis" might be called "interactive satire." It's a parody of audio self-help records as much as psychoanalysis. Back in the late '50s stores seemed to have an entire bin of "relaxation" and "self-hypnosis" discs.

Here, Close plays a German analyst. His lecture includes some mild jokes, but it's important to play along. ("No matter how filthy your thoughts are, spill them out. I am an analyst. Filthy thoughts are my life.") Throughout, he urges the listener to open up and respond to his periodic questioning:

"If you had to be painted from head to foot with kitchen enamel, what color would you choose ... Zat is the color you have chosen? Hah, you see, the more we hide, the more we reveal!"

On Side Two, Close is the patient and psychiatrist. Often subtle in its satire, this one is offbeat. Some will relish it; others will merely find it annoying and bewildering, whether they play along or simply sit and listen. But as Dr. Close notes, "Even if you remain silent, I still have plenty of material to go on!"

On "How to Speak Hip" Close tries to make straight man John Brent less square. "Dig," says Del, "I think what makes a pad different from an apartment is that every pad has a stash." "Stash?" asks the straight man, "Is it anything like a bidet?"

There are also amusing throwaways: "A nod—that's like a very hip nap."

There's also room for deeper philosophy. Says Del: "Flip out at least once. Then you wouldn't have that to worry about. Dig, once you get used to it, insanity can be the most natural thing in the world." Like Lord Buckley and Lenny Bruce, Del Close isn't just trying to show off his own hipness, but to give off the vibes of his hipness. Fans of jazz-comedy love this one; straights may give it more than a few spins, too.

Among his ensemble appearances on disc, Close is a featured cast member on the original cast album "The Nervous Set" (Columbia OL 5430) with a leering, jolly solo song, "How Do You Like Your Love?"

JERRY CLOWER

- FROM YAZOO CITY, MISSISSIPPI TALKIN' (MCA 33) *1/2 $4 $8
- MOUTH OF MISSISSIPPI (MCA 47) *1/2 $4 $8
- CLOWER POWER (MCA 317) *1/2 $4 $8
- COUNTRY HAM (MCA 417) *1/2 $4 $8
- LIVE IN PECAYUNE (MCA 486) *1/2 $4 $8
- THE AMBASSADOR OF GOOD WILL (MCA 2205) *1/2 $4 $8
- ON THE ROAD (MCA 2281) *1/2 $4 $8
- LIVE FROM THE GRAND OLE OPRY (MCA 3062) *1/2 $4 $8
- LEDBETTER OLYMPICS (MCA 3247) *1/2 $4 $8
- DOGS I HAVE KNOWN (MCA 5321) *1/2 $4 $8
- STARKE RAVING (MCA 5491) *1/2 $4 $8
- LIVE AT CLEBURNE TEXAS (MCA 5422) *1/2 $4 $8
- MORE GOOD 'UNS (MCA 5215) ** $4 $8
- OFFICER AND A LEDBETTER (MCA 5602) *1/2 $4 $8
- RUNAWAY TRUCK (MCA 5773) *1/2 $4 $8
- GREATEST HITS (MCA 3152) ** $3 $7
- CLASSIC CLOWER (MCA 42178) **1/2 $4 $8
- LET THERE BE LIGHT (MCA 42304) ** $4 $8
- AIN'T GOD GOOD (Word 8737) $4 $8

Mississippi-born Clower was a fertilizer salesman who could put over a sale with a gag. In 1971 he turned pro. His humor really doesn't travel well outside of the South and the Nashville area. On the East and West Coasts, out-of-print record shops don't get much for a Clower album. He doesn't fit comfortably into the corny country comic or the Will Rogers/rustic philosopher categories.

Clower is more a lecturer than a stand-up comic. His voice and cadence is close to that of an enthusiastic evangelist. There's good reason: he was the deacon at the First Baptist Church in Yazoo City and spoke at many Billy Graham crusades.

He tends toward a pro-rural and anti-city stance. He makes his audience feel good and take pride in a good old boy who made it big. From "Starke Raving," he talks about the difference between the country and the city. There was this hotel in the city ...

"They had four channels on the TV, and two o' them were snowy. A hundred and twenty five dollar a night room, and they ain't discovered cable TV in that big floosy-doosy dooly-wah mojo-doolah big important hotel in that downtown area where millions of smart people are supposed ta be! Now you know they look down at me and say Jerry Clower lives in a hick town. I might, but we got twenty-one channels on the TV!"

The crowd breaks out into roars, whistles, and applause. Likewise, on the "Country Ham" album he describes meeting a city slick women's libber in Philadelphia who got mad when he offered her a seat. She began to talk about women's liberation, but good ol' Jerry stopped her short: "Whoooo! I said me and Mama has been married twenty-six years. She was my childhood sweetheart, I ain't never had another date. And Mama sleeps every mornin' till she gets ready to get up ... and when Mama does get up, she can fix her own breakfast or have it brought to her ... and when Mama does get up and watches them soap operas, she can watch it in three different rooms in the house, layin' down, leanin' or propped up, whichever way she wants to do it. And when Mama gets ready to go to the supermarket, or get her hair fixed, she goes in a brand new gold Lincoln Continental. I said, 'Ms. Women Libber, Mama don't want you messin' with the deal she's got!'"

Again, the crowd laughs and applauds.

Now and then Clower simply tells a good 'un, an anecdote that most anyone can chuckle over. On the "Cleburne" album, he tells of the time he saw a hog with a wooden leg. He asked the owner about it: "Oh son, that hog's like a member of the family. When our house burned, he rushed in and saved my grandmother. And when little Eulah was drownin' in the creek he rushed in and saved her, just like a member of the family. Son, that hog's like a member of my family." I said, "But why does he have a wooden leg?" He said, "Son, when you got a hog that good, you only eat him one ham at a time."

"Classic Clower" is a good place to start, as well as "More Good 'Uns," which includes the time he paused during a funeral procession: "There's nothing funny about a funeral. Except in the South ... Southerners are naturally humorous. The funeral procession started by and everybody got quiet, put their hand over their heart, and I whispered to this ol' boy, 'Who died?' 'The one in the first car.'"

EMIL COHEN

- JEWISH STORIES AND SONGS (EMCO 1201) *1/2 $5 $10
- T'SYNAGOGUES (EMCO 1202) *1/2 $5 $10

Not to be confused with Myron Cohen, Emil was more a lecturer than a comedian, telling Yiddish stories at nursing homes and private gatherings such as the Louis Marshall Lodge of the Syracuse chapter of B'nai B'rith. The album notes include praise from Ed Sullivan ("I laughed till tears ran down my face") but his delivery is warmed over compared to the warmth and flair of most dialect comics.

These self-published albums require a good knowledge of Yiddish. Some of the old jokes may begin in English, but they end up with a Yiddish punch line. Sometimes Cohen gives the translation, sometimes not. On the first album, the highlight is Cohen's translation of "The Gettysburg Address" from English into Yiddish.

MYRON COHEN

- MYRON COHEN (Audio Fidelity 701) ** $7 $15
- THIS IS MYRON COHEN (RCA Victor LPS 6052, $10 $20
  reissue of two albums, EVERYBODY GOTTA BE SOMEPLACE (RCA Victor LSP 3534) $7 $15
  and IT'S NOT A QUESTION (RCA Victor LSP 3791, reissued on CD as DRC 1-1165) *** $8

A master dialect comedian, Cohen was originally a salesman in New York's garment district. He turned pro in 1948 and was very active for the next two decades telling inoffensive, classic stories in the Catskills and Miami resorts. Cohen's humor was as much in the (long) telling as in the gag, and his best stories make valid points about human nature.

The Audio Fidelity album is not well-recorded and not his best. Cohen takes three or four minutes for a mild punch line. It's rare when he tells a quickie, like the one about two men who meet for a loan: "Lend me twenty dollars." "Here's ten." "I asked you for twenty." "So you lose ten and I'll lose ten!"

Two cuts, "Swimming Pool Story" and "Idle Conversation," appear on the compilation album "20th Century Yiddish Humor" from the ethnic Banner Records label. For those who would like a lesson in "sweetening," the art of canned laughter, the Audio Fidelity and Banner versions make an interesting comparison. The Banner album has the originals, probably 78s recorded in a studio without an audience. To match the live cuts on the rest of their album, the Audio Fidelity engineers added a laugh track to these two studio cuts.

In 1966 and 1967, Cohen was finally persuaded to put his best stuff on a pair of RCA albums. Typical of his style, from "Everybody Gotta Be Someplace," are these funeral parlor stories, told with a great deal of sincerity and gentle warmth:

"I hope you'll think this is funny. A man calls an undertaker and says, 'You better make arrangements for a funeral, my wife passed away.' The undertaker says, 'You must be drunk, I buried your wife two years ago.' He says, 'I got married again.' He says, 'Oh, congratulations.'

"What else do you say! Speaking of undertakers, an undertaker calls a son-in-law: 'About your mother-in-law, should we embalm her, cremate her, or bury her?' He says, 'Do all three, don't take chances.'"

Cohen's two classic albums were reissued as "This is Myron Cohen," with questionably anti-Semitic or at least unflattering drawings by master caricaturist Jack Davis on front and back cover.

Cohen appears on "20th Century Yiddish Humor" (Banner BAS 1004) and "Variety Yiddish Theater" (Banner BAS 1011). Two three-minute routines, "Soup and Fish" and "Mr. and Mrs.," are on "Fun Time" (Coral CRL 57072). Again, these are studio recordings without an audience.

FRANCIS COLBURN

- A GRADUATION ADDRESS (Loren LR 1, Droll Yankees DY 11) *1/2 $4 $8
- BARN TALK (Loren LR 2, Droll Yankees DY 13) *1/2 $4 $8
- THE CAMPAIGN SPEECH (Loren LR 3) *1/2 $4 $8
- I WENT STONE BLIND (Droll Yankees DY-12) *1/2 $4 $8

Between 1962 and 1964, banquet speaker and University professor Colburn issued his albums of dry down-home Vermont humor. During his "Campaign Speech" he offers a typical remark: "My wife rather enjoyed that little car. Save for her reservations about the bucket seats. 'Francis,' she said to me, 'these bucket seats are just peachy—but it ain't everybody's bucket fits.'"

Those who wouldn't want a whole evening, or whole record, of such wit would probably agree with another of Colburn's remarks: "To understand Vermont it is extremely useful to be born there."

Colburn sometimes performed "in character" as a crusty Vermonter named "Foster Wheeler." On "Barn Talk" he joins Alan C. Bemis and Peter Kilham in swapping dusty, slightly bawdy stories further embalmed by their use of "authentic" New England accents. Colburn, Bemis, and Kilham also appear together on the "I Went Stone Blind" album.

BEN COLDER

- SPOOFING THE BIG ONES (MGM 4173) ** $5 $10
- BIG BEN STRIKES AGAIN (MGM 4421) ** $5 $10
- BEST OF BEN COLDER (MGM 4530) ** $5 $10
- GOLDEN ARCHIVE SERIES (MGM GAS 139) ** $5 $10
- WINE WOMEN AND SONG (MGM E 4482) ** $5 $10
- LIVE AND LOADED (MGM SE 4758) ** $5 $10
- WILD AGAIN (MGM SE 4674) ** $5 $10
- HAVE ONE ON BEN COLDER (MGM 4629) ** $5 $10
- WARMING UP TO COLDER (MGM SE 4807) ** $5 $10
- THE WACKY WORLD OF BEN COLDER (SE 4876) ** $5 $10
- HARPER VALLEY PTA (MGM SE 4614) ** $5 $10

Ben Colder is the pun-named pen name of Sheb Wooley, the man who hit the charts with "The Purple People Eater." Over three decades, Wooley has maintained a dual identity. In concert, "Ben" comes out in a shabby outfit to do some drunk songs and booze humor. Sheb's set has straight songs and lighter parodies. Some in the audience aren't even aware that Sheb and Ben are the same person.

Ben Colder is basically just a drunk act; he wails out boozy parodies of hit country tunes. "Golden Archives" has a lot of his better numbers. In "By the Time I Get to Phoenix" Ben talks about his plane trip: "By the time I got to Phoenix I was flyin'. Ish really ish the only way to fly. Enjoyin' the complimentary cocktails 'nd conversation. And makin' passes at the stewardi ..."

"Live and Loaded" is another better effort loaded with some of his more familiar song parodies, including "Detroit City," "Almost Persuaded," and "Folsom City Blues."

"Warming Up to Colder" includes "Help Me Fake It through the Night," "Cold Cold Heart," and "Runnin' Bare" among others. The joke is still the boozy character more than the lyrics. "Runnin' Bare" parodies "Running Bear," as the poor drunk sings about all the times he's ended up nekkid: "My girlfriend called, said, 'Hey, come around. 'Cause my husband, he's out of town.' But after a while, he walked in. I said, 'Scuse me!' And I was gone again. Runnin' bare, through the bushes. Dodging bullets from tree to tree. Runnin' bare, through the bushes. Runnin' Bare's what they call me."

Sheb Wooley recorded several "straight" albums, all for MGM, including "Blue Guitar," "Songs from the Days of Rawhide," "That's My Pa," "Tales of How the West Was Won," "It's a Big Land," and "Warm and Wooley." He has been active with more recent novelty tunes including "The Ballad of Jim and Tammy" and "Shakey Breaky Car," the latter based on the simpleminded 1992 country tune "Achy Breaky Heart." Some albums have been released especially for television mail order sales, including "Wild and Wooley." An obscure album for W International was released, titled "Sheb and Ben ... Swanging Again."

AL JAZZBEAUX COLLINS

• STEVE ALLEN'S HIP FABLES (Doctor Jazz FW 38729) ** $7 $15

Back around 1953, Steve Allen put a few children's fairy tales into "Hipsomatic," and Al Collins (the nickname spelled "Jazzbo" back then) recorded "Grimm Fairy Tales for Hip Kids," a Brunswick 45 with Lou Stein at the piano. Allen later issued the material in book form as *Bop Fables*. In 1983 Collins made this album version with Steve Allen at the piano:

"'Wow,' said the papa bear, 'somebody's been makin' it in my bed.' 'Yeah, there's been a scuffle in my pad too,' said the mama bear. 'I don't like to start idle gossip,' said the baby bear, 'but there's a chick in my sack!'"

It's still funny for hipped boppers or bopped hippies. The only flaw here is that, either to pad out the album or to genuflect to the large population in America who refuse to speak English, every line is simultaneously translated into Spanish. The assault of comic jive, followed by Spanish (as gleefully performed by Slim Galliard) is mindboggling. Then annoying.

Collectors hunt up Collins's novelty 45s, including the original "Three Little Pigs/Little Red Riding Hood" (Brunswick 9-80226), "Jack and the Beanstalk/Snow White" (Capitol F 2580), "Little Hood Riding Red/Pee Little Thrigs" (Capitol F 2773), and "The Space Man/Jazzbo's Theory" (Coral 9-61693). Four of the hip fairy tales turn up on his late '60s jazz album for Impulse, "A Lovely Bunch" (AS-9150).

BOBBY COLLINS

• ON THE INSIDE (Uproar 36652) *1/2 $8

Why did comedy clubs start folding in the late '80s? Comics like Collins. An ad-lib to a female ringsider: "Take one out, let it see the show. I love that!" The obligatory hotel soap joke: "The soap hadda be the size of an M&M. It didn't say Dial, it said duh!" And don't forget the comic from New York line: "I'm a New Yorker ... I lost my keys. I can't find my car. Get me a gun!" Collins, a club denizen once billed as "comedy's Don Johnson" for his alleged good looks, hosted a VH-1 alleged comedy cable show when this CD arrived in 1995.

PAT COLLINS

• SLEEP WITH PAT COLLINS, THE HIP HYPNOTIST (GNP Crescendo GNP 93) * $7 $15

For decades, hypnotists have invaded nightclubs and offered audiences an offbeat evening of spontaneous laughs. It doesn't even matter whether there are "plants" in the audience or not. But this "you hadda be there" comedy doesn't work on TV or here, on disc. Most of the comedy is visual, as Pat has her subjects make funny faces, sniff a bad odor in the air, and do the Can-Can.

Some celebrity guests were in the audience for the show. Sal Mineo is hypnotized into playing drums a la Gene Krupa. There's no laughs here, just two minutes of drumming. Afterward he says, "It feels weird. I remember going to the drums, but I don't remember too much ... Am I under now?"

What little verbal humor there is sounds less than spontaneous, like the man who, told that he is President Kennedy, happens to stand up and deliver a very accurate Boston accent: "I say the country must move forward. No laughter please!"

TOM COLLINS

• TWO UPROARIOUSLY FUNNY SPEECHES (Edward M. Miller, EM 1964) ** $5 $10

Sociologists who want to know what after dinner speakers were like in 1964 can listen to Collins amble along, reminding himself of humorous anecdotes. The album was either sold as a souvenir or used by his agency to solicit further business.

He opens by telling the crowd, "One thing I can promise you, that I shall have an eye on that clock that stares at me with an accusing green eye. I know what time you're supposed to be through and it's one of my prides that I'll be quittin' in time even if I'm in the middle of the word "it." Maybe this can't be any good but we can control the length of it I assure ya."

At one point he declares, "I am not up to diagnosing the ills of the world for you. I think of the doctor, a young fellow who had only opened practice, and came to his office a fellow with some kind of rash and bewildered the young doctor. He said, 'Have you had this before?' And the fellow said, 'Doc, I've had it twice before.' And the doctor said, 'Well, you've got it again.' That's about the best I can do. We've had a mess in the world in my time a couple of times and it looks like we've got it again, and I don't know much more about it than that except that I don't like it."

JERRY COLONNA

- JERRY COLONNA ENTERTAINS (Bravo K 142) *1/2 $8 $15

Colonna was known for his comical singing and his habit of histrionically holding his notes in a piercingly fierce tenor voice. He was a regular on Bob Hope's radio show and made many films (check "The Bob Hope Show" on Radiola).

The man with the popping eyes and thick mustache was a fine comedy character, but here he sings some pretty silly novelty songs like "Bowser," a song about a pet dog: "He's my friend, my pal, my buddy, yes that's the way it is. He eats the same food that I do, and sometimes I eat his." There's also the deliberately overdone "August in Azusa": "I like August in Azusa. That's the only place for-a meeeee, I like August in Azusa, underneath an orange-a treeeeee." A few cuts, like "Balling the Jack," aren't intended as comedy at all, though Colonna makes the songs personally his own ("Ah yes! That's what I call ballin' the jack!"). He issued a few other albums that were straighter, more in the mild "novelty" mode: "Along the Dixieland Hi-Fi Way" (Liberty 9004), "Entertains at Your Party" (Design 78), "He Sings and Swings" (Wing SRW 12500), and "Music for Screaming" (Decca DL 5540), a ten-incher later coupled with Decca's "Hooray for Captain Spaulding" Groucho Marx album as the British import Ace of Hearts AH 102.

COMIC'S ANONYMOUS

- WORLD'S FUNNIEST JOKES Vol 1 (Dilligaf 000032) * $7
- WORLD'S FUNNIEST JOKES Vol 2 (Dilligaf 000042) * $7
- WORLD'S FUNNIEST JOKES Vol 3 (Dilligaf 000053) * $7

Here's a cheap idea for an album: gather a bunch of amateur comics in a room, pretend they're having a "Comics Anonymous" meeting for people who can't stop telling jokes, and have them try to top each other with ancient joke book wheezes. One tries for some Black ethnic comedy now and then, one tells windy jokes in a bad British accent, and there's a woman who doesn't mind telling misogynistic gags from time to time. They all sound about college age, even if their jokes rarely reach even that level of sophistication.

There's no laugh track beyond the artificial guffaws and whoops of the other comics. From Volume One:

"This eighty-three-year-old man was caught having sex with this underaged girl. You know what he was charged with? Assault with a dead weapon."

"OK. Three old ladies are sitting on a park bench, and they're knittin' and talkin' and this flasher steps in front of them, whips open his trenchcoat, and there's a huge scary boner right in front of 'em. The first old lady is so shocked she has a stroke. The second old lady is so shocked, she has a stroke. And the third lady would've had a stroke but she couldn't reach!"

Volume Two has a bunch of lightbulb jokes for a highlight: How many Californians does it take to screw in a lightbulb? None. Californians screw in hottubs." Volume 3 has the lone female comic utter this one: "All right. I don't know if you guys know it, but there is a technical term for the useless, fleshy part around a woman's vagina. It's the woman."

Each CD is a chintzy half hour long, but the way these guys (and one amateur woman) tell 'em, two minutes is too long.

COMMERCIALS IN A PLAIN BROWN WRAPPER

- COMMERCIALS IN A PLAIN BROWN WRAPPER (Mad Ave.) $6 $12

Nobody's taking responsibility for this one. The cover is indeed a plain brown wrapper, and the back lists the contents, but no stars and no address for "Mad Ave. Records."

Several different actors and actresses perform the twenty-eight quickie fake radio commercials, and somebody took enough time to add sound effects and music. But the commercials for "Olay Potato Chips," "Praytex Girdles," and "Logeine Feminine Spray" are so obvious that the gag wears out before the minute-long bit. One of the better ones:

"Calling all bowlers. At last there's something to protect your balls: Protecto-Ball. Protecto-Ball is a finely knitted bag that fits snugly around your balls to protect them from banging together. And from nicks and scratches when you play ... If you really want to score, make sure your balls are in tip-top condition. Protect them with Protecto-Ball."

THE COMMITTEE

- THE COMMITTEE (Reprise 2023) *1/2 $10 $20

Various improv artists operated under the name of "The Committee" in the '60s. The 1963 group included Hamilton Camp, Kathryn Ish, Larry Hankin, Irene Riordan, and Dick Stahl. They were known for challenging social and political satire, most of it dated now. Their sketches of talky neurosis a la '60s greats Nichols and May and Jules Feiffer don't have strong humor. A couple of college students are involved in seven minutes of agonizing and bickering over premarital sex:

"I'm sorry. I don't love you," the girl says. "I don't care ..." the impatient boy answers. "Wait a minute, I said that wrong. The thing is, I'm not sure of my feelings. I don't know that I love you, I don't know." "I have very deep feelings for you ... we've been going together for a while ... now we've come to a point where we can share something far greater...." "Look, Cy, I just can't do it for a sharing experience ... look, what if I did share with you and then I found out I didn't love you, and I met someone else, and I had deep feelings for them too, and I shared with them. And I met someone else, and I just kept sharing and sharing...." "Look, I'm not asking you to share with anyone else...." "Cy, I'm sorry ... Gee, Cy, you're making me feel terrible." "That's okay. Please go to bed with me?" "No." "What do you mean no? No is a very abstract term...."

And on, and on, and on it goes. For ten minutes a professor and student posture and prattle about the "social, political, and cosmic ramifications of failure." There's eight minutes of forced pathos and coy humor as a straight man enters a gay bar. And finally, it's back to '60s sex hang-ups in another ten-minute routine that was once daring, as two women converse about virginity: "I lost it!" "Gee, that's great, kid, welcome to the club!" "When I came in, could you tell?" "Well, you had an aura, of womanliness...." "Uh, did this happen to you? The next day, I kept grinning!" "Oh yes."

- WIDE WORLD OF WAR (Little David LD 1007) *1/2 $7 $15

New members emerged after the first album, and others became more prominent. The key members now included Carl Gottlieb, Hugh Romney, John Brent, Chris Ross, and two men later to find fame in TV sitcoms, Howard (*WKRP in Cincinnati*) Hesseman and Peter (*The Bob Newhart Show*) Bonerz. Nothing on this album indicates which members were involved, either in writing or performance.

Although well-intentioned, the routines on "Wide World of War" are very stagy and arch. The nearly ten-minute "Clean Up" is just a typical slice of early '70s drug life as three guys talk about their troubles and get paranoid when there's a knock on the door. One guy snorts up all the drugs: "What the hell did you do, you took it all!" "I'm protecting you, man, it could be the cops." "... If you OD in my pad, that's the most inconsiderate thing of all."

The rest of the album is equally dated. The title cut, once considered daring, uses a now-stale form of parody to make its point. The horrors of war are announced in the style of a "Wide World of Sports" broadcast:

"I see a dozen oxen down and kicking on the field. And this time it looks like Napalm! It smells like Charlie's hurting down there.... Oh my God, right on top of the 101st! Field's full of penalty flags on that one.... It looks like search and destroy from here on in.... In this game the Viet Cong suffered 437 killed or injured, while the 101st's casualties were light to moderate as usual.... I know the president wanted to be here today to throw out the first grenade."

The Committee disbanded in 1973.

THE CONCEPTION CORPORATION

- A PAUSE IN THE DISASTER (Cotillion SD 9031) ** $5 $10
- CONCEPTIONLAND (SD 9051) ** * $5 $10

Following Firesign Theater's lead, several groups of comics began experimenting with studio-created "drug humor" in the '70s. This quartet, Murphy Dunne, Howard R. Cohen, Ira Miller, and Jeff Begun, are closer to *Laugh-In* than "Firesign" as they try hard to create blackouts and four-minute vignettes that are spacey but full of yocks.

When they're in their *Laugh-In* mode, doing slightly self-conscious schtick, they're pretty funny. They can imitate frantic and pointless radio commercials and TV news items, and score with bits reflecting their comic influences, like "Dial a Dirty Joke," featuring an aged vaudevillian. A few are in vibrant bad taste, like the bit on a rising star going to a "Disease Broker" so he'll have a charity to plug. Jerry Lewis has muscular dystrophy, Danny Kaye took sick children, "J. Edgar Hoover just took on paranoia," and (in a reference to his daughter's death) "We let Art Linkletter have drug addiction."

When the troupe tries to imitate their contemporaries, they fail miserably. "Searchin'," a study of a Mexican border guard strip-searching tourists hungry to score drugs, might be the boring missing link between Jose Jimenez and Cheech Marin.

1972's "Conceptionland" is now dated, but at the time was sharp. Aiding the Conception Company were J. J. Barry, Peter Boyle, Severn Darden, and Harold Ramis. There's a bit on a "Top 40" high school where dippy hippie chicks give mind-boggling talks on how to "tie-dye a tie" and a gruff Phys. Ed instructor shouts, "Arrright! Everybody meditate! One two! One two!"

Snippets from imaginary radio shows include a look at the Mike Nichols-influenced "All Night Obituary of the Air," a commercial for the corrupt "Famous Judges School," and a cut from an album by "The First Poets" (a Jewish parody on the black "Last Poets" record albums). There's a parody of Johnny Cash's "Folsom Prison Blues" and "The Late News," a news broadcast featuring dead people. The late Edward R. Murrow reports on doings in heaven. Oscar Wilde handles the gossip report: "Jesus Christ has become just impossible since he's become a superstar! And now he's moving to an unlisted cloud! Jesus Christ, Jesus!" There's an interview with the late W. C. Fields, who rambles on evocatively before mentioning, "I'll never forget the time I died! I was lying supine in my chamber when my eyes slowly closed. Next thing I knew I was in heaven ... and then there was the time I was hunting larynxes on the Serenghetti plains in Africa ..." The subliminally clever background harp music is a snippet of a Harpo solo from "Horse Feathers."

The centerpiece is the long "Conceptionland" cut, revolving around traumas, titillations, and life crises at an amusement park. Cuts like "The Amazing Dope-A-Matic," "Bummerland," and "The Ego Trip" give an idea of what to expect.

CONCERTGEBLUFF AUTHAUS ORCHESTRA SOCIETY

- BAROQUE AMERICANA (Mace 10036) ** $4 $8

In yet another example of musical transvestism, folk tunes are laced up in baroque settings. "Down in the Valley" is melded with a Handel melody, and what sounds like Bach is actually the disguised "When Johnny Comes Marching Home." Classical music fans never seem to tire of this particular game, which involves slipping a disc like this onto the turntable and carefully waiting for everyone to detect the cheat: "Why, it's a pop tune disguised as a classic!"

The limp album notes are considerably more fey than Peter Schickele's P. D. Q. Bach, but the Concertgebluffs (who get their name from the tongue-twisting Concertgebouw Orchestra of Amsterdam) do a nice job musically. Whether it's such a funny novelty over a half hour is up to fans of the genre. Some listeners may actually enjoy this as a straight album, hearing "My Grandfather's Clock," "Old MacDonald's Farm," and "Shenandoah" turned into classics.

CONFIDENTIAL COMEDIAN

- CONFIDENTIAL (Borderline B 7-8) * $5 $10

A cheaply done record of bad dirty jokes, the hook here is that "famous celebrities" are supposedly behind the microphone. The cover warns, "You must hear it to believe it ... are they for real?" And there are crude drawings of Peter Lorre, James Cagney, Cary Grant, Chico Marx, Gary Cooper, and either Warner Oland or Sidney Toler (Charlie Chan). On the back there's a cleverly worded disclaimer admitting that "through the cleverest of hidden mike techniques" the result is only "actual simulated voices of top U.S. personalities!"

The unknown mimic here is pretty bad and the wheezing "over sixteen" jokes are cornball cute at best. As Jimmy Cagney, he reads this war report: "It has officially been announced that the enemy has taken Castoria. The war office admits this, but doubts that they'll be able to hold it. Because the strain on the rear is tremendous. And they may be wiped out at any time. Because they have been caught on the run several times—while trying desperately to evacuate."

CONGRESS OF WONDERS

- REVOLTING (Fantasy 7016) **1/2 $8 $20
- SOPHOMORIC (Fantasy 7018) *1/2 $5 $10

The San Francisco based Congress of Wonders (Richard Rollins and Howard Kerr) were a little sillier than "Credibility Gap" and a lot sillier than "Firesign Theatre." Their drug-tinged humor usually has more than a dash of vaudeville in it. "Revolting" has two routines that early '70s listeners talked about: a five-minute speculation on Jerry Garcia in old age (well, fans can still speculate), and "Star Trip," a twelve-minute parody of Star Trek complete with sound effects:

"Lt. Ubangi! Where the hell did she go?" "She went to church sir." "She can't be! It's Tuesday afternoon." "It's her sect, you know." "I'm aware of her sex ... where did she go now?" "The ship's apse ..." "The ship's what? Maybe it's in here. (Sound of a door opening, heavy breathing, and a girl crying, "Oh wowee! Oh wowee! Oh wowee!") You can't do that, this is a broom closet!" "We're engaged." "Well, disengage and report to your stations!"

A typical freaked-out news item:

"Aerosol Oasis and his lovely wife Jockey accompanied by her sister Princess Lee Razafanasnatch disemboweled yesterday on their private sloop "Behemoth" for the Republic of Gotcha where they will rendezvous with former President Johnson's private yacht, "Yawl Come."

They were running out of ideas for the tedious follow-up album "Sophomoric," which includes a dull soap opera, "Sylvia Davenport"; the twelve-minute biography of "Cedro Willy"; and predictable hippie commercial announcements: "Today's episode is brought to you by Degenerate Mills, makers of Fruit Trips, a new breakfast food with a completely different texture." Corny hipsters might want the routine that begins "Good evening Ladles and Genitals...."

BILLY CONNOLLY

- AT THE ROYAL ALBERT HALL (90870) **1/2 $4 $8

Billy Connolly shaved off his beard and mustache trying to make himself more promotable for TV. Unfortunately, his two U.S. sitcom attempts failed, not helped by his Scottish accent. He returned to stand-up in Great Britain, where he had fifteen years of previous success.

This is the only album he released in America (1988). Connolly was similar to Eddie Murphy at the time—fond of cursing and anecdotal material that needs a strong personality to make it funny: "I have a dachshund. It curses when it barks! Why? You would too if you were draggin' your balls on the sidewalk." A bit of childhood recollection: "Oh yeah, my father would thrash me every now and then. And he'd talk while he did it! He'd hit me and shout, 'Have you had enough?' Had enough? What kind of a question is that? 'Why Father, would another kick in the balls be out of the question?'"

NOTES: Connolly's import albums, some of which were certified gold, include "A Big Yin" (Cambra), "The Billy Connolly Collection" (Pickwick), "Cop Yer Whack for This" (Polydor), "You Take My Photograph I Break Your Face" (Polydor), "The Pick of Billy Connolly" (Polydor), "Billy Connolly Live" (Transatlantic), "Words and Music" (Transatlantic), "Atlantic Bridge" (Polydor), "Raw Meat for the Balcony" (Polydor) and "Riotous Assembly" (Polydor). He opened for rock acts and was a rocker himself for a while. "Wreck on Tour" (Philips) is a very representative disc from 1985, featuring "Swearing," "Pubic Hair," "Men in Public Toilets," etc. "Get Right Intae Him" (Polydor) from 1975 is the pick from his early years and features monologues and songs, including country covers ("Coat of Many Colours" by Dolly Parton), his own material ("The Janny Song"), and his #1 novelty hit that year, "D.I.V.O.R.C.E."

HANS CONRIED

- PETER MEETS THE WOLF (Strand S 1001) *1/2 $7 $15
- MONSTER RALLY (RCA VICTOR) **1/2 $20 $50

Conried cultivated a comic character based on the stereotype of the grandly ridiculous Shakespearean ham. He was a favorite voice in Jay Ward cartoons and is still remembered fondly as the excitable Uncle Tonoose on *Make Room for Daddy*.

"Peter Meets the Wolf" is given a fairly straight narration. The hook here is the Prokofiev score done in a jazz style.

"Monster Rally" was released in 1959 in the midst of a monster movie fad that saw *Famous Monsters of Filmland* become a popular magazine. A comedy LP more for children than adults, "Monster Rally" contains arrangements that are as bright as Hanna-Barbera cartoon soundtracks (with a few nice sound effects, especially on the title track). The nine original tunes by Joel Herron and Fred Hertz are like cartoon themes; low on witty joke lines but strong on visual imagery and story. "Close the Door" is about a monster invasion:

"I ran into the playroom and grabbed a baseball bat, and every time I met one, I gave him this and that. It nearly drove me crazy, it had me mystified! The more and more I knocked them down the more they multiplied!"

Conreid is only on four cuts: "Flying Saucer," "Not of this Earth," "What Do You Hear from the Red Planet Mars," and the Sheb Wooley classic, "The Purple People Eater." The last two are the best, especially "Red Planet Mars," a sort of Eddie Lawrence-style nonsense tune with a ragtime beat. It's an infectious song about a homesick space nut recalling his beloved planet: "Oh, what I wouldn't give to spend another zilch in the grammis by the nalvin with the spreem!"

A catchall group called The Creatures handles a few numbers, and Alice Pearce does a few as well. She has her best moment on the old Phil Harris classic, "The Thing." Really, it's Conreid who holds the show together. "Monster Rally" is highly prized by fans who remember the album from childhood, and those who enjoy Jack Davis cover illustrations.

Conreid appears on many soundtrack albums, including stage ("Can-Can," Capitol DW 452e), TV ("Feathertop," Mars Candy 2931), and film ("Peter Pan," Disneyland 1206).

JOE CONTI

- COMEDY ALA CONTI (Elmwood ARJ-5819) ** $5 $10

There's no reason to expect much from Conti, the house comic at Mangam's Chateau in Lyons, Illinois. He spent eight years there when he recorded this souvenir album in 1960. The wife jokes: "The other day I came home, she was posing for a painter. House painter! Well, I took my brush away. Oh, clumsy, this girl. She crochets with two pickles ... the other day I says, 'Honey, we're expecting a little company this afternoon. Why don't you grab a shovel and dust up?' Ha ha ha. You know if I lose a button she sews the hole? Are you kiddin'? She starches everything I wear. The other day I sat down and broke my shorts. I try to be nice. The other day I bought her a fall outfit. A parachute ..."

TIM CONWAY

- ARE WE ON? (Liberty 7512) **1/2 $5 $10
- BULL (Liberty 7552) ** $5 $10

Conway sounds a bit like Bob Newhart trying to be Jonathan Winters on these obscure albums from 1967. Stodgy straight man Ernie Anderson plays along as Conway stammers through his deadpan put-ons, which start subtle and wry, then go off the deep end. On "Are We On," an interview with Clark Kent begins like this: "Do you mind if I call you Clark?" "Not at all, I'm mild-mannered." But Conway's penchant for deliberate silliness quickly takes over. "How is Lois Lane?" "She broke up." "Oh, you don't see her anymore." "No. She broke up. We used to have this little act we worked out at fairs in the summertime. We had a two-hundred-foot tower, she'd jump off it and I'd catch her. And this one summer, she jumped off and I missed her. So she broke up."

Things are more obvious on "Bull," which also is a series of interview sketches. From the title cut, as a drunken bullfighter: "Are you actually going to go into the ring in that condition?" "Oh I hope so!" "I guess, after all, it's not easy to get into that ring." "You know it, I got forty steps to go up, man...." "It must be pretty frightening to see a bull come charging at you." "Well you can imagine how I feel when I see two of 'em ... on a hot day I see four!"

COOK AND MOORE

- GOOD EVENING (Island ILPS 9298) *** $7 $18

Peter Cook and Dudley Moore appeared on Broadway in *Good Evening* in 1973. The album is a very mixed bag of tricks from the show. Moore solos with some silly opera parodies on the piano, Cook goes serious with a psychodrama involving a potential criminal. The latter was a little more effective onstage, with eerie lighting and his stark lone figure.

In the middle, there are parodies consisting of gleeful sickness and surly satire. Their most famous bit is "One Leg Too Few," which Peter Cook performed years before for "One Over the Eight" (available as an import disc), a revue starring Kenneth Williams. It's a cruel comedy sketch about a one-legged man trying out for the part of Tarzan in a film. Moore, bobbing up and down on one leg (the other is concealed in his long trench coat) confronts icy casting director Peter Cook. Rather than sympathy, Cook offers cool disdain for this ridiculous optimist.

"You, Mr. Spiggot," he notes with just a tad of condescension, "are a unidexter ... You, a unidexter, are applying for the role, a role for which two legs would seem to be the minimum requirement. Need I point out, that it is in the leg division that you are deficient? You are deficient in the leg division to the tune of one ... Your right leg I like. It's a lovely leg. I've got nothing against your right leg ... Neither have you."

If anyone could question the taste of the routine, it would have been Moore himself, who was born clubfooted. The evening's most outrageous sketch is about the birth of Jesus: "Three wise men arrived?" "Three bloody idiots. In they come and call themselves Maggie!"

- DEREK AND CLIVE LIVE (Island ILPS 9434) ** $5 $10

Cook and Moore had a pair of drunken alter egos, "Derek and Clive." Their records (two only available via import) are for special tastes. They're not only filled with a particularly peculiar brand of British working humor, they are also densely scatological.

The half-live, half-studio release "Derek and Clive Live" balances porno humor with sick humor. Peter Cook talks about the misery of being blind: "... deprived of sight, unable to read, this is perhaps the greatest loss to the blind person. I'm blind, but I am able to read thanks to a wonderful new system known as broil. I'm sorry—I'll just feel that again."

The two imports are "Derek and Clive Ad Nauseum" (Virgin V 2112, also on a CD with eighteen extra minutes including "Lady Vera Fart Teller" and "Sex Manual": CDOVD 162) and "Derek and Clive Come Again" (Virgin V 2094). The latter has their classic routine about Joan Crawford.

NOTES: Import albums, featuring some of their grand satires from their British TV shows, include "The World of Pete and Dud" (Decca), "Not Only but Also" (Decca), "Not Only Peter Cook but Also Dudley Moore" (Decca), "Once Moore with Cook" (Decca) and "Goodbye Again" (Decca). There's also "The Clean Tapes" (Cube), "Six Fabulous Filthy Favourites" (Krass KS 12578) and "Behind the Fridge" (Atlantic). Peter Cook and Dudley Moore appear individually on the compilation CD "Dead Parrot Society" (Rhino R2 71049), with material culled from the British albums "A Poke in the Eye with a Sharp Stick Vol. 11" and "Private Eye Presents Golden Satiricals." Cook issued the solo albums "Here Comes the Judge" (Virgin) and "Misty Mr. Wisty" (Decca). Moore has issued many musical albums.

COOL U LABORATORY PLAYERS

- CAMPUS CAPERS (Jayvee 101) *1/2 $4 $8
- MORE CAMPUS CAPERS (Jayvee 103) *1/2 $4 $8
- COLLEGE HUMOR (Party Time 105-33) *1/2 $4 $8

The Cool U group knew how to make colorful records. "Campus Capers" is on yellow vinyl and "More Campus Capers" is on green vinyl.

Inside, it's just hijinks from anonymous fugitives from Spring Break '58. The quickie cuts include songs and mini monologues, like this one from the first album, done with a bongo in the background:

"Dear Folks, Everything is cool here at school, in my first week at Old Swingin' U. I got a great room overlooking the girls' dorm. Hope you're gonna send me my binoculars. My roommate Tom plays the native drums, and he plays quite well. Matter of fact he's here on a scholarship from Nairobi Prep. My other roommate Bill is a banking major, and together we're planning a very interesting project, a small loan company for underprivileged freshmen.... Anyway, the food here is very good. If you like bread hash. I'm eating very good and I've gained twenty pounds. I now weigh 105." The third album duplicates some of the older material.

PAT COOPER

- OUR HERO (United Artists UAS 6446,
  also the title of a 1992 CD compilation from all four albums) ** $5 $10
- SPAGHETTI SAUCE AND OTHER DELIGHTS (United Artists 6548) ** $5 $10
- YOU DON'T HAVE TO BE ITALIAN TO LIKE PAT COOPER (United Artists 6600) ** $5 $10
- MORE SAUCY STORIES (United Artists UAS 6690) ** $5 $10

A strongly ethnic comedian, Cooper was popular on TV variety shows in the '60s, spouting his fast-paced routines about Italian life. These albums were recorded between 1965-68. He has the aggressive tone of Alan King (a lot of middle-aged, middle class griping) and some of the feisty frantic attitude of Jackie Mason, but little of their wit. The humor is mostly in Cooper's agitation. On "Our Hero" he describes his mother:

"I got a genuine Eye-talian mother. Four feet eleven! If they five feet they Turks! She has a bun ovah heee-ah, a knitting needle over heee-ah, a gold tooth over heee-aah. That's-a my momma!"

He explains why Italian women wear black even at a wedding: "Black dress, black stockings, and black shoes. I say, 'Poppa, why they wear black?' He says, 'In case anybody dies, they're ready.'"

Like many '60s comics, Cooper groans about child rearing in general, and teenagers in particular. From "More Saucy Stories":

"These kids today, they drive ya crazy! They know everything, you can't talk to them! They look at their mother: 'You're old fashioned, momma, what do you know about love?' She had nineteen kids, what did she know about love! I say we must explain these things to the children, our kids today don't know this kind of life ... my son, eleven years old, he threatened me! I'm thirty-nine, he threatened his father! He says, 'How do you like it, I ain't gonna

UN-APPETIZERS

The classic Herb Alpert "whipped cream" cover was turned into sour cream with The Frivolous Five. Pat Cooper got some laughs by pouring on the spaghetti sauce.

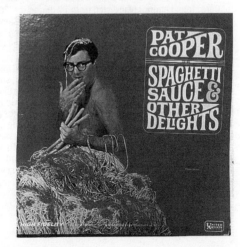

graduate unless you buy me a Stingray.' I went to the fish market, I got him one this big, I shoved it in his navel! 'Here's yer stingray!'"

REGE CORDIC

- CORDIC AND COMPANY PREFERRED (KDKA) ** $6 $12

Cordic was a morning radio personality on KDKA in Pittsburgh. KDKA, evidently responding to listener demands for copies of favorite sketches, issued this "for home use only—not for sale" album in 1961. There are the requisite parodies (now dated) of radio and TV commercials, along with some strained fake interviews and put-ons ("National Wheelbarrow Week"). Cordic isn't quite Henry Morgan or Bob & Ray, but he does have some amusing moments. An oddity is "German Gunsmoke," a sketch performed in fake German. Seems that the local bank was robbed. ("Alles de gelt geshwipin?") He takes some jabs at Pittsburgh in a nicely done fake travelogue: "Thousands of miles beyond the mountains in the East lies a grimy little town untouched by progress. This is Pittsburgh ... While street lights glow twenty-four hours a day, the gay citizens pay no mind to the constant pall of smoke that hangs in their valley. Clothing and decorations are all done in shades of gray and blue, white having been long since abandoned."

PROFESSOR IRWIN COREY

- AT LE RUBAN BLEU (Jubilee 2018) ** $10 $20
- WIN WITH IRWIN: AT THE PLAYBOY CLUB (Atlantic 1236) ** $7 $15
- WORLD'S FOREMOST AUTHORITY (Viva 6009) **1/2 $10 $20
- I FEEL MORE LIKE I DO NOW (Gateway GSLP 8502) **1/2 $5 $10

With Corey albums, the humor is as much in the windy, silly character of the professor as in the rambling monologue of prepared gags and ad-libbing. This is especially true of his first album. Corey takes plenty of time between each sentence to make gestures and faces, which makes for frustrating listening:

"After accepting (pause) the degree (pause) of the world's foremost authority (pause) it occurred to me, that it would be presumptuous of me, in one short evening (pause) but it is necessary! Since all over the world (pause) people everywhere (pause) and there are. But not here. However (pause) the government (pause) they need it. However (pause) scientists (long pause) scientists who try to classify people tell us that most people fall very roughly (pause) this is sheer carelessness. On their parts. However my topic for this evening will be (pause) the Piltdown Man (pause) and the Built-Up Woman."

"Win with Irwin" from 1961 is also filled with meandering nonsense, but the puckish professor does manage to get in a few good lines. In a Bible study: "Sodom and Gomorrah! Wicked people destroyed by a tremendous conflagration, belching forth fire, hell, and brimstone from the heavens! Wicked people stooped to debaucheries, degeneracies, and perversion. All these wonderf- all these things ... six hundred thousand souls snuffed out ... And Lot's wife looked around ... and gave one long last look at her long lost lovers—and she turned into a pillar of salt. Therefore! The moral of that story is—all girls that cheat—taste salty!"

Sensing a need for some discipline, the professor worked with a straight man on the Viva album: "Could you sum up briefly your thoughts on the juvenile delinquent problem? In ten seconds?"

"Well, not in ten seconds. I'd rather be brief ... what was the question ...?"

It's a losing battle for the straight man, but Corey fans will have a good time.

Corey found himself blacklisted from TV during the '70s, partly due to his blasts at political figures, partly due to his own irascible personality. His comeback, the 1982 Gateway album, is most welcome, even if it's a typical mishmash of old gags, double talk, and only flashes of crusading comedy. Almost a cross between Lord Buckley and Lenny Bruce, the professor can be magnetic and charismatic in his broad burlesques, dizzy flights of fancy, and winkingly hip satire. A Bible study:

"The Hebrews were slaves in Egypt for six hundred years building pyramids. There was nothing else to do! And Moses, the only illegitimate son of Pharaoh's daughter, she told her father she found it in the bull rushes. You believe that shit? There was Moses, standing on Mt. Sinai. He says, 'Here we'll build a hospital!' And there was the burning bush ... and the burning bush said, 'Moses! Moses! Go down and set my people free....' And Moses looked at the burning bush and said, 'A bush can't talk.' Little did Moses realize it was a marijuana bush. And Moses got so high he thought he was God. And he went down into the land of Egypt and marched them through the hot burning desert for forty days and forty nights ... and what did that bastard do? He turned left! If he had turned right, we would've owned the oil fields! We would've been rich people! They say that the Jews have all the money. It's true: Morgan, Mellon, Rockefeller, DuPont, Getty, Hughes, Henry Ford, Queen Elizabeth. All these Jews got money ... it's true the Jews had money. But you Christians borrowed it and never gave it back!"

Corey issued a straight album for children, "The Metric System" (on Gateway), and also turns up on the original cast album "Flahooley" with Yma Sumac (on Capitol).

BILL COSBY

- BILL COSBY IS A VERY FUNNY FELLOW ... RIGHT! (Warner Bros. W 1518, CD reissue 1518-2) *** $8

Coming just after the first wave of sick-nik comedians, Cosby was a breath of fresh air in 1963, offering warm stories about childhood, clean and cute gags on movies and TV commercials, and Mark Twain-inspired Bible humor. He was a black comic who refused to tell racial jokes. He was a "very funny fellow," period, and in doing so, he also became an important symbol of equality.

Bill's first album is not that well recorded, but it does include his famous early routine, "Noah and the Ark," his re-creation of a dutiful, if doubting, Noah wondering why he's following God's baffling instructions. After all, "what's a cubit?" The catchphrase is his put-upon answer to God's demands: "Right!"

Also on the album are quickies, including his cute TV commercial about a pro athlete so dumb that he's amazed that "little tiny hairs" grow out of his face, and the first bit Cos ever did on *The Tonight Show*, his report on "Karate." To be good, one must practice until you get a "big slab of callus on your hand. It makes your hand look like a foot. Don't laugh. This is good. Keep your hand in your pocket for nine days, then when somebody attacks you, you take a swing at 'em and even if you miss, the smell'll kill 'em."

- I STARTED OUT AS A CHILD (Warner Bros. W 1567) ***1/2 $4 $8
- WHY IS THERE AIR? (Warner Bros. W 1567) *** $4 $8

Bill's first childhood reminiscences appear on the 1964 "Child" album as he tells short anecdotes about the day he first put on "Sneakers" and what it was like to play street football with great plays like this one: "Arnie, go down ten steps, and cut left behind the black Chevy. Philbert, you run down to my house and wait in the living room. Cosby, you go down to 3rd Street, catch the J bus, have him open the doors at 19th Street—I'll take it to ya."

Memorable quick bits include a beautifully deadpan look at why "The Neanderthal Man" eats bushes, rare sick comedy on funerals (complete with a tape-recorded voice of the corpse saying, "Don't I look like myself?"), and a look at a drunken Lone Ranger and the Wolfman at the barber shop.

"Air" has his slapstick re-creation of college football ("Kamikaze play! Cosby up the middle, the whole team off the field!") and the classic admonition: "Do not touch certain areas of your bodies ... while you're out there on the football field." With his typical Mark Twain flair for the visual, Cosby also talks about his $75 car, taking Midol to cure "The Toothache," and a trauma of childhood:

"I was playing with my navel ... my mother said, 'All right, keep playin' with your navel, pretty soon you're gonna break it wide open, the air's gonna come right out of your body, you'll fly around the room backwards for thirty seconds, land, and be flat as a piece of paper, nothin' but your little eyes buggin' out.' I used to carry Band-Aids in case I had an accident."

- WONDERFULNESS (Warner Bros. W 1634) *** $4 $8
- REVENGE (Warner Bros. WS 1691) *** $4 $8
- TO RUSSELL MY BROTHER WHOM I SLEPT WITH (Warner Bros. WS 1734) ***1/2 $4 $8
- 200 MPH (Warner Bros. WS 1757) **1/2 $5 $10
- IT'S TRUE, IT'S TRUE (Warner Bros. WS 1770) **1/2 $5 $10

"Wonderfulness" is mostly about childhood. The highlight is his re-creation of "The Chicken Heart," the radio drama that frightened him. "Revenge" marks the emergence of his "gang," as he tells about Fat Albert playing "Buck Buck," a game also known as "Johnny on the Pony." Another bit of fine storytelling covers the horror-comedy of going home over the spooky "9th Street Bridge," and the wonderful title cut, where Cosby, furious over being hit with a slushball by Junior Barnes, plots to keep a snowball in his refrigerator and ambush his nemesis in the middle of the summer.

Cosby's comedies about childhood reached a peak with the twenty-six minute title cut on 1967's "To Russell." It's loaded with brotherly recognition comedy, whether fighting over having to share the same bed ("I don't want you touchin' my body because you're not really my brother anyway ... you were brought here by the police") or uniting to battle Dad, "The Giant."

Amazing considering he was now involved in the Emmy-winning *I Spy*, Cos continued to come up with new albums. His last two for Warner reflect his changing interests. Instead of childhood, "200 MPH" has a twenty-two minute rap about sports cars. Instead of his kids, he mentions his grandfather, who taught him to smoke cigars "to keep the worms away." Cosby is never less than amusing, but he doesn't get quite as much mileage out of car sound effects and a cantankerous grandfather as he did childhood.

"It's True" shows the confident Cos moving away from set routines into more observational comedy, including a loose fourteen-minute segment of anecdotes about his visit to Japan during the making of *I Spy*. The title cut refers to his glee in discovering that Japan really does have nude bathing. This early crossover album has Cosby switching from stories from a child's point of view to more mature material for the Vegas crowd, including a mild bit on trying unsuccessfully to find "Spanish Fly" in Spain, and a description of the time he went to a burlesque show: "Why do men go into a place and watch a lady take her clothes off? That's sick. If you're hungry, you don't watch a guy cook a steak! You move away from it!"

- BILL COSBY RADIO PROGRAM (Serial Number 1568) ** $7 $15

In 1968, Cosby embarked on a short-attention kid-oriented daily radio show. Each brief show featured a few minutes of sketch material and song. Nothing here rises above the kind of comedy Cos was given for guest spots on TV variety shows of the day. Along the way, Cos offers a few Soupy Sales-type words of wisdom: "Charity begins at home. Lend me a dime, mom!" This promo album, produced by Roy Silver and narrated by Frank Buxton, offers a sampling of comedy cuts plus two complete shows.

- 8:15 12:15 (Tetragrammaton TD 5100) **1/2 $7 $15

Cosby was a part owner in the ill-fated Tetragrammaton label. His two-album set is Vegas oriented, with a lot of casually paced free form ad-libbing to the ringsiders, and humor about gambling and golf: "You got the ball. You had it right there. Then ... you hit it away! And then ... you go and walk after it again! It's a dumb game!"

There are some fine moments on the leisurely record, including his advice on never challenging "Worse." "You know who's out there? Worse. Worse is out there. Yeah, worse follows everybody ... don't ever say, 'Things couldn't get worse.' Worse is rough. He followed me over to the baccarat table. Sat down with me. And I said, 'Oh man, things can't get worse.' And he said, 'WORSE!'

"I know one time, I was down to my last two hundred dollars. I mean, not to my name, but I lost all I could sign for. And I said, 'I'm gonna win somethin'. It can't get worse!' I went over to the roulette wheel ... covered the table. I mean covered the table! Red and black ... I'm gonna win something before I go to sleep. And the guy spun the ball and it fell on the floor."

- BILL COSBY: Sports (Uni 73006, reissued as MCA 552) **1/2 $4 $8
- LIVE AT MADISON SQUARE GARDEN (Uni 73082) *** $5 $10
- WHEN I WAS A KID (Uni 73100, reissued as MCA 169) ** $4 $8

Bill's debut for Uni Records in the early '70s was in a sports-oriented album with bits on basketball, baseball, track and field, etc. It had a gatefold cover and inside pictures of Bill from his Temple University days hurling the javelin and hurtling over the high jump bar. Most of the comedy is anecdotal at best, like the time benchwarmer Cos had to give up his jersey to a player with a torn one: "It was twenty degrees below zero out there. And I sat down again, my skin stuck to the metal bench, and then I started to root for my jersey! I said, 'Go ahead, jersey, get a TD!' And my jersey scored! Then I started to root for Johnson's pants. I was afraid that was next!"

The "Madison Square Garden" album has the memorable anecdotal story about "Handball at the Y," and how Bill's grouchy irritation turns to deadpan frustration over losing to an ancient old man. There's also an embarrassing, hilarious story of Cosby's visit to Ray Charles's (lightless) room. In addition, before a child-filled audience, he offers some cute stories about animals, including one about a chicken who wonders why other animals give birth to live creatures and all she gets is an egg.

"When I Was a Kid" coasts through a six-minute routine on his childhood hernia (and Fat Albert shouting "Hey hey hey, Hey hey hey" every time Cos tries to lift something). One of his weakest routines is here, a recollection of Buck Jones movies. Cosby's memory is fine, but he's forgotten to add humor. Buck was cool: "He kept chewing gum in his pocket, and whenever he got angry, and he was getting ready to hit ya, he'd reach into his pocket and get his gum." There are brief meetings with "My Brother Russell," and some meditations on "Dogs," "Frogs," and "Snakes and Alligators," but Cos is coasting here with amiable filler.

- FOR ADULTS ONLY (Uni 73112, reissued as MCA 553) *** $5 $10
- INSIDE THE MIND OF BILL COSBY (Uni 73139, reissued as MCA 554) ** $5 $10
- FAT ALBERT (MCA 333) **1/2 $4 $8

Circa 1972, Cosby was facing a kind of crisis in his stand-up. He had used up a large well of childhood comedy and the subject was getting a bit stale, especially for adults in nightclubs. He was also now a parent with many kids running around and prone to seeing things from an adult's viewpoint.

"Adults Only" isn't smutty, but there's some slightly off-color humor here as he describes how his young girls tried to emulate him—by standing up to use the toilet. He also describes visiting a hotel where there's a "Mirror Over My Bed": "I was uneasy going to sleep. When I sleep I toss and turn and when I woke up I thought I saw a naked skydiver coming at me."

"Inside the Mind" arrived at the time of his unsuccessful variety show. The prolific comic is once more running short of material. "The Invention of Basketball" is sort of Bob Newhartian as he talks about the two men who improbably began to toss a ball into a trash can and started a new pastime. Most of the album is devoted to mild, conversational domestic comedy.

There's also a lot of conversational bits on "Fat Albert," including nine minutes on dining in Italy. Cos was beginning to develop the comfortably paced "ramble," and getting away with it. He's as good as he thinks he is; a storyteller who can almost always make people laugh even with the slimmest of anecdotes. A full side of this 1973 album is stuffed with "Fat Albert" routines. There's also a rare bit of racial humor here. Cos recalls that his brother Russell had almost pink skin when he was born: "So I took him home—and put him in the oven."

- BILL COSBY IS NOT HIMSELF THESE DAYS, RAT OWN, RAT OWN, RAT OWN
  (Capitol ST 11530) **1/2 $4 $8
- DISCO BILL (Capitol ST 11683) ** $4 $8

In 1976 and 1977, Cosby experimented with comedy in music, satirizing current trends in soul and R&B. Unlike two early Warner Bros. albums that have some humorous exaggeration but can't be classified as comedy albums (see the notes section), there's no mistaking the intent here. Bill had to try something new. He hadn't released a successful comedy album in five years, and had been without a record label for three.

The first album did very well. "Yes Yes Yes," a parody of Barry White's butterfat balladeering made the charts. He croons, "My love is so deep for you, you can't find it." Other soul stars take their lumps too, notably James Brown, during Cosby's screaming "I Luv Myself Better than I Luv Myself."

The second album is just more of the same. Some cuts have better titles than lyrics: "What Ya Think 'Bout Lickin' My Chicken" and "Boogie on Your Face." An appreciation for R&B and a knowledge of the people Cos is satirizing would help the average listener.

- MY FATHER CONFUSED ME, WHAT MUST I DO? (Capitol ST 11590) *** $8
- BILL'S BEST FRIEND (Capitol ST 11731) **1/2 $5 $10

"My Father Confused Me" is a triumphant return to form that blends stories about parents and children with more general humor, including his nine-minute "Dentist" routine. Cosby has always had a talent for memorable description and scores with a recollection of his runny-nosed daughter, whose shimmering face makes her look like "The Glazed Donut Monster." In a fine series of sketches, he describes parental clichés of violence, like, "I will knock your brains out." He moans, "That's horrible, man. She's gonna hit you in the head and your brains are gonna fall out on the floor! I always wonder what would've happened if I went to the store, got some calves' brains, and when she hit me, threw 'em on the floor ... pow! Knowin' my mother, she'd say, 'Pick those brains up and put them back in your head and don't let your brains fall out of your head again! Or I will knock you into the middle of next week!'"

The follow-up from 1978 includes the nine-minute "Roland and the Roller Coaster," which never rises too high or sails too smoothly. The boy who can turn his eyelids inside out and curse cool ("Gad dang!") isn't up to the standard set by such creations as Weird Harold or Cryin' Charlie. There are some high points, though. Cosby is still a grand storyteller as he describes his battle with "Chinese Mustard," and later the problem of wet dreams during puberty: "The first time it ever happened I got scared, man ... I looked at it, I didn't know what it was. I said, 'Oh oh, I ate too much corn bread last night.' I wasn't about to show it to my mother ... so I rolled up the sheets and went down to the laundromat, did my own sheets, man. Five o'clock in the morning, nine twelve-year olds down there doin' their sheets too, man. After that day I'd get out of school ... I'd be back in bed again ... yes indeed, three glasses of water and a picture of Dorothy Dandridge and I was on my way!"

Cos developed his pontificating professor role around this time, offering cautionary tales on "Illegal Drugs" and "People Who Drink" with just enough good nature to prevent doubters from tuning out.

- BILL COSBY HIMSELF (Motown ML 6026) *** $8
- BILL COSBY/HARDHEADED BOYS (Nicetown NT 1001) ** $6 $12

Cosby was not that visible after his 1976 series bombed. When "performance" movies became successful, notably Richard Pryor's stand-up films, Cosby got his chance to jump back into the limelight. Some of the material here is duplicated from his first Capitol album. Cos talks about "The Dentist" again, but covers some new ground, demonstrating his vocal dexterity as he protrays various dental tools and drills, and does a hilarious dribbling effect pretending to have novacained lips. He also has a few parental words on drugs: "What is it about cocaine that makes it so wonderful?" "Well, it intensifies your personality." "Yes, but what if you're an asshole?"

He has a new fount of household humor from kids answering everything with "I don't know," to fights over taking a shower or having chocolate cake for breakfast. Fatherly Cos realizes, "Parents are not interested in justice—they want quiet."

In 1985 a Philadelphia record company discovered the documentary Cosby filmed at Graterford Prison in 1972. It was a look at prison life complete with interviews with convicts, and Cosby did some stand-up for the prisoners as well. These eighteen minutes are clipped out. The rest of the record is taken up by a rap group called Double Force singing tunes about ghetto life, and "Hardheaded Boys."

The liner notes call Cosby's performance "candid, humorous and real." It's not particularly humorous, filled with casual observations one might expect him to make on *The Phil Donahue Show*. He tells the cons, "No matter how big you get, you still have to answer to somebody." The question and answer segments are not too different from talk show material. The cons ask him to name his favorite fighters (Muhammad Ali is "a funny cat" but the greatest is Ray Robinson) and his favorite friends (Cos names Henry Silva and Clarence Williams III).

- THOSE OF YOU WITH OR WITHOUT CHILDREN, YOU'LL UNDERSTAND
  (Geffen GHS 24104) *** $4 $8
- OH BABY (Geffen GEFD 24428) **1/2 $8

Cos is "the old professor" on these post-*Cosby Show* albums, delivering carefully worded and paced lectures on parenting, the Bible, and anything else that William H. Cosby Jr., Ph.D. cares to pontificate about. The first album's highlight is his religious discussion: "Man invented an automobile. Called it fantastic. God did a tree—said it was *good*. The wheels fell off the car ... the tree's still up: Good." After discussing Adam and Eve, he grumbles that "be fruitful and multiply—was a punishment ... each time you multiply you get a fruit. With brain damage!'"

Cosby talks about his kids, but now they're in their teens. He recalls giving condoms to his son: "I said, 'See these, son? The next time you go out on a date, I want you to put one of those on. As a matter of fact, before you leave this house ... I want you to put it on. As a matter of fact, before you go out that door I want to see it on!'"

The 1991 "Oh Baby" is fifty minutes of anecdotal storytelling. It's divided into two parts. The long routine on skiing should certainly amuse ski buffs. The other long routine, "Oh Baby," amiably meanders through a set of marriage anecdotes. Very few stand-up comedians have lasted more than thirty years; fewer have remained in the spotlight so consistently, producing great original material.

- BEST OF BILL COSBY (Warner Bros. 1798) *** $4 $8
- MORE OF THE BEST (Warner Bros. WS 1836) **1/2 $4 $8
- BILL (MCA 8005) *** $6 $12
- BILL COSBY AT HIS BEST (MCA MCAD 20676) *** $8

- COSBY KIDS/COSBY CLASSICS (Warner Bros. 254971) *** $5 $12

Trivia fans will recognize David (Firesign Theater) Ossman's name on the "Best of" album notes. Ossman was on the Warner staff at the time. He sets the scene "It's a millennium ago ... Psychedelics haven't been invented yet" to point up how similar Cosby's storytelling is to "The Storyteller," who told his tales before the fire in the cave while "the shadowy tree-people" watched from outside. The point? "Cosby is one of the few real Storytellers of our time."

"Best of" contains some classics: "Noah and the Ark," "Revenge," "Lone Ranger," "Old Weird Harold/9th Street Bridge," "Driving in San Francisco," "Street Football," "Buck Buck." "Best of Bill Cosby Volume Two" has weaker material pulled with little thought or purpose from various early albums: "Toss of the Coin," "Conflict," "Dogs and Cats," "Smoking," "Shop," and the only two legit bests, "Karate" and "Hofstra."

When Cosby's new series became a hit, Warners went back to create a slightly more cohesive "Greatest Hits" package, and called it "Cosby Classics/Cosby Kids." The "Kids" side has the basics. The "Classics" side has "Noah," "Karate," "Driving in San Francisco," "Rigor Mortis," "Chicken Heart," and many more, but misses "Hofstra."

MCA put together a double album called "Bill" and it is uneven, with some of his best ("Handball at the Y") and least ("Buck Jones"). MCA's single CD called "Bill Cosby at His Best," isn't even close, though it has a few short sports tracks and cuts from "Adults Only," as well as "Grover Henson Feels Forgotten."

NOTES: Cosby is on several children's albums, notably "Creativity, Starring Fat Albert" (Kid Stuff KS 021), "Fat Albert's Halloween" (Kid Stuff KS 029), and "Fat Albert Rock 'n' Roll Disco" (Kid Stuff KSS 094).

Cosby released many serious albums of jazz, soul, and pop music, beginning with "Silver Throat Sings" (Warner Bros. 1709). "Little Ole Man" ("Uptight/Outta Sight") was a hit single from that one, rising to #6 in the charts. "Hooray for the Salvation Army Band" (Warner Bros. 1728) is slightly more humorous, with Cos's comically strained renditions of "I Can't Get No Satisfaction" and "Hold On, I'm Comin'," but it's still a funky "straight" album. Cosby released two albums circa 1970 with identical titles: "Bill Cosby Presents Badfoot Brown and the Bunions Bradford Funeral and Marching Band." The first, for Uni (73080) offers two long jazz instrumentals, one on each side. The second has an instrumental ballad ("I Love You Camille") along with some instrumentals and a few tunes sung by Stu Gardner. "At Last Bill Cosby Really Sings" (Partee PBS 2405) offers Bill in a comfortable baritone really trying to bring home the R&B. Cosby issued several jazz CDs in the late '80s, supervising the performing musicians: "Where You Lay Your Head" (Verve 8419301), "My Appreciation" (Verve 847812) and two volumes of "Music from the Bill Cosby Show" (Columbia CK 40270, CK 40704).

Motown's Black Forum label (B-455L) released "The Congressional Black Caucus," one side featuring a speech Cosby gave on June 18, 1971. He also issued a "Guide to Growing Up" (Silveto SPR 101). Cosby appears on "Diana" (Motown MS 719), the soundtrack to a Diana Ross special costarring The Jackson Five and Danny Thomas. He and Diana sing "Love Story" by Randy Newman, and neither sound like professional singers. The best line is at the beginning when Bill talks about his old neighborhood: "Did you ever play stickball in Detroit?" Ross answers, "Well, I did get to play once, but that was only because the fellas needed a stick." Cosby is also on "Going Back to Indiana" (Motown M 742 L), a Jackson Five soundtrack album.

A cassette tape called "After Hours" was released by CSL Ltd. in 1987 (serial number CC 1001). It was recorded live at Lake Tahoe and features some general audience bantering: "What did you have for dinner? What are you looking at him, for? Weren't you there when you were eating? A what? A vodka seven? No vegetables?" It's a brief tape and the editing is abrupt.

COUNT FLOYD

- COUNT FLOYD (RCA Victor MFL1-8501) * $7 $15

Count Floyd (Joe Flaherty) was a vampire character on the comedy show *SCTV*, and this 1982 four-cut mini album is strictly for Floyd fans. For the uninitiated, Uncle Floyd sounds like a cross between Sesame Street's silly Count and Billy Crystal's annoying "Fernando" character.

As a horror show emcee, he tells boring stories ("The Gory Story of Duane and Debbie"), assuring the kids that there's going to be "some really scary stuff" any minute. It's not much of a joke for a one-joke premise. The songs are worse. "Treat You Like a Lady" has The Count as a disco star. While the thudding music plays and a chorus warbles "Treat You Like a Lady," Count Floyd rambles out corny narration.

With self-satisfied ad-libs instead of well-constructed jokes, a tediously uninteresting character, and a set of quickly assembled songs, this record should have a stake through it to keep it off anyone's turntable.

COUSIN BUBBA

- RHINESTONE PLOWBOY (MCA 42179) ** $4 $8

Pinkard and Bowden produced the 1988 debut of country comic Cousin Bubba. He has a slightly abrasive, lecturing style, but the crowd gives him an occasional whoop and "whoaa!" when he gets off a good 'un:

"Y'all make things so complicated in the city. You use three words here we never heard of up the country. There's the word condo, and condiment, and condom. Now for goodness sake, why cancha all say apartments, rubbers, and mustard and relish. I mean to tell ya all, I plumb embarrassed myself at McDonald's the other night. They had a sign that says "Condiments on Request." I asked for a dozen! I mean, I thought it was unusual: MacRubbers? And then the very next day, a feller asked me if I wanted to share a condo with him. I said not on your life."

COYLE AND SHARPE

- ABSURD IMPOSTERS (Warner 1494) *** $10 $20

- INSANE BUT HILARIOUS (Warner Bros 1573) ** $10 $20

In San Francisco, Jim Coyle and Mal Sharpe were men in the street conducting "candid microphone" put-ons with average citizens. "Absurd Imposters" from 1963 is loaded with memorable bits. Sort of Allen Funt crossed with Bob and Ray, the men are into practical jokes that are also studies in human nature. They confront a florist with the idea of "floral humanism," trying to find a way of making flowers bloom inside their bodies. They try to talk a man into jumping off a building just for the thrill of it, and here, try to convince a clerk to sell half-eaten apples in his store:

"They've been bitten into. People have eaten, in some cases half the apple...." "If you saw a half an apple with teeth marks in it, would you buy it?" the store owner asks. "If you could get it cheaper? Yes! Be honest, wouldn't you buy it?" "No!"

"We're American Picnic Supply, we set up picnics for people, we collect what they don't eat, we sell it over ... you pick up a half-eaten apple, it's a proven apple. Somebody's eaten it ... somebody's started on, didn't finish. You know it's been selected. Hasn't somebody ever bitten into an apple and handed it to you?"

"Yes—if I know the person, I wouldn't mind."

"Better if you don't know the person! It's a question of curiosity. What other human being bit into this? Some man, some woman I'll never meet. Some animal ..."

The second album is more of the same, with reports on pack rats in an art gallery, putting fungus on an infant, and the notion of "Eating People at a Death Ritual." The very proper Englishman they've targeted announces, "I think you're trying to make me sick, actually!" They answer, "You kill insects." He replies, "Flies and things like that, surely." "Size excuses you morally," they charge. "Have you ever killed a person? You'd enjoy killing a person!" "Don't talk rubbish ... you're trying to impress me, you're trying to frighten me."

They aren't trying for big laughs, that's for sure, but they'll raise a wan smile or a disbelieving chuckle.

Some noncandid microphone routines on the album don't work as well—some silly studio sketches and a live cut where the duo pretend to be Slavic folk singers as they come onstage during a folk festival at the University of California.

Coyle died in Europe in the mid '80s. Mal Sharpe pursued the "man in the street" concept on solo albums in the '80s.

- ON THE LOOSE (213 CD CD 0005) ** $8

Though the duo's first album sold under 13,000 copies thirty years ago, here's a 1996 CD collecting moments from Coyle and Sharpe's old radio show. Sharpe's twentysomething daughter says in the liner notes that she "vaguely" remembered this stuff, "was never" a fan, and that the reissue idea was the producer's, not hers. At least she documents the duo's short-lived history, even with the ridiculous, obligatory spin-doctoring to make them relevent to the '90s: "these interviews inadvertently reveal America in the early '60s on its way to major change." Sadly, the duo that sometimes sounded like a combo of Reiner & Freberg isn't in great form here. Coyle is especially dour in exposing the gullibility of average citizens who dumbly believe him when he says he's a real werewolf, a man who plays small animals with a violin bow, an advocate of living with rats, etc., etc. Very few of these concepts have the edge and zany spirit of the original album.

CRANDALL AND CHARLES

- DON'T KNOCK IT (Beacon 309) * $5 $10

Here's a tuxedo-clad duo from the early '60s who actually open a show singing "Put down your glasses and give us a smile. Smile, smile, smile! Or drink it up fast, it burns a hole in your glass. Smile, smile, smile!" This evidently amused patrons at The Monkey Bar in New York's Hotel Elysee, The Park Lane Hotel in Denver, and The Kings Club in Dallas. Straight man Dick Crandall and Frank Charles are full of snappy patter: "They just closed the Playboy Club down." "The lesbians ate all the bunnies! There's not a hare in the joint!" "Wait a minute, Frank, I think I should sing something serious." "Why don't you sing something from Rigoletto?" "OK. La donna mobile ..." "Have you had yours today? We had ours yesterday, that's why we walk this way!"

BOB CRANE See BUTTRAM AND CRANE

GEORGE CRATER

- OUT OF MY HEAD (Riverside 841) ** $7 $18

Ed Sherman called himself George Crater. It was a semi-hip allusion to Judge Crater, whose disappearance was a great unsolved mystery at the time. They still haven't found him, but nobody's out there looking. A writer for *Downbeat*, on this early '60s studio recording he reads some of his material in a voice that sounds a bit like Lenny Bruce awakened from a sound sleep.

Crater's best bit describes wind-up dolls he has invented. They're all on jazz musicians: "This Miles Davis wind-up doll ... wears a fine Italian silk suit, but you'll never find out who the tailor was. He never tells. It's got beautiful Italian shoes on, and it carries a beautiful shiny trumpet. Dig? You wind up this doll and you put it on the table, and it turns its back on you." Other routines are similarly keyed to hard jazz fans. He talks about jazz critics, jazz night clubs, even jazz on television: "Like, if they have Louis Armstrong on television, the director is yelling, 'Get a tight close-up of that bead of perspiration on his brow ...' Every time Louis Armstrong comes on, that's it. Ed Sullivan should say, 'Next week, Louis Armstrong will sweat for you.' That's all he does, man. He gets out there with his handkerchief and they take tight close-ups of beads of perspiration. It's a drag."

After a few minutes, Crater's droning delivery and New Yawk accent begin to drag. It's sort of like listening to a jazz DJ talking to himself late at night. The "Wind-up Dolls" cut turns up on "How to Be Terribly, Terribly Funny," a Riverside compilation album.

THE CREDIBILITY GAP

- ALBUM OF POLITICAL PORNOGRAPHY (Blue Thumb BT 2) *1/2 $7 $20
- WOODSHTICK (Capitol ST 681) **1/2 $6 $15

The Gap came together in the same manner as Firesign Theater—as a Los Angeles radio team. They had their own show on KRLA in 1968. Their first LP for Blue Thumb was based on their show and featured the early Gap lineup of Richard Beebe, Lee Irwin, Thom Beck, John Gilliland, and singer Len Chandler. It's more a documentary than a comedy album—a collage of speeches by Bobby Kennedy, Lyndon Johnson and others with vintage 1968 hippie-Indian music, serious folk songs, and grim sketches with leaden ironic commentary. An asteroid named Icarus is coming toward earth. A reporter interviews a hippie about it:

"Here we are in the mile-high city, Boulder, Colorado, where cars, containing groups of Hippies, presumably loaded with STP, have been winding their way up the slopes of Sugarloaf Mountain in order to escape the possible influences of the asteroid Icarus ... Hello there." "Hi." "And how are you today?" "High ... I'm so high my beads are popping." "How do you feel about all this?" "Drugged ... (hippies singing) Who's afraid of the end of the world, end of the world, end of the world ... (bomb explodes)."

The new lineup of Richard Beebe, Harry Shearer, and David L. Lander are on the 1971 "Woodshtick." The title track is a twenty-minute satire imagining what would happen if "Woodstock" was a convention of schtick comedians instead of rock stars. It's somewhat of an inside joke to all but comedy fans: "You're the gentleman who was conducting the workshop on pratfalls in The Savoy Room?" "Yes I was, but it fell through." The album got some nasty reviews over a bit about Ted Kennedy at Chappaquiddick. It's a fake movie soundtrack that re-enacts a party, "Mary Lou" asking for a ride, and the subsequent drive home: "Look out, Mary Lou, if I recall the map correctly, there's a bad turn up ahead."

A stern announcer cuts in: "Suddenly everything went wet. What followed was a nightmare that was not as it turned out to be believed. Hemingway once defined courage as grace under pressure. But this wasn't grace under pressure, it was Mary Lou underwater. Without thinking for a moment of his own personal safety, Senator Kennedy panicked."

Kennedy actually saves Mary Lou, but she drowns going back to save the car.

The Gap LP was banned from many radio stations.

- A GREAT GIFT IDEA (Warner Bros. MS 2154, $7 $15
    reissued as Sierra 8704 with extra LP "Floats") ***1/2 $10 $20
- BRONZE AGE OF RADIO (Waterhouse 1) *** $7 $15

In 1973, the Gap (Michael McKean joining Beebe, Shearer, and Lander) made a brilliant album that should have vaulted them to the top. "Great Gift Idea" has some elements of Firesign Theater in the re-creation of radio and TV scenes using sound effects and vocal wizardry, but instead of Firesign's drifting amiable idiocy and acid casualty confusion, The Gap are disciplined enough to present strongly scripted vignettes that don't abuse the listener by trading spacey ad-libbing for well-written jokes.

"A Date with Danger," complete with a deliberately faulty 16mm projector soundtrack, is the ultimate in cautionary hygiene films. "In Someone's Sneakers" offers a fine lampoon of Rod McKuen. "16 Golden Bits" satirizes blaring K-Tel record album commercials with quick, telling impressions of Shelley Berman ("Oh? Really!"), Mort Sahl ("Right?"), Nichols and May ("You're sick" "I know"), and others. For comedy fans, the recognition humor makes it a classic.

"Where's Johnny" is a realistic copy of *The Tonight Show*, complete with rim shots, shouts of "Hi yooooo!" and shifting sound levels as Johnny suddenly talks with the off-mike Doc Severinsen. In 1973 Carson's brand of establishment comedy was a ripe target for a new generation, and he's skewered here for easy ad-libbing, funny animal segments, hokey guests, and running gags about The Fakawi Indians.

The quartet managed a single "The Night the Lights Stayed on In Pittsburgh" (on the "Rhino Royale" compilation album), but after that one shot in 1977, that was it.

In 1977, Waterhouse, a small Minneapolis company, issued an album of material from the Gap's radio days. It's a mixed bag, including some outrages like a series of ethnic radio spots.

The album's highlight is "Who's on First," an update on the Abbott and Costello routine. A rock promoter is trying to book a concert featuring The Who, The Guess Who, and Yes. And you can guess what happens. But The Gap perform it very well.

Michael McKean and David L. Lander went on to play Lenny and Squiggy on *Laverne and Shirley*. In 1979, Sierra/Briar Records, a small Pasadena label, reissued "Gift Idea" with "Floats," basically a collage of old radio material from their "Rose Bowl Parade" ad-libbed commentary on KMET-FM.

It's a one-joke album as the Gap do a sadly accurate job of imitating vapid parade announcers. There's plenty of straight-faced put-ons here: "Look at Canada ... that's a float done entirely in tundra ... oh my goodness, here come the mounted police, they've been mounted by some avid police collectors who did this with great care ... I understand the chloroform doesn't hurt at all ... the world's sleepiest police force, ladies and gentlemen! Oh, they get a big hand, everybody likes these people because nobody's ever been beaten up by these people. It's true. I have been in Montreal and you're not afraid of these people. They're good to their huskies ... but they get a big hand, oh don't they? Let's listen to that hand."

CREPITATION CONTESTANTS See WINDERSPHERE AND BOOMER

BARRY CRIMMINS

- KILL THE MESSENGER (Green Linnet GLCD 7001) ** $8

Following a promising appearance on the A&M sampler album of political comedy, "Strange Bedfellows," Crimmins turned up with this 1991 hour. His delivery is literate if bland, which means the lines must be especially sharp to sustain interest. They aren't. A liberal preaching to the already converted, he gets knowing chuckles from the elbow patch crowd as his sarcasms: "Reagan says he's gonna be very active during his retirement. Ya gotta presume that's 'cause he had so much rest during the previous *eight* years. He got sick. We were concerned. They said he had water on the brain. I said, ok, I believe the *water* part."

As for the album title, it's rather presumptuous of the virtually unknown Crimmins to consider himself such a dangerous satirist that he, "the messenger" has such deadly enemies. Some of his complaints have a familiar feel. This one sounds like Will Rogers already chewed on it: "We have a great democratic process in our country, don't we? These elections all the time. Probably the big problem with most of our elections is somebody always wins the damn thing."

NORM CROSBY

- THE FUNNY WORLD OF NORM CROSBY: SHE WOULDN'T EAT THE MUSHROOMS
  (Epic FLS 15106/FLM 13106) *** $7 $15
- NORM CROSBY LIVE FROM LAS VEGAS (Natural Light 92079) *** $10 $20

Malaprop comedian Crosby offers easygoing laughs on "Mushrooms." He reports on great men like "Sigmund Frood, who went into a lavatory and friggered out all for himself, on the sperm of the moment, that there was equalness between people." His album may not earn a "standing ovulation" from "masculine men and fennemen ladies" but he does "establish a rappaport" with his harmless antics.

Crosby isn't all malaprop humor. He has some words on the real meaning of love:

"Teenagers don't know what love is. They have mixed up ideas. They go for a drive, and the boy runs out of gas, and they smooch a little, and the girl says she loves him. That isn't love. Love is when you're married twenty-five years, smooching in your living room, and he runs out of gas and she still says she loves him! That's love!"

Crosby's promo album for Natural Light is hard to find. It features Crosby on the cover, and bottles and cans of beer on the back. It's another solid set of gentle observational humor and malaprops: "I live in L.A. We voted last year between Proposition 13 and Preparation H. They're very similar, you know. They both give temporary relief—from a pain in the ass!" As for working in Vegas with showgirls: "See how they walk around out there, did you notice when you came in, with the low cleevicles and the pasties stickin' out for God's sake. It's disgusting, grown up women with fringe on their benefits walking up and down? In a pubic place? It's disgusting. And yet you can sit here and medicate and discuss things intelligently without fear of contraception." Too much of this would be wearying, but Crosby's easy, conversational style blends malaprops, jokes, and observations into a friendly, seamless mono- logue. Underrated Norm is the only one who's been able to do it for over thirty years.

MIKE CROSS

- BEST OF THE FUNNY STUFF (Sugar Hill SH CD 1010) * $8

Cross's CD compiles songs from several previous albums, including "The Bounty Hunter," "Child Prodigy," "Born in the Country," "Rock 'n' Rye," and "Irregular Guy." Evidently those albums only had a few funny cuts each. The same could be said for this compilation. Tom Paxton, Dr. Hook, Arlo Guthrie, Harry Chapin, Oscar Brand, and any number of pickin' and singin' performers have been funnier without even trying. Cross's delivery is at the bland, tongue-in-cheek level of Paxton or Brand. Desperate fans of folkie humor might giggle now and then at "The Great Strip Poker Massacre" ("the only one left with clothes on was her") or "Elma Turl." It seems that every time Mike meets a girl, including the one named in the title, his father comes by to caution, "Son, she's my daughter." The predictable twist ending? Mike discovers from his mom: "Your daddy ain't your daddy though he thinks he is. So you can marry whoever you want to."

SCATMAN CROTHERS

- COMEDY SWEEPSTAKES (Dooto DTL 814) ** $8 $20

Scatman was a popular scat singer in the late '40s and ultimately a comic supporting actor in films. He was a bit down on his luck in 1961 when he made this album (badly recorded with a lot of echo due to microphone misplace- ment). Crothers doesn't get too earthy for the adult-oriented Dooto label: "Here's a word to you mothers. Do you have any teenage daughters? If you do, take them off to the side and talk to them. And I guarantee you'll learn plenty! As the twelve-year-old girl said: 'To bra, or not to bra, that is the question!' And speaking of bras, we have the new brassiere, the Russian brassiere. It uplifts the mass. Then we have the Salvation Army brassiere. It raises the fallen. And then we have that new honeymoon brassiere: Niagara Falsies. The bust that money can buy!"

Crothers had a warm personality, a perpetual smile and a lot of charm, but it has trouble coming through when he has to recite corny material. He issued several early '60s music albums including "Gone with the Scat Man" (Craftsmen 8036), "Scat Man Crothers and Joe Williams" (Grand Prix 419), "Four A.M." (20th Century Fox 1009), and "Rock 'n' Roll with Scatman" (Tops 1511). Two cuts from it were included on Tops's "Music for a Mad Ball," a "tribute" to the film *Operation Mad Ball*.

CROWN CITY FOUR

- SING A SONG OF SICKNESS (Pip PLP 1901) * $7 $15

This is a failed attempt to cash in on the kind of material Tom Lehrer was noted for. The bland barbershop quartet can't do much with the weak lyrics from Disney songwriter Richard M. Sherman and the old-time music supplied by Milt Larsen. Songs include "Watch World War III on My Pay TV," "Leave the Slums Alone," and "The Annual Get-Together of the KKK and NAACP." From the latter:

"Once a year they have a celebration. Down below the Mason-Dixon line. All the friendly neighbors join the jubilee. Sharin' in that Southern hospitality. Soon they're harmonizing to a Dixie band, dancin' and romancin' hand in hand. At the annual get-together of the KKK and NAACP! Banjos are a singin' all around you. Stephen Foster songs are ringin' clear ... This friendly little party is restricted, too. You'll never see a Catholic, Jap, or Jew. At the annual get-together of the KKK and the NAACP!"

Several of the songs here were used to pad out an album called "Smash Flops" by The Characters.

BILLY CRYSTAL

- MAHVELOUS! (A&M SP 5096) ** $5 $10

Crystal's even more a "Child of the '50s" than Robert Klein; in stand-up he never grew up and he remained fascinated with the era's movies and stars. Usually there's schmaltzy respect for his comic targets, like Sammy Davis Jr. and Fernando Lamas, who were regularly impersonated by him on *Saturday Night Live*. It was during his relatively brief tenure on the show that "Mahvelous" came out. He overuses the Lamas catchphrase "You Look Marvelous" in a bludgeoning disco tune, and goes back to Fernando periodically throughout the album. Another example of inane excess is "I Hate When that Happens," with Billy and Christopher Guest as two cretins: "I had nuttin' to do so I grab one of those ..." "Meat thermometers?" "Yeah, and I shoved it into my ear ... well, it only went in about three inches so I took one of those ..." "Ball peen hammers?" "Right, and gave it a few extra whacks. Boy, was that painful ... I hate when that happens. Ooooh, owww, I hate when I do that."

Mostly there's stand-up, but it's rooted in the '50s and his childlike fascination with movies, show biz, and old people who talk too Jewish and flatulate too often. He's not above going beyond sappy warm anecdotes to Whoopi Goldberg pathos as he impersonates various characters. He also does a bit as rambling hack comic Buddy Young Jr., intriguing but of limited appeal to non-comedy fans (as was demonstrated when Crystal insisted on making an entire movie about him).

Crystal is also on various "Comic Relief" compilations.

DON CULLEN, STAN JACOBSON & GARRY FERRIER

- THE DISTINGUISHED DELEGATE (Philips PHS 600-254) * $4 $8

A bunch of Canadian revue performers and writers knocked off this LP after Israel's quick victory in the Middle East in 1967. Sketches dwell on the role played by the United Nations Security Council, but centers on Israel for gags that are feeble and vaguely anti-Semitic.

An Israeli delegate, with a stereotypcical accent and lust for money, announces that "the four days of war was a terrible drain on our already hard-pressed economy. It cost us a fortune!" He continues to dwell on money woes, declaring at the punch line, "what I want to know is who's gonna pay? Ya owe, ya gotta pay!" Several other sketches drag on for a minute or two for a similar pay-off—a cheap laugh over Jewish pronunciation ("sanna-wiches!") or culture ("I've been informed these missiles are ... stale bagels!").

DICK CURTIS

- LIVE AT THE HORN (Laff 126) *1/2 $4 $8

Curtis, perhaps best known as an aggressive quiz show host on a 1964 *Dick Van Dyke Show* episode, aged into an adequate comic who could amuse an audience with racy material or anecdotes about his Indiana childhood and the Hoosier characters he used to know. He didn't belong on Laff, since very little of the album is ethnic filth. One mildly risqué down-home recollection centers on his old Uncle Charlie:

"Seventy-eight years old. I said, 'Uncle Charlie, I'm going to the drug store, can I pick you up something?' (Old old voice) 'Yeah. Yeah. Yeah. Gimme some of that stuff they used to give the soldiers in the coffee.' Seventy-eight years old! I said, 'Uncle Charles, for heaven's sake, they used to give that stuff to soldiers to kinda keep 'em from chasing after girls.' 'Well, I didn't want a lot of it. In fact all I wanted was a little pinch to snuff up my nose, kinda get the ideas outta my head.'"

BILL DANA

- MY NAME JOSE JIMENEZ (Signature SM 1013, reissued by Roulette, 25161) *** $5 $10
- JOSE JIMENEZ THE ASTRONAUT (Kapp K 1238, also released as
    JOSE JIMENEZ AT THE HUNGRY i, Kapp K 1238/KS 3238) *** $5 $10

Dana worked for Steve Allen as a writer in 1956. "Amused by his parlor-entertainment impression of a Latin-American character," Allen recalled, "I decided to have him do the voice on camera." The Jose Jimenez character was a shy, bewildered little fellow with a Hispanic accent and a catchphrase: the ingratiatingly modest, "My name ... Jose Jimenez." Though after the '60s there would be some controversy over this "stereotyped" character, the bits Dana used usually had little to do with ethnic comedy.

Steve Allen and Pat Harrington, Jr. are the straight men for Side One's clips from TV shows. The second side is prepared questions and answers at a Jose press conference. Among the questioners is Jo Anne Worley, asking: "What do you think of filter tips?" "I don't need a tip to know what kind of filter to buy. But a garbage disposal ... you got any garbage disposal tips?" This is the rarest of the Jose albums, not the funniest.

After his TV success, Dana came to nightclubs. The Kapp LP documents his first shows at The Hungry i in November, 1960. It has Dana's most famous bit, Jose the Astronaut. Straight man Don Hinkley, who cowrote this and other Jose routines, asks the questions:

"Mr. Jimenez, could you tell us a little about your space suit?" "It's very uncomfortable." "What is this called, a crash helmet?" "Oh I hope not...." "Mr. Jimenez, you must have some opinions on the race for space." "All right, I will...." "It's a very long trip into outer space ... what will you do on those long, lonely, solitary hours when you're all by yourself?" "Well ... I plan to cry a lot."

The bit became a favorite at Cape Canaveral, and when Commander Alan Shepard played it, it made news. "The Astronaut" routine became a hit single, hitting the Top 20 on Billboard's charts in September of 1961.

On Side Two Dana tries to establish his own identity as a stand-up comic, doing experimental humor on some unlikely topics. He reads a list of bizarre names, getting laughs just from the sounds. Later he asks the crowd to imagine unlikely-sounding words: "If the verb 'to love' was 'to gronge' ... and you said, 'My darling! I gronge you ... I'll gronge you to the day I die.'" Mild but different.

• JOSE JIMENEZ THE SUBMARINE OFFICER (Kapp KL 1215, also released as MORE JOSE JIMENEZ, Kapp KL 1215) ***	$5	$10
• JOSE JIMENEZ IN ORBIT (Kapp KL 1257) ***	$5	$10
• JOSE JIMENEZ TALKS TO TEENAGERS (Kapp KL 1304) **1/2	$5	$10
• OUR SECRET WEAPON (Kapp KL 1320) **1/2	$5	$10
• JOSE JIMENEZ IN JOLLYWOOD (Kapp KL 1332/KS 3332) **1/2	$5	$10
• BILL DANA IN LAS VEGAS (Kapp KL 1402) ***	$5	$10

1960's "Submarine Officer" takes routines directly from appearances on *The Steve Allen Show* and *The Spike Jones Show*, with Steve and Spike acting as straight man for Jose "The Judo Expert," "The Broadway Writer," and here, "The Submarine Officer":

"How come you stayed under water for eighty-four days?" "I didn't want to come up before the submarine...." "Tell me, did you begin to hate your friends during that time?" "One time. During the third riot." This is one of the best Jose Jimenez albums, with a variety of amusing, well-written "formula" sketches of questions and subtle but snappy answers.

When Virgil Grissom was up in space, Alan Shepard radioed a few words of encouragement: "Jose, don't cry too much!" "Orbit," the inevitable sequel to "Jose the Astronaut," is gag-filled and cute, with Dana once more playing a frightened spaceman who can't be calmed down:

"There's always the emergency escape button." "It doesn't work." "How do you know?" "'Cause I pushed it already." "When?" "On the launching pad!"

There's Jose the skin diver, rancher, and lion tamer, along with one cut that finds humor solely in Hispanic pronunciation, a song where Jose sings "Jingle Bells." The album jacket offers his lyrics: "Hingle bell, hingle bell, hingle all daht way, oh gwat fun ediss to rye in daht one orse open eslay."

"Our Secret Weapon" has the familiar formula with Jose the Coast Guardsman, paratrooper, Marine drill instructor, etc. He even works in the K-9 corps: "My name Jose Jimenez. But you can call me Spot." "I think I'll call you Jose." "OK, but I may not come...." "What is the first thing you train (a dog) to do?" "Go on the paper."

For the concept album "Talks to Teenagers," Don Hinkley consults Jose about various school and teen problems: "What do you think about teenage clothing?" "When it gets to be that age, you should throw it out." "Today's teenager is an explosive person, capable of extreme violence. Would you care to comment on that?" "What? And get killed?"

But by the time Dana released "Jose Jimenez in Jollywood," he seemed to realize that it was time to move toward more adult humor and more satire. This look at Hollywood has little to do with Jose's race or accent. Jose the Hollywood Shrink is being interviewed, and he knows all the answers:

"Good Evening—" "When you say good evening, you really want to say good-bye, because you didn't want to meet me in the first place." "Good-bye?" "There. You said it. Don't you feel better?" "Frankly no." "Well, you can't expect results right away, see my receptionist for another appointment."

This was a brave experiment; attempting a smarter type of comedy with an essentially innocent character.

1964's "In Las Vegas" was almost a "Best of," condensing some of Dana's finest routines. Andrew Duncan plays straight man to Jose the Astronaut, Spy, Judo Instructor, Skin Diver, Lion Tamer, Santa Claus Instructor, Politician, etc. The flip side is Bill Dana once again trying to go it "alone," doing a one-man character sketch about gay designer Cowboy Brucie and later interviewing himself for a "man in the street" segment on smokers:

"You quit smoking?" "Yes, and I was very, very disappointed." "Why was that?" "I found out my teeth were really brown."

Dana had issued quite a number of albums in only a few years, and had his own TV show. The Jose craze was, for the moment, over. The beloved character would be the subject of several "comebacks" in the upcoming decades.

• HOO HAH! DIRECT FROM NASHVILLE (Capitol St 464) ***	$8	$12
• JOSE SUPERSPORT (Puente P-1) ***	$5	$15
• THE BEST OF JOSE JIMENEZ (GNP-Crescendo 7001) ***	$4	$10
• JOSE CAN YOU SEE (Rhino R2 70749) ***		$9

With the success of TV's *Hee Haw*, Dana saw a chance to replace his Jose image with something closer to his roots. The Jewish parody "Hoo Hah" offered quickie, corny sketches and support from Don Knotts, Joanie Gerber, Bernie Kopell, Buck Owens, and the team of Charlie Brill and Mitzi McCall. A dialect quickie:

"Did you heard about the big airline merger? They're going to merge Varrick, El-Al and Alitalia into one big airline." "What are they gonna call it?" "Vel, Altalia!" Even quicker:

"Say Roy, why does a fireman wear red suspenders?" "How should I know, I'm in millinary!"

"Supersport" was more of a promo item than a comeback attempt, with Dana experimenting, decades later, with a less stereotypical Jose. With Gregory Sierra (best remembered as Chano on *Barney Miller*) as straight man, Jose the "King of the Surf" explains how to handle a shark attack, offering similar advice what he gave years ago as Jose "The Lion Tamer." He insists:

"If a shark comes near you, you've got to lie perfectly still. You cannot move even a little tiny muscle." "Isn't that hard to do?" "Not when you've fainted."

The formula jokes get a workout as Jose discusses bullfighting with another straight man, Fernando Escandon: "Would you believe it, the largest bull I ever faced weighed 17,412 pounds." "That's a lot of bull." "I thought you wouldn't believe it."

Some of Jose's better material is on the GNP-Crescendo disc, such as "Jose the Submarine Officer" and "The Broadway Writer" with Steve Allen, "The TV Engineer" with Pat Harrington, and "The Shakespearian Actor" with Don Hinkley. There are several cuts from the obscure "Jose Supersport" album, including "King of the Surf" with Gregory Sierra and "Jose the Bullfighter" with Fernando Escandon.

In 1991 Rhino issued a nearly seventy-minute CD subtitled "The Best of Jose Jimenez Yesterday and Today." It offers most of the familiar old Jose routines, but does dig up a rarity, the 1965 A&M single "Make Nice." It's pretty cloying (Jose and a children's chorus telling the world "Make nice, make nice, be good, be good, don't fight, don't fight"), but fans will want to hear it at least once.

Dana went into the studio to record some fresh material, mostly mild songs like "My Phony Valentine Blues." Jose is the rocking blues singer who declares: "They said you lied like a rug, so I know what to do. Since you're lyin' like a rug I'm gonna walk all over you. Your friends and all your family say I oughta toss you out. Since you lied between my teeth, babe, I'm gonna dental floss you out."

For those who'd like to hear what Bill is up to besides Jose, he offers "Look Who's Rapping" (his impressions of Bela Lugosi, Peter Falk's Columbo and Marlon Brando's Godfather set to rap music). Rap is rap and the result is obvious, but the Falk segment, with the repetitive "eck-eck-eck-eck excuse me," "am I bothering you," and "no, I'm not suspicious" is amusing, especially when the music picks up again. ("One more thing!") If he stuck to Falk alone, without the confusing combination of Lugosi and Brando, it might've gotten some airplay and rivaled the only other funny number in this genre, Joe Piscopo and Eddie Murphy's "Honeymooners Rap."

Using his own voice, Dana sings an ironic ecological folk song, "Welcome to the Yosemite National Tree," all about the last surviving hunk of wood in America: "Take a good look as you pass, but keep your fingers off the glass. Remember that's our last surviving real live tree. And when you're out in old Yosemite, don't forget to buy a can of air. And for twenty five cents additional, they'll show you the picture of the bear."

NOTES: Dana released the straight "Brand New Old Traditional Hawaiian Album" on his own label and appears on two children's albums as Jose: "The Time Machine" (Hanna Barbera HLP 2052) and "The New Alice in Wonderland" (Hanna Barbera HLP 2051). He also produced Joey Forman's lone comedy album. Sketches written by Dana appear on several Julius Monk albums, notably "Demi Dozen."

RODNEY DANGERFIELD

• THE LOSER (Decca DS 6009, reissued by Rhino Records, RNLP 012, and on CD as "What's In a Name" MCAD 22026) **1/2		$8
• I DON'T GET NO RESPECT (Bell 6040, reissued by Arista ABM 4281) ***	$5	$15

Dangerfield came by his hard luck loser character the hard way. His stand-up comedy career (using the name Jack Roy) was a failure and he retired from show business to raise a family. In his forties he attempted a comeback, and his jokes about his lack of respect rang true.

His first albums appeared in the mid '60s. From a reliable TV and nightclub comic he progressed over a decade to become one of the great stars of stand-up. In the '80s he became a movie star with *Easy Money* and the very successful summer of '86 comedy *Back to School*.

On "The Loser," recorded live at Upstairs at the Duplex in Greenwich Village, Dangerfield isn't yet the one-liner expert tossing out a nervous stream of self-abuse. He does some long routines, including a set piece on dating: "I took out a manicurist. All night she held my hand ... and while she was holding my hand, she took my other hand and put it in my drink."

A few years later, circa 1970, he recorded "I Don't Get No Respect." He'd recently opened his own nightclub, Dangerfield's, and was a TV variety show regular with clean, gag-filled loser monologues told with a hollow voice of pain and regret: "One of my problems – I don't get no respect. No respect at all. Every time I get into an elevator the operator says the same thing: basement? No respect. When I was a kid we played hide and seek. They wouldn't even look for me. The other day I was standing in front of a big apartment house. The doorman asked me to get him a cab."

- NO RESPECT (Casablanca 7167) ✶✶✶ $5 $15
- RAPPIN' RODNEY (RCA Victor AFL 14887) ✶✶1/2 $5 $15
- LA CONTESSA (Dove Audio 0787105945) ✶✶1/2 $8

Dangerfield is in his prime on the 1980 Casablanca album, his monologue loaded with pungent hard-luck gags: "The other night I felt like having a few drinks. I went over to the bartender and said, 'Surprise me.' He showed me a naked picture of my wife ... ain't got no sex life ... she cut me down to once a month. I'm lucky. Two guys I know she cut out completely. I met one of the guys, I said, 'Who told you you could play around with my wife?' He said, 'Everybody.'"

Dangerfield's 1984 album includes a rap song about Dangerfield's woes, reflecting his popularity among the young, who evidently found him a laughable example of what hard work and the American Dream does for the average man. "I'm gettin' old, it's hard to face," Rodney sings. "During sex I lose my place!" The one-liners are as sharp as ever: "My wife's an earth sign, I'm a water sign: together we make mud." At this point in Dangerfield's career, he wasn't just a sulking loser. He was angry about it, too. So he was something of a "heroic" loser. So when a heckler starts in, Rodney finishes him off. A guy cries out, "Rodney, how big's your Rod?" Rodney shouts back, "Don't you remember?" Then he growls, "It's a good thing you're wearing a mustache. It breaks up the monotony of your face!"

1995's "La Contessa" is half live, half "audio book," and pretty much half-assed. The live twenty-two-minute set was badly recorded from the stage (not on it or through the mike) so p's pop and there's a lot of echo. It's a workmanlike set at best, with some old jokes and hit or miss new ones. The first twenty-five minutes are Rodney in a studio, reading a comedy romance novel in a faux dramatic voice. It doesn't suit him, and even when he uses the correct words ("vagina," "erection,") the result is uncomfortably crass instead of liberatingly classless. Johnny Carson and Jay Leno both used the romance parody idea and did it better than this: "La Contessa was a wild woman. When she said I'll be home after five, she wasn't talking about time. Sometimes for hours she would do push-ups in her cucumber garden. Although La Contessa did have a tender side. She wouldn't hurt a fly. Unless it was open." It's hard to take twenty-five solid minutes of these formula one-liners, especially when Rodney mumbles them so unconvincingly with elevator music playing in the background. He says, "Every man has his tale of woe. Unfortunately in life there's more woe than tail." And here, more woe than comic tale.

NOTES: Rodney is on film soundtracks, including "Rover Dangerfield" (Warner Bros 267092) and "Back To School" (MCA 6175).

SLOPPY DANIELS

- LAFF OF THE PARTY (Dooto DTL 232) ✶✶ $5 $10
- SLOPPY'S HOUSE PARTY (Dooto DTL 266) ✶✶ $5 $10
- SEXMOUTH (Laff 130) ✶✶ $5 $10

Leroy "Sloppy" Daniels worked solo in the '50s and was also Leroy in the comedy team Skillet and Leroy. He gets some mileage from old stories told with boisterous charisma. From the first Dooto album: "Fellow lived next door to me, he drank all the time, I never seen a man drink like that. I went home the other night, he was so drunk, walkin' all around, he was staggering up on the porch and he put his key in the door and when he turned the key the door came open.

"He said, 'Yeah, I know I'm in the right house, 'cause this key I got jus' opened this door.' And he walked around a little bit further in the house and said, 'I know I'm in the right house now, 'cause there's that great big ol' beautiful dresser I bought for my old lady.' And he ended up in the bedroom. 'I told you I was in the right house, 'cause there's my old lady lyin' over in the bed. Look at that. I know I'm in the right house now, 'cause there I am layin' over there in the bed with her. Now I gotta figure out who the devil is this standin' up talkin'!'"

SEVERN DARDEN

- THE SOUND OF MY OWN VOICE (Mercury OCM 2202/OSC 6202) ✶✶1/2 $10 $20

An influential member of The Second City, Darden issued only one album, a 1961 release when he was thirty-two years old and the group's most promising player.

A University of Chicago student, he had been one of the major creators of "hungry intellectual" humor, his a bit more intellectual and avant garde than the kind made popular by Shelley Berman the team of Nichols and May. The album contains his most famous routine, his lecture on metaphysics and the universe, in the guise of the stereotypically accented Dr. Valter Van Der Vogelweide. "Why, you will ask me, have I chosen to speak on the universe ... well, it's very simple ... there isn't anything else!"

Darden has the audience playing along as he continues his mock lecture: "You will ask me, what is this thing called time. (long pause). *That* is time. Now you will ask me, what is space. Now this over here, is some space. However this is not all space. However, when I said that was time, that was all the time there was anywhere in the universe! At that time. Now if you were to take all of the space that there is in the universe, and cram it into this little tiny place, this would be all the space there was! Unless of course some leaked out. Which it could. And did. Hence the universe ..."

The monologue, which sometimes sounds like something Professor Irwin Corey might have done if he studied philosophy and James Joyce, stretches on for sixteen minutes. Quite some time.

Darden also appears on "From the Second City" (Mercury), "The Second City Writhes Again" (Mercury), and "Conceptionland" from The Conception Company (Cotillion). He died in 1995 at age 65.

RAY DARIANO

- ARE YOU ON SOMETHING? (Kama Sutra KSBS 2072) *1/2 $5 $10

The cover of this 1972 album imitates Bob Dylan's "Bringing It All Back Home." The inside tries to duplicate the styles of Murray Roman and Firesign Theater: mini-skits, stand-up bits, and radio commercial parodies come together in a bewildering mix. Most of it was flat then and it hasn't improved with time.

A parody of the announcers at Woodstock: "If anyone has OD'd, if you have OD'd, just lie still wherever you are and a festival coroner will pick you up. Please don't move ... hey man, there's been a birth here! Dig it, a chick named Snowflake man, just about an hour ago she gave birth to a five pound block of ice! That's far out." And that's as good as it gets in this undisciplined collection of bits that include "Thank God," "Radio Suite," "I'm Misable," and "Cheech and Ernie."

"Cheech and Ernie," incidentally, offers a comedic in-joke: Bert and Ernie (the two Sesame Street Muppets) doing Cheech and Chong's "Dave's Not Here" routine. It's a chuckle for a moment, assuming anyone cares. Dariano's big break came in 1986 when he was allowed to be a regular on Soupy Sales's NBC radio series.

KING DAVID

- BREAKFXXXING (Zoo Records) * $4 $8

A guy with a "dese and dose" delivery, King David makes Lou Cary sound classy and Marty Allen sophisticated. Evidently a homemade effort, King David recites his gags with canned laughter and applause liberally spilled all over the place.

The material probably won't seem too bad to gold-chain-wearing Long Islanders who just finished an "all you can eat for $5.95" Clam House dinner complete with a six pack of Bud. Everyone else can pass:

"I used to want a hard body. As I got older, I was willing to settle for ANY body! If this keeps up, I'm gonna end up with nobody! Even Blue Cross called me the other day. They said, 'Mr. Houlihan, what's this bill for $400 for massage parlor visits? What should I file it under?' I said, 'File it under mental health, 'cause if I don't see these women at least three, four times a week I go crazy!'" A heavy-handed delivery and that laugh track make these beauties even worse than they are.

DANNY DAVIS

- MY SON THE PRESIDENT (Strand SL 1085/SLS 1085) *1/2 $4 $10

This fairly weak concept album tried to cash in on the success of "The First Family." Here Davis plays the first Jewish president, sounding like a cross between Jackie Mason and Bullwinkle the Moose. A typical gag has the President talking with his mother: "Mom, what do you think of Red China?" "It would look nice on a white tablecloth." George Jessel evidently allowed his photo to appear on the album cover, giving the impression that the bald Davis was "his son" the President.

Davis also wrote material and appears on the album "The Shortest Day" by The Chosen Players. On February 10, 1970, the forty-one-year-old Davis was killed when a car went out of control and slammed into him at the intersection of 3rd Avenue and 59th Street in Manhattan.

DANNY DAVIS AND FRANK D'AMORE

- THE EGGHEAD AND I (Warwick W 2024) *1/2 $5 $15

A "Yul Brynner Look-Alike," Davis won an "Arthur Godfrey Talent Scouts" show. He teamed with D'Amore and later did stand-up and solo projects, but was actually more effective behind the scenes as a comedy writer. In the late '60s he contributed excellent material that helped shape the style of sad-sack comic Jackie Vernon.

This feeble album tried to cash in on the spate of sick and hip humor LPs circulating in the early '60s. It couldn't have taken long to write bits like the visit to a beatnik coffee shop ("In Zen Buddah We Trust - All Others Must Pay Up the Bread") or do a tired, obvious routine on Francis Scott Key's "Star Spangled Banner" being turned down by an agent ("They can't dance to it!").

The only reason this album is worth a listen is the peculiar last cut on the first side satirizing sick comics. Davis plays "Lenny Sahl Berman," who whines to his psychiatrist, "They keep sayin' horrible things about me, like I'm really Georgie Jessel's illegitimate son—by Don Ameche." The routine mixes cornball schtick with clumsy jabs at Lenny Bruce: "Man, I started out as a ghost writer and all my books came out on Halloween. Like I wrote "Mein Kampf" and "Das Kapital" but I got bugged man, I was makin' everybody else funny and they were gettin' the credit. Like man, yesterday I worked in front of a bad audience. All normals ... all the faggots dig me, I'm their mother figure ... last week the NAACP made me an honorary schvatza."

D'Amore later changed his name to Frank Darling and enjoyed a journeyman's success appearing at private parties, modest clubs, and conventions.

DAVIS AND REESE

- COMEDY WORLD (Laff 125) *1/2 $4 $8

A froggy-voiced Jewish comic paired with a singer/straight man, Pepper Davis and Tony Reese spent about twenty years on the snappy patter circuit, managing to get some recognizable names on their resume from the Copacabana in New York to the Royal Hawaiian Hotel in Honolulu. They were on *The Ed Sullivan Show* ten times, but they don't make much of an impression on this Laff album, recorded badly in Las Vegas at the Desert Inn.

It's standard yocks: "Hey, you're a wonderful audience. We got a lot of surprises for you. Later on we have seven girls who are gonna come out here and do the dance of the virgins. It's pretty tough to do, they have to do it from memory. We have three girls last night, couldn't remember how the damn thing started. Later on we play games. We choose up teams, go out and paint Jewish stars on Volkswagens. We got so much fun planned for tonight."

DICK DAVY

- YOU'RE A LONG WAY FROM HOME WHITEY (Columbia CL 2545/CS 9345) ** $5 $15
- STRONGER THAN DIRT (CL 2737/CS 9537) ** $5 $15

Dick Davy has played the Apollo Theater in Harlem—a club not noted for booking white comics. Remarkably, he did it in the 1960s. A Jewish New Yorker who created the character of a drawling, Arkansas comic, he sounded a little like Will Rogers or Brother Dave Gardner. The result is interesting, at least for students of comedy. Davy, the lone white playing to a black audience, is just as self-conscious and prone to making embarrassed and condescending race jokes as the early black comics were in white clubs.

On the "Stronger than Dirt" album, it's a comically jittery Davy who mumbles in front of his black audience, "Black Power comin' ta get me ... I try to help out in civil rights things as much as I can. I figure the white people been running this world a long time, it'll be the colored folks turn soon. Yeah. When the time comes I just hope some of you remember me kindly ... I go to bed every night and pray to the lord to push these freckles closer together."

Davy is sympathetic on every part of the race problem, even rioting: "Some y'all on the late night news. They talk about lootin'. That ain't no lootin', that's swappin'. White kids steal the black kids' dances, they entitled to a few suits. Fair's fair. Riots? Ain't no riots. Just some po' folks wantin' to get in the war on poverty, so they enlist. Burn down some houses full of rats and roaches. And some stores been cheatin' you, drop some bottles on policemen sassin' you and callin' you boy. That's how it is. First thing you know they send in the National Guard, shoot up the ghetto, give out swimming pools."

Davy's records are dated, his accent sounding calculated and his material often fawning and obvious. But there are a few lines now and then that have the sting of a Dick Gregory or a Will Rogers. Some jokes sound easy: "Things are better in Mississippi. Colored folks can vote there now. If they don't mind going through quicksand to the booth." But at the time, Dick Davy was daring.

DAWSON AND HARRELL

- MR. SILVER SPITZDAWSON (Dogbite 1) * $3 $8
- THINK FUZZY (Dogbite 200) * $3 $8

Lawrence Dawson and David Harrell Jr. of Arlington, Virginia liked to get together and record radio-style sketches. These albums from 1964 and 1965 are pretty boring, but it is vaguely interesting to hear how old radio dramas, Bob & Ray, and Stan Freberg influenced others besides Firesign Theater.

From the first album, a winter sketch complete with stomping footsteps through the snow and periodic blowing into the microphone to depict a storm: "If I die I want you to cremate me. I can't stand bein' in this here cold forever." "Oh, don't worry, Sam, d-d-didn't the Eskimo medicine man promise us he could end this cold spell if we brought back some unfrozen sea water to give to the Eskimo ghosts of the North Country ... hey look over there!" "By George, that's a polar bear!" "It looks like he's trying to start a fire." "He's rubbing two ptarmigans together." "What's a ptarmigan?" "It's a kind of a ptarmigan." "One of those automatic rifles." "With feathers on ..."

From the second album, an extremely self-indulgent interview with a computer expert: "Professor, where are you? I seem to have difficulty following you." "There! I got my weapon! You got to keep it handy at all times with these machines! I, Adolph von Schicklegruber, am a famous German scientist." "What do all these machines do, professor?" "My weapon! There!" "Why are you cocking it?" "You got to be ready! (sudden crashing noises) Just a minute. Got it right in the vacuum tube ... talking computer, talk to the man, computer." "Bzzz bzz bzz bzzz." "Ha ha ha!" "What's he talkin' about?" "The farmer's daughter! A dirty-minded computer ..."

DA YOOPERS

- YOOPY DO WAH (You Guys Records 71168) ** $7
- FOR DIEHARDS ONLY (You Guys Records 71169) ** $7
- ONE CAN SHORT OF A 6-PACK (You Guys Records 81170) ** $7

Somewhere in the Great Lakes area of Michigan ("Yoopers" refers to folks from the Upper Peninsula) there's a cult for Da Yoopers and their goofy polka and '50s-style rock and country tunes. They have Lawrence Welkish accents and sing happy/sappy songs that celebrate deer hunting, fishing, beer, and bowling, not to mention eating, passing wind, and doing "paperwork" in the outhouse. For those who enjoyed Tim Conway's Mr. Tudball, *SCTV*'s McKenzie Brothers, and *SNL*'s bits on Mike Ditka and the Chicago Bears, not to mention music from Dr. Hook to Ray Stevens, sampling a Yoopers album might not be a bad idea.

Song titles include "Cow Pie Song" and "Diarrhea" from the "Diehards Only" album and "Happy Birthday Fungus Face" and "Who Goosed da Moose" from "Yoopy Do Wah." 1994's "One Can Short of a 6-Pack" includes "Mighty Manly Hunting Men," a polka romp with these rhymes: "Sitting in the deer blind you don't have to go and hide just to take a whiz. Just stand out in the open, draw pictures in the snow. Wear that same old underwear two weeks in a row!" And in "Da Fishing Trip" the group cheerfully sing, with only slightly less self-satire than the Monty Python lumberjack, "We're goin' fishing, we just can't wait. We love the smell of stinky bait!"

A few other albums are available only on cassette.

RICK DEES

- HURT ME BABY MAKE ME SIGN BAD CHECKS (No-O-O Budget NBR 102) * $5 $8
- PUT IT WHERE THE MOON DON'T SHINE (Atlantic 81231-1) ** $3 $8
- I'M NOT CRAZY (Atlantic 7812881) ** $3 $8
- SPOUSAL AROUSAL (DCC DZS-091) * $8

Aggressive West Coast DJ Dees had hit singles ("Disco Duck") and even his own bomb TV talk show in 1990. His artificially bright comedy records tend to mash together novelty tunes, half-serious rock songs, and "Candid Phone" radio show segments.

The title cut on 1983's "Hurt Me Baby" is an anti-Semitic disco novelty. A speeded-up vocal whines "hurt me, baby, whip me baby, uh, uh." And what could be worse for a Jew than to be forced to "write bad checks?" Most of the album is just oafish disc jockey banter, tedious blackout sketches, and jerky fake commercials.

The first Atlantic album has a lot of smirky practical joke phone calls. They're cruel and stupid, but the targets are cruel and stupid too. Hearing about a Valley Girl who ran over a dog, Dees calls the teenager up, claiming he's from the pet funeral home. When Dees demands she pay the $600 bill, she huffs, "That's the stupidest thing I ever heard of! I'm not payin' $600 for a dog's funeral...." "There was a gigantic makeup job," Dees insists. "Makeup for a dog?" "We starched the tail ... they wanted a kind of panting look on the dog's face...." "Oh, great, great ... I don't even know this dog, OK? I'm sorry that it happened, OK? This is like the stupidest thing I've ever heard of in my life!"

The novelty songs are witless. The only mildly amusing one, "When Sonny Sniffs Glue," based on a now prehistoric Johnny Mathis hit, was the subject of a lawsuit. Dees won the landmark case in July of 1986 when it was judged that borrowing the music for parody was "fair use," and not a violation of copyright rules.

The only worthy novelty tune on "I'm Not Crazy" is the now-dated "We Are the Weird," bashing the "We Are the World" anthem of 1985. With help from Rich Little and others, Dees has gooey-voiced Julio Iglesias, flatly nasal Willie Nelson, growling Bruce Springsteen, hiccuping Cyndi Lauper, and simpering Michael Jackson sing, "We are the weird, but we're not stupid. And we're laughin' all the way to the bank." The mimicry is more fun than the lyrics. One of the better gags has a faux Stevie Wonder nattering about the "macrame pot holder" he wears on his head. The gag was filched from an earlier Joan Rivers album.

Among the cruel snickers in the "Candid Phone" segments is one in which a very stupid mother becomes tearful when Dees calls up to say her son is "definitely a homo sapien."

The 1996 CD, "Spousal Arousal," is nothing but inane radio interviews with California raisin-brains. A Valley Girl whines that her Cancun honeymoon was "bogus," then squeals with embarrassment as her boyfriend asks if her phone confessions have made her "gooey and wet." No more stupid than any couple talking to Ricki, Montel, or Rolanda—and no funnier.

WILLIAM DEFOTIS

- SATIRE IS SERIOUS BUSINESS (Centaur CRC 2237) * $7

The CD's title reflects the arrogance of the unknown DeFotis, who declares in his album notes that he's the new Tom Lehrer. After left-handed compliments about Tom's "riotous rhetorical exaggerations, as in 'Smut,' and mock seriousness as in 'The MLF Lullaby,'" and how these songs "lure us into accepting implausible or even impossible notions," Professor DeFotis presents his new (and, he likely thinks, improved) song satires.

They are so jejune and arcane (or "crappy" as we say in the real world) only a very tweedy, sherry-drunk academician could listen to more than two in a row. DeFotis is a bland vocalist, doesn't even play piano (Christine Williams offers Lehrer-esque touches to the derivative music), and writes toothless songs on easy targets: "The Politically Correct Tango," "Family Values," "Homophobia," etc.

"Some of My Best Friends Are Women" is the most obvious in Lehrer mimicry, with DeFotis taking Tom's device of the comically strained rhyme and simply removing the "comic" part. One chorus: "Some of my best friends are women. My high regard is always brimmin'. The thought of them starts my head just swimmin'." And another: "Some of my best friends are women. They are the cream so I keep skimmin'. They are the stars just never dimmin'."

The CD was issued in 1995; DeFotis's posterity-minded album notes give the places for each recording session, which include all the hottest comedy clubs: "Ewell Recital Hall, College of William & Mary, Williamsburg Va ... Wellesley College, Wellesley MA ... Cincinnati Conservatory of Music ... University of Illinois, Urbana."

THE DELEGATES

- THE DELEGATES (Mainstream MRL 100) *1/2 $4 $8

The production credits on this album go to Nick Cenci and Nick Kousaleos, but much of the album sounds suspiciously like the work of Dickie Goodman. In fact, Goodman's "Convention '72" single is on the album. Goodman was a pioneer in collage comedy, starting with "The Flying Saucer," the hit single from the '50s where interview questions were answered with snippets from pop tunes. Here, politicians at the 1972 presidential conventions are interviewed, their answers clipped from 1972 hits.

When an interviewer asks Spiro Agnew what running mate he would prefer, suddenly Jimmy Castor is heard singing "Bertha Butt! One of the Butt Sisters!" The technique becomes obvious and wearying over an entire album.

At one point, trying to break the monotony, there's a live interview with "The Godfather." Somebody speaking in a strangled whisper plays the role, with a stereotyped gay reporter adding extra yocks with lispy questions:

"Do you have any suggestions for whomever wins this presidential race?" "I sure do. Don't eat no yellow snow." It should come as no surprise that the laughter on this album is canned.

JACK DE LEON

- DE LEON ROARS (Duo 2) ** $5 $10
- THE FIRSTA FAMILY (Poppy PYS 5706) ** $4 $8

De Leon appeared in the supporting casts of many comedy albums. A stand-up in the early '60s (when "De Leon Roars" appeared) he may be best known for his recurring role as a kleptomaniacal homosexual on the sitcom *Barney Miller.*

Like Bob Newhart, Charlie Manna, and other stand-ups of the day, De Leon tried set routines in different characters. One had him impersonating a director working on the set of an epic film (on the order of *Cleopatra*). It's harmless more than humorous. The director speaks to his crew:

"I feel we are most fortunate in having the greatest cameraman in the world, Mr. James Fong Low. Mr. Low will be shooting this scene from the top of Mount Vesuvius, which arrived in crates this morning. What's that Charlie? Didn't anyone have the brains to unpack Mount Vesuvius? OK, here's what we'll do. James Fong Low, we lost Mount Vesuvius. So take your camera and set up in the middle of the Red Sea. Will someone part the Red Sea for Mr. Low please? Don't anyone know how to make a part? This picture will make Ben Hur look like a coming attraction."

"Firsta Family" is a 1972 studio album: What if The Godfather becomes President? De Leon, doing a pretty good wheezing Marlon Brando, delivers a humorless inaugural address:

"I came to this country with nothing but these two hands, ambition, and a bag of quick drying cement. You have chosen me over my worthy opponent, a man who spent millions of dollars on TV spots, newspaper advertisements— and unfortunately, he disappeared. To those people who supported me in my campaign, I say God bless you. To those who opposed me, I say God help you."

Also in the cast are Jesse White, Louise Chalmis, Ed Peck, and the team of Dick Clair and Jenna McMahon.

BOBBY DELL

- IF I INSULTED YOU IT WAS INTENTIONAL (Surprise SUR-97) **1/2 $10 $15

A kind of adults-only Pinky Lee, Dell delivers saucy burlesque jokes with a harmless lisp. In stand-up clubs in the late '50s a raunchy insult comic with an effeminate streak had to be quite a novelty. "The Boy You Know Well" Bobby Dell spent nearly four years at the 41 Club in Philadelphia, four years at The Ha Ha Club in Hollywood, Florida, and fourteen years at The Club Moroccan. He was about forty when he recorded his lone album, circa 1959, at the Club 609.

Dell uses whizbang with a minty tint: "Excuse me, I've got a frog in my throat. The first piece of meat I had all day ... I must've caught a cold. Oooh, I slept near a crack last night—and she was a mess! Windy, too ... Me with a woman? What's wrong with me!"

Reporting on his visit to a nudist colony: "I said to the woman next to me, 'Isn't that Dick Brown?' She said, 'It should be, it's been in the sun all summer!'" Well kids, I came to one conclusion: As for the men, you can see they're nuts. And the women are cracked, too."

LEO DE LYON

- LIKE, LEO'S HERE (London 5551) *1/2 $8 $15

There are a few interesting numbers on this offbeat album from the somewhat jazz-hip Leo De Lyon. A singer and cabaret comedian, De Lyon liked to imitate trumpets, trombones, and a thumping bass. He also enjoyed making animal noises. On "How About You," "Our Love Is Here to Stay," and "Cheek to Cheek" among others, the trick is underwhelming. The occasional odd noises only make him sound like Louis Prima with indigestion.

"Laura" is one of the few songs that tries to be a bit more inventive. It starts with monology: "Her long black hair. That one long black hair coming out of her left nostril ... poor girl, one day she sneezed and flogged herself to death." In a fair one-man attempt at Spike Jones, he adds his own sound effects to the lines "footsteps you hear down the hall," "the laugh that floats on a summer's night," etc., etc.

The final cut, the six-minute "Leo in Africa," is a travelogue with jungle noises, eccentric ad-libs and schtick—the kind of thing Danny Kaye might've done if he had Jack Carter's mentality. It's more strange than funny. The odd album seems true to the appraisal of himself on the liner notes: "I've had fun being a crazy guy in most parts of the world."

SALLY DE MAY

- AS MAMMY YOKUM IN SMOKE 'N HOKUM (Hokum 5556) *1/2 $8 $20

DeMay played Mammy Yokum in a stage production of "Lil Abner," and proudly quotes reviews from the *Los Angeles Herald-Examiner* and *San Francisco Chronicle* on the back cover of this 1966 album. Studio recorded, with canned laughter for artificial sweetening, De May unconvincingly recites a monologue that tries to adapt old jokes to her Mammy persona:

"I saw Stupefyin' Jones the other day molesting her cat. Why, she was shaking that cat up and down, up and down, just because she heard the poker player say, 'There was some money left in the kitty.' And did you know that Daisy Mae was so excited because she was going on a first cruise? And when she got back she done told me she had a wonderful time, except for one thing. She threw all her underwear out the porthole. She thought it was a washing machine ..."

DR. DEMENTO

- DR. DEMENTO'S DELIGHTS (Warner Bros. BS 2855) **1/2 $5 $15

Barry Hansen, owner of a master's degree in music from UCLA, is "Dr. Demento," the syndicated radio disc jockey who plays crazy tunes for a loyal and devoted listenership. Since the show seems to attract both connoisseurs of strangeness and a large number of pubescent dweebs who like anything goofy, it's not surprising that each album is an uneven mix of offbeat enjoyable dementia and detestably puerile putresence.

Demento's first collection, released in 1975, offers a G-rated side and a PG-rated side. Naturally, what one considers "a novelty" another might consider "annoying." George Rock does kiddie vocals for "Wanna Buy a Bunny," and the appropriately named Ben Gay lisps through "The Ballad of Ben Gay." Certifiable classics include Allan Sherman's "Hello Muddah Hello Faddah," Napoleon XIV's "They're Coming to Take Me Away, Ha-Haa," the 1940s jazz classic "Who Put the Benzedrine in Mrs. Murphy's Ovaltine," and the bouncy "Boobs a Lot" from The Holy Modal Rounders. There's "The Cockroach that Ate Cincinnati," done by Possum, R. Crumb's "Get a Load of This," and Doodles Weaver embarrassingly trying to wring laughs by deliberately fumbling through lyrics of "Eleanor Rigby." Evidently issued before he discovered he had so many ten-year-old listeners, Demento included drug ditties "If You're a Viper" (Jim Kweskin) and "Friendly Neighborhood Narco Agent" (Jef Jaisun).

- DR. DEMENTO'S MEMENTOS (Eccentric Records PVC 8912) ** $6 $12

This 1982 disc showcases new acts that submitted material for Demento's radio show. Demento himself tries to cut it as a novelty vocalist, while "I Get Weird" (John W. Christensen) has speeded up vocals that even Frank Zappa would've found pretentious. "My Name Is Merv Griffin" requires tremendous patience to sit through. Many of the singers here obviously have their icons (Doug Robinson on "Mediocre Mama" wishes he was Martin Mull, and Steve Lisenby wants to be Yogi Yorgesson) and they thoroughly soil the memories of the stars who came before them. "The Alphabet Song" by The Three Stooges can't save this disc, and "Harry's Jockstrap" from Dickie Goodman is actually censored (the words "fairy" and "joint" are blipped).

Tim Cavanagh's "I Wanna Kiss Her" recalls Benny Bell, as he puns, "I wanna kiss her but(t) she won't let me. I wanna whisper sweet nothings in her-rear." "Smut," by The Other Half, is just plain stupid and "The Rodeo Song" from Showdown is censored beyond listenability. Other cuts include "Space Invaders" by Uncle Vic, "My Wife Left Town with a Banana" by Carlos Borzenie, "Bodine Brown" from Purvis Pickett, "Don't Go Down to the Fallout Shelter" by Tom Fenton, "Rock and Roll Doctor" from Travesty Ltd., and "I Found the Brains of Santa Claus" by Jason and the Strap-Tones.

- DEMENTIA ROYALE (Rhino RNLP 010) ** $5 $10

Cuts include "Punk Polka" from The Toons; Fred Blassie's "Pencil Neck Geek"; "Three Drunk Newts" and "I Gotta Get a Fake ID" from Barnes and Barnes; "My Bologna" from Weird Al Yankovic; and "Davy's Dinghy" from Ruth Wallis. Once again, the accent is on giggles for eight-year-olds. "The Phantom Windbreaker" by Red Bovine is nothing more than fart noises. Marc Zydiak does "Frosty the Dope Man" and Dr. Demento gleefully but amateurishly covers Benny Bell's "Shaving Cream." Bobby Pickett and Peter Ferrara offer a parody of *Star Trek* ("Stardrek"), which should appeal to undemanding Trekkies (Captain Kirk becomes Captain Jerk, Mr. Spock becomes Mr. Schlock and Mr. Scott is Mr. Snot). The Yiddish People offer "Kosher Delight" (it isn't), Scott Beach does "Religion and Politics," and Wild Man Fischer offers the incredibly brainless "My Name Is Larry."

- THE GREATEST NOVELTY RECORDS OF ALL TIME (Rhino RNBC 490) *** $30 $75
- GREATEST NOVELTY RECORDS THE 1940s (Rhino RNLP 820) *** $5 $12
- GREATEST NOVELTY RECORDS THE 1950s (Rhino RNLP 821) *** $5 $12
- GREATEST NOVELTY RECORDS THE 1960s (Rhino RNLP 822) *** $5 $10
- THE GREAT NOVELTY RECORDS THE 1970s (Rhino RNLP 823) *** $5 $10
- THE GREAT NOVELTY RECORDS THE 1980s (Rhino RNLP 824) *** $5 $10
- DR. DEMENTO'S CHRISTMAS ALBUM (Rhino RNLP 825) ** $5 $10

The 1985 boxed set of "Greatest Novelty Records" offered six albums, each available individually.

1940s highlights "The Okeh Laughing Record," "Pico and Sepulveda" by Felix Figueroa, and "The Freckle Song" by Larry Vincent, one of those non-absurd risqué numbers ("She has freckles on her but(t) she is nice"). Hideous novelty classics include Arthur Godfrey's hamfisted "Too Fat Polka" and Kay Kyser's sap-soaked "Three Little Fishes." Country nonsense is represented by "I'm My Own Grandpa" (the best song Lonzo and Oscar ever did), "I Like Bananas Because They Have No Bones" from the Hoosier Hot Shots, and "Smoke, Smoke, Smoke that Cigarette" by Tex Williams. Other hits: Groucho Marx's "Hooray for Captain Spaulding," Billy Costello's "I'm Popeye the Sailor Man," Benny Bell's "Shaving Cream," and the theme songs for Jimmy Durante ("Inka Dinka Do") and Cab Calloway ("Minnie the Moocher").

Monsters and weird creatures dominated '50s movies, TV, and the '50s collection: "The Purple People Eater" (Sheb Wooley), "Martian Hop" (Ran-Dells), "The Flying Saucer" (Buchanan and Goodman) "The Thing" (Phil Harris), and "The Mummy," written by Rod McKuen and performed by Bob McFadden. Rarities include Tom Lehrer's fully orchestrated single version of "Masochism Tango," Jackie Gleason's "One of These Days, POW!" and the Stan Freberg "Dragnet" parody, "Little Blue Riding Hood." Some Top 40 novelty favorites are here: "The Battle of Kooka-monga" (Homer and Jethro) and "Stranded in the Jungle" (The Cadets), plus lesser cuts: "Russian Bandstand"

(Spencer and Spencer), "The Dinghy Song" (Ruth Wallis), "Eloise" (a barely tolerable Kay Thompson tune), and the amusing, once, "Sunday Driving" from Jerry Lewis.

The '60s has great if overplayed tunes: Allan Sherman's "Hello Muddah Hello Faddah," Napoleon XIV's "They're Coming to Take Me Away, Ha Ha," "Monster Mash" by Bobby Boris Pickett, and "Alley Oop" by The Hollywood Argyles. Dr. West's Medicine Show does "The Eggplant that Ate Chicago." British skiffle great Lonnie Donegan offers "Does Your Chewing Gum Lose Its Flavour on the Bedpost Overnight." Brian Hyland's gloriously idiotic "Itsy Bitsy Teenie Weenie Yellow Polka Dot Bikini" is here, along with Ray Stevens's "Gitarzan" and Tiny Tim's "Tiptoe through the Tulips." The "sick-nik" side of the '50s is represented by Larry Verne's cute "Mr. Custer" and Tom Lehrer's grimly great "So Long Mom." The line between the novel and the annoying is crossed by The Trashmen's "Surfin' Bird" and Rusty Warren's flat "Bounce Your Boobies."

The picks for the slightly humorless '70s are amusing if not exactly hilarious: Loudon Wainwright's pungent "Dead Skunk," Steve Martin's jerky jiving "King Tut," and Randy Newman's long, drawling spit at "Short People." There's the plain rocking "Time Warp" from *The Rocky Horror Picture Show*, Larry Groce's lame "Junk Food Junkie," Weird Al Yankovic's crass "My Bologna," Barnes and Barnes's dopey-cute "Fish Heads," and Ogden Edsl's "Dead Puppies." The wheezing and overbaked Shel Silverstein cautionary tale "Sarah Cynthia Stout" doesn't survive repeat listenings. "Cockroach that Ate Cincinnati" is here, "Pencil Neck Geek" (Fred Blassie) is anthologized yet again, Cheech and Chong present the painful "Earache in My Eye," and some group of dopes named "Hank, Stu, Steve and Hank" deliver "(I'm Looking Over) My Dead Dog Rover," which should only be sung by eight-year-olds on the bus going to day camp.

Like the '70s collection, there's some uneven material for the '80s. One of Weird Al Yankovic's best parodies is here, "Eat It," based on Michael Jackson's "Beat It." Also worthy: Julie Brown's "Homecoming Queen Got a Gun"; "The Curly Shuffle," Jump 'n' the Saddle's dancing tribute to The Three Stooges; and Rodney Dangerfield's "Rappin' Rodney." Weird Al returns for "Another One Rides the Bus." Hardly worth hearing: "Fast Food" (Stevens and Grdnic), "Bedrock Rap" (Bruce Springstone), "Rock and Roll Doctor" (Travesty Ltd.), "Existential Blues" (Tom Stankus), "The Scotsman" (Bryan Bowers), "Marvin I Love You" (Marvin the Paranoid Android), and "Take Off," by Bob and Doug McKenzie.

Adding an entire disc of Christmas novelties to the boxed set was pretty nasty. Those who buy it as a separate disc do so at their own risk. The only thing more annoying and detestable than having to squirm through December's radio blitz of mind-numbing Christmas songs is having to hear the coy and cloying comedy tunes of the season. "All I Want for Christmas Is My Two Front Teeth" (Spike Jones) is a known irritant. Others that should be roasted over an open fire: "Grandma Got Run Over by a Reindeer" (Elmo and Patsy), "Nuttin' for Christmas" (Stan Freberg), "Santa Claus and His Old Lady" (Cheech and Chong), and "I'm a Christmas Tree" (Wild Man Fischer). Underlining the season's greedings, Tom Lehrer offers "A Christmas Carol" and Stan Freberg adds "Green Christmas," both fairly toothless, but as fierce as times would allow. Other cuts: "Santa and the Satellite" (Dickie Goodman), "I Want a Hippopatamus for Christmas" (Gayla Peevey), "The 12 Days of Christmas" (Allan Sherman), "I Yust Go Nuts at Christmas" (Yogi Yorgesson), and "Wreck the Halls" (The Three Stooges).

- THE GREATEST CHRISTMAS NOVELTY CD (Rhino 75755) *1/2 $8
- HOLIDAYS FOR DEMENTIA (Rhino R2 72176) * $8
- DR. DEMENTO'S COUNTRY CORN (Rhino R2 72125) ** $8
- DR. DEMENTO 20TH ANNIVERSARY COLLECTION (Rhino R2 70743) *** $18
- DR. DEMENTO 25TH ANNIVERSARY COLLECTION (Rhino R2 72124) *** $16

The sixteen-tune lineup for the noxious "Christmas Novelty" CD is different from the earlier vinyl disc. The Three Stooges' "Wreck the Halls" was dropped, as well as the dated but still worthy "Santa and the Satellite" by Dickie Goodman. Stan Freberg fans will be glad to discover "Christmas Dragnet," and sadists will applaud the appearance of "I'm a Christmas Tree" (Wild Man Fischer) and the equally asinine "Jingle Bells" as yipped and yapped by The Singing Dogs. Just to prove how sappy people get at Christmas, the CD sold well enough for a sequel to appear, 1995's "Holiday for Dementia," with blandly sung, coldly calculated numbers only yuppies could laugh at: "It's So Chic to be Pregnant at Christmas" (Nancy White) and "Gridlock Christmas" (The Hollytones) are among the dreariest. As for the famous name performers, they seem to be at their most obnoxious: Ray Stevens's "Santa Claus Is Watching You" and Father Guido Sarducci's tedious "Santa's Lament." Demento includes a few Chanukah and New Year's songs. Thanks for nothing. Gefilte Joe, with a hoarse, stereotypical accent, tries for laughs by declaring: "Hanukkah comes but once a year. And when it does you know it's here." Spike Jones's "Happy New Year" can't out-noise the real thing.

The eighteen-song country CD is disappointingly tilted toward straight material: Jerry Reed's "When You're Hot You're Hot," Roger Miller's "You Can't Roller Skate in a Buffalo Herd," Johnny Paycheck's "Colorado Cool-Aid," and Jim Stafford's "Wildwood Weed." Only a few tracks are truly classic, like "May the Bird of Paradise Fly Up Your Nose" ("Little" Jimmy Dickens). "Contractual problems" evidently forced out likely material from Johnny Cash, George Jones, Shel Silverstein, Ben Colder, and Lonzo & Oscar.

Fans are bound to quibble over the choices on the 20th Anniversary two CD set (eighteen tunes on each). There are plenty of classics ("Poisoning Pigeons in the Park" and "Masochism Tango" from Tom Lehrer, "King Tut" by Steve Martin, "Der Fuehrer's Face" by Spike Jones, "They're Coming to Take Me Away, Ha-Haaa" by Napoleon XIV, "Monster Mash" by Bobby Boris Pickett, and "The Purple People Eater" by Sheb Wooley). There are also Demento show favorites like Ogden Edsl's "Dead Puppies" and Barnes and Barnes's "Fish Heads." Then there are the miseries and the obscurities: "Earache in My Eye" from Cheech & Chong, "Ti Kwan Leep" by The Frantics, "Pencil Neck Geek" from Fred Blassie, "Star Trekkin'" from The Firm, "Ballad of Irving" by Frank Gallop, and "Wappin'" from Darrell Hammond and Christopher Snell.

The double-disc "25th Anniversary" has a few legitimate collector's items here—Tom Lehrer's cartoonishly orchestrated version of "The Hunting Song" and Art Carney as Ed Norton ("Song of the Sewer"). Mostly there's overexposed novelties (Larry Verne's "Mr. Custer," Spike Jones's "Dance of the Hours," Jump 'n The Saddles' "Curly Shuffle") and tiresome nonsense (Stan Freberg's "Heartbreak Hotel," Tiny Tim's "Tioptoe Thru the Tulips," and Hank, Stu, Dave and Hank's "My Dead Dog Rover"). Obvious, childish earaches like Clean Living's polka "In Heaven There Is No Beer," Barnes and Barnes's "I Gotta Get a Fake I.D.," and "Rubber Biscuit" by The Chips don't deserve commemoration. It's impossible to tolerate West Coast radio pests Stevens and Grdnic's "Fast Food" over again. For every delightful pro like Eddie Lawrence, there's a painfully obvious amateur like John Forster. Perhaps the oddest moment is Weird Al Yankovic singing his parody of "Achy Breaky Heart." When Al declares the simpleminded country tune "the most annoying song I know," he overlooks the competition from his own catalogue.

NOTES: Demento's two-hour radio shows, circulated to stations on double-disc sets, are now circulating among collectors. Some not only feature cuts from Demento's collection, but special guests (from Martin Mull to Judy Tenuta). The doctor also issued a children's album of Mother Goose rap songs and novelties.

TOM DENNIS

- Half Loaded (Cat CT 711) * $5 $8

A pianist-singer who evidently did most of his entertaining in Westport, Connecticut, "sophisticated" bars, Dennis pounds out a few pseudo-clever satirical numbers, but most of the disc is devoted to tunes that drunks of the day appreciated, from "One for My Baby" to "Lady Is a Tramp."

The three comedy pieces rely on fast patter, the kind that might daze a tippler into giggling, but would confuse that person the morning after—when it's too late to return the "souvenir album" purchased the night before. From the aptly named "Who Cares": "Take Solomon. He had a hundred wives. And ninety-nine were doing fine and had the time of their lives. But just like that, without a further ado, the one left over saw greener clover. But Solomon had a high I.Q. He joined the rabble and learned at Scrabble new words of wisdom and woo ... what's the moral? There is no moral. And further mor-al who cares?"

JOE DE RITA

- BURLESQUE UNCENSORED (Cook 1071) *1/2 $5 $25

Joe DeRita, famed as the last "Curly" of The Three Stooges, was a burlesque comic before he joined the boys in 1958.

He was in the cast of Minsky's burlesque when the Cook label, in the guise of a "documentary" disc, recorded a performance for their "Sounds of Our Times" series. There is a stagey echo to the spoken parts, but the instrumentals come through with full brass.

Joe uses his catchphrase ("Buddy boy!") and goes through the corny jokes with steely determination:

"What do you do for a living?" "I'm a garbage man." "A garbage man?" "OK, sanitary engineer. Waddya want?" "How much do you make?" "I don't make it, I just collect it. See, I have a big truck I put it in." "I mean what is your salary?" "How much I get? Four dollars a week and all I can eat." "You mean you eat that stuff?" "Well, I certainly can't live on four dollars a week!"

Seventy-five percent of the album is stripper instrumentals, which lose something without the visuals. Three different jackets were pressed by Cook. The first has a red brick design and the back cover does not mention the performers. The second amends this oversight by handwritten notes in the margins identifying Irving Harmon, Joe De Rita, Stanley Montfort, and Peggy O'Mara. The rarest edition has a gold cover with an inch-sized photo of a topless girl at the center; it too identifies DeRita and the other stars.

The price of the album varies depending on whether dealers are aware of Stooge interest in this one.

DEREK AND CLIVE See COOK AND MOORE

ROCCO DE RUSSO

- MARY SAMPIERI (Colonial 191) $4 $8
- COMEDY DIALOGUE: I GUAY DI TONY (Colonial 691) $4 $8
- SHERZI COMICI (Colonial 771) $4 $8
- TONY LEAVES FOR ITALY (Colonial 641) $4 $8
- DIE LAUGHING WITH ROCCO DE RUSSO (Standard/Colonial 939) $4 $8
- LAUGHING MINCUCCIO (Standard/Colonial 929) $4 $8

The humor is in the extravagant Italian dialect of Rocco De Russo: one can almost see him gesticulating and pulling on his thick black mustache as he smiles and merrily carries on with his immigrant comedy. Just how funny the jokes are is hard to say, since Rocco veers into Italian most of the time, even if his straight woman, Ria Sampieri, speaks English. "Tony Leaves for Italy" contains one of their more popular routines, "Il Maestro De Lingua Italiana," with Ria trying to teach Tony simple words like "nose," "mouth," and "face," bursting into song after the lesson is complete. A little more adversarial is "Irish Wife and Charlie," with Ria trying to get him to speak English: "Go on, talk English!" "Shaddap! Nonz of you business! Me talk all-a right, please!" "Go on, you real hobo!" "You big Irish-eh!" "You crazy dirty slob!" "If you don't make-a shaddap I kick you right away!" And then he slips into excited Italian. His wife asks, "What are you mumbling about?" and so will any listeners not familiar with the language or with what the album notes refer to as "heavy Neapolitan patois, with even greater an inner tempo and with even stronger accents."

HE'S NOT SUCH A KIDDER, BUT OH, YOU KID!

With the decorative dolls on the cover, it almost didn't matter how good Don Sherman, Billy Devroe, and Hap Happy were. Many collectors want "album covers only" on similar "adults only" comedians.

WHEN GEORGE CARLIN'S IN, JACK BURNS UP

Same album, two different covers. A decade after the team of Carlin & Burns parted, their lone album was reissued sans any mention of Jack Burns! The idea was to pretend this was just an early Carlin solo album. Even the most recent version ("Killer Carlin" on CD) doesn't play straight with George's straight man.

BILLY DEVROE

- PARTY NAUGHTIES (Tampa TP 39, reissued as SEX MACHINE, Laff 110) ** $5 $10
- CENSORED (Tampa TP 31, reissued as SHE GIVES TRADE STAMPS, Laff 118) ** $5 $10
- BROAD MINDED (Tampa TP 41, reissued AS TRIP AROUND THE WORLD, Laff 119) **1/2 $5 $10

Devroe's Tampa LPs are for fans of '50s whizbang. The covers are typical of late 50s stag albums: Devroe posing with buxom, red-lipped Nugget-quality models. Devroe and his backing band use a low key approach. It sounds like Art Linkletter and The Modernaires reading "Over Sexteen."

"Party Naughties" has some wheezing song parodies. The crowd guffaws when he sings, "I wake up in the morning with a heart-ache!" And they snicker over "Casey got hit with a bucket of ... mud and the band played on! He waltzed 'cross the floor with a two legged ... girl!"

Between songs, Devroe indulges in peculiar anecdotes and corny poems. On "Broad Minded" there's a strange, elaborate tale of murder. He kills his wife by smearing petroleum jelly on the toilet seat. He describes the preparations, sounding like a cross between Woody Woodbury and Edgar Allan Poe. When the woman sits down, she slides into the water: "Fourteen years of marriage down the drain." Hearing strange sounds, Billy walls up the bathroom. Radio horror show music plays as Devroe describes his torment. He goes to the john, stares down: and there's his wife inside! She stares up at him: "She had me out of my mind! She had me nuts!"

On this one, Devroe is almost as offbeat and sap-hip as '50s sci-fi and horror films. The original Tampa albums generally get at least $10 thanks to the evocative '50s covers.

FAY DE WITT

- THROUGH SICK AND SIN (Epic LN 3776/BN 596) * $5 $20

On this disappointing disc, De Witt promises "sick" humor and an "unflinching look at the world through sardonic eyes." But it turns out to be nothing but feeble cabaret novelty numbers. Some of them are unlistenable thanks to De Witt's archly pretentious delivery. She's very trying when she attempts accents from French ("French with Tears") to Scottish ("Young Nhudanycke"). Her R-trilled and loudly fey version of "Requiem for Peace" is quite an affectation compared to the way it was recorded in a Julius Monk revue around the same time.

Some of the titles seem to promise a female Tom Lehrer: "The Old Pizza Maker," "These Ghoulish Things," and "The Insecure Tango." From the latter: "They play the tango now, and I am in his arms. I hear him praising my abundant charms. Though it appears I raise his temperature. I'm not so sure. I'm insecure!"

Some well-known songwriters contributed these throwaways, including Fred Ebb, Harold Rome, and the team of Adams and Strouse. The best cut is the last, a send-up of "Put on a Happy Face." Fay declares, "Soon the whole world will blow up. Put on a happy face. None of our kids will grow up. Put on a happy face. It isn't safe to walk the streets at night. You'll be way-laid. Even the cops don't walk their beats at night. They're too afraid ... the world's really a terrible place. So put on a happy face!"

In New York, interest from cabaret fans pumps up the price.

BARRY DIAMOND

- FIGHTER PILOT (IRS SP 70035) *1/2 $4 $8

In 1983, when this album was recorded, nightclubs had begun to fill up with such an impossible crew of hedonistic yuppies and simpleminded beerheads that most stand-up comics had to battle them with a clown's arsenel: zany faces, exaggerated gestures, cheap cursing, and aggressive insult patter. This disc is an example of just how bad things got at The Comedy Store in California.

Among the awful ploys Diamond uses here is the cliché of black dialect. For ten painful minutes he stomps around the stage as a ghetto Black: "Inside dis body is a black man screamin' to be free. Let me outta hee-yuh! Don't mess wit me, lemme out!" He doesn't miss the cliché of gay dialect either, regularly lisping in italics. He slips into a Hispanic accent to sing new lyrics to a Leslie Gore tune: "Ees my pro-blum an I cry eef I wan tu, joo would cry too eef de shit hoppen to you! Holy Shit! I try to cry and I shit!" Then the capper in a gay voice: "Oh! Oh! Spaghettios!" This witlessness actually drives the crowd wild.

SELMA DIAMOND

- SELMA DIAMOND TALKS AND TALKS AND TALKS (Carlton LPX 5001) *1/2 $5 $10

A Brooklyn-born comedy writer, Diamond wrote for Groucho Marx, Milton Berle, Sid Caesar, and others. She occasionally worked as a character comedienne, and costarred on *Night Court* until her death in 1985.

Her lone comedy album has an unfortunately accurate title. Diamond talks and talks in her distinctively broad New York accent. The fault isn't all hers; this isn't really a stand-up album. Done when she was a regular raconteur on Jack Paar's show, her anecdotal chatter was glued together sans Paar's questions or prompting. The result, intended to sound like a seamless monologue, instead seems like a self-preoccupied woman gabbing on the phone to a speechless or dead friend.

A cute gag or two comes through: "Oh, do you know about this? A lot of schools around New York keep sending school reporters over to interview me. So this little girl comes over from Girl's College the other day, and she says, 'We wanna know if a career in television as a writer compensates for marriage.' Now that's crazy. You know, on a cold night you're gonna warm your feet on the back of a typewriter? Oh, and another thing she wanted to know is, 'How old a girl should be before she goes to a prom in a strapless dress.' So I said if it stays up, you're old enough."

Diamond appears on Dave Barry's Howard Hughes parody album.

LITTLE JIMMY DICKENS

- MAY THE BIRD OF PARADISE FLY UP YOUR NOSE (Columbia CS 9242) ** $5 $10
- GREATEST HITS (Columbia CS 9351) ** $5 $10
- AIN'T IT FUN (Harmony HS 11220) ** $5 $10
- COUNTRY GIANT (Sony Special Products A 24201) ** $7

Back in 1949, Little (4'10") Jimmy Dickens had his first novelty hit. Whether it was waiting for the family to settle down for dinner, or just to keep the little kid out of trouble, his mama seemed to have only one remedy: "Take an Old Cold Tater and Wait." Over the years, especially in the '50s and '60s, he had more hits on the country charts, both novelty and straight.

Dickens doesn't have a particularly funny voice, and in performance doesn't look or act goofy either. But often his records are stashed in the comedy section, unlike Roger Miller, for example. This discography concentrates on his overtly comic albums.

In 1965, at forty, he had his biggest hit, "May the Bird of Paradise Fly Up Your Nose." Dickens sings the breezy novelty even now when he's in concert or on cable's Nashville Network.

The "Greatest Hits" compilation includes both hits plus several other toe-tappers: "Truck Load of Starvin' Kangaroos," "A-Sleepin' at the Foot of the Bed," and "Out Behind the Barn." There's also the tune that sounded slightly crude to anyone not listening closely: "Where Were You When the Ship Hit the Sand."

The Harmony compilation includes "I'm In Love Up to My Ears," "Walk Chicken Walk 'Cause You're Too Fat to Fly," "Bessie the Heifer," and "It May Be Silly but Ain't It Fun." The latter, a typical twangy rockabilly number, is all about kissin': "No matter if it's ten below or ninety in the shade, I'm always ready when there's lovin' to be made. My heart is just as frisky as a little poodle pup, so if you're ready for a kiss, I got one comin' up!"

The chintzy CD collection "Country Giant" mixes up straight tunes with his two major comic hits "Take an Old Cold Tater" and "May the Bird of Paradise."

PHYLLIS DILLER

- WET TOE IN A HOT SOCKET (Mirrosonic SP 6002) **1/2 $5 $20
- PHYLLIS DILLER LAUGHS (Verve 150256) *** $5 $12
- ARE YOU READY FOR PHYLLIS DILLER (Verve 15031) *** $5 $12
- WHAT'S LEFT OF PHYLLIS DILLER (Verve 15059) *** $5 $12
- BEST OF PHYLLIS DILLER (Verve 15053) *** $5 $12
- THE BEAUTIFUL PHYLLIS DILLER (Verve V6 15062) *** $5 $12
- GREAT MOMENTS IN COMEDY (Verve 15046) *** $5 $12
- BORN TO SING (Columbia CS 9523) $5 $10

Nearing forty, Phyllis Diller took to the stage, first as a madcap "chichi" comedienne, then as the character she's famous for today: the world's worst housewife, decked out in a fright wig and bizarre costumes, laughing at her own jokes with a trademark cackle.

The Mirrosonic album gives an idea of her early style. A bit risqué, sophisticated, and "campy," Phyllis was a chic chanteuse exuding bad taste: "My gown is by Charles ... Addams! Ha ha ha ... and he is very sick!" Among her saucy one-liners: "I can't tell you how really dedicated I am to culture ... I honestly believe that there is absolutely nothing like going to bed with a good book. Or a friend who's read one."

In between, like any cabaret performer of the period, she sang songs. Hers are mostly offbeat originals ("I'd Rather Cha Cha than Eat," "Cornflakes on the Rocks") though she covered semi-sick songs like Rodgers and Hart's "To Keep My Love Alive," about a woman who marries many men and kills them off: "... when Harry had insomnia, and couldn't sleep at night, I bought a little arsenic. He's sleeping now, all right."

"Laughs" marks the start of Diller's career. She became the first truly successful female stand-up star, not only making records, but headlining top clubs, guesting regularly on TV variety shows, and ultimately making movies and having her own sitcom. Her successful style was an interesting combination of character comedy (the cartoonish housewife) and solid one-liners delivered with a deadpan glare (Bob Hope was her inspiration).

Side One of "Laughs" contains "The New Look," "The Management," "Old Age," "Beauty Parlor," "Plastic Surgery," "Lipstick," and "New Cosmetic." On Side Two: "Moment of Truth," "Driving Downtown," "Home Maker," "Suki Yaki," "Sequel to Suki Yaki," "Cleaners," and "Insecurity."

By the time of this record, March of 1961, Diller had just about ditched her off-color material. The exception is a quickie: "Last night somebody brought a nine-year-old little boy in here. When he left he was thirty-eight." Mostly she talks about her homely home, and here, her kitchen floor: "Sections of it were moving! I thought what would I do to me if I were that filthy? So I cold-creamed it! I made a big mistake. I left the room. And HE came home! Well, he must've hit it awful fast ... You haven't seen winter sports! Nobody knows how many times he went around—before he hit the wall! And when I say hit the wall, we took him out with a torch. He broke six legs. He was carrying a dog."

"Are You Ready" has, on Side One, "Don't Eat Here," "The Way I Dress," "Beadcraft," "Hypochondriac," "Cookbook," "Household Hints," and "Cheese and Turkey." For Side Two: "Tight Wad Airlines," "Small Chest Condition," and "Labor Day."

Another very fine album of zany material, the highlight is Diller's report on the day the Food and Drug Administration came to her door: "I was making a pudding and I knew something was wrong. I couldn't get the spoon out. They wanted to stir it and the whole room went around! And then they wanted to take it to their lab to test it. They had to. One of their guys was now stuck in it. They took it to the lab and tested it. Are you ready? My pudding is bulletproof."

Verve reissued Phyllis Diller's records—twice! Collectors are advised to pick up the original two, or "What's Left" and "Best of" to avoid duplication.

"Born to Sing" does try for laughs on a few cuts. On "I Can't Get No Satisfaction," Diller puts on a breathy fake-sexy voice that will make listeners wince. She notes between refrains, "I'm such a loser if I bought a new hat they'd cancel Easter ... I wore a see-through dress and nobody looked!" Weirder is her deliberately off-key and boozy version of "One for My Baby," with jokes added: "He was so dumb. Ooh boy was he dumb. I brought him home one day. I wanted to show him to my mother. I was so humiliated, you know what she said? She said, 'Look, if you're gonna keep it, you have to feed it and walk it.'"

NOTES: Diller sings on "Nostalgia Goes Bananas" (Stanyan SR 10096), "Arthur Schwartz Revisited" (Painted Smiles 1350), and "Harold Arlen Revisited" (Painted Smiles 1345). She appears in sketch material on Bob Hope's "Still There's Hope" album (Capitol ST 11538) and Flip Wilson's "Geraldine" (Little David 1001). Verve (DJ-EPV-5074) released a promotional extended play 45 rpm version of "Phyllis Diller Laughs" (with a black and white version of the cover).

THE DIRTY OLD MAN

* AN EVENING WITH THE ORIGINAL DIRTY OLD MAN (Twi-Lite) ** $5 $10
* THE ORIGINAL DIRTY OLD MAN STRIKES AGAIN (Twi-Lite) ** $5 $10
* VERY WORST OF THE ORIGINAL DIRTY OLD MAN (Twi-Lite) ** $5 $10

Arizona-based comic Tim Adams recorded his "Dirty Old Man" albums for a Phoenix record label. His flinty, grim style in singing song parodies and reciting "Over Sexteen" type routines gives his albums a misogynistic, mean edge.

On his "Strikes Again" album, Adams tells of two brothers, one the owner of a broken-down boat that sank; the other, a recent widower. When a woman consoles the boat owner, thinking he's the widower, she's shocked by his description of the "deceased." He tells her: "She was rotten from the beginning. Her bottom was all shriveled up and she smelled like dead fish. Her gear box was full of sand and her bottom was all covered with crabs.... She had a big crack in the back and a big hole in the front, and that hole got bigger all the time. She leaked like hell, too. But that's not what finished her. Four guys from the other side of town, looking for a good time, asked if I'd rent her to 'em.... The damn fools all tried to get in her at once. It was just too much for her. She cracked in the middle."

Periodically, pianist Adams, backed by a bassist and a drummer, sings country-tinged songs that are tasteless, but not necessarily funny. "Boobie" is a switch on the depressing Kenny Rogers tune "Ruby." He mutters, "It's hard to love a man whose thing is bent and paralyzed. Or to love a man whose joint has just been circumcized. And it won't be long I've heard 'em say until I'm not around. Hey, Boobie, stop spreadin' your ass all over town."

DR. DAVE

* VANNA, PICK ME A LETTER (TSR Records TSR 852) * $3 $7

Dr. David Kolin used to be a dentist, but he wasn't inflicting enough pain on people. He became a radio comic, the ultimate in torture. This mini-album has lame sketches on one side (the kind morning DJs love to inflict on unsuspecting listeners) and the musical parody "Vanna, Pick Me a Letter" on the other. Based on the old hit "The Letter," it's just Dr. Dave reciting moronic doggerel in a Cheech Marin accent: "Vanna, I don't mean to stare, but are you wearing underwear?" Periodically the grubby Chicano shouts out things like "Arrright!" and sidewalk-level insults: "Vanna White, you beautiful, baybeeee! You an' me could play the home game!"

JOE DOLCE

* SHADDAP YOU FACE (MCA 5211) * $4 $8

The title track is a novelty tune from 1981. Using a cornball Italian accent, Dolce gently and simplemindedly repeats his momma's words of wisdom. And he repeats the words over and over in a quiet, inane sing-song refrain that could drive one slowly to drugs: "Whatsammata you ... Waddya think you do? Why-a you looka so sad? Itsa not so bad, it's a nice-a place. Shaddappa you face!" Nicola Paone he isn't.

The album is padded out with a lot of mediocre straight tunes, from bland pop ("Stick It Out") to ersatz Carpenters ("How Can Our Love Be Gone," in duet with Lyn Van Hecke). There are only two novelty cuts. Dolce sings a country twanger called "Ain't No U.F.O. Gonna Catch My Diesel," and puts his cutesy Italian accent to work on the old Jamaican novelty tune "If You Want to Be Happy."

Dolce also issued "The Christmas Album" (Montage 72002), which contains a few seasonal novelty cuts.

PAUL DOOLEY

* BOOKED SOLID (Strand SL 1018) ** $5 $15

Character comic Paul Dooley appeared in dozens of sitcoms in the '60s and even got a chance to do an album during the comedy disc boom early in the decade. It's all about books, as Dooley translates fairy tales, offers nonsense Shakespeare, and reads from "The Subway Rule Book." Most of it might read better than it sounds. From the latter, the subway system "has a point system for politeness. For example, if you step on someone's feet, you lose two points. If you hold someone's package you get four points. If you step on someone's package you get six points, if you hold someone's feet you lose eight points. And if someone holds your feet while you hold someone's package, you lose the game. Back to Times Square ... Oh listen to this, if you fall against a beautiful blonde you lose twelve points. But what's twelve points!"

EARLE DOUD

• SOUNDS FUNNY (Epic BN 598) *	$4	$12
• SCORE THREE POINTS (Capitol T 2629) **	$3	$10
• EARLE DOUD'S CELEBRITY WORKOUT (Capitol 12312) *1/2	$3	$8

Earle Doud produced or coproduced more than a dozen comedy and novelty albums, including Vaughn Meader's "The First Family." "Sounds Funny" is a series of blackout sketches keyed to sound effects. Several other performers, including Bob Prescott, made similar tiresome records. They probably were bought by early stereo fanciers who wanted an album that would show off their equipment. For example, on "The Annoying Kitten," one speaker has the meows that are disturbing Doud's sleep. Doud is on the other speaker grumbling. There's the sound of him opening a stuck wooden drawer and then throwing a can that skids from one speaker to the other. But, it misses the cat. Next, some gunshots. They also miss. Then there's the sound of him clomping downstairs, winding from speaker to speaker, until he's finally out in the yard. He's about to go after the cat when (audio punch line) there's a lion's roar.

"Score Three Points," a comical "quiz" from 1966, is very dated. From a multiple choice segment: "When Bobby Kennedy comes home in the evening, he a) has a nap, b) has dinner, c) has children."

Doud rarely spoke more than a few lines on any of his albums, and even on "Celebrity Workout," he makes only a brief appearance. He could've called more attention to this disc if he headlined one of its actual stars: Fred Travalena, Rich Little, or Julie Dees. They supply the celebrity voices on this attempt to cash in on the "Jane Fonda Workout" series. What if ... instead of Fonda, some other celebrities tried to give aerobic instruction?

A good enough idea quickly turns sour. Doud introduces his first guest instructor, Richard Nixon. As Nixon, Rich Little notes, "We used to do exercises all over the White House—running from subpoena to subpoena." "Wouldn't you like to change into some exercise clothes?" Doud asks. "These are my exercise clothes!" Nixon insists. "A blue suit?" With disco music blaring, Nixon offers such rib-tickling aerobic ideas as, "Lift your hands over your head and make a V sign." The tedious, nearly seven-minute joke is already gasping for breath by the time Julie Dees, as Jane Fonda, turns up to rant and rave at Nixon for stealing her idea. The rest of it is at the same level. When Jimmy Carter (Travalena) exercises, his mother Miss Lillian interrupts with familiar insults: "Every time I think of him, I wish birth control was retroactive."

JACK DOUGLAS

• JACK DOUGLAS AND THE ORIGINAL CAST (Columbia CL 1556/CS 8357) **1/2	$5	$20

As both writer and raconteur on Jack Paar's *Tonight Show*, Douglas gained enough fame to launch a book career (beginning with the near classics "Never Trust a Naked Bus Driver" and "My Brother Was an Only Child"), and briefly some stand-up work.

Before an evidently handpicked enthusiastic audience at The Bon Soir, Douglas isn't nearly as wild and whimsical as his writing. He's laid back, offering rambling anecdotes. Some material sounds like things Jonathan Winters might've done if he was tired or a little under the weather: "I'm on the Emergency Redi-Whip Team in New York. It's not what you think ... these jet planes, they're still having trouble with them, the landing gear ... and we get these calls in the middle of the night: grab your can. Redi-Whip comes in a can. Get out to the airport ... we spread the stuff on the runway nice and smooth, nice and deep, nice and even. We were at La Guardia and the plane landed at Idylwild."

Douglas is less well known now; the $20 that was routinely slapped down for it in the '70s is usually half that.

TOM DREESEN

• THAT WHITE BOY'S CRAZY (Flying Fish FF 70516) **	$5	$10

There are two sides to Dreesen. He's a slick comic who has opened for Frank Sinatra and has more than fifty *Tonight Show* appearances to his credit. But in addition to being a reliable middle-of-the-road comic, he has been able to play tough ghetto nightclubs, hence the title of this album. Back in the late '60s he and Tim Reid formed an interracial comedy team, working for six years until Reid landed a role on *WKRP in Cincinnati*. The Chicago-based duo cut one album as "Tim and Tom."

On this disc, recorded before a black crowd back home in the Windy City, Dreesen offers mild racial humor: "I've always felt that it was white folks that are responsible for the blues. I know you think black folks are, but if it wasn't for white folks, you wouldn't've had anything to be blue about."

ALLEN DREW

• MR. SPEAKER (Giggles) **	$5	$10
• STAG PARTY (Dooto DTL 259) **	$5	$10

Allen Drew's funky delivery is raw and likable, like the familiar jokes on the "Mr. Speaker" album:

"I've been helpin' out my neighbor's family next door. They have several children and she's got to work and take care of them herself so I've been doin' a little babysitting for her. She's got one daughter twenty years old. I'm sitting with her. Watching her is my job! And that's one job I don't mind layin' down on ... her mother's a school teacher. I was in her classroom one day. She said, 'All right kids, we have a visitor, be very studious. I want all you kids to step up to the blackboard and get your arithmetic lessons. Alice, you do number one, Phyllis you do number two. And the rest of you kids can do it sittin' in your seats. And if you need any paper just let me know.'"

"Stag Party" (with a picture of Drew and a stuffed stag head) contains "Juvenile Delinquency," "High Nuts," "Feel Funny Fanny" and others.

CHARLEY DREW

- FOR THE CONNOISSEUR (Gala 1) ** $10 $20
- ALBUM 2 (Gala 2) ** $10 $20
- ALBUM 3 (Gala 3) ** $10 $20
- ALBUM 4 (Gala 4) ** $10 $20
- CHARLEY DREW AT THE TAFT (Roulette 24324) ** $10 $15

Back in the '50s, Drew performed sophisticated risqué songs at the Tap Room of the Hotel Taft. The first of his ten-inch albums on Gala included "Blushing Bride," "Bell Bottom Trousers," "The Girls I've Loved and Lost," "Robert the Roue from Reading," "Gracie Is Socially Secure," "Lousy Louisa," "They Didn't Give the Bride Away," and "Fleet's in Today."

The second had "Phil Spitalny's Band," "Can't Put It on a Platter," "Every Girl I've Ever Known has Had One," "Cup Cakes," "Scheherazade," "The Mailman," "The Tinker, The Tailor," and "The Wedding Cake."

The third: "It's Better than Taking in Washing," "Up in the Second Mezzanine," "The Shameless Little Shed," "Lord Stuffit and Lord Stickit," "Caviar Comes from Virgin Sturgeon," "She Went to See a Man About a Dog," "You Can't Fool the Boys Behind the Desk," and "Mabel's a Glamour Girl Now."

The fourth: "Do Not Disturb," "She's Got the Biggest Kanakas on the Island," "Marie of the Follies Bergere," "I Guess I'm Not the Guy I Used to Be," "Annie's Trailer," "The Book Song," "Lady Psychaitrist," and "Gladys."

Later, Gala issued three full-size discs with a few additions and deletions. Typical is "The Mailman," a predictable set of frisky double entendres: "He gives fine daily service, and he's not one to protest. A mailman's got a route that's longer than the rest! A mailman's got the longest route in town. You'd think that such a route would get him down. But still he keeps it up, he's frisky as a pup. At each house along the way he delivers twice a day. You'd think he couldn't stand an extra pound. That this pouch would just be dragging on the ground. He's been doing it for years, yet he hasn't stripped any gears. A mailman's got the longest route in town."

Drew's lone major label release is a disappointment. It's his only live album and the crowd seems indifferent. There's constant background noise as people drink, eat, and talk. When he sings about old flame Fanny Brown ("You can all kiss my Fanny in Miami, and it won't mean a thing to me") it doesn't mean a thing to them. In fact, they're more enthusiastic when they sing along to the straight calypso tune "All Day All Night Mary Ann."

DUCK'S BREATH MYSTERY THEATRE

- OUT OF SEASON (Duck's Breath 101) * $4 $10
- BORN TO BE TILED (Rounder 3054) * $4 $10

Long after Firesign set up their Theatre, the Duck's Breath troupe began to perform, reaching San Francisco in 1976 and National Public Radio soon after. On "Born to Be Tiled," jokeless ten-minute routines like "The Invasion of the Mole People" (using the plot from "Invaders from Mars") are so tediously uninteresting it's a wonder they could write it, much less perform it. A sample of the meandering, pseudo-Firesign style in a Jacques Cousteau parody:

"I am Jacque Cocteau, welcome to my underwater world. I, with my companion Philco, have searched the waters of the world, especially central Canada, looking for things that you haven't already seen on *Wild Kingdom* ... many times people ask me questions like this: 'How is it that you, a Canadian boy from the plains of Saskatchewan, become so in love with the sea?' That's a good question. When I was a child we had no money for a bath tub. I grew up washing in the same little pan my mother used for to wash the dishes. I swore some day I would have enough water so I could stretch my feet out in it."

Even worse, their attempts at original comedy songs are not only toothless, but annoying. The most successful cut, and not that successful, is the Ernie Kovacsian "Ask Dr. Science." An interviewer and Dr. Science: "Dear Dr. Science, are cyclotrons good for making popcorn?" "No, but they make a great chocolate shake." "Dear Dr. Science, do you have to patent a cow before you can patent leather?" "Merely copyrighting the cow is enough...." "Dear Dr. Science, how come I can't look at the sun without sneezing?" "You're probably allergic to photons. Consult a physician or physicist immediately."

Various cassette tapes have collected more Duck's Breath material and the best of "Dr. Science."

DUKE OF PADUCAH

- BUTTON SHOES, BELLY LAUGHS AND MONKEY BUSINESS (Starday 148) **1/2 $8 $15

Benjamin "Whitey" Ford was "The Duke of Paducah," the country comedian with the catchphrase at the end of his shows, "I'm goin' back to the wagon, these shoes are killin' me."

The Grand Ol' Opry veteran issued only one album, a fast-paced collection of old and new gags. His brisk delivery has little of the stereotypical twang one might expect from a vintage Opry or rural comedian and many of the jokes are not Southern at all: "I see an article in the paper that says twenty-five percent of all men propose to their wives in an automobile. That's like I say. More accidents happen in a car than any other way...."

"Here's a cute story about a baby duck and a mother duck. You know, spring, and they were flying back North? And a jet went by 'em. Zoom, like that. And this baby duck said to the mama duck, 'Now that's what I call speed.' And the mama duck said, 'Yeah, well if you had four rear ends and they were all on fire, you'd fly fast, too!'"

For material like that, the album was marked "Adults Only ... Banned for Radio Broadcast Everywhere."

ANDREW DUNCAN

- THE INCOME TAX MAN (Smash SRS 67033) *1/2 $4 $8

Duncan plays a tax man named "Newbold Flound," which gives a good idea of the leaden sense of humor on this concept album.

Mr. Flound visits a variety of celebrities portrayed by Christopher Weeks, and not very accurately. Most of these are very short blackout sketches:

A visit to Jack Benny: "Mr. Jack Benny? Yes?" "Internal Revenue." "I'll send it, I'll send it already, don't hound me! Good gracious. Well!"

Here's the complete sketch on Ed Sullivan: "Let's see now. You deduct for dancing lessons, Dale Carnegie, membership to friendship clubs. I watch your television show every Sunday night. Now who are you trying to kid, Mr. Sullivan?"

One of the few bright spots is a cute quickie encounter between the tax man and Bill Dana:

"Are you Mr. Bill Dana?" "Yes sir, I am." "I'm from the income tax department." "My name Jose Jimenez!"

Ironically, not long after this record was made, Duncan would play straight man to the real Bill Dana on a Jose Jimenez album, "Live in Las Vegas."

JIMMY DURANTE

- JIMMY DURANTE (Decca DL 5116) *** $20 $35
- JIMMY DURANTE IN PERSON (MGM E 542) *** $15 $25
- JIMMY DURANTE AND GARRY MOORE (Memorabilia MLP 721) ** $5 $10
- JIMMY DURANTE ON RADIO (Radiola MR 1080) **1/2 $6 $15
- DURANTE: PATRON OF THE ARTS (Viper's Nest VN 151) **1/2 $8

Durante issued several albums of straight music and a few that included some of his snappier novelty songs. Not too many albums of his radio material have surfaced. The Radiola disc offers a complete episode of *The Jimmy Durante Show* (1947, with Charles Boyer guest star, and appearances by Peggy Lee, Alan Reed, and Candy Candido). The other side includes a meandering five-minute recollection recorded in 1972, and segments from shows recorded in 1943, 1949, and 1958, featuring Benny Rubin, Tallulah Bankhead, and his old cronies Clayton and Jackson. There's plenty of crazy and corny gags, all lifted by Durante's ebullient personality:

"The subways are too crowded." "Too crowded?" "Why, I stood in the local the other day for three stations before a lady got up and gave me her seat!" "A lady gave you her seat?" "Yes! She was reading a newspaper that was wrapped around a flounder. Suddenly she took a look at my nose and said, 'Sit down, Bud, you're carryin' a bigger bundle than I am' ... I'm as sharp as a sponge cake tonight!"

The album ends with a brief "Goodnight" song, and a final, "Goodnight Mrs. Calabash, wherever you are."

The 1994 CD from Viper's Nest compiles more radio material, both songs and a few routines. Peggy Lee, Victor Moore, Eddie Cantor, Rose Marie, and Bing Crosby are featured.

Among the various soundtrack albums and musical discs, the best for comedy fans is "Jimmy Durante" (Decca DL 5116), a rare ten-incher featuring eight songs, including some of his most energetic and silly numbers: "Inka Dinka Doo," "Jimmy the Well Dressed Man," "So I Ups to Him," "Durante—Patron of the Arts," and the exasperating monologue "Joe Goes Up—I Come Down." The humor is as much in the delivery as in the gags, as in "So I Ups to Him," Jimmy's account of a meeting with a bully who shoved him in the street: "He pushed me off the sidewalk onto the side asphalt. So I ups to him, and he ups to him, and I ups to him and I said it was his fault. He said it was my fault. I said it was his fault. He said, 'If you don't like it I'll punch you right in the proboscis!' I was so mad I was frothin' at the kneecaps ... but I don't do nothin' I just keeps my attitude, see? Then I said, 'Wait a minute, wait a minute, Mac, you might look like a lumberjack, but you can't bulldoze me!' And with that, to show him who was boss, I put a chip on my shoulder and said, 'Knock it off, knock it off.' Five minutes later the chip was still there. But the shoulder was gone!"

Also pretty good is "In Person," full of silly gags made funnier by his irresistible personality. "I'm the Guy Who Found the Lost Chord" details his struggle to make musical history. With his usual bluster, he declares, "How I struggled! I worked my head to the bone!" And "It's My Nose's Birthday" has some grotesque imagery: "My nose was born upon this day in 1893. Exactly two weeks later, the stork delivered me ... It was the first time in history that the nose outweighed the child!" Only Durante could get away with the ridiculous "I'll Do the Strutaway in My Cutaway" and "Chidabee-Ch-Ch."

DYNAMITE

- DYNAMITE (Laff 181) *1/2 $4 $8
- DYNAMITE BLOWS YOUR MIND (Laff 163) *1/2 $4 $8
- SUPER SPOOK (Laff 189) *1/2 $4 $8

There's nothing explosive about Dynamite, who ambles through recitations that rely on colorful cursing more than jokes. He'll tell the crowd that what he's got "is swell for leakin' and sweet and tender as Kentucky Fried Chicken!" And they laugh and snicker approvingly. He rarely lets a sentence or two go by without some funky adjective ("stinkin," "damn," and so on) and that's all his fans want in his descriptions of sex with his latest "ho" or "bitch."

EAST SIDE KIDS

- COME OUT FIGHTING (Murray Hill M67393) *1/2 $6 $15
- BEST OF THE EAST SIDE KIDS (Murray Hill 57385) *1/2 $6 $15

The East Side Kids, also called The Bowery Boys, were a likable group of New York-accented delinquents who supported Humphrey Bogart in the 1937 drama *Dead End*, and later went on to star in a series of low-budget comedies. Murray Hill was known for its boxed sets of old radio shows, but these aren't episodes of some mythical East Side Kids radio series. "Come Out Fighting" has the soundtracks to three of their quick, hour-long flicks: "Spooks Run Wild," "Come Out Fighting" and "Bowery Champs." "Best of" turns three more East Side Kids melodrama-comedies to wax: "The Clancy Street Boys," "Follow the Leader," and "Block Busters."

The action is not easy to follow on audio alone. Videocassettes have rendered these discs obsolete, though die-hard fans might get a chuckle or two just hearing Leo Gorcey's grousy voice and Huntz Hall's oafish joking.

HERB EDEN

- WOMEN ARE LIKE SOCKS: YOU HAVE TO CHANGE THEM EVERY DAY
  (Record Productions 3,000,006) ** $5 $10
- IN THE GARDEN OF EDEN (Lobo L 105c, also issued as FAX 105 and Laff 105) ** $5 $10

Eden is a nondescript performer, but on the poorly recorded "In the Garden of Eden" disc circa 1964, it's interesting to hear a white comic borrowing material from Redd Foxx. He opens the show with a bit on integration and how he'd like to fly over Alabama ("I wish I was a big bird with diarrhea"). He talks about a suspicious death: "They found a colored fella's body in an alley with thirty-two bullet holes in it. Coroner's report stated it was the worst case of suicide he ever saw. Integration is getting into all fields ... they're even bringing back one of my favorite radio shows, *The Shadow*. It'll be integrated. It's gonna be a gas. It'll say, 'Who knows what evil lurks in the hearts of men! The shadow do!' I met a fella from Alabama, he said, 'I ain't prejudiced. I don't mind sleepin' with 'em—I ain't goin' to school with 'em.' I found out why them damn Alabamans are afraid—they'll raise the scholastic standing and their kids'll flunk out."

To his credit, there is much more interracial humor on this disc than on most clean records of the era, and actually more clean material than one would expect from a Lobo "adults only" album recorded at "Pussycat A Go Go." Of course there's a helping of audience shpritzes that are true blue: "Uncross your legs. I don't want you to get a rash." There are familiar sex bits, some oldies, and this variation on a Lenny Bruce quip: "I like the flamenco dancers with the tight pants. They stand on the stage, keep looking back over their shoulder to see if their ass fell off."

WALKER EDMISTON

- LYNDONLAND (PS Records CB 558S) *1/2 $4 $10

Walker Edmiston is very soft-spoken as Lyndon Johnson on this topical disc. Ray Ballard is Hubert Humphrey, Peggy Doyl is Lady Bird, Harlan Del Cameron is Senator Dirksen, and Len Weinrib handles most everyone else. Some vignettes try to go beyond the standard "press conference" and "televised speech" devices. Like the odd concept of LBJ meeting with Jack E. Leonard (voice by Len Weinrib). Johnson starts, "I need some help with my style of making speeches ... what do you suggest I do?" "Get outta the business! I'm just kiddin'. Ya gotta use insult comedy ... I'll show ya what I mean: I wanna say, good evening ladies and gentlemen and welcome to the United States of Me. I wanna say you folks out there better laugh it up because you can easily be replaced by immigrants!"

OGDEN EDSL

- STUFFED (Sunburn SBLP 101) *1/2 $5 $12
- MOWER OF THE OGDEN EDSL (Oglio 81578-2) *1/2 $8

Ogden Edsl (Bill Frenzer) had a Dr. Demento radio show hit with "Dead Puppies." Using a snivelling, mock-sad voice, Ogden sings about how his puppy died and "dead puppies aren't much fun." Kids are especially fond of the tune, complete with sicko-silly verses:

"My puppy died late last fall. He's still rotting in the hall ... Mom says Puppy's days are through. She's going to throw him in the stew ... Dead puppies aren't much fun."

Unfortunately, not a single cut on the album comes anywhere near this one-shot wonder. Instead, Edsl betrays an inept fondness for the styles of Tiny Tim and the New Vaudeville Band. Worse than the sappy nonsense songs that deliberately try to be wacky are the miserable spoken passages emulating Firesign Theater. There's plenty of redundant dialogue, overdone sound effects, and put-on voices in these belabored parodies of quiz shows, radio commercials, and disc jockeys.

"Russian Roulette Giveaway" has quiz contestants gleefully risking death for various prizes such as "the latest thing in bedtime toys, the Bedtime Bondage Barbie kit ... complete with that slavish Ken doll you've heard about ... a Mack Truck made entirely out of Stuckey's Pecan Logs ... an American Tourister suitcase stuffed full of the deeds to one thousand bankrupted dustbowl farms, a legacy of misery ... and a chihuahua the size of a coffee cup."

The 1977 album was reissued on CD in 1995 from Oglio with added tracks like the dopey, obvious, reverse-racist "Only White People Dance Like That" ballooning the nonsense to nearly seventy minutes.

JONATHAN AND DARLENE EDWARDS

• PIANO ARTISTRY (Columbia CL 1024, reissued as Corinthian 104)) **	$5	$10
• IN PARIS (Columbia CL 1513, reissued as Corinthian 103) **	$5	$10
• SING ALONG WITH JONATHAN AND DARLENE EDWARDS (RCA Victor LSP 2495, reissued as Corinthian 120) **	$5	$10
• DARLENE REMEMBERS DUKE, JONATHAN PLAYS FATS (Corinthian 117) **	$5	$12
• SONGS FOR SHEIKS AND FLAPPERS (Corinthian 122, also released as THE AMERICAN POPULAR SONG, ABC 68014) **	$5	$12

Askew music is the one-joke concept for Jonathan and Darlene Edwards. Probably the first in their field, certainly the foremost, they actually had a minor hit with their first comedy album of intentionally amateurish piano playing and deliberately off-pitch singing. It was released in 1957.

One can easily imagine a sophisticated, fun-loving party giver of the '50s sneaking a Jonathan and Darlene album on the turntable and snickering as the guests suddenly notice how terribly, terribly "off" the singing and playing is. One can't imagine the record staying on much longer after the practical joke, though.

Fans marvel at the skill the duo uses in warping the originals, but for the average listener, there's a momentary chuckle hearing a pianist, backed by a struggling orchestra, trip on his own fingers as he stumbles through "Autumn Leaves," a vocalist torment "Darling, Je Vous Aime Beaucoup" with notes that warble and soar and then warp and go sore. Both are on the second album, which was keyed to the mid-50s mini-glut of "I Love Paris" instrumental discs.

The first album offers piano nightmare renditions of "Nola" and "Dizzy Fingers," as well as the now unromantic ballads "Stardust" and "Sunday, Monday or Always." 1962's "Sing Along" is intended to vaguely parody the popular Mitch Miller albums. Not only is it in stereo, it has a full chorus of bad singers. A Jack Davis caricature cover makes it more valuable.

Jonathan and Darlene were actually Paul Weston, who made many straight mood music albums, and his wife Jo Stafford, who was not only a legit singer with "You Belong To Me" in 1952, but also an old hand at novelty hits, including 1947's "Tim Tayshun" with Red Ingle's band.

Corinthian reissued the "classic" Jonathan and Darlene Edwards albums on vinyl and later on CD.

MARSHALL EFRON

• THE NUTRINO NEWS NETWORK (Polydor PD 5029) *	$3	$7

This 1972 album sounds like members of National Public Radio trying to imitate Firesign Theater. Efron, evidently influenced by Alexander Wolcott, tries for the campy intellectual approach as he leads his gang through the cloying, unfunny, and unhip sci-fi radio serial parody "The Case of the Missing Nutrino." Try this news item: "The Federal Bureau of Investigation has announced it has apprehended the suspects who dynamited the Capitol dome, tipped over the Washington monument, and threw fat on the Jefferson memorial." A jingle for "Obesi-berry Pies," sung by several cheery fellas, goes like this: "We've got cherry, we've got berry, we can hum when it comes to plum. Don't have to reach, you can each our peach, and you'll be tied when you eat our apple pie!"

RON ELIRAN

• WHAT DO YOU DO WHEN YOU'RE YOUNG AND WHITE AND JEWISH? (Capitol T 2285) *	$4	$10

Eliran, a folk singer from Israel who made many straight albums, has no voice for comedy. He sounds like a slightly less goat-like Charles Aznavour. Shel Silverstein fans might want to hear "Masochistic Bubbie," which Shel later recorded, sans Semitic minor key violin-work, as "Masochistic Baby."

Eliran sings a stupid parody of "Abilene" called "Tel-Aviv" ("People there don't treat ya mean, oh Lordy, not in Tel-Aviv! Dirty ol' falafel stand standing all alone, the grill's all greasy, ain't much of a home!") and an obscure Silverstein kiddie tune "The Monkey and the Elephant." In between cuts he tells a few jokes. He doesn't mind stealing-and-switching from Woody Allen: "My grandfather, before he died, on his deathbed, sold me this violin."

JACK ELJAN

• TOM LEHRER'S SONG SATIRES (Rivoli R 4, Audio Masterpiece 230) **	$5	$15

Jack Nagle (Eljan is "Nagle" backwards, sort of) recorded Tom Lehrer's material at a time when few people outside Boston were aware of Lehrer's comic songs.

Rivoli figured to sell copies in all the places Lehrer (still selling discs on his own label) hadn't reached. There were a few problems. Without sheet music to work from, Eljan had to guess at any lyrics he couldn't make out, and there are plenty of errors on the fast-patter "Lovachevsky" tune. Secondly, Lehrer never authorized the project and he hunted down Eljan for payment.

For an unknown, Jack Eljan does a credible job imitating the piano stylings and voice of Lehrer. No doubt some listeners at the time didn't know the difference. The Rivoli album is a ten-incher; the Audio Masterpiece version is normal size. For another twist on the Lehrer story, see the entry for Bob Peck.

LEONARD ELLIOT AND IRMA JURIST

- THE FUZZY PEACH PIE AND OTHER LUNACIES (Monitor MP 570) * $3 $7

Smug and pretentious Elliott and Jurist enjoy lampooning lieder and art singers. On "La Ploop De Ma Tante," for example, Elliott imitates French vocalists by howling in an outrageous accent. This parroting is supposed to pass for parody. On "Follow the Lieder," Elliott and Jurist decide that gutteral German sounds like coughing and wailing—so they cough and wail for three minutes.

The spoken routines include the title cut, Elliott's version of Shakespeare. He has decided that the bard's speeches are often much ado about nothing—so *he* will deflate the pomposity by giving a deliberately ridiculous Shakespearean speech. The subject is a peach pie the king is about to eat: "Oh, how gently lies this thing upon some velvet thing, that he with some succulent mouth might say, 'Tis mine, Tis mine, that I with my toothless mouth might look. Tis mine! Tis mine!' And on it goes, overacted and overbaked.

ELMO AND PATSY (and DR. ELMO)

- GRANDMA GOT RUN OVER BY A REINDEER (Epic EK 39931) * $7
- DR. ELMO'S TWISTED TUNES (Laughing Stock LS 1494) * $7

Elmo and Patsy had a hit with their irritating, simpleminded title track jingle. The black comedy aspect of it is completely sanitized and lobotomized by the cutesy production and Elmo's utterly harmless vocalizing.

The rest of this chintzy-sounding album of filler is unlistenable, and worse, mostly straight. There's a brat-chorus for "Rudolph the Red Nosed Reindeer," nauseating fiddles on "Jingle Bell Rock," and a strictly amateur female solo on "Joy to the World," not to imply that weak-voiced Elmo is much of a talent either.

The solo "Dr. Elmo" album is also annoying, with straining vocals and puerile lyrics. On "Betty Ford Clinic," Dr. Elmo is goggle-eyed over the fun of going into detox: "I got to get into the Betty Ford Clinic. I got to find a way I swear. Though I never have been strung out, I would love to say I hung out with the stars who check in there!"

ELVIRA

- VINYL MACABRE (Rhino RNLP 810) *1/2 $5 $10
- ELVIRA PRESENTS HAUNTED HITS (Rhino R2 71492) ** $8
- MONSTER HITS (Rhino 71788) ** $6
- REVENGE OF MONSTER HITS (Rhino 72179) ** $6

Elvira (Cassandra Peterson), campy queen of horror, has had a syndicated TV show, a starring film, and does endless TV commercials showcasing her decidedly un-dead top-heavy figure.

Fans of Elvira never get much of her beyond the sexy cover photos. She supplies brief introductions at the beginning and end of "Vinyl Macabre," a terrible compilation of novelty horror tunes. Only "Monster Mash" and "Purple People Eater" are classics—and they turn up on "Haunted Hits." Others veer between trashy noise ("Who is a pain in the neck? The Vegas Vampire!") and dated disco drivel ("Drac's Back! I wanna suck your ... wooooo!") Nobody, dead or undead, could listen to this ear infection from start to finish.

The other three, "Haunted Hits" and her two budget CDs, have the usual novelty songs everyone has heard over and over. "Haunted Hits" has Elvira on one track, the unfunny but horny "Full Moon." The Julie Brown influence is heavy as she goes through a lot of excited, prurient babble. Parents of kiddies will be hoping that they won't have to explain her references to "The Story of O" and "the curse of female trouble." Amid the oldies, "Monster Hits" has one fresh cut from Elvira ("Monsta Rap") and the sequel CD features her on "Haunted House" and "Zombie Stomp." Elvira thinks cheap and tacky is automatically funny—and that any quickly written lyric or introduction is good enough. As she says introducing her "Haunted House" song: "Let 'er rip. Uh-oh, it looks like my plunging neckline just took a dive." Too many jokes like that can make tolerance plummet.

CHARLES EMBREE

- ROOM AT THE BOTTOM (Embree LP #1000) ** $5 $10

Embree quietly oozes out his hip, jazz-tinged ditties and lightly drawled monologues with a quiet strum on the ukelele or a bit of cocktail piano accompaniment. His self-made album sports an endorsement from Ray Bradbury, who adds, "I never thought I would strongarm a musician-composer into performing at somebody's party, but Charlie Embree brings out the Sol Hurok in me."

The highlight selection is "Some of My Best Friends Are Shoes," sung in a mild, bluesy Phil Harris style. It's about a man driven by a woman "clear out of the world and reality. He ended up living in a world of shoes." He sings, "Oh the shoe has a tongue, but the tongue doesn't wag. The tongue of a shoe doesn't nag. A shoe tongue friend, will never give you the blues, some of my best friends are shoes...."

Other cuts are so subtle there doesn't appear to be much humor in them at all.

THE ESTABLISHMENT

- THE ESTABLISHMENT (Riverside 850) *1/2 $10 $20

In 1963, Peter Cook brought The Establishment (John Fortune, Jeremy Geidt, Eleanor Bron, and John Bird) to America, yet another "outspoken, iconoclastic, biting" comedy group to join the likes of The Second City, The Committee, and Beyond the Fringe. He cowrote the material with the rest of the group.

Much of the album is dated and dull. An eleven-minute interview with a "Minister of Defense" is not interesting, and it is matched on the flip side with a long sketch presenting Prime Minister MacMillan in an English version of the movie *Advise and Consent*.

"Crime Report" survives as a fine example of macabre British satire. Abbreviated for this sample, it's an interview with a police investigator trying to solve a brutal murder in a muddy bog, "a middle aged woman with her left arm and right leg missing." Jeremy Geidt to John Bird:

"What first made you suspect that the body had in effect an arm and a leg missing?" "Well, we conducted what we call a limb spot check ... essentially a numerical appreciation of the limbs found grouped around the body. In this case there were deficiencies...." "What do you use for these limb spot checks?" "Electronic computers ... unfortunately owing to the nature of the terrain, the computer sank into the mud...." "So on what did you fall back?" "We fell back on our hands...." "Have you got any suspects at all?" "... Through the Identikey, we get descriptions from a lot of witnesses. We built up a composite and after a lot of laborious toil, we have built up an extremely good likeness of the Archbishop of Canterbury."

"So the Archbishop is your number one suspect?" "... all I can say is he is the man we've been beating the living daylights out of...." "Is he still your number one suspect?" "No, no, I'm sorry to say the Archbishop, God bless him, no longer resembles the picture...."

The earlier album "The Establishment," released only in England (Odeon PMC 1198), features different material and has a lot of dated political references.

CALYPSO GENE FARMER

- INTEGRATION OF LODI (Dore LP 328) * $3 $8
- CALYPSO GENE ON THE SCENE (Dore LP 330) * $3 $8

Farmer's voice is bland, and these novelty tunes have the added distraction of simpleminded, faux hip calypso rhymes and music. "On the Scene" includes a foolish tune about E.S.P.: "Oh someone who is far away. Knows what you're thinking every day. Take Elizabeth Taylor and Princess Grace. If they knew what I was thinking. They would slap my face." And on astrology: "You can tell a personality. By studying their astrology. Most politicians as a rule. Must be Taurus, for they're full of bull."

FRANK FAY

- BE FRANK WITH FAY (Bally 12015) ** $6 $15

A Broadway star with a brash style that influenced Milton Berle and others, Fay was abrasive in private life and egocentric in public. When his career skidded, few felt sorry for him. Aside from caustic insults, Fay was known for his pioneering routines that analyzed (i.e., ridiculed) popular tunes.

For this attempted comeback in the '50s, Fay offers an entire album of song parodies. He sarcastically drubs, among others, "Blue Moon," "Everything I Have Is Yours" and "Stairway to the Stars." There's still some tang to the wise guy musings of this early purveyor of "attitude" comedy. As he recites "Tea for Two," he isn't impressed:

"*Just tea for two, and two for tea*—ain't that rich? Here's a guy, he's probably got enough tea for two, so he's gonna have two for tea. If a third person walks in, they stab him ... *Nobody near us, to see us or hear us.* Who wants to listen to two people drinkin' tea?..."

JOEY FAYE

- BURLESQUE WITH THE NUTS INSIDE (Jubilee JGM 2065) ** $5 $10

Veteran burlesque comedian Joey Faye (nee Paladino), leads Lew Black, Vini Faye, Sally deMay, and Ginna Carr through a set of patter routines including "The Bullfighter," "Three Men on a Spree," and "The Bells." A long variation on the old "we've only got a nickel" restaurant routine is full of old jokes:

"Here's your lobster lady." "Hey waiter, the lobster only has one claw." "Well you see, the lobsters are very fresh and they fight among themselves in the kitchen. That's how he lost the claw." "Well, take it back and bring me a winner!" "How about a nice tongue sandwich?" "I'll have you understand I never eat anything that comes out of an animal's mouth." "How about two eggs?" "Waiter, what's that fly doing in my water?" "The backstroke."

The lack of truly classic material here is a disappointment, and Faye is the only one with enough charisma to keep the belabored banter going. Recorded sans studio audience, even the laugh track is monotonous; the same ha-ha-ha yocks repeated over and over.

FRANK FERRANTE

- GROUCHO A LIFE IN REVUE (Original Cast OCR 9498) *1/2 $8

Ferrante may have been an accurate Groucho mimic at one time, but on this 1994 recording, he's way off the mark. Groucho's slurry New York accent disappears for long stretches, replaced by something all too precisely enunciated and theatrical. Ferrante's version of Groucho singing sounds more like Tom Lehrer, and the surprisingly stilted and stagey script, considering it was cowritten by Arthur "Son of Groucho" Marx, makes the fraud even worse. Anecdotes that the real Groucho told with charm (like the origin of the Marx Bros. real names) are grandiosly delivered and boring. The cabaret-style music and painfully bad supporting cast are the exact opposites of what Groucho and his brothers were all about. Reproductions of classic songs ("Hello I Must Be Going") are not only unconvincing, but obnoxiously overdone. Forget Ferrante's overly rouged mess and hunt up a video copy of Gabe Kaplan's similar one-man Groucho show, which was an HBO special.

CLIFF FERRE

- CAFE SOCIETY (Kem LP 100, also issued as LOOKS LIKE FUN) ** $4 $9

There's nothing special about this late '50s bland-voiced risqué singer. At least he had enough money to hire a band to help out on these jaunty, easygoing jazz numbers. On "Joe's Joint" the big double entendre joke is on the cafe owner: "Mothers brought their daughters in to sample Joe's desserts. The daughters just adored it and sampled till it hurts. One gal apologized for eating like a pig. 'That's fine,' said Joe, 'That's what makes the joint so big.' Lucky old Joe had the biggest joint in town." And for the reverse, the next band is about "Harry's Peacock." "Oh that peacock, oh that peacock, it's just about as small as it could get. Oh that peacock, oh that peacock. Still I've seen a cock or two that's smaller yet."

"Cafe Society" has an ordinary cartoon cover, but the "Looks Like Fun" version is on red vinyl and benefits from having a pair of photogenic cover girls.

STEPIN FETCHIT

- IN PERSON (Vee Jay 1032) **1/2 $10 $25

He said he was the first black millionaire in show business, but that prideful statement didn't mean much to blacks who disapproved of Fetchit's stereotypical movie roles. The album notes for this 1961 stand-up attempt reveal that he refused to part with his demeaning name (he was born Lincoln Perry), he let his money "slip through his fingers," and in films, his was indeed a "slow moving, drawling, droopy-eyed character." For the '60s, though, he promised comedy with none of "the material which might offend the newly nationalistic American Negro." It was just silly, old-fashioned gags stitched together:

"People don't remember me ... I used to be the Sammy Davis, Jr. of the Stone Age. Sammy Davis, he's now our great Jewish leader ... I know Sammy way back there, when he was ... so hungry, knockin' asking me for something to eat. And I was on the inside so hungry I couldn't even answer! He'd come to me and he said, 'Hey Step, I'm gonna dig us up a couple of girls.' And the one he got for me, he *must've* dug up! The girl will never live to be as old as she looked. Her face looked like it hurt. When we went to the zoo I had to buy two tickets for her...."

The album's small pressing, plus value to movie fans and those documenting black history, has made it high priced. Fetchit enjoyed some kind of amnesty late in life, returning to films in Moms Mabley's *Amazing Grace* and *Won Ton Ton* a few years before his death in 1985.

TOTIE FIELDS

- TOTIE FIELDS LIVE (Mainstream S 6123) *1/2 $8 $15

A New York-accented yenta doing self-deflating fat jokes amid her extroverted kvetching, Fields was a Catskill attraction and *Ed Sullivan Show* regular. Born Sophie Feldman, she pronounced her first name "Totie" as a child.

Fields raucously belts out songs and works the ringsiders with "am I right?" observations and patter. She spies a fashionable-looking woman and shouts, "I wonder if she ever bought Sani-Flush! You think she ever washed a toilet in her whole life? She's so rich I don't even know if she goes! You know? Well, they have servants for everything, you know. She could call in the maid: I have to make, that's it, it's over."

As for her weight: "I never let myself get over 110. I'm swollen, that's my problem. I have the same measurements as Elizabeth Taylor. Her living room is nine by twelve and so is mine ... my feet are killin' me! And it's hard to be sexy when your feet are swollen right over the shoes! You think it's easy pushing fat Jewish feet into thin Italian shoes?"

Sophie's story took a heartbreaking turn as she battled health problems to stay onstage. In 1976 her leg had to be amputated. Her courage was inspirational, but she died two years later. Nostalgia and a newfound respect for her as a pioneering woman in stand-up have raised prices here above what the comedy alone is worth.

Fields appears briefly on "Zingers from the Hollywood Squares" (Event EV 6903) with typically down-to-earth grousing. Question: "Do snails ever caress?" Totie: "I never saw a horny snail!"

W. C. FIELDS

- TEMPERANCE LECTURE/DAY I DRANK A GLASS OF WATER (Jay WCF1A) $10 $25
- Also available as ORIGINAL AND AUTHENTIC RECORDINGS, Blue Thumb S3;
    BEST OF FIELDS, Sutton SU 273; and FIELDS AND WEST, Proscenium 22,
    reissued by American Album, Tape AAT 120, and Harmony Records) ** $5 $15

Fields only made two recordings in his life. They made for a popular three-disc set of 78s from Variety Records bearing the credit "written and directed by Bill Morrow." No reissues include the set's color painting of Fields or his autobiographical notes, which include a fanciful retelling of the day he left home at age eleven: "I was digging up the yard, preparatory to planting some grass seed. Papa strolled up the yard, stepped on a shovel that I had carelessly left there and which bounced up and struck him on the leg. He patted me on the spine with it whilst I was leaning over. When I regained my breath, I conked the old patriarch on the noggin with a peach basket and took it on the lam....")

"Temperance Lecture" is couched in the great man's similar grandiose style, recited with piano backing. Combining Fieldsian delivery, inebriated logic, and bad jokes, the lecture is "classic," even if it's more lightweight than high. Among the revelations: "Ever since the beginning of time there has been a drink problem. Quite a problem. An even greater problem now is it's so scarce ... throughout the Middle Ages the use of liquor was universal, and drunkenness was so common it was unnoticed. They called it the Middle Ages because no one was able to walk home unless they were between two other fellows. I was usually the middle guy ... in my time I can remember the company of ... pink elephants with lavender dots, a bright blue ostrich with a mixmaster for a tail, and a chartreuse octopus that taught me to Samba ... a thief broke into my house one night and stole my octopus. He cut his tentacles off and used them for nonskid automobile tires. A cruel thing to do. I wish I had thought of it."

A live version of "The Temperance Lecture" appears on "W. C. Fields on Radio."

"The Day I Drank a Glass of Water," the other studio cut, is also an odd ramble, this time including some sneering byplay with a bartender: "It's election day. The bar is closed. It's the law." "Who made this law?" "The people voted for it." "That's carrying democracy too far."

The public domain records have appeared in many forms. The Jay release is a ten-incher. To fill up full-size records, Sutton uses radio segments, all of which were available on the pioneering Columbia album "W.C. Fields on Radio." Proscenium backed the Fields material with a set of Mae West songs. Blue Thumb later released their version—the same disc with only two West songs. Since there's no mention of her on the album cover, or what "Original and Authentic" recordings were inside, no doubt many Proscenium owners were suckered into buying a disc they already owned. If he was alive to collect royalties, Fields probably would've approved.

- W. C. FIELDS ON RADIO (Columbia CS 9890) **** $5 $15

In the late '60s, cult interest in Fields reached a new high, and Columbia put out this album of radio highlights. This was an honor: very few major labels ever issued a "radio" album.

There's plenty of Fieldsian cadence and delirium here, like this careening recollection: "The other evening, as I was traversing my garden in search of flora and fauna ... Flora's my cook you know ... I unexpectedly tripped, and the next thing I knew I was prostrate on terra firma. Which was not unusual in itself ... It was quite an experience. I broke my femur and fractured my decanter...."

Edgar Bergen and Charlie McCarthy are along for most of Side One. Highlights include a tipsy live reading of "The Temperance Lecture" and a pair of thirteen-minute sketches ("The Pharmacist" and "Promotions Unlimited") close in concept to Fields's movie shorts, loaded with delirious mutterings, wry asides, and hallucinatory plot machinations.

- THE GREAT RADIO FEUDS (Columbia KC 33241) ***1/2 $5 $20
- THE FURTHER ADVENTURES OF LARSON E. WHIPSNADE AND OTHER TARADIDDLES
  (Columbia KC 33240) **** $5 $20

In 1974, excellently preserved radio material from Fields's own archives were released on these two albums. "Taradiddles" is a treasure of surreal visions, whimsical recitations, inane running gags, and tangy ad-libs. The expressive Fields voice can be savored as the great man wheezes, drawls, and enunciates "Life Among the Bolivians," a travelogue of murderous natives and little known culinary delights: "... eggs boiled in elk's milk smothered with Bolivian onions." Before long he ends up with a vaudevillian ramble about a brother who was a surgeon turned lawyer: "He was pleading a case once and he was so absentminded, he sawed off the judge's leg. The jury laughed immoderately."

Other highlights include "Michael Finn" (based on his fascination with a particular brand of droll non-rhyming British Music Hall tune) and the semi-sick sketch "Fire in the Home," in which he maddeningly keeps interrupting a man who is trying to phone the fire department to prevent his house from burning down.

"Radio Feuds" is less essential. Scripts for the great man's battles with Charlie McCarthy often resort to easy insult banter. Fortunately, the sketches aren't cut to pieces like the earlier "Fields on Radio," so there are opportunities to hear Fields ad-lib, careening far from the script. There's plenty of time for Fieldsian asides. (Asked how he feels, he replies, "Highly irrelevent, incompetent ,and immaterial.") He also gets to inject one of his favorite tasteless jokes: "My father was a doctor. Yes, he treated a man for three years with yellow jaundice. Then he found out he was a Chinaman."

- POPPY (Columbia KC 33253, also released as
  LUX RADIO THEATER PRESENTS W. C. FIELDS by Mark 56 #595) ** $5 $15

"Lux Radio Theater" condensed films into sixty-minute programs. Cecil B. DeMille introduces "Poppy" with some fairly interesting biography, noting that the teenage vagabond "spent his nights under stairways, in box crates and in doorways.... The toughest brats for miles around would seek him out for a fight. Fields could never refuse a challenge and his bulbous nose was really a red badge of courage. It stands today as a radiant monument to the valor of its possesor ... he is still Fields against the world, a strange combination of cynicism and sentiment ..."

Sentiment dominates "Poppy," a Fields Broadway hit that became one of his lesser films. The best sequence features the charlatan selling patent medicine to a hostile crowd: "Step out of the gutter, boy, and let the water run ... Purple Bark Sarsparilla, one dollar a bottle ..." "I bought one bottle of that vile stuff from you yesterday. I spilled a little on the floor and my cat licked it up ... that medicine of yours killed him!" "Overdose. He should've only taken a nip. A cat nip."

- THE BEST OF W. C. FIELDS (Columbia CG 34144) **** $5 $15

This double album set uses material from the four previous Columbia albums, including a brief snippet from "Poppy." The cuts include: "The Pharmacist," "Temperance Lecture," "Snake Story," "Promotions Unlimited," "Father's Day," "The Golf Game," "Skunk Trap," "Tales of Michael Finn," "Strike Up the Band," "Fire in the Home," "Romeo and Juliet," and "Purple Bark Sarsparilla."

- W. C. FIELDS ORIGINAL RADIO BROADCASTS (Mark 56 #571) *** $6 $12

Mark 56 album covers rarely described the contents within—usually because they duplicated already released material. This one dupes Columbia's "W. C. Fields on Radio." The only reason to own this is to hear the introduction supplied by W. C. Fields, Jr. He sounds vaguely like his dad as he delivers familiar biographical material: "... his reputed dislike for dogs was real, and evolved out of early encounters with various breeds in which, unfortunately, he played a secondary role...." The disc was issued with a different cover as a promotional item by the Standard Oil Company of California.

- THE MAGNIFICENT ROGUE (Radiola MR 1049) *** $5 $15

Ten years after Fields's death, Fred Allen narrated this radio tribute featuring the recollections of directors Leo McCarey and Norman Taurog, biographer Robert Lewis Taylor, and the reclusive Baby LeRoy: "Some stories I heard were mostly publicity stories ... another old gag was he would spike my orange juice. These more than likely were a lot of publicity. My mother has pictures of him holding me. The expression on his face doesn't look like one of a man who doesn't like children."

- ORIGINAL VOICETRACKS (Decca DL 79164) *** $5 $12

In the late '60s when pop posters first appeared and nostalgia became a craze, Decca issued this LP complete with a poster inside and a pop art album cover. Despite the crass look of it and the narration by campy *Laugh-In* announcer Gary Owens, the album does a good job of collaging snippets from Fields's movies to explore the nuances of his genius. Fans can find everything from the immortal one-liner, "Never give a sucker an even break" to the tedious but indescribably funny "Carl La Fong" routine ("capital L small a, capital F, small o, small n, small g"). The parting shot offers the great man heartily inhaling the summer air and exclaiming delightedly, "What a gorgeous day. What effulgent sunshine. It was a day of this sort the McGillicuddy brothers murdered their mother with an ax."

- THE UNCENSORED W. C. FIELDS (Murray Hill M 5467X) *** $10 $20
- W. C. FIELDS (Metacom 0300334) *** $8
- THE BEST OF W. C. FIELDS (Nostalgia Lane NLR 1028) *** $5 $12

Most of the material on the Murray Hill set is available on the Columbia and Mark 56 radio show collections. The hour-long Metacom CD offers familiar material available on the Columbia collections, even if the titles change a bit (their "Romeo and Juliet at Alcatraz" was originally released by Columbia simply as "Romeo and Juliet"). A few tidbits are film clips, notably "Bartender Fields & Chicago Molly" and "Ice Cream Parlor," in which Fields grouses that the scene was supposed to be in a bar "but the censor cut it out."

Nostalgia Lane duplicates familiar material, from the long sketch "The Pharmacist" to the 78 rpm "Day I Drank a Glass of Water." The leisurely live version of "The Temperance Lecture" is different from the one on the Columbia "Fields on Radio" disc. There are four minutes with Fields, Martha Raye, and Parkyakarkus, and a real oddity, "False Arrest," performed without a live audience. This fifteen-minute show, somewhat similar to '50s TV's *Racket Squad*, chronicles confidence men at work. In this case, it's Fields wheeling and dealing as he buys a car by (bad) check, then immediately sells it for cash at a used car lot. More a public service than a comedy routine, it ends with this announcement:

"Send into W. C. Fields any unusual rackets or confidence games that have been worked on you or that you believe should be exposed ... you may prevent someone from being thousands of dollars poorer."

HARVEY FIERSTEIN

- THIS IS NOT GOING TO BE PRETTY (Plump 5904-2) ** $8

Fierstein fans get over an hour of gay in-jokes, anecdotes, and songs on this 1995 live show. The title of the CD refers to, among other things, his voice. A Totie Fields on testosterone, even without the flamboyant yenta persona, Fierstein's painfully froggy rasp is intolerable to non-devotees. Some of his gags seem like Bette Midler cast-offs (a song that begins, "I should wed a Jewish hotsy-totsy type, but I'm a sucker for the Nazi type"); others seem like vintage B. S. Pully: "I've got eight hard inches. Waddya lookin' down there for? It's in my hand." Mostly, amid the cries of "hello dahlings!" and "I'm spilling lots of dish," Harvey tosses out unremarkable observations like, "all straight men should have a gay friend" so they can dress better, and anecdotes that proudly call attention to his gayness. He recalls visiting a sperm bank: "This room is covered in Playboy pictures on the walls ... a video set with Playboy pornos. I open the door, and I said, "Excuse me ... do you have a little boy's room?"

FIRESIGN THEATER

- WAITING FOR THE ELECTRICIAN
  (Columbia CL 2718 CS 9518, CD reissue: Mobile Fidelity MFCD 762) *1/2 $4 $10
- HOW CAN YOU BE IN TWO PLACES AT ONCE
  (Columbia CS 9884, CD reissue: Mobile Fidelity MFCD 834 and Sony Legacy CK 9884) *** $5 $15
- NICK DANGER 3rd EYE: CASE NO 666 (Columbia DJS-29) *** $20 $35
- DON'T CRUSH THAT DWARF, HAND ME THE PLIERS
  (Columbia C30102, CD reissue: Mobile Fidelity MCFC 880) **1/2 $5 $10
- I THINK WE'RE ALL BOZOS ON THIS BUS
  (Columbia C 30737, CD reissue: Mobile Fidelity MFCD 785) **1/2 $4 $10

Back in the late '60s and early '70s when drugs became a major preoccupation on campus, a fun thing to do was to take a bunch of drugs, then turn on the TV, the radio, the stereo, or all three at once. The resultant mishmash could be unintentionally hilarious or profound, or just fascinatingly strange.

Basically, The Firesign Theater (Phil Austin, Peter Bergman, Philip Proctor, and David Ossman) did just that. Their records are a hallucinatory mix of overheard dialogue, bits of imaginary radio shows, commercials, and TV news broadcasts. They meld it together with a skeleton plot of dialogue to create sound collages that are by turns interesting, dull, pithy, momentarily great, and, with a lot of puns, in-jokes and wordplay, sometimes funny.

They defied description when they began at KPFK Radio on November 17, 1966. When they made their album debut two years later, fusing the vinyl style of Stan Freberg with the limitless visions inspired by Sgt. Pepper, most straight reviewers and humor fans were confused.

The first album seemed like a boring and bewildering brew of James Joyce, Samuel Beckett, and W. C. Fields. Even to Firesign fans, it's not an auspicious or funny beginning. A drawn out history lesson about the American Indian is well-meaning, including a stoned Hippie protester hanging out in front of an Indian reservation mumbling about stolen land and raw deals. Another western story is full of winking, but hardly hilarous, drug references: "Hi Ho Electric Brew, away ... give the nice horsey some sugar cubes." "Beat the Reaper," a game show parody about patients guessing their ailments, is loaded with dumb, hallucinatory pun play: "According to my careful prosthesis, this man has the plague."

Most fans agree that the next two are the classics. "How Can You Be in Two Places" offers a travelogue that takes the Firesigns all the way to Egypt and back for an examination of what makes America great: "We've got a lot of everything in this land of ours ... and a lot of places to put it in ... maybe that's where you fit in, Mr. and Mrs. John Q. Smith of Anytown, U.S.A." Druggie vaudeville includes this throwaway segment in which two teens have gone camping:

"The pup tent's right over there." (A dog barks.) "... I've lost the Lincoln Logs." "That's all right, I've got an Erector set." "Show off! Throw a towel over it!" "What are you guys doing in my car?" "The fox trot. You can have the next dance." (A cat meows.) "It is a cat-chy little number."

Side Two is a Nick Danger "radio show." It's easy to parody Sam Spade and even nontrippers can enjoy the Goon Show type opening: "Out of the fog and into the smog, relentlessly, ruthlessly — I wonder where Ruth is? — doggedly (sound effect of dogs barking) into the unknown..." comes Nick Danger.... "It all began innocently enough on Tuesday. I was sitting in my office that drizzly afternoon listening to the monotonous staccato of rain on my desktop and reading my name on the glass of my office door: Regnad Kesinn."

Avoiding too many lines like, "He was a Pisces working for scale," this one is recommended for newcomers. The Goons' Spike Milligan probably would approve of the bit where Nick Danger comes to the end of the record—and burrows through the plastic only to discover that everything on the other side sounds backwards. CD listeners may be extra confused. Columbia thought enough of the Nick Danger cut to issue it as a DJ promo album as "Case 666."

Although most comedy albums were susceptible to the "hear once, throw away" argument, it was obvious that these Dylans of comedy were intentionally layering their work with the immediate and the subtle so it would appeal to fans time and again. "Don't Crush that Dwarf" is another surreal stew studded with throwaway lines that hint at profundity (like the newscast that announces "those were the headlines, now the rumors behind the news"). There's a parody of Hardy Boys/Henry Aldrich-type radio shows and some fine, if fragmentary, moments of satire: "Howl of the Woof Movie, presenting honest stories of working people as told by rich Hollywood stars."

"Bozos," from 1971, lacks the usual quota of semi-joke wordplay, but contains some interesting authentic "theater" as the foursome duplicate the aural environment of a World's Fair or Disneyland, complete with official-sounding announcements ("Remember, the rubber lines are for your convenience and protection"). They echoingly walk through exhibits of future wonders as crowds "ooh" and "aah" over the educational dramaramas presented with corny-majestic music and solemn narration:

"For some reason, for some time in the beginning there were hot lumps. Cold and lonely, they whirled noiselessly through the black holes of space. These insignificant lumps came together to form the first union. Our sun. The Heating System. And about this glowing gasbag rotated the Earth, a cat's eye among aggies, blinking in astonishment across the face of time." There's great use of stereo in this absurdist satire of the future that includes such characters as a professional Bozo clown and a stark, computerized President.

- DEAR FRIENDS (Columbia KG 31099, reissue Mobile Fidelity MFCD 758) ** $10 $20
- A FIRESIGN CHAT WITH PAPOON (Columbia AS-41) $15 $30
- DEAR FRIENDS (Firesign Theatre 12 LPs) ** $75 $200
- LET'S EAT (Firesign Theatre 10 LPs) ** $50 $100
- NOT INSANE (Columbia KC 31585) *1/2 $6 $15
- TALE OF THE GIANT RAT OF SUMATRA (Columbia C 32730) ** $5 $15
- EVERYTHING YOU KNOW IS WRONG (Columbia KC 33141) ** $5 $10
- IN THE NEXT WORLD YOU'RE ON YOUR OWN (Columbia PC33475) ** $5 $10
- FORWARD INTO THE PAST (Columbia 34391) ** $5 $10

By 1972 Firesign Theater had momentarily worn out their welcome. Fans had figured out their formula and were disappointed by each new release. "Not Insane" was widely panned and "Dear Friends" merely collects bits from the group's syndicated radio show from 1970-71. Typical of that album's twenty-nine non sequiturs is the commercial from "The Giant Toad" supermarket, which boasts "the biggest in unhealable deep cut discounts ... Ma Rainey's moleskin cookies ... save on peach pits this week only, see our boy at the back ... talk to Charlie Kranepool, Ed's dad, at our liquor department, about choice USDA bourbon and rump roast cocktail party mix. Last and least, there's plenty of seasick fresh produce at our vegetable counter. Don't worry about the flies, we won't weigh 'em ... we give double discounted multi-identity stamps!"

"Papoon" was Proctor and Bergman's choice for president, and their promo album about their efforts to work on the campaign was the subject of an interview with KNX-FM radio personality Steve Marshal. Firesign issued their own set of radio material, the twelve-album "Dear Friends" set, highly prized by ardent fans. Likewise, when they did another series of radio shows in 1974, they also issued a ten-album set.

Firesign's latter Columbia albums, culminating in a 1976 "Best of," were predictable. Fans of Sherlock Holmes and Firesign may find some extra pleasure in "Giant Rat of Sumatra." The detective's name (Stones) gives an idea of the weak level of drug wit in this one. The dialogue is easy: "Aha!" "Oh, what's wrong, Stones?" "I sat on my pipe!"

"Everything You Know Is Wrong" is yet another sci-fi exercise loaded with obscurities and ravings: "You are now embarked upon a journey that must certainly lead you to change your life forever. If you were never a special person you are a special person now. Hello seeker ... there's a seeker born every minute."

"In the Next World You're on Your Own" mashes together "War of the Worlds" and "2001" for thirty minutes of dullness, but it picks up toward the end with some mild drug-oriented paranoia: "Beware. Your brain may no longer be the boss ... if you are beginning to doubt what I am saying, you are probably hallucinating." As usual, there are interruptions for radio commercials: "See that bear lappin' up that good old country water? Sure makes a big hairy guy like me thirsty. That's when I wrap my lips around a tall sweaty edible bottle of Good Old Country Bear Whiz Beer. As my daddy said, 'Son, it's in the water. That's why it's yellow.'"

- JUST FOLKS: A FIRESIGN CHAT (Butterfly 001) *1/2 $6 $12
- FIRESIGN WORLD (Dog and Cat WRMB 512) ** $20 $40
- FIGHTING CLOWNS (Rhino Records RNLP 018) ** $4 $10
- SHAKESPEARE'S LOST COMEDIE (Rhino RNLP 807) ** $5 $12
- CARTER/REAGAN (Rhino Records RNLP 904) ** $5 $12
- FIGHTING CLOWNS (reissue Mobile Fidelity MFCD-748) $8
- CASE OF THE MISSING SHOE (Rhino RNEP 506) *1/2 $4 $10
- CASE OF THE THE MISSING SHOE (Rhino RNEP 506, Marble Vinyl Pressing) $10 $5
- LAWYER'S HOSPITAL (Rhino RNLP 806) ** $4 $10
- THREE FACES OF AL (Rhino Records RNLP 812) ** $4 $10

In 1977 the group received some kind of "honor" by getting bootlegged like a rock group. Portions from a 1974 concert at Berkeley were released by Wizardo Records (on their "Dog and Cat" division).

The same year, Firesign issued one album on Butterfly Records. It is for ardent fans only. An odd moment on religious dietary advice: "Most creeping things are ... unclean." "How about caterpillars?" "A caterpillar doesn't have a backbone...." "How do you know? You char a caterpillar it gets real stiff." "Well I don't think the Lord meant us to eat charred caterpillars." "Pure protein, I ate 'em in the jungles ... I survived because of it, floated down in a raft. They shot at me." "Who did? The caterpillars?"

Demographics might show that college students in 1979 and 1980 were far more conservative and far less interested in LSD than the class of 1969. That, in turn, might explain the lack of interest in Firesign. Another answer might be the dullness of the Rhino releases, which mix material recorded live (and cheaply) with material already done for radio (the entire "Shakespeare" album was a radio show) and some studio moments as needed.

"Fighting Clowns" had a song about Jimmy Carter that was left off the album and issued as a seven-inch picture disc instead. When Mobile Fidelity reissued the album, the Carter song was included as a bonus track.

Fans can still enjoy the Nick Danger clever-dick satires on "Missing Shoe" and "Three Faces of Al." The former is a twelve-minute album, and yet it's shamelessly padded with music and introductions to each of its five acts. This was actually a pilot for a proposed radio series. On "Missing Shoe," Nick has problems, and so do the writers, who offer stuff like: "This heel had no soul. He probably got a kick out of booting people around."

On "Three Faces of Al," the writing is more colorful, whether it's Nick describing his miserable mood ("just a doomed dick with his dipstick on empty") or the world around him ("the moon was fat and orange like a blood-fed tic"). As always, there's recognition humor. Listeners might chuckle smugly if they know a character named Leadliver is a play on the name of the old folksinger Leadbelly. Or they might simply say, "Who cares?"

- EAT OR BE EATEN (Mercury 826452M1) **1/2 $8 $15
- BEST OF FIRESIGN: SHOES FOR INDUSTRY (Columbia Legacy C2K 52736) *** $16
- BACK FROM THE SHADOWS (Mobile Fidelity MFCD 2747) ** $18

Back on a major label in 1985, the Firesigns are involved with computer video games and a labyrinth of mazes. The problem is finding "Hawkmoth," a Nightbird-type female disc jockey. This includes a visit to a yuppie bar where the folks drink "Airhead Lite." Not a bad comeback—old fans could hail the return of "The Porridge Bird." Unfortunately, there wasn't much to attract new fans.

"Shoes" is the official "Best of" CD from the team's Columbia years. Some fans will find it sacrilege to chop out sections from albums that technically were one long saga. There's eight minutes of "Not Quite the Solution He Expected" from "Giant Rat of Sumatra," a three-minute "Army Training Film" segment from "Everything You Know Is Wrong," and a full twenty-eight-minute Nick Danger story from "How Can You Be in Two Places." Some Proctor and Bergman solo cuts are added, plus very frank album notes from the quartet, who admit that the Bozos album was "a little cold" and "Not Insane" was "incomprehensible, basically."

Nostalgic fans attended the 1993 reunion shows represented on the "Shadows" CD. The disc proves that some people could actually laugh at their stuff (mostly from their first four albums), as opposed to just sitting and grinning in a toxic haze. The group isn't at their best in a stage setting. Their deliberately overdone life-as-vaudeville schtick becomes annoying quickly and their enunciations become particularly fey and pretentious as they try to put extra spin on feeble puns. The lack of elaborate sound effects and mood doesn't help. The album notes are full of self-congratulatory palaver and PBS-speak about how they fought the good fight in the '60s and how thrilling it was to "don the motley" again.

NOTES: The original "How Can You Be in Two Places" disc has some extra appeal due to the classic "Marx and Lennon" cover. It's certainly a lithograph worth framing. The CD version from Mobile Fidelity lab reinstates it and has copious album notes from Phil Austin. Most of the CD reissues from that company featured extra notes from Firesign members. Firesign fans hunt up various radio promo items, notably 1983's double album set "Firesign Radio" from Global Satellite Network. Die-hards look for Chad & Jeremy's "Cabbages and Kings" album, which features some spoken work from the group on a few cuts.

WILD MAN FISCHER

- AN EVENING WITH WILD MAN FISCHER (Bizarre 6332) * $10 $25
- WILDMANIA (Rhino Records 001) * $5 $10
- PRONOUNCED NORMAL (Rhino Records RNLP 021) * $5 $10
- NOTHING SCARY (Rhino Records RNLP 022) * $5 $10

Larry Fischer, twice committed to mental homes by his mother, became a notorious street singer/shouter. In 1970 Frank Zappa produced a Fischer album, and in the '80s he was rediscovered by Rhino Records. Some find his repetitive yowling and moronic rhymes hilarious; others savor his dementia as a fine example of what it's like for an insane person to deal with the world—or vice versa.

The first album, with musical accompaniment added, has cuts like "Merry Go Round," which consists of Larry shouting, "Merry Go, Merry Go, Merry Go round, Boo Boo Boo" more times than most listeners will be able to tolerate. The Zappa connection explains the high price.

There's some comic pathos in Fischer as the vulnerable child-idiot. His 1977 "Wildmania" album cut "My Name is Larry" is thoroughly pathetic as he sing-songs his name over and over, as well as the names of people who tolerate him: "My name is Larry, my name is Larry, I have an uncle, his name is Bob. Hi Bob! Bob! I like you, Bob! I like you a lot ... my name is Larry, my name is Larry, I have an auntie, her name is Becky. Hi Becky! My name is Larry, my name is Larry, I have an auntie, her name is Auntie Estelle. Hi Auntie Estelle! Hi...."

For his 1984 release, "Nothing Scary," Barnes and Barnes supply electronic dashes and musical droppings to Fischer's rants, which include this tantrum: "Oh my friend Robert won't talk to me ... KNOCK KNOCK! Knock, knock, knock! Raaahbbert! Raaaaahbert! My friend Robert won't talk to me ... I knock on his door and I open his gate and I say 'RAAAAAHBERT. Raaahbert, Raaaahbert! It's Larry ... It's Larry!'"

FISHER AND MARKS

- ROME ON THE RANGE (Cameo-Parkway C 1081) ** $6 $12
- IT'S A BEATLE COO COO WORLD (Swan 514) *1/2 $8 $20

This mainstream duo appeared in the Alan Freed film *Mister Rock and Roll* as song pluggers with unlikely titles like "The Rock You Just Baked Is a Roll."

When Allan Sherman became famous with Jewish song parodies, Al Fisher and Lou Marks tried it Italian style. And if Sherman had Harpo Marx and Steve Allen for endorsements, these guys had Joey Bishop ("I laughed my head off") and Jimmy Durante ("This is a great album").

Sherman turned "Glory Halleluah" into "Glory Harry Lewis." Now it's "Glory Al an' Louise," about a vineyard: "Every day they'd go to work and get barefoot to the knees. With their stomping feet they beat and with their toes they squeeze and squeeze. Through the vermouth and chianti, muscatel and burgundy. They both keep stomping on...."

Sherman's Mexican clapping song was "Oh Boy." Here it's "Mah-Rone." And "Frere Jacques," which became "Sarah Jackman" is now "Ferrari Rocky," with question and answers: "How's your new Ferrari?" "It is paid for early." "How's your super charger?" "Sophia Loren's is larger!"

Of course, Sherman wouldn't have thought of covering some tunes. "Sorrento" becomes "No Rento" ("where I never ever spento not a one of my own cento ... where I was so contento ... and the mangia is free") and "Home on the Range" is "Rome on the Range" ("where each miss always whispers si si, where seldom is heard a discouraging word, except when they're talking to me."

When The Beatles got hot, the boys once again tried to cash in. Mild interest in any Fab Four collectible accounts for the price. The topical album about Beatlemania is a motley mix of novelty tunes and sketches. To the unlikely "On Top of Old Smokey" Fisher and Marks pretend to be The Beatles, singing: "They laughed at our accent. They laughed at our dress. They said that our hairstyles were a terrible mess. We told you our story. You Yanks we do thank. Now we do the laughing, all the way to the bank."

The duo reach for concepts, like Jack E. Leonard fielding questions as president of "The Stamping Out of the Beatles Club." Some gags: "What do you think of their hair?" "They should get dandruff and go bald...." "What do you think of their clothes?" "They should be attacked by moths...." "What do you think of their delivery?" "I think it belongs in back of a truck."

DWIGHT FISKE

- DWIGHT FISKE AND HIS MUSICAL SATIRES (Monarch 206) ** $15 $25
- SOPHISTICATED SONGS AND PATTER (Gala 100) ** $10 $25
- DWIGHT FISKE ALBUM 2 (Gala 101) ** $10 $25
- DWIGHT FISKE ALBUM 3 (Gala 102) ** $10 $25
- DWIGHT FISKE ALBUM 4 (Gala 103) ** $10 $25

- SONGS HIS MOTHER NEVER TAUGHT HIM (Jubilee 17) ** $10 $25

Dwight Fiske was an immaculately attired risqué sophisticate who played piano and offered up adult patter songs only slightly to the left of Noel Coward. He released many 78s on his own label and later these six albums, all ten-inchers from the mid-50s.

The Monarch release stresses his "song stories," monologues with piano accenting. The six specimens here include "Senorita Del Campo," "Fountain of Youth," "The Captain's Leave," "Mrs. Pettibone," "14th Wedding Anniversary," and "Case 142." His most popular tales turn up on several different albums.

The Jubilee disc offers "Senorita Margarita Del Campo," "Fountain of Youth," and "Mrs. Pettibone" again, along with "Salome," "Mr. America," and "Elizabeth and Raleigh." "Sophisticated Songs and Patter" is representative of the Gala series and features a few repeats ("Mrs. Pettibone" and "Salome") along with "Two Horses and a Debutante," "Clarrissa the Flea," "Adam and Eve," "Morning," "Ida the Wayward Sturgeon," and "The Colonel's Tropical Bird." Though a bit dated, Fiske delivers his material with an urbane flare that might appeal to some older roués.

"Ida the Wayward Sturgeon," for example, is out for "fun, fun, fun." After all, "she was only twelve, too young for Errol Flynn. So she went into a nosedive, right down to the bottom of the Gulf stream.... Fish were doing things only fish can do in Florida and get away with. Ida was dying for an affair ... she came to an information booth with a Mother of Pearl front. On the door it said, 'Love for Sale.' And she swam right in. And there on an old oyster bed, telling a group of fish how to be gay, was the world's oldest living mermaid ... now downstairs in the basement with the radio turned on was Tristan Weisenstein the Octopus, exercising his sixteen Rockette legs ... on the end of each toe was a suction cup, an invention of his own ... suddenly Ida found herself in the most terrifying embrace! Tristan was on every side, going like mad! Then she fainted and didn't know a thing until she heard the mermaid say, 'My God, Ida, you shad! It's caviar!'"

Fiske fans will find some favorites on other Gala albums. The second one includes "Seaman Dinwiddie Comes Home," "The Censored Letter," "Stella the Mouse," and "The Everglades Club." The third includes "Mr. Webster," "Mickey Finn," "Why Should Penguins Fly?" "Dr. Cinnamon," "Bella the Belle of the Beltline," and "The Hair of a Wolf." The albums are high priced thanks to scarcity and to those who collect ten-inch albums, but the number of folks who appreciate this kind of material is not great anymore.

DWIGHT FISKE AND NAN BLACKSTONE

- TONGUE WITH CHEEK (Jubilee JGM 2026) **1/2 $8 $20

Jubilee mates four Fiske cuts ("Case 142," "The 14th Wedding Anniversary," "Mrs. Pettibone," "Senorita Margarita Del Campo") with some old Nan Blackstone material for the other side. (For her own earlier ten-inch albums, her name was always spelled Blakstone.) The album has a strange cover picture, a statuesque brunette standing next to a dwarf. Naive listeners had to assume these two were Dwight and Nan Blackstone.

Nan's numbers aren't as sophisticated, the lyrics at the Ruth Wallis level. She sings about "Donkey Island" where there are plenty of asses to ride: "Of course the mayor owns an ass that nobody looks at. Yet with his wife it's a different affair. For, between you and me, she has one of the most intriguing asses ever seen on that island there...."

FANNIE FLAGG

- RALLY 'ROUND THE FLAGG (RCA Victor LSP 3856) ** $8 $15
- MY HUSBAND DOESN'T KNOW I'M MAKING THIS PHONE CALL (Sunflower SNF 5008) *1/2 $4 $8

Flagg was a young hopeful doing club work at New York's Upstairs at the Downstairs and later on-camera practical jokes on *Candid Camera*. She was one of the few women in the late '60s to attempt sketch comedy on record rather than stand-up. The 1967 RCA album is a series of sketches, including one on Lady Bird Johnson. Flagg has a Southern tilt to most of her material and obviously has no trouble with the accent. Mrs. Johnson describes being an ex-First Lady: "I had asked Mrs. Nixon to help me beautify Washington. Little did I know that Lyndon and I would be the first to go."

The 1971 album satirizes the now-forgotten political wife Martha Mitchell. The unusual supporting cast includes MacLean Stevenson and Casey Kasem. Mike Gravel, then a Senator from Alaska, supplied album notes: "I admire not only the true comedy and satire involved, but also the fact that it was done in good taste." The good taste got in the way of the jokes.

Flagg appears on Christopher Weeks's "LBJ in the Catskills" album. She later had a recurring role on *The New Dick Van Dyke Show* as Dick's sister, but is now best known for her book *Fried Green Tomatoes*.

THE FLAGPOLE SINGERS

- FOLK SONGS OF MADISON AVENUE (MGM E/SE 4234) *1/2 $4 $8

Norman Blagman and Sam Bobrick wrote the undistinguished music and easy lyrics crooned by the blandly harmonizing Flagpole Singers. Gene Klavan, a New York DJ, wrote the album notes for this 1964 release, declaring "the singers are so good ... you will be tempted to ignore the lyrical venom." The venom has long since dried on these tunes about the ad biz. They sing "The Madison Avenue Hoedown," a ballad about "Agency Image," and harmonize about their favorite pills in "Tranquilizers." They chant, "Tranquilizers, little ol' sweet tranquilizers! For a campaign that dropped dead, they're delicious on rye bread ... every morning every night, mmmm, tranquilizers! 'Cause it's cheaper than getting tight! Little ol' sweet tranquilizers!"

FLANDERS AND SWANN

- AT THE DROP OF A HAT (Angel 35797) **** $5 $15
- BESTIARY OF FLANDERS AND SWANN (Angel 36112) **** $8 $16
- AT THE DROP OF ANOTHER HAT (Angel S 36388) **** $6 $12

Portly, wheelchair-bound Michael Flanders (1922-1975) and the slight, bespectacled pianist Donald Swann (1923-1993) provided delightful humor for Broadway audiences in the '60s. Their civilized song satires were witty, Flanders's monologues wryly appealing. The two Britons looked staid, but they were far from stuffy, often raising their dueting voices as if they had been out too long in the noonday sun.

"At the Drop of a Hat," the cast album for their first show, offers eccentric delights: songs with nonsense sound effects ("The Wom Pom"); a novel idea for world peace ("In the Bath"); and a fanciful piece about "The Reluctant Cannibal" who cries, "I won't eat people, eating people is wrong!" His father offers sage advice: "Son, I admire your sincerity. Always be sincere. Whether you mean it or not." Flanders's monologue "Tried by the Centre Court" is a beautifully timed, rhymed, and executed report on a depressed tennis umpire. The duo end the evening with an audience favorite, two hippos singing cheerfully: "Mud, mud, glorious mud, nothing quite like it for cooling the blood. So follow me follow, down to the hollow, and then we shall wallow in glorious mud!" The audience gladly sings along.

The British vinyl pressing contained a few extra cuts ("Je suis le Tenebreux" and "Kokoraki"). A subsequent British extended play 45 ("More Out of the Hat!" Parlophone GEP 8636), recorded without an audience, added "Vanessa," "The Youth of the Heart," "Tried by the Centre Court," and "Too Many Cookers." All of this material in live concert versions is on the Parlophone import CD.

"Bestiary" is their lone studio album. It collects a variety of their charming animal songs. There are songs about an armadillo in love with a tank, a boring wild boar, a whale with a head cold, an elephant who suffers from schizophrenia, and a rollicking battle between a man and a spider: "my blood runs cold to meet—in pajamas and bare feet—with a great big hairy spider in the bath!" It's an epic confrontation: "For hours we have been locked in endless struggle. I have lured it to the deep end by the drain. At last I think I've washed it down the plug-hole. But here it comes a 'crawling up the chain!" The ending doesn't say much for the human race.

The Parlophone import CD includes the studio version of "The Wom Pom" (left off the American disc) plus ten bonus tracks, notably "20 Tons of TNT," "Food for Thought," "Pee Po Belly Bum Drawers," and "Bed."

"Another" marked their return to Broadway with more delightful and improbable songs, including a blues rendition of the first and second laws of thermodynamics, and a piece that matches Flanders's lyrics about the problems of playing the French horn to the intricate melody of a Mozart horn concerto. Flanders's monologue that equates olive stuffing with bull fighting is another example of educated silliness: "All is hushed. And then, in one sudden movement he brings the pick jabbing down into the heart of the olive. And a great cry goes up of "Ole! He has made an 'ole!" Before the gutted olive can fall, it's caught by the matador on his mat. It's handed over to the estufidores, of two types, the estufidores pimentos and the estufidores anchovas. Their dread work done, it is distributed among the poor...."

The Import CD for "At the Drop of Another Hat" (Parlophone CDFSB 12) adds "Built Up Area," "Sea Fever," and a fresh version of "In the Bath."

NOTES: In 1980 Swann teamed with Frank Topping for an album that was released only in England, "Swann with Topping" (MMT Records). It's lightweight fare, with "Gossip Gossip Whisper Chat" the only one approaching past glory. "And Then We Wrote" (EMI EMCM 3088) is from a radio broadcast in which the duo recall the (fairly weak) songs they wrote for British reviews (1948-1956). "Tried by the Center Court" (EMI NTS 116) is culled from private tapes friends made at Flanders and Swann concerts, and has songs that didn't make the final cut on the official albums. Most of them turn up as bonus tracks on import CDs. All three imports (two "Hats" and the "Bestiary") are available individually as well as in "The Complete Flanders and Swann" boxed set (EMI CDFSB 1), which includes a bonus thirty-six-page booklet of bio material and song annotation for those who might be glad to know the "Rustington-on-Sea" mentioned in one song is an actual place in Sussex where Flanders once lived.

HAROLD FLENDER

- CANDID TELEFUN (United Artists UAL 4075) ** $6 $10

A writer for Sid Caesar, Imogene Coca, and Bob and Ray, Flender wrote TV screenplays and a novel, *Paris Blues*. This early '60s album of put-on phone calls sometimes veers into the strange. He calls up a pet shop saying, "I'd like a monkey ... for monkey soup ... I was having dinner for twelve, and there's not much meat on a Marmoset."

The owner doesn't seem to mind the idea: "I could let you have four for $100."

"Do you have larger monkeys? A good cooking monkey?"

"Well, we have very little requests for people who want to cook them. I have a large monkey I can let you have for $85."

The results aren't always funny, but the phone calls are interesting studies in human nature. Flender died in 1975.

BUD FLETCHER

- TALL TALES (Louisanne 101) ** $4 $8
- MORE OF BUD FLETCHER (Louisanne 102) ** $5 $10
- AT THE OUTHOUSE (Louisanne 104) ** $6 $12
- GOES TO WASHINGTON (Louisanne 105) ** $6 $12
- RETURNS TO THE OUTHOUSE (Louisanne 106) ** $6 $12

- FROM THE OUTHOUSE TO WHITEHOUSE (Louisianne 116) ** $6 $12
- POLITICS AND POLITICIANS (Louisianne 120) ** $6 $12
- STANDING ROOM ONLY (Louisianne 125) ** $6 $12
- BEST OF BUD FLETCHER (Louisianne 131) ** $5 $10

Hewitt Berwyn Fletcher, a Louisiana oilman, amused folks with his imitation of a Cajun he dubbed "Cyprienne Robespierre." His Cajun dialect sounds like a cross between a Frenchman and Tim Conway's version of a Scandinavian.

Fletcher's jokes are very familiar. The dialect does help liven them up. From the "Tall Tales" album: "I see a car he come real fast and when he get right in front of the drugstore, man, he brake his car quick man, he jump out, run in the drugstore you know. Well ... that feller run in and said, 'Mac, quick, what you got good for the hiccup there?' Well the owner didn't pay him no mind, he was behind the counter moppin' the floor you know. The man say, 'Quick, what you got for the hiccup?' So he was working his way from behind the counter with the wet mop. He take a bead on his face and he swing right from the floor and catch him, man, right in the face! The man say, 'Dog gone for how come you throw me that wet mop right in the face! I just ax you what you got good for the hiccup!' The owner say, 'You don't got the hiccup now, eh?' He say, 'By joke it's not me what got the hiccup it's the ol' lady out in the car what got the hiccup!'"

ALLEN FOLEY

- VERMONT WIT AND HUMOR (Century 36247) $3 $8

Foley had the credentials to give a talk about Vermont comedy: he was a member of the Vermont legislature for years. From 1929 to 1964 he taught at Dartmouth.

It might be easier to find his books *What The Old-Timer Said* and *The Old-Timer Talks Back*, from Stephen Greene Press.

FRANK FONTAINE

- IDIOT'S DELIGHT (Guest Star G 14112) *1/2 $5 $12

Fontaine made several albums of songs (ABC Paramount), but only one full-length comedy album. For the whole disc he plays an interviewer dealing with a man on the street who offers verbose tall tales and meandering stories: "I was always a great dancer, I used to do the jitterbug. I could throw a partner straight up in the air and do twenty-two jitters and a mess of buggin' and still catch her before she hit the floor." Most any punch line is an excuse for Fontaine to do variations on his cretinous laugh routine, gurgling and coughing and sputtering.

Two compilation albums offer Fontaine's "John L. C. Savony" bit, which won him his initial fame in the '40s. It's on Capitol DT 1854 ("Comedy Hits") and Capitol T 1651 ("They're Still Laughing"). Basically, it's a laugh routine, as a tickled sweepstakes winner goes into cackling hysterics because he's struck it rich. His laugh is so goofy the audience laughs along. The gurgling laugh character evolved into goofy Crazy Guggenheim on *The Jackie Gleason Show* in the '60s.

The Frank Fontaine Show, a radio sitcom, aired on Sundays for CBS. An example of it turns up on "Five Exciting New Radio Shows," an obscure promotional album from CBS that includes snips from *Gunsmoke, December Bride, The Steve Allen Show*, and *Horatio Hornblower*. Fontaine plays a hapless dad on this show. When his kids break a window playing baseball, and a cop appears, Frank quickly assumes an ingratiating Irish accent: "Well, Begorra, officer it's fine to meet such a fine broth of soup! Begorra! Begorra!" The cop answers, "My name is Schultz."

The album has a sample of a new character Fontaine was working on, "Fred Frump" the "All-American Bore." Definitely annoying, Frump loves to sing and enjoys being "friendly" with his neighbors as he utters horrible jokes: "Maybe you know my uncle, Ferris. He's a big wheel back East!"

FORD AND REYNOLDS

- WADDA YA GONNA DO? (Jubilee 2076) * $4 $8

Second stringers to Martin and Lewis and almost any other team of the era, Ford and Reynolds play it straight man to young goofball. They use their catchphrase "wadda ya gonna do" endlessly, along with very simple gags:

"I'm a hippie, leave me alone." "You're a hippie? How'd you like a shot in the head?" "No thanks, I don't drink in the toilet!" "Are you really a hippie?" "Of course! Ha ha!" "Why do you laugh?" "Wadda ya gonna do?" "... What's your dad doing right now?" "He's doin' twenty years! Ha ha." "Why do you laugh?" "Wadda ya gonna do ... my father happens to be the greatest pickpocket in the whole world." "So what?" "So what? He's only got one finger, that's what! Ha ha ha." "One finger? How can you laugh?" "Wadda ya gonna do...."

The album notes say that Frankie and Gary played the Copa with this act. More than once?

THE FOREMEN

- FOLK HEROES (Reprise 9459932) * $7

This fat wheel of brie masquerading as a CD supposedly contains satirical songs. But all it has is a bunch of slick, self-satisfied tunes that are even more preeningly obvious and witless than The Capitol Steps. At least the Steps have better musical taste. For some reason, this foursome insist on archaic folk stylings a la The Limelighters and Kingston Trio. It couldn't have taken more than a few minutes to come up with something like "Do the Clinton," with such unoriginal lines as "Straighten up and step light, lean to the left a little, now lean to the right."

Just why Tom Lehrer supplied a few lines of praise for this is hard to fathom. He writes of the group "reintroducing literacy to comedy songs and the rhymes actually rhyme. Even if the rhymes include 'borscht' and 'divorscht.'"

Perhaps Tom was amused by some of the deliberately nose-tweeking songs like "Peace Is Out," where they seem to be alarmingly pro-war ("It's in to be in a war!"), but Randy Newman's been doing it for years, and better (as in "Political Science"). The Foremen's "Ain't No Liberal," which is supposedly about the joys of turning conservative ("The angel told me, "oh ye man of sin, open up your bleeding heart and let Pat Buchanan in") is a Mocha Frappe compared to the acid of Phil Ochs's "Love Me, I'm a Liberal." The Foremen, with their squeaky clean harmonies and archaic banjo, have learned nothing from '60s folkies or '60s satirists like Lehrer.

- WHAT'S LEFT (Warner Bros. 246246A) * $7

"What's Left" on their two-disc contract isn't much—another set of smug, obvious tunes made more annoying by cloyingly knowing vocalizing. On some cuts they've updated their sound to imitation Byrds ("Three Strikes and You're Out") but these preening harmonizers still lack the guts and humor of most anyone they could possibly have been influenced by—even Peter, Paul and Mary.

JOEY FORMAN
- BILL DANA PRESENTS JOEY FORMAN AS THE MASHUGANISHI YOGI (A&M 4144) ** $4 $8

A comic who often played cheerful small-time comedians on sitcoms, (he was Ho Ho the Clown on an episode of *Bewitched*) Forman was a regular on *The Mickey Rooney Show* of 1954, and *The Sid Caesar Show* a decade later. This would've worked better as a one-shot sketch on *The Tonight Show*, but here's a half hour of then-topical humor about the Maharishi, who was then charming The Beatles.

The humor is harmlessly silly, like the gag about not using "the full size sitar, but instead the small, eleven-inch sitar. Which I like to call The Baby Sitar." With Bill Dana doing some of the writing, the Q&A segments sound like old Jose Jimenez records: "My name is Timothy Perkins ... my friends are always trying to get me to take LSD ... but I'm afraid to take it." "You are very wise to be leery, Timothy."

Jose even drops by to ask a question: "I don't want you to be angry with me to ask you a question. My name ... Jose Jimenez. I don't want you to get sore ... Could I ask you the question?" "Yes." "How come you talk so funny?"

Forman, with Asian accent, appears on the Don Adams *Get Smart* soundtrack album (United Artists) in an amusing Charlie Chan parody segment. He lent his voice to a Dracula puppet in "Les Poupees De Paris," a 1964 World's Fair puppet show staged by Sid and Marty Krofft. He does a decent Bela Lugosi in a two-minute duet with Guy Marks as Boris Karloff on "Les Poupees De Paris" (RCA Victor LSO-1090).

TERRY FORSTER AND THE LOVEHANDLES
- FAT IS IN (Comedy Works CWLP 816) * $3 $5

In 1985, Forster, pitching for the Atlanta Braves, achieved momentary fame when David Letterman called him "a big fat tub of goo." Trying to get the last laugh, for this album he joined with some comics at Philadelphia's Comedy Works. He introduces "The Lovehandles," who rap, "Fat is in, stuff yo' face and don't be thin. Honey doll, please grow them hips. Be mah private solar eclipse!" The quickie disc is just nine minutes per side and is mostly filler having nothing to do with fat. Forster's minor league comics do cornball impressions on "Arnold, Sylvester and Clint" and none of their high school level novelty tunes are very amusing, even once.

PHIL FOSTER
- PHIL FOSTER ALIVE? (Keynote LP 1103) ** $10 $20
- PHIL FOSTER AT GROSSINGERS (Epic LN 3632) *1/2 $10 $15

A popular, very standard '50s stand-up, Foster (born Fyvul Feldman) was a sort of low class Alan King, griping about anything. From the Keynote album recorded at The Bon Soir: "We had a winter, this past winter, it was really beautiful ... seventeen inches of pure white snow on ya! Upset the mayor. He closed the city for five days. He got nervous: 'Look at all the snow that fell down here! Close the city! That's it, that's all.' He closed the city for five days. Five days they open up the city again. Same snow! They moved it from the main streets to the side streets! At the end of the year they gave a bill to the state government, twenty-six million dollars for snow clearance. Now I've heard of snow jobs, but that one was a beauty, boy."

A regular at the legendary Catskill resort Grossinger's, Foster is in his element grousing Brooklyn-style about marriage, the good old days, and kids: "You young mothers today, you bring up kids with books. Dr. Benjamin Spock ... every book has a chapter devoted to one subject: "Don't holler." Don't holler 'cause you'll give the kid a complex. Tell ya the truth, in the old days my mother didn't read, she hit. My mother's best punch was walking away from me. Think I'm lyin'? She'd walk two steps in front of me, I thought I was out of danger. That's when she let go with a shot! Wiped out all the neurotic feeling. But not you young mothers today. When the kid gets in trouble you call out the kid's name. It doesn't fit ... Michael Jeffrey, Sean, Kevin. Oh boy. Drexel. Can you picture what they call him for short? Lafayette. Can you picture the grandmother calling out Lafayetteleh?"

Foster's Brooklyn observational humor enthused Joey Bishop, who wrote the album notes, but it turned off some veteran comedians. Author John McCabe confirms that in his book *Mr. Laurel and Mr. Hardy*, the anonymous "Mr. Y" that Stan Laurel accused of rudeness was Foster, who, unlike even Jack E. Leonard for example, "lacks the occasional wit."

"Brooklyn's Ambassador to the U.S.A." often did monologues about his favorite borough. A few turn up on the Coral compilations "Do You Wanna Laugh," "Laugh of the Party," and "Fun Time." From the latter: "Don't laugh at us people from Brooklyn, 'cause we know what we're doin'. The rest of the world's mixed up...."

Foster issued a children's album, "A Day in the Life of a Dinosaur" and introduces Lenny Kent on Kent's album "The Put Down Humor of Lenny Kent." In the '70s Foster achieved national fame for his role as Frank Defazio on *Laverne and Shirley*. He died in 1985.

THE FOUR SERGEANTS

- BAWDY BARRACKS BALLADS (ABC Paramount ABC 245) *1/2 $3 $7
- BAWDY BARRACKS BALLADS VOLUME 2 (ABC Paramount ABCS 381) * 1/2 $4 $8

Around 1961, when Oscar Brand's bawdy ballads were selling, The Four Sergeants (Frank Raye, Carter Farriss, Harry Clarke, and Nelson Starr) did their versions of familiar tunes, such as "One-Eyed Reilly," "Roll Me Over," and "Hinky Dinky Parlez Vous." The arrangements sound like they came from the Walt Disney school of jolly harmony. The lyrics are incredibly sanitized. Oscar Brand got the better of "One-Eyed Reilly" when he rammed "two horse pistols up his butt and shagged his daughter." Here: "I grabbed O'Reilly by the hair, shoved his head in a pail of water, grabbed the pistols from his hand, hit him in the head, then loved his daughter."

Things don't improve on Volume Two, although the mild risqué folk tune "No Hips at All" gets more raunchy when a bouncing bass drum obscures the word "Hips," making the listener guess just what the poor wife's husband is lacking. Oscar Brand's "Sea Wolf" is included, along with "Guantanamo Bay" and a bunch of tame limericks set to music: "A lady athletic and handsome, got wedged in a sleeping room transom. When she offered much dough for release she was told: the view is worth more than the ransom."

JACK FOX

- COMMERCIALS TO CRINGE BY (MGM SE 4174) * $3 $5

Jack Fox wrote this '60s album but performs in only one of the nineteen parodies. Arthur Anderson, Pat Bright, Mary Ellen Plumber, and Marilyn Lovell do most of the work on this tedious bunch of fake commercials. An interviewer asks a housewife how she likes new "Giggle" dishwashing detergent and she giggles and giggles. An interview with a woman wearing "Leg Allure" nylons enthuses that they're perfect for women who need to hide their hairy legs: "You wouldn't believe how hairy these are! I mean really hairy! My husband says I'm a regular ape."

JEFF FOXWORTHY

- YOU MIGHT BE A REDNECK IF ... (Warner Bros. 9453142) **1/2 $8
- THE REDNECK TEST (Laughing Hyena 43) ** $7
- THE ORIGINAL (Laughing Hyena 79) ** $7
- SOLD OUT (Laughing Hyena 80) ** $7
- GAMES REDNECKS PLAY (Warner Bros. 9458562) **1/2 $8

A Southern comic who emerged from the comedy club scene at the turn of the '90s, Foxworthy easily became the most popular young comedian below the Mason-Dixon line with his blend of standard observations and the bit that brought him recognition and a series of best-seller novelty books in the South, titled *You Might be a Redneck If ...*. Although some of his Northern peers, including the cast of *Saturday Night Live*, jealously ridiculed his formulaic style and his lack of true comic charisma, Foxworthy kept racking up the sales (his first album shot to gold at a time when almost no comedy records came close) and got his own sitcom in 1995.

His Warner's discs have some lines cutting enough to make Northerners snicker, but truthful enough to amuse rather than enrage his Southern audience. "You might be a redneck," he explains on the first disc, "... if you've ever cut your grass and found a car ... if your Dad walks you to school because you're in the same grade ... if you've ever been too drunk to fish ..." There are plenty more.

He also scores with mild material on the differences between the South and every place else: "Things are just too sophisticated in L.A. Like out there, if guys fall in love, they think candy and wine and roses. Hell, in the South, we fall in love with ya, we just spray paint your name on an overpass." The second album is more of the same, including one musical cut, "Party All Night," with Foxworthy reciting some observations over the country rock: "Single people don't consider it a good party unless the cops have been there at least a dozen times...."

Foxworthy wasn't pleased when, in 1994, a series of quickly done cassette tapes from the past resurfaced on CD. They have more observational filler material. Some early material (like the spray paint bit, which is on "The Original") was used for the later Warner's discs.

REDD FOXX

- LAFF OF THE PARTY (Dooto DTL 214, Gem DTL 214) **1/2 $8 $15
- LAFF OF THE PARTY II (Dooto DTL 219) **1/2 $10 $15
- LAFF OF THE PARTY 3 (Dooto DTL 220) **1/2 $10 $15
- LAFF OF THE PARTY 4 (Dooto DTL 227) **1/2 $10 $15
- BEST OF REDD FOXX (Dooto DTL 234) **1/2 $10 $15
- LAFF OF THE PARTY 7 (Dooto DTL 236) **1/2 $10 $15
- BURLESQUE HUMOR (Dooto DTL 249) **1/2 $10 $15
- THE SIDESPLITTER (Dooto DTL 253) **1/2 $10 $15
- LAFF OF THE PARTY 8 (Dooto DTL 270) **1/2 $10 $15

- THE SIDESPLITTER 2 (Dooto DTL 270) **1/2 — $10 — $15
- THE NEW RACE TRACK (also released as RACY TALES Dooto DTL 275) **1/2 — $10 — $15
- REDD FOXX FUN (Dooto DTL 290) **1/2 — $10 — $15
- THE BEST LAFF (Dooto DTL 291) **1/2 — $10 — $15
- SLY SEX (Dooto DTL 295) **1/2 — $10 — $15
- HAVE ONE ON ME (Dooto DTL 298) **1/2 — $10 — $15
- LAFFARAMA (Dooto DTL 801) **1/2 — $10 — $15
- THE WILD PARTY (Dooto DTL 804) **1/2 — $10 — $15
- THIS IS FOXX (Dooto DTL 809) **1/2 — $10 — $15
- HE'S FUNNY THAT WAY (Dooto DTL 815) **1/2 — $10 — $15
- AT JAZZVILLE (Dooto DTL 820) **1/2 — $10 — $15
- HEARTY PARTY (Dooto DTL 828) **1/2 — $10 — $15
- NEW FUGG (Dooto DTL 830) **1/2 — $10 — $15
- LAFF ALONG (Dooto DTL 832) **1/2 — $10 — $15
- CRACK UP (Dooto DTL 834) **1/2 — $10 — $15
- FUNNY STUFF (Dooto DTL 835) **1/2 — $10 — $15
- BATTLE OF SEX (Dooto DTL 836) **1/2 — $10 — $15
- NAUGHTIES BUT GOODIES (Dooto DTL 838) **1/2 — $10 — $15
- ADULTS ONLY (Dooto DTL 840) **1/2 — $10 — $15
- JOKES I CAN'T TELL ON TELEVISION (Dooto DTL 845) **1/2 — $5 — $10
- SHED HOUSE HUMOR (Dooto DTL 846) **1/2 — $5 — $10
- FAVORITE PARTY JOKES (Dooto DTL 847) **1/2 — $5 — $10
- SANFORD AND FOXX (Dooto DTL 853) **1/2 — $10 — $15
- AND ALL THAT JAZZ (Dooto DTL 854) **1/2 — $5 — $10
- DIRTY REDD (Dooto DTL 858) **1/2 — $5 — $10
- FUNKY TALES FROM A DIRTY OLD JUNKMAN (Dooto DTL 860) **1/2 — $10 — $15

In the '50s, between being TV's Fred Sanford, and growing up plain John Sanford, Redd Foxx made a bunch of comedy records for the Dooto label. He was playing the Club Oasis on Western Avenue in Los Angeles when he agreed to record the first one for $25. These rarely were seen in the white record shops of the day, but sold well enough for Dooto to keep on going, evidently even after Foxx wanted them to stop.

Every disc is loaded with mild off-color anecdotes. This is how he opened his first album: "Have you noticed these programs they have on television? Everything is backwards. Serutan spelled backwards is nature. They have a new perfume out called "Shhhh." Spelled backwards it's "Shhhhh." Did you know motel spelled backwards is let 'em? I got a friend down the street, he's goin' backward crazy. Today on the menu in his cafe he had "Friggin' Chickasee." And "Chide Fricken." He cooked some beans backward and everyone got hiccups...."

- LAFF YOUR HEAD OFF (MF Records RF 1) **1/2 — $5 — $10
- LAFF YOUR ASS OFF (MF RF 2) **1/2 — $5 — $10
- REDD FOXX AT HOME (MF RF 3, CD reissue Right Stuff 34656) **1/2 — $5 — $8
- A WHOLE LOT OF SOUL (MF RF 4) **1/2 — $5 — $10
- AT HIS BEST (MF RF 5, CD reissue Right Stuff 34657) **1/2 — $5 — $10
- DOIN HIS OWN THING (MF RF 6, CD reissue Right Stuff 34654) **1/2 — $5 — $8
- SAY LIKE IT IS (MF RF 7) **1/2 — $5 — $10
- IS SEX HERE TO STAY (MF RF 8) **1/2 — $5 — $10
- WHERE IT'S AT (MF RF 9) **1/2 — $5 — $10
- HUFFIN AND A PUFFIN (MF RF 10) **1/2 — $5 — $10
- I'M CURIOUS BLACK (MF RF 11, CD reissue Encore 5002) **1/2 — $5 — $8
- 3 or 4 TIMES A DAY (MF RF 12) **1/2 — $5 — $10
- MR HOT PANTS (MF RF 13, CD reissue Right Stuff 34658) **1/2 — $5 — $8
- HOT FLASHES (MF RF 14) **1/2 — $5 — $10
- RESTRICTED (MF RF 15, CD reissue Encore 5001) **1/2 — $5 — $8
- SUPERSTAR (MF RF 16, CD reissue Right Stuff 34655) **1/2 — $5 — $8
- SPICE CAN BE NICE (MF RF 17, CD reissue Encore 5004) **1/2 — $5 — $8
- STRICTLY FOR ADULTS (MF RF 18) **1/2 — $5 — $10
- BLACK AND BLUE (MF RF 19) **1/2 — $5 — $10
- ELIZABETH, I'M COMING (MF RF 20) **1/2 — $10 — $15
- REDD 75 (MF RF 21, CD reissue Encore 5003) **1/2 — $5 — $8

There's a slightly smoother mix of jokes, rhymes, and patter on these '60s records for the MF label. On the first album he tells a variation on an old joke: "The woods is to find out who your best friend is. Go out with who you

DOOTO? DO TELL

There's renewed interest in the classic black comedians who were a part of Dootsie Williams's stable. That especially includes lesser knowns like Hattie Noel and Rozelle Gayle, as well as Redd Foxx and Scatman Crothers.

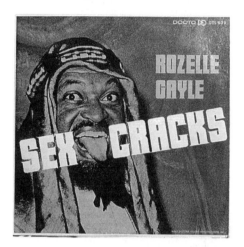

consider your best buddy and get lost in the woods, and late at night let your pants fall down. And wait till a rattlesnake bites you right back here. Now somebody has to suck that poison out. Bring your best friend with you? Here's a moment of truth...."

Foxx wasn't heavily into racial humor, but didn't avoid it. On "At Home," Foxx insists that not all Negroes carry knives: "My uncle carried an ice pick for forty-five years." And there are ad-libs like this, to a ringsider: "She's crazy about me. She thinks I'm a Negro. No, a lot of people think that, but actually folks, I'm white. This is a freckle. I figured if you're gonna have something, have a big one. My wife feels that way...." On the first album he notes that "after the nuclear war, everybody will be brown. Heat will brown your meat!"

In the '50s and late '60s Foxx was underrated for his stoic, salty delivery and his ability to knock out a seemingly infinite number of old and new gags on record, a half hour at a time. In the years before his *Sanford and Son* fame, these albums (but not the Dooto collection) were often in the $1.98 budget bin.

Foxx's "75" album has notably worse sound quality than the rest, which might indicate it's either a bootleg or outtakes, designed to cash in on the comic's newfound fame. The gags are closer to the '60s: "You know what a humdinger is. A humdinger, that's a girl who starts to hum every time she sees a dinger!"

In 1995 Encore Enterprises out of Canoga Park, California, and Capitol's Right Stuff began cheaply reissuing these Foxx albums. Many are only about a half hour per record, and should've been issued two per disc.

- IN A NUTSHELL (King 1074) **1/2 — $5 — $10
- MATINEE IDOL (King 1135) **1/2 — $5 — $10
- PASS THE APPLE, EVE (King 1073) **1/2 — $5 — $10
- BARE FACTS (King 1072) **1/2 — $5 — $10
- LIVE AND DIRTY (King NCD 2152) **1/2 — $7
- LIVE AND DIRTY (King NCD 2162) **1/2 — $7
- ON THE LOOSE (Loma 5905) **1/2 — $5 — $10
- FOXX A DELIC (Loma 5908) **1/2 — $5 — $10
- BOTH SIDES (Loma 5901) **1/2 — $5 — $10
- LIVE AT LAS VEGAS (Loma 5906) **1/2 — $5 — $10
- UP AGAINST THE WALL (Warner 1771) **1/2 — $5 — $10

Foxx recorded some good albums for King, but his best achievement was graduating to Loma, a division of Frank Sinatra's Reprise Records. This may have been the first time a major label comedy album allowed someone to actually use four letter words. Most of the humor hadn't changed much from the Dooto days.

From "Both Sides," Foxx offers "a little poem: a girl's legs are her best friend. But even the best of friends must part." And from "Foxx-a-Delic," Redd talks about a new butcher and his fussy customer. "She said, 'Bring me a Long Island duck.' The butcher gave her a duck and she stuck a finger in the duck and smelled it. She said, 'Man, this is a Michigan duck!' The butcher gave her another duck. She stuck her finger in there, smelled it and said, 'Hey, this is a Nebraska duck!' The butcher gave her another duck. She stuck her finger in, smelled it, and said, 'Now this is a Long Island duck!' She said, 'You must be new here, butcher.' He said, 'Yes, ma'am, I started yesterday.' She said, 'Where you from?' The butcher lowered his pants and bent over and said, 'You tell *me!*'"

Foxx's albums for the small King label are not easy to find. "Bare Facts," which features an unappealing cover of a nude Foxx (in modest profile) and a chunky-butted woman, offers a lot of racial humor. Many of his discs were recorded in mixed clubs, or even ones with a large white audience. Still, he could be comically reverse-racist: "I wish I liked white women. You don't have to worry about seeing me with a white woman. If you see me with a white woman, I'm holding her for the police. Thank you very much. If we ever take over, you may live! We're not gonna kill everyone, we'll need workers. Someone to harvest the melons!"

In 1993 King issued some of their Foxx material on two CDs titled "Live and Dirty" Volumes One and Two. They were budget-priced and under a half hour each.

- SANFORD AND SON (RCA Victor LPM 4739) **1/2 — $8 — $15
- WASH YOUR ASS (Atlantic SD 18157) *** — $8 — $15
- I AIN'T LIED YET (LAFF A 203, reissued as EVERYTHING'S BIG Laff 228) — $5 — $10
  reissued on CD by Loose Cannon 3145188422) ** — $7
- REDD FOXX UNCENSORED (LAFF A 210) ** — $5 — $10
- FOXX LIVE IN 85 (REDDY FREDDY RF 01) ** — $5 — $10
- REDD AND WHITE (Laff A 175) ** — $5 — $10
- REDD FOXX AND SLAPPY WHITE (Encore CD 5005) ** — $8

"Wash Your Ass" was released at the height of Foxx's *Sanford and Son* fame, and it's one of his best, though his voice is raspier than usual. Foxx was a master of cool, funky storytelling and curmudgeonly comedy, and the title cut is memorable thanks to his exasperated delivery.

"Sanford and Son" collects voicetracks from the TV series, including the reverse-racist routine that proclaims "nothing's as ugly as an ugly old white woman." Laff threw a bunch of discs into the marketplace, including one that has Slappy White on one side. The Encore CD similarly splices together ten minutes of Foxx, twenty of White, then another ten of Foxx.

Foxx's TV fame didn't last very long thanks in part to his irascible personality, and an obnoxious and arrogant circle of protecters and managers. Once he dropped from the top, few wanted to help him back up. Amid various divorces and business ventures, he ended up bankrupt. He hoped for a comeback with *The Royal Family*, a sitcom in 1991, but suffered a fatal heart attack on the set.

NOTES: The early Foxx records on Dooto have been out of print a long time and often have evocative '50s covers. There were red vinyl pressings of RF's "Laff Your Head Off" and "Laff Your Ass Off" albums. Foxx can be heard on "Zingers from the Hollywood Squares" (Event EV 6903) answering a few questions: "True or false, soccer teams in Africa have their own witch doctor." "That's true. They have a motto. If you can't beat 'em, eat 'em." "Are most stolen cars recovered?" "I had mine recovered in zebra."

REDD FOXX AND DUSTY FLETCHER

- LAUGHIN' AT THE BLUES (Savoy Jazz SJL 1181) ** $5 $10

Clinton "Dusty" Fletcher popularized the blues-novelty tune "Open the Door, Richard" in the 1940s. It's entirely a character comedy piece, as Fletcher does some funky griping and jiving as a tipsy man trying to get into his house. Many others would cover Fletcher's classic number. This 1978 compilation disc of obscure 78s includes "I'm Goin' Back There," "Gimme (Pawn Shop Song)," and "Mad Hour."

The big surprise is the reissuing of five 78s made by Redd Foxx in 1946. There isn't a single bit of gravel on Redd's tonsils here. He's amusing on the jive song "Let's Wiggle a Little Woogie," but this isn't comedy material exactly, just amusing blues.

AL FRANKEN

- RUSH LIMBAUGH IS A BIG FAT IDIOT (Dove 0787109746) ** $8

Not strictly based on Franken's successful book, this 1996 CD that goes on for over seventy minutes devotes at least ten to ruminations over the success of, criticism of, and writing of his surprise best-seller. Instead of using a cannon to put a huge hole into his giant balloon of a target, Franken needles, staples, folds, spindles, and pontificates. Only arch Limbaugh haters and those who watch C-SPAN for fun need bother.

Also see Stuart Smalley.

FRANKEN'DON

- SONGS OF ILL REPUTE (Bagel and Lox) *1/2 $3 $8

Frank Chase and Don Grey sing parodies of rock songs on this self-produced album recorded in a Vermont club. The material isn't funny, ("Another One Bites the Dust" becomes "Another One Buys a Saab") and the dirty cuts aren't interesting. It doesn't take much sniggering wit to change "Put Your Head on My Shoulder" to "Put Your Leg on My Shoulder." "Breaking Up Is Hard to Do" is now "Tying Up Is Fun to Do," with the following corn: "They say that tying up is fun to do. Now I know, I know that it's true. Our sex was boring at best. Instead of wearing women's clothes I tie you up and bite your nose ... It's so exciting when you can't move. Tying up is fun to do."

STAN FREBERG

- CHILD'S GARDEN OF FREBERG (Capitol T 777) **1/2 $6 $15
- BEST OF FREBERG (Capitol SM 2020) **1/2 $5 $10
- THE ORIGINAL CAST (Capitol SM 1424E) ** $6 $15

A pioneering satirist, Freberg's comedy singles, including "St. George and the Dragonet" from 1953, were among the first best-sellers to boost the credibility of humor at 45 rpm. These three albums collect his '50s novelties. "Garden" includes "St. George and the Dragonet," "C'est Si Bon," "Try," "Wide Screen Mama Blues," "Heartbreak Hotel," "Rock Around Stephen Foster," "Yellow Rose of Texas," "John and Marsha," "The Great Pretender," "That's My Boy," "Rock Island Line," and "Sh-Boom." The classic cut is "John and Marsha," a mock love scene from inane lovers who do nothing but whisper each other's name until they end up bellowing "Oh John ... Oh Marsha."

At the time (when *MAD Magazine* was just beginning to hit its stride) silly satire was something new. New listeners might not find anything special about "St. George and the Dragonet," but at the time it was rare to hear a well-produced and authentic parody. Freberg even took pains to have appropriate background music. The concept is more goofy than satiric, as St. George, talking like "Dragnet" detective Joe Friday, investigates a case:

"8:22 p.m. I talked to one of the maidens who had almost been devoured ... Could I talk to you ma'am? I'm St. George, ma'am, homicide, ma'am. I want to ask you a few questions, ma'am. I understand you were almost devoured by the dragon, is that right, ma'am?"

"It was terrible. He breathed fire on me, he burned me."

"How can I be sure of that, ma'am?"

"Believe me, I got it straight from the dragon's mouth!"

How is he going to catch the dragon?

"I thought you'd never ask. A dragon-net."

"Best of" duplicates a lot. It features "Yellow Rose of Texas," "John and Marsha, "St. George and the Dragonet," "Banana Boat," "Ya Got Trouble" "Tele-Vee-Shun," "C'est Si Bon," "Heartbreak Hotel, "Rock Island Line," The Great Pretender," "The Quest for Bridey Hammerschlaugen" and "Try." "The Original Cast" is another spotty reissue. It includes "Banana Boat," "Wun'erful, Wun'erful," "The Quest for Bridey Murphy," "Trouble," "Tele-Vee-Shun," "Little Blue Riding Hood," "Ba-Ba-Ball and Chain," and "Green Christmas."

There's a lot of dated material here, from a hipster urging ethnic Harry Belafonte to quiet down ("Banana Boat") to a very harmless Lawrence Welk spoof (he's caught his finger in his cheek and can't make champagne bottle pop noises on Wun'erful Wun'erful"). Freberg's sneering caricatures of '50s rock now seem wholly unhip.

"The Search for Bridey Murphy" was both a book and a 1956 documentary album about a woman who regressed into the past under hypnosis. Freberg's tame and slow parody version was evidently changed from "Bridey Murphy" to "Bridey Hammerschlaugen" to avoid legal problems. It's the same cut on every compilation.

"Green Christmas," was very controversial during the decade in which there were taboos on practically all satire. Freberg mocks "the Christmas pitch" at an ad agency, where Santa Claus is used to sell soda and cigarettes, and a chorus warbles "Deck the halls with advertising." When Bob Cratchit asks, "Can't you just wish someone a Merry Christmas for the joy of it?" An ad man answers, "What's the percentage in that?"

- STAN FREBERG COLLECTORS SERIES (Capitol CDP 7916272) *** $10
- GREATEST HITS (Curb) ** $8

Stan Freberg supplied the notes for the 1990 Capitol CD compilation. It's amusing to discover which performers liked or hated Freberg's parodies of their work. Younger fans may need the annotations explaining that "A Dear John & Marsha Letter" (the sequel to "John and Marsha") was based on a Ferlin Husky song of the day, or that "C'est Si Bon" was aimed at Eartha Kitt. Even so, many cuts are so dated that the laughter will be minimal. "Try," for example, is Freberg's perfect sendup of the overwrought mannerisms of Johnny Ray, but few will care.

Both familiar Freberg parodies and esoteric items are here. There's his #1 single "St. George and the Dragonet" (the notes say it was the fastest selling single of all time—at the time), and also the lesser known "Christmas Dragnet." In addition to the previously mentioned titles, there's "I've Got You Under My Skin," "That's My Boy," "Try," "The World is Waiting for the Sunrise," "Little Blue Riding Hood," "Sh-Boom," "Yellow Rose of Texas," "The Great Pretender," "Heartbreak Hotel," "Rock Island Line," "Banana Boat," "Tele Vee Shun," "Wun'erful Wun'erful" and "Green Christmas."

The earlier "Greatest Hits" (Curb) is skimpy, with only half the material Capitol provides.

- UNITED STATES OF AMERICA (Capitol SW 1573) **1/2 $6 $12
- UNITED STATES OF AMERICA 1 & 2 (Rhino R2 72476) **1/2 $18
- PAY RADIO (Capitol ST 2551) ** $8 $20

"United States of America" from 1961 was an ambitious, vaudevillian musical comedy written especially for disc. Freberg offers hip (for the '50s) sketches and songs with Paul Frees, Jesse White, Marvin Miller, and June Foray in the cast.

The sketches are all about historical events. One of the better ones has Columbus sailing to the New World. He hears the rumbles of mutiny (a low chorus of men going "rumble rumble rumble, mutiny mutiny mutiny"). The King of Spain has come along because, "My doctor told me I should go to Florida for the winter." Columbus arrives in the New World and meets the Indians, who describe their diet: "Berries, herbs, natural foods, and organically grown vegetables." Columbus tells of his dream "to open the first Italian restaurant in your country. Give you some real food. Starches, spaghetti, cholesterol ... that's progress!" Freberg fans still identify each other by the "rumble rumble rumble" catchphrase.

A CD version with bonus tracks arrived in 1989 (Capitol 92061). In 1996 Freberg produced Volume 2, which should delight the diehards. Freberg as Samuel B. Morse ruminates about the first message he'll send by telegraph: "Ah, I've got it.... What Hath God Wrought ... wait a minute. I'm allowed ten words ... that's only four! Wait a minute. Here we go: What Hath God Wrought, Please Advise Soonest, Sincerely Yours, Sam Morse." Amid the corn, sly satire, and dated/bouncy music, the supporting cast includes John Goodman, June Foray, Lorenzo Music, and David Ogden Stiers. Volumes 1 and 2 come as a double CD; Volume 2 was also issued separately.

Freberg's notion of records as "Pay Radio" is more amusing than the disc itself. The hit-and-miss album blends songs and sketches. Freberg gives a "Father of the Year Award" to the father of the hydrogen bomb—who says "Use it in good health."

A long sketch, "Shaft Theatre: The Flackman and Reagan," is about the efforts to "sell" Ronald Reagan as the next California governor. Based on "Batman and Robin," Reagan says things like "Holy Sacramento!" as his press agent works hard for his success. "How can I thank you?" Reagan asks. "Well, for openers you can take your foot off my cape," says Flackman.

"Digit Dialing" is a song about the change from phone exchange letters ("Remember Susquehanna?") to numbers. Other tunes include "Oh Dat Freeway System," "Poor Bobby Baker," "Dey Took Away My Diner's Club," and a slap at Beatles generation kids, "Which Is the Girl? Which Is the Boy," with the punch line, "She looks like Senator Dirksen, he looks like Joan Baez." Every now and then there's a line proving that Stan not only was, but *is* a major figure in the world of satiric comedy. In one sketch championing radio, Stan is asked, "Doesn't TV stretch the imagination?" His answer: "About twenty-one inches."

- FACE THE FUNNIES (Capitol T 1694, reissued as
   BEST OF THE STAN FREBERG SHOWS (Capitol SM 11824) ** $15 $30
- MADISON AVENUE WEREWOLF (Captiol T 1816 reissued as
   BEST OF THE STAN FREBERG SHOWS VOLUME TWO (Capitol SM11792) **1/2 $15 $30
- THE BEST OF THE STAN FREBERG SHOWS (Capitol WBO 1035) ** $20 $40
- THE STAN FREBERG SHOW (Radiola CDMR 1166) ** $8

In 1957 radio comedy was practically dead, and even Freberg's fresh approach couldn't revive it. He gave it all he had, which was mind-boggling at the time. Irreverent and hip, he created elaborate sound sketches (the twenty-minute "Incident at Los Voraces" on "Face the Funnies") that could be considered the ancestor to Firesign Theater. Another cut on the album, "Bang Gunleigh," is surreal, with a pause for unintentional drug humor in a commercial for "Puffed Grass." An astronaut mumbles, "If I didn't start off every day with a stomach full of puffed grass, I couldn't break through the sound barrier. One hundred million cows can't be wrong." Other bits on "Face the Funnies" that were excitingly new include the audio tease "The Zazaloph Family," who perform acrobatics (as if anyone can tell on radio), and the Pythonesque "Tuned Sheep," who can shake their heads and play "Lullaby of Birdland" with bells.

The "Werewolf" disc has some more accessible, silly cuts, like an interview with the Abominable Snowman:

"You are the—" "Abominable Snowman, right. I never cared for 'Abominable' but it's the nearest word translated from the original Hindustani Abomanooyamyoo, which means "The Hairy One with the Big Feet." "I was noticing your—" "Sneakers. Size 23." "That's pretty big." "Well, it's functional design, you know. Ever try to walk on snow with ballet slippers? Roller skates? I have them made up for me ... at Abercrombie and Fitch...."

A routine about high fidelity includes some imagery that was strange at the time, like a prize of "a lifesize full-color inflatable latex rubber Liberace" for anyone who can guess a particular sound, which happens to be "Benny Goodman in a skin diver's suit twenty feet underwater playing 'Danny Boy' in a kelp bed."

Capitol issued their two "Best of the Stan Freberg Shows" discs as a double-album set. There's a nice full-color photo of Freberg on the cover, plus shots of Freberg with supporting players Daws Butler, June Foray, and Peter Leeds. Prices are higher for the albums with colorful covers, like the cartoon and photo collage for "Face the Funnies" and a Charles Addams-esque drawing for "The Madison Ave. Werewolf."

Fans who already have the "Best of the Freberg Shows" on Capitol, and are curious about what the original complete Freberg broadcasts were like, get two episodes (August 4 and October 6, 1957) on the Radiola CD. The original shows turn out to be dulled by music filler (Peggy Taylor was the female singer). Desperate fans will discover some long lost (that's overly long and deservedly lost) sketches like "Lox Audio Theatre Presents Rock Around My Nose" (with Daws Butler auditioning the kid voice he later used for cartoon character Elroy Jetson). The highlights, available elsewhere, are "Lecture on Hi-Fi" and "Gray Flannel Werewolf."

NOTES: In the '60s Freberg blazed a lucrative career creating radio and TV commercials with a touch of wit and satire. Many of his fans are feverish to find the promotional albums he did for various companies. Most of them are little more than collections of somewhat amusing radio ads and promotional pitches, but it doesn't matter to the die-hards. Among the better ones: "More Here Than Meets the Ear" for the Radio Advertising Council; "The Sound of Moving" for Bekins, a moving company; "Hey Look Us Over" for CBS; "Chun King Chow Mein"; "Homogenized Commercials for Meadow Gold Dairy"; "Uncle Stan Wants You"; and "Who Listens to Radio?" With Freberg still a cult figure, albeit to a small group generally over age forty or fifty, it's not surprising to find a $20-$40 price tag on these.

"Oregon Oregon," recorded in 1959, was privately pressed for the Oregon State Centennial. Stubby Kaye costarred, with music and lyrics by Freberg. "St. George and the Dragonet" is on "25 Years of Recorded Comedy," Warner Bros. 3BX 3131.

AARON FREEMAN

- LIVE AT CROSS CURRENTS (CROSS CURRENTS RECORDS 311025X) * $3 $7

Recorded in Chicago in 1983, black comedian Freeman not only takes on Ronald Reagan, but Jesse Jackson. Instead of an "I Have a Dream" speech like Martin Luther King, Jr., Jackson declares, "I Have a Press Agent!" Unfortunately it would take more than a press agent to interest anyone in this often verbose lecture. Now and then he does a performance piece; well-acted but with a cliché character and not a lot to say.

FREEMAN AND MURRAY

- FREEMAN AND MURRAY (LAFF 165) ** $5 $10

One of the few interracial teams (Freeman King black, Murray Langston white), the duo appeared on *The Sonny and Cher Show* and made this amiably sloppy disc. Not a typically cheap and dirty product from Laff, the humor is mostly corny and clean. Murray begins: "We're proof that black and white can work together." "As long as we're getting paid." "Actually we're brothers." "I'm the white sheep of the family. To tell you the truth, I'm Jewish." "You're not Jewish!" "Wanna see my scar?..." "Oh by the way, Freeman is doing the sequel to *The Godfather*." "Yeah, it's called The Black Mother! I'd like to recommend a movie for you folks to go see. It's about the first black Dracula. It's called Blacula." "He sucks watermelon juice!" "The only way you can kill this cat is by drivin' a spare rib through his heart!"

Langston went solo and earned some notoriety as "The Unknown Comic," performing with a bag over his head.

PAUL FREES

- POSTER PEOPLE (MGM M 3489) **1/2 $5 $15
- THAT AGENCY THING (CBS Radio XTV 89549) *1/2 $10 $20

A voiceover genius, Paul Frees was behind the mike as cartoon characters Boris Badenov, Ludwig von Drake, George and John on "The Beatles," and hundreds more. He was even the Pillsbury Doughboy. As a hobby he appeared in movies, such as the original *The Thing*, and wrote the screenplay for the 1960 film *The Beatniks*. As an artist, he did the charcoal sketch of Brother Dave Gardner for Gardner's "Hipocracy" album. Frees was a nice guy who modestly avoided the spotlight, with the exception of the MGM album in the early '70s. He died in 1986.

"Poster People" mates Hollywood stars with pop hits of the day: "Mama Told Me Not To Come" (sung by W. C. Fields), "Raindrops Keep Fallin' on My Head" (Humphrey Bogart,) "Let it Be" (Warner Oland), "The Look of Love" (Boris Karloff), "Sugar Sugar" (Sidney Greenstreet), "Hey Jude" (Peter Lorre), "Games People Play" (Bela Lugosi), "Up Up and Away" (Ed Wynn), an so on. The best cuts are the most demented: "Let it Be" fractured by an inanely stereotyped Chinese accent that is hardly Oland's Charlie Chan, and "Hey Jude" done as Peter Lorre. Most numbers are cute more than funny, like "Up Up and Away" warbled by Ed Wynn (a voice Frees later adapted to "Captain Peachfuzz" on *The Bullwinkle Show*).

Frees plays the head of an ad agency on the one-sided promo album from CBS Radio Spot Sales. It's an elaborate fifteen-minute pitch intended to generate interest in radio, and features original songs performed by a chorus and supporting cast members Herschel Bernardi, Howard Morris, and June Foray. A sample of actual radio ads are included on this mildly interesting curio.

NOTES: Frees is on many Spike Jones and Stan Freberg records. A classic is "My Old Flame" sung as Peter Lorre on Spike's "Thank You Music Lovers." Paul once performed it on Spike's radio show—with Peter Lorre dropping by to listen and do his own version! It's on the Rhino CD "Spike Jones: The Radio Years."

In 1964 Frees supplied voices for an odd World's Fair puppet show, "Les Poupees De Paris." The soundtrack album (RCA LSO-1090) offers Frees for a minute and a half as "The Mad Doctor and the Creature" in a horror sketch. It's not much beyond spooky music and some growling in two different octaves.

The soundtrack for American International's "The Abominable Dr. Phibes" (AIR A-1040) features Frees in various strange guises, doing an Al Jolson-type version of "Darktown Strutter's Ball," Ronald Colman ("Over the Rainbow"), Chico Marx ("All I Do Is Dream of You"), W. C. Fields ("What Can I Say after I Say I'm Sorry"), Skinnay Ennis ("You Stepped Out of a Dream"), Dick Powell ("Charmaine"), and Humphrey Bogart ("One for My Baby.")

MICHAEL FREMER
• I CAN TAKE A JOKE (Kant-Tel KT 714) *1/2 $3 $7

This studio indulgence from a Massachusetts comic in 1976 shows the influences of Firesign Theater, *Saturday Night Live*, and radio disc jockeys. Fremer offers a lot of quickie commercials and obnoxious blackouts with overdone sound effects. His annoying voices parody old biddies, Italians, Bostonians, doped-out dopes, and other familiar types. The script is full of pseudo-spaced out punnery: "Good evening, this is Danny Hog, your news frog. This is your latex news. Stretchable. President Nixon announced the retirement of Head Pig. Excuse me, that should read F.B.I. Director, J. Edgar Hoover. Most frequently mentioned to replace the decrepit, excuse me, that should read "aging" F.B.I. leader are Gus Stoppo, former German police chief, and E. Lectro Lux, a part-time door-to-door vacuum cleaner salesman."

Simple musical parodies swipe at easy-to-imitate rockers (Bob Dylan, Neil Young, Lou Reed). The mimicry is all right, but the goofy lyrics have no edge. Sung to "Take a Walk on the Wild Side," Fremer makes fun of Lou Reed: "Lou Reed came from Wantagh in adversity. Went to Syracuse University. Had himself a real good time. Now he looks like Frankenstein. He said, 'Hey Babe, give my car a lube job ...' And the colored mechanics went: 'Do da do da do da do do da do.' Lou Reed came from Long Island. In the Velvet Underground he was almost tolerable. Then he sang like he was dead. Even had to sing from bed. He said, 'Hey babe, give my car a lube job....'"

FRIARS ROASTS
• LUCILLE BALL AND DESI ARNAZ (No Label) $25 $75
• JACK BENNY (No Label) $20 $50
• HUMPHREY BOGART (No Label, also issued as THE TESTIMONIAL,
    Martin Records, and UP YOURS Sassy Records) *** $15 $50
• HARRY JOE BROWN (see listing under George Jessel)
• GEORGE BURNS (No Label) $20 $50
• GARY COOPER (No Label) $40 $75
• LEO DUROCHER (No Label) $15 $40
• MERVYN LE ROY (No Label) $30 $75
• JERRY LEWIS (No Label) $20 $50
• DEAN MARTIN (No Label) $30 $75
• DON RICKLES (No Label, also issued as HEERE'S JOHNNY, Pornographic PP-44
    and JOINED IN THE MIDDLE, No Label) $25 $50

The Friars Club's privately issued and/or bootlegged "roasts" have been collectibles for over forty years. Those who think "family oriented" comics like Jack Benny, Maurice Chevalier, George Burns, and Alan King never worked "blue" will be surprised by these cheerfully vulgar discs. The whole point of these affairs, aside from nominally praising/insulting the guest, was to let comedians do the kind of material they couldn't do in public.

The most expensive are the three-record sets for LeRoy, Martin, and Cooper, mostly because of the extra amount of vinyl. The interest in Lucille Ball makes that two-disc set equal in value. The Benny roast, the Bogart set on Martin Records, and the original Don Rickles roast are all two-record sets.

Some events aren't as "blue" as others, depending on who the roastee is, and the nature of the event. For example, the Benny event, November 9, 1951, marking his twentieth anniversary in radio, has "straight" guests (Bernard Baruch, Adlai Stevenson, Mayor Vincent Impellitteri). The highlight is ten minutes from Fred Allen, who recalls his long association with Jack: "Mr. Benny was the only violinist after you heard him play, you felt the strings would sound better if they were back in the cat...." But later he admits: "Jack is, as I know and we all know, the best-liked man in show business today. And if our country was only fortunate enough to enjoy the status Jack enjoys, our country too would not have an enemy in the world."

For the average fan, the big-name Bogart and Rickles roasts are the place to start. Recorded circa 1955, Bogart's guests include Alan King, Charles Coburn, and Maurice Chevalier, with Red Buttons as master of ceremonies. The hit of the evening is Lauren Bacall, who manages to convulse the audience with a recorded speech (since it was a "stag" affair and she couldn't appear live). In part: "I must tell you of an incident that happened to Bogie before I met him. He was keeping company with a girl. One day while he was waiting in front of her house, she wanted Bogie to go to the store for her, so she opened the window and called out, 'Humphrey! Humphrey!' And twenty guys ran up to her room.

Boys, don't think this guy Bogie is easy to live with. When Bogie gets his script for a picture, especially where he plays a tough guy, he studies his part with so much sincerity you'd think our home was a hideout and he was really on the lam. When he has his script memorized he puts so much realism into it he really believes that he's a tough guy. Why Bogie even fights in his sleep. He wakes me up three or four times a night and says, 'Baby, hold my gun.'"

THE FRIVOLOUS FIVE

- SOUR CREAM AND OTHER DELIGHTS (RCA LSP 3663) * $3 $10

Listeners were expected to buy this one solely for the album cover. In a parody of Herb Alpert's "Whipped Cream and Other Delights," five middle-aged women smile as they pose sheathed in white goo. So what was on the disc? Old ladies singing novelty lyrics? Or singing off key? Just studio musicians doing the tunes with some off-key notes and sputtering trumpet work.

DAVID FROST

- THE FROST REPORT (Janus JLS 3005) *** $8 $15
- DAVID FROST IN LAS VEGAS (United Artists UAS 5555) **1/2 $5 $10
- THAT WAS THE WEEK THAT WAS (Radiola 1123) *** $5 $8

Now known more as a serious interviewer, in his twenties Frost was famous as the angry, bristling host of Britain's *That Was the Week That Was* and *The Frost Report*. His stable of writers included many of the "Monty Python" troupe, plus "The Two Ronnies." In the '60s he came to America for a version of his former series and, later, a talk show.

"The Frost Report" still has some amusing sketches and good writing that survives the dated references. Frost on the news: "The state of England. Mr. Harold Wilson said today the drain on Britain's gold reserves has finally stopped. They've all gone. Mr. Wilson added, 'We would all have had our backs to the wall—but we're so far behind with the building program that the wall isn't ready. Parliament is opened by Her Majesty the Queen, who would be well advised to take one quick look and shut it again.... Abroad things are done so differently. We've just heard there's going to be a general election in Greece. And we all know which Generals are going to be elected.... And a group of British M.P.'s returning from Africa report that of the African leaders they met, one of them was Haile Selassie, eight were fairly Selassie, and five weren't Selassie at all...."

Ronnie Corbett, Ronnie Barker, and John Cleese perform in the sketches and lectures.

The live Vegas set from 1972 includes a long mock-*David Frost Show* with Fred Travalena as guests Hubert Humphrey, Jim Nabors, Moms Mabley, Paul Lynde, and Truman Capote. It's competently done. Frost: "Tell me Truman, I hear you've just completed your first book since *In Cold Blood*." Capote: "Yes, it's called *In Hot Pants*. David, the F.B.I. broke into my house and stole my secret file." Frost: "What are you going to do?" Capote: "Use an emery board, silly."

Frost's "All Purpose Political Speech" is a masterpiece of weasel words and high-minded phrases signifying nothing. A segment based on his perennial question to his talk show guests (What is your definition of love?) is pure Vegas: "Love is staying awake all night with a sick child. Or a very healthy adult ... Love is spending Christmas Eve in front of the fire with your loved one. While your wife and kids are out of town ... Love is a bride and groom. The bride wears white to symbolize purity. The groom wears black."

The soundtrack material from NBC's *That Was the Week That Was* from 1964-65 (reissued on CD) pioneers territory later covered by *Saturday Night Live*'s 'Weekend Update'" and *Laugh-In*. The hour of news, songs, and sketches, compiled from various shows, include some rarities: songs by Tom Lehrer (performed by various female cast members), a brief monologue by Woody Allen, and appearances by Buck Henry, Bob Dishy, Henry Morgan, and Elliot Reid. And, yes, that's Mort Sahl introducing Lehrer's "Old Dope Peddler" tune. Frost is represented fleetingly, but there are examples of his usual dry monologues on current events.

NOTES: The 1963 British album "That Was the Week That Was" (Odeon) costars Millicent Martin and Ned Sherrin. It has a few timeless cuts, like the couple who get into a furious argument because the man's fly is open, and Frost's silly astrological report on Regella, "a very BIG star." In the early '70s Frost is on various straight documentary albums, including "David Frost on Nursing" (University Hospitals of Cleveland UH-101) and "David Frost Talks to Bobby Kennedy" (Douglas SD 800).

DAVID FRYE

- I AM THE PRESIDENT (Elektra EKS 75006) **1/2 $3 $5
- RADIO FREE NIXON, WNIX (Elektra EKS 74085) *1/2 $4 $10
- RICHARD NIXON SUPERSTAR (Buddah BDS 5097) *1/2 $4 $10

- RICHARD NIXON: A FANTASY (Buddah 1600) *** $4 $10
   (CD reissue HE'S BACK: DAVID FRYE IS NIXON, RCA 75517-49521-2) *** $8
- THE GREAT DEBATE (David Frye Productions DFP-80) *1/2 $6 $15

An intense little mimic from Brooklyn, Frye (nee David Shapiro) was hot in the late '60s with his fierce and devastating caricature style. Aside from solid vocal work, he'd twist his face into grotesque parodies of his subjects. The first mimic to go for the jugular, Frye created the definitive Nixon, making up catchphrases ("I AM the President") and visual quirks that an entire nation began imitating.

"I Am the President" follows the old "First Family" formula of blackout sketches. Mina Kolb, Chuck McCann, Tom O'Malley, and Bryna Raeburn are in the cast. Typical mild gag: Nixon, receiving the good news on election night, cries "I AM the President ... well, you can't lose them all." Leaving the White House, Lyndon Johnson asks how to get back to Texas. "I'm glad you asked me that question," says Nixon, "I have a car I'm not going to be using ... white walls, heater, low miles, easy payments." LBJ: "Buy a used car from YOU?"

But as a portent of things to come, Frye gets out his bludgeon now and then. When Nixon encounters an echo and joyfully calls out, "I am the Greatest President Who Ever Lived," the response comes back, "Sorry, I'm an echo, not an idiot!"

The initial follow-ups were just variations on a theme. "WNIX" was perfect for college radio stations, a 1971 radio show parody with Lyndon Johnson reading the farm report, Billy Graham handling an Evangel Hour, Howard Cosell reporting sports, and Nixon singing "My Way." The writing, headed by Kenny Solms and Gail Parent, is formulaic and weak. Bryna Raeburn as Julie Nixon Eisenhower in a commercial on WNIX: "Daddy, Daddy, Daddy, look, no cavities!" "No cavities? Julie, was it that new toothpaste we've been using?" "I don't know, it was either that or my new feminine hygiene spray!"

"Superstar," keyed to college kids who'd laid down a small fortune for "Jesus Christ Superstar," included a pop poster. Billy Graham narrates the sketches, which start with Nixon's momentous birth: "Mrs. Nixon, it's a boy ... one thing is remarkable. I've never seen a newborn with a five o'clock shadow...." Gabe Kaplan is credited as one of the gag writers on this hit-and-miss disc that sometimes strains to reach a punch line. Nixon on *Sesame Street* declares: "Today's show is brought to you by ... the letter W. This is not to say that the letter W is any better or worse than any other letters of our alphabet ... when I was a little lad I had an old second-hand I and a used Q. How I treasured my I.Q. It wasn't much, but it was all I had...."

"Fantasy" is just plain brutal, a 1973 release that skewers Nixon and the Watergate scandal: "I accept responsibility," says Nixon, "but not the blame ... the only way I'm gonna leave the White House is to be dragged screaming and kicking ... I love America, and you always hurt the one you love." The scalding satire fantasizes over Nixon's capture, his court trial (Raymond Burr confronts Nixon with an incriminating jowl print) and his ultimate incarceration on death row. The frantic-paced disc is loaded with eccentric "guest" mimcry appearances: Rod Steiger is the prison warden, Boris Karloff is the executioner, and Ted Kennedy turns up constantly in a morbid running joke: "And when I returned, Mary Jo and the car were gone." This was a rarity, a quickly produced topical album that worked. The writers were Gabe Kaplan, Eric Cohen, Bob Shayne, and Frye himself.

In 1996, amid a slew of Nixon movies and books, Frye's "Fantasy" album was reissued on CD with sixteen minutes added from "Superstar." In true Nixonian spirit, RCA didn't bother to explain where the sixteen minutes came from.

Frye's style was so intense it was almost self-destructive. When the hated Nixon was gone, replaced by mild fellows like Ford, Carter, and Reagan, Frye had no suitable target for his raging style. Aside from the 1980 attempt, "The Great Debate," Frye had little national exposure. This is his only live album. The title track takes up an entire side as 1980 Presidential candidates Carter, Reagan, and John Anderson feud. Frye resorts to shock comedy as Carter and Reagan insult each other: "You freckle-faced wimp!" "You jowl-faced wrinkled B-movie actor!"

Side Two offers a mean-spirited, eight-minute put-down of aging actors Kirk Douglas, Jimmy Stewart, and Henry Fonda. More creatively tasteless is his atrociously hilarious impersonation of recently deceased Nelson Rockefeller, singing "I'm in Heaven" and declaring of his scandalous demise: "A guy of seventy doing 69 with a twenty-five-year-old? It could've been worse. I could've died at twenty-five doing 69 with a seventy-five-year-old!"

NOTES: Frye's albums don't fetch high prices due to their topical nature. A "WNIX" sample is on "25 Years of Recorded Comedy" (Warner Bros. WBX 3131) and a snip of Frye's Nixon singing "My Way" appears on "The Watergate Primer" (Waterfall WFL 66), an otherwise fairly straight narrative of the events of Watergate. Frye appears on "The New First Family 1968" (see Will Jordan) doing Nixon, William F. Buckley, and Richard Burton.

LEO FUCHS

- SHALOM PARDNER (Tikva T-81) $4 $8

A star comic in Warsaw, later a Yiddish stage personality, Fuchs released this album after turning up on *The Ed Sullivan Show*, *The Danny Thomas Show*, and an episode of *Wagon Train*. The title tune is probably a humorous look at the unlikely spectacle of a Jewish cowpoke. Since the album is completely in Yiddish, it's hard to tell. Fuchs is on "20th Century Yiddish Humor" (Banner BAS 1004) singing "S'Gite Nit" in Yiddish. In the early '70s Greater Recording Co. issued "Leo Fuchs Sings Yiddish Theatre Favorites" (GRC 174).

ALLEN FUNT

- THE CANDID MICROPHONE (Columbia ML 4344, reissued by Harmony) *1/2 $4 $8
- THE CANDID MICROPHONE II (Columbia ML 4449) *1/2 $5 $10
- THE CANDID MICROPHONE Volume 3 (Columbia ML 4450) *1/2 $5 $12
- ALLEN FUNT'S CANDID CAMERA (Jubilee KS 2) *1/2 $5 $10

• CANDID KIDS (RCA Victor LPM 2679/LSP 3679) **1/2 $4 $8

Funt created "Candid Microphone" and later the long-running TV series *Candid Camera*. Funt always enjoyed documenting the stupidity of the average person. On the first album he discovers that most don't know what the word "retroactive" means: "Isn't this weather retroactive?" "Yes, it's terrible," someone answers. "You know what retroactive weather is, don't you?" "Um, very hot, without stopping."

Funt also had a sadistic streak with his practical jokes. Also on the first album, a furniture mover is ordered by Funt to remove a trunk. Inside a man moans pitifully. It takes a chillingly long time and a lot of moans before the mover finally puts down the trunk and turns down the job.

Volume Two's peculiar variation has a locksmith discovering Funt's secretary chained to her chair: "How come she's chained?" "What's so unusual about that? It's the only way to get her to do work. I let her out for lunch though." "Chainin' somebody to a desk?" "That's my business." "I know it...."

Each album's studies in human nature vary between the mildly amusing and the grimly pathetic. Sometimes the cuts are dead serious (the first album's interview with a blind war veteran and his one-legged friend) and others are just annoying teases, with Funt as a nuisance customer or obnoxious clerk.

Nothing on the Jubilee album jacket alerts customers that they are getting reissued material from the previous Columbia albums.

"Candid Kids" from 1967 was issued during the TV series and is only for very indulgent listeners. In one cute segment Funt asks the kids to fill in the last line to a famous proverb they've never heard before: "A rolling stone ... plays the guitar." "To be or not to be that is ... bad." "Man doesn't live by ... getting married." "You can't get blood ... out of a sick duck." "Fools rush in ... where the people are crowded." There are also interviews that display the essence of children's logic: "Why is the belly button there?" "To collect hair from your clothes."

ALAN GALE

• ON STAGE (Roulette R 25110) * $3 $10

Gale, once part of the trio Tracy, Gale and Leonard, worked solo in New York and later owned his own Alan Gale's club in Miami Beach. *Variety* noted, "he sometimes stayed on the floor for a minimum of three hours not repeating any gags or lines." Unfortunately, here this straw-hatted funnyman is almost a stereotype of the '50s Vegas-style comic. There are family shpritzes ("My son is a genius—he tells me!") and snappy patter ("When I was a kid I had air conditioning—on the fire escape. And I got wet and it wasn't even raining!"). It's all done in a hyper, nagging style: "I've been in this business forty-three years! No, don't applaud, I'm the Jewish Dorian Gray!" Only of interest for students wanting to hear how a nightclub veteran used to work the room. Gale was seventy-two when he died of cancer on May 26, 1980.

BOBBY GALE

• THIS IS MY LIFE (Family FLP 137) *1/2 $4 $8
• BOBBY GALE JOINS THE ARMY/NAVY (Family FLP 138) *1/2 $4 $8

Hapless Gale uses a put-upon, high, husky voice and slight Brooklyn accent to tell his mild, corny gags. He recorded for a budget ($1.98 list) label in the early '60s. Discussing his Navy days: "I'll never forget my first voyage. There was such a strong wind it was the first time in my life I spit in my own eye. Boy did I get seasick! My stomach went in and out with the tide. The voyage put color in my cheeks. Green. I looked just like my passport photos!"

MARTY GALE

• SEXY STORIES WITH A YIDDISHA FLAVOR (Cari-Gale 1) ** $5 $10
• SPICY HUMOR FOR SWINGERS (Cari-Gale 2) ** $5 $10
• MORE SEXY STORIES WITH A YIDDISHA FLAVOR (Cari-Gale 3) ** $5 $10
• RISQUE STORIES: WHAT RHYMES WITH 69? (Cari-Gale 4) ** $5 $10
• FUNFIN' AROUND (Cari-Gale 5) ** $5 $10

The late Marty Gale, brother of veteran Vegas star Jackie Gayle, released a number of sound-alike albums. Special interest goes to "Spicy Humor for Swingers" (circa 1962) for the album notes from Sally Marr, Lenny Bruce's mother. She wrote: "... he just doesn't tell risqué jokes. There is a premise underlying his comedy. There are various 'Pieces of Business' that leave you howling."

Not really. He tells the one about the Chinese daughters. One wanted to marry a husband with "three dragon on chest." Another wanted to marry a man with "two dragon on chest." But the third wanted to marry a man with "one draggin' on the floor." And then there's the one about the woman who comes to a doctor's office. He asks, "When did you have a check up?" She says, "Strictly Hungarians."

Fans of whiz-bang humor and Yiddish may be amused by Gale's Yiddisha albums (produced by partner Frank Cari). Many punch lines are in Yiddish: "I knew a fellow who went to the University of Tulane and became a tulaner." Tulaner, the Yiddish dictionary says, means "seducer."

GALLAGHER

• GALLAGHER (Liberty LT1019) **1/2 $4 $10

Before he turned into the Richard Simmons of comedy, using a pushy delivery to put over his prop-driven gags, Gallagher was a capable, semi-wacky, long-haired hippie comic, as this 1980 release proves. Not overtly campy here, nor parading props like giant tricycles or watermelons for smashing, he scores with mild observational humor based in logic ("Why do they call them 'buildings' when they're already built?") and sometimes a good sick joke:

"Blind man in a drugstore comes in, starts knocking things off the shelf with his cane. The owner says, 'Can I help you?' He says, 'No thanks, just looking.'"

WEELA GALLEZ
- GET GAY WITH GALLEZ (Duo D 4) ** $3 $7
- MY TURTLE'S DEAD (Ramco 712) ** $4 $8

Tastefully risqué, Gallez sounds a bit like a toned down Rusty Warren. She offers observation more than straight jokes and tunes. From the early '60s Duo album: "I've started a new movement, I'm so excited about it. We have a slogan: Help Stamp Out Artificial Insemination. Is anybody celebrating anything tonight? Anybody expecting to celebrate anything? Anybody worried? I asked that for a specific reason, you know ... last September I made up a whole batch of maternity wedding gowns, and I urge the girls to get them before labor day...."

FRANK GALLOP
- FRANK GALLOP SINGS (Musicor 1966) *1/2 $4 $10
- WNEW 60 SECOND SOAPS (WNEW FR-1117) *1/2 $10 $15

Announcer Gallop's ultraproper delivery provides a droll contrast to the Jewish accents on "You Don't Have to Be Jewish" (Kapp) and "Jewish American Princess" (Bell). On the Kapp album he sang "The Ballad of Irving," the laughs coming from Jewish terms pronounced in a very straight and Gentile manner. The original "Irving" song was about a "Big Bad John" of nebbish proportions:

"He came from the old Bar Mitzvah spread, schlepping a salami and pumpernickle bread. He always followed his mother's wishes. Even on the range he used two sets of dishes. Irving ... Big Fat Irving ... Big Sissy Irving. The 142nd fastest gun in the West."

The Musicor album has a sequel about Irving's effeminate son Seymour: "Seymour was dressed in boots magenta by his mother Esther, a dance hall yenta. She had one goal and he never mocked her. She dreamed he'd marry a female doctor.... Seymour. Tall sissy Seymour. Tall sissy excellent-looking Seymour. Son of the 142nd fastest gun in the West."

Other cuts, like the covers of "Cigarettes, Whiskey and Wild Wild Women" and "The Man I Love" (without changing the gender), are supposed to be funny because they're recited by a disdainfully grim and implacable announcer.

The WNEW record offers samples of "Bradley at the Bar," a sixty-second mock soap opera broadcast daily to bewilder listeners: "Bradley went to see Judge Binder and was faced with the most difficult problem he had to face in five years as a lawyer. We join them as we hear Bradley say:"

'This is the most difficult problem I've had to face in five years as a lawyer.'

"Tune in tomorrow...." No threat to similar one-joke, non-joke material from Bob and Ray.

REGINALD GARDINER
- MY SQUARE LADDIE (Foremost FMLS 1) **1/2 $6 $15

This *My Fair Lady* parody offers the very British Mr. Gardiner learning hipness from Brooklynite Nancy Walker and her friend Zasu Pitts. The trio's personality soars above the standard script and tunes. Instead of "The Rain in Spain Stays Mainly on the Plain," Gardiner must swing out with: "It's de oily boid dat always gits de woim." "On the Street Where You Live" becomes "The Block Where You Rock," and "I Could Have Danced All Night" is now "I Could Have Boozed All Night (Ain't that What Booze Is For?)"

Back in the 78 rpm era, Gardiner had a hit with the two-record set "Trains" (Decca), a mild monologue with sound effects.

BROTHER DAVE GARDNER
- REJOICE DEAR HEARTS (RCA Victor LPM 2083) **1/2 $5 $10
- AIN'T THAT WEIRD (RCA Victor LPM/LSP 2335) **1/2 $5 $10
- KICK THEY OWN SELF (RCA Victor LPM 2239) **1/2 $5 $10
- DID YOU EVER? (RCA Victor LPM/LSP 2498) **1/2 $5 $10
- ALL SERIOUSNESS ASIDE (RCA Victor LPM/LSP 2628) **1/2 $8 $16
- IT'S BIGGER THAN BOTH OF US (RCA Victor LPM/LSP 2761) **1/2 $8 $16
- BEST OF BROTHER DAVE GARDNER (RCA Victor LPM/LSP 2852) **1/2 $5 $10
- BROTHER DAVE GARDNER IN PERSON (Delta DLP 1131) $6 $15
- MOTORCYCLE STORY (Delta DLP 1130) $6 $15
- HOW YOU LOOK AT IT (Capitol ST 2055) **1/2 $5 $10
- IT DON'T MAKE NO DIFFERENCE (Capitol ST 1867) **1/2 $5 $10
- HIP-OCRACY (Tower T 5050) **1/2 $5 $10
- OUT FRONT (Tonka TLP 713) **1/2 $8 $16
- BROTHER DAVE GARDNER'S NEW COMEDY ALBUM (Four Star 4S75003) **1/2 $8 $16

Gardner was a jazz-hip Will Rogers who often appeared on Jack Paar's *Tonight Show*, and was very popular between 1958 and 1962, when he was busted for drugs. Cleared but a bit tainted, he made some more albums, but slipped back to the Southern circuit. He was making a film called *Chain Gang* at the time of his death in 1983.

Gardner's anecdotes are sometimes weak and the monologues often meander, but his audience loves him just the same. His personality is half the fun, that odd blend of jazz lingo and Gospel preaching. From "It's All in How You Look at It," Dave declares:

"Some of ye who are skeptical toward skepticism, fear not 'cause not ain't nothin' to fear no how!"

Gardner's first few RCA albums had decent-sized pressings, but at this point all are rare, especially the later ones on obscure local labels. Gardner's cult is small, but loyal enough to keep prices high. The 1969 disc for Houston's Tonka company is filled with typical one-liners: "The best way to beat the draft is to volunteer." In 1976 Nashville's Four Star label discovered he was still an interesting talker, his quick-fix theories almost pithy: "Aw shoot man, we oughta elect *everybody* this trip, so they can all watch each other.... Reason dogs are man's best friend 'cause he won't tell on ya.... I've often wondered. If an attorney practices law, when they ascend to the bench do they play?"

ED GARDNER

- DUFFY'S TAVERN (Radiola MR 1024) ** $4 $8
- DUFFY'S TAVERN (Golden Age 5026) **1/2 $4 $8
- DUFFY'S TAVERN REVISITED (Sunset LP 700) **1/2 $7 $15

Ed Gardner shot to stardom in 1940 with radio's "Duffy's Tavern." There was no Duffy, just Gardner as Archie the Bartender. His wife was originally played by his real wife at the time, Shirley Booth.

Today's listeners will be surprised to discover how closely "Duffy's Tavern" resembles Carroll O'Connor's *Archie's Place* and Jackie Gleason's "Joe the Bartender" routines. Gardner sounds like a cross between the two. His Archie, like Archie Bunker, is a malaprop specialist ("I got up at the crank of dawn"). Like Gleason's Joe, Ed's Archie had a dummy stooge pal, a Crazy Guggenheim type named Finnegan.

The Golden Age album offers two episodes, from October 19 and October 26, 1951.

Radiola offers the first full-length episode, broadcast July 29, 1940. At the time, the show had a variety feel to it. Guest/bar patron Gertrude Niesen walks in, does a bit of comedy dialogue with Archie the Bartender, then sings a number. Later Colonel Stoopnagle arrives for some byplay, unveiling his latest invention: "That's no ordinary shotgun ... it's made with one barrel on top of the other instead of side by side. It's for shooting ducks who happen to be riding piggyback."

The flip side is an episode of "My Friend Irma" starring Marie Wilson and Cathy Lewis.

"Duffy's Tavern Revisited," released in 1955, offers three excerpts featuring George Raft, Deems Taylor, and Nigel Bruce. Even gentle Nigel Bruce gets into the insult act in this typical example of radio patter, with Gardner speaking first:

"Well, old fruit, how are you?" "Uh, tip top, old bread." "Old bread?" "Would you prefer crumb?" "Jolly well put, old boy. What do you think of Duffy's Tavern here, top hole, hey?" "Rat hole, hey?" "I understand your English." "I wish I could say the same for yours!"

GERALD GARDNER See MARTIN ADAM WILLSON

IRVING GARNER

- BEST OF IRVING GARNER (Verve MGV 2078) * $3 $10

The goofy face of Spike Jones's band member Freddie Morgan adorns the album cover. Not that he pretends to be Irving Garner. No, the album notes say, "A good friend of Irving Garner's, Leonard Throat, himself an eminent and world-famous concert pianist, consented to pose for the album cover." This gag is as pointless as the one-joke disc itself, in which "Smoke Gets in Your Eyes" and other '50s melodies are overly embellished in a satire of Erroll Garner's busy right-hand technique. Only knowing jazz fans would get (or want) the joke.

MORRIS GARNER

- WORST OF MORRIS GARNER (Thunderbird TH 1958) * $3 $10

Another Erroll Garner parodist, "Morris" seems to be tweaking all cocktail tinklers as his flourishes end with clinkers and his left-hand chords stumble into each other in sick syncopation. A mild practical joke to play at a party, this was supposed to be competition for similar albums by "Jonathan Edwards" (Paul Weston).

EDDIE GARRETT

- YOU'RE INVITED (Zen 711) *1/2 $5 $10

John F. Kennedy visits Hollywood celebs on this "concept" album. Garrett's Jimmy Stewart, Boris Karloff, President Kennedy, Jackie Mason, and Peter Lorre are barely functional, and the weak script doesn't help. The most offbeat and imaginative moment has Kennedy flying with pilot Jonathan Winters. Kennedy is alarmed as Jonny veers off course, about to crash. Says Garrett/Winters, with just the right mischief in his voice, "Always wanted to scare a president!"

ROZELLE GAYLE

- LIKE, BE MY GUEST (Mercury MG 20374) **1/2 $5 $10
- SEX CRACKS (Dooto DTL 839) **1/2 $5 $15

Rozelle Gayle was as large (6'4" 250 pounds) as football player Rosey Greer. A jazz pianist with Roy Eldridge's group, he went solo in the late '40s to mix boogie-woogie piano with comedy. A bit like Fats Waller, Gayle enjoys playing, singing, and ad-libbing (or at least, *seeming* to come up with off-the-cuff gags). Gayle's neat style let him relax and be as musical or as funny as the audience wanted.

He used adult-oriented gags in clubs, though in the '50s he was a regular on *The Betty White Show*. Comedy takes a back seat to music on the Mercury disc, though an improvisation that sounds like a Greek folk tune leads him to muse: "Greece ... most of those people are backward over there. One thing, I'll stand up for the youth, they won't hold still for it ... so many of the Greek youths are leaving home. They don't like the way they're being reared. Actually they say if Russia attacks Turkey from the rear, nobody knows if Greece'll help or not."

Good-natured Gayle sticks mostly to comedy for "Sex Cracks," a pleasant romp through jokes old and new, told with a hip, if not raucous, enthusiasm.

GAYLORD AND HOLIDAY

- HI! SIMPLY HI! (VMI 71002) ** $4 $8

Ron Gaylord and Burt Holiday were traditional tuxedoed comics who played Vegas through the '60s. Their catch-phrase, "Hi, simply hi!" is based on their routine in which an angry highway cop confronts a gay driver:

"Hi, simply hi! Have you been following me, you naughty boy? Don't tell me, let me guess. I'm parked in a loading zone! I'm loaded in a parking zone." "All right, where's the fire?" "In your eyes, officer! Got ya! Got ya!" "You know I been tailin' you for twenty miles?" "Well, like the tailor said to the nudist, so what!"

Other routines, a little below Rowan and Martin and a lot above Hudson and Landry, include "Cyrano de Bergerac," "Hello Mr. Bigot," and "Black Out Quickies." The album notes are from Buddy Hackett, who used Gaylord and Holiday as an opening act.

The duo made other albums that were music more than comedy, including "Party Style," "Gaylords at the Shamrock" (Mercury), and "Second Generation" (Prodigal).

JIM GEARHART

- KINDLY DR. JOHN (Town Hall 1008) * $3 $7
- PUT HIM ON PLEASE (Award AM 31) ** $5 $10

On "Put Him on Please" Gearhart is a "funny phone caller," making over fifteen calls to unsuspecting folks, getting a few gentle chuckles along the way. A lot of the time his put-ons land on pathetic people: When he calls The Empire State Building and tells a watchman he plans to climb the building using suction cups, the dopey guy mildly agrees with the concept, but insists "you'll have to talk to my supervisor." When he calls an empty phone booth and insists, "I left some clothes ... my name is Clark Kent...." the dim-witted guy who answers doesn't seem to be paying attention.

The most successful phone calls are the ones in which the concepts are so ridiculous that they transcend the muddled response of the targets. Jim calls an A&P to complain about the "kits" they sell. He claims he bought a package of "chicken parts," and "we put it together but it won't fly ... there ain't no feathers in the kit." The straight woman calmly assures him to "bring it back and the manager will give you a different one."

Bob & Ray's influence is evident on "Kindly Dr. John," Gearhart's long, long parody of soap operas. Gearhart and supporting cast Earl Goodman, Dave Klahr, and Hamilton O'Hara, recite "zany" character names (Maude Madlin, Giuseppi Yamamoto, Freda Furbush, Prunella Prudy, etc.) and perform deliberately enigmatic sketches. The put-on rings false, the fault of the script and the unconvincing actors. The interrupting commercials are also desperately wacky: "Friends, has your life lost its luster? Do you yearn for excitement, adventure, new challenge? Have you searched for new horizons to conquer, but in the end find yourself right back in the old rut? Well, snap out of the doldrums ... now at last, you can: wrestle a giant squid! Yes, wrestle a giant squid for fun, for a change of pace, and for good, wholesome recreation. Yes, do what you've always wanted to do. Wrestle a giant squid. Imagine the thrill as you pin your giant squid with a neat step-over tentacle hold. Or the challenge of being pinned as your giant squid applies the dread Tasmanian Ten-Tentacle Crush. It's a thrill a minute...."

THE GEEZINSLAW BROTHERS

- CAN YOU BELIEVE THE GEEZINSLAW BROTHERS (Capitol ST 2570) *1/2 $4 $10
- MY DIRTY, LOWDOWN ROTTEN COTTON-PICKIN LITTLE DARLIN (Capitol T 2771) * $4 $10
- ALIVE AND WELL (Capitol ST 130) * $4 $10
- CHUBBY (Capitol ST 2885) * $4 $10
- KOOKY WORLD OF THE GEEZINSLAW BROTHERS (Columbia CS 8900) * $3 $8
- IF YOU THINK I'M CRAZY NOW (Lone Star L 4606) * $5 $10
- THE GEEZINSLAWS (Step One SOR 0052) * $8
- WORLD TOUR (Step One SOR 0056) * $8
- FEELIN' GOOD, GITTIN' UP GITTIN DOWN (Step One SOR 0074) * $8
- I WISH I HAD A JOB TO SHOVE (Step One SOR 0082) *1/2 $5 $8

Sam Allred played the mandolin, Dewayne Smith the guitar, and as the duo "The Geezinslaw Brothers," they were discovered by Arthur Godfrey. Their '60s discs on Capitol are full of mild novelty tunes. Their first album has a cover of "May the Bird of Paradise Fly up Your Nose." The second, with a lot of George Jones and Roger Miller tunes, is hardly comedy at all. The title cut is about a girl who left: "Oh my eyes are red from all the tears I've shed. And my throat is sore from all that cryin'. And my horse, of course, is hoarse, too, from crying for my dirty, lowdown rotten cotton pickin' little darlin'...."

The duo deserve some credit for staying around so long and updating their sound. In 1979 when they issued their Lone Star/Mercury album (produced by Bobby Bare and Willie Nelson), they were almost a straight country act. Like Kinky Friedman or Dr. Hook, they sang numbers that had only a dash of comic color to them. "All American Redneck" characterizes one particular specimen, but without much humor and with the curse words actually censored with a beep on the soundtrack: "He's got all the latest country-western hits. 'Cause he thinks long-haired music is a bunch of (beep). He kicks (beep) he smokes grass, he drives a '65 T-bird that runs real fast. He eats pool hall chili and drinks what you got on draft. He's got a pick-up truck. He loves to (beep). You need a woman, he'll fix you up. He's an all-American redneck, but he's got class."

In the '90s the duo has tried to liven things up with a few trendy numbers. "Feelin' Good" has a terrible rap tune, "Help I'm White and I Can't Get Down," amid the standard homely country standards like "Copenhagen," a salute to tobacco chewing: "Well, I went to the movies with my little Peggy Sue. I had a dip there in my lip just like I always do. She didn't know I's spittin' in my Coca-Cola cup. She took a great big swaller and she threw her popcorn up!" 1994's "Wish I Had a Job to Shove" mixes live comedy with the songs, which once in a while have a good concept. "Play it Backwards" insists, "If you take a country song and you play it backwards, you sober up and you don't cheat on your wife. And your dead dog comes to life...."

HERSCHEL GENDEL

- LAUGH WITH HERSCHEL GENDEL (FAMOUS FAM 1045) $3 $8

Gendel was a founder of the Artef Theatre in New York City and appeared in a variety of Yiddish-language shows in America and Israel. The album notes are mostly in English, the record label is in English, and the contents are listed in English: "Yesterday and Today," "TV Problems," "Nachas from Grandchildren," "Tales and Wisdom of Jewish Folklore." But this entire 1972 studio recording of recollections and lectures (sans audience) is in Yiddish.

Gendel died May 10, 1982. He was seventy-six.

STEVE GEYER

- SLOW MEN WORKING (Star Song SSD 8160) *1/2 $5

Geyer recorded this 1990 CD in Tulsa for a Nashville company, but the material is generic comedy club stuff, with the standard observational McDonald's jokes: "I like to mess with them. I go: 'Can I have a cheeseburger, hold the cheese please.' 'Sir, you're asking for a hamburger.' 'No man, I like the yellow paper, ok?'"

The young comic's predictable set includes reworking old gags like, "You know a man in America is hit by a car every fifteen minutes? I'm wonderin' who is this guy?"

HENRY GIBSON

- THE ALLIGATOR (Liberty LRP/3261,LST 7261,
    re-released as BY HENRY GIBSON, Liberty LST 7593) * $5 $10
- GRASS MENAGERIE (Epic FLS 15120) * $5 $15

The fey, elfish Gibson made a name for himself on Rowan and Martin's *Laugh-In* when he would march his little blonde self center stage and recite whimsical, if not downright stupid, bits of poetry. It's remarkable to think that five years earlier, Gibson was allowed to do a twenty-minute set in a smoky nightclub reciting his gentle, enigmatic a capella songs and poems. He must have had hecklers simply drop their jaws in astonishment at the sheer vulnerability of his little poetry readings.

His 1962 album for Liberty includes such perplexing recitations as "Why I Like Soap": "I like soap because ... it is lots of fun to be with. Take, for example, the bathtub. Which is a lonely enough place. In addition, it can float, and be carved into a bubble. But most of all, it is clean. There's a little bit of dirt in each of us."

Mild laughter greeted this, and other baffling numbers. The disc was reissued, and the Epic one added, during his *Laugh-In* days.

PAUL GILBERT

- CONFESSIONS OF A LAS VEGAS LOSER (Era ES 802) *1/2 $5 $10
- SPLIT PERSONALITY (HiFi R 413) *1/2 $5 $10

Is Paul Gilbert best known as a) a stand-up comic for over thirty years who was ubiquitous on *The Colgate Comedy Hour*, b) the father of *Little House on the Prairie* kid TV stars Melissa Gilbert and Jonathan Gilbert, or c) not at all?

Whatever, his albums aren't much. On "Split Personality" he works with a tense, raspy, high-strung delivery and uses every cliché in the book. Evidently, audiences at swanky joints like New York's Copacabana, Chicago's Chez Paree, and Miami's Fountainbleu enjoyed wife routines with these lines: "My wife ... ever seen my old lady? I am married to one of those big girls! A 460 pounder! You can't imagine what I have to go through!" In this, the heyday of the cocky second banana, Gilbert shoves the jokes at the audience, but does have some idea what the audience would like him to shove: "I had a request ... but the microphone is too large...."

Gilbert suffered a stroke in July 1975 and died in his sleep February 12, 1976. He was fifty-eight.

THE GREAT GILDERSLEEVE

- THE GREAT GILDERSLEEVE (Radiola MR 1020) *1/2 $4 $8
- THE GREAT GILDERSLEEVE (Mark 56# 620) *1/2 $4 $8
- THE GREAT GILDERSLEEVE (Golden Age Records GA 5024) ** $4 $8

Harold Peary was better known by the name of his most famous comic character. Most fans called him "Gildy." Peary (Harrold Jose Pereira de Faria, originally) played Throckmorton P. Gildersleeve, owner of the Gildersleeve Girdle Works on *Fibber McGee and Molly*. He was then spun off into his own show. He had a trademark throaty laugh, and a deliriously elongated gurgle of astonishment: "Eeeeeee-ehhh," that slid from tenor to baritone. TV viewers might not realize that the "Uncle Captain" character on the cartoon show *Beany and Cecil* was based on Gildersleeve's mannerisms.

The sitcom was strong on interaction between Gildersleeve and his friends and family. Radiola includes the November 20, 1949, episode in which Gildersleeve borrows his nephew Leroy's trombone and vows to start a band. His friends aren't convinced he can do it. "Chief, what did you play when you were in school?" "I played hooky." "We'll play the sweetest music this side of heaven." "Well, I wouldn't say that." The band ends up torturing "Nutcracker Suite," and afterward, torturing each other: "Floyd, as a piano player you're a good barber." "Judge, one side of the drum has a hole in it ... it would sound better with holes in both sides of it."

The quality on Mark 56's disc is slightly better than the Radiola release. Gildersleeve is upset and jealous over an old boyfriend coming to visit his current lady love. When the Judge pops by, he and Gildersleeve engage in some typical insult humor: "I don't see YOU marryin' her, you're just a dog in the manger." "I'm no dog, you dog, and don't call my house a manger." "Good night Lothario." "Good night, you money-grubbing old stupid!"

Golden Age has two episodes. The announcer says, "Starring Harold Peary," but the album notes insist that Willard Waterman is playing Gildersleeve. In 1951's "Broken Window," Gildy dreams he's in a gangster movie. The other 1951 episode is "Gildy Sells Opera Tickets." He tempts his pals by saying "Carmen" has girls so wild they "bite, they scratch, they even start to tear each others' clothes off ..." It's all predictable sitcom fare, but Peary is a hearty comic character.

STU GILLIAM

- AT THE BASIN STREET WEST (Fax 3006, reissued as THE BLACK ASTRONAUT Fax 8006) ** $5 $15
- WILD WICKED HUMOR (Fax 3007, reissued as Lobo L 3007) ** $5 $15

Originally a ventriloquist with a dummy named Oscar Pepper, Detroit's Gilliam moved to stand-up in 1952. A regular on the summertime NBC series *The Golddiggers*, his adults-only albums are mildly suggestive, closer to Cosby than Foxx. He tells long stories that finally arrive at a punch line. On "The Black Astronaut" he recalls "The 22 Year-old Virgin," a meandering tale:

"All he knew about women was what he read in the Sears and Roebuck catalogue. Twenty-two years old, handsome, masculine ... drove to the general store ... and he walked in and said, 'I'm John's boy.' They gave him a drink of that white lightnin' and he never drank that before. Two drinks and he was out cold. When he woke up, he was on the back of his wagon goin' back to his farm. And in the front seat was the town harlot. He'd been married off to her in a drunken stupor ... that night when they prepared for bed, to do what most folks do on the first night of their honeymoon, she was all decked out in one of those long flowing negligees, with the fur on the bottom to keep her chin warm. He hopped in on one side of the bed. She hopped in on the other, turned the lights out. And just as soon as her heel touched his big toe, he jumped straight up, hit the floor, ran around the foot of the bed and hopped in the other side ... she rolled over and with infinite patience, took her forty-five minutes to establish bodily contact ... once again the minute she touched him he jumped up ... she turned the light on and said, 'Fool! What's wrong with you? Don't you know what I want?' He said, 'Hell yes, you want all this damn cover, but you ain't gonna get it!'"

HERMOINE GINGOLD

- LA GINGOLD (Dolphin 7, reissued as DRG Records MRS 902) ** $8 $20

A beloved grand dame actress, the British star was described by S. J. Perelman as "an amalgam of Groucho Marx and Tallulah Bankhead." Her album of songs begins with the note, "This is the voice of Hermoine Gingold coming to you on wax in your own home. Isn't civilization ghastly?"

She emotes ironic, sophisticated tunes intended for self-consciously "smart" nightclub devotees. Titles include "Which Witch," "But the People Were Nice," "Thanks Yanks," and "The Borgias Are Having an Orgy." From "Flowers," about an admirer's attempts to woo her: "He started by sending me bluebelles, strangely enough they were gray. Each little bloom had a horrid perfume, and besides being gray, they were papier-mâché."

Campy followers will be amused. Others might be impressed by the old song "Cocaine." Gingold introduces it: "Don't you get rather depressed by films about drug addicts? I do. If we have to have films about drug addicts, why can't they be musicals? It would be so much more cheerful." And she sings, her British warble in hilarious contrast to the funky jazz arrangement: "You can take away my kisses and hugs. But don't take away my dangerous drugs! My eyes have been so swollen since my syringe was stolen at an orgy with Porgie and Elsie in Chelsea...."

Gingold, paired with Billy de Wolfe, appears on two compilation albums, "Fun Time" (Coral CRL 57072) and "Laugh of the Party" (Coral CRL 57017).

THE GINSBURG BROTHERS

- WONDERFUL WORLD OF THE GINSBURG BROTHERS (Topical 5) ** $5 $10

JACKIE GLEASON

- JACKIE GLEASON ON RADIO (Radiola MR 1057) *** $5 $15

Gleason starred in a September 24, 1944, episode of *Double Feature*, and most of it is standard. When Jackie talks about opera, the gags with straight man Les Tremayne aren't much different from radio schtick for Milton Berle or Ed Wynn:

"What an opera I wrote," Gleason exults, "it opens with a wail on the trumpet. Now all I have to do is teach a whale to play a trumpet." "What is your favorite opera?" "The Barber of Seville, the way it's sung by Uncle Fortissimo Gleason, otherwise known as Lawrence Fourbits. He sings twice as loud as Lawrence Tibbets." "How do you like Rigoletto and La Traviata?" "With meatballs and plenty of sauce."

Male ingenue Andy Russell sings four terminally wimpy tunes in the tenor style of the day. The last segment is the winner—an offbeat Gleason monologue on a love affair with a jukebox: "I looked at her and she turned green ... all the colors of the rainbow dashed through her neon veins." He knows his love affair is risky ("She only loved me for my money") but he can't resist spending all his nickels on her. He gets excited when she skips and keeps repeating, "It had to be you." But when he sees her "getting oiled" with a repairman, he knows the affair is doomed. These days, she's just "an old slot." It's on the "Golden Age of Comedy" compilation from Evolution Records.

Side Two is a mixed bag of Gleason radio appearances, including songs ("And Away We Go" and "You're a Dan Dan Dandy Bunch") and "Laura," another atypical monologue about a strange date: "I can remember her just as if it were yesterday ... our first meeting. It was in the park. She coyly dropped her handkerchief. And as I picked it up she was embarrassed. Her nose was still in it...."

- AND AWAY WE GO (Capitol 511) **1/2 $20 $50

Gleason made many albums of romantic instrumentals, but only one novelty disc. This rare ten-incher has bombast more than laughs. The cuts are "And Away We Go," "The Poor Soul," "You're a Dan-Dan-Dandy Bunch," "Reggie Van Gleason III," "Hy'A Mister Dennehy," "One of These Days, Pow!" "Here's Charlie," and "You're a Nice Man."

The title track is the kind of thing one would expect to hear as an opening for his variety show: "Everybody's singing and away we go. It's away we go everywhere ya go. You don't need a bass or baritone. You can sing this ditty all alone. Instead of singing eeny meeny miney mo, join in the fun everyone and away we go...."

The best cuts are "Reggie Van Gleason III" (just to hear the inimitable voice that Johnny Carson lovingly appropriated for his Art Fern character) and "One of These Days, Pow!" It's a Ralph Kramden ballad to Alice.

The album was reissued in 1986 on cassette (4XL-9450), but fans still want the original to get a good look at the artwork featuring portraits of six Gleason characters, plus a drawing of Gleason dancing awaaaay, elbows flexed in vaudevillian style. The album's *Honeymooners* numbers have turned up on "Greatest Novelty Records of All Time" (Rhino) and "It's Honeymooners Time" (Murray Hill 000237). Fans might want to hunt up his single "Casey at the Bat" (Capitol F 5420).

In 1996 "And Away We Go" was reissued (Scamp SCP 97062) with some comedy bonus tracks: Reggie Van Gleason's "I Had but 50 Cents" and "Casey at the Bat."

GEORGE GOBEL

- AT THE SANDS (Decca D1 4163) ** $5 $15

Gobel's brand of low-key humor made him a TV favorite with his own show during the late '50s. His lone album goes on for fifty minutes, enough time for a few songs and several long, unassuming, meandering anecdotes. They're best for Gobel fans accustomed to his puttering personality and slightly cock-eyed storytelling style. There isn't a high percentage of quotable lines, but some of his anecdotes are memorable, including the one about a fateful shower taken at a Las Vegas hotel, a classic thanks to his peculiar matter-of-fact delivery:

"I come out of the shower and I didn't have any clothes on. I take showers like that all the time. I find that it's neater that way, actually. I come out of the shower, like I say, I didn't have any clothes on ... and the room was kind of steamed up and I figured if I opened a window, that would be a pretty shrewd move...." Except that the window gives way: "My room was on the ninth floor, too. Now the fall didn't particularly bother me. It was that walk back through the lobby ..."

And after the applause and laughter dies down: "Unfortunately I'm one of those fellas that just can't walk past a crap table...."

These are mere fragments of what is a long, well-crafted routine made up of quiet asides and slightly askew observations—all deceptively simple, like George himself.

Gobel also turns up on "Zingers from the Hollywood Squares" (Event). Gobel's 1961 Broadway musical cast album for *Let It Ride* (RCA LSO 1064) is a rarity, and for good reason. Few songs are worth a listen. Dumb, misogynistic, but at least lively, is "Broads Ain't People." Gobel must be firm. Otherwise: "She'll sink you, she'll smash you, she'll chew you like a cashew...." Gobel had a decent voice, surprisingly strong in belting out the fast numbers.

WHOOPI GOLDBERG

- WHOOPI GOLDBERG ORIGINAL CAST RECORDING (Geffen GHS 24065) ** $5 $10
- FONTAINE: WHY AM I STRAIGHT (MCA 422430) * $3 $8

Introducing her, Robin Williams wrote, "when you're dealing with anyone with a name that sounds like the Hasidic inventor of artificial flatulence in a bag, all things are possible." The former Caryn Johnson was virtually unknown when Mike Nichols brought her to Broadway for this 1984 showcase.

Following in the Ruth Draper and Lily Tomlin style, Whoopi's stagey technique back then was to assume characters: a junkie, a cripple, a little girl, and a Valley Girl. As comedy, this Grammy-winning album is constantly undercut by pathos and pretentious theatrics. Every character drops the laughing mask of comedy to reveal the serious pain inside. "Surfer Chick," for example, is a ditsy Valley Girl who can't speak a line without adding "okay?" or "you know." She's into casual sex:

"The only thing, like, I really could not, like, understand ... they show you pictures of spermatazoa? And it always has on a little top hat, and flowers, and candy, right? And, like, I could not figure out how the top hat, flowers, and candy, like, come out of that little tiny hole, you know? And, like, I asked him, and he said, "Don't worry about it.' It was okay, you know, okay, okay, so like you know, he says he's gonna call me the next day, so, like, I say okay and he says okay and we say okay. Okay? And, like, I'm waiting by the phone ... days go by ... after about six weeks I figured out he's probably not gonna call...."

Whoopie manipulates the crowd shamelessly, and being the predominantly white, liberal, yuppie Broadway audience it is, it fully acknowledges that Whoopi Goldberg knows more about life's pains and pleasures than they ever will.

Based on an HBO special, MCA offers an hour of Whoopi's "Fontaine" character, a Pryor-esque character who has a supposedly hip take on everything, even "The Star Spangled Banner": "Ohh say can you motherfuckin' sing, by the dawn's early motherfuckin' light ..." With all the empty cursing, Fontaine is "streetwise" with the emphasis on "street," not "wise."

HARRY GOLDEN

- HARRY GOLDEN (Vanguard VRS 9102) *1/2 $4 $10

Golden, author of "Only in America" and "Enjoy Enjoy," is showcased on Side One giving anecdotal speeches, circa 1960. One, in front of the NAACP, includes a talk on stereotypes: "When the white men get together and talk about the race issue, they talk about how the Negroes want white women. When the Negroes get together, they talk about a linotype machine. Governor Hollings of South Carolina says, 'Those Negroes don't want integration. My maid told me so.'"

The author is well-intentioned but dull, his voice thin, his cadence sleepy. He sounds a bit like Jackie Vernon doing a bad W. C. Fields imitation. A full side of stories about New York's Lower East Side get wearying. One of the better ones describes people crashing weddings: "The strangers would eat up all the food and the guests would have nothing ... eventually the catering halls hired from Tammany Hall the bouncers. You'd go in there, say, 'I'm a guest.' The bouncer would say, 'Who do you know, the bride or the groom?' You'd take a chance. Say, 'I know the bride.' And he'd kick you right out on the sidewalk: 'Get outta here, it's a bar mitzvah!'"

JENNIE GOLDSTEIN

- MINK, SHMINK (King 534) ** $7 $15

Most of Goldstein's album is in Yiddish, the songs, including "Gin," "Mahzel," "Ich Hob Zich Gelozt," cover a range of straight material and comedy. Her best known novelty, "The Platinum Fox," is in English. It is recognition humor about a brassy yenta demanding a new fur coat from her stingy husband: "'Money,' laughed Sarah with sex in her grin, 'Don't give me that, my cookie. Use the money you lose when your horse don't come in! I'm closer to you than your bookie!'" Fans might want "Jennie Goldstein Sings 14 of Her Most Famous Yiddish Theatre Hits" (Greater Recording Co., GRC 90).

BOB GOLDTHWAIT

- MEAT BOB (Chrysalis BFV 41642) **1/2 $8 $20
  reissued on CD as Chrysalis DIDX 3167 $8

Following Sam Kinison, Goldthwait became known for his own brand of screaming and outrage, a style mixing frightened vulnerability with raging fury. He comes out quivering and stuttering, then gradually turns demonic in his rages. He evolved this style early when his hard luck routines drew jeers. "I was vulnerable," he recalled, "and people in the audience would start picking on me. So then I got kind of mean because I didn't want them to get the better of me up there."

His 1988 album/CD disappoints without his facial expressions of misery and anger. Better editing could have reduced the amount of meandering ad-libs and audience participation. Typical self-hating angst and teeth-gnashing anger: "I'll exploit my daughter for some cheap laughs. The most precious thing in my life. My bride and myself, we pounded out a baby. Pounding out a baby—I think that's pretty sensitive '80s male of me, isn't it? And I was there, um, during the delivery. I'll tell you what kind of self-centered prick I am. We had a C-section.... So this is what a self-centered jerk I am ... instead of saying, 'God, that's gonna be so painful,' I said, 'Great! I took Lamaze for nuthin'?'"

The high-end price for the original vinyl version reflects some collector interest in being able to spin the disc backwards. In parody of the "Satanic messages" to be heard on rock albums played backward, Bob planted a message at the end of the disc. Slide the turntable backward and Bob says: "Obey your parents, be nice, don't eat snacks, and go to church. Give money to Jerry Falwell."

THE GONDOLIERS

- HAVE A BLAST (RIC RLP 2001) * $4 $8

The New Orleans-based group offers meandering monologues ("Tom Dooley" takes ten minutes to be told by one of the band's funkier members) and belabored, inept versions of standard tunes, like the double entendre ditty "My

Ding a Ling." The few real jokes on this one have whiskers: "According to the script here, the number we're supposed to be doing is 'Paganini.'" "Can't you read? That's page nine!"

DR. GONZO

- THE DOC OF COMEDY ROCK (Dublab DA 104) *1/2 $4 $10

Dr. Gonzo (John Means) specialized in opening for rock acts like Huey Lewis and the News in the late '80s. This means he doesn't have to be funny as much as zany, and that drug and alcohol jokes are enough.

The Side One is studio-recorded and contains rock songs that are feel-good novelties for boneheads. "Tailgate Party" has lines like "Make sure we get a good spot, a stereo that's loud. Barbeque sauce that's too hot. We like to party proud." Faintly amusing is his reworking of Huey Lewis's "Heart of Rock and Roll" into "The Art of Telling Jokes." It turns hacking around comedy clubs into something epic: "L.A., New York, and the comedy scene ... Where else can a lonely comic hang with the hooker until a quarter to three?"

The flip side is live, and full of observational jokes aimed at people who are usually too high to observe much: "Did you ever get up in the morning: the hell with the visine, get out the Liquid Paper!"

GOODIE GOODELLE

- THE GOODIE GOODELLE ALBUM (Art ALP 2) *1/2 $8 $15

Circa 1954, Goodie, accompanying herself on the piano, recorded a collection of risqué 78s later reissued on ten-inch disc. These tunes are milder than Ruth Wallis, like "Murphy's Project," a double entendre tune about a construction worker: "Oh the ladies in the neighborhood are jealous. How they scoff. They're hoping that the government cuts Murphy's project off. But when Mr. Truman sees it, he will stand right up and say: "Murphy has the biggest project in the U.S.A."

DICKIE GOODMAN

- THE MANY HEADS OF DICKIE GOODMAN (Rori 3301) **1/2 $15 $30
- THE ORIGINAL FLYING SAUCERS (IX Chains NCS 9000) **1/2 $15 $25
- MR. JAWS (Cash CR 6000) **1/2 $10 $20
- DICKIE GOODMAN'S GREATEST HITS (Rhino RNLP 811) **1/2 $10 $20
- EVERYTHING YOU ALWAYS WANTED TO KNOW ABOUT BUCHANAN AND GOODMAN
  BUT FORGOT TO ASK (Sting S8239) **1/2 $8

A pioneer in "break ins," a form of collage comedy, Richard Dorian "Dickie" Goodman created wacky scripts and inserted snippets of pop tunes into them for shock-recognition comedy. His first trip to the charts (with early partner, Bill Buchanan) was "The Flying Saucer," released on his own Luniverse label in August of 1956.

As a solo, Goodman continued the formula of asking interview questions and letting rock song clips supply the answers. In 1961 Goodman put most of his best singles on the Rori album: "The Flying Saucer," "On Trial," "Berlin Top Ten," "Frankenstein of '59." "Frankenstein Returns," "The Touchables," "The Touchables in Brooklyn," "Flying Saucer the 2nd," "Flying Saucer Goes West," and "Santa and the Satellite."

Unlikely fan Shelley Berman provides the album notes, comparing Goodman's "The Flying Saucer" to Orson Welles's radio hoax, and declaring no other record sold "nearly two million copies" in under six weeks. He adds, "I recommend this album highly for those of you who find amusement in confusion and chaos."

As Goodman continued to have sporadic hits, he reissued them on new albums. The 1973 IX Chains disc highlighted the novelty hit single "Watergrate." The Cash album had old filler and the new hit, "Mr. Jaws." Both albums include "Santa and the Satellite 1 and 2," "The Touchables," "The Touchables in Brooklyn," and "Superfly Meets Shaft." Both also have the original "Flying Saucer" single, in which a Top 40 DJ breaks into a report on an alien landing. Slices from hit records accompany the interviews of John Cameron Cameron as he questions a man in the street:

"The gentleman with the guitar. What would you do (if you saw a UFO)?" Elvis Presley: "Take a walk down lonely street." Later, the interviewer comes upon a scientist near the saucer: "Are you there?" Fats Domino: "I hear you knockin' but you can't come in!"

On cold paper, this hardly seems hilarious. What could be more crass and calculated than set-ups for snipped-out song lines? Yet the manic combination of Goodman's goofy questions and the recognition comedy answers gave Goodman a career over three decades. The IX Chains album also includes "Watergrate," "Superfly Meets Shaft," "Convention 72," and "Ben Crazy." The "Mr. Jaws" album includes "Energy Crisis 1974" and the title track, which has an interviewer (Goodman putting on his usual crazy Walter Winchell voice) talking to a shark:

"Well Mr. Jaws, what did she say when you grabbed her?" Olivia Newton-John: "Please, Mr. Please." "What did you think when you took that first bite?" James Taylor: "How sweet it is." "Before you swim out to sea what do you have to say?" War: "Why can't we be friends?"

In the '80s there were few songs the divided (new wave, R&B, pop, country, etc.) all knew. Quiz shows like *Name that Tune* became obsolete, as did Goodman. Rhino's 1983 reissue had his classics, plus a less than popular new cut, "Return of the Jedi." The formula is the same as ever:

"When the Death Star blew up, what did it sound like?" Jackson Browne: "The mating calls of lawyers in love." "C3PO, as a robot, what is your opinion of Princess Leia?" Donna Summer: "She works hard for the money."

The 1993 CD collection from the mysterious "Sting" label (the company lists a Swedish address) doesn't have all the masters (there's surface noise on "Banana Boat Story," an obscure Luniverse single). "Santa and the Touchables," originally on the Rori label, cuts the ending, spliced down from the original 2:07 to 1:43. Still, the thirty-track compilation has all the best from Goodman, Buchanan & Goodman, and even from Buchanan & Ancell. There are a few newer attempts ("Hey E.T.") and many obscurities: "Shnonanza," "Luna Trip," and "Batman and His Grandmother." In the latter, with clips from the TV theme song, Robin cries "Something's heading right for us! Here it comes!" Rolling Stones: "Here it comes, here it comes, here comes your nineteenth nervous breakdown...."

Goodman died from a self-inflicted gunshot wound to the head, November 6, 1989.

- MY SON THE JOKE (Comet CLP 69) **1/2 $5 $15

Dickie Goodman occasionally tried to break away from the song collages. In 1970 he formed a group called The Glass Bottle. Back in 1963, he did this adults only novelty album based on Allan Sherman's "My Son the Folksinger."

This is easily the most bizarre of the many records that tried to cash in on Sherman's success. Goodman's voice is not that far from Sherman's in its homely way, as he belts out dirty folk songs.

"The Yellow Rose of Texas" becomes "Ellie Rose is Sexless," and "Sarah Jackman" becomes "Harry's Jockstrap." "Volga Boatman" becomes "Vulgar Goldman," "Alouette" is "Al and Yetta" (Allan Sherman used those names too), "Waltzing Matilda" becomes "Balling My Zelda," and "Home on the Range" ends up like this: "Moe, Moe is deranged, he plays with himself all the time. But that's not so bad. The thing that is sad—oh I wish he'd stop playing with mine."

DODY GOODMAN

- SINGS? (Coral CRL 57196) ** $5 $10

Chatty, eccentric Dody was a hit on Jack Paar's *Tonight Show* around the time she released this collection of comic cabaret tunes. She isn't much of a singer, which is supposed to be part of the gag. Several tunes accentuate Dody's ditz: "Today Will Be Yesterday" and "I Always Say Hello." From the former: "The present will be the past in the future. So make every moment bright and gay. Today will be yesterday tomorrow. So don't put off till tomorrow what you can today." She also does well as the artificially-calmed housewife of Bud McCreary's song "Tranquilizers." She's placid in times of stress: "As the dog chews the telephone receiver, I see baby is playing with the cleaver. And now my husband's crossed a wire, and he's on fire. Oh really, something should be done! I know, I'll take a tranquilizer, tranquilizer...." All but Dody fans will be taking a few, too.

THE GOONS

- GOON SHOW CLASSICS (Pye 12118) *** $5 $10
  "The Histories of Pliny the Elder" (March 1957) and
  "Dread Batter Pudding Hurler of Bexhill-on-Sea" (October 1954)
- GOON SHOW CLASSICS 2 (Pye 12122) *** $5 $10
  "Jet-Propelled Guided Naafi" (January 1956) and "The Evils of Bushey Spon" (March 1958)
- GOON SHOW CLASSICS 3 (BBC REB 245) *** $5 $10
  "Lurgi Strikes Britain" (November 1954) and "The International Christmas Pudding"
  (January 1956)
- GOON SHOW CLASSICS 4 (BBC REB 291) *** $5 $10
  "Napoleon's Piano" (October 1955) and "The Flea" (December 1956)
- GOON SHOW CLASSICS 5 (BBC Records BBC 22339) *** $5 $10
  "Treasure of Loch Lomond" (February 1956) and "The Greenslade Story" (December 1955)
- GOON SHOW CLASSICS 6 (BBC REB 366) *** $5 $10
  "Wings Over Dagenham" (January 1957) and "The Rent Collectors" (January 1957)
- GOON SHOW CLASSICS 7 (BBC REB 392) *** $5 $10
  "Man Who Never Was" (February 1958) and "Case of the Missing CD Plates" (October 1955)
- GOON SHOW CLASSSICS 8 (BBC Records BBC 22422) *** $5 $10
  "World War I" (February 1958) and "The Nasty Affair at the Burami Oasis" (October 1956)
- LAST GOON SHOW OF ALL (BBC Records 22142) *** $5 $10

The Goons were originals in the world of British comedy, today often described as the ancestors of Monty Python, or radio's answer to The Marx Brothers. But The Goons are unique, with their own fantastic world of the surreal and the silly. They were singer Harry Secombe, writer/comedian Spike Milligan, and a young actor named Peter Sellers. Michael Bentine was also in the cast early on. The trio appeared through the '50s on BBC radio and the cult has remained strong since. John Lennon was particularly influenced by Goon humor, and he reviewed a collection of "Goon Show Scripts" for the *New York Times Book Review*.

The Goons created their own world, and it takes novices a while to acclimate. At first listen, much of an average Goon half hour seems like gibberish, with eccentric voices, barrages of sound effects, and a somewhat vaudevillian script. The audience applauds and cheers seemingly incoherent running gags and the arrival of various improbable characters, the most beloved being the hero, "true blue British idiot" Ned Seagoon, the buffoon Eccles (described by Ned as "the nearest thing I'd seen to a human being without actually being one"), the spindly schoolboy Bluebottle with his yipping, idiot laugh, and the twin ancients Henry Crun and Minnie Bannister. True Goon fans smile ear to ear just hearing these creatures speak.

Typical of their nonsense is this dialogue from "Goon Show Classics #4," the "Napoleon's Piano" episode:

"Ah, good morning." "Good morning? Just a moment. (Phone dialing noises.) Hello? Air Ministry Roof? Weather report. Yes ... you're perfectly right, it *is* a good morning." "Thanks. My name is Neddie Seagoon." "What a memory you have." "Needle noddle noo! I've come to move the piano...." "Sit down. Have a gorilla." "No thanks, I'm trying to give them up." "Splendid ... sign this contract in which you guarantee to move the piano from one room to another...." "I'll sign. Have you any ink?" "Here's a fresh bottle." (Drinking noises.) "Gad, I was thirsty." "Sapristi Nuckos! Do you always drink ink?" "Only in the mating season ..."

Attempting to move the piano:

"I have an idea, we'll saw the legs off ... give me that special piano leg saw that you just happen to be carrying." (Singing) "I talk to the trees. That's why they put me away...." "There, I've sawn all four legs off." "Strange. First time I've known a piano with four legs." "Hey, I keep falling down!"

Begin with most any album except "The Last Goon Show of All," which is filled with in-jokes and audience applause based on decades of familiarity with the characters.

Actually, the best double bill is "Insurance the White Man's Burden" and "Six Charlies in Search of an Author" released only in England as "Goon but Not Forgotten," by Parlophone (PMC 7037).

NOTES: Many British albums attract big bucks from the Goon cult. There's "The Goons Unchained Melodies" (Decca LF 1332), "Goon Again" (Parlophone PMC 7062), "First Men in the Goon" (Parlophone PMC 7132), "Michael Parkinson Meets the Goons" (BBC REB 165M), and "Dark Side of the Goon" (a disappointing collection of singles, One Up 2232). Several episodes of "The Goon Show" have been released in England on CD by EMI, and a CD version of "The World of the Goons" (Eclipse 8206462) features all of the team's hilarious ("Eeh! Ah! Oh! Ooh!") baffling ("I'm Walking Backwards for Christmas") and insane/inane ("Ying Tong Song") singles. In 1995 BBC Audio issued a two-tape, four-episode audio cassette set, "Goon Show Classics: He's Fallen in the Water!" (0-553-47394-8).

Some cultists hunt up the straight, light-operatic singing albums by the knighted Sir Harry Secombe, but more cultivate the uneven solo work of Spike Milligan, including "Milligan's Wake" (Pye NPL 18104), "World of Beachcomber" (Pye NPL 18271), "A Record Load of Rubbish" (BBC RED 98M), "Live at Cambridge" (Spark SRLO 3001), and the classics "Milligan Preserved" (Parlophone PCS 3018) and "Muses with Milligan" (Decca LK 4701). There are also albums based on Milligan's books *Puckoon* (EMI SCX 6630) and *Adolf Hitler, My Part in His Downfall* (Columbia SCX 6636). Also see the entry on Peter Sellers.

STEVE GORDON AND THE KOSHER 5

- TAKE MY RAP ... PLEASE (Reflection) * $3 $7

A garbagey attempt at a Jewish rap record, Gordon can't even manage a decent accent. The humor is in an older Jew visiting a disco ("Oy the music") and becoming surprised at the sight of the disc jockey ("Meshugeneh!"). Fortunately the album is actually just a big single—four minutes of torment. A few years later the same concept actually worked for the 2 Live Jews.

BERNIE GOULD

- YOU'RE WHAT? (Jubilee 2046) *1/2 $4 $10

The Bronx's version of Dr. Spock, Bernie Gould lectures on "Toilet Training," "Bottle Feeding," "Thumb Sucking," "Nail Biting," and other problems with babies. A writer-producer (*The Jo Stafford Show*) who supplied comedy material to Milton Berle, Eddie Fisher, and other stars of '50s TV, Gould tries for the Phil Foster/Alan King approach, hoping for recognition humor based on his own aggravations. Gould's naggingly aggressive style makes the mild material worse:

"Picture your first entrance into the world as this child. Before the kid can say, 'Hello World, Here I Am!' somebody picks him up by the feet, turns him upside down, and belts him across the backside. What's with the hitting? The kid hasn't done anything yet and the doctor says, 'I'm hitting him to start him breathing.' Ya ready? The doctor is hitting him because the doctor is sore! This kid got him out of a warm bed at three o'clock in the morning...."

THE GRAND OLD PARTYGOERS

- THE REPUBLICAN RECORD? (Current Personalities CP-1) ** $3 $8

The Stone Age Capitol Steps, the anonymous barber-shop quartet offers mostly corny parodies of public domain folk songs. Of course, Mark Russell has been getting away with the same format for the past twenty years.

Targeting the Republicans (bits of Nixon speeches turn up between songs), there's "Bring Back My Checkers to Me" (sung to "My Bonnie"). One tune took a chance. "When Dick is Chancellor" implies that electing Nixon someday would be like bringing Nazi Germany to America. To an oom-pah beat version of "Sidewalks of New York": "I can't wait till Dick is chancellor. Mit all the people we distrust the jails will fairly bust. Our great leader tells us Zieg Heil's not quite politic. We'll just Americanize the term and simply say, 'Hail Dick!'"

The most interesting cut is "Requiem for Lenny Bruce, Mort Sahl, Bob Newhart, and Shelly (sic) Berman." The Republicans, to the tune "Oh Susanna," shout, "If our party is elected, how I pity Lenny Bruce. If our party gets the power, Lenny Bruce will get the noose. No more records, we're gonna shut his mouth. Oh we may not even kill him— maybe we'll just ship him south!" They connive to torture Mort Sahl by putting him in a tuxedo instead of a sweater, they complain that Bob Newhart did a parody of Lincoln and decide to stone him ("any man who mimics Lincoln has to wear a ball and chain"), and by the time they get to Berman they simply insist "no more joking. No social comedy. For there ain't no way of telling when they'll tell a joke on me!"

JUDY GRAUBART

- JEWISH AMERICAN PRINCESS (BELL 6063) *** $5 $15

A sketch album from Bob Booker and George Foster, and featuring a supporting cast of Lou Jacobi, Bea Arthur, Frank Gallop, Anthony Holland, and Bob McFadden, this 1971 satire features Judy Graubart as Judy Ann Pearlman, whose first words were "Goo goo-Master Charge."

The "Jewish American Princess" has since become the topic for endless, often viciously anti-Semitic jokes, but back in 1971, this mild album was something new. Bea Arthur, not yet famous as Maude, plays Judy's mother, who frets over her daughter's safety: "Don't open the door for anybody ... unless it's me ... I read just last night, this man attacked twelve innocent girls living alone." "Who was that?" "His name was Jack the Ripper." "Come on, mother, that was a hundred years ago." "People don't change!"

BILLY GRAY

- MY FAIRFAX LADY (Jubilee) ** $10 $20
- MANY SHADES OF BILLY GRAY (Verve V/V6 15036) ** $5 $10

Gray owned "The Band Box," a popular West Hollywood club in the '60s and '70s. Occasionally he booked himself, and here tried to jump-start his career with a Jewish parody of *My Fair Lady.*

Lerner and Loewe wouldn't allow their work to be parodied (see the Allan Sherman entry for more on this) so it's possible that the album's scarcity today is due to legal problems back then.

Billy Gray is Professor Gray, Carol Shannon plays Liza Doowhittle, and the beloved character comedian Bert Gordon (radio's "Mad Russian") turns up as Colonel Dill Pickeling, the Professor's best friend.

Gordon is a lot of fun. His musing cadence makes the straight lines a lot funnier than the jokes. His meeting with the British actress: "My name is Liza Doowhittle." "That's a nice name." "I'm a thespian." "Oh, thespian. Don't tell me about your sex life!" "Oh, you don't comprehend. I'm an actress ... I came to America to play 'Blithe Spirit' on television." "That's a nice play." "The telecast is at CBS." "Cantor's Balogna Shop?" "No, Columbia Broadcasting System." "That's a nice system."

Among the kosherized song parodies: "I have often walked on this street before. But I never knew that borscht had been a beet before. And my nostrils swell from the magic smell when I walk on the street where you eat." This ultimately leads to the strained declaration "The Chraine is Red and Plain But Both Could Stain."

For an album on Jubilee, a surprising amount of effort was put into this: real orchestrations, a mild but polished Sid Kuller script, and even The Kirby Stone Four on some chorus vocals.

Gray's monology for Verve is both Semitic and off-color. A Jewish fellow who buys a horseback riding outfit and shows it off to his wife: "This is a riding habit. I'm going cantoring." She asks, "Reformed or orthodox?" He goes out riding and comes back a half hour later all torn up and muddy: "What 'appened darling, what 'appened?" He says, "What happened! I'm cantoring past the hotel. And two fellows are standing in the lobby and one points over towards me and says, 'Look at the schmuck on that horse.' So I bent over to look...."

The 1964 album didn't do much, but The Band Box continued on for a while. Gray died on January 4, 1978, at the age of seventy-three.

TED GRAYSEN

- LAUGHS AT THE CAROUSEL (Jay Jay 1060) * $3 $7
- LAFFS AND MORE LAFFS (Jay Jay 1065) * $3 $7

The Chicago-based "clown prince of the accordion," Graysen recorded for a label specializing in Polka music. Accompanied by his accordion, he's prone to sing risqué quickies that were corny even then: "Ta Rara boom dee-ay, did you get yours today? I got mine yesterday, that's why I walk this way!" With rim shots galore, Graysen bellows the one-liners: "I got a brother so lazy they named a shoe after him. It's called a loafer!"

ROCKY GRAZIANO

- ROCKY GRAZIANO AS THE MAHARASHI YOGURT (R.I.C. 9422) * $5 $10

Rocky scored fifty-two knockouts in his boxing career and won the World Middleweight title in 1948 over Tony Zale. After consecutive losses to Sugar Ray Robinson and Chuck Davey in 1952, he retired. The subject of the film *Somebody Up There Likes Me*, Graziano made TV appearances as a comical tough guy. This quickie topical disc written by Jim Lehner and Bobby Gosh is poorly recorded, with Rocky stumbling (not always intentionally) through the question and answer script:

"What's in that bag you're carrying?" "About three quarts of champagne ..." "Sorry, Guru. I mean the other bag." "Oh, you mean this other one. That's my sitar." "The sitar is one of those very complicated stringed instruments, isn't it?" "Not only that, they're hard to play." "And they make all kinds of weird sounds when you strike them." "Which one? The bag? Or my sitar?" "I meant the sitar." "You should hear the bag."

GREASEMAN

- WHAT IT MUST BE LIKE TO BE A REAL LAWMAN (Lard Gutt) ** $8 $15

Just before he went national, syndicated into many of the same markets as colleague Howard Stern, radio redneck Greaseman issued this album loaded with sadistic cop chuckles. Like the meditation on blowing away an escaped prisoner: "He takes off running ... the kid gets smaller and smaller in the distance. You pull out your pump shotgun.

The wood feels good against your cheek. You start to salivate a little bit at the thought of pulling the trigger. You get almost a sexual stimulation as you caress that long, cold, steel barrel. The kid's got hope in his eyes now. He thinks he's beaten you. The creep thinks he's gonna get away ... and BAM. You shoot his legs out from under him ... you laugh out loud...."

THE GREAT GILDERSLEEVE See GILDERSLEEVE

BERNIE GREEN See MAD MAGAZINE

BUZZY GREENE

- ADAM STAG PARTY SPECIAL #1
  (Fax 1006, reissued as STORIES MOTHER NEVER TOLD ME) ** $5 $10
- STORIES FOR SEX MINDED MALES (Fax 1004, also known as STAG PARTY SPECIAL #5) ** $5 $10
- PARTY TIME (Laff A 124) ** $4 $10
- STAG NITE (Laff A 122) ** $4 $10
- STAG PARTY (Hudson HL 4003) $5 $10
- STAG PARTY 2 (Hudson HL 4004) $5 $10

After twenty years in burlesque, Greene emerged with a fast-paced, musing delivery that sounds a bit like Morey Amsterdam. He has Amsterdam's cadence and a slight lisp. His jokes aren't different from the rest of the late '50s and early '60s comics on small labels, but he tells them with a cheerful mildness.

From "Stories for Sex Minded Males": "Speaking of the Navy, did you hear about the old codger who goes into a grocery store and he says, 'Say, clerk, I'd like to get a roll of toilet paper.' Clerk says, 'Yes sir, what do you want, the Army or the Navy?' He says, 'Well, what's the difference?' The clerk says, 'Well, the Army paper is ordinary, but the Navy paper is four inches wider to allow for the roll of the ship.'

The crowd laughs, then begins to applaud. "It grows on ya, I know!" Buzzy says. "I admire your intelligence. So the old codger says to the clerk, 'Well, which kind do you use?' The clerk says, 'I don't think you'd be too happy about it, Pops. You'd have to use a whisk broom, I'm on a strict cracker diet, myself.'"

NOTE: Prices for Greene's Fax albums, as well as other comics on Fax, Lobo, and similar labels, can double if the cover features a topless model. Sometimes two covers were released, one with the comedian and the other with the model.

SHECKY GREENE

- 6,5,4,3,2,1, A FUNNY THING HAPPENED TO ME,
  ON MY WAY TO THE MOON (Majestic T-101) ** $10 $20
- A DAY AT THE RACES (Laff A 204) *1/2 $5 $10

Shecky Greene, one of the most popular stars in Las Vegas during the '50s and '60s, found his wild antics couldn't transfer well to disc or television. There's standard schtick here, including Ed Sullivan interviewing Ingemar Johannson:

"Tonight on our show, the brand new heavyweight champ, he's the world champion heavyweight, the weight world champeener. Change that card, will you, idiot ... Ingemar, when did you first realize that you had Floyd Patterson in real trouble?"

"I first realized it when the referee says it's over!"

"Ingemar, what blow was it that really put him away ?..."

"Well, Ed, I was jabbing him there with my left hand there, and I was feeling him out with the left hand, and I think he liked it because he bit me behind the ear, that son of a gun, and I kissed him square in the mouth! But anyway, about the third round my girlfriend Birgit give a good yell across the ring, she say, 'Go get 'em,' and I shot out my right hand!"

"You mean to tell me, Ingemar, it was your right hand that really did it?"

"No, it was my knee!"

Most of the album is minor tummling. His "showstopper" routine, a look at the rise of Danny Thomas, couldn't have meant much even when Thomas was a big name.

The Laff album from the early '70s hardly sounds much different from anybody else's Vegas routines, mixing ringsider ad-libs with standard gags of the day, like the oldie about the vaseline clerk: "Ma'am, I'm a Vaseline salesman, and I'd like to find out what you use that particular product for in the home...." "Well, we use it for medicinal purposes." "What else?" "Well, we use it for sex." "You use it for sex?" "Yeah, we rub it on the doorknob so the kids can't get into the bedroom." Also in the mix: talking parrot jokes, wife jokes, and dumb mimicry (Cary Grant, Wallace Beery, and Lionel Barrymore describing how they "go potty"). Sound quality is mediocre.

Greene once disowned this album as practically a bootleg; it was recorded for Columbia and when it was decided not to bother releasing it, somehow it turned up on Laff. He issued a local Vegas recording, "Shecky Greene in the Lounge."

EDDIE GREENSLEEVES

- HUMOROUS FOLK SONGS (Cameo SC 1031) *1/2 $4 $8

Ed Bakey billed himself as hip folksinger Eddie Greensleeves. With his folk song parodies, female chorus, and live studio audience, he uses the formula of Allan Sherman. But he sounds more like Oscar Brand. His pleasant, but uninteresting tenor voice doesn't help the mundane material.

The ancient ballad "Sweet Betsy from Pike" becomes a bland but semisatiric story of a college beatnik: "When she finished school Betsy said listen girls, before some square swine I'm not casting my pearls. Now you can all marry, but that's not my goal. Like, I'm off to Gay Paree to search for my soul." The twist is what happened to her: "Twas just five years later I happened one day. To visit the suburbs and to my dismay, twas there I found Betsy, five kids and a spouse. Two small cars, one big dog, and a split level house."

Allan Sherman turned "Matilda" into "My Zelda." Greensleeves makes it "Matt Dillon," excited because James Arness makes more money than a lawyer: "Matt Dillon he make the money with gun, not the Yale law." Dated cuts lampoon John Glenn, Newton B. Minnow, and Kennedy: "Jack be nimble, Jack be quick, or next time they will vote for Dick."

MICHAEL GREER

- TALLULAH IN HEAVEN (Riprap R 1010) ** $4 $10
  Bankhead, of course, for fans of female impersonation.

DICK GREGORY

- TALKS TURKEY (Vee Jay 4001) *** $8 $15
- TWO SIDES (Vee Jay 4005) **1/2 $8 $15
- RUNNING FOR PRESIDENT (Vee Jay 1093) **1/2 $8 $15
- MY BROTHER'S KEEPER (Gateway GLP 9007) $10 $20

After Mort Sahl and Lenny Bruce arrived, audiences were finally ready to hear truths about racial issues—as spoken by black comedian Dick Gregory. He issued many albums beginning in 1961, but retired from stand-up periodically, often for decades at a time, to devote himself to a variety of causes and programs.

Gregory's early Vee Jay albums, recorded in Chicago before evidently predominantly black audiences, have a relaxed feel. On "Talk Turkey," Gregory barely has time to begin his softspoken remarks when someone is shouting "Louder!" He comes back with "I can't talk loud— 'cause the NAACP told me not to." The album has plenty of Gregory's topical observations. He talks about seven hundred protestors jailed down South for humming: "All them kids was doin' was hummin' some hymns. Can you imagine what would've happened had they caught 'em praying? Seven hundred kids in Georgia they put in jail in one day. Can you see a little ol' hillbilly walking up to the Sarge saying, 'Sarge, put me in jail by golly, I killed my mother, my father, all my kids, and my wife.' He says, 'Cool it baby, we're overcrowded.'"

When he does observational humor about childhood, there's a lot of bitterness: "I used to listen to my mother talk to me. 'I don't want no equal rights for myself, just for you, son.' I said, 'Mom, get 'em for yourself and I know I got 'em.'" He talks about how his father wore "a stocking cap twisted around his head with a little knot in front," and how he'd "wake up in the morning and wonder why his head was hurting him." He remembers never believing in Santa Claus: "you know damn good and well ain't no white man comin' in our neighborhood after midnight."

On the "Two Sides" album, writers Ed Weinberger and Bob Orben get a credit. It was, and still is, a rare form of honesty for a comic to admit he doesn't write all his own material. "Running for President" is the least of the three, partly because the sound quality isn't perfect.

Around 1963 Gregory was actively campaigning for the relief of starving families in LeFlore County, Mississippi. He pressed thirty-seven thousand copies of "Brother's Keeper" and charged $1.60 a piece. He offered a dollar per disc to the LeFlore County Board of Supervisors, who claimed they couldn't afford $37,000 to feed the poor. The other sixty cents covered the cost of making the record. The half hour "question and answer" program has members of the audience ask Gregory for his opinion on subjects ranging from crime, Muslims, and Adam Clayton Powell, to the John Birch Society and America's treatment of the Indians. Basically a serious discussion, now and then Gregory sticks in a line from his act: "We spend billions of dollars every year on Civil Defense. We've got Civil Defense buildings all over America. And do you know they're closed on weekends? Like Khrushchev just fights a five-day week."

- EAST AND WEST (Colpix SCP 420) **1/2 $5 $15
- WE ALL HAVE PROBLEMS (Colpix SCOP 480) **1/2 $5 $15
- IN LIVING BLACK AND WHITE (Colpix SCP 417) **1/2 $5 $15

Gregory stayed with Colpix through 1964. He retained his smooth, ironic delivery style. On judges in Atlanta: "They're not formal, they're not stiff and wear the black gown or beat on the table with the gavel and holler order in the court. They just light their cross and you know court is in session." On a judge in Birmingham: "The judge said, 'Young man, you don't know how lucky you are ... eleven of the twelve on the jury are moderates.' "You know what a Southern moderate is? That's a cat who'll lynch you from a low tree."

On "We All Have Problems" there's a rare playful moment as Gregory pauses to reflect on his wife, who gave "cute rich names" to his daughters: Pamela, Paula, and Michelle. "I put my foot down. I told her the next baby we have I'm gonna name something colored. Like Beulah! Yeah, that name just slays me ... then I'll have somethin' around the house I can play with ... Pamela, Paula, what do you do with them? Paula, if you do that again I'll tell your mother ... Pamela, if you don't behave ... Michelle, Mommy gonna punish you. BEULAH GIRL, I'LL BUST THE HELL OUT YOU!"

Alex Drier tersely narrates "Black and White," using the kind of gritty delivery spoofed so well in Woody Allen's "Take the Money and Run." When he shuts up, Dick Gregory's monologues speak for themselves. One of his most famous jokes is on the album. He talks about ordering a meal in Mississippi: "I got a little hungry. I went into the 'wrong' restaurant ... they'll make you think World War II was a lawn party. But I walked in anyway. 'Cause I like lawn parties ... I sit down, a blonde waitress walked over to me. I said, 'I'd I like two cheeseburgers.' She said, 'We don't serve colored people down here.' I said, 'I don't eat colored people nowhere!'"

- LIGHT SIDE DARK SIDE (Poppy PYS 600001) ** $8 $20
- AT THE VILLAGE GATE (Poppy 40011) ** $5 $15
- ON ... (POPPY 40008) ** $5 $15
- FRANKENSTEIN (Poppy 600004) ** $8 $20
- KENT STATE (Poppy 600005) ** $8 $12
- CAUGHT IN THE ACT (Poppy PP LA 176G2) *** $10 $20
- BEST OF DICK GREGORY (Tomato 3 9001) *** $10 $20

After Gregory's Presidential run in 1968, he came back to stand-up, but more as a lecturer. "I was the only one running for the presidency," he told audiences, "the other ones were running for sheriff." His first new album in years, "Light Side Dark Side" is appropriately titled, with a slim amount of light, reflective irony and a lot of dark, angry warnings.

"I guess I spend about ninety-eight percent of my time today on college campuses," he tells the audience at Southampton College in 1969, "You young folks in America today is probably the most morally dedicated, committed group of young people as ever lived in the history of this country, bar none ... if it had not been for you, LBJ would probably still be the president today. But you young kids created an atmosphere where LBJ had to retire. Do you know how strong that is? LBJ is probably the number one tyrant that walked the face of this earth since Julius Caesar and you young kids sent him back to the ranch ... and you didn't use one missile, one fire bomb, or shoot one shot. You just got out with a pure moral dedication and he understood how powerful that was...."

In August of 1973, Gregory quit nightclubs. "Caught in the Act," his farewell performance, has its slow spots through eighty minutes (this is yet another Gregory double-album set). Gregory is amused by the predicament of Richard Nixon: "He kept his promise. He said if he got in he would take crime out of the street. He sure centralized crime, didn't he?" Watergate predominates the album: "Do you realize the best thing happened for Nixon during the whole Watergate is when Brezhnev came to the country? For about five days it wiped Watergate off the front page ... I was so sick and tired of looking at him and Nixon on television. Drunk. I mean, I looked at 'em on television they were so drunk I thought I tuned in *The Dean Martin Show.* I get scared when Nixon get drunk around Brezhnev 'cause he gives away all the food! Gave 'em all the wheat on credit. He was so drunk ... didn't even know he made the deal. NUT! And if Brezhnev had've been clever, he could've had all the soybeans, too. All he had to do was tell Dick Nixon, if you be cool and give me all your soybeans ... I'll tell the American people John Dean was a Russian spy."

Gregory isn't all political. He does a bit that sounds like early Richard Pryor, on the illogical laws against urination: "You go to jail for doin' something normal. Ain't no law against peein' in public. They get you for indecent exposure. As long as you pee and don't zip your pants down, that's normal...."

Richard Pryor, of course, seemed to take the reins when Gregory retired from stand-up, but no comedian, black or white, could match Dick Gregory in talking on the racial problem in America with directness, humanity, insight, and humor.

NOTES: Poppy's "Gregory Talks Black," was an ambitious promotional package sent out to columnists and disc jockeys. The boxed set included folded press clips, a button ("Gregory Talks Black") and two 45s, each featuring about fifteen minutes of material, from "Light Side Dark Side" and "On." Underneath each goodie was a color picture of Gregory.

JAMES GREGORY

- IT COULD BE A LAW, I DON'T KNOW (Epic EK 46080) *1/2 $8

Gregory's a fast-talking, but slow-thinking, Southern comedian who foolishly bills himself as "The Funniest Man in America." The 1991 CD covers hemorrhoids, laxatives, UFOs, and midgets: "There's three things in this life I can't stand: hatred, bigotry, midgets. I'm sorry, I just don't like 'em. Everyone in this room has seen a midget before. No one in here ever sees more than one midget at a time. You go to the mall, there'll be thousands of people. One midget. Could be a law, I don't know. Look, you've never seen a daddy midget and a mama midget and a station wagon full of midget kids. If midgets never get together with other midgets, how do we keep gettin' more midgets? It's worryin' the hell out of me."

JOYCE GRENFELL

- JOYCE GRENFELL REQUESTS THE PLEASURE OF YOUR COMPANY (DRG 5186) *1/2 $5 $10
- PRESENTING JOYCE GRENFELL (Elektra EKL 184) *1/2 $10 $15

Grenfell was influenced by Ruth Draper, who was often a guest at Grenfell's family home. A comedy star in England since the early '40s, Grenfell favored tongue-in-cheek character studies of indulgent school teachers, talkative club women, and others. She varied her act with songs, most self-penned, many of them straight. She sings them with the tame temperment of a Julie Andrews. She came to Broadway in 1955 for *Joyce Grenfell Requests the Pleasure.*

Her opening for the show: "Life, it's so exhausting just existing, and what's it all about, one longs to know? It's one long rush! And now, to top it all come dazzling wonders of television ... it's such a wrench to leave one's television

GET COMPED WITH COMPILATIONS

A great way to sample a bunch of top bananas, the "Comic Relief" series has included most of today's top young stars. From earlier eras: Steve Allen's "Man in the Street" album and the novel "My Favorite Story," featuring jokes from Groucho Marx, Bob Hope, Red Skelton, Jimmy Stewart, Lucille Ball, and many more.

SOUTHERN TRACKS

Many have no idea Andy Griffith was once a stand-up star with a hit routine on football. Jerry Clower has issued a prodigious amount of records, especially compared to the colorful "Whitey" Ford, The Duke of Paducah.

set, isn't it? May we say well done, you, for doing it? We really do appreciate it, because we know how hard it is not to look in, even when you hate it! And may we say thank you, too, for leaving your wireless and your book to come and have a look at flesh and blood? Well, it makes a change, doesn't it. Just think: real live entertainers seen in the original size and natural colors ... actually here, breathing (more or less) ready to do the show for you now...."

Grenfell teamed with Stanley Hollloway for "Bab Ballads" (Caedmon 1104) and is well represented on British imports, including HMV's "Joyce Grenfell in a Miscellany" and EMI collections "Joyce Grenfell at Home," "Joyce Grenfell Collection," "Joyce Grenfell Second Collection," and "George, Don't Do That."

ANDY GRIFFITH

- JUST FOR LAUGHS (Capitol T 962) **1/2 $5 $10
- THIS HERE'S ANDY GRIFFITH (Capitol T 1215) **1/2 $5 $10
- ANDY AND CLEOPATRA (Capitol T 2066) **1/2 $10 $15
- BEST OF ANDY GRIFFITH (Capitol T 2707) *** $8 $12
- ANDY GRIFFITH AMERICAN ORIGINALS (Capitol CDP 0777 79847624) *** $8

Griffith was a fairly succesful stand-up comic in the early '60s, and won over Broadway audiences in *No Time for Sergeants*. But to most of his fans, he's either sitcom sheriff Andy Taylor or gray-haired lawyer Matlock.

As a stand-up, Griffith's most famous routine, "What It Was, Was Football" took a bumpkin's eye view of a baffling game: "... both bunches full of them men wanted this funny little punkin' to play with ... they did, and I know friends, that they couldn't a eat it, 'cause they kicked it the whole evening and it never bust."

The bit appears on Griffith's first album, along with another typical routine, a retelling of *Romeo and Juliet*.

"... Romeo says to hisself, 'What light by yonder winder shines.' He did. And let me tell ya, Juliet stepped out of her bedroom winder onto this stoop, and she gave a soliloquy ... she says, 'Romeo, Romeo, wherefore art thou, Romeo?' And he popped up and said, 'I'm right here!' As it happened, there was this great big pea vine a growin' up to where she was a standing. And so he clum up it ... he wasn't up there for no light courtin', he wanted to get on with it...."

Griffith reworked the formula on subsequent albums through 1964. In 1992, Capitol treated Griffith to a sixty-seven-minute "Best of" CD. It features the best remembered routines ("What It Was, Was Football," "Love Poems to the Lovely Juanita Beasley," "Opera Carmen," "Hamlet," "Romeo and Juliet") as well as a few songs, including "The Midnight Special," "Preacher and the Bear," and "The Fishin' Hole," the latter being a vocal version of the famous whistling theme music to "The Andy Griffith Show."

"The TV Theme Sing-Along Album" (Rhino) also includes "The Fishin' Hole." Griffith issued four straight albums: "The Andy Griffith Show" and "Shouts the Blues" from Capitol, and "World's Favorite Hymns" and "Somebody Bigger Than You and I" for Columbia. In 1996 the new gospel CD "Precious Memories" was issued.

ELSIE AND GEUNIE GRINER

- FOCUS ON THE SOUTH (Judges' Chamber #1) ** $4 $10

"A redneck can't be cured with bleach," sings Elsie on this unusual album circa 1967. Although Southern comedy of the era, with the exception of Brother Dave Gardner, was corny and conservative, Elsie and her piano-playing brother were attempting songs and monologues satirizing "Gritzville, U.S.A." The duo billed themselves as "The Chief Jesters of the South." Geunie Griner's varied career included work as the editor and publisher of the *Nashville Herald* in Nashville, Georgia, and songwriting for a variety of publishers.

Elsie sings about moonshining ("We weren't harmin' ... just liquid farmin'") and Southern politics: "You take a corn pone politician with a fevered mind. Give him a redneck proposition, you got the winnin' kind ... no need to support a moderate sort. The far right calls him pink. I know he can't win. Darlin' I know it's a sin. You know them boys never learned how to think!"

The material is at the level of any modest revue, but coming out of Georgia in 1967, this is a surprise.

Geunie Griner died on July 21, 1975, at the age of forty-seven.

LEWIS GRIZZARD

- ON THE ROAD (Southern Tracks S004) **1/2 $5 $8
- LIVE (Southern Tracks 0007) ** $5 $8
- LET'S HAVE A PARTY (Southern Tracks 009) ** $5 $8
- LEWIS GRIZZARD LIVE (Columbia CK 48698) ** $5 $8
- ALIMONY (Intersound CDI 9140) ** $8
- ADDICTED TO LOVE (Southern Tracks STC 0011) ** $8
- ONE LAST TIME (Southern Tracks STCD 0050) ** $8
- BEST OF LEWIS GRIZZARD (Southern Tracks STCD 0025) ** $8

Very few Southern comics have broken past regional appeal. On disc, only Andy Griffith and Brother Dave Gardner have had much success anywhere but down home. Up North, the "good uns" of a Jerry Glower are greeted by mystified silence. The late columnist and best-selling author Lewis Grizzard did manage some crackerbarrel wit with crackle. He talks about the differences between Northern and Southern pronunciation:

"Naked means you ain't got no clothes on. Nekkid means you ain't got no clothes on and you up to somethin'!"

A smooth banquet speaker for many years, Grizzard is a much better performer than most humor columnists. He's adept at tossing off quickies: "Do you know what Michael Jackson and the Atlanta Braves have in common? They both wear one glove for no apparent reason." He can also chew through a shaggy dog story, or offer down-home observations on bad TV commercials: "You ladies go out and you buy Gloria Vanderbilt designer jeans. Have you got a good look at Gloria Vanderbilt lately? She's uglier than a bowlin' shoe!" And, musing on disposable douches, "Of course it's disposable! Who'd wanna keep one of those things around!"

Grizzard does have material that doesn't travel well. Gays are called "fruit flies" in a bit on how much he hates gay waiters. He reports on one "sashayin' this far off the ground. Looks like he's tryin' to carry a corn cob without usin' his hands." Eddie Murphy could probably say the same thing and get cheers, but coming from a Southerner it sounds just a tad hateful. Yuppies will also turn up their noses at ol' George. He doesn't like their fancy habit of putting mushrooms on cheeseburgers: "They're toadstools. Frogs go to the bathroom on these things."

"Live" is another collection of generally harmless Southern anecdotes. On dogs: "My dog, his name is Catfish. He drinks out of the toilet. Other day I said to him, 'Why do you go to the bathroom on my carpet?' He said, 'You go to the bathroom in my water bowl!'"

It's more of the same on the "Party" disc, with Grizzard telling some of the gags his newspaper column readers submitted to him. Like: "What is relative humidity? Is that how much you perspire when you're makin' love to your cousin?" Most of the jokes are old and familiar. He tells the one about the time he met a woman who had specific tastes in bedmates—cowboys and Jews. He introduced himself to her: "Glad to meet you ma'am, Hopalong Ginsberg." Grizzard liked this one so much he retold it on his 1991 Columbia CD: "Proud to meet you ma'am, Hopalong Ginsberg at your service."

The Columbia CD has a few tangy opinionated one-liners (love them or hate them) and an awful lot of long anecdotes about Southern family life, including "Grandma Willie's Yard" and "Mama's Old Brown Hymnal." His droning, low Southern accent doesn't give them the needed color that a true stand-up could give them. Some are corny and mildly off-color, like the drawn out one about the woman who insists her husband's erection is hard enough to support thirteen parrots. Two minutes later she confesses she may have exaggerated: "Sometimes when we put that thirteenth parrot right there on the end? It has to flap its wings to stay on!"

Grizzard had heart problems for many years, so it wasn't much of a surprise when "the big one" came. Several albums were released posthumously, including the tasteless "One Last Time," which depicted Grizzard with angel wings, a harp, and a halo—and also in a devil costume with pitchfork, just in case cynics felt he went the other way. The album offers typical wisecracks on divorce, politics, and gays: "If gay people can't reproduce, why are there so more many of 'em now than there used to be?"

Grizzard died while working on something different—the "Alimony" album, a collection of songs, most sincerely crooned and proudly mawkish ballads. Grizzard's vocalizing isn't much, but it isn't embarrassing. Half the tracks are just narrated anecdotes about "Daddy and Momma," "Grandma," or other homespun folks.

From the title track: "It's the bill you got for the thrill you got ... Now it may sound strange, and it seems a little funny, how you married her for love and divorced for money. After the magic is long gone, the alimony lingers on."

Audio books are available on various Grizzard collections, including "Elvis Is Dead and I Don't Feel So Good Myself" and "You Can't Put No Boogie-Woogie on the King of Rock and Roll."

GROUP THERAPISTS

- SICK ALONG WITH US (Strand SLP 1009) **1/2 $8 $20

Released during the "sick comedy" craze of the early '60s, the album offers sketches interspersed with classic one-liners of the day:

"Mommy, mommy, I don't wanna go to Europe." "Shut up and keep swimming." "Mommy, mommy, Daddy just fell off the cliff." "Don't make me laugh, my lips are chapped!" "Aside from everything else, what did you think of the play, Mrs. Lincoln?"

There are some good jokes here and there, even an innovative "So You Want to Be a Comic" segment where, for the first time on record, the listener gets to recite jokes from the album sleeve to a few minutes of canned laughter. Unfortunately a hunk of the material is mediocre, including a weary parody of *Gunsmoke* that couldn't even make it to the pages of *Sick* magazine.

The Group Therapists were Sandy Baron, George Eugene, and Phyllis Mercer.

GUCKENHEIMER SOUR KRAUT BAND

- SOUR KRAUT IN HI FI (RCA Victor LPM 1453) *1/2 $5 $10
- MUSIC FOR NON THINKERS (RCA Victor LPM 1721) *1/2 $5 $10

A German band of deliberately inept musicians blunder through the classics. It's a one-joke concept, but a source of offbeat humor (very, very off beat). The seven-piece band is mostly brass with the addition of a wheezing clarinet and an oomphless oom-pah drum.

On the first album, the Guckenheimers' deliberately inept German marching band perform their nauseatingly dilapidated versions of "Poet and Peasant Overture" (with a little "I've Been Working on the Railroad" for added dementia), "Skater's Waltz," and "Springtime Polka" among too many others. Excellent music to annoy neighbors with.

On the second, released in 1958, the Guckenheimers literally limp through "Raymond Overture," "Second Hungarian Rhapsody," and "Stars and Stripes," making the once-fast tunes go on endlessly.

BILLY GUY

- THE TRAMP IS FUNKY (Snake Eyes 9000) ** $5 $10

Billy Guy's version of a funky tramp is pretty cool, if not oblivious. He doesn't expend much energy with his rhymes about various "greasy" orifices full of "slick and slime." He's laconic about "a wound that'll never heal. The more you rub it the better it feels. You can talk all the soap between heavy and hell, but I'll be damned if you'll get rid of that funky smell." His anecdotal dirty stories are heavier on colorful cursing than clever punch lines. The small but enthusiastic black audience cackles and screams and shouts "right on," but it doesn't disturb Guy's peculiar serenity.

HACK AND SACK

- COUNTRY AND WESTERN NOVELTY SONGS (Diplomat) * $5 $10
- HERE COMES THE JUDGE (Ambassador 98074) * $5 $10

A budget label duo. The country album has a cover of "May the Bird of Paradise Fly up Your Nose" but their Homer and Jethro-style harmonies are bland, and the rest of the cuts are weak. "Toothache" has this chorus: "Toothache, toothache, what a horrible thing. It never starts until you go to bed. Toothache, toothache, it keeps on wriggling and sometimes makes you wish that you were dead."

BUDDY HACKETT

- THE CHINESE WAITER (Coral CRL 757422) ** $10 $20
- THE ORIGINAL CHINESE WAITER (Dot 3351, reissued as Pickwick SPC 3198) ** $10 $20

Hackett had an early hit with Catskill audiences in the '50s as the "Chinese Waiter." It's on the Coral album with other Chinese monologues (recorded in a studio, sans audience) plus a few tunes. The best is "The Songs My Mother Used to Sing to Who," a W. C. Fieldsian collection of deliberately rhymeless nonsense similar to the British Music Hall tunes Fields occasionally croaked on radio.

The Dot album also has a mix of straight material and the Chinese waiter. Though obviously dated, unlike other comics of the era from Jerry Lewis to Freddie Morgan, Hackett at least lets his Asian stereotype get in a few cracks against his Caucasian foes: "Spale lib or the egg roll. No spale lib and egg roll, spale lib OR egg roll! Yeah, you can have both, seventy-five cents extra. No, no split 'em up, I split you up you round-eyed iriot!" "What's a fly lice?" "Fly lice ... wattsamatta, can't you speak English?"

For some, the thirty-year-old ethnic comedy will have the smell of a hundred-year-old egg, but much of the disc is still cute and oddly ingratiating thanks to Hackett's unique delivery.

- THE WORLD'S FUNNIEST PRESS CONFERENCE (Bootleg) **1/2 $12 $20

In the mid-60s, Hackett, Don Rickles, and Don Adams held a press conference to discuss their affiliation with King's Castle Casino in Lake Tahoe. Hackett, clearly the leader of the gang, dominates with curse words and ad-libs.

Like Friar Roast bootlegs, there's a lot of in-jokes and "you hadda be there" lines. Hackett says that Woody Allen is also to be a partner: "I would like a more substantial type person. Woody weighs maybe a hundred twenty pounds. What are ya gonna do with him? In case a roof leaks you can't even stuff him in there." On running the shows: "You try to keep costs down and you try not to stay on the stage too long ... the one who stays on too long will have the shit kicked out of him by the others!"

NOTES: Hackett sings "Itsy Bitsy Teeny Weeny Yellow Polka Dot Bikini" on "Arthur Godfrey Time" (Contempo 3902), an album of highlights from Godfrey's radio show. Hackett sings it pretty straight, but ad-libs, "don't be a meenie! Show us your bikini!" It's also available as a single (Laurel 1014). He issued many singles including "Looey Looey" (Laurel 1017) and he stars on the Broadway cast album "I Had a Ball" (Mercury OCS 6210).

STANLEY MYRON HANDELMAN

- SPIRO T. AGNEW IS A RIOT (Cadet CCX-1) **1/2 $3 $8

This was a studio album produced by Earle "First Family" Doud. The star is mousey Stanley Handelman, a familiar guest on '60s variety shows like *The Dean Martin Show*. He wore glasses and an old fashioned cap to imitate a nerdish grown-up schoolboy. For this record, Handelman doesn't impersonate the bonehead vice president. He gives Agnew his own dronish Brooklyn accent:

"I really love America," Agnew says. "Because only in America is it possible for a person with my qualifications to become vice president. And also, in what other country than America can a person like me say to a person like you, why don't you get out of America?" There are plenty of gags based on Agnew's foot-in-mouth ethnic remarks. Here, Agnew mentions "a man of Polish extraction, but a really nice guy."

The supporting cast on this 1970 album is impressive, though none have much to do: Vincent Price, Jo Ann Pflug, Pat McCormick, Jack De Leon, and Jack Riley. Rich Little plays Nixon and Harold Oblong of *The Times Square Two* plays David Frost in a long interview sequence. Handelman's obscurity today, plus the topical nature of the album, has lessened its value.

HAP HAPPY

- CRUISING TIME (Deauville LPD 800) ** $6 $12

This "adults only" album from the early '60s sports an evocative cover: a seedy brunette in a spangled bikini being wheeled in a supermarket cart by Mr. Hap Happy, a Bud Abbott-Sidney Fields type with a sleazy pencil-thin mustache. The material is the usual whiz-bang stuff told with the laid-back, raspy delivery of a house comic who's told them time after time: "Gotta tell ya about the drunks. Two drunks sitting at the bar. One drunk says, 'Hey, did you hear about the new ice cubes with the hole in the middle?' The other drunk says, 'Waddya mean hear about 'em. I married one!'"

Collectors of campy album covers might pay more for this one, as would the ardent collector of adult comedy discs.

LARRY HARMON AND HENRY CALVIN
• LAUREL AND HARDY, THIS IS YOUR LAFF (Peter Pan 8018) *1/2 $10 $20

Harmon, creator of Bozo the Clown, bought the merchandising rights to Laurel and Hardy and began to issue comic books, toys, and even this 1963 record featuring his adequate impression of Laurel. Henry Calvin (once Sgt. Garcia on Disney's *Zorro* TV show) does an accurate Hardy. In fact, Calvin guested on an episode of *The Dick Van Dyke Show* and did a Laurel and Hardy sketch with Van Dyke. The six "stories" here are at the level of Harmon's animated cartoons, but are less interesting sans visuals. Moving a piano: "Come on Stanley, lift your end. Got it?" "Got it, Ollie!" "All right, now back up toward the door!" "Wait a second, Ollie, my end is slipping ... look out...." "YOW! My foot!" "Come on, Stanley, let's get this piano out of here before we really have to face the music." Paul Frees supplies the voices for all the supporting characters.

DOUG HARRELL
• LAUGH A SPELL (ABC-Paramount 364) ** $5 $10

Back when vinyl was cheap and recording easy, North Carolina doctor Doug Harrell talked his way through "Exsanguination Blues" a song he sold to friends and colleagues. In 1960 ABC-Paramount chanced a national pressing, padding the album with more songs and a comic lecture recorded live. "Exsanguination Blues" won't mean much to the average listener as Harrell drawls about drawing blood: "You have a lot of calculations to make to figure out how much blood it'll take and your answer comes somethin' like 100 cc. As if you didn't have no cause to act quick, some nurse is tellin' ya to get on the stick, she's waitin' to take your patient to EEG ...."

The droll, deadpan lectures take up most of the album: "One of the first things which they teach you about the doctor-patient relationship is ... never let the patient know you've changed your diagnosis, because this shakes his confidence; it's bad for rapport. Well, with this thought firmly entrenched in mind, one of my classmates started to work down in the clinic. And one of the first patients that he saw was this fellow who came in with excruciating abdominal pain.... After he finished his examination he says, 'Sir, you have what is commonly referred to as the locked bowels.' Well, the fellow ... says, 'Doctor, how can that be, I've been running to the bathroom every ten minutes all day.' My friend says, 'Get up on the table and let me check you again.' And after his second examination he says, 'Yes sir, you do have the locked bowels, but they're locked in the open position.'"

PAT HARRINGTON, JR.
• SOME LIKE IT HIP (United Artists UAI 4089) * $6 $12

In the late '50s, before his sitcom *One Day at a Time*, Pat was a stand-up comic, a favorite of Steve Allen and Jack Paar. He often performed as "Guido Panzini," a stereotypical Italian. Here he's Guido the Italian Golf Pro, talking about working at a Jewish country club. He was fired because in the shower he displayed "prima face evidence offa de New Testament."

Most other bits on this 1960 disc present Pat as a young hipster. He does a long, pseudo-cool routine on the Newport Jazz Festival, loaded with Lenny Bruce-style throwaway bits: "Ella Fitzgerald comes out in a bikini and wedgies. She does 115 pushups, closes with a hernia, walks off leaving them limp ... Duke Ellington is conducting the entire Congolese Senate ..." A la Lenny, Pat rips Lawrence Welk, imitating the unhip band leader as he wrecks the Newport Jazz Festival by introducing "Eleanor Roosevelt, doin' de 'Limehouse Blues.'"

PAT HARRINGTON, JR. AND BILL DANA
• AS GUIDO PANZINI, AS KOOKIE AS EVER
  (Signature SM 102, reissued as Roulette R 25162) ** $10 $20

Harrington's Panzini character arrived before Dana's Jose Jimenez. Pat's the star here. He does his best Guido routine as the survivor of the Andrea Doria crash. Dana plays straight:

"When did you first realize you were on a collision course?"

"The captain asked a question and somebody answered in Swedish...."

"What was the very first thing out of the captain's mouth when he knew what had happened?"

"The very first thing out of his mouth? His lunch ... I was in the bridge. I don't want to boast, but I made it to the lifeboat in 9.6. That's a maritime record ... I finished second. The captain did it in 9.4."

That last joke turns up on Dana's "In Las Vegas" album in improved form. As Jose Jimenez the lion tamer, he mentions the time he made it from the center of the cage to the exit in 9.5. "But ... the lion made it in 9.4."

Harrington's Guido doesn't survive all that well, but isn't any less redundant than Don Novello's later Father Sarducci.

Dana gets a chance to be the comic on a Jewish dialect routine and plays an embryonic Jose character, "a gentleman from Cuba" on a plane with a very right wing Harrington. Both pressings are hard to find. Since the disc has Harrington's most famous routine, plus early Bill Dana, it has some collector appeal.

BARON HARRIS

- PILLOW TALK (Dooto DTL 294) *1/2 $5 $10

Kenneth Harris, born in Kansas City and later working the circuits in Chicago and Indianapolis, isn't exactly a "Baron" of comedy. He tells the standard Foxx and Mabley jokes without much funky backspin or individuality: "(My girl and I) were walking down the street. And the people walking behind us were laughing at us. I wondered if there was something wrong ... nothing was wrong with me so I told her to run up in front of me and I immediately saw what was wrong. She had sat on a sign, perspired, and the letters had come off on the tail of the skirt, and they read something like this: Rear entrance closed for the season, main entrance around front. Admission one dollar fifty cents."

EDDIE HARRIS

- THE REASON WHY I'M TALKING S--T (Atlantic SD 18165) ** $5 $10

On this 1976 album, jazz sax player Eddie Harris offers a loose, desultory monologue on one side, four tunes on the other, each prefaced by some banter. The comedy is mostly in Harris's laid-back but moody and rude jazz attitude. He imagines how a typical couple got ready to come to his show: "He think he cool when he spray hisself with cologne. Rub all up behind, in the crack of his ass and shit ... On his way to go pick her up he forgot to brush his teeth so he buy some chewing gum. Then he goes over to pick up this lady. What she does is jump in the shower, take a seven-second shower. Didn't want to get her hair wet, you dig. She get out of the shower, put cologne all over, put a whole lotta cologne down between her legs ... She take two rolled up socks, put 'em in her bra."

A woman at ringside interrupts to shout, "I put a egg!"

Harris ponders it. "I hope you heard that. Lady say she put a egg. She look like she done fried that mother...."

PHIL HARRIS

- ON THE RECORD (RCA LPM 3037) ** $8 $15
- THAT'S WHAT I LIKE ABOUT THE SOUTH (RCA Camden 456) **1/2 $10 $15
- THAT'S WHAT I LIKE ABOUT THE SOUTH (Zodiac ZLP 5002) ** $5 $10

Harris recorded many straight songs, but the albums listed here have more of his folksy-corny novelty tunes.

Harris was influenced by Bert Williams and enjoyed reciting Bert's "Woodman, Spare that Tree." The humor is mostly in the wry attitude. Harris tells the woodman: "Look here, my friend, hold on, desist, whoa stop! Put down the forest razor. Chop not a single chop! Woodman, woodman, spare that tree. Touch not a single bough ... save Ol' Slipp'ry there, that's mine. It's the only tree my wife can't climb. Mr. Woodman, spare it for me!"

The Camden disc features "Woodman, Spare that Tree," "Darktown Poker Club," and two of Phil's best known novelties, "Goofus," a wobbly little jazz tune; and "The Thing," a risqué number that leaves the listener imagining just what "the thing" is that Phil likes to show everyone he meets. The album's title cut was one of his biggest hits, a fast recitation of the good and the ridiculous things he loves about the South.

"On the Record" is a rare ten-incher issued circa 1953 featuring "That's What I Like about the South," "Darktown Poker Club," "Ain't Nobody Here but Us Chickens," "Pappy's Little Jug," "Woodman Spare that Tree," and "44 Sycamore." The emphasis is on Phil's fast talkin' charm, evident on the Fats Waller-esque "Minnie the Mermaid," with Phil enthusing: "What a time I had with Minnie the Mermaid down at the bottom of the sea. I lost all my troubles in amongst the bubbles. Why she was as sweet as she could be. And every night when those starfish came out, I hugged and kissed her so. Oh, the time I had with Minnie the Mermaid, down in her seaweed bungalow."

Following his success as Baloo the Bear in *The Jungle Book*, Harris re-recorded some of his hits for a 1969 album that has turned up on various labels, including Zodiac and the British "Music for Pleasure." The comedy highlights are "Smoke Smoke Smoke," the Bert Williams classic "Nobody," and of course, "That's What I Like about the South."

NOTES: Harris appears on various Jack Benny records (he was Jack's swinging band leader and the subject of endless boozer jokes). He married Alice Faye in 1941 and they had their own "The Phil Harris & Alice Faye Show" (Radio Archives 101).

ROBIN HARRIS

- BE-BE'S KIDS (Wing/Mercury 841 9602) ** $8

Heavy-set Robin Harris died suddenly after a few appearances in Spike Lee movies and one HBO special. He's sort of a "you hadda be there" comic who gets big laughs playing with the audience: "Oooh eee, God damn, brother, you're a big fucker there. Look at you! Damn ... You's a big motherfucker, you know that, don't ya? Damn! Where you from, brother? New York? When you leavin'? Damn! Shit! That's the kinda nigger go to the restaurant, order everythin' on the menu except thank you please come again!" The seventy-three-minute CD could've been edited down for easier listening.

The long "Be-Be" bit isn't as funny without seeing Robin's frenzied posturing as the bratty kids. After his death, "Be-Be's Kids" was made into an animated movie.

HARRIS AND KUKOFF

- TOM EDISON'S GREATEST HITS (United Artists UAS 6547) * $4 $8

A dumb one-joke concept: Jeff Harris and Bernie Kukoff have unearthed a collection of cylinders that Edison made of famous people: Harry Houdini, Sigmund Freud, Geronimo, and so on.

Among the mediocre sketches on this 1965 disc is one claiming that on July 9, 1883, microphones were placed in a Western saloon and the actual voice of Wild Bill Hickock was captured live. Then there's the "actual recording." There's no attempt to duplicate the scratchy sound of a cylinder. Instead, in perfect studio fidelity and with sound effects, we hear glasses tinkling and a bartender ask Wild Bill what he'd like to drink. An effeminate voice calls out, "Brandy Alexander, please." Each cut is the same. An elaborate set-up and a weak punch line.

WES HARRISON

- THE ONE AND ONLY (IRC S-3330) *1/2 $6 $12
- YOU WON'T BELIEVE YOUR EARS (Philips PHM 200 103) *1/2 $6 $12

More a novelty act than a comic, Harrison tells sound-effect stories—using only his mouth to produce everything from trotting horses to jet plane and car motor noises. On these '60s discs the novelty wears thin. The aural cartoons aren't much—like the "sound gag" on the Philips album of Wes imitating a horse trotting over a bridge. There's a sudden plopping sound and then the imitation of water splashing. More than comedy fans, it's the collectors of bird calls and theremin concerts that seem to relish these and push the price up.

HARRISON AND TYLER

- TRY IT YOU'LL LIKE IT (Dore LP 327) *1/2 $5 $10
- WONDER WOMEN (20th Century Fox T 413) * $5 $10

Pat Harrison and Robin Tyler were a pair of women's lib comics with a heavy-handed sense of sarcasm and a chiding wit. Shrill even in the days when feminists tended to scream or not be heard at all, the duo flaunt some arch one-liners: "I went out and bought a women's liberation wristwatch. You wind it up and it doesn't work in the kitchen."

Rarely bringing humanity to their humor (or "womanity" as they'd probably insist) they sloganize and antagonize: "A woman marries a man for better or for worse. The guy couldn't do better and the woman couldn't do worse ... that's true, right? If God had wanted women in the kitchen he would've given her aluminum hands ... SHE would've given her aluminum hands."

In the final routine, Harrison and Tyler dare each other to say a four-letter word because, "We can't say it, male comics can say it ... they want us to do it, but they don't want us to say it!" Finally, they are completely liberated as they shout out, "Fuck it, we're free." Not many comics would end an album on a straight line.

It's more of the same on their last (1973) album: "Patti and I happen to be feminists!" "And that's not a hygiene deodorant!"

ROD HART

- BREAKEROO! (Plantation PLP 500) * $4 $8

Hart's 1976 LP was keyed to the CB craze. "C.B. Savage" is about a stereotypical lisping gay cruising for truckers: "Breakers breakers! Any takers? Hi, hi, it's me again. I'm in your chair and I love it there. Say, you truckers really know how to take a person for a ride. Speak to me, you diesel demons, I'd love to get to know your handles!" Other tunes lamely hobble over standard country fodder from ugly women ("Big Fanny") to "The Ole Town Drunk" and "Dog-Gone It Dog."

THE HARVARD LAMPOON

- HARVARD LAMPOON TABERNACLE CHOIR (Vanitas V 4401) ** $7 $20
- SURPRISING SHEEP (Epic BN 26462) * $6 $15

The 1962 Vanitas album offers parodies of rock and roll. "Teen Angel" is satirized by both "Sweet Teen-Age Cadaver" and "Sweet Earthbound Teen-Lover." The Harvard preppies were cheeky and daring in their day. On "John Foster Dulles" Christopher Cerf (the only member of the cast who went anywhere) dares to sing: "John Foster Dulles! Well he signed our rights and liberty away/Just to be alone with Mrs. K.!" And on "What Is Love," Cerf warbles the then-risqué "What is love you ask me? Now my answer is complete. It's the smile upon the face of a rhinocerous in heat."

"Surprising Sheep" from 1968 (with Christopher Cerf again) tries to satirize music trends of the day and is remarkably unhip. "Seventeen Miles from Waukegan" swipes at Bob Dylan's hallucinatory lyrics: "She seemed to be a caribou. Until the waffle farmers got a chance to lob their pickle grenade. I was going to have dinner with my horse but she lied. She denied. She alibied. Ah she cried. Never tried. Seventeen miles from Waukegan my cantaloupe died." Equally embarrassing is a white college boy making fun of Wilson Pickett by wailing a nursery rhyme: "got to got to got to eat your curds, got to eat your whey, eat your way into my heart!"

The parody vocals are tin-eared, the lyrics lame. Especially compared to what The National Lampoon would do to Dylan, John Lennon, Neil Young, and James Taylor on their first two albums.

SONNY HATCHETT

- WHY YOU MUTHA, YU MA ... (Laff 183) ** $4 $8

Here's another journeyman in the Laff stable of risqué black comics. The title refers to the punch line of a stolen Godfrey Cambridge joke about how Yuma, Arizona, got its name. It takes Sonny a meandering six minutes to tell it.

DON HAYES

- FUN EVENING (Art 63) $4 $8

JIMMY HEAP SHOW FEATURING KEN IDAHO

- LAUGH POTION (Fame 1003) *1/2 $4 $8
- LAFF FUN-TIER (Fame 1004) *1/2 $4 $8
- LAFF-A-RAMMER (Fame 1005) *1/2 $4 $8
- HERE'S TO YA (Fame 1007) *1/2 $4 $8
- BULL SHEET (Fame 1008) *1/2 $4 $8
- NUTS TO YA (Fame 1009) *1/2 $4 $8
- DO IT MY WAY (Fame 1010) *1/2 $4 $8

Heap is not the comic, just the leader of the back-up band that twangs lazy guitar and drum rim shots behind cornball Ken Idaho. These tinnily recorded albums from Texas are loaded with sloppy monology and old jokes: "I came home unexpected and there was mah wife, posin' in the nude for a painter. A house painter! Another night ... I came in unexpected, I snuck in the bedroom, and there layin' across the chair was a man's suit and his umbrella, and in the middle of the bed there was mah wife with another man! I said, 'Honey, what're ya all doin'?' And she turned and said, 'See, I told ya he was stupid.'"

WOODY HENDERSON

- LIVE IN CONCERT (Righteous Records MLK 11529) *1/2 $4 $8

Henderson was once the opening act for Gladys Knight and the Pips, Teddy Pendergrass, and The O'Jays. Of note to Trekkie fans is his predictable black version of Star Trek, complete with "Mr. Spook." He announces, "Space! The final frontier! These are the voyagers of the Star Ship Eldorado! And its five-year mission: to seek out brave new worlds! To boldly go where no nigger has gone before! Star date: 36-26-36!"

HENDRA AND ULLETT

- THE ART OF HENDRA AND ULLETT (London PS 372/LL 3372) * $10 $20

Blonde, slightly chubby Tony Hendra and dark-haired straight man Nick Ullett were seen often on *The Ed Sullivan Show*. American audiences especially loved the bit where the Englishmen played Americans and Hendra did a sketch as a typical Brooklyn baseball player. That baseball routine isn't on this album, though. Instead, the album, recorded in England, offers excruciatingly belabored routines, like the reading of a train timetable. Even Monty Python failed when they tried to satirize pretentious drones and inane dullards by becoming them.

There are terrible rock song parodies, like the classic English poem "To the Daffodils" sung with a rock beat. Another has "To Be or Not to Be" shouted as a Beatles song: "'Tis a consummation devoutly to be wished ... To Die - Yeah yeah yeah! To Sleep - Yeah Yeah Yeah." Most dialect bits (a Scottish "Folk Song") and the LP's British topical humor will be totally lost to American ears.

Oddity: The album notes are by Jackie Mason. Hendra went on to contribute some excellent material to the early National Lampoon albums. Ullett turned up with an autobiographical one-man show off-Broadway in 1994. A combination of rarity, Hendra's name, and the cult for British comedy in general pushes the price up on this disappointment.

MEL HENKE

- LA DOLCE HENKE (Warner Bros. W 1472) * $7 $15

Here's a relic from the golden era of "hi-fi," an attempt to blend cool comic dialogue with jazz, a la a hit of the day, "Kookie, Kookie, Lend Me Your Comb."

Henke's 1962 LP probably provoked a smirk from some goateed hepcat way back when. On "It's So Nice to Have a Man around the House" and "Baby It's Cold Outside," a sexy female vocalist giggles and groans through the lyrics with a wolf whistle or blast of bongo drums accentuating the fantasy of gyrating hips. "Farmer John" tries to ape Stan Freberg's "John and Marsha." To a jazz arrangement of "Turkey in the Straw" a woman mewls "John! John!" two dozen times, interrupted by pig grunts and other barnyard sounds.

There's '50s jazz behind "The Lively Ones," Herschel Bernardi's double entendre narrative about his car/girl: "Man, what a body. Dig those crazy bumpers. And that rear end suspension. Wow. What a power plant. Just right for a drag strip. Like, let's see how it feels." Nostalgic beatniks and those with an affection or affectation for the era dig this as camp cult cool (hence the inflated collector's price), but it resembles the worst of Stan Freberg, Irving Taylor, and Creed Taylor. Musician Henke wastes the vocal talents of Bernardi, Gloria Wood, and Mel Blanc.

BERT HENRY

- SHOCKING HUMOR (Fax 1012) ** $6 $10
- UNCENSORED HUMOR (Fax 3001) ** $6 $10
- POSITION IS EVERYTHING (Fax 3002) ** $6 $10
- IN THE RAW (Rax 3003) ** $6 $10
- AT THE HUNGRY THIGH (Fax 3004) ** $6 $10
- HARD WAY (Fax 3005) ** $6 $10

Bert Henry didn't have the curmudgeonly style of Redd Foxx or the Brooklyn bombast of Pearl Williams. In California clubs in the early '60s, he just whizzed through his whiz-bang gags, adding little personality to the punch lines.

On "Shocking Humor," the album notes mention his "laugh riot" rape story. Here it is, with a woman telling her tale to a judge:

"He picked me up in the bar your honor, I don't deny it. We had a few drinks. He said, 'Let's take a ride.' We're driving along, he said, 'I got a bottle in the back seat, would you like another drink?' Judge, I always like another drink. He stopped the car, I climbed in the back seat to get the bottle. That's when it happened. He grabbed my right foot, put it in that strap on the right side, my left foot, put it in that strap on the left side." At that moment in the back of the courtroom a little old man stood up and said, "Woo, Judge, if you don't mind, I'd like to pay that young man's fine. I've been driving a car for thirty years, this is the first time I ever knew what those straps were for!"

Usually Henry tells quickies, as quickly as possible. On "In the Raw" the frisky comic shoots 'em out faster than Henny Youngman: "She was a backward nurse ... she put salt in the coffee, sugar in the soup ... last night they fired her. They'd told her to prick a guy's boil.... One lady went to a psychiatrist. He said, 'Lie down on the couch. I'll lie down with you.' Ten minutes later he jumped up and said, 'Well, that solves my problem, now what the hell's yours?' I'd like to be an obstetrician. Look at all the guys you have working for ya all the time."

Collectors may pay more for Henry's blue material on blue vinyl—an added feature of early Fax pressings of "Position Is Everything," "In the Raw," and "Uncensored Humor."

LENNY HENRY

- LENNY LIVE AND UNLEASHED (Island CID 9937) *1/2 $5 $10

Often described as England's Eddie Murphy, Henry seems more strongly influenced by Robin Williams. Like Williams, he's precociously prone toward making noises and sliding into dialects, usually as a substitute for solid jokes. For nearly a minute, he shouts "Cat Flaps!" over and over and then complains, "cats have the monopoly on flaps! I hate the way they come into your house through the cat flap, lookin' at you, as if to say: Ha ha! Where's your flap then? You are flapless!"

A costar with Tracey Ullman on the British comedy show *Three of a Kind*, he also has Ullman's coy flair for impersonating a variety of different dialects—in this case, various Rastas and other black immigrants to England. Little of his comical accents or recognition humor will be recognizable to American ears. This 1989 CD goes on for over seventy minutes. Early records, including a soundtrack from *Three of a Kind* and the solo "Stand Up Get Down," are available only via import.

PAT HENRY

- PAT HENRY (Sundi) $7 $15
- SMARTIES FOR PARTIES (Sundi) $7 $15
- LOOKIN' FOR A FREEWAY (Sundi) $7 $15

Henry was a popular open act with Sinatra and others in the '50s and '60s, though he's not well remembered today. The price reflects less on Henry than on the collectability of a small pressing on a small label.

PEE-WEE HERMAN

- BIG ADVENTURE (Warner Bros. 204050 Y) ** $10 $25
- PEE-WEE HERMAN SHOW (Fatima) ** $10 $25

Pee-Wee's "scandal" of being caught in an adult movie theater may have ended his long-running kiddie-camp TV show, but it only jacked up the price on the existing merchandise, including these two picture discs.

TITO HERNANDEZ

- THE LAST FAMILY (Gema LPG 1179) *1/2 $4 $8

Recorded in Miami, this attempt at cashing in on Vaughn Meader's "The First Family" takes a look at "The Last Family," Fidel Castro's. It contains typical corny gags as an interviewer wonders about Castro's military might:

"I understand that you have commercial relations with Czechoslovakia and they send you many men."

"Yes. They send me Czechs, but they don't send me cash."

"What is your opinion about the United States?"

"Well ... it is unfair that Mr. Kennedy has so much hair, and Mr. Khrushchev has no hair at all!"

HARRY HERSHFIELD

- STORIES THAT MADE THE PRESIDENTS LAUGH (Jubilee JGM 2041) *** $8 $15

Hershfield issued dialect 78s, was a regular on radio's *Can You Top This*, and here, circa 1962, in his old raconteur mode, offers classic stories, the kind he told to Roosevelt, Truman, and Eisenhower. He sounds like he's at the dais reading from notes:

"Many of the office seekers have used this one, about the old guy dying after living a pretty careless life. Just about to breathe his last, he started to ask for forgiveness, and enumerated his many sins. 'I was a drinker, a loafer, a wife beater, a crook, and an all-around no good bum.' With that a friend leaned over and cried to him, 'Are you now ready to renounce the devil?' He said, 'Listen, this ain't no time to antagonize anybody!'"

It's a bygone style of joke telling, but many of the stories are human nature classics that should still garner a chuckle. Hershfield is also on "Old Time Radio" (Columbia 2P2m5287). Radiola (MR 1052) has an album that offers an episode from Hershfield's *Can You Top This* on one side, matched with "It Pays to Be Ignorant" on the other.

BILL HICKS

- DANGEROUS (Invasion 35001) **1/2 $8
- RELENTLESS (Invasion 35003) **1/2 $8

Bill could've inspired a headline in *Variety*: "Stix Nix Sick Hicks." The Southern comic's forte was strong social and political comedy. The liner notes on the first CD reprint an outraged review that complains about his pro-smoking, pro-abortion, pro-drugs, pro-porn routines. On the first album, he's opinionated about most everything, including the rock stars of the day: "George Michael is a big girl. If you ladies like him, you're dykes." On drugs and rock: "If drugs are so bad, how come Keith Richards outlived Jim Fixx?" From here he proceeds into a fantasy of oral sex between Debbie Gibson and Tiffany, and then Debbie's rape by Jimi Hendrix.

While many shock comics tend toward self-indulgence, Hicks didn't substitute attitude for solid lines. Behind the shock there was often motivating thought. His shock joke on flag burning: "People snapped over this! They were, 'Hey Buddy, lemme tell ya something, mah Daddy died for that flag.' Really? I BOUGHT mine." Then the point: "No one, and I repeat, no one has ever died for a flag. A flag is a piece of cloth. They might've died for freedom, which, by the way, is the freedom also to burn the frickin' flag, ok?"

It's more the same on the second disc, released in 1992: "Supreme Court says pornography is any act that has no artistic merit and causes sexual thought. That's their definition essentially. No artistic merit, causes sexual thought. Hmm. Sounds like every commercial on television, doesn't it? Ya know, when I see those two twins on the Doublemint commercial, I'm not thinking of gum. I'm thinking of chewing. Maybe that's the connection. You've all seen that Busch beer commercial. The girl in the short hot pants opens the beer bottle on her belt buckle, leaves it there and it foams over her hand and over the bottle. And the voiceover says, 'Get yourself a buuuuusssshhh!'"

In an iconoclastic Hicks set, few audience members will be in total agreement with his views, delivered with sharply satiric sarcasm one minute, blunt rage the next. Hicks had only a few *David Letterman* appearances and an HBO special under his belt at the time of his tragically early demise; interest in him had not gotten much beyond a cult following and the admiration of his peers.

NONC HILAIRE

- FOR KOONASSES ONLY VOLUME 1 (Swallow LP 7001) ** $4 $8
- FOR KOONASSES ONLY VOLUME 2 (Swallow LP 7002) ** $4 $8

Though Nonc is not one of the major Cajun comedians, there's enough interest in that brand of humor to make virtually any dialect album worth a few bucks.

BENNY HILL

- WORDS AND MUSIC (Capitol SN 12049, originally released in England
  as THIS IS BENNY HILL) *** $6 $15
- BENNY HILL ... THE BEST OF (Continuum 19206-2) **1/2 $10

British comedian Benny Hill harked back to the days of vaudeville: saucy jokes and broad comedy sketches. Like Red Skelton, Benny revitalized old jokes with an enthusiastic delivery. The Capitol album has a few spoken sketches, but is mostly songs. Benny's technique: take a bunch of jokes in a particular category, and make them rhyme.

Among the best is "Broken-Hearted Lovers' Stew," filled with puns about food: "There are nine carrots to remind me of the ring I bought for you. Some mint for all the crazy things we mint to do. A lettuce 'cause your mom and dad would not lettuce alone. I won't put in the truffles, you've got truffles of your own...."

Other cuts here include routines ("Tour Guide," "Ted"), "The Beach at San Tropez," "The Dustbins of Your Mind," and a song that offers some great advice in times of trouble: "Put your finger in your ear and go 'Ting-a-Ling-A-Loo.'"

The album was reissued in England on CD as "Ernie" (EMI 7997332) and has become a popular import item.

After his TV show was dropped for its politically incorrect cheesecake 'n' comedy, Benny dropped into Abbey Road Studios (evidently around 1991) to record the Continuum CD. The cover photo features Benny crossing that famous road. There's a mix here of old and new songs, but if Benny had lived to see it released in America, it's doubtful it would've been called "The Best of." Some of his best songs are missing.

As usual, he turns jokes into song lyrics, like this couplet from "Gypsy Dance": "Please don't blame my doggie, it's not his fault at all. Someone left a wet umbrella standing in the hall." And later in the same song: "I twirled her round the dance floor. She said 'I hate the way you're doing it.' I said 'Why?' She said, 'I've got a wooden leg and you're unscrewing it.'"

Other cuts include "Ernie," "Bianca," "Down on the Farm," "Unlucky Luke," "Pepy's Diary," "Cafe Ole," and "Older Woman."

NOTES: Fans hunt up old British imports like "Golden Hour of Benny Hill" (Golden Hour Records) loaded with songs (including "Gypsy Rock," "Harvest of Love," and "The Egg Marketing Board Tango"). Decca's "The World of Benny Hill" (also known as "Benny at the BBC") features routines from his late '60s series *Benny Hill Time* including "The Holiday King," "The Jolly Robbers," and "The Sunday Ben."

WILLIAM HIRSCH AND MAURINE DAWSON

- THE FAMILY IN THE WHITE HOUSE (Kent KLP 3010) *1/2 $6 $15

No doubt some confused fans picked up this quickly done disc instead of the one the nation was really laughing about: "The First Family." This version copies the formula exactly. There are drawn out sketches where the listener waits several minutes for the limp punch line. There is also a press conference for predictable yocks. William Hirsch puts on an Every-Bostonian's accent and Maurine Dawson's drawn out, breathy Jackie sounds (ironically enough) more like an ill Marilyn Monroe.

Every now and then there's a cute line. At one point a crowd gathers and reporters wait expectantly for JFK to give his address to the nation. The president steps forward and the crowd hushes: "My address is, uh, 1600 Pennsylvania Avenue."

While most stores put cheap price tags on dated political comedy records, collector shops often jack up the price instead, figuring that between JFK collectors and hardcore comedy buffs, somebody'll pay big for a small print knock-off of "The First Family."

GERARD HOFFNUNG

- HOFFNUNG MUSIC FESTIVAL (Angel 35500) ** $10 $20

A cartoonist, radio raconteur, and musical eccentric, Hoffnung (1925-1959) left behind a variety of books and records for his special cult. *Time* was impressed with his comic orchestrations: "The result is spectacular, a sort of highbrow Spike Jones."

At this, the first recorded concert, November 13, 1956, General Manager T. E. Bean of the Royal Festival Hall announces: "Ladies and Gentlemen, owing to circumstances over which the management of the Hall have no control, tonight's program will be given exactly as advertised." What follows are orchestral arrangements that slide in and out of key and sometimes interweave popular songs like "Pop Goes the Weasel." Various musical soloists grab their instruments and perpetrate eccentricities—tooting out weird or wavery noises. While Spike Jones, Peter Schickele (P. D. Q. Bach) and Victor Borge are more appreciated for this type of thing, the genteel and mildly scampish Hoffnung was one of the originals.

- INTERPLANETARY MUSIC FESTIVAL (Angel 35800) ** $10 $20
- THE HOFFNUNG ASTRONAUTICAL MUSICAL FESTIVAL (Angel 35828)** $5 $10
- THE HOFFNUNG FESTIVAL OF MUSIC (London 425 401-2) ** $15
- BEST OF HOFFNUNG (Angel S 37028) ** $7 $15

Recorded in November of 1958, "Interplanetary" offers Hoffnung nonsense in stereo. A highlight is "The Love of Three Oranges" played with what sound like fifes, toy flutes, and tom toms.

The passing of Hoffnung in 1959 did not end the music festivals. His widow declared of the 1961 "Astronautical" concert that it had "the very spirit and vitality of Gerard Hoffnung," and fans might agree hearing "Leonara No. 4," "Horrortorio," and "Mobile for Seven Orchestras."

The Hoffnung-less "Festival of Music" is a double CD set. Recorded in 1988 in crisply appalling digital stereo, it features British comic Bill Oddie and Donald Swann, of Flanders and Swann, on "Haydn's Surprise Symphony" and "A Grand, Grand Overture." Cuts include "The Cougher," "Leonora Overture No. 4," "Metamorphosis on a Bed-time Theme," "The Heaving Bagpipe," and "Disconcerto for Piano and Orchestra." The brilliant sonics help invigorate the coy proceedings and may even be preferable to the actual "Best of Hoffnung" album, which features "Mobile for Seven Orchestras," "Surprise Symphony," "Metamorphosis on a Bed-time Theme," "Barber of Darmstadt," and "Hosepipe and Strings."

- THE IMPORTANCE OF BEING HOFFNUNG (ABC/Westminster WBBC 8002) ** $10 $20
- HOFFNUNG AT THE OXFORD UNION (London 5606) ** $10 $20

Hoffnung was a low key, whimsical favorite on radio. The mumbling, rambling eccentric has straight man Charles Richardson prodding him:

"Mr. Hoffnung, the other day I was on top of a bus and I saw you walking along the street. You didn't see me." "Oh yes. I saw you ... I was on top of a bus." "No, no, you were walking on the street...." "Was I?" "You had on the end of a string a peculiar looking animal...." "Ohh, yes, I remember ... that was a dog. Wasn't mine. It was a friend's. I don't like dogs. I have some, ummm, horrible attraction for them and they never leave me alone." "Are you sure it was a dog? It was a very odd looking dog." "Oh yes, it's an odd dog, that. Belongs to a friend ... I've never had a dog of my own ... I had a lovely pussy you know.... A most interesting cat ... he died ... we had another puss. Well, it's actually an octopus." "Oh, oh now I think you're just joking." "I give you my word. He didn't start off as an octopus. He started off as a duopus. Two tentacles. Then later they become a triopus, quinto, sixto, and then finally an octopus. It takes them about eight years." "Does he sit at table too?" "No, no, that would be ridiculous."

The "Oxford Union" album (recorded live December 4, 1958) is a long monologue. The audience is roaring over every eccentric professorial mumble: "I was actually born when I was two (blast of laughter), and I was alone then (blast of laughter). They didn't know ... I was ... I was called Gerard Hoffnung, I was called Gerard after a cousin, uh, and I was called Hoffnung after Gerard (blast of laughter, applause). Then, my dears, (laughter), you're not writing this down are you?" (Another blast of laughter, applause.)

NOTES: Fans might hunt up British Hoffnung albums including two BBC discs, "Timeless Hoffnung" and "Short Items from BBC Archives." Hoffnung's appeal has narrowed. Older classical music fans pay for mint condition discs, but some import CDs are now available.

CHA CHA HOGAN

- BROTHER EATMORE AND SISTER FULLBOSOM (Laff 147) ** $4 $10

Hogan billed himself as "the black foxx," as if he was dirtier or blacker than Redd Foxx. The title cut is a noisily acted-out routine in which he recalls the antics of a reverend and his most devoted follower, Sister Fullbosom. He plays both parts. This attempt at funky ethnic characterization proves that Hogan is no Flip Wilson, either.

Most of the album is typically crude and rude, a la most minor Laff stand-ups.

HAL HOLBROOK

- MARK TWAIN TONIGHT! (Columbia OS 2019) *** $6 $15
- MORE OF MARK TWAIN TONIGHT (Columbia OL 5610/OS 2030) ***1/2 $6 $15
- MARK TWAIN TONIGHT (Columbia OL 6680/OS 3080) **** $6 $15

Actor Hal Holbrook and his wife began to tour high schools and Kiwanis clubs in 1948 presenting dialogues from Shakespeare and a bit where Mark Twain meets a newspaper interviewer. The duo even managed to get laughs when they played a Veteran's Hospital in Chillicothe, Ohio, working the suicide ward.

Holbrook eventually pieced together enough material for a one-man show, premiering it in 1954 and polishing it through the years, ultimately bringing it to Broadway in 1959, then TV for specials.

This first installment of Twain's wit is a bit more literary than the other records. Half of Side Two is a reading from *Huckleberry Finn.* Twain is presented as a crotchety old cuss ("I was born modest but it wore off") and he's most amusing when talking about smoking and drinking in a way that W. C. Fields must have admired: "... and to prove that I'm not a slave to the habit, I can give it up whenever I want to. I've done it a thousand times. First time I gave it up was when I was a boy. Ten or eleven ... I got scared and gave it up one day. For two or three hours."

"More of" includes some bracing Twain sick comedy: "I once interviewed the King of the Sandwich Islands. He said, 'We understand Christianity. We have eaten the missionaries.'" Later there's a Fieldsian report about a dentist's patient whose entire skeleton is pulled out along with the tooth ("they had to send him home in a pillow case") and an uncle who, on July 4th, opened his mouth "and a rocket went right down his throat. Before he could ask for a drink of water to quench the thing, it blew up and scattered him all over. Well, you know a man can't have an experience like that and be entirely cheerful the rest of his life."

Columbia 6680 is the TV version of "Mark Twain Tonight." Holbrook had added a lot more warmth and eccentricity to his portrayal by the time it reached video, including quirks of delivery (a throat-clearing hum every now and then) and a tendency to break his train of thought for seemingly ad-libbed observations. The lively talk includes a lampoon of religion: "Oh compassionate missionary! Leave China and come home and convert these Christians. Oh what a hell of a heaven it's going to be when all those hypocrites assemble there." There's a roar of approval when Mark Twain describes the Senate as "that grand old benevolent asylum for the helpless."

A highlight is another helping of Twain's pioneering sick humor. It's a story about a woman who kindly donates her glass eye to a friend. But, "it was a Number 7. And she was excavated for a 14. That eye wouldn't lay still, don't ya know. Every time she winked it would roll over. Oh, it was a beautiful eye ... painted a lovely pale blue ... didn't match the other eye, which was one of those browny-yellow eyes...."

BILLY HOLIDAY

- BILL HOLIDAY FIGHTS MENTAL HEALTH (Marca 555) ** $4 $8
- CRAZY COUNTRY COMIC (Epic KE 33421) ** $4 $8

A Louisiana-born comic, Holiday offers an easygoing act that follows Will Rogers's laid-back style. The Epic album is easier to find, released in 1975 and recorded at a Charlie Rich concert (Holiday was Rich's opening act for years). Typical observations:"Most people expect comedians nowadays to come out and do political material. I don't do political jokes. I've found lately those jokes been gettin' elected. It was old Colonel Sanders who ruined George McGovern. That's right, when he brought out that McGovern bucket, full of left wings and rear ends! I heard about President Ford talkin' about that five percent income tax raise we're gonna get ... he said they're gonna raise our income tax to keep us from buyin' things we don't need. Things like food and clothes. Lot of people believe Ford and Nixon made a deal. I don't believe that. I believe Ford gave Nixon a pardon out of the goodness of his heart. That's what I believe. I also believe in Santa Claus, the Lone Ranger ..."

Holiday worked mainly in local Southern clubs like the Minacapelli Dinner Theater in Slidell, Louisiana. He died in Slidell of a heart attack on November 13, 1984. He was forty-nine and had a wife and five children.

ROSCOE HOLLAND

- BEYOND THE REEF (Rand LPM 4731) *1/2 $5 $10
- FOR A PIECE (Dooto DTL 812) ** $5 $10

Holland played bass for various bands before soloing as a piano player specializing in bawdy songs. For some reason, the black entertainer found a warm welcome in Alaska and spent ten years there. In the early '60s he began appearing in California clubs, recording his first album live at the Kona Lanes Outrigger Room in Costa Mesa, California.

Holland offers rambling introductions to the songs, then socks out the tunes in a voice better suited to "Stagger Lee" than silly risqué novelties. "Pennies from Heaven" becomes "Bennie's from Heaven." Roscoe can't believe his son is really his: "Everytime I would ask her, she would say: Bennie's from heaven ... I took a look at Bennie, and it's plain, plain to see. That Bennie must be from heaven, because he's not from me!"

A Russian folk song called "Psonia" gives Roscoe the chance to sing: "P-sonia! P-Psonia! Don't you let them P-sonia! Don't let them P-sonia!" Even less appealing are boogie woogie nonsense songs like "Norman" and "Itsy Bitsy Girl."

It's easier to find the tinny studio album from Dooto. His belting delivery style is overkill for mild corn like "Yo Yo" and "Stick Out Your Can." His black dialect mildly helps the silly double entendre tune "Down on the Farm." He sings: "Down on the farm, they all ask for you. Down on the farm, they all ask for you. Chicken as', dog as', cat as', pigeon as', down on the farm, they all as' for you ... Spotted dog as', milk cow as', old gray mule as', plain ol' jackass, down at the barnyard, they all as' for you." Another novelty is "Foul Mule Train." Holland slips some raspberries in between the boogie woogie piano to give an idea how foul the mule train is: "cut it out, mules, watch out, you gettin' it all in mah face, watch out, plug it!" The songs "Psonia," "Stick Out Your Can," and "Bennie's from Heaven" are on both albums.

STANLEY HOLLOWAY

• HIS FAMOUS ADVENTURES WITH OLD SAM AND THE RAMSBOTTOMS (Angel 65019) ** $5 $10

Grand English character actor Stanley Holloway had a long career in the theater and in films, culminating with his role as Alfred Dolittle in *My Fair Lady*. But back in the '30s he was known as a singer and comedian in revues, and made many 78s consisting of monologues about such favorite characters as Sam Small (a Lancashireman perhaps a bit too Lancashire for American audiences to understand and appreciate) and little Albert Ramsbottom, who, in the most popular Holloway tale, is eaten by a lion a la something out of Hillaire Belloc: "Pa, who had seen the occurrence, and didn't know what to do next, said, 'Mother, yon lion's et Albert.' And Mother said, 'Eeeh, I am vexed....' The manager had to be sent for. He came and he said, 'What's to do?' Pa said, 'Yon lion's et Albert. And 'im in his Sunday clothes, too....' The manager wanted no trouble. He took out his purse right away. Saying, 'How much to settle the matter?' Pa says, 'What do you usually pay?' At that Mother got proper blazing. 'And thank you sir kindly,' said she. 'Wasting our lives raising children to feed ruddy lions? Not me!'"

These rhymed tales, with a pianist gently accentuating the lines, are gentle and amusing, though a few are slightly ghoulish. Holloway sings a song about Anne Boleyn, who haunts the Tower of London "with her head tooked oonder neath her arm." She rushes up to Henry XIII holding "her head up with a wild whoop. And Henry cries, 'Don't drop it in the soup!'"

NOTES: Holloway made many records. A charming set of British Music Hall songs for Vanguard ("Join in the Chorus") features several evocative novelties, including "Wot Cher!" and "The Galloping Major." Another set for Columbia ("Ere's 'Olloway") has more humor cuts, a highlight being the strange black humor piece "My Word! You Do Look Queer" as well as a Harry Champion medley and "I'm Shy, Mary Ellen, I'm Shy." Stanley Holloway's "Concert Party" (Riverside) is an uneven collection of mild songs and recitations including "Albert's Reunion," another verse about Albert and the lion. It seems that both Albert and the lion have missed each other! Holloway is on the original soundtrack and cast albums for "Hamlet" (RCA) and "My Fair Lady" (Columbia). His poem about Albert turns up on Riverside's compilation album "How to Be Terribly Terribly Funny." Several British albums are favorites of his fans, notably "More Monologues and Songs" and "The Original Stanley Holloway" (from EMI) and "The World of Stanley Holloway" (Argo). There are British CDs on Holloway, including "The Great Monologues" (Past CD 7021) from Flapper/Pavilion Records, which preserves (with a bit of scratch and hiss) seventeen of his old 78s.

RONNIE HOLLYMAN

• SHHH! THE QUIET MAN (King 713) ** $7 $15

English balladeer Ronnie covers a variety of classic comic tunes and folk songs. He strums his ukelele as he recites his version of "Albert and the Lion," sings "Foggy Foggy Dew," and offers up a then-new selection called "Be Prepared." None of them rival the better-known versions by Stanley Holloway, Oscar Brand, or Tom Lehrer. At least, living up to his billing, he performs without guile or much ego. The album is rare, which might intrigue die-hard collectors, but Hollyman's blandness justifies his obscurity.

HOLT AND JONAH

• ON THE BRINK (Atlantic 8051) *** $10 $20

Holt and Jonah were colleagues of both Nichols and May, and Stiller and Meara. It shows on various cuts on this 1961 album. They have Mike and Elaine's intellectuality, including this understated bit of topical satire: "Do you think that Richard M. Nixon is his real name?" "Is Richard M. Nixon whose real name?"

They aren't afraid to give their Hungry i audience something sophisticated—"The Rise and Fall of the City of Movieville," a ten-minute pseudo Kurt Weill mini-musical about Hollywood. It's loaded with nasty two-liners in song. A vicious Hollywood big shot reports, "I never wanted to be a movie mogul. All I wanted from this business was an occasional showgirl." Discovering a fallen angel, he quickly corrupts her: "I taught you how to make your habits pay ... and made you what you are today."

Like Stiller and Meara, they could favor more human and earthy material. Their best sketch in that genre is "Bertha in the Rectory," with Holt an uptight pastor, Dolly the brash chorine urging him to make the church choir more commercial: "Ya gotta sing it out so they get ya right in the last pew!" The pastor is momentarily stunned: "We're not ... Baptists." But before long, Dolly is gurgling with lusty laughter as she successfully invites the man of the cloth to an informal meeting, promising "we could have the wildest Unitarian church in the state!"

Holt, author of "Lemon Tree" (included on the album), told me he was glad to have that song become a Trini Lopez hit so he could devote himself to writing for the stage. "For me, having to perform the same thing over and over again was painful." He received an Obie for "The Me Nobody Knows."

HOMER AND JETHRO

• HOMER AND JETHRO (also issued as THEY SURE ARE CORNY, King 639)	$7	$15
• CORNIER THAN CORN (King 848)	$7	$15
• MUSICAL MADNESS (Audio Lab 1513)	$7	$15
• HOMER AND JETHRO FRACTURE FRANK LOESSER (LPM 1312) **1/2	$10	$20
• BAREFOOT BALLADS (RCA Victor LPM 1412) **	$7	$15
• WORST OF HOMER AND JETHRO (RCA Victor LPM 1560) **1/2	$7	$15
• LIFE CAN BE MISERABLE (RCA Victor LPM 1880) **	$7	$15
• AT THE COUNTRY CLUB (RCA Victor LPM 2181) ***	$6	$12
• SONGS MY MOTHER NEVER SANG (RCA Victor LPM 2286) **1/2	$6	$12
• AT THE CONVENTION (RCA Victor LPM 2492) **1/2	$6	$12

Homer Haynes and Jethro Burns were often billed as "The Thinking Man's Hillbillies." They not only offered well-etched and thoroughly "tetched" parodies of country and pop tunes, but performed them with pleasing harmonies. Their tasty arrangements often had less country corn than the fiddle-playing, guitar-twanging, dobro-weeping tunes of "straight" contemporaries.

They began achieving fame in the '50s, ending the decade by winning a 1959 Grammy for their Johnny Horton parody single "The Battle of Kookamonga." Through the '60s, when country comedy was popular and shows like *The Beverly Hillbillies* were in the Top Ten, Homer and Jethro issued countless albums (eight in 1966-67).

The boys' early albums are as polished as any, though the duo's tendency to shoot out so many discs means that each has several clinkers. Their Frank Loesser "tribute" dates from 1954 and includes "Baby, It's Cold Outside," featuring June Carter doing a Judy Canova-style cornball vocal. In 1958 they issued an early "best of" that included some of their obscure singles like the immortal "Pal-Yat-Chee," cut with Spike Jones. The duo's crude country side comes out on "How Much Is that Doggie in the Window." Now it's "How much is that hound dog in the winder, with the basketball nose on his face. You know what a basketball nose is. It dribbles all over the place.... I'll give you two bits for that hound dog. The one with the sad achin' heart. He looks so much like my girlfriend, I can't hardly tell 'em apart."

Though expensive because they are early discs, "Barefoot Ballads" isn't prime Homer and Jethro; a lot of the material features '40s hillbilly standards and well-known folk songs ("Cigareetes, Whusky and Wild, Wild Women," "[I Won't Go Hunting with You Jake But] I'll Go Chasin' Women," "The Frozen Logger"). "Life Can Be Miserable" is a 1959 low-key collection of atypical tunes about losers. "There's an empty hanger in my closet tonight," they warble on the tune of the same name, "since you took the shirt off my back."

"At the Country Club," from 1960, is an excellent live album demonstrating that Homer and Jethro were sort of the Stone Age Smothers Brothers (there's a bit of feuding over who gets to solo and who is going to start singing). There are even a few mild audience put-ons: "Why don't you stand up," Homer asks one ringsider, "Maybe somebody'll recognize ya and take ya home." Also included: live arrangements of some of their classics, from "Battle of Kookamonga" to "Let Me Go, Blubber" ("You're too fat in the first place, you know it's true. You're too fat in the second place too.") And who can forget their rendition of the ballad "Fascination?" The chubby heroine "had nine buttons on her nightgown, but she could only fascinate."

• ZANY SONGS OF THE 30s (RCA Victor LSP 2455) **	$10	$20
• PLAYING STRAIGHT (RCA Victor LPM/LSP 2459)	$5	$10
• GO WEST (RCA Victor LPM/LSP 2674) **	$10	$20
• OOH, THAT'S CORNY! (RCA Victor LPM/LSP 2743) **	$10	$20
• CORNFUCIUS SAY (RCA Victor LSP 2928) **1/2	$7	$15
• TENDERLY (RCA Victor LSP 3357)	$5	$10
• THE OLD CRUSTY MINSTRELS (RCA Victor LPM LSP 3462) ***	$10	$20
• WANTED FOR MURDER (RCA Victor LPM LSP 3673) **1/2	$7	$15
• NASHVILLE CATS (RCA Victor LPM LSP 3822) **1/2	$10	$20
• ANY NEWS FROM NASHVILLE? (RCA Victor LPM LSP 3538) **	$10	$20
• IT AIN'T NECESSARILY SQUARE (RCA Victor LSP 3701) **1/2	$7	$15
• NASHVILLE CATS (RCA Victor LSP 3822) **1/2	$7	$15
• DON'T BE CORNFUSED (Guest Star G 1428) **	$6	$12
• SONGS TO TICKLE YOUR FUNNY BONE (RCA Camden CAL CAS 948) **1/2	$6	$12
• HOMER AND JETHRO STRIKE BACK (RCA Camden CAL 707) ***	$6	$12
• THE PLAYBOY SONG (RCA Camden CAS 2315) **	$6	$12
• HUMOROUS SIDE OF COUNTRY MUSIC (RCA Camden CAL 768) ***	$6	$12
• SOMETHIN' STUPID (RCA Victor LSP 3877) **	$7	$15
• THERE'S NOTHING LIKE AN OLD HIPPIE (RCA Victor LSP 3973) **	$7	$15

- COOL CRAZY CHRISTMAS (RCA Victor LSP 4001) ** $7 $15
- LIVE AT VANDERBILT U (Rca Victor LSP 4024) ** $7 $15
- HOMER AND JETHRO'S NEXT ALBUM (RCA Victor LSP 4148) ** $7 $15
- FAR OUT (RCA Victor 4648) ** $7 $15

Through the '60s the duo continued to knock out records almost as fast as record store cashiers could sell them, at least in the South and through Nashville. The quality varies. A few albums are straight, including "Tenderly" and the all-instrumental "Playing Straight," while "Zany Songs of the 30s" offers weary novelty tunes like "The Music Goes Round and Round," "Flat Foot Floogie," and "Three Little Fishes."

A typical hit-and-miss album would be "Go West." There's some subtlety in their parody of "El Paso," which includes one-liners and a somewhat obscure reference to a hit song of the day: "Out in the West Texas town of El Paso, I spent a whole week out there in one day. I looked all over for Rosa's cantina. I think Hernando had hid it away." But there's also their preoccupation with bodily functions ("Roll On, Deodorant, Roll On").

"The Old Crusty Minstrels" offers some excellent feeble-minded balladeering ("She broke my heart at Walgreen's, and I cried all the way to Sears") and, appropriate for the Johnson era, even some solid politcal satire ("The One on the Right Is on the Left," "Charlie Cheated on His Income Tax"). They deftly switch lyrics ("That Old Piano Roll Blues" becomes "That Old Potato Peel Booze") and still demonstrate their popular tendency to repulse with style. On their version of "Red Roses for a Blue Lady": "I want some dead roses for my old lady. Send them COD or PDQ. She's like a rose to me. They smell and so does she. If you ain't got a dozen, twelve will do." Several albums were made around 1963, the time the boys had a hit with their "Ooh, that's corny" TV ads for Kellogg's cornflakes. On the "Ooh, That's Corny" album, they use the tune from the commercial, but couldn't say "corny as Kellogg's cornflakes" as in the ad, so they sing "corny as it can get." And it is: "Hey, Homer, why do cows wear bells, just tell me if ya know." "Well, Jethro, the reason cows wear bells is 'cause their horns won't blow." Other cuts are pure country corn ("I've Got Tears in My Ears from Lying on My Back in Bed While I Cry Over You") and vintage vaudeville corn ("When Banana Skins Are Falling"). The formula continues on "Cornfucius Say." Jethro had a chance to shine, starring as "Cornfucius," while Homer asks some questions set to music. "Oh, great Cornfucius, how do you keep milk from turning sour? I wish you'd tell me how." "Well, the best way to keep milk from turning sour is to keep it in the cow!"

Most every Homer and Jethro album has a few clinkers, but the duo's later albums had less highs and more lows. "Cool Crazy Christmas," for example, coasts with feeble novelties ("I Saw Mommy Kissing Santa Claus") lightly spiked with goofy grimy humor: "I saw Mommy kissing Santa Claus under the Christmas tree last night. She puckered up her lips, pleasure she did seek. She missed his mouth and kissed his nose. And the durned thing sprung a leak."

The duo sound a bit tired on 1969's "Next Album." There's no snap or enthusiasm here. At their age it might have been unseemly to try "crossover" music or add a contemporary beat like Ray Stevens. Favoring originals over parodies, they suffer through weak cuts like "There Ain't a Chicken Safe in Tennessee"; a half-hearted ragtime number, "Pennsylvania Turnpike"; and the embarrassing "I Haven't the Foggiest" (Homer trying a Cockney accent). "The Girl from Ipanema" is "The Gal from Possum Holler" and becomes another formula piece for the boys to do country ugly jokes: "Short and pale and old and ugly, the gal from Possum Holler goes walkin' and when she passes, each guy she passes goes, 'Blaaaaah.' When she walks and you see her from the back, it looks like two pigs fightin' in a tater sack, and when she passes, each guy she passes goes, 'Aaaaaaaah'"

NOTES: In many areas, Southern comedy is of limited interest, but most everyone seems to appreciate Homer and Jethro. Discs with frantic Jack Davis covers, including "Go West," "Any News from Nashville?" "Old Crusty Minstrels," and "Life Can Be Miserable," are considered art lithos by comic book collectors. A few imports have surfaced, including "Homer and Jethro Assault the Rock and Roll Era," a compilation from Bear Records. RCA issued "The Best of Homer & Jethro" (RCA 61088) in 1992.

After Homer's death, Jethro Burns issued several solo albums devoted to his fast mandolin picking. The 1980 album "Jethro Burns Live" (Flying Fish FF-072) has a few breaks for Jethro to tell some anecdotal jokes.

HOOSIER HOT SHOTS

- HOOSIER HOT SHOTS (Sandy Hook SH 2086) ** $5 $10
- HOOSIER HOT SHOTS (Sunbeam MF 10) $5 $10
- WHA HOO (Golden Tone, reissued as COUNTRY KIDDIN, Spinorama M 162) ** $5 $10
- HOOSIER HOT SHOTS (Tops 1 1541) $5 $10
- RURAL RHYTHM 1935-1942 (Columbia Legacy CK 52735) **1/2 $8
- ARE YOU READY HEZZIE (Circle CD 905) **1/2 $8

Paul (Hezzie) Trietsch and his brother Ken (Rudy) Trietsch were the leaders of this popular cornball music act. Also featured were Otto Ward and Frank Kettering. They first attracted notice on the National Barn Dance radio show in the '30s and lasted more than twenty years. The Sandy Hook album offers radio appearances.

The Hoosier Hot Shots aren't exactly a laugh riot, tossing mild Spike Jones effects (some eccentric slide-whistling clarinet playing or misplaced percussion) into their "goodtime" songs. Their best known number is a variation on "Yes We Have No Bananas," the equally silly "I Like Bananas Because They Have No Bones." That's the refrain, the chorus, and the big joke of the song, done with sprightly barbershop harmony and bouncy woodwinds. It appears on Rhino Records' "Greatest Novelty Records of All Time: The 1940s," as well as the Golden Tone/Spinorama discs and the Columbia Legacy CD compilation.

Other cuts on the Golden Tone album include the instrumental "Hog Wash," a painful version of Elvis Presley's "Hound Dog" done with searing clarinet licks and wolf howls, and a Homer and Jethro-ish song about the loveless:

"If you never cared for the rippling of a brook and if you never never peeked at the ending of a book, better stick your head in a bucket of coal. There's no romance in your soul ... If you can sit in a park after it's dark with sweethearts everywhere, while they cuddle and coo, if that means nothing to you, you should be defrosted—you're a frigidaire." Most other numbers are instrumentals.

The Columbia CD offers nearly an hour of the Hoosiers, which is too long to take at one sitting. The bouncy, cartoonish music with plenty of slide whistles should keep the toes tapping. The lyrics will keep the head shaking. Unfortunately, they rarely measure up to the promise of their titles: "From the Indies to the Andies in His Undies," "The Coat and Pants Do All the Work," "The Girl Friend of the Whirling Dervish," "Connie's Got Connections in Connecticut," and "Moving Day in Jungletown." Circle's CD preserves 25 radio transcription discs.

BOB HOPE

- THE BOB HOPE RADIO SHOW (Radiola MR 1060) **1/2 $5 $10
- THE PALEFACE (Radiola MR 1153) *** $4 $8
- CROSBY AND HOPE (Radiola MR 1044) **1/2 $5 $10

Hope was already an established Broadway star and film personality when he had his own radio show. The Radiola hour has two complete shows (October 23, 1945, and December 18, 1945). There are typically peppery monologues and silly sketches with Frances Langford and Jerry Colonna. Francis spooning with Bob: "Oh Robert, won't it be wonderful when we're married ... you helping me with the dishes, helping me with the cooking, helping me with the laundry." "I'll say. I'll even help you deliver it." Later they meet house broker Jerry Colonna. Says Frances, "In a year or two we may have a couple of little Roberts." Jerry: "Well in that case I better show you a place with trees."

Two of Hope's films were adapted to radio and are on one Radiola disc—"The Paleface" (March 3, 1950) and "My Favorite Brunette" (October 13, 1947).

Bob Hope and Bing Crosby's comic rivalry not only included the famous "road" movies, but radio work as well. Radiola couples "The New Swan Show" (November 7, 1948) with "Philco Radio Time" (January 29, 1947). The latter includes Dorothy Lamour in a sketch called "The Road to Hollywood." It's lightweight stuff with Crosby flim-flamming Hope on a trip out West ("You'll take me?" Hope asks. Says Bing: "I'm gonna try ..."). In Chicago they meet sarong-wearing Lamour. Hope: "This thing has no shoulders. What holds it up? Public opinion?" They arrive in Hollywood, but Lamour isn't sure they can make their Road pictures: "We could never make good at Paramount," she pouts, "We don't know anybody on the inside." Hope: "We don't have to, with what you've got on the outside." Later the trio warbles fresh lyrics to "The Road to Morocco" tracing their careers of late ("The villain followed Dorothy till he became a pest. So now she's doing pictures where she's practically dressed ...") The "Swan" show is more typical of radio feuds: mostly insults. "I'm on for Swan soap this year," Bob says. "Yeah, too bad it's not something you use." "Hey, Lump Lap, you've got two chins, would you like to try for one?" "Let's face it, Nostril King, before I sang my song, this show was laying a swan egg...."

- BOB HOPE IN RUSSIA (Decca 74369) **1/2 $10 $20
- ON THE ROAD TO VIETNAM (Cadet 4046) **1/2 $7 $15
- BOB HOPE'S HOLIDAYS (Spear 4700) ** $7 $15
- AMERICA IS 200 YEARS OLD ... AND THERE'S STILL HOPE (Capitol ST 11538) *1/2 $5 $10

With his reliance on topical humor and constant exposure on TV, Hope rarely made stand-up albums. The rare Decca disc was released around 1962, probably as a companion to his book *I Owe Russia $1200*. The monologues are predictable but frisky: "I got a wonderful tribute at the airport. They fired twenty-one shots in the air in my honor. 'Course it would've been nicer if they'd waited for the plane to land. They were wonderful to me going through customs. It was the first time I was ever X-rayed free.... It's a thrill to be here in Russia. I know I'm in Russia, my stomach got up two hours before I did and had a bowl of borscht.... Surprisingly enough I'm not having any trouble with the language. Nobody speaks to me."

In the '60s Hope continued his practice of entertaining the troops. The Cadet album from 1964 has fourteen cuts, each introduced by a stern announcer describing where the tireless comedian recorded it (Vietnam, Thailand, or Korea). Hope gave comfort, via comedy, to the soldiers in desperate need of a morale boost. "Since I was here last there's been some great changes of living quarters," Hope tells the men. "This looks like all fresh mud." And a definition: "Okinawa is known as the pearl of the Orient. That's because after three months you're ready to string yourself up." His praise for the soldiers: "These men are perfectly at home at land or sea. They don't care whether they're swimming or walking, as long as it's toward a girl."

"Holidays" was released in 1973, featuring quick Hope monologues on ten holidays, from Easter to Father's Day. The gags aren't memorable. The quality of the sound and the choppiness of the editing suggests that the album was culled from various Hope TV specials over the years. For July 4th: "The Fourth of July I used to refer to as Independence Day before I got married ... once on July 4th the kids tied my brother to a six-foot sky rocket and set it off. That's how he got to California twenty years before I did. When my brother went to school he had a nickname. They used to call him Aloha Hope—he was always waving his hand and leaving the room. The school saved a lot of money on my brother though. Whenever he sat in the corner they didn't need a dunce cap for him. The teacher just painted his head white."

Hope's popularity wavered in the late '60s and early '70s, the result of his right-wing stance during the Vietnam War and a less than warm comic style that was turning into a cliché. Many of his insincere TV specials were nothing more than prolonged promotions for NBC's stars and shows. Here, in 1976, an album re-creates some of the misery of a typical workmanlike Bob Hope special of the day. Gag file one-liners are shuffled into scripts and put over without conviction. Fred Travalena, Demond Wilson, Jim Backus, Arte Johnson, and Phyllis Diller are in the cast, looking back at moments in American history, from Paul Revere's ride to Betsy Ross sewing the flag. Here's Hope battling with Betsy (Phyllis Diller) over the deadline for the flag. Diller speaks first:

"Abigail Adams tore her farthingale so I'm afraid you'll have to wait." "But we can't fight without a flag." "And Abigail can't court without her farthingale." "But we'll have nothing to wave." "Abigail will."

A typical setup and thudding punch line: "Why if it isn't Bob Hope, the minuteman." "Boy those guys in the barracks can't keep a secret."

NOTES: Hope was always proud of his straight singing, which is highlighted on "Bob Hope in Hollywood" (MCA 904). He can be heard on several soundtrack albums, including "I'll Take Sweden" (United Artists UAL 4121), "The Seven Little Foys" (RCA LPM 3275), and "The Road to Hong Kong" (Liberty 16002). Hope's monologue from a 1961 TV special, "25 Years of Life," opens a *Life* magazine-produced ten-incher of the same name, subtitled "Thanks for the Memory." Hope likes *Life:* "A pile of magazines, but boy are they stacked." He's also on "Bing Bob and Judy" (Totem LP 1009) and "Philco Radio Time" (Totem LP 1002). One of the more unusual items for collectors is "The Quick and the Dead" (RCA Victor LM 1129). It's "The Story of the Atom Bomb," with Helen Hayes as Lisa Meitner, Paul Lukas as Dr. Albert Einstein, and the voices of Harry Truman, Winston Churchill, and Franklin D. Roosevelt. Hope is serious as he introduces the program and doesn't even make a pun about nuclear "fission."

GERRY HOUSE

- CHEATERS TELETHON (MCA MCAD 42341) *1/2 $7
- BULL (MCAD 10585) *1/2 $7

Country DJ Gerry House offers one-minute and two-minute studio routines from his radio show on "Cheaters Telethon," and it's a near lethal combination of annoying DJ raps and country corn. Among the dumb parodies of radio commercials: "Lee's Press On Teeth! Fine high-quality disposable incisors, molars, and bicuspids that allow you to appear fresh, healthy and have a mouth full of white chompers on a moment's notice. Lee's Press On Teeth! Simply attach to anything you have passin' for teeth now ... you won't be havin' corn on the cob for dinner, but wouldn't you rather smile and look good than eat, anyway? Lee's Press On Teeth."

Some country fans might get a kick out of some of the recognition comedy: "What is a honky tonk? It's a place where even the best of friends can get together for a fist fight. There are three forms of entertainment in a honky tonk. You got your pinball, pool, and slow dancing. The first one costs a quarter, the second one costs fifty cents, and the third one once cost me a Chevrolet truck, a mobile home, and seventeen acres in Arkansas."

Housebroken tunes dominate "Bull," a 1992 release. Typical of the predictable tunes is "My Jeans Are Too Tight," with the musical complaint, "My jeans are too tight, I can't feel my feet. If I don't keep on dancin' my legs are gonna fall asleep. My tiny buns are better known than even Vanna White. I stand all day and night 'cause my jeans are too tight."

HOUSTON AND DORSEY

- AT THE CASTAWAY (Carellen 118) *1/2 $5 $10
- LAUGH PARTY (Carellen 118a) *1/2 $5 $10
- HOUSTON AND DORSEY GOOF IT UP (Carellen 124) ** $5 $10
- AT THE WORLD'S MOST FAMOUS BEACH (Carellen 133) *1/2 $5 $10
- OUT OF THIS WORLD (Carellen 145) *1/2 $5 $10

A corny duo who recorded most of their early '60s albums at various hotels in Daytona Beach, Florida, Sonny Houston and Barney Dorsey mixed straight music in with their comedy, so most of the discs tend to stop dead for their guitar-accompanied renditions of "Hava Nagila" or the era's novelty hits like "If You Wanna Be Happy for the Rest of Your Life (Never Make a Pretty Woman Your Wife)." In their bullfighting routine on their first album "At the Castaway," they're mildly racy, but completely dumb: "Boy he's a nice lookin' bull." "Yeah, big long black horns on that thing." "He's a horny one, isn't he! A horny bull in heat ..." "The matador, he's the one that really throws the bull. In Washington they call them Sen-ators."

"Back to History" on their "Goof It Up" albums has more cornball gags: "Brigham Young ... our great Mormon leader who said, 'I don't care how you bring 'em but bring 'em young! And often!' He met a lady about ninety-two-years old ... they struck up a conversation and it went something like this. 'Are you Brigham Young?' 'I am.' 'Are you the man who came to Salt Lake City with over forty wives?' 'I am....' 'Are you the one who slept with every one of them?' 'I am.' 'I think you should be hung!' 'I am.'"

Dorsey teamed with Jimmy Clark as The Nock-a-Bouts, evidently before he met up with Houston. Their lone album (see the entry under Nock-a-Bouts) duplicates some of the songs and routines available on these discs.

BRUCE HOWARD

- MY FRIEND (Stereoddities 1902) ** $7 $15

Allan Sherman's album notes are a bit off in describing this guy as a "hilariously funny performer." Howard is a competent writer though, who worked with Victor Borge and other TV stars of the '50s, and he's able to knock off some amusing Q&A material.

A concept album on the battle of the sexes, Howard and Dolores Quinton engage in quick sketches about "The Bostonian," "The Ad Man," "The Beatnik," and other men dealing with women.

As Adam dealing with Eve: "We're the first man and woman on earth." "Well which is which?" "To tell you the truth, I haven't given it much thought. I just got here myself ... well, I'll toss you for it. Heads you're the woman, tails

I'm the man." "Put me down!" "Tails! That makes me the man...." "... you're touching me!" "But I'm supposed to touch you, see? We're married." "Mister, I don't know you from Adam!"

TOM HOWARD

- IT PAYS TO BE IGNORANT (Radiola MR 1052) **1/2 $5 $10

Tom Howard was the host of "It Pays to Be Ignorant." Combining the impatience and mock-irritation of Fred Allen and George Burns, he presided over a panel that included George Shelton, hefty comedienne Lulu McConnell, and English comic Harry McNaughton. The questions Howard asked were the jumping off point for a barrage of corny gags and digression.

When they're not answering questions, Howard and the corny crew offer whiz-bang comments about themselves and their friends:

Lulu McConnell: "My old man had an accident. He was run over by a steamroller!"

"How did they get him into the house?"

"They just slipped him under the door."

George Shelton: "I got a letter from my Uncle Webfoot this morning. He's crossing a turkey with a centipede. He says next Christmas everyone will get a leg!"

Panelist Harry McNaughton offers a poem: "There was a young lady from Eton, whose figure had plenty of meat on. She said, 'Marry me Jack, and you'll find that my back is a nice place to warm your cold feet on!'"

Fans of old-fashioned joke book comedy will also appreciate the flip side, an episode of "Can You Top This" featuring the trio of Harry Hershfield, Senator Ed Ford, and Joe Laurie, Jr.

TRUSTIN HOWARD

- GROOVE WORLD (Horoscope HLP 990) *1/2 $7 $15

The head writer during Joey Bishop's losing talk show battle with Johnny Carson in the '60s, Trustin Howard figured he could tell his formula set pieces with just as much enthusiasm as Joey. A typical bit, "How Come," would've had audiences yawning if Bishop did it free on TV:

"How come if all the world loves a lover, so many lovers have to leave by fire escape? How come when you go to a party, the ugliest guy always has a chick who looks like Elke Sommer. How come at a nightclub the exotic dance team gets laughs, but the comic gets silence. How come at the beginning of the evening your date looks like Liz Taylor, but at dawn she looks like Minnie Pearl. How come at the race track when you're tapped out and the money's gone, the horses you were gonna play start to win. How come when you go out to dinner with friends the waitress always puts the check in front of you."

Of minor interest: four sketches with Regis Philbin (back then Bishop's announcer) as the straight man. Philbin's presence and the small label give this one some modest value.

WILLIE HOWARD

- COMEDY SONGS (Gala LP 104) **1/2 $20 $35
- VAUDEVILLE MONOLOGUES (Proscenium 23) $15 $30

A Broadway legend in the '30s and '40s, Howard issued several singles, which were gathered up on these very rare albums.

The ten-inch Gala album, originally a set of 78s, offers a wide range of Howard's comedy. The laughs in the two-part "French Taught in a Hurry" come mostly from Willie's artfully mangled French-Yiddish accent. A word like "facsimile" twists and turns thanks to his Franco-Brooklynese pronunciation. There are a few malaprops ("broad chasing" for "broadcasting") along the way.

As Prof. Pierre Ginsberg, he insists, "To get the greatest benefit from the lessons, you must secure one of my textbooks entitled *French in Ten Easy Lessons, or Five Hard Ones* ... with each book I also give you a recipe: How to clean a chicken so you wouldn't lose the pipick!"

"Comes the Revolution" presents what was Howard's most famous monologue. It doesn't survive too well, but fans of dialect comedy will still be amused. A garbled soap box orator is telling "the working classes to re-wolt! Re-wolt!" He shouts, "Today the Capitalists are sleeping in silks and satins. They're living in pentshouses ... riding around in limo-zeeness ... eating strawberries and cream. Extra heavy cream. But! Comes the revolution they'll be no silks and satins ... no strawberries and cream. Comes the revolution, *we'll* eat strawberries and cream!" A heckler shouts out that he doesn't like strawberries and cream. "Iz zat so? Too sweet, eh? Comes the revolution—you'll eat strawberries and cream!"

NOTES: The most easily accessible example of Willie Howard is a mild routine with his brother Eugene on the 1983 compilation album "A Night at the Palace" (Take Two Records TT 108). His Yiddish-French lesson single turns up on "Allan Sherman and Friends" (Jubilee 1059). Howard is also on "Radio Broadcast Follies of 1935" (Louver RADCO 3500), a bootleg disc hosted by Al Jolson and Wallace Beery. He's a lot of fun as he goes through a fast-paced vaudeville routine with Eddie Moran. There's room for dialect gags: "Love is pain." "Love is pain?" "Payin' for dis, payin' for dat." "Yes, but what would you do if you happened to lose your poor wife. If your poor wife died." "Eddie, I'd go crazy." "You'd get married again?" "That crazy I wouldn't be."

HUDSON AND JUDSON

- WHO'S ON FIRST (Cream CR 1008) ** $4 $8

Following his years with Ron Landry, Bob Hudson came up with new partner Dave Judson, and on this 1978 album he reprises some of his old characters, like gay football player Bruiser LaRue. He also rewrites old Abbott and Costello routines, which is either some kind of misplaced tribute or the gall of a cultureless California disc jockey (the credit on "Who's on First" reads "PD, adaptation by Bob Hudson").

The cocktail-soaked audience titters over "improved" lines like these: "Your left fielder's name?" "Why." "Why?" "Oh he's beautiful. Bunts one-handed." "How?" "No, Why! How is our right fielder!" "How is your right fielder? Beats me, but if he's on this team he's hurtin'." "Our center fielder's a girl, you know." "Oh, is that so?" "No, Sue." "Sue who?" "That's right, our first baseman's wife...."

Taking on definitive Abbott and Costello routines? Hudson and Judson's LP is strictly for curious comedy fans who have to hear it to believe it.

HUDSON AND LANDRY

- HANGING IN THERE (Dore 324) **1/2 $5 $10
- LOSING THEIR HEADS (Dore 326) ** $5 $10
- RIGHT OFF (Dore 329) ** $5 $10
- WEIRD KINGDOM (Dore 331) ** $6 $12
- BEST OF HUDSON AND LANDRY (Dore 333) ** $4 $8
- BEST OF HUDSON AND LANDRY 2 (Dore 334) ** $5 $10

In 1969, disc jockeys Ron Landry (the slim one with the dark hair) and Bob Hudson (the fat one with the white hair) blended slick ad-libs and slapdash sketches to give KGBS in Los Angeles the number one morning radio show. During this five-year run they made their albums on the small Dore label.

Hudson and Landry's albums usually featured macabre death wish covers (drawings of a hanging or a car going over a cliff, for example). The records themselves sound embalmed, recorded poorly at a local hangout, the Pomona National Golf and Country Club. The thundering laughter from the club regulars does not seem in proportion to the airy material.

"Hanging in There" has some of the duo's better bits, including "Top Forty D.J.'s" in which two disc jockeys meet on the street and blabber fast and furiously in their obnoxious radio styles: "In ten seconds or less, Cool Daddy, try and guess what happened to me just before you ambled across the street?" "Uhh, I'm drawin' a blank, Ronnie Baby, so better lay it on me!" "A wino stumbled up and hit on me for the price of a jug." (Together) "And the HITS JUST KEEP ON COMIN!"

Most of Hudson and Landry's other bits are loaded with familiar jokes. From "Losing Their Heads": "Married are ya? You're to be pitied young man. That's an ugly woman. You should send her to Canada." "Canada?" "That's moose country. She'll fit right in."

They also enjoy belaboring the obvious, as when Landry interviews gay football player Bruiser LaRue: "You rushed 253 yards, caught four touchdown passes and picked up three fumbles—" "And a sailor!" "A sailor?" "A seaman! Yo HO, blow the man down!" "Bruiser, what do you enjoy most about football?" "Piling on, Ace! Bodies, bodies everywhere!"

The team's "Best of" album really isn't, especially without the inclusion of "Top Forty D.J.'s." It does have their Grammy nominated 1971 cut "Ajax Liquor Store," which is nothing but a boringly bad drunk routine. A man calls up the liquor store and somehow, amid the pointless byplay, begins to wonder about their listing in the phone book: "You listed in the Yellow Pages?" "Yes, we are listed in the Yellow Pages." "How come you aren't listed under Taxidermy?" "It's impossible." "Oh well, I must have a couple of pages missing in my phone book."

The audience is laughing happily. The audience is drunk.

HUDSON AND PICKETT

- THE HOLLYWEIRD SQUARES (Dore 334) *1/2 $5 $10

Bobby "Boris" Pickett of "Monster Mash" fame is Bob Hudson's partner on this mishmash made worse by poor sound quality. A toothpick in the ear would be more entertaining. In the rambling throwaway sketches, Bobby doesn't sound much different from any of Hudson's other hapless partners, though he does tend to toss in a few celebrity impressions when given the chance.

Pickett gets to solo on "The Apprentice Vampire," a demented, but not necessarily pleasant, novelty that blends the tom-tom percussion line from "They're Coming to Take Me Away" with babbling snippets of Dwight Frye in "Dracula": "Oh please Martin please ... big fat juicy spiders, Martin!" Pickett uses Frye's Renfield grinding laugh for percussion too, as the bewildered audience giggles and guffaws.

Hudson, a big fan of lispy gay stereotype humor, does his solo on a slightly rewritten version of "Big Bad John," simpering: "Somebody said he came from New Orleans, where he got into a fight over a leather queen, and a scratch in the eye from a huge right hand sent a Louisiana fella to the promised land."

When the team works in unison, the results are doubly awful. The title cut is a lame and loud version of the quiz show, with Pickett doing obvious impressions of Broderick Crawford and Truman Capote. Typical question and answer: "Most businessmen prefer musk oil, mineral oil, or baby powder." "I'd have to say baby powder. Because most guys like to get back to the womb, ya know?"

MARTIN HUGHES

- MADAM CHAIRMAN (Roto P66-2020) ** $5 $10

Sometimes priced higher; collectors of drag comedy need to have even the obscure ones to complete the collection.

CHET HUNTLEY

- BEST OF WASHINGTON HUMOR (Cameo 1044) *1/2 $7 $15

The respected NBC newsman notes a question asked of Will Rogers: "Is the field of humor crowded?" "Only when Congress is in session." Then he introduces examples of politicians who use wit and humor deliberately.

Political figures of the early '60s are heard: Senator Thurston Morton of Kentucky, Congressman Charles E. Halleck from Indiana, Senator Barry Goldwater, Adlai Stevenson, Senator Ken Keating of New York, Mortimer Caplin of Internal Revenue, President Kennedy, and Peace Corps director Sargent Shriver.

The slight humor is in forced anecdotes (the kind most any dull speechgiver would use). Among the best of the feeble wisecracks is Senator Keating's quip: "The Democrats aren't so much a party, as a treaty of mutual nonaggression." Barry Goldwater draws applause for his self-deprecating remark about being ready for the White House since "Jacqueline (Kennedy) remodeled it in an eighteenth century decor." He calls himself a conservative because there are two things that need conserving in the country: "Gold and water." Not exactly a knee slapper, but at the time, any sense of humor from a politician deserved to be encouraged. This one from Barry is still timely: "I don't apologize for being a conservative. I remember when conservative and mother were clean words."

Adlai Stevenson slips in one of the better lines, recalling the words of Joseph Pulitzer. He tells the gathered assembly, "Accuracy is to a newspaper what virtue is to a lady." Then he adds, "Except a newspaper can always print a retraction."

THE IDIOTS AND COMPANY

- IN OUR OWN IMAGE (Riverside RLP 9843/RLP 843) **1/2 $8 $20

The Idiots were Sascha Burland, a writer of commercial jingles (and creater of "The Nutty Squirrels") and Mason Adams, a radio veteran ("Pepper Young's Family") well-known for his work on TV's *Lou Grant*. This 1961 album sounds like a cross between Bob and Ray and Harold Pinter. The studio-recorded, audienceless vignettes are dark slices of life: a sportscaster crumbling when his statistician walks out on him, two couples' friendship eroding when one is caught cheating at cards, a social worker duped by her vicious juvenile delinquent charge. The duo offer excellent and varied voices as they depict various low and high societal idiots.

These satires of character and manner are not designed to provoke more than uncomfortable giggles at best. The surreal playlet "So Is Dr. Mitchell" is the highlight as two old women kibbitz while watching an adult western.

"They say," one notes of the leading man, "he's homosexual." "Well," sighs the other, "that's basic." "Oh, there's that nice girl, Gail Pender. She plays Lady Lou," one says, glancing through a movie star magazine. "Magazine says she has a butterfly tattooed." "Where was that?" "On her buttocks! She showed it at the Cannes Film Festival last year while wading in a fountain." "That's so refreshing." "Yes."

Through it all, their house companion, Fred, wanders in with somberly recited questions that are so banal as to be almost existential. Like, which is the hot and cold water tap. Ultimately he is so unable to deal with the humdrum that he sinks into a helplessness that borders on death. When he bleakly announces that he's dying of thirst, the ladies are far more interested in watching the movie, ultimately moved to tears at the plight of one of the dying screen characters: "I hate death. It's so unreal...."

Adams told me that scriptwriter Burland was influenced by Stan Freberg. The album arrived around the time Nichols and May's dark material was getting critical attention, and that may have eclipsed interest in this offbeat, small label effort. An intriguing record, ahead of its time, The Idiots' acid satire still leaves a disturbing aftertaste.

ERIC IDLE AND NEIL INNES

- RUTLAND WEEKEND SONGBOOK (Passport PPSD 98018) * $7 $15

Idle, of Monty Python, and Innes, of the Bonzo Dog Band, unite for dull and irritating satires that sound like rejects from their respective groups. They seem to enjoy satirizing stupidity and blandness—by becoming stupid and bland. A parody of meaningless TV news has an announcer droning two minutes of inanity: "Foreskin mousetrap view Mount Everest tin tray lobotomy ... lemonade enterprising apartheid rubberized plum joint ..."

In parodying The Beatles, Johnny Cash and doo-wop rock groups, they duplicate the styles without adding the satiric juice. There's no reason to chuckle when Cash (sounding more like Bob Dylan) mutters lyrics like "all the prophets of doom can always find room in a world full of worry and fear. Cigarettes and chemistry sets and Rudolph the Red-Nosed Reindeer." To quote one song, "And if it all sounds boring, if it all sounds boring, if it all sounds boring, then there's something wrong with the song."

"I Must Be in Love," is one of the better cuts, the embryonic beginning for a full-length Beatles satire that would appear two years later when Idle and Innes joined with two others to form The Rutles.

The cult for Python and/or the Bonzos has helped elevate the pricing on this one.

DON IMUS

- 1200 HAMBURGERS TO GO (RCA Victor LSP 4699) ** $10 $25
- ONE SACRED CHICKEN TO GO (RCA Victor LSP 4819) ** $10 $25
- THIS HONKY'S NUTS (Bang 407) *1/2 $15 $30

A pioneering "shock jock" since the early '70s in New York, Imus is adept at everything from put-on phone calls to glowering satire. On the title cut from 1972's "Hamburgers" he pretends to be with the army, barking out orders to a McDonald's counter man. He demands twelve hundred hamburgers for his troops within an hour. Then he twists the knife by demanding ketchup for some, mustard for others, mixing and mangling and personalizing the orders beyond most anyone's endurance. But the dumb kid from McDonald's is the perfect patsy who keeps right on taking down the order.

"Sacred Chicken" is heavy on Don's favorite character, the Evangelist Rev. Billy Sol Hargis (in the '60s Billy James Hargis and Billy Sol Estes grabbed headlines). The reverend is more concerned with commercialism than Christ:

"Say hallelujah ... from the First Church of the Gooey Death and Discount House of Worship ... Friends, it is true you work your whole life to get a little somethin' and when you go it's left for your friends and relatives to fight over ... so many people think that you can't take it with you. As a matter of fact, you can't take it with you. But it can be there when you get there ... at Billy Sol's First National Bank of Him ... send what you have or all that you have ... don't freak out and leave it to a kitty or a goldfish."

There's over twenty minutes of this. The few nonreligious cuts include "Feminine Foreplay," a series of typically obnoxious "zany" disc jockey phone calls. Imus to an anonymous girl:

"Hello, welcome to feminine foreplay. Today's question is, if you were out with a big time, sensuous disc jockey ... what would it take to get you to go all the way?" "How far are we going for all the way?" "Philadelphia." "A lot of money and a good dinner." "A lot of money and what?" "A good dinner." "I thought you said dentist."

The title of his live 1974 album attempted to cash in on Richard Pryor's hit "That Nigger's Crazy." Some of the vague racial humor is clearly Pryor influenced: "Thank you all for coming," he begins. "That's what white people say when they make love: Thank you for coming, Margaret ..." Disc jockey Imus isn't much as a stand-up. He's wooden, his cursing and funk unconvincing. The longest segment is a nineteen-minute confession from his main character Rev. Billy Sol Hargis.

Though his radio show is syndicated, the cult is strongest in New York where Imus records sometimes go for $50 or more.

AUTRY INMAN

- AT THE FRONTIER CLUB (Sims) ** $5 $10
- RISCOTHEQUE SATURDAY NIGHT VOL. 1 (Jubilee 2055) ** $5 $10
- RISCOTHEQUE SATURDAY NIGHT VOL. 2 (Jubilee 2056) ** $5 $10

Something slightly different: a bumpkin risqué comic. Little Autry Inman, who wears a toupee that looks like it's made out of molded black plastic, offers standard jokes one would expect from a Woody Woodbury or Davy Bold: "Heard about the absent-minded doctor who lost his nurse? He forgot where he laid her." They're told with an easy Southern accent. Sometimes he wanders toward slightly more offbeat humor. From his first album on Sims:

"I been little all my life. As a baby I was so little for several months my mother carried me around in her purse. And for a long, long time I thought her fountain pen was my baby brother. And I was always jealous a' him 'cause he could screw his head off and I couldn't ... But now I do!"

Inman's saucy early '60s golf parody on the first volume of "Riscotheque" recalls the clean "misconception" football routine of Andy Griffith: "I asked the instructor to teach me how to play ... he said you've got a couple of balls that we can play with, haven't you ... he said a tee is just a little bitty thing about the size of your finger. You stick your tee in the ground and put your ball down on it. He said have you got a bag? I said well, yes, of course I have. He said your balls are in it? He said do you know how to hold your club? He said you take it in both hands like this and swing it back over your shoulder. I said not me...."

To his credit, Inman doesn't play this hee-haw material too broadly. It comes out right tolerable. Black comedian Dave Turner did a similar suggestive golf routine. Inman also wrote and recorded straight country songs. Inman died September 6, 1988, at the age of fifty-nine.

THE INVESTIGATOR

- A POLITICAL SATIRE (Folkways 451 and Discuriosities LP 6834) *1/2 $5 $10

There was nothing on the front or back cover of this album to indicate who "The Investigator" was. And with good reason. This is a satire on Senator Joseph McCarthy, and when it came out, McCarthy was a dangerous personality to joke about.

The album is one long sketch in which nasty, tight-lipped McCarthy finds himself in a plane crash and brought to Heaven's gate. Before he can get in, he must sign documents and undergo an investigation. The outraged senator grumbles, "What happens if I do not get a clean bill of health from this committee of yours?"

"In that case," the angel says, "that means deportation." "To where?" "Why ... down there." "I want to state at this time that I refuse to submit to any investigation by any committee whose members for all I know may be completely unqualified to pass judgment on me!"

The ironies continue as McCarthy goes off to find such dead luminaries as Torquemada and create his own counterinvestigation. Much of the album re-creates the McCarthy environment of legal harangues and hammerheaded belligerence as "The Investigator" uses his own twisted logic to accuse Heaven's gatekeeper of subversiveness and incompetence. The morality tale is none too humorous, but survives as a sad and sober "radio play" documenting a notorious man and a frightening age in history that may one day repeat itself.

There seems to have been a good-size pressing of this one. Since the album jacket doesn't allude to McCarthy directly (times being what they were), many browsers ignore it as just another obscure comedy record. It has not attracted the attention it should as a collector's item of historical interest.

JAMES WESLEY JACKSON

- SOULED OUT! (Plum PR 301) ** $3 $8

Based in Chicago since the late '50s, Mississippi-born Jackson became an opening act for the Funkadelics and others. His style is loose, rambling, and conversational, with some prepared lines woven in throughout: "I said, 'Why aren't there more black people on TV?' They said, 'We got you on TV.' I said, 'I know it, but I get tired of watching basketball games.' I heard one of them say, 'I heard the Negroes are sweeping the country.' I said, 'Yes, it's one of the few jobs we can get.'"

MILLIE JACKSON

- BACK TO THE S--T (Jive 1186-1-J) ** $4 $8

Hot and sexy albums have been a Millie Jackson specialty for years. On this monologue and music disc, Millie poses for a comic cover photo—sitting on the toilet, panties around her ankles, eyes closed in gastrointestinal urgency.

The songs aren't that outrageous, but the live tracks should appeal to fans of funky cursing and posturing. Anybody can be a scat singer, but Millie's a shock-laugh scat riffer on literal scat subjects like "Muffle that Fart."

For women, a helpful rant on lethal diseases and condoms: "This shit is dangerous! Buy yo' own. Put 'em on yo' self. Don't even trust 'im ... You put 'em on. You know Dr. Ruth, the short white bitch? She short, but she can reach it. Dr. Ruth say: 'You take de condom, and you just go bloop, like that, and you roll it like that.' Nuthin' to it. Bloop and roll it.... Do what I tell ya."

MYLES JACKSON

- VARSITY CHEER "A History of the Western World at Half-Time" (Folkways FTS 31310) * $3 $7

In the early '70s, when "alternative" comedy albums began to appear (Conception Company, Credibility Gap, Bill Martin, Firesign Theater) even Folkways took a chance. Their entry is a collage of real audio news clips plus the campy put-ons of Jackson and his acting troupe. The shouts, chants, sloganizing, and bickering could be taking place during "halftime" at a football game—or (gasp!) "halftime" before Armageddon.

The juxtapositions are often pretentious, meaningless and unlistenable. Eavesdropping into a crowd, real and fake remarks mix: "All these guys are a bunch of fanatics." "George Washington was the biggest fanatic that ever lived." "George died of syphilis." "Shut your dirty red trap." "One man sitting with a wife so pretty, he reached out and pinched my bare brown titty." "The frame of a dame is a shame." "To war we went for God and fame."

LOU JACOBI

- YOU DON'T HAVE TO BE JEWISH (Kapp KRL 4503) **1/2 $5 $10
- WHEN YOU'RE IN LOVE THE WHOLE WORLD IS JEWISH $8
  (Kapp KRS 5506, reissued with YOU DON'T HAVE TO BE JEWISH on one CD: Rhino R2 71084) **

Beginning with this 1964 album, veteran character actor Lou Jacobi starred in a series of three Bob Booker and George Foster-produced studio albums. The casts varied slightly from record to record. This first entry features Jack Gilford, Arlene Golonka, Jackie Kannon, Joe Silver, Bob McFadden, and Betty Walker. It's short sketches filled with classic (old) jokes.

Gallop: I'm, in advertising, I'm with BBD&O.

Jacobi (in Jewish accent): I'm in women's wear. You may have heard of us. Finkelstein and O'Brien Limited.

Gallop: That's unusual.

Jacobi: "You think that's unusual? I'm O'Brien!"

The record is little more than dramatizations from a used joke book, but the actors are all first rate, giving the jokes more life than one might think possible.

On the 1966 sequel album, Jacobi is abetted by Betty Walker, Phil Leeds, Valerie Harper, Anthony Holland, Bob McFadden, and Frank Gallop. A few songs are added to the old joke mix.

Jacobi does a monologue after a rock comes crashing through his window: "It says 'Dear Mr. Shapiro, unless you deposit $10,000 in small bills in a paper bag under the old hollow tree in a vacant lot on the corner at midnight tomorrow, we will kidnap your wife. Sincerely yours, your kidnappers.' Boy, some tough cookie. I better write them a note back immediately. Let me see. Pencil. Paper. Dear Kidnappers: your rock of dis date received. I am writing to tell you I do not have $10,000. But please keep in touch—your proposition interests me."

- THE YIDDISH ARE COMING! (Verve 15058) *1/2 $5 $10
- AL TIJUANA AND HIS JEWISH BRASS (Capitol T 2596) * $4 $8

The humor in Verve's look at the 1968 Arab-Israeli war seems to come from the disbelief that Israel won. In this guilty, self-hating exercise, Jews are stereotyped as ineffective, petty, noodgy cowards. A long sketch begins with a soldier racing into headquarters, moaning "Oyyy, am I thoisty! Listen ... could I have an egg cream please? And I wouldn't die if you happened to have an extra cookie." For several minutes, he tells of the Syrian Army in the East, the Egyptian Army in the West, and the Jordanian Army to the North. The only move is to the South, but the soldier cries, "Facing us in the South is such a big black dog...."

In another long sketch, an Israeli soldier comes in evidently to volunteer. But at the end, after turning down dangerous missions, he shrugs, "On me, you shouldn't depend!"

"Al Tijuana" is a one-joke 1966 album that klezmerizes the era's hits. Ironically, only one, "A Taste of Honey," was covered by the then-popular Herb Alpert and the Tijuana Brass. The album doesn't satirize Alpert, a Jew who had hit records of Mexican music, it just takes "Downtown," "It's Not Unusual," Henry Mancini's "Peter Gunn," and other standards and adds minor key clarinets or violins, some freilach dance beats, and Jacobi's mild, occasional break-ins: "You like it, you keep asking for it, you're getting it!"

JEAN PIERRE

- JEAN PIERRE VISITS THE OUTHOUSE (La Louisianne LL 132) ** $4 $10

   Cajun comic Jean Pierre was dwarfed by labelmate Bud Fletcher, who issued ten albums for La Louisianne.

FLORENCE FOSTER JENKINS

- FLORENCE FOSTER JENKINS RECITAL (RCA Victor LM 2597) $5 $10
   reissued in 12-inch format as GLORY (???) OF THE HUMAN VOICE (RCA Victor AGM1-4808) **

   The Stone Age Mrs. Miller, Jenkins presented tone deaf opera recitals to the delight of campy classical music fans. She seems a Margaret Dumont type, a self-absorbed, solidly built, vanity-motivated matron totally oblivious to her considerable faults. She recorded in the '40s. For a moment or two her hapless high notes might raise a pained smile, but that's it. The most successful cuts are the short squealy arias from "Die Fledermaus," "Lakme," and "The Magic Flute." The 1962 twelve-inch reissue is padded out with a full side of "A Faust Tragedy" sung by Jenny Williams and Thomas Burns. The album notes have nineteen paragraphs for Jenkins, and only one for the duo, which gives you some idea of their importance.

THE JERKY BOYS

- THE JERKY BOYS (Select 261495) * $8
- THE JERKY BOYS 2 (Select 292411) * $8

   Crank phone callers, the witless Jerky Boys harangue their targets, none of whom deserve the abuse. Most of the calls are placed to companies who have placed want ads, or to service-oriented businesses (piano tuner, optometrist, laser surgery consultant) that would politely give any caller, however moronic, a few moments of their time. The Boys rarely bother thinking up a clever premise before calling. On the second album, for example, one of them shouts to a Hispanic, "Pablo, honey, come down to Florida ... are you washing your ass ... you bastard you," while perplexed Pablo keeps asking "Who is this?" after each pointless remark.

   Among the depressing calls on the debut disc, a man grousing to a doctor's receptionist:

   "I got hemorrhoids bad. My ass is killing me. I need help." "When would you like to come in, sir?" "As soon as possible." "Can you come in this evening?" "These doctors, are they reputable?" "Yes, they are." "This is tearin' the ass outta me!" "Sir, could you use the proper terminology?" "But I'm dyin' over here!"

   The woman hangs up. The man snickers with delight.

   The Jerks actually starred in their own film after the records did unexpectedly big business (and spawned many copycats). A soundtrack is available.

GEORGE JESSEL

- BEDTIME STORIES FOR GROWN-UPS (Riot R 304) *1/2 $4 $12
- JESSEL AT HIS BEST (Audio Fidelity AFSD 1706) *1/2 $5 $10
- MR. TOASTMASTER GENERAL (Palete MPZ 1019) ** $5 $15

   Jessel had a long career from silent films, including *Ginsberg the Great* and *George Washington Cohen*, to Broadway in *The Jazz Singer*. Known for both sentimental crooning ("My Mother's Eyes") and schmaltzy comedy, by the '50s he was primarily a "toastmaster" and nostalgia act. Old-time peers like Jack Benny and Groucho Marx considered him a character, with his Casanova love life and wisecracks, but in the decades before his death the general public thought him old-fashioned, were turned off by his right-wing politics, and paid him little attention.

   Jessel was often broke, which accounts for his embarrassing albums for cheap record companies. One of the shorter and more tolerable jokes on the Riot disc: "Once upon a time, a four-year-old boy was visiting his uncle and aunt. He was a very outspoken little boy and ofttimes had to be censored to say the right thing at the right time. One day at lunch, when his Auntie had company, the little boy said, 'Auntie, I want to tinkle.' Auntie took the little boy aside and said, 'Never say that, Sonny. If you want to tinkle, say, "I want to whisper."' And the incident was forgotten. That night, when uncle and auntie were soundly sleeping, the little boy climbed into bed with them. He tugged at his uncle's shoulder and said, 'Uncle, I want to whisper.' And uncle said, 'All right, Sonny, don't wake Auntie up. Whisper in my ear.' The little boy was sent back to his parents the next day." Jessel's delivery is as perfunctory and stagey as the awkward wording might suggest.

   George wasn't at his best in 1967 for the Audio Fidelity disc. Some of the shorter wheezes might provoke a mild giggle for those who are young and haven't heard them, or are extremely old and have forgotten:

   "This fellow's been in jail. He got ten years for some kind of mail fraud. He's brokenhearted, naturally, about it. His lawyer came to him and said, 'Now look, don't you worry, we've got some new evidence. You'll be out of here before you know it. In the meantime ... try to escape.'

   "And another fella told a lawyer he came home and found his wife in the arms of another man. And, uh, his lawyer said, 'What did you do about it?' He said, 'Well, I just looked at them for a little while, then I went out into the kitchen and just quietly made a pot of coffee.' And the lawyer said, 'What about the man with your wife?' And the husband said, 'Why, let him make his own coffee.'"

In his latter years, Jessel appeared often at funerals and testimonials. The Palete album offers him at affairs honoring Jack Benny, Dean Martin, Burns and Allen, etc. He's relaxed as a raconteur and ad-libber. The album has some vivid examples of "old show biz" banter. Attacking Dean Martin: "The best piece of oratory in our history is Mr. Lincoln's Gettysburg Address. And this, even if he stuttered, only takes two minutes. And I'm sure that what Mr. Lincoln said at Gettysburg is more important than any tribute to this drunken wop comedian!" The audience roared for nearly ten seconds.

Noting Jayne Mansfield on the dais: "As I look at you, Miss Mansfield, I can have only one thing on my mind: General Nasser should have them for tonsils!" The crowd laughed at this for nearly nine seconds.

GEORGE JESSEL, GEORGE BURNS, JACK BENNY, AND ART LINKLETTER

- MR. TOASTMASTER (Private Stock) * * * $10 $25

This "bootleg" record of an after dinner roast honoring Columbia Pictures executive Harry Joe Brown was hosted by toastmaster Georgie.

He does a frisky twenty minutes describing some of his actor pals, including one who recently played "the squeak in the can on the Ex-Lax show." He explains why he wears a monocle: "I have trouble with this eye. I'd rather have people say, 'Isn't he eccentric' than, 'The poor son of a bitch is going blind.'"

Burns steals the show with a salty, spry ten minutes: "I really should be in bed. I'm so tired and exhausted I probably won't remember one of the lines I was going to ad-lib tonight. Harry and I have been friends all our lives. We had good times together and we had bad times together. In fact, we both got a touch of Cupid's Eczema from the same girl. That was some girl! Harry was on first that night and I was #2. Four days later I limped into Dr. Milekson's office ... this was some office. Went there for about four months. It got so I got to know every actor by his ass. But I gotta tell ya about Harry. Harry and I were living at the Coolidge Hotel. He was going out with a girl called Gladys Trueblood. She lived on the third floor and Harry lived on the ninth. Sometimes he'd go downstairs to see her and then come up. Sometimes she'd come up to see him and then go down ... sometimes they both went down. Once when he was down there he ran into Lou Holtz ... the affair didn't last too long. Gladys went back to Oklahoma City. And Harry went back to have his throat treated."

Art Linkletter acknowledges his clean image and tries to play along ("Purely ad-lib, I called up my mother-in-law and told her to go fuck herself!"), but the surprise here is Jack Benny's six-minute dabbling in the risqué. He describes a very sophisticated British party he attended: "There was one dame there riding a Kotex sidesaddle." And then he goes on to insist: "The only word left for me tonight ... is fornicate! You know I tried that once, when I had to speak very late at a Friar's stag dinner. And I used the word fornicate; there was nothing left. I used it in a joke. And unfortunately nobody at the Friar's understood what it meant. Except Ronald Reagan."

NOTES: Jessel made many records for obscure companies, including "Seeing Israel" (Strand), "Songs My Pals Sang" (Audio Fidelity), "Tear Jerkers from the Not So Gay 90's" (Treasure), "Last of the Minstrels" (Design), and "Fiftieth Anniversary" (Cabot). "Watch the Owl" (Studio Archives) was released as "a Bicentennial Collector's Item" by Jessel's manager, and offers a few dozen long jokes and stories. He narrates clips from '30s vocalists and comics on "This Is My Show Business" (Show Biz). Jessel appears on Albert Brooks's "Comedy Minus One" album. His old "Hello Mama" bit is on "Golden Age of Comedy."

ARTE JOHNSON

- YOU'RE ON THE AIR (GNP Crescendo 2026, reissue GNP 2026) * * $5 $10

Recorded about five years before *Laugh-In*, the album was originally credited equally to the full cast (including Cliff Norton and Naomi Lewis) assembled by writer Bill Manhoff, who was evidently the big name, having written for popular sitcoms of the day (*The Real McCoys*) and Broadway's current hit *The Owl and the Pussycat*. When Johnson became popular, the album was re-released with his picture on it.

Ahead of its time as a concept disc about radio call-in shows, the problem is that now far zanier and funnier people bedevil these programs. One of the better cuts offers Johnson as a German-accented scientist calling in with a cure for the common cold. He speaks to radio DJ Manhoff:

"I captured a male and female cold germ! I lived with them intimately for a year, studying their habits, learning their language." "Wait, what language do cold germs speak?" "Cold German ... my capsule spells doom to the common cold. It says, 'Listen here, common cold, D-O-O-M!' I want to tell you the principle of my cold capsule.... I discovered that the female cold germ is ugly. Which explains why the male cold germ is so mean ... to get up in the morning and look at a puss like the one on a female cold germ, maybe YOU would go out and attack mucus membranes, too."

Johnson also appears on the *Laugh-In* albums (see listing on Rowan and Martin) and issued a single, "Very Interesting" (Reprise 0753). He reads "Newt Gingrich's Bedtime Stories for Orphans" (based on the novelty book) on Dove Audio (CD: 0787107042). The comedy is a bit self-consciously clever and winking, but there's enough wit in the parody to keep the formula from getting too predictable.

JOKEBUSTERS

- JOKEBUSTERS (LP 201) *1/2 $3 $7
- JOKEBUSTERS II (LP 202) *1/2 $3 $7

A group of Brooklyn comedians (some of them struggling pros, some of them evidently pure amateur), Jokebusters' Louis Bonomo, Dixie Dew, Nicholas Melillo, Joe Bevilacqua, and Elaine Fazio sit around swapping long sex stories that range in age and quality from Pearl Williams to Jackie Martling. The sound is bad and most can't tell a joke any better than the average high schooler.

JAMES EARL JONES

- THE ADVENTURES OF COLORED MAN (Capitol T 2597) *1/2 $5 $15

Jones is wasted on this verbose album issued around the same time as the *Batman* TV show. The script has some *Batman* ejaculations ("Holy Socks!" "Holy Cavities!") amid the tedious mini-episodes about problems in "Metro City." Since none involve racial satire, it's hard to figure why the character, from the planet Ebonite, is demeaningly called "Colored Man."

The superhero simply has to deal with various cartoonish villains. One of them has stolen daylight, leading a character to remark, "What a difference a day makes." And that's the only real joke in the entire sketch. Another episode involves Fruitman, who squirts people with lemon juice. Says one surprised victim, "Fruitman? How do you like them apples?"

RED JONES

- RED JONES STEEERIKES BACK (Motown 691) **1/2 $5 $10

Former American League baseball umpire Red Jones, pre-Bob Eucker, specialized in funny anecdotes. He appeared often on pregame broadcasts for the Detroit Tigers, which explains his appearance on the Motown label. This 1969 album is filled with evocative old-time stories, chuckle-producing classics that can be heard over and over.

Prompted by straight man Al Ackerman, Jones talks about the players of his time, such as Mule Haas, Bobo Newsome, Satchel Paige, and Hank Greenberg. On an encounter between fastballer Bob Feller and a raw rookie: "Feller ... he could throw a strawberry through a battleship. His curveball looked like an epileptic snake. And he used it as a weapon, he could frighten the hell out of a hitter with it.... I remember a little guy hitting against him ... and Feller wore a size 15-1/2 shoe, and he'd stick that foot in your face and come with the glove and the overhand fastball and the ball would come out of the white background, and it was fifteen feet before you could pick it up."

"And this kid was standing there, and here come one right down the gut. And I said, 'Strike!' And the kid turned around and said, 'My God, ump, you didn't call that pitch a strike, did ya?' I said, 'Pecker high, right down the middle, kid, didn't you think that was a strike?' He said, 'It sounded high to me.'"

With its mix of short gags and evocative anecdotes, this disc is a nice find for fans who enjoy leisurely, funny baseball conversation.

SPIKE JONES

- THE BEST OF SPIKE JONES (RCA Victor ANL1-1035e, $5 $10
    originally released as THANK YOU MUSIC LOVERS RCA Victor LPM 2224)**** $10 $20
- BEST OF SPIKE JONES VOLUME 2 (RCA Victor ANL2-2312e) ** $5 $15
- THE HILARIOUS SPIKE JONES (Pickwick ACL 7031) **1/2 $5 $10

"The Best" is indeed the best album of aural slapstick ever made; the genius of Spike Jones shines on every cut.

He was famous for taking the hot hits of the day and setting them blazingly afire with scorching brass, explosive percussion, squeamy strings, and a roaring cacophony of gunshots, animal noises, and bathroom sounds. There was always method in Spike's madness. He was a fine musician and arranger. Says Spike Jones, Jr., "One of the things that people don't realize about Dad's kind of music is when you replace a C-sharp with a gunshot, it has to be a C-sharp gunshot or it sounds awful."

Here, "Cocktails for Two," "The Glow Worm," "Chloe," "You Always Hurt the One You Love," and "Laura" all start off "straight" and, like Jekyll into Hyde, slowly go berserk as Spike's band surrounds a brave singer with unnerving sound effects.

The lyrics are usually acted out: "You always hurt (pistol shots, screams) the one you love (wolf howl) ... you always take (slide clarinet) the sweetest rose (lewd sniffing noises) and crush it till the petals fall (loud crash)." The orchestrations are at times breathtaking, like the six-note barrage in "You Always Hurt the One You Love" where, in perfect key and cadence, pistol shots, razzes, whistles, pops, glass breaking, and "the birdaphone" form a bridge from a vocal to an instrumental break.

Doodles Weaver is on hand for two of his popular word-mangling numbers: "Man on the Flying Trapeze" and "William Tell Overture." Spike, usually prone to let other band members handle the vocals, appears on "None but the Lonely Heart," a spoof on soap operas in which he and his wife Helen indulge in touching, illogical blather: "I know you have another husband. And he has another wife. And that she has another husband. And that he has another wife. And that our own child, through marriage, is now my uncle." All this is nicely spattered by an instrumental chorus of gooey squeals.

The most famous cut in this collection of 1940s singles is his first big hit, "Der Fuehrer's Face." A cartoonish German band joins Carl Grayson in a forced salute to Hitler ("Ve heil! Heil! Right in the Fuehrer's face"), each "heil" met by a rousing Bronx cheer.

"Thank You Music Lovers," in untampered mono, is available as an import item. Both albums have Jack Davis cartoon covers, but the original is much more involved and comical.

1967's Volume 2 is at times a "worst of," especially when vocalist Freddy Morgan applies his hokey Oriental accent to pop tunes ("Chinese Mule Train") and George Rock does his baby talk bit ("Bubble Gum Song"). Billy Barty scores with his Liberace parody (assuming one remembers the velvet-voiced pianist) on "I'm in the Mood for Love." Carl Grayson's "That Old Black Magic" is similar in style to "Cocktails for Two." Spike's fans will probably want it, along with nicely wrecked versions of "Love in Bloom" and "Tennessee Waltz," but the rest is disappointing, especially the tepid versions of such high-potential rousers as "Charleston" and "Yes We Have No Bananas."

MAD, MAD, MAD JACK DAVIS

Jack Davis of MAD Magazine *fame, as well as the movie poster for "Mad Mad Mad Mad World" among others, usually produced frantic and complex covers like "Monster Rally," "Dracula's Greatest Hits," and Spike Jones's "Thank You Music Lovers." He did a lot of Homer and Jethro covers, including this feverish classic with a trademark Davis babe.*

"Hilarious" is a budget compilation of songs from the two "Best of" albums.

* SPIKE JONES MURDERS CARMEN AND KIDS THE CLASSICS (RCA LPM 3128) *** $10 $35
* SPIKE JONES IS MURDERING THE CLASSICS (RCA Victor LSC 3235e) ***1/2 $5 $10

Collectors may want to hunt for the original ten-inch album, "Spike Jones Murders Carmen," with its drawing of Spike Jones in jail garb and Freddie Morgan as an unlikely Carmen, but others can enjoy the 1971 version, also on CD, which adds many more tunes. The original disc had "Carmen" on one side, and four songs on the flip: "William Tell Overture," "Dance of the Hours," "Rhapsody from Hunger(y)" and "None but the Lonely Heart."

The highlight is Spike's twelve-minute, full-blown blow-out of "Carmen," offering great musical parody and very goofy lyrics: "I can not marry you my Don, because I'm in love with another Juan. He fights the bull in the arena." "I could do that if I ate Farina." Of the tunes added to the reissue, the famous "Jones Laughing Record" is simple enough: a musician stumbles through "Flight of the Bumble Bee" and his sneezing makes the audience fall apart with absolutely insane laughter. "Nutcracker Suite" is another ambitious number, seven minutes chewing up Tchaikovsky. "Pal Yat Chee" is a cute opera nose-thumber from Homer and Jethro with some well-turned lyrics and nicely done singing ("When we listen to Palyatchee we get itchy and scratchy"). Finally, just to annoy, there's "Ill Barkio," in which a soprano duets with a yowling dog.

* DINNER MUSIC FOR PEOPLE WHO AREN'T VERY HUNGRY (Verve 4005) $10 $15
  re-released as Goldberg and O'Reilly 10010, and on CD as Rhino 70261) ** $8
* IT'S A SPIKE JONES CHRISTMAS (Verve 4000) $10 $15
  re-released as Goldberg and O'Reilly 10011 $5 $10
  issued on CD as Rhino R2 70196 * $8

Around 1957, before RCA reissued his classic 78s, Spike recorded these Verve albums. "Dinner Music" offers some new versions of his old, and at the time unavailable, hits. None match the originals. Other cuts are infantile (certainly George Rock's "Sow Song") and many are loaded with obsessive references to body odor. "Wyatt Earp Makes Me Burp" is an oddity, an ancient rap record where a chorus sing-songs the lyrics: "Wyatt Earp, that's our man, let's get him here as quick as we can." One lone vocalist constantly interrupts with a whine of "Wyatt Earp makes me burp," replete with long, disgusting burp noises. Also odd but unwarranted: "Memories are Made of This" crooned over the sound of barking dogs. Here, "Palyatchee" is not by Homer and Jethro, but Betsy Gay.

Almost a sound effects demo record, Jones introduces some of the selections and lists the different instruments on the back: the Kissing Trumpet, Ratchet, Living Coo-Coo, Klaxon, and Poontangaphone. None, alas, illustrated with a photo.

The Christmas disc has little comedy. In the liner notes, Spike Jones, Jr. asked, "Why do we have to keep changing records to get all the songs we like to sing? Why can't we have all the Christmas music we want on one record?" The result: a medley of thirty-five tunes, most rendered into fat, thanks to a choir of middle-aged men and women. George Rock does his kiddie voice for repulsive novelty tunes "All I Want for Christmas Is My Two Front Teeth" and "Nuttin' for Christmas." The only glimpse of the real Spike Jones is in "Jingle Bells," played on kazoos and sung in pig Latin.

Verve also issued a forgettable extended play single, "Spike Spoofs the Pops."

* SPIKE JONES IN STEREO (Warner Brothers B 1332) ***1/2 $15 $40

This stylish concept album from 1959 was keyed to the fad for monster movies and the popularity of *Famous Monsters* magazine. Like "Abbott and Costello Meet Frankenstein," there's comedy and some legitimate thrills. Paul Frees delivers a brilliant set of impressions, including Lugosi, Karloff, his peerless Peter Lorre, and in one sketch, Alfred Hitchcock in an interview with Edward R. Murrow:

"That armchair you're sitting in is very striking, Alfred." "It's made out of real arms...." "Alfred, what's in all those drawers along the wall?" "Well, this one, marked 'F,' is full of feet." "From here it looks like it's full of hands." "I'm sorry, Ed, I'm so untidy...." "What's in that bottle on the top shelf?" "Old Grandad. On my father's side."

Though Jones rarely lets loose with his usual fast and furious instrumentals, the Alvino Rey-produced numbers are richly orchestrated with inventive use of stereo, including a burp that seems to travel all around the room. Highlights include Paul Frees's Dracula and Luli Jean Norman's Vampira duet on "All of a Sudden My Heart Sings" and "I Only Have Eyes for You." Deep, gooey voiced Thurl Ravenscroft rocks out with "Teenage Brain Surgeon"; Frees, as Boris Karloff's Frankenstein monster, laments new lyrics to "Everything Happens to Me"; and there's an imaginative moment where Poe's "Raven" is perfectly mated to Dvorak's "Humoresque."

The album was briefly reissued by Warner Bros. in the '70s, taking some of the rare edge off the original.

* OMNIBUST (Liberty LRP 3140/LST 7140) ** $15 $30
* OMNIBUST (Liberty LRP 3140/LST 7140 Blue Vinyl) ** $15 $35
* 60 YEARS OF MUSIC AMERICA HATES BEST (Liberty LRP 3154/LST 7154) ** $15 $30
* VERY BEST OF SPIKE JONES (Liberty Records, reissued as United Artists UA 439E) ** $8 $15

Spike had his own sketch-oriented TV shows in the summers of 1960 and 1961, and "Omnibust" reflects this, an aural *TV Guide* parodying various video programs. The Japanese version of *American Bandstand*, called "Wonderful World of Hari Kari," has Freddy Morgan doing his stereotyped Oriental voice ("Ohh, today we got a clazy lock and loll show for you fans"). He accidentally anticipates the next decade's rock stars by referring to "The Japanese Beetles."

Late night movie announcers are kidded, *Captain Kangaroo* becomes "Captain Bangaroo," and Lawrence Welk is mashed together with *77 Sunset Strip* in an offbeat, but not very funny sketch. The material sounds like it was dashed off by *MAD Magazine* writers on a coffee break. A parody of jungle travelogues sounds like it never got past a first draft: "The Exoticas were a happy little tribe. They were known to love their fellow man. Medium rare. Our safari left Tanganyika Africa and it numbered nine people. Myself, a faithful guide named Mogambo, six native bearers, and a drunken elephant boy named Sabu, who was familiar with every pink elephant in the jungle."

Spike's farewell to original comedy records, "Hates Best" has a cute album cover—Spike hunkering down in front of a Victrola like the RCA dog Nipper. He offers accurate versions of ancient novelty tunes ("Hut Sut Song," "Three Little Fishes," and "Strip Polka") and a set of knock knock jokes, which was a fad way back in the Fletcher Henderson era of the '20s: "Knock knock." "Who's there?" "Duane!" "Duane who?" "Duane the bathtub, I'm dwowning!" Mild but amusing cuts include "I Kiss Your Hand Madame ('cause I can't stand your breath"), Gloria Wood sneezing through a soaked version of "River Stay 'Way from My Door," and a Vampira-Dracula duet of Irving Taylor's "Kookie Kookie Lend Me Your Comb."

Spike simply didn't record his "very best" for Liberty. To make this one more interesting, the previously unreleased "Holiday for Strings" makes its first appearance. It was from a half-finished album called "Persuasive Concussion." As expected, the pizzicato strings are replaced by clanking cans, squeaky woodwinds, and a choking car horn. Another cut, a Dixieland version of "September Song," is from one of Spike's "straight" albums, "Washington Square." Spike made four of these nonhumor Liberty albums: "Washington Square," "Spike Jones' New Band," "My Man," and "The New Band of Spike Jones Plays Hank Williams."

- FEATURING SPIKE JONES (Tiara TMT/TST 7535) * $6 $15

There are only two Spike Jones cuts on this budget label release. These are "Cherry Pink" and "No Boom Boom in Yucca Flat," which were previously issued in 1955 as a single from Starlite Records under the pseudonym "Davey Crackpot and His Mexican Jumping Beans." The former is a mild send-up of the tune, complete with burps. The latter is a dopey Belafonte-esque tune about the wind ruining a nuclear bomb test. It's not as interesting as it may sound. The rest of the disc is padded with Hoosier Hot Shots tunes and a full side of straight 1920s-type songs sung by a deservedly anonymous vocalist.

- KING OF CORN (Cornographic 1001, reissued as Glendale 6005,
    and as SPIKE JONES ON THE AIR, Sandy Hook 2073) ** $5 $10
- UNCOLLECTED SPIKE JONES 1946 (Hindsight HSR 185) * $5 $15
- AND THE GREAT BIG SAW CAME NEARER (Golden Spike GS 1754) ** $5 $15
- RIOT SQUAD (Harlequin HQCD 1) ** $8
- LOUDER AND FUNNIER (Harlequin HQCD 2) ** $8
- CORN'S A POPPIN' (Harlequin HQCD 30) ** $8

The Jones formula is predictable, so after gems like "Best of Spike Jones" and "Spike Jones Murders the Classics," it's the law of diminishing returns. The more fans hunt for rare records of radio show transcriptions, movie soundtracks, and other odds and ends, the more they run across repetition and material that should've remained buried. It does little for Spike Jones's reputation, or for a listener's enjoyment, to hear a few more '40s tunes "Spiked" in the same old way, but usually without the enthusiasm or perfection of something like "Cocktails for Two." And how many fans really want to compare radio versions of "Chloe" and "Der Fuehrer's Face" to the sharper, polished 78s?

Several record companies unearthed transcription discs that Spike made for radio use. Each album is a hit and miss collection. The Hindsight disc is mostly straight music, including instrumental versions of "I Only Have Eyes for You," "Minka," "When Yuba Plays the Rhumba on the Tuba," etc. There's a mild comic version of "Laura" and "E-Bob-O-Lee-Bop," a breezy jazz (not comedy) number sung by Helen Grayco. George Rock supplies the album notes.

Much more interesting is "On the Air" from Sandy Hook, a mix of transcriptions and live cuts offering typical Jones cacophony. There are destructive versions of "People Will Say We're in Love" (complete with birdaphone), "Besa Me Mucho" (a live version with Red Ingle), and "Jingle Bells." Most of the songs are very mild and sung by either The Nillsen Twins or Del Porter. "Wang Wang Blues" and "There's a Fly on My Music" don't sound much different from what Charlie Barnet or Fletcher Henderson did with them. Of course, it's important to remember that these are not albums of collected 78s, but collections of songs disposed of free over the airwaves. Spike can't be faulted for the posthumous release of a lot of faint fluff like "The Sound Effects Man," which has Del Porter singing about the effects and Spike acting them out.

"And the Great Big Saw Came Nearer" is disappointing, featuring barber shop quartet comedy on such tracks as the title cut, Del Porter's "Oh How She Lied to Me," and a much too coy version of "Never Hit Your Grandma With a Shovel." The weak highlights are from Red Ingle (a version of "Liebestraum") and Spike himself (he plays straight man to Luther Roundtree for corny jokes between choruses of "Camptown Races").

Harlequin is technically an import company, but these albums are easily available in America thanks to distribution via Stash Records. These CDs replace earlier, slightly different vinyl releases. The album notes are more jokey than informative and sometimes a song title is invented: "Peter Lorre's Horror Story" is simply a few minutes clipped from Spike's radio show and not even from an Armed Forces Broadcast like the rest of the CD. Along with bland, upbeat big band songs, each album has a few alternate takes of classics and obscure tunes ("You're a Sap, Mr. Jap" and "St-St-St-Stella" on the first, "Moo Woo Woo" and "Trailer Annie" on the second, "Wicked Wascal Wabbits" and "When the Midnight Choo-Choo Leaves for Alabam" on the third) to enthrall hardcore Jones fans.

- VINTAGE RADIO BROADCASTS (Mar Bren MBR 743) ** $5 $10
- SPIKE JONES (Murray Hill 947447, also known as GREATEST SHOW ON EARTH,
    MF 2054 and CRAZIEST SHOW ON EARTH, Goldberg and O'Reilly 10016) **1/2 $10 $30
- SPIKE JONES ON RADIO (Radiola MR 1010) **1/2 $5 $12

- COCKTAILS FOR TWO (Pro-Arte CDD 516) **1/2 $ 8
- THE RADIO YEARS VOLUME ONE (Rhino R2 71156) **1/2 $8
- THE RADIO YEARS VOLUME TWO (Rhino R2 71157) **1/2 $8

Spike's radio shows lasted from October 1947 to December 1948, and from January to June in 1949.

Radiola's "Spike Jones Show" has one of the worst pairings in the history of records: the wild, zany Spike show on one side; the quietly soporific "Vic and Sade" on the other. This uninterrupted half hour (June 25, 1949) is filled with corny jokes, silly filler, and some wacky music. A ten-minute opera parody called "This is Your F.B. Aida" stars Don Ameche, and contains banter such as this: "What do you think of Mascagni's Cavallera Rusticana?" "I didn't even know he bought one." "You don't know anything about opera ... how many operas begin with T?" "Trovatore, Tosca, Traviata." "How many operas begin with X?" "Excerpts from La Boheem!"

Mar-Bren offers two half-hour shows, broadcast October 17 and October 24, 1947. Music dominates, with the likes of Frankie Laine and Tex Williams. Dorothy Shay is on both programs. That leaves Spike with some mild patter along the way and only a few depreciated tunes, including "Toot Toot Tootsie."

The three-record set on Murray Hill (reissued by Goldberg and O'Reilly) has an album's worth of repeats ("Chloe," "Der Fuehrer's Face," and so on, in radio versions) half an album of the band playing it straight, and perhaps one and one-half albums worth of previously undiscovered material. There are some hits ("Holiday for Strings" done with chicken clucks, laughs, pistol shots, and bike horns) and misses ("Chantez," where someone does a weary Maurice Chevalier imitation). The sketch "Portia and the Hollywood Wolf" at least has guest star Basil Rathbone.

Pro-Arte's "Cocktails for Two" boasts the phrase "The Original Recordings" on the label, which unwary consumers might take to mean the original RCA recordings. Actually, the hour collects live radio cuts and transcription disc material. There's some duplication from the Murray Hill set, such as the same live radio version of "Der Fuehrer's Face," which ends without a final razz after the band member accidentally broke his razzer. Mel Blanc does his drunk version of "Clink Clink Another Drink."

In 1993 Rhino reissued some of Spike's radio shows on CD, two per disc. Jones wasn't much of a comedian, or even an inspired straight man, so he needed good scripts. He didn't get them, but each disc has a few bright spots. For those who've never gotten enough of Doodles Weaver's endearingly ridiculous lyric-mangling, he gets a few solo numbers. Boris Karloff and Peter Lorre guest on Volume One. Lorre good-naturedly listens to Paul Frees's frantic impression of him on "My Old Flame" and then comes up with his own version of the lyrics! Volume Two offers Frank Sinatra and Lassie. Lassie? Yes, it gives Spike a chance to dust off the howling opera parody "Il Barkio." The highlight is Frank's brief homage/impression of Doodles Weaver. He doesn't sing a comedy number with Spike, but cracks wise in a brief interview segment:

"Frank, money isn't everything. Money can't buy you love. Money can't buy you friendship. Money can't buy you happiness."

"Look, just give me the loot and I'll do my own shopping."

- SPIKE JONES AND HIS CITY SLICKERS (Jass 2) ** $10 $20

The 1986 album sports snazzy color cartoon art front and back recalling R. Crumb's style. The cover may be funnier than the record, which offers tunes Jones did for radio transcription. Some are annoying, like "Ugga Ugga Boo," a jungle nonsense song; George Rock's little brat numbers; and "Too Young," an astonishingly boring duet with mimics as Charles Boyer and Zasu Pitts.

Doodles Weaver fans will be delighted to hear a few new spoonerized and scrambled songs, "Shortnin' Bread" and "April Showers." He pauses for horrible jokes: "They have a new animal in the zoo. It's half lion, half dragon. The front half is lyin' and the back half is draggin'." There are new (but not better) versions of polished RCA classics "Rhapsody from Hunger" and "Dance of the Hours," plus a lot of mildly yocked-up razzmatazz tunes like "Five Foot Two Eyes of Blue" and "Charlie My Boy."

- WACKY WORLD OF SPIKE JONES (Pair PDC21216) *** $10
- THE SPIKE JONES ANTHOLOGY (Rhino R271574) *** $18
- SPIKED! (Catalyst 09026-61982-2) **1/2 $8

Pair, a budget label that supposedly offers two albums for the price of one, doesn't quite make it with "Wacky World of Spike Jones." The fifty-one-minute CD has every cut on "The Best of Spike Jones" except for "Laura," an irritating and pointless exclusion.

The disc has every cut on "Murdering the Classics" except for "The Jones Laughing Record," "Nutcracker Suite," "Morpheus," and the twelve-minute "Carmen." There would have been enough time on the CD to include at least four of the five missing tracks. Since these are two of Jones's best records, it makes more sense to buy them individually.

Two new compilations arrived in 1994. The two-disc, forty-song "Anthology" could have been truly definitive of the RCA years, but for no apparent reason, worthy RCA tunes are omitted for two songs taken from radio broadcasts and three album cuts from Liberty and Warner.

Every cut from "The Best of Spike Jones" is here, plus the better ones from "Best of Spikes Jones Volume 2" and the import-only "I Went to Your Wedding." Three important cuts from "Spike Jones Murders the Classics" are missing—and needn't be. At sixty minutes, the first disc could've accommodated "Carmen," and at sixty-three minutes, the other disc could have included "The Jones Laughing Record" and "Nutcracker Suite."

Lesser known cuts include "Happy New Year," "Jones Polka," "Leave the Dishes in the Sink, Ma," "Hotcha Cornia," "Barney Google," and "April Showers." The album notes give fans some fun trivia, from the identity of "beautiful Linda" mentioned in "William Tell Overture," to the mis-heard lyrics that led to a ban on "By the Beautiful Sea."

Catalyst, a pretentious division of RCA Classical, seeks to educate listeners to avant garde, sonic collage, "cutting edge," and contemporary compositions. Like educational TV networks, they'll go to something popular when they need more exposure or money. Spike receives some condescending praise and left-handed compliments in the notes, which declare his work "sassy" and his "oevre" related to "zen."

The seventy-two-minute CD includes eight tracks not previously captured on compact disc, but most are forgettable at best, annoying at worst: a collection of knock knock jokes, Paul Frees's impression of slow, gooey-voiced Billy Eckstine nodding off and snoring through "Deep Purple," and the sound of dog howls on "Our Hour." The better rarities include the original "Holiday for Strings," "I'm Getting Sentimental over You," and "Serenade to a Jerk." Two unfinished tracks come from Liberty's vaults: "Powerhouse" and "Frantic Freeway" both lack extra sound effects. The CD boasts the complete, unedited "Nutracker Suite," which was originally a three-disc 78 rpm set for kids. The edited version on "Murdering the Classics" is better, cutting out a lot of the saccharine, bland, and boring choral work.

What Spike Jones deserves is a complete boxed set of his recordings, an honor RCA has bestowed on Fats Waller, Glenn Miller, and various other jazz and pop artists.

NOTES: Various obscure domestic albums have foraged for Jones material from radio and films, including "Depreciation Revue" (Silver Swan LP 1002), "Thank Your Lucky Stars" (Show Biz 6506), and "Kraft Music Hall" (Spokane 3). Spike issued several straight albums on Liberty in the '60s (see notation under "The Very Best of Spike Jones"). Jones issued two straight ten-inch albums for RCA: "Spike Jones Plays the Charleston" (including "Varsity Drag," "Doin' the New Raccoon," and "Black Bottom"), and "Bottoms Up" (with "Sante," "Gesundheit Polka," "Drink to the Bonnie Lassies"). Fans have found rare cuts on imports; "I Went to Your Wedding" (RCA International NL 89310) has some good material unavailable on domestic pressings. Also of interest to Jones fans: the solo albums of Paul Frees, Doodles Weaver, and (perhaps) Freddy Morgan. There are still many RCA singles, as well as a Verve extended play 45, not yet available in any other format. Jones is probably the most collectible comedy performer in 78 rpm and 45 rpm.

T. C. JONES

- T. C. JONES HIMSELF (GNP Crescendo 602) ** $10 $40

Thomas Craig Jones was a very successful drag performer in the '50s and '60s. A hit in *The New Faces of 1956*, he got a chance to bring his solo show *Mask and Gown* to Broadway a short time later.

Interest from Broadway and drag fans makes this more than a comedy collectible—and more expensive. Jones's song introductions are loaded with arch throwaway lines (one song he/she claims is from "My Fair Laddie" by Loeb and Leopold). Typically odd tongue-in-somewhere one-liners: "I was up all night! It was just terrible. The phone kept ringing. It was Amelia Earhart, and she kept saying, 'Where is everybody?'"

Jones takes bitchy aim at celebrities, including Katherine Hepburn ("she's kind of a tall pink pipe cleaner with freckles") and offers Hepburn, Bette Davis, Tallulah Bankhead, Shelley Winters, and others singing pop tunes. The album's a bit dusty, but Jones's droll humor and falsies still hold up.

Jones does Tallulah on "The New Faces of 1956" original cast album and three-disc EP (RCA EOC 1025). An album based on his show *Mask and Gown* is also available (AE1-1178). Drag and cabaret interest make this one more expensive in some areas, such as New York and San Francisco.

JERRY JORDAN

- PHONE CALL FROM GOD (MCA 473) *1/2 $4 $8
- DON'T CALL ME I'LL CALL YOU (MCA 2174) *1/2 $4 $8

Circa 1975, Jordan (sporting Elvis sideburns) offered up a mix of country and religious comedy. His most popular routine is the fourteen-minute "Phone Call from God." When God calls, Jerry is stuttery and reverential: "Yessir! Yessir! I go to church ever' Sunday, I'm a faithful church member, yessir. Did I go last Sunday? I sure did. Wonderful service. What did the preacher preach? Ohhhh, well, uhh ... he talks mostly about the Bible, you know. Subjects? Oh, well, Lord, he referred to, he talked about Matthew, you know. No, I don't believe it was Matthew, Lord. It was Mark ... let's see now, I remember it. Sir? Sunday night? No, no, Lord I didn't make it Sunday night. Sir? *Bonanza*! I was *plannin'* on going, but I got to thinkin' I need my rest, to go to church all Sunday and Sunday night and go to work next morning, and ... Sir? Sunday before last? Well, you just picked on a couple of bad 'uns."

The canned laughter doesn't distinguish between the bad 'uns and the good 'uns. Aside from phone calls, Jordan offers weak anecdotes of country life. His deliberate stutters and folksy stumbles make them mighty long before the punch line.

WILL JORDAN

- ILL WILL (Jubilee 2032) *** $10 $20

Jordan influenced many '50s comedians, including Lenny Bruce. Best known as a mimic (his Ed Sullivan impression was an original, oft copied but never bettered) he often did offbeat stars (Sabu) and double mimicry (a bit where Jerry Lewis does an impression of Boris Karloff). Woody Allen paid him a tribute by asking him to appear in the film *Broadway Danny Rose*.

The cover features a demented, giant closeup of Will Jordan, his eyes popping behind his glasses, and his teeth flashing a Dwight Frye smile of insanity. Hugh Hefner's album notes report that "we've known Will as a close personal friend for several years, since before our friendships with either Mort or Lenny ..."

Evidently Jordan felt his sick comedy might hurt his image or his legit mimicry bookings. There is no mention of his last name on the album, and record catalogs simply list it as the work of "Will, III." To add insult to injury, the album is somewhat shrilly recorded with too much treble.

Listeners more familiar with Lenny Bruce might find this as a kind of embryonic Bruce album, chock full of throwaway bits that were not fully developed. Jordan madly ad-libs through wild concepts, from a gasping, inarticulate Dwight Eisenhower trying to make a speech, to the problem of reformed rabbis who put on fakely perfect diction in sermonizing about "The Tow-Rawww." There's quick shtick as Sammy Davis, Jr. calls his white wife-to-be May Britt about the guests ("Ingemar Johansson? Hmm, cross out Floyd Patterson") and the food ("smorgasbord and water-melon").

There's sick humor about a German teacher trying to conquer the world, and a heroic pilot literally flying blind into enemy territory. Similar to Bruce's "Palladium" is a fast bit on Jordan's press agent who, for his $100 a day fee, fails to get Will into the papers, but smiles and insists "They're talkin' about ya." Finally he admits that they're saying, "Whatever became of Will?"

If Lenny could do George MacReady as a child, Jordan offered up Sir Ralph Richardson fondly indulging in a penchant for Borscht Belt insult humor. When Jack E. Leonard shouts that he's a "stone-headed fag," Richardson cries out, "Fat Jack, do some more of that schtick-lach, shpritz me by all means!"

The best bit is his nine-minute "Frankenstein" routine. Like Lenny, Will introduces the bit players, ranging from Mae Clark to "Mr. Show Business himself—Dwight Frye," but outdoes Bruce with vocal sound effects (thunder, creaky coffin lids, wind, shovels, digging into the earth). In pure stream-of-consciousness, Will relates how the hunchback and Dr. Frankenstein handle grave digging:

"Fritz, are you digging?" "Oh yeah man, I'm pickin' up on all this jazz." Hip hunchback. "No Fritz. You don't understand. Take off your coat first, then you can dig better. No, no, Fritz, don't try to put the shovel through your sleeve. Look. Listen— put the shovel down. Take off your coat. No. Leave your pants alone. No, don't— all right, take your pants down. Now take out your right arm. Now take out your left arm. Now take out your ... other arm? Hold your arms up, Fritz. You know something Fritz? You're built like a fork."

This is, unfortunately, Jordan's only stand-up album.

- TAPPED WIRES (Roulette R 25204) ** $5 $10

This one rarely rises beyond the obvious, but serves fairly well as a vehicle for Jordan's mimicry. In mock celebrity phone calls, Ed Sullivan talks to Albert Schweitzer, Nehru tries to get weapons from Robert McNamara, and Fidel Castro speaks to Khrushchev. Rhoda Brown, Adam Keith, and Tina Rome help out on some of the cuts. Most of the cuts are dated (Zsa Zsa Gabor with Conrad Hilton, Eddie Fisher trying to call Liz Taylor), but a few have some good silly humor (David Susskind calls Lawrence Welk and finds that his phone number is "Lowell 1 and a 2 and a 3 and a 4"). Jordan's impressions are often fun regardless of the script (his manic Welk, his outrageous Sullivan, the inane Sabu, and a melty, raspy Nick Kenny).

- ALL ABOUT CLEOPATRA (Topical Records T 1001) **1/2 $5 $10
- THE NEW FIRST FAMILY 1968 (Verve V/V6 15054) *** $5 $15

When the papers were full of the Taylor-Burton-Fisher scandal during the making of *Cleopatra*, Jordan was asked to star in the Topical studio disc with supporting comics Sammy Petrillo and Dave Starr. Though quickly done, the LP is appealing, filled with sloppy, silly humor and ad-libs.

One crazed and corny bit stretches to imagine *Cleopatra* remade as a Western. Jordan as Marc Antony, Chief of the Texas Rangers, reports: "Been down to Egypt, herding camels ..." Cleopatra asks him about various gang members. He reports, "Cassius went with the Daltons. Brutus, an honorable man, went with the James boys." "Where's Cicero?" "In Illinois. I thought everyone knew that...." "OOOH ... where'd that bullet come from?" "A gun ... I'm going to die ... I'm dying ... I'm ... dead." "This is no time to conjugate a verb!"

Jordan zips through a variety of impressions: Jack E. Leonard, Cary Grant, Eddie Fisher, Edward R. Murrow, Richard Burton doing James Mason, Senor Wences, double-talk specialist Al Kelly, and Groucho Marx.

In 1966, Bob Booker and George Foster (the team who made "The First Family") came up with an incredible, improbable idea: an *actor* actually winning a presidential election!

Jordan plays the new President of the United States: Cary Grant. The one-joke idea doesn't exactly provide huge laughs, and the script isn't strong, but the drawing card here is an entire album devoted to mimicry. With Jordan nailing down the main role, up and coming impressionists David Frye and John Byner joined veteran cartoon-voice personality Bob McFadden to supply the rest. Ironically, the even split among the impressionists meant that Jordan's other top impressions, Ed Sullivan and James Mason, would be done by Byner and Frye. The humor is mostly from the impressions rather than the script: Jordan's Cary Grant addressing everybody three times ("Judy Judy Judy, Dino Dino Dino, Jack Jack Jack") or Byner's Robert Stack going through grim repetitions ("top secret, mum's the word, hush hush, right chief, under wraps").

NOTES: Jordan starred on a ten-inch album "Roast of the Town" (Jubilee SP 980), which also appears on the two-disc compilation "For Those Who Have Everything" (Jubilee KS 1). Introduced with both his real name, Wilbur Rauch, and stage name, he does an award show with Ed Sullivan, Martin and Lewis, Arthur Godfrey, Desi Arnaz, Wally Cox and Groucho Marx. There isn't much of a script; the humor is in the impressions, most of them perfect. Jordan issued "Bye Bye Love" as a single from Hanover.

Jordan is on "The Sickniks" (see entry under The Sickniks) and Len Maxwell's "I'd Rather Be Right than President." He narrates the Jubilee (JGs 2071) sampler "A Laughing Matter" and was Nixon on Timmie Rogers's "Super Soul Brother" album (Partee PBS 2403). He also supplied the introductions (as Ed Sullivan) for an album on the Flying

Dutchman label. He was introducing a hysterical new comedian: Spiro Agnew. The album was nothing but the vice president's speeches set to a laugh track.

JIMMY JOYCE

- YOU DON'T HAVE TO BE IRISH (MCA 174) **1/2 $5 $10

Joyce switched to comedy after ten years as a bass-baritone for the New England Opera Company and a soloist with the Boston Symphony Orchestra. He billed himself as "The Improper Bostonian." Like another singer who turned to comedy, Rudy Vallee, Jimmy Joyce simply goes through the joke files and the joke books, comes up with a seamless series of mild sure-fire anecdotes and stories, and tells them reasonably well. He doesn't add anything to them. Here he tells a few drunk jokes:

"You know the difference between an Irish wedding and an Irish wake? One less Irish drunk. This uncle of mine was on his way to a wake with a couple of fellas and they stopped in a saloon. One guy said to the bartender, 'I'll have Three Feathers.' The other guy said, 'I'll have Four Roses.' And the uncle said, 'I'll have five martinis.' They finally staggered out of there, and they were getting into the car, and one of them said to the uncle, 'Dennis, are you gonna drive?' He said, 'I'll have to, I can't walk!' They got the car on a busy one way street goin' in the wrong direction. And a cop stopped 'em. He said, 'Where are you guys going, didn't you see see the arrows?' My uncle said, 'I didn't even see the Indians.' The cop said, 'Where are you goin'?' The uncle said, 'I don't know, but we must be late 'cause everybody else is comin' back.'"

A lot of the album varies between drunk jokes and jokes about priests and Catholics. Many of them are classic, and fine enough for the uninitiated, like the one about the old lady who tries to bring "Holy Water" through customs from Ireland. The customs official is amazed because the bottle contains whiskey. "It's a miracle!" the lady cries.

Joyce died of a heart attack on January 5, 1979. He was fifty-five.

HERB JUBIRT

- LAFF ME INTO THE BIG TIME (HI SHL 32095) **1/2 $5 $10

The title of the album suggests that Jubirt knew he was still in the minor leagues. Like any young performer, he was finding his way and showing the obvious influences of his favorites (Bill Cosby and Dick Gregory). On this 1975 release for a subsidiary of the London label, Jubirt's cadence is sometimes like Cosby's. Each individual word gets its own inflection: "In 1974, the *hippest* thing was ... strrrrreakin'." But he doesn't go all the way with cartoonish imagery and acted-out stories. Sometimes Jubirt is more political and caustic, like a Dick Gregory or Lenny Bruce, rhetorically calling the audience "Jim" and deliberately using the pronunciation "Negra."

Jubirt's riffs cover everything from white and black problems to a riff on gays: "I heard two old dudes talkin' the other day. 'I hear you goin' get married. You gonna marry a virgin?' The other one says, 'Is you crazy? You don't marry nothin' till you check it out. You don't know what you gettin' nowadays. Bought that Cadillac, you took it for a road test. Hell, you see these young boys wearin' their hair out to here. You might think you've got a she and end up with a he. It happened to me in Miami. I got drunk, four o'clock Sunday morning. Copped me a she. End up with a he. I got upstairs, I got so mad I start to let 'im go. But I had me a bird in the hand, Jim! You don't give up nothin' four o'clock in the morning. Matter of fact, we had a ball!'"

Did Jubirt become more Cosby, more Gregory, or more himself? There's no second album to supply the answer.

BOB KALIBAN

- GOLF IS A FOUR LETTER WORD (For Golfers Only 101) *** $5 $10

Kaliban, a personable storyteller, collected most of the standard golfing stories and found some fresh ones for this amusing (and not dirty despite the album title) studio disc. One of the standards:

"I was hitting some horrible shots one time. It wasn't unusual for me. I turned to the old guy who was caddying for me, and I said, 'I suppose you've seen worse golfers in your time.' He didn't say a word. So I repeated my question. Almost shouting this time, I said, 'Hey! I suppose you've seen worse golfers in your time.' He said, 'I heard you the first time—I was just trying to remember when.'"

I wonder if it was the same old codger who caddied for my wife one day. She said, 'I've never played this badly before.' And he said, 'You've played before?'"

KALIL AND TAYLOR

- MY PLUMBER DOESN'T MAKE HOUSE CALLS (Capitol ST 2619) *1/2 $4 $8

Frank Kalil, a Tucson disc jockey, teamed with advertising exec Jay Taylor for this obscure release. It's all Q&A interviews as the precocious Taylor pretends to be a door-to-door taxidermist, a cosmetologist, a retired dogcatcher, a Japanese society photo-grapher, and so on. Some of the ideas are promising, but the results are mild. Taylor doesn't vary his characterizations; every interview subject has the same bland voice. Kalil interviews the door-to-door taxidermist:

"I find it difficult to believe that a person with a pet to whom they've become attached would be willing to utilize your services. You must have a tremendous closing proposition."

"We can throw in little extras. Gimmicks ... there's the two pound box of droppings. A lot of people will take those for the realism. Like, the lady will surprise her husband. He'll come home in the evening and find them in the kitchen. And he'll get a newspaper and go, 'Shame doggy! Shame!' Then there's the deluxe unit, that's the little ring in the tongue. You pull it out, they roll over and play alive, and hum 'Ave Maria.'"

MILT KAMEN

- HERE'S MILT KAMEN (Capitol W 1565) **1/2 $5 $15
- AND THE FARE KEEPS GOING UP (Sceptor 591) ** $4 $8

Kamen was a comedian's comedian, a guy other comics always enjoyed. His Capitol album was produced by Mel Brooks with liner notes by Groucho Marx: "He takes the ridiculous and makes it sublime. Just when you think you've caught up with him, he does a quick switch and with one hand tied behind his back, turns the sublime into the ridiculous." Kamen appeared in nightclubs and on *The Ed Sullivan Show* but never really caught fire. One reason was his somewhat average appearance (resembling Carl Reiner a little).

At times his delivery is close to Brooks. Offering a little looney riff on a proper English doorman, he notes, "He LIKES to be a doorman! He stands there and says, 'I'm a DOORMAN, I've been a doorman for forty years! I'm part DOOR! My son will be a doorman after me. My daughter will be a window!'"

Other times he's closer to Reiner, showing a more thoughtful sense of obsession. He reports on watching a nature film: "They showed a bee making honey ... and you feel terrible. Look at that ugly little bee. Makes honey. I'm a nice looking person and all I can do is make a little wax with my ears, that's all." Similarly, on childhood, he's mildly perturbed that his teacher "would say crazy things like parallel lines never meet. We'd get despondent. You don't tell that to kids. We'd start to cry and go in the back of the room and drink ink."

Nothing's that visceral with Kamen. Predating *Attack of the Killer Tomatoes* by a decade, he launches into a bizarre story about a giant tomato. But where a Mel Brooks or Woody Allen would seize on it for wrenching laughs, Kamen is content to simply muse. The tomato shpritzes people and "they want to fight back, but did you ever get ketchup all over your clothes? You don't care anymore, you wanna go home."

It's a nice, slightly offbeat comedy album from a nice, slightly offbeat comedian.

"The Fare ..." lampooned the Long Island Rail Road, the subway, and other forms of mass transit during the strike-ridden Lindsay administration in New York. Supporting players include Bernie Travis, Lucille Gould, and Justin Gray.

The humor here is slice-of-life, more an indictment of neurotics who ride mass transit than mass transit itself:

"I can't stand being squeezed this way."

"Yes, I feel awful funny. I think my hand is on someone's—"

"Ass, you stupid ass! Take that hand away! Driver, stop the bus! This man assaulted me!"

"OK buddy, not only are you a chiseler, you're a pre-vert ... get off the bus...."

JACKIE KANNON

- LIVE FROM THE RATFINK ROOM (Roulette SRLP 505) **1/2 $10 $15
- MUSIC FOR RATFINK LOVERS (Ratfink LP 1313) * $4 $8

A cocky little comic who specialized in raunch '60s style, Kannon opened his own "Ratfink Room" and later started a profitable novelty book business. The "Live" album gives a pretty good idea of what it was like to, heh-heh, take in a daring nightclub act in the mid-60s. Booze and bawdy belly laughs abound as Kannon plays with the ringsiders: "Fool around baby? You like horny little Jewish boys? I don't want to frighten you, sir, but your fly is open and I fall in love easily!" There are audience shpritzes, too: "Look at the size of this guy! If he fell down he'd be halfway home.... I know that broad, sir, and I hope you have a good doctor!"

The finale has Kannon encouraging tipsy audience members to sing a song loaded with innuendo. When he tries to get a lady to repeat, "Sarah, Sarah, sittin' in her Chevrolet, all day long she sits and shifts," the results are predictably rude. Or as Kannon puts it with delightful understatement, "Lady, yer fulla shit!"

The Ratfink album is a mood music novelty. After each tame tune, including "Moon River" and "Young at Heart," Arlene Golonka breaks in to say, "Oooh, you rat fink!" or make a few giggles and groans that suggest either passion or post-nasal drip.

- SONGS FOR THE JOHN (Roulette R 25187) ** $5 $10
- POEMS FOR JOHN (Swan LP 503) ** $10 $15

Kannon had a minor hit with a hardcover book of dirty jokes and poems that had a hole punched through the top, and a chain inserted so that the book could be hung up in the bathroom. He made a few albums out of it, too. "Songs for the John" is little more than whiz-bang rhymes set to music. Each side has dozens, complete with orchestra and mixed chorus—things like: "Jack be nimble, Jack be quick, Jack jumped over the candlestick. Alas, he didn't clear the flame: now he's known as Auntie Mame."

One of the better songs, simply because it really is a song, is "Tomboy," which might be an answer to Eddie Fisher's "Dungaree Doll," released a year or two earlier. With Sinatra-like crooning, Jackie sings about "Tomboy, no silken lace, no makeup face. No frilly pink chiffon. She's hard as rock and wears a jock. She even stands up in the john." Contrasting lush, jazzy romantic music with peculiar reality: "She's thirty-six and goes for chicks. That's Tomboy. She'll pull a knife and rape your wife."

"Poems for John" was recorded live, but Kannon is mostly reading from his book. Any poetry reading, even sexy ditties and limericks, can sound a bit stilted. The big surprise is that Jack E. Leonard is in the audience, briefly heckling in the background. Kannon announces a poem and Jack shouts, "Try doing it with a little humor!"

• PROSE FROM THE CONS (Roulette R 502) **1/2 $5 $10

Kannon courageously visited a prison for this experimental comedy album, offering convicts a chance to perform stand-up comedy. Recorded at Southern Michigan Prison, Kannon does a few routines and one-liners ("Bars do not a prison make, if you find a gun in your angel cake") and plays straight man to some of the cons.

There are also full-length routines from a few convicts. Using material written by Kannon and Eli Basse, Duke McKinney does a nice routine about the "ups" of prison life: "After the stick-up and having to give up" he reports that his wife "is gonna get married up. Some strange man is gonna bring my kids up. They goin' get married up before my time is up!" And, as the applause from the fellow cons dies down, he continues, "and to sum it up, the next guy that sticks a gun in my hand on a stick-up, I'm gonna say, "Take that gun and stick it – I'll see ya around."

NOTES: Kannon also appears on the album "You Don't Have to Be Jewish" (Kapp KL 4503).

GABRIEL KAPLAN

• HOLES AND MELLOW ROLLS (ABC Dunhill ABCD-815, reissued as ABC Dunhill ABCD 905) *** $5 $10

Kaplan's affectionate monologues about Brooklyn High School life resulted in his *Welcome Back Kotter* sitcom. His album was re-released to cash in, substituting a photo of the *Kotter* cast for the original color painting of stylized mellow rolls (ice cream bars).

Kaplan does well with comedy on teenage topics: "Mothers like nocturnal emissions—because for the first time, their sons make their own beds: 'Uh, ma, I made my bed already ... I washed the sheets.' I always liked that expression, because it sounds like you're doing something special ... nocturnal emission could be part of the space program: Ground Control, you're now clear for nocturnal emission ... you go first, Buzz ... It's pretty difficult to masturbate in a space capsule ... there's no gravity. Jesus Christ, put on your helmet, Neal, Leo's jerkin' off again!"

The centerpiece is the twelve-minute title cut, about class dork Arnold Horshack and his attempt to win a ranking contest. A difficult thing when his main comeback was always "Up yah hole with a Mellow Roll and twice as fah with a Hershey Bah."

The album includes what was then a classic and is now a nostalgia item, his "drunk Ed Sullivan" bit, where the variety show host becomes fried and frank: "Well, for the Jews, Myron Cohen is gonna tell you some Jew jokes ... for the Negroes, James Brown'll be out here with some soul crap ... from Italy tonight ... where's Topo Gigio, the little faggot mouse?"

Kaplan appears on several David Frye albums as both performer and writer.

STEVE KARMEN

• THIS IS A CITY? (Jubilee JGM 2048) *1/2 $4 $12

Circa 1966 this twenty-five-year-old Bronx boy hoped to be some competition for Allan Sherman. "Old MacDonald Had a Farm" becomes "Sam McDonald Sells Used Cars"; "Camptown Races" turns into "Green Stamps"; and instead of the caissons, it's "The Subways Go Rolling Along," with a few mild joke lines:

"Through the snow through the sleet, fifty feet below the street, oh the subways keep rolling along. From the Bronx to Times Square, twice a day I pay my fare. Oh the subways keep rolling along. And it's ho ho hee, I ride the I.R.T. To do this your stomach must be strong. For there we are in a human cattle car. Oh the subways keep rolling along."

This one sometimes fetches a high price on the East Coast, if the similarity to Allan Sherman's work is known.

MICKEY KATZ

• BORSCHT (RCA Victor LPM 3193) ** $10 $25
• MICKEY KATZ AND HIS ORCHESTRA (Capitol H-298 (ten inch) $10 $20
    reissued as VERY BEST OF MICKEY KATZ (Capitol T 298) ** $5 $15

At sixteen, clarinetist Katz played "Rhapsody in Blue" with the Cleveland Orchestra. He went on to work with Paul Whiteman and do some World War II tours with Betty Hutton. In 1947 with Spike Jones's band, his Yiddish version of "Home on the Range" sold more than two hundred thousand copies. He also contributed the "gluck gluck" tongue-swallowing noises to some Spike'd classics. In 1948 he created *The Borscht Capades* and toured with it till a version, *Hello Solly*, came to Broadway in 1966. By that time, his son Joel Grey was on Broadway starring in *Cabaret*. That year he looked back on the evolution of ultra Semitic comedy: "In those days, Jews were scared to be Jewish. But now it's different. Now it's in to be Jewish." As for Allan Sherman, who had shot from nowhere in 1962 to superstardom, he said, "Well, good luck to him. Some people go the hard way, other people go bango."

Mickey's Capitol disc amply demonstrates the style that was never to change: popular hit tunes twisted to include endless references to Jewish foods and expressions. From today's perspective, much of Katz's material is extremely obvious, and some of it might seem slightly anti-Semitic due to his stereotypical heavy accent and high-pitched, nasal delivery.

Unlike Allan Sherman, Katz's lyrics were not usually subtle or artful. With Mickey, "The shrimp boats are coming" becomes "Herring boats are coming"; "Come onna my house I'm gonna give you candy" becomes "Come onna my house, I'm gonna give you knishes"; and "Ghostriders" becomes "Borscht Riders." One of the cleverer parodies takes the Disney hit "Ibbidy Bobbidy Boo" and makes it "The Baby, The Bubbe, and You" (Bubbe being the Yiddish word for grandmother). There's such advice as "A glass of seltzer will straighten you out—if not, baking soda will do."

"Borscht," a ten-inch album from 1954, has plenty of energetic and boisterously loud parody, including a Yiddish-language version of "St. Louis Blues" complete with punchy brass and Spike Jones-influenced cowbells. There are three squalling versions of Latin hits: "Tico Tico" becomes "Tickle Kitzel," music from "Carmen" gets klezmerized on "Carmen Katz," and "Mañana" becomes a mishmosh of Yiddish punch lines. On this early disc the humor is mostly in the klezmerized orchestrations.

- MISH MOSH (Capitol T 1102) ** $10 $20
- KATZ PUTS ON THE DOG (Capitol T 934) **1/2 $10 $20
- MOST MISHIGE (Capitol T 1102) **1/2 $10 $20
- KATZ PAJAMAS (Capitol T/ST 1257) ** $10 $20
- COMIN' AROUND THE KATZKILLS
  (Capitol W 1307, also released as MICKEY KATZ GREATEST HITS) **1/2 $10 $20

These albums date from 1958 to 1961, which is a heavy output for so few years. "Katz Pajamas" is a collection of retold children's stories with musical backing. "Comin' 'Round the Katzkills" features some of Mickey's best jazz arrangements ("Toot Toot Tootsie," "Old Black Smidgick," and "Hermendel's Koch-a-Lain") sung in a lower, more natural style. The lyrics slip between English and Yiddish, and it's usually the latter that gets the punch lines. "Vus is a Veib" and "The Briss" are amusing, atypical anecdotal monologues told without a stereotypical accent.

"Katz Puts on the Dog" (album notes by Slapsy Maxie Rosenbloom) has a highlight in his kosherized version of "Tico Tico" (complete with the gurgling gulping fondly remembered from his Spike Jones days), and on the Yiddish version of Elvis Presley's "Hound Dog" he sings to a "doity dog" who is almost beneath contempt! Why that dog doesn't even wrap tefillin!

"You're a Doity Dog" would've fit in perfectly on one of the more eccentric albums Katz made, "The Most Mishige." Katz tries to kosherize rock songs of the day. "Rock around the Clock" becomes "K'nock around the Clock": "Yeah Manishewitz, Sweet Edelstein, we're gonna knock around the clock tonight!" Another, "Knish Doctor," has even been re-released on a "Dr. Demento" album. Katz's weird nasal voice can still be funny, or at least strange, and is effective when matched to looney lyrics: "Way down in Africa, a dotin in the Jungle. You'll find a knish doctor who looks just like your uncle ... oooh hah, ya ha ha, mendel maishe, pisha-pisha-paysha ..." Katz demolishes opera on "The Barber of Schlemiel": "Figaro, Feygeleh, Feygeleh, Feygeleh!") and does some Yiddish versions of such unlikely tunes as "Chinatown, My Chinatown," "Darktown Strutter's Ball," and "Hawaiian War Chant," even resurrecting some Spike Jones "gunkgunk" swallow noises.

"Mish Mosh" is to formula, as hit songs get pickled. Tennessee Ernie Ford's "Sixteen Tons" becomes a kvetch about toiling at a deli: "You load sixteen tons of hard salami, corned beef, rolled beef, and hot pastrami ..." Later, he relates how he first came into the world: "Mine poppa und mamma they wanted a baby. A goil for sure or a boychik maybe. When poppa saw me he said, 'Nurse, what's dis?' She said, 'Call the moil, there's gonna be a bris.'"

Katz's style, in small doses, can be a tonic. Especially for those who remember Dr. Brown's Celery Tonic. It's hard not to chuckle when he chirps, "How much is that pickle in the window, the one that's on top of the pail?"

- BORSCHT JESTER (Capitol T/ST 1445) **1/2 $10 $20
- KATZ AT THE UN (Capitol T/ST 1603) ** $10 $20
- HELLO SOLLY (Capitol W 2731) **1/2 $10 $20

For examples of Katz as a monologist, these albums offer a wide selection of classic jokes and stories. "Hello Solly," based on Katz's revue, is only one-fourth Katz. Stan Porter and Vivian Lloyd sing and Larry Best offers a monologue. Using his normal speaking voice, Katz introduces the acts and mixes a few songs with ten minutes of classic gags. He tells the one about the ninety-year-old man who went out with a woman in her '80s. She tells her friend the next morning, "I had to slap his face three times!" The friend says, "Why, did he get fresh?" She answers, "No, I thought he was dead."

"Katz at the U.N." is a concept album, not completely successful, as interviewer Len Weinrib discusses various current events with a peculiar politician: "How would you like to take a trip to the moon?" ""I wouldn't mind at all, as long as I could be back for Pesach."

"Borscht Jester" has album notes from Chico Marx, who admits that Katz's stories are old: "You may have heard some of them before, just as I had, but I'll guarantee you've never heard them told better." Chico probably never heard of Myron Cohen. Katz tells one about two old men: "They were sitting on a park bench in Prospect Park in Brooklyn. And one of them said to the other, 'To tell you the truth, I feel like a million dollars.... I got good dreams, makes me feel like a million dollars.' His friend says, 'Give me a for instance. What kind of dream you got makes you feel like a million dollars?' He says, 'Well, I had a dream yesterday that I took a walk from Prospect Park in Brooklyn down to Delancey Street, fifteen miles each way, front and back, and I feel like a million dollars!' The other guy says, 'This is a dream? I had me a dream. I had a dream that last night I took an apartment at the Waldorf-Castoria Hotel. I open the door and who's there? Marilyn Monroe! I says, "Come in, Bubbeleh, make yourself to home." She sits down. Comes another knock on the door. Oh boy! Jayne Mansfield. I said, "You sit down too, darling."' The other one said, 'You dirty dog, why didn't you call me?' He said, 'I did. Your wife told me you were taking a walk on Delancey Street!'"

- THE FAMILY DANCED (Capitol H 457) $10 $25
- WEDDINGS, BAR MITZVAHS AND BRISSES (Capitol T 1021) $10 $15
- SING ALONG WITH MICKELE (Capitol T/ST 1744) $10 $20
- SIMCHA TIME: KLEZMER MUSIC (World Pacific CDP 7243) $8

Occasionally Katz played it straight, giving his band a chance to race through bouncy dance tunes. Despite the parody cover featuring Mickey with a goatee, "Sing Along with Mickele" is actually a real Jewish version of "Sing Along with Mitch," complete with song sheets for "Hava Nagila" and other Jewish favorites. Katz introduces the selections using his normal straight voice, as opposed to his more familiar high-pitched, nasal Jewish accent.

"Family Danced" is a ten-inch album with a lot of happy tunes and folk dances, including "Keneh Hora," "Grandma's Draidel," "Mazeltov Dances," and "Trombenik Tanz," as performed by Katz and a band that includes Mannie Klein, Si Zentner, and Benny Gill on violin.

1994's CD reissue of "Weddings, Bar Mitzvahs and Brisses," now titled "Simcha Time," adds five musical tracks previously available only as singles ("Simcha Time) or never released ("Bublitchki" and "Fountainbleu Freilach" among others). There are also three music tracks from the "Hello Solly" album: "Mickey's Mishegoss," "Sunrise Sunset," and "Yiddish Folk Melody."

NOTES: Several Katz albums are available via import, including Israeli pressings from CBS. Katz fanciers should be aware of the 1993 album "Don Byron Plays the Music of Mickey Katz" (Elektra 79313-2). A black jazz clarinetist with a fondness for klezmer music, Byron re-creates the Katz instrumental style on a few joyous and brassy cuts. Eight feature fairly accurate Katz imitator Lorin Sklamberg re-creating Mickey's vocal stylings.

BOB KAUFMANN

- TRIP THRU A BLOWN MIND (LHI Records EL 12002) *1/2 $4 $8

At the time of this release, Kaufmann was known for his "Mad World" newspaper column syndicated throughout California. On this studio album, which features a supporting cast, he's not a bad performer, though his LBJ impression during a mock press conference isn't much.

For a "blown mind," he's come up with a lot of very familiar gags. A segment covers the advice columnist "Dear Scabby": "Do I have bad breath?" a questioner asks. Scabby answers: "Dear frustrated, we're really not certain, but the next time you send us a letter, would you mind using a sponge to seal the envelope?" There's easy laughs when a "Smog Conference" report turns out to be a bunch of people coughing. And this from a mock news report: "When he appeared in California to stump the state in support of Pat Brown's unsuccessful bid for re-election, Bobby Kennedy, the New York senator from Boston, was accused of being a carpetbagger. Even if Pat Brown lost, new luster was added to the brilliant Kennedy legend. Other politicians before them have tried carpetbagging, but when the Kennedys do it, they go wall to wall."

BEATRICE KAY

- HAVING A PARTY (Fax LP 108, reissued as Laff A 108) *1/2 $5 $10

The title is accurate; Kay tells anecdotes in front of a small but friendly crowd as if it were a private house party. Kay gained fame in the '50s with enthusiastic re-creations of Gay '90s hits. Her style and delivery is similar to Gwen Verdon. Many of her long stories are about her career. There's nothing very suggestive here, even if she recorded for an "adult" party label, and nothing that would be any more interesting than what she might have said on an ordinary '60s talk show. Kay issued a lot of fairly straight songs, and fans can still find them from time to time. "Naughty Nineties" (Columbia CL 6025) is a ten-incher featuring some corny novelties, including "Heaven Will Protect the Working Girl," "What You Gonna Do When the Rent Comes 'Round," and "Teasing."

DANNY KAYE

- DANNY KAYE (Decca DLP 5033) ** $5 $10
- DANNY KAYE (Columbia CL 6023) ** $5 $10
- DANNY KAYE ENTERTAINS (Columbia CL 6245) ** $5 $10
- PURE DELIGHT (Harmony HL 7012,
    re-released as BEST OF DANNY KAYE, Harmony HL 7314) *** $5 $10

The Decca and Columbia ten-inch albums, like most of Kaye's records, blend straight songs with comedy numbers. The Decca disc has the "Lobby Number" from "Up in Arms," and even without his puckish smile and coy visuals it's an amusing look at movies, with fast-paced lyrics satirizing opening credits: "Screenplay by Gluck from a stageplay by Motts from a story by Blip from a chapter by Ronk from a sentence by Dokes from a comma by Stokes from an idea by Grokes, based on a Joe Miller's Jokes ..." Most of the cuts on these ten-inchers turn up on standard-length albums.

Some of Danny's classics of sophisticated nonsense are on the Harmony album, like "Anatole of Paris": "Pa was forced to be a hobo because he played the oboe. And the oboe it is clearly understood—is an ill wind that no one blows good." There's the cautionary tale "Jenny" from "Lady in the Dark": "Jenny made her mind up when she was twelve that into foreign languages she would delve. But at seventeen to Vassar it was quite a blow that in twenty-seven languages she couldn't say no." Other fine cuts include Kaye's almost definitive version of "Minnie the Moocher"; the silly "Babbitt and the Bromide," where Danny duets with himself; and "Dinah," which derives whatever humor it has from misplaced pronunciation: "Deenah, eez there anyone feena, in the state of Caroleena?"

NOTES: Kaye made many albums of more or less straight material, including "The Best of Danny Kaye" for Decca. His original cast recordings and movie soundtracks include "Merry Andrew" (Capitol T 1016), "Court Jester" (Decca DL 8212), and "Me and the Colonel" (RCA LSO 1046). He released "Danny at the Palace" (Decca DL 8461), two ten-inch albums of Gilbert and Sullivan that include such wry patter numbers as "The Judge's Song," "My Name Is John Wellington Wells," and "When I Was a Lad" (Decca DL 5033 and 5094); children's records like "Grimm's Fairy Tales" (Golden 92); and the kiddie comic song collection "Mommy Gimme a Drink of Water" (Capitol T 937);

along with "Three Billion Millionaires," (United Artists UXL 4), which was a musical made especially for records and created for the United Nations. Kaye's gaily sophisticated style has begun to date and prices for his albums have decreased in the '90s.

GARRISON KEILLOR

- ANNIVERSARY ALBUM (Prairie Home Companion PHC 404) * $5 $10
- THE FAMILY RADIO (Prairie Home Companion PHC 606) * $5 $10
- LAKE WOBEGON LOYALTY DAYS (Virgin VC 7 91109 2) * $8

A comedian for people who have no sense of humor, National Public Radio host/satirist Garrison Keillor has a numbing and oozy baritone as creepy as sitting in syrup. His music, sort of Martin Mull on quaaludes, is a soporific affectation toward country and swing, and usually sops up about half of each show's running time. He will faux-wistfully croon from time to time, and his audience's and his own appreciation for this is akin to parents' pride in a newborn's bowel movement.

The homely down-home monologues and radio commercials about his mythical mid-American "Lake Wobegon" come off as pretentious and forced, not deserving to be mentioned in the same breath as Bob and Ray or Vic and Sade.

From "The Family Radio," reciting with all the quiet tongue-in-cheek and self-satisfied smugness of the star amateur at the local poetry reading, Keillor drones out a segment of "News from Lake Wobegon," including this announcement:

"At Our Lady of Perpetual Responsibility, Father Frank from the seminary will be subbing for Father Emil who is taking his annual vacation. He goes South, takes the same trip, goes and makes a bus tour of Civil War battlefields, and uh, he should be in Bowling Green, Kentucky, I believe, today, visiting his brother, Father Francis, who is a missionary among the Baptists down there. And in the meantime, Father Frank is in the pulpit and will be speaking tomorrow. His sermon is on "The Back 9 of Life." Father Frank is kind of an easy priest, and he's an easier confessor than Father Emil is. Father Emil who sometimes kind of heists himself up in the confessional and says "Oh, you didn't. Oh, shame on ya ..."

A cult formed for Keillor the same way mold forms on white bread, and since no commercial radio station could have survived broadcasting such dullness, it was up to National Public Radio to not only run these nudge-producing trifles, but sell endless volumes of cassette tapes via mail order. Those inclined toward knowing titters and forced chuckles can sip Keillor's demitasse wit on such double cassette collections as "Gospel Birds and Other Stories," "A Prairie Home Companion 10th Anniversary," and "Final Performance."

The only release for Keillor on a major label is "Lake Wobegon Loyalty Days" on Virgin, which is slightly more tolerable. There's less fake wistfulness and misplaced wonder in this slice-of-life recollection of freezing days in Minnesota: "Winter is the basis of Minnesota citizenship, it's the bond that holds people together in this state. Those days when they have a low of thirty below and they're forecasting a high the next day of ten below. That's when Minnesotans come to love each other, with pure affection, everybody trusts each other then. There's no crime here. Nobody locks their doors here. Doors are frozen shut, they don't need to."

Seriously damaged fans can chew over the audio granola on eight solid hours (four CDs or eight cassettes) of "The 20th Anniversary Collection," "Lake Wobegon Days," and "More News from Lake Wobegon," etc. These items are mostly sold mail order and in the lamer book shops.

AL KELLY

- FUNNY YOU DON'T LOOK IT (RCA Victor LSP 3433) ** $5 $15

Double-talk comic Al Kelly simply uses a Jewish accent for this 1966 sketch album evidently inspired by the hit Kapp Records discs featuring Al Jacobi (such as "When You're in Love the Whole World Is Jewish"). Delightful Minerva Pious (Fred Allen's Mrs. Nussbaum) is also aboard, with Gilbert Mack, Larry Alpert, Rhoda Mann, and Rhoda Brown. It's a rare album, but fetches over $10 only in some East Coast locales.

On most cuts, the one-joke gag is that a famous person (Columbus, Paul Revere, William Tell, for example) turns out to be Jewish. Robin Hood complains: "I used to rob from de rich and give to de poor. Then the poor became de rich and de rich became de poor. Den I had to rob the poor who are now the rich, and give to the rich who are now de poor ... vell to tell you the truth, the bookkeeping got so confusing now I just rob ever'body!"

A couple of Joey Adams/Al Kelly routines appear on "Do You Wanna Have a Laugh" (Coral CRL 57380).

BENNY KELLY

- MEET THE FUN MASTER LIVE AT THE OLD EAST END (USA LP 104) ** $8 $15

Similar to Moms Mabley in flavor, raspy Benny Kelly has enough personality to keep an audience amused, even though his collection of gags and stories is familiar and sometimes aged. With a rim shot or two helping him out, he guilelessly recites his lines, acting as if the unlikely stories are all true. He talks about a hazardous flight into town:

"The pilot laughed and said, 'You know, Kelly, half the people down there thought we was gonna have an accident.' I said, 'Do you know fifty percent of the people up here did?' Oh, I was so nervous I refused the service of the air limousine. I said, 'I'm going to ride the bus to the club.' And you know what the transportation situation is in Chicago today, don't you? Why, the bus I boarded was so crowded, even the men were standin'. Oh, but I saw a vacant seat. I saw a vacant seat and I gallantly pointed it out to a lady. And then raced her for it. Oh, I beat her! I beat her! Yeah ... Just then an organ grinder and his monkey got on the bus and sat down behind me. The monkey was the cutest little fella. Yeah, he started playing with me. Yes he did, he started messin' up my tie, and messin' up my hair, until

I got tired of the darn brute. I went to the motorman and I said, 'See here, I didn't know you allowed monkeys on this car.' He said, 'If you'll be quiet, no one'll know you're on here!'"

BOB KENNEDY AND RALPH ROBY

- THE NEXT FAMILY (Kanda KLP 5001) *1/2 $5 $15

The solemn combo of Kennedy and Roby sit in an empty studio in Fresno, and with an uncertain pause or stumble now and then, read their jokeless satirical script that looks forward to 1980, and "the first Negro president."

There's stark, heavy-handed irony here, as whites are forced to suffer role reversal. There are no white baseball players. Whites are refused admission to the University of Mississippi. And the Ku Klux Klan, now pushing for "total integration" under its leader, George Wallace, complains to the black chief executive that "Negro police officers have been using fire hoses, police dogs, and electric cattle prods as a means to break up the mass demonstrations staged by the white minority groups."

The black president echoes the same platitudes that white politicians were using in 1964: "We all know from experience that integration is not something that happens overnight. The white minority must not be discouraged if they do not achieve integration immediately. It is our duty as Americans to help the whites in their fight for equal status as citizens of this country. I feel that as the whites continue to show their conduct, their living habits, and their desire for better education, that they will be received by the Negro majority as equal in every walk of life."

JOHN F. KENNEDY

- THE KENNEDY WIT (RCA Victor VDM-101) *1/2 $4 $12
- THE WIT OF JOHN F. KENNEDY (Challenge) *1/2 $4 $10

RCA's 1964 tribute narrated by David Brinkley opens with Adlai Stevenson saying Kennedy's "wit was fast, audacious, impertinent." But the record doesn't capture much of the Kennedy wit or charisma. Part of the problem is that, influenced by Kennedy, many presidents began to use humor. A Kennedy press conference over thirty years later sounds no different from any politician using wisecracks:

"The Republican National Committee recently adopted a resolution saying you were pretty much a failure," someone calls out. "I'm sure it was passed unanimously," JFK retorts, to gails of laughter. "The Democratic Platform ... promises equal rights for women.... What have you done for women according to the promises of the platform?" "Well, I'm sure we haven't done enough," he answers, once more to hearty chuckles. "We ought to do better and I'm glad you reminded me of it," he adds.

Though these were the hi-fi '60s, some of the material is of worse quality than 1940s radio transcriptions. But every now and then there's a pungent one-liner: "I have the best of both worlds," he tells a Yale commencement audience, "a Harvard education and a Yale degree." At one point, someone asks Kennedy how he felt about Vaughn Meader's album, whether it was enjoyment or annoyment: "Annoyment! No ... actually I listened to Mr. Meader's record, but I thought it sounded more like Teddy than it did me. So he's annoyed."

The Challenge record opens with a narrator praising even the most mundane aspects of John Kennedy: "At social events, large and small, he was always able to enjoy himself and aid to the enjoyment of others. As a swimmer and yachtsman, he displayed, despite a troublesome back, an athletic image with vigor.... As a husband and father he had many of his greatest moments."

A half hour of excerpts from press conferences are spliced together, few of them remarkable. Asked about "a direct telephone line" to Russia, he answers, "We have communications with the Soviet Union. I think the problem is not communications, it's viewpoint. We understand each other, but we differ." The better lines turn up on "The Kennedy Wit."

LARRY KENNEY

- THE HONEST TO GOD ... VERY LAST NIXON ALBUM (Brunswick BL754201) *1/2 $5 $12

By 1972 there probably wasn't a single person in America who hadn't thrust his or her hands up in the air, pouted like a fish, and come out with a hollowly serious "I AM the President" impression of Richard Nixon. And, to judge from the interminable number of Nixon/Watergate comedy albums, most everyone in America put out a record of it.

Here, WJJD disc jockey Larry Kenney plays Nixon. The dreary blackout sketches involve Nixon going on game shows (*What's My Line*, *Let's Make a Deal*, and *Jeopardy*), trying his hand at a commercial for Comet, and in other ways hunting up new avenues for employment. Earle Doud, who had a hand in the original "First Family" album among many others, produced the disc, using the "First Family" technique of taking a single joke and belaboring it for two minutes into a mini-sketch with a punch line ending.

For nearly a minute, Nixon tries to convince people that he's trustworthy. But, for a punch line, David Eisenhower (played by Marshall Efron) turns up, asks for some money he's owed, and proceeds to untrustingly count the bills. "It's all there, David!" Nixon cries. David continues going "one, two, three ..."

At a picnic, a tedious routine ends with him defensively insisting he didn't burn the steak. But he cooked it for "twenty minutes."

The strangest thing about this little failure is that the part of Pat Nixon is played by the supernaturally glamorous Julie Newmar. With no clue about exactly how to satirize Pat, the writers give Julie some very strange lines. Pat Nixon tells reporters that she collects rust: "I have rust from all over the world. I have rust from the Great Wheel of China." "You mean the Great Wall of China.""No, the Great Wheel of China, it operates a well." "The Great Well of China?" "Yes, the Great Wheel of China operates the Great Well of China, which is right next to the Great Wall of China."

LENNY KENT

• THE PUT DOWN HUMOR OF LENNY KENT (Audio Fidelity AFSD 6198) ** $5 $10

Kent was clearly influenced by Don Rickles and the Milton Berle/Phil Foster schtick-up comics of the late '50s. Foster introduces him on the record. Kent sounds closer to Berle than Rickles as he desperately belabors a female ringsider on this 1968 album: "Have you any children in seventeen years (of marriage)? How many have you got? One? In seventeen? You know why you only have one? Because you talk too much! One child in seventeen years, that's all? Why don't you try Ovaltine. Do you play gin rummy, ma'am? Don't go for gin every hand, knock now and then, that's the idea! Look how good you look with your beautiful red hair. I see little black roots, sweetie.... Women are the stupidest dumbbell vegetables in the world. You don't believe me? You're gonna tell me women are smarter than men? Well, would a man buy a shirt that buttons in the back, Yenta?"

The Romanian-born Kent teamed with Jackie Miles from 1931 to 1937, and after World War II became a regular in Vegas. Like most Vegas comics, even at his worst he's hard to ignore—always manic, harsh, and ready to snap the crowd to attention with one-liners, some borrowed, some brawling, some basic. Examples of each: "I found a new restaurant, a Chinese-German restaurant, only a half hour later you're hungry for power." "You know what an Irishman is, don't ya? That's an English Puerto Rican." "Alimony. That's like putting a dime in the parking meter after they towed your car away."

In 1980 he retired, but chose to stay in Las Vegas, where he died of a heart attack May 1, 1985. He was seventy-two.

DAVE KETCHUM

• THE LONG PLAYING TONGUE (Sheraton 1001) ** $7 $15

Ketchum was a popular comedy character actor in sitcoms, often playing a goofy foil. He was a regular on the short-lived '60s series *Camp Runamuk* and appeared as a harried agent (usually stuffed in a garbage can or file cabinet) on *Get Smart*. On this early '60s album he plays a grumbly doctor on the golf course, a gruff boss lecturing his workers, a bureaucrat dedicating a new highway ("I would've been here sooner but I was stuck in traffic"), a yacking sports reporter giving the news, and so on. Pre-dating his *Camp Runamuk* days, he does a routine as a camp counselor who is sick of kids: "All right boys, let's settle down ... my name's Dave, and I'm gonna be your counselor. I want you to think of me as your friend and pal and your mother and father all rolled into one. But remember one thing now. When you talk to me—call me Master! Now, uh, I'm here to help you in every way, so if you have any little problems, we'll talk them over. Yes? You have a problem. Someone swiped your sleeping bag. Well, ha ha ha, don't worry about that. Somebody swiped my sleeping bag and I got another one! So figure it out for yourself."

Like the sitcoms he appeared in through the '60s, there are a few good lines mixed into the manufactured scripts. As the head of an auto factory he grandly tells employees: "I want you to look in your pay envelopes next Christmas and you'll know that I keep the Christmas spirit around here. Because in each and every pay envelope you'll find ... snow."

Ketchum plays Clyde Barrow on Gary Owens's parody album about Bonnie and Clyde.

ALAN KING

• SUBURBIA (Seeco SAW 2101) *1/2 $10 $20
• THE BEST OF ALAN KING (Seeco LP 473, reissued as Bronjo BR 109) *1/2 $10 $20

Evidently reading material from his mid-60s best-seller *Anybody that Owns Their Own Home Deserves It,* King (formerly Alan Kniberg) has no audience here, just a cocktail piano sympathetically accenting some of the lines. The Seeco album interrupts the monologues with songs ("Superb Suburban Life," "I Don't Want to Cha Cha," "Welcome Wagon Song," "I Love the City").

"The Best of Alan King" removes most of the songs, but is basically the same record. This is not the "best" of King; the compilation CD "The Sullivan Years" gives a better idea of his aggravated, scowling style. However, here one can almost imagine the curl to his lip, the look of disgust on his face, the glum shake of his head as he relentlessly enumerates the aggravations of suburban life, from lawn care to commuting. Grousing about painters: "Oh, and what money they get! We had three painters working at my house, but only two of them actually worked. One of them sat on the lawn all day. He couldn't stand the smell of paint. Then we had a paperhanger. Oh what a miserable character this was! He didn't really want to be a paperhanger, but he heard that's how Hitler started."

King sings a few songs, which is the big surprise here. These include an anti-cha-cha song where the lyrics go, "I don't join in the hoo rah-rahs ... ay ay, I don't wanna cha-cha-cha."

ALEXANDER KING

• ALEXANDER KING READS FROM MINE ENEMY GROWS OLDER (Urania UX 120) ** $8 $15
• LOVE AND HISSES (United Artists UAL 3116) *1/2 $5 $15

An artist who stole nearly fifty prints from the Metropolitan Museum, a nine-year morphine addict, a man who fluctuated between suicide (once), prison (twice), hospitals (three times), and marriage (four times), it was perhaps only natural that Alexander King would end up a colorful raconteur on Jack Paar's *Tonight Show*. Thanks to the Paar exposure, his books became best-sellers.

On the Urania studio disc, King reads four selections from his best-seller *Mine Enemy Grows Older,* one from *May this House Be Safe from Tigers,* and some miscellany. He reads his pontifications in a searing, cranky, slightly bitter and bitten Viennese accent. Some of it is self-indulgent for two reasons: 1) literary humor tends toward smugness in tone, whether it's S. J. Perelman, King, or even Woody Allen; 2) King was such an idolized raconteur he must have thought any trivia of his existence became golden simply by his caustic recollection of it.

On point two, King is partially justified.

One segment is nothing more than King's discussion of a kidney operation, but his description of finding a doctor is rich in expression and delivered with high, resonant, strident and curmudgeonly passion: "I wanted to reach a purely human level of sympathy and understanding with him first. I wanted him to like me. There you have it. I'm like an ancient iguana full of splenetic wrinkles. I wanted this character to respond to my personal charm. I covered him with the slime of my amiability until he looked webfooted. I got no response ... I became convinced ... this squat, ovoid, red-faced man permanently submerged in his urinous misgivings and speculations had finally turned into a kidney."

Other cuts cover diverse subjects from drug addiction ("I liked morphine from the start ... it made me graciously tolerant of every form of human imbecility including my own") to a meditation on women, who are just "dangling sexual giblets ... just look at a naked woman and see the sad, pear-shaped droop of her buttocks, the anomolous pubic goatee, the breasts so overtly accessible to injury and you will be looking at the most vulnerable creature that walks this earth."

"Love and Hisses" collects anecdotes one might hear from any crotchety old man:

"I couldn't get my diet and so I ate the ordinary food, and I must tell you a great secret. I'm missing nothing. Or very little. Because food has deteriorated terribly. Vegetables are no longer grown in the ground, they're grown in aquariums obviously. Our strawberries are as big as melons and they have no flavor at all. And if you've ever eaten a tomato recently they come in those little glass coffins. And the bread is so hideous, on the label it says no human hand has touched it. Well, I tell you no human hand should."

King's wife Maggie, thirty years younger, is on hand to sing four painless songs, two in Yiddish. At the end, her husband prompts her to recite Christina Rosetti's poem "Birthday of My Love," which shows the tolerance of semi-intellectual New York audiences. King, displaying a George Jessel heart under his prickly skin, listens to the poem (and flowery lines like "My heart is like a singing bird") and urges, "Love beyond your means and your heart is going to bear endless rich dividends for you."

PHILO ROCKWELL KING, III

- The Pleasure of His Company (Sister Kate SKS 230) *1/2 $3 $8

In the '60s and '70s, Rock King played piano and told jokes in various small tourist joints, mostly The Lighthouse Inn Sand Bar in Cape Cod and Sister Kate's in Stowe, Vermont. He issued several souvenir albums, either half comedy and half music or all music. This is the only pure comedy offering. There's nothing special here, just a working pro telling long anecdotal jokes, set pieces ("Cinderella" done in spoonerisms) and standard joke book defiinitions: "I'm a pseudointellectual. That means I know a lot but I can't think of it."

SAM KINISON

- LOUDER THAN HELL (WARNER BROS. 1-25503) *** $5 $15

In the late '80s, after a five-year struggle, fat and glowering ex-preacher Kinison became a comic sensation. Considered "the new Lenny Bruce" he did his best to live up to his bad boy image, both in his choice of material and his private life of sex and drugs.

Kinison literally screams out his outrageous lines on this impressive debut, which contains his exasperated put-downs of Charles Manson, who found kill messages in Beatles tunes: "You'd've gotten the same message outta The Monkees, you dickhead!" His notorious misogyny bit about an ex-wife is here: "I have to drink a six-pack of Heinekin to keep from cuttin' your f-----' head off and puttin' it in a camera bag ... I don't support wife beating. I UNDERSTAND IT!"

Kinison's demonic shock humor, punctuated by frustrated shouts of anger and comical "Oh OHHHH!" shrieks of pain, made him the most controversial comedian since Richard Pryor. In fact, Sam told me Pryor's "Bicentennial Nigger" album was the "f------ ballsiest" comedy album ever made. Like Pryor, fans could see achingly naked comic tragedy amid the furiously foaming mixture of truth, hostility, rage, and exagerrated rapping. And, like Don Rickles, most fans identified with his comic frustration, realizing it was an act. They'd walk out imitating his safety valve screams.

The album includes rare religious satire, the first potent lines since Lenny Bruce. Kinison doubts if Christ would want to come back: "I like bein' the only savior that can use his hand as a f-----' whistle." It also contains Sam's classic routine on the starving children of Ethiopia, his sense of pathos turning into a rage: "Stop sending money to world hunger organizations ... send 'em luggage! Hey, we just drove seven hundred miles with your food and it occurred to us—there wouldn't be world hunger if YOU PEOPLE would live where the FOOD IS! You live in a F----- - DESERT! Nothing grows here!... We have deserts in America, but we don't live in 'em, asshole!"

- HAVE YOU SEEN ME LATELY? (Warner Bros. 25748-1) ** $8

Kinison's simultaneous sympathy and rage, sensitivity and satire, love and hate, boiled over on either side of "the cutting edge." At times, his screams verged into self-parody, and around 1987, when he played huge venues normally reserved for rock stars, he began to pander to his new following. They weren't the hip comedy club intelligentsia, but partying heavy metal headbangers. All they wanted was gross-out humor and "outlaw" comedy for its own sake and Kinison gave it to them.

"Have You Seen Me Lately" (the cover photo of a teen Sam parodying missing kid photos on milk cartons) has his gleefully self-admitted attempt at finding the worst possible subject for humor (his choice: homosexual necrophilia). The result was histrionic enough for a few laughs, but drew angry protests from gays. Now considering himself a rock star, he offers a comic version of "Wild Thing."

In a way, Kinison was just following the Lenny Bruce instinct of taking what he considered the truth, and adding some comic hyperbole. But while his punk supporters like Billy Idol praised him, Elton John used a rock awards ceremony to brand him a pig. Sam was bewildered to find himself excoriated for the same thing he was praised for: being outrageous.

Outrageous was the word for his bit championing drunk driving. The cheering mob howls as Sam grumbles, "God, they have made such a big deal about this, haven't they?... Like you go to your car sayin', 'I hope I slide into a family of six tonight....' You're doin' your best. Don't drink and drive. Shit, we don't want to ... but there's no other way to get ... back to the HOUSE!"

The irony: On April 10, 1992, driving to a concert date in Nevada, Sam was killed in a head-on collision with a seventeen-year-old drunk driver.

- LEADER OF THE BANNED (Warner Bros 26073) ** $8

The cover picture depicting a variation on "The Last Supper" (a smirking Kinison with a bevy of lingerie clad women) showed Sam was more caught up with his own celebrity than in producing gut-wrenching belly laughs. A full side of the album is heavy metal rock, and the other has way too much coasting. His undemanding crowd is content to let him scream a lot and do audience participation bits.

He introduces Lenny Bruce's mother from the audience and tries for some Lenny tasteless prankishness with a bit about putting old people to death and by bringing out a wheelchair-bound man who tirades against Jerry Lewis: "That son of a bitch, he hasn't done a goddam thing for me! He's been doin' this goddam telethon for thirty years now!" The prank finale has Kinison calling up an audience member's ex-girl and raging to the audience, "she's a whore ... and we hate her guts!!!"

- LIVE FROM HELL (Priority P2 53863) **1/2 $8

Sam never recovered from the gay protests and the beginnings of the "politically correct" movement. He began thinking about "family entertainment" as his future (as opposed to joking about it, as he had in the past).

The best news about this 1993 posthumous CD is that it is not some bootleg-quality release tossed out to make a fast buck. Kinison intended the performance to be released, and makes several references during his act to the taping. But anyone expecting some karmic "last gasp" of outrage, some prophetic message from beyond, will be disappointed.

The CD is not divided into tracks, making it difficult to immediately get to the riffs listed in the album booklet.

GEORGE KIRBY

- NIGHT IN HOLLYWOOD (Dooto 250) **1/2 $10 $15

Black impressionist George Kirby was never that bawdy, even on this album from the adults-only Dooto label. He tells the story about the old maid who received three magical wishes: "First wish she says, 'Gee, I wish I was young and beautiful again.' Right away she turned to a gorgeous young lady. Then she thought about her second wish. 'Gee, I wish I had a lot of money....' Right away she was loaded. Then she started thinking about her third wish. While she was thinkin' she was lookin' across the room at the old tom cat been with her for years. 'Gee, I wish old Tom would turn into a handsome young man.' Right away he turned into a handsome young man. Walked over to the bed, sat down beside her, looked her in the eyes, ran his fingers through her hair and said, 'Now ain't you sorry you took me to the veterinarian when I was a kitty cat?'"

A better sample of the real George Kirby can be found on "Comedy Night at the Apollo," a compilation album from Vanguard (VRS 9093). On that one he does his famous Joe Louis and Pearl Bailey impressions and favorites like Humphrey Bogart, Edward G. Robinson, Walter Brennan, Eddie Rochester Anderson, and Peter Lorre. He tells this hotel room joke: "I heard a loving couple in their room. They were carrying on! I heard him say, 'Oh my dear, what gorgeous shoulders you have. When we get back to Manchester, I'm going to have those chiseled in stone.' A few minutes later he said, 'Oh my darling, what lovely, lovely hips you have. When we get back to Manchester, I'm gonna have those chiseled in stone.' I couldn't stand it no longer, I got up and knocked on the door. He said, 'Who is it?' I said, 'I'm the chiseler from Manchester!'"

Kirby also recorded a straight album in the '60s (Argo 4045) called "The Real George Kirby" and appears on "The Temptations Show" (Gordy GS 933) and "Porgy and Bess" (Bethlehem EXLP-1).

ROBERT KLEIN

- THE UNAUTHORIZED AUTOBIOGRAPHY OF HOWARD WHO (Caedmon TC 9100) *1/2 $3 $8
- CHILD OF THE 50's (Brut 6001, reissue by Rhino) *** $8
- MIND OVER MATTER (Brut 6600, reissue by Rhino) ** $8
- NEW TEETH (Epic PE 33535, Epic Legacy CD 33535) *1/2 $8
- LET'S NOT MAKE LOVE (Rhino R2 70750) **1/2 $8

What Alan King did for suburbanites upset over airports and doctors, Klein does for middle-class yuppies who ache over school nostalgia, sourly complain about marriage rituals, and cluck their tongues about TV commercials. Klein's early "Howard Who" can be discarded along with the studio work he did on some Solms & Parent albums of the late '60s. It's a lame Howard Hughes parody. Steve Landesberg played Henry Kissinger seeking some advice from Howard Hughes: "I'm recognized everywhere I go. That's why I'm here. You're a master of disguise. Can you suggest something for me?" "Let's see. Say, I've got it. Try wearing a nose and eyeglass set." "I am."

"Child of the 50's" is Klein at his best. With mortified anger and pained frustration in his voice, Klein relives the traumas of a regressive '50s childhood. There was H-Bomb paranoia and elementary school teacher psychosis: "No talking! Button your lips! Children no talking! Take these tags home, they are to be used in case you are burnt beyond recognition in a nuclear holocaust. And no talking during a nuclear holocaust. I want an orderly nuclear holocaust. Two lines. No talking." He reports with bitterness and disgust on childhood miseries from school lunch to teenage sexual desperation. His few bits on modern times are sharp as well, from a classic parody of throaty, intimate FM deejays, to a sound cartoon of a balky car engine. It's hard to resist an album that finally does justice to President Garfield, "shot by a disappointed office seeker."

"Mind Over Matter" from 1974 is weak, though New York listeners might be amused by his impressions of Fred Caposella, Milton Lewis, and other local TV personalities. Klein tackles current events of the day, but his hand-wringing brand of middle class whining yields little. On Spiro Agnew's corruption: "What class, huh? He was a law and order cat: There's too much permissiveness. Permissiveness. Oh my LORD! All I know—if I get caught robbing the A&P—permissive—I want the Agnew punishment please ... according to my calculations, you owe ME sixty days. I'll take it in cash, thank you ... a nice slap on the wrist ..." Desperate searches for topics to satirize led Klein to Jacques Cousteau, harmonica playing, and playing game shows with semi-celeb Phyllis Newman.

"New Teeth" (1975) is worse, with a nearly nine-minute routine on dentists, overloaded with drill noises and shrill, sarcastic observation: "You're gonna drill through the hard enamel of my teeth into the soft inner pulp, causing me agony? How much you want for that? Fifty? Certainly, well worth it." Childhood traumas (at five, being dragged into the ladies room by his mother) and problems training a puppy are both depressing. In deference to the Firesign Theater element, on the last cut Klein offers a spacey, dramatic monologue with music and sound effects, a ghost story with an astonishingly weak punch line.

Klein has more grim complaints on his 1990 CD, grumbling about buying real estate and how TV commercials for Washington and Lincoln birthday sales destroy the dignity of deceased presidents. His simmering brand of comic angst works better in an anecdotal routine on ordering kosher food on an airplane and in his description of his son's birth. There is no joy for Robert, even at this wonderful moment: "Hesitation Klein took twenty hours of labor to come out! They used a plunger at the end...."

Klein's obsession with singing, which has tended to intrude on his stand-up, continues with the title track about AIDS: "Abstinence makes the heart grow fonder. I'd rather be bitten by an anaconda ... please don't weaken my resistance, baby, baby, keep your distance." Maybe he'll issue an entire album under the pseudonym Harry Chronic, Jr.

NOTES: Klein also appears on the album "New Faces of 1968" (Warner Bros. BS 2551). Radio stations received copies of "The Robert Klein Radio Show," and some turn up in collector record stores.

J. B. KLING, JR.

- LAUGH, CAJUN, LAUGH (also known as CAJUN HUMOR ON THE BAYOU,
      Montel MX 101, reissued as Jubilee JGM 2045) ** $3 $8

TED KNIGHT

- HI GUYS (Ranwood R 8149) *1/2 $5 $12

At the time he played asinine anchorman Ted Baxter on *The Mary Tyler Moore Show*, Knight recorded this novelty album. He puts on a goofy voice and does some overacting on his cover version of "Mr. Custer" (the backing music and chorus is at least faithful to the original). Mostly he tries to sing in character, and fails, with bellowy covers of "Itsy Bitsy Teeny Weeny Yellow Polka Dot Bikini," "Who Put the Bomp," and "Cover of The Rolling Stone." The originals, trading on his Ted Baxter character, are weak: "I'm in love with Barbara Walters," he sings, "I never thought I'd love another person 'cause who's there as lovable as me?"

DON KNOTTS

- AN EVENING WITH ME (United Artists UAL 4090) ** $5 $15

Don Knotts first came to fame as one of the "Men in the Street" on Steve Allen's *Tonight Show*. It was there that viewers began to chuckle over the unhealthily gaunt, pop-eyed little man and his quivering mannerisms. He did some stand-up work (as this obscure 1961 album attests) before attaining sitcom immortality and movie roles.

Here Knotts plays several neurotic and fidgety characters, including a tongue-tied sportscaster at a football game: "He's on the louse— he's on the loose ... there's a fishing tackle. Flying tickle. Flying tackle! And downs him on the dirty clothesline! What a cackle. What a tackle. What a runner that boy is, he's been right up there in the State Pen for quite a while. Uh, Penn State ... the boys are back in the puddle. The hotel. The huddle. The ball is scrapped but the center only gains five pounds— uh, five yards ..."

Knotts turns up on Bill Dana's "Hoo Hah" album and Steve Allen's "Man on the Street" interview album. He also gets in a few lines on "Zingers from the Hollywood Squares" (Event EV 6903) answering questions: "You have trouble getting to sleep at night. Are you a man or a woman?" "That's what's keeping me up at night."

TOMMY KOENIG

- THE REAL STORY (Invasion 102) *1/2 $3 $7

Koenig, showing more chuzpah than comedy, explores "Tommy Mania" through a self-indulgent pastiche of songs and sound-effect-filled sketches that show the influences of Firesign Theater and Albert Brooks.

As a stand-up comic, the lantern-jawed Koenig can sometimes be inventive, but one wouldn't know it from this studio album. Koenig insists on doing frantic voices and a variety of characters—most of them obnoxious. The songs try more for a Sparks-like or Barnes and Barnes-ish sense of "aren't I crazy," rather than "aren't I funny." Now and then there are idiotic puns (he imitates Willie Nelson acknowledging Nelson's new version of "Honeysuckle Rose" called "Honey Suck My Nose") and thinks up bits that go nowhere (a rock DJ calling The Three Stooges, badly acted by Koenig). In trying desperately to prove his versatility, this 1984 mishmosh demonstrates little except misplaced energy.

JAMES KOMACK

- AT THE WALDORF ... DELICATESSEN (Ember ELP 800) **1/2 $8 $15

Known now as the producer of sitcoms (*Welcome Back Kotter* and *Chico and the Man*) in the '50s and '60s, Komack tried sitcom acting (Dr. Harvey Blair on Jackie Cooper's *Hennessey*), singing, Broadway musicals (*Damn Yankees*), and stand-up.

In stand-up he was unusual and oddly charismatic, a Ronny Graham hipster with perhaps a dash of Jerry Lewis in his voice. His album is short but entertaining, full of inexplicable infectious bits of business. Like Lenny Bruce, many of his lines aren't that funny, but are performed with such coolness and verve, they bear repeat listenings just for the sound. As a beat poet, he raps: "Black is the color of my true love's feet ... I woke up this morning. The sun was shining. Very depressing. Went back under the covers where it's dark ... dug my navel. The lowest. I don't think I got one. Which is the ultimate form of rejection.... Hey! These are the facts. We went down to Sak's. It's a big store we stomped on the floor. Had a ball. Wrote on the wall. A profound poem: Beverly Adland: go home!"

There's an occasional odd one-liner: "They're now desecrating the Christian Science churches. Little kids are running around writing RX." He does a jazzy minimusical version of "The Man with the Golden Arm" ("This is the first picture where the hero really gets the heroin") that seems like Lenny Bruce crossed with Louis Prima. Less effective and more typical of late '50s nightclub work is an embarrassing Oriental dialect routine that turns *Maverick* into *Mavelick*, and his biggie, a bit that imagines how a prizefight announcer would handle the play-by-play of a honeymoon night.

Komack recorded straight pop tunes, like "Inside Me" (RCA Victor LPM 1505), and appears on the Broadway cast and soundtrack recordings for *Damn Yankees* (on CD from RCA Victor1047-2-R). His oddest vinyl effort was "Clara" (Commentary Records, no number on the label). The idea was to produce an album in the style of a Broadway original cast album—with the hope that perhaps someone would want to actually stage it. Betty Garrett plays a female butcher who develops a friendship with Komack and brings him home to meet her brother and cousin (Johnny Standley and Sid Tomack). The brassy music and bland lyrics are by Leon Pober and Bud Freeman. Komack belts out the loud and barely bearable "Rootless," sings an indifferent Sinatra-esque ballad called "Think" with a melody line that meanders into fragments of "Unforgettable" and "Witchcraft," and duets pleasantly, despite the unwieldy lyrics and wobbly tune, with Betty Garrett on "It's All in Your Mind."

Komack's single "Them the Enemy" (monologue with some piano backing, all about his fascination with "women women women ... femmanims!") appears on "Laugh of the Party" (Coral CRL 57017).

THE KOSHER CLUB

- THE KOSHER CLUB (Rhino RNEP 608) * $4 $10

The Kosher Club's parodies of 1983-84 rock songs often veer dangerously past satire and into anti-Semitic ridicule. There are only four songs on this twelve-inch disc.

For "Fairfax Avenue," based on Eddy Grant's reggae "Electric Avenue," an ancient Jewish man gasps "Boogie, boogie, shmoogie down to Fairfax Avenue" and does stereotypical bris jokes and "Oy veys." Not a goodnatured laugh at the idea of an ancient Jew becoming a hip rocker, this is repulsive caricaturing.

On "Be True to Your Shul," a nasal teen whines, "Be true to your shul, like you would to your mule" and a tasteless chorus shouts the prayer, "Shma, shma, shma, shma Yisroel," emulating the Beach Boys' "Ba, Ba, Ba, Barbara Ann." The tune pokes fun at Jewish boys with a jeering sense of mockery: "I got a new cloth yarmulke embroidered in gold. It sure is bold."

"Rasta Jew" is merely idiotic as an old Jew and a Rasta man exchange sing-song stupidity: "How come you don't wear dreadlocks?" "I'm not that orthodox!" A parody of Boy George called "Yes, I Really Want to Hurt You," offers a stereotypical vicious Queens bitch insulting England's then-popular drag queen: "Gonna beat you with a club ... You'll be a sorry Limey schlub!"

Exasperating as trudging old men, wimpy schoolboys, and snotty princesses are, they don't deserve the kind of ethnic-charged sniper shots they get here. As far as getting belly laughs goes, this one should have a sticker: For Nazis Only.

ERNIE KOVACS

- THE ERNIE KOVACS ALBUM (Columbia PC 3450) **1/2 $10 $20

A pioneering TV personality, Kovacs was noted more for his visual humor, especially his surreal blackout sketches and the meaningless but lovable "Nairobi Trio," who wore ape masks and moved like robots while pretending to play a tin-whistle tune. This record pays tribute to the dry, bizarre wit and deadpan style that only he and the team of Bob and Ray seemed to have success performing in the '50s.

The tongue-in-cheek broadcast fragments includes a *Believe It or Not* parody that reports, "The wife of Paul H. Fletcher died in 1846. Her husband Paul passed away from grief seventy-four years later." There's a non-interview with forgetful Albert Gridley, an only slightly exagerrated retelling of Tom Swift, and the painfully funny poems of alum-lipped, gravy-voiced Percy Dovetonsils. Some of the material is so dry it flies away almost as it reaches the ears, but those willing to concentrate a little will chuckle over Kovacs' deceptively realistic satires.

When the album went out of print, it immediately became a collector's item for the cult. Kovacs also appears on "Golden Age of Comedy" (Evolution 3013) and "Age of Television" (Warner Bros. BS 2670).

KULLER AND WERRIS

- OUT OF THE MOUTHS OF BABES (Jubilee JLP 1057) *1/2 $5 $10

Veteran comedy writers Sid Kuller and Snag Werris assembled this album of bloopers and "darndest things" kiddies have said. The problem is that the anonymous child actors hired to "duplicate" the remarks heard on quiz shows, in school rooms, and at home are stilted and coyly rehearsed. This wrecks the few bloopers that are funny at all. A brief exception is the re-enactment of the little girl who comes home early from school. "I was making something," the moppet says. "What were you making?" "Noise."

More typical is this, a re-creation of a quiz show moment: "What is the color of your mother's hair?" "I don't know," our smartie answers, "She's still in the beauty parlor." Some of the cuts—where the little kids' fluffs and faulty malaprops are put into song form—should come with the warning label "known irritant."

KUNTZ AND KUNTZ

- VINTAGE COMEDY (A & R Records) * $4 $8

An annoyingly energetic young cornball team in plaid pants, Kuntz and Kuntz united in Cleveland circa 1956 and wandered through Colorado into Texas, where they recorded this album. Mostly they harmonize on obnoxious old novelty tunes ("Three Little Fishes," "Smile Darn Ya Smile," "Can Broadway Do Without Me?") with one man turning in a falsetto a la George Rock. There aren't many comedy cuts besides a four-minute cover of "Who's on First." Some jokes are sprinkled between the songs, including gag song titles: "Now we'd like to do 'She wanted to wear her mother's girdle but she didn't have the guts.'" Frank and Darryl's last name may sound suggestive, but there's nothing at all offensive here. As the album notes insist, "both young men and their wives are dedicated Christians."

KAY KYSER AND ISH KABIBBLE

- KAY KYSER'S KOLLEGE OF MUSICAL KNOWLEDGE (Radiola MR 1075) * $4 $10

Kyser was a soft-spoken bandleader with a corny sense of humor. He had an easygoing delivery with a North Carolina drawl, similar to Soupy Sales's speaking voice. Among his novelty hits were "Mairzy Doats" and "Three Little Fishes," with vocals by band comic Ish Kabibble (whose real name was the even less appealing Merwyn Bogue). Kyser also made some comedies, like "You'll Find Out," costarring Boris Karloff and Bela Lugosi. Time has lessened the appeal of both his big band music and his mild humor. The novelty tunes remain somewhat amusing, but none are on this record.

Side One is a complete radio show from October 11, 1944, loaded with big band tunes, quiz show filler, and a few jokes. Kyser gets some yocks from his G.I. audience over this one: "I was talking to a sailor today about San Francisco's beautiful bridges. I said, 'Think of that, five miles of span.' The sailor fainted. He thought I said Spam!" Side Two offers a long musical medley and "The Wit and Wisdom of Ish Kabibble." On an episode of the TV show *Maude*, Adrienne Barbeau asks Bea Arthur about this dim name from radio's past. "Was he funny?" Bea's answer: "Like a migraine."

Kabibble is a kind of Dennis Day character, deliberately blank, stupid, and blameless in his corny recitations. "Lady Godiva was the first woman jockey," he tells Kyser. "Did she ever win?" "No, but she certainly showed." The childlike moron (he wore Moe Howard-style bangs) was often given to verse, the kind the audience would've been happy to give back: "Oh, a girl named Lena McClean fell into a washing machine. With a slurp and a slosh it gave her a bosh, and what was left of Lena came out in the wash!" He offered essays, too: "Rocks is a very interestin' subject, which I have just writ a essay in regards to same. Now there are many kind of rocks, including small rocks, big rocks, Plymouth rocks, Clorox, 20 Mule Time Borox and Lewis Stone...."

In 1954 Kyser retired to devote his life to the teachings of Christian Science. Kabibble became a real estate salesman and wrote his autobiography.

LA GRAN SCENA OPERA CO.

- LA GRAN SCENA OPERA CO. DI NEW YORK (GS/MG 014) ** $7 $15

The transvestite opera company offers divas who scream arias and pronounce saucy one-liners with fey sexual undertones. Sylvia Bills introduces Vera Galupe-Borskh (comic diva played by company founder and director Ira Siff) by noting "Vera is known for her *disciplined* approach to her opera company, as well as to her friends."

The troupe began performing circa 1981 and is still active as of this writing. This 1985 record featuring an hour of drag queens in full howl will certainly fulfill the expectations of those anxious to hear Wagner's "Ride of the Valkyries" sung with whooping laughter and giddy squeals.

BERT LAHR

- BERT LAHR (Mark 56 # 729) ** $5 $10
- BERT LAHR ON STAGE, SCREEN AND RADIO (JJA 19765) **1/2 $10 $20

Bert's son and biographer John Lahr prefaces Mark 56's collection of Bert's radio bits with five minutes of background material in a halting, tearful voice. Lahr says his father was lured to radio only by the money, and though he had "an unusual delivery and a sense of verbal idiocy ... he rarely talked about radio, which for more than a decade fed him fees as high as $2500 per performance."

The excerpts may surprise those who only know him from *The Wizard of Oz*. The young radio comic is very much the manic, New York-accented vaudevillian, shouting "Boy oh boy," nervously repeating phrases over again ("Look it, look it," "it was awful, it was awful," "yer tellin' me, yer tellin' me"), and telling jokes about his classless pals. There's the polite one: "Say, he's so polite, when he sees an empty seat on the street car, he points it out to a lady then races her for it."

Here's more wiseguy gags and mild vulgarity:

"It's so cold out my back teeth are frostbitten." "Do you think when I go out I better wear my coat?" "Yes and your pants, too." "That reminds me, I must put some alcohol in the radiator of my car—it may freeze." "Oh, alcohol is no good for your radiator.... Alcohol's bad for your radiator, I oughta know, I'm a chemist." "Well, if you're a chemist how would you make antifreeze?" "Huh?" "How would you make antifreeze?" "Aw that's easy, I'd hide her nightgown!"

On radio, Lahr seems like a corny Ed Wynn crossed with a very street-tough and aggressive Jimmy Durante.

The JJA "private pressing" (unauthorized movie and radio clip albums never seem to be called "bootleg") has novelty songs from various movie soundtracks: "Flying High" "Just around the Corner," and "Always Leave Them Laughing." Radio clips include *The Fred Allen Show* and the "Philco Hall of Fame" with Bea Lillie. Tapes from TV shows include songs with Jimmy Durante from a 1957 special sponsored by Standard Oil. A highlight, a 1951 *Ed Sullivan Show*, has Bert doing his baseball sketch from the revue "Two on the Aisle." His delivery is a lot funnier than the material. Paul Lynde is the straight man to the garrulous Lahr: "When did you first play baseball?" "In college." "You went to college?" "Sure I went. Do I look like a diseducated bum? Went to college six years." "Why six years?" "I had a contract...." "After being so great, why did you take off your armour and cease to do active battle on the field of honor with the other knights of baseball?" "I never played night baseball! Only in the daytime ..."

Other Lahr stage tapes include songs (somebody had a tape recorder in the front row of his 1964 musical *Foxy*) and sketches ("Jealousy" with Bette Davis).

Aside from the soundtrack to *The Wizard of Oz*, Lahr fans can find a few moments of Bert Lahr on "Fleischmann's Hour" (Mark 56 #613). He's heard in a short, peculiar monologue on Radiola's "Jest Like Old Times" album. He talks about the greatness of radio, and how it brings his trademark (his famous nonsense sound of frustration phonetically rendered as "ng-ong, ng-ong ng-ong!") to millions. As a straight actor, he scored his greatest triumph in "Waiting for Godot" (Caedmon TRS 352). He can also be heard on "Two on the Aisle" (Decca DL 8040).

ARTHUR LAKE

- BLONDIE (Mark 56 # 624) ** $4 $8
- BLONDIE (Yorkshire LP 715) ** $5 $10

Arthur Lake was a hit as Dagwood Bumstead on the *Blondie* radio series, and the subsequent movie versions (beginning in 1938) and TV show (1954). Penny Singleton was the most popular "Blondie," though Ann Rutherford, Patricia van Cleve (Mrs. Arthur Lake), and Pamela Britton all played the role. On radio, Lake dominates the corny scripts with his Joe Penner-style piping voice. The Yorkshire record offers two episodes: "Dagwood Dreams about a Bank Robbery" and "The Circus." In the Mark 56 album, young Alexander is encouraged to act in a school play. Alexander: "I can't decide whether to be an actor and be famous, or be a ham and make money. Ah, what a decision. To be or not to be, that is the question. Hamlet, you know." Dagwood: "Yeah, I know. I know. I played Hamlet once myself. I walked on the stage in tights and the audience laughed. Then I bent over and they split! Then I read my line: 'Parting is such sweet sorrow.' And my pants came down with the curtain!"

ELSA LANCHESTER

- COCKNEY LONDON (Verve 6 15015) ** $10 $25
- ELSA HERSELF (Verve 6 15024) **1/2 $10 $25
- SONGS FOR A SHUTTERED PARLOR (HiFi S 406) $10 $20
    reissued as MORE BAWDY COCKNEY SONGS (Tradition 2065) **1/2 $6 $12
- SONGS FOR A SMOKE FILLED ROOM (HiFi S 405) $10 $20
    reissued as BAWDY COCKNEY SONGS (Tradition 2065) **1/2 $6 $12
- SINGS BAWDY COCKNEY SONGS (Legacy International CD 363) **1/2 $8

Best known for her dual role in 1935's *Bride of Frankenstein*, Lanchester first gained attention as a nude model and singer of risqué songs. After a long film career she returned to frisky songs with *Elsa Lanchester—Herself*, which opened on Broadway on February 4, 1961, to glowing reviews.

"Elsa Herself" offers amusing tunes, including "I'm Glad to See Your Back," describing an encounter between Elsa in her dressing room and an incoming roué: "My fingers were all thumbs, you could fancy my dismay. My cheeks I know were scarlet as I heard him say: I'm glad to see your back.... I've not forgot your promise, you see I took you up. I didn't waste a moment. I came to look you up. And since I'm here, perhaps my dear, you'll let me hook you up. I'm glad to see your back." The live album has several songs, including "Lola" and "When a Lady Has a Piazza," but also features comic introductions and several monologues of recollections ("Dancing Days and Stink-bombs" and "Freedom and All That"). A few pieces, like the peculiar "Cat's Meat," blend narrative and music and, in this case, a lot of meows.

"Cockney London" is low on comedy, though it contains some humorous songs from the British Music Halls, like "Old Kent Road" and "Burlington Bertie," a favorite of male impersonators.

Lanchester's voice recalls past mistresses of the Music Hall, such as Vesta Victoria. She wavers through her songs with a similarly carefree, lilting delivery, but has a lighter voice and a better determination to stay on key. Husband Charles Laughton supplies somewhat glum introductions to the HiFi Records originals but not the reissues. He duets with Elsa on "She Was Poor but She Was Honest," a British Music Hall standard. It's more of the same on "Songs for a Smoke Filled Room," including double entendre classics like "Linda and her Londonderry Air," "If You Peek in My Gazebo," and "Lola's Saucepan." The CD gathers material from the two albums, but again without Laughton's introductions.

NOTES: Three cuts from her old HiFi albums, "When a Lady Has a Piazza," "Catalogue Woman," and "If You Can't Get in the Corners," appear on "Turnabout: A Satirical Revue" (Pelican Records LP 142).

MURIEL LANDERS AND STANLEY ADAMS

• MARRIAGE IS FOR DINOSAURS (Big Top 121307) ** $7 $15

Here's another comic folk-song album that tried to cash in on the success of Allan Sherman in the mid-60s. "Where Have You Gone, Billy Boy" becomes "Bernie Boy," as a yenta mama complains about her son getting married: "Can she make gefilte fish, Bernie Boy, Bernie Boy? Or a hot potato knish, darling Bernie?" "She cooks ham, mother dear." "My poor baby! Vey is meer! For that woman you had to leave your mother?"

The studio audience laughs heartily at every cut, whether it's "La Donna Mobile" (now "My Wife Has Allergies") or "Three Blind Mice" ("Nag, Nag, Nag"). The original tunes are at the level of anybody's cabaret act, and that includes the title track: "Day people dig night people. And bright people dig trite people. It just doesn't seem right, people. And that's why marriage is for dinosaurs!"

Adams recorded his own solo album.

LANDRY AND BIENER

• LANDRY AND BIENER COMEDY ALBUM (Universal UVL 42280) *1/2 $3 $7

Ron Landry, formerly of Hudson and Landry, turns up for this 1989 release with new partner Tom Biener. The result isn't as tacky and broad as the earlier records, but isn't as funny either. The long interview sketches are plodding and uninspired.

A bit on smoking aboard a plane: "You'll have to put that cigarette out." "You'll have to take it from me." "Sir, I'm giving you fair warning, there's a $5,000 fine for smoking on this airliner." "I'll pay it." "You can't pay it, you'll have to put it out." "No." "Give me that!" "Take this." "You blew smoke in my face." "Of course I did, that's what happens when you corner a smoker." And on it goes without a gag line in sight, for several more minutes. Finally: "Put it out." "All right, all right ... I'll try ... I keep thinking about cigarettes...." "Think about something else, something that you like." "I like smoking." "Think about something else." "Something I like." "And keep your hands busy." "Keep my hands busy. And think about something I like...." "What are you doing? Put that away, that's indecent! What are you doing?" "What do you care, I ain't smokin'!"

CHANCE LANGTON

• 'CAUSE THAT'S THE WAY I AM (Old Green Records) * $3 $7

On this 1987 release, Langton plays a dude with an attitude; his constantly used catchphrase a smug "'cause that's the way I am." The material is minor, from desperate hokey punning ("Yoko Ono is marrying Don Ho. She's gonna be called Yo Ho!") to easy put-downs: "Michael Jackson's the singer of the year, a little boy who grew up to be a lady." Very definitely an earful of lame comedy club antics, including endless guitar parody routines, the show includes an audience sing-along of The Three Stooges' "Alphabet Song" and a whistling of *The Andy Griffith Show* theme. You hadda be there. And be very, very drunk.

SIR HARRY LAUDER

• SCOTCH SONGS (Everest/Scala SC 877) *1/2 $4 $8
• THE IMMORTAL HARRY LAUDER (RCA Camden CAL 479) ** $7 $15

Lauder was a legend in the music halls and a huge success when he appeared in America. Though some of his charisma as an ebullient entertainer filters through, it's difficult to work up much enthusiasm for him, and his outrageous burr is very hard to pierce.

The Everest album offers very early performances, circa World War I most likely, and the quality is poor. Still, some might smile as he laughs, gargles his "chs," and hiccups on the tipsy "A Wee Deoch an' Doris." Other cuts include "Roamin' in the Gloamin'," "I Love a Lassie," "The Saftest of the Family," and "Breakfast in Bed on Sunday Morning."

RCA Camden's collection has the long monologue/prefaces that delighted his fans. Evidently culled from '30s or '40s recordings, the sound is clearer, but not Harry, who laughs heartily at his own burr-stung descriptions and recollections. There are serious ballads as well as monologue-dominated novelty numbers ("I've Just Got Off the Chain"). He offers a slower, but just as hiccupy "A Wee Deoch An' Doris" as well as "Breakfast in Bed on Sunday Morning," "Soosie MacLean," and "Wee Hoose 'Mang the Heather." Only the RCA disc offers album notes. Many import albums and CDs are available, most of them with more Music Hall material than pure comedy.

LAUREL AND HARDY

- BEST OF LAUREL AND HARDY (Murray Hill M 60165) ** — $5 / $10
- WAY OUT WEST (Mark 56 #688) ** — $5 / $10
- TROUBLE AGAIN (Mark 56 #608) ** — $5 / $10
- ANOTHER FINE MESS (Mark 56 #579) ** — $5 / $10
- ORIGINAL SOUNDTRACKS (Mark 56 #575) ** — $5 / $10
- ORIGINAL SOUNDTRACKS (Mark 56 #575 Picture Disc) ** — $10 / $15
- BABES IN TOYLAND (Mark 56 #577) ** — $5 / $10
- BABES IN TOYLAND (Mark 56 #577 Picture Disc) ** — $10 / $15
- NO U TURN (Mark 56 #601) ** — $5 / $10
- NATURALLY HIGH (Douglas 10) ** — $5 / $10
- LAUREL AND HARDY ON THE AIR (Radiola MR 1104) **1/2 — $7

While Stan and Ollie do have distinctively funny voices, and it might be nice to pinpoint a particular bit of nonsense quickly on disc, videocassettes have rendered the Mark 56 collection obsolete. These discs snip moments from feature films or various short subjects ("Trouble Again" has *Below Zero* and *Busy Bodies* among others; "Another Fine Mess" includes *Scram* and *The Live Ghost*). "Original Soundtracks" at least has some tunes from the boys' films: "Blue Ridge Mountains of Virginia" and "Lazy Moon."

Murray Hill's three-record set re-releases some Mark 56 soundtracks; one entire album on *Babes in Toyland*, another for *Way Out West*, and a third featuring moments from shorts like *Going Bye Bye*, *Below Zero*, and *Pardon Me*.

The first attempt to vinylize the boys was in 1970. While Decca pop-packaged soundtracks for The Marx Brothers and W. C. Fields, Douglas went a little too far in titling their clip collection "Naturally High" and sticking a color photo of the team in front of an LSD-inspired cornucopia of multicolored flowers. Drugged out listeners could put on the record and possibly be blown away by Ollie singing "Let Me Call You Sweetheart" to a tuba accompaniment, or imagining the slapstick of hearing Ollie asking for a match, lighting an oven, and having it explode. No doubt Stan and Ollie fried a few minds with dialogue Firesign Theater might've tried to write: "How long did you say it would take us to get up there?" "Oh, just a jiffy." "How far is a jiffy?" "Oh, about three shakes of a dead lamb's tail." "Mmm, I didn't think it was so far." A few cuts, out of context, provoke suggestive humor. The "I Gave It to Him" routine from *Thicker than Water* turned up in radio ads warning against the spread of venereal disease ("She gave it to you and you gave it to him ... what do you mean you gave it to me? I gave it to you to give to him and you gave it back to me to give to him!"

Only the Radiola release (on vinyl and CD) is essential, even if half the hour is taken up with the soundtrack to their TV appearance on *This Is Your Life* (December 1954) and it's now available on video. The album features "Laurel and Hardy in London," a 1932 recording that for years was only available as a 45 through the "Sons of the Desert" Laurel and Hardy fan club. The duo's only record is cute and very mild vaudeville with typically belabored dialogue: "Listen ... here's a hardboiled egg. Just eat that and just be quiet." "Thank you, Ollie ... Ollie?" "What?" "Speak up." "What for?" "I can't hear ya." "Well, if you'd get that egg down, you'd be able to hear me much better." "I just did get the egg down." "What did you do with the egg shell?" "What egg shell?" "Don't tell me you've eaten the egg with the shell on it ... oooooh!" "Ya don't happen to have another one, do ya?" "No, I haven't." "Do you have any nuts?" "No, I haven't any nuts ... will you please stop annoying me?"

There's actually a segment that covers one of the team's rare forays into radio, a ten-minute radio fragment called "The Marriage of Stan Laurel." The script was clearly written for just about any radio comic who guested on the unnamed show. Laurel gets to deliver wisecracks instead of playing the befuddled dope. Stan, Ollie, and Patsy Moran find a Justice of the Peace in the middle of the night. When the judge complains about being wakened from a sound sleep, Laurel grunts, "What are you squawking about? *We're* up!"

Laurel fans will also be interested in the 1959 interview done by Tony Thomas. Laurel offers only a few enlightening remarks, but this is a rare opportunity to pretend to be a guest in Stan's home and hear what he actually sounded like in normal conversation. It originally appeared on "Voices from the Hollywood Past" (Delos DELF 25412) with other Thomas subjects Basil Rathbone, Harold Lloyd, Buster Keaton, Edward G. Robinson, and Walt Disney.

NOTES: Stan and Ollie's London single appears on the compilation albums "Trip to the Stars" (Monmouth MES 7031) and "Golden Age of Comedy" (Evolution 1313). There's a pathetic 45 around too, a phone interview with Stan Laurel by Don Marlow. It's nothing more than boring small talk (dominated by Marlow) on long distance time differences, the weather, and Jack Paar coming to California. Stan says, "I don't know him," and that's about as informative as it gets. Fresh, stereo versions of Laurel and Hardy film music are available, most notably in the import "Laurel and Hardy's Music Box 2" TER 1182). For "Laurel and Hardy: This Is Your Laff" see the entry under Harmon and Calvin.

LINDA LAVNER

• SOMETHING DIFFERENT (Bent) **	$5	$10
• I'D RATHER BE CUTE (Bent B 81369) **	$5	$10
• YOU ARE WHAT YOU WEAR (Bent B 33176) **	$5	$10

Lavner, working the small gay clubs in New York, offers songs that sometimes rise beyond the self-absorbed and self-indulgent level of cabaret. It makes a souvenir for the small circle of friends that would come to drink, knowingly wink, and guffaw at the recognition humor of Lavner's self-described "short, left-handed, Jewish lesbian" lifestyle.

"You Are What You Wear," from her 1988 album, tries to make a point about what people in or out of the closet are wearing these days: "You are what you wear and you wear what you are. You're yesterday's news or tomorrow's media star. We're all born stark naked. To dress is bizarre. And that's the reason why everybody's in drag!" No doubt, if this were not a studio album, there'd be cheers after the last line.

On the title cut of "I'd Rather Be Cute," Lavner laughs at well-dressed straights in their furs, crowing: "Wealth is a blessed estate, but it can't last forever. I'd rather be cute. Be cute and wear leather!" That disc has one of her better songs, the tongue-in-cheek "Oh, How I Love Cabaret," which is a collection of sarcastic vignettes about the scene. It includes sage advice: when in doubt, sing something from *Cats*. Later she sings a few lines that incorporate the names of two well-known clubs: "There's that dressing room door with the broken latch. Don't tell Mama The Ballroom has any panache. If they like you they'll kiss you. God knows what you'll catch. Oh, how I love cabaret."

LA WANDA See LA WANDA PAGE

BERNIE LAWRENCE

• IF THE PRESIDENT WUZ ... (Audio Fidelity AFSD 6279) *1/2	$4	$8

Lawrence imagines via clumsy accents what it would be like "if the president wuz" Jewish, Italian, Puerto Rican, or Black.

As the first Puerto Rican President, he announces at his acceptance speech, "See my Secretary of State—Freddy Fender! He just hand me a note, telling me when I talk to you now, in front of de tele-veeshun cameras ... Freddy Fender's note tell me my fly is open ... in conclusion, I promise a chicken in every pot, chili and tacos in every mouth, tortillas and enchiladas in every belly. And free Preparation H for everyone!"

The rest of the album is at the same level. In one routine, Lawrence plays a gay interior decorator named "Mr. Phyllis," the name copped from a gay hairdresser routine from Joan Rivers.

EDDIE LAWRENCE

• THE GARDEN OF EDDIE LAWRENCE (Signature SM 1003) ***	$20	$40
• THE OLD PHILOSOPHER (Coral 57103) ***	$10	$25

Eddie Lawrence (Lawrence Eisler) has an enthusiastic cult for his inventive audio satires that pre-date both Stan Freberg and Firesign Theater. He's also known for his exquisitely timed "Old Philosopher" hard luck monologues (with music) that shift from empathetically sad to sadistically optimistic over and over in under three minutes. There are three "Philosopher" routines on the Signature album, plus interviews with a "Kiddie Star," the birdwatcher "Wolfgang Birdwatcher," and the detective "Fleming of the Yard." There's a set of quickies ("Blackouts of 1984") and a bizarre highlight, twelve minutes on chicken plucking.

His career gained momentum with the Coral album, which had a good-size printing. On the title track, the humor is as much in the sappy voice of the optimistic, sympathetic philosopher as in the offbeat lines. "Hey there friend," he begins, "you say your radiator didn't work all winter and now that it's summer they started up again and you can't turn them off? Say your wife sent your lightweight suits to the cleaners and that means you'll have to wear your itchy tweeds this morning when they say it'll hit 106? And your shoelace just busted, and you opened a big cut on your cheek tryin' to even out your sideburns. And your daughter's goin' out with a convict? And your wife just confessed she gave your last sixty dollars as a deposit on an airplane hanger? Is that what's troublin' you, friend?"

Suddenly, stirring march music plays, and the Old Philosopher becomes inanely optimistic, shouting "LIFT YOUR HEAD UP HIGH and take a walk in the sun with that dignity and stick-to-it-iveness that you'll show the world, you show 'em where to get off, you'll never give up, never give up, never give up—that SHIP!"

Lawrence's "Old Philosopher" single made it to the Top 40 Billboard chart in September of 1956. Other cuts include startling fresh and visionary audio cartoons like "Eddie at the Opera" (a delirious fake broadcast complete with commercials), "King Arthur's Mines," "Loco Baseball," and "Gay Paree."

Sometimes Lawrence eschewed jokes in favor of subtle character comedy. "The Good Old Days" is simply two men sitting at a bar. One constantly growls his contempt for new-fangled things like rock and roll. The partner only answers with a perturbed little plaint, "Will you shut up!" The result is hilarity for fans who delight in the subtly offbeat and the sublimely ridiculous.

• THE SIDE SPLITTING PERSONALITY OF EDDIE LAWRENCE (Coral CRL 57371) ***	$20	$40
• KINGDOM OF EDDIE LAWRENCE (Coral 57203) ***	$20	$40

While there's only one "Philosopher" bit on "Side Splitting," the album makes up for it with some rare live cuts. In front of an audience, Eddie plays both parts in "Panhandling on Madison Avenue" (an argument between a pan-handler and a business man) and "Foreign Movies" (about a theater owner and an irate patron). He also recites a bewildering set of "Travel Tips" that yields giggles at some points, but clearly is too strange for most of the audience:

"If you're tall and blonde, go to Naples, you'll be a big hit. If you're short, squat and dark, go to Sweden, it will help your ego tremendously. Women will stare at you and small children will claw at your locks. And while you're at it, try the lox.... While you're in Finland you may as well keep going east and pick up a pair of cheap sandals in Afghanistan. As for me, I picked up a case of rabies in Afghanistan when a camel bit me on my smallpox vaccination."

In the parody of *Casablanca* retitled "Play the Music, Sol," Eddie puts on a Bogart voice to describe a past love: "Maggie and I was childhood sweethearts in Paris. I was twenty-eight and she was forty-two. It was puppy love, bulldog style. Those were gay, carefree days. There were twenty of 'em. Wait a minute, there was twenty-one. I forgot about that night on the roof." He also plays Maggie, imitates Peter Lorre, and plays Maggie's new lover, Oscar Rabies, the Mad Dog. There's also a full-blown parody of *The Untouchables* retitled "The Unbreakables."

The "Kingdom of Eddie Lawrence" includes "Abner the Baseball," which is almost a children's story, the saga of a baseball socked by Mickey Mantle. Also odd is "Fix Your Watch," a running (or ticking) gag about a gullible customer trying to buy a clock. The bit is slightly Pythonesque as the salesman explains his odd clocks: "A nice cuckoo clock!" "But all I got is $30." "That's OK, the cuckoo's dead ... we got a sparrow in its place." "But a sparrow don't make no noise, I'm a heavy sleeper." "This is a different kind of clock. When you want to wake up at eight o'clock, you tell the sparrow. He swoops down at eight and tickles your feet."

Another highlight is "That Holiday Spirit," in which a grouch describes his hatred for Christmas, New Year's Eve, and Halloween while the mild-mannered fellow seated next to him enunciates, "Will you shut up?" There are two "Old Philosopher" tracks.

- EDDIE THE OLD PHILOSOPHER (Coral 57155) *** $20 $40
- 7 CHARACTERS IN SEARCH OF EDDIE LAWRENCE (Coral 57411) *** $20 $40
- IS THAT WHAT'S BOTHERING YOU BUNKIE (Epic LN 24159) *** $20 $40

Eddie's "The Old Philosopher" album has four "Old Philosopher" routines. Fans of his frantic audio collages will find a highlight in "Television Highlights," a collection of commercials including this warning from an insect killing company: "Give a mosquito an inch and he'll bombard your foot." In "Memories of Louise," he talks to his old flame: "Who could predict then that from a little fibber you'd grow into a dangerous paranoiac liar ... they say the first ten are the hardest. Well, this is the tenth year, my darling, and it's murder ... ah, the way you used to stick your finger in my eye ..."

Three new "Old Philosopher" bits brighten "7 Characters," including "The Lawyer's Philosopher": "Hey there, Mouthpiece. You say you represent a man for jaywalking and they hang him? And ... you take a good look at the judge and realize he's your wife's first husband. He's still madly in love with her. And after you make an eloquent plea swearing on your record that your client is innocent, he confesses everything?... Is that what's marrin' your day, Darrow? WELL, LIFT YOUR HEAD UP HIGH AND SWAY THAT JURY IN A HIGH BARITONE VOICE.... Remember: If crime didn't pay—you'd be out of work!

Eddie's Epic record (circa 1964) includes five different "Old Philosopher" routines. There's an interview between a brat and Santa ("What Do You Want for Christmas"), an accountant and a big game hunter ("Going Ape"), and a pesty customer and a slick hat salesman ("Hats"). There's a monologue from a teenager ("Robby Prune Speaks Out"), a Karloffian report on the "Miss Transylvania" contest, and a favorite Eddie Lawrence bit, a list of "People to Stay Away From."

- THE JAZZY OLD PHILOSOPHER (Red Dragon JK 57756) **1/2 $8

After some thirty years, Eddie released this 1994 CD. Some fans may not have realized it was a new CD, since the picture on the cover was taken thirty years ago. The album was produced with Bob Thiele, who worked on the very first Lawrence album.

Older fans will find "The Old Philosopher" just as amusingly bent as ever: "He who plays "Nola" on the nose flute with a heavy cold—drowns!" Meanwhile, Eddie "The Cool Philosopher" does not neglect his younger fans—he throws in a lot of hip and current rock references: "Your grandpa's in the hospital again? He tried to make a citizen's arrest of Mick Jagger? And Barbara Walters asked Axl Rose what kind of tree he was, and he swooped down on her and screamed, 'Bonsai?' Visiting hours are from nine to six. Is that what's got you down in the dumps, Homeboy?"

Sometimes, it's a curious mix as Eddie's gags dabble on both sides of the generation gap: "Skinnay Ennis is Fats Domino ... Boy George is Sophie Tucker ... Videos that catch the imagination: Sinead O'Connor as the young Mussolini."

The routines are pretty much divided into two formats: the familiar lectures from the philosopher, and a series of irritated lists of people to "stay away from" like: "Guys with red toupees and gray sideburns, anyone who'll rough up a dwarf, anyone who'd order chopped liver in Peru, psychiatrists who come to the door naked."

The nearly hour-long CD is densely packed with Eddie's unique brand of surreal humor and silly throwaways. He'll genially toss out mind-frying nonsense with only the mildest of apology: "You know something, you take your tonsils out when you're young they'll grow back when you're old. These are just ramblings."

NOTES: Lawrence cowrote the Broadway show *Kelly*, and stars in an album of material from the show (Original Cast Records OC 8025). A few bits turn up on Coral compilations "Laugh of the Party" (CRL 57017) and "Do You Wanna Laugh" (Coral CRL 57380). "The Old Philosopher" is on "25 Years of Recorded Comedy" (Warner 3BX 3131).

Lawrence fans will be surprised by his appearance on the Major Bowes amateur radio show ("Original Amateur Hour 25th Anniversary Album," UA UXL 2). The Major refers to him as "Larry" (he was still using his real name, Lawrence Eisler) as he calls him out of the audience during a wartime broadcast to do a few impressions: Charles Boyer, Ronald Colman, Roland Young, and Clem McCarthy. He can also be heard on "Bells are Ringing" (Columbia OL 5170).

MARTIN LAWRENCE

- MARTIN LAWRENCE LIVE, TALKIN SH-T (East-West 7922892) **1/2 $8
- FUNK IT (East-West 617492) ** $8

Sitcom star Lawrence maintained a solid reputation in the soiled world of "Def Jam" comedy. The hour-long 1993 "Live" CD starts with amiable, predictable riffs on uptight whites and lampoonable news topics (i.e Michael Jackson's interview with Oprah Winfrey). Lawrence is outgoing and relaxed, and the audience is chuckling along to his street-corner riffs, although he doesn't come up with anything more witty or profound than: "If you weigh over 250 pounds, stay the f--- out of Spandex!"

Then Martin launches into twenty raunchy minutes of sex comedy. His uninhibited, slice of sex-life anecdotes are crude, but unlike most of his Def contemporaries, he offers more than simple cursing and ranting. Martin riffs on feminine hygiene, his un-stereotypically-sized circumcized penis, sex positions, and farts, and gets shock laughs discussing the literal back side of the human experience: "Some time, women can go shit at the wrong time. You're ready to make love ... she goes, 'No wait, I gotta use the bathroom, I'll be right back.' And go take a shit. Right before you get ready to make love, she go take a shit! And then come climb her shitty ass back in bed! 'I'm ready!' 'Oh, hell no you ain't!' You wake up the next morning, got shit crumbs all in the goddam bed!"

Martin, like most "bad boy" comics, found that even his mildest routines were not welcome on TV. On *Saturday Night Live* his "douche" routine was judged appalling on topic alone. Critics hoped he'd never be invited back and the producers seemed to agree. The second album, which arrived after the fiasco, isn't nearly as uninhibited. He does about twelve minutes on John Bobbitt, told with only as much comic talent as the average streetcorner homeboy telling the tale to his friends. As for his controversy, he says, "Well, women got offended ... I said how can you get offended ... how would you get offended? The only ones who would get offended are the ones that don't douche!" Excerpts from "Funk It," with curse words beeped, are on the disc jockey CD "Martin Lawrence Live" (Prcd 93332).

HARRY LAX

- THE U.N. EYE (Pulse PLP 2001) *1/2 $4 $8

Harry Lax wrote this topical album released not long after "The First Family." The album notes say he wrote "for some of the top television and night club comics" but none are named. Lax doesn't appear on the album; "The Demonstrators" do, an ensemble prone to comic overacting. They're Tony Scott, Gene Allen, Wynn Sherman, Madelyn Killeen, and Faith Lax.

The mild, formula gag routines include unlikely translations from foreign diplomats at meetings, "behind the scenes" visits to the U.N. garage and "The Entertainment Committee," and, of course, speeches. The ambassador from England: "Mr. Khrushchev can be a most irritating chap at times. Especially when he kept referring to Big Ben as "Large Bernard." On the subject of complete and general disarmament, the United Kingdom stands ready, as always, to cooperate with the United Nations. However, on the question of aerial inspection, we feel that it is in fact impractical at this present time. Bloody fog, you know."

RICK LAYNE

- FAIRY TALES (Venise 7028) ** $5 $15

Rick Layne worked the Borscht Belt in the '40s and appeared often on *The Ed Sullivan Show* in the late '50s. His dummy, first called "Willie" was renamed the Yiddish equivalent, "Velvel." The album offers four kosherized fairy tales: "Snow Weiss," "Jake and the Beanstalk," "Chinderella," and "King Midas." The humor is less in the script than in hearing a dummy piping up with a Jewish accent.

Velvel simply tells the stories to his audience as if reading from a book. Snow Weiss "saw seven beds, and on each bed was a name: Sol, Sidney, Irving, Melvin, Manny, Moe, and Jack.... Seven little fellas walked into the cabin. Vat can I tell you? They looked like the opening act on the *Sullivan Show*.... she looked at them, and dey looked at her, and dey all looked at each other. It vas a staring contest! After the initial shock wore off, they said like dis: 'Hi ho, hi ho, are you de Weiss named Snow?' And she answered in the affirmative: 'Vat else?'"

The novelty of Velvel lasts for a few minutes. The cover claims the record is in "LIVE COLOR STEREO." How can a record album be in color stereo? It's pressed on "pure golden vinyl." Vat else?

There's more of Layne, a bit more secular, on "The Original Amateur Hour 25th Anniversary Album" (United Artists UA UXL 2). From that one: "Do you know anything about history?" "A little." "Who founded Paris?" "I didn't know it was losted." "What was Louis the XIVth responsible for?" "Louis the XVth!"

LBJ MENAGERIE

- LBJ MENAGERIE (Jubilee 2068) **1/2 $5 $10

On this "break-in" album, anonymous interviewers ask the questions and the answers come from spliced tapes of Lyndon and Lady Bird Johnson, Hubert Humphrey, Richard Nixon, and so on. Each politician gets a segment for the silliness. From the brief Governor Reagan segment: "Do you like to attend wild orgies?" "Oh, I'm a team player!" The cover caricatures are by *MAD Magazine*'s Mort Drucker.

DENIS LEARY

- NO CURE FOR CANCER (A&M 3145400552) * $8

KEEP ON DRUCKIN'

One of the foremost caricaturists of the '60s, Mort Drucker's work in MAD Magazine *movie and TV parodies led to album covers like "LBJ Menagerie," Bob and Ray's Broadway cast album, and "The New First Family 1968," which is available in color and in a black and white DJ promo version.*

ORIGINAL HIRSCHFIELD LITHOGRAPHS

Al Hirschfield, known for decades as the caricaturist for *The New York Times, has an entire New York gallery devoted solely to his work. To art world collectors, his album covers would probably be considered "original lithographs," but they're still reasonably priced in record stores. Here are his fluid renditions of Alexander King, David Steinberg, and Jackie Mason.*

As the '90s began, arrogant, in-your-face attitude became hip in music (one idiot declared himself too sexy for his own shirt), commercials (Dan Cortese's Burger King ads), and briefly in comedy, where the posturing Denis Leary punctuated almost every line with a snotty "okay?"

His big routine was his punk-brave stance against no-smoking rules. Little more than Andrew Dice Clay with a trendier role model (James Dean, not The Fonz), with a rip-off of comedy club vet Colin Quinn as well, he dripped sarcasm as he abrasively ranted: "I love to smoke. I smoke seven thousand packs a day, OKAY? And I am NEVER f----- quitting, I don't care how many laws they make. What's the law now, you can only smoke now in your apartment, under a blanket with all the lights out, is that the rule now? Hah?"

"We tried to be nice to you nonsmokers. We f-----' tried, OKAY? You wanted your own sections in the restaurants. We gave ya that ... ya happy now ... Yeah, we tried to be nice to you nonsmokers but you f-----' badger us! You won't leave us alone ... I love to smoke. I love to smoke and I love to eat red meat. I love to eat RAW f-----' red meat. Nothin' I like better than sucking down a hot steaming cheeseburger and a butt at the same time. I love to smoke, I love to eat red meat, and I only eat red meat from COWS who smoke, OKAY?"

BILLIE LEE

- THE FABULOUS MR. BILLIE LEE (Deauville LPD-801) ** $5 $10

A soft-spoken, lisping gay comic, Lee was one of the few to issue an adults-only party record. He follows the standards of most early '60s comics, opening with a song ("That Old Black Magic") and then supplying the gags.

He gives the Miami Beach crowd a clue, in case they weren't sure: "I'm in a very good mood. My wife is here. She's sitting at the back of the bar with my husband." Then he offers some fairly literate risqué material: "We're gonna go cultural on Miami Beach. We really are. Right in the back room next week, we're gonna present opera. A gay opera. It's all about lesbians, called *I Eat 'er* ... the following week we're gonna do one in honor of the boys. The name of the opera is *Lik-me.*"

He's considerably more reserved than Bobby Dell, one of the few other comedians of the era to record a gay-tinged album back in the early '60s.

GYPSY ROSE LEE

- GYPSY ROSE LEE REMEMBERS BURLESQUE (Stereoddities CG-1A) $10 $20
  reissued as AN EVENING WITH GYPSY ROSE LEE (AEI 1131) ** $7 $15

The legendary stripper offers a documentary look at burlesque, written with comedy writer Eli Basse. Lee's narrative is "spiced" with pleasant if obvious gags: "I started in burlesque. I don't know how I got the job. I was only fifteen. Of course, I was big for my age. I wasn't exactly what you'd call a stripling of a girl. I was thirty-eight when I was thirteen. Minsky's on 42nd Street was a haven for the tired businessmen. Those men were tired of every kind of business but monkey business." She also sings a few songs, though her voice isn't particularly strong or sexy.

The narration is livened by sound effects and re-creations of burlesque routines (the comics are uncredited). On hearing the sketches, there's no reason for blushing, but the corn may turn the listener green:

"Hello, beautiful! May I have the honor of buying you a drink?" "I don't mind if I have two." "There's nothing wrong with the two she has now! But Miss! Won't two make you dizzy?" "The price is right. But the name is Daisy."

KATIE LEE

- SAUCY SONGS FOR COOL KNIGHTS (Specialty) *1/2 $7 $15
- SONGS OF COUCH AND CONSULTATION (Commentary CNT 01)
  reissued as Reprise R 6025 *1/2 $7 $15
- LIFE IS JUST A BED OF NEUROSES (RCA Victor LPM 2214) *1/2 $7 $15

There's still some cult interest in Katie's "Couch and Consultation" disc, a set of psychiatrist songs in which the titles are the best part: "Shrinker Man," "The Will to Fail," "The Guilty Rag," "Stay as Sick as You Are," "Hush Little Sibling," "Real Sick Sounds," "Repressed Hostility Blues," "I Can't Get Adjusted to the You Who Got Adjusted to Me," "Schizophrenic Moon," and so on.

Too bad Lee sings blandly and the lyrics are jokeless. It's up to the listener whether to chuckle with empathy or derision at this poor neurotic lady. On "The Guilty Rag" she warbles: "I love to hear the Guilty Rag, played with great authority. You don't know what it does to me ... I love to hear the Guilty Rag. Childhood dreams return to me. I tingle with anxiety when I hear that Guilty Rag."

And from "Real Sick Sounds," sung a la Julie London to a romantic beat: "I love those real sick sounds, scraping harshly through me, a weird forlorn psychotic horn can vibrate and unglue me. I don't respond to harmonies played on muted trumpets. I'm left unmoved by country songs wailed by three related strumpets."

This kind of thing was enough to get her a second, similar album for RCA in 1960. It's more facile, undistinguished pop melodies, mild lyrics, and cheerfully unconvincing vocals. Cuts include "Be Miserable," "The Ballad for Group Therapy," and "The Insecure Tango." On the latter, she wonders why her Latin lover is so passionate: "Why does he hold me close? Why does he bite my neck? Maybe he needs a loan to pay the check. What motive underlies this overture? I'm not so sure. I'm insecure!" And later: "I must protect my heart. I mustn't let it stir. He loved his mother and I look like her! I'm sure he's paranoid, my paramour. But I'm not sure I'm sure. I'm not even sure I'm insecure!"

LONDON LEE

- THE RICH KID (Philips PHS 600-322) **1/2 $8 $15

In the mid-60s, Lee was a frequent guest on *The Ed Sullivan Show*. An unusual comic stylistically, he joked about being "the rich kid," talking about his Jewish wealth: "I come from a wealthy family, I was bar mitzahed in the Vatican." Humor rarely comes from "Richie Rich" complaints, but Lee managed to succeed for a while. He looked like a sane Jerry Lewis, had a trademark nerdish chortle, and his grandson-like appeal kept him in demand at affluent Catskill resorts.

Lee, cowriting with Eli Basse, balanced his act with general humor and some weird gags: "I got a job as a short order cook. I was cooking a chicken on the rotisserie, I was turning the wheel and I was singing 'Arrivederci Roma,' and a drunk came by and he said, 'You got a nice voice but your monkey's on fire.'"

Lee issued a single, "You're So Ugly" on the Amerama label.

TOM LEHRER

• SONGS OF TOM LEHRER (Lehrer, TL 101, 10") ***	$10	$20
• SONGS OF TOM LEHRER (Lehrer, TL 101, 12") ***	$15	$25
• SONGS OF TOM LEHRER (Reprise, RS 6216) ***	$6	$12
• MORE OF TOM LEHRER (Lehrer TL 102/102S) ****	$20	$40

Harvard professor Tom Lehrer liked to parody the styles of popular tunes. His usually sick and cynical lyrics, mated to a suitably bogus folk melody, tango, march, or waltz, got enough giggles to lead him to self-pressing "Songs of Tom Lehrer" in 1953. Within years he was taking a sabbatical so he could tour the world with his songs. But ... as he told me, playing his songs over and over had limited appeal, he ran out of clear-cut issues to satirize, and there weren't even new styles of music to lampoon. Always slightly reclusive (never a photo of himself on an album cover) he simply returned to academia, teaching courses in math and music.

"Songs of Tom Lehrer" and "More of Tom Lehrer" are now the rarities in the Lehrer catalogue. That's because he elected to go with only live versions of his songs for the CD reissues.

"Songs of Tom Lehrer," first a ten-incher, then self-released in the more conventional size, has several classic songs. "Be Prepared" exhorts Boy Scouts to do their best: "Don't solicit for your sister, that's not nice—unless you get a good percentage of her price." "I Hold Your Hand in Mine" is a love song by a man who's cut off his lover's hand and bitten the fingertips. "When You Are Old and Gray" is the opposite of Browning's "grow old with me" sentiments: "I know you'll disgust me when you're old and getting fat." And "Irish Ballad" is gleefully ghoulish over a woman's killing spree: "She weighted her brother down with stones and sent him off to Davy Jones, all they ever found were some bones—and occasional pieces of skin." The masterwork is "My Home Town," a jaunty cakewalk through a hideous neighborhood where perverts and murderers teach school and work the local candy store, and priests perform unnameable acts with other men.

The album was pioneering in its use of admittedly "sick" comedy. No apologies made.

After Lehrer's later albums for Reprise became hits, the label asked him to go back and re-record his first album, since the quality of the original master wasn't up to standard. Fans will find some minor differences between the two, such as drugs being referred to as "powdered happiness" in the original but liltingly "powdered ha-ha-ppiness" in the remake.

The 1959 "More" album has some of Lehrer's sharpest songs. Literally. There's "Bright College Days," where Prof. Lehrer offers optimism to the newly graduated students: "Soon we'll be out amid the cold world's strife. Soon we'll be sliding down the razor blade of life." His classic "Poisoning Pigeons in the Park" is gaily cruel. His most savage love song is here, a parody of the era's obsession with tango songs like "Kiss of Fire." It's "The Masochism Tango," with nicely done piano accompaniment: "I ache for the touch of your lips dear," the singer cries, "but much more for the touch of your whips dear." There's also the bitter ditty about Armageddon, "We Will All Go Together When We Go": "We will all bake together when we bake, there'll be nobody present at the wake. With complete participation in that grand incineration, nearly three billion hunks of well-done steak."

• TOM LEHRER REVISITED (Lehrer TL 201) ****	$15	$25
• TOM LEHRER REVISITED (Reprise 9-26203-2) ****		$8
• AN EVENING WASTED WITH TOM LEHRER (Lehrer TL 202)	$6	$12
reissued as Reprise RS 6199 in both LP and CD versions ****		$8

"Lehrer Revisited" has the same tunes as "Songs by Tom Lehrer," but this time recorded live at M.I.T. It was released in England (Decca LK 4375) but when he decided to release it in America, he split the album up, half the songs from a Cambridge concert, the other half from an Australian concert. It was never issued on vinyl by Reprise.

The CD version has the full M.I.T. concert and includes none of the Australian versions. It also adds the pair of songs, "L-Y" and "Silent E," which he wrote and sang for *The Electric Company*. (These were previously available only on the original soundtrack "Electric Company" Warner Bros. BS 2636.) He told me that some of the students have no idea he recorded "sick" comedy, but are in awe when they learn that he wrote those beloved tunes they remember from childhood.

"An Evening Wasted," the live version of "More of Tom Lehrer," has had a more uneventful history, released first by Lehrer himself, then by Reprise on LP and CD.

The live albums have some added jokes in the introductions. "Revisited" seems to pre-date Mel Brooks's "The Producers," as Lehrer tells the audience he's currently "working on a musical comedy based on the life of Adolph Hitler." The Australian concert side of that LP has a few sly lines for Aussies only: "In Boston, Massachusetts, on the outskirts of which I live, and which is one of the oldest cities in the United States, it is considered a matter of great pride for one to be able to claim he is descended from one of the original settlers. Such I gather is not the case here."

- THAT WAS THE YEAR THAT WAS (Reprise RS 6179) **** $8

This 1965 album was actually the first Lehrer album most of the general public saw. Reprise reissued his older material later.

At the time, Lehrer's career was on the upswing thanks to the the the material he'd written for *That Was the Week That Was*, the acclaimed TV show of topical satire. Some of the songs here are outdated. Few would care about dancer George Murphy's campaign for the Senate, the world of Hubert Humphrey, or Lehrer's somewhat out of touch send-up of protest singers (he told me he had Phil Ochs specifically in mind).

The other numbers are powerful. "Who's Next" and "So Long Mom" are alternately driven and delirious in examining the number of countries that have nuclear weapons and what World War III might be like. Lehrer wrestles with racial tensions for "National Brotherhood Week": "Oh the Catholics hate the Protestants and the Hindus hate the Moslems and everybody hates the Jews." He takes on "Pollution" ("Fish gotta swim and birds gotta fly—but they don't last long if they try") and gives a rousing cheer for pornography in "Smut," a playful number that not only underlines the harmless idiocy of the average porn fan's obsessions, but offers typical Lehrer near-rhymes: "Give me smut and nothing but! A dirty novel I can't shut. If it's uncut. And unsubt-le."

The most notorious cut on the album is the outrageous "Vatican Rag." Lehrer noted that Latin was being phased out of the Catholic mass. So, "in order to really sell the product," he reasoned that the next step would be to "redo some of the liturgical music in popular forms." And so, with roaring, barrelhouse ragtime piano, he shouts out his new ragtime prayer: "First you get down on your knees, fiddle with your rosaries, bow your head with great respect and: Genuflect! Genuflect! Genuflect!"

As usual, Lehrer made no apologies for his frank nose-thumbing. The response around the nation was one of dismay, but Lehrer remained unperturbed. After all, he wasn't trying to be anti-Catholic. He was just being a wise guy.

NOTES: CD availability has cut into the high price for Lehrer's discs, but cultists (and those who hate audience laughter) will still want the now-rare studio "Songs of" and "More Songs of." True nuts would also want both pressings of the ten-inch "Songs" since the labels are differently credited to "Trans Radio, Boston Mass." and "Lehrer Records." And "Tom Lehrer Revisited" on vinyl has one full side of an Australian concert—a different audience than the CD version.

The British revue of Lehrer's songs, "Tomfoolery," was released on disc in 1980. The import (Multi Media Tapes MMT LP 001) offers eighteen Lehrer songs done by a three-man, one-woman British quartet (Robin Ray, Jonathan Adams, Martin Connor, and Tricia George). They usually avoid cloying, overacted, cabaret-style singing, but on some numbers ("Masochism Tango," "The Irish Ballad") they fail to completely refrigerate the ham. "When You are Old and Grey" is quirkily sung by two men, giving it a gay love slant. The show included only one number Lehrer never recorded, the snappily vaudevillian venereal disease tune "I Got It from Agnes," which he considered too vulgar to release back in the '50s. Lehrer revised a few songs for the revue. The very minor lyric changes (such as "light a votive candle, listen and the band'll play The Vatican Rag") can also be pondered in the songbook *Too Many Songs by Tom Lehrer* (Pantheon).

Lehrer's 45 rpm, orchestrated single of "Masochism Tango" backed with "Poisoning Pigeons in the Park" (Capricorn C-451822) turns up on Dr. Demento's CD "20th Anniversary Collection" (Rhino R2 70743). At the same session Lehrer also cut an orchestrated version of "The Hunting Song," complete with gunshots. This previously unreleased tune is on Dr. Demento's "25th Anniversary Collection" (Rhino R2 72124).

The British CD import "Tom Lehrer in Concert" (Eclipse 844-241-2) combines "An Evening Wasted" and "Tom Lehrer Revisited." It is the only package with actual photos of curly-haired Tom on the cover.

LENNY AND SQUIGGY

- LENNY AND THE SQUIGTONES (Casablanca NBLP 7149) * $5 $10

An embarrasing, half-witted mess of sloppy between-song patter and jokeless lyrics, this 1979 parody of '50s music is almost unlistenable. The hissy, nasally effeminate posturing of David Landers as Squiggy is especially irritating.

It's amazing to realize that Landers, along with his partner Michael McKean, were members of the excellent comedy foursome, The Credibility Gap. In 1975, with that troupe long disbanded, Landers and McKean were hired by pal Penny Marshall for her *Laverne and Shirley* TV series, and it was perhaps during this tenure in laugh tracked sitcomland that the duo allowed their comic sensibilities to erode. McKean later turned up as part of Spinal Tap.

JACK E. LEONARD

- ROCK AND ROLL MUSIC FOR KIDS OVER 16 (Vik LX 1080) * $7 $15
- HOW TO LOSE WEIGHT (RCA Victor LPM 2892) ** $7 $15
- SCREAM ON SOMEONE YOU LOVE (Verve V/V6 15056) ** $6 $12

"Fat Jack" was one of the originators of insult comedy as a nightclub act. With a grumbling, mumbling delivery that was a favorite of mimics, he'd stalk nightclubs and TV variety shows spewing a peculiar mix of bad jokes and gruff, but essentially harmless, and sometimes meaningless insults. He was at his best live, but oddly enough, made only studio concept albums.

The 1956 "Rock and Roll" disc is awful as the aging comic makes fun of '50s rock with noisy off-key replicas titled "Take Your Cotton Pickin' Hands off My Leather Jacket," "Get Away from Me," etc. One passable cut is "Daffodil

Rock," which puts stomping rock music to a Wordsworth poem (an idea later used by Hendra and Ulllet). This one-joke concept was a dumb idea: kids didn't want to hear Jack's mocking parody, and adults didn't want to hear the noise they hated.

The RCA album from 1964 has sketches about weight loss, with brief guest appearances by Milt Kamen, Nipsey Russell, and Jack Carter. No insults, just bad gags: "We have definite proof that overweight is hereditary. It goes back to Adam and Eve, whose parents were both very fat. Now in the Stone Age, weight naturally wasn't a problem as it is today. 'Cause in the Stone Age, it was very difficult eating stone.... The ancient Romans forced people to go on diets. It happened right after Marc Anthony tried to pick up a fat guy to throw to the lions and got a hernia in the meantime." The reaction to all this is applause, table thumping, and big laughs: a tribute more to Leonard's unique grousing, staccato delivery than the jokes.

1967's Verve release is a Booker and Foster-produced studio disc with Carol Corbett, Anthony Holland, Len Maxwell, Bob McFaddden, and Betty Walker in a mix of songs and sketches.

Most of the album is a primer on how to act nasty in various situations. At the dentist: "Root canal work is expensive. It'll come to $600." "$600? Why don't ya add a toll bridge and we'll go partners!" At the dry cleaners: "I want this cleaned, I'll pick it up tonight." "It won't be ready." "But your sign says 'Stains Removed While You Wait.'" "That's right. Can you wait seventy-two hours?"

The songs are toothless, with a harmonizing chorus cooing in the background. On "The Hostility Rag" Leonard recommends, "Stuff the plumbing at the Y, sit on grandma's raisin pie ... teach dirty words to mynah birds, drop engine sludge in momma's fudge, stick Juicy Fruit on Daddy's suit, pour minestrone on Vic Damone."

Only occasionally are there true Jack E. Leonardisms: "Your husband tells me you have a great mind. Too bad it hasn't reached your head yet ... ladies and gentlemen, if I've said anything to offend anybody here tonight, I'd like to repeat everything I've said."

Leonard also turns up on Jackie Kannon's "Poems for John" album. Fat Jack's a legend, but as his recognition continues to fade, the high price of his vinyl goes down.

SAM LEVENSON

- BUT SERIOUSLY FOLKS (Signature 1026) $6 $12

Though usually placed in the comedy section, this album is just a lecture by Levenson that lives up to its title.

JERRY LEWIS

- JERRY LEWIS COLLECTORS SERIES (Capitol CDP 7931962) ** $8

Only Lewis fans could possibly listen to fifty-five solid minutes of Jerry's jerky novelty singing. But amid the mess of cuts that sound like Danny Kaye with nasal congestion and a caffeine overdose, or Daffy Duck undergoing a bris, there are some funny or at least bizarre stand-outs.

"I Love a Mystery" is one looney tune, a manic three minutes in which Jerry manages to re-enact an entire radio murder mystery with squeals, shouts, moans, and a siren-like last note that could puncture an eardrum. "Sunday Driving" is similarly fast-paced and overpowering. For sheer sadism, there's "I Like It, I Like It," Jerry's catchphrase yowled over and over on each chorus.

Most of the collection, based on various "Bozo Approved" singles Jerry issued for Capitol (some collected for the kiddie album "The Nagger" Capitol 3267), features bold and brassy orchestrations to go with Jerry's brazen antics. Other cuts include "I Keep Her Picture Hanging Upside Down," "Y-Y-Y-Y-Yup," "I Can't Carry a Tune," "Strictly for the Birds," "I Love Girls," and "Pa-Pa-Pa-Pa Polka."

Though he didn't provide competition for Dean Martin in this category, Lewis issued several "straight" albums during his career.

JOE E. LEWIS

- IT IS NOW POST TIME (Reprise R 5001) **1/2 $10 $20

Today Lewis is better known for having a cut tongue, not a cutting tongue. A popular nightclub star of the '20s, he was brutally slashed up when he chose to move from one gangster-owned club to another in Chicago. His story was the basis for the book and film *The Joker Is Wild*. Lewis was influential in stand-up, a master of jokes, songs, and patter, using a style a generation of comics would imitate. Nightclubs remained his element and he rarely made films or TV appearances.

Recorded at the Flamingo Hotel in Las Vegas circa 1962, Lewis sounds ravaged by his legendary drinking and a long list of health problems. His voice is raspy, his delivery at first labored, but soon the adrenalin is flowing and he finds his rhythm.

These jokes may sound like standard shtick, but Lewis was the first to tell them. His style was to slide them out conversationally, not boom-boom rim shot:

"I do hope you forgive me for takin' a little drink while I'm on," he mutters. "That's just part of my act. Besides, I'm an alcoholic. I'm not a big drinker. I just put away a lotta little ones. I mean to say I'm not a steady drinker— 'cause I shake too much. My doctor is here ... he tells me if I keep drinkin' I'll never see a ripe old age. But I don't believe the dear doctor. 'Cause every night I see more old drunkards than I see old doctors ... my doctor told me I have the body of a kid. A very sick, shriveled up kid."

Lewis was also noted for his double entendre songs. From an ode to a ballerina: "As the new ballerina appeared, she did a high kick near the lights. The women all fainted but the men stood and cheered. She'd forgotten to put on her tights ... you mustn't muff your chance ... show what you're made of lass ... whirl around and show your class."

Lewis was aware of the hot new comics of the day: "Shelley Berman has two albums, one 'Inside Shelley Berman' and the other 'Outside Shelley Berman.' He has a third album called 'Up Shelley Berman.' Wonderful album."

BEATRICE LILLIE

- QUEEN BEA (DRG Archive DARC 2-1101, $12 $20
  originally available as EVENING WITH BEATRICE LILLIE (London 5212) *1/2 $10 $25
  and AUNTIE BEA (London 5471) *1/2 $10 $25
- BEATRICE LILLIE SOUVENIR ALBUM (Decca DL 5453) *1/2 $10 $20
- THIRTY MINUTES WITH BEA LILLIE (Liberty Music 1002) $15 $30
  reissued as THE YOUNG AND BEAUTIFUL AND INCOMPARABLY TALENTED BEATRICE
  LILLIE SINGS (JJC M 3003) and A MARVELOUS PARTY (AE 2103 and CD AE1-006) *1/2 $8

Time has not been kind to the great musical comedy star Bea Lillie, whom Noel Coward once called "the funniest woman of our civilization." The key word there is "civilization." Civilization has changed. Perhaps for the worst. But her civilized, oh-so-witty bits of sophisticated glitter and chic fluff sound almost as pointless as the pretentious people and manners she was satirizing.

Her most famous numbers tweak art singers and '30s and '40s music trends ("The Zither Song," "Rhythm," There Are Fairies at the Bottom of Our Garden," "I Apologize") and they are unbearably fey and unrelievedly coy. It's extremely annoying when she satirizes lah-dee-dah ladies by singing: "hey nonny no ... oh fiddle dee dee, I'm up a tree just fancy me ... la la hee hee hee."

 Some of Lillie's piquant charm and madcap sensibilities show through the dated material. One of the fresher songs that gives a hint at Bea's art is "Maud," written by Bea's sister Muriel. The worldly-wise singer wearily sings to the no-good Maud; "I said darling, look at you. And the sordid things you do. And the sordid sort of people you adore. I said Maud, you're full of maggots, and you know it ... your soul's a bed where worms queue up to breed. You don't know what life's for Maud. You're rotten to the core Maud. And Maud agreed."

Lillie not only influenced a generation of arch and aging chanteuses, but some less likely people too. Pat Paulsen recorded a version of her quick recitation "Mistaken Identity": "I was standing at the corner of the street, as quiet as quiet could be. When a great big ugly man came up and tied his horse to me."

All of the above is on the "Queen Bea" set, reissues of her 1955 and 1958 London albums. Her old 78s are on the Liberty /AEI reissues, and the quality of these old wax masters isn't good. About all one hears on "Snoops the Lawyer" is her annoying, exaggerated whoop every time she sings "Snoops." Other cuts, like "The Gutter Song," "I Hate Spring," and the once risqué "I'm a Camp Fire Girl" are antiques without much charm. Noel Coward fans might be interested in the two versions of "Mad about the Boy," one done as a school girl, the other a Cockney maid. The obscure 1954 "Souvenir Album" ten-incher is also for ardent fans only. "Clop Clip Clop," evidently intended to parody the horsey set, is unendurable in its forced cheeriness: "Clop clip clop, clop, clip, clop, giddy-up horsey, please don't stop! To the pond where the bullfrogs hop! Hee hee horsey, clop, clip, clop! Say to the bullfrog, 'What do you think? My little horsey wants a drink.' Into the water, down with his nose. Gurgle gurgle gurgle and away he goes! Isn't that cute?" Similar is the campy "Honey Ma' Love," written by Herman "As Time Goes By" Hupfeld.

Lillie appears on various Broadway cast albums and collections of Broadway-oriented material. She reads "The Mock Turtle's Song," "Jabberwocky," and several limericks on "The Nonsense Verse of Carroll and Lear" (Caedmon TC 1078), costarring Stanley Holloway and Cyril Ritchard.

GEORGE "GOOBER" LINDSAY

- GOES TO TOWN (MCA 5353) *** $5 $10

Lindsay, who spent a dozen years on *The Andy Griffith Show*, *Mayberry R.F.D.*, and *Hee Haw*, delivers his jokes at a surprisingly fast clip, using up enough material to fill three or four Jerry Clower albums. For fans of country corn, there's plenty of it. He recalls his poor lifestyle back in Jasper, Alabama: "It's not too hard to tell we was poor—when you saw the toilet paper dryin' on the clothes line.... We got two things that we're very proud of: night and day. I mean it's a small town. The Knights of Columbus and the Masons know each other's secret. They're called Mason-Knights! If you just got a year to live, move down to Jasper, buddy, it'll seem like a lifetime."

Since his blend of tall tales and quickies are told in a style that's more cheerful brawling than lazy drawling, Goober "travels" better than most Southern comics. Lindsay issued two straight song albums for Capitol in the late '60s: "Goober Sings" (Capitol St 2965) and "96 Miles to Bakersfield" (Capitol ST 230).

ART LINKLETTER

- PEOPLE ARE FUNNY (Mark 56 730) ** $5 $10
- HOWLS, BONERS AND SHOCKERS (Columbia CL 703)
  reissued as KIDS SAY THE DARNDEST THINGS (Harmony HL 7152) ** $5 $10

Linkletter, a very popular personality in the '50s and '60s, hosted his own "House Party" series on radio and daytime TV. His albums concentrate on his famous interviews with people and those "kids who say the darndest things." Typical zany antics from the kiddie album of howls and boners and shockers:

"How do you fix a fried chicken before you cook it?" "You kill it." "You kill it! What do you do after you kill it?" "Peel it." "Peel it! Nothing like peeling a chicken before you cook it!"

"Do you have any pets?" "A dog and two birds." "What kind of a dog?" "Box terrier." "A box terrier? What's a box terrier? What does he do?" "He tears up boxes."

RICH LITTLE

- RICH LITTLE'S BROADWAY (Kerr SPL 800) ** $7 $15
- POLITICS AND POPCORN (Mercury SRM 1617) ** $5 $10
- W. C. FIELDS FOR PRESIDENT (Caedmon TC 9101) *** $5 $10

Little's early studio albums, sans audience, are a bit strange. The 1968 "Broadway" album (sort of a promotional disc—Gib Kerr was his manager as well as owner of the record label) offers peculiar "twist ending" sketches. David Brinkley's newscast partner isn't Chet Huntley, but Crazy Guggenheim. Henry Fonda's volunteer soldier turns out to be Mr. Magoo. The sketches showcase Little's voices but aren't funny. More amusing are the songs: Humphrey Bogart on "Accustomed to Her Face," Ed Sullivan on "Everything's Coming Up Roses," and Jack Benny and George Burns duetting "Hey There." Little's longevity is due to his love of his stars, so here, even in a conversation between John Wayne and Liberace, the accent is on accuracy, not outrageous or vicious humor a la David Frye. He's flawless as Rex Harrison, Henry Fonda, and Claude Rains.

The Mercury LP (1971) is extremely offbeat, closer to Firesign Theater than the kind of bits Little did on TV variety shows. The stark, almost jokeless script by Sascha Burland (one of the men behind "The Idiots and Company") has one side of strange political humor (Spiro Agnew kidnapped by Walter Matthau, Rod Steiger, and Jonathan Winters in one bit). In one fantasy, Richard Nixon is drafted and stands nude before examination doctor Truman Capote. The dank script has Capote say, "Arright, bend over. That's a good soldier. Take your clothes and sit on a wooden bench till your name is called." That's carrying subtlety to an extreme. The punch line has Hubert Humphrey drafted, too. "This is very embarrassing," he tells Nixon, "Presidents and Senators don't go to war." "I know," replies Nixon, "war is for people." Side Two's re-enactments of war movies, gangster movies, and horror films are similarly hollow, deathly so without an audience. In a Western bit, Walter Brennan, John Wayne, Gary Cooper, Burt Lancaster, Kirk Douglas, and Edgar Buchanan argue about whether trains go chuggity-chug, choo-choo, toot-toot, or bibbidy-bob-bidy. When the train they want to rob rides by unscathed, Liberace appears saying, "Let's go rustle some cattle. Ya know, cattle go clompity-clomp-clomp, isn't that marvelous?" Punch line from Walter Brennan: "Aw shut up, we can't stop a train, we ain't gonna stop no cattle." This could be considered a noble experiment, but it's impossible to tell just what the experiment was.

In 1972 Little read segments from W. C. Fields's obscure 1940 book *Fields for President*. With the sound effects of cheering partisans, Fields gives speeches: the essays from the book on "How to Succeed in Business," "My Views on Marriage," "My Rules of Etiquette," etc. The Fields book itself is weak, but Little helps with a realistic performance. Rather than using a caricature of the Fieldsian cadence, and a lot of added "Ahh yes's," Little does an exact duplicate of the Fields voice as heard on the great man's 78 rpm "Temperance Lecture."

- THE FIRST FAMILY RIDES AGAIN (Boardwalk NS1 33248) ** $4 $8
- RONALD REAGAN SLEPT HERE (Dr. Dream 8708) ** $4 $8
- UNCLEAR AND PRESIDENT DANGER (Orchard Lane 9900775062) ** $8

Earle "First Family" Doud produced the two Reagan era discs. The 1981 Boardwalk album is at the same level as the original "First Family" disc. Not only are the album jackets virtually identical, the tone of the "just kidding" sketches is the same. There are the usual vice president gags (nobody recognizes who he is) and standard patter at the press conference ("At what point should a fetus be regarded as a human being?" "When it votes Republican"). Herve Villechaize is in the cast, Melanie Chartoff plays Nancy, and there are cameos from John Zacherle, Jack Riley, Shelley Hack, and ... Vaughn Meader, who is "Voice #2" for one line. When Reagan discusses jelly beans, Meader says, "Let's face it, blacks have always wound up at the bottom and whites at the top."

Little's Reagan is impeccable, but unfortunately for him, so was everyone else's. The 1987 Dr. Dream disc has impressionist Louise DuArt for all the females: Nancy Reagan, Joan Rivers, Katharine Hepburn, etc. Some unusual cameos: Chuck McCann as Admiral Poundexter, Bob Denver as Caspar Weinberger, and Julie Newmar as Mrs. Oliver North. With a cast like that, the album is at least lively, if not always funny. A predictable question and Reagan answer: "Don't you think it might be fair to say that you're a trifle uninformed about some of our current problems?" "*What* current problems?" There's even a musical number, "The Contra Rap."

The 1994 "Unclear" CD was a comeback of sorts for Little, who was long absent from late night talk shows and eclipsed in mimicry by *Saturday Night Live* mimics Phil Hartman and Dana Carvey. Rich does a fairly good Clinton with Jeannette Markey as Hillary. The hour-long script is wooden and badly paced. Many of the jokes are awfully dumb. The small studio audience doesn't have much to laugh about. Ronald Reagan is discovered on a fire escape. Why? "Well, ya see, I had to go to the men's room, but there was a line there. And fortunately I looked up and saw a sign that said, 'In case of emergency, use the fire escape.' And let me tell you, this was an emergency! Otherwise we might've had a whole new trickle down theory." Sometimes the humor gets stranger than one might expect from Little. Alfred Hitchcock discusses a new movie idea: "A giant moth attacks the girl in the shower. Here's where the suspense comes in. She's wearing a woolen bra and panties."

The quality of Little's impressions has suffered over the years, a common problem for veteran mimics who've garnered enough fame to become tired of being other people. Some are still classic (Jack Benny, George Burns) others disappointingly off (W. C. Fields, Carroll O'Connor).

NOTES: Little appears on "The New First Family 1968" (Verve), "Spiro T. Agnew Is a Riot" (Cadet), and Earle Doud's "Celebrity Workout" record (Capitol). He also issued a Reagan-era single of "The Contra Rap." His Canadian albums include "Rich Little in Concert (Much 5004), "My Fellow Canadians" (Capitol 6028), "Scrooge and the Stars"

(Capitol 6049), and "Christmas Carol" (Columbia 90580). Little's two versions of the Dickens classic differ greatly. For the Columbia album, Scrooge is W. C. Fields; in the first one, he imagined Jack Benny as Scrooge. That album also imagined John F. Kennedy as the Ghost of Christmas Past. Little had Kennedy say, "My life upon the globe is brief." The album was quickly pulled and revised. Copies of the original are collector's items.

LITTLE RASCALS

- LITTLE RASCALS (Mark 56 # 653) * $5 $10

Those charmingly stilted Little Rascals can be difficult to tolerate without the visuals. Their squeaky recitations aren't very funny and aside from Alfalfa Switzer's pained rendition of "I'm in the Mood for Love," the songs are almost unlistenable. It's hard to tell what's going on at any given time on this collage of clips. Or as one irate woman says during the rehearsal of a number by Spanky McFarland, "I don't think this is so funny."

Two CDs of *Little Rascals* soundtrack music have been issued on CD by Koch.

LOHMAN AND BARKLEY

- LOHMAN AND BARKLEY'S GREATEST HITS VOL. 7 (MGM M3F4956) *1/2 $4 $8

Al Lohman and Roger Barkley put this one out in 1974, and no, they spared the public the first six volumes. They're purveyors of disc jockey humor—sketches designed as suave time-fillers more than comedy. One three-minute routine makes fun of call-in shows by spending all three minutes telling listeners in different area codes which call-in phone numbers to use.

Several cuts offer the requisite mock interviews that sound like third-rate Bob and Ray. There's a visit with Cleveland Gordon Leatherberry, a man who can smell like anything. Then there's a session with performance artist Roscoe Bosco, who is going to do "The Dance of the Mole." How does he do it? "I dig a hole and bury myself ... dig down and down and down until I disappear."

Lohman and Barclay issued half-hour tapes on the Soap Records and Tapes label. These are tedious half-hour parodies of soap operas acted out with sound effects, organ music, and corny voices that sound like Gary Owens and Bob Eubanks trying to emulate Firesign Theater. "Light of My Life" Volume One offers two episodes: "Breath of Dr. Duncan" and "Doc in the Box." Volume Two features "The Arrest of Dr. Duncan" and "Mouse in the Hole."

In May of 1986 the duo broke up after twenty-five years on KFI in Los Angeles. Barkley jumped to KJOI-FM for his own show.

MARC LONDON AND RON CLARK

- THE PRESIDENT STRIKES BACK (Kapp KL 1322) *1/2 $4 $8
- HEAVEN ON $5 A DAY (Kapp KL 1333) *1/2 $5 $10

London and Clark were comedy writers attempting to cross over and perform. "The President Strikes Back" has some limited curiosity appeal for comedy buffs. It was released as a concept album: President Kennedy's comic answer to "The First Family." "Now gentlemen," Kennedy tells his cabinet, "here is the problem. Why wasn't I asked to make the album. I do as good a Kennedy as any of my imitators.... Never mind the applause, Lyndon. Just get me a recording contract."

The sketches are mostly about family reaction to "The First Family" and JFK's determination to record a funnier album after meeting with agents and record execs. "I was listening to that album about us," Jackie (played by Sylvia Miles) says in one sketch, "It's all in good fun." "He's misusing the language. He has me saying 'Cuber' instead of 'Cuber.' Now everybody knows there's a vast difference between 'Cuber' and 'Cuber'...." "I see what you mean Jack, and I'm behind you one hundred percent. You have the right idear."

London, a graduate of Harvard, has a good Boston accent, as opposed to a particularly accurate Kennedy impression.

Joan Rivers and Pat McCormick are in the ensemble cast of "Heaven," a concept album that pictures heaven as bureaucratic as earth. As newly arrived angels, London and Clark must line up to get their wings: "Two sets of wings, two halos, that'll be $4.50 plus tax...." "What? $4.50 plus tax? You have to pay for this?" "You don't expect us to give them away, do ya?" "We don't have any money. We always heard that you can't take it with you!" "Golly, if I heard that one once, I heard it a million times."

McCormick is heaven's social director: "This morning at ten there will be services of all faiths. Eleven o'clock in the game room, "Simon and Peter Says." After lunch there will be an intramural volleyball game: the good guys vs the bad guys ... we hope you enjoy your day, and don't forget tonight at 9 pm ... our annual "Come as You Were" party. By the way, will Vincent Van Gogh report to the lost and found department? We have something that belongs to you."

EARL LONG

- LAST OF THE RED HOT PAPAS (News 101) * $7 $15
- LAST OF THE RED HOT PAPAS 2ND EDITION (News 102) * $7 $15

Both Earl Long and his brother Huey were colorful governors of Louisiana. Until these commemorative albums came out, the closest Earl came to being on a comedy disc was when Lenny Bruce used Long's bizarre slogan, "Elect Me, I'm Not A Nut," as an album title and joked about him.

Paul Newman played Earl in the anecdotal film *Blaze*, which focused on Long's relationship with stripper Blaze Starr. Newman's version of a good ol' loudmouth from the South has a lot more charm than the original.

Following Long's death in 1960, these 1961 albums tried to commemorate him with a collage of interview clips and fragments of speeches. Though subtitled "Humor and philosophy ... his best, from pea patch to mansion," there's not much here that stands out as either humorous or philosophical.

Here's one of the better clips, featuring Long in the middle of one of his spirited, loud, raucous-voiced rants: "What we need is a four-lane highway for drunken drivers, nuts, overloaded trucks, and come what may. Then we oughta have another road for home-lovers, children, good people, business people, poor folks, rich folks, and people in all lines of endeavor who don't load up on John Barleycorn before they start up on a trip. Oh yeah!"

SHORTY LONG

• HERE COMES THE JUDGE (Soul 709) $8 $15

In 1968 Long had a Top Ten hit with a self-penned novelty song based on the Pigmeat Markham (and revived by TV's *Laugh-In*) catchphrase "Here Come de Judge."

The dance tune does have a funky chorus wailing "Here Come de Judge," but the lawyer and Judge's remarks aren't much: "Judge, I got a boy here can't dance." "Can't dance? Oh. Ninety days! Thirty days of Boogaloo. Thirty days of learning to Shingaling. And thirty more for the Afro Twist." Pigmeat Markham used similar lines on his single "The Hip Judge."

The album pads out the hit with instrumentals ("Ain't No Justice") and another seminovelty, "Here Comes Fat Albert," based on Bill Cosby's character: "Better hide all of your candy and put all your cookies away. I heard it through the grapevine: Fat Albert played hooky from school today! Hey hey hey!"

This album is usually considered comedy/novelty, not R&B, but can't really be graded for laughs. Long died in a drowning accident in 1969.

LONZO AND OSCAR

• COUNTRY COMEDY TIME (Decca 4363) ** $5 $10
• AMERICA'S GREATEST COUNTRY COMEDIANS (Starday SLP 119) ** $5 $10

This team might actually be called Lonzo, Lonzo, Lonzo, and Oscar, since there have been several replacements along the way. Ken Marvin and Rollin Sullivan were christened "Lonzo and Oscar" by singer Eddy Arnold in 1944. Within a few years, Marvin retired and was replaced by Rollin's brother John. Now "Lonzo and Oscar" were a true brother act. When John died in 1967, he was replaced by Dave Hooten.

The Starday album offers their most famous novelty song, "I'm My Own Grandpa," a right tricky tune with amusingly complicated lyrics. "When I was twenty-three I was married to a widow who was pretty as could be. This widder had a grown-up daughter who had never wed. My father fell in love with her and soon they too were wed ... my daughter was my mother 'cause she was my father's wife...." and on it goes, getting worse and worse, until the singer arrives at the song title. Another cut, timely today, is "Trouble on the Cable," about the woes of TV reception: "I just fed the chickens and they're gettin' awful skinny. You reckin' them birds are roostin' on our antenny?" "Well it may seem silly but it could be so—because now we're gettin' feathers instead of snow." Other tunes include "I've Had It," "Bare-Faced Bird Brain," "Things Look Silly," and serious cuts like "Little Talk with Jesus" and "I Lost an Angel," about the car accident that killed Rollin Sullivan's wife and another brother, Phil, but spared him.

A rarity for collectors is "Straight Songs: Lonzo and Oscar Sings 'Em," (Lonzo & Oscar Special SON 74161), which was sold only at Lonzo and Oscar's live shows. The album notes say that "in answer to numerous requests and after making 105 single recordings ... we decided to "go straight" for just one Album." Cuts include "The Time to Die," "She Thinks I Still Care," "The Fugitive," and "I'm Just Here to Get My Baby Out of Jail."

PEGGY LORD

• LUSTY TRUSTY BUSTER (Stereoddities S 1903) ** $5 $10

A "farmer's daughter" comedienne, Lord tries to combine the country charm of an Elly Mae Clampett, the likability of an Imogene Coca, and ... the desperate over-sexteen yocks of a Rusty Warren. The result isn't very funny, but it's interesting.

Just when she begins to amuse with her innocent wisecrack delivery (and a hoarse husky-sexy Blythe Danner voice) out come the crass song parodies and the dumb one- liners that she punctuates with a Rusty Warren cackle.

A typical quick ditty, accompanying herself on the guitar: "She was goin' down the hill doin' ninety miles per hour when the chain on her bicycle broke. Well she landed in the grass with the sprocket in her pocket and was tickled to death by a spoke!"

A hee-haw gag: "How about the girl who went to bed in checker board pajamas? Made two wrong moves and got jumped!"

JULIET LOWELL

• DEAR SIR (Jubilee LP 10) * $5 $15

Juliet Lowell collected comic letters for a late '50s novelty book, *Dear Sir*. This ten-inch album dramatizes them. A serious, dry, overenunciating announcer introduces the letters, which are badly acted out by various amateurs. The album was produced by Kermit Schafer, who was also responsible for endless "blooper" albums, many featuring badly re-enacted versions of TV and radio fluffs and boners.

NORMAN LUBOFF, SOLOISTS AND CHORUS

- WOLFGANG AMADEUS MOZART IS A DIRTY OLD MAN (Epic BC 1366) ** $6 $12

Long before "Amadeus," Norman Luboff issued this album calling attention to Mozart's obsession with backsides. It was intended to be placed in the comedy bin, as opposed to the various albums that classical record labels issued devoted to the instrumental "comic music" of Mozart.

The mixed choir performs these numbers without calling undue attention to the rude words. And that makes it even more surprising for listeners not sure of what they're hearing.

One lullaby bears this sweet refrain, "Good night, good night, quite plainly you're tight. Crap in bed, you're crocked. Soak your head. And get your ass to bed." Another choral work that actually sounds charming if you aren't listening to the words: "You are so coarse, you're like a horse. Who neither brains nor senses has ... You stupid lout. Stuff up your snout ... oh hurry up, be quick and kiss my ass. Oh kiss, oh kiss, oh hurry, hurry up and kiss my ass."

The novelty lasts for a few songs before the nose-thumbing, backside-raising refrains gets repetitious.

LUM AND ABNER

- LUM AND ABNER (Golden Age 5022) ** $5 $10
- AN EVENING WITH LUM AND ABNER (Mark 56 #605) ** $4 $8
- LUM AND ABNER VOLUME TWO (Mark 56 #734) ** $5 $10
- COLLECTORS EDITION (KLD Produtions 1001) ** $7 $15
- LUM AND ABNER 1940's (Memorabilia 716) ** $4 $8
- LUM AND ABNER 1950's (Memorabilia 717) ** $4 $8

Lum was Chester Lauck and Abner was Norris Goff. Their amiably-paced radio show has the kind of humor one might find on *The Andy Griffith Show*. The supporting cast included Andy Devine and Zasu Pitts. A typical sample from Mark 56's "An Evening ..." has the two men trying to raise $200:

Lum: "My only hope is to find some man that's smart enough to have made a lot of money and dumb enough to lend me some." Eventually they get involved with a finance company, and even bet on the horses: "I got good news for you ... your horse ran in the fifth race. He came in first ... in the sixth race!"

On the flip side they battle over playing checkers: "You can't move that man there, yer cheatin!" "I am not, I'm playin' just like you do." "Oh, so you admit it, do ya!"

JIMMY LYNCH

- TRAMP TIME (THAT FUNKY TRAMP) (La Val LVP 901) *1/2 $6 $12
- HE DOES IT AGAIN (La Val LVP 902) *1/2 $6 $12
- THAT NASTY FUNKY TRAMP (La Val LVP 904) *1/2 $6 $12
- THAT NASTY FUNKY TRAMP (La Val LVP 904 Picture Disc) *1/2 $8 $15
- FUNKY AND FUNNY (La Val LVP 905) *1/2 $6 $12
- BEST OF JIMMY LYNCH (La Val LVP 906) *1/2 $6 $12
- NIGGER PLEASE (Laff A 194) $4 $8
- RETURN OF THE FUNKY TRAMP (Laff A 179) $5 $8

Some adult party albums are poorly recorded. A few are nothing but curse words. And some are so ethnic that outsiders not only can't figure out the jokes, they can barely figure out what's being said. Jimmy Lynch often combines all three problems on his La Val discs.

At "the famous El Grotto bar in Battle Creek, Michigan," Lynch recorded his first album, the mildest of the lot. There are roars of laughter as he makes his way to the stage. "What did you call me?" "Tramp!" "I ain't no tramp," Lynch sulks. "I been to college. I been somewhat ed-ucated. Yes I are. You want me to spell ed-ucated, I know. E-D-D-Y-C-A-D-I-D. Now thass right. Four long years I went to college to get mah eda-cation. I got mah B.S. Mah bullshittin' degree."

On "Funky and Funny" the "nasty stinkin' delapidated ... tramp" lives up to his billing with comic insults hurled at the emcee of the show.

The number of Lynch records proves that this type of pungent cursing comedy has its fans. When he bothers to tell a joke, Lynch usually pads it to run four or five minutes, loaded with exagerrated acting and funky backspin.

PAUL LYNDE

- RECENTLY RELEASED (Columbia CS/CL 1534) *** $15 $40

A rare album recorded around 1961, Lynde was evidently Columbia's answer to the "sick comedy" best-sellers on Verve and Fantasy. Stylistically close to Shelley Berman, he's an actor who likes to enclose himself in tightly written sketches with a beginning, middle, and an ending that signals audience applause.

Most of the cuts here are complete monologue routines as he portrays a prissy lecturer fretting about the youth of America, a demented poet reciting odd odes, a battered traveler returning from a tour of Africa, and a Morticia Addams-type woman snitting at her waywardly weird son.

The African explorer bit was a favorite, one he used in "New Faces of 1952." As he prepares to show photos of his trip to an expectant audience, the feverish explorer wavers and says, "I'm gonna be all right. One of those cobra snakes struck me right between the eyes. You know how that feels, heh heh, I've been taking aspirins and doping a little." Then he launches into the black humor of a hideous trip that ended with disease, depravity, and death.

His "Addams Family" routine features a shrieking, giddy woman who cautions her monstrous son, "Did you wipe your feet? All of 'em? Now come and give mother a great big kick. Oooh that felt good!"

And his squeamy poems include a rhyme written by a headless train accident victim: "Hear the bird in my window singing his song, 'Chirrup, Cheer up, you haven't got long.'" Comedy buffs, gay cultists, and fans of "sick" humor are all in the hunt whenever this album turns up in a store. Lynde also appears on "Zingers from the Hollywood Squares" (Event) and "New Faces of 1952" (RCA Victor LOC 1008), where he appears extremely briefly as The Judge in the musical sketch "Lizzie Borden."

MOMS MABLEY

- MOMS MABLEY FUNNIEST WOMAN IN THE WORLD (Chess 1447) **1/2 — $6 — $12
- AT THE UN (Chess 1452) ** — $7 — $15
- AT THE PLAYBOY CLUB (Chess 1460) **1/2 — $7 — $15
- AT THE GENEVA CONFERENCE (Chess 1463) ** — $7 — $15
- BREAKS IT UP (Chess 1472) **1/2 — $7 — $15
- YOUNG MEN, SI (Chess 1477) ** — $7 — $15
- I'VE GOT SOMETHING TO TELL YOU (Chess 1479) ** — $7 — $15
- FUNNY SIDES (Chess 1482) ** — $7 — $15
- MOMS WOWS (Chess 1486) ** — $7 — $15
- BEST OF MOMS MABLEY (Chess 1487) **1/2 — $7 — $15
- MAN IN MY LIFE (Chess 1497) ** — $7 — $15
- MOMS BREAKS UP THE NETWORK (Chess 1525) **1/2 — $7 — $15
- SINGS (Chess 1530) — $6 — $12
- OUT ON A LIMB (Mercury 60889) ** — $6 — $12
- MOMS THE WORD (Mercury 60907) ** — $6 — $12
- AT THE WHITE HOUSE (Mercury 61090) **1/2 — $6 — $12
- NOW HEAR THIS (Mercury 61012) ** — $6 — $12
- HER YOUNG THING (Mercury 61205) ** — $6 — $12
- YOUNGEST TEENAGER (Mercury 61229) **1/2 — $6 — $12
- ABRAHAM MARTIN AND JOHN (Mercury 61235) — $5 — $10
- LIVE AT SING SING (Mercury 61263) **1/2 — $6 — $12
- BEST OF MOMS (Mercury 61139) **1/2 — $6 — $12
- I LIKE 'EM YOUNG (Partee PBS 2402) ** — $6 — $12
- MOMS' DREAM (Blues Journey SS1 783) **1/2 — $8

Beloved Jackie Mabley portrayed an outrageously dressed and feisty mom (or grandmom) for over thirty years. She made a tremendous number of records, strange considering that her raspy, raucous, half-toothless delivery requires a lot of concentration to decipher. The albums are all basically the same: a collection of familiar jokes rendered immortal by her colorful delivery. Many are keyed to her "Moms" character—the red-hot granny out after young men.

From "At the Playboy Club" here's a typical tale: "Oh I meant to tell you, about this fella, he joined the integrated church down in one of them foreign countries, Alabama or Mississippi or one of them foreign countries, and the time comes for him to be baptised, you know. So this minister ducked him down in the water, brought him up and said, 'Do you believe?' He said, 'Yessir, I believe.' Ducked him down again, held him a little longer, said, 'Do you believe?' He said, 'Y-yes, I believe!' Ducked him down there again, held him a little longer, rasied him up and said, 'Do you believe?' He said, 'Y-y-yessir, I believe. I believe you tryin' to drown me!'"

From "On Stage," another late '50s album recorded in Chicago, Moms demonstrates her philosophical side: "Anybody who acts normal nowadays, they're probably just not well! I'm tellin' you, I just don't understand. If I go too fast, I'll run into something, if I go too slow, somethin'll run into me!"

On "The Youngest Teenager" album she jokes about her old husband: "I mean old. Old as air. And twice as polluted! I mean OLD! I shouldn't talk about him 'cause he's dead. At last. He's been dead for years, but he just died lately. Talk about history. One look at him and you see history. He was old, he was, looked like six o'clock right straight up and down."

She also mentions meeting up with Richard Nixon: "I said, 'Son, you sure can't say nothin' wrong if you keep your big mouth shut.' He said, 'Mom, you know best. I would like to see you come down to Washington ... do you live in Harlem? After all, I'm white, and all the security in the world won't help my head at night!' I said, 'No, son, I live in White Plains. Don't let that fool ya. The community is black ... so if you come, would you mind comin' 'round the back?'"

Material is often duplicated from disc to disc. The "Geneva Conference" album deserves some kind of mention for having an album cover ahead of its time. Pre-Woody Allen's Zelig and Tom Hanks's Gump, here's Moms, fist raised, posing between Castro and Khrushchev, ready to lay one upside Nikita's head. The Chess albums (released through 1963) are rare, but lately the Mercury albums have almost equaled them in price. On most of the Mercury albums, the rambles are broken up with a few songs.

The CD release "Moms' Dream," culled from a performance recorded circa 1963, features a forty-minute set of songs and song parodies, all performed with the cool charisma of a female Louis Armstrong. A few are on familiar topics of old men and love, but many of them are racial, either chuckling slaps at Southern prejudice or feisty hopes for peace and integration.

To the tune of "Jambalaya" she sings: "Goodbye Joe, me gotta go, me oh my-o. I can't stand the way they treat me on the Bayou. I ain't gonna stop in Illinois or Ohio. Just send my mail in care of Adam Clayton Powell at the Harlem Y-o!" From the title track, which segues into "Georgia on My Mind": "I had a dream last night. I asked for my equal rights. Somebody said, 'Moms, you're next.' And there I stood—with a rope around my neck ... their arms reach out for me. They must want me desperately! But if I can just break free, they'd seen the last of me! In Georgia. Georgia. No peace will I find. Till I catch a plane North and put Georgia outta my mind. Ray Charles can have it, you hear me? Oh yeah!"

Moms didn't do that much strong racial comedy, at least on disc, so this album is unusual. Another important cut is "Moms' Unchained Melody," the closest she ever came to acknowledging her lesbianism. To the familiar chorus of "Two old maids, laying in bed, one turned to the other and said ..." she adds snippets from popular tunes. Like "I'm going to love you like nobody's loved you come rain or come shine," or "This is my first affair, so please be kind," or "if that isn't love, it'll have to do, till the real thing comes along!"

NOTES: In 1969 Moms actually cracked the Top 40 as a vocalist with her effective rendition of "Abraham, Martin and John." Her Mercury "Best of" was released the year before. The Partee release, from 1972, was her last. She also appears on "Comedy Night at the Apollo" (Vanguard VRS 9093).

MOMS MABLEY AND PIGMEAT MARKHAM

- BEST OF MOMS AND PIGMEAT
  (Chess 1487, re-released as MABLEY AND MARKHAM, Chess 60009) **1/2 $6 $12
- ONE MORE TIME (Chess 1504) **1/2 $6 $12

Mabley and Markham didn't appear in sketches together. These compilations have a "best of" Moms side and a "best of" Pigmeat side.

MADCAPS See ANTHONY AND ROBERTS

MAD MAGAZINE

- MUSICALLY MAD (RCA Victor LPM/LSP 1929) ** $20 $50
- FINK ALONG WITH MAD (Bigtop 12 1306) ** $15 $30
- MAD TWISTS ROCK 'N' ROLL (Bigtop 12 1305) ** $15 $30
- THE MAD SHOW (Columbia OS 2930) ** $20 $40

The 1959 "Musically MAD" is an odd mix of wry, pseudosophisticated wit from Henry Morgan, plus Bernie Green's failed attempts at Spike Jones. It's not what kid fans of the magazine would expect, and it's disappointing for adults as well.

Bernie Green's better cuts are "Concerto for Two Hands" (with Joseph Julian squeezing his hands together to create a somewhat flatulent rendition of "The Old Folks at Home") and "Anvils, of Course" (the "The Anvil Chorus" with brass and anvils, but none of the junkyard clatter Spike Jones would've added). Morgan's dry lectures include a German-accented dissection of Wagner and a discussion of light opera: "The Mikado, briefly, opens with a chorus of Japanese gentlemen on the stage rhetorically quizzing the audience as to whether one knows who they exactly are. Quote: 'If you want to know who we are, we're gentlemen of Japan,' and so forth and so on ... sometime later the Emperor appears. He is, by the grace of the Shoguns, the Emperor of Japan ... and a crashing bore. The chorus sings, quote: 'Bow bow to the Emperor of Japan' and so forth, from which I imagine we get our quaint custom of bowing to the Emperor of Japan." As for the song "Tit Willow," he insists it must be "some kind of code."

The album is highly prized by those who haven't heard it. It draws a high price because of the fine full-color portrait of Alfred E. Neuman, and audiophile interest in RCA "Living Stereo" albums.

As for the two Bigtop albums, considering the silliness and near self-parody of so many rock songs at the time, from "Itsy Bitsy Teenie Weenie Yellow Polka Dot Bikini" to "Leader of the Pack," it's no wonder they had no impact. Both were written by the team of Blagman and Bobrick, and feature the vocals of Jeanne Hayes, Mike Russo, and The Dellwoods. Ugliness, dandruff, pimples, and other teen maladies are the subject matter, handled with clod-obvious lyrics and sung fairly straight. "Fink Along with MAD" offers, among others, "When the Braces on Our Teeth Lock," "She Lets Me Watch Her Mom and Pop Fight," and "Don't Put Onions on Your Hamburger." From the latter, done in a kind of Dion and the Belmonts style:

"Baby I don't mean to bug ya, and please don't feel insecure. But though you are a walking dream, your onion lips are turning me green. Catchup, mustard, or French fries never brought such tears to my eyes. But oh, it's more than I can bear when you order one with onions medium rare!"

The "Rock 'n' Roll" album offers "She Got a Nose Job," "Let's Do the Pretzel," "When My Pimples Turned to Dimples," and "Please, Betty Jane Shave Your Legs."

Mort Drucker's artwork, illustrating the song titles, livens up the back cover for "Rock 'n' Roll." On the front cover is a color portrait of Alfred E. Neuman, who is also on the front cover for "Fink Along with MAD" (bearded a la Mitch Miller). One cut on "Fink Along" appeared as a "bonus" flexible disc in an issue of the magazine: "It's a Gas," with "vocals" by Alfred E. It's just dance music interrupted by burps.

Did parents enjoy reading *MAD Magazine*? Nope. Did young teens like sophisticated New York cabaret? Nope. That's the problem with "The MAD Show," which opened in 1966 and didn't last too long.

The stars—Paul Sand, Linda Lavin, Jo Anne Worley, and the team of MacIntyre Dixon and Dick Libertini—can't do much with the weak cabaret sketches and songs. One of the more amusing cuts is "The Boy From," Linda Lavin's breathy, robotic parody of Astrud Gilberto, not that '60s kids had any idea who this jazz artist was. "Well It Ain't," lampoons Dylan-style folk rock protestors: "I lay myself down in the gutter cryin' out against the war in Vietnam. You think it's easy to sing about misery and how the world is up a creek when you're makin' $40,000 a week? It ain't!"

Any parents bringing their *MAD*-loving kids had to cringe over some of the adult material, like the sketch about a twisted junior high schooler. When the father decides to punish the kid by making him stay home with his mother, the boy cries, "To be all alone with Mommy! Just Mommy and me, to walk like her, talk like her, wear her dresses ..." Almost as embarrassing is the song "Ecch!" It tries to meld sophisticated lyrics ("Ecch" here rhymes with "Brecht" and "Ben Hecht") with the catchword used so often in *MAD*. Ecch. Broadway cast album collectors and foolish *MAD* fans have jacked up the price on this lame failure.

NOTES: Some fans collect the *MAD* singles (33-1/3 cardboard discs) that were occasionally inserted into the magazine. A full list of these appears in the book *Completely MAD*. Another oddity is "What Me Worry?" an ABC-Paramount single attributed to Alfred E. Neuman and his Furshlugginer Five. A tired middle-age chorus sings about that "funny little fella that you all know," Alfred E. Neuman, who sings the chorus in a wimpy nasal voice: "What me worry? I don't even care. What me worry? Worry-in' can't get you an-y-where!" The flip side is an instrumental, "Potrzebie."

In 1996 Rhino (R2 72435) issued a chintzy "best of" called "MAD Grooves," offering five cuts from the Big Top and Columbia albums, five flexi-discs (mostly dull disco parodies), and two redone versions of old songs.

PENNY MALONE

• PENNY MALONE SINGS? (Jubilee LP 16) *1/2 $15 $20

Penny Malone was an ex-Miss Maryland and model. Then, sporting a crew cut, she baffled the clientele at chichi nightclubs like The Reuban Blue in New York, singing slightly suggestive tunes ("I Couldn't Say Yes," "Lady Detective," "I've Got It Hidden"). In keeping with her arch chanteuse pose, she sometimes affects accents, ranging from pseudo-operatic to dumb blonde. She has the type of act in which the pianist is obliged to underline a joke with a trill or a royal glissando.

A few songs are clean, if on "adult" subjects. One predictable number covers the new fad of the day—Freud: "Let's be neurotic together, let's have a breakdown for two. I'll exchange my neurosis for your cute psychosis, you sweet schizophrenic, you." Also deliberately offbeat is "Venus." She sings as the forlorn statue: "Oh, how I'm longing for love. Oh what goes on in my heart. But it's so hard to enfold men, when you've got no arms to hold men. Oh the things that I've done for my art ... how I long to be wed. Oh, what goes on in my heart. Is there someone in this planet who won't take my charms for granite? Oh the things that I've done for my art."

MANCOW

• BOX OF SHARPIES (Anon 7400) ** $8

Chicago's Howard Stern wanna-be, Mancow is not very original or impressive on this 1995 debut CD. There are the usual crank phone call put-ons that fall limp. One attempts to annoy aged Chicago Cubs baseball broadcaster Harry Carey. Another ends with a woman complaining to the surly crankster, "Lose my phone number, I can't stand people like you." She gets this response: "You don't even know what I'm like, lady, you've never met me so why don't you shut yer yap, why don't you shut your big, annoying, slutty yap?"

It's tough wading through seventy minutes of in-your-ear posturing and self-promotion. Along the way on this radio version of a tough man competition, there's sometimes a passable fake commercial (a minor chuckle has Tupac Shakur easily ridiculed in a spiel about a "2Pac Man" video game). Once in a while there's a call so stupid it's funny, like the few minutes Mancow spends putting on an outrageous Asian accent to belabor a Vietnamese whose name is pronounced (if not spelled in the phone book) "Bitch Bang."

HOWIE MANDEL

• FITS LIKE A GLOVE (Warner Bros. 125427) **1/2 $4 $8

Curly-haired class clown Howie Mandel's main influence is Steve Martin, which means that he's prone to doing "zany" things like putting a rubber glove over his head and doing a lot of "you hadda be there" party comedy for his delirious, seemingly indiscriminant fans. Mandel's persona is that of a manic adolescent, a nervously hyper, Hawaiian-shirted bad boy romping about the stage teasing ringsiders and using props for quick laughs. He's actually more like Shecky Greene than Steve Martin, since he leans so heavily on ad-libbed partying with the crowd.

"What do you do!" he says, charging at one ringsider. "Nothing," the man shoots back. Mandel pauses. "How do you know when you're finished?" A woman comes back from the ladies room and shouts up to Howie that there's not enough toilet paper in there. "You came back moist?" he asks. Well-edited, the album has few annoying moments of "what are they laughing at?" pantomime even if there are plenty of "what are they laughing at?" mild gags.

Sometimes Howie shoots a prepared one-liner, or one he has remembered. It's hard to figure why the guy would use a woman's joke (Judy Tenuta's, in fact) for a laugh: "I love feeding the pigeons—breast feeding them."

Sometimes there's a thinking man's gag: "You're not gonna believe this. I saw a murder, I got there like five minutes after it happened. Apparently, just from what I saw, the body fell onto a chalk line exactly the same shape!"

Mandel also appears on "Comic Relief" (Rhino 70704).

CHARLIE MANNA

- MANNA OVERBOARD (Decca DL 4159) *** $7 $15
- MANNA LIVE (Decca DL 4213) *** $7 $15
- RISE AND FALL OF THE GREAT SOCIETY (Verve 15051) *1/2 $5 $10

Charlie Manna created some classic comedy monologues during his short career (he was in his late forties when he died in 1971). His pleasant personality wasn't distinctive enough for audiences to remember him the morning after. He did sketches about submarine officers, astronauts, and life inside the human body—the kind of stuff that would've been classic coming from Jonathan Winters or Bob Newhart. It's only "nice" performed by gentle and genial Charlie.

"Overboard" features the "Inside You" bit as Charlie describes how the body works. Every organ has a different voice, from a lower lip that imitates Maurice Chevalier to a very nasal nose. They all work together when a pretty girl walks by. The central nervous system cries out, "Now hear this! All glands: secrete! Connect me with the stomach. Any butterflies down there? Connect me with the unconscious please. Well ... keep ringing." Manna's most famous routine at the time, "The Astronaut," is here. Now it sounds like Bob Newhart trying to do Bill Dana: an astronaut nervously refuses to go up in space because someone stole his box of crayons.

The petulant astronaut routine was so well known that, before takeoff, Commander Alan Shepard was handed a box of crayons as a gag. "War at Sea" is a cute and well-crafted sitcom where two submarine commanders, one American, one German, try to out-duel each other. The weirdest cut is "Hey Bud," in which a sleazy guy tries to sell a South American country from the back of his van.

"Manna Live" is seamless fun from start to finish, including "Bon Voyage," about a French travel agent briefing countrymen on how to behave in America. The Frenchman makes a mangle of explaining the sizes vs the actual value of American coins, and then reports on arriving in New York and seeing the Statue of Liberty: "Once we have passed it, we have passed French waters ... voila, New York ... and you Frenchmen remember, on many street corners there are booths. These are not what you think they are ... they are for telephone calls!" The guide also points out useful phrases to learn in dealing with New Yorkers, like "No Habla Español."

Other fine cuts: a bunch of Brooklynites tink together their "Rocket to the Moon"; a Newhart-style look at the death of Julius Caesar; a cute bit on crass Christmas tunes; and the full-blown "Alcatraz," a prison movie satire complete with original songs.

The Verve disc is a studio album of sketches, similar in tone to any Booker & Doud-Vaughn Meader disc. Some cuts are deadly dull, like the seven-minute "Park Avenue Riot" (about New Yorkers walking their dogs on the exclusive avenue) and the six-minute "Supreme Court," a wishy-washy look at pornography on trial:

"I do not understand why the author found it necessary to insert twenty full-color illustrations depicting in minute detail the intimacies ..."

"I beg the court to look at these pictures in their historical perspectives ... the educational value of the period costumes shown in these pictures."

"But they're not wearing costumes in these pictures."

"I refer in particular to their shoes and wigs, which are completely authentic."

The main cut is the eleven-minute "One of Our H Bombs Is Missing," about a possible bomb in the Central Park lake that brings out the best and worst in people, as unions, duck lovers, Park officials, cops, and civilians argue about how to remove it.

Supporting cast members include Bryna Raeburn and Bob McFadden. Manna continued to perform as a stand-up comic in clubs and on TV variety shows through the rest of the '60s. An obscure ten-inch album called "Geared for Laughs" (Dynamic Gear) features Manna and Franky Crockett. Manna also issued a single on Jubilee: "Give Me a Chance to Explain."

MARIO MANZINI'S GROOVY NEWDE REVIEW

- WE'D RATHER SWITCH (WRS 100A) * $4 $8

There's some terrible acting and muddled vocalizing from Tricia Sandberg, Yancy Gerber, Martha Wilcox, Howard Lenny, and Ron Collins on this studio album. There are plenty of straight songs and three long, uninteresting comedy sketches inspired by old burlesque routines. As one fellow says to a pair of chorines: "I got a splitting headache. Can't you girls rehearse somewhere else? Not that you need to rehearse. It's the same old crap."

MARCEL MARCEAO

- MARCEL MARCEAO (MGM S 4745) $5 $10

There's a stylized portrait of mime Marcel Marceau on the cover, but the spelling is the clue that this is just a gag album. There are pseudo liner notes from various celebrities, including Spiro Agnew: "I found this record to perfectly represent the position of the silent majority." The disc has silence on each side with a minute of polite applause at the end.

Marcel Marceau did release a noncomedy album for Caedmon, "Marcel Marceau Speaks."

BARBARA MARKAY

- HOT BOX (Hot Box FU 2) * $5 $10

In 1976, Long Islander Markay issued this studio record of coy, pandering sex songs even Sandra Bernhard would find pretentious. Somehow she got minor league skin mag *Gallery* to call her the "female Lenny Bruce." She isn't. All she does is scream and posture. She'll bang on the piano like a punkette on drugs and howl doggerel. Sometimes it's one phrase yelled over and over ("Give Your Dick to Me"), other times it's muddled nonsense lyrics: "Clark Kent had a cock of steel. Said to Lois Lane, 'Lois, how does it feel?' She says, 'Why just grand, feels just like Superman ... Cock my doodle do, doodle-ooh! And I will fondle you. You! We will bill and coo. What else is there to do? Cock my doodle do!'"

PIGMEAT MARKHAM

- THE TRIAL (Chess 1451) **1/2 $6 $12
- AT THE PARTY (Chess 1462) ** $6 $12
- ANYTHING GOES (Chess 1467) ** $6 $12
- WORLD'S GREATEST CLOWN (Chess 1475) ** $6 $12
- OPEN THE DOOR RICHARD (Chess 1484) ** $6 $12
- MR. FUNNY MAN (Chess 1493) ** $6 $12
- THIS'LL KILL YA (Chess 1500) **1/2 $6 $12
- IF YOU CAN'T BE GOOD, BE CAREFUL (Chess S 1505) **1/2 $6 $12
- MR. VAUDEVILLE (Chess S 1515) **1/2 $6 $12
- SAVE YOUR SOUL BABY (Chess S 1517) ** $6 $12
- BACKSTAGE (Chess S 1521) ** $6 $12
- HERE COME THE JUDGE (Chess S 1523, reissued 1985 as CH 9166) *** $6 $12
- TUNE ME IN (Chess S 1526) **1/2 $6 $12
- HUSTLERS (Chess S 1529) ** $6 $12
- BAG (Chess S 1534) ** $6 $12
- WOULD THE REAL PIGMEAT MARKHAM PLEASE SIT DOWN (Jewel 5012) ** $5 $10
- CRAP SHOOTIN' REV (Jewel LPS 5007) ** $5 $10

A vaudevillian for decades, Dewey Markham didn't do stand-up as much as classic sketches like "Here Come de Judge," where he played the blustery, raucous judge in a crazy courtroom of convicts. On the album of the same name, he opens with an expansive cry, "The judge is high as a Georgia pine! Everybody's goin' to jail today! And to show you I don't mean nobody no good this mornin', I'm givin' myself six months! And if I'm gonna do six months, district attorney, you can imagine what you're gonna do!"

He thunders through case after case, including the one about a man hauled in for public nudity. "I've got twelve children," the defendent pleads. He doesn't have to go any further. "This man is not a nudist ... this man hasn't had time to put his clothes on!"

Another classic, "Batter Up," appears on 1965's "If You Can't Be Good, Be Careful." An old, deaf man appears on the ball field. Pigmeat has to explain everything:

"Ball one!" "Huh?" "The man said I got one ball!!" "Ohhh, the man said you got one ball. Too bad!" "Ball two!" "What's that?" "The man said I got two balls!" "Oh, the man said you got two balls. Ain't nothin' news about that...." "Play ball ... Don't worry about it. Come on. Whee! Fly ball! I knocked up a fly!" "Say what?" "I knocked up a fly!" "Oh, you knocked up a fly. Uh-uh, it can't be done!"

Markham made it to *The Ed Sullivan Show* several times, doing clean Abbott and Costello-type burlesque bits with a straight man. He was usually billed as "Judge Dewey Markham."

In the late '60s and '70s, Pigmeat's albums went out of print. Some militant blacks insisted that Pigmeat's delivery was too close to that of Amos and Andy-type characters.

Today there is once more an appreciation for Pigmeat's brand of evocative ethnic comedy. Collectors should be aware, though, that there is some duplication on Markham's records, with variations on his most famous "Preacher" and "Judge" routines. It's also a bit frustrating to hear but not see Pigmeat and his sketch players in action.

NOTES: Pigmeat issued 78s of blues tunes, plus a few '60s singles including "Here Comes the Judge" (a Top 20 hit in 1968) and "Sock It to 'Em Judge."

GUY MARKS

- HOLLYWOOD SINGS? (ABC Paramount ABC 549) ** $5 $10
- LOVING YOU HAS MADE ME BANANAS (ABC Paramount ABCS 648) ** $5 $10

Impressionist Guy Marks, whose memorable '60s stage act included weird bird imitations, is not going for laughs on his two albums. "Sings?" is a concept album of how movie stars of the '40s would have handled their era's hit tunes. With lush orchestration, Humphrey Bogart sings "As Time Goes By," Cary Grant offers "Red Roses for a Blue

Lady," Charles Boyer croons "It Was a Very Good Year," and Clark Gable handles "I'll Be Seeing You." The mimicry is first-rate on these. There's a dash of comedy only in Bela Lugosi's frantic "Begin the Beguine," Boris Karloff's contemplative "Don't Take Your Love from Me," and James Cagney's "You Always Hurt the One You Love."

"Bananas" from 1968 has the semi-hit single, "Loving You Has Made Me Bananas." It's a ridiculous number sung in the serious deadpan style of a '30s ballroom crooner: "Oh you burnt your finger that evening, while my back was turned. I asked the waiter for iodine, but I dined all alone." At the time, "camp" was popular via Tiny Tim and others. The rest of the album is padded with a lot of genuinely hideous tunes of the era, like "The Object of My Affection," "Ti-Pi-Tin," and "Little Sir Echo."

Marks is Boris Karloff, and Joey Forman is Bela Lugosi in a minute-and-a-half duet, "Let's Be Frank, Mr. Franken-stein," on the album "Les Poupees De Paris" (RCA LSO-1090). This was the soundtrack to a 1964 World's Fair Krofft puppet show. Strangely, Marks's odd routine, in which the audio joke is hearing Gary Cooper and Humphrey Bogart speak in Indian dialect, was released only as a single: "How the West Was Really Won" (ABC 45 11148).

DANNY MARONA

- DANNY FROM BOTH SIDES (DMC) $4 $8
- DANNY MARONA LIVE (DMC) $4 $8
- DANNY MARONA LIVE AGAIN! (DMC) $4 $8

KENNETH MARS

- HENRY THE FIRST (ABC Dunhill DSD 50191) *1/2 $4 $8

Earle Doud produced this 1974 political satire on Henry Kissinger starring Mars, best known for his role as the knotheaded Nazi in "The Producers." He's more restrained here, his Kissinger rarely rising above the Secretary of State's well-known monotone. In fact, many gags rely on the contrast between lively situations and the glumly morose German accent. When a mugger rushes up and demands some bread, Kissinger calmly mutters, "Vell, I just came from de bakery, but I did not buy bread. I do have some apple shtrudel."

One moment that works well is an imagined TV commercial. The hard-headed, unemotional Mr. K. shills cigarettes: "Good evening. This is Henry Kissinger. For years I used to smoke cigarettes. Then suddenly I quit. Who needs it. I don't need it. You don't need it. Enough already. Finished."

Before the album is finished, Doud touches most of the established bases for a studio album in "The First Family" tradition, including the cliché of "politician as pop vocalist." Not quite the hit "Senator Bobby" had with "Wild Thing," Kissinger warbles "Takin' Care of Business" and "The Hucklebuck."

MARSH AND ADAMS

- THE BULLTHROWERS (Platinum 1003) ** $5 $10
- THESE JOKERS ARE WILD (Art 109) ** $5 $10

Lou Marsh was the comedian, Tony Adams the singer/straight man. Billed as "The Comedians' Comics," their album "These Jokers Are Wild" sports praise from Jackie Gleason ("Lou and Tony are the greatest"), Milton Berle ("Funny, funny guys with great timing and showmanship"), and Alan King ("My wife and I laughed till our sides hurt.") But their material, recorded at the Montmartre Hotel in Miami with many a rim shot, is just standard early '60s patter.

Lou is aggressive with his ancient whizbang: "Hey, didja see the girl I was talkin' to when you passed me?" "I didn't see her." "Tall, blonde, blue-eyed, she was gorgeous!" "Hey, that pretty?" "Yep." "What did she say?" "Nope!" "I hate to start somethin' with ya, but you missed the rehearsal." "I was downtown waitin' for a cab. There was a woman cab driver. She asked me how far I wanted to go! Hee hee hee!" "Well?" "My case comes up Tuesday! (Rim shot.) The hell with the show. Let's play a game. Call a number from one to ten, honey. Any number. What? You lose. Take off your dress! (Rim shot.)" "Hey, she's pretty. But take away that beautiful hair and what have you got?" "The sexiest bald-headed woman you ever saw! I would love to see her in 3D." "Three dimensions?" "No, my room! 3D!"

JACK MARSHALL

- MY SON THE SURF NUT (Capitol T 1939) * $7 $15

Here's stupid surf humor from the late '60s, dumb and dopey for anyone but a thirteen-year-old Brian Wilson wanna-be with a penchant for salt-water slang. One side, in front of a mumbling audience, is mock interviews with surfers, including an inventor:

"Here's a wonderful one that I call the hodad's delight. It's made of rubber and you can carry it around in your pocket. You can just blow it up and it inflates and looks like the real thing."

"Can you actually surf on that?"

"Hell no, it's just for hodads and gremmies that don't have a woodie. They can blow it up and lay it on the sand and fool all good dollies on the beach into thinking they are real surfers and not lousy greasy pseudos."

The flip side of execrable tunes includes "The Monster Surfer" (a failed combination of Bobby "Boris" Pickett and Jan & Dean) and "Some Gremmie Stole My Hair Bleach" (the big joke is that the vocalist stammers and sings off-key).

MARSHALL AND NESTOR

- CAPTAIN DINGMAR (Military Industrial Complex 13044) *1/2 $4 $8

Sandy Marshall and George Nestor attempted a radio show in New York, *Captain Dingmar: Swell Fellow*, about an effeminate superhero whose "secret identity is safeguarded by the fact that no one really cares." His voice is a combination of the Wallace Wimple character on *Fibber McGee and Molly* (similar to the "Droopy Dog" character in cartoons) and Truman Capote. His sidekick is Margo, a woman with a stereotypical Jewish accent. Their quirky dialogue is strictly for cult devotees: "Oh, Captain, my Captain, you look tres, tres delicious. That saucy peekaboo bodice! But don't you think that aquamarine snood clashes with the rest of your chic ensemble?" "Oh, and I had to listen to that female chauvinist pig, Susan Jacqueline! Stand back darling, I'm gonna fly out that window. Up, Wendy, up Tinker Bell, away!" After the sound of a crash: "Oh dear, third window this week."

BILL MARTIN
- CONCERTO FOR HEADPHONES (Warner Bros. 1856) * $5 $10

Back in 1970, Bill Martin was Warner's answer to Firesign Theater, with this LP coproduced by Harry Nilsson. The album notes on the back cover make it clear that this is supposed to be "far out" comedy. "Warning: This is not an enchilada."

There are attempts at political satire as raspy-voiced politicians and generals, Southerners and religious leaders babble and grunt at each other. The script is so full of rambling non sequiturs and obscure sound effects it's hard to tell just what is going on.

One of the few coherent moments, and one of the few to have any kind of punch line, offers two soldiers talking amid drums and machine gun fire: "report back to me by 1800. Hargrave, tell Charlie Company we'll bivuoac here for the night...." "Sir, uh, it'll be ..." "Spit it out Hargrave." "It'll be pretty bad tomorrow, won't it, sir?" "I won't lie Hargrave. It won't be easy and it won't be easy. Taking the main gate is one thing, but occupying the Dean's office is another."

KAY MARTIN
- KAY MARTIN AT THE LORELEI (Dyna 104) ** $7 $15
- I KNOW WHAT HE WANTS FOR CHRISTMAS (Fax 1005) ** $7 $15
- AT LAS VEGAS (Record Productions 3,000,004, Laff A 107) ** $5 $10
- SINGS NAUGHTY AND NICE SONGS (Record Productions 3,000,005) ** $7 $15
- KAY MARTIN AND HER BODYGUARDS
  (Roulette R-25014, and Record Productions LP 3,000,006) ** $7 $15

In the '50s and early '60s, Martin appeared in Vegas, her mild, adult-tinged songs and gags enhanced by a 38-24-37 body, strawberry blonde hair, and a tough, sexy look (from lots of makeup and mascara as typified in "men's magazines"). Generally the lyrics aren't much more erotic or amusing than Cole Porter's "Let's Do It," as in her number "S.E.X.," which is about the animal world: "They say a mink likes to think that he gets more action than a bobolink. And they say there's hardly a gnu who hasn't intimately known another gnu. When a parrot in a cage has reached a certain stage, you notice how strangely he behaves. Well, it's not a cracker he craves. It's sex!"

On the "Naughty and Nice" album, she sings "I Feel Like a New Man," with this, the most suggestive refrain: "If he's bold, I'll be bolder. If he's shy, I'll be sincere. With his head on my shoulder, he can leer at my brassiere. I feel like a new man, a motel rendezvous man. As sweet as candy, a real Jim Dandy on any handy divan. I feel like a new man!" Kay and her male bodyguards, who also sing at times, throw in straight tunes once in a while.

STEVE MARTIN
- LET'S GET SMALL (Warner Bros. BSK 3090) *1/2 $8
- A WILD AND CRAZY GUY (Warner Bros. HS 3238) **1/2 $5 $10

Martin was a sensation in the late '70s, but his records don't always capture what the fad was about. Even sociologists might not be able to explain exactly why audiences suddenly surrendered to grinning put-ons, dumb and dumber schtick like arrows through the head and balloon animal-making, or Martin's mockery of stand-up slickness, which was how he'd survived years of performing in front of bored or antagonistic audiences in small clubs and rock venues.

Melding Martin Mull's contemptuous, understated satire with brain-frying, hippie-dippy nonsense, Martin begins: "To open the show I always like to do one thing that is impossible. So right now I'm going to suck this piano into my lungs." The non-jokes continue with a report on the fun things he's buying lately: "Got me a three hundred dollar pair of socks. I got a fur sink. Oh, let's see, electric dog polisher. Gasoline powered turtle neck sweater. And of course I bought some dumb stuff, too." The one-liners are so bluntly stupid that the wit behind them is often less than evident: "If I'm in a restaurant and I'm eating, and someone says, 'Mind if I smoke,' I say, 'No no, mind if I fart?'" Then again, sometimes they aren't that witty:

"Virginia Slims, that's a woman's cigarette—what do they have, little breasts on 'em or something?

The audience is with him through all the put-ons, even the four-minute bit where he tells a joke "especially for the plumbers" in the audience, and puts them through deliberately dull technical language before the non-punch line: "'The Langstrom Seven-Inch Wrench can be used with the Finley Socket.' Just then the little apprentice leaned over and said, 'It says sprocket, not socket!'"

Seventy-five percent of the album is devoted to this anti-stand-up, along with "you had to be there" mime, and phrases like "Okay! We're really having fun now!" in the guise of a jerky pitchman. Twenty years later, it requires a lot of patience to listen to this. Even at the time, the album could have used a lot of editing.

COMEDY IS PRETTY

Sexy album covers helped spark interest in Kay Martin, Ruth Wallis, and Ava Williams. In the '60s Donna Jean Young was one of the few "cute" comics, but today there's Rita Rudner, Ellen Degeneris, Carol Leifer, and many, many more.

COMEDY IS NOT PRETTY

Getting laughs is a drag for Steve Martin, 1950s female impersonator Ray Bourbon, and Florida-based Tubby Boots.

This 1977 album went platinum. It does offer one classic Martin gag: "I gave my cat a bath the other day ... they love it. He sat there, he enjoyed it, it was fun for me. The fur would stick to my tongue, but other than that ..." But other than that ...

In 1978, Martin was not only the hottest comic in the country, but the author of a best-seller, *Cruel Shoes*. On "Wild and Crazy" he mentions some of the other hysterical books he's written: *Bad Banana on Broadway ... Renegade Nuns on Wheels ... How I Turned a Million in Real Estate into Twenty Five Dollars in Cash ... Trouble in Doggy Land ... Howdy Doody: Manor Myth ... The Apple Pie Hubbub ... How to Make Money Off the Mentally Ill*. That last made-up book is actually a good description of what Steve Martin was doing in 1978. He shared a bond with his audience. He would say nothing, the audience would laugh at nothing. Too much of the record is a non-joke ramble interrupted by non one-liners: "Is it OK to yell 'movie' in a crowded firehouse?" Martin is smart enough to know the difference between playing dumb and being dumb. He shouts: "Let's repeat the non conformist oath ... I promise to be different!" (Audience: "I promise to be different!") "I promise to be unique!" (Audience: "I promise to be unique!") "I promise not to repeat things other people say!" (Audience, realizing they are idiots, applaud and squeal delightedly). Later they give him a sixteen-second ovation just for using his catchphrase, "I am a WILD and CRAZY GUY!" There's another sixteen-second ovation for "Well EXCUUUUSE ME!"

The album has a few classic Martin bits: his routine on an embezzling cat and his semi-hit single, "King Tut," a disco rap put-on ("buried with a donkey, he's my favorite honkey").

- COMEDY IS NOT PRETTY (Warner Bros. HS 3392) **1/2 $5 $10
- STEVE MARTIN BROTHERS (Warner BSK 3477) ** $5 $10

"Comedy Is Not Pretty" has Martin in drag on the cover. His cynical non-comedy is still getting big laughs. He takes on the comedy cliché of doing a "story with sound effects" routine. The big joke is that he uses the same sound effect for everything. He does the equally old "funny names will make you laugh" routine, declaring that his real name is "Gurn Blanston," and he has several albums out, including "Gurn" and "Simply Gurn." Like a lot of Andy Kaufman's stuff, it's challenging, courageous, and funnier reported on than suffered through. A third of the album is genuinely funny in either his wild and crazy Dick Shawn style or darkly subtle Martin Mull mode. He describes a form of sex education: "I actually learned about sex watching neighborhood dogs. And it was good. Go ahead and laugh. No, go ahead. I think the most important thing I learned was: never let go of the girl's leg no matter how hard she tries to shake you off." Unlike his first two, this 1979 album is well-edited, without as much dead space or deliberately self-conscious posturing.

The last album contains a short essay on where farts go, his portrait of a silly-sounding foreign "Love God," and a mock-serious religious recitation: "I believe in going to church every Sunday, unless there's a game on. I believe that sex is one of the most beautiful, wholesome, and natural things that money can buy. And I believe it's derogatory to refer to a woman's breasts as boobs, jugs, Winnebagos, or Golden Bozos. And you should only refer to them as hooters. And I believe you should place a woman on a pedestal, high enough so you can look up her dress." Fans of Martin's banjo playing will be happy with Side Two, mostly instrumental, not mental.

NOTES: The first two albums went platinum, but the last two quickly became dollar bin specials. Now the first is on CD, which further lowers the vinyl value. The last two, thanks to smaller printings, are higher priced. Martin can be heard singing "Dentist!" on the *Little Shop of Horrors* soundtrack album. The cut was also released as a twelve-inch single. "King Tut" has been anthologized by Dr. Demento. "Pennies from Heaven Radio Special" (PRO 998) was released to radio stations.

MARTIN AND LEWIS

- DEAN MARTIN AND JERRY LEWIS (Memorabilia MLP 714) ** $4 $8
- MARTIN AND LEWIS ON RADIO (Radiola MR 1102) ** $5 $10

Both albums offer the first *Martin and Lewis Show*, broadcast December 22, 1948. Dean and Jerry teamed up just two years earlier. The first fifteen minutes finds the boys nervously waiting to do their first show. "How big an egg can we lay?" asks Dean. "Well, if we took a large hen and got it to hold back for two years ..."

When Jerry refuses to get dressed, Dean says, "You're stallin'." Jerry answers, "That's impossible, Stalin's a big man in Russia ... and he's a big important man, and if he thinks I'm impersonating him, he'll come and get me and send me to Siberia and it's full of ice and snow and sleet. And Dean ... I'm COLD!"

It continues at that level, which means only hardcore fans will want to continue listening. Guest star Lucille Ball is impressed with handsome Dean: "I'm sure you're going to be very successful!" "How about Jerry?" Dean asks. "Yeah, how about that," she deadpans.

Radiola offers an extra half-hour episode, a February 27, 1949, effort guest starring William Bendix.

- DEAN AND JERRY (Argon 101) *1/2 $10 $25
- THE CADDIE (Private Stock ML 1) **1/2 $10 $25

The prime attraction on these two bootlegs is a few minutes of the duo goofing around while cutting a radio commercial for their film *The Caddy*. The boys blow off steam at the engineers. "Was that all right, ya cocksucker?" asks Dean. The team start changing the script. Jerry: "See Paramount's *The Caddy*, it'll make ya shit." It was all pretty hilarious back in the '50s when celebrity cursing was a shock novelty.

The rest of the Argon record has anonymous actors enacting "Over Sexteen" party jokes, a few minutes of a scratchy 78 of a black group singing "Stick Out Your Can Here Comes the Garbage Man!" plus twenty minutes of that bootleg album staple, "The Crepitation Contest." The Private Stock LP has better filler, including some outtakes as radio announcers take turns making fun of a Lana Turner film, a dirty parody of "Dangerous Dan McGrew," and gay versions of a Chesterfields cigarette commercial and the show tune "I'm in Love with a Wonderful Guy." There are also monologue and dialogue cuts from anonymous adult 78s.

NOTES: Naturally, there are many albums of Dean Martin singing, and even two straight song albums from Jerry Lewis (Decca DL 8410 and Decca DL 8595). In addition, there's a pair of rare Jerry Lewis novelty song albums, "The Nagger" (Capitol J 3267) and "Jerry Lewis Sings for Children" (Vocalion 73781). An irritating (if heard more than once) Lewis novelty tune, "Sunday Driving," turns up on Dr. Demento's "Greatest Novelty Tunes of the 50's." Also see the entry on Lewis.

JACKIE MARTLING

• WHAT DID YOU EXPECT (Off Hour 30) **	$5	$10
• GOIN' APE (Off Hour 31) **	$5	$10
• NORMAL PEOPLE (Off Hour 32) **	$5	$10
• THE JOKE MAN (Off Hour 75) **1/2		$8

Martling was a journeyman dirty comic working in small Long Island nightclubs through the '70s and '80s. That's when he issued his first three records. He began writing gags for Howard Stern (and supplying on-air fake guffaws), but he still could manage little beyond local bookings. His sidelights include a dirty joke phone line and mail order sales of videos and merchandise.

Martling's early albums are hard to take due to his unpleasantly loud and leathery voice and the annoying laugh he uses to yock it up with his dead-headed audience. He also steals too many bad jokes from old sex magazines and comedy records. Here's a typical barrage from the "What Did You Expect" album:

"Little Bo Peep has lost her sheep and doesn't know where to find 'em. But a search revealed they're out in the field with Little Boy Blue behind 'em! Arrright! Haw haw haw! We're gettin' close. What's black and white and climbs the walls? A virgin penguin! There was a girl named Hortense, the size of whose breasts were immense. One day playin' soccer out popped her left knocker and she kicked it right over the fence! Ha ha ha ha ha."

Age and a decent paycheck via Stern seems to have mellowed him. On the 1993 "Joke Man" CD, his first in about a decade, he doesn't relentlessly laugh at his own gags. He comes across as an amateurish "Dice" Clay, collecting tasteless jokes and telling them with cheerfully low-class bravado:

"Guy walks in a store, he says to the salesgirl, 'I wanna buy some toilet paper.' She says, 'What color?' He says, 'White. I'll color it myself....' How can you tell the Irish guy in the hospital ward? He's the one blowin' the foam off his bedpan.... Lady catches her kid jerking off. She says, 'Son, don't do that. Save it till you're twenty-one.' By the time he's twenty-one he had nine jars.... What's the difference between a girl and a toilet? A toilet doesn't wanna cuddle after you drop a load in it."

• SGT. PECKER (Off Hours Rockers OHR 77) **	$7

It's more of the same on the 1995 "Sgt. Pecker," seventy-seven fast minutes of hit-and-miss gags and stories. Like the audience, he laughs along with the corny gags and sighs over the stinkers: "Why should an Indian wear a jock strap? Totem pole. Ha ha ha! Here's a question. In the old cowboy movies, why didn't John Wayne pull the wagons into a square? Then when the Indians turned the corners they would've fallen off the horses. No. huh. OK." Give him credit for memorizing 'em.

GROUCHO MARX

• GROUCHO MARX ON RADIO (Radiola 1072) ***	$5	$10
• GROUCHO! (Mark 56 #758) **1/2	$5	$10
• GROUCHO MARX (Nostalgia Lane NL 1021) **1/2	$5	$10
• GROUCHO MARX (Memorabilia MLP 733) **1/2	$5	$10
• YOU BET YOUR LIFE (Golden Age GA 5021) **	$5	$10

Of the many albums of Groucho's radio work, Radiola stands out thanks to the "Hollywood Agents" routine from Groucho and Chico's short-lived series, and a half-hour show featuring Tallulah Bankhead and Groucho's amusing commercial for "Plebo."

Like so many Mark 56 albums, there's no list of contents. The album is just two "You Bet Your Life" quiz shows. On Side One the secret word is "Name" and the special guests are bridge player Charles Goren, and Ernie Kovacs. It's one of Groucho's best shows. Groucho notes, "Mr. Goren, I'm impressed having you up here. Your name is a household word among millions of bridge players. But don't let that go to your head. Because Drano is a household word, too." Then Groucho goes after a sexy contestant who works as a dancer at the Moulin Rouge: "What do you do there?" "Well, actually I walk around with an hourglass figure dress." "An hourglass dress, huh. Must be the early part of the hour, huh?" Kovacs is restrained, but that's part of the fun—he refuses to play along with the quiz. On the flip side, the secret word is "Foot."

The Nostalgia Lane disc has the same Kovacs and Goran episode. Memorabilia's "You Bet Your Life" episode has odd and, thanks to Groucho, amusing contestants. A lady barber comes up: "What's the difference between male and female barbers?" "We don't talk an ear off you." "Waddya do, you just shave it off?" The flip side is the well-known fifteen-minute episode from Groucho and Chico's series. They played a pair of Hollywood agents. As Groucho aptly says, "On with the show and may the jokes have no age limit."

Golden Age has two episodes from late in the series (December 16, 1957, and February 10, 1958) and there's a bit too much quiz and not enough Groucho. They're entertaining as quiz shows go, especially when contestants make complete dunces of themselves missing easy questions (twin brothers who don't know Van Gogh's profession), but there are few moments for Groucho to bring things to life.

Stan Laurel disliked Groucho's work on "You Bet Your Life," complaining "rudeness is rudeness. I know (he) overdoes it deliberately, but I still can't enjoy it." But it's hard not to chuckle, especially when Groucho greets Wild Red Berry, the pro wrestler, with the following compliment: "I've never seen you wrestle, but I'd like to go to one of your rehearsals sometime."

- HOORAY FOR CAPTAIN SPAULDING (Decca DL 5405) **** $20 $40
- HERE'S GROUCHO (MCA MCAD 20847) *** $7
- THE FUNNIEST SONG IN THE WORLD (Young Peoples Records 10010) *** $20 $40

Groucho issued very little material on disc. His 1952 ten-incher for Decca used to be worth $50 or more, but it's reissue as part of the "Here's Groucho" CD has lessened that somewhat.

Groucho sings his favorite songs, from the title track (first performed in *Animal Crackers*) to the bent classics by Harry Ruby, "Omaha, Nebraska," "Father's Day," and "Show Me a Rose." The most impressive rarities are "Go West" (cut from the film) and "I'm Dr. Hackenbush," cut from *A Day at the Races*. From the latter:

"For ailments abdominal, my charges are nominal. Though I'm great for, I've a rate for tonsillectomy. Sick and healthy, poor and wealthy come direct to me. Ohhhhh God bless you the yell when I send them home well. But they never, no they never send a check to me!"

The arrangements are always sprightly, though the backing chorus of big band vocalists may seem a bit corny for today's tastes.

The 1995 CD has no album notes and instead of the original cover there's a "Nick at Nite" type campy shot of a '50s family watching a TV screen with Groucho on it. The six golden tracks don't run consecutively. After three, there's an interruption for the stupid, noisy mish-mash "How D'Ye Do and Shake Hands." After the next three there's the limpingly lame "Black Strap Molasses." These two sappy songs (with Groucho, Danny Kaye, Jane Wyman, and Jimmy Durante sharing vocals) were a 1951 Decca single. Neither irritating number can stand more than one listening. The CD is padded out a bit more with two "bonus" tracks from Decca's Marx Brothers voicetrack album. At thirty-two minutes, the CD could have had the whole album. The three-star rating reflects a one point deduction for the low blow of sticking one distracting track amid Groucho's great ones and releasing the album with a dull generic title and lousy artwork.

Groucho's six songs were collected on a British import (Ace of Hearts #103) with six Jerry Colonna songs on the flip side. The three liveliest songs, "Hooray for Captain Spaulding," "Go West," and "Dr. Hackenbush," appear on the British CD "Gratuitously Groucho" (Raven RVCD-30) along with a bunch of radio show clips.

In 1949 Groucho recorded a children's song released in 45 rpm (YPR-45-X-719) and 78 rpm (YPR-719) editions, which stretched over both sides of the disc. It featured a cartoon caricature of him on the cover. Ultimately the company tossed it onto an album padded out with non-Groucho material. It's the story of a monkey who wants to write "The Funniest Song in the World."

He sings a bunch of songs that make fun of a lumbering bear ("you look like a Turkish towel"), a kangaroo ("he hops around like an old bed spring"), and a giraffe ("half of the neck of one giraffe is just twice as much as it should be"). The animals object, and ultimately the monkey tries a fast-patter nonsense tune that doesn't hurt anybody's feelings. For any child in the early '50s, it certainly could have been considered "The Funniest Song in the World," and still retains its charm today. Of course, the insulting songs are almost as funny, which, despite Groucho's good intentions, only proves that grouchy insults can be fun, too.

The problem for most fans is finding any version. Old children's records rarely survive the handling a kid gives them. About ten years ago, when I was tracking this down, a woman at Young Peoples told me the master was destroyed. She asked, "Who cares about Groucho Marx anymore?"

- AN EVENING WITH GROUCHO (A&M SP 3515) **** $8 $20
- AN EVENING WITH GROUCHO (A&M PR 3515) ** ** $10 $20

Marx fans tend to be sharply divided about this album. Dick Cavett, who introduced Groucho the night of this concert at Carnegie Hall, remembers that backstage, elderly Groucho "was slumped on a couch looking more frail and papery than I had ever seen him. His voice was a hoarse whisper ... his performance consisted mostly of an unenergetic reading of his favorite anecdotes from three-by-five cards ... (but the audience) were so presold to have the time of their lives that they barely seemed to notice any difference between the all-but-drained Groucho onstage and the capering madman of the movies."

Actually, the Groucho who performs here isn't all that different from the one who often appeared on Cavett's talk show, telling many of the same anecdotes in the same frail but puckish voice. At the time, there was a certain glory to the old Groucho. If he wasn't immortal, he was certainly doing a fine, crusty job of stalling the inevitable. He was still very, very funny in his new role of semicynical sage and indulgent storyteller. The album has a lot of amusing anecdotes about his brothers, his personal life, his vaudeville years, and famous folk from Sarah Bernhardt and Winston Churchill to W. C. Fields and Greta Garbo.

Groucho manages to get through several songs, including some rarities from his early solo days. He never waxes sentimental, but there are some poignant moments. He pauses to tell one of his favorite stories. It's about Otto Kahn, a Jew who changed his religion. He was walking down the street with his friend who happened to be a hunchback. He said, "You know, I used to be a Jew." The man answered, "I know. I used to be a hunchback."

A&M PR 3515 edits the concert to one album—a picture disc.

NOTES: Three minutes of "You Bet Your Life" turn up on "Golden Age of Comedy" (Evolution 1313) as Groucho interviews a man who sells clothing in Alaska ("I thought everyone was bear up there"). He does some ad-libbing with a starlet and sings "Father's Day" on "Magic Moments from the Tonight Show" (Casablanca SPNB 1296).

An album of material bootlegged from films and appearances on TV's *Dick Cavett Show* surfaced as "I Never Kissed an Ugly Woman" (Kornyfone TAKRL). Groucho is on the interview album "Face to Face" (Decca DXD 166), and tells some golf anecdotes on the 1963 studio album "My Favorite Story" (20th Century Fox TFM 3106). "Comedy Classics" (K-Tel 30462) has a minute and a half of Groucho (the priest anecdotes from the Carnegie Hall concert).

A "You Bet Your Life" episode from March 31, 1958, turns up on "Three Funniest Hours in Radio" (Murray Hill), where Groucho plays host to Charles Goren and Ernie Kovacs. On "The Great Radio Comedians," a 5-LP Murray Hill set, an October 16, 1952, "You Bet Your Life" is included; the secret word is "water."

Groucho was a great fan of Gilbert and Sullivan, and one of his proudest moments was playing Ko-Ko in the "Bell Telephone Hour" TV production of "The Mikado." It's on Columbia Special Products (OS 2022, reissued as AOL 5480). He gets to sing the patter song "I've Got a Little List," and on "Tit Willow" tries his best to hit the high notes with appropriate sweetness and satiric melancholy. It's a wistfully charming moment.

Groucho appears on the British album "Memorial Record of Homage to T. S. Eliot" (EMI/Odeon) discussing the mutual admiration he and Eliot had for each other. It was released in 1965. A few fans might want "The East Side of Town," recorded by Groucho's daughter Melinda Marx. It was released as a single (Vee-Jay 657). She sang (and danced!) it on *The Hollywood Palace*. Too bad the flip side didn't have the duet she did with her Dad after her solo.

THE MARX BROTHERS

- COCOANUTS (Sountrak STK 108, also Sandy Hook 2059) ** $4 $8
- NIGHT AT THE OPERA (Re-Sound 7051) ** $4 $8
- MARX MOVIE MADNESS (Radiola MR 1097, CDMR 1097) *** $5 $10
- ORIGINAL VOICETRACKS FROM THEIR GREATEST MOVIES (Decca DL 79168) *** $8 $15

Videocassettes have made the Marx Brothers movie soundtrack albums less than essential. Only true devotees of Groucho, Chico, Harpo, and Zeppo (the kind of fan who not only will name Gummo as the fifth brother, but even knows that a sixth, Manfred, died in childhood) need the especially creaky-sounding "Cocoanuts."

Of more interest is "Marx Movie Madness." It collects the short, radio versions of "Duck Soup," "At the Circus," "Go West," and "Day at the Races." They were broadcast on MGM's "Leo Is on the Air" and "The Paramount Movie Parade," which were the audio equivalent of movie trailers. "Duck Soup" is the most valuable entry, offering sneak previews directly from the set. Not working from the final script, the Marx Brothers give radio listeners a few moments that ultimately did not get into the movie at all:

In the opening scene, as Groucho charges through a procession of "Freedonia" celebrants and soldiers with raised swords, he says, "All this for me? That's how you throw away your money. I'd rather have a box of good cigars. Soldiers, you may go. Keep the swords, we're gonna have roast beef for dinner!" In the movie, this is removed, and instead Groucho plays a card trick on Margaret Dumont. ("Take a card ... you can keep it, I've got fifty-one left.")

Later, the villain Trentino of Sylvania notes, "I bring you a message of good will on behalf of my president—" And Groucho interrupts, "I won't be half of the president, I'll be the whole president or nothing." This was replaced with Groucho immediately asking his rival for a loan.

There aren't many moments like this, but collectors will want this record for such morsels. The MGM clips are more advertising blather than anything else.

"Voicetracks," Decca's late '60s nostalgia and camp collection of Marx film clips (complete with "Free Pop Poster") manages to be amusing despite Gary Owens' narration and some campy music between gags. Especially useful is the segment collecting a bunch of Groucho's film insults: "You know I could rent you out as a decoy for duck hunters ... you have the brain of a four-year-old boy and I'll bet he was glad to get rid of it ... you suppose I could buy back my introduction to you ... I have a good mind to join a club and beat you over the head with it." The clips are from their Paramount films, which means no "Lydia the Tattooed Lady," but at least there's "Hooray for Captain Spaulding" from "Animal Crackers."

- THREE HOURS FIFTY NINE MINUTES FIFTY ONE SECONDS WITH THE MARX BROTHERS
  (Murray Hill 931680, also issued as THE VERY BEST OF THE MARX BROTHERS,"
  AAT Records 201-202) ***1/2 $20 $40

When this four-record set came out at the bargain price of $9.95, it was a treasure trove for Marx fans. It still is, even at double the price. It's mostly Groucho's radio sketches opposite Dinah Shore, Betty Grable, Frances Langford, Lucille Ball, Tallulah Bankhead, etc. He sings on a few shows, including the rarities "Go West" and "I'm Dr. Hacken-bush," and there's a twenty-minute segment from Groucho and Chico's short-lived radio show. It's a pleasure to hear Groucho at work, even if the sketches are just gags glued together by various radio hack writers.

Some routines have appeared elsewhere (Groucho and Chico's show and the half hour broadcast with Tallulah Bankhead), but most of it will be new to the average fan. Chico appeared regularly on a show called *The Fitch Bandwagon*, which he insists on calling "The Fishwagon," and there are three excerpts that include music and a few routines. As for Harpo, he's spotlighted in the misleadingly titled "A Conversation with Harpo." After he plays "My Blue Heaven" on the harp, Harpo remains mute. Gary Cooper appears as Harpo's "interpreter." "Well Gary, this is really a surprise. You travel around the country and do all the talking for Harpo? "Yup." "Do you have any trouble with Harpo?" "Nope." "You understand him." "Yep."

The original version is the four-record boxed set. AAT Records issued the albums as two double album sets.

NOTES: Harpo made several musical albums: "Harpo at Work" (Mercury MG 20363) and "Harpo in Hi-Fi" (Mercury MG 20232). "Harp by Harpo," a ten-inch RCA album (RCA LPM 27, also released as a set of three 45s) mixes standards ("Stardust") with semiclassical pieces (Bach's "Bouree"). The song "Guardian Angels" was cowritten by Harpo and sung by soprano Mary Jane Smith. For most fans, the full-color Harpo photos on the covers mean more than the music within. Harpo is on the cover of a Vee-Jay jazz instrumental album by his adopted son Bill Marx. Harpo speaks on "Personalities on Parade Volume One" (PP 1). "Big Bands of Hollywood" (Laserlight 15767) has seven cuts from the Desi Arnez (sic) Orchestra and seven from the Chico Marx Orchestra. Fans might get a kick out of the band's hard driving "Pagliacci" medley and Chico's piano work on "Beer Barrel Polka," but most cuts are straight and include serious big band vocalists.

JACKIE MASON

- I'M THE GREATEST COMEDIAN IN THE WORLD ONLY NOBODY KNOWS IT YET
  (Verve V 15033) **** $8 $15
- I WANT TO LEAVE YOU WITH THE WORDS OF A GREAT COMEDIAN (Verve V 15034) *** $8 $15
- GREAT MOMENTS IN COMEDY (Verve 15045) ***1/2 $8 $15

Mason's album is almost as fresh today as it was thirty years ago, with some almost Lenny Brucian arguments on sex that were ahead of their time: "There's a double standard about sex. Our father or mother becomes our father or mother. Beautiful. The arrival of a child is celebrated. But how that child was created and arrived is something that is cloaked in secrecy. They're ashamed of it. They thought it was pretty clever when they did it."

Mason's heavy Jewish accent and comic abrasiveness seemed to turn off critics who considered him more of an annoying Alan King than a satirical Mort Sahl.

Jackie's first album has such a wealth of brilliant material, he even supported part of Don Adams's act with it. Adams used some gags from this album, including the following, almost verbatim, on his "Live at Las Vegas" disc. But it really fits Mason's comical blend of self-effacing humility and prickly pseudo-arrogance: "I did a show last week in another place where the act before me was so terrible, that throughout my performance, they kept booing him! They couldn't forget how lousy he was! Some people even walked out on him while I was still performing!"

The album has his masterpiece of twisted comic logic, a visit to a psychiatrist, which suits his timing and accented cadence perfectly:

"I asked him, 'What will this cost me?' He told me $75 a visit. I said, 'For $75 I don't visit, I move in.' He said, 'What's bothering you?' I said, 'The $75 fee for the visit.' He said, 'We have to search for the real you!' I said to myself, if I don't know who I am, how would I know what I look like? And even if I find me, how would I know it's me? Besides, if I want to look for me, why do I need him? I could look myself, or I could call my friends. They know where I've been! Besides, what if I find the real me, and I find that he's even worse than I am.... The psychiatrist said, 'The search for the real you will continue at our next session. That will be $75.' I said to myself, this is not the real me. Why should I give him $75? What if I find the real me and he doesn't think it's worth $75.... For all I know the real me might be going to a different psychiatrist altogether. In fact, he might even be this psychiatrist himself! I said to him, 'What if you're the real me? Then you owe me $75.' He said, 'If you promise never to come back we'll call it even.'"

"The Words of a Great Comedian ..." has lesser material and even the sound quality isn't as good. Still, there are memorable routines ranging from an essay on double parking and cliché phrases to a long bit on luxury buildings. At the time (thirty years ago) Mason's Jewish accent offended other Jews, who didn't want such a "troublemaker" closely identified with them, especially when his self-effacing gags seemed borderline anti-Semitic: "Do you know I'm still suffering from shock from the last war? I'll tell you the truth, I was almost drafted! Luckily I was wounded while taking the physical. When I reached the psychiatrist I said, 'Give me a gun, I'll wipe out the whole German army in five minutes.' He said, 'You're crazy!' I said, 'Write it down!' I would've fought for my country, but they called me at a ridiculous time. During a war ... I'm not a pacifist. I'm not a conscientious objector. I'm just afraid."

"Great Moments" repackages bits from the two albums.

- THE WORLD ACCORDING TO ME (Warner Bros. 24603) *** $5 $10
- BRAND NEW (Columbia CK 48586) *** $8

Mason recorded, but didn't release, an album of political humor in 1980. His up and down career suddenly shot off with a one-man show that came to Broadway in 1987. He still had some audiences cringing, but most had finally caught up to him and recognized him as a compelling satirist and conversationalist. The ex-rabbi's "sermon" has some one-liners that pop like bubbles in Cel-Ray. On doctors: "In what other business could a guy tell a girl to get undressed—and send the bill to her husband?" On Reagan: "He's one of the great presidents of all time. Nobody knows it because he don't do nothing." On reducing the national deficit: "Congress and the Senate get paid whether we lose money or not. Why should they care? I say put them on commission."

The one-liners are buried in the casual conversation with ringsiders and long recognition comedy pieces like raisins in noodle pudding. Fortunately that pudding of human nature observations is tasty more than bland. He goes into great detail on Jewish vs Gentile lifestyles, including the "schmucky" way a Jewish man barely gets to pack one suitcase while his wife goes off with dozens. The voluminous material that picks up on typically Jewish behavior draws roars from the middle-class Jews who seem to make up most of the audience.

"Brand New" is another hour of prime Mason, this time from his follow-up Broadway hit from 1991. It's not that well produced. There's some problem with low microphone placement and echo, and the audience microphones are mixed loudly all around him. But Mason is still on target and hammering away at the differences between Jews and

Gentiles, with only a small portion of general humor (a routine on health and different types of food). Jackie can tell a Jew from a Gentile just by the profession: "A guy tells you he's a coal miner. A coal miner's a Gentile. Ever see a Jewish coal miner? Ever see a sign: 'Irving's Coal Mine?' I never heard a guy say, 'I'm going coal mining, then I'm going to shul for Passover.' Ever see a yarmulke with a light attached to it? You could tell by what people do for a living. Let's be honest about it. If a guy tells you he's a mugger, a mugger is a Gentile. There's no Jewish muggers, there never was, there never will be. A Jew could never make a living as a mugger. 'Cause a mugger has to say, 'Give me your money or I'll kill ya.' If a Jew said that he'd have to go to a psychiatrist for thirty years. A Jew cannot say 'I'll kill ya.' A Jew would have to say, 'Listen, you don't have to give me *all* your money. Sit down, we'll work something out, maybe you got a few dollars now, a few dollars later ... whatever ya got.' You see, there are Jewish muggers, that's a lie. But they're not called muggers. They're called lawyers."

ED MASSEY

- THE HOME-SPUN HUMOR OF ED MASSEY (NR 5586) ** $5 $10

There's a pleasant humility to the album notes on Massey's evidently self-pressed record: "The things you will hear on this record are not all original with me but things that have been handed down and picked up here and there.... For several years many of my friends have encouraged me to record some ... home-spun humor. This is my first venture in doing so...."

A speaker at local Alabama "church banquets, Civic Clubs, Professional Sales Clubs, Teachers Associations, Cattlemen's Associations," Massey loads up on familiar and harmless gags, telling them with an amateur's enthusiastic and nervous quickness. While the professional contours a monologue and removes jokes that don't fit, this type of speaker isn't about to part with anything he's clipped from a joke book (note the third gag here), even if the gender is wrong:

"One of my sisters was so poor the dogs buried that young 'un in the front yard three times—they thought she was a bone. Me and my brother dug her up, or of course she would've died. She was so thin and so poor, she could drink tomato juice and she looked like a thermometer. And if she hadn't had an Adam's apple she wouldn't had any figure at all. She'd turn sideways and stick her tongue out and she looked like a zipper. I remember one time my mama made her a beautiful striped dress out of some of that fine Jim Dandy yarn. Worked hard all day sewin' to make that striped dress for her. Well, that young 'un was so thin when she got through makin' that dress it didn't have but one stripe on it. And friend, that's really thin. She went to the doctor one time to get a physical examination. The doctor examined her; she jumped up and said, 'Well, how do I stand, doctor?' He said, 'The lord only knows! It's a miracle to me!'"

HAL MASTERS

- FUNNY SIDE OF THE STREET (Fax 101, reissued by Lobo, Bolo, and Laff) ** $5 $10

The very ordinary Masters doesn't add much personality in knocking out familiar risqué gags: "A lot of you are trying to figure out what the heck I'm drinking up here. What it is, is a new male sex hormone that we have out on the market, called Upjohn. I wouldn't laugh. This stuff's so powerful if you don't swallow fast your neck'll get hard. For those of you who are chicken and don't want to drink it, you can use it as a fly spray. It won't kill the flies but it makes 'em hornier than hell and you can swat two at a time. Fact I know a guy took an overdose of this, made it with thirty-eight chicks in a row and died. Took six undertakers three hours to wipe the smile off his face. Took six pallbearers two hours to close the damn coffin."

LEN MAXWELL

- I'D RATHER BE FAR RIGHT THAN PRESIDENT (Divine Right 50M) * $4 $10
- MEANWHILE, BACK AT THE LBJ RANCH (Power Polus 350) *1/2 $3 $7

Maxwell took no sides. One of his political comedy albums joked about Republican-conservative candidate Goldwater in 1964, and the other, winner President Johnson.

"I'd Rather Be Far Right than President" features Will Jordan as Dwight Eisenhower and Ed Murrow among others, along with Adam Keefe and Elsie Downey. Most of the gags play easily off Barry Goldwater's "eighteenth century" identity: "Senator, do you think that the momentum of tonight's triumph (winning the nomination) will carry through to election day?" "It will be almost a clean sweep of the entire nation: three states for Lyndon, ten for me!"

The Johnson album is a "break in" disc, as Maxwell asks leading questions and gets recorded answers from Johnson, Barry Goldwater, Hubert Humphrey, Nelson Rockefeller, and others. Maxwell runs into Lady Bird: "You certainly have some important people here today." "Twelve presidents, fifteen signers of the Constitution, fifteen secretaries of state, from Thomas Jefferson to Dean Rusk." "And I've noticed they've all been talking and laughing. Surely it's not matters of state. Just what is the subject they seem to be enjoying over there?" "Snide jokes about the South." "Well, this certainly is a wonderful party. Can you think of a way it might be better?" "Without my husband."

- MERRY MONSTER CHRISTMAS (20th Century Fox 3166) *1/2 $10 $20

With the "Monster Craze" still hot in 1964, Maxwell tried a somewhat cynical gambit: horror comedy geared to the Christmas gift season. Mickey Rose cowrote the studio disc, which was recorded sans audience. So nobody is laughing at the workmanlike gags constructed around monsters and Christmas, such as: a mistletoe that is really a "mistlethumb. We ran out of toes," and children hanging "their stockings on the mantle—with people still in them." Hoping for a little of Bobby "Boris" Pickett's success, there are a few novelty tunes sung as Boris Karloff, but they're as flat and feeble as a rubber bat.

EDDIE MAYEHOFF

- THE INCENTIVE PLAN (RCA LPM 3235) * $7 $15

In '50s and '60s TV sitcoms and films, Mayehoff played a variety of overbearing, throat-clearing, hearty, hand-clasping, stolid business executives, the kind who succeeded in business by being very trying. This 1955 ten-incher is very trying. On the title track he's a boss lecturing businessmen and promising a reward: "an all expense-paid evening of fun and frolic at the famous Stork Club (located at downtown Passaic) or a beautiful, large, life-like portrait of President McKinley, suitable for hanging."

On other tracks Mayehoff plays other types of annoying people—from lispy "Miss Teasy" lecturing on wayward girls to almost an entire side ("The Wages of Sin," "Revenge," and "The Recital") of off-key opera singer parodies. Even worse is "Folk Songs of the Deep Gulf States," in which Mayehoff impersonates a lisping, self-absorbed scholar who insists on breathlessly describing and then singing a capella, his favorite folk tunes: "Garbage man, garbage man, how do you do? Did you pick up a penny, did you pick up a rusty spring, did you pick up a piece of rubber?"

"The Incentive Plan" lecture is on "The Golden Age of Comedy" (RCA Victor LPV 580).

MR? BILLIE MCALLISTER

- WHAT A BIG PIECE OF MEAT (Kent KST 011) ** $5 $10

Rudy Ray Moore introduces his latest "fabalous" black transvestite comic (following Lady Reed and Mr. Jerry Walker), tank-shaped Billie McAllister. While '70s funk plays in the background, Billie blasts out the gags:

"Oh honey ... I come in town the other day, met this lovely thing. He said, 'Baby, where ya goin' ... I'll take ya for a drive.' I said, 'I love that, Daddy, I love it.' I strolled over, get into that goddamn car. Ya should've seen it. It was two years older than Christ. I don't know how the f--- it was movin' but he was movin'. I got in that car, honey, he got a mile outta town and he stopped. I said, 'What the hell ya stoppin' for?' He said, 'Bitch, waddya gonna do ... you gonna be like Chesterfields, you gonna satisfy? Or you gonna be like Camels, you gonna walk that motherf-----' mile?' I said, 'It all depends.' He said, 'It all depends on what?' I said, 'If it's king size or regular!'"

MCCALL AND BRILL

- FROM OUR POINT OF VIEW (ABC 600) * $5 $10

Charlie Brill and Mitzi McCall introduce their '60s act as "two stools and no talent." Then they prove it. In most skits Brill the bespectacled preppie has to deal with abrasive Mitzi, a "New Yawk" accented "Mighty Mouth" (Charlie's phrase).

Most of the routines involve a lot of obnoxious husband-wife kvetching. They dare to perform the wheezing "P.S. Your Cat Is Dead" routine, with Mitzi calling up and shrieking at Brill for telling her, abruptly, that her cat died. And, proving they're in some kind of hideous time warp, they perform a parody of the 1927 Jolson film, *The Jazz Singer*.

For a change of pace, and in a rare moment when she's not intent on piercing eardrums, Mitzi plays the housewife married to "The White Knight" of the laundry commercials:

"You don't look too good sweetheart, what happened?" "My lance backfired. Wait'll you hear what happened to me ... I wanna make the place a whiter, brighter place to live in? Who's the first person I run into on the street? Allen Ludden's wife, that TV personality?" "Betty White." "No, Betty Blue!" "Betty Blue? You mean—" "Zap zap and that's what happens. Of course I run into the Jolly White Giant." "No no no Honey, no. That's the Jolly Green Giant." "Not anymore ... I gotta quit the job...." "But you can't quit, you have to do a night call...." "What are you nuts? Look at it out tonight. It's raining, pouring with snow on the ground. A blizzard, a hurricane. You wouldn't send a knight out on a dog like this...."

McCall and Brill help out Bill Dana on his "Hoo Hah" album. On that one, thanks to some good jokes, Mitzi's stereotype J.A.P. accent is actually funny, and she also scores with her portrayal of a female version of George Jessel, deadly as that might seem.

CHUCK MCCANN

- SING ALONG WITH JACK (Colpix SUS 1000) ** $6 $12
- EVERYTHING YOU ALWAYS WANTED TO KNOW ABOUT THE GODFATHER BUT DON'T ASK
  (Columbia KC 31608) *1/2 $5 $10

In the '60s McCann was a beloved kiddie show host with his *Let's Have Fun* show in New York. He's also rememberd as the man behind the bathroom mirror cheerfully calling out "Hi, Guy!" in Right Guard commercials, and for playing Oliver Hardy in a variety of TV spots. A very capable actor, he won acclaim in the drama *The Heart Is a Lonely Hunter* and in the comedy *The Projectionist*.

He plays John F. Kennedy on the 1963 quickie "Sing Along with Jack." Joy Stanley is Jackie and Caroline. Crossing "The First Family" with "My Son the Folk Singer," here are folk songs with political parody lyrics. A few sketches are interspersed. McCann does a decent Kennedy. The humor is innocuous. A parody based on Stephen Foster: "I Dream of Jackie with the bouffant hair, just like a vapor floating everywhere." A twist on Gilbert & Sullivan: "I'm called little Caroline, dear little Caroline, pampered from morning to dusk. By Sorensen, Salinger, Stevenson, Schlesinger, Bundy, and Dillon and Rusk."

He's The Godfather on the 1972 Columbia album. J. J. Barry, Mina Kolb, Steve Landesberg, Dick Lord, Mike Preminger, and Marilyn Sokol are in the cast. The throaty, slow-talking thugs here are about as funny as the ones in the grim movie original. Each padded blackout sketch labors mightily before arriving at the punch line. Like the one in which a gangster gets his tools together before going out on a job, then he opens his drawer and hears "Ring around the holster! Ring around the holster!" In another tired vignette, The Godfather calls up a gangster with elaborate orders to kill a rival. Many, many moments later, the punch line is that he's got the wrong number. And there's a commercial for a record album of The Godfather's greatest hits of the '50s, which includes: "Alvin Goldstein hit in the flower shop in 1947. Louie the Blast, hit in the supermarket, 1953. Rover the Wonder Dog, hit by a car in 1958. Eddie Stanky hit by a pitched ball, 1951. And Milton Berle hit by a pie ..."

Steve Landesberg livens up the album with his German psychiatrist character, but the script does him no favors either.

McCann has been a supporting player on a variety of comedy albums through the years, including albums for Rich Little and for Minkin and Dowling.

MCCLEAN AND STANTON

- LET'S PLAY STRIKE (Roulette R 506) ** $4 $8

At one time major record companies were willing to issue albums with only regional appeal, or topical albums that could be out of date only weeks after release. Roulette's strike album had big problems. Strike one: it would only appeal to New Yorkers furious over ineffectual Mayor John Lindsay and abrasive union man Mike Quill. Strike two: the topical disc would be irrelevent once the two men got together. And strike three: how many really wanted to spend $3.98 on an album when they were complaining about twenty cents for a subway ride?

A "break-in" album, the voices of Lindsay, Quill, former Mayor Wagner, Governor Rockefeller, and Robert Kennedy are mismatched to questions supplied by Phil McLean and Betty Stanton. Part of the interview with Lindsay: "What's that little thing sticking out of your vest pocket?" "Vest pocket park." "Mr. Mayor, in the past few months New York City has suffered a newspaper strike, a water shortage, air pollution, and a total blackout. Is there anything in New York that is running smoothly?" "Transportation perhaps is the best example...." "Don't you find that when you get home at night you're too exhausted to do anything?" "Ask me wife, she'll tell you."

PAT MCCORMICK

- TELLS IT LIKE IT IS (Atco SD 33 243) *** $7 $15

Big looney Pat McCormick is a respected comedy writer who at the time of this 1968 album had written for kindred spirit Jonathan Winters and served as head writer on The Tonight Show, leading Johnny Carson to appreciate wild, wacky stuff.

A studio album with sketches and interviews, cuts range from a report on the daytime game show Humiliation to a piece on the Senior Citizens at "Wrinkle City," where they're having Olympic events like the "Hop, Skip, and Trip" and the "False Teeth Toss." There, "if everyone happens to smile at once it's automatically declared Halloween."

Pat has a report on "Inventions to Better Mankind," like a "trained mouse to work as an operator for Cuban elevator shoes." There's also an interview with a tremendously fat person who claims, "I've fallen down and not even known it ... in the winter I wear meatloaf over my ears—I even love to hear food."

It might be that a lot of this material was stuff that Winters and Carson considered just too strange to perform. At this point, some might actually find it too tame.

McCormick can also be heard on London and Clark's "Heaven on $5 a Day" album.

BRUCE MCCULLOCH

- SHAME-BASED MAN (Atlantic 827492) * $7

Only Kids in the Hall fans could deal with this depressing session of attitude and just plain creepiness. Attempted satire on this CD includes a stalker's pleasant chit chat with his equally idiotic victim: "Good to finally meet you!" "Nice to finally meet you ..." "I guess you're not gonna ask me how I've been—'cause you've been watching me. What you been up to?" "Not too much, the stalking keeps me pretty busy." McCulloch finds it clever or hysterical or hip to drone "She's a, she's a, she's a Heroin Pig" over bad Lou Reed-style music. And there's way too much faux desultory rock here. Attempts at actual one-liners sound like first drafts that he was too lazy to improve upon: "Don't trust a guy who keeps his change in his wallet."

ED MCCURDY

- WHEN DALLIANCE WAS IN FLOWER (Elektra 110) ** $5 $10
- WHEN DALLIANCE WAS IN FLOWER II (Elektra 140) ** $5 $10
- WHEN DALLIANCE WAS IN FLOWER III (Elektra 710) ** $5 $10
- WHEN DALLIANCE WAS IN FLOWER IV (Elektra 716) ** $5 $10
- SON OF DALLIANCE (Elektra M 990) ** $5 $10

Back in the early '60s, folksingers like McCurdy and Oscar Brand put out "ribald" albums of folk songs. Listeners had to strain hard to get the double entendres hidden behind archaic language and endless "fa la las." At least Ed's albums have lusty cover art as a buxom strawberry blonde (Volume II) or a brunette (Volume III) pose in negligees. His sturdy baritone makes him a more manly singer than Brand, but he performs the songs in such a leisurely, understated way that few come off as the rollicking, fun-poking ditties they really are. Nonsense refrains ("Lolly lo," "Down-Derry-Down," "Humble-dum-day") might be authentic, but are a nuisance.

Typical of the peculiar humor are these lines from "Bring Me a Lass" on the first album: "Let her face be fair, her breasts be bare, and her voice let her have that can warble. Let her belly be soft, but to mount me aloft, let her bounding buttocks be marble."

Sexual athletics are always a fun topic. "A Lusty Young Smith," also from the first album, proves to be just what one wife with a sleepy hubby craves:

"Six times did his iron by vigorous heating grow soft in the forge in a minute or so ... but the more it was softened it hardened more slow ... with a jingle bang jingle bang jingle hi ho."

The tunes tend to get repetitious. The one-joke songs on phalluses sturdy or useless, maidens virginal or bawdy, and the ultimate embarrassment of pregnancy, become predictable as each album presents tales about "A Young Man" or "The Jolly Miller" (Volume II), "The Shepherd" and "The Sound Country Lass" (Volume III), "The Miller's Daughter" and "A Maiden's Delight" (Son of Dalliance), etc. etc.

TRIVIA NOTE: Alan Arkin plays the recorder on the first album.

BOB MCFADDEN

- SONGS OUR MUMMY TAUGHT US (Brunswick 54046) ** $10 $20
- RICHARD THE 37th (Vanguard VSD 29309) *1/2 $4 $8

McFadden was a voiceover specialist who did a lot of cartoon work (he was the voice of "Milton the Monster" on that '60s series). He guested on comedy albums from "The New First Family 1968" to Vaughn Meader's "Have Some Nuts."

In September of 1959 he briefly hit the Top 40 with "The Mummy." Talking over the music, he's the squeamy-voiced little mummy who, like "Casper the Friendly Ghost," can't help frightening everyone. Amid the fake screams, he insists, "I don't try to scare people. I really came back to life to buy a copy of 'Kookie, Kookie Lend Me Your Comb.' But people run from me. Watch what happens when I walk up to somebody...." Ultimately, he meets Dor the beatnik: "I'm a mummy!" "That's cool ... I'm a beatnik." "People are afraid of me." "Yeah, I'm hip...." "Aren't you scared of me? Aren't you gonna scream?" "Yeah. Like, help!"

"Dor," better known as Rod McKuen, wrote the music and lyrics.

The follow-up album has more novelties: "I Dig You Baby," "Frankie and Igor at a Rock and Roll Party," "Son of the Mummy," and so on. The album is rare, attracting fans of monster comedy and beat generation humor, and even some McKuen fans.

McFadden got another starring album in 1969 as Richard Nixon. But he can't disguise the distinctive edge in his voice and can't lower it enough to avoid sounding more like Jack Benny. The script is standard. Nixon talking to Spiro Agnew (played by Milt Moss): "Is it Speero or Spyro?" "Call me Ted, Mr. President." "What is the origin of that name?" "... It's Greek, Mr. President." "Then you're Greek." "Not necessarily, Mr. President. Did you have something in mind?"

Also in the cast are Carol Richards, Pat Bright (as Pat Nixon) and Chuck McCann. McFadden and McCann worked together on the cartoon series *Cool McCool*.

DR. KENNETH MCFARLAND

- THE BEST OF KEN MCFARLAND'S HUMOR (Edward M. Miller Associates, Inc. EM 2010) ** $4 $8

Inspirational speaker Dr. Kenneth McFarland issued over a dozen lectures on record, from "How Is America Doing" to "Who Will Succeed in the 60's?" This album clips comical anecdotes from other records:

"One of our salesmen has a library of romantic and exotic literature: *Secrets of Winning and Wooing, Fifty Ways to Kiss a Girl*, all this sort of thing. He was at La Guardia airport sometime back. He was late ... just as you go out to the planes, right there on the left is a book shop. Well, here was a book in the window that he hadn't seen yet for his collection: *How to Hug*. Well he was late, but he rushed in there and ... fired on out to the airplane, he got on board, settled down, strapped himself in, the airplane took off. He was about to enjoy *How to Hug*. That's when he found out he bought himself volume six of the Encyclopedia Brittanica."

FIBBER MCGEE AND MOLLY

- FIBBER MCGEE AND MOLLY (Biograph BLP 2001) **1/2 $5 $10
- TALL TALES (Golden Age 5011) ** $5 $10
- FIBBER MCGEE AND MOLLY (Mark 56 #583) ** $4 $8
- FIBBER MCGEE AND MOLLY (Mark 56 #583) ** $4 $8
- FIBBER MCGEE AND MOLLY (Mark 56 #583) ** $4 $8
- FIBBER MCGEE AND MOLLY (Mark 56 #583) ** $4 $8
- FIBBER MCGEE AND MOLLY (Jeep 473) ** $5 $10
- FIBBER MCGEE AND MOLLY (Nostalgia Lane NLR 1006) **1/2 $5 $10
- FIBBER MCGEE AND MOLLY (Radiola MR 1055) **1/2 $5 $10
- FIBBER MCGEE AND MOLLY (Murray Hill 898055) **1/2 $15 $30
- FIBBER MCGEE AND MOLLY SILVER JUBILEE SHOW (NBC LKC 5900) ** $10 $20

Jim and Marion Jordan were Fibber McGee and Molly on their long-running radio show (1935-1950, with a five-minute spot on NBC's *Monitor* radio show to 1957). The supporting players included The Old Timer (Cliff Arquette), Throckmorton Gildersleeve (Hal Peary), Wallace Wimple (Bill Thompson), and Mayor La Trivia (Gale Gordon).

Most any album gives a good idea of what the sitcom was all about. Golden Age and Biograph both have "The Canoe Ride," an episode from 1946. Fibber wants to take Molly out in a canoe, but before they can get to the water, the full cast of characters appear. Golden Age has "Doc Gamble Day" on the flip side, a very ordinary sitcom episode in which McGee throws a parade for Doctor Gamble, the "Poultice Laureate of Wistful Vista." "I got this town hoppin' like a barefoot kid on a hot sidewalk," Fibber enthuses, spending a half hour working out his strategy for getting organized and making sure Doc shows up. Biograph's flip side has a hundred times more jokes, though they vary in quality. "Hunt and Peck" is about McGee's attempt at writing a great novel. Just like the inventor of the zipper, Fibber plans on using "yanky" ingenuity.

Wally Wimple, whose sad, wimpy voice is similar to cartoon character Droopy Dog, notes, "I see you're working, Mr. McGee. Novel?" Molly: "Any time McGee works, it's novel." Wally is a wordsmith too. He recites a poem about a lobster and an octopus:

"Said the oyster, watch my ball of yarn. I'm making eight argyle socks for a lady octopus." "You're such a clumsy cuss," the lobster said, "You have no hands yet you knit things for your girl?"_"Not knit," replied the oyster, "but let me show you how I pearl." They don't write 'em like that anymore.

Mark 56 isn't very generous. They're prone to stretching one half-hour episode over both sides of an album. Volume 2 is "Doghouse," broadcast January 2, 1940. It's very typical of the McGee style of humor—the character comedy of the plucky, singleminded but simpleminded Fibber, plus all of his corny wordplay.

Fibber decides to buy a dog and build a doghouse. He'll name the dog Glo-Coat, "so he won't scratch." He recalls being a dog show judge, and so good "I had to take a bow at the end of the show! I was a wow: Bow Wow McGee they called me!" The gags get worse. Fibber insists that the dog will have plenty to eat: "You know the saying: it takes a heap of liver to make a dog a home!"

This is a perfect time for Molly to give out with her catchphrase: "Tain't funny, McGee."

Jeep pairs a "Bulldog Drummond" episode on one side with a show about Fibber trying to tune his piano, breaking one string after another. Or as Molly says, "You keep that up, Dearie, and all I'll be able to play on this is Silent Night!"

Nostalgia Lane takes two shows from the latter era: March 22, 1949 (featuring a visit from The Old Timer) and July 6, 1948.

Radiola has the March 12, 1940, episode which has the "very first time the famous Fibber McGee closet was opened on radio." It also has guest star Gracie Allen: "Gracie, what's this I hear about you running for President of the United States? What's your party?" "It's my own party. The surprise party ..." "When do you expect to move into the White House?" "January 1st." "January 1st? You ain't gonna be inaugurated on New Year's Eve, are ya?" "I may not be inaugurated, but I'll be doin' pretty good!" The flip side is the December 9, 1941, episode with both comedic and historical interest. It has news bulletins on America's entry into World War II.

Murray Hill's boxed set has three discs (six hours) of material. The episodes are from October 14, 1947, January 1, 1948, and all four May episodes broadcast in 1948. Fibber is up to his old schemes in most of them. Like, "inventing a cologne for men ... men want to smell good but they also want to be masculine. So I said to myself, what's as masculine a thing as there is? Baseball, I said. So I'm whipping up a new cologne that smells like a baseball game ... if I can extract the odors of popcorn, salted peanuts, cigar smoke, and chewing gum, and add the scent of green grass and alcohol rub, I'll have me a cologne that no red-blooded American boy between the ages of sixteen and ninety-six can resist." Molly: "What are you gonna call it? Pop Fly Spray? Glove in Bloom? Or My Error?"

When NBC celebrated its 25th anniversary of radio (1926-1951), McGee and Molly hosted the show, which was issued as a promo item by NBC. Audio clips include a lot of music (Jessica Dragonette, Frank Sinatra, Jimmy Durante, for example) and some comedy moments: Amos and Andy discuss the presidency, W. C. Fields reports on killing moths, Bing Crosby parodies his own "bu-bu-bu boo" crooning, Groucho Marx is heard on "You Bet Your Life," Bob Hope jokes with Jerry Colonna, and Joe Penner sticks all his catchphrases into one minute with Rudy Vallee: "Hyuk hyuk hyuk, hello, Rudy! Wanna buy a duck?" "No, Joe, I don't wanna buy a duck...." "Maybe your brother would like to have one." "I haven't a brother." "Well, if you had one, you think he'd consider it?" "No." "Under no circumstances?" "Under no circumstances!" "You naaaaaasty man!"

A sample of Fibber McGee and Molly's brand of whimsical homey comedy appears on Radiola's "Son of Jest Like Old Times." A 1946 episode is on Murray Hill's "Three Funniest Hours in the History of Radio" three-record set. The duo issued a two-disc set for Capitol (78rpm) called "On the Night Before Christmas."

BRUCE COURTNEY MCGORRILL

• SATURDAY NIGHT IN DOVER-FOXCROFT (Melanie) * $4 $8

In 1964, McGorrill, general sales manager of WCSH-TV in Portland, recorded this collection of feeble "Yankee" stories before an audience at the Portland Junior Chamber of Commerce. Using the tight-lipped, no-sense-of-humor style of a dour New Englander, he tells long anecdotes, like the title track, about the time he bought gas at the only station open in a small town in Maine at 10:30 at night. After several rambling minutes: "Got out of the car, went into the station house where there was a teenager who was operating it at this time. He had a few of his friends with him who were probably waiting for late dates or something. As I walked in and the young fellow came up to me, wiping his hands on a cloth and he said, 'You want some gas, mister?' I said, 'Yes, would you fill it up, please?' He looked out the window and said, 'Which one's yours?' Without batting an eye, one of his friends said, 'The one that ain't moving, ya fool.'"

DION MCGREGOR

• THE DREAM WORLD OF DION MCGREGOR (Decca DL 4463) * $5 $10

A strange novelty-humor album from 1963, it collects tapes of comedy writer Dion McGregor allegedly talking in his sleep.

The album notes insist McGregor's roommate and collaborator Mike Barr would get up at seven a.m. to tape Dion's babbling. It sounds like a comedian trying to work out comedy routines while completely drunk or drugged. Whether truth or hoax, the record is hardly worth listening to except for fans of semi-nonsense. This fragment will suffice:

"Luke Harding. Yes. Runs the dairy in town. Calls it butter. Hm. It's not butter. It's yellow grease! Fly specked. We've all watched it. We all sat out there one day. He didn't know. Took notes. Took pictures. Yellow grease, not butter. Maude Slerna. Runs that little beauty parlor. Hm. You thought it was a beauty parlor. Well what do you suppose goes on there after hours? Certainly! Maude the Madam! Beautician! No sir ... Little Mary Mensa. Drove her right out of town, right out of town, said she was one of Maude's girls ... drive her out of town, drive her out of town. Wang. Boom. Pilloried. She was a pilloried girl. But Henrietta? Hmmm, she guarded her secret. She had been married twenty eight-times. Now how do you figure that out?"

HAL MCKAY

• A TREASURE OF IRISH HUMOR (Humor International LP 1000) *** $5 $10

This looks like a self-published album from a guy who might have made a few dollars doing comic lectures at schools or fraternal gatherings. McKay's delivery is average: any disc jockey, weatherman, or announcer could do as well. But the jokes are good ones—classics from the better joke books.

There's the one about the Irishman on his deathbed: "His wife was standing alongside of him. And she whispered to him, 'Do you have a last dying wish?' He says, 'Yes, you know what I'd like, Maggie dear? I'd like some of that corned beef and cabbage I smell cooking in the kitchen.' And she says, 'I'm sorry I can't do that, I'm savin' it for the wake.'"

GEORGE MCKELVEY

• A CROWD OF GEORGE MCKELVEY (American Gramophone 101) ** $6 $12

A hip folksinger from the early '60s, McKelvey's odd and quirky album doesn't hold together. The *Los Angeles Times* called him "a cross between Mort Sahl and Allan Sherman," but his songs are closer to The Smothers Brothers or Tom Lehrer. The monologue on old-time radio sounds like Jean Shepherd. When he tries for a one-man sound effects sketch as Dr. Frankenstein, the influence is Jonathan Winters.

McKelvey evidently never found his own identity or lasted long enough to correct the amateurish overacting in his monology. His songs are sometimes just fragments of ideas, or one-joke concepts. One coy tune is a romantic ballad about a visit to a deli:

"He was slicing a kosher salami. Right there in front of my eyes. I tell you it's true, I saw him and knew those rumors he's dead are all lies. He's not the same fun-loving fellow. He looks rather tired and pale. But nothing can hide that Aryan pride as he puts the corned beef on the scale. He still wears that cute little mustache. That little quaint way of combing his hair. Although he's turned gray, I saw Adolph today. Eva, you should've been there."

McKelvey appears on Dan Sorkin's folk parody album for Mercury.

BOB AND DOUG MCKENZIE

• GREAT WHITE NORTH (Mercury SRM 1 4034) * $5 $10
• STRANGE BREW (Mercury 8141041M1) * $5 $10

Only fans of Rick Moranis and Dave Thomas need listen to their albums based on the "Bob and Doug McKenzie" characters they did for the *SCTV* TV series. Bob and Doug are a pair of numbly slow-witted Canadian brothers who do very little besides shout "Ay," and "You Knob!" and "Take off!" at each other. The Cheech and Chong of beer humor, their work is boring to people who don't regularly throw up on Saturday night.

Their first album includes ambling routines and the novelty song "Take Off." Between choruses of "Take off ... to the Great White North" they dumbly bicker with each other: "This record was my idea." "Get out!" "It was ... hose head here just sorta rid on my coattails." "Why ya doin' this, it was our idea together ... aw take off."

"Strange Brew" takes the Monty Python approach to soundtrack album making—interrupting moments from the soundtrack to do some fresh material: "Okay, so good day. This album has to do with our movie. This is not our second album, it's our soundtrack album ... Okay! My brother's going through puberty now. He's got a couple of hairs comin'. Heh heh." "I might be going through puberty, but at least I don't have b.o. and you do ... okay, so let's press on then, no pun intended, ay, bein' that records get pressed ... did we forget anything?"

VAUGHN MEADER

• THE FIRST FAMILY (Cadence CLP 3060, reissued as GNP Crescendo GNPS 7002) **1/2 $3 $7
• THE FIRST FAMILY VOL. 1 AND 2 (Congressional) $10 $20
• THE FIRST FAMILY VOLUME TWO (Cadence CLP 3065/CLP 25065) ** $5 $15

Vaughn Meader had hard luck the moment he tried to record "The First Family." There was tension the night of the recording studio performance (October 22, 1962). President Kennedy had just given a speech on the Cuban missile crisis. No major label wanted the results. And when the small Cadence company released it, radio stations (as Mort Sahl discovered) refused to play any "anti-Kennedy" material.

Fortunately a few New York stations, WINS and WNEW, decided to air the "controversial" album. Suddenly the fifty thousand copies of the first pressing were gone. On November 19 the *New York Times* reported that two hundred thousand copies were sold. By Christmas, a million.

The success of "The First Family" changed the world of comedy records. Previously, hit comedy albums were live stand-up performances. Now the doors were wide open for producers to create audio sitcoms for disc. The notion that an unknown comic and a minor record label could strike paydirt spawned not just an immediate rash of copycat albums on Kennedy, but hundreds of topical and political albums in the years to come, all using "The First Family" formula of blackout sketches.

None would have the "fad" appeal of this album. This was "the original," and a surprise. Also, it seemed that people loved Kennedy so much that they viewed this very mild, very lighthearted parody as more a celebration than a slap.

The most famous cut, hardly irreverent, was the one where JFK argued over the bath toys Caroline and little John played with: "the rubber swan is mine!"

The quick copycat album was Hirsch and Dawson's "The Family in the White House." Variations include Brill and Foster's "The Other Family" (Khrushchev) and Tito Hernandez's album on Castro. "The Funniest Dream on Record" by Willie Bryant was a black version. London and Clark's "The President Strikes Back" imagined what Kennedy's reaction to "The First Family" would be. There was "Sing Along with the President" from Chuck McCann, "My Son the President" from Christopher Weeks, "The Next Family" from Bob Kennedy and Ralph Roby, plus albums from Bernie Berns, Marty Miles, and Danny Davis.

There was a sequel from Meader and company, with a supporting cast of Naomi Brossart, Norma MacMillan, Joe Silver, Barry Newman, Linda Siegel, and Stanley Myron Handelman. Like everyone else's quickie cash-in efforts, it is weak. Typically ridiculous is the nearly six-minute "Evening with JFK," in which Kennedy hosts his own TV show and sings a rap song:

"We like to keep young Caroline on an even keel. We bought her an erector set: Bethlehem Steel. The newsman that is seated there, with him I will ad-lib. I can tell with his evil eye he's from the Herald Trib!" And rapping about his wife Jackie's "White House Tour" TV special: "I haven't as yet seen my wife's TV extravaganza. How can I when it's always on opposite *Bonanza*?"

Some cuts are schizoid. In one scene Kennedy talks of his plans for the 1964 campaign. Suddenly the interviewer stops and tells him his hour is up. It turns out to be Vaughn Meader on the psychiatrist's couch! And on another cut, Meader plays all three Kennedy brothers, John, Robert, and Teddy. Says John: "I'm the older brother, I had this voice first! And I do believe that you two should find your own voices."

President Kennedy had listened to "The First Family" album and commented, "I really think he sounds more like Teddy."

Things weren't going too smoothly for Meader. A stage version of "The First Family" had bombed. For some reason nightclub and theater audiences didn't enjoy seeing the cast act out sketches radio-style in front of them.

Meader decided he'd better lose the "Kennedy imitator" tag. In an interview with the *New York Post* he talked about doing non-Kennedy material on a new album. The title of the article was "JFK Record Is Haunting Meader." The article was printed on November 22, 1963.

That afternoon newspapers were coming out with extra editions—to report Kennedy's death. A grieving nation said goodbye—and as an afterthought threw out their copies of "The First Family." Instead, they bought "John F. Kennedy, A Tribute," an album of Kennedy speeches. *The Guinness Book of World Records* had listed "The First Family" as the fastest-selling record of all time. But "John F. Kennedy, A Tribute" beat it, selling millions in under a week.

With over two million copies of "The First Family" ultimately sold, and so many disposed of, this album has been a $1 thrift shop eyesore for decades. Even now there's hardly a New York junk shop that doesn't have one. But in some places it was viewed a collector's item and in 1985 GNP Crescendo actually reissued it. (The obscure Congressional reprint, on poor quality floppy cardboard, arrived much earlier). Volume Two is the real rarity, especially in stereo.

• HAVE SOME NUTS (Verve V/V6 15042) ***	$5	$10
• IF THE SHOE FITS (Verve V 15050) **1/2	$5	$10
• TAKE THAT (Laurie LLP 2035) *	$5	$10

In early November of 1963, Meader went into the studio to record his first "non-Kennedy" album, with supporting cast Norma Macmillan, Bob McFadden, Joe Silver, Phil Leeds, and Fay De Witt. A few weeks later, Kennedy was killed. Even though Meader had been cutting down on the Kennedy material in his nightclub act, and had nothing about Kennedy on his new album, the American public saw JFK every time they saw Meader. And so "Have Some Nuts" was ignored. It's probably his best album, with not only some silly, funny sketches, but some solid satire as well. Highlights include a "John Lurch Telethon" urging citizens to turn in Commies (even red-clad Santa Claus), a look at the use of sex in TV commercials, and a seven-minute look at the high cost of funerals.

"If the Shoe Fits" isn't as tasty as "Nuts," and Renee Taylor's Queens-accented role of straight woman on some cuts doesn't help. The album opens with what seems like a sick JFK joke. As funeral music plays, Meader entones, "Dearly beloved, we are gathered here to pay our respects to a friend of this community, a man who was loved by all." Renee Taylor sobs in the background. Meader goes on and on with the eulogy, ending up by saying "When someone needed help, he was the first to give his aid. When someone wanted comfort, John Hacklemeyer was there."

Suddenly the sobbing Renee Taylor shouts, "John Hackle-moi-yahhh? Oh, Oy-am in the wrong place!"

The two best cuts are "Heel," a parody of faith healers, and "Foot in Mouth," with a speechmaker announcing a presidential candidate at a convention: "My candidate does not know the meaning of the word compromise, does not know the meaning of the word appeasement, does not know the meaning of the word cowardice—and has done quite well despite this lousy vocabulary."

"Take That" is a weak concept album about superheroes (from radio's Lone Ranger to TV's Batman). Meader's cast includes Stan Burns, Madge Cameron, and Donna Jean Young. The blackout sketches take too long to reach the punch line, like a bit with Superman doing a guest spot on *The Ed Sullivan Show*. The big joke: when he sings, it's a recording of an operatic female voice. Several gags like that are keyed to sound effects supplied by Bob Prescott.

- THE SECOND COMING (Kama Sutra KSBS 2038) *1/2 $5 $10

Following Kennedy's death and the failure of his subsequent albums, Meader dropped out, literally. He lived in a log cabin in Maine, and later drifted to Los Angeles, using LSD and living a hippie lifestyle in a tepee. And in 1971 he played Christ on this album, an attempt to cash in on *Jesus Christ Superstar*. Producer Earle Doud used Stan Z. Burns, Fred Travalina, Judy Engles, and Marshall Efron in the cast. Meader, a competent comic actor at best, really needs a good script and he doesn't get one.

The script fails time and again, as potentially sharp ideas are reduced to witless yocks. When Christ arrives on Earth, it's in Harlem, confronted by a stereotypical black: "You in trouble, Jim...." "I ask for your help, my brother, I am Jesus Christ." "Yeah, next he's gonna lay some catchy soul brother's name on us, like he's a personal friend of Bill Cosby and Flip Wilson, and he has tea with Aretha!"

Christ ends up going on TV, surrounded by gay makeup men: "Let's see that ol' Jesus smile!" He meets a women's libber: "You think that men are superior ... why aren't you the daughter of God?" He gets involved in a "Win a Week with Jesus" contest. Etc. etc.

In 1984 when Earle Doud produced "The First Family Rides Again" with Rich Little as Reagan, Meader turned up to play a reporter in one very brief sequence. He also released a musical album, "Whatever Happened to Vaughn Meader?" (Nice 006).

MELFI, VANN AND EVERLING
- WHAT MONTH WERE YOU BORN? (Fontana SRF 27566) ** $5 $10

On this 1967 album Johnny Melfi, Dorothy Vann, and Jim Everling tried to cash in on the hippie-astrology fad by dropping horoscope references into ordinary sketch material and trying to manufacture jokes about astrological signs:

"Virgo. You are practical, precise, analytical, meticulous. You are exactly like an IBM machine. Only without the charm. You are very fussy, and like everything spotless and clean. But you're lots of fun at parties—emptying ashtrays, rearranging the furniture ..."

BOB MELVIN
- CLOSER BABY, DON'T FIGHT IT (Capitol T 1575) *1/2 $6 $12

Melvin looks less like a comic than Bruce Gordon, the guy who played Frank Nitti on *The Untouchables*. He was on TV variety shows of the '60s. His deep, bland voice doesn't help his mediocre material. His catchphrase, repeated enough times to become a nagging nuisance, is "Have you got a minute?"

A dreary four-minute routine grades the audience on how well they react, he imitates a lisping Civil Defense instructor, and on the five-minute title track he mimics a sleazeball putting the make on his date while dancing: "Close, baby, don't fight, wuzzat? Am I workin'? Nah, I'm only out of the service twelve years. I'm restin'. Close, don't fight. Close. Just relax, 'at's my girl. My hand? Oh, I'll take it away. I see. You just had penicilin shots. Ay, yer all right ... close. Not too close, this is my brother's suit."

At some points, Melvin sounds like Rodney Dangerfield trying to perform Jack Carter's material. "Since 1932 I wanted to drive a caddy. That's what I drive: a '32 caddy. It's a sick car. Sick, sick, sick. I can't get gas unless I have a prescription. Have you got a minute?"

LEE ROY MERCER
- HUH! I'LL WHOOP YER (Warhead WHD 80615) * $7

Here's a redneck making prank phone calls. His idea of funny includes dialing up a gay bar to complain about queers and telling a husband that his pregnant wife has been unfaithful. Both calls degenerate quickly into anger and obscenity-filled threats. Judging from this material, Mercer's idea of true hilarity must involve pulling false alarms, setting fires, and torturing stray cats.

JULIE MEREDITH
- SONGS OF VICE AND VIRTUE (Imperial 9114) ** $6 $15

The album notes on this early '60s record insist Meredith's album "deals with folk songs and humor, and records by folk singers and humorists are the ones most sought after by discriminating buyers." But there isn't much humor here.

The "olde" folk songs here are feeble, like "Zulaika," a tune about a nymphomaniacal Persian wife who tosses her key out each night hoping for the best: "The first time she threw the key out, it fell by the old water spout. She sighed and she cried, and the door opened wide, and in walked her lover, Mahout. The next time she threw out the key, it fell by the old Banyon tree. She sighed and she cried, and the door opened wide, and in walked her lover, Ali. She threw the key out once again, expecting her lover, Sulman. She sighed and she cried and the door opened wide, and in walked a whole caravan. The caravan leader bowed low, and waited her wishes to know. 'Well, most of you stay,' Zulaika did say, 'But the children and camels must go.'"

The album was recorded live, but most of the chuckling is from Meredith when she ends each allegedly funny or spicy tune. Some cuts are straight, sung in the style of the day (a bit to the left of Judy Collins). There are more laughs on "straight" albums by folkies like The Kingston Trio and Judy Henske.

DON MEYER

• EXCUSE MY FLUFF (Rivoli RALP 1) *1/2 $4 $8

This is a very minor collection of radio bloopers, but the price is high because it's not very easy to find and it's a ten-incher.

BETTE MIDLER

• MUD WILL BE FLUNG TONIGHT (Atlantic 7812911) **1/2 $5 $10

On this 1986 stand-up album (three songs interrupt), Bette's campy-gay roots are showing. Using an archly annoying delivery that suggests Margaret Hamilton imitating Bette Davis, or maybe Katherine Hepburn doing Ed Wynn, Bette prances about assuring her worshipping male audience that she will be the bitch they wish they were: "Mud will be flung tonight!" Oooh, go girl! The script isn't really that bad—it's Midler getting too frisky before a fawning crowd. If she did these gags on *The Tonight Show* she wouldn't dare be so overbearingly fey.

She dismisses Bruce Springsteen: "I remember when his arms were as skimpy as his chord changes." The audience giggles over this mighty swipe. She revs up on Olivia Newton-John's wedding ("Everything was dyed to match the very special pink of her panties") and finally kicks into gear on Madonna: "Like a virgin? Touched for the very first time? For the very first time TODAY! Oh, pity the poor soul that has to rinse out THAT lingerie! The only thing that girl will ever do like a virgin is have a baby in a stable." Then, rolling over Prince, she notes, "When there's a sex symbol, I like to know the sex of the symbol."

These are all imposters. As Bette notes with queenly airs, "I am a STAR." The queens in the audience immediately cry out, "Yes you ARE! Yes you ARE!"

At times non-Midler fans will have something to chuckle about, if they have a short memory for '60s schtick: "I married a German ... every night I get dressed up like Poland and he invades me." It takes a pretty nervy lady to tell that oldie about the woman who gets flowers from her boyfriend: "For the next two weeks I'll be flat on my back with my legs open," she tells a girlfriend. The girl answers, "What's the matter with you, ain't you got a vase?"

MARILYN MICHAELS

• VOICES (Mew 783) ** $8

Some mimics have nothing to say, and using dozens of voices only compounds the problem. Michaels, who recorded many straight song albums in the '60s, is a good impressionist, but the novelty wears off quickly whether she simply sings songs straight as the stars (everyone from Peggy Lee to Connie Francis) or forces the laughs (Zsa Zsa Gabor, Joan Rivers, etc. doing stanzas of "12 Days of Christmas"). So many of these voices have become so familiar (Carol Channing, Barbra Streisand, Dr. Ruth) they'd try listener patience even if the lines were funny. On this CD the straight songs have little impact and the novelty numbers are designed to show off the voice without any attempt at real jokes: "Hi, I'm Dolly ... workin' nine to five and really put my heart in. Ain't no twig, my boobs are big! I'm Dolly Parton!"

JACKIE MILES

• ONE HUNDRED TWENTY POUNDS DRIPPING WET (Imperial 9154) **1/2 $10 $20
• J. SCHWARTZ, NEW YORK (Warner Bros. S 1726) **1/2 $10 $20

In the late '50s Jackie Miles was a top comic in Catskill resorts and Miami clubs. Like Myron Cohen, his delivery was slow and measured and he got a lot of mileage from humor based on human nature and a Jewish accent. Unlike Cohen, a Miles anecdote can go on for five minutes or more. Which is why near the height of his career he was bounced from London's Palladium for going on too long. The publicity didn't enhance his standing among bookers.

The Warner disc has ten long stories about a particular Jewish character, Mr. Schwartz, who has come down to Miami to enjoy the good life, always introducing himself with mock formality as "J. Schwartz, New York." Mr. Schwartz on the golf course:

"J. Schwartz, New York put a ball on the tee, and the caddy, knowing he's playing golf for the first time, very politely said to him, 'Your driver, sir, one or two or three wood.' J. Schwartz looked at him and said, 'Kid, never tell to me what or what not to do. I am J. Schwartz, New York. With branches in Allentown.' He said, 'Give me my putter.' Well, the poor kid, nice kid, he gave him the putter. My good friends, he held it at the bottom! He swung at the ball with the putter on the first try, first tee, hit that ball perfectly, believe it or not, and landed two inches away from the cup. He walked up to the green and the caddy, in amazement, said, 'What an excellent shot, sir. You may use your putter again if you like.' He said, 'Kid, never tell to me what to do, or what not to do. Now, give me my driver, three wood.' Two inches from the cup. Well, the caddy gave him his three-wood driver. He took it in one hand, and wound up with it, swung at the ball with every bit of strength he had, missed the ball completely, but the wind forced the ball into the cup! Well by this time the caddy was afraid to say or do anything. When finally J. Schwartz, New York looked at him, and he said, 'Kid, I didn't mean to yell at you, and I don't mind admitting sometimes I take advice. Tell to me, son, what club do I use to get that ball out of the hole?'"

The early Imperial album has more general material, including a few observations on golf: "You drink at a bar in the day time, people call you a drunkard. You drink at the golf course, you're a sportsman! So I get drunk like a sportsman. And it's convenient. You fall down, you land on grass, you never get hurt. If somebody hollers 'Fore!' that means two doubles."

Miles issued a single, "I'm a Rollin.'" It is character comedy as a Jewish fellow describes, via monologue, a movie in which calm Gene Autry keeps singing one tune no matter what dangers are ahead. It's on "Laugh of the Party" (Coral CRL 57017).

MARTY MILES

- MY SON THE PRESIDENT (Strand SL/SLS 1085) **1/2 $4 $8

Considering that Strand was a failed cheapie label, that the topical script was written quickly, and that amateur Marty Miles had never appeared in a club or on TV before making this album, this isn't bad. Miles, sort of a low-budget Jackie Mason, plays the first Jewish candidate for the presidency. Well, maybe not the *first*. Strand issued a Danny Davis album with almost the same album cover and the same idea. Miles plays Shapiro Finkelstein, who meets reporters to answer assorted silly questions. A drunken reporter from *The Hobo News* slurs out a question: "President Truman plays the piano. Are you also interested in music?" "Certainly. Certainly." "Then can you sing 'Melancholy Baby?'"

The script, by Miles and straight man Jack Silver, is not big on belly laughs, but it maintains a level of unpretentious chuckles. The back cover features glowing testimonials from people even more obscure than Marty Miles. Steven Garrick, who worked for Jan Murray as a music arranger, says, "I can't remember when I laughed longer and harder." Vaudevillian Arthur Pines adds, "Good luck," and singer Lori Parker chimes in, "I broke up."

DENNIS MILLER

- THE OFF-WHITE ALBUM (Warner Bros. 25780) *** $8

Miller was still the snide newscaster of *Saturday Night Live* when he released this concert album in time for Christmas 1988. The curmudgeon is sharp and mean, a bracing satirist at a time when stand-up comics were either screaming or clowning, but not always thinking. He grunts and gripes about most anything that comes to mind. On Hare Krishnas: "It says in the Bible, God created us in his own image. I just know he wouldn't wear his hair like that ... Daddy Warbucks with a f-----' Slinky hanging off the side of his head." On female gymnasts: "I love this activity since the summer Olympics. Specifically the women's uneven parallel bar event. I think I'm gonna be a little skeptical the next time a woman tells me I'm being too rough in bed. I'm watchin' these girls bang their cervix off a frozen theater rope at eighty miles per hour. You don't see men in that event, okay ... if I ever hit anything that hard with my dick I'm gonna spot weld to it." And on born again Christians: "I'm a little indignant when they tell me I'm going to hell if I haven't been born again. Pardon me for getting it right the first time!"

The album title is a mild salute to The Beatles' "White Album," utilizing the same art direction.

MRS. MILLER

- MRS. MILLER'S GREATEST HITS (Capitol ST 2494) *1/2 $4 $8
- WILL SUCCESS SPOIL MRS. MILLER? (Capitol ST 2579) *1/2 $4 $8
- COUNTRY SOUL OF MRS. MILLER (Capitol ST 2734) *1/2 $4 $8

Elva Miller, an aging, pleasantly round-faced housewife from Missouri, was struggling through a proposed album of sacred songs when somebody got the idea that she was so bad she was good. And so in 1965 "Mrs. Miller's Greatest Hits" was released, a tongue-in-cheek collection of pop tunes ("Downtown," "The Shadow of Your Smile," "A Hard Day's Night") warbled with a great deal of sincerity and soprano vibrato. The kind of vibrato that could make dogs get vicious. And some people laugh.

If the Marx Brothers' dowager Margaret Dumont had been a comic singer, she probably would have sounded like this. She's more disconcerting than funny, never intentionally veering off key or changing lyrics. The novelty wore off after a few albums; especially when it became obvious that she was in on the gag too, and didn't mind the laughs as long as she was laughing all the way to the bank. She returned home to a pleasant retirement. Or as the police say after the accident, "move along, the show's over."

NORMA MILLER

- HEALTHY, SEXLESS AND SINGLE (Laff 148) **1/2 $5 $10

A seasoned pro (she cowrote a joke book with Redd Foxx), Norma Miller alternates familiar dirty gags with racial humor.

Familiar dirty joke: "A little boy baby and a little girl baby are lying in their bassinets. Late in the morning the little girl baby starts yelling, 'Rape! Rape! Rape!' The little boy baby looked over at her and said, 'Ah, shut up and turn over. You're lying on your pacifier.'"

Racial quickie: "It makes no damn difference, black or white. Turn out that light, sweetie, it comes down to a case of who washed."

Miller's disc is marred by poor sound. The microphone was placed too far from the stage; there's tinny echo to her voice and the audience's mumbling and coughing is distractingly audible.

RICHARD MILNER

- THE CONTRACEPTIVE PUTS YOU ON (Schlock) * $6 $12

On this sloppy, self-indulgent exercise from 1969, Milner (with a guy sawing a monotone on a bass fiddle in the background, for added cool) badly overacts his amateurish hipster monologues and anecdotes. The only reasons for a high price are its rarity as a self-pressed (in Berkeley, California) "limited edition," and a bunch of nude photos collaged on the front cover.

BILL MINKIN

- THE HARDLY-WORTHIT REPORT (Parkway P/SP 7053) *1/2 $4 $8
- BOSTON SOUL WITH THE HARDLY-WORTHIT PLAYERS (Parkway SP/P 7057) ** $5 $10
- SENATOR BOBBY'S CHRISTMAS PARTY (Columbia CS 9576) ** $5 $10

"Hardly-Worthit" is a studio album satirizing the news broadcasts of Chet Huntley and David Brinkley. Bill Minkin and partner Dennis Wholey cover improbable news of the day (1966) but periodically go back in time to handle Columbus discovering America, the Lone Ranger holding a press conference, and Moses in the desert. There's no credibility to such a dumb idea, and few laughs. From the Moses bit:

"The burning bush has just flashed on. That means we have a direct report from Nancy Dickering on Mt. Sinai." "... I see Moses coming towards me. He looks happy, has a beautiful tan ... he looks like he just talked to an old, old friend. Tell me, Moses, what are those tablets you're carrying." (Lyndon Johnson accent) "Well, Nancy, these laws that I have are gonna be the laws of all mankind and part of my great promised land ... right now I'm goin' down there on the desert floor, give my speech, then we're gonna have a big ol' manna-matzoh barbecue."

Some Beatles fans might want to hear the long (six-minute) sitcom about The Beatles and Pope Paul VI arriving in New York at the same time and getting things confused: "Cardinal Spellman has just knelt down and kissed one of Ringo Starr's rings ... the Pope is waving and smiling, he's put on a pair of dark glasses ..."

Bill Minkin, billed as "Senator Bobby," issued a single imitating Senator Robert F. Kennedy doing The Trogg's hit "Wild Thing" in a flat, stuttery Boston accent. It was a Top 20 hit in January of 1967. The flip side, equal time for the Republicans, offered "Senator Everett" Dirksen doing the song in a deep, froggy baritone.

Figuring to perk up sales of "Hardly-Worthit," the album was re-released with the hit "Senator Bobby" cut on it.

Then it was time to make a new album with more politicians singing more pop songs. "Boston Soul" has "Wild Thing" again, along with Bobby trying to do "96 Tears" but ending up arguing with his recording engineer. The problem here is that some of the songs actually match what the politicians might do. William F. Buckley could certainly ooze his way through The Lovin Spoonful hit "What a Day for a Daydream" and Lyndon Johnson might have enjoyed warbling "King of the Road" in the shower. The cover of the album, a parody of "Rubber Soul," offers drawings of four men in Beatles poses. There's Johnson, Dirksen, Kennedy, and ... isn't that a bad copy of the "Blonde on Blonde" picture of Bob Dylan?

Yes, for some reason, the album of political satire ends with a parody of Bob Dylan. "Bobby the Poet," as he's called here, sings "White Christmas." It would be a good joke except that it's overproduced like the rest of the album, with recording engineer banter and other interruptions. With only three songs on each side, this a quick album.

Minkin's "Christmas Album" has some predictable sketch humor. Stretching out a joke for nearly a minute, Bobby visits his barber (Chuck McCann) for his "annual haircut." After a lot of banter, Bobby says he wants a shave, a shoe shine, and a manicure. And perhaps a haircut? "Just trim a little off the sides and throw the rest down over my face." "Oh, the usual."

Nearly half of Side Two is an oddity: "The Christmas Night Show," imagining Bobby Kennedy as host of *The Tonight Show* with Chuck McCann doing an accurate Ed McMahon and an odd Jack Benny voice for Ronald Reagan. At the time (1967) it was pretty funny hearing Bobby doing Carson monologue schtick ("this actually happened ...").

MISS DEE

- SEXARAMA (Davis 120) ** $5 $10

There's no photo of "Miss Dee." The front cover has a topless model and the back is an ad for other Davis label albums. She sings pleasantly enough on this late '50s LP as she goes through some mild risqué tunes written by Joe Davis himself, including: "It's What's Up Front That Counts," "She Sits on His Lap and Bawls," and "Hey Mister Ice Man."

These double entendre songs are set up clumsily. Like "He Broke It Off Inside of Her," which begins: "There was a careless little girl who ran a sliver in her hand. She asked her friend to get it out. He said, 'I'll do the best I can.' Now the chorus: "He broke it off inside of her, that nervous little fellow. He broke it off inside of her, and boy how she did bellow! She hollered, 'Oh please take it out, it hurts so much that I could shout!'"

BILLY MITCHELL AND HATTIE NOEL

- SONGS FOR FUN (Dooto DTL 212) ** $7 $15

It was the now forgotten Billy Mitchell who made the first records for Dootsie Williams, president of the Dooto label. Back in 1947 Williams caught Billy Mitchell's act and was amused by Mitchell's double entendre tunes "The Woodpecker" and "The Ice Man." Williams decided to record the songs for a single and call his label Blue Records. When the Dooto label was ready to go, Mitchell was already dead and gone. So "Songs for Fun" is filled out with material by Hattie Noel.

CORBETT MONICA
- FOR LAUGHS (Dot 3303) **1/2 $7 $15

An amiable nightclub comic (and still out there, opening for Steve and Eydie among others), the personable Monica was a regular on *The Joey Bishop Show* around the time he made this album. Like Bishop, he tends toward low-key conversational comedy on familiar topics. On buying a new car: "I passed a car dealership. I looked in the window and I saw the most beautiful cars. And a fellow came out and said, 'Come on in, they're bigger than ever and they last a lifetime.' He was talking about the payments."

And back when every comedian had to have an airline routine: "I'm giving up flying. I was at the airport and I saw a sign: 'Take out insurance.' I thought: if the lobby's that dangerous, imagine what it's like in the plane."

JULIUS MONK REVUES
- TAKE FIVE (Offbeat O 4013) **1/2 $20 $50

Julius Monk ran Le Ruban Bleu, which gave a start to Professor Irwin Corey in 1942 and others over the years, such as Imogene Coca, Will Jordan, James Komack, Jonathan Winters, and Arte Johnson. He moved on to supervise The Upstairs at the Downstairs, a club featuring cabaret revues. Monk assembled the best young talent in town, many emerging as stars (Estelle Parsons, Nancy Dussault, Tammy Grimes). The shows, sort of *Saturday Night Live* for sophisticates, changed once a year or so until the cabaret style, and Monk, went into eclipse in the late '60s.

Monk's "Take Five" cast featured five performers: Jean Arnold, Ceil Cabot, Ellen Hanley, and the star of the show, promising young comic Ronny Graham. The sketch "Night Heat" was cowritten by *Get Smart* writer Dee Caruso and Mr. Smart himself, Don Adams. It's a satire of Mike Wallace's powerful interview technique. A newscaster-interrogator takes on an adversary:

"In our last interview we exposed you for what you are," Matthews reports, "A crook, a liar, a thief ... but that was six months ago. Now that you're back on your feet again ... I have here your war record...."

"Every man in our outfit was proud of our record," says Graham. "We demolished a train depot, three armories, and four small towns." "That's right, and then they sent you overseas!"

"You really got a big mouth, Mike."

Graham's delivery helps save what, after several decades, is no longer a sterling example of sketch writing. Graham's monologue "Harry the Hipster" is the highlight of the show. It also appears on Riverside's compilation album, "How to Be Terribly, Terribly Funny." In this hep-smoke-a-reefer bit, Graham imagines cult jazz musician Harry "The Hipster" Gibson giving a lecture on how to smoke marijuana:

"Just for demonstration purposes let's say this is a reefer. I say let's say this is. 'Cause this is! This is not a civilian cigarette. This is standard gauge M-1. Sometimes called Progressive Pall Malls, or Left Wing Luckies, or Mexican Laughing Tobacco ..." Along the way, he sings "Cement Mixer," and tosses in lines directly from Gibson's tunes ("Hey, Stop that Dancing Up There!"). He also offers some pot-headed jazz one-liners: "How much is Rita in the Hayworth?" "I got the sun in the morning and the daughter at night." "I was walking along the ocean. That's generally where you'll find the beach. Lookin' for ashtrays in their wild state ..."

- DEMI DOZEN (Offbeat O 4015) *** $20 $40
- PIECES OF EIGHT (Offbeat O-4016) *1/2 $20 $50
- FOUR BELOW STRIKES BACK (Offbeat O 4017) *1/2 $20 $50

With "Demi Dozen," Monk expanded his cast of players to six: Jean Arnold, Ceil Cabot, Jane Connell, Jack Fletcher, George Hall, and Gerry Matthews. Still cute and clever is Bill Dana's sketch "Conference Call," about the ad world's attempts to blow smoke at the surgeon general's warnings. The team of Tom Jones and Harvey Schmidt created two seriocomic winners with the cabaret songs "The Holy Man and the New Yorker." about a downtrodden, shuffling New Yorker who looks up and sees the sky, and "The Race of the Lexington Avenue Express," sung by Jane Connell. Some cuts are brittle with age, like "Guess Who Was There," about Elsa Maxwell and her gay parties with Cole, Noel, and Tallulah.

The cast for 1960's "Pieces of Eight" features Gordon Connell, Estelle Parsons, Del Close, Jane Connell, Ceil Cabot, and Gerry Matthews. The disappointing songs range from fey to shrill and are suitable only for the die-hard cabaret fan. The satirical subjects include a love song to Mr. Clean, a semi-offensive song with Martin Charnin's lyrics decrying the amount of Asians in Broadway plays and movies (*Suzie Wong*, *Teahouse of the August Moon*, and *King and I*), and a hoity toity slap huff over *Lady Chatterly's Lover* uncensored. Jane Connell plays her: "At last I've arrived in America, and really, my dears, if you knew when a girl is no better than she should be, it's far better they don't let her through...."

Occasionally there's a decent line, if the listener can bear hearing it strained through pseudo-sophisticated rolling r's. "Radio City Music Hall," a flouncy backhand slap at the dowdiness of tap dancing and overly loud costuming, offers this snotty putdown: "It's the showplace of the nation, the mecca of the trade. There's no place in the nation where prettier girls are mounted or bigger shows are made!"

The amusing finale, "A Conversation Piece" written by Bill Dana, is a satire of David Susskind's *Open End*, renamed "Open Mouth." As a bunch of pseudo-intellectuals babble their concentric conceits, one ponders "whether man in an environment can also have surroundings."

"Four Below" and "The Son of Four Below" were Monk's first hit reviews (1956). Hence, the nostalgically named "Four Below Strikes Back," with a foursome of George Furth, Cy Young, Jenny Lou Law, and Nancy Dussault. It's a weak release with a lot of dated references in the sketches "The Constant Nymphet" and "The Sitwells." Of slight interest is "Mr. X.," a comic interview with the man who actually makes "Brand X" products for TV commercials;

and "Literary Time," a talk show parody by Tom Jones. Ronny Graham authored three very mild songs. On "Man Tan," Jenny Law gets uncomically overwrought over a then-popular brand of bronzer that's made her lover popular among all women: "Oh, Man Tan, give me back my tan man! And stop playing fan tan with my heart!" "Leave Your Mind Alone" is a dull tune about analysis, and "It's a Wonderful Day to be Seventeen," sung by Nancy Dussault, is a one-joke parody of cheery Julie Andrews tunes. Dussault does better with a straight tune by Walter Marks, "Love, Here I Am," (but would do much better in another show entirely, Marks' Broadway show *Bajour*).

Offbeat's small pressings and the enthusiasm from fans of cabaret and show tunes help make these expensive.

• DRESSED TO THE NINES (MGM E39140C) **	$20	$40
• SEVEN COME ELEVEN (Columbia 55478) **	$20	$40
• DIME A DOZEN (Cadence CLP 26063) ***	$12	$35

Monk's New York revues were popular enough in the early '60s to get major label attention, even if the songs and sketches touched on things of grave concern only to the urban, affluent, liberal audience of the era. On the MGM album this includes commuting, psychiatry, browsing in bookstores, and vacationing in Fort Lauderdale. Some cuts are silly, like Mary Louise Wilson's solo "Names" about unlikely marriages: "If Conway Twitty would marry Kitty Carlisle, then Kitty Carlisle would now be Kitty Twitty."

Things reached a peak with the Cadence album—a two-record set. But again, it was filled with references that pleased mostly a narrow section of wry New York intelligentsia. Songs include tweaks at plaid stamp collecting, the construction of Lincoln Center so close to a Puerto Rican slum, trivial items in the *New York Times* and a protest of British authors and actors on Broadway.

One sketch decries the destruction of a brownstone apartment for a new office tower for General Electric: "All glass?" "Hell yes, all glass, they're erecting a light bulb ... something about expressing the corporate image ... perhaps they'll dig a deep round foundation and screw the damn thing into place!"

Though dated, most any intellectual could still enjoy the finale—a long sketch that swipes at Ionesco, Beckett, and Albee in general and *Night of the Iguana* by Tennessee Williams in particular. Rex Robbins reports, "The plays seem to end where they began. And yet, as the curtain falls, we audiences are left repeating the same haunting phrase: either they or I am nuts! This is absurd!" Then British spinster Mary Louise Wilson meets the naked defrocked priest Jack Fletcher for some intellectual vaudeville:

"Are you the caretaker around here?"

"I think so. I mean, I read the script but I'm still not sure ... so that's your grandfather down there, the old man in the wheelchair?"

"Yes, he's stuck in the muck, I came to get help."

"He's an old one, isn't he?..."

"He's 153 this month."

"One hundred fifty-three! Looks older ..."

"... now look at him wallowing in the mud ... I've seen him in these moods before!"

"You're English, aren't you?"

"I'm a virgin if that's what you mean."

NOTES: Julius Monk recorded a solo album of music in 1959 (Offbeat OB 400). After his troupe vacated The Upstairs at the Downstairs in 1963 for the Plaza Hotel, another team moved in, produced by Rod Warren. The 1965 production *Just for Openers* with Fannie Flagg and Madeline Kahn (UD 37 W 56), and the double disc for subsequent shows *Mixed Doubles* and *Below the Belt*, featuring Madeline Kahn and Lily Tomlin (UD 37 W 56 Vol 2), were issued on the Upstairs at the Downstairs label and sold at the club.

LOU MONTE

• LIVE IN PERSON (Reprise R9-6014) **	$5	$10

In the mid '60s Monte was known for "Italian Fun Songs," several featuring Pepino the Italian Mouse, a variation on Alvin the Chipmunk. His albums seemed to mix light Italian language tunes, straight numbers, and novelty cuts.

His album "Pepino the Italian Mouse," for example, includes somewhat embarrassing dialect numbers with peppy instrumentals ("Please Mr. Columbus Turn the Ship Around"), ballads ("Eh Marie," "Mala Femmena") and the sing-song title track in which Lou chides his mouse friend: "You scare my girl, you eat my cheese, you even drink my wine, I try so hard to catch you, but you trick me all the time!"

Monte's albums are mostly placed in the pop vocals or ethnic sections of record stores except for "Live in Person," since half of one side is a monologue, "A Self-Portrait of Lou Monte at Home." Monte fans will be amused by his complaints about his family:

"If I could only get the guy who invented television! I walked up to my big boy. He's nineteen now. He just learned how to take the garbage out. I said, 'Son, I'd appreciate it very much if you kept the kids quiet and the volume down low so Daddy could get sleep!' He gets up and looks at me and says, 'Wattsamatta, you don't like it around here? We'll get rid of ya!' In the meantime the nine-year-old, he was in the garage, he was sawing the dog in half! My wife said, 'Don't hit him, don't hit him, he gets nervous....'"

PAUL MOONEY

• RACE (Step Sun 53748-3005-2) ***	$8
• MASTER PIECE (Step Sun 53728-3030-2) **	$8

With the cool poise of a Dick Gregory and a touch of the incredulous, mocking laughter that marked a Godfrey Cambridge set, Paul Mooney delivers over an hour of racial comedy on the "Race" CD. Much of it, he acknowledges, is too painful to be very funny for blacks or whites.

Blacks aren't laughing too loudly when Mooney skewers black rapper M. C. Hammer for doing a demeaning fried chicken commercial: "a nigger dancing for chicken ... that's a goddamn shame. Is this nigger's mama still alive?" And Mooney pointedly acknowledges every time a line about whites fails to get white laughter. He mocks scared "little white rabbits" who'll walk out on his show rather than take their medicine. He mimics them cringing: "'Make that nigger *stop* saying 'nigger.' I'm getting a nigger *headache*.'" White folks made up the word nigger and don't want me to say it. Ain't that a bitch?"

Mooney alternates between mockery, bitterness, and a humorless mutter of "I'm sick of the bullshit." But the set does have some broad clowning (including a look at Frankenstein movies) to break up the grimness. Even so, uneasy chuckles over unpleasant truths dominate over belly laughs.

The 1994 hour is a disappointment, the laughs coming more from blunt, opinionated ranting than wit. After a while his one-note black-note remarks on celebrities of the day become all too predictable. Barbara Walters "is a ho," John Wayne Bobbit's "white dick ... was found with a pair of tweezers," and Mike Tyson is admirably "a hard nigga" who would rather stay in jail than "apologize."

WILLIAM MOONEY

• HALF HORSE HALF ALLIGATOR (RCA Victor VDS 113) **	$5	$10

Assuming various characters, William Mooney recites American frontier stories and anecdotes, including "The Dog Who Paid Cash" by Will Rogers, "The Pious Commodore" by Charles E. Brown, "A Sage Conversation" by A. B. Longstreet, and material from Mark Twain, David Crockett, and Samuel Woodworth. The concept is similar to Hal Holbrook's "Mark Twain Tonight." The material isn't hilarious, but now and then a routine comes to life. Johnson J. Hooper's "Erasive Soap Man," written in 1851, could be an ancestor to W. C. Fields's "Purple Bark Sarsaparilla" spiel:

"I was tongue-tied but I came across this precious compound. Swallowed just half an ounce of it. And ever since to the satisfaction of my parents, myself, and an assembled world, I have been volubly, rapidly, and successfully, interminably, unremittingly, and most eloquently sounding the praises of this incomparable, ineffable, infallible, inappreciable, all-healing, never failing, spot-removing, beauty-restoring, health-giving magical radical...."

RUDY RAY MOORE

• BELOW THE BELT (Dooto DTL 808) **	$5	$10
• LET'S COME TOGETHER (Dooto DTL 850) **	$5	$10
• EAT OUT (Kent KST 001) **	$5	$10
• THIS PUSSY BELONGS TO ME (Kent KST 002) **	$5	$10
• MERRY CHRISTMAS, BABY (Kent KST 005) **	$5	$10
• COCKPIT (Kent KST 006) **	$5	$10
• DOLEMITE FOR PRESIDENT (Kent KST 014) **	$5	$10
• ZODIAC (Kent KST 015) **	$5	$10
• I CAN'T BELIEVE I ATE THE WHOLE THING (Kent KST 016) **	$5	$10
• THE PLAYER, THE HUSTLER (Kent KST 017) **	$5	$10
• RECORDED LIVE IN CONCERT (Kent KST 018) **	$5	$10
• GREATEST PARTY HITS (Kent KST 019) **	$5	$10
• THE PLAYER (Kent KST 020) **	$5	$10
• THE STREAKER (Kent KST 021) **	$5	$10
• ANOTHER CRAZY NIGGER (Kent KST 022) **	$5	$10
• SWEET PETER (Kent KST 023) **	$5	$10
• CLOSE ENCOUNTER OF THE SEX KIND (Kent KST 026) **	$5	$10
• GREATEST HITS (Right Stuff 3573523) **		$7

Moore has a cult following for his raunchy, obscure records and low budget "blaxploitation" films. He evidently had little distribution beyond record stores in ethnic neighborhoods. No doubt major record chains were especially turned off by the nude (and usually unattractive) women posing on the covers with Moore.

Moore has been called "The Godfather of Rap" for his dirty rambles done in rhyme with musical backing (beginning with "Eat Out More Often" in 1970). His backers also consider him the pioneer who blazed the trail for Richard Pryor and Eddie Murphy.

The 1995 CD "Greatest Hits" is easiest to find and does have some funky one-liners amid the orations and raps.

Moore's Kent albums have been available via reissue on cassette for quite a while, but they're hard to find outside of black record stores and black mail order catalogs.

JIM MORAN

• DON'T MAKE WAVES (London AM 48003) *1/2	$7	$15

Humorist H. Allen Smith wrote the liner notes for this one, and it's not surprising. Moran's dry comic lectures are very similar to the kind of humor pieces Smith wrote, and to some of Robert Benchley's work as well. The goateed humorist performed some of his bland lectures on talk shows of the late '50s and early '60s, including *The Tonight Show*. Here, a rumination on nature:

"The vicious, ill-tempered cassowary of New Guinea. That's a miserable bird.... Did you know a six-foot male cassowary weighs three hundred pounds, and has wattles that hang down sixteen to eighteen inches from his chin? Two bright red sacks full of hard lard swinging back and forth? It's depressing. But don't ever get a cassowary sore at you. I was weighing the wattles of a cassowary down in Queensland, Australia two years ago ... the cassowary didn't seem to be in a very good humor, so I gave him a wad of tutti-frutti chewing gum. While he was trying to figure that out, I picked up his wattles and gently laid them on the scales. I guess the weighing pan was kind of chilly because his wattles began to pucker. Well, he went hog wild and started to wattle me across the chops. And having never been wattled before, much less by an angry cassowary, I had no defense, so I got wattled. I learned a good lesson though. Never pucker the wattles of a cassowary."

LESTER "ROADHOG" MORAN

• ALIVE AT THE JOHNNY MACK BROWN HIGH (Mercury SRM 1708) **	$5	$10
• THE COMPLETE LESTER MORAN (Mercury 314-5189442) **		$8

Country comic Moran performed with The Cadillac Boys (alias The Statler Brothers). "Complete" is a CD release.

MORAN AND MACK

• THE TWO BLACK CROWS (Timestu TS 81600, TBC 1247) **	$10	$20

George Moran and Charlie Mack released four 78 rpm singles, "The Two Black Crows Part 1-8" in 1927. They were big stars with their ethnic vaudeville routines. The material is pretty corny now, and blackface humor has tainted their memory even if they tended to be more softspoken and less stereotypical (almost in the contemplative style of the only popular black stand-up of the day, Bert Williams).

Williams, like his Ziegfeld Follies friend W. C. Fields, relished the delivery as much as the gag, savoring a joke by applying exaggerated lilt and subtle flavoring. Mack tries this from time to time, but now and then his drawl oozes effeminacy, sounding like a constipated Sophie Tucker, Joe Besser at 16 rpm, or the grandfather to "Pat," Julia Sweeney's androgynous *Saturday Night Live* character.

There's a glaring Negro reference now and then (the term "boy" or an overt comment about laziness), but most of the scripts are harmless. From their first single, Mack speaking first:

"I don't feel well ... I was at the doctor and he told me what to do but I didn't do it. He told me to take one pill three times a day, but you can't do that."

"What else did the doctor say?"

"He said my veins are too close together.... He said I had very close veins."

(Moran starts playing a tune on a comb and tissue paper.)

"Boy, even if that was good I wouldn't like it."

"Boy, I play anything on this."

"Yeah? You can't play piano on that, you couldn't do that."

Moran and Mack recorded for Columbia. This record is a bootleg. The flip side has routines by Smith and Dale.

MANTAN MORELAND

• THAT AIN'T MY FINGER (LAFF A 140) **	$6	$12
• ELSIE'S SPORTIN' HOUSE (LAFF A 158) **	$6	$12
• TRIBUTE TO THE MAN (LAFF A 185) **	$5	$10

Mantan Moreland's very name connotes an era in which black comedians were the willing butt of stereotype comedy. He insisted "Mantan" was a common name down South, but in the '50s most knew it as the name for a popular suntanning product and assumed that Moreland had adopted it as a joke. Long after his "Charlie Chan" movie sidekick days, Moreland made these risqué albums for Laff.

One of Mantan's favorite routines was an interruption dialogue anticipating the straight man's questions. He'd learned it years earlier from vaudevillian Fluornoy Miller. On "That Ain't My Finger," he revives it with the assistance of straight man Livingood Pratt:

"Mantan, what's your brother doin' now?" "He's working down here for a man, they payin' him a salary—" "Can he live that cheap?" "I don't know ... He gonna get married ... the daughter of—" "She's a nice girl! Listen, let me tell you something ... one time I—" "That was her sister! I'm keepin' company with her...." "I thought she was—" "She was, but I cut him out." "Now that's funny, just the other day I was talkin' to her father and the first thing I—" "That was your fault. What you should've done—" "I did." "See that Livingood? That's why I like to talk to you. 'Cause you and I seems to agree with each other!"

That seems dumb on paper, but even in his raspy and elderly condition, Moreland makes it classic. He tries not to get too smutty. Talking about his new fishing idea, catching fish with peas: "All I have to do is take a can of peas, open it, and spread the peas all in the water." "And then what happens?" "Sit down, watch the fish come up to take a pea and hit 'em in the head!"

It's more of the same on "Elsie's Sportin' House," with Roosevelt Myles and Janet Taylor. Mantan doesn't sound quite as worn out as he did on the first album, but some of the vaudeville-style joke-sketches ("Fartin' Mule") are hard to follow without the visuals, thanks to his meandering delivery and the screams of delight from the audience. The jokes are coarser than the first album.

After his death, the "tribute" album was released, editing together moments from both previous releases.

FREDDY MORGAN

- MR. BANJO (Verve MG V 2065) $7 $15

Morgan, a conspicuously dopey looking member of the Spike Jones band, is pictured on the cover in a suitably moronic pose: toothless grin, flappy ears, Moe Howard haircut, and slightly crossed eyes. He looks very funny. The album, recorded around 1959, sports the promising note, "conceived, produced, and recorded under the personal supervision of Spike Jones."

But ... the album is just tame banjo tunes done with a slight amount of ragtime zest. Morgan was a novelty vocalist (the Oriental dialect parodies on Spike's records) but doesn't even sing here. Morgan wrote a pair of fairly well-known tunes, "Hey Mister Banjo" and "Sayonara." Neither are on the record.

HENRY MORGAN

- THE HENRY MORGAN SHOW (Memorabilia MLP 718) ** $5 $10
- THE BEST OF HENRY MORGAN (Command LP-2) ** $5 $10

The erudite and dour Henry Morgan had a cult following on radio. It wasn't a large cult because much of Morgan's work was subtle—sort of Bob and Ray with a dash of Fred Allen. Memorabilia's half-hour episode (stretched over both sides of the album) has some good examples of Morgan's eccentricity, especially his "Question Man" segment:

"From Mr. J.D. of Jackson Heights. 'I am making a study of multiple birth statistics. Can you tell me how often triplets are born?' Once. Here's a sartorial query from E.S. of Pittsburgh. 'What should I wear with a sleeveless shirt?' Shirtless sleeves. Mrs. F.B. of New York wants to know: 'When I am driving my car and wish to make a left turn, should I put my hand straight out my window?' No. First roll the window down." A long double-dating sitcom sketch features Arnold Stang.

Command excerpts 1946-47 radio shows with one entire side devoted to commercials! Morgan was known for sarcastically rewriting the ad copy. Laudible, but ten in a row is sadistic. Here's one:

"This program is sponsored by the makers of the Eversharp Shick Injector Razor, for reasons which are not quite clear to them, yet. As sponsors go, they're all right. No bargains I suppose. The only part of the program they don't like is the part in between the commercials. They're not too fond of the commercials, either. They don't think they're loud enough. Too bad about them. (Whispering) The Eversharp Shick Injector Razor and twenty blades is a dollar and a quarter. Now, if the Eversharp people don't bother me too much, next week I may do the commercial a little louder."

Side Two examines the frustrations of calling "Long Distance," satirizes "Commercial Copy Writers," and finds odd humor in "Daytime Radio for Burglars" and "Coming Attractions Theatre," promoting "*I Strangled My Brother-in-Law*. Produced by Adenoid Pictures, the Eyes, Ears, Nose, and Throat of the World."

- HERE'S MORGAN (Riverside RLP 8003) **1/2 $15 $30
- THE BEST OF HENRY MORGAN (Judson J 3016) **1/2 $12 $20
- THE SAINT AND THE SINNER (Offbeat OJ 3004) ** $10 $20

"Here's Morgan" is a ten-incher and "Best of" is full size. They're identical: a selection of the satirist's cynical lectures and silly monologues. In "The Truth about Cowboys" he enunciates his complaint:

"The average cowboy was a completely illiterate oaf. He didn't know how to read or write and his entire vocabulary consisted of about ninety-five words, of which thirty-two were Spanish as spoken by ignorant Mexicans. His job was to sit on a horse all day and stare at cows." Morgan goes on to describe cowboy food ("breakfast was some mud boiled in a rusty tomato can over a fire") and cowboy bathing habits: "You know from the movies, of course, that they wear black hats and black shirts. These originally were white." He concludes that the old-time cowboy was an "all time lummox who never heard a discouraging word." Unless he listened to this piece.

Other cuts include his familiar "Little Riding Hood Rouge" fairy tale, the esoteric "Googie Morgan on Baseball," "Dr. Heinrich von Morgan on Child Care," "The Russian Concert Commentator," and the cute and clever "Invention of Time."

The late '50s Offbeat album (also sans audience) has a few Morgan monologues interrupted by singer Isobel Robbins and her handful of forgettable tunes. There are two arch and too droll dialect variations on "Little Red Riding Hood" (French and Russian), a pair of know-it-all lectures ("Hi-Fi" and "The Morgan-Tone System") plus a cynical and curmudgeonly discussion of cats. While at a friend's home, a cat climbed into his lap. Morgan's friend enthused "She likes you!" But Morgan doesn't believe it:

"Cats sit in laps because it's warm there. They don't care if it's you or the radiator, so it certainly was a compliment when the owner said the cat liked me. Who had this cat met that it was comparing me too? The maid? Another cat? Here's an animal which can't read, that hasn't been out of the house in God knows when, lives on free milk and garbage and this bum has an opinion? Two years old, doesn't have a cent. No clothes. Owns one rotten rubber ball. For big entertainment it scratches on the upholstery ... and this green-eyed impoverished snob likes me? Thanks a group."

NOTES: Morgan's "Russian Little Red Riding Hood" routine appears on Riverside's compilation album "How to Be Terribly Terribly Funny" (Riverside RLP 7516). He also contributes monologues to "Musically MAD" (see the *MAD Magazine* entry) and recorded a pair of double album sets for a spoken arts label called Listening Library. He reads *The World of Robert Benchley* (3316-7) and *The World of James Thurber* (3318-9).

HENRY MORGAN AND MASON ADAMS

- THE LEG OF LAUGHTER (Wellman HH001) ** $6 $12

An offbeat 1967 album that falls somewhere between comedy and standard spoken word, "The Leg of Laughter" features literary works acted out with a full cast and music. These include *The Crocodile* by Dostoyevsky (nearly twenty minutes), *The Heroism of Dr. Hallidonhill* by Villers de l'Isle-Adam, and a thirteen-minute version of Edgar Allan Poe's madhouse satire, *The System of Dr. Tarr and Professor Fether* that edits out some of the liveliest passages. A few brief segments use prose by Ambrose Bierce. Folksinger Will Holt sets Thomas Hardy (*The Ruined Maid*) and Victor Hugo (*Good Advice to Lovers*) to music. Some actors tend to get grandiose and overplay their parts, but the album is somewhat droll at best.

DON MORROW

- GRIMM'S HIP FAIRY TALES (Roulette R 25146) ** $7 $15

After Steve Allen's "Hip Fables," Don Morrow (later a quiz show host) came up with this album. One side is jazz instrumentals (including Doc Severinsen on trumpet.) The other offers "Like Hansel and Gretel," "Like the Shoemaker and the Elves," and "Like Rumpelstiltskin." Morrow narrates the stories, which are acted out by Ann Thomas, Joyce Gordon, Phil Kramer, and Herb Duncan. It might still draw a giggle from older beatniks. When a shoemaker has trouble coming up with new styles, his wife nags, "Listen, Dad, ya gotta kick this square habit. The locals don't dig your brown and blacks no more. They dig cool colors. Pink shoelaces and all that jazz!"

HARRY MORTON

- LOOK OUT FOR HARRY MORTON (United Artists UAL 4104) ** $5 $10

A middle-aged average "New Yawker," Morton tells anecdotal stories rather than jokes. He manages to stretch three practical joke anecdotes over an entire side of this early '60s album. One tale, covered by many and attributed to any number of comics, is about the times he alternately syphoned gasoline into and out of his neighbor's Volkswagen. The man can't figure out what's wrong with his car. First he's getting five hundred miles to a gallon, then one mile! Punch line: eventually the guy sells the car.

Morton tells anecdotes about Buddy Hackett, Harry Ritz, and Jan Murray along the way. These stories are really no different from those any old-style comic would've told while sitting on the couch opposite Jack Paar. In fact, they're not too different from listening to the anecdotes of a middle-aged relative. The stuff is amusing—if it's free on TV, or if the album doesn't cost more than a buck or two.

GENE MOSS

- DRACULA'S GREATEST HITS (RCA VICTOR LSP 2977) **1/2 $12 $25

The monster fad of the mid-60s was in full swing at the time of this 1964 release. Bobby "Boris" Pickett's "Monster Mash" had been a hit and TV sitcoms had taken a macabre turn with *The Addams Family* and *The Munsters*. The best part of Moss's album is the Jack Davis artwork on the front and back covers, collecting a variety of famous monsters and original demons.

Moss's Lugosi/Dracula imitation is acceptable at best; about on a par with Pickett's Karloff. Taking dead aim (dumb pun intended) on Pickett's hit, "Monster Bossa Nova" opens with the same bubbling chemical sound effect as "Monster Mash," along with similar monster grunts. Dracula insists that everybody is now doing the bossa nova. Most of the songs are at the kiddie level. Dracula shouts "Kowabunga!" on "Surf Monster" and there's plenty of Halloween corn in all the lyrics. "Oh Susanna" turns into "Oh Vampire," as Dracula cries: "Oh I come from Transylvania with a black cape and a hat. And every night when I go out I turn into a bat! Oh, Vampire, don't you cry for me. 'Cause I come from Transylvania. I'm Count Dracula, you see!"

The best parody is "I Want to Bite Your Hand." It's a Beatles collector's curio, one of the first parodies of a Beatles tune. Monster fans should dig it too, just for the twisted ambiance. The familiar opening guitar riff is intact, as Dracula stiffly declares, "Oh yeah I tell you something you may not understand. But I, a thirsty vampire, I want to bite your hand! Sure! I want to bite your hand. I want to bite your hand."

Horror fans, Jack Davis collectors, and a few stray Beatles fans would want it. But don't pay too high a price unless the album contains the "15 fan cards of your favorite monsters" tucked into the sleeve.

SAM MOSS

- I AM CURIOUS JEWISH (Earth ELPS 1003) * $4 $8
- JEWISH CONNECTION PART II (No Holds Barred 30) * $4 $8
- SAM MOSS LIVE (No Holds Barred Records PLP 29) * $4 $8

Imagine Myron Cohen taking three or four minutes to tell very old and very boring sex jokes. That's Sam Moss, who uses dialect to belabor some already dying wheezes. Like the "Pope" joke. The Pope must have sex in order to help his prostate condition. There's four minutes of absolutely agonizing build-up as the Pope and his doctor share their concern. Finally the Pope agrees to do this abominable act with a lady. But first he asks, "She's gonna have big tits?"

Of course, even old jokes are new to people who haven't heard them, and Cheech and Chong dared to tell this very same joke, but on these 1970s LPs, Moss pounds them into the ground under the weight of heavy padding.

ZERO MOSTEL

- SONGS MY MOTHER NEVER SANG (Vanguard VRS 9229) *** $7 $15

Though Groucho Marx was a big fan of songwriter Harry Ruby, it was Zero Mostel who did a full LP of Ruby's whimsical tunes, including the Groucho favorite "Show Me a Rose."

Mostel's bombastic and bellowy renditions work excellently on some of the fast, Allan Shermanesque numbers. "Fight on for Tannenbaum" is a ridiculous fight song for a ridiculous college. "God Bless Everything in the U.S.A." is a recitation of every state in the union, with horrible rhymes along the way ("the morning dew sets on Vermont and Massachusetts"). The bouncy, vaudevillian "I Was an Incubator Baby and She Was the Girl Next Door" is fun and so is the epic nightmare "My Dream of the South of France."

The slower tunes don't quite work with Zero's dying walrus delivery. Groucho left his indelible stamp on the gently ironic "Father's Day," and the gloriously inane "Show Me a Rose" ("Show me a rose I'll show you a girl named Sam.... Show me a rose or leave me alone...."). Rub fans will still be happy to hear "My Love Is Waiting," "Hold Me Thusly," and the eight and a half minute operetta, "He's Not an Aristocrat." The album notes for this 1966 album are by Dorothy Parker.

THE MOVEMENT

- THE EARTHY SIDE (Pip 6804) **1/2 $5 $10

The anonymous group of roués here go under the title "The Movement to Preserve Scatalogical and Prurient Material in Its Original Form." The album collects classic bawdy songs and some jokes ascribed to such upstanding citizens as Abe Lincoln, Ben Franklin, Eugene Field, and Rudyard Kipling. To make sure that this celebration bears the "redeeming social value" tag, there are copious notes by Studs Terkel.

There's no need to be concerned about the sex gags here. The men vocalize with the same enthusiasm—and sensuality—as the group that used to sing the theme from *Davy Crockett* or *Zorro* on the old Disney TV series. And the ancient ribaldry is pretty dusty: "Here's to the game of twenty toes. It's played all over town. The girls play it with ten toes up, the boys with ten toes down!"

Terkel mentions that the main singer, a bass baritone, is also a soloist in churches. He's the best of the lot. There's some comical contrast when a deep and pious voice belts out the following: "Last night, I stayed up late to masturbate. It felt so nice. I did it twice!"

MARTIN MULL

- IN THE SOOP WITH MARTIN MULL (Vanguard VSD 79338) ** $5 $10
- MARTIN MULL (Capricorn CP 0106) *** $5 $10

These days Mull is better known as a comic actor on sitcoms (*Roseanne*) and in films, as a talk show raconteur, and perhaps for his books and cable TV specials on "White People in America." But in the late '60s, and through the '70s, he sang odd songs that were too goofy to win over Randy Newman fans, and too sophisticated for the Ray Stevens crowd.

The Vanguard album is a group effort. Mull wrote some of the cuts but doesn't sing them. Les Daniels was the main vocalist for "The Soop." Most of the songs are routine folk fare presented with sloppy, unsynchronized vocals that obscure the lyrics. Only a few have moments of wistful semi-satire. The only real portent of things to come is "Margie the Midget" (which is on Mull's first "real" album anyway) and the mildly bizarre and fairly pointless "Tuna Fish Salad" ("a latest craze is mayonaisse, it's guaranteed to stone ya").

Mull's solo debut in 1972 offers a low-key but looney mix of redneck Southern balladry, Latin ballroom dance music, jive, and wry Randy Newman-esque satire. "Ventriloquist Love" is as tender as a bunion, a wistful ballad about a love affair that didn't quite make it. Mull's lady ventriloquist prefers her dummy Charlie McNutt: "Ventriloquist love. It ain't such a groove. Whenever I kiss you your lips never move." Similarly afflicted is the fellow who goes out with "Margie the Midget," but he deals with it better. He goes "walking hand and ankle" with "her arm around my sock." After all, "She makes me feel about eleven feet tall. Heaven looks after the folks that are small." Other key cuts: "Dancing in the Nude," "I Made Love to You in a Former Life," and "Loser's Samba."

- MARTIN MULL AND HIS FABULOUS FURNITURE (Capricorn CP 0117) **1/2 $6 $12
- NORMAL (Capricorn CP 0126) *** $5 $10
- DAYS OF WINE AND NEUROSIS (Capricorn CPN 0155) **1/2 $5 $10
- NO HITS FOUR ERRORS (Capricorn CPN 0195) *** $4 $8

"Fabulous Furniture" is a live album and the between-song patter veers between homespun, deadpan, sneakily snide, and poisonously hip. Add these traits to a peculiar assortment of tunes and it's no wonder this album didn't take off, despite the novelty number "Dueling Tubas," a liver-churning version of "Dueling Banjos." There's "Licks

Off of Records," his tribute to guitarists who swipe classic riffs that still make the girls get "all warm and runny"; and the homely country ballad "How Could I Not Miss a Girl Your Size."

"Normal" is full of hummable songs about humdrum life, like "The Woodstock Samba," "Wood Shop," and his report on travel, "(I'm in) Rome and Bored." But for those who find Mull terminally subtle, there are some sharper shots. "Jesus Christ Football Star" imagines Jesus as a football hero: "So let's get Jesus Christ a football, let him even up the score. Let him run it through the crossbars and be on the cross no more." Almost as offensive is "The Blacks are Giving Me the Blues," a genially jerkish report on the plight of poor, white bread, middle-class Martin: "I never lived in no ghetto, carvin' people up in the night. That makes me think of Gepetto. That oughta prove that I'm white.... I'm just another white human tryin' to sing like the spades. It makes me sound like Randy Newman accordin' to the newsprint trades."

"Days of Wine and Neurosis" is a great title, but the album is a soporific selection of slow jazz and mild country rock. The liveliest cut is the semi-blasphemous "Jesus Is Easy." After he's tried everything from drugs to natural foods, Martin asserts, "I tried women, oh, how I tried ... I tried a poodle and a collie, Kukla Fran and Ollie, but Mary in a manger got me satisfied." Mull is amusing with the silly "Noses Run in My Family" ("nose sense cryin' over noses, let's pretend we're Eskimoses") and manages some stark satire in "Laundromat Blues," an unsympathetic look at a self-pitying lovelorn young lady: "She's at the laundromat washing out some sheets she hopes to use ... on a nice young man in thirty dollar shoes ... who'll help her count her troubles all by two's ... a guy who'll stay behind her during periods and flus and never touch a single drop of booze."

"No Hits Four Errors" is a greatest song package, the title referring to his four album tenure with Capricorn.

- I'M EVERYONE I'VE EVER LOVED (ABC AB 997) ** $5 $10
- SEX AND VIOLINS (ABC AA 1064) ** $5 $10

"Loved" is an unexceptional release, hardly an auspicious debut for a new record label. He has covered drunks, gospel music, and his own egotism better elsewhere. When the subject is sex, it's hard to be dull, so the best cuts are "The Humming Song" and "Men." In the former, Mull lightly hums over the naughty parts, so as not to offend "the squeamish." The resulting innuendo is smutty and/or funny: "hmmmmmm, pick up the soap. Hmmmm mayonnaise and rope."

"Men," bearing a resemblance to Monty Python's hearty singalongs, is about a group of stalwart sailors who chant aboard ship, happy there are no women around so they can keep the toilet seat up. The guys lustily chorus with: "Men can sweat and men can stink and no one seems to care-o, We'll throw the dishes in the sink and clog the drain with hair-o." It was cowritten with Steve Martin.

Between the songs there's some dull running dialogue, including Rob Reiner as a record exec questioning Martin's material. Billy Crystal, as Howard Cosell, introduces the album. Fans of Tom Waits, Ed Begley, Jr., Melissa Manchester, Libby Titus, Richard Tee, and Alice Playten will have to strain their ears to hear them singing and playing along on various cuts.

Mull's 1978 follow-up is his most contemplative album, loaded with lame songs about mundane lifestyles. On "Cleveland Revisited" Mull sings to an ex-love, "You've been through changes. Paris, France, and Mexico. Shortened all your dresses 'till your panties almost show." Then he realizes the years haven't been kind to him, either: "I'm in the city selling radios for Sears." "A Half Hour of Heaven" is also bittersweet, about love and sex: "They wake the next morning, he says, 'Who are you?' She looks at herself and she, too, wonders 'Who?'" The only track that tries to be hilarious is the nonsensical "Westward Ho!" written by Mull and Steve Martin, and loaded with *Blazing Saddles*-style fervor: "We eat our lunch, we shoot our meals, Grandpa's caught in the wagon wheels! See him as he spins around. Well, damn his ass, he's slowin' us down!"

- PERFECT/NEAR PERFECT (Elektra 6E 200) **1/2 $6 $12

Mull's final vinyl, released in 1979, is a return to live recording. He gets some giggles from between-song patter: "I'm wrapped up in that lawsuit. Isn't that unbelievable? My mother is suing me claiming we lived together for eighteen years even though we weren't man and wife...."

"Pig in a Blanket" is a good old-fashioned homely Mull country song about a good old boy making do with a beastly pick-up. He "drank enough till she looked good to me," though he pays the penalty. He knows that "you'd be much better off to just go home and yank it, but here I am, man and wife with a pig in a blanket."

On the other side there's "It's All Behind Me Now," a frank swing ballad about a loser at love who ruefully admits to his lady, "I've been an asshole over you." Not subtle, but it certainly makes its point.

The album lives up to Martin's opening line: "It's really a borderline thrill being here."

EDDIE MURPHY

- EDDIE MURPHY (Columbia FC 38180) **1/2 $8
- EDDIE MURPHY: COMEDIAN (Columbia FC 39005) ** $5 $10

Murphy's first album was recorded in 1982 at the height of his success on *Saturday Night Live*. It's not that much fun now. The crowd is so manic and euphoric that Eddie doesn't have to say much to excite them. Still, much of the first album is exactly what Murphy's comedy was all about: good-time put-ons and "life of the party" ad-libs. Like the class clown or the street corner cut-up, he did recognition humor imitating his friends. One could imagine most any street corner fool regaling his pals with this Murphy observation on Asians: "You know who got little tiny dicks? Chinese people. True. They got them little tiny rice dicks. That's why they be squintin' all the time, they be in the bathroom goin', 'I can't find it! I can't find it!' And the wife be goin', 'I can't see it either, you sure you got a dick?' Yeah, their dicks are small. But they work ... just tiny."

The Richard Pryor influence is still around. On a black Secret Service man, the only one who didn't try to protect President Reagan from assasination: "Fuck that shit, shootin' guns and shit, hey man, fuck that, they shot Ron, well shit man, fuck it! I'll just have to get a job in my cousin's cleaners then." Even here, where he falls into Pryor's rhythms, Murphy's attitude is lighthearted. One can almost see the good-natured smile on his face. The result is an album of material difficult to like from a comedian difficult to dislike.

"Comedian" was recorded in August of 1983 on Murphy's sold-out "Delerious Tour." Reflecting the pressures of fame and touring, as well as his anger over his limitations on *Saturday Night Live*, he's not quite his cheerful self. He opens the show announcing, "Old people that get offended easily, ya'll should just get the fuck out now!" The audience bursts into applause. "I do some nasty shit while I'm up here, and if you brought your kids down and thought I'd be up here with the Buckwheat wig on ... I don't do none of that *Saturday Night Live* shit in concert. If you want to see that shit, watch it at home for free."

The reason it's not on CD is probably his notorious anti-gay riffs: "Faggots are not allowed to look at my ass while I'm onstage. That's why I keep movin' while I'm up here ... I'm afraid of gay people. Petrified." After this kind of material, gay activists demanded a boycott of Murphy's shows.

The two better routines here, his imitation of kids dancing around because they see an ice cream truck, and his report on his shoe-throwing disciplinary mother, are better seen than heard.

NOTES: Murphy made two straight music albums when he was hot, "How Could It Be" and "So Happy" (both for Columbia) and another when he wasn't (1993's "Love's Alright" for Motown).

ROBERT MURPHY

* MURPHY'S GREATEST BITS (Q Q101-83) ** $5 $10

The morning man on WKQX-FM in Chicago, Robert Murphy offers the standard DJ schtick (phone calls and gag announcements), but isn't quite as obnoxious as the average drive-time jock. Locals will laugh more than out-of-towners. For example, the references in the mock soap opera "The Young and the Impotent," which is about "the lives and loves of Herb and Norma Finster of Buffalo Grove ... The wages of sin are high. And on Rush Street they're almost exorbitant. Try North Avenue for a better bargain. As our story unfolds this morning, the Finster children ... are in the Farkle family bathtub looking for new ways to make bubbles. Herb is listening to his favorite song, 'I've Grown Accustomed to My Fist,' as Norma heads toward the Finster family front door....'

KEN MURRAY

* KEN MURRAY'S BLACKOUTS (Mark 56 #701) * $4 $8

A vaudeville comedian, Murray staged his "Blackouts" reviews in the '40s and was a TV personality in the '50s known primarily for his home movies of celebrity pals. Murray isn't very impressive here, coming off as a mumbling, stumbling, half-baked Milton Berle. Here, with busty Marie Wilson, is a sample of his brand of unsnappy patter:

"You look beautiful tonight. You're not in that dress too far? Huh huh huh ... Where you were born?"

"Anaheim ... in a grapefruit grove."

"You were born in a grapefruit grove? Huh huh huh, that explains a couple of things anyway...."

"You really like my dress?"

"It's beautiful, it brings out your eyes, heh heh heh ... you're spitting all over me now Marie. I told you not to get those teeth through the mail. Ha ha ha. That's the only thing that's false. Ha ha ha. Huh huh huh. Ha ha ha ... (Taps microphone) Is this thing on?"

JOHN MUSACHA

* THE MUSACHA TAPES (Detonator 318242) *1/2 $7

Musacha's 1994 CD of abusive phone calls are pretty tiresome, with more cursing than comedy. Or as one annoyed recipient says, "Do you have something better to do than bother me?"

Typical of the misguided antics is when Musacha starts a crank call and then in the middle pretends to beat his wife. Then he tells the bewildered caller, "I just hit this bitch, she's out cold on the floor, and I don't know if she's gettin' up. I don't know what the fuck to do."

He's told: "Call the police and take care of your marriage...." "Listen, you were on the phone, you heard what the fuck was goin' on...."

"Call the police. I'm not going to be involved. Goodbye."

If only somebody at the record company had uttered that last line to Musacha.

MYERS AND CASS

* GO TO BLAZES (Elektra EKL 199) ** $7 $15

The idea of Tom Lehrer crossed with Noel Coward might sound intriguing, but British duo Peter Myers and Ronnie Cass are disappointing. To some forgettable Cowardian cocktail piano tunes, the bespectacled, tuxedo-wearing duo attempt lyrics a la Lehrer.

"Soho Notice Board," is about the ads prostitutes used to place semi-legally in London. While Tom Lehrer would've relished reporting all the smut, the duo stay safe and dull: "And here's a little cry for help, from somebody called Sadie. It says 'Urgent, Wanted Lyle Street flat to suit a business lady' ... and here's one here like a treasure hunt. It only gives a clue. It just says 'Delia moved to Kissold, 4-5- 7-2.' Now I often stand a 'wondering, just what does Delia do? How I love that little Soho notice board."

The duo come close to wit with "Apartheid," but it's still hopelessly hamfisted. Here, "Apartheid" is a dance: "The Apartheid, it's easy to do. You just kick the native who's nearest to you ... and if he does not keep quiet, shoot him in the back, Jack. That's a riot.... Apartheid, the dance that is bright, it's the one where two blacks never make a white."

The duo, who evidently successfully staged several West End revues, are at their brief best on "Reich Pudding." Just fifteen years after the end of World War II, England's government acceded to Germany's request to use British land for war exercises. In German accents they sing: "Ve are shocked dat ve are being maligned in de news! Ve couldn't be more liberal in our views. Two things ve can't stand: racial prejudice! And Jews!" They conclude with a splash of acid: "We hold out our hands in friendship today. The past is forgotten, so let's all be gay! Fifteen million war dead are shouting hooray. As we occupy Britain at last! Zeig heil!"

JIM NABORS

- SHAZAM! GOMER PYLE USMC (Columbia CL 2368) ** $5 $10

Nabors issued three dozen music albums (many unintentionally funny) featuring gooey, semi-operatic renditions of pop tunes of the day. Finally he issued a corny country disc using the dimwitted voice of his Mayberry, North Carolina, character Gomer Pyle. Fans of *The Andy Griffith Show* and the spin-off *Gomer Pyle USMC* finally get to hear Nabors tackle whimsical Roger Miller material ("You Can't Roller Skate in a Buffalo Herd" and "Reincarnation") as well as similar dopey originals ("Shazam!" and "Gomer Seys Hey!").

J. CARROLL NAISH

- LIFE WITH LUIGI (Radiola #15) ** $5 $10

Veteran character actor J. Carroll Naish was the star of *Life with Luigi*, the radio series about an Italian immigrant living in Chicago. Fans will be happy to hear the very first episode of the show (broadcast September 21, 1948) on this album. The flip side is an episode of *The Aldrich Family*.

Here's Luigi writing a letter home: "Dear Mama Mia, I make a promise to write you, so I write. In United States when a fellow promise to write, it's called a promisary note. In six months since I been in America my writing is already so good words don't even have Italian accent. I have a store here in Chicago just like two other businessmen, Marshall and Field. They got a same kinda store, only better location ... my line business. Old and young antiques. Everybody here is crazy for old things. Old furniture, old lamps, old chairs. Also is lots of people crazy for Old Grandad. Must be a fine man."

THE NAKED MICROPHONE

- THE NAKED MICROPHONE (Radiola MR 1163) ** $4 $8

An hour of bloopers is a bit too much, but at least they're all authentic, not re-enacted like many of the Kermit Schafer albums. Often there isn't much humor to the mistake, like the announcer who says, "Our thought for the day: he is the rich man who can avail himself of all men's facilities. That isn't quite right."

A few celebrity moments brighten the tedium, including Bing Crosby fluffing a line and declaring "my bridge is bothering me," Virginia Graham in a helpless laughing fit, and Lowell Thomas: "President Eisenhower today visited the chocolate city, Hershey, Pennsylvania ... thirty thousand or more people were cheering him, all the people who make Hershey chocolate, with or without nuts."

NINO NANNI

- PARTY MOOD (Stereoddities MN1) *1/2 $3 $8

Nanni told long bawdy stories and played semi-sophisticated songs on the piano. His brand of suave often comes across as oily thanks to his oozing low voice and maitre d's sense of class: "I like a firmly molded bust as well as the next man. But not those marble busts in the Louvre. Oh no. I like the kind that *move*."

There aren't many big laughs as Nino stumbles (but in polished shoes) toward the direction of Dwight Fiske (recitations underscored by piano chords and trills). The lyrical wit: "A married man in Iceland has a lot of wear and tear. You see, a night lasts six months up there!" He also released the straight jazz album "Chic to Chic" for Carlton.

NAPOLEON XIV

- THEY'RE COMING TO TAKE ME AWAY HA HAAA
  (Warner Bros. WS 1661 reissued as Rhino RNLP 816) **1/2 $10 $25
- CD reissue THE SECOND COMING, Rhino R2 72402 $8

In the summer of 1966, Jerry Samuels scored a hit with the literally insane novelty tune "They're Coming to Take Me Away." To a relentless, marching drum beat he sings about the degeneration of brain into cabbage. It reaches a siren-wailing crescendo on the chorus when he realizes, "They're coming to take me away, ha ha, they're coming to take me away ho ho, hee hee, haah haah, to the happy home with trees and flowers and chirping birds."

The song was banned on many radio stations. The lyrics, after all, are not exactly a laugh riot: "Remember when you ran away and I got on my knees and begged you not to leave because I'd go berserk? Well! You left me anyhow and then the days got worse and worse and now you see I've gone completely out of my mind." The humor is in the record's intensity, the speeded up vocals, and methodic march into madness.

A quickie cash-in album had such tunes as "Bats in My Belfry," "Doin' the Napoleon," and "Marching Off to Bedlam." They were saved to some extent by Samuels's production, including sound effects and jarring percussion. "I Live in a Split Level Head" is a rap record for psychopaths as the nonsense lyrics assail the listener from the left channel and right channel—and not in synch. "The Place Where the Nuts Hunt the Squirrels" is one sequel to "They're Coming to Take Me Away," using the same percussion. A third sequel, "I'm Happy They Took You Away, Ha Haah," has Josephine XV (Bryna Raeburn) declaring: "Remember when I ran away, and you got on your knees and begged me not to leave because you'd go berserk? Well, you thought you had me fooled, but I just left you anyhow because I knew you were already out of your mind!"

The 1996 "The Second Coming" is a reissue with grim album notes by Samuels describing his financial arrangements with Warners, the (humorless) intensity that drove him to create his exercise in speeded-up vocals, his disdain for fame, and his peculiar career choices, ranging from inventing and selling roach clips to his vocation over the years, singing pop tunes in retirement homes. Proof of his "one shot wonder" status are not only the original album's tracks, but the bonus cuts, including a few from an abandoned 1968 sequel album. One, "The Explorer," is a predictable aural cartoon, a few minutes of heavy breathing. Also disappointing is his 1990 single, "They're Coming to Get Me Again, Ha-Haa," with barely-updated lyrics and an inferior copy of the original's drum pattern. The 1995 tracks he has thrown in, sung a capella in a deliberately strained "zany" voice, will try any listener's patience. Samuels's annotation has nothing about insanity, betrayal, or other aspects of his hit single beyond his manic need to experiment with speeded-up vocals. It's sad to conclude from these notes that the madness behind that 1966 single was evidently just a recording engineer's perfectionism and he had no clue how to do it again.

Some collectors pay big bucks for the original Warners album, but they'd have to be crazy, now that the CD is around. Neither vinyl version has the original flip side to the single: "They're Coming to Take Me Away" played backward. It's on the CD, unlisted. It's the last track (#21). Thanks to that insane beat, even backwards "They're Coming To Take Me Away" is a winner.

OGDEN NASH

- EVERYBODY KNOWS THE TROUBLE I'VE SEEN (RCA Victor VDM 114) ** $5 $10
- FANCIFUL WORLD OF OGDEN NASH (Capitol SW 1570) ** $5 $10

Nash, once the nation's foremost humorous poet, is woefully dated, his rhymes preoccupied with the most ridiculous trifles of modern life.

Most of his albums fall into the "spoken arts" category, not the comedy bin. These include Caedmon titles "Parents Keep Out," "Reflections on a Wicked World," "Ogden Nash Reads Ogden Nash," and "Christmas with Ogden Nash." The Capitol album (very much a mainstream release) offers Nash, with background music, on such topics as ladies taking too much time before they go out for the evening; wearing eye shades and vaporizers and electric blankets to bed; the irritating way women open packages of cigarettes; and talking French in a French restaurant.

The material isn't helped by Nash's dry New England accent. Like S. J. Perelman, he pronounces "first" "foost" and he too is so erudite, everything he says comes out an impotent whine. Some of the better cuts, demonstrating both Nash's wit and whimsy, include his cheeky but heartfelt attack on boors and babblers at a "Wednesday Matinee," and the quickie "Termite," where he recites:

"Some primal termite knocked on wood, and tasted it and found it good. And that is why your Cousin Mae fell through the parlor floor today."

Slightly more painful is "The Panther":

"The panther is like a leopard except it hasn't been peppered. Should you behold a panther, crouch. Be prepared to say ouch. Better yet, if called by a panther, don't anther."

RCA's 1967 album, "Everybody Knows the Trouble I've Seen," doesn't have any music. Nash favors more recent material, including "I Never Even Suggested It," "You'll Drink Your Orange Juice and Like It," "A Man Can Complain Can't He" and "Tune for an Ill-Tempered Clavichord." There are even limericks delivered with his dainty drawl:

A handsome young rodent named Grayson

As a lifeguard became a sensation

All the lady mice waved

And screamed to be saved

By his mouse to mouse resuscitation.

THE NATIONAL IDIOTS

- DR. ROOSE (The Riot Company RT-10069) * $4 $8

The cover photo shows a guy in a badly fitting bright orange wig holding a phone in one hand and a banana in the other. That's a clue to the level of sophistication on this porn-dominated parody of Dr. Ruth Westheimer. Dr. Roose takes calls from freaks:

"Hello?" "Hello, this is Wanda the Whore." "You mean you're a prostitute?" "Yes ... I make a lot more money than you're making." "You probably are, hee-hee-hee!" "I listen to your show all the time.... Well, doctor, I can't suck...." "You choke on it? You gag ... Go and get yourself a cucumber or a banana or a sausage or something.... Put it in your mouth ... you'll get it ... don't be scared of it, that is the problem, most girls are scared of it ... don't be afraid, it's only going to spit at you. Hee-hee-hee!" "Oh this is fun. I love it. I love it! Thank you, doctor, thank you...."

NATIONAL LAMPOON

- RADIO DINNER (Banana/Blue Thumb BTS 38) *** $8 $15
- LEMMINGS (Banana/Blue Thumb BTS 6006) *** $8 $15
- GREATEST HITS OF THE NATIONAL LAMPOON (Visa 7008) **1/2 $5 $10

The *National Lampoon* magazine was started in 1970 under the supervision of Tony Hendra and Michael O'Dono-ghue. In its first years it was not only the prime humor magazine for adults, but it launched the careers of many fine comedy writers and artists. By 1972 the editors branched out with O'Donoghue supervising the *National Lampoon Radio Hour* and Hendra producing the live production of *Lemmings*. By the '80s, all the creative forces had departed. Editorial changes turned the magazine into a ratty, witless mess.

1972's "Radio Dinner" has several classics. Tony Hendra's words of wisdom for the age, "Deteriorata," parody the new age narrative *Desiderata*. Jackson Beck reads: "You are a fluke of the universe, you have no right to be here. And whether you can hear it or not, the universe is laughing behind your back." Christopher Guest plays Bob Dylan announcing a cheap mail order album of hits from "Those Fabulous Sixties," and the entire cast participates in the quiz show *Catch It and You Keep It*, in which wonderful, weighty prizes are tossed out of windows toward gleeful contestants. Firesign Theater was an influence on the patchwork collage of quickies, commercials, and sketches. The style has since been used by *Saturday Night Live* and many other programs, but at the time, "Radio Dinner" seemed very fresh, not only in humor but in concept.

The most astonishing cut on the record, "Magical Misery Tour," sung by Tony Hendra, dared to parody the public angst and primal screaming of John Lennon, and did it brilliantly. In fact, it manages to both satirize and celebrate Lennon, who could have easily sung the chorus "Genius Is Pain."

On "Lemmings," a Woodstock parody, the players once more dared to skewer the popular heroes of its audience and to cruelly parody the audience itself (the lemmings). John Belushi is the emcee who reports the uplifting news of suicidal behavior, drug freakouts, and deaths at the festival: "We all know why we came here. A million of us. To off ourselves ... if your buddy's too stoned to off himself, roll him up in a sleeping bag and drag him over to where the tractors can run him over."

The musical cuts are deadly accurate, musically and vocally. Hippies are portrayed in the title cut (as supposedly performed by Crosby, Stills, Nash and Young) as "a mighty mass of furry little mindless animals." Their flower power slogan is twisted: "We will feed our flower habit pushing daisies." Peaceful and sensitive James Taylor, whose "Fire and Rain" was a campus favorite of the day, gets ripped to pieces by Christopher Guest ("shootin' up the highway on the road map of my wrists") and Bob Dylan, flirting with country music at the time, here sings about being "up to my knees in cowshit, shovelin' my blues away." Richie Havens, Leon Russell, and Joe Cocker get theirs too, before the album ends with "Megadeath," and the lines "Living is a bummer, dying is a high."

"Greatest" relies mostly on these first two albums (including "Deteriorata," "Those Fabulous Sixties," and "Magical Misery Tour") with some very weak selections from their other discs.

- THE WHITE HOUSE TAPES (Banana/Blue Thumb BTS 6008) ** $5 $10
- GOLD TURKEY (Epic PE 33410) ** $5 $10
- GOODBYE POP (Epic PE 33956) ** $5 $10

In 1974 the *National Lampoon* troup gleefully joined the throng of comics cashing in on the trashing of Richard Nixon. Chevy Chase is featured in the Watergate Parody, which includes a version of the opening to *Mission Impossible*, now called "Mission Impeachable":

"Good morning Mr. Hunt. Several high ranking members of the Democratic Party are attempting to seize control of the government of the United States by legitimate means ... should they succeed all our efforts to repeal the Bill of Rights, intimidate the media, pack the Supreme Court with right wing morons, suppress dissent, halt social progress, promote big business, and crush the Congress will be destroyed. Your mission, E, should you choose to accept it, is to stop these men, once and for all ... you will have at your disposal electronic bugging equipment ... forged documents ... burglary tools ... five hundred loyal but clumsy Cubans.... As always, if any member of your CIA force is caught or killed, the President will disavow any knowledge of your activities. This administration will self-destruct in sixteen months."

"Gold Turkey" offers moments from the *National Lampoon*'s radio show. It's like listening to the audio of a meandering episode of *Saturday Night Live*. John Belushi, Chevy Chase, Brian Doyle-Murray, Gilda Radner, and Christopher Guest are involved in ho-hum cuts like "Terminal Football," "Front Row Center," "Flash Bazbo," "Mr. Veal Chop," "Hockey," and "The Trial." Christopher Guest sings a highlight, the "Well Intentioned Blues," about a guy who is truly liberal, wishing he was "a funky Negro" or "a wetback on a strike in a lettuce patch" or anything but white: "I wish I was an Indian, a grown-up Sioux papoose. So that when I get drunk on a beer and a half, I have a good excuse.... I sympathize with the Arab cause. I feel for the put-upon Jews. And I keep singing the middle-class-liberal-humanitarian-meaningful-dialogue-we-are-all-responsible-well-intentioned blues."

1975's "Goodbye Pop" is to formula, with sketches that become predictable after ten seconds. Bill Murray as an inane FM disc jockey is especially annoying and Paul Shaffer comes off more as a self-absorbed, pretentious, effem-inate babbler than any parody of that type. Gilda Radner lampoons feminist anthems with "I'm a Woman," and it'll please misogynists everywhere: "I'm free and up from under! Free to sing it right out loud!... I'm a woman! I'm a singer! I'm a sister!" The best song is "Southern California Brings Me Down," a superb roasting of Neil Young by Tony Scheuren. Picking up on the sensitive-but-sexist lyrics of "A Man Needs a Maid," in which Young sang about needing "someone to keep my house clean, fix my meals and go away," the new lines have him wanting "someone to live with me. To keep my bed warm. And keep my shorts clean." The humor is in recognizing the references to Young's old songs ("I gotta love you all I can—before I become an old man") and old album covers ("I need a maid to give for free. And sew patches on my jeans"). At this point, not many would want a 1977 album parodying a 1972 Neil Young tune.

- THAT'S NOT FUNNY THAT'S SICK (Label 21 IMP 2001) *1/2 $5 $10
- WHITE ALBUM (Label 21 IMP 2002) * $5 $10
- SEX, DRUGS, ROCK AND ROLL AND THE END OF THE WORLD (Passport PB 6018) * $5 $10

National Lampoon's final albums, through 1982, sink lower and lower into obviousness and obnoxiousness. In sketch after sketch, the players aggressively babble, squeal, and shout, impersonating any number of annoying geeks, yuppies, bozos, and nerds—without the humorous skills needed to parody them.

Perhaps there is someone out there who will laugh hearing the "White Album"'s radio commercial for "California Hot Tub Rectal Gonorrhea ... love hurts ... I'm talking about California Hot Tub Rectal Gonorrhea. This painful, incurable disease can make an enjoyable soak in a hot tub with family friends and dog into a literally unforgettable experience. If you catch California Hot Tub Rectal Gonorrhea, not only will you walk around feeling like you're about to pass a twisted sardine can lid, you'll also smell like a pile of burning tractor tires ... so don't jump out of the frying pan and into the hot tub, because if you get California Hot Tub Rectal Gonorrhea, it'll really burn your ass."

The "White Album"'s cast of known irritants includes Alice Playten, Rodger Bumpass, Michael Simmons, and Tia Brelis, along with brief appearances by Christopher Guest, John Belushi, and Chevy Chase.

"That's Not Funny, That's Sick" offers a better group: Brian Doyle-Murray, Bill Murray, and Christopher Guest, with cameos from Tony Hendra and Larraine Newman. Richard Belzer bores as an abrasive radio talk show host, and Bill Murray bares his soul visiting a confessional in a sketch that lives up to the album's title. The best part of the album is the Sam Gross cartoon cover.

The cover for 1982's "Sex, Drugs, Rock 'n' Roll ..." offers a semi-nude, but like the nudes in *Lampoon* magazines of the era, it can't perk up bad comedy. The cast includes Rodger Bumpass, Suzy Demeter, Barry Diamond, Mike Griffin, Tony Scheurin, and a brief appearance from Phil Proctor of Firesign Theater. Typical is this commercial: "Tonight's Colostomy Bag-Off with Celebrity Sidewinders Larry Flynt and George Wallace will not be seen tonight due to, oh, technical difficulties."

CHRISTINE NELSON

- DID'JA COME TO PLAY CARDS OR TALK? (Reprise 6209) ** $5 $15

Christine Nelson duetted with Allan Sherman on his song "Sarah Jackman." His "My Son the Folksinger" album was so hot, somebody figured Christine could score with a female version of it.

What spins on this "spin off" album are parody songs from the female point of view. Unfortunately, back in 1963, the female view was dreary: housewife grouses about the kids, driving a car badly, and playing cards with the girls. Nelson sings about Zelda, who gets headaches and leaves the card table when she's losing:

"Really I think she must be demented. She's got diseases they haven't invented. It's no wonder her hair is thinning. Every ache in the book she's got. But where does the pain go when Zelda is winning? She's healthy and wealthy when she wins a pot!" There are several more songs about card playing scattered throughout the disc.

A song about the typical female driver has lines like these: "If they would give out medals for mixing up the pedals I would have more than England's queen. Everyone on the road looks like they'll explode when I go on red and stop on green."

These obvious parodies scuttled Nelson's bid to be the female Allan Sherman. The opening cut, "Sarah Jackman," is attributed to Allan. It's just a new bunch of "Sarah Jackman" jingles. His part in the duet is taken by an anonymous woman: "Sarah Jackman, Sarah Jackman, how's by you? How's by you? How's by you your hubby?" "Getting bald and chubby." "He's nice too." "He's nice too." Other rhymes give us information about "pregnant Carol," "fatter than a barrel"; "Marvin Cooper," "he's a party pooper"; "Cousin Herschell," "very controversial"; and "Allan Sherman," "sings like Ethel Merman."

Nelson turns up in the cast of Len Weinrib's album "Have a Jewish Christmas" (Tower 5081).

BOB NEWHART

- THE BUTTON-DOWN MIND (Warner Bros. 1379, CD reissue 9456902) *** $8

An accountant whose hobby was performing comedy sketches on radio, George Robert Newhart became a star directly because of the comedy record boom in the late '50s. He was signed to Warners on the strength of some radio demo tapes, even though he'd never performed a live concert.

Newhart might be considered the link between the sick comics of 1958-1960 (Berman and Bruce) and the cute comics arriving in 1962-1964 (Allan Sherman, Bill Cosby, The Smothers Brothers).

Newhart was a deceptively satiric comedian with a sometimes grimly deadpan twist to his work (note "Ledge Psychology" on his second album). Yet, he performed with an "everyman" style so shy and self-effacing that even potentially dangerous pieces (his attack on smoking and smokers) went down sweetly. Unlike the manic "sickniks," Bob was deadpan. His phone call monologues and "nervous person" sketches seemed to put him in the same league as Shelley Berman, but he had none of Berman's angst. He never made the audience uncomfortable.

Ironically, he wasn't very comfortable himself on this first album. Stand-up was new to him, and performing live was an unpleasant chore. Here Newhart sets up each premise, presents it with an almost redundant "it would go something like this," and then does the bit. There's little patter with the audience between bits.

Some of Newhart's favorite "What if ..." devices are used here. What if people from the bygone era had to deal with modern pressures? (Abe Lincoln coached on a hard-sell "Gettysburg Address," The Wright Brothers urged to consider commercial flights). And there's the first of his "What if our ancestors had the cynicism of moderns" routines: Abner Doubleday told that baseball is a ridiculous game that will never catch on.

Newhart often played the part of an average fellow trying to hold on to his composure and normalcy under the most trying conditions. In one of his classics, "The Driving Instructor," Newhart shines in the part of the deadpan instructor quietly risking life and limb with that victim of perennial abuse in the '60s, "the female driver." A cliché now, but still amusing, Newhart counsels the woman as she makes wrong turns, backs up into traffic, and engages in a variety of miseries: "Now that was a wonderful turn ... one little thing. Uh, this is a one-way street. Well, now, now, it was partially my fault. You were in the left-hand lane, and you were signalling left, and I more or less assumed you were going to turn left.... You want to back out ... oh now we hit someone, Mrs. Webb. Remember you were going to watch the rearview mirror? The red light blinded you. The flashing red light blinded you? The flashing red light on the car you hit blinded you? Yes officer, she was just telling me about it."

- THE BUTTON-DOWN MIND STRIKES BACK (Warner Bros. 1393) ***1/2 $5 $10
- BOB NEWHART DELUXE EDITION (Warner Bros. SN/2NS1399) *** $8 $15
- BEST OF THE BUTTON-DOWN MIND (Murray Hill OP 25291393) *** $8 $15
- BEHIND THE BUTTON-DOWN MIND (Warner Bros. 1417) ** $5 $10

"Strikes Back," another 1960 best-seller, offers variations on some popular themes. Newhart has perfected his deadpan style and the deliberate use of a nervous stutter that later would actually be written into some of his TV scripts. He plays a grousing soldier annoyed at "Nutty George" Washington's illogical behavior (like throwing a dollar across the river) and a teacher at a bus driver school ("For homework tonight we're gonna mispronounce the names of streets"). There's more biting satire in "The Retirement Party," about an accountant who, slightly drunk, tells the gathered office workers, "I don't suppose it occurred to any of you that I had to get half-stoned every morning to come to this crummy job." His darkest humor appears on "Ledge Psychology." He plays a cop using a new theory on potential suicides: tease don't sympathize. "Thinking of jumping?" he nonchalantly asks the man on the ledge. "Your first time is it?" It's interesting that despite material like this, Newhart was so warmly greeted as a welcome reprieve from sick comedians. His "Grace L. Ferguson Airline" routine is not that different from "sick" airplane bits by Shelley Berman and Lenny Bruce: "If we should have to ditch, you'll receive plenty of warning, because our copilot becomes hysterical. And he'll—he'll start running up and down the aisles yelling, 'We're gonna crash.'"

In 1961 Warners issued Newhart's first two albums in a "deluxe" package complete with a souvenir booklet. Twenty years later, Murray Hill issued these two as a double album set, sans booklet.

The 1961 "Behind the Button-Down Mind" is a weak album, which is to be expected following two albums of prime material and a demand for still more. The album is dated with bits on TV commercials, Herb Philbrick, and a "Tourist Meets Khrushchev" in which a grinning fool asks the head of Russia to pose for snapshots: "Would you mind one with Little Bruce? Our eighteen-month-old son? Hand him to Nicky! Look at the face he's making! Isn't that beautiful? What's the matter? Oh Jeez, I'm sorry. Honey, you got a towel or something? Oh golly, well you know kids." The most successful bit is "The Uncle Freddie Show," with Newhart doing a good job utilizing a strained, high-pitched voice as the star of a kiddie show.

- THE BUTTON-DOWN MIND ON TV (Warner Bros. 1467) **** $8 $20
- BOB NEWHART FACES BOB NEWHART (Warner Bros. W 1517) **1/2 $8 $20

"TV," from 1962, features material used on Newhart's short-lived, Emmy-winning variety series. The infusion of a staff of comedy writers perked up Newhart's monology. The highlight is "Introducing Tobacco to Civilization," the best of his "what if" historical phone calls. He makes his satiric points gently as he plays the skeptic receiving a phone call from Sir Walter ("Nutty Walt") Raleigh, on the use for tobacco:

"You can chew it? Or put it in a pipe. Or you can shred it up and put it on a piece of paper, and roll it up! Don't tell me, Walt, don't tell me—you stick it in your ear, right Walt? Oh, between your lips! Then ... you set fire to it! Then what do you do, Walt? You inhale the smoke! Walt ... you're gonna have a tough time getting people to stick burning leaves in their mouth." Another classic is "Defusing a Bomb," in which a deadpan officer gets a call from a frantic patrolman. The officer asks, "You think that's unusual, finding a shell on the beach?" When told it's a bomb, he remains the model of muddle-headed bland efficiency in his efforts to defuse it. One of Bob's better Newhart sketches of embarrassment and discomfort is here as well, "A Friend with a Dog." He's the nervous guest pinned to the chair by a giant, vicious dog that is "perfectly harmless."

The next album is conversational, reflecting either Newhart's newfound comfort onstage, or his difficulty in creating new sketches. He talks about plane rides, his pet poodles, and his experiences as an expectant father. It's not powerful comedy, but it's fun listening, more like anecdotes related on a talk show: "If you're an expectant father you are the lowest form of life in a hospital. Even maintenance people will have nothing to do with you. People are running around with various assorted pans of one kind or another, with worried looks on their faces. I don't think they're nurses, they're just people hired to run around looking worried because it makes the father feel better."

- WINDMILLS ARE WEAKENING (Warner Bros. W 1588) *** $15 $25
- THIS IS IT (Warner Bros. W 1717) *** $10 $20

The rarest Newhart albums are his last two. Though not a strong album, a pair of cuts from "The Windmills Are Weakening" turn up on "The Best of Bob Newhart." "Returning a Gift" is a teeth-clenched study of an embarrassed man returning the toupee his wife got him. He has to explain, with great chagrin, how it fell off at a party and landed in the cheese dip. He's not happy—and the sketch isn't a laugh riot either. "King Kong" is typical of Newhart's sly satire of wimpy modern man. He imagines what would happen if a typical ineffective guard happened to be on duty the night King Kong climbed the Empire State Building. He calls his boss:

"Sir, I'm sure there's a rule against apes shaking the building. I yelled at his feet. I said, 'Shoo Ape, I'm sorry you'll have to leave, Sir.' I know how you like the new men to think on their feet, sir, so I went to the broom closet and I got a broom. Without signing out a requisition on it. I will tomorrow, yes, sir. And I hit him on the toes with it, but it didn't seem to bother him.... Did I try swatting him in the face with it? Well, I was going to take the elevator up to his head, sir, but my jurisdiction only extends to his navel."

Back before there was such a term as "wimp," Newhart was doing bits on the over-civilized timidity and impotence of modern men. Other cuts are mild and pleasant at best, including "Buying a House" (Newhart's monologue as a sleazy realtor who insists the sheet metal plant across the road doesn't make much noise), "Ben Franklin in Analysis," and "Edison's Most Famous Invention." "Superman and the Dry Cleaner" explains the premise (Superman loses his suit) and then goes on for nearly five minutes: "I brought it in this morning on one day service.... The cape is sort of a royal blue with white piping, and the leotards are kind of an off-blue. No, they're not my wife's, no. They're mine. I'm not married. What's that supposed to mean?"

"This Is It," aptly named, is also skimpy: barely ten minutes on one side, thirteen on the other. Newhart comes back to plane travel for humor, then an embarrassment sketch in which a guy walks into a topless bar and makes a shaky request for change: "uh, do you have a pair of nickels—two nickles for a dime!" There's a cute bit on the "Daddy of All Hangovers," a retelling of a classic old joke generally known as "P.S., your cat is dead," and the title track about a pair of prenatal twins waiting around to be born: "What time is it? Three thirty? Morning or afternoon? I can't tell the difference either. Boy, I got a cramp in my leg that's just drivin' me crazy. And where the hell does this cord go, do you know? I don't know, maybe we're electric! They both asleep? You sure? (Makes bashing sound.) Ha ha hah, she's gettin' him up! She said, 'The baby moved.' He's coming over to listen. Don't do anything when he comes over! That poor soul's a nervous wreck. Boy, ya forget the pill one night, it's bingo time!"

Whether Newhart intended it or not, the album follows that basic rule of show biz, "leave 'em wanting more."

- BEST OF BOB NEWHART (Warner Bros. W 1672) *** $5 $10
- VERY FUNNY BOB NEWHART (Harmony HS 11344) *** $5 $10
- GREATEST HITS (Curb-Pickwick PWKS 548) *** $8

"Best of" contains material from Newhart's first six albums, and is the only Newhart album to have remained constantly in print since its release. Cuts include Bob's classics "The Driving Instructor," "The Introduction of Tobacco," and "The U.S.S. Codfish," along with "Grace L. Ferguson Airlines," "King Kong," "Retirement Party," and "Returning a Gift." The Harmony album takes material from the later Newhart albums ("Amateur Show," "Nudist Camp," "Expectant Father," "The Man Who Looked Like Hitler," etc). The CD issued by Curb-Pickwick mixes lesser routines with the best: "The Driving Instructor," "The Introduction of Tobacco," "The U.S.S. Codfish," "Grace L. Ferguson Airlines," "Retirement Party," "Returning a Gift," and "Ledge Psychology."

NICHOLS AND MAY

- AN EVENING WITH NICHOLS AND MAY (Mercury OCM 2200) *** $10 $20

Mike Nichols and Elaine May met at the University of Chicago, where they joined the improvisational Compass Players, creating a dramatic style of comedy that was based more on character and motivation than snappy patter and gags. Their cerebral satire caught fire in New York and in 1960 they starred in their own Broadway show. Almost as quickly, the two restless talents decided to split up. Both went on to direct films. They've occasionally reteamed for charity events.

Four sketches from the team's Broadway show are presented. Two are lightweight and forgettable: a minor study of adultery and a bit about a name-dropping disc jockey. The other two throb with heavy, bruising satire.

"Mother and Son" was a pioneer in "Jewish Mother" comedy, a relentless look at the complete breakdown of a guilty, adult male into an obedient, utterly dependent child. Space technician Nichols has failed to call home, and he knows that supervising a rocket's blastoff is no excuse:

"I didn't have a second," he apologizes to his mother, "I could cut my throat. I was so busy."

His mother seizes on the guilt and rubs it in his face: "I sat by that phone all day Friday, all day Saturday, and all day Sunday ... your father said to me, 'Phyllis, eat something, you'll faint.' I said, 'No, Harry, no, I don't want my mouth to be full when my son calls me.'"

The call degenerates quickly into a tug of war between the independent son and the clinging, controlling mother. "Is it so hard to pick up a phone and call your mommy?"

The son's thin shell of adulthood flakes away. He crumbles, promising in a suddenly wavering and baby-like voice to call his mother: "I promise ... I love you Mommy." "Goodbye, baby."

There are few laughs here, just the grin produced by the chill of satire. Similarly, in "The Telephone," Nichols once more plays a modern man driven around in circles until he chokes. Having dropped his last dime in a pay phone, he's dependent on a cold, inhuman phone operator. (Elaine May's phone voice was later adapted by Lily Tomlin for her character "Ernestine.") Nichols tries his best, but the trap is set:

"Miss, try to understand what I'm saying, I'm speaking as one human being to another. Forget you're an operator—" "I'm a supervisor!" "Bell Telephone has stolen my dime! They stole it, dammit they stole it!" "... I'd be very happy to return your dime to you." "You will?" "Yes." "Thank you ... thank you...." "What is your name and address?"

"The Telephone" and "Mother and Son" represent the best of Nichols and May, along with the unreleased sketch they did about a distraught man arranging a funeral with a conniving saleswoman. It has occasionally turned up on bootleg albums.

- IMPROVISATIONS TO MUSIC (Mercury SR 60040) *** $15 $25
- NICHOLS AND MAY EXAMINE DOCTORS (Mercury MG 20680/SR 60680) *** $15 $25

Never was the term "painfully funny" better applied than to the work of Nichols and May. For "Improvisations" they went into the studio without a script and simply ad-libbed character comedy based on a prepared sentence or two: a dancing lesson, a first date, a therapist's session. Some of the improvs are just exercises and some are failures, including spies dealing with secret inane code words and a therapy session about toes, but there are some moments of aching satire on the human condition, especially as suffered by New York neurotics.

In "Bach to Bach" Mike and Elaine are two overly verbal intellectuals, frayed and afraid, coming up with thoughts that sound deep but echo shallow. Mike is so sensitive he can talk about "the ambivalence of the woman's role today."

Elaine adds, "Oh, it's incredibly ambivalent. It's so hard to resolve, it's so hard to acknowledge the fact that aggressiveness need not be hostile."

"No, Adler was no fool," Mike nods solemnly.

"No. I always thought of him as a fool, but he said some good things ... too many people think of Adler as a person who made mice neurotic. He was more, much more."

Later, Elaine listens to the music and offers another profound observation wrought from her overwrought psyche:

"There is always another dimension to music. And it's apart from life. I can never believe that Bartok died on Central Park West."

"Isn't that ugly?"

"Ugly, ugly, ugly!"

The album can't be recommended as pure comedy, despite the occasional archly satiric line: "I've taken a job as a dentist in a leper colony.... I think it's the right choice. There are good lepers and bad lepers. I don't think you can lump them together." It is, however, a challenging record, and one that influenced Lily Tomlin, Whoopi Goldberg, and others who put stark pathos into their work.

"Examine Doctors" features bits from the duo's NBC radio show *Monitor*. Because it was mainstream radio and they had to confine themselves to quick two-minute and three-minute bits, the material here is more accessible and milder than the long set pieces of the Broadway show or the grimly stark improvisations on their studio album.

A highlight is "A Little More Gauze," about a lovelorn doctor who refuses to sew up the patient until he gets an answer from his nurse: "I'm sick of this torture. I'm not gonna finish this operation until you say yes...." "Dr. Harris, this patient will die!" "I've been tortured long enough.... I don't care what lengths I go to anymore.... I will not go on with this operation until you give me your answer and it better be yes!" When the nurse capitulates, the doctor resumes the operation: "Clamp. *Darling.*"

The material here sounds frighteningly close to dialogue one might overhear in a hospital or consulting room. In fact, the sketches that don't work are the ones in which the team attempts something closer to Wayne and Shuster, like "Out of Africa," in which Elaine plays a pushy interviewer and Mike attempts a hokey German accent as Albert Schweitzer.

- BEST OF NICHOLS AND MAY (Mercury SR 60997) ** $10 $20
- RETROSPECT (Mercury SRM 2 628) *** $10 $30

Mercury has twice reissued the team's material. "Retrospect" is the one to hunt for, since it's a two-record set. Sides A and B offer the complete "Evening with Nichols and May." Side C takes four sketches from the "Doctors" album ("A Little More Gauze," "Morning Rounds," "Merry Christmas Doctor," and "Physical") and Side D clips four from "Improvisations to Music," including "Cocktail Piano," "Bach to Bach," "The Dentist," and "Nichols and May at Work."

"The Best of Nichols and May" has only one cut from "Evening with Nichols and May" ("Telephone"), two cuts from "Improvisations to Music" ("Cocktail Piano," "Bach to Bach"), and the rest from "Doctors" ("A Little More Gauze," "Physical," "The Dentist," "Merry Christmas Doctor," "Transference").

Without a "best of" CD, the '70s and '80s saw the three Nichols and May albums rise, but not high enough to dent the wallets of their affluent and intellectual fans. The 1996 reissue of "Retrospect" on one CD (CD: 314 532 373 2) has lowered the price and interest in the duo's vinyl, except for hardcore duo (and vinyl) fans.

976 GIRLS

- PHONEPHUCT (Dilligaf D00022) ** $8

These crank phone calls are from women—which makes things a bit more interesting than The Jerky Boys. The girls like cursing rants, which should titillate adolescent geeks, but sometimes there's a more elaborate practical joke. In the latter category, a girl calls up an escort service to get a job. She gets into a dizzy exchange with the dim madam. The madam speaks first:

"Are you black or white?" "I'm white. I've got red hair all the way down. Down there too, I'm naturally red." "Oh," the woman finally realizes, "you are a redhead!"

Evidently not really listening, the woman ignores the girl's description of herself as having "three teeth." So the girl puts her on with something weirder: "I only have one leg. Does that matter? It looks real. No one can tell the difference. It can come off and men really enjoy that...." "You mean a leg? You have only one leg? I see ... well, everything you're saying sounds very qualifying. We will consider, okay?" "You want me to come in for an audition?" "Well, not right at the time being."

THE NOCK-A-BOUTS

- THE TWO SIDES OF THE NOCK-A-BOUTS (Explosive E 1641) *1/2 $5 $8

Flo Dorsey teamed with Jimmy Clark for a comedy and music act circa 1958. One side is straight music, including "Malagueña," "Route 66," "Let the Rest of the World Go By" and others. On the flip side they mess around with various songs ("The Alley Cat") and, living up to their name, they knock about and yock about with risqué corn. In a bit called "Back Through History" they louse up the legend of Romeo and Juliet: "We would like to re-create—" "Is everybody happy?" "Ted Lewis, you're drunk! We'd like to re-create the balcony scene. It was one of those nights ... love is in the air, the birds are burpin'—heh heh—chirpin' and there she is, on the balcony. Sixteen years old." "Eighteen years old! I don't wanna get pinched! Eighteen...." "Romeo looks up to his Juliet ... and to his betrothed, says, 'What the hell do ya mean, yer pregnant???'"

After Dorsey and Clark parted, several albums appeared from the new team, Houston and Dorsey.

HATTIE NOEL

- THE WHOLE OF HATTIE NOEL (Dooto DTL 823) ** $8 $15
- THE BOLD HATTIE NOEL (Dooto DTL 825) ** $8 $15
- TICKLED SOUL (Dooto DTL 829) ** $8 $15
- LAFF OF THE PARTY (Dooto DTL 833) ** $5 $10

Hattie Noel first issued a few sexy singles ("Johnny's Hot Rod," "Hot Nuts," etc.) on Dootsie Williams's Blue Records label. She was his big female star, with male vocalist Billy Mitchell handling novelty tunes like "The Woodpecker Song" and "The Ice Man." When Dootsie started the Dooto comedy label, he collected Noel and Mitchell's singles for "Songs for Fun" (Dooto DTL 212).

Noel's subsequent albums offer monologue material. Noel sounds a bit like mumbly Moms Mabley. She doesn't have Moms's raw rasp, but she's in the same age bracket and just as difficult to understand.

Some of the old jokes have a little extra life thanks to Hattie's funky delivery, like the one from her "Laff of the Party" album about a lady anxious to find out what a Scotsman has under his kilt:

"She say, 'You know one thing I've always wanted to know, what was up under one of them things.' He said, 'Take a peek.' She jumped down, she took a look, she said, 'Oooooooo weeee! How gruesome!' He said, 'Take another look, it grew some more!'"

Noel may be best known to the general public for what she didn't do: get the part of Mammy in *Gone with the Wind*. Several documentaries on the making of the film include screen tests of various actresses vying for the part of Scarlett O'Hara; many of them testing with Hattie Noel as the maid.

KEN NORDINE

- WORD JAZZ (Dot 3075) $10 $20
- WORD JAZZ, VOLUME TWO (Dot 3301) $10 $25
- SON OF WORD JAZZ (Dot 3096) $10 $30
- BEST OF WORD JAZZ (Dot 25880) $10 $25
- MY BABY (Dot 3142) $10 $30
- NEXT! (Dot 3196) $10 $30
- GRANDSON OF WORD JAZZ (Snail 1003) $10 $20
- STARE WITH YOUR EARS (Snail 1001) $10 $20
- TWINK (Philips PHM 200258) $10 $20
- COLORS (Philips PHM 200224) $10 $20
- BEST OF WORD JAZZ (Rhino Word Beat RS 70773) $8

Nordine's albums are filed under comedy, spoken word, and even jazz. He was a hybrid of satirical studio comedy (a la Stan Freberg or Eddie Lawrence) and the "poetry in jazz" trend that mixed recitation, humor, and improv (listen to Lawrence Ferlinghetti and Kenneth Rexroth's "Poetry Readings in the Cellar").

The original 1957 "Word Jazz" album of bop fables, recitations, and experiments in sound include "The Sound Museum," where doors open to reveal abstract "sound paintings," some of them strange and interesting noises, others spooky and quiet. Fred Katz (best known these days for the quirky jazz score he composed for the original *Little Shop of Horrors* film), supplies the music. "What Time Is It?" raises smiles more than laughs as a *Twilight Zone*-ish story of "a regular guy, who lived a regular life. Got up 7:30 every morning. Same breakfast. Kissed the same wife goodbye every morning, went to the same office," only to become insanely obsessed with time. After practice, "he realized he knew what time it was without even looking. Not only in the important cities of this world, but in the entire universe."

The later albums vary in the amount of humor and just plain oddness. "Colors" is indeed mini-riffs on colors, backed by simple jazz. They're odd and cool more than funny or profound.

Like his contemporary Jean Shepherd and later practitioners of audio oddity (Firesign Theater), Nordine operates within his own world and his own cult. Those who put needle to the groove can sit, nod, muse, and smile; others will not get it at all.

Nordine continued on, releasing sporadic albums like 1979's "Stare with Your Ears," a collection of "talking songs," including the ooky "Angels Lament," which sounds like Leonard Cohen trying to be Eddie Lawrence; and the dazedly hip "Alphabet," which characterizes each letter in an odd way: "P is a leaking D, Q is O with its tail showing, R is a leaking P, S is a snake on edge, T is an extremely mixed up L...."

In 1992 Jerry Garcia played guitar behind Nordine's dark and deep utterances on a new album, "The Devout Catalyst" on Grateful Dead Records. It's more free association strangeness: "Mr. Slick is smooth as snake, sliding on a bellyache, slipping through some awful stuff, never ever having quite enough." The CD from Rhino offers cuts from Nordine's first four albums. Nordine fans love to hunt for any albums that feature his hip announcer's voice, finding chills and thrills in everything from his stereo demonstration disc "Sounds in Space" (RCA Living Stereo) to albums like "The Voice of Love" (Hamilton) and his straight narration hit "The Shifting Whispering Sands" (Dot).

JAY NORTH

- DENNIS THE MENACE (Colpix CP 204) **1/2 $15 $30

From 1959 to 1962 Jay North starred in the TV version of the popular comic strip *Dennis the Menace*. This 1962 album, with added narration so that it makes some sense to listeners, offers two episodes from the show: "Tenting Tonight" and "Dennis Sells Bottles." For those who have forgotten, or tried to forget, just imagine cute little dickens Dennis explaining to Mr. Wilson what happened to his window:

"Well, the day after you left on your trip ... I hit a home run.... Right through your kitchen window ... Well, the ball sorta bounced across the kitchen and turned on the water faucet.... The baseball ended up in the sink, ending up as a drain plug ... so you lost all your water on the floor. I looked through the window and saw what was happening.... I climbed up on the trellis. Dad's already fixed it ... of course we had to jimmy the back door to get in.... Boy was that door a mess!" And after all that? Why, darned if Dennis didn't break the window all over again: "I'm a regular Willie Mays!" North issued a straight album, "Look Who's Singing" (Kem 27).

NOT READY FOR PRIME TIME PLAYERS

- NBC'S SATURDAY NIGHT LIVE (Arista AL 4107) *** $8

The lone soundtrack album for *Saturday Night Live* features Dan Aykroyd, John Belushi, Chevy Chase, Jane Curtin, Garrett Morris, Laraine Newman, and Gilda Radner, plus guests Peter Boyle, Buck Henry, Richard Pryor, Paul Simon, and Lily Tomlin. Most of the material still holds up, including Tomlin's monologue of one-liners:

"I resent losing the ozone layer just so we can have Pam. Have you ever actually seen somebody laughing all the way to the bank? Why isn't there a special name for the tops of your feet? Being a New Yorker is never having to say you're sorry."

After a "Weekend Update" routine, Chase joins Richard Pryor for the kind of brash satire that made the show notorious. Chevy, testing a prospective black employee, conducts some word association:

"Dog." "Tree." "Fast." "Slow." "Rain." "Snow." "White." "Black.""Negro." "Whitey." "Tarbaby." "Ofay!" "Colored." "Redneck!" "Jungle Bunny."ker Wood!" "Burr Head!" "Cracker!" "Spear chucker!" "White trash!" "Jungle Bunny." "Honky!" "Spade!" "Honky Honky!" "Nigger!" "Dead Honky!"

Like the show itself, the record has rough spots where the actors and writers experiment with ideas that don't pay off. Still, the disc captures some of the spirit of the show's early years.

NOT THE 9 O'CLOCK NEWS PLAYERS

- NOT THE 9 O'CLOCK NEWS (BBC BBC 22400) *** $8 $15

England's *Not the 9 O'Clock News* mixed irreverent sketches, songs, and news items—and though they never reached the fame of *Monty Python*, they did do some memorable work.

There's an unlikely sketch about devil worshipping: "Cautiously, I would approve of sacrificing the odd virgin.... We believe that Satan the Prince of Darkness is lord of the universe and will destroy Jesus through infernal power.... Every full moon we go up to the heath at night, we do strip ourselves naked and ravish each other passionately till dawn." "And this summons up the powers of evil, does it?" "Who cares?"

Some bits contain British references that would baffle most Americans, and some of it is dated (this album is culled from 1979-1980 broadcasts). Then there's British comedy about British comedy as they take on the furor caused by the "anti-Christian" Monty Python film *The Life of Brian*. Here, a group of Christians have released *The Life of Python*, and are under scrutiny from Monty Python supporters who call it blasphemy: "I was apalled, that in a country that is essentially a Python-worshipping country, that a fourteen-year-old child can actually get in to see this film ... this distorted garbage." "I certainly didn't expect the Spanish Inquisition! I must emphasize, it is not about Python—" "Oh come on! The leading figure ... is quite clearly a lampoon of the comic messiah himself, our lord John Cleese. Even the initials J. C. are the same ... no, I'm sorry, this film is a highly distasteful one. Have people forgotton how Monty Python suffered for us? How often the sketches failed? These people died for us! Frequently!"

Like every show of this type, there are misfires, songs that don't pack much power (a love ballad sung to the Ayatollah), and sketches that are pat and easy (a stewardess giving foreboding instructions before takeoff). There's shock humor just to be rude (a commercial for American Express has the counter woman cheerfully asking, "Would you like to rub my tits, too"). There's even scrotum humor, "The Bouncing Song": "I like bouncing, boing, boing, boing. Up and down until I get a pain in me groin." It's still better to be shocked awake with fresh satire than fall asleep to stale sitcoms.

Various British import albums are available. The 1980 "Hedgehog Sandwich" (BBC) includes a delicious Kate Bush parody ("England My Leotard") and a Barry Manilow send-up ("Because I'm Wet and Lonely"). The double album "The Memory Kinda Lingers" (BBC) has a highlight song about a bickering "Simon and Garfunkel."

THE NUTTY SQUIRRELS

- NUTTY SQUIRRELS (Hanover HM 8014) ** $8 $15
- BIRD WATCHING (Columbia CL 1589/CS 8389) *1/2 $5 $10
- HARD DAYS NIGHT (MGM SE 4272) ** $8 $15

Sort of "The Chipmunks" for adults, Sascha Burland and Don Elliot speeded up their voices and scat sang jazz tunes and novelty items. They had a minor hit with "Uh Oh," which rose to #14 on the Billboard chart in November of 1959. They filled up their Hanover album with "Uh Oh" and such variations as "Ding Dong," "Uh Huh," "Bang," and "Zowee." Those with a bent towards the bent might be momentarily amused by these jazz Chipmunks, though playing an Ella Fitzgerald record at 45 rpm would offer about the same thing. The Squirrels tried to speed up rock and pop with their last MGM release, a persuasive plea for pest control.

LOUIS NYE

- HEIGH HO MADISON AVENUE (Riverside 842) ** $7 $12
- HERE'S NYE IN YOUR EYE (United Artists UAL 4089) ** $8 $15

Amusing character comedian Louis Nye became popular on Steve Allen's old *Tonight Show* with two different creations: an advertising man and a realistic, modern version of the stereotyped effeminate ass. The 1961 United Artists album includes his fop character as "The Choreographer." He supervises a children's play: "It's not sissy to dance!" he shouts. "It's good discipline and it prepares you for the Army!" He tries some other characters, including a "Hipster at the Bank" and here, a Jewish news reporter:

"Vell, vot kind of a day has it been? Don't ask! Dey had a day today in de Congo: you shouldn't know from it! Have ya hoid what happened on Staten Island on de ferry in de park? I can't talk about it! In Cuba today Fidel Castro signed a new alliance with Red China. He should have stomach distress from the sweet and sour pork they will serve him on official occasions! Here is a flash! Mickey Mantle finally signed. He held it out. He got what he wanted, more money and a better seat in de dugout!"

Nye's characerizations are all right, but the writing is not particularly strong.

The Riverside disc is all about Madison Avenue. Cuts include "Ode to an Ulcer," "Subliminal's Not Really Criminal," and "Think, Scheme and Plan Ahead." The studio album is mostly song satires with a few monologues thrown in, including "The Ten Commandments," a somber delivery of ad clichés:

"Thou shalt not be half-safe. Thou shalt be sociable and look smart. Thou shalt never carry more than fifty dollars in cash. Thou shalt promise her anything but give her Arpege.... Thou shalt fly now, pay later. Thou shalt ask thy local dealer. Thou shalt wonder where the yellow went. Thou shalt always think for thyself! Caveat emptor."

Both albums are a bit dated, though some in the advertising business might still get a chuckle from the Riverside album. Nye issued two singles, "Hi-Ho Steve-O" (Coral 961836) and "Roland Rockoff" (Wig 103).

CARROLL O'CONNOR

- ALL IN THE FAMILY (Atlantic SD 7210) *** $5 $10
- ALL IN THE FAMILY 2ND ALBUM (Atlantic SD 7232) ***1/2 $5 $10

All in the Family was hailed for bringing new depth to situation comedy as it dared tackle bigotry, sexual themes, war, peace, and the giant gap between the generations. The show was controversial, but the very human characters of the downtrodden Archie Bunker, his optimistic if dim wife Edith, and his argumentative daughter and son-in-law kept viewers tuning in.

In 1971, Atlantic released the first album of short two-minute and three-minute scenes from the show. The album includes a photo-filled, four-page insert with biographies of the cast and creators (Norman Lear and Bud Yorkin). The show's famous theme song (with extra lyrics) is rendered at the piano by Archie and Edith Bunker.

There's a wealth of dialogue clips, most attempting to tackle the hot topics of the day, others giving voice to Archie's working man's gripes. Some of it hasn't survived, though it was sizzlingly hot way back when:

Mike: You just got a hang-up about sex.

Archie: I ain't got no hang up about ... that.

Mike: No hangups? You can't even say the word sex!

Archie: There's women around here, ya palooka, I don't use four-letter words around women!

Gloria: Admit it, Daddy, your whole generation's afraid of sex.

Archie: Listen little girl, if I was afraid of it, you wouldn't be here. Right Edith?

Edith: I'm trying to remember.

The second album, from 1972, offers more complete sketches. There's eight minutes from the episode guest starring Sammy Davis, Jr., and the classic six-minute sequence in which Archie is stuck in an elevator with a black man (Roscoe Lee Brown) and a Puerto Rican (Hector Elizando) whose wife is expecting a baby:

O'Connor: Three ain't enough for 'em. These people don't care where, when, or how many!

Brown: They don't seem to be interested in learning modern birth control methods, do they?

O'Connor: Oh listen to this guy. If that ain't the black calling the kettle pot....

Elizando: Mr. Bunker, we are Americans, equal to you.

O'Connor: Equal to me? You ain't even equal to him!

O'Connor made two straight albums: "Sings for Old Pharts" (Audio Fidelity AFSD 6726) and "Remembering You" (A&M 4340), the latter featuring the lyrics he wrote to the end theme of *All in the Family*. He and Jean Stapleton released "Archie and Edith" (RCA APL10102) a sing-along disc. Atlantic released a single featuring a completely orchestrated, bouncy rendition of the *All in the Family* theme song sung by O'Connor and Stapleton. For those who are curious about the original British version of the show, called *Till Death Do Us Part*, there's an import album of episodes on the Marble Arch label.

TERRI O'MASON

- SONGS FOR ADULTS (Fax 1011, also available as Lobo 1011
  and released as STAG PARTY SPECIAL NUMBER 2) ** $5 $12
- BACK FOR SECONDS (Fax 1014, also available as Lobo 1014) ** $5 $12

O'Mason, to judge from the photo on the back of both albums, looked more like a stripper than a comedienne. She records her songs without an audience, so it's hard to tell just how many laughs she got (to go with the leers). There's nothing about her quiet singing style that makes her any more distinctive than her competition, including the entire Davis Records roster of unknowns. Billed as Terri "Cup Cake" O'Mason, her tune "Cup Cakes" appears on her first album. The standard double entendres are plentiful:

"He liked to nibble on my cup cakes. He just went nuts about their taste. They seemed to melt right in his mouth, I've never had complainers. They're smooth as silk, they go with milk, and he said they come in such cute containers.... He liked to nibble on my cup cakes. Just like his mother's, they're just right. And left. They're not too big, they're not too small. They fit right in his grip. They're not too hard, they're not too soft, and there's a raisin on each tip. Oh you should see my lovely cup cakes."

It's more of the same on the second album: "I got a job as a waitress. I thought I would be in the chips. But I found out my boss was not only cross, he was always pinching my tips! Ouch!"

DAVID OSSMAN

- HOW TIME FLYS (Columbia KC 32411) *1/2 $8 $15

"Entertainment." "Delay ... Testing, testing, testing. This sounds real bad, system. Can you plug the drain?" "No." "I'm out of communication." "You are." "Out." "I'm out of communication?" "Failure, failure."

There's a communication failure on this, Ossman's "hi-fi sci-fi" comedy. It features all four members of Firesign Theatre, along with Harry Shearer and Wolfman Jack, but since Firesign member Ossman wrote the whole thing, it was released in 1973 as a solo disc. Firesign fans may have the time for this self-indulgence: "This morning we're featuring real coverage of the revolt on Garbage Island."

GARY OWENS

- THE FUNNY SIDE OF BONNIE AND CLYDE (Epic 26377) * $4 $8
- THE HEXORCIST (ABC DSD50167) *1/2 $5 $10
- PUT YOUR HEAD ON MY FINGER (Pride/MGM PRD 0002) * $4 $8

Gary Owens, the ridiculously resonant and overly enunciating announcer on *Rowan and Martin's Laugh-In* is only the announcer on the "Bonnie and Clyde" album, a corny series of sketches with Joan Gerber and Dave Ketchum in the title roles and Bruce Gordon (Frank Nitti on TV's *The Untouchables*) in a supporting role. The corn:

Bonnie: You just shot off your nose.

Clyde: Now we can't pull that bank job.

Bonnie: Yeah, but we can pull a nose job.

Vaudeville also lives on in his parody of the film *The Exorcist*, costarring Pat Paulsen, Jaye P. Morgan, Patti Deutsch, and Jack De Leon. Owens plays the Devil, who makes a deal that gives "Hexorcist" author William Peatty Bladder a best-seller. Later, at the premiere of the movie, a man runs out crying, "Oh God, I'm sick! That disfigured girl with the horrible crud all over her face! How much can I guy take?" "You found the picture that disgusting?" "Picture? I'm talking about my date!"

Owens's 1972 solo for Pride is a prime example of his senseless sense of humor. He was always seriously idiotic on *Laugh-In*, spouting stupidities with deadpan urgency. Like this news item: "August 4th, 1967. National Prune and Fig Institute Devises Plan to Use Trading Cards Featuring Bob Cummings and Guy Lombardo."

This kind of jokeless nonsense wears thin very quickly, especially when the gag is just goofy names like "Norbert T. Krelk Funeral," "Foonman Home for the Perturbed News," and "The Glur Awards." Some of the cuts resemble bad Ernie Kovacs, bad *Laugh-In*, or in the case of "Win that Dwarf," awful Firesign Theater. And just when it seems that the album couldn't get more annoying, there's "Nurny Creed," in which Owens proclaims, "Any Nurny has the right to punch a Finnork right in the mouth." And the entire Mike Curb Congregation offers an a capella warble of "Nurny nurny nurny nurny nurny nurny nurny ... finnork."

JACK PAAR

- PAAR FOR TONIGHT (NBC) ** $10 $20
- THE BEST OF WHAT'S HIS NAME (Ramrod R 8001) *** $4 $15

NO NAMES, PLEASE

At the time, 1960s Tonight Show host Jack Paar's face was so well known that his name didn't need to be used on this promo disc. The small circle of friends gifted with a "Hee Larious" private pressing knew "JW" was the one and only Jonathan Winters.

MAD MEN

Alfred E. Neuman art is always collectible, from the original "Musically MAD" album from Bernie Green and Henry Morgan to Broadway rarity "The MAD Show."

"Tonight Show" host Paar never officially issued an album. "Paar for Tonight" is an obscure one-sided promo, a limited edition LP that NBC issued. It does include a few excerpts from his monologues. His Ramrod album is also a promotional item, evidently a giveaway. The back cover sports a huge ad for "Jiffy Sew," a fabric mending liquid. A box of the stuff was glued to the back cover.

One side is "Jack Paar in London," monologues culled from a series of *Tonight Shows* he did in England. Paar was noted for his conversational style. He tells many amusing anecdotes of life in a British hotel and his efforts to hide from his sometimes neurotically possessive fans by checking in using the name Primrose Magoo. He tells stories his English audience loves: "It's remarkable, we made the trip (to England) in six hours. And I was talking to an Englishman downstairs, and I said it's absolutely remarkable. In this day and age, you could fly to New York in six hours. And you know what he said? But why!"

Paar's delivery, so sincere, sometimes nervous and stuttery, was often lampooned by impressionists, some of them twisting Paar's sensitivity to the point of effeminacy. The following, even in print form, exemplifies how the vulnerable Paar would nervously babble around a joke:

"You know, I was up this morning at seven thirty. Really. I was. Truly, that's so. And I was out in the park outside the hotel, and I was there, and I was walking around, and there was a guy like Trevor Howard, you know, with tweeds on, walking the dog, and I said, 'Hello.' And he said, 'How are you?' And I said, 'I'm- I'm an American.' And he said, 'None of us is perfect.' So for the rest of the day I called myself a Southern Canadian."

"What's His Name" does not identify Paar. Perhaps this, more than the passing years, is responsible for the usual low price.

LA WANDA PAGE

- MUTHA IS HALF A WORD (Laff 142) ** $5 $10
- PIPE LAYIN' DAN (Laff 150) ** $5 $10
- BACK DOOR DADDY (Laff 156) ** $5 $10
- PREACH ON, SISTER! (Laff 173) ** $5 $10
- WATCH IT, SUCKER! (Laff 195) ** $5 $10
- SANE ADVICE (Laff 205) ** $5 $10

Page, before her fame as Aunt Esther on *Sanford and Son*, was simply billed as "La Wanda." She worked as a solo monologist, and also in sketches with Skillet and Leroy ("Back Door Daddy"). Her earthy material might surprise some fans of *Sanford and Son*.

JACKSON PAINE

- EXPLOSIVE SOUNDS (Warner Bros. W 1411) * $4 $8

In 1961, with obscure Bob Newhart suddenly a best-selling comic, Warners (and other labels) went out hunting for more obscure people to discover. Twenty-nine-year-old Paine devised this album of aural cartoons that Warners proudly called "Humor in its newest form" on the cover. The back cover teaser proclaimed, "A cerebral excursion guaranteed to keep you in stitches."

There are over thirty blackout sketches on the record, each keyed to a sound effect punch line. Not only are they obvious, but the twenty or thirty seconds it takes to reach the expected sound effect seem like an eternity. They are also poorly recorded with a booming artificial laugh track. At least Bob Prescott, another practitioner of this strained form of humor, dispensed with the fake cackles.

"Major Breakthrough" begins with a scientist lecturing: "You just happened to catch me in the middle of an experiment here. (Tittering laughter.) You see, we inject the fluid in the belly of the little chicken. (Chicken peep noises.) That's it, he doesn't seem to mind it too much. Now you'll notice how fast the little chicken is growing. (Explosion sound effect.) Now we'll try a little bit less on the next little chicken. (Hysterical laughter.)"

Bland-voiced Paine is up to his name. One sound effect to count on: a needle scratching hastily off this record.

NICOLA PAONE

- THE ONE AND ONLY NICOLA PAONE (ABC-Paramount ABC 263) ** $5 $10

Paone had a minor 1958 novelty hit, "Blah, Blah, Blah," and that's sometimes enough to file this album in the comedy bin, though most of the album is a straight mix of original ballads and upbeat tunes suitable for hand-clapping and dancing. (He also issued a second album, "The One and Only" (ABC 282), more in the pop vocal mode, and "Nicola" on his own N.P. label.) Paone's got three self-penned novelty numbers here: "Tony the Ice Man," "The Telephone Song," and "Blah, Blah, Blah." All are loaded with ethnic eccentricity, but it's the latter that has universal appeal, thanks to Paone's whimsical between-stanza patter. With muttered asides, earnest confusion, and an accent as tangy as red peppers, he describes his wife's complaining, which leads into the inevitable chorus: "Yakkity yak, blah blah blah blah, that's all I hear all day, yakkity yak, blah blah blah blah!" The album features the complete version; the single was cut by two stanzas. Even now, when ethnic humor and wife jokes are hardly timely, Paone's charm will raise a smile. Paone has spent the past thirty-five years as owner of his own Italian restaurant in Manhattan.

ANDY PARKS

- SEX, SCHOOL AND LIKE OTHER PRESSURES (Capitol ST 2799) ** $5 $10

Comedy writer Bud Freeman wrote this somewhat dated studio album for fifteen-year-old Andy. It's handled "Dobie Gillis" style, where a young, semi-hip and partially neurotic kid comes out and tells the audience his troubles. Like his embarrassment over birth control pills: "My mother, she keeps asking me if Karen takes the pill. Aw, that bugs me. I said to her, 'Mother! Man!' She's my mother and all, but that's a sensitive area."

Andy Parks's real-life parents play his parents here: Larry Parks (star of *The Jolson Story*) and Betty Garrett (Irene Lorenzo on *All in the Family*).

PARKYAKARKUS
- PARKYAKARKUS (REM 8) $10 $15

A favorite on radio with dialect routines, Harry "Parkyakarkus" Einstein issued this obscure ten-inch children's album in the '50s. Doing a straight monologue, Parkyakarkus is also on a Friar's Roast album for Lucille Ball and Desi Arnaz recorded in November of 1958. The crowd is laughing at almost every line:

"My very dear and very close friends Miss Louise Balls and Danny Arnaz, we are particularly delighted to welcome you into our club ... but you must not think that the Friar's Club is an easy club to get into. Quite to the contrary, it is most difficult.... But in spite of all this ... we have managed to put together a pretty good club made up of the very cream of show business people ... outstanding doctors, many famous lawyers, several fine judges, and quite a few defendants.... If one should be interested in nature, we have a splendid bird-watching group. No matter what time you come into our club, you'll always see two or three of our members standing around looking for pigeons."

Parkyakarkus suffered a heart attack moments after he ended his speech. The "souvenir" recording includes a preface by the evening's emcee, Art Linkletter, acknowledging the comedian's death and this, his final monologue.

JAK PARTI
- PARTY TIME (Rivoli R-6) ** $4 $12

Rivoli's answer to risqué sophisticates Charlie Drew and Dwight Fiske was "Jak Parti," the anonymous singer here. There are no credits or album notes for Mr. Parti. The photo on the cover shows a stripper wearing a set of pasties.

Parti stretches each of the seven tunes out with digressions and recitations, the subject matter covering the standard range for a roué. There's "Willie the Werewolf," "Little Johnny Guinea Pig," "Good Queen Bess," and "Old and Rare." There's the gay song "Uncle," poking fun at an odd relative: "Uncle drove his motor car with gay abandon near and far. Till he tried driving from the rear; stripped the chauffeur instead of the gear.... Now Uncle claimed he would never be in any of our jails. Till he was given twenty years for tampering with the mails."

PATCHETT AND TARSES
- INSTANT REPLAY (Decca DL 75300) ** $5 $10

Tom Patchett and Jay Tarses, better known at the time for their TV sitcom writing, are disappointing on this very standard collection of blackout sketches about football. The 1971 disc tries all possibilities. A blackout on the National Anthem features two guys imitating Sandler and Young. They stop in the middle to break into a chorus of "Dominique." There's a nearly three-minute pre-game presentation as various field judges and team captains say hello to each other. This scene imagines what goes on in a huddle:

"Okay, what have we got, fourth and two ... what do you guys feel like doing, a pass or what?" "... I gotta go check on this fried chicken franchise, see what I mean? So why don't you send me out on a fly pattern and I keep goin' right out through the tunnel?" Gay voice: "Oh gee, the fly pattern's my favorite." "Oh I'm sorry to hear these franchises are doing so lousy, Fingers, it's too bad." "Yeah, sure is a drag, man, 'cause my cosmetics are doin' great."

PAT PATTERSON
- FUNDERMOTZ: OFF THE TOP OF HIS HEAD (Fundermotz NR 3138) *1/2 $4 $8
- HAVE YOU HEARD THIS MAN? (Fundermotz 5012) *1/2 $4 $8

A disc jockey who has a bit of Don Imus's attitude (there's a picture of him and Imus on the back cover of "Off the Top of His Head"), Patterson offers minute-long studio sketches loaded with "zany" non sequiturs and hipness. At best they probably helped wake up anyone still dozing over the news and weather:

"Time now for more exciting news about Two Flags Over Fuquay, the most fantastic entertainment event between McCullers and Willow Springs. Another great new attraction on our midway: Zelda the Tattooed Lady. Yes, across her back is tattooed the Declaration of Independence. On her right leg is written Carl Yastrzemski's latest contract. On her left leg a copy of the Articles of Confederation, across Zelda's brow, a map of the Lower East Side of New York City.... It's an educational experience for one and all. And starting next week on the midway, you'll find Mandrake the Shoe Size Guesser. Yessir, Mandrake will try to guess your exact shoe size. And if he misses you get your choice of a gold-rimmed enameled ash tray emblazoned with the words "Souvenir of Miami Beach," or a genuine terrycloth beach towel, your choice of Confederate Flag or full-color rendition of 'The Last Supper.'"

PAT PAULSEN
- PAT PAULSEN FOR PRESIDENT (Rubicon/Mercury SR 61179) **1/2 $8 $15
- LIVE AT THE ICE HOUSE (Mercury SR 61251) **1/2 $8 $15

The glum, Lincoln-faced comic was a regular on *The Smothers Brothers Comedy Hour* in 1968. The boys figured he'd make a great president. The idea developed into a running gag ... but ended with a very serious Paulsen trying to score points in the New Hampshire primary. The album, narrated by Ralph Story, traces the life and times of Pat Paulsen, and takes snippets from the Smothers Brothers' show, where Paulsen would deliver "editorials" and campaign announcements. Paulsen was always funny as the crusty, deadpan, unsympathetic editorialist who rebutted angry protestors with a tart "Picky, picky, picky!" He was effective at understated satire: "Many people feel that our current draft laws are unfair. These people are soldiers."

Paulsen had his own *Half a Comedy Hour* on ABC in 1970, around the time the Ice House album appeared. Paulsen's satiric "non act" includes deliberately bad audience participation bits, such as a sing-along to a double-talk mumble tune, and a lame "finger shadows" exhibition that includes "fist with arm attached." Some of Paulsen's one-liners are bizarre: "I took biology two years in a row just to eat the specimens." Some oddities go back to Bea Lillie's era: "I was walking down the street when a very ugly man came up and tied his horse to me."

The highlight is Paulsen's self-written "Gaslight" song, a strummed monologue about a hideous evening out, half-sung in his deadpan, or rather dead-nosed, nasal voice. At one point: "We settled back to watch the show, and you settled back too far. Tipped over the girl's glass in back of you. She didn't like it and give you a punch in the kidney. So I turned around and put my finger in her nose. Then I couldn't get it out. So we left together. Walking down the street hand in nose."

Paulsen reports on his failed presidential campaign, and can't resist going serious for the song "Did I Ever Really Live?" written by Albert Hague and Allan Sherman.

He also appears on "The Hexorcist," starring Gary Owens.

MINNIE PEARL

- LOOKIN FER A FELLER (Nashville 2043) ** $5 $10
- HOWDEE (Starday 224, Sunset 1148, reissued as LAUGH ALONG (Pickwick S 6014 and MINNIE PEARL, Everest 5073)
  issued on CD as QUEEN OF THE GRAND OLE OPRY, Legacy CD 377) **1/2 $8
- AMERICA'S BELOVED (Starday S 380) ** $5 $10
- COUNTRY MUSIC STORY (Starday S 397) ** $5 $10

Born in Tennessee, Sarah Ophelia Colley was a drama instructor who developed a character called Minnie Pearl. Eventually her monologues as Minnie led her to the Grand Ol' Opry in 1940. The woman with the hearty cry of "Howdee!" became the heartland's most beloved comedienne. In 1975 she was elected to the Country Music Hall of Fame.

Her records have regional appeal, but are obscure on both coasts. A typical bit of Minnie monologue from her "Howdee" album now available on CD from Legacy: "Howdeeeee! Oh, I'm just so proud to be here. Well, sir, I'll tell ya right now, I come up here today and I thought I know I'm gonna look nice 'cause I got this dress just special to come up here. I didn't pay a lot for this dress, in fact, I got it for a bargain. I heard one fella say I musta got this dress for a ridiculous figure. Hmm. But I started in out there and there was two nice lookin' fellers standin' there and one of 'em said to the other, 'I believe that's the ugliest woman I ever seen.' The other one said, '... beauty's only skin deep.' And the other one said, 'Well let's skin her!' The other one said, 'You know, I believe I recognize her, that's that Minnie Pearl, she's been down there at the Grand Ol' Opry for 175 years. She carries on like she's from the country. I bet she don't know a goose from a gander.' I turned around and said, 'At Grinder's Switch, we don't worry about that. We just put 'em all out there together and let 'em figure it out for theirselves!'"

PEARL BOX REVUE

- CALL ME MISS-TER (Snake Eyes 9001) *1/2 $5 $20

A set of black transvestites (Jaye Joyce, Dorian Corey, Tony LaFrisky, and Clyddie McCoy) shout and posture at each other for an entire album. It may have been recorded backstage at their show, at somebody's apartment, or in the holding pen at the police station. It's just a mess of babble that would only appeal to listeners desperately curious about TV talk or excited by dirty words. They laugh and snicker, but they're the only ones.

The second album of this double-disc set is called "The Serious Side" and is at least more coherent as the foursome argue and debate the problems of straights, closet queens, drag queens, and homosexuals: "Society has always said that they don't have to deal with homosexuality because it's a minority, very small group. But they are lyin'. It's a whole lot of gay people out here in the world." "You'd be surprised how many you see on the bus that are not *women* going to do their day work but *men* going to do their day work ... drag queens that nobody knows about!"

There's no date of release on the record, but it has to be pretty old: the gals consider a good income to be $8,000 a year.

BOB PECK

- MOTH IN THE GREY FLANNEL SUIT (Jubilee JLP 1035,
  also released as SONGS THAT NEVER MADE THE HYMNAL, Jubilee JGM 2025) ** $5 $10

When Tom Lehrer first became a sensation, everyone proclaimed him "an original." What happens to an original? It's copied. Bob Peck's the copy.

Peck's voice duplicates Lehrer; the phrasing identical. Peck accompanies himself at the piano, a la Lehrer, and sings his own satires, some with a good dollop of sick humor. Where Tom Lehrer's cover lines reported on his "lyrics, his music, his so-called voice, and his piano," Bob Peck's album cleverly trumpets his "weirds and music, piano and voice(?)" They could almost have been separated at birth—Lehrer was born April 9, 1928, in New York City, and Peck on February 17, 1928, in Weedville, New York.

Comedy scholars who come across Bob Peck's disc will be thrilled, the same way a connoisseur of art enjoys detecting a sneaky forgery.

Most of Peck's ditties are mediocre, with bland music and lyrics that are well written but jokeless. General topics include the advertising world, inheriting money to shop at Abercrombie and Fitch, and trying to get a girl to stay the night. Among the cuts that try for Lehrer's sick edge is "Unsung Heroes," the stomach pumping squad: "And instead of silver medals on the chest of every lad, there are lots and lots of little spots on the men of the stomach pump squad. Be glad when they shove that tube in your mouth that the seat of the trouble is not farther south!"

Peck's "Wyatt Urp" song does have some of the bounce of Lehrer's "Old West" number: "I'm just a rootin' tootin' cowboy and I guess I'll never never learn to ride. 'Cause when I'm in the saddle, it feels as though a paddle is slapping me across the great divide."

Peck tries to find his own macabre subjects. He sings about a smoker who drops dead trying to inhale a cigarette that he's filled with filters, and it gives him the chance to use the old joke about being buried in a flip top box. Rather than poisoning pigeons a la Lehrer, he sings about dogs who die: "I always got such pleasure just to hang around and hear those cries of terror from the old dog pound." Then he segues into a joke so ancient only Benny Hill has since made it into a lyric: "Be sure to kick your puppy though it's not his fault at all. If someone's umbrella leaves some dew drops in the hall." Later it's back to the bite: "And if your doggie limps away, and he can't be found ... no more will you be kissing that puppy that you're missing ... for the gas jets will be hissing at the old dog pound!"

Peck's phrasing on the last line is pure Tom Lehrer. He stops to emphasize the word "hissing" with an emphatic "h" and by the time he gets to "old dog pound" he's going into Lehrer vaudeville: "ol' dog-ah pound!"

For connoisseurs of copycat comedy, Peck's bold forgery is worth hearing.

The only difference between the two differently titled albums is the cover. "Hymnal" sports a tired-looking woman in black sequins, fishnet stockings, and high heels, which is better than the cartoon drawing on "Gray Flannel Suit" of five look-alike businessmen watching a moth flutter away.

- SONGS THAT NEVER MADE THE HYMNAL (Jubilee LP 18) ** $5 $20

Jubilee often reissued the same record with a different title (or, in the case of The Richie Brothers, a different cover and the same title). They outdid themselves with Peck. They issued the same Peck record with different covers and titles—and used the same title over again for two different discs!

This ten-inch "Songs That Never Made the Hymnal" does not duplicate anything on the twelve-inch version. The covers are different, too. Here, the cover girl is replaced by a snarling devil mask.

Most of the tuneless tunes have risqué lyrics, usually soporific, sophomoric, and predictable. "The Ordinary Fly" tries for double entendres: "Disease is spreading right through the common fly. We opened up the fly, to see the least. We concluded right away, that it was here to stay. By the very nature of the beast."

"Homo the Range" pokes fun at the idea of a gay cowboy: "Yes, home on the range he was strange. When the cowgirls would ask for a kiss. It was seldom they heard an encouraging word. He was a prairie fairy!"

"Women and Pianos" is the best of the lot: "Women are like pianos. They're similar in brand. Some of them are upright. Some of them are grand. There are many different sizes. I can vouch for that. Some have tones that are round and full. Others are quite flat.... I have played on several. And always pleased my fans. Some you play with one finger, and others take both hands...."

The only "sick" entry is "Kind Old Dr. Brown," about an abortionist.

JIMMY PELHAM

- LAFF ALONG (Regent 6105) ** $5 $10
- SANTA WATCH YOUR CLAWS (Pel-Nor 1003) ** $5 $10
- CALLING PREZ COLLECT (Pel-Nor LPPN 1002) ** $5 $10

An N.Y.U. graduate, black comic Jimmy Pelham, as the liner notes on "Calling Prez Collect" report, "speaks articulately, blending to perfection the mellow tones of a southern accent and the rough vernacular of western culture." What that means is that Pelham can tell straight jokes in a straight voice, and when he wants, do funkier material in a funkier voice. The 1961 disc contains his most popular routine, "Calling Prez." To the delight of his black audience, he makes a phone call that hips the president to black problems.

"Give me loooooooooong distance. Yeah, I'd like to call person to person to Washington DC, I want to speak with The Prez ... no, you don't know who I am. I don't know who you are either. I know who I am. Ain't none of your cotton-pickin' business ... hang it up, I'll get another operator, you girls get too many calls anyway. No, I didn't say you was no call girl, you said that. Connect me with Washington ... give me the White House. Huh? Honey, there's only one White House there, and it's not gonna be there long, 'cause as soon as we take over we're changin' it to the Brown House."

When Pelham finally gets through, he shouts, "Hello Prez, how ya doin' baby ... Mississippi. They done locked up some of my relatives ... we know you heard about it, we want to know what in the devil you gonna do about it.... Man they got a mess of us in jail. So much of us in jail it's wall to wall US ... we put you in office, don't you forget us."

"Santa Watch Your Claws," with a blurry picture of a girl in a negligee seated next to Pelnor in a Santa suit, has some seasonal patter and novelty material, like Mel Torme's "Christmas Song," rewritten: "Hog guts roasting on an open fire. Children diggin' in their nose. Rock 'n' roll being sung by a crowd. And atha-leet's feet between your toes. Everybody knows Three Feathers and some Four Roses will help to give the season life. Little boys with their emotions all aglow will find it hard to sleep tonight. They know that Jimmy's on his way. And he's got lots o' wine and home brew on his sleigh! And every little chil' is gonna try to see if reindeers can fly when they are high!"

Pelham's first album (on Regent) is loaded with slightly blue and borrowed material, told in a cheerful, slightly affected style: "Two children are playing. The boy said, 'Sally, I'm gonna stick my finger in your belly button!' She said, 'Go ahead!' He said, 'Sure you ain't scared?' She said, 'No, go ahead.' He did. She said, 'That ain't my belly button.' He said, 'That ain't my finger!'"

RED PETERS

- I LAUGHED, I CRIED, I FUDGED MY UNDIES (Ugly Sisters 30022) *1/2 $7

Red Peters tries to juxtapose '50s crooning with double entendre lyrics, but both the words and his singing are amateurish. The band backing him and the quality of the recording aren't professional either. Red's predictable songs ("How's Your Whole ... Family" and "You Promised the Moon but I Preferred Uranus") might amuse some stray Dr. Demento fans reaching puberty. Everyone else can avoid this 1995 CD.

HANS PETERSON

- TRUST ME (GRT 8020) *1/2 $3 $7

An attempt to make a "First Family" hit off the Jimmy Carter administration (Jeff Altman also tried it), Peterson wrote and starred (only a fair job of mimicry) in this 1977 album, loaded with predictable blackout sketches and peanut jokes. Bill Conkright plays Billy and June Stewart is Rosalynn. A segment with Rosalynn, alluding to Carter's interview in *Playboy* where he admitted to lusting after women:

"I'm looking for the blue jean jacket that has the cowboy fringe on it. The one like our ambassador to France has." "Oh, Greg Allman! Honey, you never had a blue jean jacket with fringe on it." "That's right. I've lusted after one like that, though. Many times in my mind, I have seen myself wearing one. But I believe all men do." "Hush up that kind of talk now."

DAVE PETITJEAN

- MY FRANS (Kom-A-Day 5001) ** $5 $10
- CAJUN HUMOR AT ITS BEST (Kom-A-Day 5002) ** $5 $10
- HUMOR FROM CAJUN COUNTRY (Kom-A-Day 5003) ** $5 $10
- CAJUN CAPERS (Kom-A-Day 5004) ** $5 $10
- REAL AND FUNNY (Kom-A-Day 5005) ** $5 $10

Petitjean (pronounced Petty-john with a soft "j") lectures on Cajun humor and tells the standards. His accent isn't as colorful as some other Cajun humorists, but it's still odd enough to take a few moments to figure out. On "Cajun Capers" he explains "how you can tell a Cajun.... If you not sure the fella you talkin' with's a Cajun, what you do, we got plenty rice fields down here. You know that. Just take that guy to the rice field, and if he's a real Cajun, he can look at that rice field, there, and he gonna tell you how much gravy it gonna take to eat it up."

SAMMY PETRILLO

- MY SON THE PHONE CALLER (Surprise SUR-110) **1/2 $8 $15

Sammy Petrillo was a Jerry Lewis look-alike. In 1952 he and partner Duke Mitchell were the low-budget version of Martin and Lewis, starring in *Bela Lugosi Meets a Brooklyn Gorilla*. By the early '60s he was taking small parts on comedy albums (Will Jordan's "All About Cleopatra") and starring in this one produced by Dick Randall, who had cast Sammy in the 1961 sexploitation nudie comedy *Shangri-La*.

These candid phone calls are entertaining though not always funny. Petrillo confounds nurses at a maternity ward by asking for emergency instructions on how to deliver a baby gorilla:

Nurse: "If the gorilla's delivering, then you tie the cord, both sides. You have strings or something like that? Tie both sides and cut in the middle." Petrillo: "The middle of the string?" Nurse: "No, the middle of the cord!" Petrillo: "When the gorilla comes out, do I hold it by the feet and spank it?" Nurse: "Yes!" Petrillo: "Just like a regular birth?" Nurse: "Just like a regular birth!"

Many calls are supposed to be titillating and sexy, as when Petrillo talks to the owner of a lingerie shop and the box office of an adult movie theater. Twenty years and many Dr. Reubens and Dr. Westheimers later, they're merely amusing. Or, as the old Jewish man who runs a store that sells whips says, "You vanna vip yourself? Who cares!"

A double entendre call to a pet cemetery: "I have a dead ass and I'd like to have it buried. I was sitting on my ass and suddenly it died. I have to get off my dead ass and get it buried." "I don't know if they bury donkeys." "Don't they have an ass department? Can I send my ass over there and perhaps they can hold it overnight?" "I don't think so, sir."

There are some cute moments here, and that's a fine achievement from a minor record label and the passage of several decades. Petrillo's last major film appearance was in 1972's *Keyholes Are for Peeping*. Duke Mitchell fans can hunt up his singles and his album "A Tribute to Jimmy Durante."

SHORTY PETTERSTEIN

- WIDE WEIRD WORLD OF SHORTY PETTERSTEIN: MORE INTERVIEWS OF OUR TIME
  (World Pacific 1274) *** $10 $25

Henry Jacobs is "Shorty Petterstein." Fantasy coupled some Petterstein material with Lenny Bruce tracks for "Interviews of Our Times." But when that disc was subsequently promoted as a solo Lenny Bruce album, both performers were peeved.

Cultists still love his lone solo studio album released in 1958, an eccentric collection of monologues, stark vignettes, and jazz-comedy improvisations. Some of the material reflects the comic influences of Lenny Bruce or Jean Shepherd (the latter in an intimate talk about guitar chord changes), but other cuts are more like Ken Nordine's word jazz, a paranoid Lord Buckley, or the odd Creed Taylor-produced albums "Shock" and "Panic, Son of Shock" flipped toward hip hi-fi devotees.

Typical of these non-comedy cuts is "Drums in the Typewriter." A deranged narrator mutters, "drums in the typewriter, there are drums in this typewriter," as his typing turns in mad drumming. Fearing that he's going mad, he tries to call for help, but discovers that dialing information does no good: "I can't hear you! I can't hear you! Information, please? Information! What's wrong! Information, what's wrong with the telephone? What's wrong with the typewriter! I hear drums in my typewriter!" And the typing and drumming continue, louder than ever.

Side Two (dubbed "For Clinical Use Only") is almost entirely devoted to stark monologues with quirky music, weird voices, and sound effects, ending with "It's No Laughing Matter," an alarming monkey chant of mental illness. Some of the intentionally humorous cuts are beyond the reach of non-jazz listeners who won't get all the throwaway lines and insider riffs. "The Origin of Jazz Terms" is for those with a knowing, cool sense of humor:

"Dig is ... from the funerals in New Orleans. The musicians would have to dig the grave. Because these musicians were poor, you know? They'd have to play, and then later dig the grave. Well then it got switched with the music, dig the music or dig the grave...."

"But does it mean anything more...."

"It's like, uh, in the context of a funeral it would mean more, yeah."

EMO PHILIPS

- E=MO2 (Epic BFE 39981) *** $5 $10
- LIVE FROM THE HASTY PUDDING THEATER (Epic BFE 40638) *** $5 $10

In 1985 Emo Philips had a cable TV special, appeared on *Saturday Night Live* and *Late Night with David Letterman*, and issued his first album. He astonished audiences unaccustomed to seeing an adult in a jaggedly cut Dutch Boy hairstyle acting like a wide-eyed man-child. Like his contemporary Pee-Wee Herman, Philips had a cult following that appreciated both his dementia and sly satire. He describes a stroll in a park:

"I was in the park today," he says, using the sing-song, brain-damaged cadence of a five-year-old just learning how to form coherent sentences, "minding my own business, staring at people, trying to make their brains explode. You know. And I saw this old woman digging for food through a garbage can. I don't know about you folks. I have a lot of love for old women going through garbage cans. They saved my life so many times as a baby. And I thought, if I can't score with her ... hehhhhh. Oh, women, you can't live with 'em, you can't get 'em to dress up in a skimpy little Nazi costume ... beat you with a warm squash."

Emo's "Hasty Pudding" album is faster-paced; he doesn't pause quite so often or let the lines drag through his exaggerated kiddie/village idiot delivery.

He's still the bumped-on-the-head bumpkin who always gets picked on. But, like a pimple, he's liable to spit back! Much of Emo's monologue is concerned with his difficulties getting along with normal people, like his parents: "I left for college. Dad said, 'I'm going to miss you.' I said, 'Well now that I broke the sight off your rifle.' Yeah. My parents threw quite a going away party for me. According to the letter."

But you can only push Emo so far. This simpleton can be dazzlingly complex! Arrested by a highway cop, he's told, "Walk a straight line." He suddenly spouts, "Well Officer Pythagoras, the closest you could ever come to achieving a straight line would be by making an electroencephalogram of your own brain waves." He continues: "I said, 'Officer, I'm taking my mom to the hospital, she OD'd on reducing pills.' He said, 'I don't see any woman with you.' I said, 'I'm too late....' He said, 'You're under arrest. You have the right to remain silent. Do you wish to retain that right?' I thought, 'Ooooh! A paradox.'"

BOBBY "BORIS" PICKETT

- MONSTER MASH (Garpax SGP 67001, reissued as London XPAS 71063) $10 $20
  CD reissued as Deram 8441472 **1/2 $8

Bostonian Bobby Pickett was a part-time actor in a part-time rock group (The Cordials). Then the monster craze erupted in the early '60s, and *Famous Monsters* magazine, Aurora monster models, and ghoul trading cards were all over the place. Pickett put out a quickie single called "Monster Mash." It became "a graveyard smash." "Monster Mash" was originally on the Garpax label, owned by the enterprising twenty-three-year-old Gary Paxton, now a born-again religious record producer. At the time he'd already had a novelty hit, guiding "Alley Oop" to the top. In September of 1962, his tiny label had the #1 hit in the land.

Everyone knows the tune: Pickett, imitating Boris Karloff, narrates the story of "working in the lab, late one night," and having his monster rise up fearfully and start doing the latest dance craze, the Mashed Potato: "He did the Mash! He did the Monster Mash! He did the Mash! And it's a graveyard smash!" There's no point going any further with the lyrics. They're secondary to the whole incongruous tone of the song as Pickett paints a picture of singing and dancing monsters, complete with the spunky background vocals by "The Crypt Kickers."

"Monster Mash" is a four-star novelty. Boris Karloff even did a "cover version" of it when he guest starred on TV variety shows of the day. Of course, he disagreed with Pickett's mimicry, insisting, "but I don't lisp!" The tune was re-recorded and reissued in 1973 and became a hit all over again. The album, however, is what one would expect, with more deathly filler than a graveyard. Most of the rock music is terrible with Pickett ad-libbing non-jokes. Pickett and his cowriters try every type of dance tune they can think of, from "Sinister Stomp" to "Monster Minuet." Various songs refer to "Monster Mash" including "Transylvania Twist" and "The Bash," with Bela Lugosi trying to horn in on Boris's success.

Karloff: "Did you really believe by throwing this bash, your dance would replace my Monster Mash? Return to your graves, you devils with wings. This dance wouldn't make it with living things." Then Karloff mutters, "You've got a lot of nerve." And Lugosi mumbles, "Oh well, I tried."

The album has the cute "Monster Holiday," which was the next single for Pickett, released in December of 1962, but only the CD has the flip side to it, Lugosi's amusing "Monster Motion."

NOTES: The original Garpax album is a rarity. London's reissue album has a different cover and an updated photo of Pickett. The CD utilizes the original cover.

Pickett fans might want "Ticklish Tales of Terror" (Label-Aire 14005), issued around 1977. Bobby reads mild horror poems and vignettes with sound effects. A highlight is "Renfield the Madman," a scene based on "Dracula," with Pickett imitating throaty, demented Dwight Frye: "Rats! Thousands of rats! And he seemed to be saying, all of these I will give to you if you will only do my bidding." Lon Chaney, Jr., who died four years earlier, appears on the album via a few stories he recorded that were left off an album he did called "The Wolfman Speaks." Pickett was once part of a comedy team (see "Hudson and Pickett"). Pickett has issued many novelty singles including "Star Drek" (vocals by Peter Ferrara) and 1984's "Monster Rap."

CHARLES PIERCE

- For Pierced Ears (Wanda MP 2101) *** $10 $25
- Charles Pierce (Blue Thumb BTS 30) **1/2 $10 $20

Since the '60s Charles Pierce has been the unrivaled queen of drag stand-up (he prefers the term "male actress" to "female impersonator"). His concerts on both coasts, including a series of "farewell" shows in the late '80s, attracted packed houses. A video was even released, sold primarily at the performances.

On his first album for the tiny Wanda label of Belmont, California, Pierce slings gay slang along with the gags, and the code words ("brown" for anal sex) often get more laughs than the jokes. The straight lines have enough innuendo to get appreciative snickers: "I went to Judy Garland's opening."

He opens as Katherine Hepburn:

"Hello, hello, hello. I'm Katherine Heartburn, the senior citizens' Twiggy. And I came to San Francisco with a flower in my hair. Pillsbury. All you do is take this water and pour it over me and you get instant buns. Brown and serve ... I'm simply furious at Twiggy. I think her measurements are the same as mine: 10, 10, 10, and 1. She has these little teeny-tiny ankles. But I'm still thin. I was in Detroit recently and I walked unscathed through a volley of shotgun fire. What a riot. I can walk through a harp and not strike a note."

Few albums of the day offered solid jokes for transvestites: "I like that little scene with the Man from Swish, who's in church, you see, and the altar boy goes by swinging the censer. The Man from Swish peeks out of his pew and says: 'Sweetie, that's a gay drag but your purse is on fire.'"

Pierce's mimicry isn't always sharp, but the humor is bluntly sassy, as his fans would demand: "Oh, whatever happened to Rochelle Hudson? I guess she changed her name to Rock and is making millions." Pierce finds time for old favorites like Tallulah Bankhead, Bette Davis, and Mae West, but oddly enough, on the cover Pierce resembles Martina Navratilova.

The Blue Thumb release circa 1970 is easier to find. Here he avoids using a stereotypical effeminate delivery. "I'm very masculine," he insists, "I dress this way to counteract it." Nor is he particularly abusive in parodying women— a common trait among drag comics. Pierce has fun with the ringsiders, offering gags old and new: "I finally figured those three out. Four of them, they're all together. She's the lookout! These are the Rhea sisters: Gonna, Dya, and Pya. These are The Andrews Sisters: See no Evil, Speak no Evil, and Laverne. She's laughing. I love to see her laugh 'cause so much of her has a good time." Pierce spends a good portion of his set on observations and jokes, scattering a few bits of mimicry here and there. It's only in the second half that he goes to the movies for set pieces as the stars. Pierce's star impressions are uneven vocally, some definitely requiring the visuals. Still, fans will love his Tallulah Bankhead, his famous Bette Davis, and a long routine as Mae West, including one-liner recollections: "I was a lady sheriff in a picture. With four hundred gorgeous men in my posse."

PIG VOMIT

- PIG VOMIT (Oink 1063-2) ** $8

Despite the band's title, Pig Vomit is bland vocally and the music is derivative of the faceless '70s groups (the Bostons, Chicagos, etc.) these fellas grew up enjoying. The band harmonizes on topics that high school males are concerned about: farts, masturbation, and the mysteries of womanhood.

The contrast between the squeaky clean pop and oldies tunes and the "dirty" lyrics is amusing at times ("Are You Ever Going to Come?") but most of it is so targeted to the pimply that it will hardly raise an eyebrow for older listeners familiar with Billy Joel's "Only the Good Die Young," Meatloaf's "Paradise by the Dashboard Light," and the collected works of Frank Zappa. An older person listening to "She Had Her Period" will be yawning, not laughing, and maybe thinking how much the opening resembles a Shangri-Las song and how the falsetto apes Del Shannon.

But kids looking for their own version of Zappa will be cheering over the bouncy "Holy Shit, I Gotta Pee" and others. The sticker on the 1994 CD says it all: "As Featured on the Howard Stern Show."

PINKARD AND BOWDEN

- WRITERS IN DISGUISE (Warner Bros. 250571) ** $5 $10
- PG-13 (Warner Bros. 25299-1) ** $5 $10
- PINKARD AND BOWDEN LIVE (Warner Bros. 9 26057 2) ** $8
- COUSINS, CATTLE AND OTHER LOVE STORIES (Warner Bros. 9 268442) *1/2 $8

Owing a little more to Martin Mull than Homer and Jethro, the team of Sandy Pinkard and Richard Bowden offer some moderately subtle material. From the "Writers in Disguise" album: "In our little town, the dentist and the proctologist was the same guy. That was cool, as long as you scheduled your dental work first, it was no problem at all."

Just how moderately subtle the duo is depends on whether the average fan "gets" the punned title of their album.

They ride off in several directions, with originals and parodies of country classics. In parody, "Delta Dawn" becomes "Delta Dawg" and "Another Somebody Done Somebody Wrong Song" becomes "Somebody Done Somebody's Song Wrong," but these one-joke concepts are usually too short and simple to be more than momentarily amusing.

Depending on one's definition of wit, there's good times to be had on some of the originals. Bobby Braddock wrote the catchy "I Lobster but Never Flounder," loaded with soggy puns: "She was the bass I ever had, now my life has no porpoise. Oh my cod I love her yes I do.... He wrapped his line around her and they drove off in his carp.... I octopus his face in 'cause he'll only break her heart." And when it comes to pure country comedy, there's a shortie about a bird who gets eaten by a cat: "And it was bye bye birdie, you parrot-faced, finger-paintin', seed-slingin' fool!"

For some reason, Anne Murray, Steve Railsback, The Osmond Brothers, Don Henley, Glenn Frey, Jackson Browne, David Carradine, and Jennifer Warnes are on the first album, though their vocals and instrumental contributions are almost invisible.

"PG-13" from 1985 is another uneven mix of rednecked corn side-by-side with left-wing satire. The corn includes "Ballad of Dick and Jane," which has the boys chuckling how Jane's "got Dick in the palm of her hand. She likes to kiss Dick all of the time. Seems like Dick is always on her mind." The satire is on "Let's Put the X Back in Christmas" (a tongue-in-cheek number about a guy putting on a Santa Claus suit to give his wife some sexual kicks during home video taping). But with cuts like the obvious "Don't Pet the Dog" ("or the next thing you know, he'll be askin' your ankle to dance ... he'll boo-boo all over yer shoes"), there are too many "boo-boos" getting in the way of the good stuff.

The duo make little progress on their 1989 live album, which includes earlier material. The highlight for nerve, especially in front of Southern audiences, is "Elvis Was a Narc": "Elvis was a narc in rhinestones after dark. He did his best to keep Memphis drug free. He knew every pill he'd eat would be one less on the street. Elvis took 'em all for you and me." The most peculiar cut is their version of "Leaving on a Jet Plane," the main purpose being a real groaner pun: "Call my folks in Tripoli. Tell them Khadaffi made me go. I'm a Libyan on a Jet Plane. Don't know if I'll be back again." Many tunes are just dumb and pathetic like "She Dances with Meat" and their parody of Jimmy Webb's "The Highwayman," now called "I Was a Froggy."

"Cousins" is a sixty-eight-minute CD of the duo dead and alive: the songs as recorded in a studio are repeated in a live performance. The songs aren't worth hearing twice. Good parody takes a sledgehammer to pretense and flattens it with one breathtaking blow. Here, the blowhards lift the sledgehammer and drop it on their own toes. "Cocaine," which could've inspired a devastating put-down, is merely parodied as "Propane" with some gaseously silly lines: "If you wanna get warm when you're down on the farm: Propane! If you live in the sticks, and your income is fixed? Propane!"

Whether the boys are on the liberal or redneck side of an issue isn't the point. The point is satire. And here, the point is dull.

JOE PISCOPO

- I LOVE ROCK AND ROLL (Columbia 44-03254) **1/2 $5 $10
- NEW JERSEY (Columbia BFC 40046) **1/2 $5 $10

Joe Piscopo, the pug-nosed, curly-haired comic who had a few good years with *Saturday Night Live*, went solo and released "Rock and Roll," a 1982 mini-album that lasts under ten minutes. The humor is in his Sinatra voice as, swingingly unhip, he medleys rock hits by Joan Jett, Bruce Springsteen, Pat Benatar, The Rolling Stones, etc. It's a one-joke concept that manages to make it through one listening.

Piscopo's "New Jersey" has some odd moments, like a Latino impressionist doing Joan Rivers and Curly of The Three Stooges in Spanish. Equally mindboggling, Eddie Murphy joins Piscopo for "Honeymooner's Rap." It's complete with references to specific sitcom episodes and an obnoxious but funny chorus of "Nawwwton, Nawwton, naw naw naw naw naw naw Nawwton—Ralphie Boy!" There are also some fun moments in his slightly dated version of David Letterman's show.

Unfortunately, too much of the album is harsh and overpowering without humor, and when an often deliberately obnoxious comic like Piscopo takes on equally irritating celebrities like Andy Rooney and Allen Funt, the result is hard to take. Parodying Bruce Springsteen for singing overblown, rasping, pseudo-heartfelt music comes up short— when several of Springsteen's own originals are almost as silly. Piscopo's reprise of Francis Albert Sinatra singing is more a tribute than a satire, and that's not funny at all.

Cartoon fans take note: June Foray and Bill Scott briefly drop by as Rocky and Bullwinkle. Piscopo fans might want to hunt for "Joe Piscopo at Large" a radio show distributed via disc to stations around the country.

PETER AND PENELOPE POOF

- PETER AND PENELOPE POOF HAVE A PARTY (RIC M 1004) ** $4 $10

This obscure 1964 album tries to freshen up old sex jokes by creating an authentic "party" atmosphere. The result is similar to the "party" segments on *Rowan and Martin's Laugh-In* a few years later. A bunch of people just happen to be holding conversations that consist almost entirely of set-ups and punch lines.

"I'll say this much for her, she isn't easily upset." "I understand last Thursday her husband walked in and found her in bed with another man!" "What did he say, her husband I mean?" "Naturally he screamed, 'Who is this man?'" "And what did she say?" "She rolled over and said, 'That's a fair question, what *is* your name?'" "Well, I'm not surprised. She's descended from a long line her mother once fell for."

Hosts Peter and Penelope mill about, encouraging their guests to get up and sing songs ("Let's Do It" by Cole Porter, "Doin' What Comes Naturally" by Irving Berlin, and so on). This audio re-creation of a supposedly sophisticated adult party isn't poorly done, but the gags were toothless and tame even back in '64.

PORTSMOUTH SINFONIA

- PORTSMOUTH SINFONIA PLAYS THE POPULAR CLASSICS (Columbia KC 33049) * $5 $10

Dubbed "The World's Worst Orchestra," the Portsmouth troupe was formed in 1970 at Portsmouth College of Art in England. There's a slight cult that appreciates their antics, which thud somewhere to the right of Hoffnung.

With some of the brass unable to hit the high notes, and various strings hamstrung, the result sounds like an unrehearsed bunch of pathetics. Some critics insist they're satiric classical iconoclasts, punks, and nihilists.

There might be a few wincing laughs hearing them saw so forlornly and sourly through a beautiful piece like the "Air from Suite No. 3 in D Major" by Bach, but not for more than a minute. Cuts include segments from "The Nutcracker Suite," "Peer Gynt Suite," Beethoven's Fifth, "The Planets," and "Also Sprach Zarathustra."

Two cuts from this lone 1974 American release, including a clumsy kazoo-like rendition of "The William Tell Overture" appear on the CD compilation "Dead Parrot Society" (Rhino R2 71049), which also includes a previously unreleased live cut and a British single, "Classical Massacre," originally issued in 1981. Fans can hunt for the Symphonia's British import album "20 Classic Rock Classics" (Philips 9109231).

Brian Eno, who had some success with Roxy Music at the time and would later enjoy a solo career, produced the album. This broadens the album's collector interest very slightly.

TOM POSTON

- THE BEST OF BURLESQUE (MGM E 3644) * $10 $25

Poston, now best known for his portrayal of mild-mannered sitcom dimwits, starred in this 1957 tribute to burlesque. A bunch of olde-time songs like "I'm Forever Blowing Bubbles" fall flat without being able to see the Bronx-accented "Nelle's Belles" perform them.

Poston, along with Vini Faye, Nancee Ward, Emmett Rose, and Lilly White, handles the two long comic sketches, which sound pitifully hollow without a studio audience. "Higher Education" offers a feeble bunch of classroom double entendres: "It was only last week that you mislaid your bibliography." "Mislaid your bibliography? Butterfingers!" "And you hadn't been on campus three days when you lost your glossary!" "If this keeps up, kid, you'll be nothing but skin and bones!" "Floogel Street" is a classic, but not in the stark and stagey treatment here.

Poston is a lot funnier in a more typical role—as a blankly feeble-minded fellow who can't even remember his own name—on Steve Allen's album of "Man in the Street" interviews.

POTTS AND PANZY

- THAT'S MY WIFE (Laff A 143) *1/2 $4 $8

One of the more unusual black duos, Jimmy Potts was teamed with drag comedian Arthur Matthews as the hoarsely squealing "Panzy." They seldom tell jokes; just ramble and posture and mug for the audience. They turn up, unannounced and unwanted, on the flip side of "The Crepitation Contest" (Laff A 152).

OLLIE JOE PRATER

- THE RENEGADE WHITE MAN (Laff A 217) ** $4 $8

An amiable good ol' Southern comic, big Ollie Joe Prater spends a lot of time on this 1981 album happily promoting cocaine, marijuana, alcohol, and other assorted drugs. Sometimes all at once. As he tells his clapping, whistling, foot stomping audience, "Ah like to take a couple of them quaaludes ya know, drink me a coupla beers, coupla shots of tequila, four or five Valiums, and drive! Ah know ah might hit somethin', but who gives a shit?"

Later he says, "I'm a drunk. I'm not an alcoholic. I'm a drunk! There's a difference. I don't have to go to them goddam meetings!"

No surprise that Prater died young. But when folks would tell him, "You'd live a lot longer if you didn't drink so much," he liked to answer, "It would just seem longer."

THE PREMISE

- THE PREMISE (Vanguard VRS 9092) ** $10 $20

Theodore J. Flicker created The Compass Players, the famous improv group in St. Louis. Circa 1962 he brought "The Premise" to an off-Broadway theater in New York. It was a collection of sketches starring himself, Joan Darling, George Segal, and Thomas Aldredge.

Improv, the deliberate and stubborn attempt to make something out of nothing, often produces labored and stagey results. The actors have no time to live with their characters and tend to rely on stereotype and cliché.

For some reason, these faults are glaring here. Most of the routines either are dated or just sound that way, even the ones presumably polished and perfected from their original ad-libbed forms. Long routines featuring lonely neurotics and eccentrics have now become performance art cliché.

Concepts that were very fresh at the time have been used again and again since, like the routine about a-bigot meeting his maker: a black man; or the one in which Darling tells Segal that she's pregnant. His ad-libbed response: "But we never...."

A winter vignette: "Boy, you know something, I just love the snow." "Oh really? Oh, that's a very unpopular attitude you know." "I know." "Costs the city a lot of money and people couldn't drive their cars for days. All that tax money just going down the drain." "Don't you like the snow?" "Sure I do, it's my whole life." "Hey, look at that. Your nose is running." "Hey." "What's the matter?" "Hey, the sun just came out." "Oh." "Your nose is running too." "I think I love you." "Really? I love you too. You're the nicest snowman I ever met."

BOB PRESCOTT

- RUSSIAN ROULETTE AND OTHER BULLET-PROOF GAGS
    (Audio Fidelity AFLP 2103, also released as CARTOONS IN SOUND) * $4 $12

Sound effects expert Bob Prescott's 1963 album of "Sound Cartoons" is tedium relieved by moments of irritation. His twenty-three audio blackout sketches feature long setups and witless punch lines.

One sketch offers the sound of two trains. It turns out they are on the same track about to collide. Then there's a tremendous crash. The punch line: a voice says, "What a way to run a railroad." A man asks another for a match. There's the sound of the match, the sputter of flame, then the sound of fire engines racing. The punch line: a voice says, "I'm sorry I asked." A gym teacher instructs the ladies on doing calisthenics. Then suddenly there's a ripping sound.

The best one is the title cut, and that's not so hot. Two Russians are playing Russian Roulette. For an eternity they take turns with the gun: here's the sound of the cylinder spinning, the sound of the gun being slid across the wooden table and back, etc. Over and over, there's "click," "click," and "click." Finally the gun goes off. Then the punch line: "How about two out of three?"

A man goes to the barber, sits in a chair, and casually asks how the barber is doing. The barber starts chatting and babbling until his voice becomes completely speeded up. Sound effects then snip in bits of foreign languages and a cacophony of gibberish. Finally the voice slows back down to normal. His customer remarks, "I'm sorry I asked."

ROGER PRICE

- ROGER AND OVER (A.A. Records AR 1S) ** $8 $15

The bespectacled, West Virginia-accented Price was a popular satirist in the '50s, usually showcased via quiz shows. At thirty-one, he hosted 1951's *How To*, and in 1954 *Droodles*, with contestants trying to make sense of odd cartoon puzzles. Price eventually made a career out of publishing novelty books like *Mad Libs* and *Murphy's Law* for his Price/Stern/Sloan company. In 1977 he created the TV show *The Kallikaks*, and in 1979 produced the slapstick kids show *You Can't Do That on Television*.

One side of this 1960 album is live, recorded at The Village Vanguard. Price chuckles at himself from time to time, and his jittery speech pattern, coupled with a lecturing style, shows why he never made it in stand-up. He opens with some gags, talking about a man "who was born with his head on backwards. It created quite a problem actually. People would say goodbye when they met him. He was a nice fella you know, but awful messy in the bathroom." And there's another guy "who didn't know the difference between arson and incest. He set fire to his sister."

About ten or fifteen minutes is devoted to a "Theory of Names," based on his book *What Not to Name the Baby*. Members of the audience call out names and Price describes what these people are supposed to be like: "Vincent has all his clothes tailor-made and makes real terrible puns.... Ira is a guy who's sorta jerky but he doesn't know it and he acts like Cary Grant.... Arthur carries the *New York Times* around but doesn't read it. Much different from Artie. He can get you blender parts wholesale.... Pamela is a tall girl who has a job as an editor or something on a trade magazine like *Foot Digest*, and Pamela pastes covers of *The New Yorker* on her wall. And you know how with some girls you feel sorry the next day? With Pamela you're sorry when it's going on."

The second side is studio work with Sascha Burland (see The Idiots and Company and The Nutty Squirrels). The combination of Burland and Price yields dry, obscure, sometimes jokeless sketches that are hip but not funny. In a long report on the history of jazz, Price claims Insane Cadwallader invented bop: "Bop was based on a seventeen-note chromatic scale, which presented a problem as there are only twelve notes to an octave. They solved this problem by playing very rapidly." A final segment gives Price a chance to do some "Sound Droodles," in which sound effects are matched with likely captions. A clank of dropping silverware is Sir Lancelot taking his pants off.

- THE ELEPHANT RECORD (LP 100) * $4 $12

This 1963 attempt to cash in on the novelty craze for elephant jokes was cheaply recorded in a studio and would not have gotten any laughs if it was done live. A children's record performed by people who seem incapable of having them, the cloying, cabaret-style songs sung by Price, Jeff Harris, Fay DeWitt, and the others don't have the honest silliness and warmth of kiddie nonsense humor. One particularly vile track consists of the ensemble brazenly chirping a riddle over and over for nearly three minutes: "When Tarzan saw the elephants, what did Tarzan say?" "Here come the elephants, over the hill they're comin' this way. When Tarzan saw the elephants, what did Tarzan say?" Repeat, repeat, repeat.

The spoken routines are peculiarly done as stark dramatic playlets: "How many is it now, Edna?" "Fifteen days at sea Ralph, we can't hold out much longer." "Why do you have to cut an elephant's toenails?" "So you won't get scratched when you pick them up. Those look like storm clouds. I hope our little raft won't sink." "We'd be drowned instantly. What kind of deodorants do elephants use?" "They use a roll on. And on and on and on."

Too stark for kids, too inane for adults.

FREDDIE PRINZE

- LOOKIN' GOOD (Columbia PC 33562) ★★★ $5 $20

A cutie-pie ethnic comic, Prinze was almost as precocious as Bill Dana's Jose Jimenez, coming up with catch-phrases like "Is Not My Job" and the smilingly silly "Lookin' Good!" He was generally a gentle jester who talked with tolerant bewilderment about his neighborhood and the differences between Hispanics and whites.

In the early '70s, when ethnic comedy was "in," he and Jimmie Walker found themselves swept off the stand-up stage and into television. Success came quickly with his sitcom *Chico and the Man*, but in the midst of it, Prinze killed himself. The shock waves included a TV movie about him (*I Can't Hear the Laughter*) and a high price for this record. At this point, interest has subsided a bit.

The album does offer some well-constructed jokes, but the subject matter is limited to anecdotes about his tough neighborhood and gags about being Puerto Rican.

He talks about being "Hungarican," and how his Gypsy father met his Puerto Rican mother: "They were on a bus tryin' to pick each other's pockets.... My mother's always talking about the wedding: 'Oh Freddie, my wedding was so beautiful! The flowers, the orchestra playing, your father looked so handsome. You shoulda been there.' I was!"

There is the occasional bit of irony. At one point Prinze remembers his mother saying, "You can always make more money, but you can never get your life back." And, in talking about a Puerto Rican hospital in which the PA system tells doctors, "get your ass into the operating room," he tries to find directions:

"Where's the recovery room?"

"Nobody recovers here, you die!"

CORK PROCTOR

- WHAT HAVE I GOT TO LOSE? (Satyr) ★1/2 $4 $8

Proctor's Vegas act covers fast food hamburgers and other predictable subjects: "Ever see that grease? If Mario Andretti had three Big Macs in his rear end he never woulda lost that bearing, he would've gone all the way around. The worst, man ... I'm not makin' this up. 'You Deserve a Break Today.' Any wife that takes her kids out to McDonald's ought to be drawn and hamstrung. The worst. Not only that, they constipate you, those burgers. What this whole society needs is a good healthy shit. That's right. Excuse me ma'am, I didn't mean to offend you by saying 'healthy.'"

PROCTOR AND BERGMAN

- TV OR NOT TV (Columbia KC 32199) ★★ $8 $12
- WHAT THIS COUNTRY NEEDS (Columbia PC 33687) ★★ $8 $12
- GIVE US A BREAK (Mercury SRM 1 3719) ★★ $8 $12

Firesign Theater's Phil Proctor and Peter Bergman went solo in 1973. The duo favors short sketches over long, involved dramas, making their albums close in tone to the Firesign "Dear Friends" album. Most of the cuts are trifles, but some are cute enough.

Their first album, "TV or Not TV," is subtitled a "vaudeville in two acts" and does at times seem like Wayne and Shuster on acid. The corny "Declining Fall of the Roaming Umpire" has some gags that could go back to ancient Rome: "I'm hungry. Dare I eat this scroll? It's sheepskin, after all." More dialogue:

"Can we talk?" "Barely, with all these slaves underfoot." "Were we deep in Greece we'd eat them, heh heh...." "Have you come to tryst again, like we did last summer?" "My head is in another place. And where's his household's head?" "As always, down the hall to the right...." "Bruto's yet abed?" "Yet abed!" "Yuk-a-puk!" "Oh, Prolongus, he had a frightful night. He babbled like an open book. Would tell-a-vision, then fall into his dreams again back and forth, sweating like a Trojan he schlepped the night away." "I'll be a horse's ass."

Listeners can pride themselves on recognizing the references to babbling brooks, Chubby Checker, Morey Amsterdam, the Trojan Horse, etc. That's a substitute for laughing at this material.

On "Give Us a Break" a memory expert devises strange ways of remembering names:

"Bergman? Berg is a hamburger! Man, that's a guy standing on top of one. Berg-man, get it ... well, I gotta be going, I gotta give a memory lecture downtown at ... at ... downtown, that building with the clock? Doesn't matter. I was supposed to take one of those things, it's a long car with doors that open on the side? Perhaps you can help me Mr. Relishfoot."

"Relishfoot?"

"Oh yeah, my system, every time I look at you I see a man standing on a hamburger ... Mr. McDonald."

It's followed by a report from Jacques Cousteau on pollution. The serious message is camouflaged in a typical swath of Firesign wordplay: "Thousands of silvery little pop top fish spinning playfully in the currents. And here comes a family of broken brown beer bottle fish, as usual travelling in packs of six. They're cute, but beware of those jagged teeth. They can Schlitz your foot off. So remember, the next time you yell at the silent sea and she does not answer, it is not necessarily a sign that her herring has been imparied."

For those who always figured that Firesign Theater and its various members could never get laughs live, Proctor and Bergman recorded "What This Country Needs" live at The Bottom Line in 1975. Here is a segment from one of their usual commercial parodies, with audience reaction in parenthesis.

"We're brought to you this morning by Nose Brothers Coffee ... open the can, take a sniff, throw the can away, you've just had Nose Brothers Coffee (giggles). Yes, Nose Brothers Coffee is featured this week and every week in your local Giant Toad Supermarket (laughs, clapping). That's right, and specials this week: half a can of Kung Fu Beans! HY-YAHH! Half price (laughter, clapping). And, introducing the new, all-action cereal from Canada with a hockey puck in every box (laughter). "Body Chex" (laughter, applause). That's right, the kids'll have to eat all the cereal before they can get the puck out (confused silence, then giggles)."

NOTES: Back in 1960 when they were at Yale, the duo appeared in the Yale Musical Productions of *Tom Jones* (Carillon M 80P 5436/7) and *Booth Is Back in Town* (Carillon M80P-8900). "The Proctor and Bergman Report" (1977 radio material) is on eighteen albums sent to radio stations as "Hot News for the Week" from Noxema.

PROFESSOR BACKWARDS
• LAUGH WITH PROFESSOR BACKWARDS (Jumbo JLP 201) **1/2 $8 $20

Amiable Southern comic Jimmie Edmondson smoothly recites the usual corny gags in a monologue that includes some material considered mildly risqué in the early '60s: "I went in a big department store today, I asked the salesgirl, 'Do you have any notions?' She said, 'Yeah, but we have to suppress them during business hours.' I went looking around the store, I saw a sign, it said 'Ladies.' I walked in. There they were! And I found out something, fellas. They write on the walls just like we do. I went back to the salesgirl and I said, 'I'd like to see something cheap in a man's suit.' She said, 'The mirror's on the left.'"

He does his five-minute "Professor Backwards" routine, in which he takes words from the audience and immediately writes them backwards on a blackboard. Then he does a funny pronunciation that makes the crowd chuckle. "What's your word, Buddy? Polyethelene?" He spells it backwards and enunciates it: "Inny littie, ya lop!" Five minutes is just enough for this kind of novelty.

An early radio appearance by Professor Backwards appears on the double-set "Ted Mack Amateur Hour 25th Anniversary Album" (United Artists UXL 2). In 1976 three men broke into the professor's Atlanta home and held him prisoner overnight. Their initial goal was to extort money. But after he wrote a check, they shot and killed him.

RICHARD PRYOR
• RICHARD PRYOR (Dove RS 6325) **1/2 $5 $15

Pryor seemed like a "new Bill Cosby" when he first appeared on TV and in Las Vegas. Pryor admitted that he was simply imitating Bill Cosby (Cos did "Noah" so Richie did "Adam and Eve"). The Dove 1968 album is from that era. In "Girls" he uses some Cosby mannerisms as he nostalgically recalls an old girlfriend: "I used to wrestle for two hours ... you'd wrestle for two hours, and every time you'd get a grip she'd move, and you'd have to wrestle another two hours, and by the time you did, you were just too tired! (He starts breathing heavily into the microphone, exactly like Cosby doing a bit on running with sneakers.) 'I'll see ya tommorrow!' And the father would catch you (almost an exact imitation of Cosby's father voice): 'What are you kids doin' in the front room with the door locked!'" Even the father's knock on the door sounds like it was lifted from an old Cosby album.

Only one bit gives any portent of what Pryor would become. Feeling the need for a black hero, Pryor imagines what that would be: "Look! Up in the sky! It's a crow. It's a bat. It's Supernigger! Yes, friends, Supernigger. Faster than a bowl of chitlins ... Supernigger's X-ray vision enables him to see through everything—except Whitey."

• THAT NIGGER'S CRAZY (Partee 2404 reissued Reprise MS 2241) **1/2 $5 $10

In 1970, Pryor was doing safe comedy at the Aladdin Hotel in Las Vegas. Suddenly he stopped. He said, "What am I doing here?" and walked off. Another comic, George Carlin, was having similar doubts. But while Carlin found his new voice at college venues, Pryor went back to his roots, working black nightclubs and emerging with a very uncompromising style.

Pryor's jet black dialect and constant use of obscenities seemed to doom him to obscurity (and a bunch of albums from the X-rated Laff label; more on that later). But as the comic voice of the black community, Pryor found himself with hit records, newfound fame, and a lot of influence. And curious whites began to listen, too.

Like Lenny Bruce, Mort Sahl, and Dick Gregory before him, Pryor was considered to be the man with "the word."

The newfound adulation, and the willingness with which white liberals begged for more abuse, only seemed to fuel Pryor's anger. His albums would get stronger, more strident. Here, there is still a smile on Pryor's face, even though the IRS audited Richard just before the recording session for this record, cutting into him for thousands of dollars and tossing him in jail for ten days.

"YOU CRAZY!" someone shouts from the audience. But Pryor's comical madness is unstoppable as he forays into sociology and white vs black lifestyles. Both blacks and whites could be made uncomfortable as he talks about raucous blacks at home and uptight whites.

Pryor's version of *The Exorcist* is a shock delight. He figures that if *The Exorcist* was about a black girl, nobody would've tolerated the devil's takeover.

• L.A. JAIL (Tiger Lily TL 14023) **1/2 $6 $12

For this early authorized album, Pryor allowed Tiger Lily to catch one of his performances and take whatever they could get. The quality of both the recording and the comedy is pretty good. The first part of the album offers Pryor's recollections on his tough neighborhood, including the familiar bit about the cool way he ran away from trouble. But there's also some bits from his Vegas days, like the Shecky Greene-style bit on the way movie stars go to the bathroom: "John Wayne goes to the bathroom: I'm gonna go poo poo." An unusual moment: his three-minute almost rote recollection of the dialogue between Dave the astronaut and Hal the computer in *2001: A Space Odyssey*. After he finishes the slowed-down version of "Bicycle Built for Two," he just says, "I went to see *2001* today and got hung up on it." By way of apology, he launches into a surefire routine on farts.

- IS IT SOMETHING I SAID (Reprise MSK 2285, CD reissue 2285-2) **1/2 $5 $10
- BICENTENNIAL NIGGER (Warner Bros. BS 2960 and BSK 3114) *** $5 $10
- RICHARD PRYOR'S GREATEST HITS (BSK 3057) *** $5 $10

"Something I Said" isn't much. There are a few moments of fine dialect shock comedy here. "Eulogy" has some comical truth as Pryor reflects on the dearly departed, observing: "De ultimate test i' whuther or not you can survive death. That's a ultima test fo yo ass, ain't it? So far don't nobody we know have passed the ultima test. Least of all this nigger layin' here." Similarly, a thirteen-minute cut introduces "Mudbone." Pryor, who wrote for Lily Tomlin's TV specials in the early '70s, evidently was influenced by her technique of character comedy vignettes. Going more for reality than laughs, this is Pryor as a folk humorist, re-creating a favorite character filled with slice-of-life observations.

"When Your Woman Leaves You" has some vulnerability to it, with Pryor touching on some of the pain in his seemingly endless series of marriages and divorces. He stands naked for the audience: "I don't mind women leavin' me ... but they tell you why. Fuck that, just leave ... 'cause there ain't shit you can say when they're talkin' to you. You know it's true, all you can do is stand there and look silly." It was this kind of material, as well as his sizzling takes on race, that made him respected by his peers as a genius who took chances for his art.

Sam Kinison once told me that "Bicentennial Nigger" was his favorite comedy album. It has ten minutes of Mudbone and a typical Pryor rant on white women vs black women that insults both groups. The white women are portrayed as submissive princesses with babyish voices. The black women are loud bitches who "may knock you out." But his six-minute sermon about the bicentennial burns hot: "We're celebratin' two hundred years of white folks kickin' ass ... how long will this bullshit go on? How long, how long, how long will this bullshit go on ... they say in the Bible we will know how long when the angel come up out of the sea. He will have seven heads, the face of a serpent and the body of a lion. I don't know about you, but I don't wanna see no motherfucker like that." Additionally there's a chilling two and a half minute monologue, with patriotic music playing in the background, as "The Bicentennial Nigger" comes to life to talk about what America did to the black people. Pryor yucks and chuckles and giggles over every grim irony as he tells the story of the slave era: "I'm just so thrilled to be here.... I used to live to be a hundred and fifty. Now I die of high blood pressure by the time I'm fifty-two. That thrills me to death ... they brought me over here in a boat ... four hundred of us come over. Three hundred sixty of us died on the way. I just loved that ... you white folks are so good to us ... then they split us all up. Took my mama over that way, my wife over the other way ... Lord have mercy ... y'all probably forgot about it ... but I ain't never gonna forget."

"Greatest Hits" focuses on his early albums, cuts including "Ali," "Exorcist," "My Father," "Nigger with a Seizure," "Have Your Ass Home by 11," "Wino," "Craps," "Cocaine," "When Your Woman Leaves You," and "Mudbone: Little Feets."

- WANTED: LIVE IN CONCERT (2BSK 3364) *** $8 $15

Following the failure of his NBC series, and the whirlwind pace of more movies and more stand-up dates, Pryor was just about at the breaking point. New Year's Eve 1978 he'd made headlines for a wild melee at his house.

His two-record set opens with Pryor exulting: "I'm happy to see people come out, especially after all the shit I been in." He describes the New Year's Eve incident where he pumped bullets into his wife's car: "I had a Magnum, shot one of those tires ... I shot another ... and that vodka I was drinkin' said, 'Go ahead, shoot somethin' else ... man.' The police came. I went into the house. 'Cause they got Magnums too. And they don't kill cars, they kill nig-gars!"

The audience goes wild, encouraging Pryor every step of the way. Very few comedians have attempted two-record sets (Bill Cosby was one of the first, and Dick Gregory did a few). Here, with an audience supplying such giant amounts of laughter over just about everything, it's not surprising that it takes four sides before Pryor can finish his act. He does a solid eight minutes just describing the line outside the theater, with the whites who bought tickets six months in advance fearfully meeting up with blacks demanding to get in at the last minute.

There's conversational material on the Spinks-Ali fight, the difference between Chinese sex and black sex, and a solid routine ("Being Sensitive") that vividly cartoons the most intimate moments in the battle of the sexes.

He made a movie after the record was released, *Richard Pryor Live in Concert*, using a lot of the material from the set. It became a big box office hit, and this had a tremendous effect on stand-up comedy. The idea of a cheaply done one-man show making big money opened the door for other comics to do solo cable TV specials, movies, even Broadway solo productions. For the first time, a double-record comedy set went gold.

- LIVE ON THE SUNSET STRIP (BSK 3660) *** $5 $10

Pryor's erratic personal life culminated in a near-death experience. After first reporting it as a freebasing accident, he admitted he doused himself with rum and struck a match during a crazed suicide attempt. Following his painful recovery, and an attempt to stay off drugs, he had serious doubts about his ability to create. With support from Lily Tomlin, Robin Williams, and many other peers, he found his way back.

Some of the material here sounds very much like the frisky old Pryor as he talks about sex and marriage. Then he gets a little more serious: "Heartache is an education for a man. 'Cause we don't really grow up and graduate till a woman break your fuckin' heart. That's your diploma. If you come through that shit, Jack, you a man."

Equally challenging is his description of going back to Africa and ultimately discovering pride in his all-black homeland. Pryor would no longer use the word "nigger." The experience in Africa had been that powerful.

Of course, so had the experience of burning up. He wrings uncomfortable laughs in talking about his recovery. He describes the agony of taking a spongebath: "Don't touch me with that motherfuckin' sponge no more!" Then he turns it into pure comedy: "Catching on fire is inspiring.They should use it for the Olympics. 'Cause I did the 100 yard dash in about 4.6 in the underbrush! And you know something I noticed? When you run down the street on fire, people will move out of your way. They don't fuck around, they get the fuck out your way. Except one old drunk: 'Hey buddy, do you have a light?'"

- HERE AND NOW (Warner Bros. 239811) ✱✱✱ $5 $10

Pryor is in an unusually good mood for this 1983 performance, opening with his version of Lenny Bruce's "I'm going to piss on you" joke: "You sat in the right seat, 'cause if the show don't be funny, I take out my dick and piss. This is called the garden row!"

In front of a Southern audience yet, Richard is surprisingly gentle in his racial satire. "Y'all remember your ancestors used to hang us for kicks?" he asks. Then he does a mild bit on slavery that sounds more like a jiving Eddie Murphy: "It get hot down here.... I don't know how they had no slavery when it be hot down here. Slaves would've quit: Hey, fuck you. Carry that shit yourself!"

"This is a bitch," he says about quitting drugs. "I noticed something.... When I stopped doing drugs about the fourth month, I noticed my dick was smaller than I thought. Thought I had fifteen, sixteen inches. And I was in the bathroom peeing, man. I say Ayy! I been robbed! Somebody took my dick, left me with this little child's pee-wee!"

- CRAPS (Laff A 146, reissued as BLACKJACK, Laff 226) $8
- BLACK BEN (Laff 200, reissued as SHOW BIZ, 227, Reissue: Loose Cannon 3145262132) $8
- PRYOR GOES FOXX HUNTING (Laff A 170) $5 $10
- DOWN N DIRTY (Laff A 184) $5 $10
- ARE YOU SERIOUS (Laff A 196) $5 $10
- WHO ME? I'M NOT HIM (Laff A 198) $5 $10
- WIZARD OF COMEDY (Laff A 202, Reissue: Loose Cannon 3145280632) $8
- OUTRAGEOUS (Laff A 206) $5 $10
- INSANE (Laff A 209) $5 $10
- HOLY SMOKE (Laff 212) $5 $10
- REV. DU RITE (Laff A 216) $5 $10
- VERY BEST (Laff A 221) $5 $10
- SUPERNIGGER (Laff, Reissue: Loose Cannon 3145280622) $8
- LIVE (Laff A 279) $5 $10
- LIVE (Phoenix 349) $6 $12

Not long after Richard Pryor stormed off the stage at The Aladdin in Las Vegas in 1970, he got involved with Laff, a company specializing in cheap, dirty records. They eagerly added Pryor to their collection of has-beens (Mantan Moreland and Joe E. Ross). Laff recorded "Craps: After Hours" in 1971 at Redd Foxx's club. It's the most important of the Laff releases, showing Pryor's transition from "straight" set routines to uncensored, liberated comedy. Pryor slides in and out of voices, injects a few one-liners, and experiments with vulnerable humor about sex and racial problems. He talks about jail, the street, even drugs, all taboo topics for most comics at the time.

Laff and Pryor had a falling out almost immediately. Pryor got himself into a sticky contractual mire and when the smoke cleared, Laff had won the right to use the existing tapes they had on Pryor, which seems to have included ancient material from Pryor's late '60s "straight" period. Laff was able to squeeze more than a dozen albums out of the Pryor tapes and it's painfully obvious that most of them are scrapings of tapings: unpolished, poorly recorded, and sometimes incoherent. (Pryor may have thought that he'd been able to live down these records, but Loose Cannon bought the CD rights and by 1995, coinciding with the release of his autobiography, the discs were flooding the racks.)

Back in the '70s, Laff kept pace with Pryor's Warner releases, and some fans were duped into thinking that Pryor was recording fresh material for both labels simultaneously. "Are You Serious" and "Who Me?" were released in 1977, competing with Warner's "Greatest Hits." "Black Ben" and "Wizard of Comedy" of 1978 came out just before Warner's big "Wanted: Live in Concert" album in 1979, and "Insane" and "Holy Smoke" arrived in 1980.

People in the business couldn't tell the difference either. "Are You Serious?" was nominated for a Grammy, and this irritated Pryor. In January of 1978, at the height of Grammy voting, he took out trade ads protesting the record:

"An open letter to members of NARAS. When I recently received notification that I had been voted a Grammy nomination ... I was, and continue to be, appreciative of the recognition given to me.... My appreciation of the honor of this nomination is, however, tainted by my knowledge that the material under consideration was recorded ten years ago and recently repackaged and released.... Therefore, I intend to cast my vote for one of the other nominees, and I urge you to do the same."

The winner was Steve Martin for "Let's Get Small." But each year Laff material was nominated and in 1981, Pryor's "Rev. Du Rite" album did win the Grammy. The album cover is copyright 1981, but the label on the record confirms that the material is copyright 1976. It actually sounds more like 1966, since there is almost no racial humor and none of Pryor's usual swearing. Pryor sounds surprisingly like Flip Wilson at times. He does some Wilson deadpanning in a throwaway about trying to get some spare change to use a pay toilet. There's a bit of Wilson in Pryor's "Rev. Du Rite" ("But I come not here to plague you with the questions of the no answers, oh no, and you can't get to the left without the right") and he does a very Wilsonesque mock trial segment as well.

Fans who are interested in the very early Richard Pryor will find it here. It would've been nice if Laff had packaged this one as the archive item it is.

NOTES: Audio Fidelity's Pryor album is a picture disc. Pryor can also be heard on "The Living Word" (Stax 3018) and for about three minutes on the soundtrack to the film "Jo Jo Dancer" (Warner Bros. 25444). There's a short snip from Jo Jo/Pryor's early nightclub era: "Your parents always were logical ... my home, you got a beating ... My mother would always say, 'It hurts me more than it hurts you!' Yeah? Well let me beat your ass!" Another quickie lifts a heckling moment as the comic shouts to a ringsider, "Lady, I don't bother you when you're workin' Hollywood Boulevard!" One cut between the musical selections, "Burn Ward," is nothing but moans, screams, and hospital sounds.

B. S. PULLY

- FAIRY TALES (Surprise LSR 996) **1/2 $8 $20

The blustery-voiced Pully was a tough, Runyonesque character who appeared often in movies. He would take the kind of roles given to a Slapsy Maxie Rosenbloom or Allen Jenkins. He played the bouncer in William Bendix's nightclub in the film *Greenwich Village*. He was appropriately cast as Big Jule in the Broadway and film productions of *Guys and Dolls*. Sometimes he played a straight heavy. Victor MacLaglen was a fan, quoted as saying, "B. S. in real life is what I am trying to be in the movies."

In later years, Pully was known as a male Belle Barth, shocking the crowds at Miami resorts with his raunchy "venereal material" delivered in a deep, froggy voice.

Unlike Barth or Pearl Williams, Pully only made one album. The material is what one would expect: "I love all the short stories. I hate long stories. I like the one about the fella who got into a taxi cab, and there was a girl driving the cab, and he said, 'Listen, take me to the cheapest cathouse in town.' She said, 'You're in it.' I like the one about the two sharks in the ocean. One shark said to the other, he said, 'Ay, my ass burns.' The other one said, 'I told you not to eat that Mexican.' I once bought a book called *The Kinsey Report*. Cost me six and a half dollars to find out I'm a degenerate."

A poorly recorded album, there's an irritating reverberation when the audience laughs, and an extremely drunk woman was sitting very close to Pully's microphone and laughs like a cross between Desi Arnaz and a seagull.

TRIVIA: Pully's real last name was Lerman; his son Steven Lerman was the lawyer who defended infamous drunk driver/civil rights martyr Rodney King.

THE PUNCHINELLOS

- PUNCHY PUNCHINELLOS (Art 35) *1/2 $4 $8
- PUNCHINELLOS (Duo CP 1) *1/2 $4 $8

Down in Florida in the early '60s, Duke Stewart (on bass) and Ralph Michaels (with accordion) appeared in nightclubs as The Punchinellos, mixing up songs and patter. Instead of drum rim shots they punctuated gags with a thudding boost from the bass or a little squashed chord from the accordion. On the Duo album, during a Texan routine that included some hillbilly singing:

"Tex, that was so pretty it made the tears roll down my back." "What do you mean by that?" "Back-teria! Tex, I want to know one thing. Where do you hail from?" "Well, actually I'm from Louisiana...." "Louisiana? Well why do they call you Tex?" "I got tired of them calling me Louise."

MONTY PYTHON

- ANOTHER MONTY PYTHON RECORD (Famous Charisma/Buddah CAS 1049) **1/2 $5 $10
- MONTY PYTHON'S PREVIOUS RECORD (Famous Charisma/Buddah CAS 1063) *** $5 $10
- WORST OF MONTY PYTHON (Kama Sutra) **1/2 $8 $15

Up until the early '70s, most Americans might have guessed that "Monty Python" was the host of the game show *Let's Make an Eel*. But after their cult TV show arrived, followed by records taken from the soundtrack, most everyone began to recognize "Monty Python" as the collective name for a troupe of five British comedians (John Cleese, Graham Chapman, Terry Jones, Eric Idle, and Michael Palin) and American animator Terry Gilliam. Influenced by both the topical humor of David Frost and the surreal world of The Goons, "The Pythons," developed their own biting style that included a gleefully demonic streak of sadism and (nudge nudge, wink wink) sexual silliness. Their ability to perform equally well with put-on subtlety and wit as well as broad gags made them a special favorite of critics.

In 1972 the first Python albums, culled from their British TV series, began appearing in America. In many cities, their show wasn't even on local television yet. Each album is spotty, an uneven mix of titillation, top flight satire, and tedium. One of the worst traits of the Pythons is their penchant for lampooning boring lecturers or blabbery announcers by trying to be just as boring or blabbery. "Another" opens with "Apologies," nothing but two minutes of various announcers interrupting each other to apologize for each other's apologies. Highlights include the repetition song "Spam," and "Spanish Inquisition," one of the repetition routines that actually works: "Our weapon is fear. And surprise. Our two weapons are fear and surprise. And ruthless effiency. Three weapons ...." The nine-minute saga of "The Pirhana Brothers" won't mean much to non-fans. Likewise, "Gumby Theater" makes no sense if one doesn't remember the "Gumby" character from the show, a bellowing imbecile who wears a paper napkin on his head.

"Previous Record," also released in 1972, offers eighteen short bits in a faster-paced setting. There's also a better usage of stereo and sound effects than on the first album. It opens with "Embarrassment," a tastelessly amusing study in which Michael Palin tests the listener with potentially rude words ("tits, winkle, and vibraphone!") and then sound effects. Another classic is "The Argument Clinic": "I came in here for a good argument." "No, you didn't!" "An argument isn't just contradiction." "Can be." "No it can't." There are the bent tunes "Eric the Half a Bee" and "Dennis Moore" as well. There are moments that try one's patience, but a quick flick of the needle should land the listener back onto something good. The albums were later issued as a double set by Kama Sutra.

- MONTY PYTHON'S FLYING CIRCUS (PYE 12116) ***1/2 $5 $15

The mono Pye album, taken directly from the TV series, features some of the troupe's greatest routines. But it also includes the usual amount of failed experiments and material that doesn't work too well without visuals ("Flying Sheep" being an obvious example). Highlights include Eric Idle's sex obsessed "Nudge Nudge" routine, Terry Jones describing a box of disgustingly-filled candies (such delicacies as lark's vomit), Michael Palin's cheerful transvestite song about lumberjacks, and John Cleese on "The Mouse Problem," a semisympathetic piece satirizing transvestism. One of the better Python nonsense sketches, "Buying a Bed" goes on just long enough as a couple attempt to buy a bed from a salesman who can't bear to hear the word "mattress." The disc has the most famous Python sketch of all, "The Pet Shop," a masterpiece both of comic dialogue and character humor. Palin is the shifty clerk who sells prissy John Cleese a dead parrot. The piqued Cleese puts on a brilliant show as he attempts to get his money back: "It's passed on! This parrot is no more! It's ceased to be! It has expired! This ... is a late parrot ... if you hadn't nailed it to the perch it would be pushing up the daisies ... it is ... an ex-parrot!" Palin: "It's just stunned."

- MATCHING TIE AND HANDKERCHIEF (Arista AL 4039) **1/2 $15 $30

1975's Python album has a fun inner sleeve that pulls out for a fiendishly drawn joke on the cover's man in the matching tie and handkerchief.

And ... there are *two* Side Two's. Side Two has been "trick tracked," so that it contains two completely different sets of material. Cleese and Palin do a pet store sketch about "custom made" animals, like a dog fish designed by lopping off a terrier's ears, hacking its legs and adding fins. There's a "sports report" on "Novel Writing," with Palin breathlessly describing the "very good crowd" gathered to watch Thomas Hardy write *The Return of the Native*. Eric Idle complains about Australians, all named Bruce, and uses the catchphrase "No poofters!" This is far from the best of the Pythons, but it was nice of them to at least add a third side.

Even though there's an import CD available, the "trick track" vinyl makes this one valuable not only to comedy fans, but fans of quirky records in general.

- MONTY PYTHON LIVE AT CITY CENTER (Arista AL 4073) **1/2 $5 $10

This 1976 live album doesn't succeed because it's live. The Python cult is so worked up that almost every mumble is treated to a roar of laughter. Every catchphrase is greeted with a sudden shockwave of mad applause. All of this throws the actors off their timing. Even the most seasoned pro would stoop to "playing to the crowd." There's a lot of weak material here, too, including minor quiz show routines, a bit on sports commentary, and Idle's prattling about tourism that drives Michael Palin to keep crying out, "Shut up! Please shut up!"

The crowd goes wild over "Nudge Nudge," and they applaud lustily when Terry Jones describes the baby frogs and vomit contained in his chocolate assortments. Cleese and Palin engage in a screaming version of their dead parrot sketch until, with the line "this is an ex-parrot," the crowd explodes with cheers and applause. Rhythmic applause greets and ruins the finale, "The Lumberjack Song," which trails off into the Monty Python theme (actually John Philip Sousa's "Liberty Bell March.")

"Bonzo Dog" Neil Innes does some uninteresting tunes and Carol Cleveland appears in some sketches (but not, unfortunately, on the front or back album cover).

- THE ALBUM OF THE SOUNDTRACK OF ... MONTY PYTHON AND THE HOLY GRAIL
  (Arista AL 4090) **1/2 $5 $10
- LIFE OF BRIAN (Warner Bros. BSK 3396) **1/2 $5 $10
- MONTY PYTHON AND THE MEANING OF LIFE (MCA 6121) **1/2 $5 $10

With the popularity of videocassettes, there's no real reason to collect the Python soundtrack albums. The *Holy Grail* soundtrack is particularly annoying, since it attempts to convert the movie's highlights to disc via a silly and tedious series of introductions, false starts, and moments in which the projector fails and the sound grinds to a halt. Palin's irresistible "Knights Who Say Ni" routine gets ground under by this meddling. The *Life of Brian* soundtrack opens with a loud, tongue-in-cheek introduction and "Hava Nagila" played on bagpipes, not to mention the opulent stereo ballad of "Brian." *Meaning of Life*, not exactly an optimistic or encouraging film, does allow fans to instantly hear, any time they want, the rousing tune "Every Sperm Is Sacred" ("if a sperm is wasted, God gets quite irate!"), which would make a killer b-side coupled with Tom Lehrer's "Vatican Rag."

- MONTY PYTHON'S CONTRACTUAL OBLIGATION ALBUM (Arista AL 9536) ** $5 $10
- THE MONTY PYTHON INSTANT RECORD COLLECTION (Arista AL 9580) *** $5 $10
- MONTY PYTHON'S FINAL RIPOFF (Virgin 7908651) *** $18
- THE INSTANT MONTY PYTHON CD COLLECTION (Virgin 98202) *** $8
- MONTY PYTHON SINGS (Virgin 291781) *** $8

It's possible that the Python troupe did indeed knock their 1980 Arista disc together due to contractual obligation. It does contain some older material they may not have been proud of. The sketch about an insane advertising exec trying to sell useless lengths of string was written and performed on David Frost's "Frost Report" more than a decade earlier; "Bookshop" is ancient too. There are a lot of short songs, including the rousing march "Sit on My Face," a nose-tweaking tune on Henry Kissinger ("some people say you don't care, but you've got nicer legs than Hitler and bigger tits than Cher"). Also included are several impossible racial ditties that urge tolerance. One is Eric Idle's lobotomized "I Like Chinese"; another begins: "Never poke fun at a nigger, a spic or a wop or a kraut."

"Instant Record Collection" recycles, as the cover says, "the pick of the best of some recently repeated Python hits again, Volume Two." Taken from the *Holy Grail* soundtrack, and the "City Center," "Matching Tie and Handkerchief," and "Contractual Obligation" albums, the cuts include several classics: "Nudge Nudge," "Argument Clinic," "Pet Shop," "Lumberjack Song," "Sit on My Face," "Wide World of Novel Writing," "String," and "Crunchy Frog."

"Final Ripoff," is a two-disc compilation of the old material including songs ("Sit on My Face," "I Like Chinese," "Eric the Half a Bee," "The Lumberjack Song") and classic routines: "Argument Clinic," "Parrot," "Spam," "Nudge, Nudge," "Spanish Inquisition," "String," etc.

The six-CD "Instant" set, complete with a forty-page booklet, offers eight albums: "Another Monty Python Record," "Monty Python's Previous Record," "Matching Tie and Handkerchief," "Monty Python Live at Drury Lane," "Monty Python and the Holy Grail," "Contractual Obligation Album," "Life of Brian" and "Meaning of Life."

"Sings," a 1992 CD, offers nearly an hour of Python songs (twenty-five in all). There aren't many surprises for those who already have all the albums (the crisp stereo version of "The Lumberjack Song" is evidently the rare single), but it's nice to have them all on one disc. The booklet gives the credits so fans can learn which Pythons wrote each song. As it turns out, in most cases the one who sang it wrote it. The booklet also reprints all the lyrics just in case listeners can't believe they're actually hearing things like: "Isn't it awfully nice to have a penis, isn't it frightfully good to have a dong?"

NOTES: The original British pressing of "Monty Python's Contractual Obligation Album" (Charisma) contains "Farewell to John Denver," a song later withdrawn to avoid a possible lawsuit. Another import, "Monty Python Live at the Theatre Royal, Drury Lane" (Charisma) was recorded in 1974. There's a picture disk single of "The Galaxy Song" backed with "Every Sperm Is Sacred" (CBS Records). Various Pythons appear on the compilation CD "Dead Parrot Society" (Rhino R2 71049) with cuts that originally appeared on "A Poke in the Eye with a Sharp Stick" (Volumes 1 and 2), a live recording of an Amnesty International Gala in 1976.

MAE QUESTEL

- MRS. PORTNOY'S RETORT (United Artists UAS 6721) ** $5 $15

Mae Questel was the voice of cartoon heroines Betty Boop and Olive Oyl. Into the '60s she appeared in many television commercials—usually as a busybody Aunt-type, the kind who happens to know in frightening detail the exact strength and absorption properties of paper towels. Her best movie role in the '80s was as Woody Allen's mother in *New York Stories*.

When Philip Roth's *Portnoy's Complaint* became a best-seller in 1969, it seemed to be as much for his frank, pioneering depiction of obsessive masturbation as for the book's literary qualities. "Mrs. Portnoy's Retort" is the topical album that tried to cash in. The cover shows a frantic Ms. Questel cutting a salami in half with a giant knife.

Mae is in fine comic voice as she nags, moans, sputters, and squeals out her embarrassment and outrage. "The topic," she announces to the studio audience, "is a certain activity done by nonreligious boys! It begins with an "M" and ends in a mental hospital!"

The album is basically one-liners with a raucous bar mitzvah band slinging them home with freilach music: "Most kids you can trust alone with silly putty!" (Musical interlude.) "I told him to do this thing—only in one case in two does it fall off by itself." (Music.)

Mrs. Portnoy claims to have confronted her best-seller author: "I asked him, 'This is what you went to college for? To write about such a thing?' He said, 'Mom, didn't you tell me that to get ahead in this world a boy needs pull?'"

Heavy handed.

Questel can be heard on various albums doing Olive Oyl and Betty Boop ("Betty Boop Soundtracks" (Mark 56 #639), "Betty Boop Scandals" (Mark 56 #658), "Popeye's Songs" (Golden 73), "On the Good Ship Lollipop" (Harmony HL 7122), "Betty Boop" (Pro Arte CDD 440), etc. She also has a solo song of love advice in the Broadway show *Bajour* (Sony SK 48208).

QUESTION MARK

- GREAT PHONE CALLS (Amarillo AM 577) * $5 $10

No relation to Question Mark and the Mysterians (the "?" who had a hit rock single, "96 Tears" in 1966), this "?" recorded his album of crank calls in 1992 for a small San Francisco label.

The guy deserves to remain anonymous, although the back cover has the distinction of containing the most illiterate notes ever placed on a comedy album: "Great phone calls ... have been slyly captured for your exclusive entairment. Buying them. Make you side split. Great phone calls! Every one love to laugh but this album really doing the good thing."

Fans of this kind of thing might be amused by a call to a pizza joint asking for a diet pizza that substitutes the box for the crust. Another practical joke has the caller pretending to be a yock-obsessed obnoxious stand-up comic trying to book himself into a local club: "I'm Neil Hamburger! Ha ha ha ... I'm a shootin' star and you can't slow me down ... are ya there, buddy?" The booker's reply: "You're not doing yourself any good." Most of the people who get these calls have the same vaguely disgusted reaction. When Mr. Question Mark howls to one guy, "I'm a crazy motherfucker," the answer comes back: "Good for you."

GILDA RADNER

- LIVE FROM NEW YORK (Warner Bros. HS 3320, CD Reissue 9456952) *** $8

Radner's 1979 album is based on her one-woman show, a breakaway from *Saturday Night Live* and a tribute to it (the Broadway show features the characters she made famous on the TV show). Some of it is dated. Candy Slice, her parody of Patti Smith, means little if listeners don't recall Smith's obsession with Mick Jagger ("Gimme Mick") and the skimpy T-shirts that exposed a generous amount of armpit hair and more: "If you look close you can see my tits—'cause I want you to, but don't want you to know I do!"

Radner portrays Rhonda Weiss (a Streisand-Manilow-Shangri La's horror from Queens) and has a charmingly obscene bit in which she sings "Let's Talk Dirty to the Animals." Her most famous *SNL* characters are given plenty of time. Emily Litella natters about nothing before uttering her catchphrase "Never mind." And coarse Roseanne Roseannadanna, the name itself a play on New York news anchorwoman Roseanne Scammardella, describes a lunch meeting with Walter Cronkite: "All of a sudden, this wooden chair that I'm sittin' on makes a Pffft! sound on the floor. I thought I was gonna die! Cronkite says, 'Ay, did that come outta you?'"

Gilda's on the *Saturday Night Live* Arista album, and also on Rhino's "Comic Relief" where she takes a phone call from Emily Litella. Emily is eager to donate money to "Comet Relief ... we need some relief from Halley's Comet, it's a menace I tell you."

CHARLOTTE RAE

- SONGS I TAUGHT MY MOTHER (Vanguard 9004) ** $15 $25

Now primarily known for her sitcom work, often playing pudgy neurotics wavering on the verge of breakdown, Rae appeared in New York cabaret revues and chichi nightclubs in the '50s. Her studio album of songs is dated, and little of her antic charm comes through when she's forced into the standard chanteuse style of speaking like a refined kindergarten teacher to her precocious charges.

Her nightclub hit "Backer's Audition" is brittle with time, and there's not much to say for the old Cole Porter numbers ("When I Was a Little Cuckoo," "The Physician") or a monologue as Zsa Zsa Gabor, "Gabor the Merrier," by Sheldon Harnick. The better numbers are "Merry Minuet," the Harnick classic that was blackly satiric in its day, and "Modest Maid," which offers a chuckle or two as Charlotte lets raunchy lust creep into her vocalizing of a fair young maiden's folk lament. At the time, "A Nail in the Horseshoe" was a walloping punch at women who go to opera just to be seen enjoying "culture." She sings: "Carmen by Bizet is really cheese-ay, and I simply scream when I hear 'La Boheme' ... I can't stand Beethoven or Mozart nor Schubert! But I do like Victor Hubert." A spoken break praises "the opening nights, the cameras, the photographers, the lights, I love it when the baritone wears tights. I love snubbing my best friends in the hall. I love it when they take curtain calls. I love the opera hats, the opera cloaks, the opera pumps, the opera balls! The fact of the matter is I love just everything, just everything—but why in the hell do they have to sing?"

TONY RANDALL

- TONY RANDALL (Imperial LP 9090) ** $12 $20

Randall had finished his run on *Mr. Peepers* and was known for his films (*Pillow Talk* and *Will Success Spoil Rock Hunter*) and Broadway work in *Oh Men, Oh Women* and *Oh Captain* at the time this oddity was released.

His morbid fascination with rotten '20s songs is already in evidence as he salutes (and only mildly burlesques) "Little Sir Echo," "My Little Grass Shack in Kealakekua, Hawaii," and "Laugh Clown Laugh." He and Joyce Jameson duet on the once suggestive, now boring "Baby, It's Cold Outside." There are also a few songs the album notes insist were intended seriously: "Poor Little Rich Girl" and "Just a Gigolo," the latter with a chorus sung in German!

Nearly half the studio album is given over to monologues. There are several bewildering "lagniappes" (quickies), a four-minute deliberately effete and verbose lecture ("Stereo Demonstration"), and a four-minute slice of life satire called "All Night D.J." in which Randall duplicates the time-killing techniques of a professional who "jokes" with the off-mike engineer and describes everything he's doing: "I like sugar in my coffee. Don't you? How about you folks out there? You like sugar in your coffee? Yeah! Not too much, don't give me too sweet coffee, not if you want me to come back. What's that, Joe? Oh, you character! Well, okay there."

The most bizarre cut is "Nature Boy," orchestrated by Bernie Green into a droning Indian sitar ballad and featuring one of the more eccentric Indian accents any comic has ever attempted.

This one is confusing, surprising, and sometimes amusing.

NOTES: Aside from various Broadway cast and soundtrack albums, Randall issued two novelty/nostalgia discs. "Warm and Wavery" (Mercury SR 61128) has silliness ("When Banana Skins Are Falling I'll Come Sliding Back to You"), bounce ("Chinatown My Chinatown"), and nausea ("Red Sails in the Sunset"). The only modern song is the slightly jaundiced "Debutante's Ball," written by Randy Newman. "Vo Vo De Oh Doe" (Mercury SR 61108) has more campy material ("Winchester Cathedral," "Byrd: You're the Bird of Them All," and "Boo Hoo") along with a tune that turned up on an *Odd Couple* episode, "Stumbling." Randall and Jack Klugman recorded "The Odd Couple Sings" (Phase 4 XPS 903), a novelty disc that almost lets the unmusical Klugman get away unscathed ("Brush Up Your Shakespeare" yes, "You're So Vain" embarrassingly no). Randall tends to dominate and reprises "When Banana Skins Are Falling."

THE RANDOLPH SINGERS

• LAMENT FOR APRIL 15 (Composers Recordings Inc., CR-102) * $5 $10

The title cut and several more offer classical and choral humor far to the right of Anna Russell or P. D. Q. Bach. The Randolph Singers present madrigals dead seriously. The "musical joke" is that some of their choices are mundane either in lyrics or composition. The title track of this late '50s disc, according to the album notes, "achieved world wide fame." It's just income tax instructions performed by a chorale. They get worked up and start harmonizing over certain phrases. First tenor: "Mother-in-law!" Two tenors: " Mother-in-law! You can deduct your mother-in-law!" Male chorus: "You can deduct your mother-in-law!" Female chorus: "Father-in-law!" Male chorus: "Mother in law!" etc., etc.

A few numbers feature the nonsense lyrics of Edward Lear, but except for a small minority of classical music and opera fans, few listeners will be able to even understand the words through the tangle of contrapuntal sopranos, baritones, and tenors wailing away. Those inclined may indeed chuckle at hearing nonsense words (Lear's "Quangle Wangle") sung with the kind of joy reserved for Bach or Handel.

Another selection, "The Interminable Farewell," is exactly that, one man singing "so long" and "good bye" over and over, joined by females ("so nice of you to think of us, we must get home, let's meet again") and more men ("so nice of you ... come again"). The album notes explain what's so funny about it: "The text has gathered every cliché used by departing guests and by their hosts. The music is in the form of a canon, over a repeated bass figure. However with a sense of humor suggestive of Charles Addams, the composer prescribes that as each of the singers enters successively with the same melody, he or she does so in a different key! The resulting polytonality is an example of real musical wit. It might be mentioned in passing that The Randolph Singers have often used this delightful work as the final encore in their concerts. It has never failed to send their audiences home laughing."

RAYMOND AND BARKIN

• HANDWRITING IS ON THE WALL (Atlantic Sd 8178) **1/2 $4 $8

Jack Raymond and Haskell Barkin were behind this 1968 collection released during the days when some graffiti had wit. The result is a bit stilted as the duo take turns setting up each one-liner.

Narrator: "Today some of the most outspoken critics of our society are college students. And it is around the campuses of America that much of the best graffiti can be found. Among these are the protests triggered by the sexual revolution. As one graffitist chalked on the sidewalk near the library at City College of New York ..."

"Two's company. Three's a ball."

Narrator: "And this plea against progress was seen at Wellesley ..."

"Artificial insemination is so unromantic."

Narrator: "Seen at a washroom at Notre Dame ..."

"Practice abstinence. An hour a day."

BETTY REILLY

• CAUGHT IN THE ACT (Unique ULP 118) ** $6 $12

Sort of a budget Betty Hutton, excitable platinum blonde Betty Reilly runs through and runs over a lot of straight tunes from ballads ("It Ain't Necessarily So") to bombast ("Blow, Gabriel, Blow"). She also sings a number of tunes in different foreign languages. Why she was always placed in the comedy section is hard to figure at this point, though the album does open with a bizarre novelty tune, "The Saga of Elvis Presley." It cops some elements from The Cadets novelty tune, "Stranded in the Jungle." Reilly plays Elvis, lost in the jungle, who realizes that "meanwhile, back in the States," his song is a big hit. She does a frantic imitation of Presley's "Heartbreak Hotel," singing "you make-ah me so-oh lonely I could die-ie-ie-ie-ah-ah-ah!" Presley fans and novelty buffs may want to hear this brassy blonde's imitation every other stanza, plus singing cannibals. Once.

REINER AND BROOKS

• 2000 YEAR OLD MAN (World Pacific 1401) $5 $15
  reissued by Capitol ST 2981 (Rhino CD 72165) **** $8

Carl Reiner and Mel Brooks were comedy writers and performers for Sid Caesar when they began improvising "2000 Year Old Man" sketches at parties. Fans George Burns and Steve Allen urged the duo to make a record out of the material. When they did, walking into a studio, ad-libbing two hours, and then editing it all down, they had an instant comedy classic. It established the relatively unknown Brooks as a comic genius.

Most of the album is given over to some amusing, slightly dated sketches (Brooks as various patrons of a hip coffee house, a bit on rocker Fabiola, and an astronaut routine), but the twelve-minute "2000 Year Old Man" routine is priceless. "When I became him," Brooks once said, "I could hear five thousand years of Jews pouring through me. Look at Jewish history. Unrelieved lamenting would be intolerable. So, for every ten Jews beating their breasts, God designated one to be crazy and amuse the breast beaters. By the time I was five I knew I was that one."

The old man confronts mortality, fear, and the achievements of mankind. He does it with love, irony, feisty satire, and rich human nature. On this installment, he describes the Stone Age: when men first discovered women. He talks about the motivation of man ("Everything we do is based on fear"), sings the praises of nectarines, and reports on what he did for a living—like hitting a tree with a piece of stick. Later, he reports on being an early manufacturer:

"I used to make the Star of David, the Jewish stars ... as soon as religion came in, I was one of the first in that...."

"How did you make them?"

"I employed six men. Each with a point. And they used to run together in the middle of the factory. And in their great speed they would fuse the thing ... we would make two a day because of the many accidents.... I had an offer once ... a new thing ... a cross. I looked at it, and I turned it over, and I looked in all sides of it, and I said, 'It's simple. It's too simple.' I didn't know then it was eloquent.... I said, 'I'm sorry.' See, I could've fired four men! Two men run together, bang! You got a cross!"

The humor is as much in Brooks's delivery as in the jokes. On paper, it doesn't seem like much, but coming from the 2000 Year Old Man, there's pain, compassion, and deadpan comic irony in this ad-lib quickie:

"How did you feel about her being burnt at the stake?"

"Terrible."

Some have been mystified by the 2000 Year Old Man, unable to get the humor in what could be considered a simple ethnic character. It's pitiful that the old man has his problems: "I have forty-two thousand children. And not one comes to visit me!" But it's the very homeliness of the character that produces some of the finest satire. "What is the biggest change you have seen?" asks the interviewer. "In two thousand years? The greatest thing mankind has ever devised, in my humble opinion ... is Saran Wrap!"

The 2000 Year Old Man and his irreverence, wisdom, and outrageous humor could not be a "one shot wonder." In 1961 the duo were making TV appearances and ready to put out a sequel.

- 2000 AND ONE YEARS (Capitol SW 1618, Rhino CD 72166) **** $8

Once again Reiner and Brooks put together a balanced show, featuring quick interviews with "The Tax Expert" and "The Third Best Poet." They even do a twist, a report on "The Two Hour Old Baby." At first the humor is uninhibited and silly:

"Oh, I remember when I was a little tadpole! A little fetus there, swimming around."

"Do you remember having a tail?"

"Sure, oh, that was the best part. I loved the tail."

"Were you unhappy when it disappeared?"

"When I lost my tail I got a nose ... and the nose is much more important. Because ... you can't blow your tail, you know what I mean?"

But, like the 2000 Year Old Man, the Two Hour Old Baby can't help telling a few painful truths:

"What is it that makes a mother queasy or a little nauseous in the first two or three months of her pregnancy?"

"... I think it's psychological. I think the moment they realize that there's a living creature in them—they puke ... it's a frightening thing."

The fourteen-minute "2000 and Six Month Man" shows that the old man still has "peppy ways." A highlight lesson insists everything comes from fear, including songs. "Songs started when you were in trouble. You said, 'HELP!' That's a note ... fear caused singing. 'A lion is eating my foot off! Will somebody call a cop!' That's a song."

He mentions that even friendly acts like handshaking stem from fear, and recalls King Arthur, Shakespeare, and Sigmund Freud.

- AT THE CANNES FILM FESTIVAL (Capitol SW 1815) **** $8 $15

The title cut is an amusing set of improvisations with Brooks impersonating various crackpot directors at the Film Festival, including a bizarre German director named Adolph Hartler. Brooks has often injected "never again" ironic Nazi humor in his work, and this may be the first major example:

"How did you feel about ... *Judgment at Nuremberg*?"

"Unfair ... what was the picture really about? A misunderstanding, really. Look, you send people to camp, don't you, in the summer? We sent a few people to camp!"

"Sir ... how did you feel about Adolph Hitler personally?"

"He made a few errors ... losing the war...."

Very few comedians can consistently improvise and be enduringly funny. Jonathan Winters was the first stand-up to do it, and Mel Brooks was the second. One must think hard to consider a deserving third.

There's another long session with the ever aging 2002 Year Old Man. This time he talks about George Washington, Rembrandt, Cleopatra, the origin of tennis (batting a skunk), and how to tell if someone is dead (stick a finger in his nose and see if he hollers). His unique way of describing the difference between comedy and tragedy:

"Tragedy is if I'll cut my finger ... and to me, comedy is if you walk into an open sewer and die! What do I care!"

- 2013 YEAR OLD MAN (Warner Bros. BS 2741) **** $5 $10

In 1973 Carl Reiner discovered that the 2000 Year Old Man was alive and well and 2013. This welcome sequel covers both sides of the record. That gives Mel Brooks plenty of room to improvise—and for 1973 Brooks also has the freedom to inject some "GP-rated" material:

"Your long life may be attributed to the slowness of your heartbeat and the slowness of your development. Is that true?"

"Everything started slow. I breastfed for two hundred years! Loved that! I look back at that as the happiest part of my life."

"Who breastfed you?"

"I used to con a lot of ladies into doing it! They took pity on me!"

The old man also talks about masturbation, the effect of asparagus on urine, and on more general subjects: natural foods, the origin of words, great inventions, ancient poetry, and "Phil," the first god. He mentions well-known people from the past: Lord Byron, Al Jolson, Winston Churchill, Paul Revere, Jesus and the Apostles.

There are also those moments in which the old man's age-old wisdom does little to comfort modern man:

"We mock the thing we are to be. Yes, yes, we make fun of the old, then we become them. Look at that man bent over and spitting. Then we become that man bent over and spitting...."

"... sir, do you feel there's any hope for the world."

"No. As long as the world is turning and spinning we're gonna be dizzy and we're gonna make mistakes."

Around the time the record came out, some of the best from the 2000 Year old Man records were put into a new form, a half-hour cartoon special. It's now available on videocassette.

- THE INCOMPLETE WORKS OF REINER AND BROOKS (Warner Bros. 3XX 2744) **** $10 $15
- THE COMPLETE 2000 YEAR OLD MAN (Rhino R2 71017) **** $30

In 1973 the three original out-of-print Capitol albums were re-released as "The Incomplete" boxed set.

In 1994 Rhino issued a four-CD boxed set of the original albums. The accompanying booklet features an interview with the duo and virtually everything one would want to know about the origin of the 2000 Year Old Man routines and why there have not been any new releases (Reiner wants to, Brooks doesn't). There are no bonus cuts or extras. Not everyone was pleased with the high-priced chunk, so for Christmas 1995 Rhino issued the first two albums individually.

The "L.M.N.O.P. Ad Agency" piece turns up on "25 Years of Recorded Comedy" (Warner 3BX 3131). Reiner, Brooks, and Howard Morris, as "The Three Haircuts," appear on RCA's "Golden Age of Comedy" (RCA LPV 580).

JORIE REMUS

- UNPREDICTABLE (Everest LPBR 5102) ** $8 $15

Jorie Remus (Marjorie Ramos), who resembles the sister of Rondo Hatton, was a chichi chanteuse of the late '50s, notably at The Purple Onion, where she was an early co-owner. The album notes by Nat Hentoff are shockingly complimentary. The man who raved about Lenny Bruce right from the start certainly missed this time. He calls Remus "one of the more individualistic pioneers" of the "new wave of sardonic, startling, topical" satirists ... "with the verve and unerring accuracy of an indignant queen bee."

Hentoff is only accurate when he quotes another critic, who called Remus a combination of Tallulah Bankhead and Beatrice Lillie. That much is true. Jorie postures like both of them, trilling her "R's" and putting on campy airs. But on this shrilly recorded album, without her visuals, there is very little to laugh at. One of the more coherent cuts is her wry report on "Reginald," her favorite beau:

"I gave him a case of his favorite scotch and he gave me a huge bottle of joy. The detergent, that is. Valentine's Day I gave him a case of his favorite scotch. And he gave me a perfectly marvelous handmade heart-shaped bruise! On the 4th of July I gave him a case of scotch. He loved to drink. He threw a tear gas bomb in my bedroom and beat me up for crying! It was then that I began to get suspicious."

REYNALDO REY

- FLAST MUDDAH-FLUCKA (Elka 600) ** $5 $10
- FLY AWAY LITTLE BLUEBIRD (Laff 177) ** $5 $10
- THE RISING OF REYNALDO REY (Laff 201) ** $5 $10

The adult humor on Rey's Elka album is mixed with some racial remarks: "I have a warning for ... those of you who are visiting California. You got to look out for the three most dangerous things in this state. Number one is a Jew with a pawn shop, number two is a Mexican with a driver's license, and number three is a soul brother with a credit card!" There's a lot of jiving and meandering here, anecdotes acted out and padded out, but for those who tire easily, Rey has actually included a complete libretto that even spells out his sound effects: "The Texan hits the gas, skre-e-e-ech, catches the hippie at the top of the hill, over the hill they go, y-e-e-o-o-w-, down in the next valley and up the next hill, nye-e-e-eo-o-o-ow, nye-e-e-e-eo-o-ow, round the hairpin curves, skre-e-ech...."

The Laff releases are slower, with Rey taking five minutes to tell one story. His fans seem to like the way he brays and embellishes them. "Simp the Pimp" (on "Rising of Reynaldo Rey") is even in rhyme. Occasionally there's something shorter, like his report on a TV commercial: "Two girls at the locker room and they both open their locker and one girl has a little pink dainty box of deodorant tampons. The other chick got one of them ol' plain blue boxes of the nondeodorant shit. And the chick with the blue box looks at the chick with the pink box, she says, 'What does she know that I don't?' And then a voice comes out of nowhere and say, 'You funky, bitch!'"

The title track for "Fly Away Little Bluebird" won't amuse gays. It's a long story about a gay and a truck driver. The truck driver tells him, 'You remind me of a dainty little bluebird ... little bluebird, come away with me to my apartment.' Gays will not be pleased with the ending. After the evening is over, the truck driver "picked me up in his big, strong, masculine truck-driving arms and he carried me out onto the balcony. And there we were, just the two of us. Sixteen floors above the earth! And the son of a bitch dropped me off. And said: 'Fly away, little bluebird.'"

RICK REYNOLDS

- ONLY THE TRUTH IS FUNNY (Gang of Seven 74144220032) **1/2 $8

An overhyped observational humorist, Reynolds shifted from stand-up to "legitimate theater" with a one-man show. This gave him access to the critics that tittered at Spalding Gray and trembled over Eric Bogosian. The word was that since he was signed by Rollins and Joffe (who handled Woody Allen, David Letterman, and Robin Williams) he had to be brilliant. His "Only the Truth Is Funny" show became a Showtime cable TV special and this 1992 CD.

Reynolds tries to combine the storytelling of a Jean Shepherd with the twist wisecracking of early Woody Allen. A typical one-two bit where rumination leads to a pretention-saving punch line:

"My desire for fame is my bid for immortality. I fear death. I fear moving into non-existence. It's an odd, odd concept. I mean, everybody in this room knows they're going to die. I doubt if one person in this room feels they're going to die. I don't think we can come to grips with that fact. But it is something you think about a lot. You ever watch movies from the '30s and think to yourself, 'Jeez, everybody in this movie is *dead* now! I watch movies from the '70s and I think, 'Jeez, all the *dogs* in this movie are dead now!'"

More often Reynolds is way too preachy and intense, convinced the essence of the human condition lies in his anecdotes.

RICHARD AND WILLIE

- RED WHITE AND BLUE (Laff A 192) ** $5 $10
- WAITIN' FOR GAS (Laff A 207) ** $5 $10
- FUNKY AND FILTHY (Dooto 849) ** $5 $10
- LOW DOWN AND DIRTY (Dooto 842) ** $5 $10
- WILLIE AND THE RISING DICK (Dooto 843) ** $5 $10
- NASTY AND NAUGHTY (Dooto 851) ** $5 $10
- RICHARD'S FIRECRACKER (Laff 214) **1/2 $5 $10

Not too many ventriloquists are still around amusing folks with the zany antics of their snappy wooden sidekicks. The black duo of Richard and Willie rely mostly on adult comedy, the kind of things Charlie McCarthy might have known about but never told Bergen.

Of course, a young dummy doesn't know everything, as his straight man quickly discovers in this typical routine:

"Down in Texas there's a lady Sheriff." "No shit...." "First black woman sheriff ... this guy escaped from jail named Tricky Dick, and Bessie formed a posse to catch Dick." "She formed a what?" "A posse." "A posse?" "You want me to spell it?" "You can't even pronounce it! You mean she didn't have a posse? I thought every sister had a posse!" "She had to make a posse...." "You mean to tell me they're makin' posses? White men doin' everything ain't he...."

"She was known to have a good posse ... there was Long Rod, and Fat Frank, and Stiff Peter...." "How many men were in the posse?" "Thirty-six men." "Thirty-six men? In one posse...." "You don't understand, she wanted a big posse...." "Maybe that bitch had a big posse...."

The routines are a bit on the dummy side; the power of the smut taken down a peg by the high-pitched delivery.

The most interesting disc is "Firecracker," which actually satirizes Richard Pryor's self-immolation.

The album cover illustration shows a black man running down the street with his pants on fire. The ventriloquist explains on the back, "Only after knowing that Richard Pryor would fully recover from his near tragedy did I decide to do this album. I dedicate this album to Richard Pryor."

The ventriloquist drops his dummy for a while and does a routine re-enacting Pryor's freebasing accident (later revealed by Pryor to have been a suicide attempt) complete with screams. Then he does a monologue pretending to be Richard Pryor afterward:

"I first met God in 1929. Damn near met him tonight! I was outside a little hotel in Baltimore, eating a tuna fish sammitch. In 1929 you eat anything yo' ass can get! And I heard a voice, and the voice called unto me, and the voice said, 'Gimme somma that sammitch!' I say, 'You God, you make yo' own damn sammitch!' But I met God again. God came to me in a vision. And God said, 'Richard, you been fuckin' up....' And I listened to God, and I said very carefully, 'Fuck ya self!' But I met God again, in 1980! I was runnin' 'long a little street in Los Angeles with my ass on fire! And I called unto God. I said, 'God! Put out the fire!' And the same voice came unto me and the voice had holiness ... and the voice said, 'Nigger, ya didn't gimme none of the sammitch.'"

After this, Richard goes on to lampoon Pryor's drug abuse: "People say he got a monkey on his back. That ain't true. Nigger got a zoo on his back! With extra gorillas!"

It's odd to hear Pryor's style used against him; to hear another comic treat Pryor with the same combination of affection, irreverence, and grimacing contempt that Pryor used so well on his ex-wives and friends.

RICHIE BROTHERS

- POW WOW (Jubilee 2053) ** $4 $8
- BOTTOMS UP (Jubilee 2037) ** $4 $8

In the early '60s the Richie Brothers (Lou, Sal, and Rick) appeared at the Thunderbird Motel in Miami Beach. Their act is strictly whizbang. From "Bottom's Up":

"A fella put his hand on a girl's knee, she said, 'Heaven's above!' The beatnik went out with the flat-chested girl, he said, 'Like, man!' Little boy ran into the house, he told the milkman, 'You better hurry up, your horse is losing all his gas!'"

One of the brothers interrupts:

"I like a high class show!"

The other says: "Some like a high class show, some like a low class show! I'll satisfy everyone with a half-ass show!"

Fans of crass comedy will find plenty in "Powwow," as the boys spout and sing plenty of politically incorrect quickies: "Christine Jorgensen, she had a gimmick. She got rid of it! Remember her theme song? (sings) 'My Johnny Lies Over the Ocean!' And as she lay in the operating table she looked up and said, 'Doc, make it snappy.'"

Unlike the Ritz Brothers or any three-man act, there's no real teamwork here. Lou Richie tells most of the jokes. Rick does straight-man grumbling ("Get on with it!") and Sal helps out with accordion background music.

"Bottoms Up" was issued with two different album covers, the back copy remaining the same.

FAYE RICHMONDE

* A LITTLE SPICE (Davis 101) ** $6 $12
* FOR MEN ONLY (Davis 108) ** $6 $12
* GIRLESQUE (Davis 116) ** $6 $12

There's a picture of a topless brunette on the cover of the 1957 album "A Little Spice," and it would be pretty to think that it's Faye Richmonde. But, there's a completely different cover on another pressing of the album, and it's a different girl entirely. And there's a blonde on the cover of "Girlesque."

Richmonde has a pretty voice that sounds a bit like Gwen Verdon trying to imitate Billie Holiday. Her material is familiar, but fine for those who like classic Andy Razaf '20s risqué tunes sung in a casual, mildly teasing style. On "It's Smart to Be Smutty," Faye declares, "It's smart to be smutty, what the hell, we mostly are so why not you? If you make those debu-tanties laugh so hard they wet their panties, after all, what else is there to do?"

DON RICKLES

* HELLO DUMMY (Warner Bros. 1745, CD reissue 9456912) **1/2 $8
* DON RICKLES SPEAKS! (Warner Bros. 1779) **1/2 $8 $15

Rickles, the man Johnny Carson nicknamed "Mr. Warmth," was hottest in the late '60s when he made his two record albums. He was at his best in Vegas saloons and on *The Tonight Show*, where the bald-domed chunky comic sat on the couch like a kind of infected Humpty Dumpty, and cracked wise.

Rickles's shock humor has always divided the general public. As a put-upon average guy berserkly insulting everyone in sight, he strikes a chord among frustrated peers who are secretly seething. Others don't care if he's ludicrously overdoing it—they don't think that insult humor, even if everyone is attacked equally, lets off steam as much as it encourages hostility.

"Hello Dummy" presents Rickles at his best, though it's more his ranting and raving than any actual jokes that make him funny. He plays to the Vegas audience with shouts, threats, and weird sex imagery: "Got any kids? How many? One kid? Don't you fool around at all ... get yourself in heat. My wife lays in the room goin', 'Go Geronimo, Go!' Last night I was Cochise. I had to stand on top of the sink in the nude and she was in the living room with a bell on her tokus. She was goin', 'Wagon Train, comin' through the pass!' And I had to ring the bell."

Rickles pot shots all groups. To a fur-coated ringsider: "You're either a Jew, lady, or an old beaver in heat!" Then the blitz: "That was a good one, right queer? Look—the Italian guy—oil all over the table...." To a black man: "We need blacks—so we can have cotton in the drug store."

In print Rickles's wit seems non-existent, the violent insults senseless. But live, and to a lesser extent on disc, Rickles does manage some outrageous chuckles with his exasperated, nonstop whining and bullying. Often he's funniest when he spouts nonsense; so out of control and angry, his insults are comically idiotic. His catchphrase, "You hockey puck!" is an example.

The follow-up is a studio album that gives a fairly good example of the kind of humor Rickles uses on talk shows. Five panelists (Rosalind Ross, Dick Whittington, Pat McCormick, Don Richmond, and Joe Smith) ask Rickles questions and he zings back his answers. The panelists giggle and laugh as Rickles talks about television, Frank Sinatra, sports, and fellow comics. Presumably ad-libbed, but there are some sharp lines, and some typical Rickles shock non sequiturs and rambling. It's not necessarily funny, but it's hard to take the needle off and miss the next outrage:

"You're a big boxing fan ... your all time favorite fighters?"

"Joe Louis is one of my great idols ... I had a talk with him for about an hour once and didn't understand it...."

"Next week starts National Rodeo Week...."

"You know you're so annoying, I don't understand you.... Wanna go outside and look at a cowboy's sweat band? What am I gonna do with rodeos? We're gonna put a bell on your nose and ride you around for a half hour. Notice I said nose."

Rickles appears in a five-minute segment on "Magic Moments from the Tonight Show" (Casablanca SPNB 1296): "John, not lucky in love, but thank God you found the woman of your dreams. Really."

Carson answers, "Well, if you're as successful in marriage as you are in television shows, you have a lot comin' up!"

Bootlegs of a Rickles Roast hosted by Johnny Carson are available. See Friar's entry.

RIDERS IN THE SKY
- RIDERS RADIO THEATER (MCA 42180) * $4 $8
- RIDERS GO COMMERCIAL (MCA 42305) * $4 $8

Combine the worst elements of Firesign Theater and Garrison Keillor, add a dash of The Sons of the Pioneers, and you've got "Riders in the Sky." Stilted, coy, and overacted radio commercials, announcements, and barnyard noises are cemented between fey, cheesily harmonized country songs. Some of the tunes are cover versions of material done by The Sons of the Pioneers, who are probably turning over in their graves faster than tumbling tumbleweeds. Most other albums in their catalogue are mostly music.

STAN RIFKEN
- STAN RIFKEN (Windowpane) *1/2 $4 $8

A comic with a pronounced New Yawk accent and an evident lisp, Rifken acts out his jokes before a small audience in Greenwich Village:

"In this neighborhood you could walk behind a lovely young woman, checking her behind for several blocks, until you see that it's a guy. 'Oh no! I've been looking at a GUY! Get me some Visine! Wash out my eyes!' Everybody worries about their sexual identity.... We use these roles to put people down. 'Get away from me! I'm straight!' We can be omnisexual, do whatever we want ... if you see that lovely woman on the East Side, the ones that go out with the matched designer dogs, you don't have to feel bad if you're checking out the dogs instead of the woman! Omnisexuals can do whatever they want without feeling guilty! 'Oh, you're omnisexual?' 'Yes, but I don't screw animals or dead people.'"

The whole thing is conversational, though a bit on the abrasive side—expected from most any young comic trying to con the crowd.

CYRIL RITCHARD
- ODD SONGS AND A POEM (Dolphin 1) ** $10 $30

Ritchard's collection of fey cabaret songs will delight his fans and those who revel in sophisticated humor (or "humour") that sometimes dwells in the titteringly macabre.

Several tunes are very mild and archaic, and even Ritchard's self-parodying cheekiness and charming elegance can't save them: "Color Blind," "Put It Away 'Til Spring," or "You're So Much a Part of Me," the latter a duet with Elaine Dunn.

Fans who can't think of anybody but Cyril as Peter Pan's nemesis Captain Hook will enjoy "The Old Gavotte," with Ritchard hamming it up deliciously in what he calls "a rather intimate glimpse into the early life of Captain Hook," complete with stern warnings, gurgly laughs, and this refrain: "Slash her up and fore! Then pass the fingerbowl, Charlie. We'll all dip our hands in the gore!"

In a similar vein is Michael Brown's well-known cabaret tune "Lizzie Borden." As he declares, "You can't chop your poppa up in Massachusetts. Not even if it's planned as a surprise. No you can't chop your poppa up in in Massachusetts. You know how neighbors love to criticize."

"Turk in the Murkadurk" is nonsense about a woman "as fair as a prickle pear tree" who loves to drink "porcupine broth." She thinks a good sign of love is carving her name on her lover's back with a tusk. He doesn't think this is a pleasant idea at all, and lets her know this by throwing her into the nearest river.

HARRY RITZ
- HILARITY IN HOLLYWOOD (Hilarities 1-001) *1/2 $10 $20

Often called one of the most influential comics of the '40s, Harry Ritz (leader of The Ritz Brothers) released only one album, an atypical collection of five mild songs with lyrics by Mac Maurada. The rest is bland filler from Ben Yost, Skinney Ennis, Sophie Tucker, and others.

Ritz offers a few mild jokes before he sings "Don't Holler," an ordinary jazz song more suited to Louis Prima. He follows it with the silly "What the Little People Say," a collection of dumb couplets like "It may sound beastly familiar, but what can we do about it? Familiarity breeds contempt. But we can't breed without it!" Ritz's different (now cliché) dialects for each couplet don't help. The other cuts are "Who's Got Troubles" (more dialect), the brief opener "Hilarity," and the closer, "Rockabilly Wedding Day," another bland jazz rave-up that goes nowhere. There's no live audience to inspire Ritz and he goes through his paces professionally but not hilariously. There's no "Hilarity in Hollywood" here, and this was not an auspicious debut for "Hilarity Records."

BOB RIVERS COMEDY GROUP
- TWISTED CHRISTMAS (Critique/Atco 7906711, CD reissue 7906712) ** $8
- I AM SANTA CLAUS (Atlantic 825482) ** $8

A few dumb cuts on the 1987 "Twisted Christmas" have become perennials around Christmas. Most notable is "A Christmas Message from Elvis," with the bloated king talking about how "Chistmas is a time of hope, a time of joy, and a time for eating and eating and eating. Would you pass me that drumstick?" Another one is hard for Grateful Dead fans to resist. "Come All Ye Faithful" becomes: "Come All ye Grateful—deadheads to the concert. Oh come Grateful Deadheads and camp in the streets."

Rivers produced the parodies, but most of the mimicry is handled by Dale Reeves. And most are annoying, like the clunky "Wreck the Malls" ("Deck the Halls"), a brat singing "The Chimney Song," and the redundant "12 Pains of Christmas," in which various overacting grown-ups and kiddies literally yell out the things they hate. The jerky electric guitar version of "Joy to the World" is guaranteed to send shoppers racing out of stores and radio listeners climbing up the chimney.

On the plus side, curmudgeons will enjoy Rivers's forty-three second version of "We Wish You a Merry Christmas" called "We Wish You Weren't Living with Us." And racist curmudgeons will also love "Foreigners" (formerly the hymn "Gloria") in which a variety of outrageously accented illegal aliens sing about how much they enjoy coming here to "sneak across your borderlines to stand in unemployment lines."

With a larger cast and a bigger budget, the second album (1993) has a few chuckles via recognition humor. Imagine Black Sabbath's "I Am Iron Man" as "I Am Santa Claus," or Eric Burdon singing "O Little Town of Bethlehem" in the same style as "House of the Rising Sun." Or "Deck the Halls" turning into a jolly poke at Michael Jackson ("Grab your balls"). It's good for a momentary laugh, but that's it. Ten seconds into the song and the joke is tiresome. Several cuts try for deliberate tastelessness and the pushiness ruins the fun ("I Came Upon a Roadkill Deer" is overkill). The wittiest track is also the most depressing—the instrumental "O Christmas Tree" with the sound of a saw ripping into wood.

Sometimes after coming up with the parody title, the lyrics just go nowhere, as with "Walkin' in a Winter Wonderland" transformed into "Walkin' 'Round in Women's Underwear." "Teddy the Red-Nosed Senator" may be the poorest excuse for Kennedy parody ever. If the humorless song doesn't outright call him a murderer, it does end by calling him an S.O.B.

JOAN RIVERS

• MR. PHYLLIS AND OTHER FUNNY STORIES (Warner Bros. 1610) ***	$15	$25
• THE NEXT TO LAST JOAN RIVERS ALBUM (Buddah BDS 5048 reissued by Arista, BL 58096) ***	$10	$20
• WHAT BECOMES A SEMI-LEGEND MOST? (Geffen GHS 4007) ***	$5	$12

Rivers's three albums reflect the three distinct phases of her career. Back in 1965, around the time her Warner album was made, Rivers was sort of a female Woody Allen. Her improbable lifestyle included bad luck with pets: "I bought me a philodendrun ... and I put it in the kitchen and it drank my soup." Another pet, her wig, was "the runt of the litter. How can you say no to a little cross-eyed wig with love in its eyes. And the love is missing you because of the crossed eyes ... a loser wig." She did teach it tricks: "Curl!"

Like Allen, she knows the craft of one-liners, noting that her town, Larchmont, "is so tiny, there's a mirror at one end." For her fairly hip New York audience she can get a solid chuckle over the pronunciation of Leonard Bernstein. It's either "steen or styne, depending on your income level."

Joan does some typical gags for that era (airlines) and for women in stand-up (the title track about her hairdresser), but doesn't use much self-deprecatory humor here, and of course no celebrity put-downs. The closest she gets is a three-minute routine on her early years as a lonely fatty: "Nobody could get close enough to me to find out I was fun. I began to retreat very much into myselves."

After a few years of seasoning, she emerged with the Buddah album, now able to aggressively banter with ringsiders: "So? Four girls alone, what's the matter? Your mother's going crazy? How old are you. You don't know? 27? And you're single? Your mother must be going out of her mind! Jewish or Gentile. Catholic? Oh, you have nothing to worry about. Catholic mothers have an excuse: she wants to be a nun."

Abandoning any cerebral Woody Allen pretensions, the late '60s and early '70s Joan was now directing her energies toward the women in the audience, sharing her marriage and maternity experiences and having them agree with her green-eyed put-downs of dumb, but pretty, women and pert nurses:

"All men look at is looks ... men are so shallow ... they like nurses! Single, vicious good-looking girls ... little short skirts, the top button undone, always leaning over the operating room, 'Let me help, let me help.' While I was having my baby the woman in the next room died! Died, while a nurse was down the hall talking to a single man. That woman died! And she was a visitor."

Rivers established herself as the nation's top stand-up comedienne, her gut approach more contemporary than the generic bad housewife gags of Phyllis Diller. Rivers described the little hurts and miseries of womanhood with an insistent and passionate voice; and every now and then the strident cry of revenge.

By 1983, when she recorded "Legend," Rivers was the "permanent" guest host for Johnny Carson on *The Tonight Show*. She had glamourized her look and she was turning her anger outward instead of inward. Instead of self-deprecation, she joked about her peers. She came off like the house comedian for *The National Inquirer* as she joked about meeting very fallible stars. Here she mentions that Elizabeth Taylor "has more chins than a Chinese phone book" and cries "Liberace is gay. His big fantasy is having Tom Selleck as his proctologist!"

Taking advantage of the new permissiveness in comedy, Rivers tells pungent one-liners about her trampy friend "Heidi Abromowitz" and offers pungent, intimate recognition humor. Of her trip to the gynecologist's office: "My feet are in the stirrups, my knees are in my face and the door is open facing me ... can we talk here? Men don't understand ... for a woman to lie in those stirrups, is that the worst? And my gynecologist does jokes! 'Dr. Schwartz, at your cervix!' 'I'm dialated to meet you!' 'Say ahhh.' 'There's Jimmy Hoffa!' There's no way you can get back at that son of a bitch unless you learn to throw your voice."

The album is fast and furious, veering in and out of taste. Rivers's voice is now almost permanently hoarse from the gut-spilling frenzy. Her shocking style antagonized some, who considered her some kind of female Don Rickles, but it delighted many more. It was impossible to keep up the outrage, and her "hot" personality cooled. She eventually moved to daytime talk and shop programs. As for doing more comedy albums, she explained her point of view to me in three words: "Pooey on posterity!"

NOTES: Rivers is on audiocassettes reading from her autobiographies. She is also on "Zingers from Hollywood Squares" (Event E 6903): "Your baby has a certain object he loves to cling to. Should you break him of this habit?" "Yes, it's Daddy's turn." She sings on "Vernon Duke Revisited" (Painted Smiles PS 1342).

HAL ROACH

- THE BEST OF IRISH HUMOUR (Rego 14000, original title available as an import:
  I THINK I'M HAVING ONE OF MY TURNS) **1/2 $5 $10
- THE KING OF BLARNEY (Rego 21000) **1/2 $5 $10
- WE IRISH JUST TALK LIKE THAT (Rego R36000) **1/2 $5 $10
- HE MUST BE JOKING (Rego 50000) **1/2 $5 $10
- WRITE IT DOWN (Rego 28000, Irish Records International GMCD 1000) **1/2 $8

A beloved Irish comedian, Roach (not America's Hal Roach, the producer of Laurel and Hardy shorts) has spent over two decades headlining one club (Jury's in Dublin). He has crossed the Atlantic, usually around St. Patrick's Day, to play venues on the East Coast. He tells plenty of "classics," or "wheezes," depending on how many times they've been heard and laughed at.

Here are some quickies. From "King of Blarney": "My uncle Pat, he reads the death column every morning in the paper. And he can't understand how people always die in alphabetical order." "My wife converted me to religion. I never believed in hell till I married her." And from "Best of Irish Humor": "We only drink in Ireland to forget we're alcoholics."

The one-liners are usually pit stops along the journey through a long story, told in his delightful brogue. One of the shorter anecdotal tales:

"A man walks into a bar and asks, 'Is there a fella here called Rooney?' And this little fella like meself stood up and said, 'I'm Rooney. What about it?' And the big fella nearly killed him! Broke his nose, broke six of his ribs, and gave him two black eyes and dashed out of the place. When he was gone, the little fella picked himself up and said, 'I sure made a monkey out of him! Sure, I'm not Rooney at all!'"

Roach's albums were recorded mostly in the late '70s but have been in print constantly, with "Write It Down" available on CD via the Massachusettes label Irish Records. Roach's material is available from the Irish label Grainne, in import CD, cassette, and even video versions.

PADDY ROBERTS

- STRICTLY FOR GROWN-UPS (Kapp KDL 7006) *1/2 $5 $10

Roberts was a successful songwriter in England during the '50s. Evidently, much like Noel Coward, he decided to step out and sing his own material. His bland, soft, timorous, lispy crooning doesn't help his tunes at all. Perhaps a few of the gentle songs here would have more punch delivered by a professional. One number, "Lavender Cowboy," pokes fun at a gay cowboy who rides side-saddle, but Roberts's vocal coloring is pretty lavender, too.

One of the most accessible cuts is "Don't Upset the Little Kiddiewinks," a weary look at indulgent parents and their brats: "You must let each little monster do exactly as he wants to, though you know he's going to take you for a chump. You may treat each treasure to some psychiatric measure, but you mustn't dare to kick him up the rump." Another tune, "The Ballad of Bethnal Green," has a wistful opening remark: "This is a very old English folk song. I know it's a very old English folk song because I wrote it myself. When I was very young."

This album was originally issued circa 1960 on Decca in England. Roberts's other British Decca albums include "At the Blue Angel," "But Not in Front of the Children," "Songs for Gay Dogs," "Paddy Roberts Tries Again," and the compilation "World of Paddy Roberts."

ALEN ROBIN

- WELCOME TO THE LBJ RANCH (Capitol W 2423) **1/2 $4 $8
- LYNDON JOHNSON'S LONELY HEARTS CLUB BAND (Atco 33-230) *** $5 $10

Robin, the head writer of *The Tonight Show* for half a dozen years in the '60s, liked to take taped speeches of politicians—and use their words against them in spliced-up mock interviews. First with partner Earle Doud (of "The First Family" fame) and later on his own, he offered vinyl mischief from the LBJ years to Reagan and Carter.

The two LBJ albums are benign. In the "LBJ Ranch" album notes, Earle Doud wrote that he's only kidding with "people for whom we have the utmost respect," and he was unfortunately sincere. Robin's sleazy nasal voice was evidently not considered strong enough to support an album, so here he's abetted by a "panel" of respected old radio commentators: John Cameron Swayze, John St. Leger, and Westbrook Van Voorhis. There's always a solid effort made to duplicate natural conversation so that the listener isn't simply waiting for the spliced-in punch line. A White House tour with Lady Bird Johnson has her fielding many questions:

"This is one of the newer rooms isn't it?" "No." "Oh, I'm sorry." "That's all right." How would you best describe your husband?" "The brainiest, the most hardworking, most devoted—" "That's a very good description of your husband." "Yes I can hear him saying it right now." "Are those your dogs out there?" "The beagles out there under the trees." "One looks as if she's about ready to have pups. Is that possible?" "I could tell you but that's just a real personal question...." "I understood there used to be great danes, but they weren't housebroken." "Yes, the children used to walk on stilts up and down the hall."

Pop art buffs will be amused to discover the album cover's political portraits were done by sci-fi artist Frank Frazetta. Monty Python fans might be surprised to discover John Cleese laughing his head off in a back cover shot as a member of the studio audience.

1967's "Lonely Hearts" is more of the same as Robin, Earle Doud, Westbrook Van Voorhis, and John Cameron Swayze question Bobby Kennedy, Barry Goldwater, Lady Bird Johnson, Vice President Hubert Humphrey, and here, Everett Dirksen:

"What can you tell us about honesty?" "I gave it up for politics." "The senate had a lot of problems with the budget this year, how did you finally manage to cut the budget?" "We had a rabbi and what a job he did!"

- SUPERSHRINK (Janus JXS 7001) ***1/2 $5 $10
- FUNNY FARM (Courage CLP 13) *** $5 $10
- NAKED REALLY NAKED (Carrot CA 317) ** $5 $10
- THANK YOU MR. PRESIDENT (Columbia JC 36870) *** $5 $10
- WELCOME TO MY COUCH (Passport PB 6041) **1/2 $4 $8

On his own, Robin created the best of his splice and snicker albums. He started off with a new idea. Instead of just setting up the politicians as a reporter, he became "Supershrink," psychiatrist to the stars. That was a good excuse to ask all kinds of personal questions and get "honest" answers. Even his voice was well-suited to the task, the laid-back nasal drone sounding very much like that of a semi-interested psychiatrist. On the Janus album, with Richard Nixon:

"Would you care to use the couch today?" "I think I will just stand on the table." "Incidentally, I like that suit you're wearing. Who made that suit for you? "Millions of Vietnamese men, women, and children." "Where did you get that tie?" "Thailand...." "All right ... your parents, did they ever spank you and put you to bed without dinner?" "Last Friday ... I'm not afraid of 'em...." "What did you say when you needed to be changed?" "It's raining." "Did your parents have any pet names for you?" "Nixon the Rainmaker."

Other targets on this album include Hubert Humphrey, Strom Thurmond, Nelson Rockefeller, John Lindsay, Ronald Reagan, William Buckley, Spiro Agnew, Lyndon Johnson, and Chicago's Mayor Daley.

Robin tended to save and repeat his favorite jokes. The Courage and Carrot albums use material from the "Supershrink" album and are so similar, fans who find one don't need the other. Both albums contain the same targets: Spiro Agnew, Hubert Humphrey, Ted Kennedy, John Lindsay, George McGovern, Richard Nixon, and Nelson Rockefeller. Both have a segment with Hubert Humphrey complaining to the shrink:

"Two weeks ago, three weeks ago, I had reason to believe that maybe we were going to make progress. I found those hopes dashed!" "... Okay, you were telling me last week you still think you're Joan of Arc." "There isn't any doubt." "You think there's something I can do?" "Call the fire department!" "You've reached an age when a man can begin to doubt his physical magnetism. Do women still find you attractive?" "Three out of every four." "And the fourth?" "Tragically, even dangerously misguided!" "You prefer your women how?" "Naked. Really naked. Really naked, naked, naked, really naked."

Robin was fond of playing with his tapes and, as that last line indicates, repetition was a good way of jazzing up the fake interviews.

His 1980 album on the Carter vs Reagan presidential race includes a few moments with old favorites like Nixon and Kissinger. To Carter:

"Do you have a message for the American People?" "Suffer!" "With all the pressures of your office, do you still have time to be a good husband to Rosalyn?" "I will do everything in my power tonight."

To Reagan: "What did you do during the war?" "Freezing at Valley Forge." "You have been around a while. Can you think of one basic maxim that has helped make life worthwhile?" "Yes. There are physical differences between the sexes." "How is Nancy?" "You're asking me about a subject I haven't had the opportunity to look into at all."

For the small New Jersey-based Passport label in 1984, Robin worked up a satire of New York's Mayor Ed Koch. He had a lot of fun with Koch's flamboyant personality, making tape loops out of the mayor's giggles and epithets: "Garbage!" "Stupid!" No doubt Koch was at least pleased that Robin gave him a rabid sex life: "What is your technique when you meet an attractive woman, what do you say to her?" "Give give give GIVE! GIVE! Say yes! GIVE IN! Give give give give...."

LYNN ROBINSON

- YOUR GIRL FOR THE NIGHT (Ha Ha NO33) *1/2 $7 $15

On this cheaply made 1961 "adult's only" album, tinny sound matches some tacky gags: "Did you hear about the girl who bought a glass diaphragm? She wanted to have a picture window in her rumpus room." Songs outnumber jokes. Titillating titles ("Come into My Cave," "Petting My Pussy," and "Up the Canal") generally have double entendres anemic enough to be single entendres. From "Come into My Cave": "Though it may be very dark in there, you'll be happy as a lark in there. You can satisfy your soul at last. But you better make it fast." In "I'm a Girl Who Likes to Eat" she warbles: "I'm a girl who likes to eat. Especially when it's meat. No matter how hard I try I can never pass it by." Pass it by.

CHRIS ROCK

- BORN SUSPECT (Atlantic 821592) *** $8

A young black comic who moved from *Saturday Night Live* in the early '90s to *In Living Color* and movies, Chris Rock utilizes ethnic and attitude material, but doesn't exclude white audiences. In his better raps, he describes differences in the races, but underlines the humanity of one fact: all men are equally idiotic:

"Black people aren't crazy. Black people do stupid things, black people snatch rope chains and rob liquor stores. Black people generally aren't crazy. When you watch the news and hear somebody got their head chopped off, or somebody drank the blood and used the toes to play pool with, chances are that was a white guy! An old lady kicked down the stairs for a welfare check? Black guy! 'Gimme dat fo' dollah check!' Brothers be in jail for the stupidest shit. White guy in jail: 'Embezzling funds.' Black guy, what are you in jail for: 'Socks. Took me $48 worth a' socks! My feet was feelin' GOOD.'"

PAUL RODRIGUEZ
- PAUL RODRIGUEZ (Columbia BFC 40361) * $4 $8

Rodriguez, in face, voice, and attitude, is unappealing, unpleasant, and uninteresting. On California highway driving: "Mexicans! Basically our hobby is to get in the car and piss you off!" He has always overdone his ethnic jokes. His most notorius gag was a fake American Express commercial for "Mexican Express ... when I travel some people don't know who I am. That's why I always carry my Mexican Express Card!" Then he'd pull out a knife.

Here Rodriguez continues to coyly riff on racial issues, getting titters from uptight-but-liberal whites and equally edgy Hispanics. There's no real honesty or emotion (trademarks of a Richard Pryor or Lenny Bruce) just coyness, stereotype dialogue for a shock giggle, and a lot of weak prattle.

In a bit on gang fighting and war: "The biggest criticism whites have about Chicanos is (puts on a prissy white wimp voice), 'You guys never fight fair, you need like forty people with you.' Yes! Yes, we do. And you know what? I get beat up real seldom! Who wants to mess with you when you whistle and like forty people gonna go, 'Yeah, what is it!' The Israelis are bad, don't fuck with them! Somethin' about those yarmulkes! You put on those yarmulkes, you ready to kick some ass!"

ROGER AND ROGER
- DIGEST THE STARS (Dingo D-2002) *1/2 $4 $8

Roger and Roger (no last names given on this cheaply done album) offer a bunch of second-rate impressions with third-rate material. Ed Saliva (Ed Sullivan) introduces the guests, who tell one-liners. Boris Kockoff (Boris Karloff) says, "I'd like to tell you about my latest movie. It's called *The Werewolf Gets a Poodle Cut*." "Grouchy" Marx calls out, "Say the secret woid and you get fifty dollars. The secret word tonight is 'legs.' Spread the woid!"

GAMBLE ROGERS
- THE LORD GIVES ME GRACE AND THE DEVIL GIVES ME STYLE (Mountain Railroad 52779) $3 $7
- THE WARM WAY HOME (Mountain Railroad 52786) $3 $7

TIMMIE ROGERS
- IF I WERE PRESIDENT (Philips 200088/600088) ** $6 $12
- SUPER SOUL BROTHER ALIAS CLARK DARK (Partee 2403) ** $7 $15

A pioneering black stand-up (in white nightclubs he wore a suit rather than the garish clothes expected of his race), Timmie struggled through the '50s and emerged in the '60s as a popular comic, well known on *The Ed Sullivan Show* for a bubbly personality and the catchphrase "Oh yeah," which he delivered with wide-eyed intensity.

"If I Were President," his first album, is a disappointment. Instead of monologues it's blackout (no pun intended) sketches on the fantasy theme of Rogers becoming president. Some bits are well-intentioned (even the black president has to hustle and hide from angry crowds to bring his little child to a newly integrated school) while others are just obvious (jokes about "The White" House). At home with the wife:

"Hello there, you sexy Prexy. How did everything go at the office?" "Oh honey, I had a rough day. The Russians wouldn't talk to me, the British wouldn't talk to me. Even Dick Gregory wouldn't talk to me." "Why wouldn't Dick Gregory talk to you?" "When I got elected it killed his whole act...." "Well I got some good news. Mama's here for a visit." "Oh noooooo ... I'd like to put your mother on a new five-cent stamp." "Oooh, mama would be thrilled, honey!" "I'd do anything to see that face canceled out!"

The material, written by veterans like Sol Weinstein and Ron Friedman, is up to the level of a *Sanford and Son* but has few surprises. The supporting cast includes Ossie Davis, Ruby Dee, and Kenny Delmar.

"Super Soul Brother" from 1973 mixes monologue fragments and sketches in which Rogers talks with Nixon (among the costars, Will Jordan as Nixon).

Rogers issued a single on Cameo: "I've Got a Dog Who Loves Me and a Woman Who Don't," and a straight album, "Oh Yeah! It's Me Singing" (Epic 26168).

WILL ROGERS
- WILL ROGERS SAYS (Columbia ML 4604) **1/2 $10 $20
- TIMELY TOPICS (Pelican 102) ** $5 $10
- WILL ROGERS (Golden Age GA 503) ** $4 $8
- WILL ROGERS (Distinguished 3001) **1/2 $5 $10

• I NEVER MET A MAN I DIDN'T LIKE (American Heritage P11794) **1/2	$8	$15
• WILL ROGERS (Murray Hill M 51220) **1/2	$12	$25
• ORIGINAL RADIO BROADCASTS (Mark 56 # 659) **1/2	$4	$8
• THE WIT AND WISDOM OF WILL ROGERS (Caedmon TC 2046) **1/2	$8	$15

Rogers was the great topical comedian of his day, unique in his ability to not only joke about tough issues, but get away with it. He was beloved by both the people and his politician targets.

There's a lot of duplication on the various Will Rogers albums. "Will Rogers Says" is nicely put together with warm commentary from Will Rogers, Jr. The excerpts from radio shows include "On Mother's Day," "On Living in Russia," "On Flo Ziegfeld," "On the Baer-Carnera Fight," "On Making Movies in Sacramento," and "On Comedians."

The album released by Distinguished Recordings offers eight routines: "Mother's Day (May 12, 1935), "Plan Day" (April 21, 1935), "Inheritance Tax" (April 28, 1935), "The Congressional Record" (May 12, 1935), "The Dust Bowl" (April 14, 1935), "President's Day" (April 30, 1935), "Economics" (April 7, 1935), and "The Pilgrims" (April 14, 1935). The sound is clear and nicely reproduced.

The Murray Hill set offers the most Rogers for the money (three records and a budget price). Though now out of print, most stores don't raise the prices much on the Murray Hill line. Most of the familiar material is here, including "Timely Topics: Rogers Plan to Stop All Wars. Conditions in New York City" and his last broadcast, June 9, 1935. There's also a speech from the 1932 National Democratic Convention, an October 18, 1931, government sponsored address, and a ten-minute chunk from a radio appearance with Fred Stone on a July 13, 1933, broadcast: "There's been a terrible mess of governors out here lately, they're out here on vacation." "Vacation? Who's vacation, their states?" "Say, you helped herd 'em, didn't ya? Did ya ever herd a governor?" "Well, no and yes. I herded sheep once in Wyoming. It's just the same thing, ain't it?" "Well, yes and no. Herdin' Democratic governors is just like herdin' sheep, but herdin' Republican governors is more like goats." The sound quality is painfully muddled at times, not only on the radio cuts, but even on the 78 rpm "Timely Topics." Unlike other available versions (notably the American Heritage album) the cut is not remastered at all and sounds exactly as if someone stuck a microphone next to a record player trying to pick up the scratchy 78's sound.

The American Heritage album has the 78 and much more pleasing sound:

"You know these talking machines are great. When you come to a theater or movies to see some of us and you don't like our act, just outta courtesy you have to stick and see us through. On one of these if you don't like us you just stop the machine, take the record off, and accidentally drop it on the floor. Then the only annoyance is sweepin' up.

"Now folks, all I know is what little news I read every day in the paper. I see where another wife out on Long Island in New York shot her husband. Season opened a month earlier this year. Prohibition caused all this. There's just as many husbands shot at in the old days, but women were missin'. Prohibition has improved their marksmanship ninety percent. Never a day passes in New York without some innocent bystander being shot. You just stand around this town long enough and be innocent and somebody's gonna shoot ya."

The American Heritage album also features a good collection of radio broadcasts: "President's Day" (April 30, 1933), "Badwill Tour" (July 8, 1934), "Treaties" (March 31, 1935), "Supreme Court" (June 2, 1935), and "Mother's Day" (May 12, 1935). It has the last Will Rogers broadcast, June 9, 1935. His last words: "Everybody is trying to save the country. Only they are trying to do it in different ways, and it is too big, the country is too big for all of them put together to spoil anyhow. So goodbye, and I'll see you in the fall. Thank you very much."

Mark 56 duplicates material available on the American Heritage disc. Rogers describes his "plan to end all plans," the meeting between Aimee Semple McPherson and Ghandi, and the latest Presidential address: "I don't know what he's gonna talk about—maybe he's gonna talk about Mae West. Everybody else is! In fact, I'll bet he'd rather talk about Mae than some of the things he's obliged to talk about tonight."

Caedmon's double set includes broadcasts from April 7, 1935 ("Roosevelt and Taxes"), April 14, 1935 ("The Great Dust Storms of History," "Conservation," "The Pilgrim Fathers"), April 21, 1935 ("Social Security," "The Townsend Plan," "The Agricultural Plan"), and April 28, 1935 ("The Morgenthau Plan," "The Inheritance Tax," "Franklin D. Roosevelt.") Also on the record, Rogers talking about "The Congressional Record" and "Mother's Day" (May 12, 1935).

NOTES: One of the best albums for Rogers's humor is "Will Rogers U.S.A." by James Whitmore (see the entry under Whitmore). Will Rogers appears on compilation albums, including "The Old Curiosity Shop" (RCA LCT 1112), "I Can Hear It Now" (Columbia D 31366), "Ziegfeld Follies" (Veritas 107), "Calling All Stars" (Star Tone 203), and "Old Time Radio" (Columbia P2M5287).

MURRAY ROMAN

• THIS IS MURRAY ROMAN (Everest LPBR 9005) ** $5 $10

Murray Roman (born in New York in 1928) recorded his first album circa 1960. It's a theme album on skiing.

A hip comic influenced by more "swinging" humorists of the day, Roman is handcuffed by his material. Perhaps not even Lenny Bruce could've gotten much mileage out of the subject, especially over a full album. Listeners who like to ski, and have a broken leg and nothing else to do, can sit back and listen:

"Aspen, Colorado. Some pretty funny things happen here, if you have some objectivity. This is true. It frightens me, having never been a skier. Think about this town! You come up here, you spend like a hundred dollars a day. This is the greatest con in the world! They give you a room for twenty dollars a day if you got your own sleeping bag, twenty-five if you don't. For the same money in Las Vegas you get a penthouse with eight girls! But they don't have a mountain there."

• YOU CAN'T BEAT PEOPLE UP AND HAVE THEM SAY I LOVE YOU (Tetragrammaton 101) *** $7 $15

- A BLIND MAN'S MOVIE (Tetragrammaton 120) *** $10 $25
- BUSTED (United Artists UAS 5595) **1/2 $7 $15

Some Lenny Bruce imitators seemed ready to go the full route. Murray Roman was one of them. He was busted for drugs, and reportedly died of an overdose.

In 1968, forty-year-old Roman issued the first of his Tetragrammaton albums. He tried something new: a mix of live stand-up and collaged sound effects and rock music. This was the hallucinogenic '60s and Murray was going to take up where the late Lenny Bruce left off.

The album notes on the first LP are from Tommy Smothers, who writes that like "Catcher in the Rye, Lenny Bruce, Sergeant Pepper, and King Kong ... he blew my mind occasionally. He had some groovy ideas, but with this album, he suddenly just stepped out and ... became an innovator ... this record will become a classic." (Roman's daughter returned the favor years later writing the album notes for Rhino's reissue of Smothers Brothers material).

Murray/Lenny riffs on Twiggy: "Twiggy is a fag-hype on the world. A bunch of fags in London said, 'I really like Greek kids.' So they send over Twiggy who is like a stick! And chicks don't know where that is. I've watched chicks read *Vogue*, where they have sticks with a dress on. Supposedly the role of getting dressed is to attract the male bird. You can't do that by wearing the clothes that are in *Vogue*. 'Cause *Vogue* is a dyke thing! 'Cause dykes want boys too, only chicks who look like boys. Guys read *Playboy* ... all the chicks we dig have tits!"

A kind of acid *Laugh-In*, Roman offered one-liners cut between hard rock and soul vocals: "Hey, why doncha call the police department at three o'clock in the morning and speak to them in German. If they answer in German, you got 'em, babe! Oh hoooo...."

Roman's follow-up album offered more of the same, only this time with a cover Lenny Bruce would've loved. "Blind Man's Movie" had a completely black album jacket, front and back. Open it up, the gatefold's black, too.

Rock music, added to the live recording later, blazes in the background as Roman dissects the real story of Snow White: "Get high one day and read it. Sleepy would be a downer freak, into Seconals, droppin' up all day. Dopey would be a grass smoker.... Sneezy was a coke sniffer. Grumpy was a speed freak. Happy was an acid head: "I love you, I love you." Bashful was a juicer. And Doc was the connection. Dig where that is. And Snow White ... was their fantasy!" Other cuts include "The War," "Black People," "Cuba," "Black Sambo Pancakes," "Theology," and "Fuzz."

Roman's two albums were a revelation at the time, especially when there was a void left by Lenny Bruce's death. "Busted" from 1972 has a full side of previously released material. The rest centers mainly on Roman's jail experiences. With Laurel and Hardy's theme playing in the background, he talks about the trial and the incompetent lawyer. From there, he goes into the colorful characters he met in jail (played by Michael Nesmith, Bill Martin, Stu Gardner, and others). Some of it is vividly presented as theater, not intended to provoke belly laughs.

- A CHILD'S GARDEN OF GRASS (Elektra EKS 75012) * $5 $15

Roman was the only famous name in the supporting cast of this 1971 disappointment that takes the worst elements from several comedy record styles. Like Firesign Theater, there's an emphasis on sound effects and slice-of-life vignettes that try to be realistic but end up boring. Like average sketch albums, there's a tendency toward corn:

(On marijuana) "You tend to forget everything almost as soon as it happens."

"Certain thoughts seem to take on secondary, even, tertiary—"

"Hey man, what are you talking about?"

"I think I forgot."

Occasionally there may be a flash of recognition comedy, or some subliminal gag that seems amusing (back in the '70s there was a silly, but catchy, commercial for "Cresta Blanca," here parodied as "Mara Juana"). Mostly, listeners would be better off lighting up and just playing some music. It'll seem funnier. Nostalgia sometimes raises the price on this one.

HAROLD ROME

- ROME-ANTICS: SONGS OF SATIRE (Heritage H 0063) ** $7 $15

Harold Rome wrote the Broadway musicals *Fanny*, *Wish You Were Here*, *Call Me Mister*, and *Pins and Needles*. Some tunes on this 1956 album are from various lesser shows. "Cry Baby" and "French with Tears" are from *Alive and Kicking*, "Gin Rummy Rhapsody" and "You Never Know What Hit You" are from *That's the Ticket*, "Pocketful of Dreams" is from *Peep Show*.

The tunes are light and tame. "The Advertising Song" is a minor "patter" song (a la Danny Kaye) with lyrics quickly quoting from dozens of '50s ad campaigns. A song about love in The Catskills ("Ain't Love Grand") offers warpage like: "The lake sparkles like a new white tablecloth. The sand looks like fresh pumpernickel. The view is as clear as a fine chicken broth, the grass is as green as new pickle."

"Pocketful of Dreams" is not exactly Tom Lehrer, as Rome contrasts a snappy melody with what was then considered to be fairly sick humor about kiddies: "Oh the motor cars we stole, and the drunks that we did roll, and the many other carefree childish pranks. Those are my dreams on parade. Do you think that I would trade them for all the dough in all the banks?"

Rome sings them as any sophisticated lounge pianist would. They remain safely within the boundaries of what would make a chorus boy smirk, a housewife nod her head, or a very elderly lady blush.

HUGH ROMNEY (WAVY GRAVY)

- THIRD STREAM HUMOUR (World Pacific 1805) ** $10 $35
- OLD FEATHERS, NEW BIRD (Relix RRCD 2032) ** $8

It's interesting to hear Romney at work, a guy who had a cult following and was definitely in a weirder orbit than some of his contemporaries on the same cutting edge: Dick Shawn, Ronny Graham, and Severin Darden. On his 1962 album Romney has some of the grandiose enunciations of Lord Buckley and a little of Lenny Bruce's intimate whine as he touches on a variety of hip topics (Thelonious, Miles, rolling papers, blacks, and Zen).

Romney's main problem here is that he's not very funny. He's into playing with deliberately strange images and "secret visions," and at times leans toward the pretense and self-consciousness of beat poets. He also loves to swing to the sound of his own voice, registering what he thinks is profundity, elation, hipness, and word jazz with every shout, grumble, and stretched-out enunciation. In one of his better moments he describes somebody else's peculiar act:

"They had this guy onstage, and the only thing he was doin' the whole time he was onstage was snappin' his index finger against his thumb. Somethin' like this. Yeah. Somethin' like this. It seems. Like it was almost. *Yes-ter-dayyyy!* I'm just snappin' my index finger against my thumb. Lis-enn-inggg to the souuuuund. Of my index finger snappin' against my thumb! And after a while, beginning, to CON-centrate on MY *indexxxxx* finger. Noticing the dirt imbedded in my fingernail! And the *nicotine* stains *garrrnishing* my knuckle! And after a while to become, as we say in the trade, HUNG UP! AND THEN EVERYTHING BEGINS TO SPIN AND POUND, AND IT'S *black and sticky* and *strange and weird,* and I realize that I HAVE BEEN SWALLOWED by my index finger. But I don't panic. I reach down into my pocket and I take out this sterling silver drill! And I begin a drillin' from my fingerbone to my knucklebone, from my knucklebone to my wristbone, from my wristbone to my elbow bone, from my elbow bone to my shoulder bone, from my shoulder bone to my neck bone and next thing I know I'm STANDING UP INSIDE MY OWN HEAD. Whew. Are you kidding? *Quite a place I got here.* It's too bad they're gonna tear it down and build a Playboy Club."

Romney did not go the way of Lenny Bruce or Lord Buckley. He didn't age into simply an older version of himself, as Dick Shawn did. He didn't lose his Yippie/comic faith as Abbie Hoffman did. He instead transformed himself into Merry Prankster "Wavy Gravy," became the master of ceremonies at Woodstock in 1969, and became the head of Camp Winnarainbow, living on a commune in Laytonville, California. In 1992 he published a book and the same year was honored by the Ben & Jerry's ice cream company with his own flavor, "Wavy Gravy," a mixture of nuts, chocolate chunks, and caramel fudge.

His 1988 CD "Wavy" is relaxed and cheerful as he lightheartedly describes some of his current notions ("Nobody for President"), recalls "How Hugh Romney Became Wavy Gravy," and offers anecdotes of his "zany" radical life, including his appearance at a 1967 benefit for the Chicago 8:

"I come in on the airplane, I'm wearin' a WWI jumpsuit with an aviator hat ... and a duck beak that squeaked, and these Chicago police dove on my clown ass and they wanted to see some kind of ID, and the only thing I had was a picture of me in the San Francisco Chronicle dressed as a hamburger. It's true. They started to laugh. All this dust came off their head 'cause they hadn't done it in a while. Ha! They wanted to take me downtown, not to bust me, but to show me to the other cops. But I wiggled my way out of that and went into a practical joke store and got a three-foot inflatable plastic banana, and blew it up, started walkin' across Chicago. Here comes this police car, right? 'All right, what are you doing?' 'I'm walking my banana, officer.' Shrinks down in the seat and drives off. They don't wanna ask questions. Good sound advice: you ever go to Chicago, bring a three-foot inflatable banana."

PHIL ROSE

- ONE DOZEN PHIL ROSES: HILARIOUS BALLADS OF THE GARMENT BELT (Phil Rose) **1/2 $5 $10

The label declares "For Private Use Only, Not For Public Performance." Evidently this mid-60s album was a promo (the back cover says "Rose is California's most famous designer of women's sportswear and has gained international renown"). In 1960 he had published a photo-caption book called *20 Years Less 8%* about the garment industry.

This obscure album is a very pleasant surprise: well produced (many parody songs have complete orchestration) and well sung by alternating male and female vocalists Terrance and Alicia. The recognition humor will delight anyone who has a subscription to *Women's Wear Daily.*

Almost every topic is here, from a fast-paced recitation of fabrics ("I Am the Very Model of a Modern Manufacturer") to a quick tune about business goniffs ("Knock Offs") to "Herman Goldfarb of Paris," about a humble Jew who designs garments for talentless French designers who have the mystique that makes clothes sell. "Look Down that Lonesome Road" becomes the tart "Look Down Your Nose at Daddy," about a son waiting to inherit the business: "Put down, put down your father, Sonny, it's time you owned the store. Sit down, sit down, and count his money, 'cause that's what sons are for."

ELSIE ROSS AND JO LANE

- LAFF IT UP (Chaton Recordings CLR 511) * $4 $8

The soporific duo of Ross and Lane recorded this album in the mid-70s in Scottsdale, Arizona. Half of it is not comedy at all, like Jo's singing of "My Way" with sleepy organ accompaniment.

Their actual song parodies are feeble. Jo's favorite protest song, sung with marginal enthusiasm: "I ain't got a dime. I can't get in the johnny. I got lots I must lose. Most of it's booze. Woncha open the door? I ain't got much time. My panic is growing. I stand here crossing my knees. Begging you please. Woncha open the door. I've waited much too long, and it's bothering me! I checked my purse, then snarled a curse. Because I had no change, you see. Forget the dime. I fear it's too late now. Hand me the mop, I've got news. There's second-hand booze. All over the floor."

JOE E. ROSS

- SHOULD LESBIANS BE ALLOWED TO PLAY PRO FOOTBALL? (Laff A 164) ** $10 $20

Joe E. Ross began with stand-up in burlesque (he even made a film with stripper Bettie Page) and after sitcom success on *Sergeant Bilko* and *Car 54 Where Are You*, he ended up doing risqué comedy again after a disastrous teaming with Steve Rossi. He comes on like a hoarse and weakened B. S. Pully. He knows he's close to the bottom, opening immediately with his catchphrase:

"First I have to holler 'Ooh! Ooh!' Right? That's the only way anybody knows me. *Car 54 Where Are You*—anybody watch the show? Well, it's a pleasure to be working here tonight. In fact it's a pleasure to be working anyplace."

Ross's act includes a lot of familiar jokes. He talks about a man who confesses to a priest, "'Last week, I don't know what happened to me, father. My wife was bending over a sack of potatoes. I got such a sexual urge, I grabbed her and I did it....' The priest said, 'That's all right....' He said, 'You're not gonna kick me out of church?' He said, 'No, why should I kick you out of church?' 'They kicked me out of the supermarket!'"

Ross recorded an album for children during his *Car 54* popularity, "Toody Tales" (Golden LP 91), and sang "Hello Dolly," "It Had to Be You," "I Left My Heart in San Francisco," and other "Love Songs from a Cop" (Roulette 25281).

STAN ROSS

- MY SON THE COPY CAT (Delfi DFLP 1233) **1/2 $7 $20

The title is honest. Ross not only tries to come up with Allan Sherman-style material, he does a pretty fair job of imitating Sherman's voice. Folk tunes are turned Jewish. "Clementine" becomes "Clement Stein" about a "yenta ten percenta" agent, "Molly Malone" is now "Solly M. Cohen" and "Waltzing Matilda" becomes "Washing Gefilte," all about the problems of making gefilte fish. "Oh Danny Boy (The Pipes Are Calling)" is now the plumbing lament "Oh Stanley Boy" (The Pipes Are Leaking").

"I'm Called Little Buttercup" becomes the very Shermanesque "I'm Called Little Butterball." He admits to even trying drugs: "I've tried every Dexi, and yet, I ain't sexy! My legs I relaxacize sore. I drank chocolate Metracal. Grape and etcetrecal, but increased my slacks a size more!"

If Sherman could duet with Christine Nelson on "Sarah Jackman," Ross can do it with Joy Lane on "Eli Weiss" (his version of "Three Blind Mice"), about a progressive teacher not allowed to severely criticize a problem student named Eli:

"Eli Weiss, Eli Weiss, see what you've done. See what you've done. You've dumped water colors on Izzy Klein."

"I did it 'cause he ain't a freind of mine."

"I have to admit it's a striking design. But that's not nice."

Ironically Ross contributed lyrics to Christine Nelson's solo album.

ROSSI AND WHITE

- I FOUND ME A WHITE MAN (Roulette 42065) **1/2 $5 $10

Steve Rossi's brief merger with Slappy White created stand-up's first major interracial comedy team. Their style in the late '60s isn't that far removed from Allen and Rossi in the early '60s. The straight man/interviewer lobs easy lines and the comic bludgeons them into the audience. Marty Allen could've delivered a lot of these zingers:

"What do you think about all this sex in motion pictures today?" "I think sex should be confined to the privacy of the home. And I don't mind goin' from house to house!" "Where do you stand on the marijuana issue?" "Very high." "Do you stand behind Agnew?" "I won't let no Greek stand behind me!"

The racial humor is at the same level:

"Tell me, do you think a Negro could ever become President?" "Yes, if he ran against a Mexican." "I understand that Los Angeles has a number of honest policemen—" "The number is six."

The black and white teaming never gets into really touchy territory, though Steve Rossi has some moments of doubt:

"I'm lucky 'cause my wife takes the pill." "I know that!" (Audience erupts). "You mother!!!!!" "No, I mean I read that." "That's better!"

At the end, Slappy has a message for the blacks in the audience: "Don't you start that marchin'. I'm makin' a lot of money with this white man! I found me a white man, you find yourself one!"

ROWAN AND MARTIN

- ROWAN AND MARTIN AT WORK (Trey TLP 901, reissued as ATCO Sd 33-257) ** $6 $12
- THE HUMOR OF ROWAN AND MARTIN (Epic FLM 13109) *** $7 $15

Rowan and Martin's debut album released in 1960 is very mild stuff. Their famous "Spy Story" repetition routine is on it. Rowan as the spy "4X" (a brand of condom) tells dopey Dick instructions that he keeps goofing up:

Rowan: "You open the flyleaf."

Martin: "I open the fly—"

If that sounds like a slim premise for humor, it is, but Martin's character as a frisky airhead almost saves it. Another long cut is about Francis Scott Key calling up a disc jockey to announce he's written a new song, "The Star Spangled Banner."

"It's an anthem, kind of a stirring thing—" "Look, kid, look at the surveys in *Downbeat*. Kids don't dig anthems. You tell me one jukebox in town that's got an anthem on it...." "Oh, actually I didn't have it in mind for jukeboxes.... I thought it would be nice to play before baseball games...." "What do you want to play the song before baseball games?" "If the thing works like I think it should, everyone'll stand up." "What are you, some kind of nut?"

They had much better material when they were regular guests on *The Dean Martin Show*, just before they were tapped for *Laugh-In*. Cuts like "Mates, Inc.," "Birds and the Bees," and "Camp Sunny Sunshine" are based on the premise of Dick being a randy bachelor, a stupid and vapid guy who thinks he's sharp and irresistible. In the fast and silly "Birds and the Bees" he learns a few things from Dan:

"There are four ways for a flower to be pollinated." "Whee!" "One way is by the wind.... The wind blows across the top of the flower and the flower has a long, hairy stigma." "You're putting me on!" "Some flowers are pollinated by insects ... some flowers are pollinated by hand...." "Hold it, what's this one by hand?" "It's like with a gardener—" " "The gardener fools around with the flowers?" "No, no, he has 'em in a hothouse—" "Sure he does...." "The man is a horticulturist!" "I'll bet he is!" "... The most fascinating story in nature is the relationship between the bee and the flower." "The bee fools around with the flower?" "No, the bee doesn't even know it's pollinating." "I've been that drunk myself sometimes."

- ROWAN AND MARTIN'S LAUGH IN (Epic FXS 15118) **1/2 $10 $20

Rowan and Martin's Laugh-In updated old-time vaudeville and blackouts to the fast-paced new pop culture. The duo tended to play straight in their conservative suits, letting their supporting players (Goldie Hawn, Judy Carne, Arte Johnson, Ruth Buzzi, Joanne Worley, and others turn up on this album) act crazy.

For those who remember *Laugh-In*, this will be nostalgic. From ditsy Goldie Hawn: "My IQ has never been questioned. Come to think of it, it's never been mentioned."

A song from brassy Joanne Worley: "'Hava Nagila,' have two nagila, have three nagila, they're pretty small!"

Another *Laugh-In* record was issued after Rowan and Martin left the show. See the entry under Carne and Johnson. When Rowan and Martin made their first movie, they issued a single for Decca with the same title: "Once Upon a Horse."

RITA RUDNER

- NAKED BENEATH MY CLOTHES (Penguin Highbridge HBP 20619) *** $8

At the turn of the '90s, many comedians brought their stand-up to cable TV rather than records. Many, everyone from Elayne Boosler to Dennis Miller, issued these on videocassette but not in the CD format. Rita Rudner is at least represented on audio by this cassette tape. It's ninety minutes of essays condensed from her 1992 book *Naked Beneath My Clothes*.

A few one-liners are sprinkled into the mix. On pregnancy: "Life is tough enough without having someone kick you from the inside." But the essay format works against her. What is tongue-in-cheek in print can sound forced or pretentious when spoken out loud.

Fortunately Rita's style in stand-up is crisp and precise, so she can usually get away with enunciating material like this:

"Whenever my husband and I are in the car and I'm driving, he's convinced that I am out to kill us both. He has no confidence in my ability to stop. Every time we come up to a red light I see him gripping onto the side of the car as if he were hanging on to the outside of a speeding train. 'Christ! Brake, stop, stop, there's a red light,' he bellows. I know there's a red light. That's why I'm slowing down. That's what I do right before I stop. I use it as a kind of preparation. 'I tried speeding up as a preparation for a while, but it only made stopping more difficult,' I say, trying not to speed up for spite. 'You have such a heavy foot,' he says. I don't have a heavy foot. I have lots of things that are heavy. My foot is perfect."

CHRIS RUSH

- FIRST RUSH (Atlantic SD 7257) **1/2 $5 $10
- BEAMING IN (City Sounds CS 105) ** $5 $10

Chris Rush, still working the comedy club circuit in the '90s, issued his first album in 1973. At the time, his act seemed right in tune with other "hippie" comics like George Carlin and Cheech and Chong. He did endless jokes about drugs and plenty of recognition comedy with that Carlin/Cheech and Chong feel: cuts like "Sister John Damian's Virgin School," "Golden Zits of the Fifties," and "Mind Farts."

The bald-headed (and then bearded) comic's main problem is his semi-abrasive New Yawk accent, and a belaboring, sometimes histrionic delivery. Like so many minor league nightclub comics, he has enough pace and pizzazz to blitz a group of drunks, but not enough personality or unique material to push up to the big time.

The material here could certainly have grossed-out or flipped-out any group of college kids in 1973.

Even now, for those who are looking for something else to play besides old George Carlin albums, Rush could get a few shock laughs.

"Beaming In" from 1981 shows little progress since 1973. Rush still slams his observations home with screamy overacting, setting up a premise and then painting a garish visual picture.

"Grass has drawbacks," he begins. "For one thing, it makes you overly suggestive." He acts out being overly suggestive: "Hey man, ya wanna put your dick in the toaster?" "Sure!" "Grass causes laziness," he says. "Ever see two guys living in a house upstate New York with good weed?" He acts out two hippies: "Hey man, the house is on fire." "F--- it, it's gonna rain tomorrow anyway."

Again and again, he makes a remark and overacts on it. Recognition humor doesn't require a twelve-foot high day-glo poster with arrows pointing out every detail. Although many comics use the tactic of making a statement, then acting it out, it's never been as obvious a ploy as it is here.

Prices are a bit higher on the East Coast.

PIONEERING WOMEN

Jean Carroll was the first stand-up to come out doing "husband jokes" the way '50s top bananas did "take my wife" gags. Anna Russell handled musical satires. Totie Fields was really big on The Ed Sullivan Show.

ANNA RUSSELL

- SINGS? (Columbia ML 5494) **1/2 $5 $10
- SINGS AGAIN? (Columbia ML 4733) **1/2, reissued as a two-record set, $5 $10
  THE ANNA RUSSELL ALBUM, Columbia MG 31199, and in the CD format, Sony MDK 47252) $12

Anna Russell specialized in parodies of opera and classical music. Her first album satirizes coloraturas, Russian folk songs ("Da Nyet, Da Nyet"), contemporary music ("My Heart Is Red"), and folk tunes ("I Gave My Love a Cherry").

Between songs she pauses for some wry remarks: "To be a real folk song singer you have to collect the songs straight from the horse's mouth. The way to do this is to go to a village and find the oldest inhabitant and ask him to sing you the songs his mother taught me. Him I mean. Well, you'll probably find that he's deaf, and if he isn't deaf he can't sing, and if he can't sing he doesn't want to, and by the time you've persuaded him and he does sing, you won't understand a word of what he's singing about. This is how folk songs have been passed down from generation to generation."

The second LP features "How to Write Your Own Gilbert and Sullivan Opera" along with her most famous piece, a full-blown satire of "The Ring of the Nibelungs." In that one she trashes the main characters: "Wotan ... he's a crashing bore ... the Valkyries are all virgins, and I'm not the least bit surprised. Then she takes her audience through every nonsensical nuance of the plot, often uttering her catchphrase, "I'm not making this up!"

A taste for opera and classical music is mandatory, and even then, instead of hearty laughter, there will be knowing giggles.

- GUIDE TO CONCERT AUDIENCES (Columbia ML 4928) ** $7 $15

Russell guides her concert audience through a variety of numbers. She's addressing "the kind of concert audience whose wife says to him, 'Dear, put on your tuxedo because there's ... a concert by Madame Leiderkranz and you have to go.' You go, and you hate it. I know, I've seen you. Let's face it, you're always going to be dragged to these affairs ... if you have a slight clue as to what is going on you could have a gorgeous time. Because you know it isn't only on this side of the footlights where all the acting goes on." She sings a wide repertoire: "Nact and Tag," "Trink," "Oh! Night Oh! Day," "The Tender Snowdrop," "I'm Only a Faded Rose," "La Danza," "Les Cigarette," "Bagga Bagga Bona," "Spanish Rude: Guarda La Bella Tomato."

Sometimes the humor is in the way Russell injects quasi-intelligible words into the arias. On "La Donna Nannella," Anna sings out, "Belissima Zsa Zsa le darmida razza ney Barbizon Plaza" and the audience giggles appreciatively.

And there are the musical jokes, where a lugubrious example of German lieder, "Nact and Tag," actually sounds suspiciously close to Cole Porter's "Night and Day."

Other times she offers a satiric quip about the tunes: "An interesting thing is ... the things that strike you as utterly ghastly are invariably the ones chosen by the experts as the most artistic." Anna admits that even the brightest songs can only get an audience "fidgety." And she proves this by singing a high-pitched nasal Spanish folk song ("Bagga Bagga Bona") with chicken-pluck noises and fake Spanish: "Mama no no, Yoo hoo Da Da, bye bye go go! Chaka booka chaka booka chaka booka high!"

- A SQUARE TALK ON POPULAR MUSIC (Columbia ML 5036) **1/2 $10 $20
- ANNA RUSSELL IN DARKEST AFRICA (Columbia 5195) **1/2 $10 $20
- A PRACTICAL BANANA PROMOTION (Columbia ML 5295) **1/2 $10 $20

Allowing classical music fans to titter and snigger at pop music of the '50s, the title cut for "Square Talk" is a full-length lecture with Anna wryly noting, "The more your voice sounds like nothing human, the more popular you will become." She periodically interrupts her monologue to give samples of popular musical styles. Evidently she did the songs live, but decided to splice more polished, orchestrated studio versions into the finished record. She looks down her classically trained nose at seven vulgar examples of '50s pop music from the brainless swing of "Feelin' Fine" ("Feelin' fine 'cause my man is swell ... sing hallelujah, it's a lovely day!") to the blues of "Red Hot Momma" ("I'd be a red hot momma if I didn't have these varicose veins"). She even smacks "perfectly nauseating" kiddie Christmas songs like "All I Want for Christimas Is My Two Front Teeth." In her version she lisps, "Santa Claus ... bwing me a doggy." The flip side lecture, "Survey of Singing from Madrigals to Modern Opera" is more typical Anna Russell parody as she effortlessly backhands Old English folk tunes and mouldy operatic arias like "Come Lovely Death," "O Gentle Bird with Feathered Breast," and "Anaemia's Death Scene."

The cover for "Darkest Africa" shows Ms. Russell grimacing as four black natives brandish spears at her. Chances are that they heard about her operatic performances, even if they were not allowed into the Johannesburg Music Festival, where this album was recorded. One side has a somewhat arduous telling of Verdi's "Hamletto," also known as "Prosciuttino." Admitting to the audience that Verdi never did get around to creating an opera on *Hamlet*, she adds, "I'm not for a moment going to let that stand in my way." In her typically campy-haughty way, she describes how "Hamlet, Prince of Denmark is very disgusted with his mother, whom he adores, because just two months after his father dies in very suspicious circumstances, his mother married his uncle.... There would've been no story at all if Hamlet had avenged his father's death at once instead of hinkle-pinkling around! Which goes to show, that if you don't behave like you're supposed to, you're liable to be terribly interesting."

There's manic merriment when, singing Hamlet's famous "To be or not to be," she breaks into a Jimmy Durante rendition of "Didja ever have a feelin' that ya wanted to go, and still had a feelin' that ya wanted to stay!"

The flip side offers another lecture on folk music (the folk song is "the uncouth vocal utterance of the people") and one of her famous musical appreciation lectures, "How to Enjoy Your Bagpipe." She holds up the peculiar instrument and says, "I used to ask the audience to guess what! But I don't anymore, because of some of the guesses!"

"Banana Promotion" describes the time she was engaged to perform at "The Seventh Annual Food Forum" at the Plaza Hotel, sponsored by the United Fruit Company. Her ideas on banana promotion: "First of all, the first thing is to say, 'Eat Bananas.'" The flip has lectures on how to play the French horn (complete with huffs, puffs, and a few Bronx cheers) and "Poetry in the Cellar," her interpretation of "word jazz" performed by the beat generation: "I always thought that meant 'beat-up,' but it doesn't, it means 'beatific.' Of course I suppose if you get sufficiently beat up you could get 'beatific' from the point of view of being slap happy. However the whole thing is extremely existential."

Russell's album "Live at the Sydney Opera House" was released only in Australia on EMI, and a video version of a 1980's "Farewell" concert is available as well.

MARK RUSSELL

• UP THE POTOMAC WITHOUT A CANOE (Columbia CS 8572) **	$7	$15
• THE FACE ON THE SENATE FLOOR (Weet 001) **	$5	$10
• WIRED WORLD OF WATERGATE (Deep Six 0001) **	$5	$10
• ASSAULT WITH A DEADLY PEANUT (Deep Six 0002) **	$5	$10
• I'VE GOT A RIGHT TO SING THE NEWS (Madar) **		$10

Mark Russell has an obvious, bludgeoning style of satire, his jokes delivered with a carnival barker style bray. He was well known at the Shoreham Hotel in Washington D.C., where he performed for more than a decade. Later he began a series of regular specials for PBS. His first album of topical jokes was issued by Columbia circa 1960. They may have figured he could sell the same amount of albums Mort Sahl was selling for Verve.

The Columbia album is loaded with Russell's trademark, heavy-handed song satires. "In My Merry Oldsmobile" turns into a song about hijacking: "Overcome your stress and strain, come watch me hijack a plane. While the pilot's at the wheel, into the cabin we will steal. Watch and see what jolly fun, when the pilot spots my gun. 'Cause although the passengers don't know it now, old Havana here they come."

Occasionally there's a good one-liner, even a subtle and witty one, but after the earache of his brassy voice and belaboring insinuations, it's hard to raise a smile: "Here's a definition," he announces. "Definition of a sadist. A sadist is a guy who does nice things to a masochist."

From a typical later album, "Face on the Senate Floor," the results are equally hit and miss.

"In the news. A beautiful thing in the paper this week about the general in Vietnam who wants the PX's to include prostitution houses. Yeah, let's hear it for 'em. Imagine the girl answering the phone: 'Hello, this is Master Sergeant Polly Adler speaking.' Gee, that would be a new version of the Peace Corps. I can't see it. In a Quonset hut? Really this does indeed prove that an army travels on it's ... well, anyway. The girls would have a rank. Like specialist first, second, or third class. Depending on a lot of things.

"And what of Lyndon Johnson down in Texas? He has his own TV show called *Me the People*. Barry Goldwater has his own show down in Arizona, every night from seven to six-thirty."

In 1992 Russell released an hour-long studio recording featuring bass, drums, piano, and a synthesizer supplying brass. Without a live audience, Russell isn't quite so loud and blaring, but unctuous crooning isn't that much of an improvement. In churning out his topical parodies so quickly over the years, this "best of" points up Russell's weaknesses: hastily constructed lines with barely enough wit to get through a first listening.

Cole Porter's "Love for Sale" becomes "Wrench for Sale," an all too obvious tweak at Pentagon spending: "Here's our special offer now. It's a steal for seven thou. Wrench for sale."

Never one to ignore a cliché, Russell gets out his popgun to contrast John Denver's "Country Road" with new lyrics about New Jersey pollution: "My eyes are burning for the diesel engine. How I long to go home and spit that phlegm again. Take me home to Bayonne, to the place that I call home."

The CD includes Russell's favorite old songs about George Bush, Mario Cuomo, Jesse Helms, and others. He proves that there *is* something duller than yesterday's newspaper.

NIPSEY RUSSELL

• CONFUCIUS TOLD ME (Borderline/Humorsonic 701, 　　also released as HARLEM'S SON OF FUN VOLUME ONE) **	$6	$12
• THINGS THEY NEVER TAUGHT IN SCHOOL: LAFF LECTURES 　　(Borderline Humorsonic NR 702) **	$6	$12
• BIRDS AND THE BEES (Borderline/Humorsonic NR 703) **	$6	$12
• GUZZLING AND GIGGLING PARTY (Borderline/Humorsonic NR 704) **	$6	$12
• THE LIONS TALE (Borderline/Humorsonic NR 705) **	$6	$12
• SING ALONG (Borderline/Humorsonic NR 706) **	$6	$12
• YA GOTTA BE FAST (Borderline/Humorsonic NR 707) **	$6	$12
• BEST OF NIPSEY/COMEDY SAMPLER (Borderline/Humorsonic NR 708) **	$6	$12

- STAR OF THE JACK PAAR SHOW (Surprise SUR 99,
  also released as RIOT OF LAUGHS, Funn Records AAL 335) **1/2 $7 $15

Russell was a slightly risqué entertainer in the late '50s and early '60s when he made these albums. They embarrass him now, as perhaps they should. A polished performer with a literate delivery, he had to tell cornball dirt to an audience of cornball dirtbags. From the "Guzzling and Giggling Party":

"Tang. They're gonna combine it with prune juice and call it Prune Tang! Prune Tang for breakfast, how about that. You wake up in the morning, you say, 'Baby, I want bacon and eggs this morning.' She says, 'Oh no, you gonna have that Prune Tang.' Oh my ... I'll probably record for the people who make ... Man Tan. That's 'Instant Mau Mau.' Very delightful product. I never use it, and I never go to the beach and I stay brown all year 'round. And all the way down!"

On "Sing Along with Nipsey," he offers suggestive tunes with piano and bass backing. These include quickies, like this based on "Sunday Monday or Always": "Won't you tell me dear, the size of your brassiere. Twenty, thirty, or forty?" And a song about Sadie the tattooed lady, trying at least for the semi-classy patter of a Dwight Fiske:

"She decided she would like to add my picture. But she couldn't find a vacant place, you see. So she tattooed my poor face in a most undignified place—and every time she sits down she sits on me ... now you wonder why I'm feeling so lowdown, and why my attitude is absolutely wrong. I'd like to romance and kick her right square in the pants, but if I did I'd kick myself right in the jaw."

Russell's album on Surprise is a little better than the other releases (originally on the Borderline label and then reissued by Humorsonic). Demonstrating a dry style (later used by Flip Wilson),, Russell offers some satiric one-liners: "New York is a funny town. You can drown in whiskey and starve to death. Everybody says have a drink, nobody says have something to eat!" But soon enough he's giving the crowd what they want—whoopee rhymes: "I went to see my girl the other night. She came to the door in her nightie. She stood between me and the light. And Good God Almighty!"

The Funn Records version spells his name "Russel" on the front cover. He produced an album, evidently intended as a radio special, for the U.S. Department of Health, Education and Welfare. The disc "Comedy Time" (DHEW SSA 72-10732) features Nipsey introducing cuts from comedy records by Filp Wilson, Nichols and May, and others, and passing on information about medicare and social security.

THE RUTLES

- THE RUTLES (Warner Bros. HS 3151) *** $8

In 1978, Neil Innes and Eric Idle joined with Rikki Fataar and John Halsey to form The Rutles, parodying The Beatles. Their NBC-TV special was a ratings bomb despite guest spots from John Belushi, Dan Aykroyd, and Gilda Radner, along with George Harrison interviewing Mick Jagger and Paul Simon. It was something of a critical bomb, too, since the satire was subtle.

Innes's music is affectionately close to The Beatles (so close he was sued). There's recognition humor in hearing the melodies and lyrics undergoing subtle twists. "I Want to Hold Your Hand" is mirrored by "Hold My Hand," "Help" becomes "Ouch," and the accurate portrayal of John Lennon during his "I Am the Walrus" phase ("Cheese and Onions") is particularly persuasive. It has even turned up on a Beatle bootleg LP ("Indian Rope Trick").

The lyrics aren't exactly hilarious, though "Piggy in the Middle" tweaks John Lennon's hallucinogenic phase: "Walky talky man says hello hello hello with his ballerina boots you can tell he's always on his toes/Hanging from a Christmas tree creeping like a bogey man getting up my nose."

Funnier is the sixteen-page booklet of photos aping Beatle events. A lot of the humor has Monty Python-ish silliness to it. Stig O'Hara, The Rutles version of Paul McCartney, had a similar "death rumor" controversy: "He was supposed to have been killed in a flash fire at a waterbed shop and replaced by a plastic and wax replica from Madame Tussaud's.... On the song 'I Am the Waitress' the group members sing 'I buried Stig,' but actually evidence now shows he said, 'E burres stigano,' which is very bad Spanish for 'Have you a water buffalo?'"

Rhino issued the CD version, but some collectors will want the original for the larger sized booklet and photos.

SAM SACKS

- SING IT AGAIN, SAM (Arliss 3301) ** $5 $10

A male version of Mrs. Miller, off-key Sam tortures pop hits "Secret Love," "Yodel Blues," "Love Is a Many Splendored Thing," etc.

MICHAEL SAHL AND ERIZ SALZMAN

- CIVILIZATION AND ITS DISCONTENTS (NONESUCH N 78009) * $3 $7

The album notes call this "contemporary opera buffa," a term for pretentious cabaret combined with modern classical music. As the quartet of singers warble at the start of this 1981 excess: "If it feels good do it! AC/DC. E-F-G! Boogie boogie! Therapy! Really, really? Uh-uh! That's right! For sure, intense! Dynamite! Nitty gritty. Really shitty!"

MORT SAHL

- MORT SAHL AT SUNSET (Fantasy 7005) *** $10 $25

This was not the first Sahl record to be released, but it was the first to be recorded. He was taped in 1955 at the Sunset Auditorium in Carmel, California, at a jazz concert featuring Dave Brubeck. This red vinyl rarity didn't turn up in stores until after most of the Verve albums appeared.

All the trademarks of his style are here. Like his pioneering free-association verbal shorthand. He'll sketch a few comic details and it's up to the audience to be hip enough to laugh. Mort mentions an ad man who wears a charcoal gray suit "because modern science was looking for a color more somber than black ... and a large stick pin that seemed to go through the body ... crew-cut, glasses with wrought iron frames." Another example here is the one-word allusion. The audience must decode the joke: "There's a magazine of obscure poetry—called *Whither*."

Sahl isn't too political here, talking more about jazz and hi-fi (and a guy who used his house as a speaker and puts his family in the garage). His intellectual hold-up bit is the type of thing that influenced Woody Allen. An intellectual behind the counter foils robbers: "They wrote down, 'This is a hold-up. If you act normal, you won't get hurt.' He thought about it, and he wrote a rebuttal to them. He said, 'Act normal? Define your terms.'"

According to Sahl, the album was unauthorized. It was withdrawn shortly after release. A turntable with pitch control is helpful; Fantasy speeded up Sahl's voice in order to fit the complete show on a single disc.

• THE FUTURE LIES AHEAD (Verve MGV 150002) ***	$7	$15
• 1960: LOOK FORWARD IN ANGER (Verve MGV 150004) ***	$7	$15
• A WAY OF LIFE (Verve MGV 150006) ***	$7	$15
• AT THE HUNGRY i (Verve MGVS 15012) ***	$7	$15
• THE NEXT PRESIDENT (Verve MGVS 615021) ***	$7	$15
• GREAT MOMENTS OF COMEDY (Verve V 15049) ***	$7	$15

Sahl was a pioneering political satirist; he led the way for Dick Gregory and others to use a nightclub stage for more than gags. He was also the most influential stand-up comic of all time, his style completely different from guys who came onstage in a tux and machine-gunned jokes at the crowd. Sahl wore a sweater, he spoke in a conversational style of digression and free association. Lenny Bruce and Woody Allen were among the many inspired by Mort's ability to be open, honest, truthful, irreverent—and funny.

At a time when there was no Carson or Leno to comment on the day's events, Sahl was able to issue topical albums regularly. There are no bands separating the bits on Sahl's albums; each side is a free form, jittery monologue that blends anecdotes, parenthetical remarks, and one-liners.

"Future Lies Ahead" doesn't quite have the sonic brilliance to match Sahl's verbal brilliance, but there are plenty of high spots. He mentions that Vice President Nixon is getting a lot of publicity as he gears up for a possible presidential run in 1960: "He was on all these magazines, like *Time* and *Newsweek*. Every magazine but *True*." He mentions being on the bill with a folk singer, one who "was wearing a velvet shirt open to the navel. And he didn't have one. That's what I wanted to tell you about. Which is either a show business gimmick, or the ultimate rejection of mother. Right?"

Throughout, Sahl switches directions, chuckles nervously, and free associates in a style later used by everyone from Lenny Bruce to Robin Williams: "I wanted to say a few words—I have a lot of hostility tonight to bring out here—I wanted to say something on the president's press conference, and this being a primitive form of theatre—my attempts to entertain you and take your minds off the fact that there was an explosion in the shaft and we're trapped. Boy. Clichés ... right? Exciting. I wanted to say something about this press conference here...." Topics include Dave Brubeck, math and "the standard deviation," Adlai Stevenson, air raids, and his bit about an intellectual debating with hold-up men.

"Look Forward in Anger" opens with a dovetailing report on Disneyland and nuclear testing, goes on to discuss highway checks, the movie *In Love and War*, anxiety and all-night food stores, the girls of Smith College, Dave Brubeck again, atheism, and traffic reporters.

"Way of Life" includes the time he took Benzedrine for mononucleosis: "I got clairvoyance. With Benzedrine you can have a very wide view of the world, like you can decide the destiny of man and other pressing problems, such as which is the left sock?" He talks about a Vegas comic's marriage, his appearance on the Academy Awards show, Truman selling his memoirs, actors and their vegetarian diets, the differences between sorority houses and whore houses, the Yalta papers, Billy Graham, and the movie *Blue Denim*. Sahl repeats his famous remark on atheism (which originally appeared on "Look Forward in Anger"): "Most people past college age are not atheists. It's too hard to be in society, for one thing. Because you don't get any days off. And if you're an agnostic you don't know whether you get them off or not." The album has a distracting woman in the audience who gives out with squalling cackles.

"Great Moments" (with the sound quality varying) clips out material that isn't too dated: his description of touring with Brubeck in Maine, his appearance on the Academy Awards, Billy Graham rallies, the film *Blue Denim*, nuclear tests and The Mickey Mouse Club, highway driving, and taking Benzedrine for mononucleosis. The front cover, like all the covers in Verve's "Great Moments" series, has a repulsive picture of two 1962-era yuppies squinting their eyes and opening their mouths in uncontrolled laughter.

Sahl's last two albums for Verve were released in stereo. Coming home to San Francisco's Hungri i, Sahl talks about the blackouts caused by Con Edison ("power corrupts"), the marriage of Westbrook Pegler ("as part of a humanization process as yet unsuccessful"), Khruschev's visit to America, communists in America, and an ironic and salty account of the U-2 incident. He notes, "There are Russian spies here now. And if we're lucky, they'll steal some of our secrets and they'll be two years behind."

At a time when topical humor was literally unheard of, Sahl had every reason to nervously joke at show's end, "I really want to thank you all for individual perception ... and if things go well next year we won't have to hold these meetings in secret."

"The Next President" was recorded during the thick of the Nixon vs Kennedy campaign. Sahl covers the Republican and Democratic conventions. He has some time to discuss his new movie *All the Young Men*, Syngman Rhee, Che Guevara, his cover story in *Time*, and his problems with women: "She looks great, but what'll I say to her in the morning. I'm searching for the new maturity: she looks great, but I have nothing to say to her now." His liberal audience loved his description of Nixon describing life at home: "'Pat was knitting a flag in the corner, and I was studying the Constitution.' To find a loophole?"

Sahl warns, "whoever the president is—I will attack him." But when Kennedy won, and Sahl attacked—it was Mort Sahl who ended up with knives in the back, hurled by some of the same people who had supported him for being such an uncompromising satirist.

- THE NEW FRONTIER (Reprise R 5002) *** $10 $20
- ON RELATIONSHIPS (Reprise R 5003) *** $12 $25

Sahl's career took a downward skid in the mid-60s for two reasons: Kennedy was elected. Kennedy was killed. When Kennedy was elected, the Democrats and liberals who had cheered Sahl during the Eisenhower era were not prepared for anti-Kennedy jokes. On "New Frontier" Sahl tries to acknowledge and deal with the backlash. He describes people coming over to him and protesting the Kennedy jokes. "We thought this was what you wanted," they gasp. He retorts, "You didn't have to do it for ME!"

There's more than JFK jokes here. A bit on politics and movies, for example: "All bad pictures end in 'o' if you'd like a generalization. Like *Alamo, Gorgo, Vertigo, Psycho*, and so forth. That is actually derivative of another gener-alization.... *Exodus* was picketed by the American Legion because it was written by Dalton Trumbo ... they also picketed *Spartacus*, which he wrote. So you'd have to make a generalization. The American Legion will picket *Exodus*, *Spartacus* and any other picture ending in 'U.S.'"

While Vaughn Meader's gentle "First Family" LP went gold, Sahl's iconoclastic "New Frontier" album stayed in the racks.

"On Relationships" downplays the JFK jokes in favor of something everyone can understand: the battle of the sexes. For most of the album, he talks about writing a piece on relationships for *Ladies Home Journal.* In a typically neurotic, vulnerable, but lightly misogynistic moment, he recalls his problems with a female assistant from the magazine. He's bugged just shaking hands with her: "I shake hands with her, which is the worst with women. I never know what to do when I meet 'em anyway. You can't bow, that's decadent, it's European. And you have to fight 'em all the way. Your relationship hasn't grown into anything rich, so you can't touch 'em. But if you shake hands with them, their hands don't work for shaking. Have you noticed that? The hands are broken or something. Are you suggesting they're genetically inferior? No, maybe if they wear gloves....

"I met this girl ... very aggressively ... I just walked up to her and I said, 'Who are you? I have to know who you are.' It's a good opener, but you can't sustain that level of excitement. Later on chicks start complaining the relationship doesn't have that much drive anymore. You have to remind them, 'I'm the guy who ran up and said, "Who are you?"' And they always say, 'Well, you never do that anymore.' And you have to say, 'Yes, and I still don't know who you are.'"

Trivia freaks will note that the woman on the cover of Mort's album is Joan Collins.

- ANYWAY ... ONWARD (Mercury MG/SR 61112) *** $7 $20
- SING A SONG OF WATERGATE (GNP Crescendo GNPS 2070) *** $7 $15

When Lyndon Johnson became the hated tyrant leading a nation deeper into the Vietnam War, Mort Sahl was allowed to return from exile and low-paying college campus gigs to once again become the liberal media's avenging satirist.

"Anyway Onward" is in some ways one of Sahl's finest monologues. It's a cohesive performance that not only includes his usual digressions, but contains an interweaving plotline (Sahl's efforts to get a private audience with Johnson). There's even a rare running joke (the picketers outside the White House). Mort even does a bit of mimicry. As Hubert Humphrey: "This certainly is a beautiful day, just like President Johnson promised." He mentions a picketer carrying a big sign: "It says, 'Hubert Humphrey has strayed from his original commitment, and is a self-seeking opportunist.' Pretty strong. They arrested that guy. Charged him with passing federal secrets."

Mort's album on the Nixon/Watergate affair is a fine one. He offers a pungent, anecdotal history of Richard Nixon ("He was born in a log cabin in Whittier, California—in a blue suit") and takes shots at Frank Sinatra ("an interesting alloy of ignorance and power"), and Ronald Reagan running for governor: "The main thing is to keep an actor working. It doesn't matter what he does." He reworks one of his finest lines on this album:

"We've gone from Jefferson to Nixon and we've gone from Hearst to Hefner. There were four million people in the Colonies and we had Jefferson and Paine and Franklin. Fantastic. And now we have 208 million and the two top guys are McGovern and Nixon. What can you draw from this? Darwin was wrong!"

NOTES: Sahl albums are hard to appraise. To some, they're a gift from a comedy god and to others, just dated old discs. The Fantasy disc is the rarest. Sahl appears on "The Dean Martin Testimonial Dinner," a private-issue three-record set. "The Age of Anxiety" (Radiola MR 1151), an hour-long audio documentary about the '60s, includes about five minutes of Sahl, evidently from a TV appearance. Mort offers anecdotes about a visit to LBJ's White House. It's a fresh variation on material from his Mercury album: "I walked in, and the president was in his office, with this globe next to his desk, with the trouble spots marked in black. He was standing next to this black globe, is what I was getting at."

SOUPY SALES

- THE SOUPY SALES SHOW (Reprise R 6010) **1/2 $10 $20
- UP IN THE AIR (Reprise R 6052) ** $10 $20
- SPY WITH A PIE (ABC Paramount ABCS 503 reissued as Simon Says M 49) ** $10 $20
- DO THE MOUSE (ABC Paramount ABCS 517) **1/2 $10 $20

Sales was a popular kiddie show host in the early '60s when he released these albums. Reprise's owner, Mr. Sinatra, was a big fan and even stood still for a pie from Soupy.

"The Soupy Sales Show" is loaded with kiddie bop tunes about his puppets Pookie, Black Tooth, and White Fang. There's also "Soupy Sez," an instrumental interrupted with silly Soupy one-liners: "Don't bite your nails, your nails don't bite you ... Be careful crossing streets, you might get that run-down feeling ... Keep your chin up. It'll keep the milk from dripping on your clothes."

It's more of the same on "Up in the Air," as Soupy sings "It's Fun to Be Funny (and Make the People Smile)" and a few general tunes including "The Ballad of Johnny Jordan" and "My Baby's Got a Crush on Frankenstein." "Don't Kiss" could almost be a Steve Lawrence ballad, except that Soupy is singing it to his dog Black Tooth. "Doggone Doggie" and "You're a Star" are both sung to his other dog, White Fang (who offers some growling accompaniment).

Soupy's most successful album was "Do the Mouse," thanks to the novelty hit "The Mouse." It wasn't much of a song ("Hey, do the Mouse, you can do it in your house"). The fun was watching Soupy squinch his eyes, push his front teeth over his lower lip and dance around. Here was a dance any kid could do! Fun cuts include "Name Game" (a 1965 hit for Shirley Ellis) and the nonsensical "Pachalafaka" (which first appeared on an Irving Taylor album).

"Spy with a Pie" is a mild *Get Smart* type musical comedy as Soupy hunts the spies of INK (International Network of Kooks) and sings tunes like "Soupy of the Secret Service" that are amusing more for his personality than the lyrics: "I'm gonna get my man. I plan a little plan—that'll get me on his tail. Till he's in jail!"

- BAG OF SOUP (Motown S 686) $7 $15
- STILL SOUPY AFTER ALL THESE YEARS (MCA 5274) *** $7 $15

Soupy plays it pretty straight on the offbeat 1969 "Bag of Soup," his attempt to grow up along with his fans, who (to use the words on the liner notes) grew into "teenyboppers, teenagers, college kids," etc. Befitting the Motown label, Soupy tries a soulful rasp on some of the faster tunes, like "Teach Your Baby How to Dance" and "Come to Baby, Do!" His attempts at ballads are no worse than, say, Herb Alpert, whose "This Guy's in Love with You" is covered here by Soupy, along with cabaret perennial "For Once in My Life" and the sad "Tell Me What's He Got That I Ain't Got." The only real novelty cuts are an update of the oldie "Let's Think About Living" and "Muck-Arty Park," a Richard Harris parody: "Muck-Arty Park will never be the same. All the sweet young hippies blew their thing. Someone threw the cook out in the rain. It was just 11:30 when they learned his pot was dirty and he'll never have that recipe again."

The 1981 MCA album is a live concert for Soupy's fans old and new. He's still Soupy, telling plenty of corny gags, both old ("You show me a sculptor who works in the basement and I'll show you a low-down chiseler") and (for the now grown-up fans), mildly blue. Like the one about the woman who is buying hair remover to remove some ingrown hairs from her dog's ear:

"The druggist says, 'If you're using it under your arms ... take my advice, don't use any deodorant for two days, it could irritate your arms.' She says, 'It's not for my arms.' So he says, 'If you're gonna use it on your legs ... don't wear stockings for three days, it could irritate your legs.' And she says, 'I want to put it on my Schnauzer.' And the druggist says, 'In that case, don't ride a bicycle for a week!'"

Soupy also sings a few of his classic tunes ("Pachalafaka" and "The Mouse") and the crowd couldn't be happier. All that's missing is "Mumbles," the loopy jazz tune that Pookie the puppet used to "sing." It was actually a recording by jazz trumpet player Clark Terry and can be found on various Terry albums and CDs.

TIM SAMPLE
- DOWNEAST STAND-UP (Bert and I 15) $5 $10
- BACK IN SPITE OF POPULAR DEMAND (Bert and I 16) $5 $10
- THE TIM SAMPLE COMEDY ALBUM (Elephant's Graveyard 556) $5 $10

JUNIOR SAMPLES
- WORLD (Chart S 1002) *1/2 $5 $10
- THAT'S A HEE-HAW (Chart S 1021) *1/2 $5 $10
- BEST OF JUNIOR SAMPLES (Chart S 1045) *1/2 $5 $10
- BULL SESSION AT BULLS GAP (Chart CHS 1007) *1/2 $5 $10

Junior Samples was a favorite for his "big liar" character. He also got a lot of mileage out of playing dull and dumb, acting as if his brains were chitlings. By country comedy standards, he's a master of subtlety. His "World's Biggest Whopper" routine (five deadpan minutes on the big fish he caught) is on RCA Victor's "Best of Country Comedy" (LSP 4126). When he joined *Hee-Haw* there was some new interest in Samples and that yielded "That's a Hee Haw," which is monotonously terrible when he sings ("Doggone My Dog's Gone"), and just monotonous on the monologue cuts. Ralph Emery plays straight on some, trying to pry something funny out of the fat man:

"Junior, uh, do you, do you worry a lot about sex?" "Well. What do you mean about that?" "Uh, do you have a lot of sex drive, would you say? Do you think about it a lot?" "I don't know what you mean about that." "What's, what's your reaction when you see a very, very nice looking girl who looks kind of sexy?" "You know darn well I ain't gonna tell that on the radio." "Ha ha ha ha ha."

The elusive charm of Junior Samples is further showcased on the interview album "Bull Session at Bulls Gap" with Archie Campbell as straight man. His personality (or lack of it) makes the audience roar over every feeble remark he's prodded to make:

"You'd've been good at football, with your size and everything." "Size got nuthin' to do with it." "With football?" "Ain't got nuthin' to do with nuthin'. If it was, cow'd outrun a rabbit." (Laughter and applause). "Ever play golf?" "Naw." "What do you think about golf, do you think you'd like it?" "I don't know." "Doesn't make much sense, does it?" "Well, I hit a golf ball with a baseball bat one time. (Laughter.) I ain't never see'd nuthin' like it in my life. (Laughter.) It went across a three-acre cornfield. (Laughter.) They ain't never found it yet." (Laughter.)

Samples died in 1983.

ADAM SANDLER

- THEY'RE ALL GONNA LAUGH AT YOU (Warner Bros. 9 453932) * $8

It's an optimistic title for Sandler's 1993 CD. Sandler made a name for himself playing a variety of pathetic geeks and irritating nerds on *Saturday Night Live*, and obnoxious characters abound on this set of sketches and songs. Pals Rob Schneider, Conan O'Brien, David Spade, and Tim Meadows take turns playing uncool dudes who love to call each other "buddy," make crank calls to their teachers, get wasted, and in one typical sketch, add groans to a sound effect-filled minute about taking a wicked piss in the bathroom.

Sandler is aiming for the junior high school market from the start, in a bit about an assistant principal taking advantage of his job by making announcements like this: "The girls' showering facilities will be moved from the locker room into my inner office where I can watch the girls wash their breasts and buttocks while I play with myself."

Rarely can Sandler make fun of annoying people without being annoying. There's a continuing, Monty Python-inspired series of thirty-second and sixty-second sound effect-filled beatings of school personnel. He should at least get a kick in the butt for this one.

- WHAT THE HELL HAPPENED TO ME (Warner Bros 9461512) *1/2 $8

The Sandler cult won't be widened much by the follow-up 1996 CD, which has about an hour of amateurish, numbing and/or annoying spoken routines that trade on moronic characters ("The Excited Southerner Orders a Meal") and all-too-accurate imitations of young cretins (like the goofus who considers "Joining the Cult"). Kevin Nealon turns up for literal wretched excess—eight unbearable minutes on the eight-second one-joke premise of a therapist who periodically breaks wind while trying to hypnotize his subject.

A few songs interrupt. The tune "Ode to My Car" gets a few laughs as Adam mimics a Jamaican cursing over his "piece of shit" heap. But after one chorus it's overkill. Now destined to be a seasonal annoyance on FM radio, "The Chanukah Song" (despite Sandler's coy giggling and deliberately sappy rhymes) dislodges some chuckles as he celebrates who is (William Shatner and Leonard Nimoy) or isn't (O. J. Simpson) Jewish (or in the case of "not too shabby" Harrison Ford, part-Jewish). As for the cover, it's about time there was a moratorium on photos wistfully showing comedians as bright-eyed kids, implying that they weren't any less obnoxious, pushy, or troublesome before the onset of pubic hair.

FATHER GUIDO SARDUCCI

- LIVE AT ST. DOUGLAS CONVENT (Warner Bros. BSK 3440) *1/2 $5 $10
- BREAKFAST IN HEAVEN (Warner Bros. 25472) *1/2 $5 $10

Don Novello is a capable comedy writer (his first book of *The Laszlo Letters* is a classic). His comedy character of Father Guido Sarducci, who wears priest's garb, smokes cigarettes, and writes for a Vatican gossip paper, is one of the great bores of stand-up. His appeal has baffled experts.

Using a deadpan stereotype Italian accent, Father Sarducci natters on and on, stretching three or four minutes worth of jokes into a thirty-minute set. On the first album, from 1980, a bit about "The Peoples Space Program" is virtually jokeless, and there's little satire in a long, long lecture about Jesus Christ possibly being a woman. He reverses himself by concluding that, if Jesus turned water into wine, he can't be a woman because "most women can't tell good wine from cold duck."

Even the captive audience starts muttering.

The second album has a pointless discussion of the city of Doo Dah: "So many American people don't know where Doo Dah is. It's in Europe, way up in the mountains, like three hundred yards up there. You gotta take a donkey to get there. And it's named after Saint Doo Dah. And this fellow Saint Doo Dah, he became a Saint because he lived in tree trunks for fifty years. And what happened, he said to his mother, he was twenty years old, and his mother was sayin', 'Get a job,' and she said, 'What are you gonna do with your life?' And he said, 'I don't know, I don't know.' And that's his famous quote. In fact downtown Doo Dah, the main piazza, they got a statue, a marble tree trunk with this head sticking up, and underneath it says, 'I Don't Know, I Don't Know ... Saint Doo Dah.' He said, 'I'm gonna go to the woods to meditate....' He sat in the tree trunk and stayed there fifty years. And you think, why Sainthood? The miracle is you think the man would starve to death ... animals would feed him. Birds would drop him breadcrumbs and little pieces of veal."

The album also has "A medley of Beatles tunes" in which he Chico Marxes fragments of Beatles songs.

Sarducci turns up on David Steinberg's "Goodbye to the 70's" album.

SAUCY SYLVIA See SYLVIA STOUN

TONY SAVONNE

- HOLLYWOOD UP TIGHT (Laff A 123, also released on Silver Streak Records 19) *1/2 $4 $8

Obnoxious Savonne not only talks in italics but snickers at his own jokes on this tinnily recorded album of ancient material: "You know how they play strip poker in a nudist camp? *With a pair of tweezers....* They introduced me to a beautiful young girl at the nudist camp. I said, 'Pleased to see you,' and she said, *'I see!'* Then this midget was there, and this midget got flogged to death in the twist contest. I guess that's what he got for *stickin' his nose in everybody's business!"*

KERMIT SCHAFER

• PARDON MY BLOOPER (Jubilee PMB 1-PMB 8, also issued in various combinations as ALL TIME GREAT BLOOPERS by Brookville Records) **1/2	$5	$10
• BLOOPERAMA (Jubilee JUB BL 1)	$6	$12
• PARDON MY QUIZ BLOOPER (Jubilee Q PMB 10) **	$6	$12
• PARDON MY SPORTS BLOOPER (Jubilee S PMB 9) **	$6	$12
• WASHINGTON BLOOPERS (Jubilee WPMB 11) **	$6	$12
• COMEDY OF ERRORS (Jubilee 2001) **	$6	$12
• SLIPPED DISCS Jubilee (2002) **	$6	$12
• PRIZE BLOOPERS (Jubilee 2003) **	$6	$12
• SUPER BLOOPERS (Jubilee 2004) **	$6	$12
• OFF THE RECORD (Jubilee 2005) **	$6	$12
• STATION BREAKS (Jubilee 2006) **	$6	$12
• FUNNY BONERS (Jubilee 2007) **	$6	$12
• FOOT IN MOUTH (Jubilee 2008) **	$6	$12
• ONE HUNDRED SUPER-DUPER BLOOPERS (K-TEL 9320) **	$4	$8
• BEST OF BLOOPERS (Kapp 3576) ***	$6	$12
• BLUNDERFUL WORLD OF BLOOPERS (Kapp KS 3617) ***	$6	$12
• THE BLOOPY AWARDS (Kapp KS 3631) ***	$6	$12

Schafer died in 1979, but when radio or TV personalities collect "bloopers," they still mention his name as the man who popularized the word. The radio and TV producer (*The Rube Goldberg Show*, *Talent Search*, and *Quick on the Draw*) first issued a record of his collected outtakes and flubbed lines in 1953.

His eight "Pardon My Blooper" albums (in ten-inch and twelve-inch versions) are amusing enough, taken in small doses. Some of the bloopers are "re-created," not authentic. The actors aren't always convincing and often the same voices are used over and over.

Still, it's fun to hear (from Volume 5) announcers foul things up: "We take you to Central Park Mall for an appalling program of band music. I mean—appealing." Double entendres abound. A reporter on the set of a new Jayne Mansfield movie (from Volume 7) insists that, in spite of all criticism, she's actually a fine actress: "I wonder how her knockers feel now." And a newscaster notes, "After her apprehension by local authorities, Miss Ellen Benson was confined to a menstual institution for an indefinite period."

Schafer continued to reshuffle his bloopers into new packages for Jubilee, mixing in some new material as well. Kapp's "best of" albums really do offer the best, sans a lot of narration filler. "Blunderful World" offers them up non-stop, including commercials ("Do your shopping at Bloomingdale's where you'll get a free gift-rape with every purchase"), news announcements ("Vice President Hubert Humphrey is back on the campaign trail after a bout with intentional flu"), and soap opera mistakes ("Scalpel." "Scalpel." "Hemostat." "Hemostat." "Hypodeemic noodle...").

• FOR THOSE WHO HAVE EVERYTHING (Jubilee KS 1) **	$5	$10
• OVER SEXTEEN (Jubilee 2017) **	$5	$10
• OVER SEXTEEN 2 (Jubilee 2019/JGM 299) **	$5	$10
• ARE YOU CURIOUS OR YELLOW? (Audio Fidelity AFSD 1711) *	$5	$10
• GOLF PAR-TEE FUN (King 906, also released as GOLF-O-MANIA) *	$5	$10
• FAVORITE TRAVELING SALESMAN STORIES (King 901) *	$5	$10
• CITIZEN'S BLOOPERS (Commonwealth 9340) **	$5	$10

Schafer produced many comedy albums, and "For Those ..." compiles material from a few of them, including several ten-inchers: Allen Funt's "Candid Mike," and discs from Juliet Lowell and Will Jordan among others. He also produced various albums where his anonymous actors tell jokes instead of fake bloopers.

Over Sexteen was a hardcover joke book popular in the late '50s and early '60s—the ancestor to the *Playboy Party Jokes* paperbacks. These audio versions are readings from the book, sans audience. The jokes are broken up by semi-witty musical interludes.

"We know a girl who said she would do anything for a mink coat," a humorless announcer recites. "Now she can't button it."

Music: "Button Up Your Overcoat."

Dull narrators and bad actors continue to recite jokes on further Schafer anthologies. From "Favorite Traveling Salesman Stories," for example:

Announcer: In Philadelphia, an out-of-towner looking for a man named James Sexauer phoned various companies. (Phone rings.)

Man: Hello, I'm looking for some information. Uh, do you have a Sexauer there?

Woman: A what?

Man: A Sexauer.

Woman: I should say not. We don't even have a coffee break!

"Citizen's Bloopers" isn't a blooper album. It stars Dale Reeves and Gina Wilson as movie stars and politicians heard over their CB radios. They aren't bad, but the script could be better, as each of forty celebrities recite their "handle." Ted Kennedy's is "Teddy Bear," Cary Grant's is "Judy, Judy, Judy," and Howard Cosell's is "Mr. Yakkity-Yak."

"Are You Curious" is a dismal topical comedy album with some pathetic gags. An interviewer searches for opinions on the film *I Am Curious Yellow*. Aristotle Onassis declares, "It's all Greek to me." And Mao Tse Tung says he went to see the film because, "I am a curious yellow!" Sometimes actual celeb voices are spliced in, including William F. Buckley, Jr., Art Linkletter, Richard Nixon, Nelson Rockefeller, and Johnny Carson. Carson is interviewed about sexual permissiveness in motion pictures: "It's terrible." Then he's asked about the love scene in which the couple make love on the floor: "Why spend another night on an ordinary small size mattress when you can enjoy big stretch-out comfort?"

For other Schafer-produced albums see entries for Juliet Lowell, Eddie Schaffer, and Peter Wood.

EDDIE SCHAFFER

- LBJ ROAST (Atco 33 192) ** $4 $8

Catskill comic Schaffer is the "Roastmaster" at an imagined luncheon for Lyndon Johnson. A few politicians are heard in spliced up and re-edited speech fragments. Lady Bird herself applauds the "snide jokes about my husband." But, unfortunately, Schaffer is given the burden of reading the schtick-filled script himself. He regularly picks up the phone to speak to Barry Goldwater, Dean Rusk, Hubert Humphrey, and others. Only his end of the line is heard. After announcing that Goldwater is on the line, Eddie, the budget Jack E. Leonard, brays, "Of course I remember you. How can anyone forget Barry Goldfinger ... come on, Barry. The election is over. What? You want a recount? Thank you for calling, Mr. Goldwater. The President wishes you better luck next time, he's sure you're gonna make it, but not in this business!"

PETER SCHICKELE

- PDQ BACH (Vanguard 79195) **1/2 $8
- HYSTERIC RETURN (Vanguard 79223) **1/2 $8
- INTIMATE PDQ BACH (Vanguard 79335) ** $8
- PDQ BACH ON THE AIR (Vanguard 79268) ** $8
- LIEBESLIEDER POLKAS (Vanguard 79438) *1/2 $8
- BLACK FOREST BLUEGRASS (Vanguard 79427) ** $8
- A LITTLE NIGHTMARE MUSIC (Vanguard 79448) **1/2 $8
- STONED GUEST (Vanguard 6536) ** $8
- MUSIC YOU CAN'T GET OUT OF YOUR HEAD (Vanguard 79443) **1/2 $8
- PORTRAIT (Vanguard 79399) *1/2 $8
- WURST OF PDQ BACH (Vanguard 719/720) **1/2 $5 $12
- WURST OF PDQ BACH (Vanguard CD) **1/2 $8

Since 1966 Peter Schickele has been putting out albums of material from P. D. Q. Bach, who lived from 1807 to 1742 (a typical wry joke) and was the black sheep son of Johann Sebastian Bach. The long-running (predictable) gag is that P. D. Q.'s classical music contains snatches of pop music, features silly lyrics to operatic lines, and calls for unlikely musical instruments (bicycle pumps, kazoos, bottles, and so on). Cultists love their American Hoffnung, but most others will not need more than a few albums.

Schickele's first three albums were recorded in front of live audiences and blend music with fey monologues and introductory asides. These are among his better discs. The first album features "Concerto for Horn and Hardart" and "Sinfonia Concerante for Bagpipes," and "Left-Handed Sewer Flute" among others. The second has "The Unbegun Symphony" (in which "Anchors Aweigh" and "Camptown Races" somehow turn up, much to the merry laughter of the audience), "Pervertimento for Bagpipes, Bicycle and Balloons," and "Oratorio: The Seasonings," the first of the large scale operatic parodies.

"The Intimate" includes a typical Schickele lecture in which long, whimsical commentary leads to a pun. A piece "was commisioned by the Vienna Opera Company. But P. D. Q. Bach had written the entire work before he found out that the Vienna Opera Company consisted of Mr. and Mrs. Fritz Vienna and their little boy Rudy. Since there are seven different roles in the opera, P. D. Q. Bach at first gave up all hope of getting a performance, but finally Herr Vienna persuaded him to make a few revisions so that all the female parts could be sung by Frau Vienna, and all the male parts by Little Rudy, leaving the father free to play the piano, decked out in his best set of formal attire, the famous tails of Old Vienna."

Sometimes there's a variation or concept album. "On the Air" is a satire of lame classical college and/or public radio stations, this one "WOOF" in Hoople, North Dakota: "Uh-oh, well folks, I'm afraid the, uh, tape has broken on me here, but I'll have it fixed in just a jiffy. This sure is a heck of a way to start a morning, isn't it?"

"Liebeslieder Polkas" is sadistic, as a full choir shouts out the lyrics to ancient poems by Suckling, Marvell, Herrick, and so on, while the music careens between bugle calls, oompah rhythms, folk reels and, yes, beer hall polkas. "Black

Forest Bluegrass" tries to meld annoying German lieder singers to twangy folk music. Schubert fans may be faintly amused by a reference to Erl "Konig" Skruggsendorfer. "The Stoned Guest" is a "half act" opera (still too much for all but devoted fans). "A Little Nightmare Music" is an appropriate title for the one-act opera about P. D. Q. Bach. A tenor sings: "His father was a genius, 'tis true upon my word. But this man, this man is nothing but a total nerd."

Most albums have at least one or two fresh examples of the P. D. Q. formula. On "Music You Can't Get Out of Your Head," the "Howdy Symphony" somehow turns from eerie classical themes into "Hernando's Hideaway" and back, and manages to be vibrant and startling throughout. But half the album is opera ("The Civilian Barber") with a lot of dumb lyrics to titter over: "I am always being told to keep it quiet when the story is already stale and mouldy. By the way, the countess says she's on a diet; she should get a part in Tristan and Isolde."

"Portrait of P. D. Q. Bach" has the noisy chorale "Missa Hilarious" ("Kyrie Eleison" in pig latin among other yocks) and an annoying boys choir mangling "Poor Uncle John" and singing some dumb lines ("O Little Town of Hackensack") in their "Consort of Choral Christmas Carols." Fans get a lot less of "The Wurst of P. D. Q. Bach" on the CD version. The original two-disc set includes the "Unbegun Symphony," "Stoned Guest" highlights, and the twenty-two-minute "The Seasonings," all gone in order to slice the CD to sixty-three minutes.

Vanguard released other, straighter Schickele albums not in the "P. D. Q. Bach" category.

* 1712 OVERTURE (Telarc CD 80210) ** $8
* OEDIPUS TEX (Telarc CD 80239) *1/2 $8
* WTWP CLASSICAL TALKITY-TALK RADIO (Telarc CD 80295) **1/2 $8
* MUSIC FOR AN AWFUL LOT OF WINDS (Telarc CD 80307) ** $8
* TWO PIANOS ARE BETTER THAN ONE (TELARC CD 80376) ** $8

In 1989 when it seemed that the cult for P. D. Q. Bach had run its course, content with an annual live concert or two, Schickele emerged on a new record label. And even though he was doing the same old thing, he received four Grammy awards in a row for his next four releases. Were listeners that impressed with digital stereo?

The "1712 Overture" is exactly that: zany instruments adding sass, while "Pop Goes the Weasel" and other tunes suddenly chop at Tchaikovsky. There's over an hour of oratorio and opera on "Oedipus Tex," including the "Knock Knock Choral Cantata," thirteen minutes of bad jokes. As a "round," the chorus take turns singing the lines: "Knock knock," "Who's there?" "Ida." "Ida who?" "I-da-ream of Jeannie with the Light Brown Hair." This is sung, by various members of the choir, over and over for two and a half minutes.

"Music for an Awful Lot of Winds and Percussion" is more and more of the same, featuring "Grand Serenade for an Awful Lot of Winds and Percussion," etc. "Two Pianos," which opens with an extraordinarily tedious three-and-a-half-minute parody of automated phone answering machines ("if you know the opus number of the work you want to hear, enter it now") has guest pianist Jon Parker on the title cut. For "Trio Sonata" the big joke is that there's more than three players. The best (or at least, the most different) of the Telarc discs is WTWP, a welcome poke at classical radio stations "selling out" to yuppies by instructing DJs to chatter like their "Lite FM" counterparts, play only the allegro sections of symphonies, and make sure to program "greatest hits" pieces. WTWP stands for "Wall to Wall Pachelbel." There's some solid satire as the grating DJs (Donna Browne and Elliott Forrest) go overboard with ad-libs (a Red Seal record is announced, accompanied by seal barks). The actual music by Schickele, especially a pair of rock songs, is the weakest part of the album and veers between boring and bewildering.

PROFESSOR SCHNITZEL

* THE BEST OF PROFESSOR SCHNITZEL (Buch 3311) ** $5 $10

Wearing chin whiskers and glasses way down on his nose, dressed in old fashioned clothes, Professor Herman F. Schnitzel evidently performed often at local Pennsylvania festivals billed as "the foremost exponent and purveyor of Pennsylvania Dutch humor." This 1964 souvenir was done for a local label in Lincoln, Pennsylvania.

The professor points out, "I am Pennsylvania Dutch ... what we say sometimes, we mean it but the front end comes out last. Because when we translate the Dutch into English, it don't make! Take for instance, we say, 'Throw the horse over the fence some hay.' Well, now, that sounds funny, eh? But that's how we talk."

The mild lecture doesn't get much better. Sounding a bit like Victor Borge reading an old joke book, the Professor offers up many a familiar tale: "Take one of our friends, he has a daughter just came home from college. She was explaining to Pop, she says, 'Pop, the yard looks so wonderful nice this year, the flowers are so nice, the grass is so nice, how in the world did you do it?' 'Well,' he says, 'it wasn't so easy. It took a lot of hard work and twenty-four loads of manure.' Well, she didn't like this very much. She waited till Pop went out in the barnyard, and then she says to Mom, 'Mom, why don't you teach Pop to talk a little different ... Why can't you get him to say fertilizer?' Mom says, 'Shut up, it took me twenty-five years to get him to say manure!'"

TONY SCHWARTZ

* THE NEW YORK TAXI DRIVER (Columbia) *1/2 $5 $10
* THAT IS MY OPINION AND IT'S VERY TRUE (CSM 470) *1/2 $8 $15

Back in the days when New York City cabbies had Runyonesque accents, Tony Schwartz recorded interviews with them and put them out on disc. From one cabbie's diatribe: "I have to work ten, eleven hours a day. I have two growing boys—a boy going on fourteen, and a boy going on ten—they need clothes. Naturally I try to give them the things that I didn't have in my childhood. That all costs money. It's an awful thing to make a living, a lot of people look down upon you. But those people are wrong when they look down upon you because you're a cab driver. That is my opinion and it's very true."

Schwartz's radio essays appeared on WNYC radio and he issued several non-comedy albums of philosophy and sound effects for Folkways in the late '50s and early '60s, including "Sounds of My City," "Nueva York," "A Dog's Life," "The World in My Mail Box," "Music in the Streets," and "If He Asks You Was I Laughing," a collection of folk songs and prison laments recorded in concert halls and jails.

FRANKIE SCOTT

- YOU'RE IN MY ACT (Arco 501) *1/2 $7 $15

A Florida based "adults only" comedian, the thin, young Scott was often billed as "The Undernourished Comic." Potent booze must've been served in the early '60s at the "Pow Wow Room" of the Thunderbird Motel, because he got laughs and applause with this opener: "It's a pleasure to see such a big crowd here tonight. You should have been here last night. Somebody should've been here last night.... We had an overflowing crowd. The sewer backed up!" Then he goes into his song: "They call me the undernourished comic; it's because I'm so thin!" And how about those ringsider gags: "This man over here, I don't want to upset you, sir, but the hair in your nose is on fire!"

RAY SCOTT

- THE PRAYER (Checker Ck 3017) $6 $12
- JOIN RAY SCOTT IN PRAYER (Apple Juice 1000) $6 $12
- SEX IS FUNNY (Dooto 837) ** $5 $10
- RAY SCOTT LIVE (Elka LP 601) ** $5 $10

A kind of radical Redd Foxx, Scott will sometimes pause between jokes to offer bits of rambling philosophy and plenty of gratuitous cursing. He's also apt to break into straight gospel-tinged songs. He admits on the Elka record that "I steal jokes from Redd Foxx and Slappy White," and proves it with some of the old gags he uses, including the wheeze about the little boy who has to go to the bathroom: "Daddy, I got to pee." "Don't say I gotta pee, say, 'I gotta whisper,' stupid!" He goes over to his grandpa, he say, 'Grandpa, I got to whisper.' Grandpa say, 'Whisper right here in my ear.' And he did. And Grandpa said, 'I'm sure glad goddammit you didn't wanna shout!'"

Scott tells quickies ("I used to have a job in the Kotex factory—I thought I was makin' mattresses for mice") but mostly it's raunchy conversation mixed with prepared gags: "I don't like no white girls. If you see me with a white girl, I'm holdin' her for the police. So all you white fellas in here, you all think I'm lookin' at your wife's legs. Excuse me Miss, I like the way your knee grows. I like black girls. You put a black girl on the sheet and you see what you're gettin'. I put a white girl on the sheet and bit a hole in the mattress!!"

SCOTT & TODD

- SCAMARAMA (Foundation 8317372) * $8
- SCAM DUNK (Foundation 83688425) * $8

On "Scamarama" DJs Scott Shannon and Todd Pettengill offer up witless prank phone calls, self-satisfied doody humor (a fake radio ad for "Forrest Dump"), and dick jokes ("If She Could See It Now," about the reattached John Bobbitt). With very few exceptions, such as a pair of supporting players doing reasonably obnoxious impressions of Lisa Marie Presley and Michael Jackson, there's nothing on this infantile 1994 CD that would've been worth hearing for free when it was first broadcast. The same applies to "Scam Dunk," with more boring prank calls, simpleminded song parodies ("Donahue's Not Coming Back"), and ego-soaked earaches (various jingles about them and their call letters, plus poor, ancient Mel Allen reciting a "comic" tribute). No time or thought seems to have gone into any parody. The 1995 CD is so out of touch it includes a routine making fun of Paul Tsongas.

SCREWY TV

- SCREWY TV (Funko LP 1001) * $5 $10

Cursing passes for humor on this pathetic low-budget disc. Keyed to television shows, one anonymous performer (who sounds a bit like Dickie Goodman) badly imitates quiz show hosts, Walter Cronkite, Howard Cosell, Archie and Edith Bunker, and various others with the skill level one might expect from a high schooler trying to be the life of the beer party. Worse than the coarse script and bad acting is the engineering: booming laughs and applause are splattered over almost every line, even when there's nothing funny going on.

DON SEBASTIAN

- DOZ WERE THE GOOD OLE DAYS (Driftwood) $4 $8
- MY WIFE'S EXCUSES FOR LESS SEX (Driftwood) $4 $8
- WE'RE GONNA GET EVERYBODY (Driftwood S-1000) ** $4 $8

A risqué comic who played Miami Beach clubs through the '50s and '60s, Sebastian's quickies will be familiar to fans of the genre. On "We're Gonna Get Everybody," he asks, "Waddya give an elephant that's got diarrhea? Plenty of room."

His distinction is a penchant for ethnic humor, much of it Italian. There's his routine on his sister's wedding, complete with an insulting description of a typical female guest: "Four foot six, 228 pounds! Has a bun in the back of her head. Sometimes on both sides! She looks like an Italian Arthur Godfrey. Has a moustache, very light. Three or four dozen curly hairs under the chin. And she looks like she's holdin' two kids by the head. Either that or she's smuggling in watermelons."

SECOND CITY

- COMEDY FROM THE SECOND CITY (Mercury OCM 2201) **1/2 $7 $15
- THE COSA NOSTRA STORY (Smash SRS 67045) ** $5 $10
- SECOND CITY WRITHES AGAIN (Mercury SR 61224) **1/2 $7 $15
- SECOND CITY SURVIVAL KIT (Spirit 9010) ** $5 $10

The Second City was a legendary improv troupe with a varying cast. The first disc, an original Broadway cast album, features Howard Alk, Alan Arkin, Severn Darden, Andrew Duncan, Paul Sand, Mina Kolb, and Barbara Harris. The cuts are "Football Comes to the University of Chicago," "Interviews," "Blind Date," and "Museum Piece." The latter is dated but still the most lively of the stagey tracks as beatnik Arkin urges neurotic Harris to let loose and sing out her protest. "Excuse me," she says, "I'm going to say dirty words? Does everyone say dirty words?" Before long, she's chanting "freedom, freedom, freedom, rebellion, rebellion, rebellion, um ... I HATE MY AUNT! Freedom, freedom, sex, sex, SEX!"

"The Cosa Nostra Story" stars Burns and Schreiber (as Senator McClobber and Joe Valapio) along with Del Close, John Brent, and Ann Elder. There's not much to this satire of senate hearings on organized crime, especially with this kind of strained jokery:

Valapio: My name is Joseph Valapio and I am a stoolie.

McClobber: Well, you're not a stoolie, Joe, you're a remorseful misguided person doing your duty as you see it.

Valapio: Let's call a spade a spade, senator.

McClobber: I don't think we have to bring any minority groups into this."

"Second City Writhes Again" is a "best of" album with only one previously unreleased cut, "Man in the Nightclub," which has the kind of intellectual references ("Miss Ann Thrope" is a character name) that were hallmarks of The Second City in the earlier Nichols and May era.

The "Survival Kit" album is not vintage Second City, but has one of the more recent casts, featuring James Belushi and Danny Breen.

RICK SEGALL

- I LOVE YOU BECAUSE YOU'RE FAT (CASABLANCA 422 8103031) * $3 $7

The songs on this album celebrating chubby women sound quickly written, and the one-joke concept gets boring quickly.

Hoping that boyfriends of hefties would buy it (along with a box of chocolates) or that the girls themselves would be amused, Segall steers clear of insults. The parody of "Makin' Whoopie" becomes "Makin' Cookies." Segall and his lady duet: "Let's make a dozen. Well, why not two? I'll eat the first batch. Next one for you. Say what's the matter? I ate the batter! Makin' cookies...." The duo may be pleasingly plump, but the comedy is extremely lean.

PETER SELLERS

- SONGS FOR SWINGIN' SELLERS (EMI America SN 16396) ** $7 $20
- BEST OF SELLERS (Angel 35884) ** $7 $20
- PETER SELLERS AND SOPHIA LOREN (Angel 35910) **1/2 $10 $25

Sellers's style on record is completely different from the humor of his manic *Goon Show* radio days or his hit films. Americans will be completely bewildered by most of the non-joke satires and lightweight tunes.

"Songs for Swingin' Sellers," issued in America in 1986, was Sellers's first album, released in England in 1959. It features "You Keep Me Swingin'," "So Little Time," "Radio Today: Lord Badminton's Memoirs," "My Old Dutch," "TV Today," "Puttin' on the Smile," "Common Entrance," "I Haven't Told Her," "Shadows on the Grass," "Wouldn't It Be Loverly," "We'll Let You Know," and "Peter Sellers Sings George Gershwin." Some of this material also appears on "The Best of Sellers."

Typical of the deadly brand of understated British satire here is "You Keep Me Swingin'," in which a Sinatra-style vocalist is interrupted by a muttering, musing Sellers who tries his own version, strumming on a ukelele and singing flatly. Sellers thought a funny voice could save any piece of weak material. On "Wouldn't It Be Loverly" Sellers puts on his goofy Indian accent: "All I vant is a room somewhere. Fah away from de cold night air. Wid one en-orrr mous chair! Uhh would it not be loverly?"

The satiric interview material tends to be scone-in-cheek; dry and tough going. "So Little Time," for example, could be retitled "Too Much Time," as Sellers tediously skewers out of touch rock journalists, avaricious managers, and twit-like performers. Many cuts are dated and Brit-oriented, like "Putting on the Style," which doesn't mean much even if listeners don't know that Sellers is going overboard imitating "skiffle" Brit-hillbilly Lonnie Donegan.

"Best of Sellers," as issued by Angel in America in the early '60s, includes "Party Political Speech," "You Keep Me Swingin'," "Radio Today: The Critics," "So Little Time," "Wouldn't It Be Loverly," "I'm So Ashamed," "Shadows on the Grass," "Radio Today: Lord Badminton's Memoirs," "Puttin' on the Smile," "Peter Sellers Sings George Gershwin," and "Balham: Gateway to the South." The only great cut is the last, a painfully accurate soundtrack to a terrible travelogue. George Martin's production includes evocative music and sound effects. Balham's thriving industry is "exquisite workmanship—toothbrush holesmanship." An interview with a fellow who sounds very much like Bluebottle (from *The Goon Show*): "The little holes in the top, are put in manually. Or, in other words, once a year."

Sellers was infatuated with Sophia Loren when they worked on the 1960 movie *The Millionairess.* Together they did a silly little album. There are solo numbers for each. They duet on only a few cuts, including the tame "I Fell in

Love with an Englishman." Here, Sophia urges, "Take me, take all of me!" But Sellers, in parody of a particularly idiotic Englishman, can only blabber, "I say ! I say!" The best duet is "Goodness Gracious Me," a delightfully dippy flirtation between Sellers (in his dizzy Indian accent) and the pouty but pliable Sophia, whose lips must've looked inviting as she told of her heart going "boom-boody-boom-boody-boom-boody-boo." This light bit of fluff was actually a Top 5 single in England.

Loren has a nice voice for the wry femme fatale ballad "To Keep My Love Alive." Sellers is either dull (the spoken cuts) or overdone, as in the dreadfully Cockney-accented "They're Moving Grandpa's Grave to Build a Sewer."

- AN EVENING WITH PETER SELLERS (BBCS 22402) *** $7 $15

After Sellers's death, BBC Records released this excerpt from Sellers's guest spot on Michael Parkinson's British TV talk show in November of 1974. There's plenty of insightful anecdotes as Sellers describes his childhood, following his Music Hall performer parents from city to city: "I really didn't like that period of my life ... I didn't like the smell of greasepaint ... baritones with beer on their breath...." Along with the serious or conversational moments, he captivates with material from his stand-up days (imitating Olivier, Bogart, and Lorre), sings a few happy old tunes, and ad-libs a bewildering variety of dialects.

NOTES: Sellers is well represented on many British imports. "Seller's Market" (United Artists UA 6 30266) includes "The Complete Guide to Accents in the British Isles" and "The Whispering Giant." "The Songs of Peter Sellers" (MFP 5640) is a compilation featuring several eccentric gems including his singular renditions of "Help!" "Hard Day's Night," and "She Loves You."

He also turns up on the soundtrack for the film *The Magic Christian* (Commonwealth CU 6004), performing the following limerick: "There was a young lady from Exeter. And all the young men threw their sex at her. Just to the rude, she lay in the nude. While her parrot, a pervert, took pecks at her!" Fans of Sellers's Inspector Clouseau character may want the soundtrack album for *Revenge of the Pink Panther* (United Artists LA 913H). It features an amusing fractured French rendition of "Thank Heaven for Little Girls." Soundtracks for *After the Fox* and *Pink Panther Strikes Again* also include Sellers's singing.

In 1990 EMI issued "The Peter Sellers Collection" (CDP 7 92689 2) a CD with twenty cuts, including previously unavailable material. In 1981 Guild (62002) issued a four-set tribute album of Sellers and *Goon* material titled "The Voice Behind the Mask." In 1994, the ultimate "Celebration of Sellers" appeared in England (EMI 724382778127). This handsome four CD boxed set not only includes his four albums "Best of Sellers," "Songs for Swingin' Sellers," "Sellers Market," and "Peter and Sophia," but obscure singles (including his first 78s), EP material, cuts from film soundtracks, and a few previously unreleased tracks. It's nice to have so much, but unfortunately much of it will tax even Sellers's most ardent fans (including eight Beatles lyric recitations in a row where the sole joke is in Sellers's accents, including three different tries at "She Loves You"). The booklet offers notes, a complete discography, and reproductions of LP and rare EP sleeves.

Aside from the Goon Shows (see entry under The Goons) Sellers appeared with Spike Milligan and Harry Secombe on "How to Win an Election" (Philips AL 3464), and with Anthony Newley and Joan Collins in "Fool Britannia" (Ember CEL 902). Both LPs were written by Leslie Bricusse and are dryly satiric and dated. Sellers costars with Harry Secombe, Spike Milligan, and Peter Cook in "Bridge on the River Wye" (Odeon PCS 3036), a Goon-ish parody that stands up well. "He's Innocent of Watergate" (Decca SKL 5194) costars Spike Milligan and Sandra Caron. It makes for extremely odd listening. Sellers's imitation of Nixon seems crossed with his president in "Dr. Strangelove." Milligan's script views Nixon as, among other things, a lecher. He and his secretary: "Well, Rosemary dear, you can have the rest of the day off." "It's nearly midnight." "Yes. Have you seen anything like this?" "No! No! Not that! Not in the face! Ahhhhhh!"

SETTERBERG AND BORESON

- YUST TRY TO SING ALONG (Golden Crest 3079) ** $5 $10
- COLD, COLD HEART (Golden Crest 3086) ** $5 $10
- AY DON'T GIVE A HOOT (Golden Crest 3098) ** $5 $10
- HONEY (Golden Crest 31020) ** $5 $10
- YUST GO NUTS AT CHRISTMAS (Golden Crest 31021) *1/2 $5 $10
- YUST GO COUNTRY AND WESTERN
  (Golden Crest 31022, also known as SWEDE HEARTS OF SONG) ** $5 $10
- THOSE SWEDISH MEATBALLS (Golden Crest 31026) ** $5 $10

Doug Setterberg (a Seattle TV personality on KING-TV) and Stan Boreson (a Seattle native who worked on KOMO radio) teamed in 1957 for some novelty songs using a one-joke concept: popular songs with artificial Swedening.

Singing in Swedish accents is not much of a joke, but their fans don't seem to mind. To break up the monotony, the boys sometimes insert corny routines during the instrumentals. From "If You Knew Susie" on the first ("Yust Try ...") album: "You know, it's not much of a song, but it makes you think." "Yah." "It makes you think it's not much of a song! Say, that Suzie's got kind of wavy hair, huh?" "No, she doesn't have wavy hair." "She hasn't?" "Her hair is straight; it's her head that's wavy." "Oh, I couldn't tell from here. She is kinda cute but her stockings are wrinkled." "Vell, she isn't vearing stockings." "Heaven's to Betsy!"

Sometimes the boys parody tunes, acting like the Swedish version of Homer and Jethro. The title track from their "Cold Cold Heart" album takes the Hank Williams song literally: "I tried so hard my dear to show the problem I have got. But you don't seem to even care. Your hearing aid is shot. When first we met, you was so terrible sweet. How could I possibly have known that you had such cold cold feet."

Boreson issued a few solo discs. Carl Douglas Setterberg died in Seattle on April 15, 1973. He was fifty-four years old.

SCOTT SHANNON

- THE SHANNON IN THE MORNING COMEDY ALBUM (Foundation 80287) * $8

No one could endure listening nonstop to this hour of bludgeoning disc jockey humor. Shannon has some good help on the cuts featuring celebrity impressions, but few of them are bearable for more than five seconds (like Elmer Fudd singing a new version of "I'm Too Sexy for My Shirt"). The writing is mostly terrible and the slant is egocentric. Some cuts are nothing but jingles for Shannon's radio station and audio clips of celebrities mentioning his name (even if the celebrity is just a local TV weatherman). There's the requisite number of loudly overacted sketches, inane mock phone calls, and shouted references to his radio station's call letters, which could easily have been edited out to make this barrage just a tad more listenable. Much of this stuff was designed to keep bleary-eyed motorists from veering into oncoming traffic in the morning, and for a brief second, succeeds. Then annoys. See also Scott & Todd.

MAL SHARPE

- THE MEANING OF LIFE (Rhino RNLP 006) **1/2 $4 $8
- THE LAST MAN ON THE STREET (Rhino RNLP 023) * $4 $8

Long departed from his late comedy album partner Jim Coyle, Sharpe continues to plumb "man in the street" interviews for unexpected moments of comedy. The Carl Reiner-ish Sharpe has even played the role in commercials (he did "man in the street" bits in ads for *TV Guide*).

"Meaning of Life" finds that when it comes to questions of life and death, most people haven't a clue. It's the same all over the country. He asks, "What's the meaning of life here in Cedar Rapids?" A man answers, "The meaning of life is the same anywhere. The meaning of life is the people who are alive can sit around questioning the meaning of life, whereas those who are not have to lie around dead all the time."

In Tijuana he tells a Mexican that he's looking for the meaning of life. The answer: "I got it for you! Let's go take a look. Whorehouse!"

Some cuts are dumb, some serious, and on some the subjects are onto the game and try too hard to be clever.

"The Last Man in the Street" clips coy interviews he did for San Francisco's KMEL, put-ons inserted amid the rock music. A variety of oafish, self-important "I think I'm funny" imbeciles take their turns spitting their brains into Sharpe's microphone. Sometimes Sharpe nudges the comedy along; for one bit, he collars people so they can pronounce the word "Chanukah." There's no way one can keep the needle on the record when Sharpe confronts a bunch of giggling Valley Girls, hands them the mike, and lets them start howling, "Sherrr!" and "Hi mom!" Sharpe cries, "God, it's getting dumber by the minute."

Prices are slightly higher on the West Coast.

DICK SHAWN

- REACH OUT (Frankford/Wayne) **1/2 $25 $40
- DICK SHAWN SINGS WITH HIS LITTLE PEOPLE (20th Century TFM 3124) *1/2 $7 $15

Shawn, who died onstage during a performance, never issued a stand-up album. "Reach Out" features rock songs similar in style to the overwrought beatnik material he favored in "The Producers" and "Mad Mad Mad Mad World." One of the better cuts is "Hey World Baby," a desultory view of the world: "Once you were round, now you're square! Hey world, baby, what's the matter with you! You gone crazy, all the wild things you do!" "Human Race" is a gospel-tinged warning: "Human race, you're a disgrace! And you'll never get together at this pace ... why don't we conquer us before we conquer space?"

The acetate disc dubbed by the Frankford/Wayne company of Philadelphia was never commercially released.

Probably around the same time (1964), Shawn issued his album of kiddie comedy songs and novelties featuring an uncredited collection of shrill "little people." Some cuts are straight, like the slack and flattened version of Frank Loesser's "Inchworm"; others are noisy nonsense ("Hambone" and "Inka Dinka Doo").

Collectors should be aware of the single "It's Not Easy Being White" (Victory 1003).

DOROTHY SHAY

- DOROTHY SHAY SINGS (Columbia CL 6003) ** $6 $12
- THE PARK AVENUE HILLBILLIE (Capitol H 444) ** $6 $12

Shay, best remembered now for her role in Abbott and Costello's *Comin' Round the Mountain*, was a popular nightclub singer who dressed in elegant gowns to sing corn-flavored ditties. She has a lilting voice on these ten-inch albums and the arrangements are fairly tasteful. She's a lot easier to take here than in Bud and Lou's movie. One tune from the film, "Sagebrush Sadie," is on the Capitol album, along with "Why Shore," about a girl who never learned to say more than those two words: "The other kids at Nellie's house were smart as they could be. They passed the mountain education test. At twenty-one they all had reached the mental age of three. But Nellie never caught up with the rest." It's a good thing she's pretty: "And sure enough her popularity began to spread. She had the fellers hankering for romance. They never got discouraged for no matter what they said, her answer gave them all a fighting chance!"

Shay never gets wild (a la Betty Hutton) and keeps her tongue in her cheek most of the time (a la Ruth Wallis) on other tunes: "Television's Tough on Love," "Don't You Think You Should've Mentioned It Before?" "A Little Western

Town Called Beverly Hills," "If It Wasn't for Your Father," "Howlinest, Hootinest Gal," and "Sugar Plum Kisses and Vinegar Tears."

Her Columbia album collects many of the singles she began to release on that label in 1946 and 1947. "Feudin' and Fightin'" was a big hit for her. Sung by the rather sweet-voiced Shay, the song doesn't come across as harshly as one might expect from the lyrics: "Fightin' a fussin' and a feudin'—why did that sheriff keep intrudin'? He was a curious critter, yep, he was swell. It's a shame he was pushed down the well. Water, the well water, the doggone stuff don't taste like it oughta. Look here, city slicker, that's why we all drink corn liquor!" Cuts include "Say That We're Sweethearts Again," "Mountain Gal," "Efficiency," "Flat River, Missouri," "I've Been to Hollywood," "Uncle Fud," and "I'm in Love with a Married Man."

HARRY SHEARER

- IT MUST HAVE BEEN SOMETHING I SAID (Rhino R271217) *1/2 $8

Ten years of self-writing, self-directing, and self-acting a self-absorbed radio show for a PBS affiliate in Santa Monica has dulled Harry Shearer, once a member of Spinal Tap and The Credibility Gap, now best known for cartoon voices on *The Simpsons*.

On this disappointing disc some of the parody songs are so so predictable they're a yawn after a minute (like "Cops with Attitude," with its so politically correct respect for L.A.'s hoodlums). There's a boring five-minute song about morning talk show hostesses ("we love to share our oat bran with the ladies of the morning"), Even a Madonna parody falls embarrassingly flat as Shearer, sounding more like an effeminate Al Yankovic than the Material Girl, simpers inanities: "You've come a long way baby, but you haven't come far enough. Cigarettes can be sexy, mama. But how about a snootful of snuff?"

The sketches are often as droningly dull, but at least Shearer's good ear for production values hasn't atrophied completely while pandering to the tweedy tastes of public radio's listeners. With appropriate music and sound effects, "Dick Clark's Welcome Home Desert Storm Troops All-Star Party" comes closest to the old Credibility Gap style of satire, complete with an off-key Allan Thicke singing a tribute song and comic Yakov Smirnoff trying to be likable.

JACK SHELDON

- OOOO—BUT IT'S GOOD (Capitol T 1963) ** $7 $15

Jazz trumpeter Jack Sheldon used to do some comic moments as a band member on *The Merv Griffin Show* and he starred in the short-lived sitcom *Run Buddy Run*. The material on this jazz-hip early '60s LP is a bit low-key, slightly to the right of Stan Freberg. Sheldon riffs on Irving Lancelot who goes on a quest to "The Stratford-on-Avon Jazz Festival." His ride "took fourteen days and twenty-seven nights ... ooooh, but it was good!"

He sings "Born to Lose," and adds a talking bridge: "Folks, one time I lost my laundry ticket. And I had to beat up an old, crippled Chinaman to get my laundry bag. And then it was the wrong bag. It was full of some lady's lingerie. But I wore it anyway ... it's really good. Real smooth." Smooth, weirdly subtle, and a bit too cute, Sheldon is of interest only to a special breed of jazz-comedy fan.

KEITH E. SHELLEY

- THIS IS YOUR CAPTAIN SPEAKING (Kangi K 1000) *1/2 $5 $10

Shelley evidently self-produced this studio album in the early '60s, recorded at BFK Studios in Miami. With the constant whooshing sound effect of a plane in flight, a passenger offers leisurely observations about the trip and here, the captain:

"Old Smoothie, complete with the graying temples and the steel blue eyes.... The picture of a physical fitness program in uniform. Let me tell you something, friend ... fact is, he can't see worth a damn out of those steel blue eyes anymore ... listen, this guy's arches are so fallen, that he probably couldn't stand up if he didn't have these special shoes. Steel gray temples? He's lucky he's got any hair left for temples. Oh, did you see those pretty blue veins in his nose? That comes from drinking distilled water, right? Yes sir ... he's a real physical fitness program. But it looks like it might've collapsed on the way to the gymnasium."

The low-key style of sarcasm is vaguely similar to Bob Newhart, but the script is weak. The production values (sound effects, the captain's voice over the intercom, etc.) don't liven things up much.

JEAN SHEPHERD

- JEAN SHEPHERD AND OTHER FOIBLES (Elektra EKS 172) **1/2 $15 $30
- WILL FAILURE SPOIL JEAN SHEPHERD (Elektra EKS 195) **1/2 $15 $30
- LIVE AT THE LIMELIGHT (Quote 4) ** $12 $25
- DECLASSIFIED (Mercury SRN 1 615) **1/2 $10 $20

Shepherd was best known on radio, performing intimate monologues late at night for his faithful following. Later, he put out books of humor and wrote screenplays. Shepherd tells few jokes, just finely honed stories with an insistent, conversational style that establishes an intimate bond with the listener.

"Foibles," done without an audience, captures the feel of his radio days and has some of his best bits, including "Fun Funeral," "The Human Comedy," and "Monkey on My Back," his subtle and satirical report on a schoolyard addiction to Cracker Jack. He waxes philosophical about his belovedly inept (pre-pennant 1959) Chicago White Sox: "a White Sox fan measures victory in terms of defeat. Like if the White Sox lose 6-5 that's a good day." A weak cut, but noteworthy for comedy buffs, is his sour grumble over how Mort Sahl got big laughs just from one-word allusions: "Eisenhower! Golf balls!"

"Will Failure Spoil Jean Shepherd" was recorded live during his Christmas week, 1960 appearance at One Sheridan Square. Cuts include "Little Orphan Annie," "My First Blind Date," "The Playboy Syndrome," "Purgatories," and "Great American Dream." Shepherd's acolytes burst out laughing easily, which leads him to excitedly overact. A moment from "The Playboy Syndrome" that made his Manhattan audience laugh in surprise, and then applaud:

"Just beyond this curtain here, just beyond Sheridan Square, just out there in the darkness is the river. That dark old river. And on the other side of the river is *Hackensack*. Teaneck. Bergen. Jersey City, all those other sorehead cities hangin' out there. And then, just on the other side of those cities it begins. There's a great big country out there. GREAT BIG *fantastic* country that's flat and dark. At this hour. And it kind of slants away. Kind of tilts down. Wayyy, wayyy, till finally it reaches: the Pacific ocean. GIGANTIC country. Just clinging to this little island here."

The 1964 Quote disc has long pieces: "Fort Dix Wire-Laying Story," "Chicago White Sox," and "Brunner's Triangular Doughnut." The latter is the sad story of a man's get-rich quick scheme—and the horrible doughtnuts nobody wants to eat. The stories are poignant slices of ridiculous life, especially for those who enjoy storytellers over stand-ups.

"Declassified," released about five years later, is half live, half studio cuts souped up with spliced rock music, kopspeilen (music made by head thumping), jew's harp tunes, and distracting sound effects. He offers fourteen minutes on war experiences ("U.S. Signal Corps") and a cute eight-minute recollection on life with his little brother, who would only eat if he had his own trough and was told about "The Three Little Piggies." Some of Shepherd's most typical one-liners are here: "Ever look at the people around you, and say, 'How the hell did I ever wind up with these idiots!' There are also several animated, ironic commentaries on the human condition:

"The fear of discovery. Yes, how many times had your mother said to you, when you were on your way to the Warren G. Harding School (or your equivalent), 'Did you change your underwear! If you get hit by a car, I don't want them to think....' Can you imagine a Mack truck hitting this little squirt ... five minutes later, the surgeon says: 'Look at that underwear!'"

NOTES: Shepherd is a cult figure, priced accordingly. He's on "Into the Unknown with Jazz" (Abbott 5003) and "The Clown" with Charles Mingus (Atlantic 1260, also released as a twelve-minute extended play single, Atlantic 581). "The Clown" is an album of instrumentals with the exception of the title track, which features Shepherd's improvised narration, a variation on the era's "poetry and jazz" discs: "Man, there was this clown. He was a real happy guy. A *real* happy guy ... and he had just one thing he wanted in this world. He just wanted to make people laugh. That's all he wanted in this world. He was a real happy guy. Let me tell you about this clown...." This is obviously not a happy story.

Shepherd is also represented on various audio books and a six audiocassette set called "Shepherd's Pie." Each hour-long tape features a story: "Red Ryder Nails the Cleveland Street Kid," "Wanda Hickey's Night of Golden Memories and Other Disasters," etc., etc.

UKIE SHERIN

• GO MAKE FRIENDS (Imperial 9131) *1/2 $4 $8

Sherin was evidently well known as a comedy writer, his credits including *The Kraft Music Hall* and *The Bob Hope Show*. On his own he relies on some pretty old gags: "I'd like to welcome my doctor, who finally decided to come and see me here, socially. This is a wonderful doctor. If you can't afford the operation he'll touch up the X-rays. Too bad he's barred from the profession. He treated somebody for yellow jaundice for three years, before he realized it was a Chinaman." At least Sherin doesn't desperately try to sell these used wares; he goes through the motions amiably and quietly.

ALLAN SHERMAN

• MORE FOLK SONGS BY ALLAN SHERMAN (Jubilee 5019) **1/2 $10 $20

When Sherman became a big star as "My Son the Folk Singer," Jubilee came out with "More Folk Songs." All they had on Sherman was a 78 rpm single from 1951, "A Satchel and a Seck" backed with "Jake's Song." At the time Sherman seemed to be imitating the ethnic successes of Mickey Katz and Lee Tully. "A Satchel and a Seck," based on Frank Loesser's "A Bushel and a Peck," is a duet between Sherman and comedienne Sylvia Froos. They exchange warm vows of love with lots of Yiddish expressions and food references: "I love you a knaidel and a knish, a knaidel and a knish and a knippel and a kish!" In the midst of it, there's some vaudevillian Yiddish byplay: "You know darling, you sing like a regular little faygeleh," Sylvia says. "Dot's vot I am, dot's vot I am!" Allan replies happily.

"Jake's Song," based on the forgotten "Sam's Song," has Sherman imitating Frank Sinatra singing in Yiddish. The rest of the album is Jewish comedy from Jubilee's vaults: Lee Tully's classic "Essen"; "Today I Am a Man"; Harry Ross's "Tzimished," a Yiddish version of "Bewitched, Bothered and Bewildered"; and "Tennessee Frelich" from Sylvia Froos (based on "The Tennessee Waltz"). Among the monologue singles, fans will be happy to hear Fyvush Finkle do a Victor Borge-type pronunciation routine about the Yiddish language, and Willie Howard's Yiddish-French lesson.

• MY FAIR LADY (NBC Reference Recording) **1/2 $35 $75

Sherman entertained at parties with his song parodies—and ambitiously took on the score from *My Fair Lady*. He held out hope that he could record it, but Lerner and Loewe refused permission.

What survives is this one-sided "acetate" demonstration disc pressed and labeled at NBC's broadcasting studio. There's a live audience and piano accompaniment.

Sherman casually wonders what would happen if the great Broadway shows were written by Jews. Then he acknowledges, "They were." And he imagines the Jewish *My Fair Lady* with such lessons in pronunciation as: "The chrein in Spain tastes good with two cents plain!" (Chrein is horseradish). "With a Little Bit of Luck" becomes "With a Little Bit of Lox" and "On the Street Where You Live" becomes a proud recital of assimilation: "We have often walked West End Avenue. And you'll find us on a parkway known as Moshulu. Living gaily there. Like Israeli there. Oh it's grand on the streets where we live. We've got Scarsdale men. We've got Great Neck men. And just lately we've been sneaking into Darien. Strange new noses there. Friends of Moses there. Near the goys on the streets where they live...."

- MY SON THE FOLK SINGER (Warner Bros. W/WS 1475) **** $5 $10

In 1962, fired from *The Steve Allen Show* and on unemployment, writer-producer Sherman managed to interest Warner Brothers in a folk song parody album. He was given $1500 and told to choose some public domain tunes. Show biz friends Steve Allen, Jerry Lewis, Jack Benny, and Harpo Marx wrote the album notes and Allan added seven "lucky" cartoon bears to the back cover, hoping for the best.

Miraculously, this obscure comedy album from the unknown comedian caught on. Radio stations began playing it and soon everyone was asking for the plain-voiced vocalist singing those plainly hilarious folk tunes.

Almost every cut on "My Son the Folk Singer" is a gem. Warmth and good humor flow like U-bet syrup. Sherman takes exotic tunes, from the calypso "Matilda" to the Irish "Shake Hands" to the French "Frere Jacques," and makes them Jewish—proudly so, with all the gentle neurosis and "noodgery" that is part of it. His Jewish knight, Sir Greenbaum, is no putz. He'll fight dragons, even though he wishes he didn't have to: "Oh, wouldst I could kick the habit—and give up smoting for good." And a garment worker becomes a hero in "The Ballad of Harry Lewis." Sherman sings: "Oh Harry Lewis perished in the service of his lord. He was trampling through the warehouse where the drapes of Roth are stored. He had the finest funeral the union could afford! And his cloth goes shining on."

At the time, the hit of the album was "Sarah Jackman" ("Frere Jacques"), which is just a sing-song of everyday Jewishness: "How's your Cousin Shirley?" "She got married early." "How's your brother Bentley." "Feeling better mentally." "What's with Uncle Sidney?" "They took out a kidney." "How's your Cousin Norma?" "She's a noncon-forma."

Sherman's album spawned a parade of "My Son ..." comedy records as various imitators tried to get in on the gelt. The closest vocally was "My Son the Copycat" by Stan Ross, followed by Steve Karmen ("This Is a City"). "My Son the Joke" was the risqué version via Dickie Goodman. Christine Nelson was the female version. Landers and Adams offered duets ("Marriage Is for Dinosaurs") and Fisher and Marks did Italian folk songs in Sherman's style. The album also spawned a catchphrase in "My son the ..." including various "My Son the ..." albums by others, and even "My Father the Pop Singer" by Sam Chalpin.

This was an influential record for another reason—it led to dozens, if not hundreds, of albums released by unknowns convinced they could get instant airplay and an instant best-seller like Sherman.

- MY SON THE CELEBRITY (Warner Bros. W 1487) *** $5 $12
- MY SON THE NUT (Warner Bros. W 1501) **1/2 $7 $15
- ALLAN IN WONDERLAND (Warner Bros. W 1539) ** $7 $15

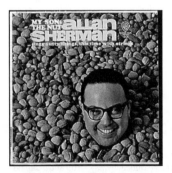

The Allan Sherman formula was set with the first album, and "Celebrity," recorded November 30, 1962 (his birthday), is more of the same, with less surprises. Some of the parodies are pointless, obviously written in a rush. The Irish tune "Harrigan" becomes "Horowitz" in a silly ode to the pianist Vladimir Horowitz ("and he plays piano good like a real piano player should, Horowitz, here here"). Spotty though the album is, many cuts are still funny, thanks more to Sherman's homely vocals than his lyrics. He turns the elegant "Tit Willow" into a clutzy ballad from a bird watcher in the Bronx; "Won't You Come Home Bill Bailey" becomes the jarringly funny one-joke "Won't You Come Home Disraeli"; and an ode to couch potatoes "Al 'n' Yetta" is more timely now than ever: "Al and Yetta always sit togetta, watch-in' TV every single night ... they're big fans a' *Gunsmoke* and *Bonanza* ... and *Ben Casey* and Dr. Jim Kildare. Third reruns of *Millionaire*. Fourth reruns of Yogi Bear."

Sherman goes happily overboard with silly punnery. On "Me," a parody of "Sorrento," he surveys his body: "Counting both feet I have ten toes. They're not lady toes they're men toes. And I keep them as mementoes for I love them tenderly."

Other cuts include "When I Was a Lad," "Get on the Garden Freeway," "Bronx Bird Watcher," "Shticks of One Half a Dozen of the Other," "No One's Perfect," and "Let's All Call Up A.T. & T."

Sporting a cute album cover of Sherman with his head poking through a sea of nuts, and an equally amusing back cover photo of the chubby-cheeked hero's face obliterated by a big microphone, "Nuts" has Sherman's lone hit, the summer camp plaint "Hello Muddah, Hello Fadduh." It's still a classic. A lot of the other cuts don't endure past a few listenings. Sherman was straining to find songs to parody. "You Came a Long Way from St. Louis" becomes "You Went the Wrong Way, Old King Louie," and "You're Getting to Be a Habit with Me" becomes "You're Getting to Be a Rabbit with Me." The songs get predictable and foolish after the first chorus. Other numbers here include "I See Bones" ("C'est Si Bon"), "Here's to the Crabgrass," "Hail to Thee, Fat Person," "Eight Foot Two, Solid Blue," and "Rat Fink" ("Rag Mop").

"Wonderland" tried for overly lush orchestrations that tend to suffocate the vocals. The show tune "Heart" turns into an ode to "Skin," with typically silly lines: "When you're sitting down it folds and looks grand. And then when you stand it's where it's been. Ain't ya glad you got skin?" "Holiday for Strings" is now "Holiday for States"—the names of all fifty states atop the famous David Rose instrumental. And "I'm Called Little Buttercup" becomes the pathetic "I'm Called Little Butterball." Sherman fruitlessly tries a bit of Victor Borge by speaking the punctuation to Cole Porter's "Night and Day": "Like the tick, hyphen, tick, hyphen, tock of a stately clock as it stands against the wall. Like the drip, comma, drip, comma, drip of the raindrops."

The better cuts are two originals, "You Need an Analyst" and "Lotsa Luck," a hard-luck tale of ironies: "Some people think a horseshoe's gonna bring 'em lotsa luck. A horseshoe is a lucky sign of course. For every set of horseshoes human beings use for luck, somewhere in this world's a barefoot horse." Others include "Good Advice," "Green Stamps," "The Drop Outs March," and "I Can't Dance."

- FOR SWINGIN' LIVERS ONLY (Warner Bros. W 1569) ** $10 $20
- MY NAME IS ALLAN (Warner Bros. 1604) * $10 $20
- PETER AND THE COMMISSAR (RCA VICTOR LSC 2773) **1/2 $10 $20
- ALLAN SHERMAN AND YOU: LET'S TALK ABOUT THE NEW ALBUM!
  (RCA Victor SP 33-3100) ** $15 $30

Sherman gets more and more predictable each time. "Grow, Mrs. Goldfarb," ("Shine Little Glow Worm") has fat gags: "Eat Mrs. Goldfarb, daily, nightly, eat though your chair is bending slightly." And "Kiss of Myer" ("Kiss of Fire") is a dopey look at romance: "He has a way that makes the ladies feel exalted. He'll take you out and treat you to a chocolate malted. Then some pistachio nuts, a nickel's worth unsalted. And after that, little girl, you're through!"

Some fans like the Stan Freberg-ish "Twelve Gifts of Christmas." And when Sherman gets really ludicrous in his homely parodies, it's hard not to chuckle. "Shine On Harvest Moon" turns into a ballad for an astronaut—with the awful pun, "Shine on, Shine on Harvey Bloom!" And in a romantic Gershwin mood, Sherman offers, "It's very clear ... your mother's here to stay."

Of some historical interest is "Pop Goes the Weasel" transformed into "Pop Hates the Beatles": "There's Beatles books and T-shirts and rings and one thing and another. To buy my daughter all of these things I had to sell her brother." Other cuts: "J.C. Cohen," "Beautiful Teamsters," "America's a Nice Italian Name," "Bye Bye Blumberg," and "Pills."

"My Name Is Allan" (parody cover photo of "My Name Is Barbra") is an astonishingly jokeless, dull album. The studio audience has nothing to laugh at. And they don't. Sherman has nothing to say—and says it anyway. "Secret Love" becomes "Secret Code." The lyrics are merely the recitation of letters: "A was B and B was G, G was K and K was J. And J was M and M was P." Allan concludes by admitting, "I don't understand my secret code." For "Call Me Irresponsible," he parrots names of famous people of the day hoping they'll call: "Dial up Liberace and while up, Joe Valacchi and tell him Lucky sends his regards." "Chim Chim Cheree" recites funny names of commercial products: "I wake up each morning a most happy man. I cover my Pico-pay with Flouristan." "That Old Black Magic" moans about a broken back scratcher: "Yes you broke it in half. Now you're too short. I tried Scotch tape as a last resort. But with Scotch tape it wasn't the same. The thrill that was wild is suddenly tame."

The better cuts are the ones in which Sherman is motivated by anger. "It's a Most Unusual Day" becomes an irritated complaint, "It's a Most Unusual Play" and "The Continental" becomes "The Painless Dentist." Other cuts: "The Laarge Daark Aardvark Song," "Go to Sleep, Paul Revere," "Drinking Man's Diet," "Peyton Place, U.S.A.," and "An Average Song."

"Peter" was recorded live at Tanglewood on July 22, 1964. It is a twenty-minute musical (with Arthur Fiedler and the Boston Pops) based on "Peter and the Wolf." Allan ambitiously wrestles with the complex problems of communism vs freedom. Peter here is trying to create his own music, but The Commissar insists on meddling.

The Commissar not only wrecks Peter's music, but insists on changing the classics. He turns Beethoven's Fifth into a Cha-Cha! Between this P. D. Q. Bach/Hoffnung stuff Sherman recites Dr. Seuss-like rhymes as the story reaches its happy ending: "So in spite of the #1 Chief Commissar, Peter was bigger than Ringo Starr. Bigger than Brahms and Shosta-kovich. Bigger than "Sing Along with Mitch."

The flip side features "How Dry I Am" (with guest hiccup from Arthur Fiedler, who wins tumultuous applause) and more classical music parodies.

"Let's Talk about the New Album" is an "open end interview" promo album containing excerpts from "Peter and the Commissar" and taped remarks by Sherman. Disc jockeys could pose questions from a script, and then play the answers on the record, pretending that Sherman was actually at the station with them. The album jacket offers extra help and advice: "Always leave your microphone open during Allan's replies to your questions and help him along with words of agreement or reaction ... it will improve the over-all sound of the interview if you interpolate natural reactions of laughter and semi-interruptions as he talks. Things like 'yup,' 'uh huh,' 'no kidding,' 'that's wonderful,' 'Oh no!' 'really?' etc."

Sherman remarks on the purpose of his "Peter" satire: "There's an old saying that a camel is a horse designed by committee. Anything that's really creative always comes out of the mind and the soul and the spirit of one single person ... I think that so many of us have a tendency nowadays to conform ... what I'm trying to encourage in here especially in kids who are listening to it, is do something creative, because everybody has something creative in him."

- LIVE (Warner Bros. 1649) ** $12 $20
- TOGETHERNESS (Warner Bros. 1684) *1/2 $12 $25
- BEST OF ALLAN SHERMAN (Rhino RNLP 005) *** $6 $12

- GIFT OF LAUGHTER (Rhino RNLP 70818) **1/2 $6 $12
- MY SON THE GREATEST (Rhino R2 75771) *** $8

Sherman's "Live" is live on a stage in Las Vegas (as opposed to live in front of a recording studio audience). That means that listeners are treated to some impromptu ad-libs during introductions to the songs. He mentions his daughter and her "Learner's Brassiere": "Well actually, she's learning real good if you wanna know! I mean the first couple of weeks it used to slide down to her ankles and trip her, but she's really getting the hang of it now."

The songs are mild. "A Taste of Honey" becomes "A Waste of Money," all about trying to lure dates with fancy gifts. "Smoke Gets in Your Eyes" becomes the obvious "Smog Gets in Your Eyes," and only ardent Sherman fans will really want yet another kosher food song as "I'm in the Mood for Love" stumbles along with lines like these: "When I'm in the mood for love you're in the mood for herring! When I'm in the mood for herring—you're in the mood for love."

Other cuts include "Second Hand Nose," "Dodgin' the Draft," "Taking Lessons," "Mononucleosis," "The Rebel," "Sorry 'Bout That," "If I Could Play Piano," and "Son of Peyton Place." Sherman also includes "Sam You Made the Pants Too Long," which for some reason he decided to improve by making the tailor Asian.

Sherman's last comedy album, "Togetherness," is lightweight but frisky—like Allan himself (he'd lost a lot of weight trying to create a new image). There's nothing great here—or particularly funny—but he sings with lots of enthusiasm. He gets worked up on "If I Were a Tishman," ("If I Were a Rich Man") for gags on the name of a prominent New York landlord: "I could realize my life's ambish ... raising rents whenever I would wish. Telling tenants, 'You can call me Pish! If I were a rich Tishman!'"

Allan sang his "Winchester Cathedral" parody, "Westchester Hadassah," on Ed Sullivan's show. It's a somewhat nasty grimace over donations: "Remember last year when you gave a masquerade ball? I came as a turnip just to see you try to squeeze my blood and all!" He also did "Strange Things in My Soup," a dull listing.

Other cuts: "Plan Ahead," "Signs," "Turn Back the Clock," "Togetherness," and "Down the Drain," a sad barbershop quartet describing forgotten things like fountain pens and double decker buses. And for New Yorkers, the World's Fair of 1964: "Where's the World's Fair? In the heart of Flushing. Where? Down the drain."

These last Warner albums had pessimistic pressings—which means their rarity makes them valuable, not their comedy.

After two vinyl "best ofs," Rhino issued the competent nineteen-song CD version, "My Son the Greatest."

NOTES: Sherman's predictable novelty single "My Son, The Vampire" turns up on "Dr. Demento Presents Spooky Tunes and Scary Melodies" (Rhino RS 71777). The refrain, a bawling "He wants blood," which comes out "He wants blawwww," makes this a painful two minutes. Diehards will want to hunt up "Music to Dispense With" (Scott 12) the one-sided promo album he did for Scott paper products (where "Makin' Whoopie" became "Makin' Coffee") and singles including an EP of songs from "The Fig Leaves Are Falling" (Warner Bros 1487). Sherman joins Jack Benny and George Burns on the souvenir record "Tom May 80th Birthday Dinner" (June 3, 1963), which boasted of special song lyrics by Sammy Cahn.

DON SHERMAN

- BACK TO COLLEGE (Jubilee JGM 2042) *1/2 $5 $10
- AT THE PLAYBOY CLUB (Roulette R 25205) ** $5 $10
- FIRST OF THE SITDOWN COMICS (Laff 186) *1/2 $4 $8
- LET THERE BE GRASS (LAFF 161) *1/2 $4 $8

Sherman's delivery is a bit like Norm Crosby's. He has a simple New York-accented plaint. The trouble is that he tends to be heavy handed and unlike Norm's "hysterical truths," Sherman's average schlub observations are very mild. From his Khrushchev-era album on Roulette:

"Now take a simple thing like war. They say war is inevitable. Well, I don't believe that, but if that's true, I say ya add one more rule. If you wanna fight a war, you hafta fight it naked. Now countries would not rush into a naked war. 'Cause this can be a chilling experience. Can you imagine two armies lining up naked. The guy says charge. And nothing happens. 'Cause they can't tell who's the friend, who's the enemy. Can't have a naked war. And where are you gonna hang the canteen?"

Sherman was an opening act for Johnny Mathis when he recorded for Jubilee, his delivery slower and more deadpan than usual as he tells his anecdotal material: "I was very unlucky in school. Whenever I knew the answer the teacher would never call on me, but if I didn't know the answer, the teacher would always call on me. I worked it out: I quit school."

Into the Laff era hadn't changed much. On "Let There Be Grass," he recalls grown-up troubles:

"I bought my first house ... one day I find out I have bad pipes. Do you know how you find out that? There's a process known as backing up. I don't know if you've ever been backed up ... it's frightening, it's like the whole world comes up at ya through every hole in your house ... and there's nothing that makes man more humble in his life than toilet trouble!"

BOBBY SHIELDS

- FIRST CUBAN AT THE U.N. (Riverside RM 7538) * $4 $10

Here, young tuxedoed nightclub comic Shields does a mediocre, shrieky Fidel Castro. His schtick could use all the help his accent doesn't give: "Now you say to me, you say, 'Fee-dell, chooowee are going to send to you de Red Cross.' Chhhhwhy you wanna do dat! Because I do not need de Red Cross. Send me de BLOOO cross. I am berry sick! Mira mira mira—on de wall. You chhhwant to send de planes over my kawn-tree, to take de peek-choores of all de mee-seel bases, and you put a blockade around de kawn-tree, and you send de Red Cross for de inspeck-shawn. Chwhat's de matter? Don't you trust me?"

CRAIG SHOEMAKER

- MEETS THE LOVEMASTER (Wildcat WLD 9202) ** $7

A pretty boy comic evidently hoping to move from suave stand-up to something better, a la Michael Keaton, Shoemaker does play-safe gags on this 1994 CD, including impressions of "Droopy Dog," an analysis of the *Jeopardy* game show, and the usual airline gags and body odor jokes: "Every airline, the meat they give you, what is that meat? I dropped it on my lap it started humping my leg.... Did you ever drive through a smelly area with somebody you don't know that well? She cuttin' the cheese? Maybe I should say something about it in case she thinks it's me!"

BROTHER SAMMY SHORE

- BROTHER SAMMY SHORE (Liberty LIB 7602) ** $7 $15

Shore wrote a book about his days as an opening act, and it's a far more useful production than his son Pauly.

On this '60s disc Brother Sammy falls short of Brother Dave Gardner and Lord Buckley when it comes to funky hipness. He does sneak in a good line during his frantic shouts and posturing as a healer and spokesman for the Lord:

"I ain't asking for the money for myself. It's for the Lord. He's broke. Because all I get out of this is salvation. That's the name of my yacht, the U.S.S. Salvation ... I had a man walk over to me the other day and he said to me, 'Brother Sam, Brother Sam! What's the answer!' I said, 'Well, what's the question?' He said, 'Where's the good times, where's happiness?' People think that happiness and good times are goin' to Las Vegas, drinking, gambling, partying, women. THAT AIN'T GOOD TIMES! It's close to it! They say that happiness and success go hand in hand. But what is success? Success doesn't come from tears, sweat, and hard work. Sucess comes from luck. Ask any failure! Rudy, a friend of mine thought he wasn't going to make it, till he started thinkin' positive. Now he's positive he's not gonna make it."

PAULY SHORE

- THE FUTURE OF AMERICA (WTG 47062) * $7
- SCRAPS FROM THE FUTURE (WTG 52788) * $7
- PINK DIGGILY DIGGILY (Priority 53881) * $7

There's no reason why fourteen-year-olds shouldn't have their own stand-up comic, even one with no reason. Everyone else, beware.

Pauly's pedigree is father Sammy Shore and mother Mitzi (who runs The Comedy Store in Los Angeles). A favorite MTV personality, Pauly's act is for teens who aren't getting enough laughs from *Beavis and Butthead*. His brand of Valley Boy babble and L.A.-speak is so grating that on *Saturday Night Live*, Adam Sandler did a parody impression that ended with a mob of people beating "Pauly" till he was bleeding.

On the 1991 "Future" album, Pauly describes what might happen if his lifestyle turns out to be the future of America: "What's it gonna be like? It'll be like: 'Sir, you can take your traffic test in English, Spanish, or Dude?' 'Shit, I'll take it in Dude, Dude. Huh-huh-heh-heh, that's the only thing I know-owwwww!' Say, like true-false on the exam'll be 'totally' or 'not even.' Instead of stop signs there'll be signs that say 'Chill.' Instead of yield signs, signs'll say 'Be Mellow.' OK, Dudes, be mell-owww."

Shore's second album literally contains "Scraps." Pauly fills up some time with amateur tape recorder bits, including an interview with his mother, who is as yammery, giggly, and woyyyny-voiced as Pauly. His minor league observational humor covers going to 7-11 for beers and shouting at the counter guy at Burger King, "Don't pop your pimple in my fuckin' fries!" For more gross-out fun, Pauly talks about uncircumcised penises ("looks like a turkey's neck chillin' on yer shaft, man") and insists, "When I was thirteen I stuck a frozen hot dog in a girl and it broke off." Then he brightly sings the "I Wish I Was an Oscar Meyer Weiner" song.

As Pauly says here, "That's cool, whatever." At thirty minutes, the CD doesn't exactly bruise the attention span of his teenage audience, but it'll be unendurable for everyone else.

1994's "Pink Diggily Diggily" is more of the same, mixing live tracks and even dumber staged bits. The crowd laughs hysterically when Pauly cleverly describes a porn star as having a "purple veiny dong." He plumbs the usual juvenile sex-obsession territory as well: "Farting on a Date," "Titty Bars," "Dildos and Stuff."

HERB SHRINER

- ON STAGE (Columbia CL 774) ** $6 $12

Popular in the '50s for his "Hoosier" wit, Shriner's album is a variety show mix of harmonica playing and anecdotal comedy. He sounds like Will Rogers with a dash of Kermit the Frog in the cadence. He recalls one of his Hoosier friends: "He was always quick. I remember he come into the barber shop, he was selling a hair oil that makes your scalp loose. It's got sheepdip in it. This was before lanolin, you know. Chicken fat and everything. It would really work. One of the boys there had his scalp so loose it was hanging over his eyes there. Sort of a hairy cap or something. But the best thing he ever sold, he come in there with a thing to keep a toupee on. It was better than glue. It was a big round hairy thumb tack. It's possible." Shriner's unassuming style made him one of the better rustic comedians, though this album doesn't contribute much to the legend. His son, Wil Shriner, is a comedian too.

THE SICKNIKS

- SICK #2 (Amy Records, also released as THE PRESIDENTIAL PRESS CONFERENCE) ** $7 $15

There was no first album—"#2" is the type of gag you'd expect from *MAD Magazine*'s second string competition in the '60s. *Sick Magazine*'s Sickniks include guest stars Will Jordan and Sandy Baron. Jordan is featured prominently on one cut, "Frankenstein," a ten-minute sketch with sound effects that comes fairly close to an aural version of a typical *Sick* (or *MAD*) parody.

The lines are silly enough, and sound like they should be captions to cartoons. Dr. Frankenstein (Jordan as Groucho Marx) has trouble with the hunchback assistant (Jordan as Peter Lorre): "Must you keep squeezing the bodies to see if they're fresh? Yech!" The script degenerates quickly as Jordan does Jimmy Stewart, Ed Sullivan and Liberace impressions. The bit is very different from the "Frankenstein" routine on Jordan's "Ill Will" album.

Another long sketch, a movie parody of *Exodus*, has a decent line now and then. Jordan: "My father, he's the head of the underground. You'll know as soon as you see him. His clothes are filthy." Mostly the humor veers toward unpleasant Jewish stereotyping. An obnoxious Jewish mother interrogates her son's Gentile date: "Shaloooom! You're a Jewish goil?" "I'm not Jewish." "You're Jewish, no?" "Well, if it'll make you happy, I'm Jewish!" "You don't look it!"

There's a press conference with Kennedy (since *Sick* was basically aimed at teenagers, the political satire is mild) and a twelve-minute finale that includes some dreadful jokes about ethnics (Italian Dean Martin, Asian Charlie Chan, French Maurice Chevalier) singing pop songs for the United Nations. Jordan's mimicry makes it bearable.

SHEL SILVERSTEIN

- HAIRY JAZZ (Elektra 176, also issued as STAG PARTY, Crestview 7804) ** $10 $20
- SHEL SILVERSTEIN SINGS HIS SONGS (Cadet LP 4052) *** $7 $15
- DRAIN MY BRAIN (Cadet LPS 4054) *1/2 $6 $12
- CROUCHIN' ON THE OUTSIDE (Janus 2JS 3052) ** $10 $20

Silverstein was a cartoonist during the Korean War, and in 1956 he issued a paperback called *Grab Your Socks*. He later shaved his head, grew a beard, and drew more satiric cartoons for *Playboy*. The Smothers Brothers covered some of his songs and he later wrote hits for Johnny Cash, The Irish Rovers, Dr. Hook, and many country stars. Periodically he recorded his own comic folk songs but his unique, raspy voice and twisted lyrics were too much for most listeners. Today, while aging hipsters know him for the records, kids love him as "Uncle Shelby," author of best-selling children's books.

The very rare 1959 "Hairy" album is strictly for Shel's die-hard fans. Most of the cuts on this sloppy quasi-Dixieland album are straight: "If I Could Shimmy Like My Sister Kate," "I'm Satisfied with My Girl," "A Good Man Is Hard to Find." The album notes by Jean Shepherd are funnier than Shel's renditions of "Kitchen Man," "Go Back Where You Got It Last Night," or "Somebody Else, Not Me."

"Sings" (recorded in October of 1965, and also known as "I'm So Good That I Don't Have to Brag") is a live album filled with wild comic folk songs for the times. Some are dated, but many are still frisky, especially the *Playboy*-oriented cuts: the boastful "I'm So Good ...," "Plastic" (describing a world where everything's artificial—even a girl's curves), and "Ever Lovin' Machine," about a robot: "She has no trouble making her mind up, for I did not give her a mind. And her heart is a clock that a wind up. So I know that she'll love me in time." He loves her shocking love techniques, but it all ends badly: "She always did what she was supposed ter, right up till this evening but then ... she had an affair with the toaster, and they ran off and left me again!"

Other cuts include "Modern Talk," "The Mermaid," "The Ugliest Man in Town," and serious numbers "I Can't Touch the Sun," "Yowsah," and "I Once Knew a Woman."

"Drain My Brain" is more straight than comedy, including ridiculous attempts at rock like "Whoo Doo Voo Doo Lady" and "My Mind Keeps Movin'." Folkie ballads include "I Can't Touch the Sun" (again) and "Rings of Brass." There's the mildly funky "Handy Man" and some dumb nonsense songs like the one about a girl who turns down his advances because she owns a "Floobie Doobie Doo": "Oh a floobie doobie doo, now what is that? It ain't no dog, and it ain't no cat. It's nine feet tall with eyes of blue. I never seen such a thing as a floobie doobie doo!" The title cut is a mildly satiric dance tune: "Baby drain my brain! Unscrew my head, take apart my heart ... ya got me talkin' to my elbow, climbin' up the wall."

The early '70s double set for Janus duplicates the Cadet albums: "Better Not Ask Me," "Floobie Doobie Do," "Modern Talk," "Ugliest Man in Town," "Plastic," "I'm So Good," "Grizzly Bear," "Workin' it Out," "I Once Knew a Woman," "Ever Lovin' Machine," "Dance to It," "Hoodoo Voodoo Lady," "Changing of the Season," "Testing the Bomb," and "Drain My Brain."

- INSIDE FOLK SONGS (Atlantic SD 8072,
    reissued as INSIDE SHEL SILVERSTEIN, Atlantic SD 8257). ***1/2 $10 $25

One of the great folk-comedy albums, and sporting a manic portrait of pop-eyed, bearded Shelby on the cover, several cuts on this low-selling but highly recommended album were later covered successfully by The Smothers Brothers. These are the short "folk jokes" like "The Slitheree-dee," "The Civil War Song," and "Boa Constrictor." Johnny Cash did a cover of his "25 Minutes to Go," an exciting, semi-humorous ballad about a convict's last moments before a hanging. His ironic Bible story, "The Unicorn," was a hit for The Irish Rovers.

The rest are pure Shel, sung to perfection in his raspy, rascally voice. "Never Bite a Married Woman on the Thigh" is a gem, a silly W. C. Fieldsian recital. "Bananas" is very similar to Stan Freberg's complaints about Harry Belafonte, and "Wreck of the Old 49" parodies the entire genre of railroad crash songs.

Many tunes cover laid-back beatnik philosophy. A guy who has seen a lot of life realizes that after you've been having steak for a long time, "Beans Taste Fine." And sometimes it's better to just sit around and "Have Another Espresso." But that lifestyle of the late '50s and early '60s is also parodied in "Bury Me in My Shades," about a hapless dude's last requests—which are ignored by his snickering friends. "It Does Not Pay to Be Hip" is the last word on the subject.

The most memorable cut is "You're Always Welcome at Our House," Uncle Shelby's cheerful report on an Addams Family-type child and his reaction to visitors: "A lady came to our house. Our house, our house ... to find out why I wasn't in school. So we asked her to come in, and we gave her some poison lemonade, and hid her in the freezer where it's nice and cool ... but you're always welcome at our house." And on it goes through many inventively ghoulish verses.

- BOY NAMED SUE (RCA Victor LSP 4192) ** $5 $10

"Who ever heard of a Jewish hillbilly songwriter?" the album notes for this 1969 album ask. Silverstein's effort to break into the record world after about seven years absence was not successful.

Like Bob Dylan, Silverstein has a voice that is expressive and at times exciting, but has weaknesses that are easily exposed by the wrong production. Chet Atkins and Felton Jarvis are not the right producers for Shel. His voice comes out pureed here as he strains against the confines of traditional and humorless country and western arrangements. Some of the songs are not intended to be funny, but a few could've been, like "Daylight Dreamer," about a guy who never finishes anything he starts, or "Pathetic Way of Getting Over Me," in which a guy insists that his girl is just trying to make him jealous by shouting "hooray I'm free" and going out with other guys. The stilted arrangements submerge the lusty, gravelly-voiced glory of Silverstein's voice.

His own version of "Boy Named Sue" has its moments (he catches fire when he finds his tormenting father and shouts "My name is Soooooo! How do you DOOOOOO!") but the tepid guitar picking arrangement fails to back Shel up. It's neither a pungent ballad (as Cash covered it) or outrageous comedy (as Shel could've covered it).

- FREAKIN' AT THE FREAKERS BALL (Columbia KC 31119) *** $5 $10

Silverstein found a perfect match with "Dr. Hook and the Medicine Show," and not only appeared with them in the Dustin Hoffman film *Who is Harry Kellerman ...*, but gave them a string of hit tunes starting with "Sylvia's Mother."

In 1972, the boys repaid Shel by sitting in on this freewheeling Ron Haffkine-produced album that has the same loose, party atmosphere that characterized the early Dr. Hook albums. Relaxed and vibrant, shout-singing and yowling out some of the most ridiculous songs of all time, Shel offers the classic "Sarah Cynthia Sylvia Stout Would Not Take the Garbage Out" (an eye-popping kiddie tune that wildly lists the repulsive contents of a garbage can) and a sly ballad for the times, "I Got Stoned and I Missed It."

Most of the tunes are semi-pornographic idiocy like "Thumbsucker," "Polly in a Porny," "Stacy Brown Got Two," "Don't Give a Dose to the One You Love Most," and "Masochistic Baby" ("ever since my masochistic baby left me I got nothin' to hit but the wall ... nothin' to beat but the eggs, nothin' to belt but my pants, nothin' to whip but the cream").

Dr. Hook covered "Freakers Ball," but Shel matches it with his good-humored gravelly rendition, enjoying a party where the chant is, "Pass that roach, pour the wine, I'll kiss yours if you'll kiss mine." The action has "FBI dancin' with the junkies, all the straights swingin' with the funkies ... plastercasters castin' their plasters, masturbators baitin' their masters."

A few serious tunes about war and astrology are out of place on this brawling disc.

- SONGS AND STORIES (Parachute/Casablanca RRLP 9007) ** $4 $8
- THE GREAT CONCH ROBBERY (Flying Fish FF 211) ** $4 $8

The 1978 Parachute album sounds like somebody doing a bad job of imitating Shel Silverstein. The overacted "Peanut Butter Sandwich" recalls "Sarah Cynthia Stout." "Someone Ate the Baby" is a variation on "Boa Constrictor" as he whispers "I simply can't imagine who would go and eat the baby." Then he burps. When he covers a number from "Inside Folk Songs," "Never Bite a Married Woman on the Thigh," it's so overdone it's hard to believe he wrote it.

About the only song here worthy of Shel is "They Held Me Down," a variation on "I Got Stoned and I Missed It" or "Daylight Dreamer" that laughs at losers who blame everyone but themselves.

It's hard to believe that Shel, and not some imitator, would dare try a sequel to "Boy Named Sue." Silverstein really trashes his hit song about the country boy who tracks down his father after leaving him as a child with a ridiculous name. Here, Shel tells the story from the father's point of view, and it becomes an odiously campy number with embarrassing gay humor.

It starts out funny enough. Dad admits that he left his kid: "That kid kept screamin' and throwin' up and pissin' in his pants till I had enough, so just for revenge I went and named him Sue." Then suddenly he meets that boy again: "Through the door with an awful scream comes the ugliest Queen I ever seen. He says, 'My name is Sue! How do you do!' And then he hit me with his purse!"

According to Dad, the boy named Sue didn't fight fair, kicking and scratching like a woman. And instead of biting off a piece of ear, Sue punches Dad in the stomach and knocks out a piece of lint. "Then out of his garter he pulls a gun. I'm about to get shot by my very own son. He's screamin' about Sigmund Freud and lookin' grim." Dad manages to explain why he named his kid Sue, and they live together. "And on the nights that I can't score ... it's a joy to have a boy named Sue."

"Conch Robbery" from 1980 is short on wit and comedy. The big joke on the guy in "Don't Go to Sleep on the Road" is that he got hemorrhoids. The grim ironic humor of "Rough on the Living" is that a famous dead singer is only remembered by a few moments of silence ("Nashville is rough on the living, but she really speaks well of the dead.") The drug satire of "Quaaludes Again" is on the girl who "fumbles and stumbles and falls down the stairs, makes love to the leg of the dining room chair. She's ready for animals, women, or men. She's doin' quaaludes again." There are a lot of fairly straight country cuts, some with squeamy fiddle playing.

- WHERE THE SIDEWALK ENDS (Columbia FC 39412) ** $5 $10
- A LIGHT IN THE ATTIC (Columbia FC 40219) ** $5 $10

Silverstein's children's books (with plenty of material for adults to enjoy, too) have become classics, including *The Giving Tree*, *The Missing Piece*, and these two whimsical collections. *A Light in the Attic* spent nearly three straight years on the *New York Times*' best-seller list.

The stories and poems take the children's side. Typical of the poems on "A Light in the Attic" is "How Not to Have to Dry the Dishes" ("if you have to dry the dishes and you drop one on the floor—maybe they won't let you dry the dishes anymore") and "The Homework Machine."

The "Sidewalk" collection includes some of Shel's most famous numbers: the "Sarah Cynthia Stout" garbage recitation, "Peanut Butter Sandwich," and "Boa Constrictor." Shel reads all of this with raspy, heavy-breathing enthusiasm—and it's entirely possible some little kids would be alarmed, if not outright frightened.

SINA

- INSIDE SINA (Charm CM 100) * $5 $10

"The Society for Indecency to Naked Animals" was a gag organization that gave Buck Henry some good publicity in the early '60s. People weren't sure if this (then-anonymous) fellow was serious or not. He appeared on the news and on talk shows with his complaint that animals should be clothed.

"Inside SINA," by Bruce Spencer, tries to bring the hoax to disc. There is nothing on the album jacket to indicate that this is a comedy album, but as Spencer begins his long lecture on SINA, including a question and answer segment, it's obvious that this is a joke. The joke wears very thin and the tinny quality of the sound doesn't help.

SINBAD

- BRAIN DAMAGED (Wing/Mercury 8419012) ** $8

A bulky, sometimes brawling comic rewarded with his own sitcom in 1993, Sinbad got his first cable TV special three years earlier. The CD version expands it to seventy-five minutes with forgettable comic rap songs, phone calls, and sound collages. Sinbad meanders through some easy targets (big butts and Mike Tyson). Admittedly influenced by Bill Cosby, Sinbad is big on observational comedy, but only rarely does he get anywhere near the universality of Cos: "When a man gets married, women suck the brain out of your head. You become severely stupid for the rest of your life!"

THE SINGING DOCTORS

- THANKS FOR THE MISERIES (American Artists 1355) ** $5 $10
- KEEP YOU IN STITCHES (American Artists 1052) ** $5 $10

The Singing Doctors performed for charity, raising money for the Scholarship Foundation of the Greene County Medical Society in Springfield, Missouri. For a bunch of amateurs, they don't do a bad job of grafting parody lyrics to popular tunes. Oddly enough, in addition to the expected jokes about hemorrhoids and psoriasis they sing some pretty insulting lyrics about doctors. On "Keep You in Stitches" one of them solos on a variation on "Foggy, Foggy Dew," singing: "You may need a specialist, complete check-up too. I'll admit that it is no fun. For the only, only thing he ever seems to do is refer you to another one. They look in every orifice. And make some new ones too. The only only time he ever speaks to you is to call you when your bill is overdue."

The Singing Doctors also released a few ten-inch albums on a private label.

RED SKELTON

- ORIGINAL RADIO BROADCASTS (Mark 56 # 699) **1/2 $5 $10
- RADIO'S ROGUE'S GALLERY (Radiola MR 1108) **1/2 $5 $10

Both albums feature Red's characters in radio sketches. Mark 56 has Sheriff Deadeye, the corrupt San Fernando Red, The Mean Widdle Kid (in "The Store"), and drunken Willie Lump Lump in a long sketch as well. Clem Kadiddlehopper is typically goofy while hard at work:

"I don't know what I'm hammerin' on but I gotta fix it! Oh, now I recognize it. It's my thumb!" "... how stupid can you get!" "Well, that's pretty hard to tell, I ain't fully developed yet!"

Radiola's full hour offers nine excerpts including some for lesser known characters Cauliflower McPugg, Boliver Shagnasty, and 42nd St. pitchman Mickey the Rat. Red even sings the classic folk tune "The Fox" semi-seriously (the Smothers Brothers covered this one twenty years later). There's a half-hour version of "The Fuller Brush Man" as well.

Skelton's scripts, whatever the character, always had a solid amount of gags, many of them genially corny. On radio, Red doesn't indulge in the deliberate breaking up and free-wheeling ad-libs that were trademarks of his television show. The results here are a little restrained, but give a pretty good idea of Red's heartland style of good-natured comedy.

NOTES: Skelton gets a full hour on the five-CD Set "Radio's Greatest Comedians" (Prime Time Nostalgia PTN 724) and can be heard on a few compilation discs, notably as the "Mean Widdle Kid" on Evolution's "Golden Age of Comedy (Evolution 3013)."

Skelton put out two straight music albums, "Red Skelton Conducts" (Liberty 7425) and "Music from the Heart," (Liberty 7477). He also made a Columbia 45 of his version of "The Pledge of Allegiance," a line by line analysis of what the words meant. On the flip side, a sentimental appreciation of circus clowns. About five minutes of Red live in concert appears on "My Favorite Story" (20th Century Fox TFM 3106).

SKILES AND HENDERSON

- DO IT DO IT DO IT (Liberty LST 7596) **1/2 $6 $12

Skiles and Henderson specialized in lighthearted mimicry. A favorite with young viewers on variety shows during the '60s, Pete and Bill had some of Jonathan Winters's skill in imitating all kinds of odd noises. Highlights here include the sound cartoon of Cole Porter trying to come up with a hit song while a repairman fixes a creaky door with oil. "Birds ..." Cole Porter muses. "Do-it!" goes the oil can.

The guys do their famous bit imitating the feedback of microphones in a giant lecture hall where Dr. Arthur Vark (Art Vark) is giving a speech. Dr. Vark is an extremely silly scientist who feeds his pet lion hay ("When he died he was already stuffed") and interrupts his interviewer for ridiculous remarks: "You have bad breath! You've been eating lizards!"

Their friendly foolery made Skiles and Henderson very much a family-oriented act along with The Smothers Brothers. This late '60s LP still has some innocent vitality to it.

SKILLET AND LEROY

- BIG DEAD DICK (Laff A 144) ** $5 $10
- THE OKRA EATERS (Laff A 174) ** $5 $10
- BURGLAR IN THE BEDROOM (Laff A 141) ** $5 $10
- TWO OR THREE TIMES A DAY (Laff A 131) ** $5 $10
- BACK DOOR DADDY (Laff A 156) ** $5 $10
- THE GOODLY SOUL (Laff A 149) ** $5 $10

Skillet and Leroy (Skillet Mayhand and Sloppy Daniels) are loud and raucous in the Pigmeat Markham tradition— and the '60s Laff albums sound even tinnier than the Markham albums from the '50s. There's plenty of funky rambling and posturing before these two get to the punch line, but that's part of their charm for fans of jiving black comedy. Their material is rarely original, but it doesn't matter for the duo's fans. On "The Goodly Soul" album, they do a soul version of a scene from Ernst Lubitsch's 1932 "Trouble in Paradise." Instead of two urbane thieves pick-pocketing each other slyly, a funky female stooge and Leroy match their thieving talents:

"Hug me baby, hug me honey," Leroy says. "I'm huggin' you, Daddy." "You got a butt, heiffer! Hug me!" "You outtasight. I heard about your reputation." "Here's yo ring," Leroy says. "Well, I'll be a son of a biscuit eater," the woman mutters. "I shake yo hand and cleaned yo butt out...." "Pretty damn slick ... yeah ... well, I don't want to beat you ... but there's yo money, baby. When I shook your hand I took your roll...." "You hugged me and got my money ... I'm a little slicker than you, honey ... you goin' outside?" "Yeah, I'm goin' outside, damn right." "It's cold out there, you know that." "I ain't catchin' no cold." "Lookie there, baby! Here's yo drawers!"

Daniels also released a solo album.

MENASHA SKULNIK

- MENASHA SKULNIK (Banner 1003) ** $4 $8

Skulnik was the most beloved performer in Yiddish theater. The album collects a lot of his old 78s, most in Yiddish. "I'm Sam the Man Who Made the Pants Too Long," veers between the two languages.

Like the later Mickey Katz, Skulnik uses a stereotypical accent and a high nasal voice that some will find annoying. Still, Skulnik's unassuming charm shows through on the one completely English language cut, "Cardova the Bronx Casinova," in which the joke is his boasts ("the girls all say I'm just their type, for every new romance I get a service stripe") contrasted with his pathetic, whining delivery.

Skulnik appears on a few Broadway original cast albums and reads "The Stories of Sholem Aleichem" (Caedmon TC 1173).

STUART SMALLEY

- YOU'RE GOOD ENOUGH, YOU'RE SMART ENOUGH (BDD BMG-353CD) ** $8

Al Franken's character of the lisping, nattering New Age nurturer Stuart Smalley became a favorite on *Saturday Night Live*. On the show, the short sketches (usually with guest star foils) were often very funny. Here, forty-eight solid minutes of Stuart is difficult to take in this satire of self help audios involving "guided visualizations" to achieve relaxation and well being.

Piano and flute provide appropriately annoying and metronomic music as Stuart offers lame instructions ("relax and surrender yourself"), babbles about "the inner child," and periodically offers up his catchphrases ("stinkin' thinkin'" "that's okay," etc.) The nurturer also has mock arguments with his sound engineer because, he whines, "I'm so terrified this tape is gonna suck!"

EFFIE SMITH

- DIAL THAT TELEPHONE (Jubilee 2057) ** $5 $10

Fans who enjoy hearing a woman complain will get plenty on this album of black character comedy. There aren't many jokes here as Effie Smith (as "Ruby Lee") makes phone calls and deals with her hubby. Listeners might find some recognition comedy in Smith's funky attitude, which pre-dates Flip Wilson's Geraldine:

"Hello? Mabel? This is Ruby Lee, honey. Guess what I gone done! Girl I done bought myself a blond wig. Watchoo mean have I lost my mind! What is Henry gon' say? Henry better not say nuthin'! Henry might tell me when to come and go and all that kinda mess, but when it comes to tellin' me what to wear on my head, somethin' gotta go ... call me later."

Later, her husband Henry appears to bicker with her:

"Woman, what in the world is that thing you got on your head!"

"It's a wig, that's what it is ... and I bought it!"

"You bought it? With my money? Woman, you ain't got no business spendin' my money on no wig! I put money in this house for bacon, eggs, po'k chops and dog food ... you ain't gonna wear that thing in the street ... you sure got a lotta nerve."

Jazz backing helps keep things going.

RALPH SMITH

- TAKE IT EASY (Monument PW 38531) ** $4 $8

South Carolina-born Smith takes a semi-Evangelical approach, punching out his material with fervent conviction. Some of the anecdotal stories are old 'uns but good 'uns. He tells the one about the wino who was drinking some Boone's Farm when a car hit him. "Yeah, hit him, knock him up against the side of the building there. I run up to him, helped him up as best I could. All of a sudden he felt something warm and wet runnin' down his leg. He looked around at me and said, 'Lord, I hope that's blood!'"

SMITH AND DALE

- AT THE PALACE (Jubilee 2035) **1/2 $20 $40
- THE GOLDEN BEST OF SMITH AND DALE
  (Timestu TS 81600, also issued as Bramal 59 and TBCSD 1247) *** $10 $20

The classic vaudevillians Joe Smith and Charlie Dale amused audiences for fifty years doing their "Dr. Kronkite" routine. This late '50s album has it recorded before a sparse but enthusiastic audience. The opening is familiar, of course:

"Are you a doctor?" "I'm a doctor." "I'm dubious." "I'm glad to know you, Mr. Dubious." And so are most of the jokes that follow it: "I have snoo in my blood." "Snoo? What's snoo?" "Nothing, what's snoo with you!"

Like "Who's on First," there's something magical about the corny routine and it's performed with endearing charm by these Jewish accented funnymen. Three more routines are included: "Shnapps and Strudel," "Tax Consultant," and "Boss and Chef." These pretty much follow the same formula. A meeting on the street:

"And how is things with you?" "How should it be?" "I'm glad to hear that. And you're making plenty of money?" "How much can I make?" "So much! What business are you in?" "I'm in every business that begins with an "A." I'm a matchmaker, a jewelry salesman, a furniture salesman...." "Who's furniture are you selling?" "So far I am selling my own!" "... how do you make a living?" "I make a living by my wits. By my Uncle Balcowitz and my Aunt Berkowitz."

Smith and Dale's easy patter may be a bit antique, but it is so deeply rooted in evocative characterization, so well polished over the years, and performed with such sincerity that it transcends itself.

"Golden Best" is a bootleg "private collectors" album. The "Dr. Kronkite" sketch here is from a TV variety show and has some additions and alterations. Another routine features Smith and Dale on an ocean voyage: "The sea gulls are here." "The Siegels are here? I thought they were still in Miami." The rest of the album is filler. The Smith and Dale side ends with an anonymous "laughing record" (a trumpeter tries to play but messes up. The audience laughs, and laughs, and laughs, and laughs.) The duo's fans will have lots of laughs here, though not as much from the flip side, a bunch of 78 rpm singles from Moran and Mack, "The Two Black Crows."

An abbreviated version of the "Dr. Kronkite" sketch appears on Evolution's "Golden Age of Comedy."

THE SMOTHERS BROTHERS

- AT THE PURPLE ONION (Mercury SR 60611/MG 20611) ** $5 $10
- TWO SIDES OF THE SMOTHERS BROTHERS (Mercury SR 60675/MG 20675) **1/2 $5 $10

Originally part of "The Casual Quintet" playing folk gigs, the brothers became a duo and found success when their between-song patter got a better response than the tunes. They soon developed more comic songs to complement the routines. Tom and Dick's fresh, child-like routines and folk songs marked a change from the previous era's "sicknik" comics and "beatnik" jazz.

The brothers are still working on their balance of straight songs and comedy on their first two albums. The humor is mostly in comic introductions on "Purple Onion." Before launching "Dance Boatman Dance," Tom stumbles over the introduction: "These boat men take their meagers weeks penances...." "No, that's not right." "Money. Weegers meeks ... uh, lousy wages ... these boatmen come into town and pick up their oars!" "Shame on you, that's enough."

THE GAY SOUND OF LAUGHTER

In the '60s and '70s Paul Lynde was one of the few gay comedians to be openly "quirky," while Charles Pierce has been a cult favorite for decades doing his mimicry of female stars.

DOES IT SOUND BETTER IN STEREO?

Some of the comedy teams that made records: Allen and Rossi, The Smothers Brothers, and Rowan and Martin. And what recording engineer thought it was so smart to stick one comic on the right channel and the other all the way on the left?

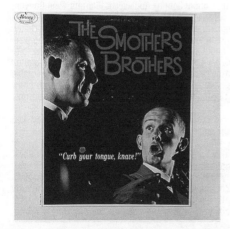

"Two Sides" literally splits routines on one side and straight songs on the other, including such awfully lightweight embarrassments as "Stella's Got a New Dress" and "If It Fits Your Fancy." The comedy side has a few classics in their song and history lecture about railroad men eating boiled "Cabbage," the song "Map of the World" (about a tattooed lady whose "chest was Bunker Hill"), and Pat Paulsen's novelty tune about falling into a vat of chocolate: "I yelled, 'Fire!' when I fell into the vat of chocolate...." "Why'd you yell, 'Fire!' when you fell into the vat of chocolate?" "Cause nobody would save me if I yelled, 'Chocolate!'"

- THINK ETHNIC (Mercury Sr 60777/MG 20777) *** $5 $10
- CURB YOUR TONGUE, KNAVE (Mercury SR/60862 MG/20862) **1/2 $5 $10
- IT MUST HAVE BEEN SOMETHING I SAID (Mercury SR 60904/MG 20904) *** $5 $10
- IT'S SMOTHERS BROTHERS MONTH (Mercury MGDJ 25) **1/2 $5 $10

"Think Ethnic" was the first real Smothers Brothers comedy album. It's loaded with silly non-song quickies, like Tom singing:

"Soap, soap, soap, soap, soap, soap, soap, soap—"
"What are you doing?"
"Singing about eight bars."

The boys begin to get into their bickering brothers character on "The Fox," where Tom insists on adding sound effects despite prissy Dick's irritated warnings. Similarly, Tom happily wrecks the story of "John Henry" with interruptions and excited overacting. There's nothing much to quote here. As Tom once admitted to me, "We were the most unquoted comics ... there were very few real jokes on our old albums. It was our attitude. It was all in the timing."

The Smothers Brothers may not have been the first to mine childhood for humor (there was Fanny Brice's Baby Snooks and Red Skelton's Mean Widdle Kid) but they were unique in portraying childlike characters. Tom told me, "we did 'puberty comedy' on the awkardness of going into adulthood."

"Curb Your Tongue, Knave" is a disappointment with only one classic cut, "Church Bells." It's a silly musical joke about the different bells in the Catholic, Protestant, and Jewish centers of worship in a little town. Other tracks include "Incredible Jazz Banjoist," "Gnus," and a fair routine about Johnny Appleseed ("American History 1a") and little known folk hero Big Ben Covington: "He had hands the size of basketballs. No fingers, just basketballs."

"It Must Have Been ..." is one of their best. While there's still bickering (a ten-minute bit about how Hiawatha went from "poverty into manhood") their songs have grown up, from the flippant "Civil War Song" and frisky "Crabs Walk Sideways" to the black-humor parody of teen love songs, "Jenny Brown." When compared to the original (see George Wood) it becomes obvious that the boys were brilliant not only in choosing but refining comic material. And Tom's underrated ability to wring laughter from personality alone is evident on many cuts here, including "Population Explosion."

"Smothers Brothers Month" was issued to radio stations in the mid-60s when the brothers starred in their first series, a sitcom. Side Two offers excerpts from the first five albums plus a few promotional skits. Side One has a "minus one" interview. There's space between the brothers' answers for the disc jockey to pose the questions (printed on the back cover). The idea was to pretend the boys were actually in town for a live interview. The boys answer many questions, from "Who cuts your hair" to "Tell us the funniest and saddest incidents of your career" to "Which other comedians do you look up to most?" The boys both answer "Jonathan Winters" to the last one.

- TOUR DE FARCE AMERICAN HISTORY (Mercury SR 60948/MG 20948) *** $5 $10
- AESOP'S FABLES (Mercury Sr 60989/MG 20989)
- MOM ALWAYS LIKED YOU BEST (Mercury SR 61051/MG 21051) *** $5 $10
- SMOTHERS COMEDY BROTHERS HOUR (Mercury/Rubicon SR 61193) *** $6 $12
- SIBLING REVELRY: THE BEST OF THE SMOTHERS BROTHERS (Rhino 70188) *** $8

The Smothers Brothers specialized in routines about American history, probably because the folk boom of the early '60s was steeped in songs about wagon trains, John Henry, and the Civil War. Kids loved these routines since they were just learning about Johnny Appleseed, Pilgrims, Paul Bunyon, and George Washington in school. On "Tour De Farce" Tommy is like a class clown, lampooning teacher Dick's discussions of the greats. Oddly, the songs have nothing to do with American History—or anything else. "Mediocre Fred" is about a dullard who turns into a throat-biting vampire at night! And "Since My Canary Died" (by the team who wrote *Fiddler on the Roof*) veers into the kind of "sick" comedy kids love. There *is* a quotable sibling rivalry joke here, with Dick getting the best of it. "Do you know why I'm mad most of the time?" he snipes. "It's difficult being an only child."

"Aesop's Fables" is a studio album intended for kids. The boys, backed by a studio band, present "The Farmer and His Sons," "The Fox and the Grapes," "The Boy Who Cried Wolf," and others. Some typical light humor in the tales. From the latter: "Oh Wolf! Here Wolf! Here Wolfie!" "What are you doing that for?" "I'm just showing them how the boy cried wolf." "He didn't cry to the wolf, he cried to the villagers!" "Sounds like a crybaby to me." "You don't understand, the boy cried wolf even though there was no wolf around, he just wanted excitement." "If that's his idea of excitement...." The moral set to music: "If you lie, you'll find this is true: the one you hurt most is really you!" The album was reissued on CD.

"Mom Always Liked You Best" has some definitive routines on the brothers' favorite subject. "Sure she liked me best!" Dick shouts. "I never knew Mom liked you best," Tom gasps. "You wanna know why Mom liked me best? Because I happen to be an only child!" "Touchy, touchy." "Touché!Touché!"

The boys recall their childhood pets (Tom had a chicken), argue to the point of futility ("You Can Call Me Stupid"), and amid all the fighting, get in one good novelty tune, the oddly cadenced and cleverly performed (on their variety show) "Last Great Waltz."

Although their variety show evolved into something satirical (and considered radical), the album was issued early in the run and most of the routines are harmless, like "Troubador Song" with Dick attempting to sing a medieval folk tune about nightingales—while Tom interrupts with chirps. The political satire turns up in a few quickies that, today, seem innocuous. Yet CBS cast a bloodshot eye when Tom described his theory on clothes and politics: "You can tell who's running the country by the amount of clothes they wear." The people who can afford less clothing are the less-ons. Who's running the country? "The more-ons!"

The boys had a tough time regaining their momentum after CBS canceled their show. Eventually they re-emerged with a balance of adult humor and childishness (Tom's yo-yo exhibitions) that made them "family entertainment" on tour, nostalgia for those who grew up with them and fun for a new generation of kids. In 1988 Rhino reissued fourteen cuts, including quirky songs ("Crabs Walk Sideways," "Mediocre Fred," "Jenny Brown") and classic feuds. The liner notes are by Shari Roman. Tom had written the notes for an album by her late father, Murray.

NOTES: A televised version of "Cabbage" is on "Here's Johnny" (Casablanca SPNB 1296). Some cuts from the first five Smothers Brothers albums are on the disc jockey-only release "The Best of the Smothers Brothers" (Mercury MGD-20).

Die-hard fans will want "The Smothers Brothers Play It Straight" (Mercury SR 61064). There are only two comedy cuts. The boys, backed by workmanlike orchestrations, offer pop pap ("Lark Day") and ordinary cover versions ("Yesterday"). Their best try is a stalwart folk version of "Silver Threads and Golden Needles." The high spot is Tom's solo on the self-penned, "Hound Dog Blues," a comic bit of scat-singing idiocy that Bill Cosby could've covered in his pseudo-singing career. The last cut "Almost," has the only spoken word comedy, with Tom predictably goofing around as the conductor who wrecks Dickie's attempt to sing a bombastic ballad.

SOCIETY'S HOT NUTS

• BULLSXXT SESSION (Wild-Hare 100) * $4 $8

Definitely not to be confused with Doug Clark's Hot Nuts, these guys don't sing, don't play instruments, and don't even tell good dirty jokes. The title of the album is accurate: this is just a taped bull session as nameless guys swap stories, braying their "woo hoo's" and "hee HEE's" every time one half-drunk joker finishes "a good one." As an aural example of street fools laughing it up in somebody's apartment, this is authentic. That's about its only value.

A typical gag that needs a bottle of Ripple to make sense: "I had a cat in my neighborhood, man, he used to tee-tee in the bed ... and his daddy made him drink some of his own tee-tee because this old lady down the street used to read palms, told him: 'I read in your son's hand where it says to stop him from tee-teeing in the bed, make him drink a can of his own tee-tee.' And the father did so! And this son has been tee-teeing ever since!"

SOLMS AND PARENT

• OUR WEDDING ALBUM (Jamie 3028) * $4 $8
• HERE COMES THE BIRD (Atco Records) * $4 $8
• I WERE A HIGH SCHOOL GRADUATE (Epic FLM 3312) * $5 $10

Kenny Solms and Gail Parent made a pair of albums lampooning the weddings of Lynda Bird ("Here Comes the Bird") and Lucy Baines ("Our Wedding Album") Johnson. They're interchangeable, obvious, and uninteresting.

From "Our Wedding Album," Lucy comes rushing in to tell Lady Bird (Fannie Flagg) about her engagement: "Oh that's wonderful, Lynda Bird." "I'm Lucy Baines." "Oh." When she tells her sister Lynda Bird (Jo Ann Worley) the results are about the same: "I'm engaged!" "It's about time, Lynda Bird." "No, you're Lynda Bird, I'm Lucy Baines."

Meanwhile Lucy's betrothed must speak to Lyndon (Robert Klein): "I'm here to talk to you about marriage." "I'm already married son." "No, I wanna marry your daughter." "Fine ... it's about time Lynda Bird settled down." "Not Lynda Bird, Lucy Baines."

The cast on "Here Comes the Bird" is lesser: Solms and Parent as bride and groom, with Carlton J. Blandert as Lyndon, Nancie Phillips as Lady Bird, and JoAnne Worley as Lucy.

Their third album is a lame collection of sketches about school days. One of the better ones is a phone call from a distraught guidance counselor: "It's about the field trip. I'm still on it." "You're still on it? You left yesterday afternoon, what happened!" "Oh everything. The bus broke down. Well, not really the bus, the bus driver broke down. He couldn't stand the singing." Robert Klein is in the cast, with Rip Taylor (billed back then as "The Crying Comedian") and Marian Mercer.

Gail Parent later went on to write a few seriocomic novels.

DAN SORKIN

• FOLK SINGING ONE (Mercury Sr 60861) *1/2 $4 $8

During the folk boom of the mid-60s, radio disc jockey Dan Sorkin put together this comic "lesson" in folk singing, featuring examples sung by "The Plucker Family," with John Brown as Father Plucker, Maxine Sellers as (you guessed it) Mother Plucker, and George McKelvey and Joel Cory as The Brothers Plucker. Chad Mitchell was the recording director.

The results are feeble, with gags that sound almost ad-libbed: "Hootenannies; named because of a famous exporter of folksingers from Terre Haute, Indiana, Edgar Hootenanny." The songs aren't much better. One is about a guy named "Three-Handed Brown," who made a name for himself at demonstrations. It ends limply: "He had one right hand, and one left hand. Folks used to ask what he called his other hand. He said he called it Fred. Now it's hard to wash a garlic press and it's hard to wear a crown. But forget about your picket line without Three Handed Brown."

ANNE SOULE

- SHE'S GONE! (New Sound NS 3001) ** $7 $15

Billed as a "song satirist," Soule recorded her lone ten-inch album for a San Francisco label. She was subtitled "The Sweetheart of Sigmund Freud," and her material recalls the arch and sophisticated style of late '50s cabaret comedy. It may amuse fans of that genre. She accompanies herself on the piano singing a happy ditty about Oedipus, vamping, "Eddie Puss! He was a sexy prexy that Oedipus Rexy; and the gods gave him apoplexy!"

Bea Lillie could've sung "Do de Do," a fey parody of cheerful ballads, sung in a babyish voice: "Where are you? Doo dee doo dee doo! I'll cheer you up if you're blue! Doo dee doo dee doo! You are my guy, my honey pie, and I am yours! Unless there really is a possibili-tee, a faint possibil-tee, that you don't love me! Doo dee doo dee doo!"

Monologues break up the songs. She lectures as the author of "Thought Patterns of the Amoeba and Their Persistence in the Republican Party Today." And in an odd vaudevillian twist, she performs Poe's "The Raven" in Jewish dialect: "Lenore. She died, ya know. All of a sudden is coming de tapping ... in is coming de raven, he's going and perching on, you should pardon de expression, de bust upon de door. He is looking at me, I am looking at him, and he don't look like much. I'm saying, 'What's your name please?' And he's saying, 'Nevermore!' What kind of name, dis?"

BRUCE SPENCER

- THE BEST OF CRAZY ADS (World Pacific WP 1407) *1/2 $4 $8

Trying to perk up riders in Minneapolis, a transportation executive named Jay Murray began sticking fake classified ads on the buses. The idea led to a novelty book and, as produced by Bruce Spencer, an album. Ya hadda be there riding the bus, because when stolid Spencer recites them to his live audience, they die:

"For sale, ferocious watch dog. Will eat anything. Very fond of children. Wanted, skilled engraver. Must be familiar with the faces of Washington and Lincoln.... Oh, this is interesting: slightly used caboose. Just painted bright red. Sleeps two. Ready to roll. One hundred feet of railroad track free. First two hundred dollars takes it. Come to Delaware and Hudson freightyard after midnight."

For another Spencer record see the entry under SINA.

SPINAL TAP

- THIS IS SPINAL TAP (Polydor CD 817846-2) ** $8
- BREAK LIKE THE WIND (MCA MCAD 10514) ** $8

Veteran National Lampoon vocalist Christopher Guest, along with ex-Credibility Gap members Harry Shearer and Michael McKean, were Spinal Tap, a heavy metal group so close to the edge of satire that their albums were often placed in the legitimate rock section of stores. After all, the group is less condescending than Frank Zappa and not as obviously comic as the Bonzo Dog Band. No doubt there were many who put Queen's "Fat Bottomed Girls" on the turntable right after Spinal Tap's ode ("big bottom, talk about bum cakes my girl's got 'em ... how could I leave this behind). And who could be sure which was serious?

The tune is on their 1984 album, which goes along with the Rob Reiner-directed *This Is Spinal Tap* fake documentary. Eight years later the band with fatal drummer problems couldn't resist one last bash with a new album, "Break Like the Wind."

But again, on that album when the boys parody misogyny ("You whine and you beg, when I'm busy you wanna dance with my leg ... gonna have to send you back to Bitch School) or devil worship ("the sugar plums are rancid and the stockings are in flames. Christmas with the Devil!") the results are so close to actual serious rock songs that it's easy to imagine the tunes covered by Alice Cooper or Black Sabbath. Those old enough to appreciate the lyrics, intentionally bad imagery ("that Rainy Day Sun") or pseudo-Medieval pomp ("the crowing of the cock, the running of the foal ... the farmer takes a wife, the barber takes a pole. We're in this together") are probably too old to want to listen to the music.

RUSS SPOONER

- YOU'VE JUST BEEN SPOONERIZED (Mega M51-5007) *1/2 $3 $7

Spooner doesn't indulge in "spoonerisms," but another odd form of humor, the prank phone call. On this 1972 disc the WMAK Nashville DJ's practical jokes rarely lead to a big laugh. Russ usually calls a halt quickly, shouting his catchphrase, "You have just been Spoonerized!" In a typical gag, he calls up an adult movie theater to pridefully announce that he's the father of one of the stars and wants to bring his family down. He's told that nobody is admitted under the age of eighteen: "There's nudity and all that stuff." "Nudity?" "It's an adult movie." "You mean ... my daughter's nude? My my! What's your name?" "Vicki Jones." "You have just been Spoonerized!"

ARNOLD STANG

- WAGGISH TALES (ABC Paramount) $5 $10
- FAVORITE FUNNY STORIES (Peter Pan 8003) $7 $15

Both albums were aimed at children. On "Waggish Tales" Stang presents his versions of "Ferdinand the Bull" and "Peter and the Wolf." On 1962's "Favorite Funny Stories" Stang impersonates "Percy the Polite Seal," "Harry the Horse," "The Elephant Who Forgot," etc. The only cut that might amuse adult Stang fans is "Schloimy the Subway Train," about a Bronx train ordered to Brooklyn. The train is soon extolling the wonderful borough. Only a powerful metal train could sing, "We stayed there until it was dark in Brooklyn's beautiful Prospect Park."

Stang has recorded children's albums as his "Top Cat" cartoon character, and lends comic support on Henry Morgan's radio albums.

DAVE STARR

- THE NEARER THE BONE (Surprise SUR 98) **1/2 $5 $10

Brooklyn-born Starr has a raspy voice similar to B. S. Pully. Like Pully, he appeared in risqué clubs and onstage in *Guys and Dolls* roles needing a hefty comic bruiser. Fans of adult comedy will probably appreciate his party jokes told one after another:

"I was out West recently, and that's where I met my first woman sheriff. I tried to get into her posse.... A fellow just graduated, and his parents decide to send him to Europe. He's over in Europe for a couple of months. He cables his father, 'Dear Dad, send me five thousand dollars. I just met a Count.' He turns to his wife and says, 'Four years in college, can't spell one word right.' These two flies are walkin' down the street. One says, 'Hey, your man's open!' The other day I saw two dogs walk over to a parking meter. One of them says to the other, 'How do you like that. Pay toilets!'"

Starr appears on the Will Jordan album "All About Cleopatra."

DAVID STEINBERG

- THE INCREDIBLE SHRINKING GOD (Uni 73013) *** $6 $12
- DISGUISED AS A NORMAL PERSON (Elektra EKS 74065) *** $5 $10
- BOOGA BOOGA (Columbia KC 32563) **1/2 $8
- GOODBYE TO THE SEVENTIES (Columbia PC 33390) *1/2 $4 $8

Steinberg was twenty-seven when he put out his first album, with liner notes from Nelson Algren: "Lord Buckley's God looked upon Man with the golden eyes of love. Lenny Bruce's stayed in a towering rage. David Steinberg's God won't answer unless you call Him Mike ... That's the nice thing about Mike—there's nothing formidable about him." Steinberg, using the exagerrated, enunciated, shouting voice of the preacher, retells Bible stories: "Moses," "Job," "Cain and Abel," etc. They may seem mild now, but back in the '60s it was radical to tell the audience, "I can't do Onan tonight—I suggest you go home and do it yourself."

It was also radical for a Jew to talk about the Old Testament—lest some Gentiles remember where they got it from. In Steinberg's story of Jonah, he tells how the hapless Jew got into the whale: "The Gentiles, as is their wont from time to time, threw the Jew overboard." He compares the Old and New Testament versions of the story: "The Judaic concept is that Jonah was swallowed by a huge whale. The New Testament—the less popular of the two— they say, 'Hold it Jews, Jonah could not have been swallowed by a whale.' They literally hold the Jews by the old Testament. They say, 'Science tells us that whales have tiny gullets and cannot swallow whole prophets.' They expostulate that Jonah was swallowed by a gigantic guppy." It was the "old Testament" crack that provoked such controversy on *The Smothers Brothers Comedy Hour*.

Unlike Lord Buckley, who just converted a Bible story into hip lingo, Steinberg was truly irreverent in the retellings. When Moses approached the burning bush, "he burnt his feet. And God said, 'Aha, third one today!' Moses swore. We're not sure what he said, but many Old Testament scholars believe to this day it was the first mention of Christ in the Bible."

The 1970 Elektra album repeats some Bible stories ("Jezebel," "Joshua," "Lot," and "Moses"). Mostly it's filled with the kind of conversational bits he used increasingly on TV talk shows. He even mentions a *Tonight Show* appearance in which he was on the panel with sex authority Dr. David Reuben. That's when he uttered perhaps his most famous one-liner: "The reason I feel guilty about masturbation—is I'm so bad at it."

Steinberg is quiet, measured, almost literary. He's so confident and compelling, the audience is respectful. And they know they can't talk among themselves because he's not going to raise his voice. They're rewarded with subtle satire, like this carefully enunciated description of a sexual encounter:

"Imagine. You have attained undreamed of horizons of virtuosity. You have devised and executed maneuvers that would mystify even Masters and Johnson. You have become to sex what Julia Child is to a chicken. And as you're lying there in the afterglow of a moment that poets devote their whole lifetimes to describe, she turns to you and says, 'Hey ... that was cute.'"

Unfortunately, by 1974's "Booga Booga," David is overloading on intellectual references for his winking brethren. Mocking commercials for rock anthologies, he imagines something for a more literate audience: a record anthology featuring Pushkin, Blake, and John Dos Passos. The audience giggles to show that they have even heard of these people. He does a long routine on taking a college test in literature.

Steinberg does some hostile humor about Jewishness (he describes his parents, who felt that unkosher food was "tantamount to kryptonite") and tells a gag that's since become a classic: "A Jewish princess is a girl who makes love with her eyes closed—because she can't bear to see another person's pleasure." On a lighter note, he sings Shel Silverstein's "Freakin' at the Freaker's Ball" as a wry connoisseur of perversion. The title track is his manic bit as a psycho psychiatrist tormenting a stooge from the audience. This LP is now on CD.

"Seventies," from 1975, is a concept album of sarcasm and cynicism based on a forseeable Arab domination of America. It misfires badly. Cowritten by Don Novello (aka Father Guido Sarducci), the grim, almost jokeless satire describes how American presidents Harland Sanders and Monty Hall were succeeded by Abdul Khalid, who punctuates every sentence with a honk on his Harpo bicycle horn and mumbles things like, "The president does not recognize questions from female reporters." Asked about economics he says, "Too many goods were stolen in consumer riots in 1975, 76 and 77. (Honk honk honk). And when people insist on living like squirrels (honk) and don't buy new products (honk) deflation snowballs (honk). Today (honk) ... I am naming deflation public enemy number 47 (honk) to help the free world curb deflation (honk) once and for all (honk)."

The "Pope Roast" cut features Don Novello; "Press Conference" includes the team of Franken and Davis. "Tears on the Dashboard," the only worthwhile cut, is a fake '50s ballad about gas shortages (an alarming problem between 1973-75): "Tears on the dashboard, gas is low. If cars went on tears our love could go. My tears, tears, tears only flow. I want you by my side, but my gas tank says no."

ELINORE STEN

- THE MENTAL BLOCKS OF ELINORE STEN (Blox Records) ** $6 $12

A Chicago-based performer, billed as "The Girl with the Mental Hernia," Sten evidently self-released this one (pressed in eye-catching gold vinyl) to sell at her shows. With cigarette in holder and tongue in cheek, she offers an odd mix of intellectual asides ("I thought Kraft-Ebing was a cheese") stitched around piano ditties sung in the low-key style of her contemporaries Dwight Fiske and Charley Drew.

Typical of her song parodies is this version of "Margie": "Orgy! I'm always dreamin' of an orgy. I'm tired of drinkin' scotch and beer and whiskey my dear. I'm so depraved that lately I've been cravin' for an orgy. Since you're my inspiration, tell you what we'll do. You bring Benzedrine and rye, and I'll bring the Spanish Fly—for a real George Orgy with you!"

SKIP STEPHENSON

- THE REAL COMEDY (Laff A 225) *1/2 $4 $8

Stephenson, best known as one of the annoyingly plastic hosts of the cloying, briefly popular *Real People* TV series, wasn't much in stand-up. On this album that couldn't be more California if it was on orange vinyl, he comes out shouting a peppy, "Thank God for 7-11!" He says, "You know the best time in the Valley is 2:15 in the morning. Go down to the 7-11 to watch all the pot heads decide on which shelf of candy they're gonna buy: 'You have any chocolate covered chili?'"

His patter to the crowd has all the sincerity of a disc jockey. "I think we oughta keep this crowd together, let's all go to my house, ya want to? We'll turn the lights up and feel around and find each other, wouldn't that be fun? Everybody wants to go? Yeah???"

Someone shouts: "What kind of drugs ya got?"

Skip does plenty of drug jokes. He also has the nerve to swipe gags from Henny Youngman: "This one guy asked me for some change. I gave him a dime, he turned around, put it in a parking meter ... the little arrow went from zero to sixty. He went, 'Oh man, I lost a hundred pounds.'" The difference, of course, is that Henny's character is drunk and Stephenson's is on 'ludes.

HOWARD STERN

- FIFTY WAYS TO RANK YOUR MOTHER (Wren 8201C) $7 $15
  reissued as UNCLEAN BEAVER (Citizen X 4202-2) * $8

Back in 1982, Stern had yet to perfect the bluntly aggressive style so opinionated, childish and/or truthful that it's actually funny. At least sometimes.

Here, he's just a shock jock with the usual corny gross-out gags and song parodies that delight kids cutting class and pinheaded menials who can keep the transistor radio on while they work. There's a commercial for "Anal Kotex, napkins for any asshole," and the title track, which starts as a parody of Paul Simon's hit song, but quickly turns into a nonstop recitation of dopey "rank" jokes: "Your mammy's like a 7-11. She's open all night, hot to go, and for thirty-five cents she'll give ya a Slurpee! Your mammy is so ugly a computer dating service set her up with the black plague! Your mammy is so ugly she's got marks all over her body from where guys were touchin' her with ten foot poles!"

Various hangers-on help Stern out when sketches require celeb impressions. Most of the material is just witless, like the parody of "I Shot the Sheriff" now called "I Shot Ron Reagan," and sung by a wimpy, squealling John Hinckley: "I shot Ron Reagan, but I did not shoot Nancy, I did not want to mess up her Gucci dress, it was so nice." "John's Revenge" has a fairly decent impression of John Lennon, but lousy lyrics aimed at Yoko Ono: "So now you think you're a financial wizard handling all of my business affairs. Do you know how many albums I have to sell to buy shampoo for all that long black hair? You got greasies too. I am the walrus. How do you do? You make me cuckoo. Cuckoo. Cuckooooo."

The 1994 reissue on CD re-edited the original ten tracks into seventeen sections, including a separate band for a bland song parody Howard happened to do about O. J. Simpson ("Baby You Can Rent a Car" based on the Beatles' "Drive My Car"). No doubt some fans thought they were getting some new or previously unreleased material.

KAY STEVENS

- NOT SO GREAT SONGS ... (Liberty LST 7309) ** $7 $15

Good concept: songs "that were left out of great movies for obvious reasons." Bad execution: the songs are dull and Kay's singing doesn't add anything to the comedy. From the love song that was left out of *Frankenstein*:

"I need you, Frankenstein, I need you much too much. I hunger for your hairy paw. I miss your clammy touch. I never knew a moment's fright, I love your sweet embracement. Until I spent that lovely night screaming in your basement. Darling! Oh, I love the way you send shivers up my spine. Though others forsake you I'd give anything to make you mine, Frankenstein!"

Songs "left out" of such movies as *Sodom and Gomorrah*, *Cleopatra*, and *The Birdman of Alcatraz* fill the disc. The sound-alike pop music is by Hal Borne. The words are by Paul Francis Webster, who won Oscars for "My Secret Love" and "Love Is a Many Splendored Thing"—neither qualifying him for comedy writing. The best he comes up with are these Allan Sherman-style rhymes on "Sodom and Gomorrah": "They went swimmin' in the nude with women. Spent three or four G's on their nightly orgies. More indiscreet-a than La Dolce Vita." Years earlier, Hal Borne wrote the delightfully pretentious "Tenement Symphony," an unintentionally funny highlight in The Marx Brothers' *At the Store*.

RAY STEVENS

- GITARZAN (Monument SLP 18115) *** $5 $10
- GREATEST HITS (MCA 5918) **1/2 $5 $10
- GREATEST HITS VOLUME TWO (MCA 42062) ** $5 $10
- COLLECTOR'S SERIES (RCA Victor 563442) * $7
- 20 COMEDY HITS (Curb D277753) ** $8
- AHAB THE ARAB (Special Music 8381692) ** $7
- GET THE BEST OF RAY STEVENS (MCA MSD 35085) *** $8
- RAY STEVENS COLLECTION (MCAD 10776) ** $8

Since the '60s Ray Stevens has had Top 40 novelty hits ("The Streak," "Gitarzan") as well as "straight" hits ("Mr. Businessman" and "Everything Is Beautiful"). The listing here is comedy-based.

Most of his tunes are silly, sort of Roger Miller acting like Jerry Lewis. The songs don't have quotable lyrics. They're cartoon pictures. Listeners can imagine Ahab the Arab racing around the desert on a camel called Clyde squealing and hollering and dancing with his lady love, or Harry the Hairy Ape jumping up and down in front of a near-sighted disc jockey also squealing and hollering, or a naked streaker just jumping up and down squealing and hollering.

"Gitarzan" was recorded live, highlighting his three best early hits ("Gitarzan," "Harry the Hairy Ape," and "Ahab the Arab") plus Coasters classics: "Yakety Yak," "Little Egypt," and "Along Came Jones." "Greatest Hits" offers the original versions of "Ahab the Arab," "Gitarzan," and "Along Came Jones" (superior to the live cuts) but misses the manic Mercury studio version of "Harry the Hairy Ape," which is one of his funnier pieces just on the vocals alone. It has three later novelty hits: "The Streak" (dumb but catchy), "Shriner's Convention" (a boring look at cornball conventioneers), and "It's Me Again Margaret" (lamebrained country comedy about a sicko yokel who makes crank phone calls saying, "Are ya nekkid ... betcha can't guess what I'm doin'").

The second volume has some of his more subtler satires: "Would Jesus Wear a Rolex" and "I Need Your Help Barry Manilow." But ... there's also real stupid stuff like "The Haircut Song," and one too many fast and furious unfunnies ("Freddie Feelgood and his Funky Little Five-Piece Band").

Curb's collection misses some hits ("Harry the Hairy Ape," "Jeremiah Peabody's Pills") and has the live "Ahab" and "Gitarzan" instead of the studio cuts. It's heavy on later material on the various Curb comic and straight albums ("Used Cars," "Barbecue," "Where Do My Socks Go?" "Tabloid News"), which leaves it up to "The Streak," "Shriner's Convention," and "Bridget the Midget" to draw fans in.

The undeservingly named "Collector's Series" 1992 CD is under thirty minutes long (only eight cuts), and mostly straight and/or uninspired, including "The Dooright Family," "Where the Sun Don't Shine," "You're Never Goin' to Tampa with Me," and "Put It in Your Ear." His "Shriner's Convention" is the only real hit, and it's available on other compilations. The MCA "Collection" has fourteen cuts but only a few classic ("The Streak," "Shriner's Convention").

"Ahab the Arab" is also a chintzy CD, only thirty-six minutes long, but it features two of his goofy greats, the original "Ahab the Arab" and "Harry the Hairy Ape." There's also two annoying polysyllabic tunes, "Further More" and "Jeremiah Peabody's Poly-Unstatured ... Pills," and a falsetto-infected serious tune called "Funny Man" that's hard to take seriously. Other numbers are too dumb for all but hardcore fans, including "The Deodorant Song" and "Bubble Gum, the Bubble Dancer."

The CD "Get the Best of Ray Stevens" has it all, twenty cuts from the vaults of Mercury, RCA, Warner, and Barnaby: "Ahab the Arab," "The Streak," "I Need Your Help Barry Manilow," and "Gitarzan." Oddly, the live version of "Harry the Hairy Ape" is here, over the original. Then there are the cuts that are knee-slappers among nitwits ("It's Me Again Margaret" among others too dumb to discuss). Fans also get Ray's two straight hits, "Mr. Businessman" and "Everything is Beautiful."

• BOOGITY BOOGITY (Barnaby BR 6003) *1/2	$5	$10
• SURELY YOU JOUST (MCA 5795) *	$4	$8
• CRACKIN' UP (MCA 42020) **	$4	$8
• BESIDE MYSELF (MCA 42303) *	$4	$8
• #1 WITH A BULLET (Curb/Capitol CDP7 959142) *1/2		$8
• RAY STEVENS LIVE! (Curb D2-77762) *1/2		$8

Stevens's albums tend to have a few chucklesome cuts and a lot of gristled filler. Casual fans should stick to the compilations. 1974's "Boogity Boogity" features Steven's big hit "The Streak," which is dated now, and was pretty silly even then: "Yes they call him the streak, he likes to turn the other cheek. He's always makin' the news, wearin' just his tennis shoes. Yes you could call him unique." Ray pays homage to The Coasters by borrowing "boogity," the nonsensical word for running they used in "Run Red Run." Most of the cuts here are more fast-paced than funny; like a chicken with its head cut off.

The "Surely You Joust" album from 1986 is embarrassing. "People's Court" describes a hokey hick calling up TV's Judge Wapner, complaining about his marriage: "Ah cain't stand that woman! Incompatible? Naw, I just hate her guts!" As usual, there is plenty of Ray Stevens's aural cartooning: "Is it true ... that you emptied out the entire contents of your ant colony into her best one-size-fits-all pantyhose that she used as workout leotards?" "... you should've seen her, Judge, made Jane Fonda look like Roy Orbison. Those little ants'll make ya some moves!"

"Crackin' Up" from 1987 has the satiric "Would Jesus Wear a Rolex." Ray is watching a TV preacher selling salvation: "Woke up this morning, turned on my TV set. There in living color was something I can't forget. This man was preaching at me. Yeah. Layin' on the charm. Asking me for twenty with ten thousand on his arm." Stevens is almost bitter (a la "Mr. Businessman") and there's nothing overtly comic about his gospel singing, which helps drive the point home more forcefully. Stevens resurrects the classic country confusion tune "I'm My Own Grandpaw" and sings the colorful Shel Silverstein oddity "Three-Legged Man." Sheb Wooley's beer ballad "The Day that Clancy Drowned" has some familiar gag lines: "When they took the dear departed over to the funeral place. Took 'em half an hour to get that big smile off his face."

1989's "Beside Myself" mixes ordinary ballads ("Another Fine Mess") with comedy cuts like the predictable "I Saw Elvis in a U.F.O." In a Bob Seger-ish groove, he wails, "I saw Elvis in a U.F.O., sittin' there with Howard Hughes! I saw Elvis in a U.F.O. Jimmy Hoffa was in there, too!"

1991's "#1 with a Bullet" has a bit of Japan bashing: "One day we're gonna lose our roots. Wear Oriental jeans and boots. Drink nothin' but Kawasaki sake, Honda wine, and Mitsubishi light beer. Ah so!" Other songs include "Teenage Mutant Kung Fu Chickens," "The Little Blue-Haired Lady" (pronounced "rittle brue-haired rady" for another Asian jab), and "Working for the Japanese."

"Live" offers a cross section of hits ("Gitarzan," "The Streak"), lessers ("Can He Love You Half as Much as I"), and straights ("Everything is Beautiful"). The slickly produced studio versions are funnier; the mild introductions and audience goofing would only be of interest as a souvenir to those who saw him at his own Branson club in the late '80s.

STEVENS AND GRDNIC

• STEVENS AND GRDNIC (Laff 220) *	$4	$8
• SOMEWHERE OVER THE RADIO (Tak 7067) *	$5	$10

Ron Stevens and his wife Joy Grdnic have made comedy into "product." They produce fake commercials, bogus interviews, and "zany" songs to be played on radio shows, including their own. Their albums seem more like industry-oriented demos than cohesive comedy records.

This commercial parody from "Somewhere Over the Radio" might raise a smile heard once. Stevens, with typical DJ exaggeration and sound effects, announces his new product:

"We're going to magnify this pimple one hundred times to show you how new Dermadrug Skin Putty fights acne pimples the natural way! Dermadrug Skin Putty doesn't cover up or dry up unsightly, ugly, juicy pimples like ordinary treatments. It bites down hard like two sharp fingernails, and squeezes till the nasty zit explodes from your face! It's the natural way to attack pimples! Now available in twenty-two exciting colors!"

Most of this hear-it-once-and-forget-it stuff is completely forgettable. Some of the short sketches are extremely annoying. "Fast Food" (on the Laff album) goes on for two minutes as Stevens shouts orders at a drive-in window. The big joke is that the response coming through the speakers is garbled. "Did you hear me?" he keeps asking, shouting the order again and again. The sketch ends with him still shouting the order again and again.

ADLAI STEVENSON

• THE STEVENSON WIT (RCA Victor VDM 107) **1/2	$7	$15

Governor of Illinois, Ambassador to the United Nations, and twice a candidate for the presidency, Stevenson was one of the great political wits of the 20th Century. Not that he had much competition. The book version of *The Stevenson Wit* is fun browsing for both silliness (bald-headed Adlai once proclaimed, "Eggheads of the world, unite, you have nothing to lose but your yolks") and wit ("An intellectual is a man who takes more words than necessary to tell more than he knows").

The record version isn't sharp sonically and isn't sharply edited. Stevenson's speeches weren't comedy monologues, so one must listen to some serious or dated talks before getting a one-liner like, "I've read the Republican Platform, which is pretty good—as a Whodunnit." The album can still be recommended to those interested in history and good humor.

CAL STEWART

- CAL STEWART AS UNCLE JOSH (Mark 56 # 797) ** $6 $12

From the turn of the century until his death, Cal Stewart (1863-1919) was one of the big stars in comedy records. His rustic monologues about life in Punkin Center appeared on cylinders for Columbia and Edison.

Today sharp listeners might find traces of Stewart in Will Rogers, Fred Allen's "Titus Moody," and even W. C. Fields. That is, if they can stand Stewart's ambling delivery, wheezing gags, and annoying laugh. His routines are loaded with archaic cracker barrel humor. A better moment from "Revival Meeting at Punkin Center" takes a Fieldsian view of good and evil:

"Obediah White, the minister of Hickory Corners was to preach to us ... I don't think I ever will forget that sermon. He said, 'Yeah verily, Satan has wonderful inducements to offer the sinner! Why brothers and sisters, hell is full of beautiful women, automobiles, fast horses, and champagne!' And just then old Jim Lawson stood up and said, 'Oh Death where is thy sting!' Ha ha ha ha! That busted up the revival meeting! Ha ha ha ha!"

There's some silly charm to Uncle Josh the codger, but this one is really for students of comedy only.

STILLER AND MEARA

- PRESENTING STILLER AND MEARA (Verve V 15038) **1/2 $7 $15
- LAST TWO PEOPLE ON EARTH (Columbia CS 9542) *** $7 $15
- LAUGH WHEN YOU LIKE (Atlantic SD 7249) **1/2 $5 $10

Jerry Stiller and Anne Meara were perennials on *The Ed Sullivan Show* in the '60s. One of the very few successful husband and wife comedy teams, they still perform together though they've both had impressive solo acting careers.

The Verve album from 1963 is filled with fairly generic "two man" mini-sketches, including an interview between a newswoman and a doctor:

"You're just coming from the operating room?" "No, I just came from the men's room. Are we on the air?" "What is the first step in admitting a patient?" "We get a check! As soon as the check clears, they're admitted. Otherwise we have to keep the baby." "That's shocking, doctor." "It is. When you consider the number of kids we have on the third and fourth floor."

They were only beginning to work on their mini-dramas with a heart, like their routines about a Jewish man and an Irish girl getting over their differences. "Wrong Number," a mellowed version of Nichols and May, is about two people shyly and self-conciously breaking down the barriers between each other when chance has brought them together.

The second album (with notes by Ed Sullivan) is the one for fans of Hershey Horowitz and his love, Mary Elizabeth Doyle. Back in the late '60s, Stiller and Meara were sort of a missing link between the humanity of *The Honeymooners* and the realism of lower class living a la *All in the Family*. There are sketches here for Hershey and Mary, and even songs. The highlight though, is "Hate." Stiller and Meara play a different type of couple for this one.

"I hate you!" Jerry begins.

"You hate me," Anne challenges. "I hate you!"

"You don't know what hate is, the kind of hate I have for you."

"Listen," Anne says, warming up, "my hate for you is such a hot hate, I hate you with hot heaping hunks of hate!"

The routine builds and builds: "If it was possible to write the word 'Hate' on each grain of sand in the Sahara Desert ... all that hate on each of those hateful grains wouldn't equal one millionth of the hate that I'm hating you with right now!"

"You know how much you hate me? Double it! That's my hate for you!"

An excellently constructed and beautifully performed little exercise, Jerry's blunt, deadpan husband is matched perfectly by Anne's tough yet fragile wife. This bit also appears on Shelley Berman's "Sex Life of the Primates" album.

1972's odd Atlantic album was recorded in a studio sans audience, which makes their sketches seem realistic, as if overheard. They play a variety of couples in the midst of seriocomic situations: A female boss dates her male employee. Mr. and Mrs. Chou En Lai are heard in a private moment. And Hershey Horowitz tries to date the Irish Mary Elizabeth Doyle:

"I couldn't come over. It's Friday. I can't eat meat on Friday...."

"Hey wait a minute, didn't they change the rule on that?"

"Sure, they changed the rule, but my family don't go along with it. See we're orthodox! Why don't you come to my house for Sunday dinner ... my mother always has a big spread, roast stuffed pork, baked Virginia ham—oh! I'm sorry! You don't have to eat any of that stuff. I'll fix you bacon and eggs."

PHIL STONE

- MAMOLOSHEN (Ethnic Productions EP 101) **1/2 $5 $10
- BAGELS AND LOX (Ethnic Productions EP 102) **1/2 $5 $10

Fans of classic Jewish dialect stories and anecdotes will get a kick out of Phil Stone's two albums, though occasionally he gets a bit risqué. And occasionally a punch line is delivered in Yiddish. The albums were recorded in Los Angeles and intended "as fundraisers, with a portion of the wholesale price to go to Israel."

From "Mamoloshen," here's the one about the "little guy busily observing the man who was sitting next to him on the subway. He said, "Friend, you're dressed terrible. Your collar is turned around backwards." The man said, "I am a father." He said, "So? I'm a father, and a grandfather, but look at me, with a nice shirt and everything. You dress terrible with the collar all turned around." The man said, "You don't understand. I am a father to thousands." The little man said, "*You* are a father to *thousands?* Better your pants should be turned around!"

On "Bagels and Lox," he tells the story of an upset mother who couldn't believe her son had been given sex education booklets at school. She called her husband and when the husband came home, "He dashed upstairs, threw open the room, and there's the kid standing there, busily masturbating. He isn't missing a stroke. The father watched him for a while and he said, 'Son, when you finish your homework, I wanna have a talk with you.'"

LARRY STORCH

- AT THE BON SOIR (Jubilee 2033) ** $10 $20

Long before he played Agarn on *F. Troop* Larry Storch was a stand-up comic. He was also a popular mimic. He confirmed for me what Cary Grant once said—that it was Storch, doing a routine about celebrities including Cary and Judy Garland, who came up with the "Judy, Judy, Judy" catchphrase.

This 1960 album doesn't have that historic bit, but it does show off Larry's impressive talents in dialect comedy. Like a multi-ethnic Myron Cohen, Storch departed from one-liners to tell stories in various character voices. His characters included an aged Latino, a twangy Southern senator, an Italian mobster, and a Jewish woman talking about her delicate granddaugther Esther: "That goil must have come down from heaven on a moonbeam ... she fell in love mit a truck driver ... a bull in a china shop! That big ape fell in love mit that girl. He proposed marriage! That poor girl, the chemistry was right and she accepted! At de wedding ceremony—well, dat big bull backed into the canopy ... when de rabbi gave him dat sacred glass of wine to drink, drank whole glass of wine, stomped on the glass, made by him such a racket that the poor delicate child had a miscarriage right there!"

Sometimes there are no jokes at all. As Dick Shawn once said, recalling these early days of stand-up, "Most of the comics were doing standard jokes. Larry was one of the first ones to do characters." Still, the lack of strong gags hurts this album—as does the harsh monaural sound.

Storch can also be heard reading the Philip Roth story "Epstein" on Lively Arts 30005.

SYLVIA STOUN

- AGENT 0069 (Jubilee 2060) *1/2 $5 $10
- SEX IS THE THING THAT STARTED IT ALL (Jubilee 2063) *1/2 $5 $10

Stoun arrived on the Jubilee roster in the mid-60s, well after Rusty Warren. Her photos look good, but she isn't much of a performer. At best she sounds like Gwen Verdon recorded a few rpm's too slow. Usually she's more like a tired Phyllis Diller wearily serving up the familiar yocks. For this stuff, from the "Agent 0069" album, she has no reason to sound enthusiastic:

"Happiness is discovering your wife needs a bigger bra. Happiness is discovering for the first time that you can do it the second time. Happiness is your mother-in-law's mah-jong group being picked up on a narcotics charge. Happiness is a $500 call girl giving you for reference. Happiness is discovering that your baby sitter is Lolita."

She does some perfunctory songs and sounds pretty bored going through the requisite limericks. These include a few that Andrew Dice Clay later covered:

"Little Miss Muffett sat on the tuffet

Eating her curds and whey

Along came a spider

And sat down beside her

And said: what's in the bowl, bitch?"

It's more of the same on the second album, but this time the limericks aren't even worth stealing by Clay:

"A hot blooded chorine named Fawn

Could make love from dusk to the dawn

She let no one slip past

But took on the whole cast

For she heard that the show must go on."

THE SUNDAY BRUNCH

- HERRING GIVES ME HEARTBURN (Era NS 807) *1/2 $5 $10

Very tolerant fans of Mickey Katz might be amused by The Sunday Brunch. They're obvious, and the singers use abrasively stereotypical accents, but there's an audience that goes into hysterics at the mention of a "fresser" or a matzoh ball. Herb Newman and Mel Levin wrote the lyrics and the forgettable music. From the title track: "Lox is so wonderful! Chopped liver is divine! Gefilte fish tastes so delish with Mogen David wine. I always get a treat from everything I eat. But herring gives me heartburn!"

GLENN SUTTON

- CLOSE ENCOUNTERS (Mercury SRM 15018) *1/2 $3 $7

On this studio album, Sutton sings his way through tame country songs: "I say Hip Hip Hooray for the E.R.A. I'll do everything I can to push it through. Hip Hip Hooray for the E.R.A. For if I gotta work I want the women workin' too. If they drove trucks just think of all them females on CB. And what a gas to have a woman doctor examine me! And if war breaks out again I'd gladly lead the battle cry, 'cause I'd rather have a woman in the foxhole than a dirty ol' G.I."

To vary the monotony, half-minute fake commercials and news items are sandwiched between songs: "This is Calvin Country with Country Music Update. Quickie Pictures announced its plans today to remake the movie *Bluebeard* with Charlie Daniels in the title role. Johnny Paycheck had been offered the part, but at the last minute refused to dye his beard blue, and flatly told the producers to take that flick and shove it."

LEE SUTTON

- NEAR MISS (Jubilee 2073) ** $7 $15

Sutton, a British female impersonator in the mid-60s, offers adult material without too much campy topspin: "Hollywood: that's the place where you can lie on the sand and gaze at the stars. Or vice versa, if you prefer. While I was out there I did another full length for Hitch. He was very grateful. It's a sequel to *The Pink Panther* called *The Bloodshot Pussy*. I never make films, I only make sequels. Did a sequel to *A Shot in the Dark*, it was called *A Bang up the Alley*.... Of course my biggest success was my first western, a sequel to *Canyon Passage* called *The Airy Prairie*. In it I played the only lady sheriff with two hundred cowboys in her posse. Well they kept on giving me bum steers. I had four leading men in that one, Mart, Art, Bart, and Fargo."

A second album was released only in England.

PAUL SYKES

- I'M NOT KIDDING YA (Horizon SWP 1611) **1/2 $6 $12
- CANDY MAN (Warner Bros. WS 1583) *1/2 $5 $10

Folkie-comic Sykes recorded his first album in 1962 at the Ice House. His offbeat, stumbling, um, um, non-patter between songs might interest fans who wonder what Tommy Smothers would be like as a solo. Introducing "House of the Rising Sun," he notes: "If it's sung by a girl, well, then it's about a house. If it's sung by a boy, it's sung about a gambling casino. With a house upstairs ... It's sung about, um, this wayward youth. He went into the gambling casino and drank and gambled and went astray. See, he went astray because he was tryin' to get upstairs and he ended up in the basement. And, uh, had the time of his life down there, but boy it was different. Um."

A few cuts on his Horizon album were later covered by The Smothers Brothers: "The Map Song," and "John Henry." And oddly, one cut is a deliberately campy version of "Tiptoe Through the Tulips" that seems to pre-date Tiny Tim by several years. Sykes's voice is similar to Smothers in the mild monologues, but becomes a tremblingly sincere tenor for the straight songs.

Sykes gets the sophomore jinx on his second album. The weak Warners disc has an intensely irritating title track as Sykes duets with himself as father and squeaky-voiced son. The lullaby lyrics about candy and gingerbread are repeated over and over. He sings many a sappy ballad ("First Time Ever I Saw Your Face," "Inch Worm," "Try to Remember") made worse by his quaveringly earnest voice. The album is mostly music, and the occasional comic introductions aren't much: "This girl came up to me in Denver, Colorado. She was very young, and she was very vivacious, and she was very bubbly. Extremely bubbly. It was all out of her mouth. That 3-2 beer, it just gets to ya. Anyway, she said, 'Excuse me, sir.' And I said, 'All right.'"

TANGERINE

- A TASTE OF TANGERINE (Laff A 162) *1/2 $4 $8

Tangerine's lone late '70s album, like label mate Tina Dixon, is full of funky swagger. Both women sound like they've been listening to a little too much of Flip Wilson's Geraldine. The poems and recitations are corny: "Here's to America, the land of the push, where a bird in the hand is worth two in the bush. But if in a bush a maiden should stand, a push in the bush is worth two in the hand. Whoooo! Right on!"

THE TAPPET BROTHERS

- BEST OF CAR TALK (Soundelux WD0002) *1/2 $8

Tom and Ray Magliozzi developed a following via "Car Talk," a public radio call-in show. The jolly duo, a pair of car mechanics, love to yock it up as they discuss the truisms of their profession: "The AMC Pacer is a nerd car.... The Dodge Aries. It's always somebody else's car. Nobody wants to admit they own one.... There is a certain kind of female driver, she has teased hair of some unidentified color, she drives a Firebird, she's always chewing gum, and she drives well above the speed limit and she's always putting on lipstick in the rear view mirror!" On this 1995 CD they narrate a selection of not always well-recorded phone-in calls from the show. The callers tend to be verbose and the hosts all too eager to chide and snicker at them and then chortle over how right they are. A few minutes of this, like a few seconds of carbon monoxide fumes, is all any noncultist would want.

HARRY TAYLOR

- TAYLOR-MADE TITTERS (Calor LC 2001) *1/2 $4 $8
- MORE TITTERS (Calor LC 2002) *1/2 $4 $8

- AN EVENING WITH HARRY TAYLOR (Calor LC 2003) *1/2 $4 $8
- LOVE (Calor LC 2004) *1/2 $4 $8

In Miami Beach circa 1960, Taylor takes the Woody Woodbury approach, telling mildly risqué gags. From the first album: "Did you hear about the Britisher who was so generous? On his wedding night he settled some two hundred pounds on his bride! And he wasn't that rich, either." There's also more than enough "drink up" lines: "Some of you folks look a little sober. The more you drink the funnier I get!"

IRVING TAYLOR

- TERRIBLY SOPHISTICATED SONGS (Warner Bros. W 1210) ** $8 $15
- THE GARBAGE COLLECTOR IN BEVERLY HILLS (Warner Bros. W 1254) ** $8 $15
- DRINK ALONG WITH IRVING (Warner Bros. W 1323) ** $8 $15
- WHIMSICAL WORLD OF IRVING TAYLOR (Warner Bros. W 1352) ** $8 $15

In 1958 and 1959 Taylor enlisted a bunch of vocalists to cover his deadpan songs aimed at suburban sophisticates. He was an Allan Sherman for those who spent most of their time getting drunk or mowing the lawn. "When the Crab Grass Blooms Again" (on both "Terribly Sophisticated" and "Whimsical World") offers a loping, easygoing western beat and lopsided lyrics: "When the crab grass blooms again, and I'm all alone and weedin' then I'll know how much I'm needin' someone like you by my side. I just can't go on this way. Why did we part? Soon I'll have a breakin' back to match my heart."

Sly, dry, and at this point, a bit dusty, Taylor was fun for fans familiar with the style of '50s pop standards. One of his better tunes is "Myrtle" (on "Terribly Sophisticated"), parodying ethereal '50s odes. Here a soprano supplies "haunting" background oohs and aahs while a baritone warbles the woman's unmusical name and less than romantic recollections: "Myrtle, Myrtle, Myrtle ... the crumbs from the roll at breakfast seems to spell out your name." Similarly, "Make It a Chocolate Soda" (on both "Drink Along" and "Whimsical World") offers a Sinatra-style "One for My Baby" bar song. It starts with fake pathos: "Oh please play number nine, it's a favorite of mine. It's a disc of Lawrence Welk's. We first heard it at the Elks." This guy's carrying a torch for a woman who overindulged in fattening drinks. How sad: after gaining a hundred pounds, and unable to fit into his sports car, she left him.

Other cuts on "Whimsical World" include "Hawaiian Worm Raiser," "Zeekie Zeekie Lend Me Your Comb," and "Pachalafaka," which became a minor hit for Soupy Sales. "Terribly Sophisticated Songs" includes "Just My Sol," "The Brooklyn Beguine," and "We Did the Samba in Shamokin." "Drink Along with Irving" is notable for guest spots by Mel Blanc on "Liquor Is Our Business," Bea Benaderet on "Sub-Bourbon Living," and both on "Separate Bar Stools." "Garbage Collector in Beverly Hills," the title song, based on "On Top of Old Smokey," goes like this: "On top of my dumptruck, I'm getting my thrills. Collecting the garbage. In Beverly Hills. No one's on a diet. In Beverly Hills. I'd hate to be paying their grocery bills."

A minor, aging cult appreciates Taylor's work. Taylor wrote a number of other novelty tunes, including "Kookie, Kookie Lend Me Your Comb" and the theme to TV's *F-Troop*.

TAYLOR AND EDWARDS

- HAVE I GOT A PROBLEM (Era E-603) * $3 $7

Bill Taylor and Brad Edwards, California radio personalities circa 1973, pretend to take phone calls. A man complains that he has "a climax" every time he sneezes. "What are you taking for it?" "Ragweed!" The duo's mimicry, from old ladies to German doctors, are stereotypical and the long setups usually have a dumb, disappointing pay-off.

VAN Q. TEMPLE

- IT'S A RIOT (Riot 1) *1/2 $4 $8
- ALLOW ME TO DEMONSTRATE (Riot 2) *1/2 $4 $8
- WE SHALL OVERCOME, I THINK (Riot 3) *1/2 $4 $8
- MISTER WALLACE, PLEASE WAIT FOR ME! (Riot 4) *1/2 $4 $8
- WOMEN'S LIBERATION (Riot 5) *1/2 $4 $8

On these early mid-60s albums from a small Georgia record company, Temple plays boisterous and feisty "Miss lula Humps." He's not exactly Flip Wilson, but he gets laughs from his local crowd. On "Mister Wallace," straight man Ray Kinnamon discusses the 1968 Democratic Convention candidate George Wallace with Miss Humps:

"Has your delegation been polled?" "Well if you think I'm gonna put that on this record, you're absolutely nuts!" "Where do you stand on George Wallace?" "You're a hard mother, aren't you? Look, since I weigh 248 pounds, anywhere I stood on George would absolutely mash him flat."

JUDY TENUTA

- BUY THIS, PIGS (Elektra 960746-1) *** $5 $10
- ATTENTION BUTT PIRATES AND LESBETARIANS (Goddess GR 94022) *1/2 $8
- IN GODDESS WE TRUST (Goddess CD 1041-2) ** $8

The eccentric "Goddess of Comedy" has acolytes who love her, and nonbelievers who simply can't stand her. It's either heaven or hell, and there's no middle ground. Which is unfortunate, because that's where the earthbound Goddess has been trying to make a living.

Devotees are dazzled by Tenuta's bewildering mix of mood swings; at any moment exhibiting campy sexiness, blustery sarcasm, or blood-curdling disgust. Her fantasy is that she's a "petite flower Giver-Goddess" here to hip the world to "Judyism." She chortles her mantra ("Oh Kyoko!") between one-liners of rare philosophical pith. When told by her mom, "You won't amount to anything because you procrastinate," she answered: "Just wait!"

The 1987 Elektra disk offers colorful descriptions of the "pigs, stud-puppets, and pseudo-virgins" she must deal with, including a date with a guy who "was going to night school to evolve a thumb." She makes fun of her Dad (who dresses in plaid) and, hoisting her trademark accordion, sings a cowboy-polka tune about the Pope: "He'd be my main man I'd be his blue nun. He'd teach me how to kiss the ground. I'd teach him how to duck from a gun. I just want a cowboy to whom I can confess. Yeah. I just want a cowboy in a long white silky dress!"

The album has her best known line: "You know what scares me?" she asks. "When you're forced to be nice to some paranoid schizophrenic—JUST BECAUSE SHE LIVES IN YOUR BODY!"

Judy was hot in the late '80s with her own Dr. Pepper commercial, a book, and some cable TV specials. By 1994 and her self-done "Attention Butt Pirates," she seemed to have gone to campy extremes, substituting attitude and audience participation for solid jokes. Ranting and prancing before a virtually all homosexual audience ("Live at the C.S.W. Gay Pride Festival") the fifty-minute show, which could've been edited down severely, is marred by "ya hadda be there" visuals. She's so caught up in her own legend that most any comic line ends with her own delighted shout of disbelief: "Oh, my God!" She overuses the desultory grunt "Hello?" way too often, and there are long stretches involving audience members dragged onstage. Sometimes there's a good one-liner ("England—nice place if you're soot") but only hardcore fans will be listening for them.

1995's "In Goddess We Trust" is an improvement, although she's still far gone with shrill cries of "Oh, my God" and gritty growls of "We're sassy tonight!" On disc, sans visuals, the voice can be piercing. The jokes? Typical Tenuta outrage, especially when a celebrity is the target. On Rose Kennedy: "She left this world. She couldn't take another one of those damn Bob Hope 'Sorry I'm Not Dead Yet' specials." On O. J. Simpson: "Did O. J. do it? Like there's any doubt! Hello? Excuse me! By now he should've been Mike Tyson's butt boy! Come on!"

TERRY-THOMAS

- JEEVES (Caedmon TC 1137s) *1/2 $5 $10
- STRICTLY T-T (London 5764) ** $8 $15
- TERRY-THOMAS DISCOVERS AMERICA (Warner Bros. WS 1558) ** $8 $15

Thomas was beloved for his British "silly ass" roles in films. His style is different on disc. The 1958 "Jeeves" disc is mild. Two Wodehouse stories are adapted to disc, "Indian Summer of an Uncle" and "Jeeves Takes Charge." Thomas does his thankless job, prattling animatedly as foolish Bertie Wooster, while Roger Livesy hoarsely rasps through the part of his manservant, the infamous Jeeves. It's much ado about English society circa 1916, and strictly for those who have acquired a taste for this mannered, antique form of humor.

The London album is loaded with understated conversational British humor. It's hard to believe that someone actually took the time to write these dreary trifles down. Several of the three-minute and four-minute cuts are padded jokes with tired punch lines. "Ram in a Jam" is an achingly long deadpan story about pills that help the virility of rams on the farm. The farmer tells the pill seller, "Well, I gave 'em them thar pills ... my goodness gracious me ... before you could say half a pound of broken biscuits, you couldn't see half the countryside for lambs. Maaaaahvelous. Tell me ... what was in them pills?" "Ay? I don't know what was in 'em, but they don't half give me horrible heartburn!" As dull as the monologues are, the songs are worse. Thomas is surprisingly excellent at mimicry as well as singing, but only his truly loyal fans will care to find out.

Far more accessible to American audiences, but generally pretty silly, "Discovers America" consists of monologue sketches. A typical sketch has him pretending to be the prissy lady who owns a dog obedience school. She's addressing a PTA meeting: "Please come to order. The refreshments will still be there after the meeting! We must set a good example for the pets! Allow me to introduce myself. I'm the principal, known to most of you as "Old Fetch." We have a guest speaker to show us color slides of bowser bags he's collected all over the world. But first I'd like to end a rumor once and for all. We are an integrated kennel! Mr. Tyson's mongrel dog we had no objection to at all. We didn't like Mr. Tyson! He had no background whatever!"

Terry-Thomas appears on the album "Three Billion Millionaires" (United Artists UTL 4) as a doctor observing a newborn babe in a serious sketch about prejudice.

THEODORE

- ENTERTAINMENT OF SINISTER AND DISCONCERTING HUMOR (Proscenium 21 ten-inch) $25 $40
  (Proscenium 21 twelve-inch) *** $20 $40
- CORAL RECORDS PRESENTS THEODORE (Coral S 7322) *** $20 $35

On his albums, he was billed simply as "Theodore." Theodore Gottlieb, a dark, sardonic performance artist (before there was such a term) was later dubbed "Brother Theodore" by Merv Griffin during talk show appearances in the late '60s. His cult expanded in the '80s when he guested with David Letterman. He doesn't work nightclubs, disdainful of noise and innattentive drunks. Mostly he has presided over midnight shows at off-Broadway theaters. Even at ninety, in 1995, he would make the painful trek down to Greenwich Village for his Saturday night show, if only to tell several hundred people that he's miserable.

Offering grand guignol with a touch of surrealist burlesque, his ruminations are as cynical as Ambrose Bierce and as fiercely intellectual as Alexander King. His rambling style, which seems like Peter Lorre crossed with Mel Brooks, is enough to give the shakes to Professor Irwin Corey.

Like Lord Buckley, Theodore deserves acclaim for being so ahead of his time and so original. The 1955 Proscenium album is recorded a bit shrilly, but contains prime material. The earlier ten-inch version has better pictures of him on the back cover. The laughter noted in parenthesis is the audience's: "Science is but an organized system of ignorance. There are more things in heaven and on earth than are dreamt of in your philsopy. What do we know about the beyond? Do we know what's behind the beyond? (Laughter.) I'm afraid some of us hardly know what's beyond the behind. (Laughter.) Creatures of twilight and delusion, we drift toward our unknown ends. And that's why I feel the best thing is not to be born. (Laughter.) But who is as lucky as that (Laughter.) To whom does it happen? Not to one among millions and millions of people. (Laughter.)"

Coral's studio disc has music, sound effects, and much more fantasy than comedy. Theodore opens with a sinister, teeth-gnashing adaptation of Poe's "Berenice," and follows this with a mild, *Twilight Zone*-ish folk tale about a poor Asian and the painting he loves. Fans will find plenty to shake their heads over as he offers frenzied lectures (over centipedes with carbonated blood) and hopeless meditations on the fate of man: "In this best of all possible worlds, everything is in a hell of a mess."

Theodore isn't thrilled with his albums. He only has a copy of the Coral disc, mostly because he happens to like the Asian folk tale. He's fond enough to have listened to it maybe once a decade. Small pressings so many years ago, and a devoted cult, have made these two albums valuable, especially in Theodore's adopted city of New York.

BUB THOMAS

- THE HAPPY DRUNK (Laff A 111) *1/2 $4 $8
- UNDERCOVER SAFARI (Laff A 112) *1/2 $4 $8
- SEVEN PLACES TO HANG A HAT (Laff A 113) *1/2 $4 $8
- LAND OF FROOTS AND NUTS (Laff A 114) *1/2 $4 $8

Thomas sounds a little like Jesse White, a fast-paced, more oily than slick, carnival sideshow barker. On these '60s albums his West Coast crowd snickers along with the risqué patter. From his "Seven Places" album: "Put the light on me, I'm the star ... look at me ... look at that body, isn't it dynamite? Of course there's only a two-inch fuse there. Would you believe I'm married? I've had five years of happy marriage. Which isn't bad out of fifteen ... she looked at me one night, said, 'Do you think I'll lose my looks when I get old?' I said, 'If you're lucky!' And her mother! Her mother's miserable. Her idea of a lot of fun is throwing a great big beer party then locking the bathroom door!"

DANNY THOMAS

- AN EVENING WITH DANNY THOMAS (MGM E 201) ** $8 $15

The only Thomas record that could be classified under comedy is this ten-incher of novelty tunes. Thomas fans will be amused by his dialect characteriziations of a Runyonesque boxer ("Toledo Dan"), an Italian immigrant ("It's a Great-a Country, America"), and "Calypso Joe," a fellow who tells silly little jokes set to music: "Mrs. Jones had triplets one day. Two weeks later she had twins they say. Don't think that your hearing has been double-crossed. It happens that one of the triplets got lost!"

HOWARD THOMASHEFSKY

- IT'S TOUGH TO BE GIFTED, JEWISH AND BLACK (Laff A 166) **1/2 $5 $10

"Star of stage, screen and Tel-Aviv," Thomashefsky's gimmick was simple enough: being a black Jew. His delivery is more Jewish than black and his gags are more black than Jewish: "My biggest problem is—I can't blush." He tells a strange assortment of jokes as he veers between both minorities: "I got a brand new 1972 Falcoon. Don't laugh! I got a second car, too. A 1972 Jiguar! Beautiful cars! Speaking of cars, did you hear what General Motors is doin'? I think it's damn white of 'em. They're building a compact Cadillac for Schzwartzes on relief."

Thomashefsky had a good way of selling this album—his day job was as a salesman for New York's Colony Record Shop.

JIMMY THOMPSON

- KING MONKEY (Laff A 213) *1/2 $4 $8

This 1980 album features two very long rap songs, one on each side, making the obscure Thompson one of the earliest of the dirty comic rappers. One is about Badd Mann Dann, and he's mean.

The rest of the disc is typical of most Laff comics, a rambling babble of old jokes freshened up by a charismatic (or for those not into funk, simply loud) delivery. Moving from sex to drugs: "Niggers be gettin' high. They didn't know nothin' about cocaine till a few years ago.... Niggers be snortin' flour, salt, bakin' soda, anything.... A nigger offered me some cocaine one night, he said, 'Say man. Come try this.' It turned out to be Massengill douchin' powder. My nose run for three days! I had to put a mini-pad on the mother!"

THE THREE STOOGES

- THE NONSENSE SONGBOOK (Coral CRL 57289) **1/2 $10 $20
  reissued as SINGS FOR KIDS (Vocalion VL 73823) and in 1985 by MCA (MCA 909) $8 $15
- MADCAP MUSICAL NONSENSE (Golden Records GLP 43) ** $10 $20
  reissued as Rhino RNEP 609 $8 $15
- MADCAP MUSICAL NONSENSE (picture disc reissue Rhino RNLP 808) ** $10 $20

- A ROCKET SHIP RIDE THROUGH TIME AND SPACE TO STORYLAND
  (Peter Pan 8019, reissued as SIX FUNNY BONE STORIES, Peter Pan 8098) ** $12 $25
- YOGI BEAR AND THE THREE STOOGES MEET THE MAD, MAD, MAD DR. NO-NO
  (Hanna-Barbera HBR 2050) *1/2 $15 $30
- CHRISTMAS TIME (Rhino RNLP 606) *1/2 $8 $15

In the '30s and '40s the Stooges were appreciated by all ages, but when their shorts were syndicated to TV in the late '50s and early '60s, it was to the daytime kiddie market. So the albums the trio sold to capitalize on their newfound fame tended to be for children. The Coral-MCA disc is the most adult, as the boys (Moe Howard, Larry Fine, and new third partner "Curly" Joe DeRita) sing novelty tunes "Mairzy Doats," "Three Little Fishies," "Aba Daba Honeymoon," and the Warner Bros. cartoon theme song, "The Merry-Go-Round Broke Down." The highlight of the album is "The Alphabet Song," which was originally in the short *Violent Is the Word for Curly*. The elderly stooges still manage to swing it: "B-a-bay, b-e-be, b-i-bickey bi, b-o-bo...." In 1986 Sex Pistols' manager Malcolm McLaren issued a thudding disco version of it, renamed "B-i-Bickie."

1959's "Madcap Musical Nonsense" has some kid stuff spiked with Stooge violence. "Go Tell Aunt Rhody" becomes "Go Tell Aunt Mary" with lines like "Go Tell Aunt Mary that Curly Joe's been bad ... he broke her window playing in the yard ... Curly Joe's been bad ... she ought to spank him, she ought to spank him, she ought to spank him 'till he's good and red." Some sketches, like "At the Circus" and "At the Toy Store," are aimed at very small kids. Now and then there's a dumb, corny joke that cracks through. At one point Moe thinks he's playing "Paganini" but it's only "Page Nine." The boys sing their version of "On Top of Old Smokey": "We're coming to your house, to have a good time ... your mommy won't like us, and neither will Dad, we're coming to your house ... ta break up the joint!"

The boys made a bunch of 45s for the Peter Pan company, but the simple fairy tales and slapstick sketches don't work too well without the visuals:

"I guess the professor must've gone out to lunch. We might as well get lunch too, huh fellas," says Curly Joe. There's a hollow clunk. "Hey, do you have to knock so much sense in? In one day?"

"What do you mean we might as well go to lunch, too?" Larry asks, "You just had breakfast!"

"This day's goin' by pretty quick, huh?"

Their 1965 encounter with Yogi Bear is faintly amusing:

Moe: How do you like that, we spend four years going to Ranger school and we wind up being a babysitter for a bear.

Yogi: Cheer up, fellas, remember: It's always darkest when the lights go out!

Moe: Don't forget, Yogi, we're here to keep an eye on you....

Yogi: Fellas! Don't you trust old Yogi?"

Curly Joe: Well, yes and no. Mostly no.

The Christmas album from Rhino, originally an extended play 45, offers six simple songs. Typical is "I Want a Hippopotamus for Christmas," sung at half speed by the elderly Stooges. At their age, it makes no sense for them to harmonize: "Pop says a hippo would eat me up but then teacher says a hippo is a vege-tari-an."

"I Gotta Cold for Christmas," with Larry on lead vocals, is fairly off-key and fairly hilarious for fans who always thought there was something funny about the lost Mr. Fine. "Jingle Bell Drag" is even mediocre, a novelty number about a junkheap sleigh and a swaybacked horse that can barely pull it: "We bought ourselves a whip. It makes a snappy sound. But everytime he hears it, Dobbin lays down on the ground."

NOTES: The Stooges made many 45s and 78s that are high priced thanks to the fanatic Stooges cult. They recorded some rarities for Epic ("Sinking of the Robert E. Lee," Epic 5 9402) and Ardee/RCA ("Three Stooges Happy Birthday Record"). Stooge fans also need to own the soundtrack album "Snow White and the Three Stooges" (Columbia CS 8450). Joe DeRita appears on the album "Burlesque Uncensored" (Cook). The Three Stooges' album on Coral/MCA was issued on CD as MCAD 22184.

TIM AND TOM

- TIM AND TOM (LMI LMI-1003) ** $5 $10

Tim and Tom were the black and white comedy team of Tim Reid (later known for his sitcom work on *WKRP in Cincinnati*) and Tom Dreesen (now a veteran middle of the road Vegas opening act). On this 1973 album they go through some predictable, heavy-handed routines. Their patter is loaded with the kind of awkward gags that acknowledge stereotyping but don't do much else:

"We worked Mancato, Minnesota, and when we were in Mancato they had a real bad black problem."

"The guy died! They don't have many brothers in Mancato. I knew I was in trouble when a white man delivered the mail!"

"I remember, seriously, one day we got on a bus, sat down together, and the whole bus got up and gave us a standing ovation. And while the people were applauding, Tim robbed the bus driver!"

JIMMY TINGLE

- JIMMY TINGLE'S UNCOMMON SENSE (LYRIC MOON LM 95042) ** $8

Once showing promise as a querulous political satirist (he was on the late '80s "Strange Bedfellows" compilation from A&M), Tingle has now moved on to the "one-man show" mode. Like Rick Reynolds, he has elevated his minor recollections and observations into the stuff of "lecture." The posturing tone doesn't work in the first half as he muses on the very idea of being a stand-up comic and then turns his youthful vices (a fondness for beer predominating) into a treatise on the human condition. When he later focuses on the vital issues of the day (prison reform, homophobia,

MORE PIONEERING WOMEN

Phyllis Diller's two Verve albums (re-released twice each!) are classics. Influenced by Bob Hope, Phyllis was the first woman with a rapid-fire one-liner style. Joan Rivers arrived just after Lenny Bruce and Woody Allen and was the first woman to use their "confessional" neurotic style. Lily Tomlin brought pathos and drama to stand-up and ended up on Broadway with a one-woman show.

immigration, and ... parking) he's logical but not exactly hysterical. On the death penalty: "You have to kill certain types of people to be eligible for death. If somebody were to kill a federal judge, that's the death penalty. If somebody were to kill a member of Congress, that's the death penalty.... Nobody's killing judges or members of Congress. The most dangerous occupation in this country is cab drivers."

LILY TOMLIN

- MIXED DOUBLES AND BELOW THE BELT (Upstairs at the Downstairs UD-37W56 Vol 2) ** $30 $75

Tomlin's appearance in the 1966 revue *Below the Belt* marked the first time she performed in stage sketches and sang with an ensemble. Unfortunately the New York cabaret scene that had flourished for the previous six years (notably with Julius Monk's revues) was sagging. There's little writing talent in this Upstairs at the Downstairs show (exceptions being Michael McWhinney, Marshall Brickman, and Rod Warren) and the cast isn't very interesting. Madeline Kahn was the featured up-and-coming star. Tomlin is in the background. She sings on a few ensemble songs and appears in an archsketch of political satire called "International Monopoly." Sample: "Oops, I've just landed on South Vietnam. Who owns it?" "I do. South Vietnam with no hotels. Rent: four hostages." The laughs are few enough to count; often there's just one enthusiastic patron snickering. The high price is due to Tomlin and Kahn's presence, and the interest of off-Broadway and cabaret show collectors.

- THIS IS A RECORDING (Polydor 24-4055) **1/2 $4 $8
- AND THAT'S THE TRUTH (Polydor PD 5023) **1/2 $5 $10

Tomlin's 1971 "This Is a Recording" is a solo album for Lily's "Ernestine" character, one of her big successes while on TV's *Laugh-In*. Bearing a vocal resemblance to Elaine May's phone operator character, here's Ernestine at work:

"Nuisance Calls, a gracious good afternoon ... you say a man has been making constant obscene phone calls to you? What is his name and address please. Oh you don't. Well, what exactly does he say when he calls ... wait a minute now ... yes ... wait, is that 'F' as in 'Frank?' I don't blame you getting upset. Making all those promises and then not even giving his name! Hello?"

"And That's the Truth," a year later, was a solo for Tomlin's brat character "Edith Ann." Unlike past brats, including Baby Snooks, Tomlin's kid is a truthful characterization, not a one-dimensional screamer. Edith Ann duplicates dialogue one might hear from any little monster: "If you love someone you can kiss them on the lips and you do not have to wipe them off. I love Junior Phillips, he's my boyfriend. He's six ... you'll never guess what happened ... Junior got twin brothers ... and Junior don't know which is the real one and which is the xerox. So he has to be mean to both of 'em."

- MODERN SCREAM (Polydor PD 6051) **1/2 $10 $20
- LILY TOMLIN ON STAGE (Arista AB 4142) *1/2 $10 $20

Now moving into one-woman shows written by her companion Jane Wagner, Lily began abandoning standard jokes for character studies. "Modern Scream" offers Lucille, a tearful alcoholic who has a rubber fetish: "At first I was careful, ya know. Door stops. Backs off the shag rugs. Tip of mother's cane ... I don't know what would come over me, I'd just jump up, run into the kitchen and eat a spatula." There's Suzy Sorority, the ultimate Valley Girl-homecoming queen; housewife Judith Beasley; and Sister Boogie Woman, who can define happiness as "When you're seventy-seven years old ... and your teeth are in a jar and those teeth are smilin'."

There are a few moments for Tomlin's one-liner observations: "The formula for water is H_2O. Is the formula for an ice cube H_2O squared? Why is it when we talk to God we're said to be praying, but when God talks to us we're schizophrenic?"

Trying to turn vinyl into an art form, this one is a collage of studio cuts with sound effects, running commentary between Lily and a reporter, and live material.

The 1977 Arista disc is based on Tomlin's Broadway show *Appearing Nitely*, a success that landed her the cover of *Time* magazine on March 28th of that year as "New Queen of Comedy." But comedy is hard to find in some of these pretentiously presented sketches. She relives a lot of childhood traumas about growing up in the '50s, some overloaded with self-obsessed details recited with chilly precision:

"My hair has been pin-curled, frizzy on the ends, parted on the side, and held in place by a red plastic two lovebirds on a stick beret. A vinegar rinse gives it red highlights and it bounces as I walk.... My new school bag slung across my chest bangs between my elbow and my waist. Inside my new Cinderella pencil box, with its own built-in sharpener. No interrupting walks to the window sill. And something I have always wanted—a big new art gum eraser with all the corners still sharp. I should feel a lot better than I do."

Even Tomlin's few one-liners, exercises in alienation and anhedonia, are testily recited: "I've actually seen a man walk up to four women sitting in a bar and say, hey, what are you doing here sitting here all alone ... Does your mind feel more and more like teflon, nothing sticks to it?"

GENE TRACY

- FUNNY FACE, FUNNY MAN (Kent CC 6003, Koala 14881) ** $5 $10
- TRUCK STOP #1: TRUCK STOP IS THE BEST PLACE TO EAT (Kent CC 6001, Koala 14868) ** $5 $10
- TRUCK STOP #2: 69 MILES TO GENE TRACY'S (Kent CC 6002, Koala 14868) ** $5 $10
- TRUCK STOP #3: GENE TRACY SERVES YOU (Kent CC 6004, Koala 14870) ** $5 $10

- TRUCK STOP #4: A NIGHT OUT WITH GENE TRACY (Kent CC 6005, Koala 14871 reissued as DOUBLE CLUTCHIN' Dingo D-2003) *1/2 $5 $10
- TRUCK STOP #5: ADULTS ONLY (Kent CC 6006, Koala 14872) ** $5 $10
- TRUCK STOP #6: GENE TRACY AND ALL HIS FRIENDS (Kent CC 6007, Koala 14873, reissued as FIRST THING IN THE MORNIN', Dingo D-2004) *1/2 $5 $10
- TRUCK STOP #7: GENE TRACY TALKS TRASH (Koala 14874) *1/2 $4 $8
- TRUCK STOP #8: THE GREAT INSULT (Koala 14875) *1/2 $4 $8
- TRUCK STOP #9: SOPHISTICATED TRUCK DRIVER (Koala 14876) ** $4 $8
- TRUCK STOP #10: RHINESTONE TRUCK DRIVER (Koala 14877) *1/2 $4 $8
- TRUCK STOP #11: GENE TRACY CLEANS UP HIS ACT (Koala 14878) *1/2 $4 $8
- TRUCK STOP #12: GENE TRACY'S TRUCK STOP (Koala 14879) *1/2 $4 $8
- TRUCK STOP #13: I LIKE DRUNKS (Koala 14880) *1/2 $4 $8
- TRUCK STOP #14: LIVE AT THE CHEETA III (Koala 14882) *1/2 $4 $8
- TRUCK STOP #15: MR. TRUCK STOP (Koala 14883) *1/2 $4 $8

A chunky country comic with a resemblance to Jackie Gleason crossed with Jerry Clower, Tracy worked colleges and fraternal organizations in the '60s with standard joke book patter pleasantly delivered. He was born Eugene Morris in Anadarko, Oklahoma, and remained best known in the South, working strip clubs in Atlanta (including the Follies and Cheetah III) until his death at fifty-two on October 26, 1979. As the titles would suggest, Tracy's discs did well at truck stops, reissued and repackaged often, most notably by Koala, a small label operating out of Hendersonville, Tennessee.

On "Funny Face, Funny Man," some typical small town gags lifted from various joke books and other comics: "... it was so small it was only open three days a week. Our phone book had only one yellow page ... the Masons and Knights of Columbus knew each other's secrets. We had an all-night diner used to close at two-thirty in the afternoon. For twenty-seven years, Howard Johnson's special flavor of the month was vanilla." The albums reissued by Dingo (a division of Laff Records) are loaded with corny dirty jokes. There are also plenty of long shaggy dog stories, the humor elusive to Northerners.

TRAVESTY, LTD.

- TEEN COMEDY PARTY (Used Records US 23) * $3 $7

The 1982 album tries for the tone of a National Lampoon album but the two dozen short routines here are hopeless "aren't we being zany and weird" radio commercials and sketches.

A commercial for Dr. Schill's Ear Spray: "Dreaded ear odor ... swabbing just isn't enough. What you need is Dr. Schill's Ear Spray ... cuts through excess ear wax fast, like molten lava cuts through a jungle village! Will not harm the ozone. Now in regular, and new spearmint!"

BERNIE TRAVIS

- THE PENTAGON PAPERS (Audio Fidelity AFSD 1712) *1/2 $4 $8

Bernie Travis may be best remembered as Lenny Bruce in the low-budget film *Dirtymouth*. This audienceless studio disc is an unsure documentary that grimly traces the path of the Vietnam War. The supporting cast includes Fred Travalena, Dave Kent, and Bob Kaliban. Stereotypical Asian voices and a mediocre imitation of Lyndon Johnson don't help in this attempt at dark satire.

Here's Johnson discussing the war with his staff: "No, gentlemen, we're here for love, peace, truth, beauty, justice, the American way, and to win this Gol-durn war. And if you guys don't pull together, I'm gonna whup your hides. Now turn on the radio and let's hear some good ol' country music. (A radio news broadcast blares protestors chanting "Ho Chi Minh is our leader! Ho Chi Minh is our leader!") That don't sound like Flatt and Scruggs to me!"

TUBE BAR See BUM BAR BASTARDS

PHIL TUCKER

- ALL TUCKERED OUT (Imperial LP 9115W) * $5 $10

Is that really a rim shot after *every* single sentence or does Phil Tucker have a malfunctioning uvula? This '60s album is almost unlistenable due to the monotonous punctuation of every feeble punch line. The fast-talking Chicago comic talks about a girl who has played the club with him:

"She owns ten percent of the club because last night in the kitchen the boss told me he was gonna give her a piece of his business (rim shot). And I believe by the end of this month she'll get the whole damn joint (rim shot). Because she's nobody's dum-dum (rim-shot). She was overseas for twelve years, I saw her discharge (rim). Papers (shot). She and her two girlfriends in the U.S.O. called themselves Martin, Barton, and *Fargo* (rim shot)."

SOPHIE TUCKER

- CABARET DAYS (Mercury MG 20046) $6 $12
- THE SPICE OF LIFE (Mercury MG 20126, re-released as Mercury Wing RW 16215) $6 $12
- BIGGER AND BETTER THAN EVER (Mercury MG 20267) $6 $12

- SOPHIE TUCKER (Mercury MG 20035) $6 $12
- GOLDEN JUBILEE (Mercury MG 20049) $6 $12
- LAST OF THE RED HOT MOMMAS (Columbia CL 2604) $6 $12
- SOPHIE TUCKER (Decca DL 4942) $6 $12
- THE GREAT SOPHIE TUCKER (Decca DL 8355) $6 $12
- HER LATEST AND GREATEST SPICY SONGS (Mercury MG 20073) $6 $12

"The Last of the Red Hot Mamas," Tucker was a lusty two hundred pounder known for straight and risqué numbers. The quota of straight to risqué varies from disc to disc. An influence on the more raucous ladies of sexual comedy (Belle Barth and Pearl Williams), Sophie was even less explicit than Mae West. She did have West's bold, liberated attitude. Her tune "I'm Living Alone and I Like It," has these lines: "If I wanna have some fun, if I get bothered and hot, I phone one of those young tall dark handsomes that I've got. So it costs me a twenty or a fifty, so what."

A recitation, "That Certain Business," offers a history of prostitution that Joe E. Lewis might have admired: "Why this business was first established by the firm of Eve and Adam. In a tiny little house that didn't even have a Madam ... it spread around the world, the stork flew like an eagle. And finally they had to pass some laws to make it legal. Like every other business when the competition is sizzling, most of it was legitimate but of course there had to be some chiseling. Hotsie Totsie babes discovered there was gold in them thar thrills. That's when the government began to print two dollar bills. According to records which I have in my possession, it's the only business in the world that's never had a depression."

Tucker's material is a bit dated (especially the schmaltzy tearjerkers) and some albums duplicate material, but the delivery and the arrangements vividly recall a bygone era.

LEE TULLY

- SELTZER ON THE ROCKS (MGM E 3695) ** $7 $15
- THE OTHER SIDE OF LEE TULLY (Jubilee JGM 2036) ** $5 $10
- JOIN THE LOVE-IN (Jubilee JGM 2070) ** $5 $10

Lee Tully's MGM and Jubilee albums present a startling change in styles. In 1943 Tully was a bright young star from the Catskills; his MGM album from the late '50s is tilted toward Jewish novelty tunes. He cowrote the best known tune, "Essen," a Danny Kaye-type patter song about nonstop gorging on resort food. Other tunes on this studio album are cowritten by Eli Basse: "Litvak Polka," "Humintash Lane," "Oomglick Blues," "Catskill Mountain Square Dance," and "Litvak and Galitz." Tully pauses now and then for a short monologue, such as "The Lone Stranger":

"Ah, Tante, dis is de place, de Vest. Vere men are men and women are women. It's a nice arrangement ... put on de television set. Ve'll vatch *Wild Bill Nudnik*. Every cockamamie's a cowboy on TV today. *Wyatt Burp*. Even Greenwich Village got a cowboy show. It's called *Wells Faygelah*. Tante, vat are we doin' in the desert! Oy vey, we're lost ... and I haven't passed water for days! And I'm dying of thirst! Seltzer! Seltzer! A malted, maybe?"

In the late '60s, Tully made a pair of "straight albums," befitting a stand-up comic appearing on *Hollywood Palace* and *The Tonight Show*. "The Other Side of Lee Tully" experiments, mildly, with the kind of monologue sketches that had made Bob Newhart and Charlie Manna popular at the time:

Imagine if a modern agent tried to counsel Shakespeare: "One more time, use a typewriter, those actors can't read your handwriting." Or a frustrated man dealing with the phone company: "Hello operator? Hello? Yes, I received my phone bill this morning and you made a mistake. No dear I don't mean you personally."

In "Join the Love-In," Tully does mild monologues about the sexual revolution. Talking about sex in the schools:

"As the pupils get older, the classes get bolder. Eventually they're gonna be taught about prostitution, homosexuality—I didn't even know about these things when I was in the army. In fifth grade one lesson actually tells the kids that human life begins when the cells of the father and the cells of the mother both unite. I can just picture two kids talking to each other, and one says: 'I just found out how I was born. My mother and father were cell mates.'"

DAVE TURNER

- LAFF OF THE PARTY WITH DON BEXLEY (Dooto DTL 238) ** $5 $10
- THE FUNNIEST NEW COMIC SINCE THE LAST NEW COMIC (Roulette 25201) ** $5 $10

Discovered by Dinah Washington, Turner was a singer in the group The Shades of Rhythm and later with Bill Doggett's combo. The Dooto album's stand-out cut is "The Golf Game." As predictable as a vaudeville sketch (note Autry Inman's white Southern version of it) it has surefire double entendres. Turner talks about a golf instructor:

"He said, 'You got balls haven't you?' I said, 'Well hell yeah! Of course on a cold morning sometime they're kinda hard to find....' He said, 'You got a bag haven't you?' I said, 'Sure.' Then he asked if my balls were in it ... then he asked me if I knew how to hold my club in both hands. After thirty years I should! And he said, 'You take your club in both hands ... and you swing it over your shoulder.' I said, 'Oh, no, not me....'" And so on and on.

Recorded live at Birdland in the mid-60s, Turner's Roulette disc has some funky jazz/hip humor to it. He tells about a wife who comes up before a judge: "She said, 'Judge, your ornery, I wanna divorce my husband.' Judge says, 'On what grounds?' She said, 'The grounds right here ... he been acting awful strange lately, judge. He come into the house last night. He had a cigarette, no label on it your ornery ... had all my kids noddin' ... he had some funny little powder in his hand. (Sniffs.) Right up his nose, judge! Tonight he ran into the house, tied up his arm, started jabbin' himself with a needle. Tell me yo' honor, waddya think about that!' The judge looked down and said, 'Crazy, baby!'"

NICK TURNER

- SONGS FROM THE TRIAL OF THE CENTURY (Quality QALCD 6733) * $7

On this quickie (twenty-seven-minute) attempt to cash in on the O. J. Simpson case, bland-voiced Turner offers uninteresting lyrics to well-known tunes. A dumb one about Robert Shapiro, sung to "Hava Nagila," proclaims: "Robert Shapiro! He is our hero. For the past year-o he's been our man. Flashing that famous smile. Always dressed up in style. Every day he's in the trial. How'd he get so tan."

Once in a while there's a somewhat amusing twist of old lyrics and appropriate new ones. "Marcia Clark," a parody of "MacArthur Park," switches "someone left the cake out in the rain" to "someone left the glove beside the wall." And the original's "striped pair of pants" now becomes a reference to O. J.'s prison garb. But Jay Leno's musical parodies during the trial were less contrived, and for free.

TWO LIVE JEWS

- AS KOSHER AS THEY WANNA BE (Kosher HTCD 3328) *1/2 $7
- FIDDLING WITH TRADITION (Kosher HTCD 3339) *1/2 $7
- DISCO JEWS (Kosher HTCD 3375) * $7

The one-joke concept: two old Jewish men from Miami singing rap, disco, etc. Eric Lambert and Joe Stone, the guys imitating "Easy Irving" and "Moisha MC," are a few trudges behind Billy Crystal in their accents. And while Crystal's affection toward his elders was always greater than his embarrassment over their behavior or accents, here a lot of the humor is jeering. On "Disco Jews," the tune "Funky Town" becomes "Bargain Town." The old men are ridiculed for their (stereotypical) obsession with getting a low price. A few songs later, there's, "She's a JAP! She shops all day! A JAP!" As deserving of parody as these targets might be, the results here are more contemptuous than comic.

"Fiddling with Tradition" is a mild reworking of songs from *Fiddler on the Roof*. The duo should've quit with the first album, which has a cute gag now and then (Easy Irving is not hiply "def," just plain deaf). In one minute, the album makes its point about strident semitic voices with the hideous chorus of yentas who squeal, "Oy, it's so humid" in a parody of various "Oooh, me so horny" rap songs. Another minute and it's overkill.

THE TWO RONNIES

- THE TWO RONNIES VOLUME THREE (BBC Records BBC 22331) *** $5 $10

"The Two Ronnies" were British comedy stars Ronnie Barker (the portly one with the white hair and glasses) and Ronnie Corbett (the little one with the black hair and glasses). Excellent comedy writers as well as performers, their work veered between bristling satire and Benny Hill-level sauce. One of their staples was an opening news and information section:

"We'll have film of the Nairsborough dustman who got married this morning. This afternoon he carried his happy bride across the threshold, but through force of habit dropped bits of her along the garden path.... Mr. Zachariah Mole, the world's untidiest man, died today. His body is now lying in a state.... Meanwhile, the search for the man who terrorizes nudist camps with a bacon slicer goes on. Inspector Lemuel Jones had a tip-off this morning, but hopes to be back on duty tomorrow."

Their mix of the literate, the lewd, and the looney may not be for everyone, but for those who enjoy Britons like Flanders and Swann and Monty Python, and want some kind of cross between the two (or rather, the two and the six) "The Two Ronnies" adds up rather nicely.

Other records were released only in England: Volume One (BBC 257), Volume Two (BBC 300), and Volume Four (BBC 393), as well as "The Very Best of Me and The Very Best of Him" (BBC 514) and a peculiar album highlighting their program's full-blown (and often hard to follow lyrically) musical comedy numbers, "The Best of the Two Ronnies" (Transatlantic, also available in Canada on Attic Records). Ronnie Barker issued solo albums, "Porridge" (BBC 270) and "Ronnie Barker's Unbroken British Record" (K-Tel 1029).

ROBIN TYLER

- ALWAYS A BRIDESMAID NEVER A GROOM (Olivia RT-3) *1/2 $4 $8
- JUST KIDDING (H&T Productions) ** $5 $10

With her partner Pat Harrison evidently moving backstage to take care of the business side of Harrison and Tyler Productions, Robin Tyler continued to try feminist humor—which tended to be arch and argumentative: "I finally liberated myself to not wearing a bra ... and I am rather large ... and some guy came over to me and said, 'You should wear a bra.' I said, 'Why?' And he said, 'Your breasts don't stand.' And I said, 'Honey, when your penis stands all the time, my breasts'll stand all the time.'"

Some of Tyler's stance may be justified, especially in the early '70s when insisting on being called "Ms" was enough to cause an argument. The 1985 "Just Kidding" album was recorded before an evidently all-woman audience. They applaud wildly when Tyler mentions, "I have two cats." She skewers political figures of the day: "Nancy Reagan. I mean, *really*. You know what I mean? All women are our sisters? Give me a break.... Now I am a lesbian, but I asked myself, if I was on an island with Nancy Reagan or Tom Selleck, I mean, I would have to think. Ya know what I mean?"

She seems to be funniest on topics outside her main areas of crusading interest. Like religion: "Jesus had to be a Jewish boy, ok? He lived with his family till he was thirty, took up his father's profession, and his mother thought he was God. Come on!"

DAVID TYREE

- FUNNIEST BLACK MAN IN AMERICA (Quality QALCD 6716) ** $8

Tyree's "test joke" for the crowd on his 1994 CD gives a pretty good idea of the rest: "So I'm trying to screw this big fat chick the other day. I reach into her panties and get a handful of cracker crumbs. I said, 'Excuse me honey, what are you doin' with cracker crumbs in your panties?' She says, 'Everything tastes better when it sits on a Ritz.'" Tyree's funky set of observations and cuss words isn't unique, but at least he doesn't take himself too seriously. Nor does he take seriously the kind of problems people go to comedy clubs to avoid: "Got a lot of homeless people out there ... lotta homeless. We gotta do something about the homeless, y'all. 'Cause we're runnin' out of shopping carts! Can't go anywhere without trippin' over them big dirty feet ... y'all got quiet like you care. Fuck you! You're right, I shouldn't talk about the homeless. But they ain't here!"

CLAY TYSON

- UP TIGHT (Frandy LP 800, reissued as Chess 1494) ** $5 $10
- CLAY TYSON DIGS THE BEATNIK (Winley WLP 6002, reissued as Up Front UPF 117) *1/2 $5 $10
- LAUGH YOUR ASS OFF (Partee 2401) ** $5 $10
- STRAIGHT FROM THE HORSE'S MOUTH (Atco 33213) *1/2 $4 $8

Tyson was toiling away in Atlanta nightclubs as early as 1953, reaching New York in 1957. A few years later he cut the Winley album (a recording company on 125th Street in Harlem), a bunch of ancient risqué stories that only a few in the tiny audience were laughing at. His major label debut in 1967 for Atco features ethnic humor no different from what many others were doing. On the space program: "Twelve time they left for the moon already, not one time they came up and said, 'Do ya'll wanna go?' We'll go. You don't have to go through college and all that stuff to go into space. Give some of us a fifth of wine, we'll go anywhere!"

More interesting, at least for fans of ethnic humor, is "Laugh Your Ass Off." Tyson works with straight man Michael Graham and goes through a number of mildly raunchy vaudeville routines:

"I used to be in show business myself." "What did you do?" "I used to play with the Ringling Sisters." "With the who?" "I used to play with the Ringling Sisters." "Aw man, you mean the Ringling Brothers." "I used to play with the Ringling Sisters." "You mean you used to play with the Ringling Brothers!" "You play with who you like, I'll play with who I like!"

UNCLE BILL

- UNCLE BILL SOCKS IT TO YA (Dot DLP 25879) ** $5 $10

When Mae West was in her late sixties, she amazed everyone with a fairly hip album of rock songs. W. C. Fields, dead for twenty years, couldn't compete. But "Uncle Bill," a look-alike and fairly decent sound-alike, could.

The result is almost at the level of Mae West's or George Burns's rock records. Imagine the Fieldsian cadence sawing through the Beatles ("A Little Help from My Friends") and Bob Dylan ("The Mighty Quinn"). Fields, as most fans know, hated singers and sang his own obscure British Music Hall songs in a somewhat sadistic wandering key. That spirit is preserved here.

For the folk tune "Bottle of Wine," Uncle Bill offers Fieldsian ad-libs: "Down with wine! I've probably downed more wine than anyone in the country." Several tunes have spoken introductions done by several writers from the *Laugh-In* TV show attempting to duplicate Fields's hallucinogenic anecdotes:

"Ah, 'giant step,' that's exactly what I took when I married my first wife, Petunia La Fong. She said if I ever went out with another woman after she passed away that she'd dig her way out of her grave and haunt me. I fooled her though, I buried her face down.... I haven't had so much fun since I bought a bear rug from an inebriated zoo keeper in downtown Azusa. Unfortunately, two days later I found out the creature was still alive. Would've been a great conversation piece, but I couldn't persuade the animal to learn English. How humiliating."

UNCLE DIRTY

- THE UNCLE DIRTY PRIMER (Elektra EKS 74097) **1/2 $6 $12

This album was made in 1971, at a time when Lenny Bruce was rediscovered and fans wished there were someone just like him alive and well and telling the truth. Uncle Dirty (Bob Altman) may have been the closest to Bruce, at least in style. Unlike Carlin, Pryor, Baron, or Roman, Uncle Dirty utilized Lenny's style of mimicry as he shot out quick studies of women, gays, Italians, blacks, and especially Jewish characters. He used Lenny's personal approach to comedy, trying to hip the audience, confess to them, and make 'em laugh about drugs, sex, and moral issues.

Like Lenny, who would toss out a line just to test censor tolerance ("Will Elizabeth Taylor be bar-mitvohed?"), Uncle Dirty likes a provocative, if idiotic one-liner: "Midget hookers for child molesters!" Lenny's riffs on carping old Jewish mothers get updated here, as Dirty recalls Jewish-sounding pets influenced by his grandmother: "My dog went, 'oy! oy!' My goldfish went, 'Goigle.' The parakeet went, 'Tvit.' There was a reason for that, my grandmother used to sing to it, 'Tvit goes de parakeet.' What does the parakeet know, eighty-nine cents from Woolworth's. My grandmother drank so much Manischewitz, when they cremated her they couldn't get the fire out.... I couldn't relate to the guys in my neighborhood because of 'Catch the Jew,' so I went to the library ... those dykes would never beat you up. Just say, 'Put the book back.'"

Uncle Dirty did the obligatory drug routines and the hip seriocomic closing, complete with a thought to take home: "I'm you and you're me. If I hurt you, I hurt me. If you hurt me, you hurt you. 'Cause not to be loved is miserable. But not to love is catastrophe. Happy everyday...."

At this point, this 1971 hippie-dippie album is certainly dated, but there are some interesting bits here. The spectre of Lenny Bruce was a very real problem at the time. Many comics wanted to be like him but didn't want to be considered an imitator or pretender. This album, aside from whatever gags, jokes and observations that have survived, clearly shows the Lenny influence and dilemma of early 70s "relevant" comics.

UNCLE FLOYD

- THE UNCLE FLOYD SHOW (Mercury 811 149 1 M 1) * $7 $15

On New Jersey's UHF Channel 68 in 1974, Floyd Vivino began his TV series, a mock kiddie show with sketches, ragtime piano music, and puppets. It was an amateur's attempt at doing *The Soupy Sales Show*, complete with hearty har-har laughter from the offstage crew. He looked more like a smaller, and more humorless John Belushi than Soupy Sales or Pinky Lee, but earned a cult following for his annoying novelty songs.

His puppet Oogie is an irritating variation on kiddie host Claude Kirschner's Clownie puppet, with a dash of Spike Jones's George Rock. His sketches recall a variety of influences. "Dull Family," for instance, apes Bob and Ray's "Slow Talkers of America," as they ooze through a numbingly slow rendition of "There's No Business Like Show Business." Only cultists need this album—and they deserve to be soaked for the highest price possible.

PETER USTINOV

- PETER USTINOV IN STEREO
  (Riverside RLP 1127, re-released as GRAND PRIX OF GIBRALTER, Fantasy MPF-4507) *1/2 $6 $12
- THE MANY VOICES OF PETER USTINOV (ABC Westminster WBBC 8000) **1/2 $7 $15

The 1961 Riverside disc requires an appreciation of Ustinov's understated British wit and an extreme fondness for sports cars and racing. Even meeting these two requirements, there's no guarantee of more than giggles, since Ustinov improvised most of this studio recording from some pages of notes.

Back then, Riverside was issuing albums about car races ("Sounds of Sebring 1959") that included engine noises and interviews with racing greats prior to the race. Here, Ustinov does all the voices himself, interviewing various drivers and reporting on the specs of each car. Unlike Jonathan Winters, Ustinov's accents and sound effects are more realistic and satirical than cartoonish and hilarious. Typical of his droll style is the German mechanic who lectures about racing while keeping an eye on Von Grips, the driver:

"Ve have a new construction of de car ... Man must be de slave of hiss machine! The man must sit on the floor, but with one leg forward and the other beckvard—naturally this needs a little training. Von Grips! It's time to blow your nose now ... Ve haff discovered after our laboratory obsercations that the best time to blow the nose to have it completely clear is seven and a half minutes before the race begins. This is important because a handkerchief carried in ze pocket would be extra weight ... which would completely destroy the balance of this revolutionary new car which we have adapted."

On March 28, 1961, Ustinov appeared on BBC-TV for an informal interview show of mannered conversation and anecdotes. In an age when fans couldn't tape such things, an album was released. Not that it's worthy of archival consideration. Ustinov isn't always hiliarious, but he's never dull. The raconteur describes his trips to Australia, West Berlin, and the Orient, where he describes being steamed and massaged in the nude. In his war recollections he talks about the military mind, or lack of same. A highlight is his recounting of a practical joke played on director John Huston. An anecdote about Arizona benefits from his deadly accurate American accents.

NOTES: Some stores try to get a high price for the original Riverside pressing, but it is the album for ABC-Westminster that's much rarer. Ustinov has recorded many narration LPs, including a popular reading of "Babar the Elephant" for Angel Records, "Baron Munchausen" (Caedmon TC 1409), and James Thurber's "Great Quillow" (Caedmon TC 1411). He has also read his own literary material ("Ustinov Reads Ustinov," CMS 524). A segment of his race car routine appears on Riverside's "How to Be Terribly Terribly Funny" compilation. Ustinov's singing parodies "Mock Mozart" and "Phoney Folklore" turn up on "Collectors' Party Record" (Belcantodisc BC 235) with various classical works from sopranos and tenors. The label specialized in historical reissues from opera singers.

JOHN VALBY

- PHILOSOPHICAL BULLSHIT (Gemsbok) ** $5 $10
- DIRT (Gemsbok) ** $5 $10
- HOTEL BUFFALO (Gemsbok) ** $5 $10
- CONCERTO (Gemsbok) ** $5 $10

A sort of young, scatological Mark Russell, Valby pounds the piano and sings simple smut songs for his small but vocal East Coast followers. The Williamsville, New York, resident released albums and CDs on his own Gemsbok label. The "Dirt" album includes a typical blues song with simple, snappy stanzas about local figures and people in the news: "I know a priest named Father Slattery. To get it off he needs a DieHard battery.... I know a polack, his name is Cliff. He puts it in the freezer to get it stiff." The crowd laughs its approval and any four-letter words get them roaring with delight.

RUDY VALLEE

- THIS IS YOUR RUDY VALLEE (Crown CLP 5204) ** $5 $10
- THE FUNNY SIDE OF RUDY VALLEE (Jubilee 2051) **1/2 $5 $10
- AN EVENING WITH RUDY VALLEE (Mark 56 #681) **1/2 $8 $15

Vallee, a quaint crooner from the '20s and a modestly amusing actor in light musicals and comedies, tried stand-up in the '60s. He used mildly risqué songs and jokes. From the 1963 Jubilee album:

"This fellow's seated at a bar. There's a very attractive girl down at the other end of the bar. He says to the bartender, 'That's a luscious dish down there.' The bartender says, 'Don't get any ideas, that's my wife.' Guy says, 'Who'd get any ideas. Give me a piece of whiskey.'"

Vallee deadpans a monologue about his girl, delivered in a style that recalls early Jackie Gleason and Jackie Vernon: "Laura, you fool, I love you. I'll never forget the first time I met you, and don't think I don't try ... you were dazed, you were trembling. Honey, you were loaded. You'd been drinking that Italian wine. One drink: Wop.... I love you, you fool, I love every hair on your lip. Those nights in the park we sat on the bench, I crossed my eyes and looked straight into yours ... I used to call you my melancholy baby. You had a head like a melon and a face like a collie. I wanted to buy a handkerchief for your birthday but I didn't know the size of your nose. You prided yourself on being fastidious. Yes indeed, your father was fast and your mother was hideous. I remember your lonely tragic youth. You couldn't go walking, your feet were too big. You couldn't go swimming, your arms were too large. And you couldn't go horseback riding. Any questions?"

Vallee never exactly caught on as a stand-up, but he was a smooth, relaxed performer. The aging star and his aging jokes might be nostalgic for the old and an education for the young.

The double set on Mark 56 appears to be the complete version of the Jubilee "Funny Side" concert, putting back the straight tunes and musical parodies left on the cutting room floor.

LARRY VERNE

- MISTER LARRY VERNE (Era EL 104) ** $10 $25

Verne had a #1 1960 novelty hit with "Mister Custer." It wasn't much, really, just a bewildered, whinin' Southern soldier wonderin', "What am I doin' here?" in the middle of an Indian attack. He pleads with Mr. Custer, "Please don't make me go!" There's also some good ol' boy humor ("Hey Charlie, duck ya head! You were a little late on that one, Charlie. Bet that smarts") and comic muttering: "Look at 'em out there. Runnin' around like a bunch of wild Injuns."

Probably the tune was one of the inspirations for the TV series *F-Troop.* Some of the show's soldiers, particularly the character Hannibal Dobbs, had a touch of Verne's chagrined attitude. The studio album of monologues (backed with music and sound effects) varies the concept as rube Larry visits a Beatnik cafe, translates the Mexican ballad "Tres Dias," and helps his friend Charlie when the poor guy gets stuck in the dryer at the "Laundromat." In the formula of "Mr. Custer," Larry alternates between shouts and asides:

"Hey Charlie! It ain't gonna open for ten minutes. Think you can hold out? Boy, look at him spin. I'll be back in nine minutes, Charlie! He's gettin' smaller. Well, I better get on with my washin'. Where's the tubs? All there is around here is TV sets. Look at that, they're all showin' *Sea Hunt.* Hey Lady, where's the tubs and washboards? What? You put the clothes in these televisions? Oh, they washers? You just put the money in 'em and they work auto-matical. Hot shot in a flyin' pot, if that isn't somethin'." And on and on (and around and around) it goes. Only a few cuts rise to the level of "Mister Custer," but fans who enjoy Verne's unique delivery will enjoy most of them.

"Mr. Custer" is available on several CD compilations, but there are evidently two versions. The "original" can be heard on Dr. Demento's "25th Anniversary" collection (Rhino). The odd "variation" can be heard on "Hard to Find Hits Vol. 1" (Curb). For the latter, Verne seems to have redone his part, adding or remixing sound effects and background shouts. The tampering may have yielded a better version sonically, but it hasn't the magic of the original.

JACKIE VERNON

- A WET BIRD NEVER FLIES AT NIGHT (Jubilee JGM 2052) *** $10 $20
- A NIGHT IN NEW YORK WITH VIC DAMONE AND JACKIE VERNON (Ethicon TB 191) *** $10 $25

Vernon was one of the pioneers of deadpan stand-up. Although well known for "dull guy" jokes based on his rotund body and pasty, sad-sack face, Vernon also favored weird one-liners and bizarre routines. The 1961 Jubilee disc is very early Vernon, notable not for dull gags but the sick humor that was very popular at the time: "I walked by a funeral parlor the other day. It had a sign in the window: 'Closed because of a birth in the family.' Someone sent me a weird gift for my birthday: a bowling ball with a thumb in it.... Just this afternoon I saw a cross-eyed woman tell a bow-legged man to go straight home."

A routine about Bela Lugosi recalls Lenny Bruce in content, but certainly not delivery: "Oh, Bela Lugosi. Fascinating man. With the VO-5 in his hair. The flamenco boots. A little of that Canoe cologne. I don't know, he had that show biz look. Can you imagine a girl going on a date with Bela Lugosi? 'Gee you kiss funny. You leave little holes.' Sort of a perforated hickey. Wouldn't it be weird if we were to find out Dracula is a Jehovah's Witness?"

Another bit with a Brucian twinge is about "The Lone Ranger." Here, it turns out that Tonto is really the Lone Ranger's mother. One of his early "dull guy" gags: "The meek shall inherit the Earth. They won't have the nerve to refuse it."

Vernon and singer Vic Damone entertained nurses at an event (February 9, 1965) at the N.Y. Hilton. On the souvenir album sent to those who attended, Vernon mixes in plenty of his offbeat and cerebral gags with more standard routines. He mentions "Wilbur Fradblatt ... poet, prophet, and philosopher. He prophesied that on May 1st, 1951, the world would come to an end. And for him it did. Because on that very day, while eating a piece of cherry pie at the Automat, the little glass door snapped down on his neck ... well you see, he didn't know you were supposed to take the food out. They rushed him to the hospital and that night he passed the crisis and died." The nurses seem especially amused. Damone takes a full side for his songs.

- A MAN AND HIS WATERMELON (United Artists UAL 3577) *** $10 $20
- THE DAY MY ROCKING HORSE DIED (United Artists UAS 6679) **1/2 $10 $20

Vernon's 1967 "Watermelon" album is studded with many excellent routines about the dull and homely. He reports on his hometown, "Ferguson, Ohio," where a big sign said "Welcome to Ferguson. Beware of the Dog," and the all-night drugstore closed at noon. He lectures on "What Is a Dull Man": "A dull guy is a fellow who usually runs away from home when he's thirty-eight ... if he has a job it's usually as a piano player in a marching band. A dull guy is a man who buys a painting of Lady Godiva because he likes horses."

The classic title cut is a surreal monologue about befriending a watermelon as a pet, teaching it tricks, and taking it out for a walk: "I figured, well, if it didn't work out I could always eat it." Like so much of Vernon's quietly bent material, it was often lost on nightclub audiences of the day. Over the decades, he tended to use more obvious material in order to maintain bookings at the standard casinos.

The 1969 "Rocking Horse" is one of the lousiest comedy albums ever recorded. The material is all right. The actual recording of it is terrible. Vernon recalled that there was a tight deadline for product and his comedy writer Danny Davis decided to try to produce it himself, splicing together two very different Vernon performances (one was recorded when Jackie was so sick he could hardly wheeze out the punch lines) and adding "extra sweetening" to the laugh track by simply playing a continuous loop of laughter and turning up the volume near the punch lines. Sometimes, in turning the laughter down again, he audibly slowed the laugh track down, turning the yocks into groans.

Jackie had some amusing loser gags: "My mother used to park my carriage in tow-away zones. On an unlisted street.... We were so poor we used to use a substitute for margarine.... We didn't have a TV set, we used to sit around and watch the mirror." Unfortunately, the arrival of the feistier Rodney Dangerfield created more problems for the gentle, offbeat performer and his star began to eclipse. Jackie's subtle humor (he reports Ponce De Leon "ended his life by dying") was simply too subtle for the average listener.

- SEX IS NOT HAZARDOUS TO YOUR HEALTH (Beverly Hills BH 1133) *** $7 $15

Around 1976 Vernon went into the studio with Tom Bosley, Marian Mercer, and Louisa Moritz to create an album of twenty-one short routines on sex—a kind of comedy album version of "Everything You Always Wanted to Know about Sex." Rather than "the dull man," Vernon plays a sex expert answering questions:

"Doctor, I have very small breasts. What should I do?" "Marry a man with very small hands." "Doctor, nowadays the streets are filled with unsavory characters. How can women best protect themselves after dark?" "They might try looking at night like they do in the morning." "Doctor, what does a sadist do?" "Beats me."

There are also man-in-the-street moments, as when Vernon comes up to Tom Bosley saying, "Please mister, I'm desperate. Give me $20. I haven't had a woman in months!" Bosley asks, "Why don't you get married?" Vernon gasps, "What? And have to beg for it every night?"

Vernon's light, bewildered delivery makes a lot of the lines funnier than they are. In fact, he breaks the audience up just by pronouncing the word "voyeur."

NOTES: Vernon appears on two promo albums: a 1967 State Farm Life Insurance disc and 1969's "Radio Plays the Plaza," a compilation from the Radio Advertiser's Bureau.

VIC AND SADE

- ORIGINAL RADIO BROADCASTS (Mark 56 # 732) ** $5 $10

From 1932 to 1944, "radio's homefolks" Vic and Sade provided fifteen daily minutes of mild human nature humor. Today's listeners might detect some similarity to Bob and Ray in the show's emphasis on the almost surreally mundane. And while *The Cosby Show* and *Seinfeld* often had "plotless" episodes geared mostly to quirks of human nature and family life, it was Vic and Sade's writer Paul Rhymer who pioneered that slice-of-life style.

Ray Bradbury believed Rhymer captured "all our inane conversations, all our bored afternoons and long evenings." Vic Gook (Arthur Van Harvey) and his wife Sade (Bernadine Flynn) still have a loyal cult to this day, though much of the goings on in "the little house halfway up the next block" are an acquired taste. Vic and Sade move slowly, and those who don't identify with their mid-American identity might find things achingly dull.

One fifteen-minute episode on the album is nothing more than Sade mildly arguing with Vic over why he doesn't write to his brother-in-law enough. Another is devoted to Vic's son describing his ideas for an upcoming party. Here's a conversation between Sade and her son as they sit in a porch swing watching townsfolk go by:

"There goes Mr. Clack. Got his little umbrella up." "Wonder why. The rain stopped." "He carries it to keep off the sun. He had sunstroke one time, been scared of it ever since ... always wears tennis shoes on account of it too ... when he was a young man working on the farm he keeled over from the heat. Affected his ankle some way. Had to wear tennis shoes ever since...." "Funny place to get sunstroke. The ankles." "That's the way it is." "Pretty nice sittin' here in the porch swing, huh? Ain't ya glad I called ya out?" "Never was so happy in my life." "You passed a sarcastic remark, huh? That's okay, I like to see a streak of fun in an individual's makeup."

The porch swing routine turns up on "Son of Jest Like Old Times" (Radiola #2). A special half hour edition of the show, broadcast October 26, 1946, is the flip side to "The Spike Jones Show" (Radiola MR 1010).

GORE VIDAL

- AN EVENING WITH RICHARD NIXON (Ode SP77015) **1/2 $5 $10

Gore Vidal does not appear on this cast album based on his pre-Watergate off-Broadway play. There are two main characters, Pro and Con, who sound like Vidal and William F. Buckley, Jr. They narrate the story of Richard Nixon, which periodically dissolves into sketches in which George S. Irving plays Nixon and Robert King attempts John F. Kennedy. Julius Monk revue players George Hall and Alex Wiph are here and, if typographically correct, an actress named "Susan Saradon." An a capella group of women, called The Saliva Sisters, provides ironic background music.

Vidal carefully researched Nixon, and all of his quotes are real: "Nothing has been invented, nothing has been taken out of context." Of course Vidal manipulates the material for ironic effect:

"At Kent State College in Ohio, National Guardsmen shot and killed three students as they viciously demonstrated against the war."

Nixon: "This should remind us all, once again, that when dissent turns to violence, it invites tragedy ... listen, the boys on the college campuses today are the luckiest people in the world. Here they are burning up the books.... Get rid of the war? There'll be another one."

Later, as The Saliva Sisters hum "The Good Ship Lollipop," Tricia Nixon is heard: "The vice president is incredible. It's amazing what he's done to the media, helping them to reform themselves. You can't underestimate the power of fear." Then Nixon: "I never called a publisher. I never called an editor. Never called a reporter. I don't care. And that's what makes them mad. I just don't care."

The album is still interesting as history and as an exercise in comic technique. Those who believe in reincarnation may be interested to hear Nixon declare, "If I had my life to live over again, I'd like to have ended up ... a sports writer."

THE VILLAGE IDIOTS

- THE VILLAGE IDIOTS (Laff A 208) *1/2 $3 $7

A comedy troupe that performed on Don Kirshner's Rock Concerts, Janice Fischer, Mark Ganzel, Robin Hunt, and Mert Rich offer pseudo-hip sketches recorded sans live audience.

 Predictable cuts include a radio commercial that starts off "High? Oh, excuse me. High," and a kiddie show parody in which the host mutters, "Took some bad drugs last night" and wonders if "mommy's upstairs getting an extra quart of buttermilk from Mr. Milkman!"

Not particularly talented or convincing actors, the foursome take aim at less hip comics (a long routine on the life and times of "Shecky Rimshot"), offer a pseudo-Python sketch about a rude French waiter ("Will you be fingering madame under the table?"), and score slightly with easy routines on commercials.

"It's the windup, it's the pitch! It's Bammo's new idea for summer fun, Kitty Ball ... yes, everybody loves Kitty Ball. Except kitty! (Sound of a cat screaming.) The Kitty Ball kit includes kitty bat, mitts, and a litter of kittens, enough to last an entire fun-filled game. And don't miss these other amazing Bammo products: Puppy Soccer and Hamster J'Alai."

BRUCE VILANCH

- OUT OF THE CLOSET (Ariola SW 50023) **1/2 $5 $15

Vilanch, a gay comedy writer who contributes material to many variety and awards shows, cowrote and costarred on this 1977 studio album. It features Steve Bluestein, Anthony Holland, Pamela Myers, Marilyn Sokol, and others. The thirteen sketches tried to find humor in various gay-gay and gay-straight situations. Like this confrontation between a woman and the man she's been going out with, who has now decided to come out of the closet:

"I'm gay!" "You're telling me!" "What do you mean?" "I've always known you were gay ... you know, like your throwing up every time we made love." "I had hoped you didn't notice." "No hard feelings. We'll split a quiche over brunch some time. If you get a chance, return my Stephen Sondheim records."

The sketches are uneven; some work, some don't. A few chide gays and lesbians while others are more patronizing. No doubt it was difficult for Vilanch to decide exactly what to do with this opportunity. There weren't many other gay comedy records at the time (a few drag albums and a sympathetic disc from straight Sandy Baron) and here he seemed to have the responsibility of speaking (comedically) for the entire gay community.

JACK WAKEFIELD

- JACK WAKEFIELD TAKES CONCORD (Legend LP 3000) ** $6 $12

Minor Catskill comic Jack Wakefield (the former Milton Fagin from Brooklyn) doesn't fit the stereotypes of a schmaltzy storyteller, a rim shot and one-liner pro, or an aggressive tummler. Perhaps that's why this 1963 album was his first and last. Recorded at the Concord Hotel, the show is a well-meaning mess of observations and joke book gags from a guy who looks a bit like Murray the Cop from *The Odd Couple*.

From an amusing, if dated, bit aimed squarely at his Jewish crowd: "Sammy Davis became Jewish. Now he can't go to the Forest Hills Tennis Club for *two* reasons. I'll tell you one thing, Sammy is the type of guy that loves people, loves to help people. We had trouble in Birmingham, Sammy went right down to Birmingham, got on the bus. The guy says, 'Sit in the back.' He said, 'I'm Jewish.' The guy said, 'Get off!' Sammy don't look to do things for publicity, he's a great great talent.... He became Jewish, they said he did it for publicity. He did not do it for publicity. Sammy Davis wanted to be a Jew. Sammy Davis proved that he would be a good Jew. 'Cause as soon as he became Jewish he married a Gentile. And he married a beautiful girl, May Britt. Thank God, it sounds like a Jewish organization. It would've been a little ridiculous if she called herself Sarah Hadassah."

DICK WALDEN

- WORLD OF COMEDY (Jubilee JGM 2066) *1/2 $4 $8

Walden evidently produced a show for up and coming comics and took it to college campuses in the mid-60s. This was recorded at Penn State with Walden introducing the hopefuls: Gene Brenner, Irwin Best, Jerry Winnick, Dave Kent, and the team of Jim and Dorothy. Nothing experimental here and no surprises. Jerry Winnick declares, "In the Midwest when we have homicidal maniacs we put them in jail. But not in New York. They give 'em jobs as cab drivers." And Gene Brenner says: "Everybody today is either a neurotic, a psychotic, or a psychiatrist. A neurotic, this is a fella who builds castles in the air. A psychotic. He lives in 'em. The psychiatrist, he collects the rent from these two fellas."

BETTY WALKER

- LOVE AND LAUGHTER (Coral 757328) ** $10 $25
- HELLO, CEIL, IT'S ME! (Columbia CS 9744) **1/2 $12 $30
- AUNT LENA AND HER FAMILY CIRCLE (Jennie 1001) ** $10 $20

Betty Walker appeared in films (*Who Is Harry Kellerman*, *Exodus*) and on Broadway (*Middle of the Night*, *Sarava*) but will always be best known for her "Hello Ceil" routines, the chatty duplication of a typical Jewish housewife's life on the phone. From the Coral album:

"Hello, Ceil? Listen, Ceil, are you still taking your course in child psychology? You are. Good. I'd like your advice on my opinion. Last night, ya hear, Ceil, last night my Marilyn and my Chickie were playing, and my Chickie got hold of a stapling machine ... and my Chickie got hold of my Marilyn's finger, and she put it right into the stapling machine. But wait a minute Ceil. She pressed down. So this is what I wanted to ask you, Ceil. Psychologically speaking, do you think my Chickie resents my Marilyn, or do you think she's mechanically inclined?"

The Coral album varies drastically in quality, between the six "Ceil" bits and a bunch of obvious, dull sketches with Dave Karr. The later Columbia album has more prime "Ceil" material for those who like New York-accented grousing. Betty's husband is sick:

"I'll tell you what's wrong with him. Emotional flu ... Hold on, Ceil, El Exigente is calling me. (Off to her husband) Warren! Sweetheart! If the vaporizer is choking you, shut it off! (To Ceil) I can't imagine how this man would carry on if he was ever pregnant. Nature knew what she was doing when she handed out the roles. Yeah ... (Off) What do you want, Warren dear? (To Ceil) Hello Ceil? He wants me to tell you a joke. You have to ask me why I know, beyond a shadow of a doubt, that Adam and Eve were Jewish. Hold On. (Off) Wait a minute Warren! I'll tell ya if she laughed in a minute! (To Ceil) Ask me. The reason that Adam and Eve were definitely Jewish is: who else says, 'Take a piece of fruit?' (Off) She didn't laugh Warren! (To Ceil) Ceil ... he wants me to rub his back ... who can talk now."

"Aunt Lena" has an endorsement from Victor Borge: "Betty is the funniest lady I have heard in thirty years." But the feisty "Aunt Lena" character can't sustain a whole album as she rambles, pontificates, and kvetches like the wife of Mel Brooks's 2000 Year-Old Man. She babbles as she bosses family members: "Jenny? Get away from de fish! Dora made de fish. Boitram, get away from de fish! Naomi, don't eat dat fish, it's gonna lay like a stone. No whitefish, no pike, nothing. Mid no bread ... Dora made de fish again dis year! So ven Nellie vas in the hospital, de nurse brought in a basket you know, Michael, de basket dat comes mit fruit, mit candy, mit a ribbon, dat basket. So ven de nurse brought in de basket, Nellie said, 'Who sent dis basket?' So dey tell her, Oiving's children. 'Oiving's children sent me a basket! If Oiving's children sent a basket, den dat means dat I am dead! 'Cause Oiving's children don't send de basket if you're living. Dey only send you the basket if you're dead.' And from de excitement, she died, from de basket!"

There's an awful lot of this, which could be either warm recognition humor or sadistic nostalgia for anyone who once knew an Aunt Lena.

NOTES: Betty Walker is on "You Don't Have to Be Jewish" (Kapp). She also has four "Ceil" cuts on "The Jest of Flair," a promo album from ABC featuring material on the syndicated Flair radio series. An interesting example of Betty's versatility is on a ten-inch 45 rpm acetate disc pressed at ODO Sound Studios in New York. It's a cabaret piece called "The British English Song," a title that doesn't seem appropriate, since it's a parody of French art songs. Walker sings well in French, providing the improbable translations: "I am a prostitute ... If you call me, I'll give green stamps."

In New York, where many over forty remember her well, prices are often double than anywhere else.

JERRY WALKER

- THE FAIRY GODMOTHER (Kent KST 003) ** $5 $10

A black female impersonator, Walker doesn't mince any worse than Little Richard, sometimes acting as tough as Moms Mabley as he goes through his mix of '60s kink and funk. He tells the howling female ringsiders, "I wear my curls, but we different kind of girls. But we girls. I may not be no real woman, but I'm fine as wine. And if the girls can get theirs in the front, ain't a damn thing wrong with my behind!"

JIMMIE WALKER

- DYN-O-MITE (Buddah 5635) * $5 $10

A stringbean with a grotesquely wide mouth, Jimmie Walker became a favorite on the sitcom *Good Times* in 1974. Some considered his role a foolish stereotype, and many were disgusted by his funky catchphrase, an obnoxiously rowdy shout of "Dyn-O- Miiiiiiite!" His costar, Esther Rolle, quit the show as "a matter of black pride." The album came out in 1975 when he was at his peak.

The rambling Walker (who in comic bravado dubs himself "The Black Prince") doesn't use many jokes. Instead, he retells anecdotes, figuring there's humor in his jivey recollections. At the time, he was justified. Just standing onstage looking ridiculous made people laugh. Recorded before a predominantly black audience, Walker does some mild racial material about the first black president:

"Prez pulls up. Eldorado, white bucket seats, bubble top. The Prez gets out. The chauffeur gets out. Prez addresses the crowd. Tilts his beaver skin hat to the side. Takes off his shades. Addresses the crowd: 'Ladies and gentlemen, brothers and sisters. I am very happy to be elected president of these great United States. And moreover I'm very happy to be elected the first buh-lack, BUH-lack, president of these great United States. Right now I'd like to give the state of the union address. But first. The number for today: 756! You got it? You're the vice president, come with me.'"

NANCY WALKER

- I HATE MEN (Camden CAL 561) ** $10 $20
- I CAN COOK, TOO (Dolphin 2, reissued DRG 909,
  and reissued as NANCY WALKER SINGS, Stet SOT 2002) ** $5 $10

Walker was a delight on Broadway (*On the Town*) long before she became known as the eccentric mother to Rhoda Morgenstern (*The Mary Tyler Moore Show*) and "Rosie," the paper towel maven in TV commercials. The Dolphin album is pretty mild stuff. As a singer she fails to bring any distinctive comic identity to songs like "Milkman Keep Those Bottles Quiet (from *Broadway Rhythm*) or "The Saga of Jenny" (from *Lady in the Dark*). She's a little more lively on "I Hate Men," which manages to collect songs that are more a stomp on the toe than a kick in the groin. These include two drolly venemous Rodgers and Hart tunes ("To Keep My Love Alive," "Everything I've Got") and Cole Porter classics "You Irritate Me So," "Most Gentlemen Don't Like Love," and the title tune, which was from *Kiss Me Kate*. Also see entry for Reginald Gardner.

WALL AND PETERSON

- BOTTOMS UP FOR SWINGERS (WP 1 3650) *1/2 $3 $7

Breck Wall and Joe Peterson produced a revue at the Flamingo Hotel and it starred an ensemble cast including Wall, Betty Waldron, Rob Barron, Mary Weintraub, Vikki Anthony, Alicia Irwin, Deeda Hymes, and others. It's a bit like *Laugh-In*, with little sketches and musical bits. Most posture too much and go on too long. A husband greets his wife and she says:

"Guess what?" "What, darling?" "I found out a new way of having sex today ... we take off all our clothes ... and then we get into bed." "Oh boy." "And then we turn back to back." "Stark naked, we turn back to back? Honey, that doesn't make any sense, back to back." "Oh, I forgot to tell you. We invite another couple!"

JAMES GARRETT WALLACE

- SINGS OF THE LAW AND LAWYERS (Association of the Bar of the City of New York) * $10 $20

A New York judge and former Assistant District Attorney in the '50s, Jim Wallace enjoyed creating comic songs that seemed to amuse his peers at banquets and other functions:

"A case was tried before me, and the lawyer was a pest. I asked a lot of questions and got some things off my chest. The jury said he's guilty. The defendant went away. The boys on 25th Street then began to have their say. Some didn't like my questions, while the others thought them cute. Two of the lads were with me but three others used the boot. This black eye that I'm wearing is a thing that I deplore. Nobody really hit me, I just struck an open door. I've got the blues. I've got the blues. I've got those appellate division blues."

Wallace sings with stout dignity. He died in 1956 and this tribute/collection arrived the following year.

RUTH WALLIS

• OLD PARTY FAVORITES (Wallis W1) **	$8	$15
• OLD PARTY FAVORITES II (Wallis W2) **	$8	$15
• CAFE PARTY (Wallis W3) **	$8	$15
• LATIN PARTY RHYTHMS (Wallis 4) **	$8	$15
• HOLIDAY PARTY (Wallis 5) **	$8	$15
• LIFE OF THE PARTY (Wallis 6) **	$8	$15
• CRUISE PARTY (Wallis 7) **	$8	$15
• AMERICA'S PARTY GIRL (Wallis 8) **	$8	$15
• TORRID LOVE SONGS (Wallis WL 9)	$8	$15
• ON THE PARTY LINE (Wallis WL 10) **	$8	$15
• SAUCY HIT PARADE (Wallis WL 11) **	$8	$15
• SAUCY REDHEAD (Wallis LPS 12) **	$8	$15
• FOR SOPHISTICATES ONLY (Wallis WL 13) **	$8	$15
• FRENCH POSTCARDS (Wallis LPW 14) **	$8	$15
• CRUISE PARTY/SAUCY CALYPSO (Wallis WL 15) **		
• SALTY SONGS FOR UNDERWATER LISTENING (Wallis WL 16) **	$8	$15
• LOVE IS FOR THE BIRDS (Wallis WL 17)	$8	$15

- HOT SONGS FOR COOL KNIGHTS (Wallis WL 18) ** ... $8 ... $15
- LIVE AND KICKING (Wallis WL 19) ** ... $8 ... $15
- HOUSE PARTY (King 507) ... $7 ... $12
- DAVY'S LITTLE DINGHY (King 987) ** ... $7 ... $12
- OIL MAN FROM TEXAS (King 991) ** ... $7 ... $12
- HE WANTS A LITTLE PIZZA (King 992) ** ... $7 ... $12
- BAHAMA MAMA (King 993) ** ... $7 ... $12
- MARRY GO ROUND (King 988) ... $7 ... $12
- RED LIGHTS (King 989) ... $7 ... $12
- UBANGI ME (King 990) ** ... $7 ... $12
- THE SPICE IS RIGHT (Jubilee 2050) ... $8 ... $15
- SAUCY HIT PARADE (Blooper 904) ... $7 ... $14
- HOW TO STAY SEXY THO' MARRIED (Mercury 61210) ** ... $10 ... $20

In the '50s and '60s, Wallis specialized in "saucy songs" loaded with double entendres. She has a pleasant, innocent delivery, with a slight hint of a country lilt. Her best known number is the silly "Davy's Dinghy": "Davy says his dinghy has been in so many ports. He's loved a lot of ladies and he's stormed a lot of forts. You'd think with just a little dinghy it could not be done. But Davy mans that dinghy like a man behind a gun."

Other "classics" include "All Night Long" ("all night long he's tryin' to do what he used to do all night long"), "Drill 'Em All" ("He's got the biggest rig in Texas and the girlies think he's swell. They all want him to show them the way he sinks a well"), and "Confidential Kitty": "Kitty, Kitty! When she made her maiden voyage it was new. Kitty, Kitty! Has sailed many times, been manned by every crew."

Over many many albums, the semisophisticated whizbang remains the same. Generally she plays the winking, easy young thing who enjoys being naughty. Once in a while, she does make fun of the men who can't keep up: "What's a large size mama gonna do with a small size papa like you ... to land a big fish ya gotta have a big worm." Kermit Schafer produced "Saucy Hit Parade," a live album.

Wallis's first eight albums are ten-inchers from the 1950s. A few times Wallis went "straight" with albums of mild, non-risqué songs, such as "Love Is for the Birds." Some of Wallis's songs have turned up on Dr. Demento compilation discs. Nelson Records issued a cassette called "Ruth Wallis Sings 20 X-Rated Songs of the 50's" which includes most of her well-known tunes.

MARSHA WARFIELD

- I'M A VIRGIN! (Laff 218, reissued on CD as THIS IS NOT GROSS,
  THIS IS IMPORTANT, Optimism OP CD 2525) **1/2 ... $8

Warfield, best known for her role on TV's *Night Court*, worked the comedy clubs for many years, perfecting her streetwise, laid-back style. Her 1981 album has plenty of observational raps on sex: "Fascinating penises. Yeah ... You look at it. And it's like: 'Put it in my what? No, I don't think so. No. If God had meant for women to do that, she would have made us toothless.' Plus I only go as far as 68. See, that's where you do me and I owe you one. But that's only if you do me until I'm through."

MIKE WARNKE

- ALIVE! (Myrrh MSA 6561) *1/2 ... $4 ... $8
- JESTER IN THE KING'S COURT (Myrrh 6589) *1/2 ... $4 ... $8
- HEY DOC! (Myrrh 6599) *1/2 ... $4 ... $8
- COMING HOME (Myrrh 6670) *1/2 ... $4 ... $8
- STUFF HAPPENS (Dayspring 7014132016) *1/2 ... $4 ... $8
- GOOD NEWS TONIGHT (Dayspring 701414801) *1/2 ... $4 ... $8

Myrrh is a religious record label from Texas, and Warnke is a "born again" stand-up. During his conversational sermonizing on "Alive" from 1976, he reports on a low point in his life:

"I tried to kill myself, oh poor pitiful Mike. I tried to kill myself, I was sitting in the Student Union building, writing a suicide note, had a gun in my waistband ... all of a sudden the doors to the room opened and three campus crusaders walked in ... they were going, 'What a friend we have in Jesus....' Now when you're gettin' ready to blow your brains out, you don't need it backed up by a gospel trio. I jumped up, pulled out my gun, stuck my gun in this ol' boy's belly and said, 'Sing, sucker.' He looked down at that gun and went, 'Well, praise the Lord.' He just stood there and waited for me to pull the trigger ... know how come? He had his insurance paid up. He was with Jesus Christ Mutual Life. And if you're looking for insurance with a dynamite retirement plan, that's it ... you don't have to worry about makin' the payments, 'cause the premiums have already been picked up by the agent. Isn't that neat? So I wasn't death to this guy, I was just a one way ticket home."

Warnke even finds humor in retelling the story of the crucifixion and the resurrection. From the 1977 "Jester in the King's Court" album: "The Devil was shaking all over ... coming striding through the corridors of hell was Jesus, that was who. It wasn't the beaten, crucified Jew of the cross, but it was the risen, glorified Lord of Glory ... man, he came striding through the ol' corridors of hell, man, and all the people were with him and they were all shoutin' 'Hallelujah' and 'Praise God,' and ol' Jesus walked right up to Corruption and he threw him that way, and he grabbed ol' Death around the neck and threw him that way, and he reached out and grabbed the Devil by the front of his shirt, shook him three times real good and hard and said, 'Hand over them keys, turkey!'"

Warnke also released a few obscure albums on the Dayspring label, "Good News Tonight" and "Stuff Happens."

ROBERT WARREN

- INSANITY (Rodney RP 827) ** $5 $10

A seventy-year-old man trying to be Tom Lehrer? That's Robert Warren, big band arranger and songwriter ("Number Ten Lullaby Lane"). After retiring he began turning out topical ditties. Mitch Miller took him into the recording studio in 1976. Fred Gwynne drew the symbolic album cover of Don Quixote riding a piano with a windmill in the background. And then Robert Warren died.

His songs aren't hilarious, his vocals just about hang in there, and the music is only functional, but Warren's lyrics are opinionated, and with enough outrage to give a few smiles. On Dr. Ruth:

"Who dared to whet the nation's carnal appetites? By raising sexploitation to undreamed-of heights? Like putting masturbation under civil rights! Dr. Ruth, Dr. Ruth."

Parodying yuppies:

"You won't find us fillin' our tummies with burgers. Tuna on white is a cardinal sin. We lay in gourmet from the neighborhood shops; if it wasn't for take-out we'd never eat in!"

And kicking the moral majority:

"We are the fundamentalists, the moral majority, and if you don't team up with us you're gonna miss the bus ... there's nothing wrong with child abuse if they belong to us."

RUSTY WARREN

- SONGS FOR SINNERS (Jubilee JGM 2024) *1/2 $5 $10
- KNOCKERS UP (Jubilee JGM 2029, released as GNP 2 2079
  as a double set with SONGS FOR SINNERS) *1/2 $5 $10
- BANNED IN BOSTON (Jubilee JGM 2045) *1/2 $7 $15
- BOUNCES BACK (Jubilee JGM 2039, re-released as GNP 2 2090 with SINSATIONAL added) *1/2 $5 $10
- IN ORBIT (Jubilee JGM 2044) *1/2 $7 $15
- PORTRAIT ON LIFE (Jubilee JGM 5025) $5 $10
- SEX X PONENT (Jubilee JGM 2054)*1/2 $7 $15
- SINSATIONAL (Jubilee JGM 2034) *1/2 $7 $15
- MORE KNOCKERS UP (Jubilee JGM 2059) *1/2 $5 $10
- BOTTOMS UP (Jubilee JGM 2069) *1/2 $7 $15
- LOOK WHAT I'VE GOT FOR YOU (Jubilee JGM 2074) *1/2 $5 $10
- KNOCKERS UP '76 (GNP Crescendo 2088) *1/2 $5 $10
- SEXPLOSION (GNP Crescendo 2114) *1/2 $5 $10
- LAYS IT ON THE LINE (GNP Crescendo 2081) *1/2 $5 $10

Rusty Warren (formerly Ilene Goldman) gained some fame with her mild risqué songs and brassy audience participation patter.

From the 1958 "Knockers Up" album, she describes a first date in a car: "You girls ... remember some of the things he said to you before he married you? Remember when you were in the car? Ah yes. There you were, sitting in a car with—him! A kind man. Up to a point. A generous man. Sometimes. But right now you were alone with him. And you thought you'd be playful. Most women are that way. Curiousity they call it. And maybe you got too playful, and he looked at you and said, 'Ay baby, prove to me ya love me!' And she looked at him, 'Oh, I'm not that kind of a girl.' And he married you. Sick boy! But he doesn't regret it. Because she still remembers those words he said in passion: 'Marry me baby and I'll give it to you every morning, every afternoon, every night, and twice on Sundays!' Am I right girls? After fifteen years you're lucky to get it! And when you do it's a present! He brought it all the way home from the office for you! On the bus! Under his hat!"

The "Knockers Up" album also has the boob jokes that were her trademark and the ridiculous song of the same title. At the piano, shouting like Rose Marie crossed with Phil Silvers, she shouts: "Knockers Up! Knockers Up! Ladies get your knockers up! Come on girls, throw those shoulders back! Get those shoulders back, get those knockers up! Now doesn't that make your navel tingle! Throw your knockers up and out! Up, two, three, four! Up, two, three, four! Up, up, up, up, up! There we go! Ladies, get up and march through the room, knockers high! Are you ready to commence the march of the knockers? Ladies! March! Hut, two, three, four! Ladies, you're not marching!"

This kind of bombast might have made Warren notorious and exciting live, but it falls flat on disc. Most Warren albums follow the same formula of ringside ad-libs, songs, and standard gags. On "Rusty Rides Again," she talks about a guy who'd rather gamble than pay attention to his wife:

"A wild, beautiful weekend in Las Vegas, and you don't get any! I know a woman who got so damn mad, ran naked into the gambling room, laid stark naked on the crap table. Her husband's at the other end saying, 'Lady, would you move your knocker, you're on my point.'"

Crashing into the '70s, and now on GNP, "Rusty Warren Lays It on the Line" still plumbs the same depths as the comic whips a tittering group of drunken drones into a frenzy: "What's the favorite word of the men! SEX! All the girls in the audience who really like SEX, holler 'I LIKE SEX!'

"When I look around, when I see these magnificent ladies with boobs galore (drum rim shot) I say to myself, why them and not me! Just once before I die I wanna know what it's like to be inside a body that has REAL BIG BOOBIES! (Rim shot.) Just once I wanna feel the pain of a bra strap cutting into my shoulder blades! (Rim shot.) And when I lay flat on my back I wanna know that something just fell under my armpit! (Rim shot, cymbals.) Oh great magnificent boobs! (Rim shot.)"

The Julie London of sex comedy records, her album covers ("Sinsational," "Rusty in Orbit," or "Rusty Rides Again") were attractive enough to sell the record. Especially compared to Belle Barth. "Portrait on Life" was an attempt to go "straight," something comedy fans didn't seem too eager to hear. "Look What I Have for You" is a compilation.

WARSAW PLUMBERS SHAKESPEARIAN PLAYERS

- THE OFFICIAL POLISH COMEDY ALBUM (Samada 4631) **1/2 $5 $10

For those who missed the paperback *Official Polish/Italian Joke Book*, here's the album version, the gags recited out loud by a variety of actors. They don't do a bad job and for those who like this kind of thing, there's plenty of it. From the Polish joke side:

"Hey doctor." "Yes, Mrs. Wasnicki?" "Those birth control pills you gave me ain't gonna work too good." "But Mrs. Wasnicki, I just gave them to you a week ago, how can you be so sure they're not going to work?" "Because every time I stand up they fall out."

And from the Italian joke side, performance credited now to "The Rigatoni Repertory Actors":

"All right, Maria, you may begin-a you confession." "Father, on the night of June 22nd, I make a big-a sin when I go to bed with-a Frankie Germino, who happened-a to be a married man. We go to a hotel with a bottle of wine and I got-a undressed...." "Wait a minoot, Maria, that happened forty-three year ago, and you-a tell me the same story every week." "I know, Father, but I like-a so much to talk about it!" "Get outta the box." "That's what I should-a told Frankie Germino."

WAVY GRAVY See HUGH ROMNEY

JEFF WAYNE

- IT'S OK TO BE A WHITE MALE (Uproar 36632) ** $7

There's nothing very memorable about this 1995 comedy club performance. Wayne needs curse words to help punch up the punch lines on his predictable observations. His piping, bland voice makes him sound like a pipsqueak Rush Limbaugh as he tries to champion "politically incorrect" causes that would appeal to fun-loving clubgoers. He naturally approves of drunk driving, smoking, and red meat, and has plenty of complaints about dizzy ex-wives who prattle about their yeast infections and headaches. On red meat vs exercise: "I want a steak so goddam thick it stops my heart when I'm eating it ... cut my heart open and shove a baked potato in there ... these people who work out. What the hell's that all about ... what is that? That's where you pay money to lift heavy things!"

WAYNE AND SHUSTER

- IN PERSON COMEDY PERFORMANCE (Columbia CS 8231) ** $8 $15
- SHORT SUBJECTS (Columbia CL 1636) ** $8 $15

Frank Wayne and Johnny Shuster were Ed Sullivan's favorite comedy team. In fact, he booked them more often than anyone else, making their vaudeville-style schtick inescapable. They were professional, but that's about it. They looked ordinary, their ability at character comedy was functional at best, and their scripts were written to a formula.

The "In Person" album documents their style in four long routines done in a studio with music, sound effects, and supporting players. They re-enact the death of Julius Caesar and turn it into a Mickey Spillane murder drama. They present a modern adult western complete with a "Frontier Psychiatrist." They also perform their classic "Shakespearean Baseball Game." In the bottom of the ninth:

"A very palpable hit!" "Foul ball!" "Fair it was indeed!" "That ball was foul." "So fair or foul I have not seen! A cursed knave with heart as black as coat you wear upon your back, get thee to an optometrist ... thy head is emptier than Ebbets Field!" "One more time at bat do we have to win the game. Who's next ... see how the valiant Yogi stands at the plate." "But soft, here is the wind-up. Here is the pitch!" "Ooooh!" "The ball did strike his head! The pitcher bean-ed him! He staggers from the plate and rolls his eyes. He comes this way. I cannot look!" (Dizzily singing) "Take thou me to the ball game!" "Oh, his noggin hath taken a floggin' ... concussion thou hath made its masterpiece ... with this bucket shall I pour water on his pate." "Oh! Good fortune smiles upon our club again! The game has been called off on account of rain!"

Those who might wish for shorter, less labored sketches could try "Short Subjects," an album collecting twenty-two bits on everything from "The Whipped Cream Diet," "A Sheik in New York," and "Home with a Vampire" to "Dog Psychologist":

"What kind of problems do dogs have?"

"I had a patient the other day, a dog, I can't mention the dog's name ... ethics ... he was always chasing cats."

"That's not very abnormal, most dogs chase cats."

"This was Mr. Katz. And Mrs. Katz was very upset."

CHARLIE WEAVER

- LETTERS FROM MAMA (Coral 57458) *** $10 $20
- CHARLIE WEAVER SINGS (Starlite ST 6003) $15 $35
     also issued as SINGS FOR HIS PEOPLE (Columbia CL 1345) *** $10 $20

THE SONG REMAINS INSANE

Musical comedy albums generally have a longer shelf life than stand-up because "you can hear them over and over." And get brain damage: Spike Jones, Ray Stevens, Allan Sherman, and Charlie Weaver.

Cliff Arquette was a radio actor who specialized in lovable old codgers, including the Charlie Weaver character. In the '50s, he became a popular guest on *The Tonight Show* reading his whimsical "Letters from Mama," reporting on the doings in the homely little town of Mount Idy. The Coral album offers the transcripts of eight appearances with Steve Allen, who adds his own commentary now and then. One letter describes Mama's car:

"You never saw such an old car. Why even the hair in the upholstery had already turned gray. And it rode with a limp.... When we got home your father parked it on the street and was immediately arrested as a litterbug. Your father thinks our new car is pretty hot. The police knew it is.... The speedometer's been turned back so many times the car runs sideways."

The 1959 Grammy-nominated Columbia album offers songs about Mt. Idy's denizens, and that adds a new level of dementia to the proceedings. It's tragic that an album with cuts like "It's Cumquat Time in Mt. Idy," "They're Draining Snyders Swamp in the Morning" "Gomar, Come Out of the Sewer," "Who'll Sign the Pardon for Wallace Swine," and "Fight for Subnormal U." is out of print. Weaver's voice trembles like a shivering goat coughing up popcorn. The music, featuring a tiny band led by a frenzied mandolin, complements him like a cracked mirror.

The anthem "These Are My People" describes all of the Weaver favorites: "There they go, a-marching by. The crowd lets out a cheer. There's Gomar Cool a-cutting up with a bull ring in his ear. There's Elsie Crack, hair down her back. But none upon her head." Charlie ends up crying out, "With heads held high, and steps so firm, I really must confess. These are my people—they are a most sick, miserable mess."

NOTES: The rare Starlite edition includes a red vinyl pressing. It has a different cover photo (a black and white picture of Charlie leading a band of dressed up mannequins) and, being a ten-incher, it is missing a few cuts, notably "These Are My People." Weaver recorded "Let's Play Trains" (Harmony HL 9513) and appears on the "Zingers from the Hollywood Squares" album (Event V 6903). He was the spry old guy always ready with a droll quip: "On the average Miss America, would her bust be larger than her hips?" "Out at the home we have one of the first Miss Americas. Her bust meets her hips." Charlie turns up describing "Danny the Dragon" on the souvenir album "Freedomland" (Columbia 1484). "Freedomland" was an early '60s attempt at a patriotic Disneyland, filled with exhibits of Americana. Unfortunately it was located in the Bronx.

DOODLES WEAVER

- FEETLEBAUM RETURNS (Fremont M 5074) ** $5 $20

This album was a disappointing "return" for elderly Doodles (yes, uncle of Sigourney) Weaver, the beloved cornball comic who guested on Spike Jones albums with fast-paced racing routines and spoonerism-filled songs.

Doodles reprises both his racing routines ("Dance of the Hours" and "Feetlebaum"), but they don't move very fast. The spirit may be willing, but the dentures are weak. The spoonerism songs aren't bad. Doodles messes up "Home, Home on the Range," and even though it's pretty slow, it's nice to hear Doodles slugging away and interrupting himself with awful jokes:

"Home, home on the stove. Home, home on the waffle iron. The frying pan. The, the, something that had to do with a range ... that's it. The range. The mountain! I used to work on Lookout Mountain. I sat on top of one mountain, and if another mountain got too close I'd shout, 'Look out, mountain!'"

His other parody choice is the haunting Beatles ballad, "Eleanor Rigby." "All the lonely people, where do they all come from" becomes "All the bony people. No. All the ornery—all the ugly people—publy reeple. I'm a people. Go climb a steeple." It's as funny as it reads.

One spoken routine on this studio record might amuse fans. It's his version of the Fred Allen/Red Skelton boozing announcer routine, "Gentry's Gin." The rest is filler, including three duets with a woman named Pattie Barham. For the brief "Interview with the World's Smartest Idiot," Doodles embarrassingly imitates what appears to be a dying retard. Pattie asks the questions:

"What's your name." Uhhhhh George." "How old are you?" "Thirrrrty-two." "How long have you been here, George?" "Three years." "Where are you from?" "George." "Do you like America?" "Thirrrty-two." "What's your favorite song?" "Three years." "Do you like ice cream?" "George!" "What kind of car do you drive?" "Thirrrrty-twoooo." "What's your favorite sport?" "Three years."

The "Eleanor Rigby" cut is on "Dr. Demento's Delights" (Warner Bros. 2855). Doodles's best early work is on "The Best of Spike Jones" and other RCA compilations. The low or high price reflects whether the connection between Weaver and Spike Jones is known.

TONY WEBSTER

- MARRIAGE COUNSELOR (V/V6 15040) *1/2 $5 $10

Three times an Emmy winner, Webster wrote comedy for Art Carney, Bob and Ray, and *Your Show of Shows*. His studio album, featuring George Coe, Lovelady Powell, Joan Darling, and Rex Robbins is quite a disappointment given his credits and the glowing album notes from Carl Reiner. Most of the twenty-five blackout sketches are formula obvious. From the marriage counseling skit:

Mrs. R : John has been drifting away from me and the children. For one thing, every night he has to spend all that time commuting from the city to the suburbs ... it's ruining our marriage.

Counselor: ... Why do you think your husband's commuting from the city to the suburbs is any worse than any other family?

Mrs. R : Because the children and I live in the city.

Even worse:

Counselor: ... What is it that's endangering your marriage?

Woman: You tell him, Hon.

Counselor: Well, I certainly have great hope of saving your marriage if you can still call your husband Hon.

Woman: I don't call him Hon because I like him. That's his name. Attila the Hun!

CHRISTOPHER WEEKS

- MY SON THE PRESIDENT (Clan 1501) *1/2 $5 $10
- LBJ IN THE CATSKILLS (Warner Bros. W 1662) ** $5 $10

If the "The First Family" could be a hit, and "My Son the Folk Singer," how about a Kennedy album with songs? "My Son the President" has plenty of silly sketches, including this Jack Benny rip-off as Fidel Castro is questioned about "The First Family" album:

"Do you like it?" "Sí." "What would you do if someone made an album called "My Son the Dictator?" "Me?" "Sí." "Sue." "Sí." Then there's Caroline joking with he father: "Knock Knock." "Who's there?" "Nixon." "Nixon who?" "See, you forgot him already." "That's a very old joke from such a young girl." "So what."

Periodically JFK pauses to sing folk songs. "On Top of Old Smokey" becomes "On Top of Old Rocky." Kennedy wonders about the 1964 election and Nelson Rockefeller:

"On Top of Old Rocky, who seldom unbends. I'll keep a sharp lookout. To find me new friends ... I can't fight him with money. Since he's loaded too. For each million that I got. I'm sure he's got two. On Top of Old Rocky, that's where I must be. Or else next election. Nelson will stop me."

A mildly funny in-joke has JFK talking to Jackie (played by Fran Stacy). She wonders if he can do an impression of Vaughn Meader and he says, "Of course." Then he warbles "Racing to the Moon ..." a la Vaughn Monroe.

Weeks went on to do a Lyndon Johnson album. Both his Kennedy and Johnson impressions are fine, and here, the material is slightly better. With Fannie Flagg as Lady Bird, the angle is a visit "on August 18, 1966" to the Catskills, where LBJ's Texan personality contrasts the area's Jewish clientele. Johnson takes dance lessons:

"Ah think I'm gettin' it now. How am ah doin'?"

"You're doing fine, but that secret service man you're dancing with is out of step."

He takes in a Catskill resort breakfast:

"Uh, waiter, you brought my Wheatena, but you didn't bring the hot milk." "I'm sorry, you didn't order hot milk. You ordered Veetena vit-out milk." "I distinctly remember sayin' with hot milk." "Dots vat you said, vit-out milk!" "I think I'll go out for an airing." "You don't have to go out for a herring, I got some right here. One herring coming up."

Christopher Weeks supplied some celebrity voices for an album called "The Income Tax Man," but straight man Andrew Duncan got the star billing.

LEN WEINRIB

- HAVE A JEWISH CHRISTMAS (Tower 5081) **1/2 $7 $15

Trivia buffs may note that "Len Weinrib" was adopted by Woody Allen for his sportswriter character name in *Mighty Aphrodite*. But some thirty years earlier, it was soley the property of a young comic trying to get ahead in the business.

Weinrib narrates this good natured selection of corny sketches and mild songs about how Jews deal with Christmas. Or to quote the opening number: "Jingle Bells, Jingle Bells, Jingle night and day. It's Yo ho ho and mistletoe and Santa's on his way. Jingle bells, jingle bells, it's tragic but it's true. There's joyous fun for everyone—but what's a Jew to do?" In a sketch, a Jewish family proudly finds a compromise when their children want to celebrate Christmas like everyone else: "From the top of the tree instead of the Star of Bethlehem, we got a Jewish star." "A Jewish star? The Star of David?" "No, a picture of Elizabeth Taylor."

The supporting cast includes veteran comic Benny Rubin.

LEN WEINRIB AND JOYCE JAMESON

- THE FIRST NINE MONTHS ARE THE HARDEST (Capitol T 2034) **1/2 $7 $15

Weinrib and Jameson costarred on *The Spike Jones Show* in 1960, and subsequently made this record together. They had slightly better success solo. Stand-up Weinrib played a Catskill comic in an episode of *The Dick Van Dyke Show* and Jameson guested on sitcoms and lent her buxom presence to the Peter Lorre and Vincent Price films *Tales of Terror* and *Comedy of Terrors*.

This album is sort of a *Dick Van Dyke Show* episode on pregnancy. It is directed by Carl Reiner, and written by the Van Dyke team Bill Persky and Sam Denoff. What's missing is Dick Van Dyke and Mary Tyler Moore. Weinrib and Jameson simply don't have strong personalities. Most sketches have the expected quota of quick conversational jokes.

When mother-to-be Joyce mentions she's practicing "Breath Control" Len quips, "Isn't that a little late?" In "Morning Sickness," an anxious Len confronts whining Joyce:

"Aw honey, are you sick again? What makes you nauseous?" "This conversation!" "Look, I bet it's mind over matter. Wanna try something? I'm gonna mention a whole lotta foods—" "Please don't. Besides it's not only food." "Aha! What else makes you sick?" "You."

MARV WELCH

- DOUBLE SHOT (Wild Records) *1/2 $4 $8
- SPICE ON THE ROCKS (Wild Records) *1/2 $4 $8

Coming on like a Jackie Kannon on speed, second banana Welch aggressively plays the sleepy room at the Metropole Supper Club in Windsor, Ontario. The jokes are no different from what's available on anyone else's party record, but Welch's bludgeoning salesmanship underlines the crudity. The following is from the "Spice" album:

"Figure 'em out as we get this thing goin' right off the bat. No sense foolin' around," Welch begins. "Right. The old lady walks into the drugstore and says, 'Do you handle urinary specimens?' 'Yes we do.' 'Then wash your hands and make me a malted.' I say to my doctor, 'Who do you think I'm kiddin', I'm a nervous wreck, I'm a nervous wreck. Look at me, I gotta have something.' He says, 'Relax, I'll write you a prescription.' So he reaches in his pocket for a pen and pulled out a rectal thermometer, and says, 'Son of a gun, some ass has my pen.' See, that's where we get rid of the Baptists right away and get down to the whole thing ... it's like the little Italian girl sittin' in the back seat of the rented car: 'It's a Hertz.' But anyhow...."

FRANK WELKER

- ALMOST SOLD OUT (Down the Hall in a Meeting DHIM-0001) ** $4 $8

Welker does commercials ("Crackle" in Rice Krispies ads) and cartoons ("Slimer" in *Ghostbusers* and "Baby Kermit" in *Muppet Babies*). The 1988 record was an attempt to branch out.

At Pasadena's "Ice House" his routines rise and fall on the skill of his impressions. The audience seems happy just hearing Tatoo from *Fantasy Island* say "De plane! De plane!" and roars when Welker does "Bullwinkle the Moose." He takes requests from the audience. They ask for Gomer Pyle and he obliges with a faithful, "Shazam."

Welker's Julia Child, Jimmy Stewart, and John Wayne are like anyone else's, but his Bob Hope has nice detail on Hope's dentalized s's, and for Archie and Edith Bunker he duplicates both the voices and distinct cadences of the two stars. His rambling Cosby is pretty good, too.

Side Two has the long, studio-produced "Answering Machines of the Rich and Famous." Generally, Welker has trouble with raspy celebrities (W. C. Fields especially) and is better suited to soft-voiced stars Gregory Peck and Jimmy Carter. He could probably do a great Robert Klein since he sounds like him when he grimly announces the next impression he is about to do.

ORSON WELLES

- THE BEGATTING OF THE PRESIDENT
  (Media Arts 41-2, re-released as United Artists UAS 5521) *1/2 $5 $10

At several stages during his career, Welles would do almost anything to finance his movies, including this satire of the Lyndon Johnson era. Far funnier are the bootleg tapes around of Welles's grumbling bloopers during the recording of other narration work. Here, with ponderous background music, Welles drones the one-joke premise: modern history written in the style of the Bible:

"In the beginning LBJ created the great society, and darkness was on the face of the Republicans ... and LBJ said, 'Let us make war on poverty.' And lo, there were welfare checks fallen upon the land, and on them was it writ: fold not, nor yet shall ye spindle nor mutilate. And LBJ saw that it was good."

Everything from the war to Johnson's attempt at re-election is treated in the same weary way, until a new king arises, Richard Nixon. Welles urges, "Let us pray."

MAE WEST

- VOICETRACKS (Decca DL 79176) *** $8 $15

The "Voicetrack" album splices Mae's songs and wisecracks together. Unlike Decca's W. C. Fields and Marx Brothers sets, there's no campy Gary Owens narration. A bad '60s rock music soundtrack plays between collages, trying for some kind of pseudopsychedelic effect. After a few minutes this becomes pretty obnoxious. Listeners get all her classics, though: "When I'm good, I'm very good—when I'm bad, I'm better." "It's not the men in your life that counts, it's the life in your men." "Don't let a man put anything over on ya—except an umbrella." There are some extended dialogue segments (two clips from *My Little Chickadee*) as well as a few songs from her movies.

- MAE WEST ON THE CHASE AND SANBORN HOUR (Radiola MR 1126) **1/2 $5 $10
- MAE WEST ON RADIO (Mark 56) **1/2 $5 $10
- MAE WEST ON THE AIR (Sandy Hook SH 2098) **1/2 $5 $10

Mae West appeared on Edgar Bergen's radio show in one sketch about Adam and Eve (December 12, 1937) and was promptly "banned from the air." Well, for a little while.

The Radiola and Mark 56 albums both have the notorious "Adam and Eve" routine. With a script by Arch Oboler, Don Ameche plays a lethargic Adam, and Mae the restless Eve who sits "under a spreading fig tree."

"Listen, tall, tan, and tired," Mae huffs, "ever since creation I've done nothin' but play double solitaire. It's disgustin' ... a girl's gotta have a little fun once in a while."

"Let me sleep, will ya...."

"Adam, you don't know a thing about women!"

"Oh, you apparently forget. You were originally one of my ribs." "A rib once, but now I'm beefin' ... months of peace and security and a woman's bored all the way down to the bottom of her marriage certificate ... Adam, my man, give me trouble!"

Ameche tries to boss her:

"Do you realize I'm Man number one?"

"Yeah, but are you Number One Man?"

That's really as suggestive as the material ever gets.

The Sandy Hook album includes material from radio appearances with Perry Como in 1949 and 1950. Como is an odd choice for her straight man since he's so mild and unflappable. Fans should enjoy their sketches together, "Romeo and Juliet" and "Little Red Riding Hood." The flip side features an appearance on *The Dean Martin Show* in 1959 and a guest spot on *The Red Skelton Hour* in 1960. An opening segment provides some double entendres that, given modern slang, are now triple entendres:

"About your book, Miss West...."

"*Goodness Had Nothing to Do With It* ..."

"About those men in your life, Miss West, have you included all of them in your book?"

"Oh please, the book is only 271 pages...."

"Now, how about a real exclusive for our television audience. Could we hear about the men who don't appear in your book?"

"Oh, stand by, we're about to start a telethon!"

"Miss West, I simply meant, we'd like to hear about some of the unusual men, the men who are offbeat."

"Well, a smart girl never beats off any man."

• ALBUM OF MAE WEST SONGS #1 (Mezzotone 1)	$30	$50
• ALBUM OF MAE WEST SONGS #2 (Mezzotone 2)	$30	$50
• FIELDS AND WEST (Proscenium 22, also released as SIDE BY SIDE, Harmony HS 11405)	$6	$12
• MAE WEST AND HER GUYS (Caliban 6036)	$5	$10
• WAY OUT WEST (Capitol St 5028)	$15	$30
• FABULOUS MAE WEST (Decca 9016, reissued as MCA 2053E)	$8	$15
• WILD CHRISTMAS (Dagonet 4, reissued as MAE IN DECEMBER, AEI 2104 and UNDER THE MISTLETOE, Round RS 100)	$8	$15
• GREAT BALLS OF FIRE (MGM SE 4869)	$10	$25
• SINGS SULTRY SONGS (Rosetta RRCD 1315)		$8
• COME UP AND SEE ME SOMETIME (Mastersound 113)		$8
• MERMAN, ROBERTI, WEST (Sony CSP 2751)	$5	$10

West's musical albums can't really be rated, since they aren't intended as pure comedy. There is certainly an element of good dirty fun on them as well as self-parody. The Mezzotone albums are ten-inchers from 1952, including "Page 54," "My Man Friday," "That's All Brother That's All," and others. A few were reissued on half of the Proscenium album (with W. C. Fields on the flip side).

1955's "Fabulous Mae West" is vintage West with renditions of classics "Frankie and Johnny," "Criswell Predicts," and "A Guy That Takes His Time." She slips in wisecracks now and then. On "Sin" she hears a soloist and cracks, "Awww, this guy's got somethin' solid ... ahhh, this is sin, you're in like Flynn!"

The early '60s were probably the slowest years in West's career, restricted mostly to nightclub work. She issued her Christmas album in 1963 with predictable cuts including "Put the Loot in the Boot, Santa" and "Santa Come Up and See Me."

In 1967 West recorded mildly suggestive rock songs for Tower, including her renditions of "Day Tripper" and "When a Man Loves a Woman." She was pretty hip to cover a then-obscure Dylan tune, "If You Gotta Go, Go Now." Some tunes have a one-liner or two. On "You Turn Me On" she remarks, "A man in the house is worth two on the street." The 1972 disc for MGM is campier with "Great Balls of Fire," "Whole Lotta Shakin' Goin' On," and "Light My Fire." The latter ends with a guy crying out "Where's the fire!" And Mae answering, "In your eyes!" West could still primp and posture during the age of free love with her own antique version of it.

The Rosetta, Sony, and Mastersound entries are CDs. Rosetta is notable for digging up public domain tracks, film soundtracks, and oddities including "Easy Rider," "My Old Flame," "They Call Me Sister Honky Tonk," "I'm an Occidental Woman," "That's All Brother," and "My Daddy Rocks Me."

West songs are on many compilation albums. A few rock numbers turn up on Rhino's "Golden Throats" first two volumes. Fans can try to dig up the rare 45s, including "Songs Teacher Never Taught" (Monogram 111), "He's a Bad Bad Man" (Plaza 506), and "Hard to Handle" from the "Myra Breckenridge" soundtrack (20th Century Fox 6718).

IAN WHITCOMB

• COMEDY SONGS (I.T.W. ITW 009) *	$7

Whitcomb has issued many albums, but this is the only one that turns up exclusively in the comedy category. Having an affection for risqué ditties and novelty 78s of a bygone era, Whitcomb offers his versions of "Lucky Jim," "You Don't Like It, Not Much," "I Go So Far with Sophie and Sophie Goes So Far with Me," and "When Ragtime Rosie Ragged the Rosary."

Unfortunately his smirking nudge-nudge, wink-wink feyness ruins the fun. He even adds some witless campy asides and his own badly done sound effects. Numbers that thrive on a light, tongue-in-cheek touch, from Harry Roy's "My Girl's Pussy" to "My Dead Dog Rover," are destroyed by Whitcomb's cloying clowning.

JIM WHITE

- HOSPITAL VACATION: 41 BUCKS A DAY (Loco M 2301) *1/2 $4 $8

Back when $41 a day seemed expensive, White went into a Boston recording studio and read his essay on being a patient. The album has no audience, but does have continuous generic "zany" music that sounds like it was clipped from old '50s sitcom reruns, and White's distracting Boston accent that turns "forty-one" into "fotty-one" and "potato" into "pid-day-dough."

The one-liners have the right construction, but weak punch lines and the observations, like the patient, just lie there: "For supper we had Southern fried chicken. And let me tell you something. I believe that chicken *was* fried down South. That night the nurse came in with some Valley-of-the-Dolls. I said, 'Do I have to take those pills all at once?' She said, 'Leave the driving to us.' I said, 'I would honey, but this is not a Greyhound terminal! And in the second place, I don't believe you got your license!'"

NELSON C. WHITE

- CONNECTICUT CHARACTERS REMEMBERED (Bert and I 4) * $5 $10

White, a trustee at a museum in New London, Connecticut, offers a very dull collection of long, long anecdotes. He insists on acting them out utilizing a variety of annoying New England dialects. It's sort of like listening to dialogue clipped from the Cabot Cove, Maine, episodes of *Murder She Wrote*, sans Angela Lansbury. It's murder by droning.

White recites: "Tiptoe Gardiner had a small farm in the back country near New London, Connecticut. He had let it run down to a point where the front yard was a cemetery of old farming tools, plows, logging chains, and old boards. The only help Tiptoe could get were the town paupers. And so it was that Henry Schofield came to work at the farm. He used to say, 'Mr. Gardiner cooks the meals and he is so dirty I hate to eat after his hands. His wife, Mrs. Gardiner, has been sick in bed and the roof leaks so she don't know but what she'll wake up and find herself drownded before mornin'.'"

SLAPPY WHITE

- THE FIRST NEGRO VICE PRESIDENT (Brunwsick 754146) **1/2 $7 $15
- THE FIRST (SLAPPY) WHITE ASTRONAUT (Brunswick 754132) *** $7 $15
- AT THE PLAYBOY CLUB (Mercury MG 20692) *** $7 $15
- AT THE CLUB HARLEM (Chess 1481) **1/2 $7 $15
- SLAPPY WHITE FOR VICE PRESIDENT (Laff A 190) **1/2 $5 $10
- JUST FOR LAUGHS (Bull B-10, also released as PARTY GAGS) **1/2 $8 $20
- JUST FOR LAUGHS 2 (Bull B-11, also released as PARTY GAGS, 2) **1/2 $8 $20

Mel White was part of several comedy teams (at one point he costarred with Redd Foxx) but went out solo in 1951 on the bill with Dinah Washington. White appeared often on variety shows in the '60s, and in an interesting move teamed with Steve Rossi (See Rossi and White.) A capable storyteller a la Flip Wilson, and a literate comedian who was at Chicago's Playboy Club just after Dick Gregory, White is a neglected funny man who never seemed to catch fire with the general public.

His early albums on Bull are "adults only," but more silly than dirty: "When I finish here I'm goin' on a hunting trip up in Alaska. Be goin' out there and try and hunt some polar bear. I guess you all know how to hunt polar bear. All you need is a hatchet and a can of peas. You take the hatchet, cut a round hole in the ice and sprinkle peas around the top of the hole. And every time a polar bear come up to take a pea, kick him in the ice hole!"

White's later albums for Laff were a return to risqué comedy, but he was never as blatant as others on the label: "Three girls go to confession. One girl goes up to the priest and says, 'Father,' she said, 'you know a man kissed me on my lips.' The priest said, 'Well go over there and put some holy water on your lips.' The second girl said, 'Father, I put my hand on a man's penis.' He said, 'Go over there and wash your hand in that holy water.' The third girl said, 'That's all right, Father, I'll just go over and gargle.'"

White's prime albums were for Brunswick and Mercury in the '60s. "White Astronaut" has varied gags that anyone from Moms Mabley to Red Skelton could tell, but the opening is pure Slappy: "Hear the way Rocky introduced me? Here's Slappy White, folks. That was the first time I was ever called 'White Folks.' You might not believe it but I'm a Negro. And it's tough these days being a Negro. I woke up the other day, I didn't know whether to vote, integrate, go to school, or march. So I turned over and went on back to sleep!"

On the "Playboy Club" album, White offers some satirical one-liners ("Times are hard, times are so hard right now people who don't intend to pay ain't buyin'") and slips in a few racial jokes now and then ("I did one television show in the Congo. It was called 'Eat the Press'), but his fame in the racial area is for his famous closing poem. He puts on a white glove and a black glove and says, "If the white man and the black man would work hand in hand they could make this whole world a promised land. You've got George Washington. We've got Booker T. You've got congressmen in congress and so have we. Einstein split the atom, no ifs, ands, or buts. Look what Dr. Carver did with the little peanut. We will forget about slavery, you forget about the Indian raids. We quit calling you ofays, you quit calling us spades. Together we'll wipe out poverty, hatred, and we'll conquer outer space. So why don't we get together and let America win the race."

JAMES WHITMORE

- WILL ROGERS' USA (Columbia SG 30546) **** $14

After Hal Holbrook's successful portrayal of Mark Twain in a one-man show, several actors followed suit with their own shows on everyone from Edgar Allan Poe to Lyndon Johnson. James Whitmore's resurrection of Will Rogers is a triumph. Will Rogers, Jr. said, "Listening to him I can see my father."

Will Rogers was one of the nation's greatest humorists, but his work has not been well preserved. His records and early '30s radio tapes are in poor condition. Rogers also had one of the worst deliveries of any stand-up comic: he'd chew gum and mumble. It was part of Rogers's endearing, self-effacing style, and it worked well enough at the time.

Here, Whitmore distills all the best of Will Rogers, picking through his voluminous writings for topical satire that remains biting. He captures the flavor of Rogers's easygoing delivery, judiciously including a touch of rambling here and there or a whimsical aside. This album, released while the Vietnam War continued to rage, offers Rogers reporting on another war in Asia, but with the same effect:

"Youth for Peace March. I've been readin' a lot about that lately. The kids don't want us in the Syno-Japanese War. They're marchin' to keep us from war. Seems they're gettin' the same training as they would in the military. But folks, if you're gonna travel seven thousand miles to find a war, you really have to be looking. 'Course the thing we do worst in this country is mind other folks' business. But the joke's on the kids anyway. We say we ain't got no war, and the other side says we ain't got no war. Of course the guys gettin' shot say it's the best imitation they've seen yet. But don't worry, we got the best politicians in this country that money can buy."

There's some biographical material as Rogers recalls his childhood, his Indian heritage, and his schooling: "There's one thing I have regretted all my life. And that is that I never took a chance on the fifth grade." And he talks about college: "Does college pay? Of course. If you're a halfback or a basketball player they pay you very well, I understand. College athletes are always saying to me, 'When should I turn pro,' and I say, 'Not until you've earned all you can in college.'"

DICK WHITTINGHILL

- WHITTINGHILL AND ARBOGAST AT CARNEGIE HALL (Dot DLP 3500) * $5 $10
- HELEN TRUMP: A LOTTA WOMAN (Republic REP 501,
    also released as THE ROMANCE OF HELEN TRUMP, Dobre DR 1062) ** $5 $10

Whittinghill was a disc jockey at KMPC in Los Angeles when he recorded this 1966 album. Bob Arbogast helps him out on this studio-recorded set of twenty-five mini-sketches, most of them dull and/or obvious, all of them leaving the listener impatient for the punch line.

They put on voices that sound vaguely familiar to characters used by Stan Freberg and Bob and Ray.

This blackout sketch with war noises is typical:

"Morning, Lieutenant." "Morning, Maloney." "Looks like they mean business this time, don't they, Lieutenant?" "Who's that, Maloney? Who means business?" "Why, the enemy, Lieutenant?" "What?" "The enemy, sir. Those guns, those tanks. Shells." "What? I thought we were just on maneuvers. Mommy! Mommy!"

Like Bob and Ray, Whittinghill liked to parody the old *Helen Trent* radio soap opera on his own show. The album version is loaded with unsubtle double entendres and formula gags. Dick might deserve some credit for doing them in 1961, a few years before this became part of Johnny Carson's late night arsenal. ("One guy romancing Helen is old." "How ... old ... is he?" "He was caught sniffing prunes.")

With organ music playing in the background, various men (Dr. Titus Tittman, D. Dewey Dedderwick, Barton Kissel Von Keister, Freddie Fondleheinie, etc.) recall their dalliances with loose Helen Trump: "She'd gone to a party in a low-cut dress and sure enough, she won a prize as the best couple. Why, this woman is so stacked the city had to rope her off as a hard hat area. Women have been heard to say she wears next to nothing. Men don't agree, they know that what she wears is next to plenty. She's so sexy her chest X-rays have been sold as French postcards. Even her voice is sexy. Once a Peeping Tom was caught looking down her throat."

The album was originally released in 1961. The Republic Records label was distributed by Warner Bros.

WILDMAN STEVE

- MY MAN (Raw 7000) *1/2 $5 $10
- WILD WILD WILD (Raw 7001) *1/2 $5 $10
- KING OF THEM ALL (Raw 7002) *1/2 $5 $10
- DO NOT DISTURB (Dick-er D 70) ** $7 $15
- EATIN' AIN'T CHEATIN' (Laff 181) *1/2 $5 $10
- WHEN YOU'RE HOT YOU'RE HOT (Laff 191) *1/2 $5 $10
- IS IT GOOD BABY (Dealer's Choice 777) *1/2 $7 $15
- DID HE REALLY SAY THAT (Dealer's Choice 780) *1/2 $7 $15
- LOVE TO MAKE A' UGLY M.F. LAFF (Ichiban ICH 11632) * $8

Steve Gallon began his career as a disc jockey in the '60s, earning the nickname "Wildman" around 1965. He appeared on stations in Boston and Miami. He isn't merely "Wildman." On his records he refers to himself as "Wha-ha-ha-ha-haaaald Man!" Most of his early albums on Raw are high on meandering raunch, but low on jokes. He's energetic, happy but sappy on his first album, which includes some odd racial humor as much as sex jokes.

"Do Not Disturb" was issued around 1972, his self-produced bid to move up to the lucrative Richard Pryor/Redd Foxx level. It's his best. With a delivery akin to a preacher, Wildman shouts out his observations: "The things I say shouldn't embarrass ya no way! The only type of person who would be embarrassed at what the Wha-hild Man has to say, is the type of man who gets out of the shower to take a piss, or the woman who eats a banana sideways!"

Some of the jokes are almost classic. He tells the story of the boy who is half black and half Jewish. He goes to his mother and asks, "Am I more black or more Jew?" She tells him, "Son, I've always told you over and over again, just remember that you're part of the human race." But he says, "Ma it's so important! I wanna know!" She says, "If you want to ask a foolish question like that, ask your daddy!" He comes to his father and asks, "Am I more black or more Jew?" The father asks, "Why do you want to know?" He said, "A little boy down the street got a bicycle. And he want eighteen dollars for it. I wanna know if I should try and get him down to fourteen dollars and ninety five cents—or steal the mother."

The earthy, mirthy Wha-ha-ha-hild Man turned up on Laff for two albums in 1973 and 1976. The influence of Richard Pryor evidently lead him to slightly more racial rambling, though the corny sex gags are still there.

Wildman's later albums on Dealer's Choice give the impression that he's some kind of legend. The album notes for "Did He Really Say That" insist his first record "sold over a million copies" and he "became the first black comedian to have a party album on the National Record Charts for over 26 weeks." Inside, he points out a difference between himself and a more popular comedian. "Somebody said to me, 'Wildman Steve, if you didn't talk so dirty and talk so nasty you could be like Dick Gregory. Why don't you be like Dick Gregory and go out and demonstrate?' I am NOT going to do like Dick Gregory, starve myself to death for a bunch of niggers sitting home eating pork chops! I got more sense than that!"

In 1993 Wildman Steve issued a skimpy (half hour) CD. Influenced by rap rhythms and "Def Jam"-style younger black performers, Steve wails and cries out repetitive curse-filled rants while relentless drum beats and music clatter in the background. There's more rapping than joking here.

LARRY WILDE

- THE JOKER IS WILDE (Dot DLP 25753) *1/2 $5 $10

Blandly pleasant Larry Wilde offers an extremely lightweight album of material just about at the level of what other comics were doing on TV in 1964. Wilde does satires of television commercials: "How about the one where the woman is smelling her clothes? They smell as fresh as all outdoors! Is that ridiculous? Do you realize what all outdoors smells like? If she lived in New York she'd cough for twenty-two minutes." And there's this Alan King-style report on going out: "How about this, you go to a swanky nightclub, and they got a bandit there, does nothing else but show you to your table. Jesse James in a tuxedo. They call him Maitre 'D. I found out that's a French expression for 'Stick 'em up.'"

It's all delivered in a voice with the emotional range of Monty Hall. The celebrity endorsements on the back are mildly surprising: Art Linkletter and ... Tina Louise (who says "I dig his sense of humor ... at last, I now have someone to keep me laughing during those long days and nights on *Gilligan's Island).* Evidently looking for much needed advice, Wilde interviewed a dozen comedians for the book, *Great Comedians Talk About Comedy.* He never made another album, but did turn out paperback joke anthologies.

AVA WILLIAMS See AVA

BERT WILLIAMS

- NOBODY (Folkways RBF 602) **1/2 $7 $15

The legendary black vaudeville comedian Bert Williams was called the greatest by everyone from Eddie Cantor to W. C. Fields. Sadly, his charm and charisma are almost buried under the dust and scratches of these poorly preserved recordings. Indifferent novelty tunes, from 1914's "You Can't Get Away from It" to 1917's "He's a Cousin of Mine," must be listened to very closely to savor the humor of Williams's musing delivery. Even the 1918 Fieldsian half-sung, half-spoken "O Death, Where Is Thy Sting?" requires some patience.

Fortunately a fairly decent recording survives of his major hit, "Nobody," even though it's his earliest (1913). There are delightful nuances to Bert's performance as he sings of his bad luck. Every refrain of "Nobody" is spoken with a Chaplinesque sense of humorous irony: "When summer comes all cool and clear and my friends see me drawing near, who says there, 'Come in, have some beer.' Nobody. When I was in that railroad wreck, and thought I'd cashed in my last check, who took the engine off my neck? Not a soul!" And on it goes, with Bert's chorus reflecting on the situation: "I never done nothin' to nobody. I never done nothin' for nobody no time. Until I get something from somebody sometime I'll never do nothing for nobody. No time!"

BERYL WILLIAMS

- GIGGLES FOR GUZZLERS (Lobo L 103) ** $6 $12

Williams has memorized the standard gags and tells them reasonably well, his voice having a little Jesse White salesman's nasality to it:

"My wife looked at me one night and said, 'Do you think I'll lose my looks when I get old?' I said, 'If you're lucky.' And her mother! There is the one! That miserable broad. Her mother's idea of a lot of fun is throw a great big beer party and lock the bathroom door. But I think marriage is a very wonderful thing. I don't think there's an unhappy marriage. Living together afterward! But the marriage itself is very happy."

In the '70s Williams was often booked for cruise ships and appeared at the "Vive Les Girls" show at the Dunes Hotel in Las Vegas. He died of cancer on March 11, 1978, at the age of fifty-nine. One version of the album has Williams on the cover, another a topless nude. Obviously, one gets a higher price than the other.

HANK WILLIAMS

- KAW-LIGA AND OTHER HUMOROUS SONGS (MGM SE 4300) ** $8 $15

Williams is best known for his stark country moans ("I'm So Lonesome I Could Cry" and "Cold, Cold Heart") but here's the flip side. Homer and Jethro's parodies of Hank's serious ballads are funnier, but there are some chuckles here. The title cut is a novelty tune about a wooden cigar store Indian who falls in love with a wooden Indian maid in an antique store. Poor Kaw-Liga never told her how he felt: "Too stubborn to ever show a sign, because his heart was made of knotty pine. Poor old Kaw-Liga he never got a kiss. Poor old Kaw-Liga he don't know what he missed. Is it any wonder that his face is red? Kaw-Liga, that poor old wooden head!"

KENNETH WILLIAMS

- WHAT'S HIS NAME'S GREATEST HITS (Stanyan 10038) *** $10 $20

Williams was a British comic best known for his roles in the endless *Carry On ...* film series. A radio star (*Hancock's Half Hour, Beyond Our Ken, Round the Horne*) he created the character of "Rambling Syd Rumpo," a balladeer sporting an obscure regional accent, a lisp, and a distinct nasal effeminacy. Here, on Rod McKuen's record label (the Stateside release of the British album "Best of Rambling Syd Rumpo"), he sings fifteen short folk songs that are all pretty much the same. They're all double entendre nonsense songs: "Pewter Wogglers Bangling Song," "Runcorn Splod Cobbers Song," "The Ballad of the Wogglers Moulie," etc. From "The Sussex Whirdling Song":

"Will you still love me Mary-O. When my grossets be bending low. When my orbs grow dim and my pubes grow white—and my cordwangle makes an ugly sight?"

There are few songs here that don't mention cordwangles or grossets, or someone who enjoys a good whirdle. Williams is feyly parodying the entire antiquated olde school of "dearie-o!" balladeering, though most of the Marty Feldman-Barry Took lyrics seem to aim below the belt in doing so.

Many will find this album repetitious, irritating, and completely devoid of humor, but others with an eccentric bent will be driven to helpless giggling over Williams's effeminate exaggerations and the sincerity of his ludicrous euphemisms.

Williams died of a barbiturate overdose in 1988. He was beloved by fans and had a fascinating personality (a homosexual virgin), and he was soon the subject of a biography. In 1993 a book of his letters and a huge collection of diary entries were published.

British imports of Williams include an early revue with Maggie Smith called "Share My Lettuce" (Nixa NPL 18011), in which he performs with various cast members ("Trapped," "Sez We"). On the original cast album "Pieces of Eight" (London 5761) he stars in several Peter Cook-written sketches including "Not an Asp," "If Only," and "Buy British." The sequel, "One Over the Eight" (Decca SKL 4133) includes more sketches by Peter Cook, including "Hands Up Your Sticks," a rather atypical vaudevillian turn with Williams playing an annoying robber who nervously speaks in spoonerisms and conundrums. Another key cut is "One Leg Too Few," the "sick" routine that was the hit of Cook and Moore's Broadway show. His solo "On Pleasure Bent" (Decca SKL 4856) offers peculiar musical satires in various styles, including the vaudevillian "Boadicea" plus "A Boiled Egg," "A Runcible Episode," and "Itty Bitty Hitty Potamus." "The World of Kenneth Williams" (Decca SPA 64) compiles sketches and songs.

PEARL WILLIAMS

- A TRIP AROUND THE WORLD IS NOT A CRUISE (After Hours LAH 70) *** $7 $15
- 2ND TRIP AROUND THE WORLD (Surprise SUR 75) *** $7 $15
- PEARL WILLIAMS AT LAS VEGAS (Riot R 303) *** $6 $12
- ALL THE WAY (Riot R 307) *** $6 $12
- YOU'LL NEVER REMEMBER IT, WRITE IT DOWN (Laff A 128) *** $5 $10
- BAGELS AND LOX (Laff A 127) *** $5 $10

Williams (Pearl Wolfe) had a Brooklyn delivery that blended Mae West with a touch of Leo Gorcey. Her first album, recorded in 1962, features her behind the piano, punctuating the lines with rollicking minor key chords:

"Definition of indecent. If it's long enough, hard enough, and in far enough, it's in decent!"

The audience is gleefully shocked. Pearl grunts, "Get used to me, doll. I get broads come in here, they sit in front of me and they stare at me. Everything I do, they stare at me. Then they walk out saying, 'She's so dirty!' They're so refined how come they understand what I'm saying ... it takes them two or three hours to find out I'm dirty? Then these rat bastards walk out, get into their cars, and eat everything but the steering wheel.... I know a guy married a broad half Greek half French, didn't know which way to turn!"

The second album is more of the same: "Hear about the broad who walks into the hardware store to buy a hinge? The clerk says, 'Madam, would you like a screw for this hinge?' She says, 'No, but I'll blow ya for the toaster up there....' Hear about the Scotchman, found a fifty-cent piece? He married her.... Honey, you know what they call falsies in Chicago? The Unsuckables.... Clever?"

Clever or not, Pearl's delivery puts them over. Along with rival Belle Barth, she worked Miami and added plenty of Jewish accented risqué stories and a Yiddish word or two. The Riot albums are a bit tinnily recorded, but the material is as brassy as ever.

Pearl's last albums are only slightly mellowed. Pearl felt that the sexual revolution was actually turning audiences off to dirty jokes, so she used less vulgarity and some cuter material. From "Write It Down": "Sir, did you hear what the cow said to the farmer: 'How come you always pull my tits, you never kiss me!'"

"Bagels and Lox" is similarly toned down: "How about the girl who woke up in the wheat field and cried, 'My God, I've been reaped!'"

Pearl manages to avoid dirty words by using the names of Jewish foods instead: "You're from Montreal? Ahh, those French Canadians ... they're the only guys who know what your belly button is for. That's where they leave their gum on the way down! They put ice cubes in your knish and eat you on the rocks! When I worked Montreal I used to douche with vinegar. They like pickled knish!"

Pearl rarely tells anecdotes, but here's one of the best she has told: "This actually happened. About eighteen years ago, Tallulah Bankhead was working in a Broadway show, the *Ziegfield Follies*. One night a real imbecilic, moronic, idiotic chorus girl came up to her and says, 'Tallulah, would you believe I've been in show business for five years and I still have my cherry!' Tallulah looks at her and says, 'Darling, doesn't it get in your way when you're fucking?'"

ROBIN WILLIAMS

- REALITY, WHAT A CONCEPT (Casablanca NBLP 7162) ** $5 $10
- THROBBING PYTHON OF LOVE (Casablanca 811 150 1M1) *1/2 $5 $10
- A NIGHT AT THE MET (Columbia FC 40541) *** $4 $8

For the past decade, film work has been more of a preoccupation for Robin Williams than stand-up. He seemed to reach a peak with his one-man show at The Met in 1986 and there probably was nothing else to accomplish.

His first two albums document the way he dazzled the drunks and druggies at comedy clubs. Constantly compared to his idol Jonathan Winters for his off-the-wall improvisations, here he's fast-paced, shifting in and out of characters at rapid speed, stabbing at ringsiders with quick pantomime and ad-libs, going "full tilt bozo." All that's missing is purpose.

When the first album came out in 1979, it was criticized by parents who thought they were going to get a cute disc of comedy for their children who loved *Mork and Mindy*. But even Williams's adult fans can't be pleased with this one. "Wait," Williams says at one point, "you're laughing at nothing now." Most of the album is nothing. What was dazzling in person falls flat on disc. There are stretches of pantomime and too many "ya hadda be there" gags aimed at the euphoric ringsiders. It's a strain to listen and piece together what's going on. Especially when Robin is throwing out non sequiturs and mimcry: "Before we go on, a brief joke for any psychics in the audience. We know who we are, don't we. (Peter Lorre voice) "Look, the fog's coming in!" (Whistles "Hall of the Mountain King.") Nobody's seen that movie. Good. We're all set? Time for some culture now. My first poem: Red sand between my toes from a vacation in outer space. That was Martian haiku ... now a poem for those who've taken Evelyn Wood speed reading: IP!"

The album includes a parody of *Mister Rogers Neighborhood* and Williams's Shakespearean "Meltdowner's Nightmare."

1982's "Python" occasionally has a subtle and satiric line (he reports on his teacher at Julliard, John Houseman: "Mr. Williams, the theater needs you. I'm going off to sell Volvos") but much of this is comedy club cliché, no matter how fast he presents it. There's the gratuitous, easy impression of Jack Nicholson as Hamlet, saying, "To be or not to goddam be," an impression of Elmer Fudd singing Bruce Springsteen, and way too many dumb dick jokes about "Mr. Happy." On top of everything else, the record is shrilly. Williams's attitude may be summed up in one of the lines on this disc: "Joke 'em if they can't take a fuck, okay?"

In 1986 Williams appeared at the Metropolitan Opera House in New York for a bravura performance. It's more impressive in the video version than on record, but it's still a brilliant show.

Williams's one liners are still cheap and easy on cold vinyl. Like the Henny Youngman-type shout, "How do you like the play, Mr. Lincoln? Duck!" And then there's the Jackie Mason-ish line about ballet at the Met: "Men wearing pants so tight you can tell what religion they are!"

Of course, one-liners aren't what Williams is about. They are really just the bones on which he hangs his rubber faces and elastic body. They mark time between his exhausting bursts of blood, sweat, and tears that go into his different voices, actions, and characters.

One can overlook such familiar bits as Sylvester Stallone as Hamlet: "To be, or what?" And one can even forget about his cornball tendency to shift into black dialect for added hipness. Because throughout the show Williams is in an emotional frenzy—bleeding, crying, and sweating—racing through quick riffs on marijuana, alcohol, and cocaine to an exhausted, agonized cry against the insanity of Reagan, Khadafi, and the useless United Nations whom he pictures as "a traffic cop on Valium: 'Staaahhhp, staaahhp.' Best thing for the UN to do is go condo! It's scary times!"

After a hilarious psychodrama about a battle between a man and his urges, he moves into recollections about his wife's pregnancy: "She's screaming like crazy ... 'You have this myth you're sharing the experience. Unless you're passing a bowling ball, I don't think so! Unless you're circumsizing yourself with a chainsaw, I don't think so! Unless you're opening an umbrella up your ass, I don't think so!'"

NOTES: Collectors will find a few brief monologues on the soundtrack album for *Good Morning, Vietnam.* Robin sings on the soundtracks to *Popeye, Aladdin,* and others. With backing music by Ry Cooder, Williams narrates a children's CD, "Pecos Bill" (Windham Hill WD 0709). He is on many "Comic Relief" CD compilations.

MARTIN ADAM WILLSON

- HE'S IN CHARGE HERE (Atlantic 8074) * $5 $10

Through the '60s Gerald Gardner scored with novelty photo books that stuck funny captions in the mouths of politicians. The album is billed as "Gerald Gardner ... presents: He's In Charge Here."

But it's Willson who is the star, doing a doleful imitation of John F. Kennedy on what is essentially just another attempt to cash in on "The First Family." In monologue sketches we overhear Kennedy dictating letters and making phone calls, Typically: "Hello, mother? Sorry I missed your call, I was speaking at an A.M.A. luncheon. No I didn't. Well, mother, I can't always brush after every meal. Yes, mother, it was a good speech. Yes, I encouraged the doctors to support Medicare ... they're sending me an alternate proposal. In the A.M.A. plan if you're over sixty-five and you need an operation but you can't afford it, the doctors will retouch your X-rays. Yes, mother, we'll work it out. Goodbye, mother."

FLASH WILSON

- FLASH WILSON ARRIVES (Jamie SLP 3030) ** $5 $10

A black comic from the '60s, Flash Wilson doesn't have a Flip delivery; he's more like Moms Mabley as he rasps out some gags about his wife: "This chick look like an accident gonna happen. She got lips on her that look like bicycle tires with no tred on! Darlin', let me tell you about mah old lady. She dietin' and she told me the other day, 'Honey, I done lost ten pounds.' I said, 'Look behind ya, baby, you'll find 'em.' This woman is messed up! I ain't lyin'!"

The most notable thing about Wilson's set is his use of the term "Mr. Charlie." For a '60s album intended for general audiences (Philadelphia's Jamie label saw white comedy team Solms and Parent and guitarist Duane Eddy supplying hits) it's very unique. When earlier black comics Dick Gregory or Godfrey Cambridge used racial humor the term "white folks" was enough.

Wilson relates an anecdote about the old days in Georgia. "There was a time when Mr. Charlie controlled everything ... the mayor, the judge, and he had the only grocery store in town. And every time you would walk in Mr. Charlie's store, you'd have to say, 'Hello, Mr. Charlie, can I get me a pound of pork chops?' 'If what, boy?' 'If you please?' That's how you got 'em ... one day a cat drove up in front of Mr. Charlie's store with a low slung Cadillac with New York plates! Suede cap, suede coat, suede pants, suede shoes, gold tooth, and dark glasses! Lookin' good! Eased into the store ... this cat eased over to the counter. 'Say baby, gimme a pack of Camels.' Mr. Charlie say, 'If what, boy?' And this cat pulled out a 45, stuck it in Mr. Charlie's face and said, 'If you got 'em, baby!'"

FLIP WILSON

- FLIP WILSON'S POT LUCK (Sceptor 520, re-released as
     FUNNY AND LIVE AT THE VILLAGE GATE Springboard SP 4004) *** $5 $10
- FLIPPIN (Minit 24012) $6 $12
- COWBOYS AND COLORED PEOPLE (Atlantic ATS 8149) **1/2 $5 $10

Clerow Wilson got his nickname while in the air force, when his mock-Shakespearean clowning had fellow soldiers saying, "he flippith his lid!" His early albums were recorded for adults only, but Wilson never worked too blue. On "Pot Luck" he says, "This morning I caught my wife in a lie ... I'm sitting there in the kitchen, having some coffee, bisquits, some jelly. And I'm rollin' up a few reefers to bring to work with me tonight. About 11:30 my old lady came in, and her wig was amuss. All mussed up. Her blouse was torn to shreds, you could see the imprint of fingers ... this really threw me off. So I asked her, 'Where the hell have you been?' And she said she spent the night with her sister. You dig it? I knew she was lyin' because I had spent the night with her sister."

Even this early, Wilson's style is set. He tells long joke-stories, some of them pretty shaggy. He tells a long one about a guy who entices a girl back to his room so they can listen to Ray Charles records. She turns out to be an embryonic version of his drag character Geraldine as she shouts out her praise for "Raaaay Charles!" Eventually they get in bed, and the man discovers she has a wooden leg. He unscrews it, drops it, and it breaks. He rushes across the hallway: "And coming up the hall is a drunk guy. He rushes up to him and says, 'You gotta help me ... man, I got a broad in my room and I got one of her legs apart and I can't get it back together.' Drunk guy said, 'Don't worry about it. I got a broad in my room with both legs apart and I forgot the room number.'"

1967's "Cowboys" was nominated for a Grammy and contains three of his well-known routines: a retelling of Columbus discovering America (the queen thinks "He gonna find Ray Charles! What you say!"), his version of "David and Goliath," and the title cut, Wilson's clever racial comedy switching the pressure to ... Indians. "Ladies and gentlemen, we gotta do something about the Indians. The Indians aren't ready yet ... do you want to build a $50,000 home and have some guy put a wigwam next to it? I'm not against Indians."

- YOU DEVIL YOU (Atlantic SC 8179) *** $5 $10
- THE DEVIL MADE ME BUY THIS DRESS (Little David LD 1000) *** $7 $15
- THE FLIP WILSON SHOW (Little David LD 2000) *** $5 $10
- GERALDINE (Little David LD 1001) **1/2 $7 $15

"You Devil You" has seventeen short tracks including "Herman's Berry," a shaggy dog story with a terrible pun ending that must be heard to be believed. "Days of the Knights" turns Geraldine into a damsel in distress. And another highlight is his classic joke about a woman who is riding on the train with an ugly baby. Another passenger can't help telling her, "'That's a bad lookin' baby, lady.' The woman took this as an offense. She pulls the emergency cord, the train stops ... the conductor comes in. The lady says, 'This man just insulted me.' The conductor says, 'Now calm down lady. The railroad will go to any extent to avoid having differences with the passengers. Perhaps it would be to your convenience if we were to rearrange your seating. And as a small compensation from the railroad, if you'll accompany me to the dining car, we'll give you a free meal. And maybe we'll find a banana for your monkey.'"

On Wilson's first release for his own Little David label (distributed by Atlantic) he presents funkier material than ever before. The title cut is a classic of characterization, as Wilson plays a reverend's wife (very much like Geraldine) who squeals out an elaborate set of excuses for buying that dress: "I said Devil stop it! Please! Then he made me try it on! Devil pulled a gun, made me sign your name to a check...." Other cuts include the seven-minute "Go-Rilla" story involving Reverend Leroy, "Ruby Begonia," and a set of "Great Quotations" including the greatest quotation ever made by a woman. It was funky Sarah Johnson shouting at an airport, "If you can fly dis plane six hundred miles in the air in the dark and find Los Angeles you can find mah bag!"

The Flip Wilson Show, premiering in 1970, marked the first time that a comedian and a television network were able to offer strong ethnic comedy free from major complaints on either side of the issue. Flip's Geraldine and Reverend Leroy were liberated in being able to use slang and talk funky. Nobody seemed to bring up the spectre of Amos and Andy in these broad comic characters and it also seemed that Wilson was able to walk in the middle of the road, not prone toward pointed racial satire (Dick Gregory) or ignoring the subject (Bill Cosby).

It was only after Flip Wilson that other shows, like The Jeffersons and Sanford and Son came on the scene. His Grammy-winning 1971 album of cuts from the TV show offers segments for Reverend Leroy and an interview with Geraldine, done by special guest David Frost: "Would you care for a cigarette?" "I don't drink, I don't smoke, and I don't do windows ... Honey, lemme tell you, nobody can tell Geraldine what to say. I listen to what everybody has to say about everything, but Geraldine'll say what she want to say. And it's my opinion that the cost of living's goin' up and the chance of living's goin' down."

There's plenty more of Flip's drag alter ego on the "Geraldine" album. Geraldine Jones became a dominant character on his show, and he often performed in very convincing drag to make Geraldine come alive. This 1972 album of "Geraldine" sketches from his TV show includes guest stars Phyllis Diller, Billy Eckstine, Tony Randall, Ruth Buzzi, and Tim Conway. The humor in these throwaway TV sketches is predictable, relying on catchphrases and Wilson's ability to deliver a funky line. With Bing Crosby and Playboy Bunny Geraldine: "Here's lookin' at you." "Look all you want! What you see's a lot more than what you gonna get! Don't touch me! You gotta lotta nerve, honey! You don't know me! You can't come in and GRAB someone. They got rules against bunny touchin'! Just because I'm dressed like this doesn't mean I'm a (snaps fingers) loose woman ... You guys are all alike! You come in here and say you want love. All you want is—a shallow friendship ... watch out! Back off, Jack! Back off."

JUSTIN WILSON

- HUMOROUS WORLD (Ember 801, reissued as Tower 5183) ** $5 $10
- I GAWR-ON-TEE (Project 8001, reissued as Tower 5008) ** $5 $10
- "WONDERMUS" HUMOR (Project 804, reissued as Tower 5010) ** $5 $10
- HOW Y'ALL ARE (Tower DT 5090) ** $5 $10
- ACROSS THE USA (Tower DT 5179E) ** $5 $10
- HUMOROUS WORLD (Tower DT 5183) ** $5 $10
- ME I GOT A FRIEN' (Tower DT 5011E) ** $5 $10
- WHOOOO BOY (Tower DT 5039E) ** $5 $10
- WILSONVILLE USA (Tower DT 5009E) ** $5 $10
- BROUGHT YOU SELF WIT' ME (Tower DT 5133) ** $5 $10
- JUSTIFYIN (Capitol SVBB 11379) ** $5 $10
- CAUGHT DEM FISH (Delta 1119) $5 $10
- JUSTIN'S PICK (Delta DLP 1125) $5 $10
- TRUCKIN' (Delta DLP 1129) $5 $10
- A CAJUN CHRISTMAS (Paula 2222, also released as CHRISTMAS CAJUN STYLE, Delta 1120) $5 $10
- HUNTING (Paula 2214) **1/2 $5 $10
- KEEP IT CLEAN (Paula 2223) **1/2 $5 $10
- MEETS JOHN BARLEYCORN (Paula 2221) **1/2 $5 $10
- OLD MASTER STORY TELLER (Paula 2219) **1/2 $5 $10
- PASS A GOOD TIME (Paula 2210) **1/2 $5 $10
- IN ORBIT (Paula 2229) **1/2 $5 $10
- THE SPORT (Paula 2227) **1/2 $5 $10
- FOR TRUE (Paula 2232) **1/2 $5 $10
- CHRISTMAS STORIES (Paula 2231) $5 $10
- OL' FAVORITES (Delta 1121, reissued as Great Southern GS 11013, in both LP and CD versions) $8

- HUNT DEM DUCK (Great Southern GS 11014) $5 $10

The Louisiana-born Wilson released many albums for Tower in the '60s and for the Paula label between 1972 and 1975. Some of the Paula titles were also issued on the Kom-a-Day label. These days many fans know him for his Cajun cooking show and are surprised to learn he made so many stand-up albums.

His humor is mostly in the telling; his Cajun dialect adds spice to old and familiar stories. His albums, especially the slightly more warm and relaxed Paula releases, are especially fine for indulgent listeners who would like to hear colorful anecdotes and tall tales told by a wry and foxy humorist.

Here's an accessible quickie for most anyone, from the "How Y'all Are" album:

"Not long ago, there was a little Cajun boy that brought himself in the house. And like all little boys, first thing he did he yell, 'Mamma, ho, Mamma!' She say, 'What it is, you yell like that.' He says, 'Poppa done hung himself out there in the garage.' She said, 'What you said?' He said, 'Poppa done hung himself in the garage, that what I said.' She said, 'Did you cut him down?' He said, 'Hell no, he waddn't dead yet.'"

On the "I Gawr-On-Tee" album he explains what a Cajun is: "About two hundred year ago, in Nova Scotia there was a place call Arcadia. And England took it over and all them French people living there would not swear allegiance to the King of England, they would just swear at him all the time. So they say you got to leff here. They wouldn't leff real good so they put them on this sailing vessel and brought them down the Eastern seaboard to Virginia, North Carolina, Georgia, but most of them had sense enough they brought themself to Louisiana. And they are most prolific people, I gaw-ron-tee. And there was some other French and Spanish people, but them Arcadian people absolved them. Arcadian became Cajun in English. Of course you Texans have another name for some of us."

Each album has one or two stories that could become a "favorite" to listen to again and again or play for a friend. "The White Mule" story from "Pass a Good Time" is typical, a five-minute yarn about a man who has a beautiful garden and decides to buy a mule. He spends $150 on the mule but ... "next day, he come back in his pickin' up truck with his trailer. The fella meet him at the gate, say, 'You know that white mule ... it broke my heart to tole you this. He haul off and dropped dead....' 'That's bad. But how about helping me load that ol' dead mule into this trailin' truck I got here, hah?' He say, 'What you gonna did with a dead mule?' He say, 'I'm gonna raffle him off, that's what I'm gonna do.' He say, 'A dead mule?' He say, 'Hell yaaaas. Help me load him up.' He say, 'I'll help ya, but I ain't gonna have no part o' them raffle....' Well, he helped him load him up. He didn't see him for four or three week, and he ran into him and say, 'Did you raffle that old dead mule off?' He said, 'You doggone right I did, I sold a thousand tickets, a dollar a chance, I made $850 less the tickets!' He say, 'Maaaan. I bet you made a lot of people mad, hah?' He say, 'Only one.' And he say, 'I gave him his money back.'"

LONNIE "PAP" WILSON

- THE PLAYBOY FARMER (Starday SLP 217) ** $4 $10

Raspy Wilson takes his time delivering anecdotal old country stories like this one:

"We rode on a little ways and come to a place they call a bus stop or rest stop. I wasn't tired, but they stopped anyway. We all got off the bus and everybody runnin' to the building. Of course I had a little curiosity. I followed them. I run in through the doors and run up to a door there. It had 'Ladies' marked on it. I opened it up and sure enough, there they was. I found out one thing, boys, they write on the walls, just like we do.

"We stopped just outside of town here, and the bus driver stopped and picked up a lady and a little boy. The lady asked the bus driver what the fare was. The bus driver said, 'Well, it'll be a quarter for you and a quarter for the little boy.' The lady said, 'Now wait just a dad burn minute. Yesterday I got on this bus, that little boy just paid half fare. What's the matter?' The bus driver said, 'I know ya lady, but yesterday you got on here, the little boy had on short pants. He paid half fare. Today he's got on long pants, he pays full fare. Short pants half fare, long pants full fare.' 'Bout that time some ol' big gal back of the bus said, 'Whoopee! Here's where I ride this bus fer nuthin'.'"

MARIE WILSON

- MY FRIEND IRMA (Radiola MR 1024) ** $5 $10
- MY FRIEND IRMA (Anonymous) ** $6 $15

A favorite "dumb blonde," pretty Marie Wilson was a costar on "Ken Murray's Blackouts" (see album entry for Ken Murray) before becoming a hit as "My Friend Irma" on radio, films, and briefly TV. There's only one episode of "My Friend Irma" on the Radiola disc; the flip side offers "Duffy's Tavern" starring Ed Gardner. There are probably enough light and dizzy lines scattered throughout the script to amuse fans: "Irma, do you like to travel?" "Oh yes, it's really the only way to get anyplace." Likewise, the "My Friend Irma" album from an anonymous label flips a February 3, 1952, episode with an "Our Miss Brooks" show on the other side.

TIM WILSON

- WAKING UP THE NEIGHBORHOOD (Southern Tracks CD-0043) *1/2 $7
- LOW CLASS LOVE AFFAIR (Southern Tracks CD-0059) *1/2 $7

Aggressive redneck Tim Wilson offers country rock and novelty songs as well as standard observational comedy about his native Georgia and environs. On the first album from 1994 he recalls his "grandaddy" who sat on his front porch and groused about the people passing by: "That Jones boy, he ain't worth a damn. He ain't had but one job, and that's givin' blood. He's just like his daddy—couldn't find his butt with both hands."

WINDERSPHERE AND BOOMER

• THE CREPITATION CONTEST (Laff A 152) ***	$5	$10
• THE CONTEST (Audiophile NG-1) **1/2	$6	$12
• GONE WITH THE WIFF (Borderline 6) **1/2	$6	$12
• FART: THE ONE AND THE ONLY WORLD FAMOUS CONTEST (Traf 1000) **1/2	$6	$12
• THE CREPITATION CONTEST (Beacon 308) $6$12		

One of the classics of low, if not foul humor, "The Crepitation Contest" was an anonymous recording that often appeared on plain-label records and bootleg tapes. Legend has it that the first version was created in the 1940s at a Canadian radio station. William Karl Thomas, in the book *Lenny Bruce: The Making of a Prophet*, insists Lord Buckley created it and issued it anonymously. Whoever originally did it inspired several others to re-record versions, all anonymous. None of the versions reviewed here are from recognizable comedians or actors.

The scripts don't vary much. "The Crepitation Contest" is always presented in the form of a "live radio broadcast" of a farting contest between Australian challenger Paul Boomer and champ Lord Windersphere. Laff's album label calls him "Lord Winderspere" and Audiophile lists "Lord Windersmere." The name is pronounced differently from record to record.

The Laff version is the best, though the flip side is terrible ("Potts and Panzy," a black drag comedy team). With sound effects and eloquent description, the announcer describes the setting, reports on the two men preparing for combat, and even offers color commentary on the uniforms the men wear:

"The trunks are powder blue with red trim. These trunks are similar to ones worn by wrestlers, with one important difference. There's a hole about six inches in diameter removed from the seat. This is called the "finesse debris," literally translated, "the zephyr window." Mr. Boomer's finesse debris has a scarlet trim around its perimeter, giving a provocative air to this genial Australian backside."

With tension and excitement, the announcer analyzes each man's work, describes the point totals, and reports on each blast of "windbreaking virtuosity" that requires control and expertise to release. There is the "single flutter-blast," the "trelblow," a "plotcher," and "fragrant fuzzes." All of these are matched by the appropriate sound effects.

Pungently written, breathtakingly well acted, and bursting with that most ancient tool of laughter (the fart), "The Crepitation Contest" should release embarrassed laughter from anyone who hears it.

Traf offers the same contest. The sound quality is a bit better, and not as speeded up, but "shit" is scissored down to "sh-" which disqualifies it. The flip side offers several risqué songs, including one from a gay-tinged pianist. "The Contest" (Audiophile NG-1) boasts of being "Full-Speed Mastered," as if there's some benefit to hearing fart noises recorded at "a tape speed of 30 inches per second ... free of tape hiss normally found in analog recording." It sounds just like everybody else's mono version, though there is a touch of echo on the farts. The flip side has six straight pub songs (including "My Darling Clementine" and "Down at the Old Bull and Bush") sung by a bland male chorus with honky-tonk piano.

"Gone with the Wiff" (Borderline 6, also released on Borderline 24) favors a more hushed delivery, as if to talk louder would cause the contestants to lose concentration. Connoisseurs who favor the "silent but deadly" approach might like this over the more raucous Laff version. There's censorship here, though. The punch line to the windy contest is a toned down "oooh, he sh-defecated" rather than a lusty shout of "Ooooh, he shit!" The flip side is the long monologue "The Hip Chinaman." On it someone puts on a Buddy Hackett-type Asian accent to talk about be-bop. It's be-boring.

• THE CREPITATION CONTEST (Encore 5012-2) **	$7

Encore's chintzy (twenty-two-minute) CD version is a modern re-creation (the announcer talks about "whether or not to admit women into open competition" due to a petition from the "women's lib movement"). To pad out what is basically about a seven-minute contest, there's an awful lot of boring pre-interviews with participants and guests. Encore tries for some of the old radio ambiance (it's in mediocre-quality mono) and the anonymous performers don't overdue the fart noises or try to "improve" the script too much. But some accents are too fake to be believed (there's a Beatle-esque Liverpudlian player) and there's not much comic flair to the ending. The announcer walks all over the punch line and repeats it several times.

PAUL WINTER

• A WINTER'S TALE (Offbeat 4010) *	$4	$8

Winter's arch, preening, pseudointellectual cabaret songs are made worse when he puts on an "upper class" accent: "Here" becomes "hee-uh," and r's are casually trilled. For effete hipsters he drops references to Stalin and Trotsky, Hegel and Schopenhauer (two different songs, of course).

A few tunes sound like failed Tom Lehrer. On "Fallout" he sings about his mutated girlfriend: "I'm in love with a girl with a lovely blonde curl in the middle of both of her foreheads. She could neatly disguise her numerous eyes if she had a couple more heads." For "Actor's Studio" he uses a country and western melody to trash method actors: "Let's mumble just a little bit, like Marlon taught us to. That's what we call our "method" to get the smash review. We got to live all the roles we're portrayin'. Life for us is deep and hard and mean. Kazan calls for death, so it goes without sayin' we'll simply follow Jimmy Dean."

JONATHAN WINTERS

• WONDERFUL WORLD OF JONATHAN WINTERS (Verve MGV-15009) ** 1/2	$10	$20
• DOWN TO EARTH (Verve MGV-15011) ***1/2	$10	$20

One of the most influential stand-ups of all time, Winters was a complete original when he arrived on the comedy scene in the late '50s. Able to caricature American characters and color his stories with sound effects, he was both a childlike funster and an angry satirist, wildly uninhibited, yet also serious and conservative. He did it all, and everyone from Johnny Carson to Burt Reynolds to Robin Williams learned lessons from him in attitude, delivery, and style.

Jonny's first album isn't his funniest, but it's filled with bizarre characters and quirky lines: "Have you ever undressed in front of a dog? It's the wildest. You know they can't talk, but it's the way they look at ya!" There's more strange humor in "Used Pet Store," a bit that way was ahead of its time: "That's an owl, but you wouldn't know it, he ain't got no feathers on his body ... incidentally, don't put your finger in that bowl. Oh! Took your finger off, didn't he! Oh God, it's a funny thing, you don't have to feed that fish nothin'. There's always some clown like yourself puttin' his finger in the bowl ... bet that smarts!"

Audiences got the impression Winters was way out—and he admitted it. He opened the album by acknowledging his confinement to a sanitorium: "I'm still a kid. Proved that a few months ago. Said I was John Q from Outer Space and left the mother ship—and they caught me. Terrible thing. But it was fun, playing checkers all day ... man, I'm out. I'm out, that's what counts ... I had six psychiatrists with pads: 'Why did you say that?' 'Oh, I don't know. I'm a robin red breast!'"

"Airline Pilots," an early improv with sound effects, was the kind of thing that really delighted fans. At the time, comics did set pieces and one-liners. Improvisation was almost unheard of. George Burns came up to him after the performance when this first LP was recorded and said, "Winters, you're unique and that ad-lib was sensational ... nobody can ever steal your act because no man can ever do it."

On his follow-up, "Down to Earth," Jonny draws a back cover that shows a gasping comedian with frayed nerve endings for fingers. The theme of the album is stability: "I'm still a rebel without a cause, but I've cooled it. I don't get into the flying saucer anymore." But this one has some of his wildest and most inventive routines. "Horror Movies" wonderfully re-creates every cliché, every sound effect, and every golden moment in "mad doctor" movies. "Scratchy" is a low-key but slyly satirical report on old Westerns. One of his finest bits, "Prison Scene," takes the Lenny Bruce "Father Flotski" theme a step further. Winters's priest turns out to be lethal!

Jonathan looks to the stage, too, performing his own "Broadway Musical" and an achingly realistic "Amateur Show" with a set of pathetic singers, including fidgety Willis Mumphert. The emcee notes: "His dad, Mr. Mumphert, has the taxidermist shop in the village. Did a nice job on your brother. Put bunny eyes in him! Come out, Willis."

Winters's whimsical cartooning sometimes veiled his mordant satire. He mentions having a casual talk with a businessman and asking him, "'Don't you think most men are little boys?' And he said, 'I'm no little boy! I make $75,000 a year.' And I said, 'Well, the way I look at it, you just have bigger toys.'"

• HERE'S JONATHAN (Verve MGV-15025) ***	$10	$20
• ANOTHER DAY ANOTHER WORLD (Verve V6-15032) ***	$10	$20
• HUMOR AS SEEN THROUGH THE EYES OF JONATHAN WINTERS (Verve V-15035) ***1/2	$10	$20
• WHISTLE STOPPING (Verve V 15037) **1/2	$10	$20

The showpiece of this album is "Oldest Airline Stewardess," the first routine on that wild oldie, Maude Frickert. It's strange and wonderful humor, as Maude talks to an interviewer, here describing her demented relative trying to learn how to fly:

"He was a little off, I think is the term. He never hurt nobody, but he used to wander a lot. He used to run up to a groundhog in May and say, 'It's the first of February!' He had a funny sense of humor. One day he said to me, 'Maudie, I'm gonna fly....' I said, 'I believe ya can, Maynard, I've seen ya do a lot of wild things.' We went up to Willard's Bluff ... he Scotch taped a hundred forty-six pigeons to his arms...."

At this, the audience is so broken up Winters can't continue for a full thirty seconds.

"He said, 'I know I can do it Maudie, I know I can.' I said, 'Don't repeat yourself, just do it....' He was airborne for a good twenty seconds. Then some kid came from outta nowhere, threw a bag of popcorn in the stone quarry and he bashed his brains out."

Today's listeners, accustomed to hearing "weird" jokes in Johnny Carson's monologues or the outrages of '80s comics like Emo Philips, Judy Tenuta, or even Winters-influenced "sick" comic Richard Lewis, will probably miss the full impact of Winters. At the time, he was breaking through all barriers and literally creating an entire new genre of stand-up comedy. Even so, bits like "The Oldest Airline Stewardess" are not only classic, they are still very potent.

Other cuts include several excellent sketches that offer slightly subtle satire: a well-done parody of "High Noon" type Westerns ("Billy the Kid"); and an unusual piece blending comedy and pathos, "Thoughts of a Turtle," about a turtle trying to cross a highway to meet his girlfriend. Lesser but still amusing fun: "Test Flight," "Child Psychiatrist," and "New Flying Saucer."

"Another Day" is Winters's most balanced album, a blend of anecdotes, improv, and movie parodies. Half the set is conversational comedy and for a change of pace centers on personal recollections. Two excellent long set pieces allow him to create an entire story complete with sound effects. Monster movie parody "Igor and the Monster" offers an affectionate Karloff imitation as a scientist ignores a horny, drooling assistant and tons of bizarre-sounding equipment as he attempts to make an eighteen-foot tall monster. "The Lost Island" satirizes jungle movies. At one point in the show Jonny even tells a one-liner: "An Episcopalian: that's a Catholic that flunked his Latin."

The 1962 "Humor As Seen Through the Eyes of ..." marks a move toward more improvisation. Perhaps that was what the album's pretentious/obvious title was supposed to mean. A lot of the comedy here is in Winters's unique characters, not jokes. He does a nine-minute bit on "Terry Thai," a Thailand folk singer, who tells a fairy tale about "a ugly little prince" and the little girl who wants to be his friend. It wouldn't seem like much written down, and sometimes Winters seems to be groping for the next line, but it's still charming and a wonderful flight of fancy.

Equally elusive (hysterical for some, but not for others) is the lengthy monologue Winters's rube character Elwood P. Suggins offers in describing his new automobile: "It's a car everyone in America will love. And some Europeans." The humor in a piece about sissy Captain Arnold hunting Moby Dick is mostly in Jonny's delivery, not the lines, whether it's a fussy demand ("Where are my harpoons?) or hissy impatience: "I just don't know where to begin. You stick it in the tail, they go crazy!" "Chief Running Fox," is a quick, ironic study of Indians on a reservation and "Maude Frickert and the Funeral" is a classic of "sick comedy," the fiesty, fearless old lady fighting with a low-key funeral director over the job they've done on her nephew.

"Whistle Stopping" was written by Pat McCormick. He plays straight to Winters on a few cuts keyed to the 1964 presidential race. A concept album with writing at the level of his short-lived CBS variety show, Winters covers a a gay liberal (Lance Lovegard), a farmer (Elwood P. Suggins), a conservative (Tick Bitterford), a teenager (Melvin Gohard), an American Indian (Chief Crying Trout), and Maude Frickert. McCormick, who would soon become head writer of *The Tonight Show* and supply Johnny Carson with "weird" lines, has the best time talking with Maude Frickert:

"What's it like living here in this old folks home?"

"Look at the veins in my hand ... they tell a story."

"What is that man doing down by the brook?"

"What is he doing down by the brook! Shame on you, Eddie! That's what's killing all the fish."

• MAD MAD MAD MAD WORLD (Verve V 15041) ✳✳✳	$10	$20
• BEST OF FRICKERT AND SUGGINS (Verve 15052) ✳✳✳	$10	$20
• MOVIES ARE BETTER THAN EVER (Verve 15057) ✳✳✳	$10	$20
• GREAT MOMENTS IN COMEDY (Verve 15047) ✳✳✳	$10	$20

Verve repackaged and reissued their catalogue of albums often, but at least they made them collectible. "Mad World" has a frantic Jack Davis cover and "Movies are Better than Ever" has a cute cover painting of Winters as various movie characters.

• WINGS IT! (Columbia CS 9611) ✳✳1/2	$6	$15
• STUFF 'N' NONSENSE (Columbia CS 9799) ✳✳1/2	$6	$15
(Both albums were reissued as JONATHAN WINTERS LAUGHS LIVE, Columbia PG 31985)	$10	$20

Winters tired of prepared sketches and preferred audiences to help him "wing it" with their suggestions. Improv demonstrated Jonny's skill and it was more interesting and challenging for him than mouthing the same old lines, but the consequence was a lot of failed experiments. While virtually anything he did was exciting for his core of fans, a lot of it was bewildering to the masses.

"Wings It" has some very mild four-minute routines ("Maude Frickert Explains the Birds and the Bees," "Deer Hunters," "King Kwazi of Kwazi Land," "Necking in a '38 Ford"), but eighty percent of the album was ad-libbed. The results are benign and cute. Even Maude Frickert on sex doesn't quite have the teeth in. Her daughter asks her, "How do birds do it?" and Maude snaps, "Very fast. And high in the air, idiot! Sometimes in trees, smart aleck ... you're getting to that dangerous age when you'll be playing around! Ohhhh! Now let's get back to the birds. I blew it on the birds. There's a father bee and a mother bee. And they meet. And sting! Mmmmm, and then there're little bees. And honey. And life is sweet ... there's me and your Dad ... when you kids are in your pads, we're in our pad. Now he's your Dad ... big stud ... and there's me, frail, 120. But fun! Ha ha ha ... your Dad kisses me. Strange way, right in the ear. Which drives me right out of my gourd. And I kiss him. That's it ... ain't it beautiful?"

His last album, "Stuff 'n' Nonsense" has Winters creating instant bizarre characters and producing strange slices of life, but it doesn't always provoke big laughs. Winters fans will be giggling all the way through, just hearing him riff on "John Wayne Landing on the Moon," "A Mouse Just Caught in a Trap," "Elderly Gentleman Seeing a Flying Saucer," and "Maude Frickert's Nursery School." And when asked to impersonate a man confronting the Abominable Snowman:

"Hi there. I'm Fred Kipter, I represent the press. Nice of you to come down the slope here. You're the Abominable Snowman, right? Well, bless your heart ... (Growling). Well a lot of the villagers are scared to death of you. There was a guide here a minute ago. I guess the minute you did that 'Grrrrr' he was frightened. But I'm not frightened, because I see the zipper there, see?"

• IT'S HEE-HEE-HEE HEE LARIOUS (No Label) ✳✳✳	$20	$50
• RHAPSODY FOR BAR USERS (Columbia CS 786)	$10	$25

Subtitled, "a collectors item of JW FROM WITHOUT," "Hee Larious" was evidently a private pressing, a gift from Winters to a select group of friends, circa 1960. There's just a white label on the disc and no album notes. The cover shows a space creature parachuting to Earth.

Sort of an audio notebook, Winters has assembled snips from hours of private ad-libs, conducted alone, with an anonymous friend prompting him, or in the company of four or five laughing observers. Quick turns involve golf broadcasts, perverted relatives at Christmas, an interview with a German, a hulking flasher visiting old Maude Frickert, and some strange racial satire playing in the same territory as Lenny Bruce's "nigger" routine about using offensive names over and over.

Winters himself admits some of the ideas "are pretty sick," including a commercial from a bigoted Southerner for a salve that will "free" the black man's kinky hair. One of the few completely formed routines here is a narrative version of Little Red Riding Hood: "She went through the forest one day and she was tired, run down. In ill health, so to speak, boys and girls. She was skinny, she weighed forty-seven pounds. In fact she dragged herself across the forest floor. She finally got into this little nothing house, it was typical F.A.K. type of thing, a real fuzzy house; strange, boys and girls. She went in there and sat down at this table full of hot porridge. Common, ordinary grits. Oh, she went through maybe fifteen, twenty bowls, and then she threw up, boys and girls. There's a little message there. Don't be greedy and stuff yourself or you'll throw up. Then after she done that it left a rather terrible aroma about the house. Consequently the bears smelled this ... they came back and what they did with her: first the little bear tore her one arm out, and then the other bear tore her other arm out, and they put her in a little tiny cigar box. Threw it in a gravel pit. Heh heh heh heh. That's it, boys and girls."

One segment features some blooper tapes and outtakes he collected, including odd moments from Della Reese, Freddie Cannon, and Phyllis Diller: "What do they call a man who shovels cement with a pitchfork? A mortar-forker! Ha haaaaaa haaaa."

The Columbia LP was a promotional album for Republic Steel. One side is a gift of music, including songs by Columbia's musical stars The Mormon Tabernacle Choir, Mitch Miller, Robert Goulet, etc. On the flip side Jonathan presents humorous facts about Republic Steel. In Jim Lehner's corporate-sponsored script, the jokes are incidental to the commercial announcements.

At one point, Frickert says Republic Steel produces "everything we need in carbon, alloys, and special metal bar products. In fact, if you can dream up something they ain't got, they'll figure a way to steel it for ya! A ha ha, that's a little funny!"

- PETER AND THE WOLF (EMI CDC 7 499182) **1/2 $8
- THE BEST OF JONATHAN WINTERS (Dove Audio) *1/2 $8
- CRANK CALLS (Audio Select 80010) ** $8

Winters is respectful to the composers of "Peter and the Wolf" and "Carnival of the Animals." For each poem in "Carnival of the Animals," he uses a different bizarre voice or accent. "Peter and the Wolf" gets duck quacks and wolf growls plus a few ad-libs. While Peter is hunting in the woods, there's a gunshot: "Gee Bob, I'm sorry. I thought I unloaded it." Though previous comic narrators (from Hermoine Gingold, Rob Reiner, and Al Yankovic to Michael Flanders, Sterling Holloway, and Zero Mostel) are on Peter's side, Winters is sympathetic when the wolf is captured. He imitates a snarling wolf, then mutters, "Well, if anybody ever tried to do this to you, you'd try to get loose. Think about it, gang."

Winters issued several tapes for Dove, which were sold primarily in bookstores. The 1993 CD compilation is brief (thirty-two minutes), the sound quality is just passable (since the tracks are taken from Winters's incoming and outgoing phone machine messages), and calling this a "best of" is misleading.

On the positive side, diehard fans can enjoy the vicarious thrill of hearing what it's like to call Winters and get his answering machine, or what would happen if Winters called up and left a message. Sometimes Winters is surprisingly no better than any other joker assuming a corny voice and letting his mind wander. Accompanying an unconvincing Bogart imitation: "This is Rick calling about the passports. I know that you got 'em and I'll be picking 'em up ... I've got some contacts. We'll crawl through some sewer pipe in order to get in on the Canadian side. I don't want to take any chances with those stiffs at the gate, ya know. They say, 'Can I have some identification please.' I don't need that! So we'll crawl through the pipe, then we're on our way. Well, that's all for now."

The 1995 "Crank Calls" offers forty-five minutes of phone antics. Seems Jonny called his friend J. B. Smith quite a bit—and Smith was rarely home. Though the messages Jonny leaves are strange more than hilarious, fans will be intrigued. He mulls over getting Smith's machine: "... you're missing the most important thing in your life. That is your dear friend and talent, former star Jonathan Winters. Brighter side, two words: who cares. You know, we're only visitors. Bye bye, and remember the Prince of Darkness is with us twenty-four hours a day regardless of light. The Prince of Darkness can deal with it. Heavy." It's tough to take a lot of these since each segment includes Smith's tedious "Thanks for calling, I'm sorry I can't be here, leave a message" preamble.

NOTES: Winters has recorded several children's albums, old "The Little Prince" (Pip Records 6813) and newer "Paul Bunyan," a CD for Windham Hill (WD 0717). He had a straight announcer's role on the ten-inch promotional disc for Scandinavian Air Lines, "European Holiday" (Columbia 2586). He does five minutes of improv with Bob Crane on "Laffter and Profane" (see Buttram and Crane entry). On the promo disc "Motorola Presents 3-Channel Stereophonic High Fidelity," Winters is briefly interviewed as Sir Trafalger Whitley, Maude Frickert, and B.,B. Bindlesstiff. He is also on a rare promo from Fiat. He turns up on "Jest of Flair," a 1960 promotional album for the ABC radio series interviewing himself as stuntman "Casualty Mumphert," lisping Lance Loveguard, Madison Avenue's "Tic Bitterford," and as big game hunter Sir Trafalger Whitley: "It was only a month ago, I was being charged by a bull elephant. I side-stepped the elephant only to be bitten by a cobra. But what really scared me was seeing Lady Whitley swinging through the trees yelling, 'There'll always be an England.' She has the most perverted sense of humor at times."

At the turn of the '90s Winters issued two cassettes for the Dove "books on tape" company ("Finally Captured" and "Into the 90's," which were nominated for Grammy awards).

REVEREND BILLY C. WIRTZ

- DEEP FRIED AND SANCTIFIED (Hightone HCD 8017) *1/2 $6
- BACKSLIDER'S TRACTOR PULL (Hightone HCD 8024) *1/2 $6
- A TURN FOR THE WIRTZ (Hightone HCD 8042) *1/2 $6
- PIANIST ENVY (Hightone HCD 8051) *1/2 $6

South Carolina-born Wirtz's country-swing songs, sung in a deep dull baritone, veer between slightly warped and numbingly predictable. The typical "Food Chain of Fools" on "Turn for the Wirtz" (released in 1992) is a corny food fight: "Walked in the kitchen and there was weird noises comin' from the Frigidaire. I said Lord have mercy something's going on in there ... the black-eyed peas were out for a stroll. And little Sara Lee was on a big roll. Mr. Arm and Hammer banged out a beat on a month-old package of mystery meat." Wirtz tries for the unusual and strains himself. On "Pianist Envy" he sings about Elvis coming back to earth as kiddie fave Barney the dinosaur: "Now the king of rock and roll got a new day job, bigger than he was before. He's packin' 'em in down at the local mall, he ain't nothin' but a purple dinosaur.... So the next time you see Barney on the TV set, remember he's not some annoying reptile, he's the King we'll never forget."

WITS END PLAYERS

- GONE WITH THE WITS (Wits End 72870) ** $7 $15
- SOME OF MY BEST FRIENDS WATCH TV (Century 20097) ** $7 $15

A satirical comedy troupe from Atlanta, the Wits were evidently the city's equivalent of the Second City (Chicago) and Julius Monk revues (New York). Philip Erickson and his wife Nancy were the mainstays. Trivia fans will note that previously Erickson spent seven years teamed with Dick Van Dyke as the pantomime duo The Merry Mutes.

The Century album features album notes by Dick Van Dyke. The music was written by Jack Holmes, and one of the tunes here, "Thor," turns up in Julius Monk's revue "Dime a Dozen." Only a few of the mild, dated cuts actually satirize TV, like "Funanza," a complaint about the lack of women on *Bonanza* where "everybody loves his Hoss." The highlight, "A House Is Not a Home," a Polly Adler parody, still has a few laughs as a madam talks about her Atlanta bordello: "Tell me, do you have trouble with the police?" "All the time. They never want to pay the full price." Cast members include George Ormiston, Nancie Phillips, and Kay Mason.

The Ericksons join Bill Sims, Janet Wells, Sally Street, and Kay Mason for the sketches and fey songs on the Wits End record. Some of the tunes try for a little bite (a cheerful song about "Your Friendly Liberal Neighborhood Ku Klux Klan"). The sketches include Adam talking to Eve, and a female sky diver interviewed about her hobby: "It's a pleasure to drop in...." "You've had some famous falls in your time, haven't you?" "We were up in the plane at three thousand feet. I jumped out of the plane, reached for my ripcord, and pulled my bra strap instead." "Oh, that is dangerous." "I almost smothered." "How'd you come out of it?" "Made a four point landing!" "Four point?" "My feet touched, too!"

GENE WOOD

- WHAT WOULD HAVE HAPPENED IF? (Coral CRL 57428) *1/2 $5 $10

Following his teaming with Bill Dana, Gene Wood (later a quiz show announcer and host) made this early '60s record of fairly simple sketches. With a supporting cast, he rewrites history (the Boston Tea Party, David and Goliath, the Louisiana Purchase, and so on). The results aren't too interesting. A blackout sketch on Charles Lindbergh: "Contact!" (Sound of a motor idling repeatedly.) "Oh, it was a crazy idea anyway!"

GEORGE WOOD AND KATIE

- THE SPECIAL WORLD OF GEORGE WOOD AND KATIE (AVA AS 17) ** $5 $10

Fans of the Smothers Brothers will be familiar with two of George Wood's best songs: "Church Bells" and "Jenny Brown." It shouldn't come as any surprise that the Smothers' versions are 100% funnier than the originals sung by the bland folkie Wood with background cooing and harmonies from his wife Katie. Wood, betraying his roots in old folk tunes and madrigals, uses a warbling voice, archaic phrasing ("preserve-ed"), and archaic words ("Twas"). It's to the Smothers' credit that they saw through the defects in Wood's "Johnny Brown" and turned it into a '50s rock parody "Jenny Brown," switching olde English ("On his hand I marked a ring") to teen anguish ("On her hand a high school ring") in telling the story of a deathly practical joker.

The other tunes here are sing-song silly, from a tune about Caroline Kennedy rocking her rocking chair so hard she goes into orbit, to one about Dwight Eisenhower hitting a golf ball extremely far: "The ball sailed high way up in the sky until it was gone from the human eye. It sailed across the ocean blue and across the European continent too." The flip side of this 1962 album is filled with serious songs like "The Witching Willow" and "Song of an Orphan."

PETER WOOD

- THE CENSOR (Jubilee JGM 2043) * $4 $8

On a studio album produced by Kermit Schafer, Wood vaguely tries to lampoon television censorship. The Censor is previewing a new talk show and finds it appalling. Listeners will find it trying as Wood interviews himself in various uninspired guises. His mimicry runs to dialect voices (some in very questionable taste), put-on gruffness, fey lisping, etc.

With Schafer producing, the result is even more obvious and artificial than if Wood did his act live. The canned laughter is turned on and off like a faucet and zany noises are tossed in, too. Wood introduces an African leader sitting in the audience next to Arkansas Governor Faubus. The African says, "If you can't beat 'em—eat 'em!" And suddenly there's a lot of snarling and eating sound effects. Faubus shouts, "Get your cotton pickin' hands off me, boy! I can't wait till I get you in Little Rock!" And the canned laughter explodes.

WOODY WOODBURY

• LOOKS AT LOVE AND LIFE (Stereoddities MW 1) **	$5	$10
• LAUGHING ROOM (Stereoddities MW 2) **	$5	$10
• BOOZE IS THE ONLY ANSWER (Stereoditties/BITOA) **	$5	$15
• CONCERT IN COMEDY (Stereoddities MW 3) **	$5	$10
• SALOONATICS (Stereoddities MW 4) **	$5	$10
• THE SPICE IS RIGHT (Stereoddities MW 5) **	$5	$10
• BEST OF WOODY WOODBURY (Stereoddities MW 6) **	$5	$10
• THROUGH THE KEYHOLE (Stereoddities MW 7) **	$5	$10

Woodbury, best known in Florida clubs, had a few chances at national exposure, first when he took over as host of Johnny Carson's quiz show *Who Do You Trust* in 1963, and in 1967 when he briefly had a syndicated talk show. His last album of "adult" material was released in 1964.

Rather gentle for a booze and off-color joke comedian, Woodbury was a likable guy who could banter mildly with his fun-loving audience, do a few jokes, then sit down at the piano for a parody or two. He tells one-liners occasionally, this from "Laughing Room": "I love those slow-talking Southern girls. I was out with a Southern girl last night, took her so long to tell me she wasn't that kind of girl, she was."

Mostly, though, he tells anecdotal stories. From "Looks at Life," Woody's drunk jokes: "I like stories about drunks the best.... As a rule I don't drink. As a habit I do, but as a rule I don't. I like the story about the two drunks who went out to play golf.... This one drunk turned to the other and said, 'Fred, I'm going up and tell those two women up there to either get the devil off this golf course or let us play through....' So he ran up, got almost up to 'em and ran back. He said, 'Good heavens, Fred, I almost got trapped. One of those girls is my wife and the other's my mistress. Boy, what a close call.' Second one says, 'I'm new around here, I'll go tell 'em.' Well, the second one races up, he gets almost up to them, turns around and runs back and says, 'By God, John, it's a small world, isn't it!'"

Woodbury delivers these stories as if there is some charm to drunkenness. This, coupled with his celebration of booze (one of his catchphrases is the toast "Booze is the only answer") may repel some listeners.

Woodbury favors humor for couples, which makes him a bit different from the usual "stag" oriented risqué comic. From "Spice Is Right": "What's the first thing a wife says to her husband in the morning? 'No, dammit, you'll be late for work.' What's the second thing she says in the morning? 'See honey, I told you you'd be late for work.' The Woodbury formula doesn't vary much from disc to disc. "Spice Is Right" has a few more songs than the others, written by Eli Basse. "Booze Is the Only Answer" is a boxed set with a record, a paperback book, and booklets.

JAY WRAY

• IT'S WARM INSIDE (Jacco) *1/2	$5	$10
• HAVE A FUNDERFUL EVENING (Jacco 2770) *1/2	$5	$10

Wray performed at the Tale o' The Tiger Lounge in Ft. Lauderdale in the early '60s. He tepidly tells his tired gags with a slightly gay tinge to his voice. The anecdotal adult material is straight. From the "Funderful" album: "I bought a dog two weeks ago. The cutest little dog you ever saw in your life. He's just a dog dog. I only paid $2.50 for him. And then I spent $196 building a fence in the back for him. I tried to figure out a name for him, something real different, you know? So I got hold of a real good one. I call him Sex. Heh heh. I said, 'Come on, Sex ...' and he ran away from me. So I'm lookin' for this stinker, you know, heh heh, all over town, and four o'clock in the morning I'm in this blind alley. And this cop comes up to me. He said, 'What are you doin' here?' And I had to answer him, I said, 'Well, I'm looking for Sex.' My case comes up about two weeks from Saturday. And then I understood that I had to have a license, so I went down to the license bureau and I said, 'I'd like to have a license for Sex.' And he said, 'So would I.' But I said, 'No, no, this is for a dog.' He said, 'Well I don't care what she looks like.'"

STEVEN WRIGHT

• I HAVE A PONY (Warner Bros. 1-25335) ***1/2	$5	$10

In the late '80s, at a time when "zany" was the word in comedy clubs, deadpan Steven Wright emerged as a cerebral alternative. His one-liners recall the surreal lines of Jackie Vernon and the offbeat concepts of Woody Allen—both big influences. He offers deadpan that detonates, verbal cartoons spoken in a hollow, sleepy voice that suddenly explode in the listener's head:

"I saw a subliminal advertising executive. But just for a second." "I just got out of the hospital. I was in a speedreading accident. I hit a bookmark." "If I melt dry ice can I swim without getting wet?"

Wright's 1985 album is pretty much an unconnected series of odd notions and disjointed gags. While Jackie Vernon and Woody Allen often performed complete routines, even after ten years Wright rarely seemed ambitious enough to put the gags together into a sustained (and more memorable) storyline.

ED WYNN

• THE FIRE CHIEF (Mark 56 #621) **1/2	$6	$15

A star in vaudeville and *The Ziegfield Follies*, Wynn switched to radio where his frantic, cornball style and cracked, yodeling delivery endeared him to millions. Possessing such a unique voice probably led him to his famous remark, "A comic is a man who says funny things—a comedian is someone who says things funny." Wynn found his style out of favor in the '50s (though his disciple, Red Skelton, was following in his footsteps), but he became successful in straight acting roles.

Keenan Wynn supplies the strangest introduction to any comedy album as he haltingly narrates his father's life story as if trying to recall a bad dream. Music that sounds like it could have come from *The Twilight Zone* wavers in the background. The drama ends with this summation: "I would say my father was a very gentle man who was put under great stress by everybody. He tried to do the best he could ... he really tried ... My father would perform in the men's room if somebody would recognize him ... he was a very sad man ... he had achieved such great success, monumental success, and he would be in a room with the door closed and say, 'Why am I not happy?'"

The radio material here is loaded with corny jokes and silly puns told with a euphoric, good-time giggle. Describing animals, he says, "I like skunks! They're noted for their fur—the fur away from them the better!"

"... Well anyhow ... the waiter is in the restaurant and a customer enters.... The customer says, 'I want some Chicken Okra Soup.' The waiter says, 'I'm very sorry, but we do not carioca!' See? Ha ha! I love puns, you know ... then the waiter says, you know, 'The last man who was in the restaurant ate twenty-seven hotcakes right off the griddle. And the customer says, 'How waffle!'"

All this is greeted with laughter and outbursts of applause from the happy studio audience. Wynn, known for years as "The Perfect Fool," achieved perfection for his kind of foolishness. Samples of Wynn's silliness appear on "Jest Like Old Times" (Radiola #1) and "Golden Age of Comedy" (Evolution 3013). Wynn also made six children's fantasy albums for Riverside as "Grandpa Magic." He appears on the soundtrack album for the 1966 animated film *The Daydreamer* (Columbia OS 2940).

PAUL WYNN

- SONGS BY PAUL WYNN (Cocktail 1) **1/2 $7 $15

An album of off-color favorites and nonsense tunes including "The Automobile Song," "Noses Run in My Family," "The Tattooed Lady," and of course, "Shaving Cream," which became a hit decades after its original release (see "Shaving Cream" by Benny Bell).

NOEL X

- FOLK SONGS FOR CONSERVATIVES (Toad TRLP 8) * $4 $8

As "Noel X and His Unbleached Muslims," Noel Parmentel, Jr., Marshall Dodge, Mike Childs, and a few others, sing rewritten folk songs in an annoyingly fey barbershop quartet style. Those expecting some kind of forceful racial satires or some other reason for alluding to Malcolm X will be disappointed.

Dated now, there was nothing very amusing about this one when it first arrived. The lampoons of conservatives include revised lyrics for "We Shall Not Be Moved," declaring: "They say we are dogmatic, but we shall not be moved. Because we're not pragmatic we shall not be moved ... we're standing by Goldwater! We shall not be moved!" "Aura Lee" is now "Orally," a protest against fluoridation in drinking water: "Don't put fluorides in our streams. Don't spray our willow tree. It's a Commie plot, it seems. To get us orally." And "Glory Hallelujah" becomes an attack on Earl Warren: "Hang Earl Warren to a soul apple tree. His impeachment still won't fill the bill for folks like you and me. We'll soon cast off the yoke of his judicial tyranny, as we go charging off!"

"WEIRD" AL YANKOVIC

- WEIRD AL YANKOVIC (Rock 'n' Roll BFZ 38679) **1/2 $5 $10
- IN 3-D (Rock 'n' Roll FZ 39221) *** $5 $10
- DARE TO BE STUPID (Rock 'n' Roll FZ 40033) *1/2 $5 $10
- POLKA PARTY (Rock 'n' Roll FZ 40520) ** $5 $10
- WORSE (Rock 'n' Roll 834 770-2) ** $8
- OFF THE DEEP END (Rock 'n' Roll DGCD 24425) *1/2 $8
- ALAPALOOZA (Scotti Bros. 72392 7544152) * $8
- THE FOOD ALBUM (Scotti Bros. 754212) *1/2 $7
- THE TV ALBUM (Scotti Bros. 75432) ** $7
- GREATEST HITS (Scotti Bros. 754562) ** $7
- AL IN THE BOX: THE PERMANENT RECORD (Scotti Bros. 54512) ** $25
- BAD HAIR DAY (Scotti Bros. 75500) ** $8

"Weird Al" listened to dumb songs on Dr. Demento's radio show and in 1979 submitted his own: a screamy, accordion-accompanied version of The Knack's "My Sharona" called "My Balogna." The rest is history, sort of.

Yankovic's raw first album still has some high points. "Ricky" is a double pronged poke in the ears. It not only sends up Toni Basil's original hit, but twists it into an ode to *I Love Lucy*, complete with Tress MacNeille's devastatingly accurate whines as Lucy. The last lines, sung by Lucy, cut a little deeper than the usual Yankovic lyrics: "Oh Ricky, what a pity, don't you understand, that every day's a rerun and the laughter's always canned." Another worthy early hit is "Another One Rides the Bus," about a variety of obnoxious bozos onboard. Al's thin, rangeless yelling doesn't help predictable kid stuff like "My Balogna" and "I Love Rocky Road."

Most of Al's early tunes are, like eight-year-olds, preoccupied with food. In 1984 he scored big with the Michael Jackson parody "Eat It," complete with an MTV video. It's on 3-D along with another winner, "I Lost on Jeopardy" (complete with a cameo from announcer Don Pardo jeering, "You made yourself look like a jerk in front of millions of people ... YOU don't even get a lousy copy of our home game"). "Polkas on 45" wretchedly runs hits of the day through the bellows of Al's accordion. (No, Al is not related to accordionist Frankie Yankovic, but having the same last name did inspire the choice of instrument). Al would use the polka medley/meddling device on other albums.

"Dare to Be Stupid" is an accurate title. Like Allan Sherman, by the third album his parodies held to a formula. Madonna's "Like a Virgin" should've yielded something more potent than "Like a Surgeon": "Like a surgeon, cuttin' for the very first time. Got your kidneys on my mind." Huey Lewis's "I Want a New Drug" becomes the equally witless "I Want a New Duck." "Girls Just Want to Have Fun" is another boring food song, "Girls Just Want to Have Lunch." Weird Al's originals, never a highlight, are sledgehammer obvious here.

"Polka Party" from 1986 is even less interesting: "Living in America" becomes "Living with a Hernia," "Ruthless People" is "Toothless People," and "Addicted to Love" becomes yet another food list, "Addicted to Spuds." Who cares: "You planned a trip to Idaho just to watch potatoes grow. I understand how you must feel. I can't deny they've got a peel." Yankovic's originals at least try for something more grown up. One cut has some Tom Lehrer starkness: "... it's Christmas at Ground Zero and if the radiation level's okay I'll go out with you and see all the new Mutatations on New Year's Day."

"Worse" (than Michael Jackson's "Bad") has better vocals from Al, who must've realized that a less grating singing voice would help prolong his career. "This Song's Just Six Words Long" isn't a bad response to George Harrison's hit cover of the repetitive "I Got My Heart Set on You." On "Fat," yet another authorized (thereby toothless) Michael Jackson parody, the jokes are broad, including the borrowing of a Joan Rivers gag about Liz Taylor ("I've got more chins than Chinatown"). Other jokes are even older: "When I go to get my shoes shined, I gotta take their word." This 1988 disc marked the cooling down of Al's shooting star.

Weird Al's hiatus ended with "Off the Deep End" in the summer of 1992. The cover parodied a Nirvana album jacket; Al floating nude in a swimming pool. That drew more attention to the disc than it deserved. By this time there was such a fractioning of the pop charts (between heavy metal, progressive, rap, etc.) that it was hard finding a program of songs to satirize that all listeners would even know. Food parodies—again? Yep: "Taco Grande," based on "Rico Suave." Equally pointless is M. C. Hammer's "U Can't Touch This" becoming a protest about bad TV, "I Can't Watch This." "Smells Like Nirvana" is a harmless take on Nirvana's "Smells Like Teen Spirit," with Al whining: "What is this song all about? Can't figure any lyrics out. How do the words to it go? I wish you'd tell me, I don't know."

Predictably, in 1993 Weird Al tried to cash in on *Jurassic Park* but his anemic parody on "Alapalooza," crossing dinosaur references with the fossilized tune "MacArthur Park," is deader than old bones: "Jurassic Park is frightening in the dark. All the dinosaurs are running wild." Yankovic's originals are, as usual, blandly weak, like the doughy "Waffle King," that urges, "believe in the power of the waffle." "Livin' in the Fridge" (based on "Livin' on the Edge") is yet another stupid food song: "You can't stop the mold from growin. Livin' in the fridge!" Amusing (at least once) is Al's swat at the dumb country hit "Achy Breaky Heart." After listing Barry Manilow, New Kids on the Block, Vanilla Ice, Debbie Boone, Zamfir, and Tiffany, Al insists "Achy Breaky" is "the most annoying song I know." Quite a remark, considering his own catalog.

Al recycled his food tunes ("The Food Album") and TV parodies ("The TV Album") to keep product flowing. He did a version of "Peter and the Wolf" with synthesizer wiz/synthesized woman Wendy (nee Walter) Carlos. He tossed in a greatest hits CD and ultimately a 1994 Christmas gift box: fifty-two songs on four CD's, plus a sixty-four-page color booklet.

The 1996 "Bad Hair Day" requires an MTV addict's mentality to even recognize the numbers being parodied (Coolio, TLC, and Presidents of the United States of America). A "Weird Al" fan's mentality is also needed to find humor in songs about the Amish and Forrest Gump. While he still seems prone toward safe nonsense for preteens, the good news here is that Al's originals aren't bad, with a harder edge to the music and less kiddie-vaudeville in the lyrics. He actually rises to the level of what Cheap Trick was doing in the '70s, which isn't necessarily a bad trick. "Alternative Polka," *polking* fun at recent hits, is one of his better medleys thanks to Spike Jones sound effects. Al sees "the edge" and goes overboard, raising the sap level on Sheryl Crow's airheaded "All I Wanna Do" and even squeezing a laugh out of Alanis Morisette's real serious whine "You Oughta Know." Al's work has always been as spotty and slapdash as a pizza with everything on it, which means that some have to pick their way along to find the good nuggets while others with strong stomachs can swallow it whole.

THE YEADLES

• REBBE-MANIA (Rich Tone 119124) *1/2 $7 $15

"Not the Beatles," the album cover says, "These guys are Jewish." And they're putting new, Jewish lyrics to Beatles melodies. Not exactly Allan Sherman, only a few songs seem out for laughs. More often the intent is to provide young Jewish listeners with something rocking and religious. "I Get By with a Little Help from My Friends" becomes "I Get By with a Little Faith in Hashem." "I Saw Her Standing There" becomes "I Felt God's Presence There," and "Nowhere Man" becomes "Chutzpanik" with these lines: "He's a real Chutzpanik, giving us his Chutzpah schtick. Thinking he's so righteous. But he isn't. Oy, the smarts he hasn't got. Speaks from where he sits a lot. Wasting so much time of his. And ours."

YOGI YORGESSON

• YOGI YORGESSON'S FAMILY ALBUM (Capitol H 336) *1/2 $10 $20

- THE GREAT COMEDY HITS (Capitol T 1620) *1/2 $7 $15

Yogi (Harry Stewart) used to sing pop songs in dialect, often favoring a corny Swedish accent. A typical tune like "The Object of My Affection" gets snickers from the stereotypical vocals, and sometimes a bit of monology over the instrumental break: "My sweetheart Lillian—on her poppa's farm I'm the hired man.... I scrape off the dinner dishes for Lillian, I get rid of the table scraps as quick as a wink. Her poppa put in a new garbage disposal. He keeps a pig under the kitchen sink ... side by side, Lillian and me milk the cow together ... we was milking together when I slipped our engagement ring on Lillian's finger. That is, I thought it was her finger. It felt like her finger. But I know now that for twenty minutes one night I was engaged to the brown and white Jersey cow."

Stewart sometimes recorded tunes as the Japanese "Harry Kari." "Family Album" is a ten-inch disc. His novelty tunes turn up on various compilation albums, including "Comedy Caravan" (Capitol T 732).

COUNTRY YOSSI AND THE SHTEEBLE-HOPPERS

- WANTED (House of Menorah Men 707) ** $6 $12
- STRIKE AGAIN (House of Menorah Men 4000) ** $6 $12

Circa 1984, Country Yossi offered country and western and folk music with a Jewish twist. Typical from "Wanted" is "The Cholent Song," with this chorus: "Cholent is its name, heartburn is its game. It looks so innocent it's deadly just the same. If I had my way, I'd ship it all away. And drop it on the Arabs. They'd be gone in a day." Another highlight is their version of "Big John," now called "Big Moish." Moish is quite a mensch. A yahrtzeit candle tips over in the shul and he's right there to save a minyan of worshippers and the Torah.

On "Strike Again," they rework "The Purple People Eater" into "Flyin' Lukshin-Kugel Eater" complete with speeded up vocal parts; rework "Monster Mash" into "The Shteeble Hop"; and turn "A Boy Named Sue" into "A Boy Named Zlateh." Angry Zlateh meets his father in a restaurant and they get into a fight: "He just smashed that soggy pizza all over my face, so I reached out to a paper dish and I come up with a potato knish. And I held it high and chased him all over the place."

ALAN YOUNG

- MISTER ED (Colpix CP 209) *** $15 $35

In 1950 Alan Young starred in his own TV show, which ran for several years. He was on radio and also made films. But as pleasant straight man to a grouchy talking horse, he's achieved his greatest fame. 1961's *Mister Ed* continues on in rerun. This album offers two connecting episodes of the show, "Ed the Song Writer" and "Mr. Ed's Blues," and as well as being fine examples of wholesome, mild TV sitcoms of the era, they include some songs.

Western star Rocky Lane was the voice of Mister Ed, and here he gets a chance to sing. In the first episode, Ed casually hums a tune that is so catchy Wilbur picks it up. When he hums it, and an anxious record producer demands to put it out with lyrics, Ed becomes a pop star. In the second, he has to duplicate the feat while distracted by a neighbor's cute filly. Not only do listeners get to hear the famous *Mister Ed* theme song, there's "Empty Feed Bag Blues" and the immortal "Pretty Little Filly": "Got a date a little later. When the moon is on the trail. With the cutest triple gaiter, mah pretty little filly with the ponytail!"

DONNA JEAN YOUNG

- LIVE FROM EAST MCKEESPORT (Epic BN 26366) ** $8 $15

Sort of stand-up's answer to Mary Ann on *Gilligan's Island*, Young was a well-scrubbed, bright-eyed girl who talked about small town living: "It's such a little town, when I was a kid we used to play Monopoly on it." The late '60s album manages to make it through both sides without getting too calculatedly coy.

JAMES YOUNG

- YOUNG AT HEART (London International TW 91468) ** $5 $10

In the '60s, when James Young was probably also in his '60s, he issued over a half-dozen albums in Ireland on the Emerald label. Titles include "It's Great to Be Young," "Ulster Party Pieces," "Behind the Barricades," "James Young's Fourth," "Young and Foolish," and "The Young Ulsterman." In 1966 this became the only one to be imported. Young's Ulster accent is difficult to penetrate, especially when he meanders anecdotally to reach a mild gag at the end. Some cuts require a slight knowledge of Scots customs. Like the tale of a Scotsman who baffles an Irish woman who thinks he's keeping a dog in his room. He proudly announces, "That's my sporran." Her punch line: "You know I wondered why he wouldn't take a biscuit."

HENNY YOUNGMAN

- PRIMITIVE SOUNDS (NRC LPA 10) *** $10 $20
- THE BEST OF THE WORST (Certron CS 7009) *** $5 $10
- AND A LITTLE BARBECUE ON THE SIDE (Youngman LP 115) *** $10 $20
- HORSE AND AUTO RACE GAME (Urania UR 9014) ** $10 $20
- TAKE MY PROJECT PLEASE (Ryerson and Haynes) ** $10 $20

"The King of the One-Liners," Henny Youngman's style was telling one joke after the other—quantity if not quality. The non sequitur style was unintentionally funny and his guileless desire to please made him welcome for fifty years. The early '60s "Primitive Sounds" album repeats his catchphrase twice within a minute: "I can never understand women. Now take my wife. Please!" Then he segues effortlessly: "As you get older you need less sleep 'cause you dream more. Last night I had a dream that Marilyn Monroe and my wife had a fight over me and my wife won. And the funny thing is my wife looks like the closest thing to Marilyn Monroe. She looks like Arthur Miller. Marilyn Monroe. Take away her long blonde hair and what have you got? The sexiest bald-headed woman in the world. I've been married for thirty-one years and I'm still in love with the same woman. If my wife ever finds out she'll kill me. Now you take my wife. Please."

Youngman insisted that it doesn't matter how often you tell a joke, if someone hasn't heard it before, it's new. And, as the above proves, Youngman will tell a joke over again within a minute and a half, just in case anyone in the audience is senile.

It's easy to poke fun at the way Henny Youngman pokes fun, but the brief quote from Red Skelton on the back cover says it all: "With the kindness of one-line comedy as told by Henny Youngman, it becomes classic, unoffensive and an expression of true American humor."

In 1970, with *Laugh-In* resurrecting Henny by offering one-liners and the catchphrase "Oh, THAT Henny Youngman," Henny issued "Best of the Worst" for a small Nashville company. A woman's voice opens the album saying "Oh ... THAT Henny Youngman." And THAT Henny Youngman starts knocking out the one-liners: "Two guys meet. One says, 'What's the latest dope on Wall Street?' He says, 'My son.' The album is also known as "Sol Hurok Does Not Present ... The Best of the Worst of Henny Youngman."

Youngman issued a few odd custom records as promos for companies and for himself. "Barbecue on the Side" (which also opens with a woman's voice calling "Oh, THAT Henny Youngman") has a set of barbecue jokes sprinkled throughout ("And now, let's get back to the barbecue"). A few gags aren't quite as ancient as usual, like:

"A holdup man walks into a Chinese restaurant. He says, 'Give me all your money.' The Chinaman says, 'To take out?'"

But to balance this, Youngman tells one joke twice: "I told my mother-in-law my house is your house. So she sold it!"

The album was recorded before a sparse crowd of what sound like Florida retirees. Henny tells a quickie: "I got this parrot for my wife—that was a good trade." And audible amid the sparse snickers, some woman remarks, "Very cute!" Another woman's squeaky chirp of a laugh is distractingly audible about two dozen times during the album.

The Urania disc is a peculiar novelty record, evidently one of the first "trick-tracked" albums marketed, Youngman narrates (complete with sound effects) a horse race on one side and an auto race on the other. Each race takes about three minutes.

When you put the needle down, you really don't know which of the five "entrants" is going to win: it all depends on which track the needle hooked. There are a few mild jokes along the way: "Nashua springs out of the gate and goes back in again! That's the first time I saw a horse start from the kneeling position."

"Take My Project" is a one-sided disc done for a North Miami real estate company. About half the gags are keyed to real estate in one way or another:

"A developer shows a man an apartment. He says, 'Well, how do you like the high ceilings?' The man says, 'They don't look so high to me.' The developer says, 'Well, that's because the floors are so high. The guy underneath you wants high ceilings too.'"

"I spent so much on my apartment I had to hock my watch. I had to tell time by my fiddle. I practiced in the middle of the night and the neighbors would shout, 'Fine time to practice the violin, three o'clock in the morning!'"

"I got a brother Lester, he lives in a condo. He tells people he's a diamond cutter. He mows the lawn in Shea Stadium!"

- TAKE MY ALBUM, PLEASE (Waterhouse 4, K-TEL CD reissue 32832) *** $8
- 128 GREATEST JOKES (Rhino RNLP 011) *** $8 $15

In 1978, the tiny Waterhouse record company of Minneapolis hired the seventy-two-year-old Youngman to try to spring their label into national prominence. At the time, Henny's act had transcended itself. No longer did critics complain about his old jokes. No more did the audience shift uncomfortably over a wheeze. Now, Henny had become "in" and even "campy." The crowd on the Waterhouse album is really alive, roaring over nearly every joke.

"Ladies and gentlemen, while I'm making this album, I want you to know, this week you're looking at a guy who's been married to the same woman for forty-nine years. This week. Where have I failed? In love with one woman forty-nine years. If my wife finds out she'll kill me." The wife jokes continue: "All she does is shop all day. Once she was sick for a week. Three shops went under. She has housework. I bought her an electric iron, electric dishwasher, electric dryer. She said, 'Too many gadgets around, no place to sit down.' What did I do? Bought her an electric chair. She ran after the garbage man, 'Am I too late for the garbage?' He said, 'No, jump in.' Take my wife. Please!"

Hearing that catchphrase, the crowd erupts with thirteen seconds of whistling and applause. Youngman does try to freshen his act—with some sick jokes and Polish jokes:

"There's a whole new world today. Ethnic jokes. There's a new Polish jigsaw puzzle. One piece.... They sent a Polish terrorist to blow up a car. He burned his lips on the exhaust pipe.... On Halloween two Polish guys had burned faces. They were bobbing for french fries. Are you Polish? I'll talk slower."

The 1980 "128 Greatest" has the "trick track" gimmick of offering four different three-minute routines stamped into the vinyl on one side. Fans will have to keep setting the needle down over and over to connect with all four variations. But anyone who's heard Youngman over the years will be used to hearing the same jokes over and over.

The other side offers a complete twenty-two minute set. On the trick track side, the needle will come down and hit one of these four jokes:

1) "Who would think I just had a physical. I said, 'Doc, how do I stand?' He said, 'That's what puzzles me.'"

2) "And now folks it's barbecue time. I'm gonna give you some real handy hints ... start barbequing immediately. In no time at all you'll be surrounded by dozens of people offering you advice. Ask one of them to save you."

3) "Say there's two boys—I forgot the joke! There's two truck drivers applying for a job. One says, 'I'm Sam, this is Nero, he's my partner. When I drive at night he sleeps.' The man says, 'All right, I'll give you an oral test. Suppose you're driving at three in the morning. All of a sudden you see a trailer coming towards you, you can't get out of the way, what would you do?' 'I'd wake up my partner Nero.' 'Why?' 'He's never seen a wreck like this before!'"

4) "A guy goes to a doctor, he says, 'Look doc, I got a dime in my ear.' The doctor says, 'What, you got a dime in your ear?' 'Yes I've had it for ten years.' 'Why didn't you have it taken out?' 'I didn't need the money.'"

NOTES: Short Youngman routines turn up on the compilation albums "Golden Age of Comedy" (RCA Victor LPV 580), "Fun Time" (Coral CRL 57072), and "Laugh of the Party" (Coral CRL 57017). For "Comic Relief" (Rhino 70704) he gets a polite response from the crowd telling four minutes of classics, one or two semisick for the '80s: "I'm sitting in a bar having a drink, over here is a man ... he falls down three times, I pick him up three times. I say, 'Bartender, you know where this man lives? I'll give him a lift home....' I grab the guy, pull him down to the car, he falls down. I get to the address ... he falls down three more times ... I knock on the door: 'Mrs. Welzer, I brought your husband home.' 'Where's his wheelchair?'"

JOHN ZACHERLE

- MONSTER MASH (Parkway P 719, also available as Wyncote SW 9050) **1/2 $15 $30
- SCARY TALES (Parkway SP 7023) ** $15 $30
- SPOOK ALONG WITH ZACHERLEY (Elektra 190/7190,
  also issued as ZACHERLE'S MONSTER GALLERY, Crestview 803/7803) **1/2 $20 $40
- DEAD MAN'S BALL (Tristique 38312) ** $8

In 1954, Philadelphia TV announcer John Zacherle was asked to host a horror movie show. Turning up with his hair parted in the middle, cheeks sunken with gray makeup, his eyes wild and his teeth set in a skullish grin, he was soon known as "Zacherley," and quickly developed a following for his cheerful sick humor and his Ernie Kovacsian tendency to suddenly insert himself in the midst of moldy old movies for some added laughs. He moved to New York for a cult children's show and in 1958 invaded the Top Ten with a pre-"Monster Mash" novelty recitation, "Dinner with Drac." He had paperback horror story anthologies out and was a cover-ghoul for *Famous Monsters* magazine. In 1960 Zacherley issued his Elektra album, which was reissued on Crestview three years later.

Since both are expensive collector's items, cost-conscious fans will have to decide which version to get. "Spook Along with Zacherley" has a photo of the cool ghoul on the cover and liner notes on each song. "Zacherle's Monster Gallery" drops the "y" in his name, and replaces his cover photo with a manic drawing by Jack Davis of various comically gruesome fiends (with Zach as the pied piper leading the way). The art direction ("Zacherle's Monster Gallery" in huge letters) removes all liner notes from the back.

Like "Monster Rally" by Hans Conreid (also sporting a Davis cover), the original songs are a bit kid-oriented, but Zach's personality makes them fun. On "Sure Sign of Spring" he happily sings, "When the fungus starts in spreadin' and the werewolves start their sheddin' it's a sure sign of spring ... everywhere there's excitement in the air as creatures stir from their gloom. Fangs get polished, capes get pressed, and claws get freshly groomed."

His little asides are often funnier than the tunes: "My dear, since I first laid my eyes on you I can't get them back in the sockets."

When "Monster Mash" arrived, Zach covered the tune on his Parkway album, adding the previous "Dinner with Drac," and its silly horror limericks: "For dessert there was batwing confetti. And the veins of a mummy named Betty. I first frowned upon it, but with ketchup on it, it tasted very much like spaghetti!"

Parkway filled the album by stripping the existing vocals off their various hit records (like "The Bristol Stomp") and adding Zacherle's revised lyrics (and ad-libbed laughing and muttering). In the new version every kid in Bristol carries a pistol: "Each time you have to do The Pistol Stomp, protect yourself at all times! I'm not gonna help ya! Ha ha ha! When they start gunnin' everybody's jumping. No use runnin.' Everybody around here stomps, so join the fun." Zacherle continued the formula of corny horror humor over several albums, and cultists still love his snickering laugh and "Cool Ghoul" persona. Since he worked mainly for eight to thirteen-year-olds (who grew up to hunt for these albums all over again) it's not surprising to find a kiddie novelty slant to some discs, especially 1963's "Scary Tales," which includes revised fairy tales (Red Riding Hood is a vampire who eats the wolf), a children's chorus on several tracks, and many a sing-song tune: "Now we know our ABC's, kindly stop this record, please!"

For Halloween 1995, Zach came back with a new CD, but most fans didn't know since the small and/or inept label failed to get it placed in a single chain store even in his New York stronghold. There are remakes of old songs (including "Dinner with Drac") and new ones that are '60s simple musically, but a little more disgusting for today's gore fans. "Grave Robbing Tonight," one of the better entries, has a good beat and beat up imagery: "I dragged that coffin up from the pit. It smelled real bad 'cause it leaked a bit. The thing inside that should be dead just smiled at me and grabbed my head! Now it wants to take a bite! 'Cause I went grave robbing tonight!" But trust Zach to get the last licks, murdering the fiend and eating it: "It cooked up fast and tasted just right. And I went grave robbing tonight ... Hey hey hey now, if you should catch a whiff of bowel, don't forget it's nice to share. It ruins my breath, but I don't care. I have a motto I repeat: you really are just what you eat! Ha ha ha ha...." A knowledge of Zacherle's shows and persona give this stuff a boost that his voice alone might not—which holds true for the fragments from his old TV shows that are interspersed between the songs and poems.

NOTES: "Dinner With Drac" has turned up on several compilation albums including "Funny Bone Favorites" (Ronco). "Monster Mash" has been anthologized on "Oldies by the Dozen" (Parkway P 7037). Fans hunt for various 45s including "Monsters Have Problems, Too" on Colpix and "I was a Teenage Caveman" on Cameo.

BOB ZANY

- HI HOME, I'M HONEY (Laff A 231) * $4 $8

The title tells it all on this 1985 example of mediocre comedy club entertainment. Chubby Bob Zany, evidently weak with laughter, can barely force out the jokes in a tired voice that has an element of California Valley Boy to it. As lame as the material is, he giggles after almost every joke he recites: "Stole a dollar from a liquor store. Got caught the next day when I tried to spend it? I forgot to take it out of the frame! I had a lot of pet fishies when I was a kid. And like, when one of 'em died? My mom would say flush 'em down the toilet. Burial at sea, what a strange thing to do! The other day the cat died. I got in really big trouble. We had to call the plumber. It was a mess!"

THE ZOO

- THE 93Q MORNING ZOO GREATEST HITS (Arista AL 8 84141) *1/2 $5 $10
- THE Z-100 MORNING ZOO GREATEST HITS (Arista AL 8 8413) *1/2 $5 $10
- THE Z-100 ZOO'S GREATEST HITS II (Arista AL 8451) * $5 $10
- BEST OF THE Z-100 NEW YORK MORNING ZOO TAPES 1989 (Arista ARCD 8636) * $5 $10
- THE Z-100 MORNING ZOO NEW YORK: LAST 100 YEARS (Arista ARCD 8664) * $8
- BEST OF THE MORNING ZOO Volume VIII (Arista 18717-2) * $8

Disc jockey "drive time" humor, obnoxious, pseudo-hip, and obvious though it may be, does have a following. "The Zoo" features an entire roster of "zany" folks, all hell-bent on being awesomely wacky.

The 93Q Zoo in Houston and Z-100 in New York sometimes shared the same pool of performers for the studio-done sketches, song parodies, and fake commmercials. Among the main irritatants is an ex-dentist named Dave Kolin, who thinks he can do impressions of Dr. Ruth Westheimer and others, and the usual hyperactive motor mouths, including Scott Shannon, John Lander, Ross & Wilson, Gary Bryan, and Ross Brittain. (See separate entries on Kolin and Shannon.)

All the albums are loaded with self-promotion and fast-paced redundancy. The DJs never tire of hearing their own voices and seem to love writing long, involved routines for themselves. They come off like a McDonald's version of Monty Python, grinding it out too fast, too obvious, and too smugly slick.

Typical of the easy gags to be found on the Z-100 "Greatest Hits" album is this quickie commercial: "You'll be hungry like a wolf for Duran Duran's Wild Rice ... and watch for Ike and Tina Tuna!" Very lame sketches include a parody of *Miami Vice* called "Miami Mice," and a visit to "Chez Rat" where all the food is ratty.

Predictable bits of ear filler include this zany phone call on the "Best of" 1989: "Hello, and thank you for calling the Bijou Triplex Theater, conveniently located a half mile from the State Mental Institution. This week is sequel week at the Bijou. In Theater 1, we are proud to present Robin Givens in *Rocky V.* Robin plays the part of Rocky's wife who then drains the champ of his money, makes his life a living hell, and then runs off to her mother played by Diana Ross. In Theater 2, we're proud to present Billy Idol, Sean Penn, and Sgt. Slaughter in *Three Men and a Baby Part Two*, and in Theater 3, we are proud to present Bette Midler and Barbara Hershey. You loved them in *Beaches*, now enjoy the sequel as the two stars give birth to boys in *Sons of Beaches*. Thank you for calling the Bijou Triplex Theater."

Each album may have one or two good bits amid all the poorly collaged together filler and corrosive DJ blather. On the "Best of" dubbed "The Lime Green Album," there's a few seconds dubbed here and there so dumb they're funny (the rap song "Me So Horny" switched to "Oh! Woody horny!" sung by a stereotyped Asian girl), but these moments are usually ruined when a gag is milked to headache-producing lengths. An Amy Fisher sketch, idea stolen from *Saturday Night Live*'s land shark routines a decade earlier, has Amy knocking at Mary Jo Buttafuoco's door: "Telegram for Mary Jo." "Uh, no thanks." "Flowers for Mary Jo." "Uh, that's okay." "Candygram for the wife of my pimp!" "Nobody here by that name...." "Thirty-five caliber bullet through your face for the woman whose husband I'm sleeping with." "Uh, okay." (Gunshot).

Top Ten Most Valuable Comedy Records

1. *Lord Buckley "Friends, Romans, Countrymen" (RCA)*
2. *Lenny Bruce "Lenny Bruce Is Out Again" (Philles)*

   Collectors have paid up to $200 for both these albums. I confirmed that The Jazz Record Center in New York recently sold a copy of the Buckley ten-incher for $125. Most any record shop would consider this a "wall item," proudly displayed for a big price.

   Both Lenny Bruce fans and collectors who want all of producer Phil Spector's catalog (he owned Philles) want "Lenny Bruce Is Out Again." Two hundred dollars is not unheard of, while some collector shops easily rate it $50-$100.

3. *Bob and Ray "Bob and Ray on a Platter" (RCA Victor)*
4. MAD Magazine *"Musically MAD" (RCA Victor)*

   These two titles are sought after by both comedy fans and collectors of Living Stereo releases. Fifty dollars each for diehards in either category. Some shops might be merciful and mark Bob & Ray down to $40, since the duo's fan base is older and fewer.

5. *Friars Roast Albums*

   Virtually any limited edition pressing from the Friars is worth at least $20 and the usual asking price can go up to $50 or even $100.

6. *Jonathan Winters "It's Hee-Hee-Hee Hee Larious"*
7. *Lenny Bruce "Testimony"*
8. *Allan Sherman "My Fair Lady"*

   Each comedian has a cult following and each of these albums was pressed expressly for his cult. It's hard to say how many copies of each record exist.

   Literally living up to the words on its plain white cover, the Jonathan Winters album is "a collectors item of JW," from Jon to his fans and friends circa 1960. It's a collection of home tape recordings, ad-libs, and at the end, some of his favorite risqué outtakes and gags.

   Lenny Bruce's album collects material used at his trial, and only portions of it resurfaced on the Douglas "What I Was Arrested For" album.

   Allan Sherman's "My Fair Lady" parody was never released thanks to quibbling from Lerner & Lowe. He recorded samples from it before a live audience, and there's an NBC Reference Recording acetate. But how many did NBC press?

9.

10. *(TIE) Eddie Lawrence and Brother Theodore*

    Both cult figures can get up to $40 per disc if not more. In the same range are "cast" albums from Julius Monk revues. Other albums in this book have a $40 high end price, in some cases higher, but the ones listed above are consistently selling at high prices.

Top Ten Unusual Comedy Album Castings

1. Mel Blanc as President Gerald Ford
    ("Henry the First," with Kenneth Mars)

2. Bob Denver as Caspar Weinberger
    (on Rich Little's "Reagan Slept Here")

3. Julie Newmar as Pat Nixon
    ("The Last Nixon Album," just a bit odder than her role as
    Mrs. Ollie North for Rich Little's "Reagan Slept Here")

4. Stanley Myron Handelman as Spiro Agnew
    ("Spiro Agnew Is a Riot" with Vincent Price as his straight
    man)

5. Buck Henry as President Richard Nixon
    ("At Home with the Other Family")

6. George Segal as Khrushchev
    ("At Home with the Other Family")

7. Mae "Betty Boop" Questel as Mrs. Portnoy
    ("Mrs. Portnoy Retorts")

8. Vaughn Meader as Christ
    ("The Second Coming")

9. Robert Klein as President Lyndon Johnson
    ("Our Wedding Album" with Solms & Parent—edging out
    Klein as Howard Hughes on Caedmon's "Howard Who?"
    album)

10. Larry "Al Jolson" Parks and Betty "Irene Lorenzo" Garrett
    (as Father and Mother, even though they were, on Andy
    Parks's lone comedy album)

Top Ten Non-Comedian Comedy Album Appearances

1. MUHAMMAD ALI, back in his Cassius Clay days, did an album of novelty poems about himself titled (of course) "I Am the Greatest." Honorable mention to Rocky Graziano for pulling punch lines on his own solo disc.

2. LON CHANEY, JR, good-natured monster, tried to get howls of laughter from doing a cover of Bobby "Boris" Pickett's "Monster Holiday," a single reissued on the "Christmas Comedy Classics" CD. Honorable mention to Vincent Price's British-only single of "Monster Mash."

3. ADLAI STEVENSON, twice defeated by Eisenhower for president, was one of the first politicians to deliberately stick witty one-liners into his speeches. Some are on the "Stevenson Wit" album. The bald-headed Adlai declared his motto was "Via ovum cranium difficilis est." That's: "The way of the egghead is hard."

4. LAUREN BACALL, wife of Humphrey Bogart, but still not allowed at a "men only" stag roast for him, prerecorded a monologue to be played on the dais. As the bootlegs prove, the guys all puckered up their lips—and laughed. Honorable mention to various stars on Friar's bootlegs, including Bogie himself.

5. PETER FONDA, with evidently nothing better to do, played the minor role of "3rd Translator" on the Kenneth Mars "Henry the First" album. The oddness of this edges out honorable mentions Bruce Gordon (who went from playing Frank Nitti on *The Untouchables* to "Frank Nitty-Gritty" on a Gary Owens's "Bonnie and Clyde" parody disc), and Karl Malden (who played George Washington in a sketch on a Bob Hope album for Capitol).

6. JOAN COLLINS, fortunately not attempting any jokes, simply appears on the cover of Mort Sahl's "On Relationships" album.

7. PETER LORRE, who had a fine sense of humor offscreen and on, tangled with Lorre mimic Paul Frees on a Spike Jones radio show (Rhino CD) and chilled out Abbott and Costello on one of their shows (on the "Treasury" double record set from Nostalgia Lane). Honorable mention to Boris Karloff dueling Jack Benny (on the boxed set MF 214).

8. BASIL RATHBONE, showing some of his funny bone, sings a mock radio commercial on a Fred Allen show: "When you're buying frozen fruit, what's the fruit that's sure to suit? It's a frosted goodie, the fastest selling: Fagel's Frozen Watermelon!" It's on both Radiola MR 1146 and Mar Bren 741.

9. THE NORMAN LUBOFF CHOIR, well-known and respected in the '60s, unexpectedly released "Wolfgang Mozart Is a Dirty Old Man," wolfing down naughty novelties like "Kiss My Behind."

10. PRISONERS 91494, 74828, 68776, 101505 and 75558, all at Southern Michigan Prison, got a chance to try for a second career in comedy via Jackie Kannon's "Prose from the Cons" album.

Top Ten Odd Liner Note Writers

1. Sally Marr, Lenny Bruce's mother, chose to praise "Over Sexteen"-style schtick comic Marty Gale.

2. Pat Buttram's "We Wuz Poor" sports laudatory album notes from ... Richard M. Nixon. But just to be on the safe side, in case nobody remembered him, there's also ... Lorne Greene.

3. Ray Bradbury showed a spacy sense of humor by endorsing an album of mild tunes by Charles Embree.

4. Writer, columnist, and humorist Dorothy Parker wrote the album notes for Zero Mostel's album.

5. Gossip columnist Louella Parsons offered a little squib for black comic Dave Turner: "I invited him to my house to perform for some of my friends. I like him, he's really good."

6. Three-Way Poet Tie: Marianne Moore lent her seal of approval to the comic doggerel of Muhammad Ali—back when he was "Cassius Clay" and issued a comic album of sketches and verse; Louis Untermeyer waxed poetic for "A Personal Appearance" by Shelley Berman; Langston Hughes praised "Comedy Night at the Apollo."

7. Tina Louise and Art Linkletter praised Larry Wilde.

8. Writer Nelson Algren analyzed David Steinberg's "Incredible Shrinking God."

9. Ed Sullivan put his finger on Jackie Mason as a bright new star ("I Want to Leave You with the Words of a Great Comedian"). Later, myopic, dirty-minded Ed thought Jackie gave the finger during a TV show appearance and it was years before "the feud" between the two was resolved.

10. Larry King was enthused over a Kermit Schafer-Eddie Shafer break-in album called "LBJ Roast."

Comedians Supporting Comedians

(A selection of albums and the comedians who wrote the liner notes)

Mickey Katz "Katz Puts on the Dog"	Slapsy Maxie Rosenbloom
Mickey Katz "Borscht Jester"	Chico Marx
Milt Kamen (Capitol)	Groucho Marx
Allan Sherman "My Son the Folk Singer"	Harpo Marx, Jack Benny, Jerry Lewis, Steve Allen
Bruce Howard	Allan Sherman
"Bill Cosby Is a Very Funny Fellow Right!"	Allan Sherman
Tony Webster	Carl Reiner
Reiner and Brooks "2000 Year Old Man"	Steve Allen
Pat Harrington (Roulette)	Steve Allen
Pete Barbutti (Vee Jay)	Steve Allen
Godfrey Cambridge "Ready or Not"	Steve Allen, Abe Burrows
"An Evening with Groucho"	Woody Allen
Will Jordan (Jubilee)	Hugh Hefner
Dickie Goodman (Rori)	Shelley Berman
"Inside Shelley Berman"	Mort Sahl
"Lenny Bruce in Concert" (1 disc UA)	Paul Krassner
"Jean Shepherd Live"	Paul Krassner
Jean Shepherd "And Other Foibles"	Shel Silverstein
Shel Silverstein "Hairy Jazz"	Jean Shepherd
Norm Crosby (Epic)	Johnny Carson
Sandy Baron "Race Race"	Dick Gregory
Sandy Baron "How I Found God"	Joan Rivers, Richard Pryor
Pete Barbutti "Sahara"	Buddy Hackett, Shecky Greene, Rich Little
J. S. Bork "Musical Menopause"	Gary Owens
Gary Owens "Bonnie and Clyde"	Don Rickles, Rowan and Martin, Don Adams
Don Adams "Get Smart"	Bill Dana
McCall and Brill	Bill Dana
"Mabley: Funniest Woman in the World"	Redd Foxx
"Best of Moms Mabley"	Bill Cosby
Foster Brooks "Lovable Lush"	Bill Cosby
Joan Rivers "Mr. Phyllis"	Bill Cosby*
"Best of Bill Cosby"	David (Firesign Theatre) Ossman
Henny Youngman	Red Skelton
"Bob Newhart Faces Bob Newhart"	Don Knotts
"Orson Bean at the Hungri i"	Henry Morgan
Hendra and Ullet	Jackie Mason
Pigmeat Markham "Here Come the Judge"	George Kirby
Jack E. Leonard "Rock and Roll"	Jackie Gleason
Marsh and Adams "Jokers Wild"	Jackie Gleason, Alan King, and Milton Berle
David Tyree	Rodney Dangerfield, George Wallace (the stand-up, not the governor)
Smothers "Mom Always Liked You..."	Jack Benny
Smith and Dale	Harry Hershfield
Solms & Parent: "Here Comes Bird"	Carol Burnett
Larry Kent	Phil Foster, Gary Marshall
Murray Roman "You Can't Beat..."	Tom Smothers
Lou Alexander	Joey Bishop

*This asterisk could probably be applied to several discs here. Bill's notes were actually written by Roy Silver, who managed both Cosby and Joan Rivers at the time. No doubt several other comedians were called upon to supply praise as a favor, or just their signatures to someone else's notes.

Album Title List

Some comedy albums are better known by title, not comedian. These, as well as radio shows and TV soundtracks, are listed below. In parentheses is the name of the comedian the album is filed under:

ALL IN THE FAMILY (Carroll O'Connor)
AT THE DROP OF A HAT (Flanders and Swann)
BEGATTING OF THE PRESIDENT (Orson Welles)
BEST OF WHAT'S HIS NAME (Jack Paar)
BEVERLY HILLBILLIES (Buddy Ebsen)
BEWARE OF GREEKS BEARING PRESENTS (Anspach and Silver)
BLIND MAN'S MOVIE (Murray Roman)
BOY AM I GLAD WE JOINED THE INDIANS (Bologna and Taylor)
BROTHER THEODORE (Theodore)
BURLESQUE: BEST OF BURLESQUE (Tom Poston)
BURLESQUE LIVE (Dick Bernie & Co)
BURLESQUE UNCENSORED (Joe DeRita)
BURLESQUE WITH THE NUTS INSIDE (Joey Faye)
THE BUTTON-DOWN MIND (Bob Newhart)
CAMPUS CAPERS (Cool U Laboratory Players)
COLLEGE HUMOR (Cool U Laboratory Players)
COMMERCIALS TO CRINGE BY (Jack Fox)
CONTRACEPTIVE PUTS YOU ON (Richard Milner)
CREPITATION CONTEST (Windersphere and Boomer)
CYPRIENNE ROBESPIERRE (Bud Fletcher)
DEMI DOZEN (Julius Monk)
DENNIS THE MENACE (Jay North)
DR. ROOSE (The National Idiots)
DUFFY'S TAVERN (Ed Gardner)
THE EARTHY SIDE (The Movement)
EVERYTHING YOU WANTED TO KNOW ABOUT THE GODFATHER
     (Chuck McCann)
FARTING CONTEST (Windersphere and Boomer)
FAWLTY TOWERS (John Cleese)
FIRST FAMILY (Vaughn Meader)
FIRST FAMILY RIDES AGAIN (Rich Little)
FIRST NINE MONTHS ARE HARDEST (Weinrib and Jameson)
FIRSTA FAMILY (Jack De Leon)
FRIAR'S ROASTS (Johnny Carson, Lucille Ball, George Jessel)
FUNNY FONE CALLS (Steve Allen)
FUNNY YOU DON'T LOOK IT (Al Kelly)
GONE WITH THE WIFF (Windersphere and Boomer)
HAIL TO THE TEETH (The Harris Brothers)
HARDLY-WORTHIT REPORT (Minkin and Wholey)
HELLO DERE (Allen and Rossi)
HERE COMES THE BIRD (Solms and Parent)
HE'S IN CHARGE (Martin Willson)
HEXORCIST (Gary Owens)
HILARITY IN HOLLYWOOD (Harry Ritz)
HONEST TO GOD: THE LAST NIXON ALBUM (Larry Kenney)
HOW TO SPEAK HIP (Del Close)

THE INCOME TAX MAN (Andrew Duncan)
JEWISH AMERICAN PRINCESS (Judy Graubart)
LAMENT FOR APRIL 15th (The Randolph Singers)
LAUGH-IN (Rowan and Martin)
LAUGH-IN 69 (Carne and Johnson)
LBJ IN THE CATSKILLS (Christopher Weeks)
LIFE WITH LIZ AND DICK (Bright and Baxter)
LYNDONLAND (Walker Edmiston)
LYNDON JOHNSON'S LONELY HEARTS CLUB BAND (Alen Robin)
MAN FROM TANTE (Brill and Foster)
MEANWHILE BACK AT THE LBJ RANCH (Len Maxwell)
THE MISSING TAPES (Marty Brill)
MOM ALWAYS LIKED YOU BEST (Smothers Brothers)
MR. ED (Alan Young)
MR. TOASTMASTER (George Jessel)
MUSICALLY MAD (*MAD Magazine*)
MY FRIEND IRMA (Marie Wilson)
MY NAME JOSE JIMENEZ (Bill Dana)
MY SON THE COPY CAT (Stan Ross)
MY SON THE FOLKSINGER (Allen Sherman)
MY SON THE JOKE (Dickie Goodman)
MY SON THE PHONE CALLER (Sammy Petrillo)
MY SON THE PRESIDENT (Danny Davis)
MY SON THE PRESIDENT (Marty Miles)
MY SON THE PRESIDENT (Christopher Weeks)
MY SON THE SURF NUT (Jack Marshall)
MY SQUARE LADDIE (Reginald Gardiner)
NEW FIRST FAMILY 1968 (Will Jordan)
OFFICIAL POLISH/ITALIAN COMEDY ALBUM (Warsaw Plumbers)
OTHER FAMILY (Brill and Foster)
OUR WEDDING ALBUM (Solms and Parent)
P. D. Q. BACH (Peter Schickele)
PARDON MY BLOOPER (Kermit Schafer)
PENTAGON PAPERS (Bernie Travis)
PHONE CALLS
    (Harold Flender, Question Mark, Jerky Boys, Sammy Petrillo, Steve Allen)
THE RICH KID (London Lee)
SANFORD AND SON (Redd Foxx)
SATURDAY NIGHT LIVE (Not Ready for Prime Time Players)
SCORE THREE POINTS (Earle Doud)
THE SHORTEST DAY (The Chosen Few Players)
SMASH FLOPS (The Characters)
THAT FUNNY SMOKING ALBUM (Barrett Clark)
THAT HONKY'S NUTS (Don Imus)
THAT NIGGER'S CRAZY (Richard Pryor)
WATERGATE COMEDY HOUR (Burns and Schreiber)
WHEN YOU'RE IN LOVE THE WHOLE WORLD IS JEWISH (Lou Jacobi)
WHY NOT? (Dayton Allen)
YIDDISH ARE COMING (Lou Jacobi)
YOU DON'T HAVE TO BE IRISH (Jimmy Joyce)
YOU DON'T HAVE TO BE JEWISH (Lou Jacobi)
YOU'RE GOOD ENOUGH, YOU'RE SMART ENOUGH (Stuart Smalley)

Compilation Albums

The following important albums feature assorted routines by a variety of comedians. Many comedians who never issued a full-length album are at least represented by a few minutes on one of these:

- **ALL TIME COMEDY HITS (Capitol T 1854) **1/2**

  A sampler from various Capitol albums by Reiner and Brooks, Frank Fontaine, Stan Freberg, Andy Griffith, Johnny Standley, and Yogi Yorgesson.

- **AMERICAN COMEDY BOX 1915-1994 (Rhino R271617) ******

  Though the notes take the elbow-the-ribs, "yuk yuk" approach and the box cover has to have the ultra cliché fake nose, glasses, and mustache logo on it, here's four CDs that try to cover the bases. The 1995 set actually delves into 78s (Cal Stewart, Barney Bernard, Moran & Mack, Sam 'n' Henry) and has some now hard-to-find material (Smith & Dale's Jubilee "Dr. Kronkheit" sketch) before sampling the standards: Shelley Berman, Andy Griffith, Bill Cosby, George Carlin, Robin Williams, etc.

- **BEST OF COMEDY (MCA D 20581) ** 1/2**

  A CD collection featuring Bill Cosby, Buddy Hackett, Jerry Clower, Foster Brooks, and others.

- **BEST OF COUNTRY COMEDY (RCA Victor LSP 4126) **1/2**

  Cuts from RCA's albums by Archie Campbell, Bob Corley, Don Bowman, Junior Samples, Dave Gardner, Homer and Jethro, and Fannie Flagg.

- **CATSKILLS ON BROADWAY (Dove Audio) ****

  The 1992 Broadway show offered grousing Freddie Roman, Mal Z. Lawrence (who manages the feat of elegant kvetching), plus Dick Capri and an out-of-place Louise Duart, whose stagy routines filled with mimicry seem to baffle the crowd.

- **CHRISTMAS COMEDY CLASSICS (Priority CDL 9306) *1/2**

  Obnoxious (Mel Blanc, St. Nick) and familiar (Chipmunks, Stan Freberg) novelty cuts with only one honest rarity, Lon Chaney, Jr.'s cover of Bobby "Boris" Pickett's "Monster Holiday."

- **CHRISTMAS COMEDY CLASSICS VOL. 2 (Priority P2 53682) *1/2**

  Chintzy twenty-five-minute CD of yawn-producing standards and filler from Allan Sherman, Stan Freberg, Tom Lehrer, The Jingle Cats, Mel Blanc, Bob and Doug McKenzie, Weird Al Yankovic, The Chipmunks, and The Cowtown Chorus.

- **CHRISTMAS WITH EDDIE G (Columbia CK 46919) ****

  A mixed bag of rock novelties and comedy from Eddie Lawrence ("Merry Old Philosopher"), Tony Rodelle Larson, Debbie Dabney, Detroit Junior, Augie Rios, Louis Prima, George Jones, and Tammy Wynette.

- **CLASSIC COMEDY (MCA D 20671) **1/2**

  A CD collection featuring Bill Cosby, Buddy Hackett, Albert Brooks, Jerry Clower, Rodney Dangerfield, and Jerry Jordan.

- **COMEDY CARAVAN (Capitol T 732) **1/2**

  Featuring Andy Griffith, Stan Freberg, and less easily available Capitol roster comics Harry Kari, Yogi Yorgesson, and Johnny Standley.

- **COMEDY CLASSICS (Era BU 3890) ***1/2**

  Including George Carlin, Abbott and Costello, Jonathan Winters, Redd Foxx, Rodney Dangerfield, Lily Tomlin, Burns and Allen, Richard Pryor, and Myron Cohen.

- **COMEDY CLASSICS (K-Tel 30462) **1/2**

  A CD collection with The Smothers Brothers, George Carlin, Henny Youngman, Burns and Allen, Foster Brooks, Hudson & Landry, Flip Wilson, Redd Foxx, Groucho Marx, and Rodney Dangerfield.

- **COMEDY CONCERT (United Artists UAL 95) **1/2**

  Cuts from UA's albums by Pat Harrington, Don Knotts, Louis Nye, Alexander King, Kaye Ballard, and phone caller Harold Flender.

- **COMEDY TONIGHT (K-Tel/Dominion BU4660) ****

  With Marty Cohen, Marsha Warfield, Jeff Altman, Johnny Dark, Elayne Boosler, Jay Leno, Arsenio Hall, George Miller, Lenny Rush, Mink Binder, Steve Bluestein, and Eugene Libowitz

- **COMEDY'S GREATEST HITS (HF Records HF 1801) **1/2**

  Bootleg 78 rpm and 45 rpm singles and radio cuts offer "Who's on First," "Cohen on the Telephone," and more from Abbott and Costello, Barney Bernard, Moran and Mack, Jim Backus, Johnny Standley, Robert Benchley, Beatrice Kay, and Red Ingle.

- **COMIC RELIEF (Rhino 70704) *****

  Excerpts from the cable TV telethon starring Billy Crystal, Whoopie Goldberg, Robin Williams, Garry Shandling, Henny Youngman, Carl Reiner, Sid Caesar, George Carlin, Firesign Theater, Gilda Radner, Howie Mandel, Dennis Miller, Dick Gregory, and others.

- **COMIC RELIEF 2 (Rhino 70707) *****

  The 1987 concert highlights with Cook and Moore, Bob Goldthwait, Roseanne, Richard Lewis, Robin Williams, Marsha Warfield, Steven Wright, and others.

- **COMIC RELIEF 3 (Rhino R2 70893) *****

  Robin Williams, Billy Crystal, Steven Wright, Garry Shandling, and Richard Lewis are the top laugh-getters, along with Elayne Boosler, Arsenio Hall, Paul Reiser, Paula Poundstone, Louie Anderson, and others.

- **COMIC RELIEF '90 (Rhino R2 71010) *****

  George Carlin, Rita Rudner, Joan Rivers, Dennis Miller, and Bob Goldthwait add something fresh while the familiar faces Steven Wright, Louie Anderson, Whoopi Goldberg, Paula Poundstone, and Robin Williams do their thing.

- **COMIC RELIEF V (Rhino R2 71165) ***
  Rita Rudner, Dennis Miller, Bob Goldthwait, and Paula Poundstone are the attractions, with cable TV perennials like Paul Rodriguez, Sinbad, Jake Johannsen, and Jim Carrey adding "ya hadda be there" goofs. Garry Shandling, Richard Lewis, Whoopi Goldberg, and Billy Crystal (as "Lester") also perform, with Robin Williams having less time than ever before.

- **COMIC RELIEF VI (Rhino R2 71692) ***
  Garry Shandling, Brett Butler, Dennis Miller, and Bill Maher present the challenging comedy amid the sap (Bob Saget) and crap (Paul Rodriguez). Alan King, David Chappelle, and Kevin Pollak are on hand, and Robin Williams performs. Aside from dull introductions, hosts Whoopi Goldberg and Billy Crystal were edited out.

- **COUNTRY COMEDY CLASSICS (K-Tel 30952) ****
  A 1993 CD compilation with Homer and Jethro among many others.

- **CRA-A-ZY HITS (MCA MCAD 22028) ****
  A 1990 CD compilation of ten tunes, some classic novelties (Pigmeat Markham, Johnny Cymbal, Nervous Norvus), most just trivia (Surfaris, Irish Rovers, Royal Teens, Bill Haley).

- **THE CRAZY ALBUM (Manic Music) ****
  A double set of mostly obscure novelty tunes from Big Boomer, Elvin Boyd, The Crawlers, etc. and cover versions of novelty tunes from The Duke of Waterloo, Borris Norris, Roy Shield, Morey Gory, and so on.

- **DEAD PARROT SOCIETY (Rhino R 271049) ***
  CD British comedy anthology featuring many cuts previously unavailable in America from Monty Python group members, Peter Cook, Dudley Moore, Eleanor Bron and John Fortune, The Portsmouth Sinfonia, and Neil Innes.

- **DO YOU WANT TO HAVE A LAUGH (Coral CRL 57380) **1/2**
  Singles and Coral album cuts from Buddy Hackett, Betty Walker, Phil Foster, Joey Adams, Al Kelly, Betty Walker, Eddie Lawrence, and Phil Foster.

- **FLY BUTTONS (Capitol) **1/2**
  Cuts from Capitol albums by Stan Freberg, Reiner and Brooks, Kalil and Taylor, and the title track by Millicent Martin and Roy Kinnear from the British TV series *That Was the Week That Was*.

- **FUN ROCK (Ronco P-12629) ****
  A 1975 compilation of novelty tunes from Sheb Wooley, Ray Stevens, Sam the Sham, Brian Hyland, Shirley Ellis, and Johnny Preston, along with too many general upbeat songs by Ohio Express, The Monkees, 1910 Fruitgum Company, and others.

- **FUN TIME (Coral CRL 57072) **1/2**
  Novelty singles from Buddy Hackett, Henny Youngman, Bob and Ray, Steve Allen, Myron Cohen, Phil Foster, Billy de Wolfe and Hermoine Gingold, Harvey Stone, Tom D'Andrea, and Hal March.

- **FUNNIEST FUNKIEST FILTHIEST (Laff A 211) ****

  A 1980 grab bag of black sex rants from minor label talents Dynamite, Tangerine, and Tina Dixon plus old regulars Wildman Steve, Skillet & Leroy, Richard & Willie, Redd Foxx, and Reynaldo Rey.

- **FUNNIEST ROASTS OF THE CENTURY (Laugh Dome LD 2201-2) ****

  A 1996 CD with salty clips from Friar's and other roasts as performed by Milton Berle, Pat McCormick, Jackie Vernon, Pat Buttram, Henny Youngman, Slappy White, and Dick Shawn.

- **FUNNY BONE FAVORITES (Ronco R 2210) *****

  Featuring novelty tunes performed by Ray Stevens, John Zacherle, Shirley Ellis, Buzz Clifford, Clovers, The Olympics, Little Jimmy Dickens, The Coasters, David Seville, Debbie Reynolds, Hollywood Argyles, The Cadets, Phil Harris, Reunion, Ray Stevens, Larry Verne, and Rick Dees.

- **GOLDEN AGE OF COMEDY (Longines Symphonette LS210A) *****

  Five albums narrated by George Burns. Most of the material is familiar stuff from radio shows (Burns and Allen, Ed Wynn, Fred Allen, Jack Pearl) and albums (Betty Walker, Dick Gregory, Jonathan Winters, The Smothers Brothers). A few comics are represented with cuts from unreleased albums or roasts (Leonard Barr, Morey Amsterdam) and for some (like radio star Bob "Bazooka" Burns, or Jack Gilford) this is the only popular source for a sampling.

- **GOLDEN AGE OF COMEDY (RCA Victor LPV 580) *****

  Album cuts and 78s from Weber and Fields, Fanny Brice, Eddie Cantor, Amos and Andy, Henny Youngman, Abbott and Costello, Judy Canova, Eddie Mayehoff, Wally Cox, Alice Ghostley, Myron Cohen, Bob and Ray, Lord Buckley, and The Three Haircuts (Caesar, Reiner, and Morris).

- **GOLDEN AGE OF COMEDY (Evolution 3013) *****

  Includes Eddie Cantor, Fibber McGee and Molly, Abbott and Costello, Fred Allen and Jack Benny, Jackie Gleason, Sid Caesar and Imogene Coca, George Burns and Gracie Allen, Groucho Marx, Ernie Kovacs, Milton Berle, Red Skelton, Oscar Levant, Jack Pearl, Bob and Ray, Tallulah Bankhead, George Jessel, Ed Wynn, Smith and Dale, and Laurel and Hardy. Some cuts edited for time. CD is available via import (On the Air OTA 101901).

- **GOLDEN THROATS: GREAT CELEBRITY SING OFF (Rhino R1 70187) *****

  Unintentionally bad or campy vocals from Leonard Nimoy, Sebastian Cabot, William Shatner, Jack Webb, Mae West, Andy Griffith, Jim Nabors, and others.

- **GOLDEN THROATS 2 (Rhino R2 71007) **1/2**

  Uneven collection where older vocalists strain to become hip and current, including Mel Torme, Sammy Davis, Jr., Bing Crosby, Jack Jones, Mae West, and Mitch Miller. The real amateurs are more reliably funny: William Shatner, Sen. Sam Ervin, and Sebastian Cabot.

- **GOLDEN THROATS 3 (Rhino R2 71867)** ***

  Subtitled "Sweethearts of Rodeo Drive," this one spotlights attempts at country songs by Goldie Hawn, Leonard Nimoy, Jack Palance, Carol Channing, Merv Griffin, Rod McKuen, Living Marimbas Plus Voices, Telly Savalas, etc. Plus oddities like Lorne Greene reciting his hit "Ringo" in French.

- **GOOFY TUNES (Ronco R 2150)** ***

  Novelty songs by Allan Sherman, Larry Groce, Sam the Sham, Sheb Wooley, Little Anthony, The Ohio Express, Tom Glazer, The Cadillacs, Jim Stafford, Bobby Boris Pickett, The Playmates, Royal Guardsmen, 1910 Fruitgum Company, The Detergents, Brian Hyland, The Coasters, and Chuck Berry.

- **GREAT RADIO COMEDIANS (Murray Hill M 5419x)** ***

  Five-album set of half-hour shows by Groucho Marx, Amos and Andy, Fred Allen, Edgar Bergen, Eddie Cantor, Jimmy Durante, Ed Gardner, and The Great Gildersleeve, plus a routine from Smith & Dale.

- **GREATEST COMEDY STARS OF THE GRAND OLE OPRY (Guest Star GS 1475)** **

  Budget disc with one early track for Homer and Jethro, one song from Lonzo & Oscar, and the rest of the songs by the less well known solo acts Brother Oswald and Cousin Jody.

- **HERE'S JOHNNY: MAGIC MOMENTS FROM THE TONIGHT SHOW (Casablanca SPNB 1296)** ***

  With Johnny Carson, Ed McMahon, Groucho Marx, George Carlin, Lenny Bruce, The Smothers Brothers, Jack Webb, Lucille Ball, Dean Martin, Buddy Hackett, Jack Benny, Jerry Lewis, Joey Bishop, George Burns, and Don Rickles.

- **HOLLYWOOD HI-FI (Brunswick BRU 81013-2)** **

  Some collectible (Jayne Mansfield, Jack "Jimmy Olson" Larson, Steve Allen) if not always listenable (Joe E. Ross, Ted Cassidy) novelty singles plus the usual celeb singing attempts that provide a wincing smile (Sissy Spacek, Anthony Quinn) or a grimace (Joey Bishop, The Brady Bunch, Robert Mitchum).

- **HOLLYWOOD PARTY (Pelican LP 130)** **

  Novelty 78s and film clips offer movie stars singing, including comics Gracie Allen, Groucho Marx, Clifton Webb, Eddie "Rochester" Anderson, Joan Davis, and Charles Chaplin.

- **HOW TO BE TERRIBLY TERRIBLY FUNNY (Riverside 7516)** **1/2

  Including Ronnie Graham's "Harry the Hipster" plus cuts from Riverside albums by Louis Nye, Peter Ustinov, Stanley Holloway, Henry Morgan, and George Crater.

- **JEST FOR LAUGHS (K-Tel PNU 5160) ****

  Novelty tunes by Bob and Doug McKenzie, Frank and Moon Zappa, Frankie Smith, Meri Wilson, Flying Lizards, Weird Al Yankovic, Joe Dolce, Bruce Baum, The Jimmy Castor Bunch, Jim Stafford, Henhouse Five Plus Too, and St. Nick.

- **JEST LIKE OLD TIMES (Radiola #1) ******

  Including Bert Lahr, The Happiness Boys, Jack Pearl, Stoopnagle and Budd, Ed Wynn, Amos and Andy, Bergen and McCarthy, George Burns and Gracie Allen, Joe Penner, Abbott and Costello, and Fanny Brice.

- **THE JEST OF FLAIR (ABC Paramount, Promotional Item) **1/2**

  Including Dick Van Dyke, Jonathan Winters, Betty Walker, Wayne and Shuster, and Milt Kamen. *Flair* was a short-lived ABC radio series "for the young adult woman with a flair for living and a flair for fun."

- **JOKERS AND WILDCARDS (Risky Business/Sony AK 66395) ****

  A dozen country novelties, including rare singles, from Shel Silverstein, Johnny Cash, Lonzo & Oscar, Leroy Pullins, Johnny Bond, and others.

- **JUST FOUR LAUGHS (Sceptor SPS 5105) ****

  Compiles routines from Bill Cosby, Dick Gregory, Redd Foxx, and Flip Wilson.

- **KINGS OF COMEDY (K-Tel NU 1180) *****

  Including Joan Rivers, Albert Brooks, Hudson and Landry, David Brenner, Richard Pryor, George Carlin, and Robert Klein.

- **KINGS OF COMEDY (Longines Symphonette SYS 5282) **1/2**

  George Burns narrates clips on Abbott and Costello, Will Rogers, Jackie Gleason, Jack Benny, Smith and Dale, and Groucho Marx. A "quickies" segment offers forty more comics, including Morey Amsterdam, Bert Gordon, Godfrey Cambridge, Pete Barbutti, Ed Wynn, Jonathan Winters, Milt Kamen, Leonard Barr, Harry Hershfield, Red Skelton, Woody Woodbury, Stiller and Meara, Moms Mabley, Ed Gardner, Joan Rivers, and Ernie Kovacs.

- **LAUGH OF THE PARTY (Coral CRL 57017) **1/2**

  Novelty singles from Steve Allen, Buddy Hackett, Phil Foster, Harvey Stone, Tom D'Andrea and Hal March, Bob and Ray, Jackie Miles, Henny Youngman, Jimmie Komack, Hermoine Gingold and Billy de Wolfe, and Eddie Lawrence.

- **A LAUGHING MATTER (Jubilee JGS 2071) ****

  Will Jordan narrates segments from Jubilee albums, including his own, and ones from Rusty Warren, Jackie Vernon, Saucy Sylvia, Lee Tully, Richie Brothers, and Autry Inman.

- **LAUGHING STOCK OF THE BBC (BBC LAF1) ****

  A sample of BBC albums with The Two Ronnies, The Goons, Monty Python, Kenneth Horne, and Tony Hancock.

- **LIVE AT THE IMPROV (The Comedy Label) ****

  There are a dozen different albums in the series. Each collects gags on a specific topic ("Dating," "Work," "Pets," and so on). Comedians on the first release, "Relatives," include Drake Sather, Fred Stoller, Ronnie Shakes, and Jerry Seinfeld. The same company has a similar series titled "Jokes to Go" and one for adult humor called "Comedy After Hours."

- **A MAINE POT-HELLION (Bert & I 2) ***

  Some pretty dull examples of anecdotal New England humor are on this 1960 compilation, as told by Alan Bemis, Steve Graham, Horace Stevens, Peter Kilham, Lawrence Kilham, George Allen, Walter Kilham, Betty Brown, and William Lippincott.

- **MY FAVORITE STORY (20th Century Fox TFM 3I06) ****

  Anecdotes recorded in a studio without an audience. Includes Lucille Ball, Jack Benny, Joey Bishop, George Burns, Bob Hope, George Jessel, Art Linkletter, Groucho Marx, Phil Silvers, Red Skelton, and Danny Thomas.

- **MY PUSSY BELONGS TO DADDY (Beacon LP 305) ****

  Mild off-color songs from the Beacon and Davis label singers Faye Richmond, Saul T. Peter, Angelina, and Miss Dee. The best part is the title and the cover shot of a topless redhead holding her pet cat.

- **NOSTALGIA RADIO: COMEDY GREATS (Metacom 0700-439) *****

  Four hour-long CDs, one each for W. C. Fields (the usual clips) Abbott and Costello ("Who's on First" and other familiar items), Burns and Allen, and Jack Benny (the latter two feature complete half-hour shows).

- **NUMBER ONE IN FUN (Stereoddities DJ 332) ****

  Intended for disc jockeys: clips from Woody Woodbury, Gypsy Rose Lee, and Eli Basse albums.

- **OLD TIME RADIO COMEDY FAVORITES (Smithsonian 1-57019-015-1) *****

  Four CDs offering five hours of old time radio shows, including Jack Benny, Burns and Allen, Edgar Bergen, Eddie Cantor, Fibber McGee, Fred Allen, *The Bickersons*, *The Aldrich Family*, *Our Miss Brooks*, *Great Gildersleeve*, *Duffy's Tavern*, and *Life of Riley*.

- **ORIGINAL AMATEUR HOUR 25TH ANNIVERSARY ALBUM (United Artists UXL 2) ****

  Very early radio appearances by Eddie Lawrence, Stubby Kaye, Ricky Layne, and Professor Backwards. The double set has more straight music cuts from Phil Ramone, Pat Boone, Jan Bart, etc.

- **ORIGINALS: MUSICAL COMEDY 1909-1935 (RCA LPV 560) **1/2**

  Vintage 78s from Gallagher and Shean, Beatrice Lillie, Eddie Cantor, Elsie Janis, plus others more musical than comedy.

- **PARTY SNATCHES (Surprise 105) **1/2**

  Risqué sampler taken from the Surprise discs of Belle Barth, Pearl Williams, B. S. Pully, Nipsey Russell, Dave Starr, and Bobby Dell.

- **RADIO'S GREATEST COMEDIANS
(Prime Time Nostalgia/Cimino Publishing Group) *****

   Five-CD set with an hour each for Fred Allen, Jack Benny, Red Skelton, Burns and Allen, and Edgar Bergen. Instead of complete shows, each CD has five to ten different radio clips.

- **RADIO'S GREATEST SITCOMS
(Prime Time Nostalgia/Cimino Publishing Group) **1/2**

   Five-CD set with an hour each for *The Bickersons*, *Duffy's Tavern*, *Ozzie and Harriet*, *Our Miss Brooks*, and *The Phil Harris-Alice Faye Show*.

- **RHINO BROTHERS' CIRCUS ROYALE (Rhino RNLP 007) *1/2**

   Novelty tunes by Ogden Edsl, Big Daddy, Kazoos Brothers, Gefilte Joe and the Fish, Captain Sticky, Suzie Seacell, Barnes and Barnes, and KGB Chicken.

- **ALLAN SHERMAN AND FRIENDS (Jubilee 5019) ** 1/2**

   Fifties novelty songs and monology from Allan Sherman, Lee Tully, Harry Ross, Sylvia Froos, Fyvush Finkle, and Willie Howard.

- **SILLY SONGS 1922-1934
(ABC 836-169-2 Marketed in the U.S. by D.R.G.) *****

   Sixteen tunes enhanced into "digital stereo," most of them from British artists including Durium Dance Band, Tessie O'Shea, Noel Coward, Jack Hylton, Ross & Sargent, Six Jumping Jacks, and Jack Hodges.

- **SILLY SONGS (K-Tel 30362) **1/2**

   A twenty-six-minute CD of ten novelty hits about chewing gum, bikinis, lost meatballs, and so on, from Brian Hyland, Lonnie Donegan, Tom Glazer, Shorty Long, Napoleon XIV, The Detergents, Tiny Tim, and others.

- **SNAPS (Big Beat 92611-2) ***

   Comedy's answer to rap music: snappers gather in a studio to insult each other, as music keeps a beat in the background. Based on book collections of put-downs, the audio result doesn't have the ring of true spontaneity, but fans won't mind. Performers are Biz Markie, Coolio, A. J. Johnson, Ricky Harris, and others.

- **SON OF JEST LIKE OLD TIMES (Radiola #2) ***1/2**

   Including radio broadcasts by Fibber McGee and Molly, Ed Gardner, Vic and Sade, Jimmy Durante and Eddie Cantor, Jack Benny, and Fred Allen.

- **STRANGE BEDFELLOWS (A&M/Blue Rose 5219) *****

   Live concert of four young political comics in 1988: Will Durst, Barry Crimmins, Randy Credico, and Jimmy Tingle.

- **THE SULLIVAN YEARS: COMEDY CLASSICS (TVT 9432-2) *****

   Routines from Ed Sullivan's TV variety show, most from the late '60s and early '70s, by Robert Klein, Joan Rivers, Stiller and Meara, Alan King, Burns and Schreiber, George Carlin, Flip Wilson, and Reiner and Brooks.

- **THEY'RE STILL LAUGHING (Capitol T 1651) **1/2**

  Introduced by George Jessel. Classic routines from Frank Fontaine, Jack Pearl, Lou Holtz, Joey Faye and Jack Albertson, and Sid Marion and Julius Tannen as Weber and Fields.

- **THREE FUNNIEST HOURS IN THE HISTORY OF RADIO (Nostalgia Lane WNRL 130) *****

  Half-hour shows with Groucho Marx, Fibber McGee and Molly, Jack Benny, Abbott and Costello, and Burns and Allen.

- **TWENTIETH CENTURY YIDDISH HUMOR (Banner BAS 1004) **1/2**

  A selection of old 78s from Billy Hodes, Leslie Brothers, Myron Cohen, Larry Best, George Jessel, Leo Fuchs, Myron Cohen, and The Radio Aces.

- **TWENTY FIVE YEARS OF RECORDED COMEDY (Warner Bros. 3BX 3131) ******

  A three-LP set culled from the albums of Nichols and May, Shelley Berman, Lenny Bruce, Bill Dana, Jonathan Winters, Stan Freberg, Kermit Schafer, Allen and Rossi, The National Lampoon, Lily Tomlin, Monty Python, Vaughn Meader, David Frye, Gabriel Kaplan, Reiner and Brooks, The Firesign Theater, Cheech and Chong, Eddie Lawrence, Richard Pryor, and Allan Sherman.

- **THE UPROAR TAPES (Antilles AN 7084) ****

  Experimental humor and "performance art" from Eric Bogosian, Ann Magnuson, David Cale, Ethyl Eichelberger, Richard Price, and Karen Finley.

- **VARIETY YIDDISH THEATRE (Banner BAS 1011) ****

  Mostly in Yiddish, the cuts feature Miriam Kressyn, Molly Picon, Myron Cohen, Leo Fuchs, Benjamin Fishbein and Mintz, Marlin Sisters, Malavsky Family, Burton Sisters, Fraydele Oysher, Max Wilner, Menasha Skulnik, and Seymour Rexsite.

- **VAUDEVILLE PERFORMANCES (Mark 56 #798) ****

  Cylinders and 78s, including "Gasoline Gus and His Jitney Bus," "Cohen on the Telephone," and others from The Two Dark Knights, Billy Murray, Steve Porter, Ernie Hare, Al Bernard, Julian Rose, and George L. Thompson.

- **VOICES FROM THE HOLLYWOOD PAST (Delos DELF 25412)**

  Six interviews with Hollywood personalities. A half-hour (one full side) features Tony Thomas's talks with Harold Lloyd, Buster Keaton, and Stan Laurel. Not intended as comedy, but certainly of interest to fans.

- **WHITE MEN CAN'T (W)RAP (Rhino R271750) **1/2**

  Familiar repackage of unintentionally funny numbers by Jack Webb and Sebastian Cabot, plus spoken novelty tunes from Napoleon XIV, Lorne Greene, C. W. McCall, Commander Cody, Lenny Bruce, Jimmy Dean, Phil Harris, Tex Ritter, Rex Harrison, and Abigail Mead.

- **WOMEN OF THE NIGHT (A&M/Blue Rose 5220)** **

  Live concert from three comedy club performers in 1988: Diane Ford, Cathy Ladman, and Paula Poundstone.

- **ZINGERS FROM THE HOLLYWOOD SQUARES (Event EV 6903)** ***

  Clips from the *Hollywood Squares* TV quiz show, featuring short quips from Marty Allen, Mel Brooks, Dom DeLuise, Totie Fields, Redd Foxx, George Gobel, Buddy Hackett, Alan King, Don Knotts, Harvey Korman, Rich Little, Paul Lynde, Freddie Prinze, Don Rickles, Joan Rivers, Rose Marie, David Steinberg, McLean Stevenson, Charlie Weaver, and Demond Wilson.

Grammy Awards

The Grammy is awarded by the National Academy of Recording Arts and Sciences.

1958: The award for "Best Comedy Performance" didn't distinguish between a single or an album. Nominated albums were "Best of the Stan Freberg Shows," Mort Sahl's "The Future Lies Ahead," and Nichols and May's "Improvisations to Music." Also nominated, Stan Freberg's single, "Green Christmas." The winner was the novelty single "Chipmunk Song" by David Seville.

1959: There were two comedy award categories this year. "Best Spoken Word Comedy" was won by "Inside Shelley Berman," with other nominee albums "Sick Humor" by Lenny Bruce, "Look Forward in Anger" by Mort Sahl, "Stan Freberg with the Original Cast," and the single, "Hamlet" by Andy Griffith. "Best Musical Comedy" saw album nominees "A Party with Comden and Green," "Charlie Weaver Sings for His People," "Monster Rally" by Hans Conreid and Alice Pearce, and "Musically Mad" from Bernie Green. The winner was a single, Homer and Jethro's "Battle of Kookamonga."

1960: Up against "Harry Belafonte Returns to Carnegie Hall," was "Nice 'n Easy" by Frank Sinatra, "Puccini: Turandot" by Erich Leinsdorf, "Wild Is Love" by Nat King Cole, and "Brahms: Concerto No. 2 in B Flat" from Sviatoslav Richter. Bob Newhart won "Album of the Year" for "The Button-Down Mind." In the "Best Spoken Word Comedy" category, it was Newhart for "Button-Down Mind Strikes Back." The other nominees were: "2000 Year Old Man" by Reiner and Brooks, "The Edge of Shelley Berman," and "The Wonderful World of Jonathan Winters." In the "Best Musical Comedy" category, "Jonathan and Darlene Edwards in Paris" by Weston and Stafford was the winner, with "Homer and Jethro at the Country Club" and "An Evening Wasted with Tom Lehrer" the nominated albums and Stan Freberg's "Old Payola Roll Blues" and the Chipmunk's novelty "Alvin for President" the nominated singles. "Old Payola Roll Blues" won in the obscure "Engineering Contribution: Comedy" category against "Spike Jones in Hi-Fi," and the Larry Verne's single "Mr. Custer," among others.

1961: "Best Comedy Performance" went to "An Evening with Nichols and May," up against "Here's Jonathan" by Jonathan Winters, "Jose Jimenez the Astronaut," "2001 Years with Carl Reiner and Mel Brooks," and "Stan Freberg Presents the United States of America." Freberg's album won "Best Engineering Contribution: Novelty" up against such competition as Bob Prescott's "Cartoons in Stereo" and "The Soupy Sales Show" album.

1962: Vaughn Meader's "The First Family" won "Album of the Year" up against "I Left My Heart in San Francisco" by Tony Bennett, "Jazz Samba" from Stan Getz, "Modern Sounds in Country and Western Music" from Ray Charles, and Allan Sherman's "My Son the Folksinger." "Best Comedy Performance" was also won by "The First Family" against "Another Day Another World" by Jonathan Winters, "Beyond the Fringe," "My Son the Folksinger," and "Nichols and May Examine Doctors." "My Son the Folksinger" and "The First Family" were nominated, but did not win in the "Best Album Cover" and "Best Engineering: Novelty" categories. The latter went to "The Civil War Volume One."

1963: "Best Comedy Performance" went to Allan Sherman for his single, "Hello Mudduh, Hello Faddah." Nominees were "Think Ethnic" by The Smothers Brothers," "I Am the Greatest" by Cassius Clay, "Carl Reiner and Mel Brooks at the Cannes Film Festival," and "Bill Cosby Is a Very Funny Fellow, Right!" The "Best Engineering: Novelty" category was changed to "Special or Novel Effects," and was won by "The Civil War, Volume Two." Reiner and Brooks's Cannes album, with a tattooed female torso, was nominated for "Best Album Cover" and lost to Barbra Streisand's face.

1964: Starting his never-duplicated winning streak, Bill Cosby won for "I Started Out As a Child," beating Allan Sherman's "For Swinging Livers Only," "Whistle Stopping with Jonathan Winters," "Ready or Not Here Comes Godfrey Cambridge," and "Woody Allen." "The Kennedy Wit" lost in "Best Documentary" to "The BBC Tribute to John F. Kennedy."

1965: Bill Cosby won for "Why Is There Air?" against The Smothers Brothers ("Mom Always Liked You Best"), Godfrey Cambridge ("Them Cotton Pickin' Days Is Over"), and two concept albums, Lou Jacobi's "You Don't Have to Be Jewish" and Alen Robin's "Welcome to the LBJ Ranch."

1966: Bill Cosby won for "Wonderfulness," against three country albums (Don Bowman's "Funny Way to Make an Album," "Have a Laugh on Me" from Archie Campbell, and Homer and Jethro's "Wanted for Murder") and a novelty item, off-key Mrs. Miller's "Downtown."

1967: Bill Cosby's "Revenge" won the award now known as "Best Comedy Recording" (as opposed to "Performance") against competition from Archie Campbell's "The Cockfight and Other Tall Tales," "Cowboys and Colored People" by Flip Wilson, "Take Offs and Put Ons" by George Carlin, and the posthumous "Lenny Bruce in Concert at Carnegie Hall."

1968: Bill Cosby won for "To Russell, My Brother." The other nominees were "W. C. Fields Original Voice Tracks," "Flip Wilson, You Devil You," "Rowan and Martin's Laugh In," and Don Rickles's "Hello Dummy."

1969: Bill Cosby won for "Bill Cosby," his first album on Uni, beating out "W. C. Fields On Radio," "Laugh-In 1969," "Don Rickles Speaks," and "Lenny Bruce: The Berkeley Concert." Shel Silverstein's comic novelty "Boy Named Sue" won "Best Country Song" and the song, as sung by Johnny Cash, won "Best Country Vocal," though it lost "Record of the Year" to "Aquarius-Let the Sunshine In" by The Fifth Dimension.

1970: Flip Wilson won for "The Devil Made Me Buy this Dress." The other nominees were Orson Welles for "The Begatting of the President," Homer and Jethro for "Daddy Played First Base," "I Am the President" by David Frye, and Bill Cosby's "Live at Madison Square Garden."

1971: Lily Tomlin won for "This Is a Recording." The competition was "When I Was a Kid" by Bill Cosby, "The Flip Wilson Show," "Cheech and Chong," and the single, "Ajax Liquor Store" by Hudson and Landry. James Whitmore's "Will Rogers' U.S.A." lost in the "Spoken Word" category to Les Crane's "Desiderata." Bill Cosby won an award for "Best Recording for Children" with "Bill Cosby Talks to Kids About Drugs."

1972: George Carlin won for "AM and FM." Coming up short were "All In the Family," "Geraldine" by Flip Wilson, "And That's the Truth" by Lily Tomlin, and "Big Bambu" from Cheech and Chong. The two-record original cast album "Lenny," with Cliff Gorman, won "Spoken Word" honors, and the "Lenny Bruce at Carnegie Hall" three-record set reissue lost "Best Album Notes" honors to "Tom T. Hall's Greatest Hits." Bill Cosby won a Grammy as a member of the cast for *The Electric Company*, in the "Best Recording for Children" category.

1973: Cheech and Chong not only won for "Los Cochinos" as "Best Comedy Recording," but the Ode Records art department won for "Best Album Package." Other nominations for "Best Comedy Recording" were Bill Cosby for "Fat Albert", George Carlin's "Occupation Foole," Robert Klein's "Child of the 50's" "Richard Nixon: A Fantasy" by David Frye, and "National Lampoon Lemmings."

1974: Richard Pryor won for "That Nigger's Crazy," against "Booga Booga" by David Steinberg, "Mind Over Matter" by Robert Klein, "Cheech and Chong's Wedding Album," and "The Missing White House Tapes" from National Lampoon. Peter Cook and Dudley Moore won in the "Spoken Word Recording" category for their Broadway hit "Good Evening." It was not nominated for "Original Cast Show Album" honors.

1975: Richard Pryor won for "Is it Something I Said?" Other nominees: Lily Tomlin for "Modern Scream," Albert Brooks for "A Star Is Bought," Monty Python for "Matching Tie and Handkerchief," and George Carlin for "An Evening with Wally Londo." Ralph J. Gleason won a "Best Album Notes" award for "The Real Lenny Bruce."

1976:   Richard Pryor won for "Bicentennial Nigger" against Bill Cosby's "Not Himself These Days Rat Own" album, "Goodbye Pop" from National Lampoon, "Sleeping Beauty" by Cheech and Chong, and Redd Foxx's "You Gotta Wash Your Ass."

1977:   Steve Martin broke Richard Pryor's three-in-a-row streak with "Let's Get Small." Pryor was nominated for "Are You Serious?" along with "The Ernie Kovacs Album," "On the Road" by George Carlin, and "Saturday Night Live."

1978:   Steve Martin won with "A Wild and Crazy Guy" against Richard Pryor's "The Wizard of Comedy," Martin Mull's "Sex and Violins," Lily Tomlin's "On Stage," and "All You Need Is Cash" from The Rutles.

1979:   Robin Williams won for "Reality, What a Concept" against Steve Martin's "Comedy Is Not Pretty," Richard Pryor's "Wanted," and two musical numbers, "Rubber Biscuit" by The Blues Brothers, and "I Need Your Help Barry Manilow" by Ray Stevens.

1980:   Rodney Dangerfield won for "No Respect," with respectable competition: "Monty Python's Contractual Obligation Album," "Live from New York" from Gilda Radner, "Live at St. Douglas Convent" from Father Guido Sarducci, and Richard Pryor's "Holy Smoke."

1981:   Richard Pryor won for "Rev. Du Rite" against two movie soundtracks ("Airplane" and "Mel Brooks History of the World Part I"), a single ("The Inquisition" by Mel Brooks), and a novelty disc ("Urban Chipmunk").

1982:   Richard Pryor won for "Live on the Sunset Strip" with the other nominees including "The Steve Martin Brothers," "Eddie Murphy," "Great White North" by Bob and Doug McKenzie, and "A Place for My Stuff" by George Carlin.

1983:   Eddie Murphy won for "Eddie Murphy Comedian" against "Bill Cosby Himself," "Monty Python's Meaning of Life," "Throbbing Python of Love" by Robin Williams, and "What Becomes a Semi-Legend Most" by Joan Rivers.

1984:   Weird Al Yankovic won for his hit single "Eat It" from his "3D" album. The competition was "Here and Now" by Richard Pryor, "Hurt Me Baby" by Rick Dees, "Three Faces of Al" from Firesign Theater, and the single "Rappin' Rodney" from Rodney Dangerfield. Shel Silverstein won a children's recording grammy for "Where the Sidewalk Ends."

1985:   Whoopi Goldberg won for her original cast album. Two singles were nominated: "Born in East L.A." by Cheech and Chong and "Honeymooners Rap" from Joe Piscopo and Eddie Murphy. Also nominated: "You Look Mahvelous" by Billy Crystal and "Dare to Be Stupid" by Al Yankovic. Dick Cavett was nominated for "Best Spoken Word" recording, reading "Huckleberry Finn."

1986: Bill Cosby won for "Those of You with or without Children..." For the first time, an audiocassette was nominated ("Bob and Ray: A Night of Two Stars") along with a single ("Twist and Shout" by Rodney Dangerfield) and three albums: "I Have a Pony" by Steven Wright, "Mud Will Be Flung Tonight" by Bette Midler, and "Playin' with Your Head" by George Carlin.

1987: Robin Williams won for "A Night at the Met." Other nominees were Realart's tape "The Best of Bob & Ray Vol. 1," "Polka Party" by Weird Al Yankovic, "The World According to Me" by Jackie Mason, and Ray Stevens's "Would Jesus Wear a Rolex."

1988: Robin Williams's soundtrack recording "Good Morning Vietnam," which featured a few snippets of monologue material, won over "Even Worse" by Weird Al Yankovic, "Fontaine" from Whoopi Goldberg, "Jonathan Winters Finally Captured" (a Dove audio book on tape), and George Carlin's "What Am I Doing in New Jersey?"

1989: Peter Schickele won for "1712 Overture." The other nominees: "Dice" by Andrew Dice Clay, "Motherhood," an Erma Bombeck book on tape, "Wild Thing," a single by Sam Kinison, and Sandra Bernhard's "Without You I'm Nothing."

1990: Peter Schickele won for "Oedipus Tex," edging "The Best of Bob and Ray: Selections from a Career Vol. 4," "The Best of Comic Relief '90," the Dove book on tape "Jonathan Winters into the ... 90's" by Jonathan Winters," and "More News from Lake Wobegon" by Garrison Keillor. George Burns won "Best Spoken Word" for his audio book on tape, "Gracie: A Love Story."

1991: Peter Schickele won for "WTWP, Talkity-Talk Radio." He beat Jackie Mason's "Brand New," Garrison Keillor's tape "Local Man Moves to the City," "Parental Advisory" by George Carlin, and "When You Look Like Your Passport Photo ..." an audio book from Erma Bombeck.

1992: Peter Schickele won for "Music for an Awful Lot of Winds and Percussion." Other nominees: "Naked Beneath My Clothes" (Rita Rudner audio book), "An Evening with George Burns," "Jonathan Winters Is Terminator 3" (audio book), and "Off the Deep End" (Weird Al Yankovic).

1993: George Carlin won for "Jammin' in New York," and the category title changed from "Best Comedy Album" to "Best Spoken Comedy Album." Other nominees: Garrison Keillor ("Lake Wobegon USA"), Leslie Nielsen (his audio book pseudo-autobiography "The Naked Truth"), Erma Bombeck ("A Marriage Made in Heaven" audio book) and Al Franken ("You're Good Enough, You're Smart Enough ...").

1994: Sam Kinison won for "Live from Hell," over "Attention Butt Pirates and Lesbetarians" by Judy Tenuta, "Jerky Boys 2," "They're All Gonna Laugh at You" by Adam Sandler, and "The Official Politically Correct Dictionary," an audio book from Christopher Cerf.

1995: Jonathan Winters won for "Crank Calls."

RIAA Gold Awards

The Recording Industry Auditors of America began issuing "gold album" certificates in 1958, and "platinum" honors in 1976. According to the RIAA, "From 1958 until January 1, 1975, the requirement for a Gold Album certification was a minimum of $1 million in manufacturer's dollar volume (wholesale price) based at 33 1/3% of list price of each LP and/or tape sold. Since then, the requirement has been a minimum sale of 500,000 units ... a further requirement is that the manufacturer's dollar volume be at least $1 million based at 33 1/3% of the list price of each record and/or tape sold."

Platinum Awards are given to albums that sell one million copies (minimum) and clear $2 million. For an album to be eligible for a Gold or Platinum Certificate, there must be an audit to verify the sales totals.

The first comedy album to go "Gold" was Bob Newhart's "Button-Down Mind" on March 1, 1962, followed by Allan Sherman's "My Son the Folksinger" and Vaughn Meader's "The First Family," though there had been top-selling albums earlier, notably "Inside Shelley Berman," "Outside Shelley Berman," "Jose the Astronaut" by Bill Dana, "Rejoice Dear Hearts" by Brother Dave Gardner, and several albums by Mort Sahl. Some "adults only" albums, like "Knockers Up" from Rusty Warren and "Woody Woodbury Looks at Love and Life," have allegedly attained big sales figures. It's possible that some of the above may have qualified for "Gold" status, but nobody from the record company's sales department thought to apply (or wanted an audit).

It's also possible that some comedians claiming "Gold Record" awards in the early '60s referred to honors bestowed by other organizations, such as NARM, the National Association of Record Merchandisers, but for the past thirty years the RIAA has become the recognized standard. For many comedy albums, the award reflects cumulative sales. For example, "Jerry Clower's Greatest Hits" was released in 1979 but went gold in 1992.

Gold Winners (Platinum winners are in italics):

George Carlin: "AM and FM" (Little David), "Class Clown" (Little David), "Occupation Foole" (Little David), "Toledo Windowbox" (Little David)

Cheech and Chong: "Cheech and Chong" (Ode), "Big Bambu" (Ode), "Los Cochinos" (Ode), "Wedding Album" (Ode)

Jerry Clower: Greatest Hits (MCA)

Bill Cosby: *"I Started Out as a Child"* (Warner Bros.), *"Wonderfulness"* (Warner Bros.), "Why Is There Air?" (Warner Bros.), *"Bill Cosby Is A Very Funny Fellow"* (Warner Bros.), "Revenge" (Warner Bros.), "To Russell My Brother" (Warner Bros.), "200 MPH" (Warner Bros.), *"Best of Bill Cosby"* (Warner Bros.) "Those Of You..." (Geffen)

Jeff Foxworthy: "You Might Be a Redneck If..."

Jerky Boys: Jerky Boys (Atlantic), Jerky Boys 2 (Atlantic)

Steve Martin: *"Let's Get Small"* (Warner Bros.), *"Wild and Crazy Guy"* (Warner Bros.), "Comedy Is Not Pretty" (Warner Bros.)

Vaughn Meader: "The First Family" (Cadence)

Eddie Murphy: *"Eddie Murphy"* (Columbia), *"Eddie Murphy Comedian"* (multi-platinum; Columbia), his "straight" music "Party All the Time" went platinum, as did the "Beverly Hills Cop" soundtrack

Bob Newhart: "The Button-Down Mind of Bob Newhart" (Warner Bros.), "Button-Down Mind Strikes Back" (Warner Bros.)

Richard Pryor: *"Was It Something I Said?"* (Warner Bros.), Bicentennial Nigger (Warner Bros), "Wanted Live" (Warner Bros.), *"Greatest Hits"* (Warner Bros.), "That Nigger's Crazy" (Warner Bros.)

Allan Sherman: "My Son the Folk Singer" (Warner Bros.)

Smothers Brothers: "Think Ethnic" (Mercury), "Two Sides of The Smothers Brothers" (Mercury), "Smothers Brothers at the Purple Onion" (Mercury)

Ray Stevens: He Thinks He's Ray Stevens (MCA), I Have Returned (MCA)

Flip Wilson: "The Devil Made Me Buy this Dress" (Little David)

Weird Al Yankovic: "Weird Al in 3D" (Epic), "Dare to Be Stupid" (Epic), *Even Worse* (Epic), Alapalooza (Scotti Bros), Off the Deep End (Scotti Bros.)